Handbook of Distance Education

The third edition of this award-winning handbook continues the mission of its predecessors: to provide a comprehensive compendium of research in all aspects of distance education, arguably the most significant development in education over the past three decades. While the book deals with education that uses technology, the focus is on teaching and learning and how its management can be facilitated through technology. Key features include:

- Comprehensive coverage that includes all aspects of distance education, including design, instruction, management, policy, and a section on different audiences.

- Chapter authors frame their topic in terms of empirical research (past and present) and discuss the nature of current practice in terms of that research. Future research needs are discussed in relation to both confirmed practice and recent changes in the field.

- A unique review of the theories that support distance education pedagogy.

- A focus throughout on contemporary applications, online and e-learning.

This book will be of interest to anyone engaged in distance education at any level. It is also appropriate for corporate and government trainers and for administrators and policy makers in all these environments.

Michael G. Moore is Distinguished Professor of Education at The Pennsylvania State University, where he specializes in the study of distance education.

Handbook of Distance Education

Third Edition

Edited by

Michael Grahame Moore

The Pennsylvania State University

Routledge
Taylor & Francis Group

NEW YORK AND LONDON

Third edition published 2013
by Routledge
711 Third Avenue, New York, NY 10017

Simultaneously published in the UK
by Routledge
2 Park Square, Milton Park, Abingdon, Oxon OX14 4RN

Routledge is an imprint of the Taylor & Francis Group, an informa business

© 2013 Taylor & Francis

First edition published 2003
Second edition published 2007

Library of Congress Cataloging in Publication Data
Handbook of distance education / edited by Michael Grahame Moore. — 3rd ed.
   p. cm.
   Includes bibliographical references and index.
   Distance education—Handbooks, manuals, etc. I. Moore, Michael G.
   LC5800.H36 2012
   371.35'8—dc23
   2012018509

ISBN: 978-0-415-89764-8 (hbk)
ISBN: 978-0-415-89770-9 (pbk)
ISBN: 978-0-203-80373-8 (ebk)

Typeset in Minion
by EvS Communication Networx, Inc.

Printed and bound in the United States of America
by Edwards Brothers, Inc.

CONTENTS

LIST OF FIGURES AND TABLES

Figures

Tables

PREFACE

MICHAEL GRAHAME MOORE

This volume is about research and other scholarship in distance education and is organized in five parts:

Part 1. Historical and conceptual foundations
Part 2. Learners, learning, and learner support
Part 3. Design and teaching
Part 4. Policies, administration, and management
Part 5. Audiences and providers

This structure is only slightly modified from that of previous editions, and its purpose remains the same, to provide access to a broad selection of the scholarly and research literature, organized in a way that will enable students and practitioners to identify sources relevant to their particular needs, as the first step leading to their personal, in-depth, follow-up literature research. It was the perceived need for such a compilation that led to the publication of the first edition of the *Handbook of Distance Education* in 2003, at a time when it had become apparent that distance education had emerged to be one of the most significant developments in education of the previous quarter century. The need for an updated edition is no less acute, as distance education continues to make inroads into the mainstream of educational and training practice at all levels, and in virtually every field of learning. Across this wide educational spectrum, it is the subject of increasing attention by policy makers and administrators as well as teachers and students. Its traditional role of opening opportunity for learners and its more recent role of adding to the quality of teaching are roles now widely recognized, as much by professors in universities and community colleges as by trainers in corporations and the armed forces, in continuing professional education of teachers, physicians and nurses, public accountants and pharmacists, leaders of voluntary organizations, managers in the corporate boardroom, and workers seeking new skills on the factory floor. Thankfully, what I described in the first edition as the "recent frenzy" of precipitant innovation driven by excitement about Internet technology, has subsided to a considerable extent, as those who got caught up in that early excitement discovered for themselves the challenges as well as the benefits offered by the technology. Communication through computer technologies, the Internet and the Web has long ceased to be an innovation for most teachers, and they have settled down to confront the more interesting work involved in acquiring the skills needed for designing and delivering quality programs through those technologies. More cautiously perhaps, an increasing number of the leaders of their institutions have also begun to confront the different management and administrative changes needed to accomplish good quality distance teaching. Most difficult among these are changing the allocation of resources in order to produce mediated programs with quality, and the particularly difficult job of channeling their faculty into roles more appropriate for the information age than those they have been accustomed to performing in the classroom. So far, in this regard, timidity still overshadows boldness and considerable more education for leaders is called for. However, it is the students who are learning new ways, faster than either teachers or administrators, growing from childhood to be at ease with the technologies, accustomed to learning informally out-of-school, online, and inducted from an early age into the rewards that follow the effort of distance learning. Our students, of course, are also driving their teachers to explore the most recent wave of new technologies, the situation of recent years being perhaps worth calling a second wave of frenzy! This is the spread and adoption of mobile technologies, and their application as vehicles for so-called social networking—for which, let it be noted, only minimal educational benefits have yet been realized.

In this environment of further maturing in understanding about distance education, as it becomes increasingly part of the educational mainstream, accompanied by continuing volatility in the invention and spread of information and communication technologies, a growing number of students are looking for the opportunity of academic study of this field, and a growing number of educational institutions offer programs of study, particularly at graduate level. Evidence of this can be seen, for example, in the growth in the number of doctoral dissertations that include the terms "distance education" or "distance learning" in their title, averaging, at the most modest estimate, about 100 each year since the beginning of the decade. As editor for the past 26 years of *The American Journal of Distance Education* I am aware of the enormous increase in interest by university and other faculty in publishing research in this area, resulting in a frequently overwhelming supply of article submissions. I also note the growth in the number of new journals, especially online journals that are able to absorb what the more established journals cannot publish. The extent of this growth in scholarship of distance education becomes even more apparent when we take into account the many research studies and published works that focus on one or other of the component parts of this field, or one of its many applications—reported in terms such as distributed learning, tele-learning, e-learning, open learning, blended learning, and flexi-learning. Each of these subsets of distance education has generated its own following of specialists, some with their own journals, conferences, and an evolving corpus of literature—a natural development in this, as in any, maturing field.

This splitting of the field into component specialties does, however, bring with it one problem, which is that by focusing on what is published using the terminology of one part of the field, students might be distracted from relevant knowledge that is packaged under the label of one of the other of the field's component parts. In this handbook, it is intended that the reader will acquire an understanding of the breadth of the field through the chapters in Part 1, and acquire some conceptual tools that will enable recognition of both the specific trees in this forest, as well as the woods of which they are a part. Here, just to underscore how critically important it is to recognize how broad is the field before tackling any of its components, I will repeat the definition of distance education: "—teaching and planned learning in which the teaching normally occurs in a different place from learning, requiring communication through technologies, as well as special institutional organization" (Moore & Kearsley, 2012, p. 2). Three key words here are worth emphasizing. The first is "normally," which should remind us of that in distance education the use of communications technology is *not* an option but is a defining characteristic of the teaching-learning relationship, unlike its use in the classroom where the same technology is ancillary to the teacher's presence. The second word to emphasis is "planned" as in "planned learning," for in this age of ever-ready search engines, and global exchanges of information through social networks, we need to remember that our study is of *education,* and education is always a two-sided transaction, learners on one side and a teaching agency on the other, having the resources to make learning more effective and efficient than when it is entirely self-directed. That is not to detract from the importance of self-directed, informal, independent learning, but it is important to avoid the muddled thinking that we sometimes encounter in the social media in which informal, even serendipitous, learning is spoken of as synonymous, even sometimes replacing, education. Third, the word "organization" reminds us that our field includes—as well as study of information and communications technologies and questions regarding the design of teaching programs and facilitation of learning—study of the administrative, organizational and policy issues associated with the provision of such educational programs. Broad too are the research methods that should be brought to bear on those questions, employing techniques from all research traditions—experimental, case study and ethnographic, comparative and historical. The aim of all such activity is the acquisition of empirically based knowledge, organized in a body of literature, and sometimes synthesized into a theory that will act, in turn, to point the way to further empirical research.

It is the five topical areas of study and research listed in the opening paragraph that provide the themes around which this handbook is organized. Following Part 1, that introduces the history of the field and some of its widely recognized theoretical foundations, introducing such core ideas as "systems approach" and "independent learning," subsequent parts of this volume provide reviews of learning and learners; course design and teaching; policies, administration, and management; and the main client groups and institutional providers, including a closing essay to remind us about changing perspectives about learning, in the global context.

RATIONALE FOR THIS HANDBOOK AND HOW TO USE IT

The motivation for producing the handbooks has two roots. First, as the editor of *The American Journal of Distance Education* for more than a quarter century and as adviser of doctoral students during that same period, I have noted that one of the most common causes of difficulty and failure for researchers as well as students is a too-common view that research is nothing more than mere empiricism. From this perspective, the focus, indeed the beginning and end of the research process, is gathering, analyzing and reporting data; I might almost say "grabbing at data." The "literature review" that typically is the second chapter in a doctoral dissertation or comprises the opening section of a research article is too often approached as a tedious chore imposed by convention that has to be got through as quickly as possible before getting to the "real thing"—which is to gather and report data. These data may be the results of a survey or a case study, or—too seldom—an experiment. However much of this data gathered and submitted for publication, and even reported in some dissertation studies, has little or no value. This is simply because the research question that the data is supposed to address has little or no connection with the previous state of knowledge, as reported in the literature. I have found it so sad for many years to see students (and others who should know better) investing time and energy to design a study and collect data that addresses questions that have already been answered—or that are unanswerable, given the present state of knowledge. Not quite so seriously, I see other studies based on a review of a too-narrow set of literature that fall short of their potential by not linking to a wider literature, in other words, a more general theoretical framework. A common example is the research question that addresses teaching and learning through a specific technology, grounded in a review of the research of that technology, but missing a wealth of relevant knowledge on the same question that was conducted in programs using a different technology.

My sympathy lies with the student, confronted by what must seem an almost impossibly confused and anarchic body of literature, with hundreds of journals with titles suggesting possible relevance to the distance education study. What help can be provided? In our view the best help is to address the problem as already stated, that research will fail unless it is based on a good foundation of knowledge of previous research. And therefore it is to meet this need, to provide a structured guide to what is already known about distance education, and thus help better-grounded research, that the handbooks have been written.

The second root motivation for this collection is closely related to the first. Experience as a consultant to a wide range of institutions, states, national governments, and international agencies over several decades has led to the conclusion that a similar impatience for moving to action without adequate comprehension of previous experience characterizes not only the research, but virtually all practice in this field also. Just as it is hard to imagine that in any other field of inquiry researchers could set out to gather data without knowing what research had been previously undertaken, so it is hard to imagine that other professions would set up departments, design courses, recruit teachers, invest millions of dollars, make appearances before Congressional committees, and so on, without first acquiring a substantial knowledge of previous practice in their field; without a thorough knowledge of what had succeeded and what had failed, and the reasons for those successes and failures. Yet in distance education, it happens all the time. University professors, generally knowledgeable in an academic subject, and skilled in lecturing to rows of students in a classroom, are driven into designing courses for delivery on the Web or by video-conference with little or no knowledge about how to design programs suitable for learning in what is, still, a more individual mode of study, requiring the special skills of facilitating interaction with content, learners and instructors through information and communication technologies. The same could be said about teachers in K-12 schools, and trainers in business and other corporate settings.

Thus this book is intended to be a source of information for students and researchers to help them *know what is known* before they begin a search for new knowledge, and to help practitioners and policy makers **know what is known** before they plan, design, and deliver new programs. It should be emphasized, especially to the researcher that this is *only* a key. No synthesis or summary of other people's research can be a substitute for the knowledge provided by that research itself, and so each of these chapters should be regarded as merely pointing the way to the literature that has to be studied in depth. Our approach in compiling this book, showing also the way we expect the book to be used, can be explained by quoting the following instruction, given our authors when their contributions were commissioned: "To provide the reader, particular the student, with a reference source for study and research in the author's specific field, and therefore takes the form of a comprehensive, thematically structured review of the research and other literature published up to and including 2011. The chapter is not a report on the author's particular research or opinion except as is reasonable to include as part of such a comprehensive literature review. One way of conceiving the chapter is as a bibliographic essay." I should say immediately that a few authors strayed from the narrow path laid out for them, and there are, in a few chapters, what can only be described as authors' opinions, some of which are quite polemical; where they survived the editorial review it was for their merits in offering issues for discussion as well as, I hope, provoking research. It should also be explained that for the new edition, it was expected that authors would carry over many of the references from earlier editions because they represent what is known and needs to be known, but add literature of the past five years, so that this edition can entirely replace the earlier ones. To accommodate the additional contents, the length of each chapter was increased by one third, and to compensate for this, the number of chapters, compared to previous editions, was reduced.

Our recommendation to students is that early in your studies, you should skim the whole book, and subsequently, after deciding on an area for research, take the relevant chapters as the starting point for identifying the literature in that area. The next step is to locate each of the items listed in the references of the chosen chapters, and using them thus dig deeper and deeper into the literature until mastery is achieved. Lest that seems too easy, it has to be repeated that knowledge in this field, like most others, does not lend itself to water-tight compartmentalization and it is *vital* to be aware that something of value for any research question can be found within a chapter having a principal focus that is quite different from the question one is focused on. In this book, for example, we have chapters about historical research in Part 1, but references to history will be found in several chapters in other parts of the book. Similarly it is impossible to separate important references to learning from those of teaching, while much that is addressed to administration is relevant to both. The process of literature research is not easy, but there can be no doubt that time and effort spent in this foundation work will result in better research and better practice.

In this volume, as in previous editions, we have assembled some of the most respected authorities in the North American field of distance education as well as some rising stars. In extending our invitations, we aimed to deal with another problem commonly encountered in advising students and in reviewing research. This is the problem of *authority*. Along with my plea to give more attention to building a solid theoretical foundation for their research and practice (i.e., knowing what is known), I would like to remind students (and other readers) of the importance of developing a critical perspective on what is published, recognizing that not all that is published is of equal value. In this age of Facebook, Twitter, blogging, and so-called open source materials it is a bigger problem than ever before to identify what is trustworthy, and the search engines that make it easy to gather whatever is published on the Web give no reliable clues about its the handbook. Moore's theory of transactional distance, probably the most widely cited theory specific to distance education, is the subject of one of the four remaining chapters in Part 1. It follows a chapter by another of the most highly regarded scholars in our field, Farhad Saba, who masterfully describes the foundation concept of the systems approach, and its historical evolution in distance education theory and practice, set in a macro-level, global theoretical framework. An intriguing feature of Saba's chapter, unique among all the chapters in the book, is his references to other chapters of this book as illustrations of his "hierarchy of nested systems." Elaborating on this idea, he points out that transactional distance is itself a component of a larger system, and in so doing paves the way for Moore's update in Chapter 5 of some of the research of recent years that has been grounded in his theory. The concept of learner autonomy derived from Moore's theory features heavily in the next chapter, in which William Anderson explains the relationship of distance education to the even broader theory of adult learning, and shows how recent scholars have revisited earlier ideas about adult self-directed learning represented by Knowles and Tough. Anderson's summary of research on learner autonomy and student outcomes points to a later chapter (in Part 3), in which Hill, Domizi, and Kim, discuss " Teaching and Learning in Negotiated and Informal Environments" as well as Allen, Burrell, and Timmerman's in Part 2 that discusses student satisfaction. His review of research on meta-cognition introduces themes that will also be picked up later, particularly by West and colleagues (Chapter 8). To conclude Part 1, Anderson is followed with an update of another widely cited theory, this in Garrison and Akyol's account of The Community of Inquiry Theoretical Framework.

An ideal way of negotiating these four chapters of theory would be to read Moore's explanation of the evolution of the theory of transactional distance, recognizing the link to Wedemeyer, as explained in their chapters by Black and Diehl and especially the connection with Wedemeyer's idea about independent learning and also, importantly, the early experiments in a systems approach to teaching and learning. Turning back to Saba's chapter, one should find this helpful in "joining the dots," at least at a preliminary level, recognizing the evolution of the seminal ideas "autonomy," "structure," and "dialogue" into their modern forms as they are promised to appear in later chapters. Apart from the Hill, Domizi, and Kim chapter and its relevance to "autonomy," every chapter in Part 3 has some relevance to issues associated with "structure" and some (Kuskis and Friesen, for example) with "dialogue." Finally, for Part 1, you should be able to reflect further on dialogue, as Garrison and Akyol pull the focus firmly into the Web 2.00 age, with their emphasis on social presence, complementing the more long-standing elements of cognitive and teacher presence. This, like Transactional Distance is, as Saba would explain, a high-level, global theoretical structure. Therefore, as with the chapter on transactional distance, the student is strongly recommended to refer back to the Garrison and Akyol chapter as well as the Saba chapter when studying subsequent chapters throughout the book, especially those in Parts 2 and 3. After reading these later chapters, some of the insights about teaching and learning at a distance that are of necessity only summarized in the theories, should become more fully understood.

1

A HISTORY OF SCHOLARSHIP
LINDA M. BLACK

This chapter presents the origins and development of distance education scholarship. It is organized by seven principal topics: (1) pioneer research; (2) research centers; (3) trends in the late 20th century; (4) professional development of distance educators; (5) professional associations; (6) lectures, seminars, symposia, workshops, and conferences; (7) publications and other media.

PIONEER RESEARCH

Among the first people to encourage research in distance education were William H. Lighty, and John S. Noffsinger; the latter recorded the first systematic description of American correspondence study in 1926 (Moore, 1987a). Other early advocates for research were Gayle B. Childs of Kansas State University (Almeda, 1988) and Charles A. Wedemeyer of the University of Wisconsin-Madison (Moore, 1987b).

After he wrote his doctoral dissertation on correspondence education in public schools, Childs (1949) received a grant from the Ford Foundation (Wright, 1991, p. 43) and performed one of the first studies of educational television. Urging the National University Extension Association (NUEA) to support research, Childs (1966) participated in a milestone study of correspondence education completion rates. The study gathered data on 42,068 college enrollments in 32 institutions and on 17,520 high school enrollments in 24 institutions.

During the 1960s, the Correspondence Study Division (CSD) of the NUEA and the National Home Study Council (NHSC) collaborated in the Correspondence Education Research Project (CERP), a national survey of correspondence study in higher education in the United States. CERP was the first study to report evidence that correspondence instruction could be as effective as face-to-face classroom instruction (MacKenzie, Christensen, & Rigby, 1968, pp. 104–105).

Charles Wedemeyer, as University of Wisconsin-Madison correspondence director during the 1960s, conceived and implemented the Articulated Instructional Media Project (AIM) at the university. He demonstrated that by deconstructing the teaching process into specialties, employing specialists to work as members of teaching teams, and connecting (i.e., "articulating") a variety of communications media to deliver programs produced higher quality programs than programs produced by individuals working alone, or programs produced and delivered by only one communications medium (Wedemeyer & Najem, 1969). Of monumental historical importance, Wedemeyer's ideas were incorporated into the design of the then-revolutionary Open University of the United Kingdom (UKOU), the first publicly funded, national autonomous degree-granting distance teaching university. Refer to Diehl's chapter in this volume and Diehl (2011) for further coverage of Wedemeyer's importance to open and distance education.

In Europe, early scholarly writing based on empirical, systematic research, is associated with two pioneers: Börje Holmberg in Sweden and Otto Peters in Germany. Holmberg's (1960) "On the Methods of Teaching by Correspondence," as described by Larsson (1992), initiated the first European awareness of correspondence study as a pedagogical methodology (p. x). Peters, first a researcher at the Education Center of Berlin and later at the German Institute for Distance Education Research (DIFF) at the University of Tübingen, inventoried distance education institutions in more than 30 countries and analyzed their systems. His research resulted in the development of a theory that compared distance education to "industrialized education" (Peters, 1967, 1973; Keegan 1994). In the previous edition of the *Handbook of Distance Education,* Moore (2007b) includes chapters delineating Peters' ideas about "The Most Industrialized Form of Education" and Holmberg's conceptualization of "A Theory of Teaching-Learning Conversations."

In the United States, during the decade of the 1970s, Wedemeyer published his ideas about his definition of "independent study" (1971). Influenced by Wedemeyer's (and also Gleason's) ideas, Michael G. Moore (1972) published his research on a theory of "learner autonomy" and incorporated this in his 1976 dissertation about self-directed learners who use correspondence study. By the 1980s Moore's theorizing evolved into the well-known theory of "transactional distance" (Moore, 2007c). Refer to Black's (2004) dissertation and to Diehl's chapter in this volume for more descriptions of Wedemeyer's influence on theorists Holmberg, Moore, and Peters; and also refer to Bernath and Vidal (2007).

EMERGENCE OF ORGANIZED RESEARCH CENTERS

The second half of the 20th century saw a number of phenomena lead to growing interest in research; these included favorable research findings about effectiveness of distance education; educational reforms and socio-economic justifications for distance education, especially in developing countries; increased funding for research; and the birth of large single-mode distance institutions employing specialist academic researchers. This resulted in the growth of distance education research centers. Some important ones were: the University of Wisconsin-Extension, United States; the Institute of Educational Technology (IET) at the UKOU; the Education Center of Berlin in collaboration with the DIFF at Tübingen; the Central Institute for Distance Education Research (ZIFF) at the FernUniversität, Hagen, Germany; the Centre for Distance Education (CDE) at Athabasca University, Canada; and the American Center for the Study of Distance Education (ACSDE) at the Pennsylvania State University, United States.

The earliest research topics in the United States were typically limited to comparison studies of results of conventional face-to-face classroom compared with mediated distance delivery, and comparisons of the effectiveness of different technologies and media. Popular topics, internationally, went beyond comparison studies, with a major focus on survey research. For example, UKOU's research arm investigated students' characteristics and attrition rates, under-representation of society's disadvantaged segments, and resistance to distance education as well as instructional effectiveness (Glatter & Wedell, 1971; McIntosh, Calder, & Swift, 1976).

In 1988 the First American Symposium on Research in Distance Education, which brought together by invitation 50 American distance education leaders and sponsored by the ACSDE, aimed to set a national research agenda. Moore's (1990) book, *Contemporary Issues in American Distance Education*, carried edited papers from the symposium and provided the first compilation of American scholarly articles reflecting the state of distance education research. With the focus on international research, a similar 1990 event, "Research in Distance Education: Setting a Global Agenda for the Nineties" was sponsored by the ACSDE in collaboration with the International Council of Correspondence Education (ICCE). Representatives from five continents proposed a global research agenda comprised of (a) research on computer conferencing; (b) meta-analyses of researchers' values and assumptions; (c) comparative institutional studies; (d) analyses of students' life experiences; (e) methods and technologies of small island countries; (f) representation of women in distance education materials; and (g) influences of planning and personal, institutional, instructional contexts on student performance (Paulsen & Pinder, 1990, pp. 83–84).

Beginning in 1995, a number of factors—including less generous funding, the retirement of founding pioneers, the co-option of distance education research questions by a wider population of academic specialists such as computer scientists and information technologists—impacted the research centers. The DIFF reorganized to become a broad-based education research center and donated its distance education materials to the ZIFF (Black, 2004). In 2005 the ZIFF closed and its personnel were assigned quality control tasks (http://www.fernuni-hagen.de/ZIFF/index.htm). The IET now helps manage the OUUK's Jennie Lee Research Laboratories (http://www8.open.ac.uk/iet/main/core-services/jennie-lee-research-labs) and partners with the United Kingdom's Centre for Research in Education and Educational Technology (CREET), established in 2004 to employ multidisciplinary research teams. In 2002 Moore left the directorship of the ACSDE. The early centers are important for establishing distance education as a field of study, and new centers have sprung up to carry on the work. Prominent ones are the Learning Resources Development and Support (LRDS) Center, formerly the Distance and e-Learning Centre (DeC) at the University of Southern Queensland, Australia; the Center for Research in Distance Education (ASF) at the Carl von Ossietzky University of Oldenburg, Germany; the Norwegian Center for Distance Education (SEFU); and the South African Institute for Distance Education (SAIDE). Of course, many open universities have research centers. Some examples are the Canadian Institute of Distance Education Research (CIDER) coordinated by the Centre for Distance Education Research at Athabasca University, Canada; the Research Institute of Open and Distance Education at the China Open University; the Staff Training and Research Institute of Distance Education (STRIDE) at the Indira Gandhi National Open University (IGNOU), India; the Center for Research in Distance and Adult Learning at the Open University of Hong Kong; the Institute of Distance Education at the Korea National Open University; and the Knowledge Media Institute (KMi), UKOU, created in 1995 to research the convergence of knowledge media—the cognitive and learning sciences, artificial intelligence and semantic technologies, and multimedia—associated with the UKOU's educational systems. For lists of international research centers, refer to Moore and Kearsley (2012, pp. 300–304).

TRENDS IN THE LATE 20TH CENTURY

Throughout the remainder of the 20th century, many studies continued to focus on one particular research question (Moore & Kearsley, 2012, pp. 225–226): Which learning environment or which delivery technology or media is more effective when the outcome variable is the average scores of two or more groups of learners? It might have been argued that the question was already answered in Dubin and Taveggia's (1968) seminal study, in which they analyzed data from 7 million academic records and concluded that it is *not* difference in instructional method that determines student performance. Three decades later, citing a 1928 dissertation as the earliest study found, Russell (1999) once again summarized research studies that show "no significant difference" in the effectiveness of face-to-face compared to distance education systems (http://www. nosignificantdifference.org/).

In 2010, Davies, Howell, and Petrie summarized trends in North American distance education research after they analyzed graduate students' dissertations and theses, 1998 to 2007. Consistent with Naidu's (2005, as cited by Davies, Howell, & Petrie, 2010) observations, they found that most research consisted of descriptive, self-reports, i.e., studies which addressed the perceptions, concerns, and satisfaction levels of various stakeholders within a single, particular distance education experience.

For another recent illustration of progress in research, in 2010 de Oliveira Neto and dos Santos analyzed the methods and research topics in a sample of Brazilian distance education publications, 1992 to 2007, and in a sample of articles from the *American Journal of Distance Education*, 1987–2006. The predominant research paradigm used in the Brazilian research was qualitative, with the predominant research method exploratory and the second-most predominant case study. The most-researched Brazilian topic was management, and the most-researched topic in the *American Journal of Distance Education* was evaluation.

Via a Delphi study, Zawacki-Richter (2009) examined experts' opinions on categories of research areas in distance education, their importance, and the most neglected areas of distance education research. He reported the opinion that access and equity, the role of distance education in developing areas, student support services, evaluation, educational technologies, and instructional design are still of major importance. Given the globalization of education, Zawacki-Richter argues for more research pertaining to access, equity, and ethics. With 80% of all articles originating in five countries, a review of articles published from 2000 to 2008 in five leading distance education journals was completed by Zawacki-Richter, Bäcker, and Vogt (2009). They found research was strongly dominated by instructional design issues and individual learning processes. Important topics, e.g., innovation and change management or intercultural distance learning phenomena, were dreadfully neglected. They noticed a significant trend towards collaborative studies and qualitative research.

Based on what has been done, and more importantly *not* done, Berge and Mrozowski (2001), Moore and Kearsley (2012), and Zawacki-Richter et al. (2009) advocated more research on policy and management, innovation and change, technology selection and adoption, and cost-benefit/value for investment. Zawacki-Richter et al. emphasized the need for studies on educational globalization and cross-cultural aspects of learning. To raise awareness about the importance of globalization, Moore (2011a) published two articles in the 25th anniversary issue of the *American Journal of Distance Education*. One article presented an American higher education perspective and the other a French viewpoint.

Moore (2011b) also has observed, referring to the United States, that we need research on continuing and professional development, since only a scant amount has been published, primarily about nursing, accounting, librarianship, and engineering. Continuing and professional education is addressed by Kuhne and Krauss (2007) and by Kuhne in this volume.

In 2009 Cavanaugh, Barbour, and Clark reviewed open access literature in K-12 online learning. They reported on a content analysis of the documents, past research topics and current trends, and recommended future research that establishes best practices for online teaching strategies, identifies strategies for ensuring learner success and/or adequate remediation, and encourages increased interaction between online and face-to-face students.

PROFESSIONAL DEVELOPMENT OF DISTANCE EDUCATORS

Before the 1960s, the private United States Hadley School for the Blind was one of the few correspondence institutions to provide its instructors in-service professional development. By the 1960s the previously mentioned pioneers were delivering professionalizing programs. Holmberg participated in creating training courses for the European Association of Distance Learning (EADL); Peters created "Weekly Information Sheets" for DIFF professors and also for *Funkkolleg,* a radio college; Wedemeyer organized faculty lectures on correspondence teaching and developed the first graduate seminars in independent study offered in the adult education program at the University of Wisconsin-Madison. Michael. G. Moore, Wedemeyer's research assistant, continued the seminars at Wisconsin from the mid-1970s to the mid-1980s. After moving to The Pennsylvania State University in 1986, he developed a three-course graduate program and certificate in distance education, still taught through the university's online World Campus. Moore's early experiments in the late 1980s used computer- and audio-conferencing technology to deliver his certificate program to students in Mexico, Finland, and Estonia as well as the United States.

Beginning in the 1960s, professionalizing courses were delivered face-to-face for third world countries by the German Foundation for International Development, Bonn; the International Extension College (IEC), London; the Swedish Authority for Work in Developing Countries (SIDA); the University of Wisconsin Extension Department; and the International Council for Correspondence Education (ICCE) (Black, 2007). Other entities also delivered professionalizing courses via correspondence and other technologies and media. Among them were Australia's South Australia College of Advanced Education, Canada's Open Learning Institute of British Columbia, West Germany's FernUniversität, Sweden's Hermods Correspondence School, the United

Kingdom's Open University, and in the United States, the University of Wisconsin and The Pennsylvania State University. Not only because of research and theorizing but also because of the professionalizing academic programs about study at a distance, by 1987 Holmberg was able to assert, "It is evident that a research discipline of distance education has emerged" (p. 20).

In 1993 The Bangkok Project, sponsored by the International Council for Distance Education (ICDE), successfully demonstrated online networking could provide cost-effective, yet meaningful, interactions among distance education professionals (Anderson & Mason, 1993, p. 15). By 1996, master's degrees in distance education existed in several countries around the world, including Australia, India, and the United Kingdom (Scriven, 1996). Today, highly regarded professional development programs include: Master's degrees in distance education at Athabasca University, Canada, and the University of Maryland University College (UMUC) in partnership with the University of Oldenburg, Germany; the Penn State graduate certificate in distance education delivered by Penn State's World Campus as part of the adult education master's program; certificate programs at the University of Wisconsin-Madison and the State University of West Georgia; courses with Indiana University's School of Continuing Studies; and programs with the UKOU. According to Fahlman (2009), the first North American doctoral program in distance education was launched at Athabasca University in 2008. A MarylandOnline inter-institutional project to train higher education adjunct faculty to teach online is reported by Shattuck, Dubins, and Zilberman (2011).

Two important international associations that support distance education professionalizing projects are the Commonwealth of Learning (COL) and the United Nations Educational, Scientific and Cultural Organization (UNESCO). COL is a resource for training in the policies, methodology, and practice of open, distance, and technology-mediated learning in developing countries. COL has established a network of Honorary Chairs in Open and Distance Learning, often in collaboration with UNESCO, which operates a Chairs Programme across a range of disciplines (refer to http://www.col.org/about/pages/unesco-colchairs.aspx). UNESCO has set policies regarding distance education for international development and has created some courses of its own. For example, UNESCO's Institute for Integrating Technology in Education (IITE) sponsored a course "Information and Communication Technologies in Distance Education" (http://unesdoc.unesco.org/images/0012/001293/129395e.pdf) to teach professionals in developing regions of the world. Recently, UNESCO published case studies in a report "ICT: Case Studies from Asia and the Pacific" (http://www.icde.org/filestore/Resources/Reports/ICTforHEUNESCO.pdf). A source of basic information on UNESCO and COL is Gutierrez (2010).

Professional Associations

To promote sound practices among correspondence and home study schools, two associations—the National University Extension Association (NUEA), which represented university correspondence *independent study* educators, and the National Home Study Council (NHSC), which represented for-profit correspondence *home study* schools, stand out as pioneering organizations. The NUEA held its first meeting in 1915 at the University of Wisconsin (Watkins, 1991, p. 17) and in 1924 codified its standards for correspondence study. The NUEA in 1980 became the National University Continuing Education Association (NUCEA). The NUCEA in 1996, to incorporate international educators, dropped the word national and became the University Continuing Education Association (UCEA). To reflect changes in member programs, the name was changed in 2010 to the University Professional and Continuing Education Association (UPCEA). UPCEA encourages good practice through its Distance Learning Community of Practice and quality awards.

The Correspondence Study Division (CSD), a powerful NUEA subgroup, established correspondence (i.e., independent study) as a distinct field of practice within university continuing education; created the first criteria for standard practice, published the predecessor of *Peterson's Guide* to identify reputable programs, and researched the effectiveness of the correspondence format (Pittman's interview with Powell, 1991). Nudged by Wedemeyer, the CSD in 1969 became the Independent Study Division (ISD), a title which emphasizes the learner rather than the educational delivery mechanism (Moore, 2007c, p. 90) and which reflects the many types of technologies being used in addition to print-based correspondence (Feasley & Bunker, 2007, p. 18). The title held until 1998, when NUEA abolished divisions (Pittman, 1998). CSD/ISD leaders included G. B. Childs, Nebraska; J. L. Davies, Iowa; B. Powell, Georgia; A. Rowbotham, California; and C. A. Wedemeyer, Wisconsin.

"With the help of a grant from the Carnegie Corporation and the National Better Business Bureau" (Ludlow's, 1987, interview with Lambert, p. 67), the NHSC (whose first director was Noffsinger) was a trade association formed in 1926 by some of the reputable proprietary for-profit schools (Pittman, 1990, p. 68). The NHSC aimed to set standards for home study, i.e., correspondence instruction delivered by private institutions. In 1959, the United Stated Office of Education recognized the NHSC as a national accrediting agency (Feasley, 2003, p. 39), and today the Council for Higher Education (CHEA) also recognizes the NHSC as an accrediting agency. To reflect the incorporation of newer technology, the NHSC in 1994 became the Distance Education and Training Council (DETC). Today, through its Accrediting Commission, it accredits the more than 60 main for-profit home study schools.

Two other more recently established professional associations that stand out as important are the American Association for Collegiate Independent Study (AACIS), which in 2010 became the Association for Distance Education and Independent Learning (ADEIL), and the United States Distance Learning Association (USDLA). Formed about 20 years ago, AACIS advances the interests of independent study professionals, focused on distance learning by individuals rather than distance learning in groups, and initially supported mainly continuing professional education. For a decade, AACIS (now ADEIL) has continued to perform and publish a yearly survey, a survey originally conducted by the UCEA, of independent study programs in the United States. Among other things, enrollment data is studied. The 2009 report of independent study programs (http://www.aacis.org/sites/default/files/research/AACIS%20Survey%20Report%202009.xls) showed a decline in the use of text-based correspondence teaching and a preference for online delivery. ADEIL annually evaluates, selects, and awards quality distance programs and courses. Created in 1987, the USDLA, which promotes professionalizing activities, currently encompasses international as well as national members and includes K–12 education, higher education, continuing education, corporate training, military and government training, home schooling, and telemedicine. The USDLA involves senators and representatives in its conferences and national policy forums and aims at including state and federal government participation in the association. Its annual awards have been reported in the journal *Distance Learning* (Anonymous, 2010) and are listed online at http://www.usdla.org/2010-award-winners/.

A relatively new professional association, established a decade ago, has the potential to be important in K-12 distance education. The International Association for K-12 Online Learning (iNACOL) "facilitates collaboration, advocacy, and research to enhance quality K-12 online teaching and learning" (http://www.inacol.org/about/index.php). The current president, Susan Patrick, formerly was the Director of the Office of Educational Technology at the U.S. Department of Education.

At an international level, in 1938 Canadian and U.S. visionaries created the International Council of Correspondence Education (ICCE). ICCE (now International Council for Open and Distance Learning ICDE) represents public and private schools, colleges/universities, adult and continuing educators, and university extension. ICCE provides a structure, forum, and network to facilitate information exchange and idea development; sponsors emerging regional conferences; provides non-formal professional development; and provides a vehicle for evaluating practice and systems. Decades ago, ICCE established a research committee and supports research and disseminates findings.

Referred to as the International Linking Organization by Feasley and Bunker (2007), ICCE has played a key role in the networking of distance educators around the world. According to Holmberg, Peters, and Moore (Black, 2004), from its inception, ICCE helped develop a community of scholars, "a family of experts," who emotionally and socially as well as intellectually supported one another. In fact ICCE, globally, ended the isolation imposed on correspondence study leaders by traditional face-to-face educators. Known for building an international network, Wedemeyer, ICCE president from 1969 to 1972, moved ICCE forward. He created the first ICCE newsletter, accomplished UNESCO recognition, generated the first computerized membership list, and initiated a modest research and training project.

Beginning in 1965 ICCE leadership and conference attendance shifted dramatically (Black, 2004, pp. 223–224; Bunker 2003) when representatives of European mega open universities began attending ICCE conferences. Evans and Nation (2003) deemed this the "distance education renaissance," where newcomers joined and worked beside early correspondence study pioneers. The open universities' diverse academic specialists, e.g., instructional designers, information technologists, and media experts, began to dominate. To reflect its changing membership, in 1982 ICCE dropped the term *correspondence* from its name and added *open* and *distance*, becoming the International Council for Open and Distance Education (usually referred to as ICDE). In 1988 ICDE established a permanent secretariat in Oslo, Norway, with a full-time paid Secretary General. ICDE has regional memberships and sponsors conferences around the world. An example of an ICDE member institution that recently launched an Open Educational Resource forum in the Asia region is Wawasan Open University, Malaysia, the youngest among Asia's 70 open universities (http://www.icde.org/Launch+of+OER+Asia.b7C_wJjUYk.ips). ICDE's 2011 awards for excellence can be found at http://www.icde.org/ICDE+Prize+of+Excellence+winners.b7C_wJjUXj.ips.

As distance education evolved, professional associations continued to emerge. A typical association is the Open and Distance Learning Association of Australia (ODLAA), which had been known as Australian and South Pacific External Studies Association (ASPESA) until 1993. Another is the Canadian Association of Distance Education (CADE); since 2005 CADE has been known as the Canadian Network for

Innovation in Education (CNIE). Some other important associations are the United Kingdom's Council of Educational Technology (CET); the European Council for Education by Correspondence (CEC) established in 1963; the European Home Study Council (EHSC) established in 1968; the European Association of Correspondence Schools (AECS), a merger in 1985 between two the CEC and the EHSC.

A sampling of relatively new associations includes the Asian Association of Open Universities (AAOU); the European Distance and eLearning Network (EDEN) and COL. EDEN appears "to have recognized the need for more and better research and scholarship in Europe and has taken on the challenge of stimulating and nurturing a scholarly as well as the practitioner's interest in distance education" (Moore, 2007a, p. 55). COL was established in 1988 to support distance education scholarship, research, and outreach/service for the group of nations known as the Commonwealth, including Australia, Canada, Great Britain, India, New Zealand, and Pakistan. COL, which frequently partners with UNESCO, is important for setting distance education research agendas for developing countries. COL and UNESCO have directed their attention to understanding the cultural differences and promoting cross-border collaboration in distance education (Gutierrez, 2010). For example during the 24th ICDE World Conference, October, 2011, the Open University of China and the University of Maryland University College, United States, signed a cooperation agreement (http://www.icde.org/Cooperation+agreement+between+ICDE+members+from+China+and+USA.b7C_wJjUZl.ips). UNESCO and COL have published a set of guidelines for the use of Open Educational Resources (OER) in higher education (http://www.icde.org/Guidelines+for+OER+in+Higher+Education+institutions.b7C_wJjU1I.ips).

For more on the histories of distance education associations, refer to Black (2004), Feasley and Bunker's (2007), and Chen (2009). For a list of open and distance learning professional associations, refer to COL's website (http://www.col.org/resources/otherResources/Pages/proAssn.aspx).

Lectures, Seminars, Symposia, Workshops, and Conferences

A marginalized group in higher education, correspondence educators depended on networking among themselves to enjoy mutual support. In 1891, the First National Extension Conference brought together educators interested in correspondence study (Watkins, 1991, p. 4). The CSD/NUEA activities of the 1950s and 1960s and the ICCE conferences of 1948 and 1953 lifted correspondence instruction's status within higher education, stimulated an international movement, and established some United States correspondence educators as international leaders.

With Wedemeyer and Childs as keynote speakers, the 1962 Conference on New Media, funded by the United States Department of Education (Erdos, 1992, pp. 68–72), brought together specialists in audio-visual media, programmed instruction, field service bureaus, motion picture, radio, and television production, and correspondence study. During the 1970s, specialists from other fields and from developing countries attended distance education conferences in larger numbers. In fact, authors from third-world countries submitted the majority of the papers considered for the 1979 UKOU's 10th anniversary conference (Neil, 1981). During the 1980s, European regional conferences were funded by various groups, e.g., the EHSC and the European Association of Distance Teaching Universities (EADTU), the European Union (EU), the United Kingdom's CET and the European CEC. In the United States, the University of Wisconsin-Extension, sponsored its First Annual Conference on Distance Teaching and Learning in 1985 with Michael G. Moore as keynote speaker. ICDE world conferences grew in size and frequency and remained important to the development of scholarship. Bunker (2003) and Feasley and Bunker (2007) describe ICDE conferences from, 1938 to 2001. The appendices of Moore and Kearsley (2012, pp. 293–304) identify current conferences.

Publications and Other Media

Among early publications that helped lay the foundation for study and scholarship are the newsletters of NUEA (NUEA, 1952, as cited in Wright, 1991, p. 42) and the *Home Study Review* by NHSC. Also important are Wedemeyer's 1963 film *The Postage Stamp Classroom*, a story about correspondence study; Wedemeyer's (1963, 1966) *Brandenburg Essays on Correspondence Instruction*; Wedemeyer's ICCE's newsletters, first published in 1971; and the CET's *Open Learning Guides* of the 1970s, created by the United Kingdom's National Extension College (NEC) (Lewis & Paine, 1985, p. vii).

Three bibliographies of significance are those by Childs (1960), Mathieson (1971), and Holmberg (1968, 1977). Two reports of historical value are Wedemeyer's (1968) reports on the University of South Africa and on the AIM Project (Wedemeyer & Najem, 1969). Important documents include the ICCE conference proceedings and occasional papers by Australia's Deakin University, the Netherlands' Open Universiteit, the *Broadsheets on Distance Learning* by the United Kingdom's International Extension College; and publications of Spain's Universidad Nacional de Education a Distancia (UNED). Prominent among American documents of historical importance are the American Center for Study of Distance Education (ACSDE)'s monographs, research reports, and books of readings.

Early journals published articles aimed at improving practice rather than scholarship. Examples include: the NHSC's *Home Study Review*; *Epistolodidaktika*, first published in Germany in 1963 and subsequently by the EHSC; and the UKOU's *Teaching at a Distance*, published beginning in 1975, renamed *Open Learning* in 1986, and today renamed *Open Learning: The Journal of Open, Distance, and e-Learning*.

During the 1980s, several new journals reported on research and theory rather than only on practice. Most important are *Distance Education*, started in 1980, by ASPESA and today the official journal of the ODLAA; the *Journal of Distance Education*, started in 1986 by CADE and currently published under its new name CNIE, and the *American Journal of Distance Education (AJDE)*, founded in 1987 by Michael G. Moore. The *AJDE* paved the way for greater external visibility and recognition of distance educators by the higher education community in the United States and abroad, and provided budding U.S. distance education scholars—often a marginalized group in higher education—a place to publish, "increasing the opportunity for the exchange of ideas and information" (Almeda's interview with Childs, 1988, p. 70).

Other important journals and publications originating in recent years include Athabasca University's *International Review of Research in Open and Distance Learning*, West Georgia University's *Online Journal of Distance Learning Administration*, the *Quarterly Review of Distance Education*, the *Turkish Online Journal of Distance Education*, and the Sloan Foundation's *Journal of Asynchronous Learning Networks (JALN)*. Moore and Kearsley (2012, pp. 296–298) provide a list of current journals and directories. Also, refer to Olgren's (2011) list of journals and periodicals found at http://depd.wisc.edu/html/mags3.htm.

Two of the first books about correspondence education, both published in 1926, are *The University Afield* by Hall-Quest and *Correspondence Schools, Lyceums, Chautauquas* by Noffsinger. Published in 1933, Bittner and Mallory's *University Teaching by Mail*, illuminates correspondence study's origins and its integration into American universities. Three decades later, several more books contributed to emerging scholarship in the United States (Pittman, 1990, pp. 69–71): *Correspondence Instruction in the United States* (MacKenzie et al., 1968); *New Perspectives in University Correspondence Study* (Wedemeyer & Childs, 1961); *The Changing World of Correspondence Study: International Readings* (MacKenzie & Christensen, 1971); and Wedemeyer's (1963, 1966) *The Brandenburg Memorial Essays.*

Catalyzed first by the emergence and proliferation of the open universities in the 1970s and 1980s, and then by the advent and increasing popularity of online delivery, the quantity of books about distance education has exploded. Among the most valuable books for studying scholarship are *Learning at the Back Door: Reflections on Nontraditional Learning in the Lifespan* (Wedemeyer, 1981) and *Distance Education: International Perspectives* (Sewart, Keegan, & Holmberg, 1983, 1988). Three other valuable books in the study of history are: *The Distance Teaching Universities* (Rumble & Harry, 1983); *The Ivory Towers Thrown Open* (Reddy, 1988); and *Distance Education in Canada* (Mugridge & Kaufman, 1986).

In the United States, Moore's (1990) anthology *Contemporary Issues in American Distance Education* reported on the state of scholarship and practice. Another anthology, Garrison and Shale's (1990) *Education at a Distance: From Issues to Practice*, includes a history by Moore's student Sherow co-authoring with Wedemeyer. Their chapter "Origins of Distance Education in the United States" includes a brief explanation of Wedemeyer's AIM system and its relationship to the UKOU and the influence of both AIM and the UKOU on distance education.

An outstanding book is *The Foundations of American Distance Education* (Watkins & Wright, 1991). According to historian Von Pittman (2003), the Watkins and Wright book "represents the single most important contribution to the history of collegiate correspondence study" (p. 23). Watkins and Wright's history begins in 1882 with the founding of the University of Chicago's correspondence study program and covers the next 100 years of achievements, ideas, issues, and research in collegiate distance education.

Renee Erdos, the first distance educator awarded a Fulbright Scholarship and President of ICCE in the late 1960s, studied the educational systems at 18 correspondence study institutions in Asia, Canada, Europe, and the United States. Erdos (1992) reports her impressions and findings in *Teaching Beyond the Campus.* A more recent, valuable book is Sarah Guri-Rosenblits' (1999) *Distance and Campus Universities.*

Peters' ideas became well-known to English-speaking scholars through Keegan's (1994) *Otto Peters on Distance Education: The Industrialization of Teaching and Learning* and eventually through Peters' own writing, e.g., *Learning and Teaching in Distance Education* (Peters, 2001), *Distance Education in Transition*, 4th edition (Peters, 2004), and Peters' (2007) chapter "The Most Industrialized Form of Education" in Moore's (2007b) *Handbook of Distance Education.*

A standard textbook in the United States is Moore and Kearsley's (1996, revised in 2005) *Distance Education: A Systems View.* The textbook, in addition to English, is available in Chinese, Korean, Portuguese and Japanese. Published again in 2012, the textbook is now titled *Distance Education: A Systems View of Online Learning*. Similar to Moore and Kearsley (2012), is the 2011 fifth edition of *Teaching and Learning at a Distance: Foundations of Distance Education* edited by Simonson, Smaldino, Albright, and Zvacek.

With their descriptions of research intended to stimulate and support better research and improved practice, the *Handbooks of Distance Education* (Moore, 2007b; Moore & Anderson, 2003) have become definitive scholarly reference books. Extolling the importance of the 2007 *Handbook*, Beaudoin (2010) refers to it as "a sort of *magnum opus* in the field" (p. 58) and points out the *Handbook* includes "a valuable global perspective" (p. 58). Edited by Martine Vidal, Monique Grandbastien, and Pierre Moeglin, a 2009 issue of a leading French journal *Distances et savoirs* published a synopsis of the 2007 *Handbook of Distance Education*. According to Moore (2009), *Distances et saviors* purposes were "to introduce our French colleagues to the American research literature" and "to prepare the ground for future exchanges of ideas and information between Anglophone and Francophone scholars and students in our field" (p. 536). Beginning with its 25th anniversary issue in 2011, Moore (2011a) in the *American Journal of Distance Education* reprinted the bibliographic essays—summaries of the various sections of the 2007 *Handbook of Distance Education* complemented by a contrasting French view.

Important but much neglected topics—distance education planning, costing, management, and decision making—were reported at an international level in the 2008 book *Economics of Distance and Online learning: Theory, Practice and Research* edited by Bramble and Panda. Because of increasing globalization and its multi-cultural impacts; also important, with its first section devoted to "Diversity in Distance Education," is the *International Handbook of Distance Education* (2008), edited by Evans, Haughey, and Murphy.

Within the past five years, many books of value to both scholars and practitioners have been published. One is the second edition of the *Encyclopedia of Distance Learning* edited by Rogers, Berg, Boettcher, Howard, Justice, and Schenk (2009). Its four volumes and more than 100 chapters written by international contributors from many countries cover distance learning issues, concepts, trends, and technologies. A second is *Contemporary Perspectives in E-Learning Research* edited by Conole and Oliver (2007). A third book, *Web 2.0-Based E-Learning: Applying Social Informatics for Tertiary Teaching* edited by Lee and McLoughlin (2010), presents strong research-based findings and thus contributes to our Web 2.0 e-learning knowledge base.

Michael Beaudoin (2010) identified five of the "significant contributions to the field" (p. 60) to end his five-year tenure as the *American Journal of Distance Education*'s book editor. Two of the five are especially important for historians. The first is Moore's (2007b) *Handbook of Distance Education*, which contains several chapters devoted to history. The second is Burge's (2007) *Flexible Higher Education: Reflections from Expert Experience*. Her book provides "insights, through reflection and commentary, on what has worked and why, based on the careers of these true believers and shapers of the field" (Beaudoin, 2010, p. 59).

Prominent editors such as Desmond Keegan, Fred Lockwood, Michael G. Moore, and Uli Bernath are important for creating whole series of publications on distance education that have promoted and advanced scholarship. Another prominent publisher is Tony Bates, who is the author of nine books and whose research groups at the UKOU, Open Learning Agency of British Columbia, and University of British Columbia, published "over 350 papers in the area of distance education and the use of technology for teaching" (Awalt, 2007, p. 105).

In the United States, under Moore's leadership the ACSDE published more than 20 monographs between 1987 and 1997 (e.g., Moore & Thompson, 1990, 1997; Munro, 1998; Wagner & Koble, 1998). The ACSDE also published historically important edited books such as Moore & Shin's (2000) collection of reprinted interviews (interviews first published in the *American Journal of Distance Education*) with distance education leaders of the 1980s and 1990s and a special original interview with pioneer Michael G. Moore (pp. 214–221). From 1987 to the present, the *American Journal of Distance Education* has published interviews referred to as "Speaking Personally" with pioneering leaders, e.g., Charles A. Wedemeyer, Michael P. Lambert, Gayle B. Childs, Betsy Powell, Tony Bates, and Börje Holmberg (to name a few). The interviewees have "lived" distance education's history; thus via first-person research data, the collection of interviews illuminates 25 years of distance education history.

One of the earliest comprehensive databases (published in German) of international distance training and education systems was created in the 1960s by Peters as part of his comparative research and theoretical work (Keegan, 1993, pp. 2–3). Another of the earliest, large, centralized databases—the International Center for Distance Learning (ICDL)—was established at the UKOU (Harry, 1986, 1992). One of the first online databases of information, ideas, and discussions, the DEOS-L listserv was developed at Moore's ACSDE in 1991, had 4,000 participants in 60 countries by 1996 and is still running.

Moore (1998) describes working with the World Bank in 1997 to create a database, Global Distance Education Network (GDENet or DistEdNet), designed to provide information about distance education to developing countries. The database, later administered by COL, consisted of a World Bank core site and regional global sites, e.g., the East Asia Global Distance Education Net (http://www.ouhk.edu.hk/cridal/gdenet/) designed and produced in collaboration with the Open University of Hong Kong's Centre for Research in Distance & Adult Learning. Today, another database of interest is UNESCO's Higher Education Open and Distance Learning Knowledge Base (http://portal.unesco.org/education/en/ev.php-URL_ID=22306&URL_DO=DO_TOPIC&URL_SECTION=201.html). Gutierrez (2010) describes the Global Learning Development Network created by the World Bank as an educational effort, which links resources and knowledge to reshape the future of distance education that will provide a way to achieve and sustain an equitable education for many who would not be able to otherwise achieve it.

Important doctoral dissertations of the 1960s to the 1970s include: *William Henry Lighty: Adult Education Pioneer* by Axford (1961), which according to Pittman (1990) "stands alone as a comprehensive account of the career of a seminal figure in collegiate correspondence study" (p. 72); *Die Didaktische Struktur des Fernunterrichts. Untersuchungen zu einer Industrialisierten Form des Lehrens und Lernens (The Didactic Structure of Distance Education: Inquiries into an Industrialized Form of Teaching and Learning)* by Peters (1973); *Investigation of the Interaction Between the Cognitive Style of Field Independence and Attitudes to Independent Study Among Adult Learners Who Use Correspondence Independent Study and Self-Directed Independent Study* by Moore (1976); and *College-Sponsored Correspondence Education in the United States: A Comparative History of Its Origins (1873–1915) and Its Recent Developments* by Gerrity

(1976), a dissertation that Pittman (1990) states, "is arguably the best single historical work on collegiate correspondence education" (p. 70).

From 1995 to 2006, the number of doctoral dissertations and master's papers about distance education exploded, comprising a valuable body of unpublished secondary literature (Pittman, 2003). According to Black (2007) April 5, 2006, search of UMI Dissertation Abstracts Online by keyword "correspondence study" produced only 40 citations, 20 which were dated from 1981 to 2001, and 20 from 1932 to 1976. On the same date, a search by keyword "distance education" produced 1,178 citations with 947 of the citations dated 1995–2006, and 231 dated 1981–1994. The earliest data-based publication under "distance education" was dated 1981. An analysis of North American theses and dissertation, 1998 to 2007, by Davies, Howell, and Petrie (2010) showed that the number of North American dissertations and theses has remained fairly stable. Whether quantity is exploding or leveling off, a past problem continues today, which is that much research is a-theoretical! The field needs more research that is theory-based, grounded in what we already know about education at a distance, and also is carried out by applying rigorous methodologies (Davies, Howell, & Petrie, 2010; Moore & Kearsley, 2012).

REFERENCES

Almeda, M. B. (1988). Interview: Speaking personally with Gayle B. Childs. *The American Journal of Distance Education, 2*(2), 68–74.

Anderson, T., & Mason, R. (1993). International computer conferencing for professional development: The Bangkok Project. *The American Journal of Distance Education, 7*(2), 5–18.

Anonymous. (2010). USDLA award winners. *Distance Learning, 7*(3).

Awalt, C. (2007). Interview: Speaking personally with Tony Bates. *American Journal of Distance Education, 21*(2), 105–109.

Axford, R. (1961). William Henry Lighty: Adult education pioneer (Doctoral dissertation). *Dissertation Abstracts International.* (ADD X1961, AAT T-07764)

Beaudoin, M. (2010). Book review: A retrospective of recent books. *American Journal of Distance Education, 24*(1), 57–61.

Berge, Z., & Mrozowski, S. (2001). Review of research in distance education. *American Journal of Distance Education, 15*(3), 5–19.

Bernath, U., & Vidal, M. (2007). The theories and the theorists: Why theory is important for research. *Distances et saviors, 5*(3), 427–458.

Bittner, W. S., & Mallory, H. F. (1933). *University teaching by mail: A survey of correspondence instruction conducted by American universities.* New York: Macmillan.

Black, L. M. (2004). *A living story of the origins and development of scholarship in the field of distance education* (Doctoral dissertation). Dissertation Abstracts International (DAI-A 65/12, p. 4496. AAT 3157520)

Black, L. M. (2007). A history of scholarship. In M. G. Moore (Ed.), *Handbook of distance education* (pp. 3–14). Mahwah, NJ: Erlbaum.

Bramble, W. J., & Panda, S. (Eds.). (2008). *Economics of distance and online learning: Theory, practice and research.* London: Routledge.

Bunker, E. L. (2003). The history of distance education through the eyes of the International Council for Distance Education. In M. G. Moore, & W. G. Anderson (Eds.), *Handbook of distance education* (pp. 49–66). Mahwah, NJ: Erlbaum.

Burge, E. (2007). *Flexible higher education: Reflections from expert experience (Society for Research into Higher Education).* Maidenhead, UK: Open University Press.

Cavanaugh, C. S., Barbour, M. K., & Clark, T. (2009). Research and practice in K-12 online learning: A review of open access literature. *International Review of Research in Open and Distance Learning, 10* (1). Retrieved Nov. 20, 2011, from http://www.irrodl.org/index.php/irrodl/article/view/607/1182

Chen, I. (2009). History of distance learning professional associations. In P. L. Rogers, G. A. Berg, J. V. Boettcher, C. Howard, L. Justice, & K. D. Schenk (Eds.), *Encyclopedia of distance learning – 4 volumes* (2nd ed., pp. 1079–1087). Hershey, PA: IGI Global.

Childs, G. B. (1949). Comparison of supervised correspondence study pupils and classroom pupils in achievement in school subjects (Doctoral dissertation). *Dissertation Abstracts International*, (ADD W1949)

Childs, G. B. (1960). *An annotated bibliography of correspondence study 1897–1960*. New York: National University Extension Association, Committee on Research, Correspondence Study Division.

Childs, G. B. (1966). Review of research in correspondence study. In C. A. Wedemeyer (Ed.), *The Brandenburg memorial essays on correspondence instruction – II* (pp. 126–141). Madison: The University of Wisconsin– University Extension.

Conole, G., & Oliver, M. (Eds.). (2007). *Contemporary perspectives in e-learning research*. New York: Routledge.

Davies, R. S., Howell, S. L., & Petrie, J. A. (2010). A review of trends in distance education scholarship at research universities in North America, 1998–2007. *International Review of Research in Open and Distance Learning, 11* (3). Retrieved November 2011 from http://www.irrodl.org/index.php/irrodl/article/view/876/1602

de Oliveira Neto, J. D., & dos Santos, E. M. (2010). Analysis of the methods and research topics in a sample of the Brazilian distance education publications, 1992 to 2007. *American Journal of Distance Education, 24*(3), 119–134.

Diehl, W. C. (2011). Diehl, W. C. (2011). *Learning at the back door: Charles Wedemeyer and the evolution of open and distance education* (Unpublished doctoral dissertation). The Pennsylvania State University, University Park.

Dubin, R., & Taveggia, T. C. (1968). *The teaching-learning paradox: A comparative analysis of college teaching methods*. Eugene, OR: Center for the Advanced Study of Educational Administration. ERIC Document ED 026 966.

Erdos, R. (1992). *Teaching beyond the campus*. Glebe, New South Wales, Australia: Fast Books, a Division of Wild and Woolley Pty. Ltd.

Evans, T., Haughey, M., & Murphy, D. (Eds.). (2008). *International handbook of distance education*. Bingley, UK: Emerald Publishing.

Evans, T., & Nation, D. (2003). Globalization and the reinvention of distance education. In M. G. Moore, & W. G. Anderson (Eds.), *Handbook of distance education* (pp. 777–792). Mahwah, NJ: Erlbaum.

Fahlman, D. (2009). The first doctoral program in distance education in North America. *International Review of Open and Distance Education, 10* (6). Retrieved November 20, 2011, at http://www.irrodl.org/index.php/ irrodl/article/view/711/1431

Feasley, C. (2003). Evolution of national and regional organization. In M. G. Moore, & W. G. Anderson (Eds.), *Handbook of distance education* (pp. 37–47). Mahwah, NJ: Erlbaum.

Feasley, C., & Bunker, E. L. (2007). A history of national and regional organizations and the ICDE. In M. G. Moore (Ed.), *Handbook of distance education* (pp. 15–29). Mahwah, NJ: Erlbaum.

Garrison, D. R., & Shale, D. (Eds.). (1990). *Education at a distance: From issues to practice*. Malabar, FL: Robert E. Krieger.

Gerrity, T. W. (1976). *College-sponsored correspondence education in the United States: A comparative history of its origins (1873-1915) and its recent developments (1960–1975)* (Doctoral dissertation). Dissertation Abstracts International (DAI-A 37/02, p. 4496. AAT 7617282)

Glatter, R., & Wedell, E. G. (1971). *Study by correspondence*. London: Longman Group.

Guri-Rosenblits, S. (1999). *Distance and campus universities*. Oxford, UK: Pergamon.

Gutierrez, I. P. (2010). Global Perspectives in open and distance learning and open learning resources [online publication]. *Distance Learning, 7*(1).

Hall-Quest, A. L. (1926). *The university afield*. New York: Macmillan.

Harry, K. (1986). The International Center for Distance Learning of the United Nations University: Resources and services. *Journal of Distance Education, 1*(1), 77–79.

Harry, K. (1992). The development of information and documentation work in distance education. In G. E. Ortner, K. Graff, & H. Wilmersdoerfer (Eds.), *Distance education as two-way communication: Essays in Honour of Börje Holmberg* (pp. 210–224). Frankfurt, Germany: Peter Lang.

Holmberg, B. (1960). *On the methods of teaching by correspondence*. Lund, Sweden: Lunds Universitets Arsskrift.

Holmberg, B. (1968). *Studies in education by correspondence: A bibliography*. Malmö: Sweden: European Council for Education by Correspondence (CEC).

Holmberg, B. (1977). *Distance education: A survey and bibliography*. London: Kogan Page; New York: Nichols.

Holmberg, B. (1987). The development of distance education research. *American Journal of Distance Education, 1*(3), 16–23.

Keegan, D. (Ed.). (1993). *Theoretical principles of distance education*. London: Routledge.

Keegan, D. (Ed.). (1994). *Otto Peters on distance education: The industrialization of teaching and learning*. London: Routledge.

Kuhne, G. W., & Krauss, G. E. (2007). Continuing professional education. In M. G. Moore (Ed.), *Handbook of distance education* (pp. 531–542). Mahwah, NJ: Erlbaum.

Larsson, H. (1992). Living eulogy—Börje Holmberg: Scholar, teacher, and gentleman. In G. E. Ortner, K. Graff, & H. Wilmersdoerfer (Eds.), *Distance education as two-way communication: Essays in honour of Börje Holmberg* (pp. viii–xi). Frankfurt, Germany: Peter Lang.

Lee, M. J. W., & McLoughlin, C. (2010). *Web 2.0-Based e-Learning: Applying social informatics for tertiary teaching.* Hershey, PA: Information Science Reference.

Lewis, R., & Paine, N. (1985). *Open learning guide 6: How to communicate with the learner.* London: Council for Educational Technology.

Ludlow, J. (1987). Interview: Speaking personally with Michael P. Lambert. *The American Journal of Distance Education, 1*(2), 67–71.

MacKenzie, O., & Christensen, E. L. (Eds.). (1971). *The changing world of correspondence study: International readings.* University Park: Pennsylvania State University Press.

MacKenzie, O, Christensen, E. L., & Rigby, P. H. (1968). *Correspondence instruction in the United States: A study of what it is, how it functions, and what its potential may be.* New York: McGraw-Hill .

Mathieson, D. E. (1971). *Correspondence study: A summary review of the research and development literature.* New York: National Home Study Council/ERIC Clearinghouse on Adult Education.

McIntosh, N., Calder, J., & Swift, B. (1976). *A degree of difference. A study of the first year's intake to the Open University of the U.K.* Gulidford, UK: Society for Research in Higher Education.

Moore, M. G. (1972). Learner autonomy: The second dimension of independent learning. *Convergence, 5*(2), 76–88.

Moore, M. G. (1976). *Investigation of the interaction between the cognitive style of field independence and attitudes to independent study among adult learners who use correspondence independent study and self-directed independent study.* (Doctoral dissertation). Dissertation Abstracts International (DAI-A 37/06, p. 3344. AAT 7620127).

Moore, M. G. (1987a). Editorial: Words of welcome and intent. *The American Journal of Distance Education, 1*(1), 1–5.

Moore, M. G. (1987b). Interview: Speaking personally with Charles A. Wedemeyer. *The American Journal of Distance Education, 1*(1), 59–64.

Moore, M. G. (Ed.). (1990). *Contemporary issues in American distance education.* New York: Pergamon Press.

Moore, M. G. (1998). Editorial: The Global Distance Education Network. *American Journal of Distance Education, 12*(3), 1–3.

Moore, M. G. (2007a). Editorial: Meeting the theorists in Europe. *American Journal of Distance Education, 21*(2), 55–59.

Moore, M. G. (Ed.). (2007b). *Handbook of distance education* (2nd ed.). Mahwah, NJ: Erlbaum.

Moore, M. G. (2007c). The theory of transactional distance. In M. G. Moore (Ed.), *Handbook of distance education* (pp. 89–105). Mahwah, NJ: Erlbaum.

Moore, M. G. (2009). Foreword. *Distances et saviors, 7*(1), 533–536.

Moore, M. G. (2011a). Editorial: Our twenty-fifth anniversary. *American Journal of Distance Education, 25*(1), 1–4.

Moore, M. G. (2011b). Editorial: Corporate and professional continuing education. *American Journal of Distance Education, 25*(3), 133–134.

Moore, M. G. (Ed.). (2012). *Handbook of distance education* (3rd ed). Mahwah, NJ: Erlbaum.

Moore, M. G., & Anderson, W. G. (Eds.). (2003). *Handbook of distance education.* Mahwah, NJ: Erlbaum.

Moore, M. G., & Kearsley, G. (1996). *Distance education: A systems view.* Belmont, CA: Wadsworth.

Moore, M. G., & Kearsley, G. (2005). *Distance education: A systems view* (2nd ed.). Belmont, CA: Wadsworth.

Moore, M. G., & Kearsley, G. (2012). *Distance education: A systems view of online learning* (3rd ed.), Belmont, CA: Wadsworth-Cengage Learning.

Moore, M. G., & Shin, N. (Eds.). (2000). Speaking personally about distance education: Foundations of contemporary practice. *Readings in Distance Education No. 6 of the American Center for the Study of Distance Education (ACSDE).* University Park: The Pennsylvania State University, ACSDE.

Moore, M. G., & Thompson, M. M. (1990). The effects of distance learning: A summary of literature. *Monograph No. 2 of the American Center for the Study of Distance Education (ACSDE).* University Park: The Pennsylvania State University, ACSDE.

Moore, M. G., & Thompson, M. M. (1997). The effects of distance learning. *Monograph No. 15 of the American Center for the Study of Distance Education (ACSDE).* University Park: The Pennsylvania State University, ACSDE.

Mugridge, I., & Kaufman, D. (Eds.). (1986). *Distance education in Canada.* London: Croom Helm.

Munro, J. S. (1998). Presence at a distance: The educator-learner relationship in distance learning. *Monograph No. 16 of the American Center for the Study of Distance Education (ACSDE).* University Park: The Pennsylvania State University, ACSDE.

Neil, M. W. (1981). *Education of adults at a distance: A report of the Open University's Tenth Anniversary Conference.* London: Kogan Page in association with the Open University Press.

Noffsinger, J. S. (1926). *Correspondence schools, lyceums, chautauquas.* New York: The Macmillan Company.

Olgren, C. H. (2011). Journal and magazines. University of Wisconsin-Madison: Distance Education Certificate Program. Retrieved November 22, 2011, from http://depd.wisc.edu/html/mags3.htm

Paulsen, M. F., & Pinder, P. W. (1990). Workshop report: Research in distance education: Setting a global agenda for the nineties. *The American Journal of Distance Education, 4*(3), 83–84.

Peters, O. (1967). *Das Fernstudium an Universitaten und Hochschulen: didaktische Struktur und vergleichende Interpretation: Ein Beitrag zur Theorie der Fernlehre* [Distance education at universities and higher education institutions: Didactical structure and comparative analysis—A contribution to the theory of distance education]. Weinheim, Germany: Beltz.

Peters, O. (1973). *Die didaktische struktur des Fernunterrichts. Untersuchungen zu einer industrialisierten form des lehrens und lernens* [The educational principles of distance education: Research into an industrialized form of teaching and learning]. Weinheim, Germany: Beltz.

Peters, O. (2001). *Learning and teaching in distance education: Analysis and interpretations from an international perspective* (rev. ed.). London: Kogan Page. (First published in German as Didaktik des fernstudiums by Luchterhand Verlag, 1997)

Peters, O. (2004). *Distance education in transition: New trends and challenges* (4th ed.). Oldenburg, Germany: Bibliotheks – und Informationssystem der Universitat Oldenburg.

Peters, O. (2007). The most industrialized form of education. In M. G. Moore (Ed.), *Handbook of distance education* (pp. 57–68). Mahwah, NJ: Erlbaum.

Pittman, V. (1990). Correspondence study in the American university: A historiographic perspective. In Michael G. Moore (Ed.), *Contemporary issues in American education* (pp. 67–80). New York: Pergamon Press.

Pittman, V. (1991). Interview: Speaking personally with Betsy Powell. *The American Journal of Distance Education, 5*(1), 67–71.

Pittman, V. (1998). Low-key leadership: Collegiate correspondence study and "campus equivalence". *American Journal of Distance Education, 12*(2), 36–45.

Pittman, V. (2003). Correspondence study in the American university: A second historiographic perspective. In M. G. Moore & W. Anderson (Eds.), *Handbook of distance education* (pp. 21–35). Mahwah, NJ: Erlbaum.

Reddy, G. R. (1988). *The ivory towers thrown open.* India: Stosius Inc., Advent Books Division.

Rogers, P. L., Berg, G. A., Boettcher, J. V., Howard, C., Justice, L, & Schenk, K. (Eds.). (2009). *Encyclopedia of distance learning – 4 volumes* (2nd ed.). Hershey, PA: IGI Global.

Rumble, G., & Harry, K. (1983). *The distance teaching universities.* London: PalgraveMacmillan.

Russell, T. (1999). *The no significant difference phenomenon: A comparative research annotated bibliography on technology for distance education.* Retrieved from http://www.nosignificantdifference.org

Scriven, B. (1996). Book review. *Distance Education, 17*(2), 412–413.

Sewart, D., Keegan, D., & Holmberg, B. (Eds.). (1983). *Distance education: International perspectives.* London: Croom Helm.

Sewart, D., Keegan, D., & Holmberg, B. (Eds.). (1988). *Distance education: International perspective* (rev. ed.). New York: Routledge.

Shattuck, J., Dubins, B., & Zilberman, D. (2011). Maryland Online's inter-institutional project to train higher education faculty to teach online. *International Review of Research in Open and Distance Learning, 1* (2). Retrieved November 20, 2011, from http://www.irrodl.org/index.php/irrodl/article/view/933/1669

Sherow, S., & Wedemeyer, C. A. (1990). Origins of distance education in the United States. In D. R. Garrison, & D. Shale (Eds.), *Education at a distance: From issues to practice* (pp. 7–22), Malabar, FL: Robert E. Krieger.

Simonson, M., Smaldino, S. F., Albright, M., & Zvacek, S. (Eds.). (2011). *Teaching and learning at a distance: Foundations of distance education* (5th ed.). Boston: Allyn and Bacon.

Vidal, M., Grandbastien, M., & Moeglin, P. (Eds.). (2009). A la croisee des recherches/autour du Handbook of Distance Education. *Distances et saviors, 7*(4), 529–735.

Wagner, E. D., & Koble, M. A. (1998). Distance Education Symposium 3: Course design. *Monograph No. 14 of the American Center for the Study of Distance Education (ACSDE).* University Park: The Pennsylvania State University, ACSDE.

Watkins, B. L. (1991). A quite radical idea: The invention and elaboration of collegiate correspondence study. In B. L. Watkins, & S. J. Wright (Eds.), *The foundations of American distance education: A century of collegiate correspondence study* (pp. 1–35). Dubuque, IA: Kendall-Hunt.

Watkins, B. L., & Wright, S. J. (Eds.). (1991). *The foundations of American distance education: A century of collegiate correspondence study.* Dubuque, IA: Kendall-Hunt.

Wedemeyer, C. A. (1963). *The Brandenburg memorial essays on correspondence instruction – I*. Madison: The University of Wisconsin–University Extension.

Wedemeyer, C. A. (1966). *The Brandenburg memorial essays on correspondence instruction – II*. Madison: The University of Wisconsin–University Extension.

Wedemeyer, C. A. (1968), No. 302763, Assessment Report of February, 1968. *University of South Africa (UNISA): Report and recommendations*. Pretoria, South Africa: UNISA..

Wedemeyer, C. A. (1971). Independent study. In L. C. Deighton (Ed.), *The encyclopedia of education, vol. 4* (pp. 548–557). New York: Free Press.

Wedemeyer, C. A. (1981). *Learning at the back door: Reflections on non-traditional learning in the lifespan*. Madison: The University of Wisconsin Press.

Wedemeyer, C. A., & Childs, G. B. (1961). *New perspectives in university correspondence study*. Chicago: The Center for the Study of Liberal Education for Adults.

Wedemeyer, C. A., & Najem, R. E. (1969, August). *AIM—From concept to reality: The Articulated Instructional Media Program at Wisconsin*. Syracuse, NY: Syracuse University: Publications in Continuing Education.

Wright, S. J. (1991). Opportunity lost, opportunity regained. In B. L. Watkins & S. J. Wright (Eds.), *The foundations of American distance education: A century of collegiate correspondence study* (pp. 37–66). Dubuque, IA: Kendall-Hunt.

Zawacki-Richter, O. (2009). Research areas in distance education: A Delphi study. *International Review of Research in Open and Distance Learning, 10* (3). Retrieved November 20, 2011, from http://www.irrodl.org/index.php/irrodl/article/view/674/1260

Zawacki-Richter, O., Bäcker, E. M., & Vogt, S. (2009). Review of distance education research (2000 to 2008): Analysis of research areas, methods, and authorship patterns. *International Review of Research in Open and Distance Learning, 10* (6). Retrieved on November 20, 2011, from http://www.irrodl.org/index.php/irrodl/article/view/741/1433

2

UNIVERSITY CORRESPONDENCE STUDY
A Revised Historiographic Perspective

VON V. PITTMAN

For several generations, correspondence study stood alone as a medium of distance teaching and learning in postsecondary institutions in the United States. It provided not only an impetus for electronically assisted distance education formats, but an initial administrative home for many of them. Also, in many universities, correspondence study programs provided the funds and expertise that facilitated the pursuit of innovative—but sometimes foolish or ill-conceived—telecommunications schemes.

In spite of correspondence study's long and contentious presence in the American university, historians of higher education, scholars whose task it is to analyze and illuminate, have to this point given little attention to it, even though hundreds of thousands of college students have used one or more correspondence courses to further their progress toward graduation. This lack of interest is regrettable.

In 1990, an anthology edited by Michael Moore, entitled *Contemporary Issues in American Distance Education*, surveyed the state of scholarship and practice in distance education. It included my essay on the historiography of correspondence study (Pittman, 1990). In it, I pointed to the lack of reflective historical treatments of collegiate-level correspondence courses, enumerated extant secondary works, and pointed to some obvious gaps.

In a second bibliographic essay, published in the 2003 first edition of this *Handbook of Distance Education*, edited by Michael Moore and William Anderson, I went beyond published secondary works to point out dissertations, master's theses, "fugitive" (uncataloged) literature, and oral history projects (Pittman, 2003). These works and collections offer scholars of correspondence study valuable evidence and arguments.

This chapter will update my previous anthology chapters. It will note recent contributions to the scholarly literature on postsecondary correspondence study that have appeared since the *Handbook's* first edition. It will also raise the issue of university operated high school correspondence study programs, note the paucity of extant research on them, and suggest sources for further research.

RECENT DEVELOPMENTS IN THE HISTORIOGRAPHY OF CORRESPONDENCE STUDY

Social and Intellectual Context

The historiography of correspondence study continues to lack systematic analysis. Such works as Bittner and Mallory's *University Teaching by Mail* (1933) and Wedemeyer and Childs's *New Perspectives in University Correspondence Study* (1961) remain among arguably the best books ever written on the subject. For all their merit, however, they are descriptive rather than reflective. While invaluable to the historian as resources, they are not works of history. They are snapshots of the practice of collegiate correspondence study with some narrative background, and offer little in the way of analysis. And, they are *old*. No book-length interpretive history of the field has yet been written. However, scholars have begun to take a more serious look at correspondence/independent study.[1]

The best interpretation of independent study's place in American higher education is contained in Joseph Kett's *The Pursuit of Knowledge Under Difficulties: From Self-Improvement to Adult Education in America, 1750–1990*, which appeared in 1994. Kett took his title from an 1830 book by George L. Craik. First published in Britain, Craik's collection of inspirational biographical sketches of worthy and persevering autodidacts became extremely popular in the United States, complementing the widespread belief in self-help, as well as the ideology of Jacksonian democracy. Kett's book, a social and intellectual history of adult and continuing education in the United States, places university extension and continuing education programs—including correspondence study—squarely in this tradition of voluntary self-improvement. Universities became one of many providers of education intended to promote self-improvement, along with proprietary correspondence schools, community evening classes, lyceums, traveling chautauquas, and other providers.

Kett (1994) describes how extension programs, including correspondence courses, developed in universities—mainly public—while never really becoming part of their missions (in spite of frequent statements to the contrary). It was a poor fit, he maintains. Many other extension programs, and most correspondence study departments, became self-supporting small businesses operating within tax-supported public institutions. Kett explores the association of correspondence courses with an alleged lowering of standards that caused professional academics to regard them skeptically. Yet, by 1960, university adult education programs came to hold "a secure but marginal niche in American education" (p. xviii). While it deals with much more than independent study, *The Pursuit of Knowledge Under Difficulties* is essential to any serious study of this form of instruction.

The publisher's blurb on the back cover of Kett's (1994) book proclaims it the "first history of nontraditional education in America." This is not precisely the case. Charles A. Wedemeyer's *Learning at the Back Door: Reflections on Non-traditional Learning in the Lifespan* (1981) has a better claim to that distinction. Like Kett, Wedemeyer stresses the voluntary nature of nontraditional education and places correspondence study and other forms of distance education in the context of a larger self-improvement movement. Whereas Kett takes the position that the institutions of higher education absorbed and accommodated some of the adult education programs and methods, however grudgingly, Wedemeyer sees nontraditional education as a revolt against the elitism of the established education system. Neither Wedemeyer nor Kett deals extensively with correspondence education, but both books provide valuable historical and intellectual context.

History by Anthology

Since the publication of *Contemporary Issues in American Distance Education* (1990), a number of anthologies on the general subject of distance education have appeared. A fair number have included one or more chapters with an historical orientation.

In terms of the early history of distance education, the most important of these books is *The Foundations of American Distance Education: A Century of Collegiate Correspondence Study*, edited by Barbara Watkins and Steve Wright (1991). The Independent Study Division (ISD) of the National University Continuing Education Association (NUCEA) produced this anthology to celebrate the first 100 years of collegiate distance education (dated from the founding of the University of Chicago and its correspondence program in 1892).[2] It arguably represents the single most important contribution to the history of collegiate correspondence/independent study.

The first two chapters, one each by editors Watkins and Wright, survey correspondence study's history within the American university. Chapters on two specialized areas of collegiate programming—high school (Young & McMahon, 1991) and courses offered without college credit (Rose, 1991)—follow. Another examines the unending controversy over the academic quality of correspondence study within a university setting (Pittman, 1991). Van Kekerix and Andrews (1991) contribute a particularly useful piece on early attempts by university independent study departments to incorporate electronic technology within their instructional formats.

Other anthologies have included chapters on the history of correspondence study, either as background for discussions of more modern programs and events, or as token representations of one of the smaller areas of scholarship within the larger field of distance education. Rothe's chapter in *Distance Education in Canada* (Mugridge & Kaufman, 1986), published prior to *CIADE*, is an example of the former type of writing. Rothe notes the earliest Canadian correspondence programs, describes the development of institutions based in whole or in large part on distance education, and ends with a discussion of early electronic formats. A chapter entitled "Origins of Distance Education in the United States," by Sherow and Wedemeyer, serves the same purpose in *Education at a Distance: From Issues to Practice*, edited by Garrison and Shale (1990). This piece is almost certainly the last signed work of Charles Wedemeyer's distinguished career.

"Harper's Headaches" (Pittman, 1995) focuses on administrative and policy issues within in a more general research monograph (Duning & Pittman, 1995). The author compares—and points to parallels—between today's administrative problems and those faced by the University of Chicago's founding president, William Rainey Harper, who is generally regarded as the founder of collegiate correspondence study.

Institutional Histories

Institutional histories of major American universities rarely mention correspondence or independent study. Only the excellent—but dated—history of the University of Wisconsin (Curti & Carstensen, 1949) gives it substantive treatment. Histories of extension and continuing education divisions—often written and published in-house—frequently are useful, but they, too, tend to be quite old and limited in scope. On the other hand, scholars researching the history of correspondence education will find several books on other postsecondary institutions quite helpful.

Gene Getz's *MBI: The Story of Moody Bible Institute* (1986) recounts the history of an institution that is, among other things, a two-year college. Moody initiated its correspondence program in 1901, placing it among the pioneers of this teaching method. Moody then built a program with huge enrollments and developed a worldwide reach.

Regents College: The Early Years (Nolan, 1998) is the story of an innovative external degree institution. Renamed Excelsior College, Regents College of the University of the State of New York (not the same thing as the State University of New York, confusingly enough) grew out of the practice of granting college credit by examination. In 1972, it began awarding external degrees, the first to be granted in the United States since the 19th century. Correspondence courses were one of several teaching-learning formats regents students could use to acquire credit hours. For many years, it offered no distance education courses of its own. Regents students enrolled in other independent study courses in such great numbers as to have an impact on virtually every university program in the United States. Because it is so unconventional, Regents/Excelsior's story is as confusing as it is interesting. Donald Nolan, who served as a member of its founding board of directors, recounts it deftly.

The Province of Alberta founded Athabasca University in 1970. Originally intended to be a conventional institution, Athabasca later developed along lines influenced by the British Open University. It began using teams of content specialists, instructional designers, and editors to develop "home study" courses in 1975. It is now a mature and innovative university, committed entirely to distance education. T. C. Byrne's *Athabasca University: The Evolution of Distance Education* (1989) offers a comprehensive history.

New Critics

Books by Thorstein Veblen (1918) and Abraham Flexner (1930) presented the major early critiques of correspondence/independent study from within academia. While dismissive and scornful remarks have always been common on campus, thoughtful, detailed criticism has been rare. But this is not necessarily good news. It could be argued that despite evidence to the contrary, a preponderance of academics consider independent study inferior by definition, not worthy of research. However, a few thoughtful critics have weighed in. Some have not been opponents of distance education, but rather proponents of other formats.

Reflecting on major university independent study divisions, Duning (1987) worries not so much about the format itself as about the state of its leadership. The prevailing generation of independent study directors at the time failed to appreciate the potential of electronically enhanced formats, she argues. By not embracing electronic delivery enthusiastically, independent study directors risked becoming irrelevant to the future of distance education.

In an unpublished, but widely disseminated paper, Carla Montgomery, associate dean of the Graduate College at Northern Illinois University, uses negative assumptions about correspondence study to damn electronic formats. After all, they might be "the electronic equivalent of the correspondence-course-by-mail" (1993, p. 2). Thus, she says, graduate schools simply refuse to accept them as transfer credit, due to unspecified "questions" about academic integrity and quality.

By far the most flamboyant academic critic of distance education in the past decade was David Noble, a history professor at Toronto's York University. Noble is particularly critical of online education, which he warns is corrupting the faculty-centered model of university governance and control of curriculum (Noble, 2001).

Professor Noble's essentially Marxist critique, rails against an unholy alliance of "dot.com" companies and university administrations combining forces to teach more students at a lower cost, thus oppressing the faculty by eliminating positions and constraining their autonomy (Noble, 2001). Indeed, his criticism is reminiscent of Veblen's (1918), who—though not a Marxist—railed against William Rainey Harper and other university presidents who he sarcastically called "captains of erudition" for their proclivity for fund-raising among captains of industry.

Noble damns university-level correspondence study's history and origins and describes its work as essentially equivalent to the crasser commercial schools. Their purpose was simply to raise cash, he contends. He notes that University of Wisconsin president Charles Van Hise and Louis Reber, among the founding fathers of the university extension movement, were educated as engineers, and were thus committed to meeting the training needs of American commerce and industry, rather than the liberal arts (Noble, 2001). Noble wrote his piece as a cautionary tale, preceding it with one hackneyed warning about the lessons of the past from Santayana and ending it with Marx's equally trite quotation on the same subject. He contends that the lessons of correspondence study's history provide an ominous warning of the consequences of online education.

Professor Jack Simmons, of Savannah State University, echoes Noble, characterizing distance education as "a means by which universities may reduce their costs while increasing their enrollments" (2000, p. 4). Ironically, Simmons disseminates his message on the Internet. He says that the standardization involved in asynchronous learning presents a significant threat to academic freedom. However, Simmons's argument also exhibits a strong concern about how changing modes of teaching could affect the teaching roles of professors. Thus, his apprehension of an altered faculty lifestyle rivals his loftier appeal to academic freedom.

Vanishing Resources

The original records and in-house publications of university correspondence programs are disappearing rapidly. This problem is not new, of course. Charles Wedemeyer, who had an acute appreciation of the need to preserve the history of independent study, told a colleague about a collection he had developed in the Extension Library at the University of Wisconsin:

> I requested all NUEA institutions to send three representative correspondence courses to our library of materials on correspondence study, along with any materials developed by each institution on course development, teaching, revision, production, and other aspects of the field. (Letter to B. Holmberg, June 25, 1984)

Wedemeyer said that the University of Wisconsin gave him no resources for extending this collection, and that its development ceased with his retirement in 1976. In the early 1990s, the University of Wisconsin-Extension closed its library. Some of its materials were transferred to the university's archives, but many items, particularly those gathered from other institutions, were discarded.

Among the materials held by the Wisconsin-Extension library were products of the day-to-day operations of individual independent study departments. Others originated with professional associations. Items such as course writers' guides, statistical compilations, directors' handbooks, and the like formed a minor—but important—body of unpublished, uncataloged writings, often called "fugitive literature." Recent trends in the reorganization or elimination of independent study, other forms of distance education, and continuing education divisions in general have accelerated the loss of these resources. Many of the offices that once housed such artifacts have been merged with larger departments or dispersed, and their staffs reassigned.

Oral History Collections

Two oral history collections offer useful accounts taken from correspondence program directors, editors, association members, and others. The NUCEA's Independent Study Division (ISD) collected the structured reminiscences of 27 persons active in the field, mainly in the 1950s, 1960s, and 1970s. Gayle Childs, the retired director of the University of Nebraska's program and a preeminent figure in the field, began work on a monograph based on the typescripts of these oral histories. However, ill health ended this effort; Dr. Childs died in 1997.

This project essentially ended due to yet another reorganization and renaming of the NUCEA, now the UCEA (University Continuing Education Association). The organization terminated the Independent Study Division. No oral histories have been added to the Penn State Libraries collection since that time. However, the documents that were collected represent a rich source of data for scholars. In addition, Loyola University (Chicago) independently collected the oral history of its long-time director, Mary Lou McPartland, who served during the same time as the NUEA interviewees.

At about the time the NUCEA/ISD project ceased collections, a new organization, the American Association for Collegiate Independent Study (AACIS—later changed to ADEIL, Association for Distance and Independent Learning) began an ongoing oral history project. AACIS collected interviews of its founding generation and each outgoing president. Typescripts of these interviews are held in the Special Collections Room of the Ohio University Library, in Athens, Ohio.

Fortunately, the *American Journal of Distance Education* (*AJDE*) provides another source of first-person data. Since 1987, it has recorded the experiences, perspectives, and insights of working professionals in distance education through its "Speaking Personally" interviews. The American Center for the Study of Distance Education, headquartered at Penn State, issued a collection of all those published from 1987 through 1999 (Moore & Shin, 2000). Anyone interested specifically in independent study will find the interviews with Charles Wedemeyer, Gayle Childs, Michael Lambert, and Betsy Powell particularly interesting and informative. Scholars and professionals in all areas of distance education owe *AJDE* thanks for collecting and publishing these pieces.

The NUCEA/ISD partnered with the Penn State Libraries to establish an archival collection. The parties signed a contract for the deposit of materials shortly thereafter. In the years immediately following, many university independent study offices sent large collections of records, handbooks, study guides, annual reports, and other artifacts to Penn State. The shelf list quickly grew to more than sixty pages. The collection is an invaluable resource. However, this project has languished. Nothing has been deposited in this collection in at least a decade. Indeed, since one of the parties to the contract no longer exists, further development seems unlikely.

AACIS arranged for the deposit of its papers with the Ohio University Library. However, it is extremely unlikely that this collection will ever rival the ISD archives in breadth. Unlike UCEA, AACIS has no institutional members. Its members join as individuals, not as representatives of colleges or departments. Therefore, they do not control the documentary records of their offices to the extent that the ISD membership once did.

Refereed Journals: An Embarrassing Absence

The most remarkable—and disappointing—facet of the historiography of collegiate correspondence/independent study is its absence from scholarly, peer-reviewed education and history of education journals. Few articles have been published in refereed journals. And such publications are the coin of the academic realm, the most important factor in promotion and tenure, at least at the university level. The content of its scholarly journals, it can be argued, reveals higher education's areas of greater and less research interest.

Since the 2003 publication of the first edition of the *Distance Education Handbook*, only a handful of articles have appeared in refereed higher education journals. Robert Hampel (2001) compared the business models of the Columbia University and University of Wisconsin correspondence programs with those of the proprietary schools in the prestigious *Teachers College Record*. Burton (2010) and Pittman (2009) published biographical articles on Charles Wedemeyer and Helen Williams, respectively, in *Vitae Scholasticae*, the journal of the International Society for Educational Biography. Pittman also published another biographical article on Helen Williams (2006) and one on the decline and abolition of the University of Chicago's correspondence program (2008) in *The American Educational History Journal*.

Given the length of correspondence/independent study's history in the American university, its identification with the ideological commitment to democratic access to higher education, and its status as the initial format of distance education, the paucity of publications on the subject in the refereed education journals can only be called embarrassing. However, the small number of active researchers in the field provides opportunities for younger scholars, or even older ones who might be looking for a change of areas. There are few competitors.

UNDERUSED AND UNDERAPPRECIATED: UNPUBLISHED AND OBSCURE SOURCES

The Dissertation Literature

The small number of peer-reviewed articles on the history of postsecondary correspondence study does not mean that there has been no significant research from primary sources. A sizeable number of dissertations make up a valuable body of unpublished secondary literature. Indeed, Thomas Gerrity's Teachers College (Columbia University) dissertation, *College-sponsored distance education in the United States* (1976) remains one of the best historical works on collegiate correspondence education. It is one of a handful of dissertations that should have been published in whole, as a book, or in parts, as refereed articles. For some reason—probably several reasons—the authors apparently did not follow up after they received their degrees.

Dissertations give us the best picture of three early correspondence programs. Illinois Wesleyan University offered courses and degrees—from the bachelor's to the Ph.D.—on an *in absentia* (non-resident) basis using correspondence study, well before the University of Chicago's program opened in 1892. Henry Allen did a masterful job telling this story in his 1984 thesis, written for his doctorate from the University of Chicago. Richard Bonnell's dissertation, *The Chautauqua university* (1988), is the only secondary work on the Chautauqua Institute that gives detailed attention to its academic credit-granting arm. Like Illinois Wesleyan, the Chautauqua University depended largely on correspondence study. Sheila Sherow (1989) tells the story of a 19th-century correspondence program created by a major university. In 1892, the Pennsylvania State College (now Penn State) designed the "Chautauqua Home Reading Course in Agriculture." Initially modeled after the Chautauqua Literary and Scientific Circle's courses—but totally unrelated to the CLSC—this program evolved into a group of rigorous, credit-bearing correspondence courses.

It seems strange that there still is no full biography of William Rainey Harper, one of the seminal figures in the history of American higher education. However, it turns out that there is a rich vein of dissertation literature on Harper, his American Institute of Sacred Literature, and his vision for the University of Chicago. While none of these works is primarily a biography, and only one is specifically devoted to university extension, all contribute to understanding Harper, his commitments as an educator, and his vision of higher education.

Lars Hoffman (1978) deals primarily with Harper's association with other Baptists. In a more ambitious work, James Wind (1983) provides a thorough exposition of Harper's theological position and demonstrates its relationship to his commitment to the diffusion of knowledge. Wind makes a persuasive case for the close relationship between Harper's religious beliefs and his development of the Extension Division at the University of Chicago. Reed (1980) also depicts Harper's commitment to both Baptist theology and educational innovation.

A less analytical study, without a religious dimension, can be found in Engle's 1954 thesis. Engle is particularly informative when describing Harper's role as a promoter of the university. Plath (1989) also details Harper's promotional skills as part of a study of leadership style, including his ability to compromise, and frequently to prevail, despite entrenched opposition. Two dissertations relate more peripheral aspects of Harper's presidency at Chicago. Blake (1966) recounts the development of the science curriculum and Cook (1993) describes the Extension Division in her thesis on the development of evening classes in the city of Chicago.

Beginning in 1880, at the Baptist Union Theological Seminary in Morgan Park, Illinois, Harper developed his famous correspondence courses in Hebrew, which he took along to Yale, then brought back to Chicago as the core of the University's Home Study Department. Kenneth Beck (1968) tells this story in his dissertation on The American Institute of Sacred Literature, an institution often overlooked in the history of adult education.

Two early dissertations describe the integration of the Extension Division into the organizational structure of the University of Chicago. Clem Thompson (1932) uses data generated in the first large-scale review of the university in his thesis on the operation of the Extension Division. A decade later, William Haggerty (1943) explains Harper's original vision, then subsequent changes in organization after his death. For the most part, Storr's *Harper's University* (1966) supersedes these works. All of these dissertations place Harper in a much larger context than his involvement in correspondence study. Still, scholars of correspondence study will find them useful.

Several other dissertations merit mention because they are treatments of subjects rarely encountered in the existing body of published secondary works. Lorenzo Timmons (1930) makes an early examination of the controversial problem of awarding and accepting transfer credit for correspondence courses. Collegiate correspondence/ independent study programs have long suffered from comparison with proprietary schools. Andrew Hadji (1931) describes the rapid rise—and the shortcomings—of some of these schools in his University of Chicago dissertation.

Almost all secondary works on correspondence education describe the programs of state flagship and land-grant institutions. Thus, Thomas Jenkins's 1953 study of the correspondence programs offered by teachers colleges stands alone. Indeed, absolutely nothing else about this sector of postsecondary correspondence study seems to exist.

Two additional doctoral dissertations deserve a look. In 1974, Roger Young, already a veteran practitioner in the field, took the pulse of university administrators with respect to correspondence/independent study programs. Like Gerrity (1976), Young concluded that the 1970s presented great opportunities for expansion and innovation. Marv Van Kekerix's 1986 dissertation on the State University of Nebraska (SUN), an early telecourse program, is particularly noteworthy. Scholars and especially practitioners of distance education have traditionally written success stories. SUN, however, was the prototype and immediate predecessor of the mightily hyped University of Mid-America (UMA), which turned out to be one of the most notorious flops in the history of distance education. Van Kekerix adroitly chronicles its rise and fall.

Anyone who has ever written a dissertation knows the odds of publishing it as a book, at least without extensive revision, are long. As time passes, the prospect becomes extremely unlikely. Housed in only one library and catalogued by University Microfilms, they generally pass into obscurity. This is unfortunate. In the field of correspondence/independent study, much of the best available scholarly work can be found in them.

One new dissertation provides a superb example of the kind of work that ought to be published. Will Diehl wrote *Learning at the Back Door: Charles Wedemeyer and the Evolution of Open and Distance Education* (2011) under the direction of Michael G. Moore. This biographical treatment is critical to an understanding of Wedemeyer's seminal role, not only in independent study, but in all of distance education. Like some of the dissertations cited above, this one deserves to be published. We must hope that it will be, preferably as a book, rather than a series of articles.

Other figures from the field of correspondence/independent study merit biographical treatment. We can hope that younger scholars will take a look at the career of Gayle Childs, at the University of Nebraska. Ripley Sims, longtime head of the United States Armed Forces Institute (USAFI) played a critical role in expanding the use of correspondence study throughout the military. Among other career correspondence educators deserving of scholarly attention come to mind, including—but certainly not limited to—Betsy Powell, of the University of Georgia, and Roger Young, who led innovative programs at the University of Nebraska, University of Minnesota, and University of Missouri.

Some "Classics" of Fugitive Literature

"Fugitive literature" consists of unpublished, uncataloged, and for the most part, uncollected documents. Such materials as reports, in-house organs, manuals for course authors, and study guides tell us a great deal about the craft of correspondence/independent study. Historians would consider some of these works primary sources, others secondary. The Independent Study archives at Penn State contain numerous such documents; others reside in various independent study departments and continuing education divisions. A very few university archivists have shown some interest in maintaining a sample of materials from the programs at their schools. For the most part, however, the ephemera of independent study are being discarded.

A sample of the fugitive literature should illustrate value of this body of material. These examples are not intended to be exhaustive, but simply to provide insights into the value of such artifacts in examining distance education's past.

Unlike doctoral dissertations, master's theses are generally not catalogued—except perhaps in the library of the schools at which they were written—making it impossible to sort and search for them by title or subject matter. Yet, some of them can be helpful for examining particular departments or universities at specific points in time. Grace Donehower's master's thesis (1968) examines the relationship between operational policies and their effects on correspondence study enrollments at the University of Nevada between 1963 and 1965. Some theses are available in archival collections; a few others may be found in the continuing education offices at the universities where they were produced.

Documentation of the success or failure of innovative programs or approaches, for the most part, can only be found in the offices where they originated. In the early 1950s, the University of Wisconsin conducted its Rhinelander Center Project (University of Wisconsin-Extension, 1955). The report on this project is important because it documents a major university's early experiment with an external degree. Yet, documents such as this one are often either consigned to obscurity or discarded, disappearing without a trace.

Almost all independent study departments regularly produced—and constantly updated—handbooks for course authors and instructors. Collectively, these documents illustrate changes in the design, mechanics, style, and instructional philosophy of the independent study format and the administration of courses. Individually, they can shed light on the programs they represent. Two examples should suffice. The design and content of a manual from the University of California (Lawson, 1994) reflected its Center for Media and Independent Study's dependence on a scattered, adjunct faculty, none of whom were full-time university employees. Therefore, it reads quite differently from handbooks designed by departments that employed mainly the faculty and graduate students of their own institutions. The University of Iowa's manuals for its course authors have always reflected that program's commitment to clear and engaging prose and to capturing the individual voices of its faculty. As one issue said,

> We believe it is important for you [course authors] to find a voice in your written materials that is informal, engaging, and clearly interested in helping students master the course content. The material you are preparing is, after all, a *guide*, not merely a workbook. (1994, p. 17)

Manuals from other institutions may exhibit a greater concern for standardization or overall course design, and these preferences and values can change over time. Therefore, this sub-genre of fugitive literature could be of considerable value to the researcher.

Perhaps the most detailed instructional material for authors of correspondence courses can be found in a study guide on developing and teaching courses, written by Joseph Kleiner (1966) at the University of Wisconsin-Extension. Kleiner wrote it to walk faculty through the course development process, offering feedback as they finished the course's eight units. He also wanted to help faculty understand how students experienced the correspondence format. This study guide contains such lessons as "Correspondence Study Learning Theory" and "Designing the Correspondence Lesson." This unusual study guide was once filed in the Wisconsin-Extension Library. Whether it survived the dismantling of that facility is unknown.

The NUEA/UCEA's Independent Study Division (ISD), which operated from the late 1960s through the late 1990s, produced some useful—but now generally forgotten—documents of potential historical interest. The ISD was an unusual entity. It was one of an ever-changing number of NUEA/NUCEA divisions. Unlike the others, however, it also functioned as an autonomous organization. Throughout its life, it promoted professional development and the creation of standards of practice. In April 1972, the ISD held a workshop in Columbia, South Carolina for the purpose of discussing and selecting materials that would help new directors adopt the best practices of their craft. After further refinement and editing, the ISD produced the *Handbook for Independent Study Directors* (Division of Independent Study, 1975). While it once was shelved in every university's independent study department, by now most copies have disappeared.

The growing variety of distance education media and formats caused concern within the Independent Study Division, as did ambiguities and occasional conflicts resulting from its de facto status as an autonomous organization within a larger group. In 1989, in response to these issues, the ISD appointed a Task Force on the Status of the Division. After grappling with its members' concerns, the Task Force issued a report (1990) that provided a number of recommendations for future organizational changes. The significance of this report has increased with the opportunities and problems that have subsequently emerged in the greater field of distance education. Distributed to all members of the ISD, an indeterminate number of copies are scattered around the country.

These six examples represent many non-catalogued artifacts that provide information and some valuable insights about the practice of independent study in American universities. They are prime examples of the sort of documents now disappearing mainly as a result of major organizational changes in college-level distance education. The loss of this fugitive literature of the field will hinder or detract from larger studies of distance education in the future.

TOPICS MERITING FURTHER RESEARCH

Professional Organizations

Anyone with an interest in the history of distance education—especially independent study—will find a wide choice of significant questions that merit serious consideration. The role of the various professional organizations that involved themselves with correspondence/independent study is an obvious example. Two articles on the NUEA's early years provide a start. Edelson (1991) described the organization's determination to earn respect for the correspondence and extension lecture programs of their universities. As an organization, it set and articulated standards of quality, carefully separating itself from less prestigious types of institutions, such as teachers colleges. It advanced the principle of "campus equivalence," in hopes of having the courses of its members' schools achieve a stature comparable to that of on-campus classes. Pittman (1998) also looked at the NUEA's efforts at setting standards for correspondence study, but concluded that its ambitions, though commendable, were flawed from the beginning. Additional studies of this group's impact on the growth of distance education would be useful, along with studies of competing or complementary organizations.

Early Uses of Electronic Media

Considering the current enthusiasm for electronic distance education formats, the early attempts to combine correspondence study with telecommunications provide another obvious topic. Yet little work has been done in this area. Carroll Atkinson's *Radio Extension Courses Broadcast for Credit* (1941), the best treatment of attempts to use broadcast radio for instruction is over 70 years old. E. B. Kurtz, a professor of engineering at the University of Iowa, compiled a book (1959) on the first experiments with instructional television 40 years ago. While still useful, in spite of being very old, both of these books are entirely descriptive, and provide little in the way of insight or analysis.

The 1950s and 1960s saw serious new attempts to develop television as a distance education format. Purdy (1980) contributed a brief overview of these early efforts. Van Kekerix and Andrews's (1991) anthology chapter on the same subject is more detailed and thoughtful, and more firmly linked to independent study. Some areas lack even short descriptive treatments. For example, the use of the telephone in teaching, especially in Wisconsin, has not been described adequately.

Broadcast telecourses, with their huge budgets, splendid video productions, and large enrollments generated a lot of ink in the 1960s and 1970s. Despite claims to the contrary, they were a variant of traditional independent study. Their history has not yet been subjected to scholarly scrutiny. It is particularly disappointing that the Annenberg/Corporation for Public Broadcasting telecourse project receives no mention (although the film series for a single course does) in two recent studies of public television (Day, 1995; Jarvik, 1997).

The graduate programs of some of the nation's finest engineering colleges provide a twist on the usual manner in which technology has been combined with independent study. In the late 1960s, Stanford University began transmitting some of its courses to industrial sites via Instructional Television Fixed Service (ITFS). With the advent of videocassette recorders, and at the request of students, the faculty began to allow students to view their lectures on tape, rather than in real time. Schools of the caliber of the Massachusetts Institute of Technology, the University of Illinois, and many other first-rank engineering colleges adopted this format. Its popularity led to the creation of the National Technological University (NTU).

Over the years, students and their employers pressed for less and less structure and synchronicity. For example, students initially had to gather to view the tapes in groups, in the presence of a "tutor," and follow a strict week-by-week schedule. Few schools now insist on either of these formalities. The usual trend in distance education has been that new technologies have been used to make independent study more closely resemble the conventional classroom. The engineering programs, on the other hand, dispensed with structure and thus increasingly came to resemble traditional independent study. The story of this teaching format is as obscure as it was successful. To the extent that its story has been recorded at all, it has been primarily in contemporaneous publications and promotional materials. It deserves better.

Excess and Corruption: Big Time Sports and Correspondence Study

An examination of the often-unsavory association of independent study and intercollegiate athletics is long overdue. As big-time college sports have corrupted numerous other aspects of university life, they have occasionally had a pernicious effect on independent study. Athletic department staffs have sometimes used independent study's unique administrative practices—such as off-cycle registration and completion—as loopholes when trying to maintain the eligibility of their "scholar-athletes." To date, there has been no scholarly work on this problem. For anyone who might be interested, however, Wolff and Yaeger's 1995 story in *Sports Illustrated* provides an excellent starting point.

University Programs and High School Instruction

Perhaps the most overlooked aspect of the history of collegiate correspondence/independent study programs is the fact that many of them offered courses at the postsecondary level. At some universities, the correspondence programs included high school instruction from the beginning—1892 for the University of Chicago, 1913 for the University of Missouri, for example. Initially, the high school courses were intended to help students erase deficiencies and qualify for admission to college (Storr, 1966; University of Missouri, 2010). Over time, however, numerous university programs, most notably in the Midwest and South, moved toward providing courses students could apply toward their diplomas. Postsecondary institutions were never alone in offering high school correspondence courses. Public high schools and state departments of education began programs, also. Between 1923 and 1930, more than 100 high schools offered their own correspondence courses. However, the universities tended to have more staying power than the other providers. Young and McMahon (1991) provide a useful—but brief—overview of this period.

The University of Nebraska's high school correspondence program is the most important from a historical viewpoint. No other program is documented to the same extent. J. J. Van Arsdall (1977) tells its story, beginning with Carnegie Corporation grant-funded experiments in the late 1920s and continuing through its accreditation as a high school by the North Central Association, and its achievement of the status of a full, diploma-granting high school. Unfortunately, there are no other extant historical studies of university high school programs.

During the 1930s, the United States Office of Education, then housed in the Department of the Interior, took notice of the Nebraska innovations and other correspondence programs. It promoted further development of high-school level correspondence study as a means of economizing, thus making secondary education more accessible, especially in rural areas. Various New Deal agencies, like the Civilian Conservation Corps (CCC) and the Works Progress Administration (WPA) subsidized university correspondence study at the high school level within their programs (Gaumnitz, 1933). A good deal of documentation of this effort is contained in government publications, which historians of education could use to good effect.

Gayle Childs summarized developments in high school programs offered by universities in the renowned *Brandenberg Memorial Essays* (1963). The contribution of Roger Young and Monty McMahon in *The Foundations of American Distance Education* (1991) has already been noted. It appears to be the last piece written on the history of university-operated high school correspondence programs. This is surprising, given that these programs served substantial numbers of students. In 1958-1959, for example, 35 university sponsored high school programs enrolled more than 58,000 students for one or more courses (Childs, 1963).

Acknowledgements or descriptions of high school correspondence/independent study programs have not appeared even in works where they might reasonably have been expected. For example, a 1997 anthology on K-12 distance education (Moore & Koble), did not include an article on correspondence/independent study—because no article on K-12 independent study meeting the selection criteria existed at the time. In a more recent anthology (Berge & Clark, 2005), the editors defined non-electronic instruction out of "virtual education." However, they did include a chapter on a university correspondence program then in the process of converting its high school courses from the correspondence format to online delivery (Smalley, 2005).

Through state-level "virtual schools" and other agencies and vendors, distance education high school courses and enrollments are increasing rapidly. Their future seems assured. However, it must be remembered that high school distance education was not invented yesterday. It has a long, but regrettably obscure, history.

CONCLUSION

There is no shortage of topics for historical narrative and analysis in the history of correspondence/independent study. Resources for such work are rich and varied, if erratic. When dissertations are considered, the body of useful secondary sources grows dramatically. However, while several excellent collections of primary sources are available for study, two of the best are stagnant. The acquisition of primary source materials has come to a halt for the NUEA papers filed in the Adult Education archives at Syracuse University as well as for the Independent Study Division's collection at Penn State. The closure of the University of Wisconsin-Extension's library has resulted in the dispersal of an excellent body of research materials.

An even greater loss of resources is ongoing. The closures, reorganizations, and mergers within the continuing education offices and other units that manage distance education are having a devastating effect. Records are being scattered, discarded, and or destroyed. The fugitive literature that illuminates the day-to-day work of professionals in the field can be found only in a few university libraries and one or two private collections. Veterans of the field, many of whom made significant contributions, are retiring and passing away without having left *memoirs*, while the collection of oral histories has almost been abandoned.

Unless more young scholars investigate distance education's past, beginning with correspondence study, the collection and archiving of primary resources may come to a complete halt. Today's promoters of distance education will believe themselves vindicated in their belief that the field was born yesterday.

NOTES

1. Early collegiate-level correspondence study was often called "home study," to distinguish it from the product of proprietary schools. For much the same reason, colleges and universities began to call it "independent study" beginning in the late 1960s. The three terms will here be used interchangeably, with preference given to the label in general use during the chronological period under discussion.
2. The National University Extension Association (NUEA) was founded in 1915. It changed its name to National University Continuing Education Association (NUCEA) in 1979. In 1996 it dropped "National" and became simply the University Continuing Education Association (UCEA). Recently, it effected yet another name change, to The University Professional Continuing Education Association. This essay will employ all four names and abbreviations, with each usage determined by the chronological period under discussion.

REFERENCES

Allen, H. C., Jr. (1984). *History of the non-residential degree program at Illinois Wesleyan University, 1873–1910: A study of a pioneer external degree program in the United States.* Unpublished doctoral dissertation, University of Chicago.

Atkinson, C. (1941). *Radio extension courses broadcast for credit.* Boston: Meador.

Beck, K. N. (1968). *The American Institute of Sacred Literature: A historical analysis of an adult education institution.* Unpublished doctoral dissertation, University of Chicago.

Berge, Z. L., & Clark, T. (2005). *Virtual schools: Planning for success.* New York: Teachers College Press.

Bittner, W. S., & Mallory, H. F. (1933). *University teaching by mail: A survey of correspondence instruction conducted by American universities.* New York: Macmillan.

Blake, L. C. (1966). *The concept and development of science at the University of Chicago, 1890–1905.* Unpublished doctoral dissertation, University of Chicago.

Bonnell, R. K. (1988). *The Chautauqua University: Pioneer university without walls, 1883–1898.* Unpublished doctoral dissertation, Kent State University.

Burton, G. C. (2010). Opening the Great Gate at "the Palace of Learning": Charles A. Wedemeyer's pioneering role as champion of the independent learner. *Vitae Scholasticae, 27*(1), 26–43.

Byrne, T. C. (1989). *Athabasca University the evolution of distance education.* Calgary, Canada: University of Calgary Press.

Childs, G. B. (1963). Supervised correspondence instruction. In C. A. Wedemeyer (Ed.), *Brandenburg memorial essays, Vol 1* (pp. 22–33). Madison: University of Wisconsin Extension.

Cook, S. A. (1993). *The origins and development of evening undergraduate education in Chicago.* Unpublished doctoral dissertation, Loyola University of Chicago.

Craik, G. L. (1830). *The pursuit of knowledge under difficulties.* London: Knight.

Curti, M., & Carstensen, V. (1949). *The University of Wisconsin: A history (Vols. 1–2).* Madison: University of Wisconsin Press.

Day, J. (1995). *The vanishing vision: The inside story of public television.* Berkeley, CA: University of California Press.

Diehl, W. C. (2011). *Learning at the back door: Charles Wedemeyer and the evolution of open and distance education.* Unpublished doctoral dissertation, The Pennsylvania State University.

Division of Independent Study. (1975). *Handbook for independent study directors.* Madison: University of Wisconsin-Extension.

Donehower, G. M. (1968). *Variables associated with correspondence study enrollments at the University of Nevada, 1963–1965.* Unpublished master's thesis, University of Nevada-Reno.

Duning, B. S. (1987). Independent study in higher education: A captive of legendary resilience? *The American Journal of Distance Education, 1*(1), 37–46.

Duning, B. S., & Pittman, V. V. (Eds.). (1995). *Distance education symposium 3: Policy and administration.* University Park, PA: American Center for the Study of Distance Education.

Edelson, P. J. (1991). Codification and exclusion: An analysis of the early years of the National University Extension Association (NUEA) 1915–1923. *Continuing Higher Education Review, 55*(3), 176–188.

Engle, G. W. (1954). *William Rainey Harper's conceptions of the structuring of the functions performed by educational institutions.* Unpublished doctoral dissertation, Stanford University.

Flexner, A. (1930). *Universities: American, English, German.* New York: Oxford University Press.

Gaumnitz, W. H. (1933). High-school instruction by mail: A potential economy. *Bulletin 1933, No. 13,* U. S. Department of Agriculture, Office of Education. Washington, D. C.: Government Printing Office.

Hampel, R. (2010). The Business of education: Home study at Columbia University and the University of Wisconsin in the 1920s and 1930s. *Teachers College Record, 112*(9), 2496–2517.

Garrison, D. R., & Shale, D. (Eds.). (1990). *Education at a distance: From issues to practice.* Malabar, FL: R. E. Kreiger.

Gerrity, T. W. (1976). *College-sponsored correspondence instruction in the United States: A comparative history of its origins (1873–1915) and its recent developments (1960–1975).* Unpublished doctoral dissertation, Columbia University Teachers College.

Getz, G. A. (1986). *MBI: The story of Moody Bible Institute.* Chicago, IL: Moody Press.

Hadji, A. G. (1931). *Private correspondence schools: Their growth and marketing methods.* Unpublished doctoral dissertation, University of Chicago.

Haggerty, W. J. (1943). *The purposes of the University of Chicago.* Unpublished doctoral dissertation, University of Chicago.

Hoffman, L. (1978). *William Rainey Harper and the Chicago Fellowship.* Unpublished doctoral dissertation, University of Iowa.

Jarvik, L. (1997). *PBS, behind the screen.* Rocklin, CA: Prima.

Jenkins, T. S. (1953). *Correspondence course instruction: An investigation of practices, regulations, and course syllabi as developed in state teachers colleges.* Unpublished doctoral dissertation, University of Oregon.

Kett, J. F. (1994). *The pursuit of knowledge under difficulties: From self-improvement to adult education in America, 1750–1990.* Stanford, CA: Stanford University Press.

Kleiner, J. L. (1966). *An introduction to the method of correspondence study.* Unpublished study guide, University of Wisconsin-Madison.

Kurtz, E. B. (1959). *Pioneering in educational television, 1932–1939.* Iowa City: State University of Iowa.

Lawson, J. (1994). *Handbook for instructors.* Berkeley: University of California Extension Center for Media and Independent Learning.

Montgomery, C. W. (1993). *Some issues in the remote delivery of graduate course work and programs.* Paper delivered at the Illinois Association of Graduate Schools.

Moore, M. G. (Ed.). (1990). *Contemporary issues in American distance education.* New York: Pergamon Press.

Moore, M. G., & Anderson, W. G. (2003). *Handbook of distance education.* Mawah, NJ: Erlbaum.

Moore, M. G., & Koble, M. A. (1997). *K-12 distance education: Learning, teaching, and teacher training.* University Park: The Pennsylvania State University.

Moore, M. G., & Shin, N. (Eds.). (2000). *Speaking personally about distance education: Foundations of contemporary practice.* University Park, PA: American Center for the Study of Distance Education.

Mugridge, I., & Kaufman, D. (Eds.). (1986). *Distance education in Canada.* London: Croom Helm.

Noble, D. F. (2001). *Digital diploma mills: The automation of higher education.* New York: Monthly Review Press.

Nolan, D. J. (1998). Regents College: The early years. Virginia Beach, VA: Donning.

Pittman, V. V. (1990). Correspondence study in the American university: A historiographic perspective. In M. G. Moore (Ed.), *Contemporary issues in American distance education* (pp. 67–80). New York: Pergamon Press.

Pittman, V. V. (1991). Academic credibility and the "image problem": The quality issue in collegiate independent study. In B. L. Watkins & S. J. Wright (Eds.), *The foundations of American distance education: A century of collegiate correspondence study* (pp. 109–134). Dubuque, IA: Kendall/Hunt.

Pittman, V. V. (1995). Harper's headaches: Early policy issues in collegiate correspondence study. In B. S. Duning, & V. V. Pittman (Eds.), *Distance education symposium 3: Policy and administration* (pp. 19–31). University Park, PA: American Center for the Study of Distance Education.

Pittman, V. V. (1998). Low-key leadership: Collegiate correspondence study and campus equivalence. *American Journal of Distance Education, 12*(2), 36–45.

Pittman, V. V. (2006). Out on the fringe: Helen Williams and early correspondence study. *American Educational History Journal, 33*(1), 107–116.

Pittman, V. V. (2008). "An alien presence": The long, sad, history of correspondence study at the University of Chicago. *American Educational History Journal, 34*(1), 123–134.

Pittman, V. V. (2009). Correspondence study and the "Crime of the Century: Helen Williams, Nathan Leopold, and the Stateville Correspondence School. *Vitae Scholasticae, 26*(2), 5–28.

Plath, P. J. (1989). *The fox and the hedgehog: Liberal education at the University of Chicago.* Unpublished doctoral dissertation, University of Illinois at Urbana-Champaign.

Purdy, L. N. (1980). The history of television and radio in continuing education. In M. N. Chamberlain (Ed.), *New directions for continuing education, number 5: Providing continuing education by media and technology.* San Francisco: Jossey-Bass.

Reed, J. E. (1980). *A study of William Rainey Harper's educational principles: Modifications and innovations in an era of change.* Unpublished doctoral dissertation, New Orleans Baptist Theological Seminary.

Rose, S. L. (1991). Collegiate-based noncredit courses. In B. L. Watkins & S. J. Wright (Eds.), *The foundations of American distance education: A century of collegiate correspondence study* (pp. 67–92). Dubuque, IA: Kendall/Hunt.

Rothe, J. P. (1986). An historical perspective. In I. Mugridge & D. Kaufman (Eds.), *Distance education in Canada* (pp. 4–24). London: Croom Helm.

Sherow, S. (1989). *The Pennsylvania State College: A pioneer in non-traditional agricultural education.* Unpublished doctoral dissertation, Pennsylvania State College.

Sherow, S., & Wedemeyer, C. A. (1990). Origins of distance education in the United States. In D. R. Garrison & D. Shale (Eds.), *Education at a distance: From issues to practice* (pp. 7–22). Malabar, FL: R.E. Krieger.

Simmons, J. (2000). The future of Academic freedom: Educational technology and academic freedom. *DEONEWS, 10*(3). Retrieved December 8, 2000, from http://www.ed.psu.edu/acsde/deos/deosnews/deosarchives.asp

Smalley, K. D. (2005). The University of Missouri-Columbia High School: From independent study to accredited diplomas online. In Z. L. Berge & T. Clark, T. *Virtual schools: Planning for success.* New York: Teachers College Press.

Storr, R. J. (1966). *Harper's university: A history of the University of Chicago.* Chicago: University of Chicago Press.

Task Force on the Status of the Division of Independent Study. (1990). *The status of independent study: 1990 and beyond.* NUCEA.

Thompson, C. O. (1932). *The extension program of the University of Chicago (Illinois).* Unpublished doctoral dissertation, University of Chicago.

Timmons, L. Z. (1930). *A study of correspondence study, for college credit, in Texas colleges and universities.* Unpublished master's thesis, Texas Technical College.

University of Iowa. (1994). *Faculty guide for developing and instructing guided correspondence study courses.* Iowa City: University of Iowa.

University of Missouri. (2010). A century of Distance Learning, University of Missouri course bulletin: High School-Middle-Elementary, 4–7.

University of Wisconsin. (1955). *Experiments in correspondence study.* Unpublished report, University of Wisconsin Extension Division.

Van Arsdall, J. E. (1977). *The stated and operative objectives of the University of Nebraska extension high school program, 1929–1975.* Unpublished doctoral dissertation, University of Nebraska-Lincoln.

Van Kekerix, M. J. (1986). *The SUN experience: A historical analysis of the state university of Nebraska program utilizing the organizational life cycle perspective.* Unpublished doctoral dissertation, University of Nebraska-Lincoln.

Van Kekerix, M. J., & Andrews, J. (1991). Electronic media and independent study. In B. L. Watkins & S. J. Wright (Eds.), *The foundations of American distance education: A century of collegiate correspondence study* (pp. 135–157). Dubuque, IA: Kendall/Hunt.

Veblen, T. (1918). *The higher learning in America: A memorandum on the conduct of universities by business men.* New York: B. W. Huebsch.

Watkins, B. L. (1991). A quite radical idea: The invention and elaboration of collegiate correspondence study. In B. L. Watkins & S. J. Wright (Eds.), *The foundations of American distance education: A century of collegiate correspondence study* (pp. 1–35). Dubuque, IA: Kendall/Hunt.

Watkins, B. L., & Wright, S. J. (Eds.). (1991). *The foundations of American distance education: A century of collegiate correspondence study.* Dubuque, IA: Kendall/Hunt.

Wedemeyer, C. A. (1981). *Learning at the back door: Reflections on non-traditional learning in the lifespan.* Madison: University of Wisconsin Press.

Wedemeyer, C. A., & Childs, G. B. (1961). *New perspectives in university correspondence study.* Chicago: Center for the Study of Liberal Education for Adults.

Wind, J. P. (1983). *The bible and the university: The messianic vision of William Rainey Harper.* Unpublished doctoral dissertation, University of Chicago.

Wolff, A., & Yaeger, D. (1995). Credit risk. *Sports Illustrated, 83*(6), 46–55.

Wright, S. J. (1991). Opportunity lost, opportunity regained: University independent study in the modern era. In B. L. Watkins & S. J. Wright (Eds.), *The foundations of American distance education: A century of collegiate correspondence study* (pp. 37–66). Dubuque, IA: Kendall/Hunt.

Young, J. R. (2000, March 31). David Noble's battle to defend the 'sacred space' of the classroom. *Chronicle of Higher Education.* Online Edition. Retrieved December 8, from http://chronicle.com

Young, R. G. (1974). *A critical analysis of the views and opinions of university administrators toward university correspondence study.* Unpublished doctoral dissertation, University of Nebraska-Lincoln.

Young, R. G., & McMahon, M. (1991). University-sponsored high school independent study. In B. L. Watkins & S. J. Wright (Eds.), *The foundations of American distance education: A century of collegiate correspondence study* (pp. 93–108). Dubuque, IA: Kendall/Hunt.

3

CHARLES A. WEDEMEYER

Visionary Pioneer of Distance Education

WILLIAM C. DIEHL

In Chapter 1 of this volume on the history of scholarship, Linda Black introduced Charles A. Wedemeyer and mentioned some his achievements, noting in particular his pioneering advocacy for empirical research in distance education. Considered by many to be the father of modern distance education, Wedemeyer's influence is examined in greater detail in this chapter. The chapter is organized by these topics: (1) Wedemeyer as an innovator; (2) his professional journey; (3) his impact on the Open University of the United Kingdom (OUUK); (4) his influence on Holmberg, Moore, and Peters; and (5) his legacy.

INTRODUCTION—CHARLES A. WEDEMEYER: INNOVATIVE CHANGE AGENT

Charles A. Wedemeyer (1911–1999) devoted his life to the field of education, and in particular, distance education. Recognized as an innovator, leader, and authority by his contemporaries, he was one of the first educators to advocate for scholarship in what had been known as the field of correspondence study.

Wedemeyer's primary vision was to develop a systems approach in the emerging field of distance education as a way of addressing the opportunity gap that exists for non-traditional adult students, or as he referred to them, "back door learners" (Wedemeyer, 1981, p. 19). He developed a concept for cradle-to-grave "open" education that in contrast to the popular Behaviorism of his day, applied technology to meet the goals espoused in Humanistic psychology.

Following such principles, Wedemeyer believed that the goals of education should include emphasis on student-centered learning. Students should be taught the values and skills required to become independent learners, so that they could pursue lifelong learning at any point in their lives. In 1971 he published his definition of "independent study." The Wedemeyer (1971a) definition of Independent Study is various forms of teaching-learning arrangements in which teachers and learners carry out their essential tasks and responsibilities apart from one another, communicating in a variety of ways, for the purposes of freeing internal learners from inappropriate class pacings or patterns, or providing external learners opportunity to continue learning in their own environments, and developing in all learners the capacity to carry on self-directed learning, the ultimate maturity required of the educated person. Independent Study programs offer learners varying degrees of freedom in the self-determination of goals and activities, and in starting, stopping and pacing individualized learning programs which are carried on to the greatest extent possible at the convenience of the learners. (p. 3)

In addition to placing emphasis on the learner, the definition introduced the idea of a domain of education in which teachers and learners "carry out their essential tasks—apart from one another," a defining characteristic of distance education. Wedemeyer's idea of Independent Study referred to both *internal study* and *external study*, and that Independent Study could be applied both in campus face-to-face traditional and nontraditional and distance education programs. Lifelong learning could best happen via open and flexible educational systems. Two innovative systems were designed, based on his ideas; these were the Open School system (Wedemeyer, 1971c; Wedemeyer & Ghatala, 1971; WHA, 1970) for the State of Wisconsin (which did not come to fruition) and the Articulated Instructional Media Program (AIM). As will be discussed in the following section, based on the AIM experience, Wedemeyer went on to play a leading role in the development of the Open University in Great Britain, consequently impacting the world of higher education.

BIOGRAPHICAL: WEDEMEYER'S PROFESSIONAL JOURNEY (1930s THROUGH THE 1980s)

In the 1930s and early 1940s, Wedemeyer demonstrated his first abilities to adopt and apply new technologies to education. During that period, he wrote scripts and hosted the radio show *Literature Then and Now* for the Wisconsin College of the Air. By the 1950s, he had become the chairman of the National University Extension Association (NUEA) correspondence study division committee on radio and TV.

During World War II, Wedemeyer designed, developed, and edited course books used for teaching armed services' personnel on ships at sea and in other unconventional learning environments. After the war and through the mid-1950s, he was director of Correspondence Study at the University of Wisconsin, one of the largest correspondence study programs in the world. Over 8,500 students were enrolled in more than 400 courses and over 85,000 men and women in the Air Force, Army and Navy took courses in a program that linked Wedemeyer's program with the United States Armed Forces Institute (USAFI). The number of USAFI related lessons grew to 300,000 at its peak (UWEX, 1956).

In early 1958, Wedemeyer and the University of Wisconsin announced their plan for combining television with college-level correspondence study, a pioneering experiment in the use of multiple media for teaching-learning activities, requiring teaching by a team of specialists working together to design, develop, deliver, and assess the project.

The course was designed for 2,500 to 10,000 enrollees who would be "given tests and projects by the UW Extension Division" which would also "handle grading of papers and other administrative functions" (Bauder, 1959). In 1959, with Wedemeyer acting as correspondence advisor and teaming with Professor Percy H. Tannenbaum of the Mass Communications Research Center, the first graduate course using television and correspondence education for credit for students across the United States was announced by University of Wisconsin Extension (UWEX, 1959).

In the 1960s, Wedemeyer's experimentation with multiple types of media and the use of course teams continued in a particularly groundbreaking experimental program, The Articulated Instructional Media Program (AIM). Towards the end of this period, Wedemeyer pioneered another significant development in education—the application of satellite technologies.

When the use of satellites was in its earliest stages of development, Wedemeyer worked with colleagues such as Richard G. Lawson at the University of Wisconsin to develop an experimental program called the Educational Diffusion and Social Application of Satellite Telecommunications (EDSAT). Situated on the Madison, Wisconsin campus, the project was a joint program with the Space Science and Engineering Center, UNESCO, and ICCE.

In 1975 as a consultant for the U.S. State Department, Wedemeyer conducted educational satellite demonstrations during a trip through Indonesia, Malaysia, Singapore, Thailand, and Japan. During his tour, he demonstrated the potential of teaching over vast distances by facilitating his regular seminar at the University of Madison Wisconsin via satellite.

This brief chronological description of Wedemeyer's professional life illustrates some of the diversity of his activities. Throughout this period he also held leadership positions in several professional associations. For example, he served as president of and a member of the executive boards of the International Council of Correspondence Education (ICCE) and the National University Extension Association (NUEA). He was a director of the Correspondence Study Division for the NUEA, and at USAFI he was Director of Instruction and Evaluation. Later, at Wisconsin, he was Director of AIM and the AIM Board, and he held the William H. Lighty Professor of Education Chair. Wedemeyer was the recipient of numerous awards, including the Gayle Childs Award for Distinguished Service and an honorary doctorate by the OUUK. He was also honored with a variety of public appointments. For example, he became the First Kellogg Fellow at Oxford University and served on the Wisconsin Governor's Commission on Education and the Governor's Educational Advisory Committee.

WEDEMEYER'S IMPACT ON THE REVOLUTIONARY OUUK

In 1965, several years before the Open University of the United Kingdom (OUUK) was launched, Wedemeyer, as the first Kellogg Fellow at Oxford University, shared his experience, ideas, and lessons learned from the AIM Project in lectures and informal conversations with several key individuals who would become the OUUK's planners (Wedemeyer, 1968, 1971b).

A few years later, one of those individuals, Walter James, the new Director of Studies of the OUUK, wrote to Wedemeyer, emphasizing that it had been their conversations in 1965 at Nottingham that had shaped the ideas and plans he was going to implement as one of the first senior appointees at the new OUUK. James asked Wedemeyer for additional assistance, and Wedemeyer (1969c) told him that he would "help in any possible way." What was at first known as *University of the Air* shared several of the characteristics of Wedemeyer's AIM project. However, it also benefited from what Wedemeyer recognized as weaknesses in AIM. The Wisconsin project had not owned its own production facilities nor, more importantly did it have organizational autonomy in finances and awarding of credits and degrees, and it was these weaknesses, as Wedemeyer perceived them, that he urged should be avoided in the design of the new British institution (Diehl, 2011a). Even the *course team* (which years later, First Vice-Chancellor of the OUUK Walter Perry (1976) credited the OUUK with innovating) had in fact been developed by Wedemeyer as early as 1959.

In April of 1969, Anastasinos Christodoulou, the Secretary Designate of the Open University Planning Committee contacted Wedemeyer and arranged a meeting for the two of them together with the Vice-Chancellor of the new university, Walter Perry (Wedemeyer, 1969a). After the meeting, Perry invited Wedemeyer to become a consultant and to stay with him at Swan Cottage, his home in Milton Keynes, where the new OUUK campus would be located. In October 1969, the offices of the OUUK moved from London to Milton Keynes, where renovations and the first phases of administrative and course development began in earnest (Perry, 1976; Stabler, 1986; Tunstall, 1974).

For two months, Wedemeyer worked with Perry and with various teams of academic and media specialists in the development of mediated instructional materials, and also shared ideas with administrative and supportive services personnel. This work included weekly lectures on theory and media instructional processes, faculty development seminars, a seminar for London based BBC producers and directors, meetings with various other teams, and consultations with individuals who were associated with the OUUK and BBC (Wedemeyer, 1969a, 1971b).

After returning to the United States, Wedemeyer carried on correspondence with the OUUK planners throughout 1970 until the OUUK opened its doors in 1971. In 1972, Wedemeyer returned to London and interviewed colleagues Walter Perry and Walter James about the early days at the OUUK in a the BBC broadcast titled *Conversations*. The success of the new institution and its attraction as a model was reflected in comments by the British Prime Minister Harold Wilson, who was responsible for providing top-level political leadership in pushing through the idea of the nation-wide experimental OUUK program. Wilson wrote that he had been "besieged by University Presidents, Senators, Congressmen, and Presidents of the U.S. to tell them more about the achievements of the Open University" (1976, p. xii).

In 1975, with the OUUK firmly established, Wedemeyer was invited to become the third recipient of an honorary doctorate, putting him in the company of former recipients Paulo Friere and Lady Plowden. During the award ceremony, Professor Walter James (1975) spoke about Wedemeyer's contributions to the OUUK:

> What's to come in open independent study for the adult learner is still unsure. What is sure is that Chuck Wedemeyer, who more than any other person secured lift-off for the vehicle, will be developing its guidance and control systems, and sending it further into the unknown, beyond the limit of its present orbit. Those whom such education has reached out to and touched owe more than they know and far more than they can repay to him. The Open University—an inheritor of

his inspiration, a beneficiary of his advice, and a learner from his wisdom—has the privilege of offering a token on their behalf.

In his 1981 book *Learning at the Back Door: Reflections on Non-Traditional Learning in the Lifespan*, Wedemeyer (p. 60) identified "non-traditional, distance, open or independent learning" as "a single great new development in education" that would be a vehicle for a new era in higher education. Nearly three decades later, Moore (2009) emphasized two "watershed events" which were the "beginning of a global, worldwide paradigm shift in higher education." The two events were AIM and the Open University.

WEDEMEYER'S INFLUENCE ON THREE PIONEERING THEORISTS: HOLMBERG, MOORE, AND PETERS

Of the hundreds of distance educators that Wedemeyer corresponded and interacted with during his career, three are especially important—Börje Holmberg, Michael G. Moore, and Otto Peters—each of these practitioner-scholars has become recognized as a major contributor to theory and scholarship in the field of distance and open education. Chapters by Peters and Holmberg appeared in earlier editions of this handbook (Holmberg, 2003, 2007; Peters, 2003, 2007). A look at the evolution of Wedemeyer's relationships with Holmberg, Moore, and Peters provides us with further insights into the history of the field of distance education as well as explaining how Wedemeyer's ideas came to live on around the world.

Wedemeyer and Holmberg

As a distance education theorist, Börje Holmberg is known for the development of what he described as "a predictive theory" that applies an instructional methodology grounded in using a teaching-learning conversational style and in making use of "empathetic emotions" (Bernath & Vidal, 2007, p. 430). Just how significant was Holmberg's contribution is indicated by the date (1960) when he first published his ideas in On the methods of Teaching by Correspondence and referred to his theory as "guided didactic conversation" and, later, as "teaching-learning conversations" (Holmberg, 2003, p. 79). His "approach to distance education … is based on the very general observation that feelings of personal empathy and personal relations between learner and teacher support motivation for learning and tend to improve the results of learning" (Holmberg, 2007, p. 69).

As Wedemeyer prepared for a trip to Europe in the summer of 1961, he wrote to Holmberg for the first time. Wedemeyer had just finished reading Holmberg's (1961b) article in *Home Study Review*, and wrote,

> I have read with great interest your article … entitled "On the methods of Teaching by Correspondence." The information is of great help to me as I prepare to visit the major correspondence schools of Europe.… Enclosed for you is a small book describing correspondence instruction in American universities. (Wedemeyer, 1961a, 1961b)

Thanking him for sending this book *New Perspectives in University Correspondence Study* (Wedemeyer & Childs, 1961), Holmberg arranged to meet during Wedemeyer's visit to Sweden in 1961, and they continued a lifelong correspondence, sharing publications such as Hermods' monthly newsletter *Korrespondens* and myriad course materials (Holmberg, 1961a, 1963). In July, 1963, Holmberg visited Wedemeyer in his Madison, Wisconsin, office and furthered their personal friendship and a professional alliance. In 1964, Holmberg was focused on the upcoming Correspondence Education Conference (CEC) which was to be held in Malmo, Sweden, and Wedemeyer was working on the second volume of the *Brandenburg Memorial Essays* (Wedemeyer, 1963, 1966b). Wedemeyer invited Holmberg to contribute to the second volume, suggested that topics from the CEC would be valuable, and indicated he wanted to include writings from authors who were from outside the United States. Holmberg agreed to contribute and added that he would look forward to June of 1965 when Wedemeyer was scheduled to give the keynote speech at the ICCE conference in Stockholm. During this time, Wedemeyer had also been invited to be Oxford's first Kellogg Fellow during April and May, and immediately following, he traveled directly to Stockholm for the June ICCE.

About two years later, Holmberg (1967b) finished his book *Correspondence Education* and told Wedemeyer that "Lots of things are happening here.... We are giving more and more attention to and spending more money on developing our methods and products and we have certainly learnt a lot from American research and experiences.... All over the world people talk about the multi-media project that you are in charge of in Wisconsin. I wonder if you can let me have some rather detailed information on it?" (Holmberg, 1967a). Holmberg was referring to Wedemeyer's AIM program, and even though Hermods was experimenting with television, radio, and telephone courses, Holmberg told Wedemeyer that "this is a mere beginning and I understand you have reached much further."

Wedemeyer and Holmberg continued their correspondence throughout the rest of the next two decades and worked together in ICCE and CEC. When Wedemeyer was President of ICCE, he appointed Holmberg to a key role in negotiations with UNESCO that led to a strengthening of ties and a raise in ICCE's status, which also raised Holmberg's status and leadership role within ICCE, and he succeeded Wedemeyer as president of that organization.

Holmberg is well known for his belief that quality student support is a primary basis for successful programs, and as previously noted, his theory of teaching-learning conversations that is based on the importance of "personal relations, study pleasure, and empathy between students and those representing the supporting organization" (Holmberg, 2007, p. 69). Wedemeyer's analysis of programs such as the University of South Africa (UNISA) and AIM show that, like Holmberg, Wedemeyer also believed that student support was a critical aspect for successful programs. Clearly, the two men influenced one another; Holmberg certainly drew upon Wedemeyer in the development of his theoretical and practical work, and Wedemeyer drew upon Holmberg's ideas and practice.

Recommended publications for further insight into Holmberg's influence and ideas can be found in Bernath and Vidal (2007), Black (2004, 2007, this volume), Diehl (2011a, 2011b), and Holmberg (Holmberg, 2003, 2007).

Wedemeyer and Peters

Otto Peters is known for the theory which describes distance education as an industrialized form of education. In the early 1960s, Peters examined correspondence educational systems and concluded that in a post-industrial society, distance education incorporated teaching as an "objectified process" which includes "professional planning and preparation, formalization, standardization, mechanization, automation, digitalization, rationalization, division of work, mass production, repeatability, and centralization" (Peters, 2007, p. 58). While many researchers have focused on this organizational dimension, Peters (Bernath & Vidal, 2007; Peters, 2007) has stressed that his theory also addresses the historical, economic, cultural, sociological, anthropological, and most significantly, the important and unique pedagogical dimensions of the phenomenon of distance education. According to Peters (Bernath & Vidal, 2007, p. 435), "The change of the very nature of knowledge is a product and consequence of industrialized learning" and the focus of his theory is "on these radical changes, which had never been experienced before."

In 1965 Wedemeyer and Peters met for the first time at the ICCE in Stockholm. Wedemeyer gave the keynote address, *Correspondence Education in the World of Today*. The ICCE conference in 1965 was more international than it had ever been, with over 220 participants from about 30 countries. Peters was the Chief Educational Adviser for the Federal Republic of Germany's Educational Centre in Berlin at this time (ICCE, 1965).

Wedemeyer, like Peters, shared an interest in surveying the world's correspondence institutions. In 1966, Otto Peters (1966a) wrote to Wedemeyer to tell him that "Der Fernunterricht" had been published and that it contained "a description of correspondence instruction in 11 countries...." Peters, working on *Correspondence Instruction in Teacher Training*, sent Wedemeyer an institutional survey to complete. Wedemeyer (1966a) responded with congratulations and told Peters that the publication would "most certainly be a substantial contribution to our knowledge of correspondence education." In the survey that Wedemeyer returned, he provided information about teacher motivations as well as the use of television combined with correspondence study, radio, and small group correspondence methods. Wedemeyer also sent Peters a list of all of the NUEA institutions that offered correspondence to teachers and thus might be helpful to him. Additionally, Wedemeyer enclosed a copy of the *Brandenburg Memorial Essays I* (Wedemeyer, 1963) and a promise for a copy of the upcoming *Brandenburg Memorial Essays II* (Wedemeyer, 1966b). Over the following months, Peters sent requests for additional information and Wedemeyer arranged to have research materials delivered to him.

In the autumn of 1966, Otto Peters and three other German educators visited the United States. In Madison, Peters met with Wedemeyer and arrangements were made so that he could also meet with Dr. Ripley Sims (director, Division of Instruction with USAFI) and with Dr. William Brothers (assistant director for Developing Correspondence Programs—Innovated Processes).

Following his tour, Peters (1966b) penned *Report about the International Teacher Development Program,* in which he recommended that the United States should develop a single national center for correspondence courses, citing USAFI as a possible model. After returning to Germany, Peters (1967) wrote to Wedemeyer, told him about a new book *Texte Zum Fernstudium* that he was going to publish, and asked him to contribute. Requesting that Wedemeyer write about AIM, Peters stated it was "the best and most advanced development of university correspondence study!" As the publication date neared, Peters (1968) wrote to tell Wedemeyer that he believed Wedemeyer's and collaborator Dr. Bern's contribution would be "the best chapter of the book." Additionally,

Peters told Wedemeyer that he had been invited to make a presentation at the upcoming ICCE in Paris, something that Wedemeyer had suggested to then President Renée Erdos earlier in the year.

Peters also invited Wedemeyer to visit Berlin to participate in a West German conference to present on "The Changing Role of Teachers." Wedemeyer (1967) believed that in the end, "the AIM experiment would shed light on the changes that innovation require" and that

> these challenges and changes impel a serious educator to undertake innovations, one result of which is a radical shift in the role of the teacher. But this role change is implied in the challenges and changes, and must be confronted there before the implementation through innovation. Indeed I think that if the role change is seen only as a result of innovation, innovation and change will be resisted vigorously. The 'revolution' in education is not, then, merely technological, although the technological elements are most visible.

Wedemeyer and Moore

Michael G. Moore is known for his theory of Transactional Distance, which is covered elsewhere in this volume.

After a seven-year career in adult education in Kenya in East Africa, Moore became Wedemeyer's research assistant and graduate student at the University of Wisconsin in Madison in July 1970. He was immediately immersed in ideas about open and distance education as he provided research data for the Wisconsin Open School Project, an endeavor led by Wedemeyer on behalf of the Wisconsin Governor's Commission on Education. This project was an innovative program that would have created a cradle-to-grave centralized system of education using communication technologies across the whole State of Wisconsin, systematically similar to the national Open University in the UK. The plan never got off the ground and was abandoned after years of planning under political pressure from within and outside the state university (Diehl, 2009, 2011a; Gibson, Moore, Burton, Hardy, & Bonk, 2009; Moore & Kearsley, 2012).

Moving from Madison in 1973 to become a professor at St. Francis Xavier University in Antigonish, Canada, and still building on Wedemeyer's independent study theory, Moore published his second article, "Towards a Theory of Independent Learning and Teaching" (Moore, 1973b) and together with Wedemeyer expanded some of the ideas about distance education in Speculations on a Definition of Independent Study" (Moore, 1973a) at the Conference on Independent Learning in Vancouver, Canada.

While teaching at St. Francis Xavier University, Moore (1976) completed work on his doctoral dissertation, *Investigation of the Interaction Between the Cognitive Style of Field Independence and Attitudes to Independent Study Among Adult Learners Who Use Correspondence Independent Study and Self Directed Independent Study*. In this study he measured learning attitudes, field independence, and examined and measured the "psychological characteristics of correspondence students" in two professional adult education programs. The study's significance, according to Moore (1976, p. 14), was that it represented "the first investigation of the field independence cognitive style of students in an adult education program" but also contained the basic ideas about dialog, structure and learner autonomy that a few years later were reworked into a theory called transactional distance. "A Model of Independent Study" was published in the

European journal *Epistolodidactica* in 1977, and Moore continued to work on building theory pertaining to independent study (Moore, 1980a, 1980b). Wedemeyer had established graduate seminars related to distance education and independent learners, and as Wedemeyer approached his retirement, Moore came to Madison as a visiting professor to teach them. At the time, they were the only courses in the world on this topic (Moore, 1999). After leaving Canada, Moore worked for nine years at the OUUK, and, in 1986, he accepted a professorial position in the Adult Education Program at The Pennsylvania State University. There he founded the American Center for the Study of Distance Education (ACSDE) as well as the Distance Education Online Symposium (DEOS). He also started a national research symposium and designed and taught the first full program of graduate courses in distance education. In 1986 Moore launched what became an important journal for the developing field of distance and open education, *The American Journal of Distance Education* (*AJDE*). The first issue included an interview with Wedemeyer, which was appropriate, since the founding of the *AJDE* brought another of Wedemeyer's dreams to fruition. Decades earlier, Wedemeyer had planted a seed regarding a professional journal. In 1969 he suggested "a need for a correspondence instruction journal to help workers in the field identify with others in the field as well as to develop and maintain a competency in the field," but he was "pessimistic that a correspondence instruction journal could be supported in the U.S." (Wedemeyer, 1969b).

Wedemeyer and Moore remained in contact via correspondence through the remaining years of Wedemeyer's life and in face-to-face meetings when Moore attended the Annual Conference on Distance Teaching and Learning in Madison, Wisconsin (which he had been instrumental in establishing in 1986). At that conference, beginning in 1987, an important award in honor of Wedemeyer was initiated—the Mildred B. and Charles A. Wedemeyer Award, and Michael G. Moore presented the first award to Farhad Saba in Wedemeyer's presence (see Figure 4.1 in the next chapter).

REFERENCES

Bauder, D. (1959, November 11). TV-correspondence course carrying graduate school credits, Feature Story, *U.W. News Service*.

Bernath, U., & Vidal, M. (2007). The theories and the theorists: Why theory is important for research. *Distances et savoirs, 5*(3), 427–458.

Black, L. (2004). *A living story of the origins and development of scholarship in the field of distance education* (unpublished doctoral dissertation). The Pennsylvania State University, University Park.

Black, L. (2007). A history of scholarship. In M. G. Moore (Ed.), *Handbook of distance education* (2nd ed., pp. 3–14). Mahwah, NJ: Erlbaum.

Conversations. (1972). BBC program. London: BBC.

Diehl, W. C. (2009). *A glance back at Charles Wedemeyer: Excerpts from an interview with Michael G. Moore, Ph.D.* [Video]. Retrieved from http://vimeo.com/29200626

Diehl, W. C. (2011a). *Learning at the back door: Charles A. Wedemeyer and the evolution of open and distance learning* (Unpublished doctoral dissertation). The Pennsylvania State University, University Park.

Diehl, W. C. (2011b). Speaking personally — with Börje Holmberg. *The American Journal of Distance Education, 25*(1), 64–71.

Gibson, C., Moore, M. G., Burton, G., Hardy, D. W., & Bonk, C. (2009). Lessons from history and the continuing mission of distance education: Who is still at the back door? *The Annual Conference on Distance Teaching and Learning*. Retrieved from http://mediasite.ics.uwex.edu/mediasite5/Viewer/?peid=a863be1f5bc348bbb1c875366dafe581

Holmberg, B. (1960). *On the methods of teaching by correspondence*. Lund, Sweden: C.W.K. Gleerup.

Holmberg, B. (1961a, June 10). *Letter To Wedemeyer*. Wedemeyer Archives. Steenbock Memorial Library, Madison, WI.

Holmberg, B. (1961b). On the methods of teaching by correspondence. *The Home Study Review, 2*(Spring).

Holmberg, B. (1963, May 20). *Letter To Wedemeyer.* Wedemeyer Archives. Steenbock Memorial Library, Madison, WI.

Holmberg, B. (1967a). *Correspondence education. A survey of applications, methods and problems.* Malmö, Sweden: Hermods-NKI.

Holmberg, B. (1967b, September 28). *Letter to Wedemeyer.* Wedemeyer Archives. Steenbock Memorial Library, Madison, WI.

Holmberg, B. (2003). A theory of distance education based on empathy. In M. G. Moore & W. G. Anderson (Eds.), *Handbook of distance education* (pp. 79–86). Mahwah, NJ: Erlbaum.

Holmberg, B. (2007). A theory of teaching-learning conversations. In M. G. Moore (Ed.), *Handbook of distance education* (2nd ed., pp. 69–75). Mahwah, NJ: Erlbaum.

ICCE. (1965, June). *Proceedings Seventh International Conference of The International Council on Correspondence Education,* Stockholm, Sweden.

James, W. (1975, April). *Remarks on the occasion of the honorary doctorate for Charles Wedemeyer.* Open University Commencement. Nottingham, United Kingdom.

Moore, M. G. (1973a). *Some speculations on a definition of independent study.* Paper presented at the Kellogg Seminar on Indpendent Learning in the Health Sciences, Vancouver, Canada, University of British Columbia. Vancouver, Canada: W.K. Kellogg Report No. 7. pp. 25ˉ41. ERIC #ED285573.

Moore, M. G. (1973b). Towards a theory of independent learning and teaching. *Journal of Higher Education,* (44), 661–679.

Moore, M. G. (1976). *Investigation of the interaction between the cognitive style of field independence and attitudes to independent study among adult learners who use correspondence independent study and self directed independent study* (Unpublished draft of doctoral dissertation). University of Wisconsin, Madison.

Moore, M. G. (1980a). Independent study. In R. Boyd & J. Apps (Eds.), *Redefining the discipline of adult education* (pp. 16–31). San Francisco, CA: Jossey-Bass.

Moore, M. G. (1980b). On a theory of independent study. *ZIFF, Papiere No. 16.* Hagen, West Germany: Fern Universitat.

Moore, M. G. (1986). Speaking Personally — with Charles Wedemeyer. *The American Journal of Distance Education, 1*(1), 59–64.

Moore, M. G. (1999). Editorial: Charles Wedemeyer, In memorium 1911–1999. *The American Journal of Distance Education, 13*(3), 1–6.

Moore, M. G. (2009). The scholarship of distance education: A story of which we can be proud! *The Annual Conference on Distance Teaching and Learning.* Retrieved from http://mediasite.ics.uwex.edu/mediasite5/Viewer/?peid=505b5517421a4f91a4db0de736f05254

Moore, M. G., & Kearsley, G. (2012). *Distance education: A systems view of online learning* (3rd ed.). Belmont, CA: Wadsworth.

Perry, W. (1976). *Open university: A personal account by the first vice-chancellor.* Milton Keynes, United Kingdom: Open University Press.

Peters, O. (1966a, March 25). *Letter to Wedemeyer.* Wedemeyer Archives. Steenbock Memorial Library, Madison, WI.

Peters, O. (1966b). *Report about the international teacher development program — Special German project — September 30–December 23, 1966.* Berlin, Germany: Padagogisches Zentrum.

Peters, O. (1967, May 3). *Letter to Wedemeyer.* Wedemeyer Archives. Steenbock Memorial Library, Madison, WI.

Peters, O. (1968, October 31). *Letter to Wedemeyer.* Wedemeyer Archives. Steenbock Memorial Library, Madison, WI.

Peters, O. (2003). Learning with new media in distance education. In M. G. Moore & W. G. Anderson (Eds.), *Handbook of distance education* (pp. 87–112). Mahwah, NJ: Erlbaum.

Peters, O. (2007). The most industrialized form of education. In M. G. Moore (Ed.), *Handbook of distance education* (2nd ed., pp. 57–68). Mahwah, NJ: Erlbaum.

Stabler, E. (1986). *Founders: Innovators in education, 1830–1980.* Edmonton, Alberta, Canada: University of Alberta Press.

Tunstall, J. (1974). *The Open University opens.* Amherst: University of Massachusetts Press.

UWEX. (1956, March 30). Press release, *University of Wisconsin Extension News.*

UWEX. (1959, November 11). Press release, *University of Wisconsin Extension News.*

Wedemeyer, C. (1961a, June 1). *Letter to Gadden.* Wedemeyer Archives. Steenbock Memorial Library, Madison, WI.

Wedemeyer, C. (1961b, June 1). *Letter to Holmberg.* Wedemeyer Archives. Steenbock Memorial Library, Madison, WI.

Wedemeyer, C. (Ed.). (1963). *The Brandenburg memorial essays on correspondence instruction I.* Madison, WI: University of Wisconsin, University Extension.

Wedemeyer, C. (1966a, April 5). *Letter to Peters.* Wedemeyer Archives. Steenbock Memorial Library, Madison, WI.

Wedemeyer, C. (Ed.). (1966b). *The Brandenburg memorial essays on correspondence instruction II.* Madison, WI: University of Wisconsin, University Extension.

Wedemeyer, C. (1967, November 14). *Letter to Peters.* Wedemeyer Archives. Steenbock Memorial Library, Madison, WI.

Wedemeyer, C. (1968, March 29). *Letter to Stafford.* Wedemeyer Archives. Steenbock Memorial Library, Madison, WI.

Wedemeyer, C. (1969a, March 18). *Letter to Christodoulou.* Wedemeyer Archives. Steenbock Memorial Library, Madison, WI.

Wedemeyer, C. (1969b, April 3). *Letter to MacKenzie.* Wedemeyer Archives. Steenbock Memorial Library, Madison, WI.

Wedemeyer, C. (1969c, April 10). *Letter to W. James.* Wedemeyer Archives. Steenbock Memorial Library, Madison, WI.

Wedemeyer, C. (1971a). Independent study. In L. C. Deighton (Ed.), *The encyclopedia of education* (Vol. 4, pp. 548–557). New York, NY: Free Press.

Wedemeyer, C. (1971b). *Letter to Florence Anderson.* Letter. Wedemeyer Archives. Steenbock Memorial Library, Madison, WI.

Wedemeyer, C. (1971c). The open school. Supplement to the final report of the Govenor's Commission on Education (Kellett Commission). Madison, WI: Governor's Commission on Education.

Wedemeyer, C. (1981). *Learning at the back door: Reflections on non-traditional learning in the lifespan.* Madison: University of Wisconsin Press.

Wedemeyer, C., & Childs, G. B. (1961). *New perspectives in university correspondence study.* Chicago, IL: Center for the Study of Liberal Education for Adults.

Wedemeyer, C., & Ghatala, M. (1971). Wisconsin's Proposed "Open" School. *Audio Visual Instruction* (January).

WHA (Writer). (1970). The open school (with Professor Wedemeyer), *Accent on living.* [Radio broadcast]. Madison, WI.

Wilson, H. (1976). Foreword. In W. Perry (Ed.), *Open University: A personal account* (pp. xi–xii). Milton Keynes, UK: The Open University Press.

4

BUILDING THE FUTURE

A Theoretical Perspective

FARHAD SABA

INTRODUCTION

While the practice of distance education is rapidly growing, its theoretical base is not, and is in need of further articulation. Questions to be addressed in this regard include:

- In a field that is growing rapidly in the number of institutions, practitioners, and students, what is the most appropriate approach for theory building?
- In a discipline that has spawned several subfields, how can we understand the relationships between different—and at times seemingly unrelated—ideas, research results, and practices?
- As complex and colorful as distance education is, and may become in the future, how can we cast a net wide enough to capture its key attributes in parsimonious theoretical principles?

The task is daunting. The literature in the field is immense and increasing in volume rapidly. In this volume, Black has documented how scholarship in distance education has exploded since 1995, with increasing numbers of researchers in professional organizations and graduate programs contributing to the knowledge-base in journal articles, books, monographs, master's theses, and doctoral dissertations. Online databases have also been established by organizations such as the World Bank, each of which includes thousands of documents and resources. Although this surge in publishing is a welcome development, it has created some challenges for the theoretician.

    1. Confusing Terminology. A major factor that has made the task of theory building perplexing is the emergence of terms and phrases in the current literature that have received acceptance among different groups of practitioners, while they remain poorly defined, or undefined. Throughout the literature, authors widely use terms, such as, online education, eLearning, or Web-based learning/education while ascribing different meanings to them. Moore, Dickson-Deane, and Galyen. (2010) conducted a survey in which respondents were asked to define selected terms, such as, distance education, eLearning and online learning and describe their connotations. The study confirmed "conflicting responses" about the meaning of these terms. The authors concluded: "The findings show great differences in the meaning of foundational terms that are used in the field, but also provide implications internationally for the referencing, sharing, and the collaboration of results detailed in varying research studies" (p. 134). Inevitably, this lack of consistency impacts researchers that like to build upon existing findings, which is a necessary process for developing a discipline based on a unified paradigm.

More specifically, and concentrating on only one widely used term, Guri-Rosenblit and Gros, (2011) conducted an analysis of the term *e-Learning* and its different connotations in the literature. They aptly focused on the first letter "e" in e-Learning and the varied electronic technologies to which it can refer. The authors concluded:

> This confusing terminology stems from the fact that the variable technological abilities are rich and complex. It does not seem possible at this stage to aggregate the multiple [technology] terms into one accepted term, to be used by all practitioners and researchers in this field. It is most likely, that new terms will enter the discourse on technologies in learning/teaching processes as new technologies and new technological applications continue to develop. (p. 55)

This lack of consistency in key conceptual terms has brought general confusion about distance education to the minds of novice students as well as administrators and decision makers who may not be familiar with the history of distance education and its conceptual evolution.

2. Lack of Historical Perspective. Reading some of the articles, even in peer reviewed journals, one comes to the inevitable conclusion that their authors, editors, and reviewers are not familiar with the historical origin and conceptual growth of the field of distance education. For some, history starts from when they become interested in the field. Depending on the initial period of their focus, some authors attempt to reduce the entire field of distance education to a narrow view defined by a particular medium of communication (e.g., web-based learning) or mode of information transmission (e.g., online learning). This reductionist approach to understanding the field is in sharp contrast to the holistic systems approach that is essential for developing a comprehensive theory of the field, as it will be shown in this chapter.

3. Absence of Construct Validity. Even if we accept such crude constructs as e-Learning or online learning, one is hard pressed to find studies that have validated them empirically. As shown above in the example of e-Learning, some of these concepts cannot even stand the test of face validity. Nevertheless, for inclusion of these concepts in a theory of distance education, at the minimum, such constructs must be validated in experimental empirical studies. To illustrate how these constructs can be put to the test of verification, an example will be presented in this chapter. It will demonstrate how:

- *Distance* in education was defined in the context of the construct *transactional distance*,
- *Transactional distance* was measured in terms of the two related constructs of dialogue and structure, and

- *Transactional distance* was empirically verified in an experimental data-based study.
- Similar demonstration of verification and establishment of validity is necessary for such terms as *eLearning, online learning/education, web-based education,* and *mobile learning* if they are to be taken as serious theoretical constructs.

4. The Postmodern Turn. Tests of validity have become even more important during the current turn from modernism to postmodernism as graduate students as well as more seasoned researchers elicit constructs in exploratory studies. As needed and important as these studies are, their results are seldom subjected to experimental data-based research for determining the validity of newly surfaced constructs beyond their initial exploration. European postmodernism tends to search for the *different* in a seemingly endless process of deconstructing tenets of established disciplines. When a discipline is fragmented in this way, the question becomes: is there an approach to bringing seemingly unrelated concepts into a coherent picture and presenting them in a form that would make sense to the novice and the expert alike? At the dawn of the 21st century, when it seems we are leaving the epoch of the modern and stepping into the postmodern, while it is useful to take a fresh look at disciplines and search for the *different* to make the hitherto invisible visible, it is important to balance such deconstruction with the American approach to the postmodern. The origin of American postmodernism is embedded in the thoughts of pragmatic philosophers Dewey, Pierce, and James, thinkers who rejected the dogmatism of established disciplines and re-opened the door to hermeneutics and paralogy. But the core of their approach—especially that of William James—was the idea of webs of relationships among different or even ostensibly unrelated concepts, what we would call a systems approach. Choosing a systems approach for bringing key concepts of a field to an understandable whole, however, should not be misconstrued as an attempt in *totalizing*. It is not the aim of the systems approach to make everyone behave the same or impose a pre-defined agenda on research and exploration without offering alternatives to thought or action. As will be demonstrated, open dynamic systems provide for formation of new ideas as well as their testing and validation both at the instructional level for the learners and instructors and at the theory building level for the researchers. As James illustrated, to explore a phenomenon in as many of its aspects as possible is similar to walking in a hotel corridor in which opening a door leads to other doors.

A DISCUSSION ABOUT RELATIONSHIPS

This chapter, therefore, is about relationships. A systems approach to understanding a phenomenon relies on exploring the relationships among its constituent parts. It focuses on the process of:

- Identifying key concepts in a system; i.e. distance education in this case;
- Making educated guesses (hypotheses) about how the constructs are related;
- Experimentally validating such constructs, and their relationships.

Therefore, in the remainder of this chapter I will:

1. Propose the systems approach as a robust philosophy, methodology, and technology.
2. Demonstrate that American postmodernism offers the philosophical underpinnings for taking a holistic approach to understanding complex phenomena, such as distance education.
3. Justify the necessity of a systems approach for building a comprehensive contemporary theory of distance education.
4. Describe the initial steps taken by Saba (1988), and Saba & Shearer (1994) in developing a systems theory of distance education by experimentally verifying the relationships among key theoretical constructs of transactional distance proposed by Moore (1973, 1983).
5. Extend the application of systems methodology to empirically verify and validate other key concepts.

The ultimate purpose here is to present philosophical underpinnings, research methods, and technical means for theory building, research, and practice in distance education that are appropriate for the postmodern era.

Why the Systems Approach?

In broad terms, the traditional scientific method based on the Cartesian dictum has been to "break down every problem into as many separate simple elements as might be possible" (Weinberg, 2001, p. 183). However, in fields concerned with human behavior, including education, it is not enough to merely observe and report about isolated parts. For example, observing the behavior of individuals within an educational organization might reveal what each does for an organization. However, it is clear that the result of their collective behaviors is more than the sum of their individual actions. In other words, organizations as a whole are far more complex than the actions of each individual within them. As Capra (1996) put it, the "great shock" of 20th-century science was that reality could not be understood merely by Cartesian analysis. Understanding the *relationships between components* of a phenomenon is at least as important, if not more so than understanding each part separately, particularly when living systems and human organizations are concerned.

Systems Science. A systems approach to research and development was conceptualized in the 1930s (Bertalanffy, 1968). As explained by Skyttner (2002), classical science, due to partitioning and specialization, became incapable of solving complex problems ranging from the spread of communicative diseases to over-bureaucratization in social services. He explained, "The interaction of system-variables are so interlinked to each other that cause and effect can seldom be separated. One separate variable thus can be both cause and effect. An attempt to reduce complexities to their constituent and build an understanding of the wholeness through the knowledge of its parts is no longer valid" (p. 33). In explaining the systems approach, Skyttner added, "General systems theory is a part of the systems paradigm which complements the traditional scientific paradigm ... with a kind of thinking that is better suited to biological and behavioural realms" (p. 50).

In the recent past, scientists from a wide range of disciplines including physics (Capra, 1982), biology (Wilson, 1998), psychology (Damasio, 1994), and education (Banathy,

1992), to name a few, have questioned Cartesian reductionist thinking (Appleyard, 1993). Capra (1982) has suggested:

> The new vision of reality we have been talking about is based on the awareness of the essential interrelatedness and interdependence of all phenomena-physical, biological, psychological, social and cultural. It transcends current disciplinary and conceptual boundaries and will be pursued within new institutions. At present there is no well established framework, either conceptual or institutional, that would accommodate the formulation of the new paradigm, but the outlines of such a framework are already being shaped by many individuals, communities, and networks that are developing new ways of thinking and organizing themselves according to new principles. (p. 265)

SYSTEMS THINKING IN DISTANCE EDUCATION

1. Origin. Systems thinking in distance education is not new. Moore (1999) and Moore and Kearsley (2005, 2012) place its origin to Wedemeyer's founding of the Articulated Instructional Media (AIM) project in 1969 at the University of Wisconsin-Madison. The project not only broke "the ancient mold of extension adult, and higher education," it created an integrated approach to the use of media for educating mature learners. Moore and Kearsley (2005) explained:

> Wedemeyer's idea regarding students was that using a variety of media meant that not only content could be better presented than through any one medium alone, but also meant that people with differing learning styles could choose the particular combination that was most suited to their needs. To bring together the expertise needed to produce such integrated multimedia programs, AIM invented the idea of the course design team, formed of instructional designers, technology specialists and content experts. (p. 33)

We take multimedia for granted today, and can see on the horizon the wide acceptance of adaptive systems that can differentially respond to learner preferences that can accommodate their emergent behavior. However, it was the pioneering effort of Wedemeyer some five decades ago that brought systems thinking to the use of media at a time when each medium was touted as the effective solution for responding to educational problems.

2. Relationships of Key Constructs. Building on Wedemyer's holistic approaches to distance teaching, Michael G. Moore in some of his early studies, brought systems thinking to theorizing. In 1984, while resuming my research in the field after 10 years of managing distance education programs, I came across two of his articles (Moore, 1973, 1983). In these articles he had set forth structure, dialogue, autonomy, and transactional distance as key constructs in independent adult learning. While reading these articles I noticed the obvious dynamic relationships between these constructs. Moore explained that variability in dialogue and structure indicates four types of programs for individual learning:

1. Programs with no dialogue and no structure (-D -S)
2. Programs with no dialogue, but with structure (-D +S)

3. Programs with dialogue and structure (+D +S)
4. Programs with dialogue, but no structure (+ D -S)

Looking at these types of programs and the operation signs (i.e., + and -) assigned to them, I had one of those rare "aha!" moments that leads to creative work. Moore, by defining the relationship between dialogue and structure in mathematical terms, had already started the preliminary development of a system dynamics model. It was all right there in front me! How could I possibly ignore the opportunity to test Moore's hypotheses by not developing a system dynamics model? This brainstorm led me to formalize Moore's hypotheses in terms of system dynamics. I presented the results in an article submitted to the *American Journal of Distance Education* (Saba, 1988). It was with great surprise that I received a call a few months later. I was informed that I would have the great honor of being the recipient of the Charles A. Wedemeyer award for a research article. In a rare historic event, standing next to Dr. Moore, I received the award from Dr. Wedemeyer in Madison, Wisconsin. This system's particular causal loop had come full circle (see Figure 4.1).

In recent years, Shearer (2010, this volume) has continued this line of research, with a critical analysis of the concept of dialogue in transactional distance that has moved this key concept to a higher level of theoretical clarity. Also, in the context of instructional design, Shearer has demonstrated the relationship of dialogue with affordances of technologies employed in distance education (this volume).

3. Systems in Practice. In recent times, Moore and Kearsley (2012) reiterated their systems view of distance education:

> Because distance education requires using a range of technical and human resources, it is always best delivered in a system, and understanding a distance education program is always best when a systems approach is used. A distance

Figure 4.1 Michael G. Moore, Charles Wedemeyer, and Farhad Saba at first Wedemeyer award ceremony in Madison, Wisconsin, August 1987.

education system consists of all the component processes that operate when teaching and learning at a distance occurs. It includes learning, teaching, communication, design, and management. (p. 9)

They also presented a conceptual model of distance education, which includes primary components such as teaching, learning, program/course design, technology, management, policy, and organization, and defined the relationship between these components and the broader educational system in which these components operate. These broader systems include economics, psychology, sociology, history, culture and philosophy (Moore & Kearsley, 2012).

They augmented this conceptual model with a systems model in which main components and processes were defined. These include:

- A source of content knowledge and teaching (i.e., an educational institution, with faculty and other resources for providing content);
- A course design susbsystem to structure this into materials and activities for students;
- A subsystem that delivers the course to learners through media and technology;
- Instructors and support personnel who interact with learners as they use these materials;
- Learners in different environments;
- A management subsystem to organize policy, needs assessment and resource allocation; to evaluate outcomes; and to coordinate other subsystems. (p. 12)

Embedded in this model are elements that instructional designers have been using since the 1970s to develop new programs, courses, and instructional materials. The Instructional System Design (ISD) model follows a linear process that begins with identifying and analyzing the needs of the learner. Such analyses enables the instructional designer to design, develop, and implement instruction, as well as to evaluate the results in terms of learning outcomes. Ideally, the instructional designer leads a team of other specialists, such as, programmers, videographers, graphic desingers and writers and is often guided by a subject matter expert.

Other scholars have also contributed to systems thinking:

- Spector (2000); de Jong,(2006); Komis, Ergazaki, and Zogza (2007); Thompson and Reimann (2009); Bravo, van Joolingen, and de Jong (2009); Nuhog˘lu (2010); Gonzalo and Dutt (2011) have applied system dynamics to study various aspects of designing intruction.
- Concentrating on public policy, Pacey and Keough (2003) presented a model that offers feedback between policy goals and objectives (input) and intended/observed outcomes (output). Components influencing the behavior of the model are content, resources, and activities.
- Shaffer (2005) proposed a model of the socio-economic environment of distance education. He claimed that "much research is published as disembodied pieces of information that lack coherence" (n.p.) and called for the development of a standard model.

DIMENSIONS OF SYSTEMS THINKING

Systems thinking in these studies include three dimensions that must be explained if we are to develop a comprehensive view of how it can illuminate future theory building. These dimensions are:

1. Systems philosophy and theory
2. Systems methodology
3. Systems technology for research and practice

1. Systems Philosophy. Premodern philosophy viewed the universe as one cohesive entity, comprised of interdependent parts. As modernism gained influence this holistic view was replaced with an atomistic vision. Today, a new systemic view of the world is reemerging and defining the postmodern era. Table 4.1, based on Laszlo (2001), shows a comparison of the modern atomistic view of the world with a reemerging postmodern systemic view.

Distance education in the postmodern systemic view is composed of many interrelated components and processes that include functions related to managing organizations and offering programs, providing funding and other social support for each enterprise, as well as designing, developing, distributing and evaluating courses. These processes and components are embedded in a global context in which distance education is implemented via various technologies, such as the World Wide Web, and telecommunications satellites, which have made geographic borders transparent for most countries.

2. Systems Methodology, If the idea of the traditional scientific approach was to isolate one element in order to study its effect on another, the purpose of systems science

Table 4.1   Comparison of the Modern Atomistic View of the World with the Postmodern Systemic View

Modern Atomistic World View	Postmodern Systemic World View
Classical world view was anthropocentric. Man is perceived as mastering and controlling nature.	Man is an integral part of nature.
Nature is a giant machine with intricate but replaceable parts.	Nature is endowed with irreplaceable elements and an innate but non-deterministic purpose for choice, flow, and spontaneity.
People and objects are viewed as separate from their environments and from one another.	People and objects are perceived within the context of their environments and in relation to one another. Interconnectedness, communication, and community are emphasized.
All things are distinct and measurable material entities.	Matter is conceived as a configuration of energies that flow and interact. It allows for probabilistic processes, self-creativity, and unpredictability.
The purpose of life is the accumulation of material wealth through competition.	Acquiring knowledge is the purpose of life. Education, communication, human services, and cooperation are emphasized.
Science and technology are Eurocentric.	Valid contributions of people from other regions of the world are welcome.

is to study a phenomenon in relation to its environment. In defining a field, the theorist must identify the boundaries of a system by determining its key components and defining how components relate to each other. Determining and defining these key components are the most important tasks of a theorist who is building a model for a relatively young field of study such as distance education. Relative to one another, and collectively in relation to their environment, these components constitute a system that ideally would represent the field of practice. Examples of such components are:

- Management systems of an entire organization, such as, the Open University, UK or Athabasca Univeristy. An example on a smaller scale would be the management system for a department in a university which offers distance education courses;
- The instructional design process for creating courses in these organizations;
- Components that are responsible for dissemination of courses;
- Evaluation of courses and programs;
- Hardware and software technologies used.

The current literature on distance education is replete with verbal descriptions of how distance education is organized in a certain university or corporation, but very often these descriptive studies lack a formal and precise account of how components of such an organization relate to one another; are affected by each other and affect each other. Occasionally an author might provide a diagram that clarifies the relationships among selected components of a distance education system in an institution. However, although identifying components of a system, articulating their functions, and depicting the relationships among them in a graphic model are necessary, they are not sufficient. Such relationships must also be expressed in mathematical equations because only the model in its mathematical form has the potential to be empirically validated by collection of qualitative and quantitative data.

A. The Modeling Process. Previously, I explained how I first came across Moore's theoretical statements on how several components of distance teaching and learning relate to each other and that I decided to formalize them in system dynamics equations. Moore (1983) hypothesized that transactional distance in education is determined by two variables: structure and dialogue. Consequently, I articulated the relationships between these components in the following hypotheses: (a) when structure increases, transactional distance increases and dialogue decreases; (b) when dialogue increases, transactional distance decreases and structure decreases. By now, Rick L. Shearer had joined me as a research colleague. Together we proceeded by illustrating these hypotheses in the causal loop diagram shown in Figure 4.2.

Notice that these statements imply a dynamic relationship between system components. That is, the mathematical values of system components increase or decrease as time progresses. Time is an inescapable reality affecting our lives. We cannot avoid its progression. Yet, research in education is often oblivious to the impact time has on phenomena. A robust theory of distance education must take the dynamic (i.e. time-based) nature of teaching and learning into consideration.

Once the causal loop diagram was completed, we turned our attention to developing system equations. In system dynamics, components are mainly of two kinds: *levels* and *rates*. (There are others, but for simplicity's sake we will discuss only these two primary and most important components.) Let's use an analogy to understand the concepts of

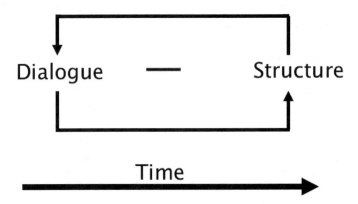

Figure 4.2 Causal loop of transactional distance.

levels and rates. A level is analogous to the amount of water in a pool at any given point in time. A rate is analogous to the the amount of water per unit of time (e.g., second, or minute) that may pour into the pool or drain out of it. Water may pour into a pool while some may drain out simultaneously. However, the water level at any single point in time is determined by: (a) the water level in the pool immediately prior to opening the faucet or the drain; and (b) the rates at which water pours into the pool and drains out of it once the faucet and drain are opened.

If we conceptualize transactional distance as a level, as in our study (Saba & Shearer, 1994), structure would increase the mathematical value of transactional distance, and dialogue would decrease its value. But our work was not done yet. One more step had to be taken. This particular relationship between structure and dialogue needed to be expressed in an algebraic equation as in the following:

TransactionalDistance (t) = TransactionalDistance (t – dt) + (structure – dialogue)(dt)

In this equation, the level of transactional distance at any point in time [TransactionalDistance (t)] is equal to its prior level [TransactionalDistance (t - dt)], plus the rate of structure, minus the rate of dialogue [structure - dialogue], multiplied by the time interval (dt). This equation, along with a few others, constituted a system that could be computer-simulated and tested. Data to show the rate of dialogue and structure in an instructional session could be collected in terms of speech acts iterated per minute by instructors and learners. The model could then be run based on actual empirically observed and collected data to test and verify its validity. This was demonstrated in Saba & Shearer (1994).

B. Analyzing the Model. Ideally, model analysis is an iterative process. After new data are collected, a model should be retested. Sometimes anomalies are observed in retesting a model that may lead to its further refinement. Such refinements may ultimately result in a paradigm shift (Kuhn, 1970). However, in the field of distance education few if any studies are replicated. Rather than building upon existing concepts and frameworks many researchers begin anew by:

• Developing a different terminology, often for existing concepts, and;

- Creating models without clarifying the similarities or differences of the components incorporated in them with those that are included in the existing models.

This lack of concern with existing knowledge should be a major concern for theorists and researchers in our field and an embarrassment for academic advisers and others responsible for the research process. We must adopt the practice of the traditional scientific method of replicating published research studies. Replication allows gaps in the existing knowledge to surface and be articulated in precise terms so that theorists and researchers will be able to work towards bridging them. Replicating studies is a major research strategy that eventually will reduce conceptual confusion when it is conducted often on a regular basis; it is a practice that can benefit our field immensely.

To summarize the process of model building, Roberts, Andersen, Deal, Garet, and Shaffer (1983) presented the following guidelines:

1. Problem Definition. At this stage the "problem" (developing a theoretical model of distance education, in this case) is defined.
2. System Conceptualization- Components of the system are identified and their relationships are formalized in mathematical equations (e.g., transactional distance, structure, dialogue).
3. Model Behavior. The behavior of the theoretical model is observed in a test performed on the computer running hypothetical base data.
4. Model Evaluation, The theoretical model is evaluated and refined based on observation of the results of its behavior.
5. Model Analysis. Data is collected in empirical observation of distance education teaching and learning and the theoretical model is tested based on running actual data.

TRANSACTIONAL DISTANCE IN ITS LARGER CONTEXT

So far the discussion of model building has revolved around transactional distance—the level of which is dependent on the rate of autonomy and dialogue. The hypothesis was that the learner's behavior is based on his or her need for dialogue while the instructor strives to maintain a certain rate of structure to ensure that learning objectives are achieved; thus, the dynamic of interaction between the learner and the instructor determines the level of transactional distance at each point in time. Transactional distance is the central construct in the theory of distance education, as well as in this model because it explains the relationship between the teacher and the learner, which is paramount in any educational system.

However, transactional distance resides within a larger system, and it is to this we now turn our attention.

1. Hierarchy of Nested System Levels. According to Ahl and Allen (1996), "*Complex systems* are defined as those which require fine details to be linked to large outcomes. Forging this link in a way that allows predictability requires addressing multiple levels of analysis simultaneously. Examples are as diverse as a telecommunications satellite, or a poem" (p. 11). An example of such hierarchy in nature is Cell → Organism → Population → Community → Ecosystem → Landscape → Biome → Biosphere (Ahl & Allen, 1996).

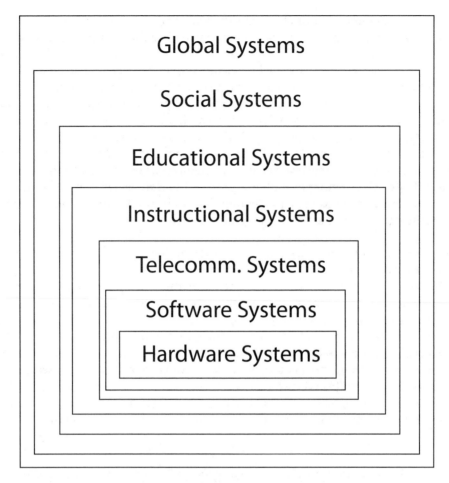

Figure 4.3 Hierarchical model of nested systems in distance education.

Figure 4.3 above depicts distance education as a hierarchical complex system of seven nested levels.

A. Complexity Within Each Level. In this model, transactions between learners and the instructor, with which we have been concerned so far, take place at the Instructional Systems Level. However, there are other subsystems in this level, including at least two other subsystems: the interaction among learners and the interaction of learners with learning materials. Open systems, by definition, behave in response to their environment, and therefore, one can hypothesize that transaction between a learner and the instructor affects the interaction among the learners, which in turn will have an effect on the interaction between the instructor and each of the learners.

B. Complexity Between Levels. Each nested system level also affects other levels and are affected by them. For example a change in Software Systems Level may affect how learners can communicate with their instructor. In fact, each chapter of this handbook elucidates numerous important dimensions of the field of distance education revealing the complexity of the systems related to one or more of the levels depicted in the above model. As evident from the research presented in this *volume, each* of these nested system levels is complex, but relatively and cumulatively they increase in complexity from the core to the outer layers. Each system level is further examined below briefly.

Hardware Systems are the necessary equipment needed to produce instructional materials, establish and maintain communication between the instructor and learners, and establish communication among learners. Since the communication industry has become digital, the computer, or other hardware that operate with a microprocessor, are widely used for production of instructional materials and significantly affected communication between the instructor and learner. Currently, a new generation of mobile devices is dramatically changing affordances for the field.

Software Systems consist of the array of proprietary or open source computer programs needed to convey instructional messages to students or to maintain synchronous communication between instructor and learner and among students. They range from email to more complex programs such as Internet-based video conferencing systems (e.g., Adobe Connect) and learning management systems (e.g., Blackboard). A new generation of adaptive learning system software is emerging now that is capable of differentially responding to learners, making learning more dynamic, personalized and individualized, and allowing for a learner's emergent behavior to manifest in less structured (low transactional dsitance) environments.

Telecommunication Systems are necessary to connect the instructor with learners, and provide connection among learners. The signal generated on a computer might go through a network of coaxial cable, as well as ordinary or structured twisted pair cables before reaching a trunk line made of fiber optics, and then through a microwave relay or a telecommunication satellite before reaching its destination on another set of cable systems. Rapidly, however, wireless telecommunication is augmenting and in certain cases supplanting wired communication as such networks become ubiquitous in cities and even some less populated areas.

Instructional Systems are courses, modules, learning objects and supporting elements such as databases that include the instructional design and content for each subject, knowledge domain, skill set, and competency taught and learned. Professionals who work at this system level are instructors, instructional designers, subject matter experts and evaluators. They work closely with those who are in the Software System Level to produce instructional materials and prepare them for students. As complex adaptive learning systems continue to emerge and provide for personalized learning, the learner may also be added to the list of such "professionals" because many decisions previously determined by instructional designers in advance will now be made by the learner dynamically.

Educational Systems represent a collection of courses that form a discipline, usually offered by an academic department or the training division of a corporation or government agency. As education becomes decentralized (e.g., home schooling), this system level may include programs and courses offered by a variety of organizations, ranging from museums and theme parks to business and industry; including textbook publishers who are already major contributors to this system level.

Societal Systems consist of individuals who work in government agencies or private organizations that create the legal and financial basis for distance education to function. Laws governing accreditation, telecommunication, and copyright greatly influence the practice of distance education. Also, allocating public and private funds to distance education has a crucial impact on the availability of programs to learners.

Global Systems consist of a network of institutions and international associations that make distance education viable throughout the world. In recent years, major structural changes in the relations among nations has fostered direct institution-to-institution, and person-to-person collaboration in distance education as well as improved collaboration among governments, and non-governmental organizations. The effect of the Internet (Telecommunications Systems Level) on the Global Systems Level has been substantial in making person-to-person collaboration possible to the point that elementary school students can hold video conferences with their peers across the globe.

C. Application of the Model. The complexity of distance education cannot be fully articulated in this short description of the hierarchical system model. In fact each edition of the *Handbook of Disatnce Learning* is devoted to explaining important dimensions of the history, theory, and practice of our field; aspects that must be formally incorporated in this model. One of the uses of the model, therefore, is to depict the intricate network of many components gleaned from the studies in this handbook as well as other authoritative sources. A few examples from this volume illustrate the point.

- Hardware, Software, and Telecommunications Systems Levels. Several studies in this volume focus on constructs that are related to these systems levels. Two are presented as examples:
  - In Chapter 19, Kim, Kozan, Kim, and Koehler discuss the concept of technology integration at different levels (i.e., micro, macro and teacher community; a level between micro and macro) as this construct relates to other concepts, such as learner-technology interaction, as well as learner-learner and learner-instructor interaction.
  - In Chapter 20, Moisey and Ally, in their analysis of the concept of learning objects, indicate how these Software Systems have profound ramifications for Instructional and Educational Systems Levels.
- Instructional Systems Level. Three chapters directly related to this level are:
  - Chapter 5 in which Moore documents a series of studies published since 1988 wherein researchers have contributed to further analyzing and articulating the concept of transactional distance. To fully demonstrate the dynamic components involved in the idea of transactional distance, the results of these studies in the Instructional Systems Level, should be subjected to the iterative model building process described above.
  - Chapter 16 in which Shearer demonstrates the intricate relationships that exist between dialogue, structure, and autonomy in transactional distance in the context of design specifications for course development. He also emphasizes that affordances of technologies of distance education (Hardware Systems, Software Systems, and Telecommunications Systems) affect design decisions.
  - Chapter 8 in which West, Hannafin, Hill, and Song present several constructs at the Instructional Systems Level, including prior knowledge, motivation, cognitive demands, metacognition, and scaffolding, which greatly influence the design of instruction. The effect of these constructs on the other components

of the Instructional Systems Level, including transactional distance must be studied.

- Educational Systems. All chapters in Part 4 and most of those in Part 5 of this volume are directly related to constructs that are active at this systems level. The authors of these chapters highlight the complexity of managing distance education systems.
- Societal Systems Level
  - In Chapter 30, O'Brian explains the various Societal Systems in the form of organizations, policies, and procedures that are involved in accreditation of higher education institutions in the United States—each of which is a candidate for system modeling—to explain the powerful effect that the process of accreditation has on both Educational and Instructional Systems levels.
- Global Systems
  - Visser's Chapter 44 is directly related to this systems level. However, Gunawardena' Chapter 12 also demonstrates the complexity of the Global Systems.

Future researchers might consider how to place all the constructs discussed in this volume in the model proposed here and suggest how they impact constructs in other systems levels, by developing causal loop diagrams and writing equations to formalize them. Here we have demonstrated how the proposed system model highlights the vast area of research that needs to be conducted at each system level. In following Dubin's (1978) requirement for scientific model building, the complexity of each of these levels must be articulated in submodels. As such, the model building process in Saba and Shearer (1994) that articulated one submodel of the Instructional Systems Level (i.e., transactional distance) must be extended to articulate submodels in each of the other system levels. Each system level must be analyzed for defining its constituents and the relations among them.

Theory Building vs. Prescriptive Models. As Dubin (1978) argued, modeling for theory building should not be confused with offering prescriptive approaches to practice. Models developed by the systems dynamic method described in this chapter are intended for building theories of distance education that are inspired by current knowledge, research, and practice. Practitioners may adopt them to guide program development, implementation, and evaluation. Progress in our field and the development of sound models for practice require that there be a close and iterative relationship between theory building and developing and testing of practical applications.

Systems as Technology

In traditional sciences, the laboratory is the place where experiments are conducted. In systems science, the computer is the instrument as well as the virtual place for research and theory building. Skyttner (2002) posited, "When creating theories regarding the information world and complex living systems, different kinds of virtual worlds are necessary. There, the computer works as a laboratory and in its digital universe artificial intelligence and artificial life is created" (p. 38). Computer models for theory building and research occupy substantial space within these virtual worlds. These models are capable of simulating various contingencies based on hypothetical scenarios or actual data. A growing number of simulation software has entered the market, especially since the advent of the personal computer. The computer has brought the laboratory to the desktop. In building a systems theory of distance education, I have used system dynamics in most of my work. Unlike in the 1970s when running system dynamics models were only possible on mainframes involving cumbersome and time-consuming processes, in recent years software programs enabling simulations of system dynamics models have been developed for the personal computer. What used to take hours or even days to accomplish is now possible in minutes or seconds on a PC. Surprisingly, the most challenging part of producing and running a model is not the actual building on the computer by programming the required mathematical equations; it is conceptualizing the model itself, determining its components, articulating their functions and specifying their relationships to each other. Today, software such as STELLA and Vensim make it relatively easy to construct system dynamics models. With built-in equations and a graphic interface, model builders can focus their efforts on the conceptual integrity of their models and spend less time on writing equations or tweaking the software.

SUMMARY AND CONCLUSION

Growth in the volume of literature in the field and an expanding community of practice has introduced new challenges in building a theory of distance education. Piecemeal approaches to conceptualizing the field without considering its theoretical knowledge-base and the history of its conceptual development, have, at times, created more conceptual confusion. Clarifying the nature of a multifaceted field with constructs at varying levels of complexity is a daunting task. These constructs range from learner autonomy in relation to the instructor's need for imposing structure, to the application of distance education on the global stage along with diverse cultural constructs that practice across borders may introduce to an educational program.

The systems approach as a philosophy, methodology, and technology concerned with relationships among phenomena was proposed to encompass a wide variety of theoretical constructs in a hierarchical model. This model can accommodate developments at the global level as well as less complex levels, for example, hardware systems as shown in Figure 4.3. Transactional distance was presented to illustrate how a dynamic model can be constructed consisting of key concepts such as autonomy and structure. Transactional distance, however, is itself a component of the Instructional Systems Level. The same theory building process that was used to test the validity of transactional distance should be applied to identify and model theoretical components and their behaviors at each system levels.

Implementing a systems dynamic research program is likely to lead to a unified theory of distance education with the flexibility to assimilate future theoretical ideas as they may emerge. As new ideas and concepts are developed, they can be incorporated into the systems model, and their integrity and validity can be tested. A systems approach to distance education provides the breadth necessary to understand a field that includes theories and methods of praxis from various disciplines. Yet it also represents elements of everyday practice that range from the management of complex hardware at one system level to the intricacies of different cultures working together at another system level. The task is enormous, but systems-thinking is the path that offers the greatest potential.

REFERENCES

Ahl, V., & Allen, T. F. H. (1996). *Hierarchy theory: A vision, vocabulary and epistemology.* New York: Columbia University Press

Appleyard, B. (1993). *Understanding the present: Science and the soul of modern man.* New York: Doubleday.

Banathy, B. H. (1992). *A systems view of education: Concepts and principles for effective practice.* Englewood Cliffs, NJ: Educational Technology Publications.

Bertalanffy, L. V. (1968). *General system theory: Foundations, development, applications* (rev. ed.). New York: George Braziller.

Bravo, C., van Joolingen, W. R. , & de Jong, T. (2009). Using Co-Lab to build system dynamics models: Students' actions and on-line tutorial advice. *Computers & Education, 53,* 243–251.

Capra, F. (1982). *The turning point: Science, society and the rising culture.* New York: Simon and Schuster.

Capra, F. (1996). *The web of life: A new scientific understanding of living systems.* New York: Anchor Books.

Damasio, A. (1994). *Descartes' error: Emotion, reason and the human brain.* New York: G. P. Putnam's Sons.

de Jong, T. (2006). Computer simulations — Technological advances in inquiry learning. *Science, 312,* 532–533.

Dubin, R. (1978). *Theory building* (rev. ed.). New York: The Free Press.

Komis, V. Ergazaki, M., & Zogza, V. (2007). Comparing computer-supported dynamic modeling and 'paper & pencil' concept mapping technique in students collaborative activity. *Computers & Education. 49,* 991–1017

Kuhn, T. S. (1970). *The structure of scientific revolutions* (2nd ed.). Chicago: University of Chicago Press.

Laszlo, E. (2001). *The systems view of the world: A holistic vision for our time.* Cresskill, NJ: Hampton Press.

Moore, J. L., Dickson-Deane, C., and Galyen, K. (2010). e-Learning, online learning, and distance learning environments: Are they the same? *Internet and Higher Education, 14,* 129–135

Moore, M. G. (1973). Toward a theory of independent learning and teaching. *Journal of Higher Education, 44*(9), 661–680.

Moore, M. G. (1983). The individual adult learner. In M. Tight (Ed.), *Adult learning and education* (pp. 153–168). London: Croom Helm.

Moore, M. G. (1999). Charles Wedemeyer, In memoriam. *The American Journal of Distance Education, 13*(3), 1–6.

Moore, M. G., & Kearsley, G. (2012). *Distance education: A systems view of online learning* (3rd ed.). Florence, KY: Wadsworth, Cenage Learning.

Moore, M. G., & Kearsley, G. (2005). *Distance education: A systems view.* Belmont, CA: Thomson Wadsworth.

Nuhog˘lu., H. (2010) The effect of the system dynamics approach on understanding causal relationship skills in science education. *Procedia Social and Behavioral Sciences 2,* 3614–3618.

Pacey, L., & Keough, E. (2003). Public policy, institutional structures, and strategic implementation. In M. G. Moore & W. G. Anderson (Eds.), H*andbook of distance education* (pp. 401–416). Mahwah, NJ: Erlbaum.

Roberts, N., Andersen, D., Deal, R., Garet, M., & Shaffer, W. (1983). *Introduction to computer simulation: A system dynamics modeling approach.* Reading, MA: Addison-Wesley.

Saba, F. (1988). Integrated telecommunications systems and instructional transaction. *The American Journal of Distance Education, 2*(3), 17–24.

Saba, F., & Shearer, R. L. (1994). Verifying key theoretical concepts in a dynamic model of distance education. *The American Journal of Distance Education, 8*(1), 36–59.

Shaffer, S. C. (2005). System dynamics in distance education and a call to develop a standard model. *International Review of Research in Open and Distance Learning.* Retrieved December 10, 2005, from http://www.in·odl. org/contentlv6.3/shaffer.html

Shearer, R. L. (2010). *Transactional distance and dialogue.* Saarbrücken: Germany: VDM Verlag.

Skyttner, L. (2002). *General systems theory: Ideas & applications.* Singapore: World Scientific.

Spector, J. M. (2000). System dynamics and interactive learning environments: Lessons learned and implications for the future. *Simulation and Gaming, 31*(4), 528–535.

Thompson, K., & Reimann, P. (2009). Patterns of use of an agent-based model and a system dynamics model: The application of patterns of use and the impacts on learning outcomes. *Computers & Education 54,* 392–403.

Wilson, E. O. (1998). *Consilience: The unity of knowledge.* New York: Knopf.

5

THE THEORY OF TRANSACTIONAL DISTANCE

MICHAEL GRAHAME MOORE

TRANSACTIONAL DISTANCE THEORY:
HISTORICAL SIGNIFICANCE

The publication of this edition of the *Handbook of Distance Education* coincides with the fortieth anniversary of the first appearance of what became known as the theory of transactional distance (Moore, 1972, 1973).

To most readers of this volume, now living in a world in which distance education and its offspring, e-learning, online learning, and blended learning—among others—are such familiar co-habitants, it is hard to imagine a world like that of the 1970s and 80s, when the idea that students might learn as well apart from their teachers as in a classroom was, to the vast majority of mainstream educators, a preposterous idea. There was, of course, correspondence teaching, a form of distance education that had opened doors for millions of otherwise deprived "backdoor learners" as has been described in an earlier chapter of this handbook, and there were educational programs broadcast by radio and television too. However so despised and derided by the educational establishment were these, that it would be a very adventurous professor of education who would deign to mention them when lecturing on teaching methodology, or countenance their representation in the theories about education that appeared in the textbooks studied by teachers in training. Because there was no theory framing such out-of-classroom practice, there was no academic research either. That is not to say there was no research, as has been described also in a previous chapter, for it was left to leading practitioners like Charles Wedemeyer and Gayle Childs to create a research agenda, derived from their need to evaluate the effectiveness of their correspondence and broadcast education. Scholarly research, in the sense of research driven by theory and contributing to theory, was impossible, simply because there was no theory to start with. All scholarly research in education was grounded in the almost universally accepted assumption that "instruction refers to the activity which takes place during schooling and within the classroom setting" (Association of Supervision and Curriculum Development, 1971).

It was as an attempt to establish the identity of the *other* form of teaching and learning, i.e., teaching and learning that did *not* take place in classrooms that the concept of distance education was first proposed, and developed into what became referred to as the theory of transactional distance. What had hitherto been an activity on the far margins of educational practice was given a name, called, for the first time in English, distance education. It was then defined in terms of three sets of variables that have proven to be sufficiently robust to enable subsequent research and further theorizing by an ever-growing number of students and academics, and for the concept to enter into the mainstream of educational discourse, as has the practice of distance education also entered the mainstream of education and training at every level. As a result, whatever specific issues might be the cause of disagreement among scholars of our present generation, it is only by rather convoluted and even bizarre argument that any contemporary writer would argue that there is no such field of research and study as distance education. True, there are those who cause confusion by failing to recognize the full breadth of the field and its multi-dimensional nature, as they focus on one or other of its component parts or one of its many applications—expressed in terms such as distributed learning, tele-learning, online learning, and e-learning—and others who by accident or design conflate distance education and "contiguous" (Moore, 1972, p. 76) education, using such terms as "open learning," "blended learning," and "flexi-learning." However, even such muddling of concepts does not detract from the general recognition that there *is* a universe of educational programs and practices that are distinctly different from those where teachers and learners work in the same space and time, a field worthy of study and research, and the practice of which is also worth study and training. It is this recognition and acceptance that distance education has its own identity and distinguishing pedagogical characteristics that is the first claim of transactional distance as an educational theory.

To further appreciate the historical significance of the theory, it is the *character* of that identity that must be understood, for this was the first American theory to define the field in *pedagogical* terms. By 1970, as already noted, education outside the classroom had existed in practice for almost a hundred years, beginning as correspondence study through the mail and later supplemented by radio and television programs, the use of telephone and the earliest computers. As long as this practice was defined solely by the technology, the few research questions that were generated were also stated as studies of the technology—usually how education through that technology might best resemble "real" teaching, i.e., teaching in classrooms. This began to change with the theory of transactional distance, which showed that teaching and learning in separate locations is better understood not as an aberration from the classroom, but as a significantly different pedagogical domain.

ORIGINS OF TRANSACTIONAL DISTANCE THEORY

The argument for legitimizing, identifying and researching this kind of teaching and learning and the need for developing its own theory was argued in the following terms in a 1972 presentation to the World Conference of the International Council for Correspondence Education (ICCE):

> As we continue to develop various non-traditional methods of reaching the growing numbers of people who cannot or will not attend conventional institutions but who choose to learn apart from their teachers, we should divert some of our resources to the macro-factors, i.e. describing and defining the field … discriminating between the various components of this field; identifying the critical elements of the various forms of learning and teaching, in short building a theoretical framework which will embrace this whole area of education. (Moore, 1973, p. 661)

In that presentation, distance education was first defined. It was defined as: "the family of instructional methods in which the teaching behaviors are executed apart from the learning behaviors … so that communication between the learner and the teacher must be facilitated by print, electronic, mechanical, or other device" (Moore, 1972, p. 76). The "critical elements" mentioned in the extract from the ICCE presentation above, were identified through a process of empirical research, a content analysis of a large selection of program descriptions and other literature. This analysis produced three sets of "macro-factors" and it was these that, it was argued, should define the field in three dimensions. The first of these, derived from analysis of the curricula taught through the technologies of the day was described as the teaching-learning program's "structure"; the second, derived from analysis of communications between teachers and learners— mostly at that time by mail but also by telephone—is the "dialogue" in the program. The third described the roles of learners, in terms of the extent to which they exercise degrees of "autonomy" in deciding what to learn, how to learn, and how much to learn. The pervasive requirement in all distance education environments for learners to exercise degrees of self-management was reflected in Wedemeyer's (1971) definition of independent study as well as informed by the (then) radical writings of Carl Rogers (1969), Abraham Maslow (e.g., Maslow, 1968), and other "humanistic" psychologists.

The term "distance education" originated at the University of Tübingen in Germany, where researchers in the 1960's wrote about *fernstudium* (distance study) to describe how certain industrial principles, such as division of labor and use of technology, could be applied in the craft of teaching. The terms "dialogue," "structure," and "transaction" originated with adult education professor Robert Boyd. The term "dialogue" was chosen deliberately in preference to "interaction" in recognition of Boyd's argument that the latter term includes relationships that are manipulative and negative and that an alternative term should define the kind of helping, constructive, and positive exchanges that are required in a teaching-learning relationship. Boyd's teaching theories were heavily influenced by Gestalt psychology, and it was from this that the importance of identifying programs according to their 'structure" originated. The term "transactional distance" was first used in Boyd and Apps' 1980 *Handbook of Adult Education*. Originating with John Dewey, the concept of transaction "connotes the interplay among the environment, the individuals and the patterns of behaviors in a situation" (Boyd & Apps, 1980, p. 5). Thus the transaction in distance education is the interplay of teachers and learners in environments that have the special characteristic of their being spatially separate from one another. As the concept of transactional distance was refined, what emerged was a typology of educational programs having this distinguishing characteristic of separation of learner and teacher. A typology, as a heuristic device should accommodate all possible types, and in this case accommodates programs at one extreme that

are relatively highly structured and quasi-industrial, owing a lot to behaviorist and cognitivist theories of learning, as well as those—at the other extreme—that reflect the
humanists' (and nowadays, constructivists') perspective of a learner-centered pedagogy,
in which learners engage in a relatively high degree of dialogue with a more-or-less
supportive tutor. (It should be noted that the terms "relatively," "varying degrees," and
"more or less" are very significant, since transactional distance theory describes the full-
est range of *all possible* degrees of structure, dialogue, and autonomy.) Because this is a
point that is often overlooked, it bears repeating that transactional distance is relative
rather than absolute. Teaching-learning programs are *not* dichotomously either "distance" or not "distance," but they have "more distance" or "less distance." One has more
dialogue than another, less structure than another, or allows greater learner autonomy
than another. Commenting on the significance of this, the distinguished German
scholar Otto Peters (one of the Tübingen group mentioned earlier) says: "by showing
the transactional distance not as a fixed quantity but as a variable, which results from
the respective changing interplay between dialogue, the structured nature of the teaching program being presented, and the autonomy of the students, it (the transactional
distance theory) provides a convincing explanation of the enormous flexibility of this
form of academic teaching. It also provides an insight into the pedagogical complexity
of distance education" (1998, p. 42).

MORE ABOUT STRUCTURE, DIALOGUE, AND AUTONOMY

More about Structure

An educational course consists of one or more lessons, each containing such elements
as: learning objectives; presentations of information, case studies, images, possibly
audio and video recordings; activities and exercises, questions for discussion, advice
about study, projects, and tests. Each of these might be very strictly specified by the
designer(s), leaving little room for a student or instructor's deviation. You only have to
imagine the content of courses designed for medical, nursing, military, or other technical training to see how such rigid standardization would be appropriate. To arrive at the
structure that would be most effective, an instructor or design team might test parts of
the course on a pilot group of students, to find out, for example, precisely how long it will
take each student to accomplish each objective and the suitability of the test questions
aimed at evaluating performance; they might measure the reading speed of the sample
of students and then tailor the number of pages of reading required for each part of the
course. Where more than one instructor is to be employed (which in better distance
education systems is usually the case), to ensure all students achieve precisely the same
degree of competence, instructors may be provided detailed marking schemes. During
the instruction, they may monitor the progress of each student very frequently and give
regular feedback and remedial activities for those that need them, and so ensure that
every student has accomplished each step of the course in a tightly controlled sequence.
Each student might have to follow the exact same sequence of reading and activity; audio
and video materials may be synchronized very tightly and linked to specific pages in a
study guide or Website; synchronous discussions may be carefully organized minute by
minute to ensure participation by each student, according to a carefully scripted plan.
A recorded video program for example is usually highly structured with virtually every

activity of the instructor and every minute of time scripted and every piece of content pre-determined. There is little or no opportunity for any student to deviate according to personal needs from what the instructors have planned for that period of time. All this describes a course or program that has a high degree of structure. By comparison, other courses are designed with a loose structure in which students can follow any of several different paths, or many paths, through the content or may negotiate significant variations in the program with the instructor(s). Such a course might allow students to surf the Internet, browse YouTube, or a loosely determined set of Websites, or view a CD or DVD or podcast at their own speed, choose from a library of recommended readings, and only submit written assignments when they feel ready. They may be told to call an instructor if, and only when, they need advice. Such would be a course with much lower structure than the one described before. Since structure expresses the rigidity or flexibility of the course's educational objectives, teaching strategies, and evaluation methods, it describes the extent to which a course can accommodate or be responsive to each learner's individual needs and preferences.

More about Dialogue

Dialogue is a particular kind of interpersonal interaction, and it happens after a course is designed, as teachers exchange words and other symbols with learners, aimed at the latter's creation of knowledge. Interaction is not always constructive, but dialogue by definition is. Dialogue has a synergistic character, as each party in the exchange builds upon comments of the other. In dialogue, "each party … is a respectful and active listener; each is a contributor and builds on the contributions of the other party or parties" (Moore, 1993, p. 26).

Courses of instruction may allow almost continuous dialogue between students and teachers or none, and there is a range of variations between the extremes. The extent and nature of dialogue in any course is determined by numerous factors, and overarching all is the *structure* of the course. For example, a teaching institution using synchronous video conferencing on the Web (a potentially highly dialogic medium) but holding the view that the role of the student is to assimilate information by listening and taking notes, might design its courses with highly structured lessons and dialogue limited to asking factual questions of the teacher and receiving answers. Obviously, another particularly important variable affecting dialogue is the medium of communication. In a correspondence course in which communication is through postal services, although there is the potential for each learner to engage in a relatively highly dialogic relationship with the instructor, the pace of such dialogue is slow when it is conducted by traditional mail. If the same course was delivered on the Web, even though communication is in text, a greater degree of dialogue is likely, as there can be rapid and frequent responses by teacher to student. A tutorial between an instructor and a single student conducted in real-time by audio online is likely to be a highly dialogic process, while a similar online teleconference between groups would probably have a lower degree of dialogue (for each student). Some courses, such as those using CDs or "teach yourself" books, are not only very highly structured, but have virtually no dialogue with a live instructor. Other determinants of the extent of dialogue in a course or lesson are the subject matter of the course, the personality of the teacher, the ability of a learner to competently participate in the dialogue, and cultural and language differences between instructors and students. Dialogue is, of course, also powerfully affected by the abilities of students to manage their side of the process. Highly autonomous learners are able to cope with a lower degree of dialogue but less autonomous need a relatively high degree of dialogue.

Transactional Distance Is a Function of Dialog and Structure

In the typical recorded video podcast instructional program, the teaching is highly structured and there is minimal teacher-learner dialogue (we have to say "minimal" because there is a kind of vicarious dialogue between the learner and the instructors who prepared the recordings as the learner experiences what Holmberg [1981] called an "internal didactic conversation"). With such a high degree of structure and little or no dialogue, the transactional distance is high. By comparison a virtual class meeting in Second Life could experience considerable dialogue, though with some restriction from the technology, and less structure, so the course would have, and the student's experience, less transactional distance. It should be clear that the extent of dialogue and the degree of structure varies from course to course. It is not simply a matter of the technology, though that definitely imposes limitations, but also depends on the teaching philosophy of the instructor, the capacity of learners, and the nature of the subject.

For these reasons, online distance education programs vary enormously in the extent of both structure and dialogue. A common cause of failure, or at least of courses falling short of expectations, is failure to design the balance of structure and dialogue that is appropriate for a particular student population and subject field.

How the variables of dialog and structure interact to determine transactional distance can be seen in a simple two-dimensional graph (Figure 5.1).

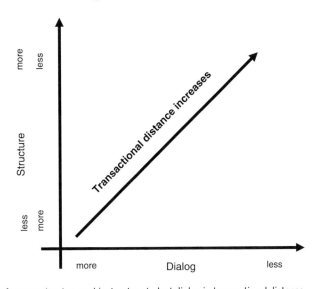

Figure 5.1 Relation of course structure and instructor-student dialog in transactional distance.

More on Learner Autonomy

The Humanistic psychologists, particularly Carl Rogers (1969), were responsible for establishing the idea of "learner autonomy," supported by empirical research, notably that of Alan Tough (1971), that demonstrated that students have, in different degrees, the ability to develop a personal learning plan, to find resources for study in their work or community environments, and to evaluate for themselves when progress was satisfactory. During the research that led to the development of the theory of transactional distance, it became apparent that some programs allow or demand the greater exercise of learning autonomy than others and that there are conditions under which greater learner autonomy may be exercised and others where a lower degree of autonomy is more appropriate.

Thus it was hypothesized, and demonstrated, that teaching-learning programs can be organized, not only according to the extent of structure and dialogue, but also according to the extent of self-management, or learner autonomy, permitted by each program.

Here is how the idea was first explained, in 1972:

> In our efforts to explore various aspects of learner autonomy in distance teaching and learning programs, we have tried to prepare a system that makes it possible to order programs according to the kind and extent of autonomy the learner is expected or permitted to exercise. We are placing programs in appropriate positions on a continuum, with those permitting the exercise of most autonomy at one extreme and those permitting the least at the other. For every program, we seek to identify the relationship between learners and teachers, and where control of each instructional process lies, by asking:
>
> > Is learning self initiated and self-motivated?
> >
> > Who identifies goals and objectives, and selects problems for study?
> >
> > Who determines the pace, the sequence, and the methods of information gathering?
> >
> > What provision is there for the development of learners' ideas and for creative solutions to problems?
> >
> > Is emphasis on gathering information external to the learner?
> >
> > How flexible is each instructional process to the requirements of the learner?
> >
> > How is the usefulness and quality of learning judged?
>
> By this subjective, inductive method we can put together a typology of distance teaching programs, classified by the dimension of learner autonomy. (Moore, 1972, p. 83)

Applying these criteria, programs were classified on a range from AAA meaning the learner had full autonomy in deciding what to learn (Goals) how to learn (Execution) and how much to learn (Evaluation) at one extreme, and NNN at the other extreme, describing a program in which the learner had absolutely no freedom to make any decisions about the learning program. These are only theoretical constructs, because no one is entirely without freedom or absolutely without constraint. Between these

Degrees of learner autonomy. Programs vary from those allowing learner to decide what to learn, how to learn and to self-evaluate (AAA) to those in which all decisions are taken by others (NNN) and various combinations.

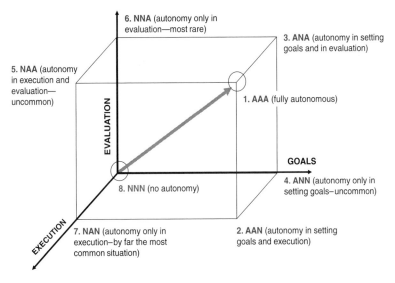

Figure 5.2 Degrees of learner autonomy in determining what to learn, how to learn, and evaluating learning.

theoretical poles lie all teaching-learning programs. This can be illustrated in a model (Figure 5.2)

Since this has sometimes been misunderstood, it should be noted that it was not suggested that all learners are fully or even highly autonomous. It is recognized that learners vary in their ability to exercise autonomy, and might want to have greater autonomy in some courses than others. It is very appropriate for educators to allow the exercise of more or less autonomy. Also, it is not suggested that highly autonomous learners do not need teachers. It is the relationship of such learners to teachers that is different than that between teachers and less autonomous learners, with the latter needing more emotional support from the teacher and the former only needing instrumental support, i.e., information and the advice necessary to get the job done.

Relationship of Autonomy and Transactional Distance

In a course with low structure and high dialogue, i.e., low transactional distance, learners receive information and guidance through on-going dialogue with their instructors and through instructional materials that allow modifications to suit their individual needs, learning style and pace. Such a program with a lower degree of transactional distance is invariably more attractive to those learners who are less secure in managing their own learning. On the other hand, more autonomous learners are more comfortable with less dialogue, receiving instruction through more highly structured course materials, comfortable with finding information and making decisions for themselves about what to study, when, where, what ways, and to what extent. In other words, the greater the transactional distance the more the learners have to exercise autonomy. This relationship is illustrated in Figure 5.3.

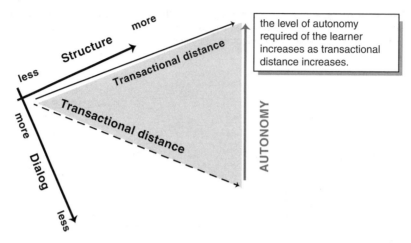

Figure 5.3 Relation of dimensions of transactional distance and learner autonomy.

Transactional Distance Theory at Work in Research, 1988–2005

Since the publication of the second edition of this handbook, the theory of transactional distance (TD) has entered even further into the mainstream of discourse about distance education. Indeed, it is frequently used even when the three-dimensional theory it represents has been neither identified nor recognized. Occasionally such uncited use is deliberate, but usually the failure to reference the literature is because the idea of transactional distance is now so much a part of the general knowledge of the field that the source is either not known, or not considered noteworthy. Leaving such cases aside, we can provide here a brief mention of some of the dissertation and other studies in which the theory has been formally acknowledged as the basis of the research.

Although the term transactional distance first appeared in print in 1980 (Moore 1980), the first major researcher to recognize its potential, and subsequently to contribute significantly to the development of transactional distance theory was Farhad Saba. In pioneering the use of computer simulation, Saba and colleagues developed a model based on principles of systems dynamics that operationalized dialogue, structure, and autonomy (Saba, 1988; Saba & Twitchell, 1988), and tested the hypothesized changes in each of these that resulted from changes in others. In a subsequent project, Saba and Shearer (1994), used discourse analysis to identify 10 categories of teacher-learner transactions and again demonstrated how changes in dialogue, structure, and teacher/learner control effected changes in each of the others. Saba and Shearer's instrument has been adapted for use by others, as for example by Shinkle (2001) in an analysis of dialogue by e-mail in a doctoral distance education program. Enhancements and modifications of dialogue and structure have been proposed, as, for example by Braxton (1999) in what she called a "refined theory of transactional distance." Along with Saba and Shearer and others, Braxton also attempted to create an instrument to measure transactional distance. An instrument developed by Zhang (2003) measured transactional distance in Web-based courses, not only between student and teacher, but also student and student, student and content, and between student and interface procedures. Based on an analysis of 58 research articles in five distance education journals, Jung (2001) suggested that in Web-based instruction, the dialogue variables include academic, collaborative, and interpersonal interaction, while the structure variables are content expand, content adaptability, and visual layout, and learning variables are learner autonom collaboration. Gallo (2001) used transactional distance theory in an attempt to iden- tify the competencies needed for success as distance learners, and proposed a training program to develop these competencies. Shin (2001) expanded the idea of transactional distance by postulating and testing a concept of transactional presence. Caspi, Gorsky, and Chajut (2003) developed what they called a "restructured model of transactional distance" consisting of four kinds of dialogue, and used it to examine the effect of group size on students' behavior in asynchronous discussion groups.

Bischoff (1993) and Bischoff, Bisconer, Kooker, and Woods (1996) reported the effect of electronic mail in lowering transactional distance in public health and nursing courses delivered by video-conferencing. In what were probably the first cross-cultural studies, Gayol (1996) and Bunker, Gayol, Nti, and Reidell (1996) examined transactional distance in courses delivered by audio-conferencing and electronic mail to students in four countries. The effects of differences in culture on transactional distance among foreign graduate students in the United States was studied by Walker Fernandez (1999), and effects of cultural differences on transactional distance in computer science courses delivered on the Web have been reported by Lemone (2005). M. H. Moore (1999) used transactional distance theory in a study of the effects of changing a training program from an individual, self-directed package to a group method using videoconferenc- ing. Vrasidas and McIsaac (1999) studied course structure and dialogue in computer mediated instruction, and found that quality of dialogue is significantly affected by prior experience. In a study of mathematics taught on the Internet, Anderson (1999) found that students and faculty reported that their dialogues were meaningful, though they were relatively highly structured, and that while these courses facilitated learner autonomy, for some students the level of autonomy was uncomfortable and they wanted more dialogue with instructors. Atkinson (1999) described instructor strategies such as humanizing and the use of visual techniques as ways of increasing dialogue to reduce transactional distance in video based courses. Hopper (2000) found that students who reported a perception of high transactional distance did not think it impeded their achievement or satisfaction with their learning experience. Transactional distance was among variables examined by Rovai (2000) to see what makes a sense of community in asynchronous learning networks, and later (2002) he described steps to increase a sense of community by facilitating dialogue. Y. J. Chen (2001) found that in a Web-based course, previous experience with distance education and in-class learner support had no effect on students' perception of the transactional distance but the learner's skill in using the Internet and the extent of the dialogue that occurred between instruc- tor and learners and among learners had significant effects. Clouse (2001) found that transactional distance in an online course was lower in a chat mode and higher in a threaded discussion. Dron (2002) reported an online course explicitly designed to have a high degree of dialogue, in which an unanticipated reversion by instructors to increased structure occurred, with negative effects on both quality and quantity of dia- logue. Subsequently, Dron and colleagues (2004) discuss how students' self-organiza- tion (i.e., the exercise of autonomy) in a highly structured learning environment can lead to increased dialogue, and thus a program in which both structure and dialogue are high. Williams (2003) includes implications for transactional distance theory in a dis- cussion of research on retention and barriers to success in an online graduate program.

Wikeley and Muschamp (2004) developed a model for the delivery of professional doctorate programs at a distance, arguing that dialogue might be increased through a structure that allowed greater adaptability of content by instructors. Edstrom (2002) discussed transactional distance in the classroom, and how it can be reduced through use of information and communication technologies. Wheeler (2002) concluded that transactional distance can explain why "remote students expect a great deal more from their instructors than their local peers in terms of social and practical support ..." (p. 425). Lee and Gibson (2003) concluded from a study of adult learners taking a computer mediated course that instructors should encourage dialogue, allow for structural flexibility, encourage critical reflection, and permit students to take on some degree of control. Witte and Wolf (2003) in a study of mentoring recommended that instructors " ... should consider the perceived transactional distance as well as keeping the various types of mentoring interaction, facilitation, and structured student collaboration in mind when organizing materials and assignments" (pp. 98-99). Lowell (2004) found that significant predictors for perceived distance among students in online courses were dialogue, social presence, and fluency. Pruitt (2005), in a study of students in three delivery modalities (Internet, telecourse, compressed video), found dialogue, structure, and learner autonomy to be significant in predicting self-ratings of performance and grades. Stein, Wanstreet, Calvin, Overtoom, and Wheaton (2005) concluded that satisfaction with the course structure and with dialogue led to satisfaction with perceived knowledge gained. Dupin-Bryant (2004) identified teaching behaviors necessary to account for transactional distance in a survey of 225 instructors at nine land grant universities. Aviv, Erlich, Ravid, and Gava (2003) evaluated dialogue in two Open University of Israel courses, one more structured than the other, and found that high levels of critical thinking were more evident in the structured environment. Also at the Open University of Israel, Gorsky, Caspi, and Trumper (2004) investigated dialogue in a physics course and Gorsky, Caspi, and Tuvi-Arid (2004) in a chemistry course. Gorsky and Caspi concluded that transactional distance could be explained primarily in terms of dialogue, though they also said that dialogue was supported by "structural resources" such as "instructional design, group size and accessibility of students and instructors" (2005, p. 140). Offir, Lev, Lev, Barth, and Shteinbok describe how an analysis of verbal and nonverbal interactions revealed the strategies teachers use to reduce transactional distance. They report that "data, indicating significant cross-context changes in teacher-student interaction patterns validate Moore's (1972, 1993) transactional distance theory"; they believe their "empirical evidence of changes in specific categories of interaction also expands the conceptualization of the dialogue variable" (Offir et al., 2004, p. 101).

Among enquiries that focus primarily on learner autonomy, Munro's (1991) study reported a relationship between dropping out of distance learning programs and perceived deficiencies in dialogue. Emulating, though not replicating, Moore's (1976) study of learner autonomy and the cognitive style of field dependence-independence, Brenner (1996) investigated field dependence-independence of learners who studied by video and text, and found no relationship between field independence and achievement. Richardson (1998) also failed to find a relationship between students' field independence, their course evaluations, preference for independent learning, course completion, or level of autonomy. In her study of learner autonomy among nurses returning to college, Thompson, (1998) used questionnaires based on Baynton's (1992) derivation of transactional distance theory, and concluded the distance learners did not show greater autonomy than traditional students, which she believed was probably due to the high degree of structure in both their programs. Y. Chen (1997) and Y. Chen and Willits (1998, 1999), who studied teaching strategies in videoconference courses, concluded that "the more independent the students reported themselves to be, the more frequently they indicated in-class interaction" (Y. Chen & Willits, 1999, p. 54). This finding of a positive relationship between dialogue and autonomy was later confirmed by Huang (2000), who gathered data about Web-based courses. Kanuka, Collett, and Caswell (2002) investigated the effects of integrating asynchronous Internet communication into distance courses and wrote: "Finally, in terms of Moore's theory of the relationship between structure and dialogue versus learner autonomy, the outcomes of this study not only support this idea, but also provide additional insights and clarification. While structure is a relatively straightforward concept that tends not to be in need of further clarification, in agreement with Garrison and Baynton (1987) we find that autonomy is a complex and multifaceted construct. However, while Garrison and Baynton describe autonomy in terms of power, control and support, the participants in this study referred to autonomy in terms of flexibility" (p. 165).

Transactional Distance Theory at Work in Research 2006–2011

As mentioned above, the terminology of transactional distance is widely used, even when the actual theory it represents has been neither identified nor recognized. The number of studies that use the term in this loose atheoretical manner is so large and there is so little coherence in such use that there is no point in trying to include them in our literature review. More helpfully, we are able to point to examples of studies that *are* grounded in the theory, either as the principal source of the research question—the more important—or in which TD played a supportive role to some other theory. Perhaps most interesting and valuable is a third set of studies, those in which the researcher has set a goal of refining, developing, adding to or criticizing the theory itself.

What is of special interest perhaps in this new edition of the handbook is the extent to which in all these studies, a theory that was conceived in the days of correspondence education, television, and radio broadcasting, is now employed in formulating researchable questions about teaching and learning carried by Web 1.0 and even Web 2.0 technologies.

2006–2011 STUDIES IN WHICH TD FEATURED AS THE PRINCIPAL OR A DOMINANT THEORY

The following is a selection of recent studies in which TD featured as the principal or a dominant theory:

Falloon (2011) analyzed the effects of using a virtual classroom in graduate teacher education, and identified positive effects (creating dialogue) and negative (diminishing learners' sense of autonomy).

Belair (2011) determined how regular phone calls by teachers contributed to the work habits of students in a virtual high school.

Mathieson (2011) examined Shearer's (2009) idea of "dialogue towards understanding" in a study of audiovisual feedback as a supplement to text feedback in a graduate online course.

Watts (2010) studied online dialogue, contrasting participants in baccalaureate radiologic sciences and in the English department.

McLaren (2010) asked, to what extent does transactional distance affect learner satisfaction in online Masters courses?

Veale (2009) interviewed students in an online Radiologic Science baccalaureate program and analyzed results for emergent themes that increase students' feelings of connectedness and decrease transactional distance.

McBrien, Jones, and Cheng (2009) studied the use of Elluminate Live! and identified themes related to dialogue, structure, and learner autonomy.

Deng and Yuen (2009) studied the use of educational blogs in higher education.

Bajt (2009) investigated relationships between dialog, structure, support, and satisfaction among "Millennial" online students, and found a positive relationship between structure and satisfaction.

Benson and Samarawickrema (2009) used cases from two Australian universities in applying TD to discuss design of courses using Web 2.0 technologies.

A study by Wang and Morgan (2008) investigated student perceptions of using instant messaging for online discussions in a graduate teacher educational technology course.

Murphy and Rodriguez-Manzanares, (2008) collected data regarding TD in the context of Web-based high school distance education

Seok (2008) reviewed instructional contents, assessment strategies, and digital libraries in e-Learning. Stewart (2008) studied online synchronous dialogue.

Dron (2007) extends the theory to the social software, such as blogs, wikis, tagging systems, and collaborative filters.

Beasley (2007) studied the effects of instructor behaviors on student perceptions of the online learning experience.

Steinman (2007) addressed transactional distance: (a) learner-to-instructor; and (b) learner-to-other-students in online learning courses.

Lenear (2006) compared mentor-protégé interaction, transactional distance, structure, satisfaction, and support in Internet-based mentoring.

Mulhollen (2006) demonstrated that interpersonal intelligence was predictive of attitude toward independent learning, supporting the theory regarding autonomy and transactional distance.

Kuskis (2006) described the social dynamics in asynchronous online higher education courses, and concluded that the dialogue between learners as well as instructor-to-learner dialogue, also reduces transactional distance for learners.

Wallace, Grinnell, Carey, and Carey (2006), in one of the relatively few experimental designs, compared two instructional strategies, and found that students taking quizzes in the lower transactional distance format performed significantly better.

Aceves (2006) questioned the relevance of the university's traditional tasks and missions in the newly emerging online environment.

2006–2011 STUDIES CONTRIBUTING TO EVOLUTION OF THE THEORY

Every study that uses a theory contributes to the evolution of the theory. However, some studies go further than others in refining, developing, adding to, or criticizing the theory itself—as compared with those studies listed above in which the purpose of the theory was to guide the formulation of the research question. The following is a selection of recent studies in which the researchers articulated the evolution of the theory as one of the purposes of their research:

Horzum (2011) is one of several who have attempted to develop a scale to measure transactional distance. A scale consisting of 38 items and 5 subfactors was used to measure perception of transactional distance in a blended learning environment.

Hughes (2010) also developed an instrument, the Multivariable Transactional Distance Survey to explore the effects of disseminating educational messages via email to nurses.

Park (2011) postulated four types of mobile learning, with varying degrees of transactional distance.

Shearer (2009) proposed a scheme for classifying dialogue, drawing on the philosophical work of communication theorist Burbules.

Rabinovich (2009) developed a 46-item Scale of TD for synchronous Web-extended learning environments.

Giossos, Koutsouba, Lionarakis, and Skavantzos (2009) drew on the work of John Dewey to link TD theory with the epistemological framework of "realism."

Whitesel (2009) offered a phenomenological rendering of transactional distance in exploring teacher presence in learning based in technology.

Sahin (2008) concluded that the three dimensions of transactional distance may be linked with Kolb's two dimensional views of individual learning styles.

Kang and Gyorke (2008) compared TD with cultural-historical activity theory and noted areas of compatibility as well as contradictions.

Wheeler (2007) concluded that the effects of transactional distance could be analyzed more deeply if two subvariables of dialogue were recognized, social presence and immediacy.

Wolverton (2007), seeking to sharpen the focus of TD that he describes as a "grand theory," proposes a "middle-level" theory of Internet education.

Jung (2006) studied students in videoconferencing classrooms and developed what he claimed to be a superior operational definition of transactional distance.

Sandoe (2005) designed an instrument to measure structure in the online environment and tested it on 20 courses, finding it to excel in comparison to other instruments.

2006–2011 STUDIES IN WHICH TD THEORY PLAYED A COMPLEMENTARY ROLE

The following are examples of the third type of research study, in which the theory is cited but not necessarily as the principal source of the research question, illustrating the wide range of subject areas in which researchers find some value in the theory.

Boster (2009) grounded a study of social issues facing online students in the theories of social development as well as transactional distance.

Logsdon (2008) applied both TD theory as well as a model of conflict resolution to identify factors leading to student-to-student conflict in online courses.

Pettazzoni (2008) surveyed students who completed world literature classes online to evaluate attitudes including that to transactional distance.

Kennedy and Cavanaugh (2008) focused on the contributions of the course's design elements to the students' perceptions of transactional distance in an online teacher education course.

Cavanaugh and Cavanaugh (2008) attempted to reduce students' sense of transactional distance by using interactive geographic maps as a form of dialogue.

Heindel, Smith, and Torres-Ayala, (2007) applied TD theory to the analysis of how Blackboard tools are used across different disciplines

Talvitie-Siple (2007) looked at perceptions of transactional distance as well as social presence in evaluating students' motivation to learn mathematics in a virtual high school.

Her (2006) investigated students' media preferences within a foundational mathematics course in blended and online enhanced face-to-face learning environments.

Ehrlich-Martin (2006) studied teaching of American sign-language, and said she found her central finding supported by transactional distance theory.

Urban (2006) compared using computer-based distance education (CDE) and traditional tutorial sessions as ways of providing supplemental instruction for at-risk students.

Papadopoulos and Dagdilelis (2006) used TD theory in a study of students learning geometry in a traditional classroom.

Sargeant, Curran, Allen, Jarvis-Selinger, and Ho (2006) interviewed 50 physicians in an attempt to ascertain how to overcome the transactional distance in online continuing medical education.

Hendry (2005) measured student satisfaction with various facets of an online biology course.

CONCLUSION: HOW TO USE THIS LITERATURE

Transactional distance theory provides the broad framework of the pedagogy of distance education. It allows the generation of almost infinite number of hypotheses for research into the interactions between course structures, dialogue between teachers and learners and the student's propensity to exercise control of the learning process. It is as a framework for such a scientific approach, as contrasted to the haphazard "wouldn't it be nice to know …" approach that is unfortunately too prevalent in education, that transactional distance theory, like other theory, is most valuable.

This chapter has summarized the genesis of the theory, and listed some of the research projects it has spawned, which now serve to point the way for future research. Before proceeding in that direction, potential researchers should look more closely at some of the studies reviewed above, and then when results are in, they will be able to report them with reference to this literature, and in terms of the underlying theory.

REFERENCES

Aceves, R. (2006). *Input quality in Internet delivered education at a large comprehensive university* (Doctoral dissertation). Retrieved from ProQuest Dissertations and Theses Database. (304941419).

Anderson, D. S. (1999). *Mathematics and distance education on the Internet: An investigation based on transactional distance education theory* (Doctoral dissertation). Retrieved from ProQuest Dissertations and Theses Database. (304500155).

Association of Supervision and Curriculum Development. (1971). Criteria for assessing the formal properties of theories of instruction. In R. Hyman (Ed.), *Contemporary thought on teaching* (pp. 123-130). Englewood Cliffs, NJ: Prentice-Hall.

Atkinson, T. R. (1999). Toward an understanding of instructor–student interactions: A study of videoconferencing in the postsecondary distance learning classroom (Unpublished doctoral dissertation). Louisiana State University, Baton Rouge.

Avive, R., Erlich, Z., Ravid, G., & Geva, A. (2003). Network analysis of knowledge construction in asynchronous learning networks. *Journal of Asynchronous Learning Networks, 7* (3). Retrieved from http://www.sloan-c.org/publications/jaln/v7n3/index.asp.

Bajt, S. K. (2009). *Preferred distance learning modalities of millennial community college students* (Doctoral dissertation). Retrieved from ProQuest Dissertations and Theses Database. (304894997).

Baynton, M. (1992). Dimensions of "control" in distance education: A factor analysis. *The American Journal of Distance Education, 6*(2), 17–31.

Beasley, S. (2007). *Influence of instructor behaviors on student perceptions of the online learning experience* (Doctoral dissertation). Retrieved from ProQuest Dissertations and Theses Database. (3282352).

Belair, M. (2011). *The investigation of teacher communication practices in virtual high school* (Doctoral dissertation). Retrieved from ProQuest Dissertations and Theses Database. (897921887).

Benson, R., & Samarawickrema, G. (2009). Addressing the context of e-learning: Using transactional distance theory to inform design. *Distance Education, 30*(1), 5–21.

Bischoff, W. R. (1993). *Transactional distance, interactive television, and electronic mail communication in graduate public health and nursing courses: Implications for professional education* (Unpublished doctoral dissertation). University of Hawaii, Honolulu.

Bischoff, W. R., Bisconer, S. W., Kooker, B. M., & Woods, L. C. (1996). Transactional distance and interactive television in the distance education of health professionals. *The American Journal of Distance Education, 10*(3), 4–19.

Boster, M. (2009). *Social implications facing online learners: A case study of undergraduate multimedia students* (Doctoral dissertation). Retrieved from ProQuest Dissertations and Theses Database. (305080477).

Boyd, R., & J. Apps (Eds.). (1980). *Redefining the discipline of adult education.* San Francisco: Jossey-Bass.

Braxton, S. N. (1999). *Empirical comparison of technical and non-technical distance education courses to derive a refined transactional distance theory as the framework for a utilization-focused evaluation tool* (Unpublished doctoral dissertation). George Washington University, Washington, DC.

Brenner, R. J. (1996). *An analysis of the transactional distance in asynchronous telecourses at a community college using the group embedded figures test* (Unpublished doctoral dissertation). East Tennessee State University, Johnson City.

Bunker, E., Gayol, Y., Nti, N., & Reidell, P. (1996). A study of transactional distance in an international audio-conferencing course. *Technology and Teacher Education Annual* (pp. 40–44). Phoenix, AZ: Association for the Advancement of Computing in Education.

Caspi, A. P., Gorsky, & Chajut, E. (2003). The influence of group size on non-mandatory asynchronous instructional discussion groups. *The Internet and Higher Education, 6*(3), 227–240.

Cavanaugh, T., & Cavanaugh, C. (2008). Interactive maps for community in online learning. *Journal of Computers in the Schools, 25*(3–4), 235–242.

Chen, Y. (1997). *The implications of Moore's theory of transactional distance in a videoconferencing learning environment* (Unpublished doctoral dissertation). The Pennsylvania State University, University Park.

Chen, Y. J. (2001). Dimensions of transactional distance in World Wide Web learning environment: A factor analysis. *British Journal of Educational Technology, 32*(4), 459–470.

Chen, Y., & Willits, F. (1998). A path analysis of the concepts in Moore's theory of transactional distance in a videoconferencing learning environment. *Journal of Distance Education, 13*(2), 51–65.

Chen, Y. J., & Willits, F. K. (1999). Dimensions of educational transactions in a videoconferencing learning environment. *The American Journal of Distance Education, 13*(1), 45–59.

Clouse, S. F. (2001). *The assessment of student performance and satisfaction outcomes with synchronous and asynchronous interaction methods in a student-centered distributed learning environment* (Unpublished doctoral dissertation). University Of Montana, Missoula.

Deng, L., & Yuen, H. K. (2009). Blogs in higher education: Implementation and issues. *TechTrends, 53*(3), 95–98.

Dron, J. (2002). *Achieving self-organisation in network-based learning environments* (Unpublished doctoral dissertation). University of Brighton, Brighton, UK.

Dron, J. (2007). Designing the undesignable: Social software and control. *Educational Technology & Society, 10*(3), 60–71.

Dron, J., Seidel, C., & Litten, G. (2004). Transactional distance in a blended learning environment. *ALT Journal, 12*(2), 163–174.

Dupin-Bryant, P. (2004). Teaching styles of interactive television instructors: A descriptive study. *The American Journal of Distance Education, 18*(1), 39–50.

Edstrom, R. (2002). *Flexible education in the upper secondary school: Extended classrooms and a decreased transactional distance* (Unpublished doctoral dissertation). Uppsala University, Uppsala, Sweden.

Ehrlich-Martin, S. (2006). *A case study of an American sign language course taught via videoconferencing* (Doctoral dissertation). Retrieved from ProQuest Dissertations and Theses Database. (305355708).

Falloon, G. (2011). Making the connection: Moore's theory of transactional distance and its relevance to the use of a virtual classroom in postgraduate online teacher education. *Journal of Research on Technology in Education, 43*(3), 187–209.

Gallo, J. A. (2001). *A distance learning and training model* (Unpublished doctoral dissertation). The Pennsylvania State University, University Park.

Garrison, D. R., & Baynton, M. (1987). Beyond independence in distance education: The concept of control. *The American Journal of Distance Education, 1*(3), 3–15.

Gayol, Y. (1996). The use of computer networks in distance education: analysis of the patterns of electronic interaction in a multinational course. In C. C. Gibson (Ed.), *Distance education symposium 3: Learners and learning* (pp. 61–70). University Park, PA: The American Center for the Study of Distance Education.

Giossos, Y., Koutsouba, M., Lionarakis, A., & Skavantzos, K. (2009). Reconsidering Moore's Transactional Distance Theory. *European Journal of Open, Distance and E-Learning, 2*(II), 1–6.

Gorsky, P., & Caspi, A. (2005, March). Dialogue: A theoretical framework for distance education instructional systems. *British Journal of Educational Technology, 36*(2), 137–144.

Gorsky, P., Caspi, A., & Trumper, R. (2004). University students' use of dialogue in a distance education physics course. *Open Learning, 19*(3), 265–277.

Gorsky, P., Caspi, A., & Tuvi-Arid, I. (2004). Use of instructional dialogue by university students in a distance education chemistry course. *Journal of Distance Education, 19*(1), 1–19.

Heindel, A. J., Smith, G. G., & Torres-Ayala, A. T. (2007). Blackboard tool usage across different disciplines: Interaction and transactional distance. In T. Bastiaens & S. Carliner (Eds.), *Proceedings of World Conference on E-Learning in corporate, government, healthcare, and higher education 2007* (pp. 1866–1873). Chesapeake, VA: AACE.

Hendry, S. R. (2005). *Student perceptions: Importance of and satisfaction with aspects of an online biology course* (Doctoral dissertation). Retrieved from ProQuest Dissertations and Theses Database. (305435299).

Her, M. H. Y. (2006). *An investigation of students' media preferences in learning mathematical concepts* (Doctoral dissertation). Retrieved from ProQuest Dissertations and Theses Database. (305335299).

Holmberg, B. (1981). *Status and trends of distance education.* London: Kogan Page.

Hopper, D. A. (2000). *Learner characteristics, life circumstances, and transactional distance in a distance education setting* (Unpublished doctoral dissertation). Wayne State University, Detroit.

Horzum, M. (2011). Developing transactional distance scale and examining transactional distance perception of blended learning students in terms of different variables. *Educational Sciences: Theory and Practice, 11*(3), 1582–1587.

Huang, H. (2000). *Moore's theory of transactional distance in an online mediated environment: Student perceptions on the online courses* (Unpublished doctoral dissertation). Seattle Pacific University, Seattle, WA.

Hughes, W. G. (2010). *Transactional distance theory: The effect of disseminating educational messages to frontline registered nurses in an acute care hospital setting* (Unpublished doctoral dissertation). Louisiana State University, Baton Rouge.

Jung, H. Y. (2006). *Transactional distance and student motivation: Student perception of teacher immediacy, solidarity toward peer students and student motivation in distance education* (Doctoral dissertation). Retrieved from ProQuest Dissertations and Theses Database. (304968352).

Jung, I. (2001). Building a theoretical framework of Web-based instruction in the context of distance education. *British Journal of Educational Technology, 32*(5), 525–534.

Kang, H., & Gyorke, A. (2008). Rethinking distance learning activities: A comparison of transactional distance theory and activity theory. *Open Learning, 23*(3), 203–214.

Kanuka, H., Collett, D., & Caswell, C. (2002). University instructor perceptions of the use of asynchronous text-based discussion in distance courses. *The American Journal of Distance Education, 16*(3), 151–167.

Kennedy, K., & Cavanaugh, C. (2008). Student perceptions of transactional distance in online teacher education courses. In K. McFerrin, R. Weber, R. Carlsen, & D. A. Willis (Eds.), *Proceedings of Society for Information Technology and Teacher Education international conference 2008* (pp. 485–490). Chesapeake, VA: AACE.

Kuskis, O. A. (2006). *Facilitation and community in asynchronous online courses: Views and practices of expert practitioners* (Doctoral dissertation). Retrieved from ProQuest Dissertations and Theses Database. (304926057).

Lee, J., & Gibson, C. C. (2003). Developing self-direction in an online course through computer-mediated interaction. *The American Journal of Distance Education, 17*(3), 173–187.

Lemone, K. (2005). Analyzing cultural influences on ELearning transactional issues. In G. Richards (Ed.), *Proceedings. World Conference on E-Learning in Corporate, Government, Healthcare, and Higher Education 2005* (pp. 2637–2644). Chesapeake, VA: AACE.

Lenear, P. E. (2006). *The effect of an Internet-based mentoring program on the transactional distance and interaction between mentors and proteges* (Doctoral dissertation). Retrieved from ProQuest Dissertations and Theses Database. (305331326).

Logsdon, Jr., D. (2008). *A quantitative study of student perceptions of factors likely to produce student-to-student conflict in the online learning environment* (Unpublished doctoral dissertation). TUI University, Cypress, CA.

Lowell, N. (2004). *An investigation of factors contributing to perceived transactional distance in an online setting* (Unpublished doctoral dissertation) University of Northern Colorado, Greeley.

Maslow, A. H. (1968). Some educational implications of the humanistic psychologies, *Harvard Educational Review, 38*(4), 685-696.

Mathieson, K. (2011, August). *Screencasting: Results of a pilot study and practical applications.* Presentation at the 27th Annual Conference on Distance Teaching and Learning. Madison, WI.

McBrien, J., Jones, P., & Cheng, R. (2009). Virtual spaces: Employing a synchronous online classroom to facilitate student engagement in online learning. *International Review of Research in Open and Distance Learning, 10*(3), 1-17.

McLaren, A. C. (2010). *The effects of instructor–learner interactions on learner satisfaction in online masters courses* (Doctoral dissertation). Retrieved from ProQuest Dissertations and Theses Database. (231235132).

Moore, M. G. (1972). Learner autonomy: The second dimension of independent learning. *Convergence, 5*(2), 76–88.

Moore, M. G. (1973). Towards a theory of independent learning and teaching. *Journal of Higher Education*, (44), 661–679.

Moore, M. G. (1976). *Investigation of the interaction between the cognitive style of field independence and attitudes to independent study* (Unpublished doctoral dissertation). University of Wisconsin, Madison.

Moore, M. G. (1980). Independent study. In R. Boyd & J. Apps (Eds.), *Redefining the discipline of adult education* (pp. 16–31). San Francisco: Jossey-Bass.

Moore, M. G. (1993). Theory of transactional distance. In D. Keegan (Ed.), *Theoretical Principles of Distance Education* (pp. 22–29). New York: Routledge.

Moore, M. H. (1999). *The effects of two instructional delivery processes of a distance training system on trainee satisfaction, job performance and retention* (Unpublished doctoral dissertation). The Ohio State University, Columbus.

Mulhollen, C. (2006). *The relationship between multiple intelligences and attitude toward independent learning in a high transactional distance environment* (Doctoral dissertation). Retrieved from ProQuest Dissertations and Theses Database. (305281548).

Munro, P. (1991). *Presence at a distance: The educator–learner relationship in distance education and dropout* (Unpublished doctoral dissertation). University of British Columbia, Vancouver.

Murphy, E., & Rodriguez-Manzanares, M. (2008). Revisiting transactional distance theory in a context of Web-based high-school distance education. *Journal of Distance Education, 22*(2), 1–13.

Offir, B., Lev, Y., Y. Lev, Barth, I., & Shteinbok, A. (2004). An integrated analysis of verbal and nonverbal interaction in conventional and distance learning environments. *Journal of Educational Computing Research, 31*(2), 101–118.

Papadopoulos, I., & Dagdilelis, V. (2006). The theory of transactional distance as a framework for the analysis of computer-aided teaching of geometry. *International Journal for Technology in Mathematics Education, 13*(4), 175–182.

Park, Y. (2011). A pedagogical framework for mobile learning: Categorizing educational applications of mobile technologies into four types. *International Review of Research in Open and Distance Learning, 12*(2), 78-96.

Peters, O. (1998). *Learning and teaching in distance education Analysis and interpretation from an international perspective.* London: Kogan Page.

Pettazzoni, J. E. (2008). *Factors associated with attitudes toward learning in an online environment: Transactional distance, technical efficacy, and physical surroundings* (Doctoral dissertation). Retrieved from ProQuest Dissertations and Theses Database. (AAI3346551).

Pruitt, D. (2005). *Transactional distance and learner autonomy as predictors of student performance in distance learning courses delivered by three modalities* (Unpublished doctoral dissertation). Tulane University, New Orleans.

Rabinovich, T. (2009). *Transactional distance in a synchronous Web-extended classroom learning environment* (Doctoral dissertation). Retrieved from ProQuest Dissertations and Theses Database. (304845866).

Richardson, J. T. (1998). Field independence in higher education and the case of distance learning. *International Journal of Educational Research, 29*(3), 241–250.

Rogers, C. (1969). *Freedom to learn.* Columbus, OH: Charles E. Merril.

Rovai, A. P. (2000). Building and sustaining community in asynchronous learning networks. *The Internet and Higher Education, 3*(4), 285–297.

Rovai, A. P. (2002, April). Building sense of community at a distance. *The International Review Of Research In Open And Distance Learning, 3*(1). Retrieved from http://www.irrodl.org/index.php/irrodl/article/view/79/1526

Saba, F. (1988). Integrated telecommunications systems and instructional transaction. *The American Journal of Distance Education, 2*(3), 17–24.

Saba, F., & Shearer, R. (1994). Verifying key theoretical concepts in a dynamic model of distance education. *The American Journal of Distance Education, 8*(1), 36–57.

Saba, F., & Twitchell, D. (1988). Research in distance education. A system modeling approach. *The American Journal of Distance Education, 2*(1), 9–24.

Sahin, S. (2008). The relationship between student characteristics, including learning styles, and their perceptions and satisfaction in Web-based courses in higher education. *Turkish Online Journal of Distance Education, 9*(1), 123–138.

Sandoe, C. (2005). *Measuring transactional distance in online courses: The structure component* (Doctoral dissertation). Retrieved from ProQuest Dissertations and Theses Database. (305421786).

Sargeant, J., Curran, V., Allen, M., Jarvis-Selinger, S., & Ho, K. (2006). Facilitating interpersonal interaction and learning online: Linking theory and practice. *Journal of Continuing Education in the Health Professions, 26*(2), 128–136.

Seok, S. (2008). Teaching aspects of e-learning. *International Journal on E-Learning, 7*(4), 725–741. Chesapeake, VA: AACE. Retrieved from http://www.editlib.org/p/24323

Shearer, R. (2009). *Transactional distance and dialogue: An exploratory study to refine the theoretical construct of dialogue in online learning* (Doctoral dissertation). Retrieved from ProQuest Dissertations and Theses Database. (AAI3399706).

Shin, N. (2001). *Beyond interaction: Transactional presence and distance learning* (Unpublished doctoral dissertation). The Pennsylvania State University, University Park.

Shinkle, A. (2001). *Interaction in distance education: A study of student–student and student–teacher interaction via an electronic distribution list* (Unpublished doctoral dissertation). University Of Wyoming, Laramie.

Stein, D. S., Wanstreet, C. E., Calvin, J., Overtoom, C., & Wheaton, J. E. (2005). Bridging the transactional distance gap in online learning environments. *The American Journal of Distance Education, 19*(2), 105–118.

Steinman, D. (2007). Educational experiences and the online student. *TechTrends, 51*(5), 46–52.

Stewart, S. (2008). *A study of instructional strategies that promote learning centered synchronous dialogue online* (Doctoral dissertation). Retrieved from ProQuest Dissertations and Theses Database. (3347372).

Talvitie-Siple, J. (2007). *Students' motivation to learn: An evaluation of perceptions, pedagogy, and design in one e-learning environment* (Doctoral dissertation). Retrieved from ProQuest Dissertations and Theses Database. (304842369).

Thompson, B. (1998). *An investigation of professional nurse autonomy and learner autonomy among female registered nurses enrolled in distance education and traditional baccalaureate programs* (Unpublished doctoral dissertation). Widener University School of Nursing, Chester, PA.

Tough, A. M. (1971). *The adult's learning projects.* Toronto: Ontario Institute for Studies in Education.

Urban, C. Q. (2006). *The effects of using computer-based distance education for supplemental instruction compared to traditional tutorial sessions to enhance learning for students at-risk for academic difficulties* (Doctoral dissertation). Retrieved from ProQuest Dissertations and Theses Database. (304916833).

Veale, B. L. 2009. *Transactional distance and course structure: A qualitative study* (Doctoral dissertation). Retrieved from ProQuest Dissertations and Theses Database. (304940869).

Vrasidas, C., & McIsaac, M. S. (1999). Factors influencing interaction in an online course. *The American Journal of Distance Education, 13*(3), 22–36.

Walker Fernandez, S. E. (1999). *Toward understanding the study experience of culturally sensitive graduate students in American distance education programs* (Unpublished doctoral dissertation). Florida International University, Miami.

Wallace, T., Grinnell, L., Carey, L., & Carey, J. (2006). Maximizing learning from rehearsal activity in Web-based distance learning. *Journal of Interactive Learning Research, 17*(3), 319–327. Retrieved from http://www.editlib.org/p/6311

Wang, L. C., & Morgan, W. (2008). Student perceptions of using instant messaging software to facilitate synchronous online class interaction in a graduate teacher education course. *Journal of Computing in Teacher Education*, 25(1), 15–21.

Watts, L. K. (2010). *The role of dialogue in distance education: A qualitative study* (Doctoral dissertation). Retrieved from ProQuest Dissertations and Theses Database. (250697391).

Wedemeyer, C. A. (1971). Independent study. In L. C. Deighton (Editor-in-Chief), *The encyclopedia of education* (Vol. 4, p. 548–557). New York: MacMillan.

Wheeler, S. (2002). Student perceptions of learning support in distance education. *Quarterly Review of Distance Education, 3*(4), 419–429.

Wheeler, S. (2007). The influence of communication technologies and approaches to study on transactional distance in blended learning. *ALT-J: Research in Learning Technology, 15*(2), 103–117.

Whitesel, C. H. (2009). *Virtualizing the teacher: The lived experience of teaching within technology* (Doctoral dissertation). Retrieved from ProQuest Dissertations and Theses Database. (304924476).

Wikeley, F., & Muschamp, Y. (2004). Pedagogical implications of working with doctoral students at a distance. *Distance Education, 25*(1), 125–142.

Williams, K. T. (2003). *Factors affecting student retention in an online graduate certificate program: A grounded theory study* (Unpublished doctoral dissertation). University of Florida, Gainsville.

Witte, M. M., & Wolf, S. E. (2003). Infusing mentoring and technology within graduate courses: Reflections in practice. *Mentoring and Tutoring, 11*(1), 95–103.

Wolverton, R. (2007). *Internet education: A middle-range theoretical model for overcoming transactional distance* (Doctoral dissertation). Retrieved from ProQuest Dissertations and Theses Database. (304787027).

Zhang, A. (2003). *Transactional distance in Web-based college learning environments: Toward measurement and theory construction* (Unpublished doctoral dissertation). Virginia Commonwealth University, Richmond.

6

INDEPENDENT LEARNING

Autonomy, Control, and Meta-Cognition

WILLIAM ANDERSON

In reviewing the area of independent learning in distance education, the term "independence" is used initially because of its connection to the beginnings of the modern practice and study of distance education through Wedemeyer's (1971) work on independent learning. This review will pull together threads of discussion from several related areas, each of which contributes in its own way to our understanding of the ways in which learners are seen as independent. The fields of distance education and adult education, the field from which much of the early theoretical work in distance education arises, provide three dominant descriptors for this area: self-directed learning (SDL), autonomous learning, and independent learning. These descriptors are often used with a considerable degree of equivalence. Tight (1996), for instance, suggests that the concepts of independent and SDL are so closely linked that they are essentially synonymous, while Moore (1986), in describing one type of educational transaction, explained them by saying "This is autonomous, or self-directed learning" (p. 12). These areas and the various concepts that have coalesced around each in relation to distance education, form the basis of the literature from which this chapter draws.

As early as the 1960s, personal autonomy and freedom of choice were identified as key aspects of adult learning (Boyd, 1966; Rogers, 1969), this approach developing out of the humanistic psychology of Maslow and Rogers. Boyd wrote, for example, that adult learners:

> approach subject matter directly without having an adult in a set of intervening roles between the learner and the subject matter. The adult knows his own standards and expectations. He no longer needs to be told, nor does he require the approval and reward from persons in authority. (p. 180)

Tough's (1971) work on adult learning projects was seminal, and Knowles' (1975) engagement with and popularisation of the notion of SDL supported the concept of andragogy that was at the core of his approach to adult education. These writers tended to focus on the design of learning activities, with Knowles writing that adult learners will take the lead "in diagnosing their learning needs, formulating learning goals, identifying human and material resources for learning, choosing and implementing appropriate learning strategies, and evaluating learning outcomes" (p. 18).

In the field of distance education, Wedemeyer (1971) chose to focus on the idea of independent learning, drawing his inspiration from the independent study system that had developed on some U.S. campuses for "superior students" who were on-campus. He did this to move distance education from its strongly teacher or institution directed approach to one that gave more freedom and choice to learners. Moore (1972) provided the link between Wedemeyer's ideas and considerable authority in distance education, and the emerging ideas about self-direction in learning within the field of adult education, imbuing the field of distance education with a conceptual foundation that still has considerable influence.

Moore (1972) set out an argument that independent study comprised two dimensions—distance teaching and learner autonomy. Distance teaching had two principal characteristics that Moore named individualization (later to be called structure) and dialogue. In explaining the second dimension, Moore describes the autonomous learner as one who has learnt how to learn; as one who "knows how to proceed through each of the instructional processes" (p. 81). The autonomous learner is also a person who draws on a range of resources. When these resources include teachers, the autonomous learner is "surrendering temporarily some of his learner autonomy … However, if he is a truly autonomous learner, he will not give up overall control of the learning processes" (p. 81). Moore (1980) notes that autonomous learners may at times be instrumentally dependent on teachers but they will not be emotionally dependent on them.

Through the 1980s, changes in the conceptualisation of SDL within distance education mirrored those occurring in adult education. In the latter area, a more complex picture of SDL emerged. There was concern particularly for the need to capture learner characteristics that were internal to individuals, alongside consideration of the social context in which learning occurs. In distance education, there was some concern that in applying the early conceptualisation of SDL too great an emphasis was placed on learner autonomy. The concern is strongly evident in the work of Garrison (1987) and is also seen in Morgan's (1985) critique of independent learning. Morgan was particularly concerned about what he saw as the total nature of learner control in conceptualisations of SDL and the lack of consideration for a sharing of control between the student and the institution. Garrison's concerns were about the role of the teacher as a facilitator of learning, and the need to make SDL relevant to formal educational contexts. Moore (1980) had previously acknowledged that learners differed in their ability to learn autonomously but he continued to advocate for a strong version of learner autonomy. Moore (1986) argued that institutions should modify their teaching to give learners a chance to exercise their autonomy, citing Ljosa and Sandvold's (1983) comment that "Through a long series of personal conscious choices the student will make his/her own course" (p. 21). Alongside this he recognised that teachers would work as "joint enquirers" with students and act as a "resource person, a procedural specialist, and a co-inquirer" (Moore, 1986, p. 12). The key issue at this time was the balance of control between teacher and student.

The role of the teacher was highlighted in Candy's (1991) work on SDL. Candy differentiated between learner control and autodidaxy as distinct domains of self-direction, saying that in the first, the learner maintained primary ownership of learning although "there is still a residue, albeit small, of teacher-control" (p. 18), while in the second no teacher is present. It is the first that has relevance to distance education, for, even if only through the presence of a voice within prepared study material, a teacher's part in the educational transaction is always evident, and learning is acknowledged as the purpose of student activity.

Learners capable of and motivated to undertake SDL may, however, choose not to do so. Knowles made this point in 1980, and the argument is supported by Candy (1991) and Brockett and Hiemstra (1991). Candy suggested that four major variables influence the extent to which a learner decides to engage in SDL: commitment to learning at the current time, sense of competence as a learner, familiarity of the subject matter, and technical skills related to the learning process. Even a learner who is capable of SDL to a considerable extent may choose to engage in a highly teacher-directed educational setting in, for example, the initial stages of a learning project, or for convenience. Responsibility for learning is something that is shared between teacher and learner, although the orientation of this approach sees learners ceding control of the learning process and aspects of the design of learning activities as they wish, rather than fighting for them.

Questions of control in educational transactions surfaced in Garrison's attempts to overcome what he regarded as the lack of conceptual clarity in the use of the term "independence." Garrison (1989, p. 27) wrote that "Control is concerned with the opportunity and ability to influence and direct a course of events. Control not only implies having choices and making decisions, but includes the capability to effect change." Control is valuable in the educational process because "(w)ithout substantial control (i.e. information and communication) in the educational process learners are less likely to realize their potential" (p. 39).

Building on Garrison's work, Garrison and Baynton (1987) described control as a crucial and central concept in distance education. Their focus in relation to control was on the nature of the interaction between teacher and student, and they linked control with communication. They said, "Clearly, communication is the process that makes an educational transaction possible. Two-way communication provides the means for negotiation and dialogue. This in turn determines the balance of control which will maximize educational development" (p. 14). Anderson and Garrison (1998) also suggested that the reciprocal component of educational communication moves the balance of control of the educational transaction toward the student, shifting the emphasis from an institution being the determinant of control in the learning situation to recognition of the role of learners.

Analysis of the concept of control in relation to educational transactions in distance education needed to be underpinned by a firmer and coherent understanding of SDL that accounted for the transactional nature of education. Garrison (1997) proposed such a model based on three interconnected dimensions to account for both the external factors of learning (what, where, when, etc., to learn) and internal factors (cognitive, metacognitive, and motivational aspects). His approach also adopted a collaborative perspective that "has the individual taking responsibility for constructing meaning while including the participation of others in confirming worthwhile knowledge" (p. 19).

Garrison's (1997) proposed three dimensions were self-management (task control), with a focus on the enactment of learning goals and the management of learning resources and support, self-monitoring (cognitive responsibility), which addresses cognitive and metacognitive processes, and motivation (entering and task), relating to initiation and maintenance of effort. The dimension of motivation was tied to the concept of control. Garrison argued that intrinsic motivation was necessary if students were to achieve quality educational outcomes, and that "to encourage intrinsically motivated learning, students must see opportunities to share control and to collaborate in the planning and implementation of the learning process" (p. 29). Motivation was also seen as having a mediating effect on the dimensions of self-management (task control) and self-monitoring (cognitive responsibility) which Garrison describes as "integral and reciprocal constructs" (p. 21) in this model of SDL.

More recently, the notion of autonomy, of self-direction in learning, has come under renewed scrutiny. Brookfield's (2009) critical review of the nature of self-directed learning highlights six areas of critique, but most notable is his discussion of the notion of the self in regard to self-direction. Key to his discussion is recognition that "the 'self' that is involved in conducting learning is culturally formed and bound" (p. 2620), and he argues that reflection on the way in which culture helps shape a learner's needs is an important aspect of self-directed learning. Part of this cultural critique emphasises the importance of the collective, interdependent nature of learning. The concept of "self" has been revisited by others, who have reached related conclusions. In acknowledging that individuals are embedded in a range of relationships and groups at various levels, Boucouvalas (2009) brings a cultural dimension to autonomy alongside its more individualistic notion, arguing for interaction and collaboration as the basis of interdependence, and a move "from an exclusive focus on the *me* of self direction to inclusion of the *we* of self-direction" (p. 7, italics in original). Similarly, Eneau (2008) develops a perspective on the self that places relationships and relating to others at the centre of the development of autonomy. The growth in the concept of autonomy involves a change from the concept of the bounded autonomous self in interaction with others to one which stretches the boundary to acknowledge autonomy as inclusive of interactions.

With this view of autonomy, the issue of control of one's learning, described by Brookfield as "being at the heart of self-direction" (p. 2621) seems problematic. Brookfield rightly notes the importance of learners exercising control over educational decisions—questions of goals, resources, methods, and criteria for success—as the basis of self-direction. With an inclusive concept of autonomy that encompasses relationships with others, how is such control developed and exercised? This question is important for distance educators seeking to integrate an expanded conception of autonomy with the nature of distance education in the connected, online and sometimes more informal contexts appearing worldwide.

Ding's work in the area of distance language learning provides one answer. Ding (2005) argues for an intersubjective version of collaborative autonomy, defined as "a version of autonomy that not only stresses the 'virtues' of collaboration as a means of facilitating autonomy but also argues that promoting autonomy necessarily entails complex relations of interdependence" (p. 41). This approach draws on the concept of intersubjectivity, the idea that knowledge and thought are social and dialogical in nature. In terms of control, Benson (1996, cited in Ding, 2005, p. 42) argues that

> Greater learner control over the learning process, resources and language cannot be achieved by each individual working alone according to his or her own preferences. Control is a question of collective decision-making rather than individual

choice. Yet collective decisions are also arrived at by individuals achieving consensus and acting in concert.

Control, conceived in this way, "is not just seen as the power that individuals have to give effect to their wishes, but also acknowledges the relations of power within which individuals exist and takes account of the range of forces that impact on their ability to attain their goals" (Anderson, 2006, p. 109).

The concept of control has been used increasingly in place of autonomy, perhaps reflecting Garrison's (2003) concern that autonomy may have connotations which reflect a false ideal of what learners are. When autonomy is used in the sense of a personal quality in line with what McLaren (1993) describes as "the magnificent Enlightenment swindle of the autonomous, stable and self-contained ego" (p. 121), there is some point to the critique. However, the distance education literature more often uses autonomy as a characteristic of adult learning rather than of adults. Thus Moore's 1994 discussion of autonomy as "the potential to participate" (p. 2) in adult learning, ties in with the Dron's (2007) description of autonomy as a variable quantity within the learning process. In this sense, having autonomy in learning is synonymous with learner control. We see this in the similarity that exists between Dron's statement, in a brief section entitled "The Centrality of Control" that

> flexibility of choice also implies that learners should be able to evaluate in any given circumstance whether it is wise to relinquish their freedom of choice and to allow another (whether in person or by proxy, e.g. through a book) to guide them. (2007, p. 45)

and Garrison's argument that "only by accepting the mediation of others and developing the ability to make critical judgements between a range of alternatives can autonomy be exercised over learning" (1987, p. 311). In exercising more or less autonomy within the learning process, learners are taking or ceding more control.

The recent work of Dron (2007) responds to the question of control by proposing a focus on a concept called "transactional control," which he describes as being concerned with choices saying "some choices are made by teachers and some by learners. The extent to which those choices are dictated by particular individuals determines their level of transactional control at any moment" (Dron, 2006). Dron develops this concept through an examination of the work of Candy, Garrison and Baynton, Moore, Saba and Shearer, and also highlights the dynamics of control in relation to the possibilities provided for learning by new technologies. He focuses on the use of dialogue as a means of making choices and negotiating control but argues that it is only one of the ways in which a learner might gain control. Alongside discussion of control comes recognition of the importance of constraint and of scale. Constraints can both enhance and impede choice making, and scale considers the level at which choices can be made. Dron sees close parallels between his ideas and those of Garrison and Baynton.

The insight that Dron provides relates to how transactional control informs discussions of the pedagogical properties and uses of social software. He recognises that in social software use "the group is a first class object that has an existence in its own right, mediated through the environment just as interactions between individuals are mediated" (Dron, 2006), and that because of its emphasis on the group social software allows user control and delegation of control simultaneously. Social software he says, "appears to offer the best of both worlds, assisting dependent learners through the provision of structure, yet enabling autonomy at any point" (Dron, 2006). There are strong parallels here with the intersubjective view of autonomy discussed earlier.

Transactional control is a concept that suggests particular approaches to the design and use of online environments for learning and teaching and may well make a significant contribution to the theory and practice of distance education. In particular it may have potential to support more rigorous discussion of connectivism (Siemens, 2005). Siemens proposes connectivism as a learning theory with particular application to the digital age and the (online) connectivity that enables. In a review of the nature of connectivism and its critiques, Kop and Hill (2008) suggest that the digital age does indeed bring new opportunities for learning that must be carefully considered and utilised by educational institutions. They conclude that connectivism "plays an important role in the development and emergence of new pedagogies, where control is shifting from the tutor to an increasingly more autonomous learner" (p. 11). Their recognition of the ongoing centrality of control as a key feature within the new pedagogies highlights the usefulness of Dron's re-vitalisation of the concept and his alignment of it with the affordances of new technologies.

As a recent excursion into the area of adult learning and online learning environments, the concept of transactional control has yet to inform a body of empirical research. In contrast, the dimensions of self-management and self-monitoring arising from Garrison's (1997) work provide a useful starting point, one that is supported by Peters' (1998) discussion of autonomy as comprising a psychological dimension (self-management) and a pedagogical dimension (self-monitoring). The two sections that follow will consider these two dimensions more thoroughly through a review of empirical studies undertaken in distance education contexts. Because the first will be considered primarily by reviewing work that has been based on Moore's theory of transactional distance, the term "learner autonomy" will often be used in the text to be largely consistent with the studies being reviewed. The second will be developed through a review of work that directly considers cognitive and metacognitive processes in relation to distance education students and will use the term "self-monitoring" from Garrison.

MANAGING EXTERNAL ACTIVITIES

Moore's theory of transactional distance hypothesises that students with a greater degree of autonomy as learners would be comfortable with courses where transactional distance was greater; and students who were less autonomous in their learning would prefer courses where the combination of structure and dialogue meant that transactional distance was less. Moore conducted an empirical study that provided some evidence in support of this hypothesis, using field dependence/independence as the indicator of autonomy. Since Moore's original work, a small number of studies have explicitly considered the nature of the variables involved in the transactional distance theory and their relationship to each other and to other relevant educational variables such as student satisfaction and course learning outcomes.

What Is Learner Autonomy?

The cognitive style variable of field dependence/independence was used by Moore, in his original study, to indicate the level of learner autonomy. Three subsequent studies have used factor analysis as the basis for investigation of the nature of learner autonomy in distance education contexts.

Following Garrison and Baynton's (1987) theoretical investigation of learner control, Baynton (1992) undertook an empirical test of the model of learner control primarily using exploratory factor analysis of student responses to a questionnaire. Responses to a small number of open-ended questions were also gathered from the study participants to widen the scope of the analysis. Baynton suggested that control could be conceptualised as the interaction of three categories or complexes of factors—a predispositional category of factors that "predispose the learner and/or the teacher/tutor to enter the distance learning situation" (p. 26), an operative category that relates to factors "that are interactive and operate within the context of communication … during the planning and instructional phase of learning" (p. 28), and an environmental/contextual category of factors that "contribute to the enhancement or inhibition of the amount of control experienced by the learner" (p. 28). In addition, she indicated that the analysis reinforced the interdependence of student and teacher in the teaching-learning process.

In a study that defined learner autonomy as "the learner's perception of both independent and interdependent participation in a learning activity and involves both the student's ability to learn individually/self-directedly and his or her preference or need for collaborative learning" (p. 48), Chen and Willits (1999) attempted to empirically investigate the nature of learner autonomy. In the study, independence referred to items such as the ability to develop a personal learning plan, to find resources for study and to learn without lots of guidance; items related to interdependence referred to learning as a member of a team, preferring to learn in a group, sharing effort and responsibility with classmates. A two-factor solution, in which students described themselves as both independent and interdependent learners was generated. These factors "were not contrasting poles of the same continuum but rather represented separate and distinct attributes" (p. 57). Chen and Willits concluded that autonomy must thus be a combination of independence and interdependence. Pruitt (2005) replicated the Chen and Willits (1999) study, using a slightly modified version of their survey as the basis for his data collection, with similar results. He obtained a two-factor solution for learner autonomy with the factors of independence and interdependence.

The use of factor analysis serves to summarise data by grouping together variables that are correlated, in this case survey items. Interpretation is reliant on the conceptual framework and definitions that were used to develop the original items. Since Chen and Willits and Pruitt built interdependence into their definition of learner autonomy from the outset, the finding that it emerged as a factor is not surprising. Moore (1994) appeared to separate learner autonomy from interdependence whilst recognising their closeness. He defined learner autonomy as "the potential of distant learners to participate in the determination of their learning objectives, the implementation of their programs of study, and the evaluation of their learning" (p. 2) and wrote, with regard to his observation of a teleconference course, that "successful groups exhibit a high degree of interdependence among relatively autonomous individuals" (p. 3).

More recently, in a study designed to develop qualitative understanding of the relationships between autonomy, structure, and dialogue, Kostina (2011) showed how autonomy is a multi-dimensional, multilevel construct. Drawing from literature in the area of language learning Kostina argues that autonomy has interactive and interdependent components as well as acknowledging its individual nature. Her work, a mixed methods examination of the relationships between autonomy, structure, and dialogue in distance language learning classes, demonstrates that interactions with peers and instructors shape autonomy, and describes autonomy as being the result of a climate in which teachers and learners shape autonomy through their interrelationship.

Autonomy relates to control and includes the ability to choose to cede control, since as Dron (2006) says, "the simple fact of being a learner implies a lack of knowledge and consequently requires control to be delegated to one who posses that knowledge and is willing to communicate it, whether directly or mediated." The inclusion of interdependence as an aspect of learner autonomy is consistent with an understanding of the individual as not "metaphysically independent of society" (Taylor, 1985, as cited in Wertsch, 1991, p. 69). It reflects the view of education as a transactional practice, at the heart of which lies a process described by Mercer (1995) as "the guided construction of knowledge" (p. 1). Engagement with others is intrinsic to education and seems especially salient when distance education practice utilises technologies that expand dialogic possibilities and may include software tools that enhance interaction in the service of learning. Garrison (2003) prefers the notions of control and responsibility in discussions such as this suggesting autonomy may be the wrong concept to employ because of its connotations of separateness. While that may once have been the case, recent developments have emphasised the manner in which autonomy is usefully regarded as a concept inclusive of interdependence. Whatever name it is given, the concept of learners managing external aspects of their learning activity must account for their ability to work with others in that activity.

THE RELATIONSHIP BETWEEN LEARNER AUTONOMY AND OUTCOMES FOR STUDENTS

Learner achievement and satisfaction are examples of educational outcomes that are relevant to educational policy makers and administrators. Several studies investigate the relationship between learner autonomy and such outcomes. In transactional distance theory, learner autonomy does not relate directly to outcomes. The theory hypothesises that there is a positive relationship between transactional distance and learner autonomy (Moore, 1993, p. 83). What does this relationship imply? Several possibilities present themselves. Perhaps students with greater autonomy as learners will be disproportionately represented in programs characterised by greater transactional distance because of the congruence between their skill as autonomous learners and the requirements of the program, although Willen (1988) disputes this possibility. Levels of student satisfaction with a program may be related to the match between measures of transactional distance and learner autonomy. Perhaps, indirectly through the degree of match between those measures, learning achievement may also be affected. Transactional distance theory does not extend to hypotheses about the success of students in distance education, although Moore (1993) suggested there were "recognizable patterns of personality characteristics among student who preferred, or who succeeded in, teaching programmes that were more highly dialogic and less structured, compared with those who preferred, or succeeded in, less dialogic and more structured programmes" (p. 31). In addition to the work described earlier, Pruitt (2005) and Chen and Willits (1998) used exploratory factor analysis to create variables representing the concepts of transactional distance theory (including autonomy with the factors independence and interdependence), and both studies then used multiple regression techniques to determine the extent to which the variables predicted learning outcomes. Chen and Willits used a measure of perceived student learning in which students were asked to indicate how much they thought they had learnt during the course, while Pruitt's study used instructor assigned final course grades as the dependent variable in the regression analysis. Chen and Willits indicated that learner autonomy had neither direct nor indirect effect on perceived learning outcomes.

Pruitt (2005) noted interaction between independent variables in describing effect on grades. In particular he reported an interaction concerning the variable "learner autonomy-independence." When learner autonomy-independence was low, course grades improved if levels of in-class dialog were high; when learner autonomy-independence was high, course grades dropped if levels of in-class dialog were high. Within a given course structure, increasing the level of dialog will decrease transactional distance (and vice versa), thus Pruitt's finding provides some support for the possibility of successful attainment of course learning outcomes being correlated with the degree of fit between transactional distance and learner autonomy viewed as independence. Pruitt also reported two interaction effects for learner autonomy-interdependence—with number of distance courses taken and with mode of delivery. High levels of interdependence predict lower grades for students both in independence-demanding environments (as Pruitt describes the Internet delivery option in his study) and when they have some experience (two or more courses) in distance education study. If we accept Pruitt's assertion that one type of delivery demanded greater independence of students, we see in that result additional support for a mediated relationship between autonomy and course outcomes.

In his original work, Moore used the Group Embedded Figures Task (GEFT), assessing the cognitive style variable field dependence/independence, as a measure for learner autonomy. Using the GEFT, De Ture (2004) hypothesised that the cognitive style scores, representing the level of autonomy of learners, would predict student success as measured by grade point average (GPA). A second predictor in the study was online technologies self-efficacy. Neither variable was found to predict GPA. De Ture's work reported on results collapsed across five courses with clearly differing requirements for interaction and with different course structures. Unfortunately, no attempt was made to examine GPA levels in relation to interactions between levels of autonomy and transactional distance.

Parcels (2008) also investigated the relationship between field dependence (FD)/independence (FI) and learning outcomes in asynchronous online distance education. The study focused on the effect of matching, or not matching, design of lessons with the FD and FI cognitive styles. In effect, lessons designed to match the FD style were designed to include structure designed to support FD learners. There was a significant positive impact on achievement for both FD and FI learners matched to lessons designed for the FD learners. However there was no such positive impact for FI learners whose instruction was designed to match their cognitive style. This small study supports the argument that autonomous learners, while not needing the additional structure of lessons designed for FD students, will use and may benefit from such structure in achieving learning outcomes.

Investigations of the impact of learner autonomy on educational outcomes other than learner achievement have also been undertaken. Drennan, Kennedy, and Pisarski,

(2005) investigated factors (including locus of control as a measure of autonomy) that affect student satisfaction with flexible online learning. Wheeler (2005) focused on perceptions of social presence as a dependent variable, arguing its importance in electronically mediated contexts, and used structural equation modelling to create path models that show the relationships between variables (including a measure of learner autonomy) used to predict the degree of social presence in four different learning modes—face-to-face, telephone, email, and videoconference. In both cases findings suggest a place for learner autonomy as an important variable in the prediction of the outcome being investigated.

Changes in the level of satisfaction with perceived knowledge gained were explored by Stein, Wanstreet, Calvin, Overtoom, and Wheaton (2005) using the independent variables of learner satisfaction with course structure, learner satisfaction with interaction and technical expertise. Courses from which participants were drawn were either web supported (up to 50% online delivery) or Web-delivered (90%–100% online). The authors found that satisfaction with structure was a major predictor of satisfaction with perceived knowledge gained, and they argue for course design that allows fluidity at the outset of a course so that "autonomous learners can identify their learning needs and work with the instructor to develop criteria for successful achievement" (Stein et al., 2005, p. 115).

Lee and Rha (2009) argue a contrary viewpoint. Their study considered differences in the outcomes of achievement and satisfaction as a function of online course designs developed to emphasise either (a) self-learning with well-structured materials or (b) learning in a highly interactive course without well-structured materials. Among other results, they argue that the nature of the course design has a greater impact on both achievement and satisfaction than do learner characteristics.

These studies highlight the potential to confuse delivery mode with the nature of the course. Equating delivery type with the nature of a course ignores the socially constructed nature of courses with the myriad, though not endless, possibilities for course design that brings. For example, the Drennan, Kennedy, and Pisarski (2005) findings implicate mode of delivery in an indirect relationship between autonomy and satisfaction, and Wheeler (2005) uses mode of delivery as the basis for developing different path models, but the subtext in each case is that it is the nature of the course that is of interest. Drennan et al. refer to flexible learning as placing the onus on students to use study material and learning options as they deemed suitable (p. 337), and Wheeler discusses telephone and email modes of delivery in terms of dialogical possibilities. The important research variables must be those that characterise courses, not technologies. However, different technologies will bring different affordances to their use. This creates the likelihood that courses using a particular technology will have similar pedagogical characteristics (see for example, Oliver & McLoughlin, 1997), and be markedly different pedagogically from those that take advantage of other technologies. Wheeler's (2005) work discusses the impact on outcomes of the role of learner autonomy in relation to the affordances of different technologies, especially with regard to their dialogic capability. This is an interesting line of research and worthy of further development.

Learner autonomy has also been suggested as a factor influencing student persistence in, or its obverse, dropout from distance education. Sweet (1986) and Parker (1999) both hypothesised locus of control as one predictor of dropout. Both studies suggest a direct effect of locus of control, but Sweet's path model predicts only 19% of the variance in dropout. These results illustrate a difficulty with persistence studies highlighted by Woodley (2004), who is highly critical of research into dropout rates, citing the difficulty of adequately testing the general models of dropout that have been developed theoretically. However, more recently, Holder (2007) has suggested that learner autonomy has a particular role to play in dropout from online courses. Holder's study surveyed 259 learners studying by distance in associate, bachelors, and masters degrees to obtain measures of several predictors of persistence identified in the literature. Using a measure of autonomy that emphasises an individualistic view, Holder found that a student scoring highly on the scale of Learner Autonomy was almost twice as likely to drop out of an online course as a student obtaining a low score on this scale. Recognising that this finding runs counter to other studies on persistence, he suggests by way of explanation that the interdependent nature of online learning may lead many students high in learner autonomy to drop out, and writes that "The hypothesis that the cohort model could be a sustainer of compliant learners, while at the same time a contester of independent learners, bears further study. Further research of institutions using the cohort model of online instruction is warranted" (p. 258).

Developing Autonomy (skill)

It is often argued that study by distance fosters the development of independent or autonomous learners. Paul (1990) proposed such a link, and Morgan (1993) also noted the challenge of developing in learners the self knowledge and skills that are characteristic of the autonomous learner. The development of autonomous learners has been noted as a goal of the education of adults (Merriam & Caffarella, 1999, p. 290) either formally or incidentally. A small number of studies suggest that for students who learn in a distance education context, the ability to learn autonomously improves over time.

Ching (1998) reported the results of a study into changes in the level of field dependence/independence of students enrolled in a distance education nursing programme. The study involved both cross-sectional (obtaining data from students new to a distance education program and graduates of that program) and longitudinal (obtaining data from new students at the beginning and end of the program) samples. Ching reported significant overall change toward field independence in both samples but noted especially that field dependent students become more field independent as they progress through a course of distance study. McFerrin (1999) examined the incidental learning that occurs in a graduate level asynchronous online distance education course, and noted the increase in time management ability, self directive behaviour, self confidence and self-discipline, while Anderson (1999) reported student perceptions that Internet-based courses facilitated learner autonomy. Rickwood and Goodwin (2000) and Vanijdee (2003) both develop a case for the growth in learner autonomy over time in distance education courses.

The lesson that these studies leave us with, albeit one that requires greater substantiation, is that development of autonomy, in the sense of developing the skills required to make appropriate choices about one's learning, should not be left to chance. The area of distance language learning has addressed this issue quite fully. Although Hurd (2005, p. 4) suggests that distance learning contexts require learners to have a measure of autonomy to function, she also acknowledges the need to support autonomy development and that there are considerable difficulties balancing the development of autonomy with the constraints of distance education contexts (Hurd, Beaven, & Ortega, 2001).

Murphy discusses autonomy based on reports of (a) the impact of an intervention designed to enhance student decision-making and critical reflection (2005), (b) support provided for the development of autonomy by tutors (2007) and (c) by course material (2008). She makes the case that the development of autonomy requires careful work in the design of course material, alongside pedagogical dialogue and interaction. She argues that teachers must create environments in which learners are able to experience autonomy in order to become more autonomous and discusses how appropriate course design can help learners develop decision-making, reflective and metacognitive skills. Although her conclusions are drawn from the specific context of distance language learning, they have an evident transferability to the field as a whole.

Summary

Modern conceptions of learner autonomy challenge researchers to develop more sophisticated responses as they attempt to determine the impact of that concept on educational outcomes. Much of the work reported here is from an era in which there was, as Merriam (2001) says, "little or no acknowledgement that every person has been shaped by his or her culture and society" (p. 7). That acknowledgement has gradually occurred through the work of, for example, Evans and Nation (1989), Garrison and Baynton (1987), and Gibson (1998). A brief article by Nah (1999) demonstrates the importance of this wider view of autonomy in a cultural sense. The ongoing development of the concept is essential.

The research reported here does not provide conclusive evidence for direct or indirect relationships between learner autonomy and outcomes for students. There is some evidence of potential for study by distance education to foster the development of independent or autonomous learners. If one considers that a goal of education is to help students become autonomous learners, this is a valuable finding, but one in need of further verification. It also suggests that students who initially do not prefer distance study may find that as their distance education experience grows and their autonomy as learners develops they are more satisfied with or more capable in an increasing range of courses characterised by increasing transactional distance. Verifying this possibility may be an interesting direction for research.

DISTANCE EDUCATION AND SELF-MONITORING

This section reviews the psychological dimension of Peters' (1998) definition of learner autonomy through a discussion of self-monitoring and the role of cognitive processes and metacognition in relation to distance education students. Metacognition is a form of cognition which involves active control over one's cognitive processes, or more briefly, a "person's cognition about cognition" (Wellman, 1985, p. 1). Questions that could be considered here might ask about the extent to which distance students use cognitive and metacognitive strategies and whether that level of use differs from face-to-face students, whether use of cognitive and metacognitive strategies by distance students impacts on learning outcomes and about whether and, if so, how distance education courses can be designed to foster the development of cognitive and metacognitive skills and knowledge.

Early work by Marland, Patching, and Putt (1992), Bernt and Bugbee (1993), and Koymen (1992) represented the first empirical exploration by distance educators of cognitive strategy use and metacognition. Marland et al. focused on determining study strategies of 17 students who were studying text and used a stimulated recall interview technique to elicit information about the extent and nature of strategy use. The Bernt and Bugbee and Koymen studies reported that although distance students do employ learning and study strategies, and high achievers report greater use of those strategies, there appeared to be no differences in strategy use between distance and face-to-face students.

The next major work in the area was by White (1995, 1997, 1999). White's thorough initial study was based on a large-scale questionnaire on learner strategies and a verbal report procedure with a smaller number of participants to gather accounts of cognitive and metacognitive strategy use. A second study used a similar verbal report procedure to obtain accounts of learners' metacognitive knowledge. The first study sought to compare strategy use by undergraduate foreign language learners in distance and classroom learning contexts, the second to develop a more detailed picture of the nature of metacognitive knowledge of distance foreign language learners and explore the role of metacognitive experiences in their learning.

Broadly, White's first study (1995, 1997) showed that distance learners made considerably greater use of metacognitive strategies than classroom learners, especially in the areas of monitoring and evaluation. In particular the strategy of self-management was the most important strategy in differentiating between groups. The apparent importance of self-management that relies on learners' knowledge of how they learn best, was the driver for White's second study (1999). In this study she conceptualised metacognitive knowledge as comprising knowledge of self, task, strategies and goals and found that knowledge about self and strategies was more influential than knowledge about task and goals.

Hurd's (2006) research also involved students undertaking distance language learning. Hurd's study involved intervention at four points during a year-long course, investigating student perceptions of a number of affective factors in the distance language learning setting and also attempting to determine whether there were beneficial changes in students' approaches to learning as the course progressed. In both a survey and post-course interviews with a small number of participants, students reported higher levels of metacognitive awareness and improved self-management, with around three quarters of participants feeling their learning approaches had improved as a result of learning a language at a distance.

In contrast with White's conclusions, Jegede, Taplin, Fan, Chan, and Yum (1999) report that their study of 712 distance education students "did not show that the students engaged in meaningful metacognitive strategies to monitor, organise and reflect upon their information processing" (p. 268). They suggest this indicates a reliance on distance learning material as prepared and this was supported in later interviews where students indicated they rarely questioned ideas presented in the study material. Jegede et al. suggest that cultural or environmental factors may have come into play in determining this result. They do note however that there was evidence that high achievers monitor, organise and reflect on strategy use to a greater extent than low achieving students.

Jegede et al.'s (1999) article and work from the distance language learning field provide major studies of cognitive strategy use and metacognition in a distance education context, and gives rise to a number of questions about this important aspect of learning. White's (1995) first analysis suggested that cognitive strategy use was related to language being studied. Does strategy use, cognitive or metacognitive, also differ according to subject area, or level of study? In contrast with Jegede et al.'s suggestion that students rely on distance material as prepared and use it in an unproblematic way, White (1995) argues that student inability to regulate the degree of complexity of study material might well prompt them make greater use of self-monitoring. The cultural background of students is suggested as an explanation of this difference.

The impact of mode of technology employed in a distance education context should be investigated. White's studies were conducted with students who were undertaking study with little ongoing contact with other students. Self-paced, technology-based corporate instruction was the context for Dobrovolny's (2006) study of the use of learning strategies. Students in this study were also relatively isolated from their peers. This was a relatively small-scale phenomenological study in which data were gathered from interviews and participant journaling. Dobrovolny found that self-paced technology-based learning starts with and is sustained by metacognitive activity in the form of self-assessment and suggests that in such contexts designers must design to allow for such activity and for the ability to undertake self-correction. In both White's and Dobrovolny's studies, students had little opportunity to have others help them monitor understanding of course material. Do the more socially interactive modes of technology used in distance education impact on the extent to which metacognitive strategies are used?

In work in the area of approaches to study, Anderson, Lee, Simpson, and Stein (2011) examined of the nature of study orchestrations amongst distance learners. Similar studies with on-campus students have shown that students with dissonant study orchestrations, that is, those showing an inability to satisfactorily match the content, context and processes of learning, are likely to have difficulties in the use of metacognitive skills and lower levels of achievement (Cano, 2007; Lindblom-Ylänne, 2003; Long, 2003). Anderson's et al.'s study involving 176 participants studying distance courses at undergraduate and postgraduate levels, identified the existence of a sizeable group of students with dissonant study orchestrations alongside other anticipated and theoretically coherent study orchestrations. Anderson et al. provide evidence for the commensurability of on-campus and distance students involved in such studies and argues for an increasing awareness of the metacognitive abilities of students involved in distance study as a way of enhancing learner achievement.

The last study to be considered in relation to cognitive and metacognitive processes is interesting for its implications in a world that is increasingly moving to distance education using online communication, and to making some post-compulsory education in that manner a requirement. Smith (2000) undertook an investigation of the use of flexible online delivery for vocational education and training (VET) in Australia. Smith reports that a sample of over 1,200 VET learners had a strong preference for learning contexts where instructors provide leadership of learning and where it is clear what is to be learnt and how. A small sample of students was interviewed and identified restricted or rare use of the strategies of analysis and strategy planning and cognitive monitoring. Smith concluded, "apprentices are generally not ready for the self-directed learning demanded by flexible delivery. They do not have a preference for self-directed learning and they appear not to have developed the learning strategies needed."

Smith's study is valuable for the way it highlights two important factors. First is the notion that use of distance education methods, especially in an online form, is growing relative to classroom-based education. Second, as we have already noted, this brings an increasingly diverse range of students, including many more who may not wish or prefer to undertake study at a distance, and who do not bring with them the range or level of cognitive or metacognitive skills appropriate for distance study. Cognitive and metacognitive strategy training within distance education contexts can thus be seen to be essential. Such training goes beyond the use of support devices embedded in text as investigated by Martens, Valcke, Poelmans, & Daal (1996) and into a specific focus on cognitive and metacognitive strategy development as in the work outlined by McLoughlin and Hollingworth (2002). Metacognitive training for school-age students in face-to-face contexts has been researched reasonably extensively, but there is considerable scope to investigate the complexities of metacognitive strategy training across a range of subject matter for adult students in distance education contexts employing differing technologies.

These studies all suggest the importance of cognitive and metacognitive strategy use in distance education, but also allude to the difficulties that can arise when learners who are not self directed undertake study in a mode that is not preferred or not consistent with cultural or environmental factors. Given the increasing prominence of courses delivered online, awareness of the cognitive and metacognitive strengths required of learners is essential. Additionally, it will be important to ensure that course materials and interactions are consistent with and help to foster the goal of individual development in the use of study and metacognitive skills. When students have little or no choice but to study at a distance, supporting their development in this area is paramount.

CONCLUSION

Garrison (1997) conceptualised self-directed learning as comprising three dimensions. The correspondence between two of those dimensions and aspects of autonomy as discussed in the distance education literature provided the basis for the review of self-management and self-monitoring (to use Garrison's terms) in distance education. That review has highlighted some areas where little is known, or not known with sufficient certainty, and others where the complexity of the area is becoming apparent and requiring further investigation.

Distance education occurs in many forms. To be of value to the area of distance education, the concept of self-directed learning must pertain to them all. For instance, online forms of distance education bring with them considerable social affordance. Newer methods of enabling social interaction such as blogs, wikis, and other social software tools are becoming more common in online learning and are appearing in learning management systems. The concept of self-directed learning must account for the collaborative and interdependent nature of learning as much as the independent. It must be able to show how distance learners within their social milieu shape their learning environment and control their learning within the educational transaction and thus, as Garrison (1997, p. 167) said, "become a powerful concept, capable of illuminating and shaping the field (of distance education)."

REFERENCES

Anderson, B., Lee, S., Simpson, M., & Stein, S. (2011). Study orchestrations in distance learning: Identifying dissonance and its implications for distance educators. *International Review of Research in Open and Distance Learning, 12*(5), 1–16. Retrieved from http://www.irrodl.org/index.php/irrodl/article/view/977/1886

Anderson, B. (2006). Writing power into online discussion. *Computers and Composition, 23*, 108–124. doi:10.1016/j.compcom.2005.12.007

Anderson, D. S. (1999). Mathematics and distance education on the Internet: An investigation based on transactional distance theory. *Dissertation Abstracts International* — A, 60/05, p. 1488. (UMI No. 9930678)

Anderson, T., & Garrison, D. R. (1998). Learning in a networked world: New roles and responsibilities. In C. C. Gibson (Ed.), *Distance learners in higher education* (pp. 97–112). Madison, WI: Atwood.

Baynton, M. (1992). Dimensions of "control" in distance education: A factor analysis. *The American Journal of Distance Education, 6*(2), 17–31. doi: 10.1080/08923649209526783

Bernt, F. M., & Bugbee, A. C. (1993). Study practices and attitudes related to academic success in a distance learning program. *Distance Education, 14*(1), 97–112. doi: 10.1080/0158791930140108

Boucouvalas, M. (2009). Revisiting the concept of Self in self-directed learning: Toward a more robust construct for research and practice in a global context. *International Journal of Self-Directed Learning, 6*(1), 1–10. Retrieved from http://www.sdlglobal.com/IJSDL/IJSDL6.1-2009.pdf

Boyd, R. (1966). A psychological definition of adult education. *Adult Leadership, 13*, 160–162.

Brockett, R. G., & Hiemstra, R. (1991). *Self-direction in adult learning: Perspectives on theory, research and practice.* New York: Routledge.

Brookfield, S. (2009). Self-directed learning. In R. Maclean & D. Wilson (Eds.), *International Handbook of Education for the Changing World of Work* (pp. 2615–2627). Bonn, Germany: Springer.

Candy, P. C. (1991). *Self-direction for lifelong learning: A comprehensive guide to theory and practice.* San Francisco: Jossey Bass.

Cano, F. (2007). Approaches to learning and study orchestrations in high school students. *European Journal of Psychology of Education, 22*(2), 131–151. doi: 10.1007/BF03173518

Chen, Y.-J., & Willits, F. K. (1998). A path analysis of the concepts in Moore's theory of transactional distance in a videoconferencing learning environment. *Journal of Distance Education, 13*(2), 51–65.

Chen, Y.-J., & Willits, F. K. (1999). Dimensions of educational transactions in a videoconferencing learning environment. *The American Journal of Distance Education, 13*(1), 45–59. doi: 10.1080/08923649909527013

Ching, L. S. (1998). The influence of a distance learning environment on students' field dependence/independence [Online version]. *Journal of Experimental Education, 66*(2), 149–160. doi: 10.1080/00220979809601401

DeTure, M. (2004). Cognitive style and self-efficacy: Predicting student success in online distance education. *The American Journal of Distance Education, 18*(1), 21–38. doi: 10.1207/s15389286ajde1801_3

Ding, A. (2005). Theoretical and practical issues in the promotion of collaborative learner autonomy in a virtual self-access centre. In B. Holmberg, M. Shelley & C. White (Eds.), *Distance education and languages: Evolution and change* (pp. 40–54). Clevedon, UK: Multilingual Matters.

Dobrovolny, J. (2006). How adults learn from self-paced, technology-based corporate training: New focus for learners, new focus for designers. *Distance Education, 27*(2), 155–170. doi: 10.1080/01587910600789506

Drennan, J., Kennedy, J., & Pisarski, A. (2005). Factors affecting student attitudes toward flexible online learning in management education. *Journal of Educational Research, 98*(6), 331–338. doi: 10.3200/JOER.98.6.331-338

Dron, J. (2006). *Social software and the emergence of control.* Retrieved from http://www.brighton.ac.uk/cmis/research/publications/icalt2006.pdf

Dron, J. (2007). *Control and constraint in e-learning: Choosing when to choose.* London: Ideas Group.

Eneau, J. (2008). From autonomy to reciprocity, or vice versa? French Personalism's contribution to a new perspective on self-directed learning. *Adult Education Quarterly, 58*(3), 229–248. doi: 10.1177/0741713608314135

Evans, T., & Nation, D. (Eds.). (1989). *Critical reflections on distance education.* London: Falmer.

Garrison, D. R. (1987). Self-directed and distance learning: Facilitating self-directed learning beyond the institutional setting. *International Journal of Lifelong Education, 6*(4), 309–318. doi: 10.1080/0260137870060404

Garrison, D. R. (1989). *Understanding distance education: A framework for the future.* London: Routledge.

Garrison, D. R. (1997). Self-directed learning: Toward a comprehensive model. *Adult Education Quarterly, 48*(1), 18–33. doi: 10.1177/074171369704800103

Garrison, D. R. (2003). Self-directed learning and distance education. In M. G. Moore & W. G. Anderson (Eds.), *Handbook of distance education* (pp. 161–168). Mahwah, NJ: Erlbaum.

Garrison, D. R., & Baynton, M. (1987). Beyond independence in distance education: The concept of control. *The American Journal of Distance Education, 1*(3), 3–15. doi: 10.1080/08923648709526593

Gibson, C. C. (1998). The distance learner in context. In C. C. Gibson (Ed.), *Distance learners in higher education.* Madison, WI: Atwood Publishing.

Holder, B. (2007). An investigation of hope, academics, environment, and motivation as predictors of persistence in higher education online programs. *The Internet and Higher Education, 10*(4), 245–260. doi:10.1016/j.iheduc.2007.08.002

Hurd, S. (2005). Autonomy and the distance language learner. In B. Holmberg, M. Shelley, & C. White (Eds.), *Distance education and languages: New perspectives on language and education* (pp. 1–19). Clevedon, UK: Multilingual Matters.

Hurd, S. (2006). Towards a better understanding of the dynamic role of the distance language learner: Learner perceptions of personality, motivation, roles, and approaches. *Distance Education, 27*(3), 303–329. doi: 10.1080/01587910600940406

Hurd, S., Beaven, T., & Ortega, A. (2001). Developing autonomy in a distance language learning context: Issues and dilemmas for course writers. *System, 29*(3), 341–355. doi: 10.1016/s0346-251x(01)00024-0

Jegede, O., Taplin, M., Fan, R. Y. K., Chan, M. S. C., & Yum, J. (1999). Differences between low and high achieving distance learners in locus of control and metacognition. *Distance Education, 20*(2), 255–273. doi: 10.1080/0158791990200206

Knowles, M. (1975). *Self-directed learning: A guide for learners and teachers.* New York: Association Press.

Knowles, M. S. (1980). The modern practice of adult education: From pedagogy to andragogy (2nd ed.). New York: Cambridge Books.

Kop, R., & Hill, A. (2008). Connectivism: Learning theory of the future or vestige of the past? *International Review of Research in Open and Distance Learning, 9*(3). Retrieved from http://www.irrodl.org/index.php/irrodl/article/view/523/1137

Kostina, M. V. (2011). *Exploration of student perceptions of autonomy, student-instructor dialogue and satisfaction in web-based distance Russian language classrooms: A mixed methods study* (Doctoral dissertation, University of Iowa). Retrieved from Iowa Research Online http://ir.uiowa.edu/etd/1003

Koymen, U. S. (1992). Comparison of learning and study strategies of traditional and open-learning-system students in Turkey. *Distance Education, 13*(1), 108–117. doi: 10.1080/0158791920130109

Lee, H.-J., & Rha, I. (2009). Influence of structure and interaction on student achievement and satisfaction in web-based distance learning. *Journal of Educational Technology & Society, 12*(4), 372–382.

Lindblom-Ylänne, S. (2003). Broadening an understanding of the phenomenon of dissonance. *Studies in Higher Education, 28*(1), 63–77. doi: 10.1080/03075070309306

Long, W. F. (2003). Dissonance detected by cluster analysis of responses to the approaches and study skills inventory for students. *Studies in Higher Education, 28*(1), 21–35. doi: 10.1080/03075070309303

McFerrin, K. M. (1999, February 28–March 4). *Incidental learning in a higher education online distance education course.* Paper presented at the 10th Society for Information Technology and Teacher Education International Conference, San Antonio, TX.

McLaren, P. (1993). Multiculturalism and the post-modern critique: Towards a pedagogy of resistance and transformation. *Cultural Studies, 7*(1), 118–146. doi: 10.1080/09502389300490101

McLoughlin, C., & Hollingworth, R. (2002, June 24–29). *Bridge over troubled water: Creating effective online support for the metacognitive aspects of problem solving.* Paper presented at the ED-MEDIA 2002 World Conference on Educational Multimedia, Hypermedia & Telecommunications, Denver, CO.

Marland, P., Patching, W., & Putt, I. (1992). Thinking while studying: a process tracing study of distance learners. *Distance Education, 13*(2), 193–217. doi: 10.1080/0158791920130204

Martens, R., Valcke, M., Poelmans, P., & Daal, M. (1996). Functions, use and effects of embedded support devices in printed distance learning materials. *Learning and Instruction, 6*(1), 77–93. doi:10.1016/S0959-4752(96)80005-3

Mercer, N. (1995). *The guided construction of knowledge.* Clevedon, UK: Multilingual Matters.

Merriam, S. B. (2001). Andragogy and self-directed learning: Pillars of adult learning theory. In S. B. Merriam (Ed.), *The new update on adult learning theory* (pp. 3–14). San Francisco: Jossey-Bass.

Merriam, S. B., & Caffarella, R. S. (1999). *Learning in adulthood* (2nd ed.). San Francisco: Jossey Bass.

Moore, M. (1972). Learner autonomy: The second dimension of independent learning. *Convergence, 5*(2), 76–88.

Moore, M. G. (1980). Independent study. In R. Boyd & J. Apps (Eds.), *Redefining the discipline of adult education* (pp. 16–31). San Francisco: Jossey-Bass.

Moore, M. G. (1986). Self-directed learning and distance education [Online version]. *Journal of Distance Education, 1*(1), 7–24.

Moore, M. G. (1993). Theory of transactional distance. In D. Keegan (Ed.), *Theoretical principles of distance education* (pp. 22–38). London: Routledge.

Moore, M. G. (1994). Editorial. Autonomy and interdependence. *The American Journal of Distance Education, 8*(2), 1–5. doi: 10.1080/08923649409526851

Morgan, A. (1985). What shall we do about independent learning? *Teaching at a Distance, 26,* 38–45.

Morgan, A. (1993). *Improving your students' learning: Reflections on the experiences of study.* London: Kogan Page.

Murphy, L. (2005). Critical reflection and autonomy. A study of distance learners of French, German and Spanish In B. Holmberg, M. Shelley, & C. White (Eds.), *Distance education and languages: New perspectives on language and education* (pp. 20–39). Clevedon, UK: Multilingual Matters.

Murphy, L. (2007). Supporting learner autonomy: theory and practice in a distance learning context. In D. Gardner (Ed.), *Learner autonomy 10: Integration and support* (pp. 72–92). Dublin, Ireland: Authentik Language Learning Resources.

Murphy, L. (2008). Supporting learner autonomy: Developing practice through the production of courses for distance learners of French, German and Spanish. *Language Teaching Research, 12*(1), 83–102. doi:10.1177/1362168807084495

Nah, Y. (1999). Can a self-directed learner be independent, autonomous and interdependent? Implications for practice. *Adult Learning, 11*(1), 18–19, 25.

Oliver, R., & McLoughlin, C. (1997). Interactions in audiographics teaching and learning environments. *The American Journal of Distance Education, 11*(1), 34–54. doi: 10.1080/08923649709526950

Parcels, B. (2008). *Matching instructional design to field dependent and field independent learners: Implications for online design in distance education* (Doctoral dissertation). ProQuest Dissertations and Theses database. (UMI No. 3314063)

Parker, A. (1999). A study of variables that predict dropout from distance education [Online version]. *International Journal of Educational Technology, 1*(2), 1–10.

Paul, R. (1990). Towards a new measure of success: Developing independent learners. *Open Learning, 5*(1), 31–38. doi: 10.1080/0268051900050106

Peters, O. (1998). *Learning and teaching in distance education.* London: Kogan Page.

Pruitt, D. (2005). *Transactional distance and learner autonomy as predictors of student performance in distance learning courses delivered by three modalities.* (Doctoral dissertation). ProQuest Dissertations and Theses database. (UMI No. 3170380)

Rickwood, P., & Goodwin, V. (2000). Travellers' tales: Reflections on the way to learner autonomy. *Open Learning, 15*(1), 47–56. doi: 10.1080/026805100115461

Rogers, C. (1969). *Freedom to learn.* Columbus, OH: Charles E. Merrill.

Siemens, G. (2005). Connectivism: A learning theory for the digital age. *International Journal of Instructional Technology and Distance Learning, 2*(1). Retrieved from http://www.itdl.org/Journal/Jan_05/article01.htm

Smith, P. (2000, September 11–13). *Developing strategies for effective workplace use of flexible delivery for training.* Paper presented at the ICDE Conference "Distance education: An open question?", Adelaide, SA, Australia. Retrieved from http://www.unisanet.unisa.edu.au/cccc/papers/refereed/paper47/Paper47-1.htm

Stein, D. S., Wanstreet, C. E., Calvin, J., Overtoom, C., & Wheaton, J. E. (2005). Bridging the transactional distance gap in online learning environments. *American Journal of Distance Education, 19*(2), 105–118. doi: 10.1207/s15389286ajde1902_4

Sweet, R. (1986). Student dropout in distance education: an application of Tinto's model. *Distance Education, 7*(2), 201–213. doi: 10.1080/0158791860070204

Tight, M. (1996). *Key concepts in adult education and training.* London: Routledge.

Tough, A. (1971). *The adult's learning projects.* Toronto: Ontario Institute for Studies in Education.

Vanijdee, A. (2003). Thai distance language learners and learner autonomy. *Open Learning, 18*(1), 75–84. doi: 10.1080/0268051032000054130

Wedemeyer, C. (1971). Independent study. In R. Deighton (Ed.), *Encyclopedia of education (Vol. 4)* (pp. 548–557). New York: MacMillan.

Wellman, H. (1985). The origins of metacognition. In D. L. Forrest-Pressley, G. E. MacKinnon, & T. G. Waller (Eds.), *Metacognition, cognition, and human performance*, Volume 1 - Theoretical perspectives (pp. 1–31). New York: Academic Press.

Wertsch, J. (1991). *Voices of the mind.* Cambridge, MA: Harvard University Press.

Wheeler, S. (2005, November 11). *Creating social presence in digital learning environments: A presence of mind?* Paper presented at the TAFE Conference, Queensland, Australia.

White, C. (1995). Autonomy and strategy use in distance foreign language learning: Research findings. *System, 23*(2), 207–221. doi:10.1016/0346-251X(95)00009-9

White, C. (1997). Effects of mode of study on foreign language learning. *Distance Education, 18*(1), 178–196. doi: 10.1080/0158791970180112

White, C. (1999). The metacognitive knowledge of distance learners. *Open Learning, 14*(3), 37–46. doi: 10.1080/0268051990140306

Willen, B. (1988). What happened to the Open University - in brief. *Distance Education, 9*(1), 71–83. doi: 10.1080/0158791880090105

Woodley, A. (2004). Conceptualizing student dropout in part-time distance education: Pathologizing the normal? *Open Learning, 19*(1), 47–63. doi: 10.1080/0268051042000177845

7

THE COMMUNITY OF INQUIRY
THEORETICAL FRAMEWORK

D. RANDY GARRISON AND ZEHRA AKYOL

Theoretical interests and developments in the field of distance education have progressed from a preoccupation with organizational and structural barriers to transactional (teaching and learning) concerns (Garrison, 2000). This transformational shift is the result of advances in communications technology coupled with a focus on collaborative-constructivist learning theories (Garrison & Archer, 2000). The transactional era of distance education has been made possible by the capabilities of information and communication technologies (ICT) to create and sustain communities of learners at a distance. The emergence of new asynchronous and synchronous communications technology has made possible collaborative distance education experiences.

Online learning now represents the post-industrial era of distance education with the focus on designing context specific collaborative educational experiences (Garrison & Cleveland-Innes, 2010). Integrating ICT, online learning creates both independence and interaction enabling the creation of learning communities. Online learning has been utilized extensively to enhance classroom learning as well as to increase access to educational experiences at a distance. Articles on the educational uses of computer mediated communication (CMC) in general and asynchronous computer conferencing in particular began appearing in the 1980s. One of the first articles to cause distance educators to take note was by Roxanne Hiltz (1986). She argued that CMC could be used to build a "virtual classroom." At about the same time, Paulsen and Rekkedal (1988) discussed the potential of CMC and stated that "the most exciting challenge in the long run will be to apply the new technology to create new and more efficient learning situations, rather than replicate the traditional classroom or distance learning environment" (p. 363). These insights were prescient.

This same message was carried forward by Kaye (1987, 1992; Mason & Kaye, 1989), another early researcher in online learning. Kaye (1987) rightly noted that CMC is "qualitatively different from other interpersonal and group communication media" (p. 157). Kaye (1992) recognized that computer conferencing represented a new form of collaborative learning that goes beyond information exchange and necessitated moderated critical discourse to realize new and worthwhile learning. Lauzon and Moore (1989) were the first to recognize that the potential of computer conferencing represented a new generation of distance education characterized by networked, asynchronous group communication. Like her contemporaries, Harasim (1987, 1989, 1990) argued strongly "that on-line education … represents a unique domain of educational interaction" (Harasim, 1989, p. 50). She argued for instructional designs to accommodate collaborative online learning, thus adopting constructivist learning approaches. From a research perspective, Henri (1992) advocated and provided a framework to systematically study computer conferencing. She identified both cognitive and social dimensions of computer conferencing that enhance learning outcomes. This may have been the first coherent theoretical approach to studying the methodologies of CMC and computer conferencing.

A THEORETICAL FRAMEWORK

Much of the research and practice associated with online learning during the 1990s focused on and took advantage of the social and democratic features of the technology (Gunawardena, 1991, 1995; Harasim, 1990). Some researchers attempted to broaden the focus to include cognitive elements and focused on the ability of this medium to support higher-order learning (Garrison, 1997; Newman, Johnson, Cochrane, & Webb, 1996). Another key area of research was the role of the moderator as facilitator of the learning process (Fabro & Garrison, 1998; Feenberg, 1989; Gunawardena, 1991; Kaye, 1992). It is these three essential elements (social, cognitive and teaching) that form the core of the framework outlined next.

Garrison, Anderson, and Archer (2000) constructed a comprehensive conceptual framework designed to capture the educational dynamic and guide the study of online learning effectiveness in higher education. The first assumption was that an educational experience intended to achieve higher-order learning outcomes is best embedded in a community of inquiry composed of students and teachers (Lipman, 1991). Lipman (2003) argued the necessity of a community of inquiry for the operationalization of critical or reflective thinking and as an educational methodology. This assumption was also consistent with the educational philosophy of Dewey (1959), who described education as the collaborative reconstruction of experience. The context for this study was a collaborative-constructivist learning experience within a community of inquiry. An educational community of inquiry is a group of individuals who collaboratively engage in purposeful critical discourse and reflection to construct personal meaning and confirm mutual understanding. There is both independence and interaction (co-regulation) in a community of inquiry.

This was a sharp departure from theories of distance education that idealize student independence. It was the early work of Moore and Garrison, among others, who focused on communication (i.e., transactional) dynamics between teacher and student and attempted to clarify the concept of independence. Moore focused on the dimensions of structure, dialogue, and independence, while some early work of Garrison and Baynton (1987) explored the concept of control consisting of power, support, and independence. Suffice to say here, the central role of dialogue/discourse in this work was seen to be central to the distance education experience. Moreover, the issues of structure and autonomy in Moore's theory have their parallels in terms of the affordances of technology and design/organization in the community of inquiry framework. While the focus here is not to explore these connections, such an endeavor would be worthwhile to better understand the evolution of distance education and whether the field has fully embraced the interactive potential of new and emerging ICTs (Garrison, 2009a).

An educational community of inquiry is defined as "a group of individuals who collaboratively engage in purposeful critical discourse and reflection to construct personal meaning and confirm mutual understanding" (Garrison, 2011, p. 2). The Community of Inquiry (CoI) theoretical framework embraces deep approaches rather than surface approaches to learning and aims to create conditions to encourage higher order cognitive processing. Relative to many distance education theories, the CoI framework is grounded in specific philosophical and epistemological assumptions and learning theories (Garrison, 2012). In this regard, the CoI theoretical framework represents a process of creating a deep and meaningful (collaborative-constructivist) learning experience through the development of three interdependent elements—social presence, cognitive presence and teaching presence (Figure 7.1). A sense of being (i.e., presence) is created through interpersonal communication. In order to provide an effective inquiry process and achieve higher order learning, all three presences must be developed in balance (Akyol & Garrison, 2008).

Before describing each presence in detail, it is important to mention the theoretical development of the CoI framework. A decade of CoI research has provided the empirical evidence that the CoI framework represents a coherent set of articulated elements and

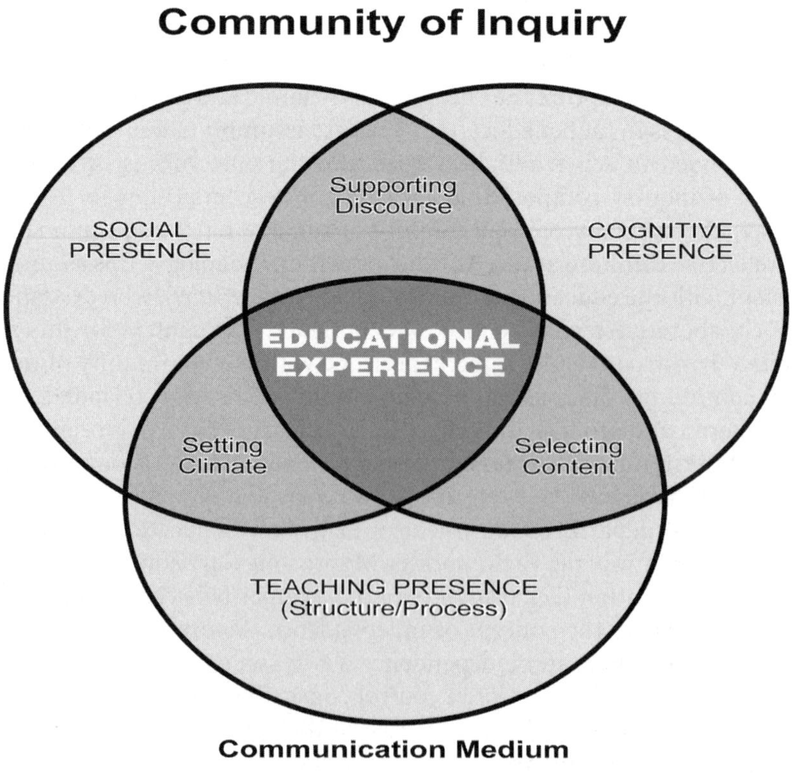

Figure 7.1 The Community of Inquiry theoretical framework

respective models describing a higher learning experience applicable to a wide range of learning environments (from face-to-face to online, from K-12 to higher education). It also provides the means to understand and explore the relationships among the elements and learning, and it has the ability to generate hypotheses and provide the theoretical context to interpret findings. These developments verify that the CoI framework has sufficient coherence and explanatory power to be considered a theory (Garrison, 2011). Therefore, the terminology has been shifted from the CoI framework to the CoI theoretical framework in this new edition.

Social Presence

Within the community of inquiry framework, social presence was initially defined as the ability of learners to project themselves (i.e., their personal characteristics) socially and emotionally, thereby representing themselves as "real" people, in a community of inquiry (Rourke, Anderson, Garrison, & Archer, 2001). Establishing relationships and a sense of belonging is important. However, the role of social presence in a purposeful learning community is to support critical inquiry and the achievement of educational outcomes. Social presence does not mean supporting engagement for purely social purposes; it means creating a climate that supports and encourages probing questions, skepticism, expressing and contributing to ideas. As Rogers and Lea (2005) indicate when individuals identify with the group and the purpose, the group is more productive (as opposed to simply creating interpersonal bonds). To reinforce this, Jahng, Nielsen, and Chan (2010) found that increased social communications reduced cognitive presence. Therefore, in order to emphasize the mediating role of social presence to collaboration and critical discourse, the definition of social presence has been revised as the ability of participants to identify with the group or course of study, communicate purposefully in a trusting environment, and develop personal and affective relationships progressively by way of projecting their individual personalities (Garrison, 2009b). The new definition suggests that social presence should be developed naturally and progressively through the purposeful and collaborative inquiry process (Garrison, 2011).

Three broad categories of social presence, along with indicators of these categories, were identified through a review of the literature (Garrison et al., 2000). Through the analysis of the transcripts of online courses, adjustment, and re-application, these categories and their associated indicators were refined by Rourke et al. (2001). The resulting construct was used to detect and quantify levels of social presence in different online courses. The categories of social presence that were derived from this research are affective communication, open communication and group cohesion. However, after a decade of research into the community of inquiry theoretical framework, it would appear that affective responses may not be the defining characteristics of social presence. Affective interpersonal communication may describe the initial conditions that establish a community of inquiry. Affective expression using emoticons, capitalization or punctuation, self-disclosure, and use of humor are indicators of the interpersonal communication aspect of social presence. Open communication encourages critical reflection and discourse through a process of recognizing, complimenting, and responding to the questions and contributions of others. Interpersonal and open communications contribute directly to the third category of social presence—group cohesion. Group cohesion is achieved when students identify with the group and perceive themselves as a part of the community of inquiry. Cohesive communication begins with activities such as addressing others by name and continuous with using inclusive pronouns such as we, our as the next level. Group cohesion increases the capacity for collaboration; the discourse (the sharing of meaning) and the quality of learning will be optimized when there is a cohesive community.

The natural progression or development of these three categories over time raises the issue of the dynamic of social presence. Theoretically, it was predicted that open communication will be high at the beginning and diminish slightly over time while group cohesion and interpersonal indicators will increase (Garrison, 2011). The research of Akyol and Garrison (2008) confirmed this when the data showed a decrease in open communication and an increase in group cohesion over time. Moreover, it should also be noted that the development and progression of social presence categories may vary depending on the instructional design of the course, the technology used for communication, or the level of teaching presence (Nippard & Murphy, 2007; Shea et al., 2010; Swan & Shih, 2005). For example, Shea et al. (2010) found a rise or fall in student social presence with the rise and fall of instructor teaching presence. This research also confirms the interrelatedness of the CoI elements.

 When social presence is established, collaboration and critical discourse is enhanced and sustained. Studies have found a relationship between social presence and learning outcomes (Caspi & Blau, 2008; Lui, Gomez, & Ye, 2009; Swan & Shih, 2005) and social presence and satisfaction (Akyol, Garrison, & Ozden, 2009; Arbaugh & Benbunan-Fich, 2006; Richardson & Swan, 2003). Recently, research has shown a significant relationship between social presence and retention (Boston et al., 2009). The authors concluded that social interaction remains a crucial factor for retention. Further research is required to better understand the influence of social presence on learning variables and retention.

COGNITIVE PRESENCE

The second element in the framework is cognitive presence. We define cognitive presence "as the extent to which learners are able to construct and confirm meaning through sustained reflection and discourse in a critical community of inquiry" (Garrison et al., 2001). The concept of cognitive presence is grounded in the critical thinking literature and derived specifically from Dewey's (1933) reflective thinking model. According to Dewey, reflective or critical thinking deepens the meaning of our experiences and is therefore a core educational aim. Critical thinking both authenticates existing knowledge and generates new knowledge suggesting an intimate connection with education. Critical thinking is integral to inquiry and viewed as an inclusive process of higher-order reflection and discourse. Cognitive presence is operationalized by the Practical Inquiry (PI) model that, as noted previously, has its genesis in Dewey's phases of reflective inquiry (Figure 7.2). One key characteristic of this model is the interplay between the public and private worlds which is particularly relevant to the e-learning experience in an asynchronous and text-based environment. The model has two dimensions that reflect inductive/deductive and divergent/convergent processes of critical thinking. The vertical axis, the deliberation-action dimension, represents constructive and collaborative activities. It reflects the rigorous process of integrating induction (arrival of generalizations) and deduction (employment of generalizations). The horizontal axis is the perception-conception dimension which reflects the point of fusion of the shared

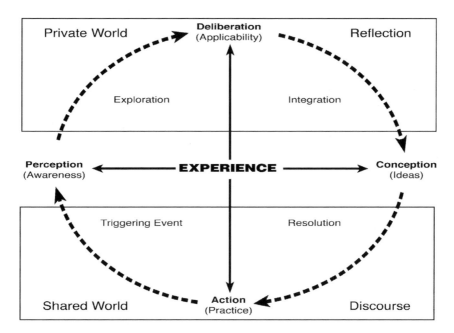

Figure 7.2 Practical Inquiry model.

and private worlds. At one extreme is the divergent process of perception and analysis of facts or events; at the other extreme is the convergent process of insights and understanding associated with ideas and concepts.

The PI model is comprised of four phases of critical inquiry, which are idealized and, as such, are not sequential or immutable. The four phases are the triggering event, exploration, integration, and resolution. The first phase, the triggering event or initiation associated with conceptualizing a problem or issue, should be a well-thought through activity that ensures students' engagement and generates curiosity and questioning. The exploration phase includes understanding the nature of the problem and then searching for the relevant information and possible explanations. At this phase, students iterate between the reflective and shared worlds as ideas are explored collaboratively and individuals try to make sense of complexity and confusion. The third phase, integration, moves into a more focused and structured phase of constructing meaning where students are intimately engaged in critical discourse that will shape the understanding. In this phase, participants begin resolving the dilemma or problem at hand by constructing a meaningful framework or discovering a contextually specific solution to a defined problem. The final phase is settling on a solution and vicariously or in reality testing the solution through implementation.

Although the PI model represents the inquiry *process*, it has been compared to other models such as Bloom's taxonomy in terms of its potential to measure learning outcomes (Buraphadeja & Dawson, 2008; Cotton & Yorke, 2006; Meyer, 2004; Schrire, 2004, 2006). Buraphadeja and Dawson (2008) indicate that the PI model has been widely cited as suitable for assessing critical thinking. Moreover, Schrire (2004) found that the PI model is "the most relevant to the analysis of the cognitive dimension and represents a clear picture of the knowledge-building processes occurring in online discussion" compared to Bloom's and SOLO taxonomies (p. 491).

Cognitive presence is at the core of a community of inquiry and requires engaging students in all phases of practical inquiry. However, most early studies yielded low level activity on integration and resolution phases (e.g., Garrison, et al., 2001; Kanuka, Rourke, & Laflamme, 2007; McKlin, Harmon, Evans, & Jone, 2002; Meyer, 2003, 2004; Pawan, Paulus, Yalcin, & Chang, 2003; Picciano, 2002; Vaughan & Garrison, 2005; Stein et al., 2007). Several possible explanations were made. In the review of the CoI framework by Garrison and Arbaugh (2007), it was argued that inquiry becomes more demanding as it moves to the resolution phase. The inability to move students to the latter phases of inquiry was explained as a function of teaching presence in terms of the design of the task, the need to provide crucial information, and moving the discussion forward in a timely manner. Not surprising, therefore, tasks designed to achieve resolution and directed toward that end are more likely to lead to integration and resolution phases (Stein et al., 2007). Perhaps taking into consideration these arguments, recent research have yielded greater activity at the integration and resolution phases (Akyol & Garrison, 2008, 2011b; Richardson & Ice, 2010; Shea & Bidjerano, 2009b). It should also be kept in mind that online discussions seldom provide sufficient time to reach resolution (Richardson & Ice, 2010) and major projects generally reach resolution off-line (Akyol & Garrison, 2008; Archer, 2010: Shea et al., 2010).

In order to create cognitive presence and higher-order learning outcomes consistent with intended goals and expectations of the educational experience, there is a need for a moderator (i.e., teaching presence) who can assess the nature of the discourse continuously and proactively shape it following the critical thinking cycle. Students should be encouraged to relate the ideas and concepts to societal contexts, which increases the likelihood to move the discourse to integration and resolution phases. Moreover, metacognitive understanding of critical thinking and practical inquiry greatly supports the development of cognitive presence. That is, when students understand the inquiry process and what is required at each phase, they can exhibit the skills to ensure progression through the phases to resolution. Kuhn (1999) reinforces this point when she argues "the development of metacognitive understanding is essential to critical thinking because critical thinking by definition involves reflecting on what is known and how that knowledge is justified" (p. 23). Initial research into metacognition has provided evidence of its role in practical inquiry in an online context (Akyol & Garrison, 2011b). Work is currently focusing on validating a metacognitive instrument consistent with the PI model.

Teaching Presence

We now turn to teaching presence, the third element of the framework. As alluded to previously, teaching presence is crucial for realizing intended learning outcomes. It is the key element in integrating social and cognitive presence during the inquiry process. Simply stated, teaching presence is what the participants (usually the instructor) do to create a purposeful and productive community of inquiry. Teaching presence is formally defined "as the design, facilitation and direction of cognitive and social processes for the purpose of realizing personally meaningful and educationally worthwhile learning outcomes" (Anderson, Rourke, Garrison, & Archer, 2001, p.

5). Main responsibilities of teaching presence are identifying relevant societal knowledge, designing experiences that facilitate reflection and discourse, and diagnosing and assessing learning outcomes. Results from this definition and validation work, the functions of teaching presence are organized into three categories: design and organization, facilitating discourse, and direct instruction. A set of indicators correspond to each of these categories.

Design and organization involve macro level structure and process. In an e-learning context, design and organization could be more demanding considering the technology related issues and the need to redesign the approaches to teaching and learning to maximize the capabilities of the e-learning medium. In a collaborative constructivist e-learning process, students must have influence in what is studied and how it is approached. Therefore, design should not be separated from delivery. This is best accomplished when both design and organization allows for effective responsiveness to developing needs and events. The second category, facilitating reflection and discourse, recognizes the role of the community of inquiry as enabling and encouraging the construction of personal meaning as well as shaping and confirming mutual understanding. Facilitating discourse involves pedagogical, interpersonal and organizational issues. Teaching presence must be as concerned with cognitive development as with a positive learning environment, and it must see content, cognition and context as integral parts of the whole. The third category, direct instruction, is associated with specific content issues, such as diagnosing misconceptions. The need for direct instruction challenges the "guide on the side" concept. While a guide or facilitator is integral to teaching presence, in and of itself, it is limited as an educational approach to e-learning. It suggests an artificial separation of facilitator and content expert and causes the potential distortion of an educational experience due to the exclusion of the influence of a pedagogical and content expert. Teaching presence in an educational context is not possible without the expertise of an experienced and responsible teacher who can identify the ideas and concepts worthy of study, provide the conceptual order, organize learning activities, guide the discourse, offer additional sources of information, diagnose misconceptions and interject when required. *[handwritten margin note: Importance of teaching presence]*

There is growing evidence supporting the crucial role and impact of teaching presence in an educational community of inquiry. Research has shown that teaching presence is important for perceived learning and satisfaction (Akyol et al., 2009; Richardson & Swan, 2003; Swan & Shih, 2005), for the acquisition of knowledge (Paechter, Maier, & Macher, 2010), for ensuring participation and quality of responses (An, Shin, & Lim, 2009; Bliss & Lawrence, 2009; Gorsky, Caspi, Antonovsky, Blau, & Mansur, 2010), and for the development of the community of inquiry (Brook & Oliver, 2007; Ice, Curtis, Phillips, & Wells, 2007; Shea, Li, & Pickett, 2006). Teaching presence provides the structure (design) and leadership (facilitation and direction) required for effective interaction and discourse, which leads to higher-order learning. As stated earlier, metacognition is gaining increasing emphasis in relation to effectively managing and monitoring learning. In this regard, teaching presence must also help students recognize the developmental progression of the inquiry process. For example, activities should be designed and moderated so as to focus on the appropriate phase of critical thinking, ensure that learners progress to the next phase, and that the learners gain a metacognitive understanding of the process they are engaged in (Garrison, 2003).

To this point the community of inquiry theoretical framework has been introduced along with a detailed description of each element. The next section focuses on the application of the framework presenting the principles and guidelines in order to develop an effective community of inquiry.

APPLICATION OF THE COI THEORETICAL FRAMEWORK

To date, e-learning has been largely technology driven. Ubiquitous and inexpensive Internet and communications technology has influenced the display, the interaction, the cost, and the design of educational transactions. Some of the new technologies, commonly labeled as Web 2.0 tools, are increasing the possibilities to create fully engaged learning communities in the relativity of space and time. However, an educational technology is innovative only when it improves the effectiveness of an educational experience. Even though emerging instructional technologies have allowed educators to adopt online and blended learning, their motivations for adopting this technology are mixed and are not often based upon sound educational and pedagogical reasoning. The power and potential of the technology may be enormous but realizing this potential will depend on conceptual models and principles, and well-founded guidelines and techniques.

The focus and challenge here is to understand pedagogically the use of online and blended learning to achieve higher-order learning objectives. This means going beyond enhancing course packages and using email to contact tutors, or putting videos of lectures online. The premise is that educators must first understand that online and blended learning both have unique properties that make it possible to create a critical community of learners not constrained by time or place. Second, we must be able to develop pedagogical principles and guidelines that will directly facilitate deep and meaningful approaches to teaching and learning. In other words, we must ensure that we encourage critical thinking online and have as the outcome of the educational experience critical thinkers who have learned to learn.

While there are numerous guidelines and suggestions as to how to conduct online learning (e.g., Berge, 1995; Paulsen, 1995; Salmon, 2000), these are generally disparate methods for ensuring participation. However, the use of online learning in pedagogically sound ways that make optimal use of its unique properties means using it for more than merely participating in an optional discussion forum or accessing information more efficiently. As Fraser (1999) suggests, the extent to which we have not taken advantage of the "expanded horizons for communicating ideas ... is the extent to which you have done nothing of pedagogical value by using the Web" (p. B8). According to Fraser, doing anything with these new media that does not expand our horizons is "pedagogically pointless."

The challenge facing researchers and teachers in distance education is the development of a more sophisticated understanding of the capabilities of new technologies and how we might harness this potential to enhance critical thinking and higher-order learning. As important as critical thinking is as an educational process and goal, educators often fall far short of achieving it (Garrison et al., 2001). Reasons include a lack of metacognitive understanding of the inquiry process and a lack of purposeful and sustained commitment to facilitating and directing critical discourse and reflective thinking. In this regard, there is an absence of systematic empirical research into how to facilitate critical thinking and inquiry (Kuhn, 1999). In terms of fostering critical thinking skills Kuhn states:

> … teachers have been offered remarkably little in the way of concrete examples of what these skills are—what forms they take, how they will know when they see them, how they might be measured. (p. 17)

The CoI theoretical framework has been a viable theory in understanding the complexities of technology enhanced learning environments and to address the challenge mentioned above by its emphasis on critical thinking and the inquiry process. The CoI theoretical framework has a high adoption rate and has been quite influential in explaining and prescribing the effective conduct of online and blended learning experiences (Arbaugh et al., 2008; Garrison & Arbaugh, 2007; Swan, 2010). There is a growing body of evidence on the potential and success of the framework to create a learning environment where deep and meaningful approaches are employed to reach higher order learning outcomes (Akyol & Garrison, 2008, 2009, 2011a; Barber, 2011; Bidjerano, 2009a; Conrad, 2005; Garrison & Vaughan, 2008; Jezegou 2010; Stein et al., 2007; Vaughan & Garrison, 2005).

In a large scale study, it was reported that the epistemic engagement approach is more fully articulated and extended through the CoI theoretical framework (Shea & Bidjerano, 2009a). Students were able to engage in reflection and dialogue that provided further opportunities to extend their understanding. In a subsequent study, Shea and Bidjerano (2009b) found that a majority of the more than 5,000 students surveyed reported that they were able to achieve high levels of cognitive presence in online and blended courses.

From another perspective, a series of studies have provided insights into blended learning regarding the development of a community of inquiry. The study of Akyol et al. (2009), which compared online and blended communities of inquiry, yielded higher perceptions of all three presences, and an increased frequency of cognitive presence at the integration phase, in the blended course compared to the online course. In another study, students expressed that they preferred the face-to-face environment to initiate discussions and the online environment to expand and sustain discussions (Vaughan & Garrison, 2005). Having the strength of both media, blended learning would appear to better serve teaching and learning needs and provides an easy transition to distance education for educators (Garrison & Kanuka, 2004; Garrison & Vaughan, 2008; Palloff & Pratt, 2007). That said, more research is needed to further explore the dynamics of a blended learning approach.

While each element is essential, teaching presence is the unifying force in developing a community of inquiry. There is always a need for an instructor to structure, shape and assess the learning experience, whether it is online, blended or face-to-face learning. Moreover, the literature suggests that a stronger teaching presence is required, especially in online learning (Garrison & Cleveland-Innes, 2005; Meyer, 2003; Shea et al., 2006; Swan & Shih, 2005). Unfortunately, the simple adoption of technology does not resolve issues related to the teaching of critical thinking and inherent metacognitive understanding. Moreover, it does not fundamentally change approaches to teaching and learning for the better. It has been argued elsewhere that technology can have both a strong and weak influence on the educational transaction (Garrison & Anderson, 2000).

The weak approach is to enhance and, thereby, reinforce existing teaching practices. On the other hand, the

> stronger influence of technology on teaching would fundamentally change our outcome expectations, and thereby, how we approach the teaching and learning transaction.... Here the focus is on the quality of learning outcomes (i.e., developing critical thinkers) and adopting approaches to teaching and learning that are congruent with such outcomes. (Garrison & Anderson, 2000, p. 25)

Here, the guidelines are approached from the perspective of teaching presence and its three sub-elements or categories: design and organization, facilitating of discourse and direct instruction. The first challenge to develop an effective community of inquiry is to develop a comprehensive understanding of the properties of online and blended learning, and the implications for supporting an educational community of inquiry using these media. To help identify the process, Garrison (2011) presents seven principles that reflect the pedagogical approach for creating and sustaining a community of inquiry:

- Plan for the creation of open communication and trust;
- Plan for the critical reflection and discourse;
- Establish community and cohesion;
- Establish purposeful inquiry dynamics;
- Sustain respect and responsibility;
- Sustain inquiry that moves to resolution;
- Ensure assessment is congruent with intended processes and outcomes.

The second challenge is that the transition to an e-learning context requires a significant adjustment for both instructors and students. It can be even more challenging for first time online students who need to adjust to both communicating online and participating in a community of inquiry. Some general design considerations to ease the adjustment are to make explicit adjustment challenges, provide technological support, and ensure greater instructor involvement at the beginning (Cleveland-Innes, Garrison, & Kinsell, 2007). Other specific guidelines and suggestions for practice associated with design and organization include establishing curriculum, indentifying resources, defining clear expectations and goals, addressing technological concerns, structuring collaborative and individual activities, setting the time frames and devising assessment processes and instruments. At this stage, the activities to develop social presence should focus on creating trust and respect that will not discourage skepticism and constructive criticism. Instructors' modeling is crucial to depict the appropriate communication. Specific activities to establish social presence could be to send introductory email to students, develop students Web pages with their bios, discuss and negotiate expectations in small groups, create an informal coffee discussion board and make explicit the netiquette and code of conduct. From a cognitive presence perspective, two issues stand out: content and assessment. The PI model (i.e., cognitive presence) could be utilized both to design learning and assessment activities that are congruent with content and to ensure the discourse move to integration and resolution phases. It should be made clear that greater cognitive presence is expected as the course progresses. Students should be encouraged to consider their cognitive level during the discussions and assignments.

Some of the specific activities suggested are designing question driven or problem based learning activities, using small breakout groups, and creating a Web platform to collaboratively search, analyze, and synthesize information.

Facilitating discourse is a key responsibility in creating and managing educationally worthwhile discourse. The activities for facilitation include both social and cognitive presence issues as personal communication and critical discourse are not separable. The focus here is managing the process and monitoring the depth of understanding. Through open communication, instructors can reveal thought processes, provide appropriate insights and information when needed, seek common understanding and encourage students to participate actively. In order to move the discourse to the latter phases of inquiry, instructors again should be aware of the PI model to use as a guide in progressing through the phases. Students should also be given an opportunity to moderate the discussions which can shift the authoritative influence of an instructor and encourage freer discussion.

Direct instruction is the responsibility of the instructor to provide intellectual and pedagogic leadership. Students need feedback and direction throughout the process but they also must feel comfortable respectfully challenging instruction. Enabling this requires particular care. Some suggestions for social presence are to shape the discussion without dominating, to provide feedback with respect, to be open to negotiation and providing reasons, and to deal with conflict quickly and privately. Cognitive presence issues associated with direct instruction should be approached with the intent of taking the students to higher levels of cognitive development. Some suggested instructional behaviors are to offer alternative ideas and perspectives for analysis and discussion, respond directly to and elaborate on inquiries for all to absorb, and acknowledge uncertainty where it exist.

Finally, it should be kept in mind that in a collaborative constructivist approach, design must be inherently flexible and adaptable to unpredictable and individual learning needs as they arise. Design and redesign continues throughout the educational experience enabling students' input through shared teaching presence. The guidelines and practical suggestions are discussed here briefly and described more extensively elsewhere (Garrison, 2011; Garrison & Vaughan, 2008; Vaughan, Cleveland-Innes, & Garrison, in press). More research is needed regarding the application of the CoI theoretical framework to different contexts. As suggested by Akyol and Garrison (2008), the development and progression of the CoI elements may vary according to the context. Some of the roles and responsibilities mentioned above may not be needed to the same degree, or additional roles and responsibilities may be required as a result of the particular context.

CONCLUSION

During the past decade of e-learning, there was an extensive focus on technology which hindered educators and researchers from giving enough consideration to the pedagogical practices. However, without adequate pedagogical transformation, these technological innovations have created more uncertainty and dissonance. We are now in a post-industrial era of distance education in which contextual and structural constraints are greatly diminished (Garrison, 2009a). The emerging Internet and communications technologies have made communities of inquiry possible allowing students to interact where and when they choose and collaboratively engage in a purposeful and cohesive group environment (Garrison & Cleveland-Innes, 2011). As a result, there is a growing awareness and responsibility in terms of applying technology with greater understanding and purpose.

The community of inquiry theoretical framework introduced and discussed here has important theoretical and practical implications for online and blended learning—and distance education in general. Over a decade of research has confirmed that the CoI theoretical framework has enormous potential to design, guide and assess e-learning approaches, strategies, and techniques—notwithstanding that much work remains to validate the dimensionality of the elements and the dynamics of the CoI theoretical framework. As a comprehensive guideline, the framework has been a successful catalyst to understand the complexities of online and blended learning. The paramount implication is that the CoI framework has guided the extensive study of how we can use online learning to support and facilitate critical thinking and higher-order learning outcomes. For example, most recently the community of inquiry theoretical framework has been used to provide a model of metacognitive awareness and regulation of discourse and reflection online (Akyol & Garrison, 2011b). Without such awareness, there is a serious question as to whether researchers will have the means to systematically study the complexities of communities of inquiry and whether students will have the cognitive map within which to learn how to learn and become self-directed, cognitively autonomous learners.

REFERENCES

Akyol, Z., & Garrison, D. R. (2008). The development of a community of inquiry over time in an online course: Understanding the progression and integration of social, cognitive and teaching presence. *Journal of Asynchronous Learning Networks, 12*(3), 3–22.

Akyol, Z., & Garrison, D. R. (2009). Community of inquiry in adult online learning: Collaborative-constructivist approaches. In T. T. Kidd (Ed.), *Adult learning in the digital age: Perspectives on online technologies and outcomes* (pp. 52–66). Hershey, PA: IGI Global.

Akyol, Z., & Garrison, D. R. (2011a). Understanding cognitive presence in an online and blended community of inquiry: Assessing outcomes and processes for deep approaches to learning. *British Journal of Educational Technology, 42*(2), 233–250.

Akyol, Z., & Garrison, D. R. (2011b). Assessing metacognition in an online community of inquiry. *Internet and Higher Education, 14*(3), 183–190.

Akyol, Z., Garrison, D. R., & Ozden, M. Y. (2009). Online and blended communities of inquiry: Exploring the developmental and perceptual differences. *International Review of Research in Open and Distance Learning, 10*(6), 65–83.

An, H., Shin, S., & Lim, K. (2009). The effects of different instructor facilitation approaches on students' interactions during asynchronous online discussions. *Computers & Education*, 53, 749–760.

Anderson, T., Rourke, L., Garrison, D. R., & Archer, W. (2001). Assessing teacher presence in a computer conferencing context. *Journal of Asynchronous Learning Networks, 5*(2), 1–7.

Arbaugh, J. B. & Benbunan-Fich, R. (2006). An investigation of epistemological and social dimensions of teaching in online learning environments. *Academy of Management Learning & Education, 5*(4), 435–447.

Arbaugh, J. B., Cleveland-Innes, M., Diaz, S., Garrison, D. R., Ice, P., Richardson, J., … Swan, K. (2008). Developing a community of inquiry instrument: Testing a measure of the Community of Inquiry framework using a multi-institutional sample. *Internet and Higher Education*, 11, 133–136.

Archer, W. (2010). Beyond online discussions: Extending the community of inquiry framework. *Internet and Higher Education, 1*(1–2), 69.

Barber, T. C. (2011). The online crit: The community of inquiry meets design education. *Journal of Distance Education, 25*(1). Retrieved August 11, 2012 from http://www.jofde.ca/index.php/jde/article/view/723/1188

Berge, Z. L. (1995). Facilitating computer conferencing: Recommendations from the field. *Educational Technology, 35*(1), 22–30.

Bliss, C. A., & Lawrence, B. (2009). From posts to patterns: A metric to characterize discussion board activity in online courses. *Journal of Asynchronous Learning Networks, 13*(2), 15–32.

Boston, W., Diaz, S. R., Gibson, A., Ice, P., Richardson, J., & Swan, K. (2009). An exploration of the relationship between indicators of the community of inquiry framework and retention in online programs. *Journal of Asynchronous Learning Networks, 13*(3), 67–83.

Brook, C., & Oliver, R. (2007). Exploring the influence of instructor actions on community development in online settings. In N. Lambropoulos & P. Zaphiris (Eds.), *User-centered design of online learning communities* (pp. 341–364). Hershey, PA: Idea Group.

Buraphadeja, V., & Dawson, K. (2008). Content analysis in Computer-mediated communication: Analyzing models for assessing critical thinking through the lens of social constructivism. *American Journal of Distance Education, 22*(3), 130–145.

Caspi, A., & Blau, I. (2008). Social presence in online discussion groups: testing three conceptions and their relations to perceived learning. *Social Psychology of Education, 11*(3), 323–346.

Cleveland-Innes, M., Garrison, D. R., & Kinsell, E. (2007). Role adjustment for learners in an online community of inquiry: Identifying the challenges of incoming online learners. *International Journal of Web-Based Learning and Teaching Technologies, 2*(1), 1–16.

Conrad, D. (2005). Building and maintaining community in cohort-based online learning. *Journal of Distance Education, 20*(1), 1–20.

Cotton, D., & Yorke, J. (2006, December). Analyzing online discussions: What are the students learning? In *Proceedings of the 23rd Annual Conference of the Australasian Society for Computers in Learning in Tertiary Education: "Who's learning? Whose technology?"* Sydney, Australia.

Dewey, J. (1933). *How we think* (rev. ed.). Boston: D.C. Heath.

Dewey, J. (1959). My pedagogic creed. In J. Dewey, *Dewey on education* (pp. 19–32). New York: Teachers College, Columbia University. (Original work published 1897)

Fabro, K. R., & Garrison, D. R. (1998). Computer conferencing and higher-order learning. *Indian Journal of Open Learning, 7*(1), 41–54.

Feenberg, A. (1989). The written word: On the theory and practice of computer conferencing. In R. Mason & A. Kaye (Eds.), *Mindweave: Communication, computers and distance education* (pp. 22–39). Oxford, UK: Pergamon Press.

Fraser, A. B. (1999). Colleges should tap the pedagogical potential of the World-Wide Web. *The Chronicle of Higher Education, 48,* p. B8.

Garrison, D. R. (1997). Computer conferencing: The post-industrial age of distance education. *Open Learning, 12*(2), 3–11.

Garrison, D. R. (2000). Theoretical challenges for distance education in the 21st century: A shift from structural to transactional issues. *International Review of Research in Open and Distance Learning, 1*(1), 1–17.

Garrison, D. R. (2003). Cognitive presence for effective asynchronous online learning: The role of reflective inquiry, self-direction and metacognition. In J. Bourne & J. C. Moore (Eds.), *Elements of quality online education: Practice and direction* (Vol. 4, pp. 29–38). Needham, MA: The Sloan Consortium.

Garrison, D. R. (2009a). Implications of online learning for the conceptual development and practice of distance education. *Journal of Distance Education, 23*(2), 93–104.

Garrison, D. R. (2009b). Communities of inquiry in online learning. In P. L. Rogers, Berg, G. A., Boettcher, J. V., Howard, C., Justice, L., & Schenk, K. D. (Eds.), *Encyclopedia of distance learning* (2nd ed., pp. 352–355). Hershey, PA: IGI Global.

Garrison, D. R. (2011). *E-Learning in the 21st century: A framework for research and practice* (2nd ed.). London: Routledge/Taylor and Francis.

Garrison, D. R. (2013). Theoretical foundations and epistemological Insights. In Z. Akyol & D. R. Garrison (Eds.), *Educational communities of inquiry: Theoretical framework, research and practice* (pp. 1–11). Hershey, PA: IGI Global.

Garrison, D. R., & Anderson, T. (2000). Transforming and enhancing university teaching: Stronger and weaker technological influences. In T. Evans & D. Nation (Eds.), *Changing university teaching: Reflections on creating educational technologies* (pp. 24–33). London: Kogan Page.

Garrison, D. R., & Arbaugh, J. B. (2007). Researching the community of inquiry framework: Review, issues, and future directions. *Internet and Higher Education, 10*(3), 157–172.

Garrison, D. R., & Archer, W. (2000). *A transactional perspective on teaching and learning: A framework for adult and higher education.* Oxford, UK: Pergamon.

Garrison, D. R., & Baynton, M. (1987). Beyond independence in distance education: The concept of control. *American Journal of Distance Education, 1*(3), 3–15.

Garrison, D. R., & Cleveland-Innes, M. (2005). Facilitating cognitive presence in online learning: Interaction is not enough. *American Journal of Distance Education, 19*(3), 133–148.

Garrison, D. R., & Cleveland-Innes, M. (2010). Foundations of distance education. In Cleveland-Innes, M. & Garrison, D. R. (Eds.), *Understanding distance education in the 21st century: Transition to a new era* (pp. 13–25). London: Routledge.

Garrison, D. R., & Kanuka, H. (2004). Blended learning: Uncovering its transformative potential in higher education. *The Internet and Higher Education, 7*(2), 95–105.

Garrison, D. R., & Vaughan, N. (2008). *Blended learning in higher education.* San Francisco: Jossey-Bass.

Garrison, D. R., Anderson, T., & Archer, W. (2000). Critical inquiry in a text-based environment: Computer conferencing in higher education. *The Internet and Higher Education, 2*(2-3), 87–105.

Garrison, D. R., Anderson, T., & Archer, W. (2001). Critical thinking and computer conferencing: A model and tool to assess cognitive presence. *American Journal of Distance Education, 15*(1), 7–23.

Gorsky, P., Caspi, A., Antonovsky, A., Blau, I., & Mansur, A. (2010). The relationship between academic discipline and dialogic behaviour in open university course forums. *International Review of Research in Open and Distance Learning, 11*(2), 49–72.

Gunawardena, C. N. (1991). Collaborative learning and group dynamics in computer-mediated communication networks. *Research Monograph of the American Center for the Study of Distance Education* (9) (pp. 14–24). University Park: The Pennsylvania State University.

Gunawardena, C. N. (1995). Social presence theory and implications for interaction and collaborative learning in computer conferences. *International Journal of Educational Telecommunications, 1*(2/3), 147–166.

Harasim, L. M. (1987). Teaching and learning on-line: Issues in computer mediated graduate courses. *Canadian Journal of Educational Communication, 16*(2), 117–135.

Harasim, L. M. (1989). On-line education: A new domain. In R. Mason & A. R. Kaye, (Eds.), *Mindweave: Communication, computers, and distance education* (pp. 50–62). New York: Pergamon.

Harasim, L. M. (Ed). (1990). Online education: Perspectives on a new environment. New York: Praeger.

Henri, F. (1992). Computer conferencing and content analysis. In A. R. Kaye (Ed.), *Collaborative learning through computer conferencing: The Najaden papers* (pp. 117–136). Berlin, Germany: Springer-Verlag.

Hiltz, S. R. (1986) 'The "virtual classroom": Using computer mediated communication for university teaching' *Journal of Communication, 36*(2), 95–104.

Ice, P., Curtis, R., Phillips, P., & Wells, J. (2007). Using asynchronous audio feedback to enhance teaching presence and students' sense of community. *Journal of Asynchronous Learning Networks, 11*(2), 3–25.

Jahng, N., Nielsen, W. S., & Chan, E. K. H. (2010). Collaborative learning in an online course: A comparison of communication patterns in small and whole group activities. *Journal of Distance Education, 24*(2), 39–58.

Jezegou, A. (2010). Community of inquiry en e-learning: A propos du modele de Garrison et Anderson. *Journal of Distance Education, 24*(2), 1–18.

Kanuka, H., Rourke, L. & Laflamme, E. (2007). The influence of instructional methods on the quality of online discussion. *British Journal of Educational Technology, 38*(2), 260–271.

Kaye, T. (1987). Introducing computer-mediated communication into a distance education system. *Canadian Journal of Educational Communication, 16*, 153–166

Kaye, T. (1992). Learning together apart. In T. Kaye (Ed.), *Collaborative learning through computer conferencing* (pp. 1–24). New York: Springer-Verlag

Kuhn, D. (1999). A developmental model of critical thinking. *Educational Researcher, 28*(2), 16–25.

Lauzon, A., & Moore, G. (1989). A fourth generation distance education system: Integrating computer-assisted learning and computer conferencing. *The American Journal of Distance Education, 3*(1), 38–49

Lipman, M. (1991). *Thinking in education.* Cambridge, UK: Cambridge University Press.

Lipman, M. (2003). *Thinking in education* (2nd ed.). Cambridge, UK: Cambridge University Press.

Lui, S., Gomez, J., & Yen, C. (2009). Community college online course retention and final grade: Predictability of social presence. *Journal of Interactive Online Learning, 8*(2), 165–182.

Mason, R., & Kaye, A. R. (1989). *Mindweave: Communication, computers, and distance education.* New York: Pergamon.

McKlin, T., Harmon, S. W., Evans, W., & Jone, M. G. (2002). Cognitive presence in web-based learning: A content analysis of students' online discussions. *American Journal of Distance Education, 15*(1) 7–23.

Meyer, K. A. (2003). Face-to-face versus threaded discussions: The role of time and higher-order thinking. *Journal of Asynchronous Learning Networks, 7*(3), 55–65.

Meyer, K. A. (2004). Evaluating online discussions: Four different frames of analysis. *Journal of Asynchronous Learning Networks, 8*(2), 101–114.

Newman, D. R., Johnson, C., Cochrane, C., & Webb, B. (1996). An experiment in group learning technology: Evaluating critical thinking in face-to-face and computer-supported seminars. *Interpersonal Computing and Technology, 4*(1), 57–74.

Nippard, E., & Murphy, E. (2007). Social presence in the web-based synchronous secondary classroom. *Canadian Journal of Learning and Technology, 33*(1). Retrieved July 29, 2011, from http://www.cjlt.ca/index.php/cjlt/article/view/24/22

Paechter, M., Maier, B., & Macher, D. (2010). Students' expectations of, and experiences in e-learning: Their relation to learning achievements and course satisfaction. *Computers and Education, 54*(1), 222–229.

Palloff, R. M. & Pratt, K. (2007). *Building online learning communities: Effective Strategies for the Virtual Classroom* (2nd ed.). San Francisco: Jossey-Bass.

Paulsen, M. (1995). Moderating Educational Computer Conferences. In Z. Berge & M. Collins (Eds.), *Computer mediated communication and the online classroom* (pp. 81–90). Cresskill, NJ: Hampton Press.

Paulsen, M. F., & Rekkedal, T. (1988, August). Computer conferencing: A breakthrough in distance learning, or just another technological gadget? In D. Sewart & J. S. Daniel (Eds.), *Developing distance education* (pp. 362–364). Unpublished papers submitted to the 14th World Conference, Oslo, Norway.

Pawan, F., Paulus, T. M., Yalcin, S., & Chang, C. (2003). Online learning: Patterns of engagement and interaction among in-service teachers. *Language Learning & Technology, 7*(3), 119–140

Picciano, A. G. (2002). Beyond student perceptions: Issues of interaction, presence, and performance in an online course. *Journal of Asynchronous Learning Networks, 5*(2), 18–35.

Richardson, J. C., & Swan, K. (2003). Examining social presence in online courses in relation to students' perceived learning and satisfaction. *Journal of Asynchronous Learning Networks, 7*(1), 68–88.

Richardson, J. C., & Ice, P. (2010). Investigating students' level of critical thinking across instructional strategies in online discussions. *Internet and Higher Education, 13*(1-2), 52–59.

Rogers, P., & Lea, M. (2005). Social presence in distributed group environments: The role of social identity. *Behavior & Information Technology, 24*(2), 151–158.

Rourke, L., Anderson, T., Garrison, R., & Archer, W. (2001). Methodological issues in the content analysis of computer conference transcripts. *International Journal of Artificial Intelligence in Education, 12*(1), 8–22.

Salmon, G. (2000). *E-moderating the key to teaching and learning online.* London: Kogan Page.

Schrire, S. (2004). Interaction and cognition in asynchronous computer conferencing. *Instructional Science, 32,* 475–502.

Schrire, S. (2006). Knowledge building in asynchronous discussion groups: Going beyond quantitative analysis. *Computers & Education, 46*(1), 49–70.

Shea, P., & Bidjerano, T. (2009a). Community of inquiry as a theoretical framework to foster "epistemic engagement" and "cognitive presence" in online education. *Computers and Education, 52*(3), 543–553.

Shea, P., & Bidjerano, T. (2009b). Cognitive presence and online learner engagement: A cluster analysis of the community of inquiry framework. *Journal of Computing in Higher Education, 21,* 199–217.

Shea, P., Hayes, S. Vickers, J., Gozza-Cohen, M., Uzner, S., Mehta, R., … Rangan, P. (2010). A re-examination of the community of inquiry framework: Social network and content analysis. *Internet and Higher Education,* 1-2, 10–21.

Shea, P., Li, C. S., & Pickett, A. (2006). A study of teaching presence and student sense of learning community in fully online and web-enhanced college courses. *The Internet and Higher Education, 9*(3), 175–190.

Stein, D. S., Wanstreet, C. E., Glazer, H. R., Engle, C. L. Harris, R. A., Johnston, S. M., … Trinko, L. A. (2007). Creating shared understanding through chats in a community of inquiry. *The Internet and Higher Education,* 10, 103–115.

Swan, K., & Shih, L.F. (2005). On the nature and development of social presence in online course discussions. *Journal of Asynchronous Learning Networks, 9*(3), 115–136.

Swan, K. (2010). Teaching and learning in post-industrial distance education. In M. Cleveland-Innes. & D. R. Garrison (Eds.), *Understanding distance education in the 21st century: Transition to a new era* (pp. 108–134). New York: Routledge.

Vaughan, N. D., Cleveland-Innes, M., & Garrison, D. R. (in press). *Teaching in blended learning environments: creating and sustaining communities of inquiry.* Athabasca: Athabasca University Press.

Vaughan, N. D., & Garrison, D. R. (2005). Creating cognitive presence in a blended faculty development community. *Internet and Higher Education,* 8, 1–12.

Part 2

Learning, Learners, and Learner Support
An Overview
MICHAEL GRAHAME MOORE

In Part 2 we focus specifically on a selection of topics that address research issues about some of the characteristics of learners that should be taken into account in the quest for successful distance teaching, especially online, and some of the special issues to be considered in supporting these distance learners.

The opening chapter by West, Hannafin, Hill, and Song introduces learning, with a range of studies drawn from the field of cognitive psychology. The chapter begins with a review of the theory of learning as information processing, then moves to research on prior learning and its value in teaching, and four specific information processing constructs, i.e., motivation, cognitive demands, meta-cognition, and scaffolding. This opening chapter's focus on psychological research is followed by three that address questions about student responses, one with its primary focus on their satisfaction, the second persistence and the third achievement.

Student satisfaction is reviewed through the technique of literature meta-analysis, in Allen and colleagues' Chapter 9, which focuses especially on studies reporting differences in satisfaction when learning in face to face environments and at a distance. Clearly, everything known from cognitive psychology, the chapter preceding, as well as the best practices in design and teaching, subject of Part 3, must be considered among the explanations for what cause some students to be optimally satisfied and successful, and other not. The causes of such satisfaction and achievement are very elusive, the variables so many, and shifting with each change of content, teacher and student, but what can be said with some confidence, as has been demonstrated so many times, is that what determines satisfaction (and achievement) is seldom the delivery environment itself, whether at-a-distance or face-to-face. Rather it is the qualities in the course design, instruction, and within the learners themselves.

The capacity to persist on the part of the student is one such learner characteristic, and, following the discussion about satisfaction, the next chapter deals with student persistence. It is a closely related phenomenon, of course, to satisfaction, for students who are satisfied are likely to persist, and those who persist are likely to succeed—and usually be satisfied! This question of persistence has often, in the past been expressed as a question about drop-out, and is one that has exercised distance educators from the earliest years. As with satisfaction, there are many variables that contribute to drop-out or persistence, and in their review in Chapter 10, Stavredes, and Herder introduce some of the best-known models that have been developed to represent this multivariate phenomenon. They go on, for most of the chapter, to discuss the response of educators, asking what approaches and techniques are learners most likely to find supportive, and thus to enable them to sustain persistence and complete their study. Among the many variables under consideration, several of the most important have already been encountered in earlier chapters, particularly cognitive presence and social presence, community of inquiry, and cognitive scaffolding in various forms. (The reader might recall the advice given previously, to revisit earlier chapters especially those dealing with theory, and reconsider them, in light of new understanding resulting from this and other later, more in-depth chapters.)

Following Stavredes and Herder, the next chapter, by Cavanaugh, reports several meta-analyses of literature of effectiveness, but in this case, specifically of effectiveness for young, K–12 students. Repeating the well-supported conclusion, "student learning on average in well-designed online elementary and secondary environments appears to be equivalent to learning in a well-designed classroom environment," Cavanaugh proceeds to offer vitally important advice—researchers must move past such broad syntheses and look for what she calls the "fine-grained trends." The chapter proceeds to focus on some of these, in each of the main areas, i.e., student characteristics, course design, instructional strategies, teacher preparation and development, course facilitation, and technological approaches. As with every chapter, this one anticipates themes in many that follow, but, here Cavanaugh's statement: "teacher quality is among the most important contributors to student achievement," points forward particularly to Shattuck's chapters about faculty participation and the faculty's motivation to support the distance learning enterprise.

To complete Part 2, three chapters fall within the broad theme of learner support. In the first, Chapter 12, Gunawardena explains the significance of culture and cultural differences in the teaching-learning relationship, with special attention given to how culture plays a role in learning online, especially the processes involved in social construction of knowledge, how it relates to social presence and group process, and language and discourse. This is followed by a discussion of the implications of culture for course designers. Throughout the chapter are numerous implications for those who provide student support, helping deal with the special problems facing different cultures arising from the content of courses, differences in learning and teaching styles (for example, the suggestion that students of some cultures might not understand, or prefer, the collaborative over independent study pedagogies that we discussed in earlier chapters). Academic student support is the subject of Curry's Chapter 13, a revision of that in the 2nd edition of the *Handbook of Distance Education*, reporting several important new developments in this area, such as the development by the National Academic Advising Association of a set of standards for advising distance learners. Among eye-catching studies reported here, one includes students' responding to the importance of no fewer than 64 different support services for distance learning. Staying with the theme of student support, in Chapter 14, Chrichton and Kinash address the needs of disabled students and the support services needed by this special group—a population that has traditionally looked more than the general population to distance education to provide opportunity that was often unavailable in the general educational system because of their disabilities; reference in Chapter 1 to the Hadley School for the Blind is just one reminder of the special part that distance education has played over many decades in serving the disabled student. The authors here follow in that tradition, asking specifically, how can educators "promote universal design in distance education by disrupting the traditional dependency on text with the thoughtful addition of visual and auditory interfaces which tend to be more inclusive," and they add a very Web 2.0 generation question, "how might the emergence of tablet devices supplement and, in some cases, replace assistive technologies?" Their response includes a review 53 recent publications.

To conclude Part 2, another vital student support area is addressed, that of the library. Few areas in the university, college, school, or training institute have been more transformed as a result of the development of information and communication technologies than the library. And, for certain, the opening of access to library resources wherever a student lives or works has been one of the most significant (though widely overlooked) contributors to the renaissance of distance education in the past decade. Advanced degree students in particular, having to undertake research, were seriously disenfranchised when having to travel to a local library or send for books by mail. Today, access to the library is little more difficult in the proverbial lighthouse that is part of the distance education mythology than it is for the student on the Harvard or Berkeley campuses. The new prominence of the academic librarian's profession is represented by Johnson and Fabbro's Chapter 15, consisting of a review of the literature in the following areas: (a) connecting with users by promoting awareness of the library, providing reference services, assessing library services, and meeting the needs of diverse teachers and learners; (b) providing access to resources, particularly through e-resources, electronic course reserves, and document delivery; and (c) promoting information literacy by establishing institutional support, delivering information literacy instruction, developing relevant pedagogical approaches, and assessing information literacy skills.

8

COGNITIVE PERSPECTIVES ON ONLINE LEARNING ENVIRONMENTS

RICHARD E. WEST, MICHAEL J. HANNAFIN, JANETTE R. HILL, AND LIYAN SONG

Cognitive psychology is a pervasive influence in teaching and learning research, theory, and practice (see overview by Winn, 2004) and has shaped designs for technology-mediated teaching and learning environments (see, for example, Koenig & Atkinson, 2009; Rieber, 2009; van Merrienboer, Sweller, & Paas, 1998). As online learning environments (OLEs) have evolved, they have generated a predictable but important debate: To what extent are empirically-derived, cognitive principles applicable to online learning environments? Do alternative perspectives warrant, or require, different approaches? How do the affordances of technologies and contextual demands influence the applicability of cognitive principles?

Several principles have been extrapolated from past research to online learning environments (see, for example, Clark & Hannafin, 2011; Doolittle, Terry, & Mariano, 2009; Low, Jin, & Sweller, 2009; Mayer, 2005), suggesting that many time-tested cognitive constructs apply to online learning. At the same time, varied perspectives on the use of technology tools to support individual processing indicate that our applications of many cognitive constructs may be modified via technology's affordances. For example, recent perspectives have departed significantly from classic cognitive theory, leading some to suggest that the quest for a single, "correct" psychological paradigm may be fruitless (see, for example, DeSchryver and Spiro, 2009; Hannafin, West, & Shepherd, 2009). Rather, we suggest the utility and applicability of different cognitive principles and perspectives must be aligned, or grounded, in corresponding psychological and pedagogical approaches (Hannafin, Hill, & Glazer, 2011; Kim & Hannafin, 2008, 2009).

The evidence suggests potential variations in both the underlying assumptions about the nature and mechanisms of cognition and their associated implications for technology-enhanced teaching and learning. Since one chapter cannot address all possible cognitive psychology variations, the purposes of this chapter are to: (a) introduce background related to information processing-related perspectives; (b) review and critically analyze research on four specific cognitive constructs in the context of online learning environments; and (c) describe implications of these cognitive perspectives for online learning research, theory, and practice.

INFORMATION PROCESSING PERSPECTIVES

Information processing perspectives, rooted in objectivist epistemology, assume meaning exists independent of the individual; individuals acquire and comprehend this meaning to become knowledgeable and productive with that knowledge. Historically, information processing models were characterized as "mind as computer" (Atkinson & Schiffrin, 1968) and "microscopes of the mind" (Massaro & Cowan, 1993). The individual mediates what is valued, acted upon, remembered, recalled, and generalized based on unique prior knowledge, needs, and interests. Information processing, in effect, involves the exchange of signals between external stimuli and internal mental processes such as sensory registers, selective perception, short-term memory (STM), and long-term memory (LTM) (Doolittle, Terry, & Mariano, 2009).

Schema theory is commonly used to characterize how we presume information is processed. Donald Norman (1982) described the organized networks of prior knowledge as schemata, or variables, "slots," and associations among knowledge that collectively define how a given individual knows or performs a task. As we acquire, update, and revise new knowledge, the number and strength of associations and representations increases. The process of updating schema "spreads" as representations are retrieved and modified through activity (Anderson & Pirolli, 1984).

Accordingly, sensory registers detect external stimuli, which are then selectively filtered (often with little or no conscious awareness). This culls the amount and type of information and signals information to be processed more deeply. Information initially perceived is processed temporarily in STM, where it is selectively filtered. Since STM, or working memory, has limited capacity, much of the information is rapidly discarded while other data is retained and selectively further processed based on prior knowledge and new incoming information.

For information processing, therefore, durable learning is the transfer of encoded information from STM to LTM. Subsequent retrieval involves recalling "learned" knowledge from LTM to working, or short-term, memory where it is compared with new information. Precisely what is learned and how well it is retrieved depends on how knowledge is represented: the more richly knowledge is encoded, the more likely it will be activated under appropriate conditions, retrieved (decoded), and applied or transferred to related situations. Information processing theory hinges on several important and mediating constructs, including the roles of prior knowledge, cues and cuing, coding and representing knowledge, and acquiring and deploying knowledge.

Mediating Constructs

Prior Knowledge. Ausubel (1968) was among the first cognitive theorists to underscore the primacy of prior knowledge in learning. Prior knowledge provides both the conceptual foundation (schema) and the links or associations between and among "nodes" or discrete sets of ideas. As prior knowledge is more richly, deeply, and broadly connected, learners more readily acquire new knowledge and integrate it with existing understanding. In effect, to the extent an individual has acquired knowledge about a to-be-learned concept—even if naïve or incomplete—a basis is established for selecting new stimuli, elaborating with current knowledge, and refining existing conceptions. In addition, as prior knowledge and associations increase, the more motivated, capable, and strategic learners become in seeking, evaluating, and self-regulating new learning (Tobias, 1994).

Prior knowledge has played a significant role in learning and retention across a wide range of learning environments. For example, Clark and Mayer (2007) extrapolated "proven" design and learning strategies and guidelines based largely on their analysis of prior research. These authors cited numerous references to psychological research underlying their guidelines, including, but not specifically related to, online learning. Other scholars also documented the role of prior experience in influencing learning during online instruction. Song (2005), for example, noted that experienced online graduate learners tended to be more strategic in time-management and soliciting support, such as raising questions during online chats that the instructor could address quickly. Experienced online learners also reported spending less time in bulletin board discussions, focusing instead on their particular interests and discussions. In contrast, first-time online learners reported reading nearly all bulletin board postings as they attempted to stay current with and understand course content.

Prior knowledge of the online system also appears to influence how available affordances are accessed and used. In one study, prior system knowledge was found to have a stronger impact on performance than prior subject knowledge. Hill and Hannafin (1997) examined the decisions made by 15 current and future K-12 teachers enrolled in a technology for teachers course who searched the Web to identify materials for a to-be-taught classroom topic of their choosing. Novice users were far more likely than experienced system users to become frustrated and disoriented in their attempts to locate resources, and thus less strategic and successful in their searches. In contrast, those with high system knowledge reported more confidence, persistence, and success in their search strategies.

Prior online learning experience also appears to influence how individuals perceive and use online tools and resources. In a series of studies, Sharma and Hannafin (2004, 2005, 2007) noted different patterns of use among college students who perceived online tools as helpful and productive versus those who did not. Similarly, Song, Singleton, Hill, and Koh (2004) indicated that whereas novices often struggle during their first online learning course, experienced online learners tend to develop strategic knowledge about the use of system affordances, manifest greater metacognitive awareness of their distance learning strengths and needs, and persist in the face of confusion or frustration.

Cues & Cuing. The nature, content, and structure of cues are especially significant for information processing. External cues both represent to-be-learned concepts and provide the means through which internal mechanisms are invoked (selectively perceived), acted upon in STM, coded richly and appropriately, transferred to LTM, and subsequently recalled and transferred as needed. Gagne's *Events of Instruction* (1984) linked external (instructional) events to specific internal (cognitive) events to ensure a link between how external stimuli were organized and presented and the associated requisite cognitive processes. The co-mediation between external events and cognitive processes establishes a fundamental tenet of information processing perspectives.

Coding & Representing Knowledge. Paivio's (1971) believed in his dual coding hypothesis that information coded multiple ways (e.g., verbal and imagery) is better stored and retrieved. This has been empirically validated, but more stimulation does not necessarily improve learning because it can often interfere as well. In a comprehensive review of numerous studies involving school-aged students using multiple representations (such as pictures accompanying text or video with accompanying narration), Pressley (1977) found that combined verbal-visual representations improved learning when they were complimentary in nature, but interfered when they were not. Similar research findings have repeatedly supported the complementary versus competing potential of visual and verbal stimuli across ages, grades, and domains (Fleming, 1977). Cognitive resources are well-used and effective when complementary information is conveyed simultaneously, but become quickly overtaxed when learners attempt to simultaneously decode non-congruent information presented across modalities.

A variety of explanations have been tendered as to how knowledge is ultimately represented (Rummelhart & Ortony, 1977). Representation is commonly characterized in terms of propositions, productions, and associations. Knowledge representations comprise simple propositions (knowing what) and productions (knowing what to do). Connections, both within and between types of knowledge, are established during initial encoding and modified through successive experience, creating associations of varied richness and depth based upon individual differences.

Acquiring & Deploying Knowledge. According to information processing theorists, encoding and retrieving are inextricably tied and influenced by factors such as depth of processing, extensiveness of coding, and richness of association. Information that has been processed deeply in STM—for example, by comparing and contrasting with similar information, analyzing closely for similarities and differences, and relating to prior knowledge—tends to be encoded more richly, activated more readily, and retrieved more quickly (Anderson, Reder, & Lebiere, 1996). Craik and Tulving (1975) examined the time needed to answer "deep" (semantic) questions as well as the retention of key terms to assess depth of processing effects. They concluded the quality of a word's encoding determines retention at a comparable level to when the questions were salient, suggesting that depth reflects the degree of elaboration during encoding. Similarly, Anderson and Pirolli (1984) described "spread of activation" as the rate with which knowledge can be associated according to relevancy. Simply summarized, where relevancy is high, spread of activation is rapid; where low, activation is low and likely to decay rapidly.

COGNITIVE CONSTRUCTS & OLEs

Based on this understanding of basic cognitive perspectives, we now present recent research evidence on how four specific information processing constructs apply to online learning environments (OLEs). While there are other relevant constructs we cannot discuss in this chapter, we will review research related to motivation, cognitive demands, metacognition, and scaffolding.

Motivation

According to cognitive perspectives, motivation (classified as either extrinsic and intrinsic) involves initiating and sustaining a desirable behavior in accordance with defined goals (Driscoll, 2000; Schunk, 1990). Course requirements often serve as extrinsic motivation by establishing an external incentive to which the learner strives (Laszlo & Kupritz, 2003), while intrinsic motivation pertains to goals unique to the individual because of personal interests (Lim & Kim, 2003). In this section, we first discuss some of the research into motivation in online learning, including the evidence that learners with different goal and self-regulatory orientations have very different levels of learning motivation. We then discuss research indicating how different technological and pedagogical approaches may affect a students' motivation to learn.

Motivation has consistently been considered an important construct for successful online learning, and has been widely studied. For example, Bures, Amundsen, and Abrami (2002) examined student motivation and computer conferencing. During one study, they observed 167 students in 10 different courses using varying levels of computer conferencing technology and found that both intrinsic (personal task relevance and beliefs) and extrinsic elements (task attractiveness) predicted satisfaction. They further reported that students with a personal learning orientation (intrinsic motivation) participated more in CC activities, had higher grades, and benefited more from the CC environment.

In another study on goal orientations, Ng (2008) tested the hypothesis that learners with various types of multiple goals would have different learning patterns. Ng surveyed 1,200 (797 responded) undergraduate distance learners at the Open University of Hong Kong on their achievement goals, learning strategies, self-regulatory strategies, beliefs, and attitudes regarding their courses. Cluster analyses categorized participants into four types of learners: mastery-focused learners, multiple-goal learners with a work focus, multiple-goal learners with a performance focus, and multiple-goal learners with multiple foci. MANOVA analyses indicated that students with these different goal orientations differed in their use of various learning and regulatory strategies motivational beliefs and course attitudes. In other words, students with different goal orientations differed in how they learned online.

Using naturalistic case methods to investigate the relationship between self-regulation and motivation, Whipp and Chiarelli (2004) studied six graduate students using Lotus Notes/Learning Space during an instructional technology and assessment course. Based on their analysis of interview transcripts, course documents, and student reflective journals, the researchers reported that students' motivations for self-regulated navigation depended upon the extent that they were able to manage both technical and social environments of the course. Although the sample size was small, the findings from this study suggested that personal and system-related aspects of experience may influence motivation in online environments and the effectiveness of self-regulated learning.

Researchers have suggested various ways to increase students' motivation in OLEs. For example, Huett, Kalinowski, Moller, and Huett (2008) studied the use of attention, relevance, confidence, and satisfaction (ARCS)-based emails to increase the motivation of undergraduate students in an online computer application course. Student participants in the treatment group received emails constructed according to Keller's ARCS model, including the following components: introduction, goal reminders, words of encouragement, and multiple points of contact. These researchers found statistically significant differences in motivation between the treatment group and the control group suggesting that well-designed communications can help increase students' motivation in online courses.

Emerging forms of technology can also increase motivation in OLEs (Mei-Mei, 2005). Hee Jun and Johnson (2005) reported a significant difference in learners' motivation for video-based instruction and text-based instruction. In their quasi-experimental, post-test-only study, 16 online masters' students were provided both video- and text-based instruction within an online module, then asked for perceptions of understanding and motivation for each. Results indicated a significant difference for perceived learning and motivation, with participants reporting that the video-based instruction was more appealing and memorable. While Clark's (1994) cautions concerning novelty effects must be heeded, these findings suggested that online, context-based videos may provide additional extrinsic motivation for students to engage online instruction.

Some research has indicated that student perceptions of the (OLE design structures can influence their motivation. One study (Furnborough & Truman, 2009) shed light on the relationship between students' perceptions of assignment feedback and their abilities to maintain their motivation. This qualitative study examined how distance language learners at the Open University in the United Kingdom perceived assignment feedback and how this affected their perceived achievement. From students' interviews and surveys, Furnborough and Truman concluded that the more students perceived feedback as a formative learning support, the more likely they persisted to the next level. In cases where students considered feedback as a judgment on their progress, they were less motivated.

Hsinyi, Chin-Chung, and Ying-Tien (2006) found gender-based differences in motivation, reporting that male undergraduates demonstrated more positive Internet attitudes than females. In addition, students who perceived the Internet as a leisure tool reported more positive attitudes and higher self-efficacy than students viewing the Internet in only a functional role. In effect, Hsinyi et al. suggested that fostering an informal, exploratory, and leisurely attitude towards the Internet may improve students' motivations toward learning in OLEs.

Others, however, have suggested motivation may actually decline following online learning. For example, Schrum, Burbank, Engle, Chambers, and Glassett (2005) studied the motivation and beliefs of 22 higher education faculty from eight different colleges and universities enrolled in an online professional development course. They concluded that difficulties sustaining the learning community and learning new technologies decreased learner morale. Schmeeckle (2003) also reported a significant negative impact on learner motivation in quantitative studies where trainees in the classroom group reported both higher motivation and more positive feelings about learning than did the online group.

These findings reinforce the conclusion that there may perhaps be nothing inherently motivational about online learning. Indeed, evidence suggests that due to the increased technical and interpersonal complexity of many systems, motivation to engage may decline in many instances. Well-designed and supported instruction will generally increase motivation to engage and learn, while cumbersome, problematic instruction will not. Consistent with general learning environment research, several more fundamental cognitive and design factors seem to influence student motivation (cf. Clark, 1994).

Cognitive Demands

Total cognitive load, or the demands on mental processing while attempting to learn, has been conceptualized as comprising intrinsic, extraneous, and germane cognitive load (Gerjets & Scheiter, 2003; van Merrionboer & Ayres, 2005). In this section, we first briefly define the three different kinds of cognitive load, and then discuss basic approaches to researching cognitive load, as well as studies into how to decrease extraneous load and increase helpful, germane load in OLEs. We then conclude discussing the need for future research in the area of cognitive load in online learning.

Intrinsic load, the number of elements that need to be processed in working memory (STM), is influenced by individual expertise and the inherent task complexity in to-be-learned material. For example, learning from a biology text may present a higher intrinsic load than reading a children's story to the everyday person, but not to a scientist (Pollock, Chandler, & Sweller, 2002). Since a great deal of to-be-learned knowledge and skill made available at a distance is designed for non-experts, intrinsic load is especially relevant to OLEs.

Extraneous load is influenced by the mental resources required to engage a learning environment. Well-organized information, instructions, and tools tend to minimize extraneous load, while poorly organized information and tools engender higher extraneous load. In effect, to the extent the learner must expend cognitive resources simply to locate and access content, extraneous load (and effort) increases, possibly leading to learner disorientation in online environments, and the sense of being "lost in hyperspace."

Germane load is defined as the amount of working memory needed to create new or activate existing schemas to learn desired or required concepts (Gerjets & Scheiter, 2003; Renkl & Atkinson, 2003). Germane load involves the allocation of cognitive resources that are appropriate for processing the task. Increasing germane load may help improve the efficiency of future learning, while increasing extraneous load may prove inefficient, ineffective, and overwhelming (van Merrienboer, Schuurman, de Croock, & Paas, 2002).

Researchers have often studied cognitive load through posttreatment questionnaires, where learners self-report their mental effort (Paas, van Merrienboer, & Adam, 1994; Paas, Tuovinen, Tabber, & Van Gerven, 2003) or rate the difficulty of the material they learned (Kalyuga, Chandler, & Sweller, 1999). However, Brunken, Plass, and Leutner (2003) argued for direct, objective measures of cognitive load. Thus far, few direct measures of cognitive load have been developed, leaving us still unsure of how to improve helpful, germane load and decrease inefficient, extrinsic load in online learning.

Researchers have suggested that hyperlinking may increase extraneous load (Oliver & Hannafin, 2000). In a study of 39 undergraduate students in an educational computing course, Niederhauser, Reynolds, Salmen, and Skolmoski (2000) tested the impact of different navigational patterns on learning using hyperlinked text. They used surveys to assess students' reading abilities, domain knowledge, and backgrounds using computers. Computer software helped measure the time spent reading each screen and navigation patterns, and a posttest questionnaire and essay assignment measured learning. As expected, they found that reading comprehension, background knowledge, and reading time were positively related to learning. They were surprised to learn, however, that using hyperlinked material to compare and contrast concepts had a negative influence on learning. The authors concluded that the increased cognitive load in the hypertext environment negatively impacted student learning.

Similarly, Eveland and Dunwoody (2001) divided 219 students into five groups taught via different online materials. One group browsed a Website using linear navigation buttons, while another group browsed a site with links embedded throughout the material to encourage students to explore the content nonlinearly. A third group used nonlinear links with linear navigational guides; the remaining students served as a paper-based and independent task control group. All groups were given 15 minutes to study the material, and then rated their motivation, Web expertise, and the difficulty of the learning. The paper-based control group outperformed two of the three Web-based groups, suggesting that Web-based hyperlinking, in the absence of advice, increased extraneous cognitive load.

Consistent with Hill and Hannafin's (1997) finding related to prior system knowledge, limited technology familiarity may also increase extrinsic load. Clarke, Ayres, and Sweller (2005) assigned 24 Australian ninth graders into four groups based on their experience using spreadsheets and mathematics abilities. They compared one group that received technology instruction prior to domain instruction with a second group that received simultaneous instruction in both and measured their math and spreadsheet abilities as well as their subjective ratings of cognitive load. These researchers reported that initial technology instruction followed by domain instruction was most effective for students with low prior spreadsheet abilities, rather than teaching both concurrently. Concurrent instruction in technology and domain content apparently increased extraneous, while decreasing germane, cognitive load.

One way to reduce extraneous cognitive load is with graphic organizers. Chen, Hirumi, and Zhang (2007) studied the use of two types of advanced organizers (graphic and text) on undergraduate students' performances in a fully online health-related ethics course. While no statistical significant differences were found between these two types of advanced organizers, participants reported that the advanced organizers helped scaffold the materials, indicating a need for further research and clarification.

Many researchers reported benefits from providing students with worked examples (problems showing an example along with the step-by-step solution process); likewise, self-explanation may help to increase schema creation (Gerjets, Scheiter, & Catrambone, 2004; Paas, 1992; Paas & van Merrienboer, 1994; Reed & Bolstad, 1991; Renkl, Atkinson, & Grosse 2004; Renkl, Stark, Gruber, & Mandl, 1998; Sweller, 1988). Other methods for increasing germane load include the use of example elaboration and example comparison (Gerjets, Scheiter, & Catrambone, 2004), and fading procedures (Renkl & Atkinson, 2003; Renkl et al., 2004). As a result of highly developed mental models, students may better transfer learning (Paas & van Merrienboer, 1994). Since the goal is to minimize extraneous load while increasing germane load, these strategies hold considerable promise for organizing, structuring, and supporting online learning.

Research on developing, instantiating, and inducing mental schemas may also influence the cognitive load of to-be-learned concepts. In a study by Eveland, Cortese, Park, and Dunwoody (2004), two groups of participants (college students and nonstudents) explored for 20 minutes health topic Websites designed with either linear navigation or nonlinear navigation. The researchers then posttested participant understanding of factual information using a questionnaire and asked them to list and rate relationships among remembered concepts (knowledge structure density). Whereas participants learned factual information best from linear sites, nonlinear sites improved knowledge structure density, which they interpreted to be more transferable knowledge. The researchers also suggested that nonlinear sites may increase germane load (positive load). However, in a previous study by the same researchers, nonlinear sites increased extraneous (negative) load (Eveland & Dunwoody, 2001), indicating this issue is not yet fully understood.

Finally, some researchers have examined the specific relationship between cognitive load and learners' success online. For example, McQuaid (2010) found that learner's confidence was the single most important factor determining e-learning success. McQuaid focused on the cumulative and task-specific cognitive loads experienced by e-learners resulting from the five major tasks required in the asynchronous course. The National Aeronautics and Space Administration-Task Load Index (NASA-TLX) was employed to measure the cognitive load experience by e-learners in this asynchronous course. The measured cognitive load was compared against each of those five tasks. The correlational analyses indicated that the more confident the learners were, the less cognitive load they would experience; the higher the learners' self-efficacy level, the lower their experienced cognitive load level. In other words, learners' self-efficacy and confidence were found to be critical factors affecting the level of cognitive load that learners would experience in asynchronous courses.

The inconsistencies in some of these findings indicate that there is still much to be learned and understood about managing extrinsic and germane load, particularly in online learning. In addition, while several studies have examined extraneous load in OLEs, little research exists about intrinsic load. However, research from information literacy studies may provide interesting insights. Jones, Ravid, and Rafaeli (2004) reported a trend towards high intrinsic load in informal online spaces based on an analysis of more than 2.65 million postings in over 600 Usenet newsgroups over a six-month period. They found that the higher the intrinsic load, the lower the participation by the users. In another study, Huang (2011) examined the impact of online, game-based learning environments on learners' goal-setting activities and cognitive loads. The results from this study indicated that students reported significantly higher levels of intrinsic load than the germane load due to the novelty of the subject matter, implying a relationship between learners' intrinsic load and the subject matter and/or instruction delivery method. More research on how varying levels of expertise impacts intrinsic load in OLEs could help understand learners' adaptive learning in OLEs (Federico, 1999).

Metacognition

Metacognition refers to one's awareness of, and ability to manage, one's own cognitive processes (Flavell, 1977) and involves the ability to anticipate, detect, and correct or "repair" understanding needs as they emerge (Schraw & Dennison, 1994). Like many cognitive phenomena, metacognitive awareness and skill are influenced by prior domain knowledge, experience, and expertise. As individuals become increasingly knowledgeable and experienced, they increase in metacognitive awareness and skill. Metacognition may be especially relevant to learning from and during OLEs. Indeed, Dobrovolny (2006) found in a phenomenological study of seven participants in online corporate training that knowledge construction began with metacognition as learners assessed their own knowledge gaps, and then was mediated by metacognitive strategies. In this section, we first review some of the evidence connecting metacognition to successful online learning, discuss some research into how to effectively scaffold and improve online metacognition, and conclude with current efforts to develop ways to measure metacognition in OLEs.

Zion, Michalsky, and Mevarech (2005) gave insights into why metacognition may be particularly relevant online, as they argued that asynchronous learning networks (ALNs) allow students to review digital records of constructed learning, enabling students to better monitor their learning and making cognition more visible while they develop metacognitive skills. The authors conducted a 2 × 2 experiment involving 407 Israeli 10th-grade microbiology students, and found that ALN students with metacognitive scaffolding performed significantly better than those in the face-to-face group with no scaffolding. No significant differences were found between the ALN students without metacognition help and the face-to-face group with the scaffolding, indicating that metacognition was the most effective method. This finding is in accord with authors such as Workman (2004), who suggested that the repetitive nature of self-paced computer-based education, where learners interact with material presented via CD-ROM and structured sequentially with multi-model instruction followed by review, provides cognitive cueing and supports metacognitive awareness "by prompting learners to reflect on their learning progress and allowing them to repeat material at critical junctures if needed" (p. 520).

Metacognitive proficiency in OLEs may be related to ability and prior knowledge, or at least intrinsic motivation for the learning material. Oliver and Hannafin (2001), for example, reported that middle school students lacked even basic metacognitive activity while attempting to solve science problems using Web-based resources. In their study, students aged 12–14 years of age relied on scaffolds to provide explicit direction rather than to induce metacognitive reflection as designed.

Smidt and Heigelheimer (2004) conducted a qualitative study of nine adult English as a Second Language (ESL) learners as part of a larger study on the use of Web-based video for a vocabulary and listening comprehension course. The researchers interviewed high, middle, and low-performing students regarding their learning strategies, which were categorized as either cognitive or metacognitive. Advanced learners exhibited both metacognitive and cognitive learning strategies, but intermediate and lower-level learners used mainly cognitive strategies, suggesting greater metacognitive awareness and utilization among advanced students. They also reported that males were more likely to use metacognitive strategies, while females used more cognitive strategies in their learning. However, a later study (Tsai, 2009) found no gender differences, leaving the question unanswered.

Besides ability and prior knowledge, Artino (2009) found in his study of 481 service academy undergraduates that students' perceptions about a course and their motivations for the material was related to their metacognition. Through logistic regressional analysis, Artino reported that students who completed an online course in aviation physiology, and who were planning to become aviators themselves, reported a greater use of metacognitive strategies.

Land and Greene (2000) found that metacognitive knowledge can sometimes compensate for limited system or domain knowledge. In their qualitative study, the authors studied undergraduate preservice teachers working alone, in pairs, or in groups in an online instructional technology course. For two of the four cases studied, metacognitive knowledge seemed to build off of system and domain knowledge. However, for teachers who struggled with low domain/system knowledge, their metacognitive knowledge compensated and helped them complete tasks successfully. This suggests the importance of providing scaffolds to develop and regulate metacognitive knowledge and support

Chen, Hirumi, & Zhang (2007). Investigating the use of advanced organizers as an instructional strategy for web-based distance education. *Quarterly Review of Distance Education, 8*(3), 223–231.

Clark, R. E. (1994). Media will never influence learning. *Educational Technology Research and Development, 42*(2), 21–29.

Clarke, T., Ayres, P., & Sweller, J. (2005). The impact of sequencing and prior knowledge on learning mathematics through spreadsheet applications. *Educational Technology Research & Development, 53*(3), 15–24.

Clark, R. E., & Hannafin, M.J. (2011). Debate about the benefits of different levels of instructional guidance. In R. Reiser & J. Dempsey (Eds), *Trends and issues in instructional design and technology* (3rd ed., pp. 367–382). Upper Saddle River, NJ: Merrill/Prentice-Hall.

Clark, R. C., & Mayer, R. (2007). *E-learning and the science of instruction: Proven guidelines for consumers and designers of multimedia learning* (2nd ed.). New York: Wiley

Conrad, D. (2009). Cognitive, instructional, and social presence as factors in learners' negotiation of planned absences from online study. *International Review of Research in Open and Distance Learning. 10*(3), 1–18.

Craik, F. I. M., & Tulving, E. (1975) Depth of processing and the retention of words in episodic memory. *Journal of Experimental Psychology: General, 104*(3), 268–294.

Dabbagh, N. (2003). Scaffolding: An important teacher competency in online learning. *TechTrends, 47*(2), 39–44.

DeSchryver, M., & Spiro, R. (2009). New forms of deep learning on the Web: Meeting the challenges of cognitive load in conditions of unfettered exploration in online multimedia environments. In R. Zheng (Ed.), *Cognitive effects of multimedia learning* (pp. 134–152). New York: Information Science References.

Dobrovolny, J. (2006). How adults learn from self-pace, technology-based corporate training: New focus for learners, new focus for designers. *Distance Education, 27*(2), 155–170.

Doolittle, P., Terry, K., & Mariano, G. (2009). Multimedia learning and working memory capacity. In R. Zheng (Ed.), *Cognitive effects of multimedia learning* (pp. 17–33). New York: Information Science References.

Driscoll, M. P. (2000). *Psychology of learning for instruction* (2nd ed.). Boston, MA: Allyn & Bacon.

Eveland, W. P., Cortese, J., Park, H., & Dunwoody, S. (2004). How Web site organization influences free recall, factual knowledge, and knowledge structure density. *Human Communication Research, 30*(2), 208–233.

Eveland, W. P., & Dunwoody, S. (2001). User control and structural isomorphism or disorientation and cognitive load? *Communication Research, 28*(1), 48-78.

Federico, P.-A. (1999). Hypermedia environments and adaptive instruction. *Computers in Human Behavior, 15*(6), 653–692.

Flavell, J. H. (1977). *Cognitive development.* Englewood Cliffs, NJ: Prentice-Hall.

Fleming, M. (1977). On pictures in educational research. *Instructional Science, 8*, 235–251.

Furnborough, C., & Truman, M. (2009). Adult beginner distance language learner perceptions and use of assignment feedback. *Distance Education, 30*(3), 399–418.

Gagne, R. (1984). *The conditions of learning and theory of instruction* (4th ed.). New York : Holt, Rinehart and Winston.

Gerjets, P., & Scheiter, K. (2003). Goal configurations and processing strategies as moderators between instructional design and cognitive load: Evidence from hypertext-based instruction. *Educational Psychologist, 38*(1), 33–41.

Gerjets, P., Scheiter, K., & Catrambone, R. (2004). Designing instructional examples to reduce intrinsic cognitive load: Molar versus modular presentation of solution procedures. *Instructional Science, 32*(1), 33–58.

Hannafin, M. J., Hannafin, K. M., Land, S., & Oliver, K. (1997). Grounded practice in the design of learning systems. *Educational Technology Research and Development, 45*(3), 101–117.

Hannafin, M. J., & Hill, J. R. (2007). Epistemology and the design of learning environments. In R. Reiser & J. Dempsey (Eds.), *Trends and issues in instructional design and technology* (2nd ed.). Upper Saddle River, NJ: Merrill/Prentice-Hall.

Hannafin, M. J., Hill, J., & Glazer, E. (2011). Designing grounded learning environments: Linking epistemology, pedagogy, and design practice. In G. Anglin (Ed.), *Instructional technology: Past, present, and future* (3rd ed., pp. 179–189). Santa Barbara, CA: Libraries Unlimited.

Hannafin, M. J., West, R., & Shepherd, C. (2009). The cognitive demands of student-centered, web-based multimedia: Current and emerging perspectives. In R. Zheng (Ed.), *Cognitive effects of multimedia learning* (pp. 194–216). New York: Information Science References.

Hee Jun, C., & Johnson, S. D. (2005). The effect of context-based video instruction on learning and motivation in online courses. *American Journal of Distance Education, 19*(4), 215–227.

Hill, J. R., & Hannafin, M. J. (1997). Cognitive strategies and learning from the World Wide Web. *Educational Technology Research and Development, 45*(4), 37–64.

Hsinyi, P., Chin-Chung, T., & Ying-Tien, W. (2006). University students' self-efficacy and their attitudes toward the Internet: The role of students' perceptions of the Internet. *Educational Studies, 32*(1), 73–86.

Huang, W-H. (2011). Evaluate learners' motivational and cognitive processing in an online game-based learning environment. *Computers in Human Behavior, 27*(2), 694–704.

Huett, J. B., Kalinowski, K. E., Moller, L., & Huett, K. C. (2008). Improving the motivation and retention of online students though the use of ARCS-based emails. *American Journal of Distance Education, 22*, 159–176. doi:10.1080/08923640802224451

Jones, Q., Ravid, G., & Rafaeli, S. (2004). Information overload and the message dynamics of online interaction spaces: A theoretical model and empirical exploration. *Information Systems Research, 15*(2), 194–210.

Kalyuga, S., Chandler, P., & Sweller, J. (1999). Managing split-attention and redundancy in multimedia instruction. *Applied Cognitive Psychology, 13*, 351–371.

Kaufman, D. F. (2004). Self-regulated learning in web-based environments: Instructional tools designed to facilitate cognitive strategy use, metacognitive processing, and motivational beliefs. *Journal of Educational Computing Research. 30*(1 & 2), 139–161.

Kim, H., & Hannafin, M. J. (2008). Grounded design and Web-enhanced, case-based reasoning. *Educational Technology Research and Development, 56,* 161–179.

Kim, H., & Hannafin, M. J. (2009). Web-enhanced case-based activity in teacher education: A case study. *Instructional Science, 37*, 151–170.

Koenig, A., & Atkinson, R. (2009). Using narrative and game schema acquisition techniques to support learning from educational games. In R. Zheng (Ed.), *Cognitive effects of multimedia learning* (pp. 312–339). New York: Information Science References.

Land, S. M., & Greene, B. A. (2000). Project-based learning with the World Wide Web: A qualitative study of resource integration. *Educational Technology Research and Development, 48*(1), 45–67.

Laszlo, F., Jr., & Kupritz, V. W. (2003). The identification of online learning motives in use by undergraduate students. *Delta Pi Epsilon Journal, 45*(1), 63–72.

Lim, D. H., & Kim, H. (2003). Motivation and learner characteristics affecting online learning and learning application. *Journal of Educational Technology Systems, 31*(4), 423–439.

Low, R., Jin, P., & Sweller, J. (2009) Cognitive architecture and instructional design in a multimedia context. In R. Zheng (Ed.), *Cognitive effects of multimedia learning* (pp. 1–16). New York: Information Science References.

Massaro, D., & Cowan, N. (1993). Information Processing Models: Microscopes of the Mind. *Annual Review of Psychology, 44*, 383–425.

Mayer-Kress, G., & Barczys, C. (1995). The global brain as an emergent structure from the worldwide computing network, and its implications for modeling. *The Information Society, 11*(1), 1–27.

McQuaid, J. W. (2010). Using cognitive load to evaluate participation and design of an asynchronous course. *American Journal of Distance Education, 24*, 177–194. doi:10.1080/08923647.2010.519949

Mei-Mei, C. (2005). Applying self-regulated learning strategies in a Web-based instruction: An investigation of motivation perception. *Computer Assisted Language Learning, 18*(3), 217–230.

Ng, C.C. (2008). Multiple-goal learners and their differential patterns of learning. *Educational Psychology, 28*(4), 439–456.

Niederhauser, D. S., Reynolds, R. E., Salmen, D. J., & Skolmoski, P. (2000). The influence of cognitive load on learning from hypertext. *Journal of Educational Computing Research, 23*(3), 237–255.

Norman, D. (1982). *Learning and memory.* San Francisco: W.H. Freeman & Co.

Oliver, K., & Hannafin, M. J. (2001). Developing and refining mental models in open-ended learning environments: A case study. *Educational Technology Research and Development, 49*(4), 5–33.

Oliver, K., & Hannafin, M. J. (2000). Student management of Web-based hypermedia resources during open-ended problem solving. *Journal of Educational Research, 94*(2), 75–92.

Paas, F. G. W. C. (1992). Training strategies for attaining transfer of problem-solving skill in statistics: A cognitive-load approach. *Journal of Educational Psychology. 84*(4), 429–434.

Paas, F., Tuovinen, J. E., Tabber, H., & Van Gerven, P. W. M. (2003). Cognitive load measurement as a means to advance cognitive load theory. *Educational Psychologist, 38*(1), 63–71.

Paas, F. G. W. C., & van Merrienboer, J. J. G. (1994). Variability of worked examples and transfer of geometrical problem-solving skills: A cognitive-load approach. *Journal of Educational Psychology, 86*, 122–133.

Paivio, A (1971). Imagery and verbal processes. New York: Holt, Rinehart, & Winston.

Pimentel, E. P., & Omar, N. (2008). Formative assessment in distance learning education with cognitive and metacognitive measurements. *International Journal of Information and Communication Technology Education, 4*(3), 39–58.

Pollock, E., Chandler, P., & Sweller, J. (2002). Assimilating complex information. *Learning and Instruction, 12*(1), 61–86.

Pressley, M. (1977). Imagery and children's learning—putting the picture in developmental perspective. *Review of Educational Research, 47*, 582–622.

Reed, S. K., & Bolstad, C. A. (1991). Use of examples and procedures in problem solving. *Journal of Experimental Psychology: Learning, Memory, and Cognition. 17*(4), 753–766.

Rieber, L. (2009). Supporting discovery-based learning within simulations. In R. Zheng (Ed.), *Cognitive effects of multimedia learning* (pp. 217–236). New York: Information Science References.

Renkl, A., & Atkinson, R. K. (2003). Structuring the transition from example study to problem solving in cognitive skill acquisition: A cognitive load perspective. *Educational Psychologist, 38*(1), 15–22.

Renkl, A., Atkinson, R. K., & Grosse, C. S. (2004). How fading worked solution steps works: A cognitive load perspective. *Instructional Science, 32*(1), 59–82.

Renkl, A., Stark, R., Gruber, H., & Mandl, H. (1998). Learning from worked-out examples: The effects of example variability and elicited self-explanations. *Contemporary Educational Psychology, 23*, 90–108.

Rummelhart, D., & Ortony, A. (1977). The representation of knowledge in memory. In R.C. Anderson, R.J. Spiro & W.E. Montague (Eds.), *Schooling and the acquisition of knowledge* (pp. 99–135). Hillsdale, NJ: Erlbaum.

Salmon, G. K. (2004). E-moderating: the key to teaching and learning online. Londonk: Routledge Falmer.

Salmon, G., Nie, M., & Edirishingha, P. (2010). Developing a five-stage model of learning in Second Life. *Educational Research, 52*(2), 169–182.

Schmeeckle, J. M. (2003). Online training: An evaluation of the effectiveness and efficiency of training law enforcement personnel over the Internet. *Journal of Science Education & Technology, 12*(3), 205–260.

Schraw, G., & Dennison, R. S. (1994). Assessing metacognition. *Contemporary Educational Psychology, 19*, 460–475.

Schrum, L., Burbank, M. D., Engle, J., Chambers, J. A., & Glassett, K. F. (2005). Post-secondary educators' professional development: Investigation of an online approach to enhancing teaching and learning. *Internet & Higher Education, 8*(4), 279–289.

Schunk, D. H. (1990). Goal setting and self-efficacy during self-regulated learning. *Educational Psychologist, 25*,71–86.

Schwartz, N. H., Anderson, C., Hong, N., Howard, B., & McGee, S. (2004). The influence of metacognitive skills on learners' memory information in a hypermedia environment. *Journal of Educational Computing Research, 31*, 77–93.

Sharma, P., & Hannafin, M. J. (2004). Scaffolding critical thinking in an online course: An exploratory study. *Journal of Educational Computing Research, 31*(2), 181–208.

Sharma, P., & Hannafin, M. J. (2005). Learner perceptions of scaffolding in supporting critical thinking. *Journal of Computing in Higher Education, 17*(1), 17–42.

Sharma, P., & Hannafin, M. J. (2007). Scaffolding in technology-enhanced learning environments. *Interactive Learning Environments, 15*(1), 27–46.

Smidt, E., & Heigelheimer, V. (2004). Effects of online academic lectures on ESL listening comprehension, incidental vocabulary acquisition, and strategy use. *Computer Assisted Language Learning, 17*(5), 517–556.

Song, L. (2005). *Adult learners' self-directed learning in online environments: Process, personal attribute, and context* (Unpublished doctoral dissertation). The University of Georgia, Athens.

Song, L., Singleton, E. S., Hill, J. R., & Koh, M. H. (2004). Improving online learning: Student perceptions of useful and challenging characteristics. *Internet & Higher Education, 7*(1), 59–70.

Sweller, J. (1988). Cognitive load during problem solving. *Cognitive Science, 12*, 257–285.

Tobias, S. (1994). Interest, prior knowledge, and learning. *Review of Educational Research, 64*(1), 37–54

Tsai, M.-J. (2007, July). *A pilot study of the development of the Online Learning Strategies Scale (OLSS).* Paper presented at the ICALT2007 conference, Niigata, Japan.

Tsai, M-J. (2009). The model of strategic e-learning: Understanding and evaluating student e-learning from metacognitive perspectives. *Educational Technology and Society, 12*(1), 34–48.

van Merrienboer, J. J. G., Schuurman, J. G., de Croock, M. B. M., & Paas, F. G. W. C. (2002). Redirecting learners' attention during training: Effects on cognitive load, transfer test performance and training efficiency. *Learning and Instruction, 12*(1), 11–37.

van Merrienboer, J. J. G., & Ayres, P. (2005). Research on cognitive load theory and its design implications for E-Learning. *Educational Technology Research & Development, 53*(3), 5–13.

van Merrienboer, J., Sweller, J., & Paas, F. (1998). Cognitive architecture and instructional design. *Educational Psychology Review, 10*(3), 251–296

Vygotsky, L. S. (1978). *Mind in society.* Cambridge, MA: Harvard University Press.

Whipp, J. L., & Chiarelli, S. (2004). Self-regulation in a web-based course: A case study. *Educational Technology Research and Development, 52*(4), 5–22.

Winn, W. (2004). Cognitive perspective in psychology. In D. Jonassen (Ed.), *Handbook of research on educational communications and technology* (2nd ed.). Mahwah, NJ: Erlbaum.

Wood, D., Bruner, J. S., & Ross, G. (1976). The role of tutoring in problem solving. *Journal of Psychology and Psychiatry. 17*(2), 89–100.

Workman, M. (2004). Performance and perceived effectiveness in computer-based and computer-aided education: Do cognitive styles make a difference? *Computers in Human Behavior, 20*(4), 517.

Yeh, S.-W., & Lo, J.-J. (2005). Assessing metacognitive knowledge in web-based CALL: a neural network approach. *Computers & Education, 44*(2), 97–113.

Zheng, R. Z., Flygare, J. A., & Dahl, L. B. (2009). Style matching or ability building? An empirical study on FD learners' learning in well-structured and ill-structured asynchronous online learning environments. *Journal of Educational Computing Research, 41*(2), 195–226.

Zion, M., Michalsky, T., & Mevarech, Z. (2005). The effects of metacognitive instruction embedded within an asynchronous learning network on scientific inquiry skills. *International Journal of Science Education, 27*(8), 957–983.

Zumbach, J., Reimann, P., & Koch, S. C. (2006). Monitoring students' collaboration in computer-mediated collaborative problem-solving: Applied feedback approaches. *Journal of Educational Computing Research, 35*(4), 399–424.

9

SATISFACTION WITH DISTANCE EDUCATION

MIKE ALLEN, KIKUKO OMORI, NANCY BURRELL, EDWARD MABRY, AND ERIK TIMMERMAN

Estimates suggest that upwards of 20% of all undergraduate students have enrolled in a distance education course (U.S. Department of Education, 2011). Clearly, the distance learning (DL) format, which we define as instruction in which there is no expectation for the physical copresence of the learner and instructor, is popular when students to register for courses. What is less clear is the degree to which these courses satisfy the expectations held by the students enrolling in them. To address this issue, the present chapter focuses on student satisfaction with distance education and the implications of various technological applications.

Student satisfaction constitutes an evaluation by students about the quality of the education experience. The issues of student evaluation of the quality of instruction has received much attention from scholars over the years (see meta-analyses, Allen, 1996; Feldman, 1979, 1983, 1984, 1986, 1987). The growing use of new technological formats for implementing distance learning constitutes an ongoing source of concern as technology evolves and the delivery of DL changes. A comparison between the level of satisfaction students report when using distance learning to what is normally experienced in face to face (f2f) formats is essential, but the question is now complicated by the need to compare differing formats and methods of DL instruction. The very evolution of technology means that improves in DL must be compared now to other forms of DL as well as f2f formats for education.

The profound impact that technological innovations are having in all facets of education focuses attention on assessing the changing practices of instruction. Understanding the impact of technologically driven differences between traditional classrooms and DL contexts is clearly appropriate (Althaus, 1997; Greene & Meek, 1998; McHenry & Bozik, 1995; Verduin & Clark, 1991; Whittington, 1987). Phipps and Merisotis (1999) as well as Traphagen et al. (2010) have concluded that current research, while rapidly accumulating, generally lacks systematic comparisons of factors that differentiate traditional classroom and distance learning outcomes. This sentiment is present in the continued calls for more research on the consequences of mediated communication technologies in instructional settings (Institute for Higher Education Policy, 2000; Kuehn, 1994;

143

Traphagen et al., 2010). In addition, the construction of Second Life and other forms of avatars or social presence complicates the notion of classroom and presence (Traphagen et al., 2010). The more fundamental problem is that such distinctions rapidly provide little distinction when the "traditional" classroom can incorporate technological applications that reduce the distinction between a DL and f2f classroom experience.

This chapter does not consider the issues of technology used in the f2f classroom or computer assisted instruction (for a meta-analytic review see Timmerman & Kruepke, 2006a, 2006b). Blends of f2f and distance learning in "hybrid" formats are possible. The net result is that distance learning, in a practical sense, may only be used for part of an entire course or the use of technology as a supplement to what might be called a "normal" f2f classroom. The line distinguishing the use of technology for DL separate from f2f applications continues to blur and erode as the use of technology is blended with f2f instructional settings.

The available meta-analyses reviewed in this chapter do not include "blended" courses that combine f2f and DL approaches. Current reviews only examine studies comparing levels of student satisfaction in a DL course to students in a f2f format. This limitation provides for a fruitful future area of investigation beyond the scope of this chapter, particularly as the number of alternative institutional formats expands.

One aspect of a DL course delivered in an online format is the question of a student's ability to participate when compared to a f2f course. A part of the attractiveness of a DL format for students is the ability to participate meaningfully in a class discussion. Consider that a f2f course of 50 minutes with 25 students provides an average participation of 2 minutes per student per session. The f2f format means that many students will not even get an opportunity to participate and that the total length of participation remains limited. This is contrasted with a DL format using the typical discussion posting provides an unlimited potential for interaction, and threading the discussion means that many discussions can simultaneously take place on divergent topics. However, an online DL format provides a means for discussions among students with more extensive possibilities (however, if the DL format is synchronous the same limitations would exist as in a f2f classroom). This means that students can think, edit, research, and post on a topic, even a couple of days after the original post. Unlike the dynamics of a temporal f2f discussion, hesitation or pondering is not penalized. A topic shift does not make it necessary for the student to go back to a previous oral statement in the f2f setting but the DL setting is not limited by the same temporal dynamic. The change in format means that students can feel more satisfied and able to participate meaningfully in a discussion. A part of the reason for some students preferring DL formats is related to that ability to participate in the discussions that continue.

Issues expressed in Tinto's (1975, 1982, 2004) model of student satisfaction predict that the level of satisfaction with the institution reflects largely the students' feeling of connectedness to the university. Serious questions are raised about maintaining this feeling when the communication becomes mediated (Sweet, 1986). The importance of discussion or other participatory practices may increase the sense of connection to the material, the course, and the institution in general. A central question is whether the students in a DL environment feel "connected" to the learning experience. The requirement and impact of the instructional immediacy requires consideration (Allen, Witt, & Wheeless, 2006; Hackman & Walker, 1990a, 1990b; Walker & Hackman, 1992, Witt, Wheeless, & Allen, 2004).

Shin's research (2003) on transactional presence indicates that both achievement and satisfaction for DL learners is associated with the sense of the availability and connectedness of a student with peers, the instructor, and institution. Research examining online teaching (Bozkaya & Aydin, 2007; Chang & Smith, 2008) indicates that the perception of the social presence of the instructor through immediacy behaviors contributes to increases in satisfaction with the learning experience (see Garrison & Akyol, Chapter 7, this volume, for a more extensive review). The research indicates that instructors can generate an environment that creates a transactional presence with a feeling of participation in the course and interaction with other students and the instructor. The "connectedness" of the student to the course creates a virtual presence in an ongoing active dialog or interaction viewed as participatory, encouraging, and supportive.

USING META-ANALYSIS TO UNDERSTAND THE DL SATISFACTION LITERATURE

Meta-analysis provides a means of synthesizing vast amounts of literature using quantitative methods. Meta-analysis represents a method of quantitatively synthesizing results across a number of studies. The goal is to provide an average estimate across the data combined over a set of studies. What the average permits is an understanding of what the entire body of literature provides for the estimation of any parameter. What meta-analysis provides is a means of literature synthesis that is more systematic, comprehensive, and accurate than more traditional narrative reviews. Essentially, rather than reviewing the more than 100 empirical investigations of student satisfaction individually, meta-analysis permits summarization to represent the sample of studies more systematically. Shachar (2008) argues that traditional narrative reviews fail to systematically handle issues in empirical literature and concludes that meta-analysis should be the preferred method for assessment of distance learning issues and calls for the development of a common database that researchers could use to analyze for useful conclusions.

The reason for this improved accuracy is a reduction in sampling error (combining sample sizes reduces the confidence interval), corrections for sources of bias and error (regression to the mean, attenuated measurement, dichotomization of continuous variables, restriction in range, halo effects, construct validity, etc.) as well as the evaluation of potential moderator variables (Hunter & Schmidt, 2004).

A series of meta-analyses exist that consider DL outcomes (Allen et al., 2002; Allen, Timmerman, Bourhis, Mabry, & Burrell, 2002; Bernard et al., 2004; Machtmes & Asher, 2000; Williams, 2006). These reports consider the issues of DL student satisfaction compared with traditional f2f instruction, student performance comparing DL to f2f instruction, and finally the relationship of learning styles of a student to the reported level of satisfaction with DL. Various compilations of existing literature served as a place to collect information for these reports (Russell, 1999; Stickell, 1963). The results from the various meta-analyses will report three basic statistical properties: (a) average effect measured in the metric of a correlation-positive correlation favors DL compared to f2f, (b) the number of studies or investigations contributing to the estimate or k, and (c) the combined total sample size used to make the estimate or N. The larger the number of studies and sample size the less sampling error in the estimate of the population parameter.

RESULTS CONSIDERING STUDENT SATISFACTION

The overall analysis from Allen, Bourhis, et al. (2002) demonstrates that students only have a slight preference for a live course when compared to distance learning environments (*average r* = -.031, *k* = 25, *N* = 4702), replicated by Bernard et al. (2004) (*average r* = -.045, *k* = 154, *N* = 21,047). The two meta-analyses essentially reach identical conclusions about the comparison of satisfaction between f2f and DL classrooms, that students exhibit slightly higher levels of satisfaction with a f2f environment.

One study (Köymen, 1992) functions as an outlier in Allen, Bourhis, et al. (2002) where the effect favoring DL was large (r = -.239) (Bernard et al., 2004 did not perform an outlier analysis so no comparison between meta-analyses is possible). Köymen reports that the university used overcrowded classrooms with poor lighting and inadequate heating and/or cooling. Students preferred DL because the quality of the instructional environment was viewed as a superior experience to live, overcrowded, and unpleasant classrooms. Köymen illustrates that while students do indicate a small preference for the live classroom, that preference can be mitigated or even reversed if the live environment is less than optimal (stuffy, crowded, lacks or has poor technology). The findings should therefore not be interpreted as a blanket statement of preference for one setting over another and indicate a general sense of preference that is subject to changes in circumstances. The research findings may change as technology improves and students of the current generation become increasingly focused on using technology like smart phones, ipads, and social media, shifting away from more traditional f2f methods of social interaction.

Another consideration in pedagogical design is the selection of the channels of communication (video, audio, and written). The structuring of our understanding of the relationships among the channels is that video messages include audio and written communication and that audio messages include written communication. The Allen, Bourhis, et al. (2002) meta-analysis (Bernard et al., 2004, do not report this analysis) examined three distinct methods of delivery: (a) video, (b) audio, and (c) written. However, there were not enough studies using strictly audio communication to form a separate group. This comparison was restricted to written and video channels. The comparison of f2f and DL courses using video channel only results in a small correlation favoring the DL course (*average r* = .006, *k* = 23, *N* = 4,277). The results indicate no difference between video DL and f2f courses in terms of student satisfaction. When comparing courses conducted entirely using a written channel, f2f courses demonstrate higher levels of satisfaction (*average r* = -.247, *k* = 4, *N* = 255). Not surprisingly, the addition of sensory information slightly increases the level of satisfaction reported. Students demonstrate a higher level of preference for video DL courses versus written courses compared to a f2f version of the same course. This finding provides support for those arguing that the level of sensory input is related to the level of student satisfaction with a particular course format.

One feature of DL courses is the degree to which interaction with the instructor is possible. Interaction is defined by whether or not synchronous message transmission between instructor and student or student to student is expected. For example, during a live broadcast, a two-way audio/visual signal, telephone, or written interactive system may be employed. One question is whether employing and incorporating such synchronous feedback improves satisfaction with the course expressed by the student

(Fulford & Zhang, 1993). The research must address whether the inclusion of some form of interaction provides a social as opposed to a physical presence that creates a better relationship between student and instructor (Gunawardena & Zittle, 1997). Obviously, the requirement of simultaneous communication would reduce the potential flexibility of a DL format when compared with something like a videotaped, correspondence, or some formats for online instruction. There were only enough studies to conduct this examination using courses with a combination of video and audio channels. The Allen, Bourhis, et al. (2002) meta-analysis divided the studies into three groups: (a) full and live interaction, where the students and instructor could communicate immediately and simultaneously; (b) limited interaction, where students and instructors could communicate either by a restricted means (telephone or computer) or was limited to a few times; and (c) where no direct interaction was provided for the course.

The expectation would be that the most satisfying experience would be that with full interaction, followed by the limited interaction, and then no interaction conditions. Contrary to expectations, there exists a slight trend indicating a greater difference between f2f and DL courses based on channel and availability of information.

The fully interactive audio/visual course had the largest contrast effect favoring f2f (*average r* = -.078, *k* = 12, *N* = 2,476), followed by the limited interaction format (*average r* = -.049, *k* = 3, *N* = 421) and then the no-interaction courses favors DL (*average r* = .029, *k* = 5, *N* = 674). This trend of effects indicates is that the addition of information levels in the DL format led more favorable satisfaction for the f2f version of the course.

The results reported by Bernard et al. (2004) provide a comparison for synchronous and asynchronous formats. The results reported by the authors replicate the earlier Allen, Bourhis, et al. (2002) findings. Synchronous format DL courses have a correlation favoring the f2f format (*average r* = -.092, *k* = 83, *N* = 9,483). However, comparing f2f to a DL course employing an asynchronous format reports the same level of satisfaction (*average r* = -.002, *k* = 71, *N* = 11,624). This indicates the analyses reported by Allen, Bourhis, et al. (2002) and Bernard et al. (2004) are in agreement.

One possible explanation lies in the relatively primitive technological systems at the time of the studies. Many studies using multi-channel instructional methods and settings used delivery systems that required the cobbling together of various means of communication that were not integrated. New distance learning technologies permit and require a lot more potential for interaction. The implication of new technology is to entirely rethink the approach to education and a new generation of research is required to consider evolving technology. For example, Yamada (2009) believes that the loss of social presence in computer-mediated communication reduces educational effectiveness. However, this potential loss is not inevitable; Johnson (2008) points out that a central conclusion of the Bernard et al. (2004) meta-analysis is that the quality of the instruction provided, not the nature of the technology determines the outcome. This view provides a need to consider how to evaluate the quality or qualities of the educational approach of a particular course in how the technology has been utilized.

Another aspect of the issue is the relationship of learning style to student satisfaction in the context of DL (the results of a meta-analysis reported in Allen, Timmerman, et al. (2002). The critical question is whether the level of satisfaction experience in a DL or f2f course is a consequence of student learning style. The findings indicate that students with a preference for social learning (learning with and in the presence of others) demonstrate greater satisfaction for f2f instruction, *average r* = -.148, *k* = 6, *N* = 1,166.

Similarly, results demonstrate that students preferring the use of technology to learn are more satisfied with distance learning situations, *average r* = .221, *k* = 5, *N* = 872. This finding is not surprising since a preference for technology should be associated with the satisfaction with a comparable educational format. Learner autonomy, while not directly explored, should generate similar outcomes in predicting the success for a DL environment where a student that requires more autonomy to learn can find the environment more suited to that style of learning. What this may indicate is a greater need to match a student's learning style with the means of instruction. For some students, a more traditional f2f instruction would be preferred to maximize both satisfaction and achievement where as many students may maximize educational effectiveness using a DL format, not to mention possible combinations of various approaches. This may indicate that the educational system should perhaps be more flexible in the approach to educational delivery to maximize the best possible outcome for the student.

SATISFACTION WITH CHANGING COMMUNICATION TECHNOLOGIES

Besides the issue of student satisfaction, an equally pressing question is whether *instructors* are relatively satisfied with the experiences in distance education (Whittington, 1987). In an observation of an interactive television distance education class, McHenry and Bozik (1995) noted substantial variability in classroom climates which evolved at different instructional sites. However, the variability did not appear to undermine students' relatively positive orientation toward the class. Thus, we must delve more deeply into the question of how students perceive the experience of distance education.

In addition to perceptions of technologies, various human factors (e.g., personality, attitudes, skill) emerge to influence user reactions to communication technologies in distance education. Early research on computer-mediated communication conferencing systems showed that user attitudes toward the technology, prior use experience, and skill positively affected user satisfaction with participating in computer conferencing (Kerr & Hiltz, 1982). Application of similar technologies to the university classroom (creating the so-called *virtual classroom*), with more experienced and extensively oriented students, produced strong relationships between evaluation attributes about the experience and learning outcomes (Hiltz, 1986). User experience played a similar role in Althaus's (1997) study of students involved in online electronic mail discussion groups used in supporting traditional classroom instruction. Students with more computer experience were more likely to use the online discussion groups and perceive them as beneficial. Cody, Dunn, Hoppin, and Wendt (1999) reported a similar connection between the extent of mentoring experiences used in training and subsequent use of the Internet in a group of elderly adult learners. Scott and Rockwell (1997) noted opposite trends for self-reported likelihood of use of new communication technologies and both computer apprehension and communication-bound apprehension. Higher scores on the anxiety measures were negatively correlated with technology usage preferences. A decade later, Traphagen, et al. (2010) find similar results when using a text-chat learning environment without visuals (TeachNet) for a course. The model developed by Traphagen et al. points out that the first critical factor for educational computer-mediated communication is consideration of the tool used. Familiarity with the tool or approach increases engagement and diminishes resistance. The other critical factors involve how the educational opportunity will permit an instructor to demonstrate presence (social and teaching) to accomplish the tasks and facilitate group cohesion.

Clearly, both user and technological efficacy are involved in the success of new communication technologies when they are applied in learning contexts. A critical question is whether DL opportunities can provide a consistent level of satisfaction for students. One theoretical approach to the issues surrounding the diverse set of communication channels that comprise communication technologies (e.g., electronic mail, audio, interactive video) is the perceived message *richness* (complexity of message stimuli) contained in a mode of communication that delivers an intact message.

Media richness theorists (Daft & Lengel, 1986; Trevino, Daft, & Lengel, 1990) sought to explain the effectiveness and desire to communicate using particular channels on the basis of a match between the features of a medium and the complexity of the instructional message. Media richness theory has been valuable in explaining the interplay between mediated messages and distance education effects (Timmerman & Kreupke, 2006a). The application to computer-mediated-communication (CMC) indicates some issues deserving consideration in the context of DL. Essentially, persons will choose media to reflect the various needs for types and amount of information. Media lacking that information may be evaluated as unsuitable or undesirable. For the practice of DL, the chosen means of delivery of materials should relate to the level of satisfaction with the experience in the course. One way to express this in the educational environment is the issues of transactional or social presence when using a particular technology to communicate.

Many satisfaction issues operate before student enrolls for a particular type of course. For example, students with computer apprehension or the need to have an instructor physically present remain unlikely to enroll in a course taught entirely online. The impact of self-selection in the context of DL limits the amount of dissatisfaction by removing the persons most likely to have negative experiences with the course. Liu (2010) points out that ease of use for the technology plays a major factor in increasing student motivation for participation in a course. Any frustration or difficulty due to either lack of preparation, little prior experience, or poor instructions can reduce the desire of the student to participate and/or complete the course. This creates an interesting dilemma for instructors, using the most recent or advanced technological application only provides maximum benefits if the student population is capable of easily using the application. Brand new applications are likely to have bugs and students with little prior experience using, working against the supposed advantages of the technology.

Sherblom (2010) in a review of the computer-mediated classroom literature points out that the changing nature of society, with the incorporation of "social media" indicates a need to reconsider educational practices. Boase (2008) points out that persons now rely in their personal lives on a variety of technological means of communication to accomplish both social and employment tasks. The use of Facebook has gone from personal connections between individuals to use by corporations and organizations to build networks and distribute information to persons. But not all outcomes are considered beneficial, Rice and Markey (2009) in a review conclude that CMC experience can both be positive or negative for persons, echoing Lazzari's (2009) concluding that scholars remain divided about the impact of technological applications in education. The continued evolution of technology and the applications to education will increase this problem and provide difficulty in the evaluation of how such changes will impact on student satisfaction with DL courses.

Solving this challenge ultimately requires the development of a theoretical system to evaluate the connection between technology and student satisfaction. Understanding how the learning process is changed by evolving technology requires a generative model that permits predicting how changes in technology should be expected to impact student satisfaction. A theory that permits a dynamic understanding will provide prescriptions for the instructor about how to use the technology within a course format. Current attempts, like transactional presence (Shin, 2003), Sherblom's five factors (2010), or media richness (Timmerman & Kreupke, 2006b) provide potential templates to begin establishing such a framework. The goal should be the generation of a model that can understand how changes in applications of technology to DL teaching will impact on student satisfaction. Failure to generate such a model means that with each succeeding change in technology there would be a requirement to replicate the literature because the ability to predict the impact of such changes would not exist.

CONCLUSIONS

The essential conclusions of the current meta-analyses comparing DL and f2f instructional contexts is there exists little difference in outcomes when one considers levels of student satisfaction. The results associated with these meta-analyses demonstrate that the expectation that distance learning outcome differs from traditional education appears unwarranted. Two independent meta-analyses of the literature (Allen, Bourhis, et al., 2002; Bernard et al., 2004) report almost identical findings for the same literature. While the number of estimates exceeds 150 in the Bernard report and over 50 in Allen, additional work is warranted in understanding a number of issues addressed below.

Additional research continues to support the conclusion of the meta-analyses that distance education and f2f education produces similar satisfaction levels (e.g., Chang & Smith, 2008; Nora & Snyder, 2008–2009; Reeves & Osho, 2010). The new body of research requires a new meta-analysis designed to focus on comparing various technological applications rather than to traditional f2f classrooms. The problem is that various technologies possess both strengthens and weakness in the context of DL. Sherblom (2010) argues that five factors (medium, presence, interaction, identify, and relationship) moderate the relationship of the CMC classroom. An evaluation of each of the factors both with original research and using meta-analysis is warranted in determining the impact (potentially the conditional impact) on the satisfaction of students in that experience.

What is a bit surprising is that synchronous classrooms with simultaneous communication report less satisfaction than asynchronous approaches to DL. We believe that one possibility for this finding across the investigations involves expectations about communication. Technology is limited, uncertain, and sometimes difficult in a synchronous environment. The problem of failed expectations may result is slightly higher levels of frustration than that in a conventional f2f classroom. Bray, Aoki, and Dlugosh (2008) document that satisfaction is predicted by student perception that the technology is easy to use. The research results indicate the importance of making sure that DL applications are both easy to use and a complete set of instruction about the technology is provided. One forgets that in the f2f classroom many students are frustrated with the inability to participate in classroom discussion (due to time limits, the need for time to formulate and express a thought) and online discussion boards provide the ability to participate in a manner that can be reflective and prepared and has no limit on time or the desire of the instructor to "move on" to other matters.

The most interesting finding about student satisfaction is the association of learning styles with the method of instruction. Not surprisingly, results indicate students report higher levels of satisfaction when the preferred learning style matches the attributes of a pedagogical structure (Bray et al., 2008). DL provides the possibility of many different potential styles existing simultaneously in the same course to be pursued in whatever combination that a student finds most beneficial. The learning experienced by the student can, in many ways, be self-designed to increase the level of satisfaction with the method of instruction.

The same finding is true for measurements involving issues of performance (see Allen et al., 2002). Students perform better in educational environments where the structure of the instruction matches the preferred learning style (see Lee & Rha, 2009, for an example of how the structure of course impacts satisfaction/learning outcomes). This finding is important to both DL and f2f instructional contexts. The finding implies that instructional environments may require modifications to accommodate learning styles, and tracking students into DL contexts may be one effective way to accomplish this outcome.

The findings of the meta-analyses reviewed do not indicate a broad preference favoring either DL or f2f instruction. A more fundamental understanding of how students learn in general is required. There exists some evidence to argue for a kind of student-context match such that the learning style of the student should be matched to the appropriate educational format to maximize student satisfaction. Future research should target an understanding of why, on the surface, what would appear to be very different formats do not differ in student satisfaction.

The long-term implications of using DL education deserve consideration. Why do students stay in a program? Does DL instruction have higher levels of attrition (Fjort-fort, 1995, 1996)? Most educational programs are not simply a single course but require the completion of an entire degree program to be considered fully successful. Bernard et al. (2004), indicate only slightly higher levels of attrition in DL formats (*average r =* .028, $k = 103$, $N = 3,735,050$). When separated by whether the DL format was synchronous (*average r = −.003*, k = 17, $N = 3,604$) or asynchronous (*average r = .047*, $k = 53$, $N = 10,435$). This finding indicates that synchronous communication does slightly increase student retention, supporting the arguments about the impact of media richness. However, the differences are small and do not indicate a fundamental challenge to or preference for either format.

All the authors of this chapter continue to teach online courses in college. We find the process challenging, requiring constant updating and adaptation to a changing technological environment. We have been doing this for over a decade and find that the ability and willingness of the students to operate in this environment continues to improve. Continued changes in technology make operating at a distance easier and provide increasing flexibility in options. The next generation of instructors can begin to focus more on excellence in materials and content and less on instruction about how to use the technology or struggle to gain acceptance with students or administrators. When we first started teaching using DL, extensive efforts had to be made to "teach" students about technology and how to operate in a virtual environment. Current students have, in our view, reversed, to a large extent, this presumption, many current students prefer the DL format because the reliance on flexible technology matches the way they approach many tasks. Student satisfaction with technological means of accomplishing tasks has gone from the need from extensive institutional support for students and instructions to instead a pressure by students for faculty and institutions to provide more adaptive and powerful technological applications.

The next challenge will involve identifying those means most successful for instruction and training to implement those techniques. Distance learning offers a challenge to thinking about educational formats and resources. This challenge seeks to determine how best to incorporate new tools into the educational system. The problem of relying on a "one size fits all" philosophy for instruction may not be maximizing the potential of individual students. Instead, the need may exist for some diagnosis and matching of pedagogical formats to the ability of students to achieve maximum instructional benefits. This new orientation provides an opportunity for DL approaches to be enlisted in fulfilling educational missions. The admonition is that most effective educational practice is going to require a combination of both f2f and DL approaches to maximize the potential of every student in higher education.

REFERENCES

Allen, M. (1996). Research productivity and positive teaching evaluations: Examining the relationship using meta-analysis. *Journal of the Association for Communication Administration, 7,* 77–97.

Allen, M., Bourhis, J., Burrell, N., Mabry, E., Emmers-Sommer, T., Titsworth, S., … Wells, S. (2002). Comparing student satisfaction with distance education to traditional classrooms in higher education: A meta-analysis. *American Journal of Distance Education, 16*(2), 83–97. doi:10.1207/S15389286AJDE1602_3

Allen, M., Bourhis, J., Mabry, E., Burrell, N., & Timmerman, E. (2006). Comparing distance education to face-to-face methods of education. In B. Gayle, R. Preiss, N. Burrell, & M. Allen, M. (Eds.), *Classroom communication and instructional processes: Advances through meta-analysis* (pp. 229–244). Mahwah, NJ: Erlbaum.

Allen, M., Timmerman, E., Bourhis, J., Mabry, E., & Burrell, N. (2002, November). *Distance education: A meta-analysis of how learning styles influence outcomes.* Paper presented at the National Communication Association Convention, New Orleans, LA.

Allen, M., Witt, P., & Wheeless, L. (2006). The role of teacher immediacy as a motivational factor in student learning: Using meta-analysis to test a causal model. *Communication Education, 55,* 21–31. doi:10.1080/03634520500343368

Althaus, S. L. (1997). Computer-mediated communication in the university classroom: An experiment with on-line discussion. *Communication Education, 46,* 158–174. doi:10.1080/03634529709379088

Bernard, R. M., Abrami, P. C., Lou, Y., Borokhovski, E., Wade, A., Wozney, L., … Haung, B. (2004). How does distance education compare with classroom instruction? A meta-analysis of empirical literature. *Review of Educational Research, 74,* 379–439. doi:10.3102/00346543074003379

Boase, J. (2008). Personal networks and the personal communication system. *Information, Communication, & Society. 11,* 490–508. doi:10.1080/13691180801999001

Bozkaya, M., & Aydin, Î.E. (2007). The relationship between teaching immediacy behaviors and learners' perceptions of social presence and satisfaction in open and distance education: The case of Anadolu University Open Education faculty. *Turkish Online Journal of Educational Technology, 6*(4), Article 7.

Bray, E., Aoki, K., & Dlugosh, L. (2008). Predictors of learning satisfaction in Japanese online distance learners. *International Review of Research in Open and Distance Learning, 9*(3), 1–24.

Chang, S. H., & Smith, R. A. (2008). Effectiveness of personal interaction in a learner-centered paradigm of distance education class based on student satisfaction. *Journal of Research on Technology in Education, 40,* 407–426.

Cody, M. J., Dunn, D., Hoppin, S., & Wendt, P. (1999). Silver surfers: Training and evaluating internet use among older adult learners. *Communication Education, 48,* 269–286. doi:10.1080/03634529909379178

Daft, R. L., & Lengel, R. H. (1986). Organizational information requirements, media richness and structural design. *Management Science, 32,* 554-571.

Feldman, K. (1979). The significance of circumstances for college students' ratings of their teachers and courses. *Research in Higher Education, 10,* 49–172. doi:10.1007/BF00976227

Feldman, K. (1983). Seniority and experience of college teachers as related to the evaluations they receive form students. *Research in Higher Education, 18,* 3–124. doi:10.1007/BF00992080

Feldman, K. (1984). Class size and college students' evaluations of teachers and courses: A closer look. *Research in Higher Education, 21,* 45–116. doi:10.1007/BF00975035

Feldman, K. (1986). The perceived instructional effectiveness of college teachers as related to their personality and attitudinal characteristics: A review and synthesis. *Research in Higher Education, 24,* 139–213. doi:10.1007/BF00991885

Feldman, K. (1987). Research productivity and scholarly accomplishments of college teachers as related to their instructional effectiveness: A review and exploration. *Research in Higher Education, 26,* 227–298. doi:10.1007/BF00992241

Fjortoft, N. (1995, October). *Predicting persistence in distance learning programs.* Paper presented at the Mid-Western Educational Research Meeting, Chicago, IL. (ERIC ED 387 620)

Fjortoft, N. (1996). Persistence in a distance learning program: A case in pharmaceutical education. *American Journal of Distance Education, 10,* 39–48. doi:10.1080/08923649609526940

Fulford, C., & Zhang, S. (1993). Perceptions of interaction: A critical predictor in distance education. *American Journal of Distance Education, 7,* 8-21.

Greene, B. & Meek, A. (1998). *Distance education in higher education institutions: Incidence, audiences, and plans to expand* (Report no. NCES-98-132). Washington, D.C.: U.S. Government Printing Office.

Gunawardena, C., & Zittle, F. (1997). Social presence as a predictor of satisfaction within a computer-mediated conferencing environment. *American Journal of Distance Education, 11*(3), 8–26. doi:10.1080/08923649709526970

Hackman, M., & Walker, K. (1990a, April). The impact of system design and instructional style on student reactions to distance education. *Research in Distance Education, 37,* 7–9.

Hackman, M. Z. & Walker, K. B. (1990b). Instructional communication in the televised classroom: The effects of system design and teacher immediacy on student learning and satisfaction. *Communication Education, 39,* 196–206. doi:10.1080/03634529009378802

Hiltz, S. R. (1986). The "virtual classroom": Using computer-mediated communication for university teaching. *Journal of Communication, 36,* 95–104. doi:10.1111/j.1460-2466.1986.tb01427.x

Hunter, J. E., & Schmidt, F. L. (2004). *Methods of meta-analysis: Correcting for error and bias in research findings* (2nd ed.). Thousand Oaks, CA: Sage.

Institute for Higher Education Policy, (2000). *Quality on the line: Benchmarks for success in Internet-based distance education.* Washington, DC: Author.

Johnson, G. M. (2008). The effectiveness of distance education vs. classroom instruction: A summary of Bernard's meta-analysis with implications for practice. International *Journal of Instructional Media, 35*(2), 137–144.

Kerr, E. B., & Hiltz, S. R. (1982). *Computer-mediated communication systems.* New York: Academic Press.

Köymen, U. (1992). Comparisons of learning and study strategies of traditional and open-learning-system students in Turkey. *Distance Education, 13,* 108–117. doi:10.1080/0158791920130109

Kuehn, S. A. (1994). Computer-mediated communication in instructional settings: A research agenda. *Communication Education, 43,* 171–183. doi:10.1080/03634529409378974

Lazzari, M. (2009). Creative use of podcasting in higher education and its effect on competitive agency. *Computers & Education, 52,* 27–34. doi:10.1016/j.compedu.2008.06.002

Lee, H. J., & Rha, J. (2009). Influence of structure and interaction on student achievement and satisfaction in web-based distance learning. *Educational Technology & Society, 12*(4), 372–382.

Liu, X. (2010). Empirical testing of a theoretical extension of the technology acceptance model: An exploratory study of educational wikis. *Communication Education, 59,* 52–59. doi:10.1080/03634520903431745

Machtmes, K., & Asher, J. (2000). A meta-analysis of the effectiveness of telecourses in distance education. *American Journal of Distance Education, 14*(1), 27–46. doi:10.1080/08923640009527043

McHenry, L. & Bozik, M. (1995). Communicating at a distance: A study of interaction in a distance education classroom. *Communication Education, 44,* 362–371. doi:10.1080/03634529509379025

Nora, A., & Snyder, B. P. (2008–2009). Technology and higher education: The impact of E-learning approaches on student academic achievement, perceptions and persistence. *Journal of College Student Retention, 10,* 3–19. doi:10.2190/CS.10.1.b

Phillips, G., Santoro, G., & Kuehn, S. (1988). The use of computer-mediated communication in training students in group problem-solving and decision-making techniques. *American Journal of Distance Education, 2,* 38–51. doi:10.1080/08923648809526607

Phipps, R. A. & Merisotis, J. P. (1999). *What's the difference? A review of contemporary research on the effectiveness of distance learning in higher education.* Washington, DC: American Federation of Teachers and National Education Association.

Reeves, T. C., & Osho, G. S. (2010). The satisfaction of community college students regarding distance education versus traditional education. *National Forum of Applied Educational Research Journal, 23*(3), 1–13.

Rice, L., & Markey, P. M. (2009). The role of extraversion and neuroticism in influencing anxiety following computer-mediated interactions. *Personality and Individual Differences, 46,* 35–39. doi:10.1016/j.paid.2008.08.022

Russell, T. (1999). *The no significant difference phenomenon.* Raleigh: Instructional Telecommunications, North Carolina State University.

Shachar, M. (2008). Meta-analysis: The preferred method of choice for the assessment of distance learning quality factors. *International Review of Research in Open and Distance Learning, 9*(3), 1-17.

Scott, C. R., & Rockwell, S. C. (1997). The effects of communication, writing, and technology apprehension on likelihood to use new communication technologies. *Communication Education, 46,* 44–62. doi:10.1080/03634529709379072

Sherblom, J. C. (2010). The computer-mediated communication (CMC) classroom: A challenge of medium, presence, interaction, identity, and relationship. *Communication Education, 59,* 497–523. doi: 10.1080/03634523.2010.486440.

Shin, N. (2003). Transactional presence as a critical predictor of success in distance learning. *Distance Education, 2003, 24,* 69–86. doi: 10.1080/01579103200006634.

Stickell, D. (1963). *A critical review of the methodology and research comparing televised and face-to-face instruction* (Unpublished doctoral dissertation). Pennsylvania State University, State College.

Sweet, R. (1986). Student dropout in distance education: An application of Tinto's model. *Distance Education, 7,* 201–213. doi:10.1080/0158791860070204

Timmerman, C. E., & Kruepke, K. A. (2006a). Computer-assisted instruction, media richness, and college student performance. *Communication Education, 55,* 73–104. doi:10.1080/03634520500489666

Timmerman, C. E., & Kruepke, K. A. (2006b). Computer assisted instruction and student performance. In B. Gayle, R. Preiss, N. Burrell, & M. Allen, M. (Eds.), *Classroom communication and instructional practices: Advances through meta-analysis* (pp. 77–98). Mahwah, NJ: Erlbaum.

Tinto, V. (1982). Limits of theory and practice in student attrition. *Journal of Higher Education, 53,* 687–700. doi:10.2307/1981525

Tinto, V. (2004). *Student retention and graduation: Facing the truth, living with the consequences.* Retrieved January 15, 2006, from http://www.pellinstitute.org

Traphagan, T. W., Chiang, T. V., Chang, H. M., Wattanawaha, B., Lee, H., Mayrath, M.C., ... Resta, P. E. (2010). Cognitive, social and teaching presence in a virtual world and a text chat. *Computers and Education, 55,* 923–936. doi:10.1016/j.compedu.2010.04.003

Trevino, L. K., Daft, R. L., & Lengel, R. H. (1990). Understanding managers' media choices: A symbolic interactionist perspective. In C. Steinfield (Ed.), *Organizations and communication technology* (pp. 71–93). Newbury Park, CA: Sage.

U.S. Department of Education, National Center for Education Statistics. (2011). *The Condition of Education 2011*(NCES 2011-033), Indicator 43. Washington, DC: Author.

Verduin, J. R., & Clark, T. A. (1991). *Distance education: The foundations of effective practice.* San Francisco, CA: Jossey-Bass.

Walker, K., & Hackman, M. (1992). Multiple predictors of perceived learning and satisfaction: The importance of information transfer and non-verbal immediacy in the televised course. *Distance Education, 13,* 81–92. doi:10.1080/0158791920130107

Whittington, N. (1987). In instructional television educationally effective? A research review. *American Journal of Distance Education, 1,* 47–57. doi:10.1080/08923648709526572

Williams, S. L. (2006). The effectiveness of distance education in allied health science programs: A meta-analysis of outcomes. *American Journal of Distance Education, 20,* 127–141. doi:10.1207/s15389286ajde2003_2

Witt, P., Wheeless, L., & Allen, M. (2004). A meta-analytical review of the relationship between teacher immediacy and student learning. *Communication Monographs, 71,* 161–183.

Yamada, M. (2009). The role of social presence in learner-centered communicative language learning using synchronous computer-mediated communication. *Computers & Education, 52,* 820–833. doi:10.1016/j.compedu.2008.12.007

10

STUDENT PERSISTENCE—AND TEACHING STRATEGIES TO SUPPORT IT

TINA M. STAVREDES AND TIFFANY M. HERDER

Learners often choose online learning because they may select a school or program that fits their educational goals rather than choosing one based on the best options available in their geographic area. However, online learners must overcome many challenges to persist and successfully achieve their goals. Persistence refers to learners' actions to continue their education from the first year until degree completion. Evidence suggests that dropout rates among distance learners are higher than traditional, campus-based learners (Allen & Seaman, 2009). Therefore, it is critical to understand the factors that contribute to learners dropping out and to develop effective strategies to support learners persist in learning. A review of persistence models appropriate for the online learner population provides the foundation for understanding important academic factors that impact learner persistence. Then, we will consider how building a community of inquiry and providing appropriate scaffolding to support online learners can support them academically to achieve their educational goals.

PERSISTENCE MODELS

Persistence models provide valuable insight into important variables to consider when developing online courses. William Spady, Vincent Tinto, and Ernest Pascarella, are three prominent researchers who studied learner persistence and retention. Their models address the traditional student in a land-based institution. When studying persistence of non-traditional students who work full time, live away from campus, have families, and belong to social groups not associated with their college, the question arises whether persistence models such as Spady (1970), Tinto (1975), and Pascarella (1985) are true for non-traditional students. Bean and Metzner's (1985) persistence model and the Rovai (2003) model of persistence, on the other hand, specifically address distance learning students.

Bean and Metzner's Persistence Model

Bean and Metzner (1985) identified students being over the age of 24 as a common variable of learner attrition. These learners commonly work full time and have family responsibilities that prevent them from attending school full time, and these issues affect their ability to persist. They proposed a model grounded on Tinto's (1975) model of persistence and earlier psychological models to explain attrition of nontraditional students. Their model predicts student persistence. Factors that affect persistence include academic variables such as study habits and course availability and background including age, ethnicity, educational goals, and prior GPA. Environment variables include finances, hours of employment, family responsibilities, and outside encouragement. Finally, psychological variables such as stress, self-confidence, and motivation can impact learners' ability to successfully complete a program of study online.

Rovai Model of Persistence

Alfred Rovai (2003) evaluated several persistence models relevant to non-traditional learners and developed a composite model to explain persistence of online learners. His model includes learner characteristics and skills prior to admission and external and internal factors after admission.

He integrates Bean and Metzner's (1985) learner characteristics prior to admission including age, ethnicity, gender, intellectual development, academic performance, and preparation. He also includes skills distance learners require to successfully navigate the online environment including computer literacy, information literacy, time management, reading and writing skills, and online interaction skills. He argues that if learners lack these skills and do not overcome these deficiencies, it can lead to attrition.

Once learners begin a program of study, additional factors both external and internal to the institution affect learners' persistence. According to Rovai (2003), external factors include issues with finances, hours of employment, family responsibilities, the presence of outside encouragement, opportunity to transfer, and life crises such as sickness, divorce, and job loss. Internal factors include variables researched by Tinto (1975), Bean and Metzner (1985), Workman and Stenard (1996), and Kerka and Grow (1996, as cited in Rovai, 2003).

According to Tinto (1975), social and academic integration, goal commitment, institutional commitment, and the development of a learning community are internal institutional factors affecting persistence. Workman and Stenard (1996) found online needs include consistency and clarity of online programs, policies, and procedures, strong self-esteem, identifying with the institution and not feeling like an "outsider," developing interpersonal relationships with peers, faculty, and staff, and accessing academic support and services.

A predictive model to explain persistence is essential to understand how to support online learners. A key theme in the persistence literature is the need for learners to be able to integrate academically and socially and the greater the level of academic and social integration, the greater chance students will persist in a program of study. Developing presence online can provide a structure for social integration and cognitive scaffolding can support academic integration. These factors can provide important insight to begin to develop a model for predicting online learner success.

DEVELOPING PRESENCE IN THE ONLINE ENVIRONMENT

The development of presence in the online environment is essential for learning to occur and for learners to persist (Bean & Metzner, 1985; Rovai, 2003; Tinto, 1975; Workman & Stenard, 1996). Garrison, Anderson, and Archer's (2000) community of inquiry model provides a framework for integrating social, cognitive, and teaching presence to support learners' persistence online. Because you have already been introduced to the community of inquiry model, the following serves as a brief review. Social presence includes the affective dimension of feelings, beliefs, and values as well as the need for open communication and group cohesion. Cognitive presence supports the construction of meaning through sustained discourse and reflection. Teaching presence includes the design and organization of the online environment as well as the facilitation of discourse and direct instruction. The structure of the online learning environment should consider the interaction of social, cognitive, and teaching presence. These dimensions of presence can help us understand important factors to consider in the design, organization, and facilitation of an online course to increase the probability of learners persisting from course to course to complete a program of study.

Interaction is related to student perception of presence, which is a predictor of student satisfaction in computer-mediated environments (Picciano, 2002). Garrison and Cleveland-Innes (2004) found that interaction, both socially and cognitively, presented the greatest student adjustment challenge to online learning. Interestingly, their study established that peer interaction shaped social presence more heavily than instructor interaction. Teaching presence in the form of facilitation, however, was crucial to successful higher-order learning. Rovai (2002) found a positive relationship between learners' sense of community and cognitive learning. May (1993) elaborates and suggests simply increasing learner interaction is not enough. Developing quality interactions to create of sense of community to help learners achieve their educational goals must be the focus. Picciano (2002) also made a distinction between interaction and presence. He states that interaction does not necessarily mean a learner is engaged in inquiry and cognitively present.

Social Presence

Social presence establishes learners as individuals and, through the process of relationship building, allows learners to engage in a community of inquiry (Garrison et al., 2000). The more learners establish themselves with other learners and the instructor, the more trust they build. Trust helps learners feel comfortable with sharing their thoughts and ideas without the fear of criticism. As the level of interaction increases, a greater sense of community can occur where learners share their divergent thoughts and perspectives to construct knowledge and understanding.

Gunawardena and Zittle (1997) define social presence as the degree to which a learner is perceived as a real person. In their research, they found social presence to be a strong predictor of satisfaction in computer-mediated conferencing (CMC) environments.

An American Public University study used a community of inquiry survey with 28,877 students enrolled in bachelors or associates level courses. The study found that responses to the phrase "Online or web-based communication is an excellent medium for social interaction" accounted for over 18% of the variance associated with whether a student returned to study in the semester subsequent to completing the survey (Boston et al., 2009). In another study comparing the highest and lowest disenrollment quartiles of all courses at American Public University (Ice, Gibson, Boston, & Becher, 2011), teaching presence and cognitive presence were found to be significant predictors of student satisfaction in both quartiles. For the lowest disenrollment quartile, predictors included instructional design and organization for the teaching presence dimension and the initiation of the triggering event for the cognitive presence dimension. For the highest disenrollment quartile, the lack of follow-through in the facilitation of discourse and cognitive integration were found to be negative predictors of student satisfaction. The two studies together demonstrate the importance of all three types of presence.

Cognitive Presence

Cognitive presence is "the extent to which the participants in any particular configuration of a community of inquiry are able to construct meaning" (Garrison et al., 2000, p. 89). It is important to recognize that cognitive presence focuses on higher-order thinking processes as opposed to specific individual learning outcomes (Garrison, Anderson, & Archer, 2001). Critical thinking skills provide learners a solid foundation to engage in a community of inquiry and reason through concepts and ideas to construct knowledge.

Asynchronous discussion questions set the stage for developing and integrating the high level cognitive skills needed to develop critical inquiry. Garrison et al. (2001) propose a four-phase critical inquiry model, which includes a triggering event, exploration, integration, and resolution. Triggering events motivate learners by posing problems or asking questions to provide direction for and enhance discourse. Exploration allows learners to conduct research to solve or make sense of given problems. Integration occurs when learners solve problems and connect their ideas with the multiple perspectives and ideas of other learners. Finally, resolution allows learners to critically evaluate their solution to test its validity.

Bullen (1998) examined the degree to which online discussions facilitate knowledge building and critical thinking. His research found that course design and instructor interventions were critical factors in promoting critical thinking in online environments. According to Muilenburg and Berge (2000), instructor interventions should include the use of higher level questions as initial prompts for online discussions and formative feedback from the instructor. They recommend a wide range of question types including controversial questions, critical incidents, case studies, problems, and role-plays. They also recommend follow-up questions to stimulate learners' thinking and expose them to multiple perspectives to develop deeper thinking and understanding.

Wilson-Robbins (2006) recommends a model for critical thinking be defined and conceptualized at the beginning and intentionally promoted throughout a course to be effective. This includes incorporating the chosen model into instructional strategies and providing learners with opportunities to demonstrate their critical thinking skills. Yang, Newby, and Bill (2005) recommend the use of Socratic questioning to stimulate thinking to enhance critical thinking skills. Stavredes (2011) recommends using a scoring guide that incorporates the elements of the implemented critical thinking model in the grading criteria to provide alignment between the thinking process learners are expected to use during discourse and the methods of evaluation.

Chang (2002) found critical thinking can be promoted with authenticity, community, reflection, and multiple perspectives in the online environment. Authenticity is an indicator of a constructivist approach in the design of an online course. Community is developed through interaction and collaboration using discussion boards. Reflection supports learners' consideration of their learning processes and construction of thoughtful responses to discussions. Finally, multiple perspectives promote critical thinking by helping learners understand alternative views, previously held assumptions, and the interpretation of new information. Based on these four constructs, Chang concludes that the following conditions need to exist to promote critical thinking in the online environment: use of constructivist learning theory in the design of an online course, cooperative and collaborative learning opportunities, critical reflection activities, and opportunities to engage with and understand multiple perspectives.

Teaching Presence

Teaching presence is critical in facilitating interactions to help learners develop social presence and cognitive presence. The role of teaching presence includes designing the course to help students achieve stated learning outcomes. According to Anderson, Rourke, Garrison, and Archer (2001), it is the instructor's responsibility to facilitate effective learning with a clear purpose and focus on goals and outcomes. Garrison, Anderson, and Archer (2001) describe the essential responsibilities of the instructor— setting the curriculum, designing instructional methods, establishing time parameters, utilizing the medium effectively, and establishing netiquette. They identified six indicators for facilitating discourse—identifying areas of agreement and disagreement, seeking to reach consensus and understanding, encouraging, acknowledging, and reinforcing student contributions, setting the climate for learning, drawing in participants and prompting discussion, and assessing the efficacy of the process. Also, instructors should provide direct instruction, which includes presenting content and questions, focusing the discussion on specific issues, summarizing the discussion, confirming understanding, diagnosing misperceptions, injecting knowledge from diverse sources, and responding to technical concerns.

Shea, Li, and Pickett (2006) studied the relationship of teaching presence for developing a learning community in an online environment. Their survey instrument was devised to assess effective instructional design and organization, facilitation of productive discourse, and direct instruction as described in the community of inquiry model (Garrison et al., 2000). They found a significant link between learners' sense of learning community, effective instructional design, and the instructor use of directed facilitation.

Garrison and Cleveland-Innes (2004) focused on the nature of online interaction and found that course design and teaching approach influenced how students approached their study and whether learning occurred in a deep and meaningful manner. Teaching presence appears to contribute to the adoption of a deep approach to learning that interaction by itself does not promote.

Delotell, Millam, and Reinhardt (2010) discussed the relationship of deep learning to student retention. They concluded that the key to retaining students and achieving deep learning within the online environment is high student engagement, which is a product of instructional content and quality of social interactions. They proposed that discussion forums can be used effectively to drive engagement through the use of motivation strategies and setting the stage, which are elements of teaching presence as well as the use of problem and case-based learning, which is an element of cognitive presence.

A study on teaching presence by Shea, Fredericksen, Pickett, and Pelz (2003) and a follow-up study by Shea, Pickett, and Pelz (2003) correlated students' opinions on teaching presence with their reported satisfaction with their course and learning outcomes. The results demonstrate a strong correlation between the teaching presence of instructors, student satisfaction, and perceived learning.

It is clear from the literature that the development of presence in the online environment is essential for learning to occur and the lack of it can cause learners to become dissatisfied and eventually drop out. Cognitive presence, social presence, and teaching presence are critical building blocks to support online learners' engagement and achievement of their educational goals. The research indicates that interaction is related to students' perception of presence; however, simply increasing the amount of interaction in the course is not enough. The quality of the interaction to create a sense of community to help learners achieve their educational goals must be the focus along with cognitive presence to help learners construct meaning. In addition, teaching presence is a critical factor in learner satisfaction and deep learning. Focus must be paid to the design and organization of the learning environment to support deep learners including the use of instructional strategies to encourage thinking, exploration, reflection, and integration. Teaching presence should support learners in being able to connect with the course topics, find value in them and see how they can be applied in the real world.

Cognitive scaffolding is another effective strategy for providing learners support to successfully engage in the online environment, effectively learn, and persist.

COGNITIVE SCAFFOLDING TO SUPPORT PERSISTENCE

Many learners enter the online environment without the prerequisite skills outlined by Rovai (2003) such as computer literacy, information literacy, and time management. They also lack strategies to plan, monitor, and evaluate their thinking and learning (Stavredes, 2011). Other learners may lack prior knowledge and need support in learning new content areas and competencies. Many institutions support students using individualized tutoring and supplemental instruction; however, this can be costly if student need is high. Cognitive scaffolding provides a strategic way to provide the appropriate support for a diversity of needs to help learners persist. In the previous section, we discussed instructional design and organization as a key component to teaching presence. Cognitive scaffolding can be used in the design of an online course to support learning as well as in teacher interactions to support learners' just-in-time needs.

Cognitive Scaffolding Defined

Cognitive scaffolding was born out of Vygotsky's sociocultural theory and zone of proximal development. Vygotsky believed that "individual development could not be understood without reference to the social and cultural context within which such development is embedded" (Driscoll, 2005, p. 247). Vygotsky (1978) also studied the process by which this development might occur and developed the zone of proximal development. He defined this zone as:

> The distance between the actual developmental level as determined by independent problem-solving and the level of potential development as determined through problem-solving under adult guidance or in collaboration with more capable peers. (p. 86)

Cognitive scaffolding, is meant to support learners in this zone—in the gap between what they can accomplish on their own and what they can accomplish with the assistance of an individual with more advanced knowledge and skills. Wood, Bruner, and Ross (1976) discuss several scaffolding functions in their seminal research. These functions include gaining the learners attention, simplifying the learner's role in completing the task, keeping learners focused on the task, emphasizing relevant features of the task, alleviating frustration, and modeling the task (p. 98).

The key to incorporating cognitive scaffolding strategies is to use the right amount of scaffolding to support learners in their zone of proximal development. Dabbagh (2003) writes:

> … too much scaffolding could result in dampening students' efforts to actively pursue their learning goals, causing them to lose their momentum or drive towards meaning making and self-directed learning efforts, and too little scaffolding could result in students' inability to successfully complete or perform certain tasks and instructional activities, leading to anxiety, frustration, and finally loss of motivation and attrition. (p. 40)

The use of the term *scaffolding* alludes to the nature of this strategy. Over time, cognitive scaffolding is reduced until learners can complete the task or function independently (Greenfield, 1984). This also propels them into a new zone of proximal development in which new strategies may be used to support further learning. Ultimately, if applied over time, this helps learners to become self-regulated—able to motivate themselves, plan their learning process, assess their progress and adjust strategies, and locate and use resources to support their learning (Schunk & Zimmerman, 1994).

Cognitive scaffolding may be implemented in a static, or fixed, manner, or in a dynamic and collaborative way (Sharma & Hannafin, 2005). Static scaffolding focuses on anticipating needs in advance and designing the instruction to support all learners. This may include thinking about common misconceptions or difficult subject matter or reflecting on previous experiences teaching specific concepts and where learners may have had difficulty. Dynamic scaffolding, on the other hand, can be used to support the facilitation of activities and may be used for individual learners or the group. This dynamic scaffolding may operate on many levels at once. Joyce E. Many (2002) discusses how an intended scaffold for one learner may impact another learner as a different scaffold. For example, she explains how affirming a learner's understanding may also serve as a model for another learner and a prompt for a third learner (p. 401). Li, Price, and Fu (2011) present a model that blends the two approaches. They discuss the creation of a repository of resources created during course design that the instructor then modeled the use of and referred specific learners to, as needed, throughout the semester. This approach allowed more advanced learners to self select needed resources and the opportunity for the instructor to provide more guidance and personalized scaffolding for developing learners.

Hannafin, Land, and Oliver (1999) categorize scaffolding into four types—conceptual, metacognitive, procedural, and strategic. *Procedural scaffolding* guides learners about "how to utilize resources and tools" (p. 133). This may include orientations to a system or tool, such as an online courseroom, or just-in-time tutorials or explanations. *Metacognitive scaffolding* helps guide learners about "how to think" (p. 131). This may include specific strategies for working through content such as using a critical thinking model or the scientific method. It can also include more general strategies such as prompts to reflect on goals, to link concepts to prior knowledge, to evaluate progress, and to determine specific resource needs. *Conceptual scaffolding* guides learners about "what to consider" (p. 131). This includes helping learners work through complex problems, correcting common misconceptions, and identifying key concepts and ideas related to the task at hand, for example, through concept maps or content trees. Finally, *strategic scaffolding* guides learners on "approaches to learning tasks or problems" especially focusing on multiple alternative approaches. This may include strategies for identifying, evaluating, and relating information to existing knowledge, providing questions to consider, and expert advice (pp. 132–134).

While Hannafin et al. (1999) focused on the application of these categories within the open learning environment (OLE), Stavredes (2011) reinterprets and adapts these categories to fit the online learning environment. She explains *procedural scaffolding* as supporting navigation in the online course environment and explaining how to engage in learning activities. She also divides procedural scaffolding into three types: orientation, expectation, and resource. *Metacognitive scaffolding* is explained as support for "the development of general academic skills to help learners manage their learning" (p. 103). She expands on metacognitive scaffolding by categorizing them into planning, monitoring, and evaluating scaffolds to support learners' thinking processes as they engage in learning activities. She explains *conceptual scaffolding* as focusing on supporting learners when they "encounter new information or information that is difficult to understand" (p. 103). Finally, she explains *strategic scaffolding* as emphasizing "alternative learning pathways that can be applied to the learning context to meet the diverse needs of learners" (pp. 149–150). She recommends using strategic scaffolding to support individual learning needs and provide just-in-time support to help learners persist.

The functional categories presented by Hannafin et al. (1999) and further refined by Stavredes (2011) help to simplify the application of the complex concept of scaffolding. They also provide a strategy for identifying the underlying instructional purpose of course activities and lessons and integrating specific scaffolds to support critical learning needs. The following paragraphs provide an in-depth look at these categories and current applications present in the literature.

Procedural Scaffolds

Stavredes (2011) describes procedural scaffolding as guiding learners as they learn how to navigate the online course environment and engage in learning activities (p. 150). She explains that learners may have difficulty understanding where to start in an online course especially given the diversity in how online content may be delivered online, the variety of resources available, and new expectations for participating in a course (p. 112). She describes three types of procedural scaffolds that can help the learner persist— orientation, expectation, and resource scaffolds.

Koutsoubakis (1999, as cited in Rovai, 2003) demonstrated increased persistence with the use of an orientation. Palloff and Pratt (2003) suggest an orientation include Internet basics, basic computer skills, strategies for success (such as time management), an explanation of the role of interaction, how to provide feedback, the rules of netiquette, and support contacts (p. 67). Based on their research, Tomei, Hagle, Rineer, Mastandrea, and Scollon (2009) recommend an orientation include the following information at minimum: bookstore link, course syllabus, login information, technical contacts, and necessary technical competencies (p. 82). These suggestions incorporate many of the student skills and needs Rovai (2003) includes as essential for learner success in the online environment.

Shapiro (2008) focused on the use of scaffolding within the context of hypermedia design. Although specific to hypermedia aided learning environments, these principles may also further support orientation scaffolding strategies in online courses. She centered on grounding hypermedia design in learners' experience working toward learning goals rather than usability principles or common sense (p. 41). For learners with low prior knowledge, she suggests using hierarchies or other well-defined structures to organize hypertext, site maps, notating links, and emphasizing important links. For learners with high prior knowledge, she suggests connecting to existing knowledge, providing minimum cues, and allowing maximum learner control. These strategies help learners to easily navigate the hypermedia environment and access the resources and tools they need to succeed. She also discusses embedding scaffolding in the structure of the hypermedia to make the support invisible to learners which she argues helps make fading the support and adapting to individual learners' needs more seamless (pp. 30–31).

MacGregor and Lou (2004–2005) focused their research on the use of scaffolding in WebQuests, a resource-based learning strategy that supports and organizes the use of Web resources (p. 161). They argue that the usability and navigation of the sites used in the WebQuests may be thought of as procedural scaffolds (p. 173). In their study of scaffolding pre-service teachers' design of WebQuests, Wang and Hannafin (2009) found that procedural scaffolds, including templates with a structure and description for each design component and the demonstration of technical skills related to design, were helpful to learners. They also found that procedural scaffolds helped learners reduce their cognitive load for the task and improve the output of their work, in this case, their WebQuest designs.

Yelland and Masters (2007) discussed scaffolding in novel problem solving using computers. Their research included an initial project to observe children solving mathematical problems independently and then used their findings to develop scaffolding techniques. The procedural scaffolding included in the activity was an introductory conversation that modeled a task the children then completed. Although their research study focused on children in a face to face setting, the example provided in the research may be a model for incorporating scaffolding into online learning activities.

Puntambekar and Stylianou (2005) conducted a two part study to examine the types of support learners need in a hypermedia environment. The first study followed 74 middle school students as they navigated through an instructional environment called CoMPASS. They focused on the paths students took to navigate through the environment and the impact those paths had on learning. They found that learners need metacognitive strategies to assist with navigation through the system. They use the term *metanavigation* to define this type of support "designed to enable students to reflect upon and monitor their link selection while navigating through a hypertext system" (p. 469). In the second study, they designed, implemented, and tested these metanavigation cues. They found that students who received a tailored metanavigation aid provided better and richer explanation of the content and improved connections among concepts. This study seems to indicate a type of hybrid scaffolding. Although the prompts were used to support navigation, indicating a procedural scaffold, they were done so within the framework of metacognition, the next type of scaffolding discussed.

Metacognitive Scaffolds

Metacognitive scaffolding supports learners' thinking processes and management of their learning (Hannafin et al., 1999; Stavredes, 2011). Bannert, Hildebrand, and Mengelkamp (2009) focused on the use of metacognitive scaffolding to prompt learners to use metacognitive skills they previously developed in prior learning experiences (p. 830). They used an experimental research design with 56 university students. The experimental group received instructions on the use and value of a metacognitive support device and was prompted to use the device during learning activities. The control group did not receive the instruction and prompts but were instructed on how to organize their study space. They found that the experimental group reported more metacognitive activities and cognitive organization activities; however, there were no significant differences in cognitive elaboration and rehearsal. They also did not find significant differences in recall, however, there was a significant different in task transfer (p. 833). They conclude that these finding were in line with previous research and that performance on transfer tasks should be the evaluation criteria for the educational effectiveness of metacognitive interventions (p. 834). Their methods incorporated both paper-based and computer-based supports and they indicate that further research into online measures would be an important addition to this research. Although they outline many limitations and stipulations in their study, they posit that their research provides a confirmation of the need for metacognitive support in electronic learning environments.

Reingold, Rimor, and Kalay (2008) studied the relationship between instructor feedback and learners' metacognitive processes in an online course on democracy and multiculturalism. They analyzed 700 postings, written by 68 students based on the Meta Cognitive tool for Students' Reflections (MCSR) that analyzes learners' reflections based on metacognitive dimensions and categorizes them as personal, task, or strategy reflections. They also developed the Tool for analyzing Instructor's Online Scaffolding (TIOS) to analyze the types of scaffolding support instructors provide including technical, content-centered, procedural, and metacognitive (p. 142). They found a significant positive correlation between instructor's scaffolding efforts and students' metacognition. In discussing the results, they posit that appropriate instructor responses can emphasize learning through reflective and metacognitive processes. These efforts include "the presentation of the rationale for the task, fostering the integration across various course readings and course objectives, supporting reflective writing, differentiating between conclusion, fact, opinion and hypothesis, supervising text comprehension, focusing on the process of learning and encouraging interactions among the participants" (p. 147).

Pifarre and Cobos (2010) studied the use of peer scaffolding of metacognition in a collaborative knowledge-building system. As part of the course, instructors and learners collaborated to develop guidelines for working in the system and supporting peer review which included "content adequacy, personal elaboration of the ideas, organization of the ideas, presentation strategies, and conclusions" (p. 244). They noted that these guidelines assisted learners in their own work as well as guiding peer scaffolding. Their results showed improvement of metacognitive skills, especially in planning where learners asked for new approaches and processes. They also noted increases in "keeping clarity" over time which included asking for structural improvements and asking for explanation, clarification, and illustration (p. 248). Overall, they found that the explicit use of peer review and notes enhanced "social metacognitive regulation" (p. 250).

Sharma and Hannafin (2005) define three main activities for implementing scaffolding in practice: (1) establishing the goal of the activity at the beginning, (2) continuing to refine the goal throughout the activity, and (3) leveraging appropriate support and communication strategies to enable the achievement of the goal (pp. 19–20). This helps to situate the learning activity within a goal, helps learners to internalize and adapt the goal, and, finally, to achieve the goal. They connect these goals to Tharp and Gallimore's (1988, as cited in Sharma & Hannafin, 2005) position that the goal of scaffolding is metacognitive control of learning (p. 19). They created six instructional design activity documents to help facilitate deep reflection, metacognition, and critical thinking with five graduate learners enrolled in an online instructional design course. They also provided Socratic questioning, modeling, and externalization as additional scaffolding strategies. They found that learners' use of the scaffolding and learning and metacognition varied, but in most cases, deeper reflection and analysis was the result (p. 28). Their results confirm the importance of goals in implementation and the clarification of the purpose of scaffolding early on in an activity.

CONCEPTUAL SCAFFOLDS

Conceptual scaffolding guides learners about "what to consider" during learning especially in the case of complex concepts (Hannafin et al. 1999). Advance organizers, study guides or questions, definitions, graphical organizers, outlines, and hints are examples of conceptual scaffolding strategies (Stavredes, 2011).

Knowledge maps are another effective type of conceptual scaffolding. O'Donnell, Dansereau, and Hall (2002) define knowledge maps as "node-link representations in which ideas are located in notes and connected to other related ideas through a series of labeled links" (p. 72). They explain that knowledge maps scaffold learning by reducing cognitive load, facilitating the representation of relationships, providing many paths for knowledge retrieval, supporting learners with low verbal skills, and supporting the communication of knowledge (p. 74). In their review of recent literature on knowledge maps, they discuss four major findings. First, learners remember more central ideas using knowledge maps than with text. Second, learners with low verbal ability or prior knowledge benefit the most. Third, learners who support interaction with the use of knowledge maps, learn more effectively. Finally, using gestalt principles to design knowledge maps, results in better recall (p. 81). They discuss, however, that these results have differed according to the content of the knowledge map and that study of the influence of different content types is needed.

As previously mentioned, MacGregor and Lou (2004–2005) studied the use of scaffolding with WebQuests. In addition to their findings with procedural scaffolding, they found that "providing a study guide that identified what information to extract and a concept map that provided cues for organizing and synthesizing their information were helpful in keeping students on task and facilitated high-order learning" (p. 172). In Wang and Hannafin's research, a grading rubric with specific requirements and points for a WebQuest design activity was considered a conceptual scaffold and was found very useful.

Harris (2008) focused on the application of scaffolding in reflective journaling. Her formal scaffolding included an introduction to reflective journaling which she found to be appropriate and successful. Included in her introduction was a discussion about reflective journaling including its value and implementation, potential difficulties including timing, effort, and maintaining effort, and generic example entries (p. 316). She also created an assignment guide which included a rationale, suggested framework, and an organization and time structure to further scaffold the reflective journal process. In addition, she implemented a writer-responder critique and a student self-evaluation form. These scaffolding examples could be applied in a variety of tasks to help focus learners on the most important concepts related to their learning task.

Strategic Scaffolds

Strategic scaffolding supports learners in completing specific learning tasks or problems, specially focusing on multiple alternative approaches (Hannafin et al., 1999). Stavredes (2011) focuses strategic scaffolding as a just-in-time strategy for supporting individual learner performance (p. 147). In the online courseroom, this just-in-time approach requires frequent dialogue, which is a major theme in cognitive scaffolding literature.

Palincsar (1986) argues that "dialogue has a critical role to play in scaffolded instruction, facilitating the collaboration necessary between the novice and expert for the novice to acquire the cognitive strategy or strategies" (p. 95). Many of the insights she provides are still relevant in today's online classroom. She discusses the importance of supporting learners' contributions, linking learners' ideas to new ideas, providing focus and direction, making instruction explicit, and moving learners' responses from negative statements to more constructive statements (p. 96).

Many (2002) also addresses the use of cognitive scaffolding in face to face dialogue, or what she calls instructional conversations. She discusses how scaffolding may be integrated throughout discussions as opportunities arise in the form of direct assistance, using questions and prompting statements, and monitoring and affirming learners' understanding. Whipp and Lorentz (2009) discuss specific suggestions for online instructors that parallel Many's (2002) study. These include the use of challenging questions, prompts for elaboration of ideas, and sharing knowledge from personal and professional experience and resources (p. 187).

Lee (2009) focused her study on the use of experts in monitoring group discussions in a foreign language teaching methods course. In addition to an instructor, the online, asynchronous discussions included expert language teachers who taught foreign language in the five years prior to the study (p. 214). She explains that the expert went beyond information sharing, clarification, and explanation but also challenged learners to critically reflect on the topics (p. 222). Many of the learners expressed that the experts enhanced their reflection and discussion of the topics but others expressed feelings of information overload. Lee cautions that "the role of the expert is to monitor, not to dominate the discussion" (p. 223).

In addition to dialogue strategies such as prompts and probing questions, Stavredes (2011) discusses the uses of worked examples and expert advice as effective strategic scaffolding applications. Clark and Mayer (2011) also discuss the effectiveness of worked examples in building knowledge for long-term memory. They define a worked example as a "step-by-step demonstration of how to perform a task or solve a problem" (p. 224). Based on their review of empirical research, they recommend that worked examples replace some practice exercises for beginning learners, use principles regarding effective media, are realistic and diverse, and help learners explain the examples in their own words.

Further Research on Cognitive Scaffolding

Lajoie (2005) discusses the shift of cognitive scaffolding from primarily facilitated by instructors to newer research in computer-based scaffolding. An example of this shift is the work of Najjar (2008), who proposes a framework of scaffolding adaptive feedback based on a knowledge representation model using an artificial tutor in virtual laboratories.

Lajoie (2005) also examines the expansion of scaffolding from a cognitive focus to conative, affective, and motivational scaffolds. Yelland and Masters (2007) discuss the use of three types of scaffolding—cognitive, technical, and affective that may relate to this expanded focus. *Cognitive scaffolding* is used to distinguish assistance with conceptual and procedural understandings, *technical scaffolding* relates to strategies to support the interaction with computers, and *affective scaffolding* focuses on support to keep learners on task and encourage critical and strategic thinking. Although out of the scope for this review, this expansion and an in-depth review of these new categories may help to further support learner persistence by taking a more holistic view of learners and their specific needs and challenges in learning. Research studies focused primarily on the correlation of cognitive scaffolding and persistence factors related to a specific persistence model would also help strengthen the case. A range of studies may also be completed to identify specific cognitive scaffolding strategies that best enable learners' persistence in online learning.

CONCLUSION

With the massive growth of online learning, it is critical to understand factors that contribute to learner success. From the review of literature, we found a number of factors that impact leaners' ability to persist. Although many factors are beyond the control of the institution, engagement appears to be an important factor that contributes to student success. Research indicates that structuring activities to develop social, cognitive, and teaching presence can support engagement and deep learning. Cognitive scaffolding can be incorporated into the design of the online course and used by instructors to support learners individually to help them navigate the online environment, plan, monitor, and evaluate their learning, develop understanding of concepts, and strategically support learners just-in-time. This can reduce stress and help them develop effective academic skills to support their learning. Together, these strategies assist online instructors in addressing many variables that effect persistence and provide them with valuable tools to support learners in achieving their educational goals and completing their program of study. For practitioners, these strategies can be used in the design and organization of the online environment to scaffolding learning. In addition, they offer guidelines for how to provide meaningful facilitation and direct instruction to motivate and engage learners, which can lead to deep learning.

REFERENCES

Anderson, T., Rourke, L., Garrison, D. R., & Archer, W. (2001). Assessing teaching presence in a computer conferencing context. *Journal of Asynchronous Learning Networks*, 5(2), 1–17.

Allen, I. E., & Seaman, J. (2009). *Learning on demand: Online education in the United States.* Retrieved from http://www.sloanconsortium.org/publications/survey/pdf/learningondemand.pdf

Bannert, M., Hildebrand, M., & Mengelkamp, C. (2009). Effects of a metacognitive support device in learning environments. *Computers in Human Behavior, 25,* 829–835.

Bean J. R., & Metzner, B. (1985). A conceptual model of nontraditional undergraduate student attrition.*Review of Educational Research, 55,* 485–650.

Boston, W., Diaz, S. R. Gibson, A. M., Ice, P., Richardson, J., & Swan, K. (2009). An Exploration of the Relationship Between Indicators of the Community of Inquiry Framework and Retention in Online Programs. *Journal of Asynchronous Learning Networks, 13*(3), 67–83.

Bullen, M. (1998). Participation and critical thinking in online university distance education. *Journal of Distance Education, 13*(2), 1–32.

Chang, E. A. (2002). The efficacy of asynchronous online learning in the promotion of critical thinking in graduate education (Doctoral dissertation). Retrieved March 3, 2009, from Dissertations & Theses: Full Text database. (Publication No. AAT 3052867).

Clark, R. C., & Mayer, R. E. (2011). *E-Learning and the science of instruction: Proven guidelines for consumers and designers of multimedia learning (3rd ed.).* San Francisco, CA: Pfeiffer.

Dabbagh, N. (2003). Scaffolding: An important teacher competency in online teaching. *TechTrends, 47*(2), 39–44.

DeLotell, P. J., Millam, L. A., & Reinhardt, M. M. (2010). The use of deep learning strategies in online business courses to impact student retention. *American Journal of Business Education. 3*(12), 49–55.

Driscoll, M. (2005). *Psychology of learning for instruction (3rd ed.).* Boston, MA: Pearson.

Garrison, D. R., Anderson, T., & Archer, W. (2000). Critical inquiry in a text-based environment: Computer conferencing in higher education. *The Internet and Higher Education, 2*(2–3), 87–105.

Garrison, D. R., Anderson, T., & Archer, W. (2001). Critical thinking, cognitive presence, and computer conferencing in distance education. *The American Journal of Distance Education, 15*(1), 7–23.

Garrison, D. R., Cleveland-Innes, M. (2004). Critical factors in student satisfaction and success: Facilitating student role adjustment in online communities of inquiry. In J. Bourne & J. C. Moore (Eds.), *Elements of quality online education: Into the mainstream* (Vol. 5, pp. 29–38). Needham, MA: The Sloan Consortium.

Greenfield, P. M. (1984). A theory of the teaching in the learning activities of everyday life. In B. Rogoff & J. Lave (Eds.), *Everday cognition* (pp. 117–138). Cambridge, MA: Harvard University Press.

Gunawardena, C. N., & Zittle, F. J. (1997). Social presence as a predictor of satisfaction within a computer-mediated conferencing environment. *The American Journal of Distance Education, 11*(3), 8–26.

Hannafin, M., Land, S., & Oliver, K. (1999). Open learning environments: Foundations, methods and models. In C. M. Reigeluth (Ed.), *Instructional-design theories and models: A new paradigm of instructional theory* (Vol. 2, pp. 115–140). Mahwah, NJ: Erlbaum.

Harris, M. (2008). Scaffolding reflective journal writing: Negotiating power, play and position. *Nurse Education Today, 28,* 314–326.

Ice, P., Gibson, A. M., Boston, W., & Becher, D. (2011). An exploration of differences between community of indicators in low and high disenrollment online courses. *Journal of Journal of Asynchronous Learning Networks, 15*(2, 44–69.

Lajoie, S. P. (2005). Extending the scaffolding metaphor. *Instructional Science, 33,* 541–557.

Lee, L. (2009). Scaffolding collaborative exchanges between expert and novice language teachers in threaded discussions. *Foreign Language Annals, 42*(2), 212–228.

Li, S., Price, D., & Fu, Y. (2011). The impact of the teacher-made online learning resources. *The Business Review, Cambridge, 18*(1), 35–40.

MacGregor, S. K., & Lou, Y. (2004–2005). Web-based learning: How task scaffolding and web site design support knowledge acquisition. *Journal of Research on Technology in Education, 37*(2), 161–175.

Many, J. E. (2002). An exhibition and analysis of verbal tapestries: Understanding how scaffolding is woven into the fabric of instructional conversations. *Reading Research Quarterly, 37*(4), 376–407.

May, S. (1993). Collaborative learning: More is not necessarily better. *American Journal of Distance Education, 7*(3), 39–50.

Muilenburg, L., & Berge, Z. L. (2000). A framework for designing questions for online learning. *DEOSNEWS, 10*(2). Retrieved September 30, 2011, from http://www.emoderators.com/moderators/muilenburg.html

Najjar, M. (2008). On scaffolding adaptive teaching prompts within virtual labs. *International Journals of Distance Education Technologies, 6*(2), 35–54.

O'Donnell, A. M., Dansereau, D. F., & Hall, R. H. (2002). Knowledge maps as scaffolds for cognitive processing. *Educational Psychology Review, 14*(1), 71–86.

Palincsar, A. S. (1986). The role of dialogue in providing scaffolded instruction.*Educational Psychologist, 21*(1 & 2), 73–98.

Palloff, R. M., & Pratt, K. (2003). *The virtual student: A profile and guide to working with online learners.* San Francisco, CA: Jossey-Bass.

Pascarella, E. T. (1985). College environmental influences on learning and development: A critical review and synthesis. In J. C. Smart (Ed.), *Higher education: Handbook of theory and research* (Vol. 1, pp.1–61). New York: Agathon.

Picciano, A. G. (2002). Beyond student perceptions: Issues of interaction, presence and performance in an online course. *Journal of Asynchronous Learning Networks, 6*(1), 21–40.

Pifarre, M., & Cobos, R. (2010). Promoting metacognitive skills through peer scaffolding in a CSCL environment. *Computer-Supported Collaborative Learning, 5.* 237–253.

Puntambekar, S., & Stylianou, A. (2005). Designing navigational support in hypertext systems based on navigation patterns. *Instructional Science, 33,* 451–481.

Reingold, R., Rimor, R., & Kalay, A. (2008). Instructor's scaffolding in support of student's metacognition through a teacher education online course: A case study. *Journal of Interactive Online Learning, 7*(2), 139–151.

Rovai, A. P. (2002). Building sense of community at a distance. *International Review of Research in Open and Distance Learning, 3*(1), 1–16. Retrieved September 30, 2011, from http://www.irrodl.org/content/v3.1/rovai.html

Rovai, A. P. (2003). In search of higher persistence rates in distance education online programs. *Internet and Higher Education, 6,* 1–16.

Shapiro, A. M. (2008). Hypermedia design as learner scaffolding. *Education Technology Research Development, 56,* 29–44.

Sharma, P., & Hannafin, M. (2005). Learner perceptions of scaffolding in supporting critical thinking. *Journal of Computing in Higher Education, 17*(1), 17–42.

Schunk, D. H., & Zimmerman, B. J. (1994). *Self-regulation of learning and performance: Issues and educational applications.* Hillsdale, NJ: Erlbaum.

Shea, P. J., Fredericksen, E. E., Pickett, A. M., & Pelz, W. E. (2003). A preliminary investigation of "teaching presence" in the SUNY Learning Network. In J. Bourne & J. C. Moore (Eds.), *Elements of quality online education: Practice and direction* (pp. 279–312). Needham, MA: Sloan Center for Online Education.

Shea, P., Li, C. S., & Pickett, A. M. (2006). A study of teaching presence and student sense of learning community in fully online and web-enhanced college courses. *The Internet and Higher Education, 9,* 175–190.

Shea, P., Pickett, A., & Pelz, W. (2003). A follow-up study of teaching presence in the online program. *Journal of Asynchronous Learning Networks, 7*(2), 61–80.

Spady, W. (1970). Dropouts from higher education: An interdisciplinary review and synthesis. *Interchange, 1,* 64–85.

Stavredes, T. M. (2011). *Effective online teaching: Foundations and strategies for student success.* San Francisco, CA: Jossey-Bass.

Tinto, V. (1975). Dropout from higher education: A theoretical synthesis of recent research, *Review of Educational Research, 45,* 89–125.

Tomei, L. A., Hagle, H., Rineer, A., Mastandrea, L. A., & Scollon, J. (2009). Do orientation materials help students successfully complete online courses? *International Journal of Information and Communcation Technology Education, 5*(2), 73–89.

Vygotsky, L. (1978). *Mind in society.* Cambridge, MA: Harvard University Press.

Wang, F., & Hannafin, M. J. (2009). Scaffolding preservice teachers' WebQuest design: A qualitative study. *Journal of Computer Higher Education, 21,* 218–234.

Whipp, J. L., & Lorentz, R. A. (2009). Cognitive and social help giving in online teaching: An exploratory study. *Education Technology Research Development, 57,* 169–192.

Wilson-Robbins, C. L. (2006). Assessing critical thinking in asynchronous online learning: A case study of two community college online courses. *Dissertation Abstracts International 67*(06), A. (UMI No. 3223879).

Wood, D., Bruner, J., & Ross, G. (1976). The role of tutoring in problem solving. *Journal of Child Psychology and Psychiatry, 17,* 89–100.

Workman, J. J., Stenard, R. A. (1996). *Student support services for distance learners,* DEOSNEWS, 6, 3. Retrieved September 30, 2011, from the Distance Education Online Symposium Website: http://www.ed.psu.edu/acsde/deos/deosnews/deosnews6_3.asp

Yelland, N., & Masters, J. (2007). Rethinking scaffolding in the information age. *Computers & Education, 48,* 362–382.

Yang, Y. C., Newby, T. J., & Bill, R. L. (2005). Using socratic questioning to promote critical thinking skills through asynchronous discussion forums in distance learning environments. *The American Journal of Distance Education, 19*(3), 163–181.

11

STUDENT ACHIEVEMENT IN ELEMENTARY AND HIGH SCHOOL

CATHY CAVANAUGH

OVERVIEW OF K–12 ONLINE LEARNING

This chapter is a review of research on teaching and learning online by children in elementary and high schools, commonly referred to in the United States as grades K–12. This span encompasses primary and secondary levels from kindergarten to high school graduation. Online learning programs for K–12 students offer instruction and content in the form of synchronous or asynchronous Web-delivered courses, also known as virtual schools. The majority of the U.S. states have statewide supplemental and full-time K–12 online learning programs, and online courses are offered by schools or districts in every state (Watson, Murin, Vashaw, Gemin, & Rapp, 2011), with the most rapid growth occurring in school district-operated and blended programs. The largest publicly funded virtual school programs each enroll over 200,000 students, a scale afforded by the predominant asynchronous Web-based mode of delivery for K–12 distance learning courses (Watson et al., 2011). As of 2007, more than 20% of postsecondary students enrolled in at least one online course (U.S. Department of Education, 2011), and in 2010 that figure had risen to 30% (Allen & Seaman, 2010). Thus far, only 1%–2% of K–12 students have taken online courses (Watson et al., 2011). However, several states have enacted legislation requiring online courses or experience for graduation (Davis, 2011).

EFFECTIVENESS OF K–12 ONLINE LEARNING

Meta-Analyses of Research in K–12 Online Learning

In recent years, eight meta-analyses have included data from studies of K–12 distance education (Table 11.1). Cavanaugh's (2001) meta-analysis reviewed telecommunications technology in use for courses and supplemental educational programs in the 1980s and 1990s at the K–12 level. The small positive effect size fell within the confidence interval, resulting in a finding of no significant difference in academic achievement between distance and classroom programs. However, the few online programs included in the synthesis showed higher effect sizes than the audio and videoconferencing programs.

Table 11.1   Meta-Analyses of K–12 Distance Education, 2001–2009

Author(s), Date	Focus	Delivery System	N of Studies	Effect Size; 95% CI
Cavanaugh (2001)	Academic achievement of K–12 students	Analog and digital	19	+0.015; −1.113 to 1.407
Shachar & Neumann (2003)	Student achievement of postsecondary and K–12 students	Online	86	+0.37; 0.33 to 0.40
Ungerleider & Burns (2003)	Networked and online learning in postsecondary and K–12 programs	Online	16	Near zero; NA
Bernard, Abrami, Lou, Borokhovski, Wade, Wozney, Wallet, Fiset, & Huang (2004)	Student achievement, attitude, retention of postsecondary and K–12 students	Online	232	+0.0128; −0.0068 to 0.0325
Cavanaugh, Gillan, Kromrey, Hess, & Blomeyer (2004)	Academic achievement of K–12 students	Online	14	−0.028; −0.116 to 0.060
Zhao, Lei, Yan, & Tan (2006)	Effectiveness of postsecondary and K–12 courses	Online	51	+0.10; −0.01 to 0.223
Bernard, Abrami, Wade, Borokhovski, Tamin, Surkes & Bethel (2009)	Achievement of postsecondary and K–12 students	Online	74	+0.38; NA
U.S. Department of Education (2009)	Achievement of postsecondary and K–12 students	Online	50	+0.20; NA

The Shachar and Neumann (2003) synthesis found a significant positive effect for distance education programs delivered between 1990 and 2002. Detail about the ages of the students and the delivery systems used in the courses was not included in the meta-analysis, preventing conclusions about the relative effectiveness of online programs for K–12 students. In contrast, Ungerleider and Burns (2003) restricted their analysis to networked and online distance education programs. Two out of the 12 studies were conducted at the secondary level, and the others were conducted at the postsecondary level. No significant difference was reported for student achievement, and a small positive effect size was found for satisfaction in classroom courses.

The meta-analysis of 232 studies of online and video-based learning in K–12 and postsecondary students by Bernard et al. (2004) resulted in a small positive effect size for achievement in online learning, although online learners had lower retention rates. Bernard et al. followed with a meta-analysis in 2009 that refined the focus on K-adult achievement resulting from levels and types of interactions in courses, showing that stronger interaction in courses corresponds to significantly higher levels of achievement.

The single meta-analysis that focused solely on the K–12 online learning delivery systems representative of today's virtual schools was by Cavanaugh, Gillan, Kromrey, Hess, and Blomeyer (2004). This synthesis found an effect size near zero, and because it was limited to 14 studies, it did not differentiate achievement levels by student characteristics or course features. Zhao, Lei, Yan, Lai, and Tan (2005) conducted a meta-analysis of 51 studies, only one of which included precollege learners, finding a small positive effect for distance education on student achievement. Of note, strong positive effects were found in courses that combined synchronous and asynchronous interaction, as well as for courses that included some face-to-face instruction in the online experience. This finding in support of blended course designs was echoed in the 2009 U.S. Department of Education meta-analysis of 99 studies of learning in distance education courses, five of which focused on K-12 learners.

The uniformity of the results across these meta-analyses and other distance education studies (Russell, 1999) suggests that as distance education is currently practiced, student learning on average in well-designed online elementary and secondary environments appears to be equivalent to learning in a well-designed classroom environment. Such broad syntheses tend to mask fine-grained trends and have to date offered little illumination of the practices that contribute to student success. To address what works in K–12 online learning, numerous studies of individual online programs have been published over the past ten years. These studies will be examined in the following section.

EFFECTS ON K–12 STUDENT OUTCOMES OF THE FEATURES OF ONLINE DISTANCE EDUCATION

The examination of the literature regarding the effects on K–12 student outcomes of online distance education is organized thematically to focus on student characteristics, course design, instructional strategies, teacher preparation and development, course facilitation, and technological approaches. The knowledge base in each theme serves to guide online program administrators, course designers, and instructors toward effective practice, and it points policymakers and researchers toward developing initiatives that will advance the field to better serve students.

Student Characteristics

With the increase of actual and projected use of online teaching, it becomes essential that online instructors and course designers apply a thorough and current understanding of K–12 learners in their practice (Oliver, Kellogg, Townsend, & Brady, 2010). For example, a necessary characteristic for success as a distance learner is autonomy, which is present at different levels in children and adults. As discussed by Anderson in Chapter 6 of this volume, most adults have acquired a degree of autonomy in learning, whereas younger students require more scaffolding in their distance education experience. Adult learners approach expertise in their learning and in their ability to learn independently, as a result of their extended experience with the concepts and with metacognition. In contrast, children are relative novices. Experts organize and interpret information differently from novices, and these differences affect learners' abilities to remember and solve problems (Bransford, Brown, & Cocking, 1999), and their ability to learn independently. Children develop metacognitive skills gradually and with guidance. Learners need to be supported in the development of autonomy throughout their schooling. A focus on time-management skills is particularly important in online courses, which "provide opportunities to increase learners' motivation, support the development of independent learning skills, and help students take responsibility for their learning" (Lewin et al., 2008, p. 5).

A second characteristic of successful distance learners that differentiates K–12 distance learners from adult learners is locus of control. Learners persist in an educational endeavor when they have developed an internal locus of control (Rotter, 1989). Older children have more internal locus of control than younger children (Gershaw, 1989).

Additionally, a learner's social and emotional maturity may play a role in academic success in the dynamic and interactive online environment, requiring a higher level of teacher or mentor mediation than is provided in postsecondary online courses (Picciano & Seaman, 2007). This design and instruction challenge is especially urgent given growth in online dual enrollment courses that place secondary students in college courses, and given the trend toward proficiency- or competency-based pathways through high school that may result in younger students who are academically ready for college before they are socially ready (Sturgis & Patrick, 2010).

The range of students enrolling in online learning opportunities is expanding (Barbour & Mulcahy, 2008; Dickson, 2005; Ferdig, Papanastasiou, & DiPietro, 2005). The composition of online students differs significantly from the general population of K–12 students (Glick, 2011; Kinash & Crichton, 2007) in that online programs serve higher numbers of female students and lower numbers of Black, Hispanic, Asian, exceptional, and English language learner (ELL) students. In an examination of factors that bring students into online courses and support their persistence in the courses, Rauh (2010) identified the students' economic situation, motivation, parents' involvement, and technology skills as contributing factors, stating that in one state's virtual public school a significant difference in poverty indices distinguished students who completed courses from those withdrawing. Cavanaugh and Liu (in press) confirmed the importance of student socioeconomic status (SES) in a study of 950 online middle school (grades 6–8) students which found that SES was the most significant predictor of course grade among eight factors examined. In seven of fourteen courses examined, students not participating in free or reduced lunch programs performed significantly better academically than those eligible for the programs.

While each virtual course and program has unique features that intersect in different ways with different types of students, findings of research on the characteristics of successful virtual school learners suggest a common set of characteristics likely to result in successful virtual learning.

Several online programs have shown that online learning can improve school retention rates (Ferdig, 2010; Repetto, Cavanaugh, Wayer, & Liu, 2010; Talvitie-Siple, 2007). However, emulating classroom-based approaches "often replicates the negative behavioral, affective, and cognitive outcomes of at-risk students" (Ferdig, 2010, p. 3). One approach to increasing graduation rates is to design learning environments that serve students with disabilities and other risk factors through the "5Cs" known to increase school completion: connect, climate, control, curriculum, and caring community (Repetto et al., 2010). Virtual school programs aligned with the 5Cs have closed achievement gaps and increased completion rates among students with disabilities. Further research-based practices for online programs serving at-risk learners were proposed by Archambault et al. (2010):

1. Individualizing instruction;
2. Providing professional development for teachers;
3. Providing support structures;
4. Using online orientation programs;
5. Translating current pedagogy into instructional strategies;
6. Capitalizing on early identification, screening, and data collection.

Instructional design strategies recommended to ensure online courses meet the special needs of students with disabilities (Keeler & Horney, 2007; Rose & Blomeyer, 2007) include assurance of accessibility to the information for students with disabilities and the supports in course materials and learning activities needed by these students. Virtual courses that accommodate students with disabilities also benefit all learners under the framework of Universal Design for Learning principles (Rose & Blomeyer, 2007). For accelerated and gifted students, an appropriate balance of structure and autonomy matters as much as for struggling learners, although the balance may vary. An online gifted course should be designed to lead students in a planned progression from structured to open learning (Wan & Nicholas, 2010). An effective course design allows students a choice of topics and peer groupings, and includes a display of work where peers and instructors can provide support (Nicholas & Ng, 2009).

A key to success for adolescents, both online and offline, appears to be motivation, according to a study of Oregon's CyberSchool (Weiner, 2003). While identifying discipline and self-motivation as critical factors, Weiner emphasized that at the secondary level students are still learning how to learn and they were often able to develop responsibility and organization through participation in a structured online course. While both novice and experienced online teachers appear to be effective in motivating students through supporting their attention to learning and the relevance of their learning, more teacher experience has been associated with higher levels of student confidence and satisfaction (Carpenter, 2011). The study of an online high school English course found that students perceived the most motivating factors to be instructional practices including timely, constructive feedback, flexibility, and frequent instructor-student communication.

In recent years, student use of technology in the act of multitasking has received attention in the education and research communities (Foehr, 2006; Lenhart, Purcell, Zickhur, & Smith, 2010). Students can learn effective multi-tasking skills that support their online course completion; however, engagement in frequent non-academic digital gaming has been associated with lower levels of online course completion (Crawford, 2009). Further support for the interplay of technology and learning comes from studies of personality, cognitive tempo, and information processing tendencies that reveal students enrolled in online courses want control over the timing and pacing of their learning (Scheick, 2007).

These studies provide evidence that strong academic skills, motivation, discipline, and course structure compatible with one's learning preferences are conducive to success in K–12 online learning. Factors such as these have been accounted for in a student success prediction instrument developed specifically to identify secondary level students who are likely to succeed in virtual school courses. Roblyer, Davis, Mills, Marshall, and Pape (2008) developed and evaluated the Educational Success Prediction Instrument (ESPRI-V2), finding that the four factors measured by ESPRI-V2, technology use/self-efficacy, achievement beliefs, instructional risk-taking, and organization strategies, can predict student success in online courses. The combination of prior knowledge, cognitive characteristics such as self-efficacy and achievement beliefs, and factors such as Internet access and technical support can predict student online success.

Course Design Factors

Knowledge of factors that contribute to student success in virtual courses has implications for the types of support services provided to students, particularly counseling, study-skill development, and course design. A need has been articulated for more exploration of the factors that account for K–12 student success in distance education in the form of design research approaches (Barbour & Reeves, 2009). The following studies have focused on elements of online course design for secondary learners.

An online science program for deaf high school students in three schools was found to foster independent learning through a collaborative project-based design (Barman et al., 2002). Students worked in teams with peers from the other schools to develop a hypothesis, conduct Web-based literature searches, perform hands-on experiments, and critique the work of other teams. Students valued the models of portfolios and problem solving produced by other students for helping them develop their own science and technology abilities.

Weiner's (2003) study of cyber-school students found that structure in courses was critical to student success. Components of structured courses were clear expectations, concrete deadlines with some flexibility, outlines of course requirements, time sheets, and study guides. A meaningful curriculum was also cited as an important contributor to student success in a virtual course, as was the opportunity for rich interactive collaboration among students and teachers. In fact, students felt frustration and isolation when interaction was limited. Students advocated for a design that allowed them to complete course activities at the pace that was comfortable for them, with due dates that reduced procrastination, and that maximized communication among students working at the same pace.

Barker and Wendel (2001) reinforce the need for flexible timetables for students who select virtual schooling because these students need more control over the pace of their learning. Their report states that the combination of flexibility, independence, and experience with online tools resulted in improved critical thinking, research, and computer skills, as compared to learners in conventional schools when measured by standardized exams. Virtual school students also showed greater improvement in problem solving, creative thinking, decision making, and time management, had equivalent performance in reading and science, and exhibited lower performance in listening and speaking.

The expanded learning time afforded by a flexible online course timeline has shown success in raising student achievement (Cavanaugh, 2009). Indeed, time was identified as the most significant factor in student success in 11 of 15 high enrollment high school level online courses examined in a large virtual school (Liu & Cavanaugh, 2011). This finding encourages the design of courses to engage and motivate students to spend more time in the system. Specifically, Liu and Cavanaugh (20011) observed that the frequency with which students accessed an online course related to achievement in ways that seem to depend on the complexity of the course, in that more log-ins corresponded to higher achievement in introductory level high school courses, while fewer log-ins for longer sessions corresponded to higher achievement in advanced courses.

Virtual course designs have many strengths, but they have not so far compared well with traditional settings for auditory production and reception skills among other forms of performance. A study of an online instrumental music course (Bond, 2002) showed that distance between teacher and student had "negative effects on quality of performance, level of engagement, and development and refinement of skills and knowledge" (p. 5), even though the course design included audio, video, guided practice, and additional resources. Similarly, music students in videoconference-delivered instrument lessons experienced more teacher modeling, off-task time, performance time, and eye contact than the site-based comparison group (Orman & Whitaker, 2010), resulting in equivalent levels of learning across the delivery modes.

Course design for K–12 online learners is a specialized craft that should account for analysis of learners as well as demands of content and affordances of technology systems (Cooze & Barbour, 2007). In an investigation of general approaches to K–12 online course design, students in courses following a learner-centered design completed the first semester at a statistically higher rate than control students in courses that did not adhere to this design (Hannum, Irvin, Lei, & Farmer, 2008). After long-term study of virtual course design, Schnitz and Azbell (2004, p. 165) propose the following guidelines for materials used in virtual schools. Online materials must be visual and dynamic, downloadable and printer-friendly, randomly accessible and manipulable, conducive to production/interaction, documented to model appropriate permissions and copyright alignments, instructionally aware of and prepared for remote use, aware of the audience, assessable and accountable, and easily updatable.

Teacher Preparation and Development

It has been established that in elementary and secondary education, teacher quality is among the most important contributors to student achievement (Darling-Hammond, 2000). Because most K–12 online courses are moderated in part or in full by a teacher, teacher preparation, professional development, and supportive instructional practices are essential foundations of effective virtual courses. To date, the majority of online teachers have transitioned from or are bridging across face-to-face classroom teaching, and they have the dispositions of valuing engagement and community, seeking innovative and challenging teaching situations, and wanting to apply their knowledge in adapting learning materials for students (Archambault & Crippen, 2009). Specialized supports and skills are needed to assist these teachers in navigating multiple learning environments.

On the basis that virtual students and practices differ from students and practices in conventional schools (Barbour, Kinsella, Wicks, & Toker, 2009), Davis and Roblyer (2005) developed a model to prepare virtual school teachers with the unique knowledge, skills, and dispositions they will need to become effective online teachers. Online, teachers need to work differently in time and space and they need to be able to engage students using communications technology. The model used guided observations, mentoring in K–12 online courses, and design of virtual course materials to prepare new teachers to transition to online teaching to ensure that new teachers left their teacher-preparation programs with the skills to begin teaching online (Compton, Davis, & Mackey, 2009). A well-rounded teacher education program that prepares preservice teachers for online practice should include courses in online pedagogy, online courses in the certification areas, and professional development for online teachers (Smith, 2009). Further, state boards of education are advised to implement virtual school internships and online teacher certification in order to adequately prepare teachers for virtual schools (Kennedy, 2010).

To meet their demand for online teachers and to prepare teachers for the unique context of each virtual school, many virtual schools have developed their own professional-development programs. Professional development for online teachers has been shown to have an effect on teacher ability and on student perceptions. The Virtual High School instructor preparation program was seen to have an effect on the participating teachers even after they returned to classroom teaching (Lowes, 2005). Following initial preparation in course design and instructional practices, mentoring or peer coaching (Rice & Dawley, 2009) and teacher inquiry or action research (Dana, Dawson, Krell, & Wochenhauer, 2012) are recommended as ongoing professional development approaches for virtual school teachers.

Student perceptions of their learning environment may be related to the amount of professional development their teachers receive in technology (Hughes, McLeod, Brown, Maeda, & Choi, 2007). In their study of online algebra students, Hughes et al. found that teacher professional development appeared to have a positive effect on students' perceptions of cohesiveness. Teacher technology skill was identified as a "significant factor affecting pedagogical success" (n.p.) in an evaluation of Australia's Virtual Schooling Service Pilot (Kapitzke & Pendergast, 2005).

Course Facilitation

Standards for effective online teaching have been developed by professional organizations, but they have been characterized as lacking a basis in research on best practices and over reliance on research from face-to-face education and higher education (Ferdig, Cavanaugh, DiPietro, Black, & Dawson, 2010). The standards also generalize online teaching without accounting for the variety of models of virtual schooling and the range of effective content-specific approaches (Roblyer et al., 2008). The studies outlined in this section are beginning to fill this gap.

K–12 online course completion and academic performance are influenced by instructional approach and setting. The role of online course mentor in support of the certified content teacher has been described as an essential contributor to a high-quality learning experience (DiPietro, 2010). Course facilitators or mentors who are in the same physical location with students during part of their online learning time contribute to student persistence, as do facilitators who guide students with self-management and motivation (Hannum et al., 2008). Student achievement tends to benefit when site-based facilitators have this as their full-time professional role (Roblyer, Freeman, Stabler, & Schneidmiller, 2007) for which they are trained, when they have frequent contact with the online course teacher (Lewis, 2011), and when they practice learner-centered support that demonstrates interest in their students (De la Valle, Keane, & Irvin, 2010). A quasi-experimental study of online algebra classes examined student performance and the role of the teacher (Kleiman, Carey, Bonifaz, Haisted, & O'Dwyer, 2005). In this model an in-class coach worked with the online students during the school day, while they completed the work assigned by the online teacher. The "frequency with which the in-class teacher worked with small groups of students and observed individual student work related positively to student achievement" (p. 39). Achievement also improved "when online and in-class teacher teams collaborated frequently on planning" (p. 39).

How teachers enact their skills in the virtual classroom affects student satisfaction and achievement. Singh and Dika (2003) found that a blend of academic and social support from adults resulted in positive outcomes in terms of educational aspirations, academic effort expended, and academic self-concept. Teachers who made more connections between their online course and other content areas had students who performed at measurably higher levels in a study of a state-wide Spanish course, as did teachers who showed higher levels of student engagement, valuing the course, and community (Rockman et al., 2007). In the same study, more adult use, student use, and interpersonal authentic practice of the target language related to higher student performance, while closed-ended and paper-based activities related to lower levels of performance.

Interaction is at the heart of online learning. Frequency of interactions in an online course among learners, the course interface, and the instructor has been associated with significantly higher course achievement (Rockman et al., 2007; Beldarrain, 2008). Communication with and feedback from instructors were identified as the most valuable aspects of online courses in a study of students with specific learning disabilities (SLD) and students with attention deficit hyperactivity disorder (ADHD) in a virtual school (Smouse, 2005). In a study examining the nature of teacher-student interaction in an asynchronous, statewide, self-paced virtual high school, significant differences were found between course completers‘ and non-completers‘ perceptions of teacher-student interaction. However, there were minimal differences between students based on grade awarded and teacher-student interaction (Hawkins, 2010).

The ways an online teacher uses interaction tools influence how students encounter and master concepts in a course. Zucker's study at the Virtual High School (2005) focused on student-student interaction in a discussion board. The majority of students valued inter-student communication within courses. However, student satisfaction, amount of communication, persistence in the course, and course grade were not affected by more heavily weighting student postings to discussion boards in randomly selected classes. Murphy and Coffin's (2003) study of an online high school French class showed that "simultaneous use of a number of tools in combination" (p. 244) enabled group collaboration, one-to-one coaching, oral practice, and other strategies that compensate for the lack of visual cues online.

Technological Approaches

New technologies and tools are adopted in virtual courses to decrease the constraints of the online environment and increase affordances for learning. Recent advances in online learning technology provide solutions to some of the most important and perplexing issues in K–12 education today: teaching core literacy skills, teaching complex math and science skills, teaching problem solving in authentic contexts, and facilitating performing arts instruction.

As virtual course designs vary the balance between synchronous and asynchronous online communication technology, guidance is needed regarding the optimal blend of these learning environments for each course. Videoconferencing has been recommended as a supplement to rather than a primary means of applied music instruction (Dammers, 2009), for example. A review of the environments used in academic subjects found no significant difference in student performance between synchronous and asynchronous high school courses, but higher course completion rates in synchronous courses (Roblyer, Freeman, Donaldson, & Maddox, 2007).

When learning in complex and ill-structured domains, a range of media and communication tools may be advantageous. Support for complex learning has been documented in student use of Personal Learning Environments (PLEs) for science, in which students applied the processes of practicing digital responsibility, practicing digital literacy, organizing content, collaborating and socializing, and synthesizing and creating (Drexler, 2010). The PLEs consisted of ebooks, open education resources, social bookmark tools, widgets, blogs, wikis, microblogs, and other tools and resources in an aggregated interface where students accessed their content materials.

Games, simulations, and augmented reality (AR) environments are finding their way into online courses at primary and secondary levels. The predominant educational problem that AR games for primary and secondary learners has undertaken to address is the cognitive load associated with learning about complex interactive natural systems or processes. Research into the uses of AR games as educational platforms demonstrates the strengths and areas for continued development in the application of augmented reality games for childhood learning in formal and informal settings. AR games may be more efficient for learning than other forms of electronic games due to their more "platformless" nature. A review of 12 AR games for school-age learners found that they supported engagement in learning and understanding of complex scientific concepts (Cavanaugh, 2008).

Game-based learning environments and virtual worlds are in use in primary and secondary virtual school courses. The Florida Virtual School's *Conspiracy Code: Intensive Reading* is a game-based high school course. An independent study found the course to effectively support reading skill development of struggling students across demographic subgroups at levels significantly better than control group students (Haydel, Farr, & Munroe, 2010).

In the high-need fields of mathematics and science, the focus for advanced high school courses is teaching abstract concepts and problem solving. Symbolic representations of mathematical concepts can be made more concrete for students in online courses through the use of virtual manipulatives. A study of online algebra classes compared the performance on graphing linear equations of students who used online graphing tools to students who did not (Cavanaugh, Gillan, Bosnick, Hess, & Scott, 2008). Students using the tools showed larger gains between pretest and posttest scores, but the differences were not significant.

Just as students can feel isolated as online learners, online teachers also experience isolation as professionals. In addition, online teachers face challenges in networking with peers because the numbers of online K–12 teachers are still low. Carroll, Neale, and Isenhour (2004) studied a technological approach to teacher collaboration. The Collaborative Critical Incident Tool was used with a group of virtual school teachers as a problem-and-solution database. Teachers who taught a similar curriculum joined in a focused online forum to report critical incidents in their teaching and threaded discussion of the critical incident reports among the teachers and others involved in the program. The tool was found to be effective "at evoking usability evaluation information, as well as reflective analysis of usability issues from diverse points of view" (p. 215).

RECOMMENDATIONS FOR RESEARCH, POLICY, AND PRACTICE

Even after nearly two decades of exponential growth, research on K–12 online learning still lags relative to adult online learning. The field has made strides in identifying effective practice as the community of practitioners and researchers has grown, but much work remains. A critical step in moving the field forward is consensus on the goals of K–12 online learning. This need is more acute as the forms of K–12 online learning diversify with the increase in blended models and competency-based pathways in school, and as the learners served in K–12 online courses diversifies. Without agreement on these goals, evaluation directed at assessing progress toward the goals cannot happen. If the primary goal is increasing educational equity and access to alternate learning opportunities, then it is likely that online courses judged as "as good as" classroom courses made available to large numbers of students will be sufficient for achieving the goal. If, however, the goal is to offer high-quality education using materials and practices that may not be possible in a classroom, then the nature of instruction, course designs, program models, and student outcomes will differ dramatically. In a re-envisioned K–12 education landscape in which learning environments are combined in personalized ways for the development of each student, access and scalability are lower priorities than interaction, flexible pathways, and individual student needs and capacities. In practice, the goals will vary depending on needs and resources, and the goals will evolve as media and our understanding of learning evolve.

Identifying the Needs and Abilities of Learners

It is imperative that all decision makers in K–12 online learning better understand the students who take courses online, so the level of scaffolding can be adapted for all student populations and to enable multiple pathways for students with different learning preferences. In particular, research should focus on the optimal combinations of student needs, course structure, and support services. Predictive instruments, diagnosis, and prescription of services and scaffolds could enhance every student's chance of success while increasing the efficiency of teachers. Advances in cognitive science can be important contributors to a multidisciplinary research agenda in K–12 online learning. An initiative that would benefit online and offline learners would be the development of programs or course modules that foster the abilities known to result in success: self-discipline, motivation, responsibility, and organization.

Designing Courses and Programs for All Learners

Based on the research demonstrating that online learning can strengthen K–12 students' teamwork skill, problem-solving abilities, creativity, decision-making proficiency, higher-order thinking skills, and success in higher education, virtual schools can design courses to highlight and evaluate these skills. By reporting success in these areas, virtual schools can distinguish themselves as vanguard institutions in education of citizens prepared for participation in a democracy. Long-term research in methods of promoting these skills online and tracking their effects will inform stakeholders and the public. Detailed study of the demands of the content areas will enable course designers to supplement auditory and performance-based courses with the appropriate media, synchronous tools, and offline materials. Such study should result in course design standards and job aids for designers that account for intended learning across domains and in concrete guidance for the design of competency-based pathways with multiple feedback points.

Student-centered Teaching and Technology

State or federal definitions for highly effective online teachers should be articulated to teacher education and professional-development providers. New online teachers require preparation with mentors and practice with the media and methods that work in an environment that they may not have experienced as learners. Study of the teacher preparation and professional development practices that produce exemplary teachers is needed, as are standards. Research is also needed to inform instructors about the most effective interaction types, tools, and frequency for the learners and tasks in a course. Online courses seem to work best for well-defined knowledge domains and pose greater challenge for ill-defined learning and complex skills. Research is needed to develop tools in psychomotor subjects and abstract, complex subjects.

Supportive Administration and Policy

Standards are needed for reporting outcomes of online learning programs. For the first time in education, immense amounts of detailed data are available in course-management systems, but standards do not exist that allow data to be shared, synthesized, and analyzed. A common descriptive system and metrics should be created and refined to ensure that outcomes from online programs can be accurately compared and combined. Such a learning analytics system would streamline processes such as developing cost-benefit rubrics to determine course sustainability, the feasibility of developing in-house courses as compared to purchasing courses, and the most effective and efficient student-teacher ratios. Ultimately, knowledge resulting from standardized data will result in improvements in student success.

Instructional leadership practices in online programs that foster student success have not been well-studied or documented. As the number of organizations entering the field of K–12 online learning grows, the demand will soar for leaders who exemplify the qualities and possess the specialized skills needed for new and dynamic programs. Institutional cultures, work environments, the nature of the work, and tools of leadership that characterize online programs vary from traditional education organizations in important ways. Qualities practiced by leaders that enhance the social interactions at the heart of an online program include managerial skills, embracing diversity, political awareness, and motivation for innovation. Research and case studies are needed that explicate the specific skills and forms known to be successful in various virtual school models.

REFERENCES

Allen, I. E., & Seaman, J. (2010). *Class differences: Online education in the United States, 2010.* Babson Park, MA: Babson Survey Research Group.

Archambault, L., & Crippen, K. (2009). K–12 distance educators at work: Who's teaching online across the United States. *Journal of Research on Technology in Education, 41*(4), 363–391.

Archambault, L., Diamond, D., Brown, R., Cavanaugh, C., Coffey, M., Foures-Aalbu, D., … Zygouris-Coe, V. (2010). *Research committee issues brief: An exploration of at-risk learners and online education.* Vienna, VA: International Association for K–12 Online Learning.

Barbour, M., Kinsella, J., Wicks, M., & Toker, S. (2009). Continuing change in a virtual world: Training and retraining teachers [Special issue]. *Journal of Technology and Teacher Education, 17*(4), 437–458.

Barbour, M. K., & Mulcahy, D. (2008). How are they doing? Examining student achievement in virtual schooling. *Education in Rural Australia, 18*(2), 63–74.

Barbour, M., & Reeves, T. (2009). The reality of virtual schools: A review of the literature. *Computers & Education, 52*(2), 402–416.

Barker, K., & Wendel, T. (2001). *E-learning: Studying Canada's virtual secondary schools.* Kelowna, BC: Society for the Advancement of Excellence in Education.

Barman, C., Stockton, J., Ellsworth, M., Gonzales, C., Huckleberry, T., & Raymond, S. (2002). Evaluation of the soar-high project: A web-based science program for deaf students. *American Annals of the Deaf, 147*(3), 5–10.

Beldarrain, Y. (2008). *Engaging the 21st century learner: An exploratory study of the relationship between interaction and achievement in the virtual high school* (Unpublished doctoral dissertation). Capella University, Minneapolis, MN.

Bernard, R. M., Abrami, P. C., Borokhovski, E., Wade, C. A., Tamim, R. M., Surkes, M. A., & Bethel, E. C. (2009). A meta-analysis of three types of interaction treatments in distance education. *Review of Educational Research, 79*(3), 1243–1289.

Bernard, R. M., Abrami, P. C., Lou, Y., Borokhovski, E., Wade, A., Wozney, L., … Huang, B. (2004). How does distance education compare with classroom instruction? A meta-analysis of the empirical literature. *Review of Educational Research, 74*(3), 379–439.

Bond, A. (2002). *Learning music online: An accessible program for isolated students.* Leabrook, South Australia: Australia National Training Authority.

Bransford, J., Brown, A., & Cocking, R. (Eds.). (1999). *How people learn.* Washington, DC: National Academies Press.

Carpenter, J. (2011). *An exploratory study of the role of teaching experience in motivation and academic achievement in a virtual ninth grade English I course* (Unpublished doctoral dissertation). University of Florida, Gainesville.

Carroll, J., Neale, D., & Isenhour, P. (2004). The collaborative critical incident tool: Supporting reflection and evaluation in a Web community. In C. Cavanaugh (Ed.), *Development and management of virtual schools* (pp. 216–243). Hershey, PA: Information Science.

Cavanaugh, C. (2001). The effectiveness of interactive distance education technologies in K–12 learning: A meta-analysis. *International Journal of Educational Telecommunications, 7*(1), 73–78.

Cavanaugh, C. (2008). Augmented reality gaming in education: Authentic and engaged blended learning. In R. Ferdig (Ed.), *Handbook of research on effective electronic gaming in education* (pp. 83–95). Hershey, PA: Idea Group.

Cavanaugh, C. (2009). *Getting students more learning time online: Distance education in support of expanded learning time.* Washington, DC: Center for American Progress.

Cavanaugh, C., Gillan, K. J., Bosnick, J., Hess, M., & Scott, H. (2008). Effectiveness of interactive online Algebra learning tools. *Journal of Educational Computing Research, 38* (1) 67–95.

Cavanaugh, C., Gillan, K., Kromrey, J., Hess, M., & Blomeyer, R. (2004). *The effects of distance education on K–12 student outcomes: A meta-analysis.* Naperville, IL: Learning Point Associates.

Cavanaugh, C., & Liu, F. (in press). Virtual middle school courses to support anytime, anyplace learning. In C. Mouza & N. Lavigne, (Eds.), *Emerging technologies for the classroom.* New York: Springer.

Compton, K.L., Davis, N.E., & Mackey, J. (2009). Field experience in virtual schools—To be there virtually [Special issue]. *Journal of Technology and Teacher Education, 17*(4), 459–478.

Cooze, M., & Barbour, M. K. (2007). Learning styles: A focus upon e-learning practices and pedagogy and their implications for successful instructional design. *Journal of Applied Educational Technology, 4*(1). http://www.eduquery.com/jaet/JAET4-1_Cooze.pdf

Crawford, D. (2009). *Characteristics leading to student success: A study of online learning environments* (Unpublished doctoral dissertation). Texas A&M University, Commerce

Dammers, R. (2009). Utilizing Internet-based videoconferencing for instrumental music lessons. *Update: Applications of Research in Music Education, 28,* 17–24.

Dana, N. F., Dawson, K., Krell, D., & Wochenhauer, R. (2012, April). *Using action research in professional development for virtual school educators: Exploring an established strategy in a new context.* Paper presented at the annual meeting of the American Educational Research Association, Vancouver, BC.

Darling-Hammond, L. (2000). Teacher quality and student achievement: A review of state policy evidence. *Education Policy Analysis Archives, 8*(1). http://epaa.asu.edu/epaa/v8n1/

Davis, M. (2011). No longer optional. *Education Week, 5*(1), 27–29.

Davis, N., & Roblyer, M. (2005). Preparing teachers for the "schools that technology built": Evaluation of a program to train teachers for virtual schooling. *Journal of Research on Technology in Education, 37*(4), 399–409.

de la Varre, C., Keane, J., & Irvin, M. (2010) Enhancing online distance education in small rural US schools: A hybrid, learner-centred model. *Research in Learning Technology, 18*(3), 193–205.

Dickson, W. (2005). Toward a deeper understanding of student performance in virtual high school courses: Using quantitative analyses and data visualization to inform decision making. In R. Smith, T. Clark, & B. Blomeyer, (Eds.), *A synthesis of new research in K–12 online learning* (pp. 21–23). Naperville, IL: Learning Point Associates.

Dipietro, M. (2010). Virtual school pedagogy: The instructional practices of K–12 virtual school teachers. *Journal of Educational Computing Research, 42*(3), 327–354.

Drexler, W. (2010). The networked student model for construction of personal learning environments: Balancing teacher control and student autonomy. *Australasian Journal of Educational Technology, 26*(3), 369–385.

Ferdig, R. (2010). *Understanding the role and applicability of K–12 online learning to support student dropout recovery efforts.* East Lansing: Michigan Virtual University.

Ferdig, R. E., Cavanaugh, C., DiPietro, M., Black, E. W., & Dawson, K. (2010). Virtual schooling standards and best practices for teacher education. *Journal of Technology and Teacher Education, 17*(4), 479–503.

Ferdig, R.E., Papanastasiou, E., & DiPietro, M. (2005). *Teaching and learning in collaborative virtual high schools.* Report submitted to the North Central Regional Educational Laboratory as part of the K12 Online Learning Initiative.

Foehr, U. G. (2006). *Media multitasking among American youth: Prevalence, predictors and pairings.* Menlo Park, CA: Henry J. Kaiser Family Foundation.

Gershaw, D. (1989). *Line on life: Locus of control.* Retrieved from http://virgil.azwestern.edu/dag/lol/Control-Locus.html

Glick, D. (2011). *Demographics of online students and teachers in the US: 2010–2011.* Maplewood, MN: David Glick and Associates.

Hannum, W. H., Irvin, M. J., Lei, P. W., & Farmer, T. W. (2008). Effectiveness of using learner-centered principles on student retention in distance education courses in rural schools. *Distance Education, 29*(3), 211–229.

Hawkins, A. (2010). *We're definitely on our own: interaction and disconnection in a virtual high school* (Unpublished doctoral dissertation). Brigham Young University, Provo, UT.

Haydel, E., Farr, R., & Munroe, K. (2010). *Conspiracy code: Intensive reading efficacy study.* Bloomington, IN: Educational Research Institute of America.

Hughes, J. E., McLeod, S., Brown, R., Maeda, Y., & Choi, J. (2007). Academic achievement and perceptions of the learning environment in virtual and traditional secondary mathematics classrooms. *American Journal of Distance Education 21*(4), 199–214.

Kapitzke, C., & Pendergast, D. (2005). Virtual schooling: Productive pedagogies or pedagogical possibilities? *Teachers College Record, 107*(8), 1626–1651.

Keeler, C. G., & Horney, M. (2007). Online course designs: Are special needs being met? *American Journal of Distance Education, 21*(2), 61–75.

Kennedy, K. (2010). *The essence of the virtual school practicum: a phenomenological study of pre-service teachers' experiences in a virtual school* (Unpublished doctoral dissertation). University of Florida, Gainesville.

Kinash, S., & Crichton, S. (2007). Supporting the disabled student. In M. G. Moore (Ed.), *Handbook of distance education* (pp. 193–204). Mahwah, NJ: Erlbaum.

Kleiman, G., Carey, R., Bonifaz, A., Haistead, E., & O'Dwyer, L. (2005). A study of the effectiveness of the Louisiana Algebra I Online Project. In R. Smith, T. Clark, & B. Blomeyer, (Eds.), *A synthesis of new research in K–12 online learning* (pp. 36–39). Naperville, IL: Learning Point Associates.

Lenhart, A., Purcell, K., Zickhur, K., & Smith, A. (2010). *Social media and mobile internet use among teens and young adults.* Washington D.C: Pew Internet & American Life Project.

Lewin, C., Whitton, N., Cummings, J., Roberts, B., Saxon, D., Somekh, B., & Lockwood, B. (2008). *MILO: Models of innovative learning online research report.* London: BECTA.

Lewis, S. (2011). *Local implementation of online high school German courses: The influence of local support on student achievement* (Unpublished doctoral dissertation). Oklahoma State University, Stillwater.

Liu, F., & Cavanaugh, C. (2011). Online core course success factors in virtual school: Factors influencing student academic achievement. *International Journal of E-Learning 10*(4) 43-65.

Lowes, S. (2005). Online teaching and classroom change: The impact of virtual high school on its teachers and their schools. In R. Smith, T. Clark, & B. Blomeyer (Eds.), *A synthesis of new research in K–12 online learning* (pp. 24–26). Naperville, IL: Learning Point Associates.

Murphy, E., & Coffin, G. (2003). Synchronous communication in a Web-based senior high school course: Maximizing affordances and minimizing the constraints of the tool. *The American Journal of Distance Education, 17*(4), 235–246.

Nicholas, H., & Ng, W. (2009). Engaging secondary school students with extended and open learning that are supported by online technologies. *Journal of Research on Technology in Education, 41*, 305–328.

Oliver, K., Kellogg, S., Townsend, L., & Brady, K. (2010). Needs of elementary and middle school teachers developing online courses for a virtual school. *Distance Education, 31*(1), 55–75.

Orman, P., & Whitaker, J. (2010). Time usage during face-to-face and synchronous distance music lessons. *American Journal of Distance Education, 24*(2), 92–103.

Picciano A. G., & Seaman, J. (2007). *K–12 online learning: A survey of U.S. school district administrators.* Needham, MA: Sloan Consortium.

Rauh, J. (2010). Online education as a toll good: An examination of the South Carolina virtual school program. *Computers & Education* doi: 10.1016/j.compedu.2010.11.014

Repetto, J., Cavanaugh, C., Wayer, N., & Liu, F. (2010). Virtual high schools: Improving outcomes for students with disabilities. *Quarterly Review of Distance Education, 11*(2), 91–104.

Rice, K., & Dawley, L. (2009). The status of professional development for k-12 online teachers: insights and implications. *Journal of Technology and Teacher Education, 17*(4), 523–545.

Roblyer, M. D., Davis, L., Mills, S., Marshall, J., & Pape, L. (2008). Toward practical procedures for predicting and promoting success in virtual school students. *The American Journal of Distance Education, 22*(2), 90–109.

Roblyer, M. D., Freeman, J., Donaldson, M. B., & Maddox, M. (2007). A comparison of outcomes of virtual school courses offered in synchronous and asynchronous formats. *The Internet and Higher Education, 10*(4), 261–268.

Roblyer, M. D., Freeman, J., Stabler, M., & Schneidmiller, J. (2007). *External evaluation of the Alabama ACCESS Initiative: Phase 3 report.* Eugene, OR: International Society for Technology in Education.

Rockman et al. (2007). *ED PACE Final Report* (Evaluation of the West Virginia Dept. of Education Virtual School Spanish Program). San Francisco, CA: Author.

Rose, R., & Blomeyer, R. (2007). *Access and equity in online classes and virtual schools.* Vienna, VA: International Association for K–12 Online Learning.

Rotter, J. B. (1989). Internal versus external control of reinforcement: A case history of a variable. *American Psychologist, 45*, 489–493.

Russell, T. (1999). *The no significant difference phenomenon.* Montgomery, AL: International Distance Education Certification Center.

Scheick, A. J. (2007). *Virtual vistas: High school students describing their experiences in online courses* (Unpublished dissertation). University of Central Florida, Orlando.

Schnitz, J., & Azbell, J. (2004). Instructional design factors and requirements of online courses and modules. In C. Cavanaugh (Ed.), *Development and management of virtual schools* (pp. 158–177). Hershey, PA: Information Science.

Shachar, M., & Neumann, Y. (2003). Differences between traditional and distance education academic performances: A meta-analytic approach. *The International Review Of Research In Open And Distance Learning, 4*(2), Article 4.2.9. http://www.irrodl.org/index.php/irrodl/article/view/153

Singh, K., & S. Dika. (2003). The educational effects of rural adolescents' social networks. *Journal of Research in Rural Education 18*(2), 114–28.

Smith, R. D. (2009). Virtual voices: Online teachers' perceptions of online teaching standards. *Journal of Technology and Teacher Education, 17*(4), 547–571.

Smouse, T. (2005). *Students with either specific learning disabilities or attention deficit hyperactivity disorder: Perceptions of self as learning in online courses at Florida Virtual School and in the traditional learning environment* (Unpublished doctoral dissertation). University of Central Florida, Orlando.

Sturgis, C., & Patrick, S. (2010). *When failure is not an option: designing competency-based pathways for next generation learning.* Vienna, VA: International Association for K–12 Online Learning.

Talvitie-Siple, J. (2007). *Students' motivation to learn: An evaluation of perceptions, pedagogy, and design in one e-learning environment* (Unpublished doctoral dissertation). The University of North Carolina at Chapel Hill.

Ungerleider, C., & Burns, T. (2003). *A systematic review of the effectiveness and efficiency of networked ICT in education: A state of the field report.* Council of Ministers Canada and Industry Canada. Ottawa, ON: Industry Canada.

U.S. Department of Education, National Center for Education Statistics. (2011). *The Condition of education 2011*(NCES 2011-033). Washington, DC: Author.

U.S. Department of Education, Office of Planning, Evaluation, and Policy Development. (2009). *Evaluation of evidence-based practices in online learning: A meta-analysis and review of online learning studies.* Washington, D.C: Author.

Wan, N. G., & Nicholas, H. (2010). A progressive pedagogy for online learning with high-ability secondary school students: A case study. *Gifted Child Quarterly, 54*(3), 239–251.

Watson, J., Murin, A., Vashaw, L., Gemin, B., & Rapp, C. (2011). *Keeping pace with K–12 online learning: An annual review of policy and practice.* Evergreen, CO: Evergreen Education Group.

Weiner, C. (2003). Key ingredients to online learning: adolescent students study in cyberspace — the nature of the study. *International Journal on E-Learning, 2*(3), 44–50.

Zhao, Y., Lei, J., Yan, B., & Tan, R. S. (2005). What makes the difference? A practical analysis of research on the effectiveness of distance education. *Teachers College Record, 107*(8), 1836–1884.

Zucker, A. (2005). A study of student interaction and collaboration in the virtual high school. In R. Smith, T. Clark, & B. Blomeyer (Eds.), *A synthesis of new research in K–12 online learning* (pp. 43–45). Naperville, IL: Learning Point Associates.

12

CULTURE AND ONLINE DISTANCE LEARNING

CHARLOTTE N. GUNAWARDENA

Online distance learning (ODL) has become a global phenomenon transcending national, political, and geographical boundaries challenging distance educators to re-examine notions of teaching and learning and issues of culture inherent in cross-border delivery of online courses and programs. Rogers, Graham, and Mayes (2007) note that the sheer amount of learning content being developed in the West (defined for this chapter as Eurocentric, North American, Australasian) and exported via the Internet to other countries highlights the crucial need to explore questions of culture more thoroughly in our online course designs to provide a more equitable learning experience for all. Global universities are faced with the choice between continuing to expect all students to adjust to traditional English-Western academic values and uses of language, or changing their processes to accommodate others (Pincas, 2001).

Moore (2006) addresses the challenges and privileges that distance educators are faced within this context and states that rather than addressing international students who have removed themselves from their own culture to be in the culture of the teacher, distance educators are now addressing students who remain physically and socially within their own culture, a culture that is foreign to, and mostly unknown, to the teacher. The educational culture that is transmitted can be very different from the educational culture that adopts the program and can become a dominating force. Moore poses questions for us to consider such as: whose ideas are being shared or incorporated into the local culture, how will this incorporation affect the local culture, how does the instructor react to the student at a personal level, and how does the instructor integrate the student into the dominant culture of the online class. Carr-Chellman (2005) argues that making a single online course that is available worldwide is efficient, but culturally and contextually bankrupt. In order to make a product truly marketable globally, it is necessary to homogenize it. "Isn't learning necessarily contextualized in our own cultures and contexts?" (pp. 9–10). The potential of ODL will be frustrated as long as educators in more technologically developed countries fail to understand the needs and perspectives of students in other countries, and the potential to learn from the perspectives of people in other countries will be lost for students in more technologically developed countries (Moore, Shattuck, & Al-Harthi, 2005). Therefore, in order to provide quality education to diverse audiences, distance educators need to be sensitive to hegemonic perspectives, "the imposition of cultural values and practices" (Latchem, 2005, p. 189), educational differences, and the social, cultural, and language assumptions embedded in online courses and programs.

Several researchers have pointed out the dearth of studies on culture and ODL (Rogers et al., 2007; Uzuner, 2009; Zawacki-Richter, 2009). This could be partly due to the fact that developing definitions of "culture" for the online context, framing questions related to culture, and conducting cross-cultural research studies are challenging. Zawacki-Richter (2009) in his Delphi study of research areas in distance education noted that the role of culture and cultural differences in global distance learning programs should receive much more attention.

This chapter examines the significance of culture and its impact on communication, and the teaching and learning process in ODL. I will begin by attempting to define culture for the online learning context and will explore cultural factors that impact learning, the sociocultural context, group process, language and discourse in ODL. I will conclude with a discussion of implications for designing ODL with culture in mind by presenting an instructional design model we developed that can be used to address cultural factors in learning design.

I address issues of culture, drawing on the emerging body of interdisciplinary research on globalization, the Internet, online learning, technology-based language learning, and virtual communities, and from my own previous discussion of culture and online distance education (Gunawardena & La Pointe, 2007; Gunawardena & La Pointe, 2008; Gunawardena, Wilson, & Nolla, 2003), and research studies conducted in China, Mexico, Morocco, Spain, Sri Lanka, Turkey, and the United States.

DEFINING CULTURE IN THE CONTEXT OF ONLINE DISTANCE LEARNING (ODL)

Many of the studies that have examined the role of culture in ODL (Gunawardena et al., 2001; Moore et al., 2005; Uzuner, 2009) have defined culture employing the four dimensions of nationally held cultural values: individualism-collectivism, power distance, uncertainty avoidance, and masculinity-femininity, developed by Hofstede (1980, 1986) and based on a factor analysis of business-oriented cultural values and dimensions of contextual information, high and low context communication styles advanced by Hall (1973, 1990).

Ess (2009) provides a considered critique of the applicability of Hofstede's framework to the online context and notes that what interests CMC researchers is how national, as well as other cultural identities such as ethnicity, youth culture, and gender, etc., interact with intercultural communication online; that is already removed from the face-to-face setting. Very often those who communicate online identify with multiple frames of reference. They note that Hofstede's framework (1980) and, to a lesser extent, Hall's (1973, 1990) conceptualization of culture appear to be limited to national cultural differences and thus less well-suited for understanding and researching the multiple cultural differences within nation-states, including the third or hybrid identities that are themselves fostered by the cultural flows facilitated by the Internet and the Web. Our research (Gunawardena, Idrissi Alami, Jayatilleke, & Bouacharine, 2009) supported this view by showing that although Sri Lankan and Moroccan societies would be classified in Hofstede's framework as high power distance societies, participants from these countries look to the online medium as a liberating medium that equalizes status differences, thereby providing them with a level playing field. Therefore, their interactions online will not necessarily reflect high power distance communication, even though their culture would be classified as high power distance. On the other hand, we found Hall's (1973, 1990) conceptualization of high context and low context communication styles, and implied indirect and direct communication styles, useful for analyzing cultural differences in communication online. Context is important to understanding a message and its connotations in both Moroccan and Sri Lankan cultures. Many Moroccans and Sri Lankans adopt indirect communication styles in face-to-face communication. Therefore, Hall's conceptualization helped us to analyze if there were changes in communication styles when participants interacted online, or whether they were using the same communication styles online as they would use face-to-face (Gunawardena et al., 2009).

Goodfellow and Hewling (2005), and Goodfellow and Lamy (2009), like Ess (2009), critique the essentialist frameworks developed by Hofstede and Hall to describe national cultural characteristics as inappropriate to understand culture in transnational online learning contexts. Goodfellow and Hewling (2005) move from an "essentialist" to a "negotiated" perspective to conceptualize culture as being negotiated in online discussions. This stance on seeing culture as negotiated is similar to Hall's definition of culture as communication "Culture is communication and communication is culture" (Hall, 1990, p. 186). Raffaghelli and Richieri (2012) note that "Networked learning should emphasize Bruner's idea about education as *forum* where culture is not transmitted but generated through interaction" (pp. 102–103) leading to new learning cultures.

Goodfellow and Lamy (2009) undertake the task of problematizing the very notion of culture in connection with online learning environments and move on to develop the concept of "learning cultures," which takes account of the emergence of "new" cultural and social identities in virtual learning communities which draw on cybercultures of the Internet as well as systems of cultural relations inherited from conventional educational or corporate settings. They note that the emergence of "learning cultures" might transcend both the institutional cultures of learning in which the resources originated and the cultural learning styles predominant in the sites where they were taken up: "It is characteristic of online learning cultures that the negotiation of personal and social identities is integral to learning, just as a critical awareness of culture is integral to a nonhegemonic model of online learning … The identities of participants become part of the knowledge constructed as well as the means of construction" (Goodfellow & Lamy, p. 176).

Therefore, one can come to terms with the complexity of culture in online courses, by defining it from the perspective of the Internet as a culture in its own right, blurring the boundaries between the real and virtual worlds. Creating and participating in new communities is one of the primary pleasures people have interacting online, and these communities develop their own conventions for interaction, and for what is acceptable and not acceptable behavior online (Baym, 1995). "This web of verbal and textual significances that are substitutes for and yet distinct from the networks of meaning of the wider community binds users into a common culture whose specialized meanings allow the sharing of imagined realities" (Reid, 1995, p. 183). Ess (2009) expands this line of thought further by exploring the notion that technology itself is culturally produced and thus is also a culturally shaped artifact in contrast to the notion that technology is culturally neutral or just a tool and hence its design and implementation requires no attention to its cultural origin. He discusses how digital environments can create "third cultures" where identity can be constructed and negotiated through interaction with other participants.

Thus, subscribing to a view of culture as negotiated online, I have adopted the definition of culture as an "idioculture," a concept developed by Gary Alan Fine and cited by Cole and Engestrom (2007), in my own work (Gunawardena et al., 2009) as an appropriate definition of culture online:

> An idioculture is a system of knowledge, beliefs, behaviors, and customs shared by members of an interacting group to which members can refer and that serve as the basis of further interaction. Members recognize that they share experiences, and these experiences can be referred to with the expectation they will be understood by other members, thus being used to construct a reality for the participants. (Fine, 1987, p. 125)

This definition accommodates the idea of culture as a locally emerging activity system involving a briefer stretch of history (Cole & Engestrom, 2007) and includes multiple cultural selves and hybrid identities on the Internet that interact with each other cross-culturally to form unique cultures of their own. The definition allows for the development of culture through dialogue, negotiation, and the sharing of experiences. The definition fits well with the ephemeral, fluid nature of the Internet which fuels the development of cybercultures, cultures that emerge among those who use the Internet to communicate, developing its own etiquette, norms, customs, ethics, and mythology, just as an idioculture does.

With this understanding of culture online, I next explore a selection of research studies on culture and ODL.

RESEARCH ON CULTURE AND ONLINE DISTANCE LEARNING (ODL)

Although there are many ways in which culture impacts ODL, in the following section, I have selected to focus my discussion to examine how culture plays a role in (a) online learning specifically social construction of knowledge, (b) the sociocultural environment, specifically social presence and group process, and (c) language and discourse.

Learners and Preferred Ways of Learning

How one learns and what one learns is culturally determined. People reared in different cultures learn to learn differently (Matsumoto, 1996; Merriam, 2007). Some do so by pattern drill, memory, and rote as explained by behaviorist theory; some work in groups learning through interaction with others to cross the zone of proximal development (Vygotsky, 1978). Generally, the primary theory of knowledge construction underlying most emerging online course designs emphasizes the exchange of ideas, expressions of agreement and disagreement to construct meaning.

Biesenbach-Lucas (2003), in her survey of the differences between native and non-native students in their perceptions of asynchronous discussions, found that both groups of students tended to avoid "challenge and explain cycles" where they had to do more than demonstrate knowledge by also agreeing and disagreeing in non-abrasive ways. She notes that non-native speakers, particularly students from Asian countries, consider it far less appropriate to challenge and criticize the ideas of others. In addition, they may not know how to express disagreement appropriately in English. This view is supported by Zhao and McDougall's (2008) when they note that Chinese students "may post fewer messages in online discussions, because they are not accustomed to discussion-based learning and hesitate to contradict their peers and instructors in a public forum" (p. 75). Cultures which value interpersonal harmony may refrain from critical comments in text conferencing to avoid tension and disagreement (Hu, 2005). Rye and Støkken (2012) made a similar observation in their study of online collaboration in a global master's program. They point out that the African (Ghanian and Ugandan) students were surprised by the Norwegian students' very direct and critical communication with the academic staff and fellow students, which was seen as impolite behavior in an academic setting. This situation made them uncomfortable, as respect for the teacher's authority is a deep-rooted value in most African societies. "Thus, the first months of global online collaboration was for many of the African students characterised by observation and by wondering about how they might be able to function as a real member of the online community" (p. 200). Biesenbach-Lucas notes that this lack of challenge and disagreement of ideas is troubling as it is the "resolution of such areas of agreement and disagreement that 'results in higher forms of reasoning' because 'cognitive development requires that individuals encounter others who contradict their own intuitively derived ideas'" (p. 37).

The point we need to consider here is whether such challenges to ideas expressed by others in online discussions is a necessary condition for higher forms of reasoning and knowledge construction or whether it is merely an expectation from a western academic point of view, particularly American. Further, we should consider whether higher cognitive reasoning and knowledge construction can happen without such open disagreement of ideas. The following discussion of two studies from Mexico and Sri Lanka provide a different perspective.

Lopez-Islas (2001), in his analysis of knowledge construction in online discussion forums at Monterrey Tech-Virtual University in Mexico using the Gunawardena, Lowe, and Anderson's (1997) Interaction Analysis Model (IAM) that describes five phases in the process of knowledge construction: (1) Sharing, comparing and agreement, (2) cognitive dissonance or disagreement of ideas, (3) negotiation of meaning and co-construction of knowledge, (4) testing and modification of proposed co-construction, and (5) application of newly constructed meaning, observed that cognitive dissonance (phase two) was not evident in his data as open disagreement with ideas expressed by others is not appropriate in the Mexican cultural context. Participants moved to knowledge construction (phase 3) without moving through the cognitive dissonance phase as specified in the IAM model.

In our studies that employed the IAM model to examine the impact of cross-cultural e-mentoring on social construction of knowledge in inquiry-based asynchronous discussion forums between American e-mentors and Sri Lankan protégés (Gunawardena et al., 2008; Gunawardena et al., 2011) we found a similar result. The Sri Lankan participants did not openly disagree at the level of ideas but moved to negotiation of meaning and co-construction of new knowledge based on consensus building. Therefore, we had to re-define dissonance as specified in the IAM model in cultural terms. In further exploration of the online asynchronous interactions in the course, we found that while the academic discussion was very polite and lacked open disagreement of ideas, strong opinions and disagreements were expressed by the same participants in the informal "virtual canteen," where they engaged in a heated debate about gender issues. This finding made us reflect on the role of culture in academic online discussions. It is possible that collectivist traits in both the Sri Lankan and Mexican cultural contexts may have transferred to online group interaction in an academic setting where open disagreement of ideas would make the participants uncomfortable. Yet, it also shows that these very same participants as noted in the Sri Lankan context would engage in a heated debate in an informal discussion space. So, the context of the discussion, whether it was formal or informal, is key to the expression of open disagreement. This is an interesting cultural difference that should be explored further in other online cross-cultural communication contexts.

Weinberger, Clark, Hakkinen, Tamura, and Fischer (2007) have observed the issues and challenges involved in argumentative knowledge construction in cross-cultural interactions and state that there is little knowledge on the question of how learners from different cultures engage in and ultimately benefit from argumentative knowledge construction. They note that more research needs to be conducted on interaction patterns of collaborative learners within various cultures and propose examining the use of collaboration scripts that will support learners to engage in argumentative discussions.

From his study of a global e-mail debate on intercultural communication, Chen (2000) showed that differences in thinking patterns and expression styles influence student reactions to teaching methods. The debate format caused orientation problems for some participants as the debate is a product of low-context culture that requires a direct expression of one's argument by using logical reasoning. Students who come from high-context cultures in Asia and Latin America find an argumentative format uncomfortable in an academic context, and this discomfort is exacerbated when the debate is facilitated through a medium devoid of non-verbal cues. Kim and Bonk (2002), in their cross-cultural comparisons of online collaboration between Korean, U.S. and Finnish students using the Curtis and Lawson's (2001) coding scheme, found differences in online collaborative behaviors: Korean students were more social and contextually driven online, Finnish students were more group-focused as well as reflective and, at times, theoretically driven, and U.S. students more action-oriented and pragmatic in seeking results or giving solutions.

Through in-depth online interviews, Shattuck (2005) attempted to understand how non-American students, primarily Asian, perceive the values related to study in an American distance learning program, and found that these students felt marginalized within the e-learning environment. She notes that online learning designs based on constructivist pedagogy and a high level of interaction can be a lonely and uncomfortable place for an international online learner whose cultural experience is different than the dominant educational culture (cited in Moore, Shattuck, & Al-Harthi, 2005).

In our study using nine instruments to analyze preferred ways of learning in Hispanic adult learners in a Northern New Mexico community college (Sanchez & Gunawardena, 1998), we found that these learners showed a preference for collaborative over competitive activities; reflectivity in task engagement; and a preference for an action-based, active approach to learning. For these learners, we recommended designing real world problem solving or case-based reasoning tasks in asynchronous learning environments that provide opportunities for reflection and active collaborative learning. In general, it is best to design alternative activities to reach the same objective and give students the option of selecting activities which best meet their culturally adapted ways of learning.

Gibson (1998) makes a plea for understanding the distance learner in context (for example, in relation to classroom, peer group, workplace, family, culture, and society) and the impact of their learning on those who share their lives in the multiple interacting contexts that contain them. "Our challenge as educators is to consider how the context might be seen as a partner in teaching and learner support" (p. 121). Based on their interviews with Ghanian, Ugandan, and Norwegian students on how the every day life of these students influence their participation in online collaboration in a global online master's program, Rye and Støkken (2012) showed the importance of recognizing the students' local context as a significant part of their educational space. Their exploratory case study showed how the influence of the students' local context creates an online learning space characterized by inequality. They note that how the local life of students interacts with their global interconnectedness has not yet been widely researched, although these relationships are increasingly characteristic of online higher education. Taking into consideration the local context, culture, and needs as we design learning can avoid the trap of the dominant provider and the dependent receiver in online global programs (Mason, 1998).

THE SOCIO-CULTURAL ENVIRONMENT AND SOCIAL PRESENCE

Tu (2001) conducted a study of how Chinese perceive social presence in an online environment and found that three dimensions: social context, online communication, and interactivity affected Chinese students' perceptions of social presence, and observed that engaging Chinese students in a more interactive online learning environment will increase social presence. In addition, online privacy and public/private issues impacted the level of social presence. Chinese students perceived online communication as a more comfortable medium to express their thoughts due to lack of confrontation and face-saving concerns, but, on the other hand, they were concerned that their messages may appear in public areas that may cause them to lose face and privacy.

In a cross-cultural study of group process and development in online conferences in the United States and Mexico, we (Gunawardena et al., 2001) found that social presence emerged as a theme addressed by both U.S. and Mexican focus group participants. U.S. participants felt that social presence is necessary to the smooth functioning of a group, to provide a sense that the group members are real people. Social presence built trust and led to self-disclosure. Building relationships enhanced online civility. The Mexican focus group participants, however, felt that having personal information about the participants was unimportant. For these participants, how peers contribute to the conference is more important than knowing their personal information. The differences in the way that U.S. participants and Mexican participants perceived social presence could be attributed to cultural differences related to power distance (Hofstede, 1980) in the two societies. In a high power distance society like Mexico, computer-mediated communication was seen as equalizing power and status differences present in society. Therefore, participants did not want their peers to interject social context cues that would take away the equalizing power of the online environment.

To further examine social presence from a cultural perspective, we undertook a study (Gunawardena, Bouachrine, Idrissi Alarmi, & Jayatilleke, 2006) to generate a theoretical model of social presence from the perspective of two sociocultural contexts—Morocco and Sri Lanka—by examining the communication conventions and processes employed by Internet chat users who develop online relationships with people they do not know. Employing qualitative ethnographic analysis and grounded theory building, this study explored cultural perspectives on "social presence" and properties related to the construct "social presence" in online communication. Preliminary results showed that social presence played a key role in the communication patterns of Internet chat users. Properties associated with social presence in both cultural contexts include: self-disclosure, building trust, expression of identity, conflict resolution, interpretation of silence, and the innovation of language forms to generate immediacy.

Al-Harthi (2005) conducted in-depth telephone interviews with Arab students in order to understand how they perceived the values related to study in an American distance learning program and found that for Arab students the lack of physical presence in the online environment was seen as a positive feature because, in addition to accessibility advantages recognizable to Western students, it provided a reduced risk of social embarrassment. Female Arab students in particular felt more comfortable studying online as it allowed for an easy conformity with the separation of genders that is traditional in Muslim culture. Moore (2006) notes that this sensitivity to what other people think is more foreign to American students, but for people of more collectivist (as contrasted with individualist) cultures, a form of communication that gives ways of saving face has value that may outweigh some of what the Western student might consider drawbacks. Al-Harthi's study identified several ways in which Arab students dealt with problems differently than their American colleagues. These findings provide insight into the social dynamic of ODL and the cultural factors we need to consider as we design.

GROUP PROCESS AND CONFLICT RESOLUTION

Chan (2005), in his study of 59 tutors at the Open University of Hong Kong and their 1,106 students, found that four dimensions: renqing (humanized obligation, carrying with it a continued expectation for mutual favor exchanges), face, harmony, and leadership, promoted group effectiveness. Tutors who brought face and saved face were considered more effective in creating harmony and balance in relationships. This study reflects the social obligation to help others within the social group.

In Morocco, communication patterns are more high context and less direct than in the United States. There are many taboos, and *hchouma*—that can be translated as shameful. Many questions do not get answered because Moroccans cannot be very direct and tell things to the face of the other. This opens up room for interpretation and sometimes miscommunication (Gunawardena et al., 2009). The notion of "shame" was also a factor in Al-Harthi's (2005) study of Arab distance learners for whom guarding family reputation is key. One of the Arab female participants reported that she would log off an online discussion when joined by a fellow student who was acquainted with her family to avoid the risk of saying anything that would reflect negatively on her family. This shows how social conventions that exist in the real world are also translated into online interaction.

In their study of synchronous chatting, Gunawardena et al. (2006), noted that anonymity is a factor in the attempt to resolve conflict. If the person who insults is a stranger (and anonymous), either he or she will be ignored or insulted back. Cultural perceptions and social status seem to influence the way insults are handled. Attempts to resolve conflict depend on the strength of the relationship that has been built and the reality of the other. Face-saving strategies are adopted when there is a bond and when there is an interest in maintaining the relationship. If not, in the real-time world of chat, the general tendency is to close the window and forget the person. A study of face saving strategies employed in asynchronous online communication showed that all 16 participants representing six different ethnic groups would post a message in reply, saying that they had been misunderstood or that their discussion had been misinterpreted (Walsh, Gregory, Lake, & Gunawardena, 2003). These studies show that attempts to resolve conflict are different in synchronous and asynchronous environments, and depend on the relationship that has been established.

Language and Discourse

Martin and Nakayama (2003) distinguish language from discourse. While language refers to a method of communication, discourse refers to how language is used by particular groups of people, in particular contexts, and for particular purposes. The grammar of each language voices and shapes ideas, serving as a guide for people's mental activity, for analysis of impressions, and for synthesis of their mental stock in trade (Whorf, 1998). Language also reinforces cultural values and worldviews.

Although it is increasingly recognized as the international langua franca, using English to learn, rather than one's native language, puts learners at a disadvantage. Often English is a learner's third or fourth language with little opportunity to actually use English daily. Communicating in English requires Asian and Arabic speakers to enter individual letters, one stroke at a time, on a keyboard while frequently referring to online dictionaries. English as a Second Language (ESL) learners need additional time for reading and need content provided in a variety of formats—written lectures, audio recordings, and concept maps.

Goodfellow and Lamy (2009) note that research into telecollaborative projects for language learning carries many stories of full or partial failure, not in the use of code (French, Spanish, or Japanese, etc.) but in the partner's understandings of each others' cultural styles and genres. When computer users from different cultures communicate with each other they may not be aware of each other's genre (discourse type or discourse style) that is appropriate for the exchange. Kramsch and Thorne's study (2002) offers a good example of how miscommunication in an intercultural asynchronous online dialogue between American and French students was caused, not so much by deficient individual linguistic styles, but mostly by a lack of understanding "cultural genres" in each other's discourse.

In our study of informal synchronous chatting in Morocco and Sri Lanka (Gunawardena et al., 2009), we found innovations in language forms to adapt to communication via chat. While the predominant language of chat in Morocco was French and in Sri Lanka, English, participants interjected the native language using the Latin keyboard to increases their level of social presence and connectedness when they were chatting with people who understood the native language. Chatters had developed unique forms of textual language and visual expressions to communicate their ideas and feelings through a new medium. Users bring with them the conventions of their native language, which embody cultural traits as well as their prior use of the second language, English or French. This implies that as online learning cultures develop, students and facilitators have to adjust to new modes of communication and interaction.

Smith (2005) found that a lack of awareness of cultural differences and generalizations about others who use English as a second language may lead learners from dominant cultures to unknowingly de-authorize non-native group members that, although well intended, limit opportunities for participation. Groups assigned minimal responsibilities to their non-native English-speaking members because they felt these learners face unusual challenges of adapting to the United States and completing their studies. These non-native-English speakers then feel uncomfortable and unproductive. This crystallized the recognition of difference among group members; non-native speakers were perceived as "others" and treated as a threat to the group in ways that mirror hierarchical structures within larger society, creating unsafe learning spaces (Smith, 2005). Therefore, providing access to mainstream group discourse has to be managed diplomatically so as to not silence the voices of non-native speakers.

La Pointe and Barrett (2005), who taught English at a distance to Taiwanese and Mainland Chinese students, found that although students recognize the need to study English through materials from the target culture, when they have no prior experience with the content of the materials, they cannot participate. When the topic was considered too far away, it did not generate the intended level of critical thinking as would a topic that more directly affect students' lives. This study showed that many students feared speaking English with native speakers. Students, particularly adults, seek a safe place to speak. The Internet provides that safe space through the removal of visual cues; informants reported that they are more willing to try to speak English when they cannot see either other students who they perceive to be better English speakers, or the teacher's dismay as they are speaking. They also feel safer participating from their homes.

IMPLICATIONS FOR DESIGNING
ONLINE DISTANCE LEARNING (ODL)

Moore (2006) asks: how to set up a course and manage it "so as to induce the different forms of understanding that lie in the culture represented by each student, to the greater benefit of the whole class?" (p. 4). Germain-Rutherford and Kerr (2008) review design guidelines for culturally inclusive online teaching and learning. Rogers et al. (2007) examine the cultural competence of instructional designers. Parrish and Linder-VanBerschot (2010) developed the Cultural Dimensions of Learning Framework to address issues of culture when designing multicultural instruction. Given the discussion in this chapter of the myriad ways in which culture plays a role in online communication and learning, I now present an instructional design model that we developed and currently use to design online learning for diverse audiences.

The Wisdom Communities (WisCom) instructional model that we developed (Gunawardena et al., 2006) and have used to design and deliver online graduate courses at U.S. and Venezuelan universities and an online faculty professional development program in Sri Lanka is flexible in accommodating opportunities to design for cultural inclusivity. WisCom is most suitable for designing learning outcomes that require the exchange of multiple perspectives, problem solving, negotiation of meaning, and social construction of knowledge, where there are no right or wrong answers. Based on socio-cultural and socio-constructivist learning philosophies (Vygotsky, 1978) and distance education principles, WisCom aims to facilitate transformational learning by fostering the development of (a) a wisdom community, (b) knowledge innovation, (c) and mentoring and learner support to aid knowledge innovation and community building. It is based on a Cycle of Inquiry module design, as recommended by Bransford et al. (2004) in their research of how people learn. Their module design mirrors authentic learning and starts with a learning challenge—a question, a problem, or case to be solved—moving a group of learners through a process of exploration, gathering, and sharing of resources and experience to address the learning challenge, discussing points of view with peers to learn from multiple perspectives, and concluding with the creation of a knowledge artifact (such as a concept map) that provides a solution to the learning challenge. This knowledge artifact is preserved in an online format for future learners. The module helps learners to transform their perspectives through self-reflection and reflection on the community's learning process, which is documented in online journals. A detailed explanation and visual representation of the WisCom design model is found in Gunawardena et al. (2006). I discuss below how we have used WisCom to design culturally inclusive online learning.

Developing a Wise Community

Bleyl (2000), after an extensive review of literature from diverse cultural perspectives, concluded that wisdom appears to be an integration of cognition, affect, and reflectivity. Reflective learning is a significant aspect of perspective transformations, the instructional goal of the WisCom model. WisCom is community centered. Based on the notion that culture is created and negotiated online in a learning community and subscribing to the view of "idioculture" discussed earlier, we believe that in designing for cultural inclusivity it is essential that we develop a learning culture that can take advantage of the diversity present among its members, a culture where each member has a voice. One of the initial activities the community undertakes is identity negotiation, where members have the option of either presenting him or herself or another to the online community. Trust building, self-disclosure, and face negotiation were important aspects in the expression of identity and the generation of social presence (Gunawardena et al., 2009). Self-presentation is difficult and uncomfortable in many cultures, and therefore, in a cross-cultural telecollaboration, we undertook with a Chinese university, we paired students so that the American students introduced the Chinese students, and vice versa, which overcame the difficulty the Chinese students had in presenting themselves online. Students either uploaded a photograph or an image that represented them. During the first two weeks, students engaged in community building activities and shared and described an important personal artifact.

To situate the learning context, the learning philosophy, and local flavor of the course, we adopt the metaphor of giftedness from the Keresan Pueblo communities in New Mexico as a core value, where giftedness (or the Western concept of intelligence) is defined as the individual's ability to contribute or "give back" to the well-being of the entire community (Romero, 1994). The individual is seen in relationship to the learning community. In large classes, students work in peer support groups so that they have voice and opportunity to contribute. As Furstenberg, Levet, English, and Maillet (2001) have advocated, we to try to make culturally hidden semantic networks explicit by structuring course discussions around enabling students to situate themselves in relation to others, to perceive similarities and differences in personal opinions and reactions within the group, and start identifying the complex factors influencing their attitudes so that they may become aware of how the content and manner of what they say is relevant to their immediate situation and to a given context. Communication protocols that describe how to participate in academic discussions, how language and discourse are used, what is negotiable and non-negotiable, and institutional expectations are posted at the beginning of the course. Guidelines are provided for leading and moderating online discussions to facilitate knowledge and community building. Social rules and conventions of communication are vital to understanding the norms according to which we carry out conversations and judge others. For instance, cultural variations in the use of silence might well lie behind lack of participation in online discussions. As Ishii and Bruneau (1994) have pointed out, the Japanese culture nurtures silence, reserve, and formality, whereas Western cultures place more value on speech, self-assertion, and informality.

When WisCom was implemented in an online faculty development forum in Sri Lanka, we found through our regression model that interaction (learner-learner and peer interaction) was a strong predictor of learner satisfaction among 53 participants explaining 50.2% of the variance in Learner Satisfaction (Gunawardena et al., 2007). This finding showed that if learning environments are designed for cultural inclusivity, then, interaction becomes a key vehicle for learning and satisfaction, thus dispelling the myth that South Asian students are reluctant to interact online.

Mentoring and Learner Support

WisCom utilizes mentoring as a mechanism for people supporting people as knowledge is created, and thereby contributing to building a community of wisdom. Mentoring aids in supporting new members and in the inclusion of diverse members into the community and diversity contributes new perspectives and wisdom to the community. Matching a novice or inexperienced learner with a more experienced counterpart facilitates the zone of proximal development (Vygotsky, 1978), which refers to achieving a learner's optimal developmental potential, with assistance from an expert. Peer mentoring is utilized to support learning in peer groups and distributed e-mentoring brings in e-mentors from the community who share their expertise with specific groups or the entire class. In our study of cross-cultural e-mentoring, where American e-mentors supported social construction of knowledge in Sri Lankan protégés (Gunawardena et al., 2011), several e-mentor roles emerged, such as setting the context and expectations, facilitating and creating a momentum for the discussion, and facilitating of metacognitive activity amongst protégés. In addition to facilitation, there was evidence of the e-mentor taking a supportive role when issues arose with the technology used by groups. E-mentors initiated the learning activity by setting the context and clearly defining the expectations even though they were based in a different country.

Learner support is designed to empower learners and honor diversity. Cultures differ in problem recognition, the problems for which help is sought, and attitudes and readiness to seek help. Understanding cultural and gender differences in help seeking enables us to design a learner support system that addresses diverse learner needs (Gunawardena & La Pointe, 2007).

Knowledge Innovation

In online learning, a key feature of knowledge creation is discourse. Learners progress through the Cycle of Inquiry in WisCom exploring multiple perspectives through discourse. The Cycle of Inquiry utilizes the pre-existing knowledge of the learner by asking the learner to determine what they know and do not know about the learning challenge they have to address. This provides the opportunity for each learner to contribute his or her prior knowledge and perspectives. Through dialogue with the instructor, mentors, and peers, students are able to negotiate learning activities to reach the same objectives. The Cycle of Inquiry is flexible enough to balance learning activities and media formats to provide opportunities to learn in preferred ways and activities that challenge the learner to learn in new or less preferred ways. While social construction of knowledge is an important goal, challenges to other ideas, or open disagreement, is not emphasized as crucial to knowledge construction. Learners negotiate within their peer groups, how they will address the learning challenge, the resources they will seek and share, and the type of collaborative activities they will engage in. Learning activities in the community are designed to develop a learning culture incorporating the diversity inherent in the class. Learners reflect on, share, and present their cultures' answers to problems through their chosen means—photos and videos, drawings, storytelling, animation, song, scholarly text and poetry. Learners work in their small peer support groups to complete assigned tasks and reflect on the experience in the online journals. Course grades reflect contributions to both knowledge building and community building.

Exploratory studies conducted with graduate students in a Southwestern university in the United States in 2010, and in a Venezuelan university in 2005, and 2006, showed that the WisCom instructional design model was effective in building an online learning community, and supporting social construction of knowledge leading to transformative learning (Gunawardena & Layne, 2011). Additional research with diverse learners in various other cultural contexts is necessary to validate the efficacy of the WisCom design model.

I have presented one model that has helped me to design online learning for diverse audiences. However, what counts as sound educational practice in one context in all likelihood presents a form of cultural bias on the part of the person or institution promoting that educational practice. We as distance educators need to be cognizant of our own positionality and communicate our world views clearly in our designs, and through rigorous evaluation and research determine which designs work best in specific contexts for specific learners. The field is wide open for quality research on questions of culture and online learning. I hope this chapter helps you to begin that quest.

ACKNOWLEDGMENT

It is with deep gratitude that I acknowledge the significant contributions made by Deborah K. La Pointe (1952–2009) to our collaborative writing on issues of culture in previous publications.

REFERENCES

Al-Harthi, A. S. (2005). Distance higher education experiences of Arab Gulf students in the United States: A cultural perspective. *The International Review of Research in Open and Distance Learning, 6*(3). Retrieved from http://www.irrodl.org/index.php/irrodl

Baym, N. K. (1995). The emergence of community in computer-mediated communication. In S. G. Jones (Ed.), *CyberSociety: Computer-mediated communication and community* (pp. 138–163). Thousand Oaks, CA: Sage.

Biesenbach-Lucas, S. (2003). Asynchronous discussion groups in teacher training classes: Perceptions of native and non-native students, *Journal of Asynchronous Learning Networks, 7*(3), 24–46. Retrieved from http://sloanconsortium.org/publications/jaln_main

Bleyl, M. (2000). *The wise ones: A multi-cultural perspective* (Unpublished doctoral dissertation). The University of New Mexico, Albuquerque.

Bransford, J., Vye, N., Bateman, H., Brophy, S., & Roselli, B. (2004). Vanderbilt's AMIGO project: Knowledge of how people learn enters cyberspace. In T. M. Duffy & J. R. Kirkley (Eds.), *Learner-centered theory and practice in distance education: Cases from higher education* (pp. 209–234). Mahwah, NJ: Erlbaum.

Carr-Chellman, A. A. (Ed.). (2005). Introduction. In *Global perspectives on e-learning: Rhetoric and reality* (pp. 1–16). Thousand Oaks, CA: Sage.

Chan, B. (2005). From West to East: The impact of culture on personality and group dynamics. *Cross Cultural Management, 12*(1), 31–43.

Chen, G. M. (2000). Global communication via Internet: An educational application. In G. M. Chen & W. J. Starosta (Eds.), *Communication and global society* (pp. 143–157). New York, NY: Peter Lang.

Cole, M., & Engestrom, Y. (2007). Cultural-historical approaches to designing for development, in J. Valsiner & A. Rosa (Eds.), *The Cambridge handbook of sociocultural psychology* (pp. 484–507). New York, NY: Cambridge University Press.

Curtis, D. D., & Lawson, M. J. (2001). Exploring collaborative online learning. *Journal of Asynchronous Learning Networks, 5*(1), 21–34.

Ess, C. (2009). When the solution becomes the problem: Cultures and individuals as obstacles to online learning. In R. Goodfellow & M. N. Lamy (Eds.), *Learning cultures in online education* (pp. 15–29). London, UK: Continuum.

Fine, G. A. (1987). *With the boys: Little League Baseball and preadolescent culture.* Chicago, IL: University of Chicago Press.

Furstenberg G., Levet S., English K., & Maillet K. (2001). Giving a virtual voice to the silent language of culture: The cultural project. *Language Learning & Technology, 5*(1), 55–102.

Germain-Rutherford, A., & Kerr, B. (2008). An inclusive approach to online learning environments: Models and resources. *Turkish Online Journal of Distance Education, 9*(2), 64–85. Retrieved from https://tojde.anadolu.edu.tr/tojde30/index.htm

Gibson, C. C. (1998). The distance learner in context. In *Distance learners in higher education: Institutional responses for quality outcomes* (pp. 113–125). Madison, WI: Atwood.

Goodfellow, R., & Hewling, A. (2005). Reconceptualising culture in virtual learning environments: From an "essentialist" to a "negotiated" perspective, *E-Learning, 2*(4), 355–367. doi:10.2304/elea.2005.2.4.355

Goodfellow, R., & Lamy, M. N. (Eds.). (2009). *Learning cultures in online education.* London, UK: Continuum.

Gunawardena, C. N., Bouachrine, F., Idrissi Alami, A., & Jayatilleke, G. (2006, April). *Cultural perspectives on social presence: A study of online chatting in Morocco and Sri Lanka.* Paper presented at the Annual Meeting of the American Educational Research Association, San Francisco, CA.

Gunawardena, C. N., Fernando, S., Kulasekere, C., Lamontagne, M. D., Ekanayake, M. B., Thaiyamuthu, T., & Jayatilleke, B. G. (2007, June). *Online tutor mentor development through community building: A case study from a transitional nation.* Paper presented at the Third International Conference on Open and Online Learning, Universiti Sains Malaysia, Penang, Malaysia.

Gunawardena, C. N., Idrissi Alami, A., Jayatilleke, G., & Bouacharine, F. (2009). Identity, gender, and language in synchronous cybercultures: A cross-cultural study. In R. Goodfellow & M. N. Lamy (Eds.), *Learning cultures in online education* (pp. 30–51). London, UK: Continuum.

Gunawardena, C. N., Keller, P. S., Garcia, F., Faustino, G. L., Barrett, K., Skinner, J. K., … Fernando, S. (2011, December). Transformative education through technology: Facilitating social construction of knowledge online through cross-cultural e-mentoring. In V. Edirisinghe (Ed.), *Proceedings of The 1st International Conference on the Social Sciences and the Humanities, 1,* 114–118. Peradeniya, Sri Lanka: Faculty of Arts, University of Peradeniya.

Gunawardena, C. N., & La Pointe, D. (2007). Cultural dynamics of online learning. In M. G. Moore (Ed.), *Handbook of distance education* (2nd ed., pp. 593–607). Mahwah, NJ: Erlbaum.

Gunawardena, C. N., & La Pointe, D. (2008). Social and cultural diversity in distance education. In T. Evans, M. Haughey & D. Murphy (Eds.), *International handbook of distance education* (pp. 51–70). Bingley, UK: Emerald.

Gunawardena, C. N., & Layne, L. (2011, October). *Building a knowledge-based society through online wisdom communities: An Instructional Design Model.* Paper presented at the 24th ICDE World Conference on Open and Distance Learning, Bali, Indonesia.

Gunawardena, C. N., Lowe, C. A., & Anderson, T. (1997). Analysis of a global online debate and the development of an interaction analysis model for examining social construction of knowledge in computer conferencing. *Journal of Educational Computing Research, 17*(4), 395–429.

Gunawardena, C. N., Nolla, A. C., Wilson, P. L., López-Islas, J. R., Ramírez-Angel, N., & Megchun-Alpízar, R. M. (2001). A cross-cultural study of group process and development in online conferences, *Distance Education, 22*, 85–121.

Gunawardena, C. N., Ortegano-Layne, L., Carabajal, K., Frechette, C., Lindemann, K., Jennings, B. (2006). New model, new strategies: Instructional design for building online wisdom communities. *Distance Education, 27*(2), 217–232.

Gunawardena, C. N., Skinner, J. K., Richmond, C., Linder-Van Berschot, J., La Pointe, D., Barrett, K., … Padmaperuma, G. (2008, March). *Cross-cultural e-mentoring to develop problem-solving online learning communities.* Paper presented at the 2008 Annual Meeting of the American Educational Research Association, New York, NY.

Gunawardena, C. N., Wilson, P. L., & Nolla, A. C. (2003). Culture and online education. In M. Moore & B. Anderson (Eds.), *Handbook of distance education* (pp. 753–775). Mahwah, NJ: Erlbaum.

Hall, E. T. (1973). *The silent language.* New York, NY: Anchor Book Editions.

Hall, E. T., & Hall, M. R. (1990). *Understanding cultural differences: Germans, French, and Americans.* Yarmouth, ME: Intercultural Press.

Hofstede, G. (1980). *Culture's consequences: International differences in work-related values.* Beverly Hills, CA: Sage.

Hofstede, G. (1986). Cultural differences in teaching and learning. *International Journal of Intercultural Relations, 10*(3), 301–320.

Hu, G. (2005). Using peer review with Chinese ESL student writers. *Language Teaching Research, 9*(3), 321–342.

Ishii, S., & Bruneau, T. (1994). Silence and silences in cross-cultural perspective: Japan and the United States. In L. A. Samovar & R. E. Porter (Eds.), *Intercultural communication: A reader* (7th. ed., pp. 246–251). Belmont, CA: Wadsworth.

Kim, K., & Bonk, C. J. (2002) Cross-cultural comparisons of online collaboration, *Journal of Computer Mediated Communication, 8*(1). doi:10.1111/j.1083-6101.2002.tb00163.

Kramsch, C., & Thorne, S. (2002). Foreign language learning as global communicative practice. In D. Block & D. Cameron (Eds.), *Globalization and language teaching* (pp. 83–100). London, UK: Routledge.

Lopez-Islas, J. R. (2001, December). *Collaborative learning at Monterrey Tech-Virtual University.* Paper presented at the Symposium on Web-based Learning Environments to Support Learning at a Distance: Design and Evaluation. Asilomar, Pacific Grove, California.

La Pointe, D., & Barrett, K. (2005, May). *Language learning in a virtual classroom: Synchronous methods, cultural exchanges.* Paper presented at the meeting of Computer-Supported Collaborative Learning, Taipei, Taiwan.

Latchem, C. (2005). Towards borderless virtual learning in higher education. In A. A. Carr-Chellman (Ed.), *Global Perspectives on e-learning: Rhetoric and reality* (pp. 179–198). Thousand Oaks, CA: Sage.

Martin, J. N., & Nakayama, T. K. (2004). *Intercultural communication in contexts* (3rd ed.), New York, NY: McGraw-Hill.

Mason, R. (1998). *Globalising education: Trends and applications.* London, UK: Routledge.

Matsumoto, D. (1996). Culture and psychology. Pacific Grove, CA: Brooks/Cole Publishing.

Merriam, S. B., & Associates (2007). *Non-Western perspectives on learning and knowing.* Malabar, FL: Krieger.

Moore, M. G. (2006). Questions of culture [Editorial]. *The American Journal of Distance Education, 20,* 1–5.

Moore, M. G., Shattuck, K., & Al-Harthi, A. (2005). Cultures meeting cultures in online distance education. *Journal of e-Learning and Knowledge Society, 2*(2). Retrieved from http://je-lks.maieutiche.economia.unitn. it/index.php/Je-LKS/index

Parrish, P., & Linder-VanBerschot, J. A. (2010). Cultural Dimensions of Learning: Addressing the Challenges of Multicultural Instruction. *International Review of Research in Open and Distance Learning, 11*(2). Retrieved from http://www.irrodl.org/index.php/irrodl

Pincas, A. (2001). Culture, cognition, and communication in global education. *Distance Education, 22*, 30.

Raffaghelli, J. E., & Richieri, C. (2012). A classroom with a *view*: Networked learning strategies to promote intercultural education. In L. Dirckinck-Holmfeld, V. Hodgson, & D. McConnell (Eds.), *Exploring the Theory, Pedagogy and practice of networked learning* (pp. 99–119). New York, NY: Springer.

Reid, E. (1995). Virtual worlds: culture and imagination. In S. G. Jones (Ed.), *CyberSociety: Computer-mediated communication and community* (pp. 164–183). Thousand Oaks, CA: Sage.

Rogers, C., Graham, C. R., & Mayes, C. T. (2007). Cultural competence and instructional design: exploration research into the delivery of online instruction cross-culturally. *Educational Technology Research and Development, 55*, 197–217.

Romero, M. E. (1994). Identifying giftedness among Keresan Pueblo Indians: The Keres study. *Journal of American Indian Education, 34*(1), 35–58.

Rye, S. A., & Støkken, A. M. (2012). The implications of the local context in global online education. *International Review of Research in Open and Distance Learning, 13*(1), 191–206. Retrieved from http://www.irrodl.org/index.php/irrodl

Sanchez, I., & Gunawardena, C. N. (1998). Understanding and supporting the culturally diverse distance learner. In C. Campbell Gibson (Ed.), *Distance learners in higher education: Institutional responses for quality outcomes* (pp. 47–64). Madison, WI: Atwood.

Shattuck, K. (2005). *Cultures meeting cultures in online distance education: Perceptions of international adult learners of the impact of culture when taking online distance education courses designed and delivered by an American university* (Unpublished doctoral dissertation). Pennsylvania State University, University Park.

Smith, R. O. (2005). Working with difference in online collaborative groups. *Adult Education Quarterly, 55*(3), 182–199.

Tu, C. H. (2001). How Chinese perceive social presence: An examination of interaction in online learning environment. *Education Media International, 38*(1), 45–60. doi:10.1080/09523980010021235

Uzuner, S. (2009). Questions of culture in distance learning: A research review. *International Review of Research in Open and Distance Learning, 10*(3), 1–19. Retrieved from http://www.irrodl.org/index.php/irrodl

Vygotsky, L. S. (1978). *Mind in society: The development of higher psychological processes*. Cambridge, MA: Harvard University Press.

Walsh, S. L., Gregory, E. M., Lake, M. Y., & Gunawardena, C. N. (2003). Self-construal, facework, and conflict styles among cultures in online learning environments. *Educational Technology Research and Development 51*(4), 113–122.

Weinberger, A., Clark, D. B., Hakkinen, P., Tamura, Y., and Fischer, F. (2007). Argumentative knowledge construction in online learning environments in and across different cultures: a collaboration script perspective. *Research in Comparative and International Education, 2*(1), 68–79.

Whorf, B. (1998). Science and linguistics. In M. J. Bennett (Ed.), *Basic concepts of intercultural communication: Selected readings* (pp. 85–95). Yarmouth, ME: Intercultural Press.

Zawacki-Richter, O. (2009). Research areas in distance education: A delphi study. *International Review of Research in Open and Distance Learning, 10*(3), pp. 1–17. Retrieved from http://www.irrodl.org/index.php/irrodl

Zhao, N., & McDougall, D. (2008). Cultural influences on Chinese students' asynchronous online learning in a Canadian university. *Journal of Distance Education, 22*(2), 59–80.

13

ACADEMIC ADVISING IN DEGREE PROGRAMS

ROBERT F. CURRY

Good academic advising contributes to a caring environment, students' academic and career development, and a positive public image through satisfied students (Greenwood, 1984). Academic advising is the one function that covers both academic and student services; it deals with students from their first day at the institution to graduation (Gordon, 1992).

Support mechanisms readily available to on campus students are often lacking in distance education programs. Even highly motivated and self-directed students can find the experience lonely, difficult, and overwhelming (LaPadula, 2003). Academic advising provides an opportunity for distance students to connect with a concerned college staff or faculty member who can contribute to their academic success (Steele & Thurmond, 2009).

Since the publication of the *Handbook of Distance Education*'s second edition, standards and models have been developed for advising distance students, and are described in the next section of this chapter. That description is followed by a review of the research on academic advising published in 2005 or earlier, then a review of more recent research. There will be a section on recommendations for further research before a conclusion of the chapter.

STANDARDS AND MODELS

In 2000, the National Academic Advising Association (NACADA) established an interest group for Distance Education Advising. This group included NACADA members who wanted to focus on distance advising, but it had no formal governance role in the national organization. In 2008, the group moved to commission status and was charged with providing resources to advance the professional development of members (NACADA, n.d.). The Distance Education Advising Commission wrote Standards for Advising Distance Learners detailed below (NACADA, 2010).

Those standards were developed to address many of the categories in the Academic Advising CAS standards (CAS, 2005). The Council for the Advancement of Standards

Institutions engaged in distance education are expected to:
• Adhere to all applicable federal, state, and accrediting agency regulations and policies.
• Offer a minimum set of core services which assist distance learners in identifying and achieving their education goals.
• Employ a myriad of technologies in the delivery of distance education and related services.
• Provide leadership and an organizational structure that supports students, faculty, and advisors.
• Offer appropriate professional development activities and support for staff and faculty advisors.
• Engage in continuous evaluation of program quality by reviewing factors such as educational effectiveness, student learning outcomes, student retention, student/faculty satisfaction, etc.
• Commit sufficient technical and financial resources on a continuing basis in the delivery of services to distance learners.
• Present the programs and services available accurately in marketing materials.
• Assess applicants to ensure that students have the knowledge and technical skills needed to undertake the program.
• Provide an orientation to introduce new students to the distance learning environment.
• Provide appropriate student support services for distance learners as they would for students on campus.
• Provide a single point of contact for the services commonly accessed by distance learners.
• Create opportunities for connection and community with the institution, faculty, staff, and other students.
• Respond to the unique needs of distance learning students, rather than expecting them to fit within the established organizational structure.

Figure 13.1 Standards for Advising Distance Learners (Reprinted with permission from NACADA: The Global Community for Academic Advising www.nacada.ksu.edu).

in Higher Education (CAS) is a consortium of over 35 professional organizations, with the goal of promoting standards in various areas of higher education to foster student learning and development, quality assurance, and professional integrity. Guidelines for Academic Advising were developed by CAS and endorsed by NACADA (White, 2006).

For online students, the design of an institution's Website is especially important. Burnett (2003) identified a means to evaluate Web services, with four distinct generations in the way information is organized. Generation I is the Institution View, with information organized by departments and written in a style consistent with print materials. Generation II is the Customer View, with information grouped by the student's interest or audience; for example, sections for current students and prospective students. Generation III is the Web Portal with sections such as my home page, my interests, and my transactions. It integrates each student's information; text is written to support student tasks and goals, avoiding jargon. Generation IV is High Touch and High Tech with interactive text, decision criteria, and guided step by step processes. Personalized and relevant communication is sent to each student, including actions required related to advising, registration, financial aid, and other university functions (Burnett, 2003).

Steele and Thurmond (2009) compared the four generation model with the DIKW model, commonly used in the information sciences and knowledge management fields.

DIKW stands for data, information, knowledge, and wisdom, a hierarchy of cognitive processing. For example, Generation II is parallel to information, with data in meaningful categories and Generation III is parallel to knowledge, drawing on different sources of information and focusing on the student. This cognitive processing is critical for helping students in conjunction with new technological tools (Steele & Thurmond, 2009).

Web-based student services provide increasingly powerful means to encourage greater complex cognitive processing for students. Use of GPA calculators and degree audits relieve students and advisors from doing these tasks manually. The tools allow time for advisors to help students understand the information available to them and provide individual support based on student needs (Steele & Thurmond, 2009).

An institution's various Web-based student services are not likely to proceed at equal pace through the levels. Having all services at Generation IV is probably unobtainable, requiring a single portal for all administrative functions requiring action by a student. The focus for advising is on stages two and three, the differences between Web-based and portals. The shift from Generation II to III is the greatest change for student cognitive processing and tasks that are the core of good academic advising (Steele & Thurmond, 2009).

Means of communication for academic advising include email, smart FAQs, telephone, and Web conferencing. Although email is one of most commonly used, it can be relied on too heavily. Email is designed for shorter information responses, but advisors may attempt to answer complex questions. Another disadvantage is the time spent answering the same questions from students. This repetitiveness takes time that could be devoted to higher-order dialog (Steele & Thurmond, 2009).

Smart FAQs are interactive lists of frequently asked questions that are usually included in customer relationship management systems. Responses are at the informational level, but can contain links to other sections of the Website to guide students. They can also link to an email address or phone number if a different answer or further explanation is needed. The Smart FAQs can allow students to evaluate effectiveness of responses; revisions can be made based on this feedback (Steele & Thurmond, 2009).

Telephone conversations provide a means for advisors to ask probing questions and listen to responses. Web-conferencing has tools that can allow high level of discussion with visual information to support the voice communication. The advisor can show where tools and services are located on the Web and assess nonverbal cues. Compared to email, the disadvantage of telephone and Web conference is the synchronous communication; there may be scheduling difficulties between students and advisors (Steele & Thurmond, 2009).

Advisors need to critically review and assess the institution's Website and student portal. They should also evaluate the communication tools used for effectiveness and efficiency in facilitating high-level cognitive interactions needed for students to prepare successful academic and career plans (Steele & Thurmond, 2009).

RESEARCH, 2005 OR EARLIER

In the second edition of the *Handbook of Distance Education*, the most recent academic advising study reviewed was from 2005. Some studies in this section were also included in the second edition, while others were omitted from the earlier edition due to space restraints. While the earlier editions included studies from several countries outside of

North America, only research conducted in the United States or Canada is reviewed in this edition.

Studies of One Institution

Clark (2003) studied students in a distance education associate's program in early childhood care and education. Qualitative and quantitative data was collected from a pool of 64 matriculated students in this program, all women. The questionnaires included closed and open-ended questions. Response rate was 41%; 89% of respondents lived more than 50 miles from main campus. Semi-structured interviews were done with a sample of eight students, chosen from survey respondents and non-respondents.

In a list of recruitment and enrollment services, students rated most important general information, advice on course selection, information on technical requirements, assistance with course registration, and help with admission process. One point of contact, an orientation to course delivery format, and assessment of prior learning were also rated as important (Clark, 2003).

In open-ended questions, the most frequently mentioned theme of what most assisted students in the distance learning experience was a personal touch demonstrated by instructors and staff. They also expressed appreciation in having a designated and consistent point of contact to help interpret confusing information and serve as intermediary with other college officials. Data from interview participants was consistent with the survey results; one point of contact and responsive, friendly and personalized assistance were important in the distance learning experience (Clark, 2003).

Some students indicated the academic counseling process was a challenge by distance; it was unclear what was needed and appropriate to discuss with administrators on the phone. Several students cited getting conflicting advice on course selection. Students recommended having more extensive orientation to the distance learning process, either on campus or with step by step videos (Clark, 2003).

During the study, there was not a highly developed system of support services at the institution The author concluded that institutions need ongoing assessment of distance learner support needs to assist in institutional planning and decision making (Clark, 2003).

Libron-Green (2004) sent a survey to all 579 students enrolled in Internet-based classes during the fall 2001 semester at a large Mid-Atlantic state community college; 92 students completed the survey for response rate of 15.89%. Of the respondents, 79.3% were familiar or very familiar with academic advising services, but only 33.8% used academic advising often or very often. There was not a statistically significant relationship between utilization of academic advising or other support services with the final grade received (Libron-Green, 2004).

At the time of LaPadula's study (2003), New York Institute of Technology (NYIT) online students had limited access to orientation for new students, academic advising, personal counseling, career counseling, transcript evaluation, or diagnostic testing. Research was undertaken to aid in implementation of online student support services (LaPadula, 2003).

About 500 online students at NYIT were emailed a survey; 92 surveys were returned for a response rate of 18.4%. In the first part of the survey, participants were asked how satisfied they were with several online student services. In the second part, they were asked what additional type of student services they would like to have (LaPadula, 2003).

Participants were 85% to 90% satisfied with academic advising services. However, 50% to 69% reported interest in additional services such as online degree maps, career planning seminars, and online tutoring (LaPadula, 2003).

With student services in the early stages of development during their studies, research by Clark (2003), Libron-Green (2004), and LaPadula (2003) provided insights to administrators at the three institutions. Knowledge was gained on distance learning students' needs and their awareness of available student services. With each study at only one college, however, results cannot be generalized to a broad distance learning population.

Studies of More than One Institution

Paneitz (1997) identified 10 two-year institutions for her research. All had an associate's degree program available at a distance, but varied in their use of technology for providing advising, counseling, and library/media services. A total of 183 out of 400 questionnaires (randomly distributed at each institution) were returned, for a response rate of 46%.

For the study, Paneitz (1997) made the following distinction in level of technology:

1. No technology—Students must come to the main campus for advising.
2. Low technology—Advising is done with the assistance of a toll-free telephone number and/or a facsimile.
3. High technology—Students have access to a toll-free number and a facsimile for advising. In addition, technical assistance for advising includes at least one other means such as voice mail, email, computer bulletin, or videotapes.

Students were asked to rate their satisfaction with advising services. The majority of students were satisfied or very satisfied with the assistance in recommending remedial and study skills classes, assistance with initial degree planning, and assistance with transfer to four-year institutions. There were no significant differences in satisfaction based on level of technology in providing the services (Paneitz, 1997).

Academic advising was considered the most essential student service by distance students. Thirty-nine percent ranked it first, while 31% ranked it second in importance when compared with library/media services, career counseling, tutorial services, and personal counseling (Paneitz, 1997).

Paneitz concluded that academic advising is the most essential student service for distance students in two-year institutions. She also concluded that technology will play a larger role in future years in providing student services to distance students (Paneitz, 1997).

The questionnaire sent by Paneitz (1997) to distance students provided valuable data on the use of advising services and student satisfaction with the services. A strength is that the survey was completed by students at multiple institutions, with varied delivery models for academic advising. Although the response rate was not very high, the randomness of the selection offsets this fact for a valid study.

For a doctoral dissertation, Curry (1997) conducted a national survey of academic advising in distance education. Institutions selected for the sample had a least one baccalaureate degree program available at a distance, using primarily electronic means of instruction. While only 89 institutions met the study's sample criteria, 73 surveys were returned for a response rate of 82%. Results from the Academic Advising in Distance

Education Survey were compared to data from American College Testing's (ACT) Fourth National Survey of Academic Advising (Habley, 1993). With these data, Curry compared and contrasted current practices of distance education programs with those of institutions as a whole.

Academic practices were found to be similar for distance education and institutions as a whole in that faculty advisors were the most frequent deliverers of advising services. There were differences in other practices, with less utilization of group advising, institutional reference materials, and advising evaluation in distance education (Curry, 1997).

Most respondents indicated it was likely that advisors and distance education students would develop personal relationships. In Fielstein's (1989) study, 83% of students indicated it was a priority advising activity that advisors be personally acquainted with their students. A respondent who reported that a personal relationship was likely qualified the answer with the statement, "if indicating a satisfactory comfort level in their interactions as opposed to a social type relationship" (Curry, 1997).

From the dissertation results, an article was published focusing on academic advising practices specifically for distance education students (Curry, Baldwin, & Sharpe, 1998). When asked about the top three means of communication between advisors and distance education students, institutions reported telephone conversations in real-time most often (94%), followed by in-person (61%), written correspondence by mail (55%), telephone conversations through voice mail (33%) and computer conferencing out of real-time such as electronic mail (33%).

At the time of this writing, the dissertation (Curry, 1997) and article based on it (Curry et al., 1998) remain the most comprehensive national data on academic advising in distance education. The high response rate resulted in a valid study despite the small population at the time. With considerably more distance education programs and technologies now available, however, the results are not indicative of current practices.

J. T. Brown (2004) studied the differences between student service satisfaction for traditional versus distance learning students. The population was undergraduate and graduate students enrolled in a residential or distance program at two universities. Both universities were small, private institutions with a religious affiliation, located in the eastern United States. All students at both institutions were asked to participate; with a total of 17,685 students, 8,697 were traditional and 8,988 were distance. The request came by email from the student's home institution. The instrument was the Student Satisfaction Inventory Version Two (SSI-2) by Noel Levitz. With 5,292 students completing the online survey instrument, the response rate was 29.9%. The majority of distance and traditional students who responded were undergraduates (Brown, 2004).

The distance learning students were more satisfied than traditional students in most student services, including the following: recruitment and financial aid, academic advising, registration, library services, tutoring, counseling, career services, and the new student program. Traditional students were more satisfied than distance with campus services and spiritual activities. J. T. Brown (2004) speculated that a higher level of satisfaction was because the distance learning students were more advanced developmentally, with an average age 10 years greater than the traditional students. However, there may be other factors in the student's lives that were not investigated. The researcher encouraged student services personnel to question what services should be offered online and to whom, whether online services can meet the developmental needs of each students, and how community can be formed among online students (J. T. Brown, 2004).

Because the institutions in the study were so specialized, the research has limited generalizability (J. T. Brown, 2004). For the population studied, additional insights could have been gained if the undergraduate and graduate student data had been separated.

Dunn's study (2005) was undertaken to provide a richer understanding of some key issues in providing services to distance students. Student service administrators in Canadian postsecondary institutions were asked to participate in a descriptive survey of their programs, and answer open-ended questions about their experiences with issues related to counseling and advising services to distance students.

Potential participants were directors of advising and counseling centers in Canadian universities, colleges, and technical institutes. Purposeful sampling was used to determine 100 directors from 53 institutions that offered a significant number of programs through distance colleges; 31 agreed to participate (Dunn, 2005).

Dunn (2005) used thematic analysis, searching for common threads through an entire set of interviews. She identified six major themes.

1. Technological and practical challenges
   There was low comfort level of students and faculty, with difficulty in establishing contact.
2. Institutional challenges
   There was lack of resources and awareness of services among students and staff.
3. Professional challenges
   Advisors lacked nonverbal cues from students, which could indicate confusion or other concerns. Confidentiality was at risk with the potential of email messages being seen by the wrong students.
4. Attempted remedies
   Respondents recommended adding new modes of communication, providing better information about services on the Website, providing unique services, and increasing accessibility of services.
5. Distance learner needs
   Respondents discussed the importance of tailoring services to student needs and the expectation by students for immediate service. They also discussed the need for distance students to be motivated and resourceful.
6. Delivery-Mode Approximation
   There were attempts to find existing models of counseling and advising services in distance learning and determine best practices.

Dunn's study (2005) provides valuable information for administrators involved with counseling and advising for distance learning students. The common themes she identified through interviews with administrators from multiple institutions are factors that should be considered by all individuals providing advising and counseling for distance learning.

RESEARCH, 2006 OR LATER

Studies of One Institution

Collins (2007) sought to identify the key issues and needs for online student support services at a community college in the southwest United States. She surveyed students enrolled in business and computer information systems classes, online and on campus. Of the 66 students who completed the survey, 58% lived 25 or less miles from campus; over 50% had taken an online course. Having one point of contact for general assistance was rated the most important academic support service. In response to open-ended questions, students recommended having more knowledgeable and available advisors, a help desk available 24 hours daily/7 days a week, and a single point of contact for questions. At the time of this study, online services were limited, and students were not always aware of the services that were available (Collins, 2007).

In addition to the survey of students, Collins (2007) interviewed selected student services support staff. Knowledge of an available online service was generally exhibited only by individuals in that specific area. Consistent with student responses, staff indicated a central point of contact for students' questions was needed (Collins, 2007).

Collins (2007) studied students and student services staff, a strength of the research. Results identified the need for better internal communication, so students are aware of the services and staff members are knowledgeable enough to refer students to appropriate services.

Axelson (2007) surveyed students enrolled in online classes at the University of Wyoming. Of these 1,154 students, 526 responded, for a response rate of nearly 46%; 57% lived outside of Laramie, where the main campus is based; 16% lived outside of Wyoming. At the time of this study, academic advising was not provided in an online or other distance format.

From a list of proposed student services, academic advising received the highest percentage (51%) of students indicating they would use it if available. Career advising was the second highest cited, by 38% of students. Academic advising was also cited most often as one of the three most important student services, with 51% of students mentioning it. Career advising was cited by 25% of the students (Axelson, 2007).

There were four open-ended questions to probe student reasons for previous responses. A common theme was that support services contribute to the success of students because they assist them in navigating administrative offices and course delivery requirements at the university. Students appreciated the convenience of online student support services (Axelson, 2007).

Axelson (2007) recommended assigning students an advisor who would also serve as case manager, directing students to the appropriate faculty advisor or other student service. This was a valid study with a large sample and good return rate.

Hernandez (2007) used the Academic Advising Inventory (AAI), designed primarily for conducting formative and summative evaluations of academic advising programs. Participants were recruited from the approximately 2,500 psychology majors at the University of Central Florida. They received invitations to participate in advisement sessions by the department's advising newsletter listserv. Students were randomly assigned to face-to-face in-seat or a face-to-face via Web camera advising sessions. The sample consisted of 102 psychology students with 51 assigned to the control group and 51 assigned to the experimental group. The Likert scale for the AAI was: (1) strongly disagree, (2) disagree, (3) neutral, (4) agree, and (5) strongly agree (Hernandez, 2007).

Both groups reported being satisfied in general with the academic advising received. The in-seat control had a mean of 4.53, while the Web experimental had a mean of 4.65. Both results were very high, with no significant difference. Similar results were achieved for having: accurate information about courses, programs, and requirements through academic advising; sufficient prior notice about deadlines related to college policies and procedures; access to advisors when needed; and sufficient time available during advising sessions (Hernandez, 2007).

Hernandez (2007) mentioned the importance of having a personalized relationship between advisors and students. The Web sessions provide an opportunity for immediate feedback in an interactive discussion with an advisor. The advisor can watch for visual cues from students with video that would not be accessible from a phone conversation. Video also provides a means for sharing text. Although security is a concern, students can show identification for verification before personal material is discussed (Hernandez, 2007).

While a small sample, this is rare example of an experimental study related to advising in distance learning. It demonstrates that satisfactory results can be achieved in a two-way video advising format.

J. M. Brown (2011) conducted a study to determine the effectiveness of a Web-based career development workshop at a midsized multi-campus community college in the southeastern United States. If effective for undecided community college distance learners, the evidence could justify the inclusion of similar workshops in various academic and career advising services. The population consisted of 420 students enrolled in distance learning sections of a freshmen college success course in fall 2010. In the first week of the semester, all 420 students were asked to participate voluntarily. Despite an initial email to all students in classes, a follow-up email, and the possibility of winning gift cards, participation rate was very low. Initially, 29 students agreed to participate, randomly assigned to one of two groups. Complaining of technical difficulties and inability to open or submit documents, ten students dropped out of the study, leaving nine students in Group I and ten students in Group II (J. M. Brown, 2011).

Group I used a Web-based system identified as the State Education and Career Planning System (SECPS). It was launched in March 2009 to help users explore majors, colleges and associated costs, and careers. Group II also used SECPS, but had additional modules to provide opportunities for more study of the career decision making process and in-depth exploration.

The Career Decision making Difficulties Questionnaire (CDDQ) developed by Gati, Krausz, and Osipow (1996) was used as pretest and posttest for each group. Three variables are:

- Lack of readiness (lack of motivation, indecisiveness);
- Lack of information about the process, self, occupations, and additional resources;
- Inconsistent information—unreliable information, internal conflicts, external conflict.
- Neither Group had statistically significant changes in those three variables from the pretest to posttest (J. M. Brown, 2011).

J. M. Brown (2011) indicates a comprehensive online career guidance system could be incorporated into academic advising, giving students opportunities to make the connection between academic and career information. She encourages students to seek academic or career advising to discuss assessment results received from an online tool. Although these ideas seem logical and appropriate, this study did not demonstrate that online workshops improve career readiness.

Long-Goding (2011) did a study to determine if improving advisor knowledge of online learning would increase retention in online courses. The study was conducted at one community college in Massachusetts. Retention was defined as a student who was enrolled in an online class at the end of institution's drop-add period and who earned a grade of A, B, C, or D at the end of semester. This data was obtained from the College's Office of Institutional Research.

All 21 professional advisors and 109 faculty advisors at the community college were sent a letter of invitation to their home addresses. Their participation in the study was an online professional development activity regarding online learning. The researcher developed an instrument to assess advisor knowledge about online learning at a community college. Each participant had two weeks to review class materials before taking the posttest. Although the posttest covered the same basic content, some wording was changed and some questions were reordered from the pretest (Long-Goding, 2011).

With 28 faculty and 11 professional advisors completing both tests, the response rate was 30%. The mean score of the pretest was 75.14. After the professional development activity, the mean score on posttest was 79.86, which was a statistically significant difference. This data answered a subquestion of the study concerning the change in knowledge base about online learning after completion of a professional development activity (Long-Goding, 2011).

The retention rate was 69% for online courses in spring 2010 and spring 2009. Therefore, the study was not able to demonstrate that increasing advisor knowledge about online learning would improve retention (Long-Goding, 2011).

There are several limitations to the study. Although knowledgeable academic advisors may be a factor in retention, there are clearly other factors such as teaching strategies, course design, instructional technology, student characteristics and life events. In addition, advisor participation in the professional activity was voluntary. Even for those who agreed to participate, the researcher does not know if advisors completed the online materials before taking the posttest. Also, student advising for non-matriculated students is not required. It is not known from the study which of the students enrolled in the online classes met with an advisor who had taken full advantage of the professional development activity (Long-Goding, 2011).

Long-Goding (2011) recommended a longitudinal study to provide more evidence that a formal program of professional development activities enhance knowledge of advisors regarding the rigors of online learning. Unlike her own study, Long-Goding (2011) stated a systematic means of measuring post-participation knowledge gains should be included in this recommended study.

Research: Studies of More than One Institution

Cunningham (2006) did a study to establish a rating of the essential support services used by institutions in developing online support services infrastructures. Distance education faculty in Texas were contacted and 302 completed the study's survey; 299 of their distance education students completed the same survey. Thirty-seven different Texas private and public colleges were represented. Respondents indicated how important 64 different support services are for distance learning. The Likert scale used was (1) not important, (2) slightly important, (3) somewhat important, (4) very important. Services related to advising, and mean ratings of faculty and students, are on Table 13.I. The highest mean rating by faculty (3.74) was for

Table 13.1 Rating of Online Support Services

Service	Mean Rating For Faculty	Mean Rating for Students
Information during registration on the nature and technical requirements of the course.	3.74	3.63
Expert advisement on matters of transfer evaluation and credit awarding.	3.64	3.72
A "one stop shopping" point of contact that provides general assistance to distance learners.	3.20	3.25
Individual liaisons assigned to first-time students to monitor academic process and resolve problems.	2.75	3.01
Career counseling by phone.	2.53	2.82
An ombudsperson to investigate problems and resolve complaints.	2.78	3.17
Access to self-assessment tools that help students understand their learning preferences.	2.97	3.26
Program planning tailored to the student's specific needs and interests.	2.79	3.42
Pre-admission advisement to assess student's educational goals and prior learning experience.	3.42	3.30
Instruction on the techniques and methods for studying effectively at a distance.	3.45	3.27
A "real" person contact to help students through the process of admitting from a distance.	3.47	3.49
A distance learner's guide containing information on instructional policies and procedures, academic program requirements, and available resources.	3.56	3.51

Note. Adapted from "College and university faculty and student rating of distance learning support services." (Doctoral Dissertation). by G.L. Cunningham, (2006).

"Information during registration on the nature and technical requirements of the course." The highest mean rating by students (3.72) was for "Expert advisement on matters of transfer evaluation and credit awarding."

Cunningham (2006) indicated an essential support service model can assist administrators in determining priority for existence and funding for services in the distance learning program. This was a good study with a large sample including faculty and students from 37 different institutions in Texas.

Klukas (2006) did a study to examine and describe the need, availability, importance, and accessibility of online student services for distance students in Wisconsin's 42 public two- and four-year colleges and universities as perceived by student service administrative personnel. With 29 surveys returned, the response rate was 69%. All 29 colleges and universities had been offering distance and online courses for at least three years (Klukas, 2006).

Respondents were questioned about 12 student services; five of these related to academic advising. They were asked to rate the importance of these services on the following Likert scale: (1) unimportant, (2) of little importance, (3) moderately important, (4) important or (5) very important. The mean importance level for the five relevant services was academic advising (4.41), career services (4.11), orientation to distance learning (4.68), basic information (5.0), registration (5.0) (Klukas, 2006).

Although only 19 of the 29 institutions provided academic advising through distance learning, all but one planned to offer it in the future. The survey included rating effectiveness of the services, but only two respondents reported that information for academic advising. Perhaps the student services administrators were not familiar enough with academic advising for distance students to rate it (Klukas, 2006).

Klukas (2006) concluded that administrators are having difficulty with developing and providing effective student services in distance education. She indicated research into best practices in advising, tutoring, and career services would be beneficial to administrators.

Research by Klukas (2006) provides information on perceived importance of services by Wisconsin student affairs administrators. With a good response rate and diversity of institutions studied, the results can also provide guidelines for administrators at institutions outside of Wisconsin. Contrary to results on importance of services, the results regarding effectiveness of the services were not valid. Especially on the issue of academic advising, the number of responses was too small.

Betts and Lanza-Gladney (2010) wrote an article about the Online Human Touch (OHT) concept used in Drexel University's online Master of Science in Higher Education (MSHE) Program. OHT includes (1) student engagement, (2) community development, (3) personalized communication, (4) work-integrated learning, and (5) data driven decision making. An Online First-Year Experience was developed using the OHT concept. Over 75% of students surveyed indicated the Online First-Year Experience was important to student engagement and 66% indicated it was important to student retention. When asked which factors were most important to the overall MSHE experience, students included quality of academic advising and accessibility of academic advisors. Authors indicate academic advising is essential to providing a sense of community and connecting online students to the institution. Although the article has interesting points, it lacks details regarding research methodology to demonstrate whether the results are valid.

RECOMMENDATIONS FOR FURTHER RESEARCH

Studies consistently show academic advising is considered important by students and administrators (Axelson, 2007; Clark, 2003; Collins, 2007; Cunningham, 2006; Klukas, 2006; Paneitz, 1994). Studies are needed that focus on academic advising, however, rather than just inclusion among many services being researched.

For comprehensive data, a national survey of distance education students should be conducted. This study of academic advising needs would provide quantitative data from the student perspective, including modes of advising delivery that are consistent with the needs and types of students served. Associate, baccalaureate, and graduate students should be surveyed, with data reported for each of the degree levels. Information based on solid research will help advisors develop appropriate advising techniques, processes, and programs.

Based on the study by Hernandez (2007), Web cam technology can be used effectively to provide advising. She recommended studies to address advisor roles and the technological support tools that provide opportunities to have more effective and efficient advising. She also recommends observational and reflective studies of advising encounters to provide understanding of effective practices (Hernandez, 2007).

A case study focusing on students' perceptions of advising throughout their academic careers is needed. A longitudinal study would be ideal, but researchers can also study separate groups of students concurrently as long as some are beginning a program, taking courses about midway through the program, and nearing completion of the program. Graduates of the distance education program should also be included in this study. In-depth interviews of students and graduates would be the primary method of data collection.

Although online services are very appealing to campus-based students, they also have access to campus-based programs not available to students located far away from the institution. In studies of distance advising, it is important that location be clearly identified and data reported separately for groups such as (a) on campus, (b) in region off campus, (c) out of region, but in same state, (d) out of state, and (e) out of the country. There may differences among these subgroups in perceived effectiveness and satisfaction with similar advising services when an online service is the only means of obtaining a service compared with just one of several options.

Studies should be done based on NACADA standards for advising distance learners (NACADA, 2010). For example, do advising administrators and students believe the guidelines are being followed? A national study would be most beneficial to the field's knowledge base, but individual institutions may also find a similar study helps identify areas of success or need for improvement. A qualitative study could provide considerable insight on ways to build a sense of community for distance students. A study assessing different means of providing orientation sessions is also needed.

CONCLUSION

As in the first and second editions of the *Handbook of Distance Education*, it must be said that research on academic advising is not extensive. Fortunately, the NACADA's Commission on Distance Learning now has a research committee. A study on academic advising at institutions offering online, blended, and on-campus programs is planned (K. Betts, personal communication, September 19, 2011).

NACADA Standards for Advising Distance Learners (NACADA, 2010) are helpful for institutions in developing and assessing advising programs. In addition, they provide guidance to individual advisors. Steele and Thurmond's article (2009) describes how advisors can make use of technology to help students reach higher levels of cognitive processing in their academic and career planning.

Technology has advanced considerably in the 21st century. For Paneitz (1997), toll-free numbers, fax, email, and voice mail were considered high tech and high touch, but now those tools are common. More sophisticated and interactive technologies are available. Hernandez (2009) studied advising using a Web camera technology which provides an advising experience close to a traditional face-to face encounter.

With additional national and institutional studies, knowledge will advance in the field of academic advising in distance education. While distance education programs and services are diverse, some issues are relevant for advising of any student at a distance. Advising must be accessible, personalized, user-friendly, accurate, and consistent. As advisors examine knowledge in the field and practices that have been successful, they can choose the advising strategies that will be accessible and helpful to their own distance education students.

REFERENCES

Axelson, S. L. (2007). *The use and value of student support services: A survey of undergraduate students in online classes* (Doctoral dissertation). Retrieved from ProQuest Dissertations and Theses database. (AAT 3259798)

Betts, K., & Lanza-Gladney, M. (2010). Academic advising: Ten strategies to increase student engagement and retention by personalizing the online education experience through online human touch. *Academic Advising Today, 33*(1). Retrieved from http://www.nacada.ksu.edu/ePub/AAT33-1.htm

Brown, J. M. (2011) *Utilizing a Web-based career development workshop to address career decision-making difficulty among community college distance learners* (Doctoral dissertation). Retrieved from ProQuest Dissertations and Theses database. (AAT 3455286)

Brown, J. T. (2004). *Student service satisfaction: Differences between traditional and distance learning students* (Master's thesis). Retrieved from ProQuest Dissertations and Theses database. (AAT 1425242)

Burnett, D. J. (2003). Web service generations. Paper presented at the McSCU E-Student Services Meeting. Retrieved from http://www.mnonline.project.mnscu.edu/vertical/Sites/%7BDF3FAE8D-FD97-4C7A-A66D-778FC8DAFB25%7D/uploads/%7B7D5558DC-0F14-4A58-8F0D-524FF5181143%7D.PDF

Clark, M. S. (2003). *Student support for academic success in a blended, video and Web-based distance education program: The distance learner's perspective* (Doctoral dissertation). Retrieved from ProQuest Dissertations and Theses database. (AAT 3120878)

Collins, L. D. (2007). Online *student support services: Perceived problems and strategies to affect change* (Doctoral dissertation). Retrieved from ProQuest Dissertations and Theses database. (AAT 325085).

Council for the Advancement of Standards in Higher Education (CAS). (2005). *Academic Advising programs: CAS standards and guidelines.* Retrieved from http://www.cas.edu/getpdf.cfm?PDF=E864D2C4-D655-8F74-2E647CDECD29B7D0

Cunningham, G. L. (2006). *College and university faculty and student rating of distance learning support services* (Doctoral dissertation). Retrieved from ProQuest Dissertations and Theses database. (AAT 3227512)

Curry, R. F. (1997). *Academic advising in distance education.* (Doctoral Dissertation). Retrieved from ProQuest Dissertations and Theses database. (AAT 9722676)

Curry, R. F., Baldwin, R. G., & Sharpe, M. S. (1998). Academic advising in baccalaureate distance education programs. *The American Journal of Distance Education, 12*(3), 42–52.

Dunn, S. (2005) A place of transition: Directors experiences of providing counseling and advising to distance students. *Journal of Distance Education, 20*(2), 40–57.

Fielstein, L. L. (1989). Student priorities for academic advising: do they want a personal relationship? *NACADA Journal, 9*(1), 33–38.

Gati, I., Krausz, M., & Osipow, S. H. (1996). Taxonomy of difficulties in career decision making. *Journal of Counseling Psychology, 43,* 510–526. Retrieved from Psych ARTICLES database.

Gordon, V. N. (1992). *Handbook of academic advising.* Westport: CT: Greenwood.

Greenwood, J. D. (1984). Academic advising and institutional goals: A president's perspective. In R. B. Winston, Jr., T. K. Miller, S. C. Ender, & T. J. Grites, *Developmental academic advising* (pp. 64–88). San Francisco: Jossey-Bass.

Habley, W. R. (1993). *Fulfilling the promise? Final report: ACT fourth national survey of academic advising.* Iowa City, IA: The American College Testing Program.

Hernandez, T. R. (2007) *Academic advising in higher education: Distance learners and levels of satisfaction using Web camera technology* (Doctoral dissertation). Retrieved from ProQuest Dissertations and Theses database. (AAT 3276365)

Klukas, G. M. (2006) *Online student Support Services at Wisconsin Colleges and universities* (Doctoral dissertation). Retrieved from ProQuest Dissertations and Theses database. (AAT 3204907)

LaPadula, M. (2003). A comprehensive look at online student support services for online learners. *The American Journal of Distance Education, 17*(2), 119–128.

Libron-Greene, D. M. (2004) *Awareness and utilization of institutional support services by Internet-based learners* (Doctoral dissertation) Retrieved from ProQuest Dissertations and Theses database. (AAT 3177197)

Long-Goding, J. L., *Will enhancing academic advisor knowledge about online learning increase retention in distance education?* (Doctoral dissertaion). Retrieved from ProQuest Dissertations and Theses database. (AAT 3465885)

NACADA. (2010). *NACADA standards for advising distance learners.* Retrieved from http://www.nacada.ksu. edu/Commissions/C23/documents/DistanceStandards.pdf

NACADA. (n.d). *Commission and interest group Division information.* Retrieved from http://nacada.ksu.edu/ CandIGDivision/cigdivinfo.htm

Paneitz, B. (1997). *Community college students' perceptions of student services provided when enrolled in tele-courses* (Doctoral dissertation). Retrieved from ProQuest Dissertations and Theses database. (AAT 9735008)

Steele, G. E., & Thurmond, K. C. (2009). Academic advising in a virtual university. *New Directions for Higher Education, 146,* 85–95.

White, E. R. (2006). *Using CAS standards for self-assessment and improvement.* Retrieved from http://www. nacada.ksu.edu/Clearinghouse/AdvisingIssues/CAS.htm

14

ENABLING LEARNING FOR DISABLED STUDENTS

SUSAN CRICHTON AND SHELLEY KINASH

Educators and researchers have struggled with questions stemming from the intersection of distance delivery and technological affordances for students with disabilities (Kinash & Crichton, 2007). Central to these questions is how the prevalence of distance education might increase access to students with disabilities, what services are most important in supporting distance learners, and what standard accommodations and innovations specifically encourage diverse learners (Kim-Rupnow, Dowrick, & Burke, 2001, p. 37). In attempting to answer these core questions, additional issues arise, including, but not limited to; how educators can promote universal design (Burgstahler & Cory, 2008; Connell et al., n.d.; Rose & Meyer, 2002) in distance education by disrupting the traditional dependency on text with the thoughtful addition of visual and auditory interfaces which tend to be more inclusive; and how might the emergence of tablet devices supplement and, in some cases, replace assistive technologies.

A further intersection rests in the promise afforded by the emerging technologies that support innovations in distance and more recently in blended learning. Garrison and Archer (2007, p. 83) suggest the "attractiveness of blending face-to-face and online learning is the assumption that designers can organically integrate the best of each mode" to suit both the needs of the students and the intent of the learning experience. Pedagogical application of blended learning might well answer the mainstream questions posed above. Blended learning also has the potential to meet the needs of learners and teachers with disabling conditions by recognizing the potential of multimedia to support multiple learning styles and needs and the ease by which handheld/tablet devices and their app-based interfaces enable immediate engagement (Crichton, Pegler, & White, 2012).

Addressing these concerns is critical as research indicates disability affects 15%–20% of the population (Employer Forum on Disability, n.d.), suggesting, conservatively, in 2007, there are "at least 650 million people with disabilities worldwide" (UN Web Services, ¶1). For example, in India alone, that percentage would translate into approximately 100 million people (Mehta, 2008). Exact incidence and prevalence statistics are difficult to obtain for a number of reasons. There are a diversity of ways of establishing, classifying, and identifying disability. Few countries have adequate means of identifying adult onset disability, which is a significant issue in the context of an aging global population. Disability is often documented from self-report, which is error-prone for various reasons. In this chapter, focusing on issues of distance education and disabled students, a disability is defined as a barrier "due to physical, sensory, or cognitive impairments as well as learning disabilities" (Kinash & Crichton, 2007, p. 193).

A SURVEY OF THE FIELD

Moore (2007, p. xii) states, we need "'to know what is known' before searching for new knowledge." Further, he suggests practitioners and policy makers need to know what is known before they plan, design, and deliver new programs." In the 2007 edition of *The Handbook of Distance Education*, a review of the literature overlapping the areas of disability and distance education reported 67 publications (journal articles, government and newspaper reports, and full-article conference proceedings). These publications reflected three main areas: (a) the promise and potential of distance education to help "level the playing field" for disabled students through the use of multimedia to support speech, text and audiovisual materials (Negroponte, 1995; Mayer, 2001); (b) the use, by all students, of "electronic curb-cuts"—a metaphor used to describe the affordances made for a specific population and then found to be helpful to the general population (Coombs & Banks, 2000; Jacobs, 2004); and (3) the increasing adoption of universal design for learning (UDL) criteria in course and content design (North Carolina State University, 1997).

Reprising our 2007 approach (Kinash & Crichton, 2007) for this chapter, we reviewed publications intersecting the areas of disability, distance learning, blended learning, UDL, assistive technology, and accessible learning. The search yielded 53 publications focusing specifically on those search areas. Articles referring only to those topics in general or peripheral ways were excluded from the review. The majority was journal articles (45) and the remainder included research reports (4), dissertations (2), newsletters (1), and one opinion piece. Thirty-nine of the publications addressed areas included in the previous review, specifically UDL, potential and promise of distance education to provide increased accessibility for disabled learners, the role of assistive technology to support disabled learners, and the need for specific accommodations and support services to prompt inclusion.

The articles addressing UDL focused on the benefit of ICT enhanced content design and multiple media content, accessed through assistive technologies, to support disabled learners, Whitney et al. (2011) reviewed 25 years of training and education, suggesting attention to *Design for All* supported digital inclusion and provided a significant alternative education route. Zeff (2007) suggests UDL enhances student access through management of learner tasks and the creation of learning opportunities. Fichten et al. (2009) report on a study of students with disabilities located on 58 campuses. They sent online questionnaires to the 223 students, 28 professors, and 33 e-learning professionals on Canadian campuses to determine problems/concerns with Websites and e-earning courses. Predictably, problems rested with accessibility of Websites, consistent availability of multimedia options for course content, lack of adaptive technologies, and poor course design. Armstrong (2009) echoes these findings in her work with vision-impaired students, noting most e-learning course design is predominately vision-centric with few or no alterative tag descriptions to alert students or explain what the media is illustrating. Keeler and Horney (2007) further refine the issue of UDL suggesting that while many new courses address the basic needs of students with disabilities, they fall short of accommodating concerns of those with specific barriers or limitations (Richardson, 2010).

The articles discussing the potential and promise of distance education to provide increased accessibility presented a mixed view of actual practice. Newell and Debenham (2009) note unless courses are well designed with attention paid to principles of UDL, distance education, like the technology that supports it, can be as disabling as enabling. In a delightfully entitled chapter, *Magic Fairies and Accessibility Dust*, Seale (2006, p. 1) cautions that while educators know they should make their e-learning courses accessible, few do unless prompted by a student who requires it. She questions, "despite the presence of a multitude of tools, why do … practitioners appear … to be waiting for a magic fairy to miraculously transform all e-learning material with one wave of her magic wand?" Lewis, Yoder, Riley, So, and Yusufali (2007, p. 31) suggest the solution rests with the need for "more training and awareness of accessibility issues by developers of online instructional sites whether they are faculty, administrative assistants, designers, or others."

Articles discussing assistive technology and the need for specific accommodations and services to support disabled learners predictably focused on institutional decisions concerning ICT infrastructure and academic support centres. However, Ladner (2010) comments, "Assistive technology is really a redundant term because, in some sense, all technology is assistive, making tasks possible or easier to do" (p. 25). He suggests:

> The social model of disability dictates an empowering approach to assistive technology research and development where consumers are given the power to configure and even create technology to suit their own needs and desires. The technology that comes from this approach is called accessible technology, rather than assistive technology, emphasizing its role in making human activities more accessible. (p. 25)

Burgstahler, Anderson, Slatin, and Lewis (2008) note when campuses use technologies that are not designed with accessibility in mind, they actually create additional barriers that a lack of IT intervention would not have created.

EMERGING TOPICS

Emerging topics identified in this review include accessibility as a legal/human right, disability and learning styles, changing distance education learner profiles, use of simulations to prompt empathy and understanding, and advances in assistive technologies.

Accessibility as a Human Right/Legal Issue

In many countries civil laws provide anti-discriminatory legislation concerning disability and issues of accessibility (Schlosser & Simonson, 2009). "Disability" is defined as "having a physical or mental impairment that substantially limits one or more major life activity including walking, seeing, hearing, speaking, breathing, learning, working, caring for oneself and performing manual tasks" (p. 210), disability legislation states a *reasonable effort* must be made to make "content and facilities available to all individuals regardless of cognitive or physical impairments or geographic locations" (p. 86). Schlosser and Simonson offer an example of this when discussing of how blind students might use a screen reader to access content from a Web site. They identify three critical aspects: (a) audio excerpts be accompanied by text transcripts; (b) tags be placed in the Web design which describe elements/content on the site allowing the screen reader to access the descriptions; (c) screen pages be kept short—more linked pages rather than long pages are best for the screen reader. Along with tips for heightened accessibility, the authors provide a link to the Web Accessibility Initiative (WAI) that has developed a disability simulator that tests a site for accessibility concerns (http://www3.org/WAI and http://www.bl.uk/aboutus/accessibility/index.html).

Perlin (2011) describes the impact of regional and international human rights courts and tribunals on disabilities—especially in the field of mental disability law. He notes there are no such bodies in many regions of the world, such as Asia or the Pacific region, suggesting this reduces the enforcement of international legislation especially since the passing of the Convention on the Rights of Persons with Disabilities (UN Web Services Section, 2006). This United Nations convention consists of 50 articles identifying specific issues impacting the disabled globally, including their ability to receive education and access information. Notably, "The convention marks a shift in thinking about disability from a social welfare concern, to a human rights issue, which acknowledges that societal barriers and prejudices are themselves disabling." Further, the convention states,

> The more obstacles there are the more disabled a person becomes. Persons with disabilities have long-term physical, mental, intellectual, or sensory impairments such as blindness, deafness, impaired mobility, and developmental impairments. Some people may have more than one form of disability and many, if not most people, will acquire a disability at some time in their life due to physical injury, disease or aging.

Specifically, Article 2 provides definitions and identifies a range of both traditional and emerging forms of communication and technologies that must be afforded disabled persons.

For the purposes of the present convention:

> *Communication* includes languages, display of text, Braille, tactile communication, large print, accessible multimedia as well as written, audio, plain-language, human-reader and augmentative and alternative modes, means and formats of communication, including accessible information and communication technology;

> *Language* includes spoken and signed languages and other forms of non spoken languages;

> *Discrimination on the basis of disability* means any distinction, exclusion or restriction on the basis of disability which has the purpose or effect of impairing or nullifying the recognition, enjoyment or exercise, on an equal basis with others, of all human rights and fundamental freedoms in the political, economic, social, cultural, civil or any other field. It includes all forms of discrimination, including denial of reasonable accommodation;

Reasonable accommodation means necessary and appropriate modification and adjustments not imposing a disproportionate or undue burden, where needed in a particular case, to ensure to persons with disabilities the enjoyment or exercise on an equal basis with others of all human rights and fundamental freedoms;

Universal design means the design of products, environments, programmes and services to be usable by all people, to the greatest extent possible, without the need for adaptation or specialized design. *Universal design* shall not exclude assistive devices for particular groups of persons with disabilities where this is needed.

Article 24 addresses issues related to education, stating persons with disabilities have a right to education without discrimination and with equal opportunity. Article 24 mandates an inclusive education system at all levels and life long, noting that education is essential for the "full development of human potential and sense of dignity and self-worth, and the strengthening of respect for human rights, fundamental freedoms and human diversity." On a pragmatic note, the convention notes the economic loss to a country that ignores its disabled population suggesting there is both a loss of their creative and productive talents but also a drain on the social infrastructure in terms of supports such as government assistance through welfare payments for socio-economic sustainability. Therefore, one might argue the degree of inclusion within a society is a measure of its openness and freedom.

To enact the Convention on the Rights of Persons with Disabilities, governments must take appropriate measures to employ teachers, including teachers with disabilities, who are qualified in sign language and/or Braille, and to train professionals and staff who work at all levels of education. Such training shall incorporate disability awareness and the use of appropriate augmentative and alternative modes, means and formats of communication, educational techniques and materials to support persons with disabilities. (UN Web Services Section, 2006)

This is an approach that many articles and reports included in this literature review suggests is missing and inconsistent in distance education initiatives reported. The majority of articles reviewed were in developed country settings in North America and the United Kingdom. Perlin (2011, p. 2) states, "The research is clear.... persons with mental disabilities especially those institutionalized because of such disability are uniformly deprived of their civil and human rights." He argues for the creation of a Disability Rights Tribunal noting it "would be a bold, innovative, progressive and important step on the path toward realization of those rights."

Rothstein (2010) conducted a 50-year retrospective of the judicial, statutory, and regulatory developments affecting students with disabilities (1960 to 2010). In particular, her article notes

emerging issues including documentation of disabilities, students with psychological impairments, the impact of the 1990 Americans with Disabilities Act (and the 2008 amendments), emotional support animals, access to technology, programs abroad and field placements, and the relationship of professional education programs to the professional licensing process.

She concludes:

> Students with disabilities in postsecondary education have come a long way in the past 50 years. From a time when there were virtually none of them, they now make up over eleven percent of the student body. Along the way, higher-education institutions have learned to define what is essential about their educational programs, they have developed offices to provide disability services on virtually every campus, and they have faced numerous complaints to OCR and in the courts. Ideally, most college and university attorneys have guided the administrators and educators on their campuses to become proactive in addressing these issues, thus avoiding costly and time-consuming litigation and dispute resolution. Those institutions that have a positive and proactive attitude and approach are more likely to avoid confrontations in the first place and to fare best in litigation and other disputes that do arise. (2010, p. 876)

Helms, Jorgensen, and Anderson (2006, p. 190) note that while attention to accessibility and compliance to legislated standards are required in all educational settings in North America, what is "Less clear are judicial interpretations related to making technology accessible and to the disclosure by programs of information about students' disabilities during licensing." They concluded the gap rests in a need for profession-wide standards of competencies and skills in addressing accessibility issues for disabled learners and a dialogue between educators and state licensing bodies as to the roles and responsibilities that will lead to ensuring appropriate and reasonable accommodations are afforded and pedagogical practices are developed to seamlessly support those accommodations.

Changing Learner Profiles and Recognition of Learning Styles

Noticeable in the recent literature was a growing recognition that disabled students are individuals who reflect different experiences. Prior to 2006, the majority of the literature appeared to classify the students by their disability alone rather than as individuals within the classification of blind, deaf, etc. Possibly due to increased attention paid to disability by legal and human rights legislation and the raising numbers of individuals impacted by war and conflict, publications appeared to narrow their scope by reporting on veterans, millennial generation students, and those in developing contexts.

Ruh, Spicer, and Vaughan (2009, p. 67) observe,

> Veterans with disabilities constitute a vast, capable, deserving, and under-utilized workforce, and many successful hiring campaigns have targeted the employment of veterans. Colleges offering comprehensive, individualized transitional services have proven successful in supporting veterans with disabilities reentering the civilian workforce. With the incorporation of learning models and reasonable academic adjustments to educational pedagogies and policies, veterans can be poised to successfully transition from college to the workforce.

They propose, in the United States, the deployment of Disability Service (DS) offices to bridge the disability and career transition needed to help people move from the military to school or to civilian employment. The American Community Survey (2006) reports, "more than 6 million veterans have a disability, and more than 700,000 are unemployed in any given month" in the United State alone; figures for veterans and civilian survivors of civil conflicts in developing countries are not easily available. In addition, many of those who are employed are actually drastically under-employed. The United States Department of Labor (2008) has predicted that in coming years over 200,000 veterans with disabilities will find a civilian job as they leave the military. The question for educators is how many would benefit from accessible education and training that would enhance their fulltime employability and job satisfaction.

Also mentioned in the literature were concerns about the impact learning styles might have among disabled learners. Noticeable in these publications is the manner in which students with disabilities are treated as a block—suggesting students with a particular disability might also present with the same learning styles and learning needs. Heiman (2006) reports students with learning disabilities (LD) tended to need support in obtaining self-regulation strategies that would allow them to control their individual learning process in terms of orientation, planning, and monitoring of their studies within their skills sets, learning preferences, and abilities. In a later study (2008), Heiman suggests students with learning disabilities found online learning environments to be less supportive and academic supports more limited than their fellow students without labeled disabilities. She does comment that further research is needed to help institutions better support the academic needs of LD students, noting online learning environments are not designed to be inclusive, which requires specific attention to accommodations and UDL.

It is interesting to note the increasing mention of disabled learners as a diverse population rather than a single collective. Publications focused on the millennial generation, cultural and linguistic groups, and non-traditional students. Specifically, Rothstein (2008, p. 870) notes, "The enrollment of 'millennials' (students born after 1982 and who have grown up with the technology culture), has brought new challenges" for institutions attempting to provide accommodations for disabled students. She explains that post-secondary education must recognize millennial students come to campuses with expectations developed from their K-12 contexts in which schools complied closely with legislation enforcing inclusion and providing assistive technologies. Further, students come "into higher education with behaviors that reflect their experience with instant communication and the use of technology" that personalizes content and is increasingly social and interactive.

In addition to differences among generations and learning styles,

> The field of education now faces an increasingly diverse student body that includes English as second language speakers, those with physical as well as psychiatric disabilities, and multiple representations of races, ethnicities, and religions. Traditionally, postsecondary faculty have thought of students as 'normal' or 'disabled' and have taught in a uniform manner using predominately lectures that rely on verbal media of voice and text, leaving diverse students on their own to adapt to the course. (Grabinger, Aplin, & Ponnappa-Brenner, 2008, p. 63)

Therefore, the traditional lecture or the transfer of the lecture into threaded discussions and podcasts in distance education are not adequate and educators / instructors must learn to leverage new technologies better and offer more differentiated learning experiences. Leake et al. (2006, p. 149) argue students with disabilities "who are of culturally and linguistically diverse (CLD) heritage often face additional barriers to success compared to their non-CLD peers with disabilities, in many cases due to the effects of simultaneous membership in two minority groups (CLD and disability)." They suggest "postsecondary education personnel involved in supporting students with disabilities need to become aware of the issues that are particularly relevant for those of CLD heritage," recognizing the "cultural competency; social support networks; mentors and role models; attitudes, skills, and knowledge" these students will need to be successful in postsecondary education success, in addition to access to assistive technology and funding supports to support their attendance due to mobility issues and other factors.

Battista, Forrey, and Stevenson (2008, p. 1) remind readers while "Distance education provides many nontraditional students with the opportunity to pursue a college education not possible through traditional brick and mortar education," educators must think beyond their traditional approaches and design learning activities "to help promote a stronger connection between the classroom and university community." They suggest possibilities including the use of Second Life, student created media, changing instructor / student roles, academic coaching and mentoring, and many others—all conducted online and consistent with the title of their article—*It Takes a Virtual Community: Promoting Collaboration through Student Activities*.

Repetto, Cavanaugh, Wayer, and Liu (2010, p. 91) echo the need for community with their work on the 5C model. They suggest:

> Individual and social benefits accrue when high school graduation rates increase. One approach to increasing graduation rates is to design learning environments that serve students with disabilities through the 5Cs known to increase school completion: connect, climate, control, curriculum, and caring community.

Their findings suggest online programs that "align with the 5Cs … have closed achievement gaps and increased completion rates among students with disabilities."

Simulations and Advances in Assistive Technologies

The literature, both academic and popular, recognizes that as technology continues to develop, it both helps and hinders access to information and education for disabled learners. Assistive technologies, such as adaptive hardware that support various accommodations, have become more sophisticated and specialized while Web-based technologies provide solutions and problems of their own. Gray, Harrison, Sheridan-Ross, and Gorra (2008, p. 67) describe a computer-based training tool

> to raise awareness among university academic staff of some common experiences faced by people with visual, mobility, hearing and cognitive difficulties when using a computer. This test simulates experiences of disabled students who use computers and take computer-based tests, and provides advice and guidance to university teaching staff on how they may best cater for the needs of such students.

Hayman (2010, p. 453) describes "efforts at University of Technology, Sydney (UTS) to acknowledge disability within the overall experience of student life." The UTS Website provides students with opportunities to have "personal experiences of studying and disability." It address both practical and cultural dimensions of disability "Its underlying ethos is to reflect, encourage and generate a multiplicity of ways of relating to the all-too-often unpacked phenomenon of student life as it plays out in relation to disability."

> UTS AccessAbility is an attempt to generate a space within a large higher educa-tion institution in which a multiplicity of nuanced understandings of disability can be explored. It is intended to be a readily consumable framework of ideas, support and provocation, through which users self-navigate. Co-authored by intended users, it has been infused with an eclectic mix of political, practical, academic and cultural engagement to encourage a dialogue which moves beyond general understandings of disability. Generalist assumptions about disability are further fractured and made thoughtful by introducing ideas drawn from disabil-ity scholarship. (p. 465)

Miller, Doering, and Scharber (2010) challenge designers, researchers, teachers, stu-dents, and parents to re-assess and re-envision the value of technology-mediated feed-back and e-assessment by examining the innovative roles feedback and assessment played in the design of three contemporary Web-based learning environments. These environments include (a) an e-assessment system for postsecondary American Sign Language learners; (b) a hybrid environment for teaching geography through the use of geospatial technologies; and (c) a progress-monitoring environment for reading, writ-ing, and language development with deaf or hard-of-hearing students.

Of particular interest in their work is the reliance on Web-based tools as assistive technologies, which parallels the work of Hayman (2010), Whitney et al. (2011) and Rothstein (2008, 2010). Common among these publications is the depiction of accom-modations/assistive supports being increasingly drawn from mainstream technolo-gies—a trend that will be discussed in a case study presented in the following section.

An Example of Recent Changed Practice—Questioning Tablets as Hype or Help?

Ladner (2010) explores assistive technology from the view of the consumer. He suggests:

> Consumers of assistive technology follow the social model of disability, that is, persons with disabilities are part of the diversity of life, not necessarily in need of cure or special assistance. Their identity does not revolve around being a patient or client, but focuses on their human desires to work, play, and associate with others. The social model of disability dictates an empowering approach to assis-tive technology research and development where consumers are given the power to configure and even create technology to suit their own needs and desires. The technology that comes from this approach is called accessible technology, rather than assistive technology, emphasizing its role in making human activities more accessible. (p. 25)

A promising technology is the tablet. Duncan Stewart, the dean of tablets for Deloitte Canada Research, comments, "the tablet has made computing more interactive because of its touch screen. Removing the keyboard also has eliminated a psychological bar-rier, making the tablet a more personal experience than a so-called personal computer" (Magder, 2011). "Just touching a tablet is a more intimate experience than using a com-puter," Stewart said. "We hold tablets right up to our bodies, and so it comes into our personal zone of intimacy."

According to Magder (2011), there were 12.1 million tablets in North America in 2010, and 70 million worldwide. Of those devices, 75% were iPads—the popular tablet from Apple, Inc. In November 2011, it was reported the industry of application (app) and game development had grown to $15.1 billion, disrupting the video game industry by increasing the use of mobile and social games accessed through handheld, Internet-enabled tablet devices and smartphones.

The Association of American Publishers notes sales for eBooks in the United States in 2010, increased by 116% in 1 year, resulting in $70 million in sales. McGill University, ranked one of the top 100 universities in the world, reported its holdings for 2011 at 50,000 print titles and 400,000 eBooks. It holds 10,000 journal articles, 60,000 electronic journal articles and 800,000 eBooks.

When one listens to the recent advertisement for the iPad, the potential of universal design for learning seems, literally within the grasp of disabled students without needing to rely on often cumbersome, expensive assistive technologies. Students can now "watch a newspaper, listen to a magazine, see a phone call, hold a bookstore in our hands, and touch the stars" (Apple Inc., 2011). Previous practice suggests over 53 technologies used in the mainstream were actually originally designed for or by the disabled ("The Electronic Curb-Cut Effect," n.d.), the iPad promises to be the opposite. While designed for personal use by the general public, "it's poised to change the learning landscape" (Apple, Inc., 2011) by providing access and opportunity for disabled students by enabling equitable participation. Of concern is whether the potential of the tablet is more hype than help.

Hedman and Gimpel (2010) define hyped technologies as being "distinct from other innovations and product launches because they are surrounded by extravagant publicity" (p. 161). Further, they note that once the "hype declines, the products become part of the normal everyday landscape" (p. 162), and identify five values that underlie consumer choice: functional value, social value, epistemic value, emotional value, and conditional value. Simply put, functional value relates to how an item meets a need; social value relates to the image connected with the item; epistemic value relates to curiosity about the item; emotional value is tied to wanting the item for its aesthetics; and conditional value is related to a specific context or need. Hedman and Gimpel determined that functional value has "little impact on the adoption of technologies that are surrounded with significant hype" (p. 161).

Therefore, a question for educators, students, and parents must be, is the emergence of tablet devices a boon for access or a trap for institutions wrestling to provide relevant assistive technologies and appropriate accommodations for their disabled learners? Currently, one challenge is the lack of empirical data to balance the hype of the advertisers. The following section shares initial findings from a pilot distribution of iPad devices within a large urban school board in western Canada.

A Case of Actual Practice—Deploying iPads within a K–12 Settings

Since the release of the first generation iPad, a team of education specialists within a large urban school board in western Canada has researched the promise and potential of these devices in a variety of settings. Due to the hype surrounding the launch of the iPad, school administrators pressured the school board to purchase the tablets for student and teacher use. The board was understandably reluctant and initiated a pilot project, placing class sets of iPads in eight schools—five with significant disabled populations, including children with autism and Down Syndrome in inclusive settings (K Pegler & P. Auld, personal communication, November 9, 2011).

Initial findings have been extremely positive, suggesting the tablets are living up to the hype concerning ease of use, customization/personalization, pedagogical support, and inclusion. While the pilot has not been without challenges, the school board is considering purchasing additional iPads and rethinking its plans for evergreening (updating) existing computer lab and classroom technology and technology supports for students in their distance delivery programs.

The iPads have proven to be easy for disabled students to use—even those with significant physical and cognitive issues. Students with limited mobility can swipe the screen with one finger and access an entire desktop of applications. Each app has both an icon (picture) and word title that supports diverse learning needs. As Magder (2011) notes, the intuitive interface only requires users to point, tap and do. The iPads, in the pilot project, have been added to an external network within each school. This network was created for student-owned devices, and it does not allow access to printing services or other intranet options other than access to the password protected Internet. Because the iPads can easily be re-synced and the apps restored, there is no security on the devices themselves, ensuring ease of access without requiring students to type in a login identification and password. The settings on the devices support accessibility options including voice-over for audio support and auto-text, zoom to increase font/icon size, white-on-black for enhanced visibility, increased audio levels, and assistive touch to increase or decrease sensitivity of the touch control.

Key to adoption has been the students and teachers' ability to customize and personalize the tablets. Each group has taken pains to select a personal background screen and to arrange the app icons in groupings that suit their tastes. After thoughtful conversation, students have been able to add apps and music on their individual tablets, and classes have researched apps they think might be appropriate and negotiated their inclusion within shared class sets of devices. An unexpected aspect of personalization has been a pleasant change in orientation enabled by these devices when working collaboratively. Researchers have noted instead of sitting facing a computer, a teacher and student can now sit face-to-face with the tablet between them and maintain eye contact. This physical shift allows the teacher to support and offer reassurance through a smile or a nod, something more difficult in a computer lab or when sharing a laptop or desktop computer while sitting side-by-side. This physical shift holds true for distance education as well, since the iPad has both a front and rear facing camera, teacher/student relationships can be developed and supported through a more realistic presence.

In addition to comments suggesting the iPads are engaging and motivating, an interesting observation from the pilot project has been increased collegiality among teachers. An online community of practice was created in the district's learning management system to sustain the face-to-face professional development activities. Teachers have been actively sharing successes and challenges in greater numbers and frequency of postings than in other professional development opportunities. The teachers have shared apps, annotating suggestions as to how they best support a particular student need or curriculum outcome. Teachers have utilized the *assistive apps* available from iTunes, and many report that they are happy to simply customize the *regular* apps identified within

the *education* category by using the assistive settings on the iPad. The ability to use and modify student access to free or reasonability priced apps translates into significant savings for the school boards as assistive technology software is quite expensive and often requires specialized hardware and training. Parents, within the pilot schools, are beginning to purchase iPads for their children after seeing the benefit from the school devices. However, this introduces a concern about affordability and accessibility for less affluent disabled students and their families.

Teachers' comments about the pedagogical value for the tablets tend to fall into four categories: (a) the usability of the tablet and intuitive design of the apps encourage collaboration; (b) students appear to interact more with both fellow students and students online; (c) the technology is socially acceptable and the students with disabling conditions, who were unwilling to use assistive technology due to stigma (Goffman, 1963), are willing to use the iPads; and (d) because of the ease of use, teachers report they can focus on the learning as they are less frequently called upon to trouble shoot problems with more complex assistive hardware and software. These comments bode well for distance learners, as lack of technical support is often a concern reported by online learners and a barrier for participation.

As mentioned in categories b and c above, teachers report increased feelings of inclusion and pride among the disabled students. When students with disabling conditions engage with their peers using an iPad, there appears to be a social cache to having access to the device. Teachers report that some students who were reluctant to venture beyond special education classrooms have joined the inclusive settings afforded through use of the iPads. This is particularly important as schools adopt more blended learning approaches in their programs. Specifically, junior high school students commented that they felt "normal" when using their devices. Blind students and learners with low vision use app chat with other students, and link their iPads to the classroom interactive whiteboards thereby allowing them to participate in discussions and activities. The read aloud options and ability to enlarge text in iBooks was also highly valued.

While it is early days for the research into the use of iPad devices with disabled learners, both in face-to-face and distance settings, the initial results are promising and the devices appear to be living up to some of the hype. Tablets running Android software rather than proprietary Apple apps are also enjoying success in diverse settings (Crichton & Onguko, 2010). Currently, the main challenge in the Android environment is the scarcity of educational apps compared to the Apple environment.

Deployment of tablets within educational settings is not without challenges. The devices, whether Apple or not, are designed for personal, individual use. Most institutional settings deploy them in a shared way, having multiple users sharing one tablet and a classroom sharing one application library account (e.g., iTunes). At this point, the majority of concerns focus on ways of sharing/turning in student work from the device; determining in advance the most appropriate apps and downloading them before the students use them; creating a generic classroom account in iTunes or the Google app store; and finding time to explore/locate new apps that are appropriate for specific learning needs (Crichton et al., 2012). It is interesting to note that absent from the list of concerns is learning to use the device or the apps—something not common for those wrestling to master many other assistive technologies, both hardware and software.

CONCLUSION

Emerging topics reflected in the convergence of the fields of disabled students and distance education include disability education as a human right, a recognition that the profile of disabled learners is changing, and that technology advances are changing the tools available to disabled students and their teachers. Specifically, the introduction of tablet devices supported by a range of applications is showing potential and promise.

While legislation continues to mandate inclusive practices for disabled learners, actual practice remains challenging and patchy. Blended learning approaches offer promise for accessibility within traditional environments, and distance education continues to be recognized by the United Nations and institutions—both K-12 and post-secondary, as a way to increase educational opportunities.

Questions for further research include, but are not limited to (a) whether the increased use of blended learning within formal learning offers promise or increased challenges for disabled students, (b) whether tablet devices will live up to their hype, and (c) whether faculty and staff will embrace the need to incorporate principles of universal design for learning (UDL) into their courses as common practice rather than as a retrofit to course materials when they determine there is a disabled student in their class.

REFERENCES

American Community Survey. (2006). *Veteran status*. Retrieved from http://www.census.gov/acs/www/library/by_year/2006/

Armstrong, H. (2009). Advanced IT education for the vision impaired via e-learning. *Journal of Information Technology Education, 8*, 243–256.

Apple Inc. (2011). *Now*. Retrieved from http://www.apple.com/ca/ipad/videos/#play-guided-tours-ads

Battista, L., Forrey, C., & Stevenson, C. (2008). It Takes a Virtual Community: Promoting collaboration through student activities. *Online Journal of Distance Learning Administration, 11*(2).

Burgstahler, S., Anderson, A., Slatin, J., & Lewis, K. (2008). Accessible it: Lessons learned from three universities. *Information Technology and Disabilities, 12*(1). Retrieved from http://www.freepatentsonline.com/article/Information-Technology-Disabilities/198354433.html

Burgstahler, S. E., & Cory, R. C. (2008). *Universal design in higher education: From principles to practice*. Cambridge, MA: Harvard Education.

Crichton, S., Pegler, K., & White, D. (2012). Personal devices in public seetings: Lessons learned from an iPod Touch/iPad project. [Special Issue] *Electronic Journal of e-Learning* (http://ejel.org).

Crichton, S., & Onguko, B. (2010, November). Colorboard — Product and process to enable quality education for all. *Proceedings of the Commonwealth of Learning PCF 6*. Indira Gandhii University, India.

Connell, B., Jones, M., Mace, R., Mueller, J., Mullick, A., Ostroff, E., ... Vanderheiden, G. (n.d.). The principles of universal design. *Center for Universal Design*. Retrieved from http://www.ncsu.edu/project/design-projects/udi/center-for-universal-design/the-principles-of-universal-design/

Coombs, N., & Banks, R. (2000, March). *Distance learning and students with disabilities: Easy tips for teachers*. Retrieved from http://www.csun.edu/cod/conf/2000/proceedings/0119Coombs.htm

Employer Forum on Disability. (n.d.). *Realizing potential: Disability worldwide*. Retrieved from http://www.realising-potential.org/stakeholder-factbox/disabled-people-worldwide/

Fichten, C., Ferraro, V., Asuncion, J. V., Chwojka, C., Barile, M., Nguyen, M. N., ... Wolforth, J. (2009). Disabilities and e-Learning problems and solutions: An exploratory study. *Educational Technology & Society, 12*(4), 241–256.

Garrison, D. R., & Archer, W. (2007). The theory of community of inquiry. In M. Moore (Ed.), *Handbook of distance education - second edition* (pp. 77–88). Mahwah, NJ: Erlbaum.

Goffman, E. (1963). *Stigma: Notes on the management of spoiled identity*. Englewood Cliffs, NJ: Prentice Hall.

Grabinger, R., Aplin, C., & Ponnappa-Brenner, G. (2008). Supporting Learners with Cognitive Impairments in Online Environments. *TechTrends, 52*(1), 63–69. doi:10.1007/s11528-008-0114-4

Gray, J, Harrison, G., Sheridan-Ross, J., & Gorra, A. (2008). Using a computer aided test to raise awareness of disability issues amongst university teaching staff. Computers Helping People With Special Needs Lecture Notes. *Computer Science, 5105*, 198–206. doi:10.1007/978-3-540-70540-6_29

Hayman, E. (2010). Re-thinking disability in public: The making of the "UTS AccessAbility" website project. *Discourse: Studies in the Cultural Politics of Education, 31*(4), 453–467.

Hedman, J., & Gimpel, G. (2010). The adoption of hyped technologies: A qualitative study. *Information Technology and Management, 11*(4), 161–175.

Heiman, T. (2006). Assessing learning style among students with and without learning disabilities at a distance-learning university. *Learning Disability Quarterly, 29*(1), 55–63.

Heiman, T. (2008). Females with learning disabilities taking on-line courses: Perceptions of the learning environment, coping and well-being. *Journal of Postsecondary Education and Disability, 2* (1), 4–14.

Helms, L., Jorgensen, J., & Anderson, M. (2006). Disability law and nursing education: An update. *Journal of Professional Nursing, 22* (3), 190–196.

Jacobs, S. (2004). *The electronic curbcut effect.* Information technology technical assistance and training centre (ITTATC). Retrieved from http://ideal-group.org/articles/ECC_1_6.htm

Keeler, C., & Horney, M. (2007). Online course designs: Are special needs being met? *The American Journal of Distance Education, 21*(2), 61–75.

Kim-Rupnow, W. S., Dowrick, P. W., & Burke, L. S. (2001). Implications for improving access and outcomes for individuals with disabilities in postsecondary distance education. *The American Journal of Distance Education, 15*(1), 25–40.

Kinash, S., & Crichton, S. (2007). Supporting the disabled student. In M. Moore (Ed.), *Handbook of distance education — second education* (pp. 193–204). Mahwah, NJ: Erlbaum.

Ladner, R. (2010). Accessible technology and models of disability. In M. Mitsuko, K. Oishi, I. M. Mitchell, & H. F. M. Van der Loos (Eds.). *Design and use of assistive technology* Part 1 (pp. 25–31). doi:10.1007/978-1-4419-7031-2_3

Leake, D., Burgstahler, S., Rickerson, N., Applequist, K., Izzo, M., Picklesimer, T., & Arai, M. (2006). Literature synthesis of key issues in supporting culturally and linguistically diverse students with disabilities to succeed in postsecondary education. *Journal on Postsecondary Education and Disability, 18*(2), 149–165.

Lewis, K., Yoder, D., Riley, E., So, Y., & Yusufali, S. (2007). Accessibility of instructional web sites in higher education. *EDUCAUSE Quarterly, 30*(3), 29–35.

Magder, J. (2011, November 20). Tablets tap into our intuitive side. *The Vancouver Sun.* Vancouver, British Columbia. Retrieved from http://www.vancouversun.com/news/Tablets+into+intuitive+side+with+video/5738905/story.html

Mayer, R. (2001). *Multimedia learning.* New York: Cambridge.

Mehta, K. (2008). Digital divide-challenges for the disability sector in India. *Welingkar Research Journal, 7*(2), 5–11.

Millennium Development Goals (n.d.). Retrieved http://www.un.org/millenniumgoals/index.shtml

Miller, C., Doering, A., & Scharber, C. (2010). No such thing as failure, only feedback: Designing innovative opportunities for e-assessment and technology-mediated feedback. *Journal of Interactive Learning Research, 21*(1), 65–92.

Moore, M. (2007). *Handbook of distance education — second edition.* Mahwah, NJ: Erlbaum.

Negroponte, N. (1995). *Being digital.* New York: Vintage.

Newell, C., & Debenham, M. (2009). Disability, chronic illness, and distance education. In P. Rogers, G. Berg, J. Boettche, C. Howard, L. Justice, & K. Schenk (Eds.), *Encyclopedia of distance learning, second edition* (pp. 646–655). doi:10.4018/978-1-60566-198-8.ch092

North Carolina State University, Center for Universal Design. (1997). *About universal design.* Retrieved from http://www.ncsu.edu/cud/about_ud.htm

Perlin, M. (2011). Promoting social change in East Asia: The movement to create a disability rights tribunal and the promise of international online, Distance Learning. *NYLS Legal Studies* Research Paper No. 10/11 #17

Realising potential - Disabled people worldwide. (n.d.). Retrieved November 12, 2011, from http://www.realising-potential.org/stakeholder-factbox/disabled-people-worldwide/

Repetto, J., Cavanaugh, C., Wayer, N., & Liu, F. (2010). Virtual Schools: Improving Outcomes for Students with Disabilities. *Quarterly Review of Distance Education, 11*(2), 91–104.

Richardson, J. (2010). Course completion and attainment in disabled students taking courses with the Open University UK. *Open Learning, 25*(2), 81–94.

Rose, D., & Meyer, A. (2002). *Teaching every student in the digital age: Universal design for learning.* Alexandria, VA: ASCD.

Rothstein, L. (2010). Higher education and disability discrimination: A fifty year retrospective. *Journal of College and University Law, 36,* 843–874.

Rothstein, L. (2008). Millennials and disability law: Revisiting Southeastern Community College v. Davis. *Journal of College and University Law, 34*(1).

Ruh, D., Spicer, P., & Vaughan, K. (2009). Helping veterans with disabilities transition to employment. *Journal of Postsecondary Education and Disability, 22*(1), 6–74.

Schlosser, L., & Simonson, M. (2009). *Distance education: Definitions and glossary of terms.* Charlotte, NC: Information Age.

Seale, J. (2006). *E-Learning and disability in higher education: Accessibility research and practice.* New York: Routledge.

The Electronic Curb-Cut Effect. (n.d.). Retrieved from http://www.icdri.org/technology/ecceff.htm

UN Web Services Section. (2006). *Convention on the Rights of Persons with Disabilities.* Retrieved from http://www.un.org/disabilities/convention/conventionfull.shtml

U.S. Department of Labor (2008). *Employment situation of veterans: 2007*(USDL 08-045): Washington, DC: Author.

Whitney, G., Keith, S., Bühler, C., Hewer, S., Lhotska, L., Miesenberger, K., & Sandnes, F. (2011). Twenty-five years of training and education in ICT design for all and assistive technology. *Technology Disability, 23*(3), 163–170.

Zeff, R. (2007). Universal design across the curriculum. New directions for higher education [Special Issue]. *Managing for Innovation, 137,* 27–44.

15

THE ROLE OF ACADEMIC LIBRARIES

KAY JOHNSON AND ELAINE FABBRO

This chapter offers a guide to current, key literature pertaining to the provision of distance learning library support in higher education. The literature is grouped into a number of core areas: (a) connecting with users by promoting awareness of the library, providing reference services, assessing library services, and meeting the needs of diverse teachers and learners; (b) providing access to resources, particularly through e-resources, electronic course reserves, and document delivery; and (c) promoting information literacy by establishing institutional support, delivering information literacy instruction, developing relevant pedagogical approaches, and assessing information literacy skills. An overview of professional resources is provided at the end of the chapter to assist in further exploration of key issues in the provision of library support to distance learning communities.

CONNECTING WITH USERS

The "access entitlement principle" is a core principle of the highly influential *Standards for Distance Learning Library Services* which evolved from the frequently revised *Guidelines* first introduced by the Association of College & Research Libraries in 1963 (ACRL,2008). All members of a higher education institution must have equitable access to its library services and resources, and have direct communication with library staff, regardless of their location. One of the greatest challenges for distance librarians is bridging the distance between remote users and their libraries. To meet this challenge, librarians must find creative ways to make their libraries more visible and present to distance learning communities and ensure they are meeting their needs.

Promoting Awareness of the Library

Librarians recognize that promoting library resources and services is crucial in creating successful programs, courses, and students, and this topic is discussed extensively in the literature. In distance education, the issue is perhaps more critical because faculty and students may not have physical access to campus resources and services. Dermody

(2005) captures the complexity of marketing library services to distance learners in the title of her article "We Cannot See Them, but They Are There." She notes the importance of multifaceted marketing, and of collaboration with faculty and other institutional partners, to ensure distance learners are aware of the library support available to them. Shelton (2009) points to the importance of outreach to distance faculty to ensure that they are aware of library support, and can pass this information on to their students.

By promoting the library's online resources and services, librarians help to ensure that distance learners are not disadvantaged in completing assignments and courses. Librarians use a variety of techniques to promote the library, including online newsletters, participation in social media such as Facebook and Twitter, and library training sessions or orientations for staff and students. In many cases, librarians choose to market specific resources such as e-resources (Fry, 2010; MacDonald, Vanduinkerken, & Stephens, 2008); however, for the distance learner, it is especially important to also market services such as reference and instruction, as these services can help to initiate a communications link between the institution and its distance students, and provide much needed personal support. While promotional efforts do not necessarily require a significant amount of money, developing a marketing plan and identifying clearly in advance the audience and expected outcomes of the promotional initiative can help ensure success (Tremblay & Wang, 2008). Often the best way to promote the library to distance students is through embedded or integrated librarian programs in which librarians participate in online courses as co-teachers or resources for students, and provide information literacy instruction and reference services within the context of the discipline and the curriculum (Tucci, 2011; Tumbleson & Burke, 2010).

Providing Reference Services

Providing reference services in a distance education environment can pose challenges for both students and librarians. An introduction to the provision of reference services in distributed learning can be found in Cantagallo, Dennis, and Reeg-Steidinger (2011). Where in a face-to-face reference transaction the reference interview can be conducted in a relatively expedient fashion, reference assistance provided over email can take more time, and may involve a number of conversations before the student's "true" question is revealed (Jones, 2008). In recent years, libraries have begun offering reference services using instant messaging. This not only has the potential to increase the speed by which a student's question is answered, but can also provide quality services to distance learners (Meulemans, Carr, & Ly, 2010). Opportunities to co-browse Web pages allow for a stronger level of personalized service (Jones, 2008).

Assessing Library Services

Assessment plays a crucial role for distance learning librarians striving to meet the research and information needs of their communities, and to provide library support equivalent to what is experienced on campus. Distance libraries make collections of online resources available, and offer a variety of services, but how do students perceive their value and ease of use, and how do they use these resources and services? ACRL's *Standards for Libraries in Higher Education* (2011b) advocates for assessment that employs both qualitative and quantitative methods, and notes that assessment may take a number of forms. Needs assessments assist in planning by determining gaps in services. Outcomes assessments can evaluate the effectiveness of library practices in

relation to the library's stated goals and objectives, and the extent to which students are learning library skills (ACRL, 2008). Sometimes assessment of distance learning library services is performed to demonstrate compliance with the standards of accreditation bodies (Lewis, 2011). Most libraries supporting distance learning tend to perform some form of assessment, typically surveys of library users that are initiated annually or at longer intervals. Nichols (2006) has suggested the use of monthly library surveys to facilitate continuous improvement in removing barriers for distance learners.

Increasingly, academic libraries are being asked by their institutions to demonstrate their value to student learning, and professional organizations such as ACRL are investing significant time and energy in attempting to assist their members in formulating a response. Megan Oakleaf's (2010) report, *Value of Academic Libraries,* is one such example.

Meeting the Needs of Diverse Teachers and Learners

Distance education enables a teaching and learning environment that brings together widely dispersed teachers and students. Such communities may include considerable diversity—socio-economically, culturally, demographically, and in terms of learning styles. Librarians supporting distance learning seek to meet the needs of their diverse populations, including facilitating the extensive research needs of graduate students and faculty, supporting international students, and removing barriers for students with disabilities.

Brahme and Walters (2010) developed a study to compare the research practices and preferences of doctoral distance students with those of their residential counterparts. They found that the distance students were 40% more likely than residential students to want "easier contact" with the university librarians and, although the groups appeared equally knowledgeable about using the library, the distance students expressed much less confidence about their research skills. Schrnehl Hines (2006) examined studies of what distance faculty want from their libraries and found a need for better marketing of services to faculty, help with copyright, and outreach through library handouts and tutorials. Kvenild and Bowles-Terry's (2011) needs assessment of distance faculty at the University of Wyoming concluded that distance educators needed more familiarity with available library services, and that the librarians needed to attend more to marketing to faculty.

Key trends affecting higher education and distance education include increasing globalization and internationalization (Walsh, 2009). A growing number of students are engaging in distance learning through online or site-based programs that cross national boundaries. Academic libraries are directing attention to how best to support the academic success of international students, and address challenges these students may face such as language and cultural barriers. In 2009 ACRL (n.d.) initiated the Academic Library Services to International Students Interest Group which maintains a collection of resources for providing quality library support to international students. The Society of College, National and University Libraries (SCONUL, 2008) in the UK offers guidelines and best practices for supporting international students. Although these resources do not focus specifically on distance learners, there are many areas of overlap, such as designing library Web pages especially for international students, avoiding jargon, and providing library staff with diversity training (SCONUL, 2008). Providing library support to international distance learners includes additional challenges related to technology, time zones, bureaucratic hurdles, and the logistics of delivering resources and services. Helpful research has come out of Nova Southeastern University in Florida, including Ramdial and Tuñón's (2007) survey of international distance learners in Jamaica and the Bahamas.

To meet the needs of persons with disabilities, academic libraries must attend to issues such as resource accessibility, universal design principles, inclusivity, assistive technologies, appropriate reference and instruction services, broader institutional supports and policies, and relevant acts, laws and regulations at national and local levels. Such issues are discussed within ACRL's Universal Accessibility Interest Group (2011), and SCONUL has provided a detailed report for the UK on access for library users with disabilities (Robertson, 2007). ACRL's *Standards for Distance Learning Library Services* (2008) draws attention to the need to ensure equivalent access for distance users with disabilities. Black's (2004) examination of implications for librarians supporting distance learners with learning disabilities is particularly helpful, as is the literature on issues related to accessibility of library Web sites and electronic documents, such as Vandenbark (2010) and Thompson (2009). More on the challenge for supporting students with disabilities will be found in Chrichton and Kinash (Chapter 14, this volume).

PROVIDING ACCESS TO RESOURCES

The information and communications environment has changed dramatically since the days when reliance on telephone, fax, the postal system, courier, satellite library locations, and reciprocal borrowing arrangements dominated the distance learner's experience of the library. Technology provides access through online journal databases, e-book collections, digital repositories, electronic course reserves, and electronic document delivery.

E-resources

The move toward expanding electronic resources in academic libraries continues. Many database providers now include substantial full text content in their databases and allow subscribing institutions to provide remote access to content through proxy servers. In addition, available full text content now often includes access to older articles from journals indexed in databases. As a result, content that previously was available only in the physical holdings of large research libraries is now available electronically anytime/anywhere, and this has helped to ensure the equivalency of access for distance learning communities.

An increasing number of scholarly resources are being published in open access formats which do not require subscriptions and are freely available to anyone. The availability of open online resources provides both opportunities and challenges for distance users and librarians. The ease of access to these resources—the fact that they usually do not require a login and are often accessible through a Web search—allows users greater access to scholarly sources. However, the sheer volume of information and sources can be overwhelming. Whereas scholarly resources were once available only from library collections, now these resources are available through countless online sources such as institutional repositories and open access initiatives, which may or may not be familiar to users and librarians. While tools such as Google Scholar can facilitate access to some of these open resources (Hartman & Bowering Mullen, 2008), more can be done by distance libraries to provide greater access to these resources (Hutton, 2008). Many

There are a number of standards documents which can assist in the development of institutional support, including the *Information Literacy Competency Standards for Higher Education* (ACRL, 2000) and the *Standards for Distance Learning Library Services* (ACRL, 2008). These documents identify the role of higher education in promoting information literacy, but also remind us that an important goal of higher education is fostering lifelong learning, of which information literacy is a component. The references to information literacy in the criteria established by accreditation bodies can be useful in increasing the prominence that information literacy has on campus at the administrative level, but faculty must also recognize its importance so as to more consistently allow for curricular integration in pedagogically appropriate ways.

Faculty/librarian collaboration is crucial in establishing institutional support. The literature provides an abundance of suggestions for best practices in establishing a collegial working relationship between faculty and librarians, and examples of effective collaboration efforts (Held, 2010; Pritchard, 2010; Sterling Brasley, 2008). As trust and respect are two crucial elements of collaboration, common goals and common understanding are important. Ideally, collaboration should result in alignment with the strategic goals of the institution thereby encouraging further institutional support for information literacy initiatives (Sterling Brasley, 2008). Owens and Bozeman (2009) suggest a number of strategies for developing relationships with faculty, including attending faculty presentations, offering to conduct a library orientation for students, and participating in faculty committees. In becoming a known and thoughtful presence, the foundation for collaboration is being built.

Delivering Information Literacy Instruction

Collaboration between faculty and librarians is necessary for the delivery of effective and equitable information literacy instruction to distance students (Owens & Bozeman, 2009). Determining the best way to deliver this instruction can be extremely challenging due to a range of factors that may vary substantially. Distance librarians may have difficulty developing a clear understanding of learner needs and limitations and, as is recommended in the *Standards for Distance Learning Library Services,* must be able to provide services in a wide range of formats (Nicholson & Eva, 2011).

Information literacy instruction for distance students is provided in a variety of ways using different technologies. While some libraries are able to offer in-person information literacy training to their distance students in the form of so-called one-shot sessions, institutional factors may preclude this approach. In addition, some literature questions the efficacy of these sessions in a distributed environment, recommending instead point of need information literacy instruction that is directly relevant to specific assignments or tasks (Kenney, 2008; Mery, Newby, & Peng, 2011; Tuñón & Ramirez, 2010).

As a result, librarians and their institutions are exploring the use of alternative methods to provide information literacy instruction to their distance learners. These methods include the use of technologies such as Skype (Nicholson & Eva, 2011) and Second Life to deliver instruction sessions (Sterling Brasley, 2008), and the creation of tutorials customized for distance learners and meant to address specific needs. Online tutorials must meet the needs of students with diverse learning styles and, as a result, may be animated, text- or activity- based. In recent years, there have been efforts in the library community to establish best practices for creating and updating tutorials especially given the increasing number of online students and availability of electronic resources. However, creating online tutorials can be onerous if staff members are unfamiliar with

HTML (Gonzalez & Westbrock, 2010). Many academic libraries are using technologies such as LibGuides, which allow for easy creation and maintenance of tutorials that can include a range of different media types, and allow for student interactivity. Tutorials should be seen as complementary to other information literacy activities rather than as stand-alone tools. Increasingly, they are being integrated into learning management systems, and into assignment instructions or the assignments themselves.

Embedded librarian programs, in which the librarian participates in course conference boards and acts as a resource for the students within the course to answer questions, provides another option. In some circumstances, embedded librarians are team or co-teachers (Tucci, 2011; Tumbleson & Burke, 2010). While this has proven an effective means of providing information literacy instruction, there can be serious workload implications, especially in an environment of decreasing staff and funding (Tumbleson & Burke, 2010). Another frequently used method is the development of for-credit online information literacy courses designed to teach students about the different facets of the information landscape (Mery et al., 2011; Morrison & Garcia, 2011). Librarians can also work closely with faculty to build information literacy instruction into their courses and assignments. Ultimately, the integration of information literacy skills instruction directly into the curriculum provides the context needed to help students understand the relevance of these skills (Fabbro, 2009; Jacobs & Jacobs, 2009; Sterling Brasley, 2008; Tuñón & Ramirez, 2010).

Developing Relevant Pedagogical Approaches

Careful consideration of pedagogical approaches, learning theories, and instructional design helps ensure that information literacy instruction meets the needs of distance learners. Mestre et al. (2011) note the need for librarians to meet the challenge of engaging students effectively in online learning environments if students are to become information literate. Understanding how students perceive and process experiences can help librarians and educators develop effective online tutorials that meet differing learner needs. Mestre (2010), in assessing the effectiveness of online tutorials in accommodating diverse learning styles, points to the need for learning objects that address multiple modalities: visual, auditory, and kinesthetic. Learning objects is a topic discussed extensively by Moisey and Ally (Chapter 20, this volume).

Information literacy instructors are increasingly recognizing the limitations of a disconnected, fragmented skills focus. Many alternatives can be found in the literature. By engaging with pedagogical practices from the field of writing and rhetoric librarians can move information literacy away from skills taught in isolation and towards a process-oriented, recursive approach (Norgaard, 2003). Ovadia (2010) applied "Writing in the Disciplines" concepts to an online research class in which students used writing as a means to learn and demonstrate information literacy. Inquiry-based learning taps into natural human curiosity to engage students in the act of inquiry as they formulate questions, build new knowledge, gain deeper understanding, and develop solutions. Librarians at the University of Calgary developed an online, inquiry-based, information search process tutorial to support blended learning (Rutherford, Hayden, & Pival, 2006). Søk & Skriv (Search & Write), an online information literacy tutorial for distance learners in Norway, uses a social-constructivist approach to "promote student learning by doing and reflecting," and to encourage knowledge construction within the context of social interaction (Skagen et al., 2008, p. 89). Duke, Ward, and Burkert (2010) have combined understandings from critical pedagogy, and its focus on the importance of raising critical consciousness and creating empowerment, with information literacy instruction for teachers in a distance-delivered Master's program in Special Education. Aims of the program include raising awareness of social injustices, preparing "teachers as researchers" capable of locating and evaluating sources for the benefit of those they teach, and encouraging culturally responsive approaches and advocacy, all in the context of the teachers' work as special educators in rural Alaska.

With increasing demands on them to develop online learning objects and courses, deliver online instruction, and collaborate with faculty, librarians are finding a need for more knowledge and training in pedagogical theory and instructional design. A number of resources have been developed to help librarians improve their knowledge in this area. The Online Learning Toolkit, developed by the Online Learning Research Committee of the ACRL Education and Behavioral Sciences Section (EBSS), provides a collection of pedagogical resources for librarians involved in online instruction (ACRL, 2011). *Practical Pedagogy for Library Instructors: 17 Innovative Strategies to Improve Student Learning* uses case studies, covering behavioral to cognitive to constructivist approaches, to help librarians use pedagogical theory to inform their instruction in the classroom and online (Cook & Sittler, 2009).

By supplementing the library literature with research, theory, and educational philosophy from the fields of distance education and adult education, distance learning librarianship can develop a robust and relevant approach to information literacy instruction.

Assessing Information Literacy Skills

Are students learning the necessary information literacy skills? Is an institution's information literacy program effective? What do we need to know to improve such programs? *Information Literacy Competency Standards for Higher Education* (ACRL, 2000) lists outcomes that can be used as guidelines for developing local methods for measuring students' information literacy skills within the context of an institution's mission. The ACRL standards note the importance of assessing not only basic information literacy skills, but also discipline-related information literacy that reflects understandings around how knowledge is created and disseminated within particular disciplines. The *Standards for Distance Learning Library Services* (ACRL, 2008) note the importance of measuring students' library knowledge, and the assessment of student learning is an important concern of U.S. accreditation bodies. There is a considerable body of literature on information literacy assessment in general, and some studies focus on assessing distance learners' information literacy skills using pre- and post-assessment (Hufford & Paschel, 2010; Ivanitskaya, DuFord, Craig, & Casey, 2008; Shaffer, 2011).

PROFESSIONAL RESOURCES

For librarians and others seeking information and research about library support for distance learning there are many valuable professional resources, including databases, bibliographies, citation and content analyses, conferences and their proceedings, and professional organizations.

Three of the best databases for research within the field of library and information science are Library Literature & Information Science Full Text, Library and Information Science Abstracts (LISA), and Library, Information Science & Technology Abstracts with

Full Text (LISTA). Relevant research can also be found in education databases such as ProQuest Education Journals and ERIC (Education Resources Information Center), and in other databases such as Emerald Full Text and Taylor & Francis Online. These databases are available by subscription, but EBSCO Industries (2011) offers a complimentary LISTA index and ERIC is available at no charge through its sponsor, the Institute of Education Sciences of the United States Department of Education (n.d.). The *Journal of Library & Information Services in Distance Learning* is particularly notable within the journal literature as its primary focus is provision of library services and resources in distance learning. This peer-reviewed, quarterly publication provides articles, essays, reviews, and research reports addressing a variety of issues in distance learning librarianship with an international scope.

Although bibliographies quickly become dated, they are very useful for discovering core subjects and literature, and for acquiring historical and contextual perspective. *Library Services for Distance Learning* is a key bibliographic tool in distance learning librarianship. This free, online annotated bibliography continues the work of the three print bibliographies (Latham, Slade, & Budnick, 1991; Slade & Kascus, 1996, 2000) and is available as *The Fourth Bibliography* (ACRL Distance Learning Section, 2006–2008), which is continued by *The Fifth Bibliography* (ACRL Distance Learning Section, 2008-2010). *Library Services for Distance Learning* organizes research and other literature in a number of broad categories, including bibliographies, general works, the role of libraries, organizational issues, managing e-resources, document delivery, information literacy, interlibrary cooperation, surveys, user studies, and case studies.

Citation and content analyses offer another important guide to the professional literature, providing insights into key subjects, issues, trends, authors, journals, and research methodologies. One of the more recent studies comes from Susan Herring (2010), who analyzed the citations, abstracts, and subject indexing of 472 articles focused on library services in distance education published in English from 1999–2009. Earlier studies include Reiten and Fritts (2006) and Slade (2004).

Conferences and their proceedings are one of the richest sources for sharing ideas and research in the field. Distance Library Services (formerly known as Off-Campus Library Services) is one of the most important conferences for practitioners and administrators of distance learning library services. This biennial conference, sponsored by Central Michigan University, was first held in 1982. Past conference proceedings are available from the University in digital form for free, or print form for a fee, and the proceedings have been published in special issues of the *Journal of Library Administration*.

Conferences from the fields of librarianship and distance education, such as the American Library Association Annual Conference and the Annual Conference on Distance Teaching & Learning, sponsored by the University of Wisconsin, often regularly include presentations, workshops, or proceedings of relevance to the provision of distance learning library services. There are also topic-specific conferences such as the International m-Libraries Conference, the first of which was hosted by The Open University in partnership with Athabasca University in 2007. M-Libraries focuses on sharing expertise around library support within the context of the growing ubiquity of mobile and hand-held devices (Needham & Ally, 2008). There are a number of excellent conferences dedicated to information literacy including the annual LOEX (Library Orientation Exchange) conference in the United States, the annual WILU (Workshop for Instruction in Library Use) conference in Canada, and the Librarians' Information Literacy Annual Conference (LILAC) in the United Kingdom.

Professional organizations are an important source of communication, professional development and leadership. Established in 1991, the Distance Learning Section (DLS) of ACRL is the most prominent professional organization in distance learning librarianship in North America. Perhaps the most significant contribution of the DLS has been its development of the *Standards for Distance Learning Library Services,* which provides important direction to academic libraries serving distance learning users (ACRL, 2008). The DLS performs many functions through its different committees and projects, including publishing the *Library Services for Distance Learning* bibliography. DLS facilitates communication and research among distance education librarians through the DLS Discussion Group and programs at conferences, and the work of the Research Committee in encouraging research activities and in identifying areas where research is needed.

ACRL's Regional Campus Libraries Discussion Group provides another venue for exchanging information and networking, with a focus on physical and virtual regional campuses. In addition, the Distance Learning Interest Group of the Library & Information Technology Association (LITA) offers professional development resources in distance librarianship, with a particular focus on the application of technologies to the provision of distance learning library services and resources. The OFFCAMP listserv, from the University of Tennessee Knoxville, is a predominant resource for discussions amongst distance librarians. Other valuable professional development resources can be found within groups that are not specifically dedicated to distance learning librarianship such as the Instruction Section of ACRL which is responsible for the ILI-L Discussion List, a tool for facilitating the exchange of information about information literacy and library instruction among librarians.

CONCLUSION

This is a challenging but exciting time for academic libraries supporting distance learning. As they face significant funding constraints, distance librarians find themselves trying to do more with less, working with staffing shortages, and needing to make important strategic decisions about services and resources. This is at a time when the number of distance learning graduate programs is growing; universities are positioning themselves to meet the educational needs of greater numbers of international students; a generation of students that is used to always being connected, networked, and mobile is working its way through higher education; and awareness of the value of the academic library in relation to student success and retention is increasing. The boundaries between serving distance learners and on-campus students are blurring as, regardless of location, students increasingly use libraries remotely due to the availability of extensive, full-text online collections and virtual reference and instruction services. Macauley and Green (2008) refer to this phenomenon as "the convergence of off-campus and on-campus library services" (p. 368).

Faced with these complex realities, those involved in distance learning librarianship will now more than ever need to access the knowledge gained through research and experience, and contribute to this knowledge base, to ensure an informed and innovative approach to meeting the needs of diverse distance learning communities. The literature surveyed in this chapter provides examples of the creativity and flexibility of distance librarianship in facilitating successful teaching and learning experiences by connecting distance users with their libraries, meeting their needs for research and learning resources, and providing them with opportunities to develop their information literacy abilities.

REFERENCES

Association of College & Research Libraries. (2000). *Information literacy competency standards for higher education*. Chicago, IL: Association of College & Research Libraries. Retrieved from http://www.ala.org/ala/mgrps/divs/acrl/standards/standards.pdf

Association of College & Research Libraries. (2008). *Standards for distance learning library services*. Retrieved from http://www.ala.org/ala/mgrps/divs/acrl/standards/guidelinesdistancelearning.cfm

Association of College & Research Libraries. (2011a). *Online learning toolkit*. Retrieved from http://wikis.ala.org/acrl/index.php/Online_Learning_Toolkit

Association of College & Research Libraries. (2011b). *Standards for libraries in higher education*. Retrieved from http://www.ala.org/acrl/standards/standardslibraries

Association of College & Research Libraries. Academic Library Services to International Students Interest Group. (n.d.). *Home page*. Retrieved from http://www.acrl.ala.org/international/

Association of College & Research Libraries. Distance Learning Section. (2006–2008). *Library services for distance learning: The fourth bibliography*. Retrieved from http://caspian.switchinc.org/~distlearn/resources/4thBibliography/BibliographyHome.html

Association of College & Research Libraries. Distance Learning Section. (2008–2010). *Library services for distance learning: The fifth bibliography*. Retrieved from http://caspian.switchinc.org/~distlearn/resources/5thBibliography/BibliographyHome.html

Association of College & Research Libraries. Universal Accessibility Interest Group (2011). Home page. Retrieved from http://www.ala.org/ala/mgrps/divs/acrl/resources/leadership/interestgrps/acr-igua.cfm

Behr, M. D. (2008). Streamlining document delivery and interlibrary loan services for distance learners. Survey and case study. *Journal of Interlibrary Loan, Document Delivery & Electronic Reserve, 18*(2), 129–139. doi:10.1300/10723030802097289

Behr, M. D., & Hayward, J. L. (2008). Do off-campus students still use document delivery? Current trends. *Journal of Library Administration, 48*(3/4), 277–293. doi:10.1080/01930820802289318

Black, N.E. (2004). Blessing or curse? Distance delivery to students with invisible disabilities. *Journal of Library Administration, 41*(1/2), 47–64. doi: 10.1300/J111v41n01_05

Blankenship, B. L., & Wood, P. S. (2009). Electronic reserve on a regional campus: The evolution of the service. *Journal of Interlibrary Loan, Document Delivery & Electronic Reserve, 19*(2), 131–135. doi: 10.1080/10723030902776170

Brahme, M., & Walters, L. (2010). While technology poses as the great equalizer, distance still rules the experience. *Journal of Library Administration, 50*(5/6), 484–514. doi: 10.1080/01930826.2010.48859

Burgstahler, S. (2002). Distance learning: The library's role in ensuring access to everyone. *Library Hi Tech, 20*(4), 420–432.

Cantagallo, C., Dennis, M., & Reeg-Steidinger, J. (2011). Examining reference assistance in support of distributed learning. In S. G. Almquist (Ed.), *Distributed Learning and Virtual Librarianship* (pp. 147–174). Santa Barbara, CA: ABC-CLIO.

Cheung, O., Thomas, D., & Patrick, S. (2009). *New approaches to e-reserve: Linking, sharing and streaming*. Oxford, UK: Chandos.

Clark, J. (2011). Distributed learning copyright issues. In S. G. Almquist (Ed.), *Distributed Learning and Virtual Librarianship* (pp. 175–228). Santa Barbara, CA: ABC-CLIO.

Clayton, S. (2008). The impossible takes a little longer: Implementing a copyright policy for electronic reserves. *Journal of Access Services, 5*(1-2), 243–250. doi:10.1080/15367960802198770

Clumpner, K. E., Burgmeier, M., & Gillespie, T. J. (2011). Embedded course reserves: Piecing the puzzle together. *Computers in Libraries, 31*(4), 10–14.

Cook, D., & Sittler, R. L. (2009). *Practical pedagogy for library instructors: 17 innovative strategies to improve student learning*. Chicago, IL: Association of College and Research Libraries.

Dalton, J. T. (2007). Electronic reserves and the copyright challenge in Canada. *Journal of Interlibrary Loan, Document Delivery & Electronic Reserve, 17*(1/2), 97–120. doi:10.1300/J474v17n01_11

Dermody, M. (2005). We cannot see them, but they are there: Marketing library services to distance learners. *Journal of Library & Information Services in Distance Learning, 2*(1), 41–50. doi:10.1300/J192v02n01_04

Drew, C., & Flanagan, P. (2007). Bypassing e-reserves with durable links to subscribed content: Efficient access and how to enable it. *Journal of Interlibrary Loan, Document Delivery & Electronic Reserve, 17*(3), 117–127. doi:10.1300/J474v17n03_15

Duke, T. S., Ward, J. D., & Burkert, J. (2010). Preparing critically conscious, information literate special educators for Alaska's schools. In M. T. Accardi, E. Drabinski, & A. Kumbier (Eds.), *Critical library instruction: Theories and methods* (pp. 115–131). Duluth, MN: Library Juice Press.

EBSCO Industries. (2011). *Library, information science & technology abstracts*. Retrieved from http://www.libraryresearch.com

Fabbro, E. (2009). *Athabasca University Library: Information literacy across the curriculum*. Retrieved from http://library.athabascau.ca/about/libdoc.html

Fry, A. (2010, November). Boost your use: Promoting E-resources to students and faculty. Paper presented at the *Brick and Click Libraries: Proceedings of an Academic Library Symposium,* Northwest Missouri State University, Maryville.

Giustini, D., Hooker, D., & Cho, A. (2009). Social cataloguing: An overview for health librarians. *Journal of the Canadian Health Libraries Association, 30*(4), 133–138. Retrieved from http://pubs.chla-absc.ca/doi/pdf/10.5596/c09-039

Gonzalez, A. C., & Westbrock, T. (2010). Reaching out with LibGuides: Establishing a working set of best practices. *Journal of Library Administration, 50*(5/6), 638–656. doi:10.1080/01930826.2010.488941

Goodson, K. A., & Frederiksen, L. (2011). E-Reserves in transition: Exploring new possibilities in e-reserves service delivery. *Journal of Interlibrary Loan, Document Delivery & Electronic Reserve, 21*(1/2), 33–56. doi:10.1080/1072303X.2011.557976

Hartman, K. A., & Bowering Mullen, L. (2008). Google Scholar and academic libraries: An update. *New Library World, 109*(5/6), 211.

Held, T. (2010). Blending in: Collaborating with an instructor in an online course. *Journal of Library & Information Services in Distance Learning, 4*(4), 153–165.

Herring, S. D. (2010). Research on libraries and distance education: An analysis of articles published 1999–2009. *Journal of Library & Information Services in Distance Learning, 4*(3), 137–146. doi: 10.1080/1533290X.2010.503494

Hosburgh, N., & Okamoto, K. (2010). Electronic document delivery: A survey of the landscape and horizon. *Journal of Interlibrary Loan, Document Delivery & Electronic Reserve, 20*(4), 233–252. doi:10.1080/1072303X.2010.502096

Hufford, J. R., & Paschel, A. K. (2010). Pre-and postassessment surveys for the distance section of LIBR 1100, Introduction to Library Research. *Journal of Library Administration, 50*(5/6), 693–711. doi:10.1080/01930826.2010.488956

Hutton, J. (2008). Academic libraries as digital gateways: Linking students to the burgeoning wealth of open online collections. *Journal of Library Administration, 48*(3/4), 495–507.

Ivanitskaya, L., DuFord, S., Craig, M., & Casey, A. M. (2008). How does a pre-assessment of off-campus students' information literacy affect the effectiveness of library instruction? *Journal of Library Administration, 48*(3/4), 509–525. doi:10.1080/01930820802289649.

Jacobs, H., & Jacobs, D. (2009). Transforming the one-shot library session into pedagogical collaboration: Information literacy and the English composition class. *Reference & User Services Quarterly, 49*(1), 72.

Jones, M. F. (2008). Internet reference services for distance education. *Internet Reference Services Quarterly, 9*(3/4), 19–32. doi:10.1300/J136v09n03_03

Kenney, B. (2008). Revitalizing the one-shot instruction session using problem-based learning. *Reference & User Services Quarterly, 47*(4), 386–391.

Kvenild, C., & Bowles-Terry, M. (2011). Learning from distance faculty: A faculty needs assessment at the University of Wyoming. *Journal of Library & Information Services in Distance Learning, 5*(1/2), 10–24. doi:10.1080/1533290X.2011.548239

Latham, S., Slade, A. L., & Budnick, C. (1991). *Library services for off-campus and distance education: An annotated bibliography*. Ottawa, ON: Canadian Library Association.

Lewis, J. S. (2011). Using LibQUAL+® survey results to document the adequacy of services to distance learning students for an accreditation review. *Journal of Library & Information Services in Distance Learning, 5*(3), 83–104. doi:10.1080/1533290X.2011.605935

Li, X., & Demers, D. (2010). Improving electronic reserve services: A collaborative effort. *Journal of Interlibrary Loan, Document Delivery & Electronic Reserve, 20*(4), 263–269. doi:10.1080/1072303X.2010.507134

Long, D. (2009). Going the extra mile: Designing a delivery service for remote borrowers. *Journal of Library & Information Services in Distance Learning, 3*(3/4), 182–191. doi:10.1080/15332900903182697

Macauley, P., & Green, R. (2008). The transformation of information and library services. In T. Evans, M. Haughey, & D. Murphy (Eds.), *International handbook of distance education* (pp. 367–382). Bingley, UK: Emerald Group.

MacDonald, K. I., Vanduinkerken, W., & Stephens, J. (2008). It's all in the marketing: The impact of a virtual reference marketing campaign at Texas A&M University. *Reference & User Services Quarterly, 47*(4), 375-385.

McCaslin, D.J. (2008). Processing electronic reserves in a large academic library system. *Journal of Interlibrary Loan, Document Delivery & Electronic Reserve, 18*(3), 335–346. doi:10.1080/10723030802186348

Mery, Y., Newby, J., & Peng, K. (2011). Why one-shot information literacy sessions are not the future of instruction: A case for online credit courses. *College & Research Libraries.* Advance online publication. Retrieved from http://crl.acrl.org/content/early/2011/08/26/crl-271.short

Mestre, L.S. (2010). Matching up learning styles with learning objects: What's effective? *Journal of Library Administration, 50*(7-8), 808–829. doi:10.1080/01930826.2010.488975

Mestre, L.S., Baures, L., Niedbala, M., Bishop, C., Cantrell, S., Perez, A., & Silfen, K. (2011). Learning objects as tools for teaching information literacy online: A survey of librarian usage. *College & Research Libraries, 72*(3), 236–252.

Meulemans, Y. N., Carr, A., & Ly, P. (2010). From a distance: Robust reference service via instant messaging. *Journal of Library & Information Services in Distance Learning, 4,* 3–17.

Morrison, R., & Garcia, L. (2011, March-April). From embedded to integrated: Digital information literacy and new teaching models for academic librarians. Paper presented at the *ACRL National Conference 2011.*

Needham, G., & Ally, M. (Eds.). (2008). *M-libraries: Libraries on the move to provide virtual access.* London: Facet.

Nichols, J. T. (2006). Monthly check-up: Using a monthly survey to monitor and assess library and information services for distance learners. *Journal of Library Administration, 45*(3/4), 387–395. doi: 10.1300/J111v45n03_05

Nicholson, M. H., & Eva, M.N.C. (2011). Information literacy instruction for satellite university students. *Reference Services Review, 39*(3), 497–513.

Norgaard, R. (2003). Writing information literacy: Contributions to a concept. *Reference & User Services Quarterly, 43*(2), 124–130.

Oakleaf, M. (2010). *Value of academic libraries: A comprehensive research review and report.* Retrieved from http://www.ala.org/acrl/sites/ala.org.acrl/files/content/issues/value/val_report.pdf

Oakley, B., Pittman, B., & Rudnick, T. (2008). Tackling copyright in the digital age: An initiative of the University of Connecticut Libraries. *Journal of Access Services, 5*(1/2), 265–283. doi: 10.1080/15367960802198978

Oliver, A. (2008). Current practices and philosophy on electronic reserves, course management systems, and copyright compliance: A Survey of the Council of Public Liberal Arts Colleges Libraries. *Journal of Interlibrary Loan, Document Delivery & Electronic Reserve, 18*(4), 425–437. doi:10.1080/10723030802181711

Ovadia, S. (2010). Writing as an information literacy tool: Bringing writing in the disciplines to an online library class. *Journal of Library Administration, 50*(7/8), 899–908. doi:10.1080/01930826.2010.488990

Owens, R., & Bozeman, D. (2009). Toward a faculty-librarian collaboration: Enhancement of online teaching and learning. *Journal of Library & Information Services in Distance Learning, 3*(1), 31–38. doi: 10.1080/15332900902794898

Poe, J., & McAbee, S. (2008). Electronic reserves, copyright, and CMS integration–six years later. *Journal of Access Services, 5*(1/2), 251–263. doi:10.1080/15367960802198879

Pritchard, P. A. (2010). The embedded science librarian: Partner in curriculum design and delivery. *Journal of Library Administration, 50*(4), 373–396. doi:10.1080/01930821003667054

Ramdial, S., & Tuñón, J. (2007). Equivalent library services for international students?: A comparison of student responses in Jamaica and the Bahamas with the results of a university-wide survey. In C. Peltier-Davis & S. Renwick (Eds.), *Caribbean libraries in the 21st century: Changes, challenges, and choices* (pp. 291–302). Medford, NJ: Information Today.

Reiten, B. A., & Fritts, J. (2006). Distance learning librarianship research over time: Changes and the core literature. *Journal of Library Administration, 45*(3/4), 397–410. doi:10.1300/J111v45n03_06

Robertson, L. (2007). *Access for library users with disabilities.* London: Society of College, National and University Libraries. Retrieved from http://www.sconul.ac.uk/groups/access/papers/

Rutherford, S., Hayden, K. A., & Pival, P. R. (2006). WISPR (Workshop on the InformationSearch Process for Research) in the library. *Journal of Library Administration, 45*(3/4), 427–443. doi: 10.1300/J111v45n0308

Schlipp, J. (2011). Electronic reserves and information delivery. In S. G. Almquist (Ed.), *Distributed Learning and Virtual Librarianship* (pp. 229–262). Santa Barbara, CA: ABC-CLIO.

Schrnehl Hines, S. (2006). What do distance education faculty want from the library? *Journal of Library Administration, 45*(1/2), 215–227. doi: 10.1300/J111v45n01_12

Shaffer, B. A. (2011). Graduate student library research skills: Is online instruction effective? *Journal of Library & Information Services in Distance Learning, 5*(1/2), 35–55. doi: 10.1080/1533290X.2011.570546

Shelton, K. (2009). Library outreach to part-time and distance education instructors. *Community & Junior College Libraries, 15*(1), 3–8. doi:10.1080/02763910802656812

Skagen, T., Torras, M. C., Kavli, S. M. L., Mikki, S., Hafstad, S., & Hunskår, I. (2008). Pedagogical considerations in developing an online tutorial in information literacy. *Communications in Information Literacy, 2*(2), 84–98.

16

THEORY TO PRACTICE IN INSTRUCTIONAL DESIGN

RICK L. SHEARER

In distance education, there is an underlying acknowledgement or understanding that a particular technology or group of technologies is being utilized to bridge the distance between the student, the instructor, and learning organization. Key to any one of the technologies chosen is how it allows or does not allow the other elements of the course to behave in a systems environment.

Further, before a designer considers technologies, there exists a multitude of factors (cost, audience, etc.) that must be examined in the design of a course before one examines the learning goals and objectives. In many instances, these factors dictate the technologies used, frequency of revisions, and the level of customization allowed before each offering. It is important to understand that online learning is just a subset of the distance education world and it should not be automatically assumed that the technologies used in distance education will be internet based, or that any of the students will be located in the same physical location as the instructor.

Today, there is no single technology that addresses all the needs of learners or the results expected by the constituents involved in the distance education enterprise. Also, how we view content and the production of content is changing with the introduction of open education resources (OERs) and Web 2.0 tools. In essence, content as we have viewed the written work in the past, may no longer be king in our design. Although in a recent study by Miyazoe and Anderson (2010), it is shown that student–content interaction is still highly valued in distance education online courses.

It is also evident in today's distance education courses that the integration of rich media, a focus on accessibility or universal design, and an accreditation focus on learning outcomes across the curriculum, requires a team of experts to develop all aspects of a quality distance education course.

This chapter will explore key design factors in distance education and look at how these factors may impact today's online course designs. The chapter will also briefly review the theory of transactional distance and the Community of Inquiry (COI) model in order to connect the design factors to the theory and model.

THEORETICAL FRAMEWORK

Without going into a full review of the theory of transactional distance (see Chapter 5, this volume), it is important to briefly review the theory in order to form a framework for the key design factors. Moore's (1980) theory of transactional distance remains one of the central theories to the field of distance education and has a profound impact on instructional design for distance education courses. Supplementing Moore's theory, the COI model by Garrison, Anderson, and Archer (1999) (see Chapter 6, this volume) provides an enhancement to the theory of transactional distance framework in terms of social presence and cognitive presence.

Transactional Distance

Moore explored his ideas for the theory of transactional distance throughout the 1970s, as he examined numerous distance education courses. The resultant outcome was a proposed system of linkages between three key variables: (a) dialogue, (b) structure, and (c) learner autonomy, with transactional distance being the outcome of the interplay between these variables. As Shearer (2010) states in his work on dialogue in transactional distance "transactional distance in learning environments is an educational exchange that happens at a distance. The effectiveness and efficiency of the exchange depends on dialogue, structure, and autonomy, and is affected by a psychological dimension of connectedness" (p. 2).

Dialogue, at the time the theory was introduced, was viewed as a subset of the communications between the student and the instructor that led to the construction of knowledge or advanced a student's understanding of the material being studied. Structure was viewed as the amount of freedom a program provides the student in determining pace, sequence, learning objectives and outcomes, and assessment strategies; learner autonomy, looked at the degree of dependence the student needed with the learning organization or learning environment to be successful.

In general, the theory of transactional distance is the resultant of the interaction between the three variables, dialogue, structure, and autonomy (see Figure 16.1). On one

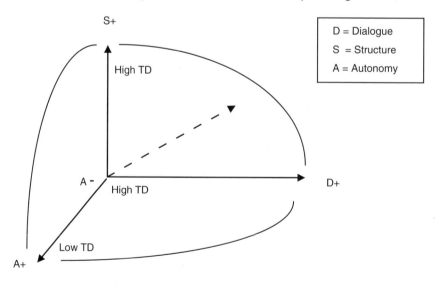

Figure 16.1 The three dimensions of transactional distance.

dimension, the theory looks at how structure and dialogue interact. As diagrammed by Saba (1989), in a systems model, as dialogue increased, transactional distance—or the psychological separation of the learner from the instructor and effectiveness of the transaction—decreased. Or simply stated, the more efficient the dialogic exchange the lower the perceived distance in the educational transaction, and the possibility for miscommunication is reduced.

Also, as shown in Figure 16.1, it may be possible to have high learner autonomy and low dialogue and still have low transactional distance based on the reduced need of the student for dialogue. Thus, the theory outlines three key design factors that interrelate and impact our designs for distance education courses.

Community of Inquiry

Garrison et al.'s (1999) COI model presents a means of analyzing and planning online learning, and presents three key factors: cognitive presence, social presence, and teaching presence. Garrison and Anderson (2003) in their book *E-Learning in the 21st Century* depict the model as three overlapping circles of presence, with the area that is common to all three circles representing the Educational Experience. Garrison and Anderson (2003) define the three variables or presences as:

Cognitive Presence—the extent to which learners are able to construct and confirm meaning through sustained reflection and discourse in a critical community of inquiry (p. 28). The indicators of cognitive presence are based on the practical inquiry phases of triggering event, exploration, integration, and resolution.

Social Presence—the ability of participants in a community of inquiry to project themselves socially and emotionally as "real" people (p. 28). Short, Williams, and Christie (1976) introduced the idea of social presence in their work on the social psychology of telecommunications and looked at the impact of different media on the construct of social presence. Further, Gunawardena (1995) indicates that in the absence of face-to-face non-verbal cues such as head nodding, smiling, gesturing, etc., participants in an online learning environment make up for the lack of these observable cues by increasing "... overt social-emotional expressions such as greeting, and paralinguistic cues ..." (p. 155).

Teaching Presence—the design, facilitation, and direction of cognitive and social processes for the purpose of realizing personally meaningful and educationally worthwhile learning outcomes (Garrison &Anderson, 2003, p. 29). In describing teaching presence, they state, "teaching presence brings all the elements of a community of inquiry together in a balanced and functional relationship congruent with the intended outcomes and the needs and capabilities of the learners" (p. 29).

When comparing the key variables of the theory of transactional distance with the ideas presented in the COI model, there is apparent overlap. For example, cognitive presence is similar to the idea of dialogue and is related to the development of knowledge within an individual or group through open and trusted dialogue and reflection. Teaching presence is similar to the construct of transactional distance where it is the interplay of the variables and the amount of structure, dialogue, autonomy, and social presence that is afforded in the design and teaching that facilitates students being able to meet the required learning outcomes. While social presence is not a part of the theory of transactional distance, the recent work of Swan (2002), Picciano (2002), Tu (2002), Shearer (2010), and others show its importance in the online and distance education spectrum in terms of a sense of psychological connection that may lead to increased motivation and increased satisfaction with an educational experience. Although how it is related to increased learning outcomes needs to be reviewed.

DESIGN FACTORS

As instructional designers approach course design in distance education, the key elements of the theory of transactional distance and the COI model should inform many of their design decisions. The following outlines five key design factors and their relationship to the theory of transactional distance and the COI model.

Learner Autonomy/Learner Control

Students involved in distance education are, in general, isolated geographically from the instructor and institution, and must behave in a more autonomous manner in order to meet their learning goals and those of the institution. The amount of control that the design of a distance education course provides these learners is critical to their successful completion. If one provides too much structure within pacing, sequencing, and timing of assessment, then the learner, with competing life demands, may be forced to drop out. If a student is provided too little structure, then the learner may feel cut off and flounder through the course. Also, the type of control referred to here is not simply the control over how one interacts with the course and the instructor, but as Garrison and Baynton (1989) argue, control is a dynamic balance between independence, power, and support. Where power is a psychological dimension of the learner and involves the learner's motivation, cognitive style, emotional maturity, and attitude. Support refers to the support of family, financial support, the administrative processes of the institution, and so forth.

The variables structure and learner autonomy in the theory of transactional distance are in play when we consider learner control. If we assume that they are negatively correlated, then as learner autonomy increases, structure decreases. Thus, as one thinks about course design, the designer needs to think about the students they are trying to serve. Are they independent adult learners who are highly autonomous, or are they more traditional, aged students? Or is the course design trying to meet multiple audiences; which is never an easy task. In Moore's (1983) work on the theory of transactional distance, he developed a table that examined the types of programs in relation to the idea of learner autonomy and dependence or independence. In the table, he looked at who determined the learning objective, who decided what material to use, and who set the assessment strategies. He also depicted a learner as being in less control of the learning environment if all three of these aspects of dependence or independence were set by the teacher or learning institution. Within the COI model, teaching presence can be associated with learner control and structure as it is within teaching presence that the instructor balances these to assure a successful learning experience and outcome.

While the construct of learner control may seem subtle, it is vital to reflect on the construct in terms of how one designs courses for distance education. When thinking about how courses are structured in higher education, how many leave it up to the student to determine objectives, material, and assessment? The answer is few, which leads one to consider that even if our audience is one of highly autonomous learners, we have traditionally taken away the ability for them to act in an independent fashion. However, with the adoption of a variety of Web 2.0 tools in our designs, control and autonomy

(p. 73). Where the first two types of utterances represent a form of closeness and the latter two represent a sense of separation.

In today's courses, the addition of video for faculty introductions, student presentations, synchronous collaboration through Elluminate Live/Blackboard Collaborate or Adobe Connect, and Web 2.0 tools provide for an enhanced sense of presence not previously available to students in many distance education courses. This enhanced ability to be "real" in a virtual environment may provide for increased satisfaction and a perception of reduced transactional distance as it is related to psychological separation. Whether it reduces the possibility of miscommunication, which is the other key factor in decreasing transactional distance, still needs to be explored.

Further, the idea of immediacy in social presence is closely related to the idea of psychological distance/connectedness presented in the theory of transactional distance. This construct leads credence to the postulate that it may be social presence speech acts that reduce psychological separation or transactional distance instead of the construct of dialogue as discussed in the previous design factor section. However, more research needs to be conducted to examine these relationships.

Design Factor: Access

Making learning opportunities available to the disenfranchised has been a primary goal of distance educators and adult educators for over a century; however, access has many attributes. For example, throughout the past decade there was no shortage of articles and news stories on the technology aspect of the digital divide, but this is just one way of looking at the concept of access. Access issues in education can be viewed in terms of gender, culture, financial, geographic, supply and demand, disabilities, preparedness (entrance exam qualifications), motivational (self-esteem), language, and a number of other ways. To view access strictly as a concern of geographic separation, or simply as a concern of technology access, is too limiting a view. To design distance education courses and curriculums of study without acknowledging the variety of access issues that the intended audience may face can lead to the exclusion of many who may otherwise be interested in or need the course of study.

Traditionally in distance education, we have thought of access primarily as an issue of geographic separation of the learner and the instructor. In many ways, the technologies we have employed in the delivery of courses have been used to address this concern; however, technologies such as print, radio, and TV (with closed captioning) have also addressed a range of disabilities, as well as cultural and financial issues of access. These are technologies that can reach broad audiences, are relatively inexpensive to receive, are often readily available in most countries, and can address the needs of those who have special visual or auditory needs. Today, in countries across Asia and Africa, where traditional access to the Internet is limited, studies are highlighting the broad adoption of cell phones (Motlik, 2008) as a necessary means of providing access to information and education. In the Philippines and Mongolia there has been considerable work done with the use of SMS (short message service) to expand access to education and informal learning (Librero, Ranga, & Lambert, 2007). The adoption of cell phones, which have a huge market presence in these countries at a low cost of entry, is expanding the reach of education in the same way as radio did in the past. However, it brings up questions of access for those with disabilities or language barriers.

Internet and Technology Access

In 2005, the Pew Internet & American Life Project Report "Digital Division" (Fox, 2005) reported that 68% of American adults use the Internet. A similar study by the Pew Internet and American Life Project (Smith, 2010) reports that in 2010, 66% of American adults now have high-speed Internet access with the biggest growth over the past year in the African American demographic. The report indicates a leveling off of high-speed Internet adoption. In the report, respondents indicate that 31% feel that the lack of broadband access is a disadvantage to learning new things, while 63% do not feel that the lack of high-speed access is a disadvantage to learning new things. Also, the report indicates that 21% of adults still do not use the Internet with only one in ten indicating they would start. In other Pew Internet & American Life reports (2011b, c) the data shows that 92% of American adults use the Internet primarily for email and search with 6 in 10 doing so daily. Also, from 2005 to 2010 usage of social network sites has grown from 5% for adults to 65%, with heaviest usage among women, young adults under 30, and parents. Women between 18 and 29 are the power users, with 89% of this demographic using social networks; 69% daily. However, the data does not reflect how the uses of social networks are related to any educational purpose. Further, Pew Internet & American Life report (2011a) indicates that 35% of adults now use smartphones, with the United States now seeing an 89% adoption of cell phones.

Thus, over the past 10 years there has been a narrowing of the gap between the haves and have-nots in relation to traditional Internet access and the new gap appears to be developing around access to smartphones. However, is this a detriment in America for access to distance education or are smartphones just a convenience factor? As the Pew Internet and American Life studies highlight, in the United States it is usually those in the higher socioeconomic classes and those with higher levels of education that are the earlier adopters of new technologies.

Internationally, a report by WRI Research (Wired Digital Inc., 2000) indicated that 80% of the world population was being left out of the global communications system, and a report by the Commonwealth of Learning (2005) stated, "millions of children in commonwealth countries lack access to basic education." Recent reports from International World Stats (2011) and UNESCO (2007, 2011) indicate that Internet penetration in Africa is only 11%, in Latin America/Caribbean it is 36.2%, and in Asia it is 23.8% (with Asia representing 44% of all Internet users worldwide). However, within Asia many countries still fall below 10% of penetration in their populations and Africa still accounts for more than 43% of the world's out of school children and 38% of the adults still lack basic literacy. In the 2008 Education for All Global Monitoring Report (UNESCO, 2007), it was estimated that 774 million adults worldwide lack basic literacy; 64% are women, and gender equity issues remain high for women's access to education.

For designers and faculty, national and international statistics are critical to consider when undertaking the design and development of courses offered at a distance. They need to know the institutional mission, the audience(s) intended to be served, and their access to technologies. When various technologies are integrated into distance education courses, they may be disenfranchising a large portion of the population, and/or increase the cost of education to the student. This increase in cost is not only through the need for information technology access, but is associated with the cost of developing technology-rich courses, which may drive up the fee or tuition structure for technology-rich courses. Also, it is important to consider issues of access related to disabilities, as well as supply and demand for education when the Internet and other computer technologies are integrated. The idea of universal design or ADA compliance is extremely critical; especially as distance education has become more mainstream over the past five years. With more non-traditional students turning to distance education to meet their educational goals, institutions are seeing an increased awareness and scrutiny by entities like the American National Federation of the Blind, who are actively exposing institutions that do not approach their course designs with an eye to disability compliance.

As designers look at incorporating new and innovative technologies into their course designs, they need to examine how or if the technologies provide greater overall access to education and a sense of control for students in how they interface with their courses and their peers in the courses. Also, is dialogue enhanced through SMS or other social networks, and what is the impact on social presence? As learning management systems add social media capacities within courses and across curriculums, researchers will need to explore the impact on dialogue/cognitive presence and on social presence and locus of control.

Design Factor: Costs

Costs of designing and developing courses for distance education have been associated with high fixed costs of development and low delivery (variable) costs in order to fulfill the mission of making education opportunities broadly available to the general public. This has essentially been the rationale behind the high expenditures that distance education providers have put into the production of education television and radio broadcasts, as well as traditional print correspondence courses; however, each technology used in delivering a distance education course has its own unique cost structure.

For designers, it is important to understand the unique cost implications for each technology for both the student and the institution. As technology is added to a course, it not only drives up the costs of development, but potentially drives up the costs to the students for delivery. If one reviews the cost analysis that has been conducted at the Open University of the UK and other distance education institutions (Hülsmann, 1999), it highlights that the benchmark media other distance education courses are measured against is print. This is not surprising, as print has a relatively low cost for production per hour of study usage, and distribution of print-based courses tends to be low. Also, courses developed in this medium have a long shelf life before they are in need of revision.

Once one moves up the technology continuum, development costs are added. Changing the printed narrative of the course author(s) into audio, video, or a host of other interactive technologies increases production costs. The studies presented by Hülsmann (1999), which used a measure of "development cost per student learning hour by medium," indicate that other technology costs are measured in terms of a ratio to print. Development for educational television is roughly 180 times that of print, CD-ROM 40 times that of print, and audio (cassette tapes) is 34 times that of print. What is important to note is that all these technology forms are canned productions meant to have long shelf lives and to be accessible by a large student population. Further, in Shearer's (2004) report. *The Distance Education Balance Sheet*, a series of tables illustrate the impact on a course's bottom line when class size is altered, or yearly revisions are required, when compared to a traditional rolling enrollment course. This analysis highlights how the mission of the institution and how an institution implements distance education can impact a unit or organization's return on investment (ROI).

The concept of long shelf life and delivery to a large student audience is what allows for economies of scale. What is unclear since the adoption of Internet technologies and the World Wide Web is whether one can design a course that will have a long shelf life and be available to a large number of students. Most distance education institutions now incorporate Internet communication technologies into their courses in order to provide a greater sense of connectedness between the learners and the instructor and institution. With the addition of these tools it is hoped that a greater sense of community, timeliness of feedback, and a sense of social presence is provided; however, what is not clear is to what extent this limits the number of students who can enroll in a single section of a course. As designers add greater interactivity between the student and the instructor, this limits the number of students a faculty member can effectively interact with. For institutions that have moved to semester-based online distance education courses, this aspect of connectedness can be quite limiting in terms of the number of students who can take an individual section of a course; and obviously, the more individual course sections an institution needs, the greater the variable costs in terms of instructor salaries and course section set up costs. Even the addition of Internet communication technologies into open enrollment courses adds limitations in terms of the level of instructor–learner interaction that a single instructor or tutor can handle. While increased interactivity is positive in terms of transactional distance, it may have negative consequences in regard to costs and scale.

Flexibility of design must also be examined in terms of impact on course shelf life and ROI. Learning management tools like Angel,™ Blackboard,™ Desire2Learn,™ and others along with open education resources (OERs) allow faculty and authors a great degree of flexibility in terms of updating and revising courses. With this flexibility and ability to make minor revisions each time the course runs, we lose a degree of shelf life that will dramatically impact the economies of scale. If an institution is constantly revising courses, then additional development costs are incurred that reduce even the positive monetary impact of a large student audience. This logic, however, assumes that a traditional relationship between the design team and the faculty author continues to exist after the initial development of the course. If after the initial development, the task of maintaining the course and integrating changes falls to the individual faculty, then the ROI equation changes depending on faculty pay model. In a scenario like this, the added faculty time might not be captured as an ongoing cost, and the impact of the constant tweaks and revisions will be viewed as minimal to the unit's or organization's bottom line.

With the vast array of technology tools available to instructional designers in today's highly digital and connected world, it is more difficult to achieve a long shelf life for distance education courses. The constant need to remain current with technologies makes it hard to maintain a standard course over more than a year. Further, the integration of rich media is increasing the cost of production and truly requires a design team with specialists in media production. Thus, as production costs rise for online distance education courses, scale may actually be decreasing.

Instructional designers need to take into consideration the ROI goals of the institution or unit of distance education. If the model is one where the design team handles all initial development and revisions, and the institution is looking for a strong ROI, then they want to strive for content presentation that can be stable for three to five years to ensure a certain degree of shelf life. The degree of shelf life one achieves will depend on establishing a balance between the desire for continuous improvement of academic quality, the integration of new technologies, and the need for ROI. Therefore, a decision needs to be made between what content can exist in a fixed form for three to five years and what aspects of the course can to be updated each semester or year through other technology means such as: electronic postings to the LMS discussion boards, the use of asynchronous tools like Adobe Connect or Elluminate Live/Blackboard Collaborate,™ or integrated social media tools. The instructional designers must also weigh the impact of high levels of interaction between the students and the teacher on the ROI. The more interactive the course, the lower the number of students a faculty member can effectively communicate with. Other factors that may impact costs are associated with new government regulations for tracking and monitoring progress and for adherence to accessibility requirements for students with visual or other disabilities.

The analysis of costs associated with delivering courses at a distance is complex, as demonstrated by Keegan (1996), where he examined several formula-based approaches to the topic. There are several factors in the cost equation, and each must be viewed in a systemic manner, as there is no simple cause-effect relationship. For designers, it is important to be cognizant of how decisions about distance education course design impact both development and delivery costs—which affects both the students' and the unit's or organization's bottom line.

TECHNOLOGY'S IMPACT ON DISTANCE EDUCATION

Over the years technologies have been used in various ways to address the distance education design factors outlined above. The previous section has briefly touched upon print and other early technologies (see *Handbook of Distance Education* [2nd ed.], for a broader review of print, educational TV, and two-way interactive video) related to issues of learner autonomy, interaction, access, social presence, and costs. This section will briefly examine how the Internet, and the new Web 2.0 tools provide for or diminish these design factors.

The Internet and the World Wide Web

Today, when one thinks of the Internet, concepts of Web 1.0, Web 2.0, OERs, Social Media, Social Networks, Mobile Learning, and more are forefront in our thoughts. There is a vast array of tools and applications or apps that provide designers with new and innovative ways to address design challenges associated with helping the learner meet the learning objectives. However, due to the vastness it also leads to the tool of the day approach. Institutions and designers continue to be caught up in the abilities to present information online and build elaborate communication environments, sometimes with little thought about how the technologies will impact students and instructors. While there is no doubt that the Internet has improved our capability for more immediacy of feedback, assessment, collaboration, and social presence, it has, at the same time, limited access due to constantly evolving technology requirements, the constant need to learn new tools, and in developing countries just the need to have access to the Internet through the older landline infrastructure.

As discussed in the section on access, America has seen a leveling off of Internet access growth, and many parts of the world may ultimately access the Internet through cell phones, thus by-passing older landline technology. Further, the data highlights a rapid adoption of smartphones in the U.S. and around the world. How we design for smartphones or the newer tablets is still very much a question. Also, what is the role of OERs in our designs and the impact of such on cost reduction? The emergence of content repositories like Pearson's Equella open up opportunities to reduce the cost of development by making learning objects and lessons readily reusable, and organizations like the Khan Academy (2011) and other enterprises open the door to learning in new ways not previously available. But what are the business models for these enterprises that will assure continued existence? Also, with the vast array of tools and options available to designers and the vast amount of information available to students, it is possible that the new digital divide is not technology, culture, or other aspects of access, but the new construct of information literacy (Katz, 2007), where it is not about how to use technology, but how to make sense of all the information flowing at students. What is reliable, what is peer reviewed, and what should be ignored? This is the new cost to the Internet for students, institutions, and faculty. Thus, the new Internet tools and applications can have a tremendous negative impact on the accessibility by individuals to distance education, not in the traditional sense of access to the technologies, but in terms of how to cope and handle the vast array of information.

As designers look at integrating new social media tools into distance education courses, they must consider the new view of information literacy and how comfortable the student audience is with the technologies. How do designers help the students navigate the various technologies without the students feeling lost and confused about where to go in the course in order to do what is required. How much structure is needed versus learner control? Further, given all the ways to communicate, how do we assure that the learning involves critical reflection and deep learning in our courses. As discussed by Schreck (2011), distance education is not currently seeing deep levels of learning or critical thinking in online discussion forums, partly due to the curricula approach of a new topic each week, and partly due to the variety of places students need to go to post or respond to posts. As referenced earlier, Shearer's (2010) work on dialogue in distance education indicates that only about 50% of the posts could be considered dialogic, while other posts fell into the category of dialogue towards conversation related heavily to the idea of social presence.

It is very important in today's course designs that instructional designers look closely at aspects of dialogue, learner autonomy and learning control, and structure. What is the correct mix in our designs, and how will that mix impact decisions around the technologies integrated into courses? What is the learning curve for students every time we introduce a new tool, and what is the time commitment to learn the new technologies? Further, does it lead to greater learning outcomes than existing technologies? Institutions and designers must resist the urge to chase the tool of the day. The approach to the adoption of new technologies needs to be more measured through research and testing, and informed by the literature of the field.

The student characteristics are also critical to consider when we design online courses. Is the design for adult learners or is it for traditional age students? The latter may have more of an affinity to learning new technologies and more time to explore various tools. Also, many institutions have attempted to model their distance education offerings after the traditional campus-based semester system. While this fits well within existing policies and within the normal faculty contract timeframes, it may not work well for the independent learner. The question remains whether the traditional structure assists students in completing their course work or if it adds to increased drop out. The inability of some adult students to work in such a structured environment, which competes for their time with work, family, and other social commitments, needs to be considered. In many ways we may be establishing pace, sequence, interaction requirements, and technology requirements that eliminate the ideas of anytime and anyplace. Aspects of pacing, sequence, and meeting times of semester based distance education courses may resemble the traditional classroom model so closely that we have in fact negated, to a large degree, any feelings of independence and learner control. Thus, a key question to be answered by distance education providers is what audience are they attempting to address when they develop courses delivered online. Some may argue that institutions are designing distance education courses to fit within the policies and procedures of the traditional university structure and not to address the unique needs of learners at a distance. This is especially true of institutions moving to a hybrid course format in order to meet flexibility requirements of resident students and to capitalize on physical plant usage. This focus on hybrid courses may require that designers now develop courses to meet both the needs of true distance education students and resident instruction students who are looking for more flexibility in their course scheduling to allow time to work part time. This is a very difficult design task.

CONCLUSION

Since the second edition of the *Handbook,* there has been a dramatic change in the technology available to designers, especially around social media, the variety of ways one can allow for interaction and dialogue, and the integration of rich media. However, the underlying theories, models, and design factors, presented in this chapter, remain valid for the field of instructional design in distance education.

Instructional designers of distance education courses and programs must make a series of conscious choices each time they design and develop a course to be delivered to distant students. In some cases, the decisions are made for pedagogical reasons, at other times the decisions are made for access reasons, and yet at other times the design decisions are based on costs. Each time a designer decides to use a particular technology or combination of technologies, they need to be very clear on why the chosen technology is being used, and for what purpose. Knowing and understanding the strengths of each technology, whether the latest Internet tool or an old faithful such as print, is critical to defending and implementing our design decisions. It is critical that designers, faculty, and institutions take a systems view of how the technologies chosen impact all the components of a distance education delivery system.

In the development of distance education courses, there is no one best technology, rather it is usually a combination of technologies that produces the best course to assist the student in meeting the educational objectives. Over the years print has been the most dependable means for the delivery of content, but this may be changing with the rapid adoption of cell phones around the world. Also, delivery and production costs must be in the forefront of instructional design decisions, for if as designers, the design decisions are driven by the goal of reduced delivery costs to an international audience, then one may decide to provide the study guide or content by means of a downloadable PDF (portable document format) file, or a short video podcast. It is also important to understand when technology adoption adds value or simply passes a cost onto the students.

It is essential, therefore, that designers of instructional material for distance education courses understand the strengths and weaknesses of a vast array of technologies and how the older technologies have been deployed in the past to address the multitude of design factors, and how their decisions are supported by the literature and underlying theories and distance education models. How and why we integrate certain technologies into our designs is the key to the success of our distance education students, courses, and institutions.

REFERENCES

Bates, A. W. (1995). *Technology, open learning, and distance education.* London: Routledge.

Burbules, N. C. (1993). *Dialogue in teaching* (Vol. 10). New York: Teachers College Press.

Commonwealth of Learning. (2005). ODl for teacher and school development. Connections, 10(2), 8. Retrieved July 1, 2006, from http://www.col.org/colweb/site/pid/3040

Fox, S. (2005). *Digital divisions. Pew Internet and American Life Project.* Washington, DC: Pew.

Garrison, D. R., & Anderson, T. (2003). *E-Learning in the 21st century.* London: RoutledgeFalmer.

Garrison, D. R., Anderson, T., & Archer, W. (1999). Critical inquiry in a text-based environment: Computer conferencing in higher education *The Internet and Higher Education, 2*(2–3), 87–105.

Garrison, D. R., & Baynton, M. (1989). Beyond independence in distance education: The concept of control. In M. G. Moore & G. C. Clark (Eds.), *Readings in principles of distance education* (pp. 16–28). University Park, PA: American Center for the Study of Distance Education.

Gunawardena, C. N. (1995). Social presence theory and implications for interaction and collaborative learning in computer conferences. *International Journal of Educational Telecommunications, 1*(2/3), 147–168.

Gunawardena, C. N., & Zittle, F. J. (1997). Social presence as a predictor of satisfaction within a computer-mediated conferencing environment. *The American Journal of Distance Education, 11*(3), 8–26.

Hillman, D. C. A. (1999). A new method for analyzing patterns of interaction. *The American Journal of Distance Education, 13*(2), 37–47.

Hillman, D. C. A., Willis, D. J., & Gunawardena, C. N. (1994). Learner—interface interaction in distance education: An extension of contemporary models and strategies for practitioners. *The American Journal of Distance Education, 8*(2), 30–42.

Hirumi, A. (2002). A framework for analyzing, designing, and sequencing planned e-learning interactions. *The Quarterly Review of Distance Education, 3*(2), 141–160.

Holmberg, B. (1983). Guided didactic conversation in distance education. In D. Stewart, D. Keegan, & B. Holmberg (Eds.), *Distance education: International perspectives* (pp. 115–122). New York: St. Martin's Press.

Hülsmann, T. (1999). The costs of distance education. In K. Harry (Ed.), *Higher education through open and distance learning* (pp. 72–84). New York: Routledge.

IJsselsteijn, W. A., Ridder, H., Freeman, J., & Avons, S.E. (2007). *Presence: Concept, determinants and measurement* [Electronic Version], 1–10. Retrieved July 22, 2007, from http://www.ijsselsteijn.nl/papers/SPIE_HVEI_2000.pdf

International World Stats. (2011). *Usage and population stats.* Retrieved October 15, 2011, from, http://www.internetworldstats.com/stats.htm

KhanAcademy. (2011). Retrieved October 28, 2011, from http://www.khanacademy.org/

Katz, I. R. (2007). ETS research finds college students fall short in demonstrating ICT literacy: National Policy Council to create national standards [Electronic Version]. *College and Research Libraries News.* Retrieved October 24, 2011 from http://crln.acrl.org/content/68/1/35.full.pdf+html

Keegan, D. (1996). *Foundations of distance education* (3rd ed.). London: Routledge.

Librero, F., Ranga, A .I., & Lambert, D. (2007). Uses of the cell phone for education in the Phillippines and Mongolia. *Distance Education, 28*(2), 231–244.

Miyazoe, T., & Anderson, T. (2010). The interaction equivalency theorem. *Journal of Interactive Online Learning, 9*(2), 94–104.

Moore, M. G. (1980). Independent study. In R. D. Boyd, Aps, J. W., & Associates (Eds.), *Redefining the discipline of adult education* (Vol. 5, pp. 16–31). San Francisco: Jossey-Bass .

Moore, M. G. (1983). On a theory of independent study. In D. Stewart, D. Keegan, & B. Holmberg (Eds.), *Distance education: International perspectives* (pp. 69–94). New York: St. Martin's Press.

Moore, M. G. (1989). Three types of interaction. *The American Journal of Distance Education, 3*(2), 1–7.

Motlik, S. (2008). Technical evaluation report 63: Mobile learning in developing nations [Electronic Version]. *The International Review of Research in Open and Distance Learning, 9.* Retrieved October 14, 2011, from http://www.irrodl.org/index.php/irrodl/article/viewArticle/564/1039

Neff, B. D. (1998). Harmonizing global relations: A speech act theory analysis of PRForum. *Public Relations Review, 24*(3), 351–376.

Pew Research Center. (2011a). 35% of American Adults own a smartphone [Electronic Version]. *Pew Internet & American Life Project.* Retrieved October 15, 2011, from http://pewresearch.org/pubs/2054/smart phone-ownership-demographics-iphone-blackberry-android

Pew Research Center. (2011b). Search and email still the most popular online activities [Electronic Version]. *Pew Internet & American Life Project.* Retrieved October 14, 2011, from http://pewresearch.org/pubs/2079/-email-internet-search

Pew Research Center. (2011c). 65% of online adults use social networking sites [Electronic Version]. *Pew Internet & American Life Project.* Retrieved October 14, 2011, from http://pewresearch.org/pubs/2088/social-networking-sites-myspace-facebook-linkedin

Picciano, A. G. (2002). Beyond student perceptions: Issues of interaction, presence, and performance in an online course. *Journal of Asynchronous Learning Networks, 6*(1), 21–40.

Rourke, L., Anderson, T., Garrison, R. D., & Archer, W. (1999). Assessing social presence in asynchronous text-based computer. *Journal of Distance Education, 14*(2), 50–71.

Saba, F. (1989). Integrated telecommunications systems and instructional transaction. In M. G. Moore, & G. C. Clark (Eds.), *Readings in principles of distance education* (Vol. 1, pp. 29–36). University Park, PA: American Center for the Study of Distance Education.

Saba, F., & Shearer, R. L. (1994). Verifying key theroretical concepts in a dynamic model of distance education. *The American Journal of Distance Education, 8*(1), 36–59.

Schreck, R. (2011, March). *Continuing education, critical thinking, and virtual collaborative learning.* Paper presented at the University Professional Continuing Education Association, Toronto, Canada.

Searle, J. R. (1969). *Speech acts: An essay in the philosophy of language.* Cambridge, UK: Cambridge University Press.

Shearer, R. (2010). *Transactional distance and dialogue: An exploratory study to refine the theoretical construct of dialogue in online learning.* Stuttgart: Germany: VDM.

Shearer, R. L. (2003). *Interaction in distance education* (special report). San Diego, CA: Distance-Educator.com.

Shearer, R. L. (2004). *The distance education balance sheet: What are the measures of success for institutions and students?* (special report). San Diego, CA: Distance-Educator.com.

Short, J., Williams, E., & Christie, B. (1976). *The social psychology of telecommunications.* New York: Wiley.

Smith, A. (2010). *Broadband 2010: A big slowdown* [Electronic Version]. Pew Internet & American Life Project. Retrieved October 14, 2011, from http://pewresearch.org/pubs/1694/broadband-adoption-slows-dramatically-except-african-americans-little-interest-among-non-users

Swan, K. (2002). Immediacy, social presence, and asynchronous discussion. In J. B. J. C. Moore (Ed.), *Elements of quality online education* (Vol. 3, pp. 157–172). Needham, MA: Sloan Center for Online Education.

Tu, C. (2001). How Chinese perceive social presence: An examination of interaction in online learning environment. *Education Media International, 30*(1), 45–59.

Tu, C. (2002). The measurement of social presence in an online learning environment. *International Journal of E-Learning, 1*(2), 34–45.

UNESCO. (2007). *EFA global monitoring report 2008: Education for all by 2015: Will we make it?* [Electronic Version]. Retrieved October 15, 2011, from http://unesdoc.unesco.org/images/0015/001548/154820e.pdf

UNESCO. (2011). *Facts and figures: Sub-Saharan Africa's education progress and challenges.* Retrieved October 15, 2011, from http://www.unesco.org/new/en/education/themes/leading-the-international-agenda/education-for-all/single-iew/news/facts_and_figures_sub_saharan_africas_education_progress_and_challenges/

Wired Digital Inc. (2000). *On creating digital dividends.* Retrieved March 21, 2001, from http://www .wired.com/news/technology/

17

INSTRUCTIONAL DESIGN MODELS FOR OPTIMAL LEARNING

SOM NAIDU

PRINCIPLES AND PROCESSES OF INSTRUCTIONAL DESIGN

In conventional educational settings, the design of teaching and learning has always been the role and responsibility of the individual teacher in the classroom. But in distance education, teachers-in-charge, largely as subject matter experts, could no longer be responsible for the entire teaching and learning transaction. The development of printed and other types of study materials for self-study by distance learners required a team effort with significant input in the educational process from instructional designers and media producers. This brought into the educational process the need for specialized skills in instructional design and media production, and in supporting learning in noncontiguous educational environments.

The critical role of instructional design in distance education perhaps received greatest prominence from the development of the team approach to course design and development at the United Kingdom Open University. This team approach comprised the participation of a group of specialists in the design and development of courses for distance education. These specialists included subject matter experts, media producers, and instructional designers (see Kelly, 1994). They would bring to the course design and development process specialist skills and knowledge in the design and development of a range of study materials for distance education including print, audio and video materials, and television programs.

The focus of instructional design knowledge in this process was on a range of learning and teaching issues. These included analyzing and understanding learners and their learning context; developing goals and learning outcomes; analyzing, sequencing, and synthesizing subject matter content; activating learning and engaging learners with the subject matter; supporting learning with socialization and interaction among learners; selecting appropriate media; assessing learning outcomes and providing feedback; and evaluating the learning and teaching process.

Understanding Learners and Their Learning Context

In most educational settings, very little attention is paid to analyzing and understanding learners and their learning context before any learning and teaching occurs. A great deal about learner characteristics, their learning styles, and approaches to study, is quite often presumed. This is especially true in classroom-based educational settings. However, distance education with its policy of open access opens up opportunities for a wide range of learners from young and old, to those in full- or part-time employment, and those with families to support and with little or no pre-requisites (Moore, 1987). This means that the distance education course design and development process needs to pay particular attention to distance learners, their styles and approaches to studying, and their special learning contexts (see Kember & Harper, 1987; Richardson, 2000).

Developing Goals and Learning Outcomes

Generally, in most educational settings, the development of instructional goals and learning outcomes is considered a chore as neither teachers nor students give it much attention, and also because these goals and outcomes are not closely aligned with the learning and assessment activities. In distance education settings specifically, carefully designed instructional goals and learning outcomes can serve a critical role for learners who are studying independently and without a great deal of opportunity to interact with their peers and tutors (see Garrison & Baynton, 1987; Mager, 1984).

Analyzing, Sequencing, and Synthesizing content

In both distance education and conventional classroom-based educational settings, selecting, analyzing, sequencing, and synthesizing subject matter content is where much of the thinking about learning and teaching has generally begun. This process comprises selecting the relevant subject matter content, analyzing, and representing it in a suitable form (see Jonassen, Hannum, & Tessmer, 1989; Scott, Clayton, & Gibson, 1991), and then representing it to the learner to enable an efficient and effective learning process (see Reigeluth, 1983, see chapters 6 and 10; Van Patten, Chao, & Reigeluth, 1986). Failure to effectively carry out this critical design task makes the learning task very difficult for the distance learner and causes problems such as lack of motivation and attrition. For this reason, there has been growing interest in approaches to representing subject matter content that is more goal-directed, problem-oriented, and embedded in the context of the subject matter content (see also Barrows & Tamblyn, 1980; Brown, Collins, & Duguid, 1989; Schank, 1997; The Cognition and Technology Group at Vanderbilt, 1990, 1993).

Engaging Learners with the Subject Matter

Engaging learners with the subject matter content and their learning activities involves the selective use of learning and instructional strategies to activate and support learning (see Lockwood, 1998; Rigney, 1978). In the distance education context, these strategies include a range of self-assessment activities embedded within the study materials that serve to scaffold and assist learning (see Bernard, & Naidu, 1992; Bernard, Naidu, & Amundsen, 1991; Jonassen, 1988; Naidu, 1994; Naidu & Bernard, 1992).

Learners can be also kept engaged with the subject matter and their learning activities with a range of collaborative and cooperative learning techniques to support learning and socialization (see Koschmann, Kelson, Feltovich, & Barrows, 1996; Slavin, 1990, 1994). In distance education contexts, many of these cognitive supports can be made available through face-to-face meetings at local or regional study centers, and increasingly now, via computer-mediated communications technologies such as email, bulletin boards, and mailing lists, and a range of social networking tools (Bernard & Naidu, 1990; Naidu, 1989; Salmon, 2002, 2004).

Selecting Media for Learning and Teaching

A critical instructional design task is the selection of appropriate media or delivery system for the teaching and learning of a particular body of subject matter content or skill. A great deal of care and consideration needs to be given to selecting the media that will enable the achievement of the intended learning outcomes and at an affordable price. The most current and fashionable or the cheapest media might not necessarily offer the best match for the subject matter, the learners, the intended learning outcomes, and the learning context especially in distance education settings.

There has been a great deal of discussion on the instructional effects of media on learning. Thomas Edison, for instance, claimed that the use of the moving image for teaching and learning would make schools more attractive and motivating for students (see Heinich, Molenda, & Russell, 1993). Marshall McLuhan saw media as extensions of humans, which allowed them to influence other people who were not in face-to-face contact with them. This view led McLuhan to claim that the "medium is the message" (McLuhan, 1964). McLuhan was referring to the societal impacts of electronic media such as television, film, and telephone on the lives of people (Campbell, 2000).

Neither Edison's nor McLuhan's premonitions were realized as they had been projected. However, more recently, Clark (1983, 1994) argued that instructional media do not influence learning achievement. He suggested that media are like vehicles that deliver instruction and they cannot influence learning achievement any more than the truck that delivers our groceries can cause changes in our nutrition. While Clark's view on the role of media in learning achievement remains contentious, the main point of his argument is that it is the instructional method (i.e., the pedagogical approach) and not media, per se, that is mostly responsible for learning achievement. He argues that the selection of appropriate media for learning and teaching needs to be based on the intended learning outcomes, the nature of the subject matter, and the learning context (see Reiser & Gagné, 1983). In distance education settings, the learning context takes on a special significance in the choice of appropriate instructional media.

Assessing Learning Outcomes and Providing Feedback

The assessment of learning achievement is foremost in the minds of both the teachers and the students in any educational setting. The teachers are concerned about how best to ascertain if their students have acquired the desired level of knowledge and capability in the subject matter, and the extent to which they have accomplished the intended learning outcomes. Students, on the other hand, are concerned about how their learning achievement will be assessed, when, where, and against what criteria. They are also very eager to know what opportunities there are for receiving feedback and advice on their work. The flexibility and openness afforded by distance education contexts further complicates procedures and processes for all of these issues. Instructional designers and teachers have to be particularly vigilant about assessment of learning achievement in the most valid, reliable, equitable, and secure manner (see Grondlund, 1985). They need to also ensure that there is ample opportunity for students to receive appropriate amounts of feedback in a timely manner (see Bangert-Drowns, Kulik, Kulik, & Morgan, 1991; Kulhavy, 1977; Kulik & Kulik, 1988; Schimmel, 1983).

Evaluating the Efficacy of Learning and Teaching

A systematic approach to the instructional design and development process also comprises evaluation of the efficacy of the process as well as the impacts of the learning and teaching processes (see Dick & Carey, 1994; Gagné, Briggs, & Wager, 1992; Smith & Ragan, 1993). However, despite the importance of gathering data on the instructional design, development, and implementation process, evaluation of learning and teaching is often poorly carried out or completely neglected from most educational settings. To ensure a high quality of learning and teaching experience, it is critical that evaluation is considered as an integral component of the instructional design, development, and implementation process (see Flagg, 1990; Guba & Lincoln, 1989; Kirkpatrick, 1994). Moreover, it is important that evaluation is considered proactively and not something that is carried out at the end of the entire process (see Sims, Dobbs, & Hand, 2002). In addition, a range of approaches and data-gathering instruments ought to be used to obtain various types of data (see Patton, 1990; Shulman, 1988).

RECONSIDERING LEARNING DESIGNS FOR DISTANCE LEARNING

While there is growing evidence to suggest that delivery media (including print) offer tremendous opportunities for building rich, resourceful, and highly interactive learning environments (see Dede, 2000; Edelson & O'Neill, 1994; Lockwood, 1998; Pea, 1994; Schank, 1997), it has been also suggested that media alone can have little impact on the quality of teaching and learning (see Clark, 1983; Kozma, 1991). As such, careful attention must be paid foremost to the instructional method (i.e., the *pedagogy* of the learning and teaching transaction). This is especially critical in distance education settings where a greater degree of independence is required from learners due to their separation in time and place from their teachers or educational organization.

Paying attention to the instructional method or pedagogy means looking after the design architecture of the learning and teaching environment, which incorporates, inter alia, definition of the learning outcomes, what the learners will do, how learning will be supported with the available media and resources, what will comprise formative and summative assessment, and how feedback will be provided to the learners. In distance education contexts, these considerations take on an added degree of complexity due to the asynchronous nature of much of the learning and teaching transaction.

Careful integration of the instructional media and the instructional method (i.e., the pedagogy) is a core instructional design function. It requires careful reconsideration of our approaches to teaching and learning to ensure that we are making the most of the delivery technologies that are available to us (see Burgess & Robertson, 1999; French, Hale, Johnson, & Farr, 1999). This incorporates shifting the role of the classroom teacher from one of being a "sage on the stage" to that of a "guide on the side" who is responsible for carefully choreographing and stage-managing all learning and teaching activities. It comprises a more learning-centered focus in which the role of the teacher or tutor is critical and central, not as a presenter of subject matter content, but as a source of expertise and guidance.

Contemporary information and communications technologies, including the Internet, the Web, mobile technologies and applications, and social networks, which are able to place a great deal of resources within easy reach of teachers and students, have a significant role to play in supporting these foreshadowed changes in the nature of teaching and learning (see French et al., 1999). They are also critical in promoting learning and teaching environments that are resource- and activity-based, in which learners are allowed and expected to develop understanding by engaging in authentic learning tasks. These are called situated learning environments as they are grounded in the context and culture of the learning environment (see Brown et al., 1989).

Situated learning environments are based on constructivist learning theory (see Wilson, 1996). They are less heavily dependent on the acquisition of subject matter knowledge and more on "learning by doing" (see Schank, 1997; Schank & Cleary, 1995; The Cognition and Technology Group at Vanderbilt, 1991).

The concept of learning by doing is at the heart of pedagogical designs that have the potential to engage students in the learning process better and retain their interest and motivation in learning. These pedagogical designs are better suited for distance education settings as they focus more heavily on the learning activities and less so on the declarative subject matter content. They include designs such as scenario- and problem-based learning, case study-based learning, role play-based learning, and design-based learning (see also Naidu, 2002). Their common trait and strength is their learner-centered focus and the greater degree of attention to learner engagement in the learning and teaching process (Hmelo, 1998; Williams & Hmelo, 1998).

For a fuller discussion of a range of strategies for learning through problem solving, readers are encouraged to consult *The Journal of the Learning Sciences* [Special Issue]: *Learning Through Problem Solving* (Williams & Hmelo, 1998b).

SUPPORTING STUDENTS IN DISTANCE LEARNING

Student support in conventional distance education settings often comprised assistance that was provided to the learner beyond what is available in their study materials (see Tait & Mills, 2003). This kind of support normally comes by way of local center and tutorial support, and increasingly now online via contemporary information and communications technologies. A major disadvantage of this disposition towards student support is that it is a regressive approach because it approaches student support as an afterthought and as something that needs to be taken care of because of an endemic problem with the existing instructional system. The argument that is proffered in this chapter promotes a proactive approach to student support by emphasizing the need to conceptualize all learning and teaching support activities as part of the instructional design process (see also Naidu, 2004b).

Instructional designs such as scenario-based learning and problem-based learning are embedded with ample opportunities for feedback and intervention throughout the learning process (see Brown et al., 1989; Collins, Brown, & Holum, 1991). In so doing, they are much better able to scaffold and support students' learning activities, leading to better learning outcomes.

A learning scaffold is a transitional support strategy. It provides learners with supports that they are unable to afford on their own or without assistance (Pea, 2004). It comprises carefully targeted support for a range of learning activities such as learning of the subject matter content and also learning how to learn (see Azevedo & Hadwin, 2005b). Effective learning scaffolds are those that are accessible to the learner at the time, place, and pace they are most needed, and those that are appropriately matched to, and directed at, the task or problem at hand.

The provision of this kind of scaffolding is a very complex task. A good place to start integrating this kind of scaffolding is with the intended learning outcomes of the subject. The learning outcomes will help determine the kinds of learning activities that learners will be required to undertake as part of their learning and assessment activities. Once these are developed, it will become abundantly clear what kinds of tools and cognitive supports learners will need to accomplish these tasks. For instance, in a study of a school curriculum, if learners are required to survey teachers' perceptions of an aspect of the school curriculum, they will need tools to ascertain that. In this case, the tool for ascertaining teachers' perceptions serves as an essential scaffold. Will this tool need to be available in print form, or in electronic form, online or offline? Answers to these questions will determine the exact nature of this tool, and where, when, and how it will need to be provided to the learners (e.g., see Naidu, Menon, Gunawardena, Lekamge, & Karunanayaka, 2005).

There has been considerable work on developing and integrating learning scaffolds in computer-based learning materials for conventional educational settings (see Azevedo & Hadwin, 2005a). With the growth of online distance education across all sectors of education, many of these computer-based learning materials will soon enter the self-paced and self-instructional online distance education environment. With a different set of learner and learning needs in online distance education settings, several of these learning scaffolds are quite likely to be found not as effective because they had not been developed to cater for the needs of online distance learners. There will be a need to develop learning scaffolds that can address the unique needs of online distance learning. The obvious opportunities for these would be when incorporating information and communications technologies and collaborative learning with problem-based learning (Koschmann et al., 1996; Kirschner, Kreijns, Beers, & Strijbos, 2005). Other opportunities for scaffolding learning in online distance education settings would be in moderating computer conferencing and other forms of online discussions (see Salmon, 2002, 2004).

For a fuller discussion of a range of issues to do with scaffolding learning, readers are strongly encouraged to consult two very reputable journals in the field of learning and instructional sciences which have produced two special issues on the subject of scaffolding. These are *Instructional Science: An International Journal of Learning and Cognition* [Special Issue]: Scaffolding Self-regulated Learning and Metacognition: Implications for the Design of Computer-based Scaffolds (Azevedo & Hadwin, 2005b). The other is *The Journal of the Learning Sciences* [Special Issue]: Scaffolding (Davis & Miyake, 2004).

MODELS OF SITUATED LEARNING DESIGNS

The following is a selection of instructional designs that stand to optimize the distance learning experience. They are grounded in constructivist learning theory and principles of situated cognition, and furthermore, they promote an action-based approach to student-centered learning that is situated within meaningful contexts.

Scenario-based Learning

Scenario-based learning is a pedagogical design in which a real or contrived scenario forms the basis of all learning, teaching, and assessment activities (see Naidu et al., 2005). The best scenarios are those that are extracted from real-life settings as they are likely to contain the complexity that is needed to address the full range of skills and knowledge that needs to be covered. An effective learning scenario looks like a good story (Naidu, 2004a). It will have a context and characters. However, the important thing about a good learning scenario is that it will have a precipitating event and a goal for the learner to pursue in order to address the problem or issue in the precipitating event (see Schank, 1990, 1997).

A precipitating event is a trigger for a chain of events. A good example of a precipitating event is as follows. A patient is brought into a hospital where you are working. The patient needs immediate attention and care. Your goal in this contrived situation is to deal with this case and resolve it, hopefully with the best results. In order to do this, you will need to follow hospital procedures and consult with your colleagues. The aim of putting you through this activity is to enable you to acquire the knowledge and skills for managing such cases in real life (see Naidu, Oliver, & Koronios, 1999). It is designed to be inherently motivating and also able to afford you the opportunity to learn by doing. Such a learning scenario is organized around "performance" skills and the result is a student who can perform the specified task (Schank & Cleary, 1995). This contrived, but authentic, learning scenario offers students an opportunity to also learn by making mistakes in a safe environment, as mistakes offer real opportunities for learning when these are accompanied by timely and potent feedback.

Problem-based Learning

Problem-based learning (PBL) is a pedagogical design in which a contrived, but authentic, problem provides the anchor for all learning, teaching, and assessment activities (see Barrows, 1994; Barrows & Tamblyn, 1980; Schmidt, 1983). It is different from scenario-based learning in that in PBL a problem situation is used to contextualize and anchor all learning activities (see Naidu et al., 1999). In scenario-based learning, the anchor for all learning, teaching, and assessment activities need not be a problem situation. It could be an event, such as a visit to your school by a parent or an official. It could be a legislation, such as one that requires you to deal with some aspect of curriculum reform in a school where you are teaching (see Naidu et al., 2005).

Beyond this essential difference, PBL is very similar to scenario-based learning in the remainder of its operations. It also incorporates a precipitating event or trigger and a goal which learners are expected to pursue in order to address the problem at hand. Learners work in groups and also individually over a defined period of time to address the presenting problem (see Evensen & Hmelo, 2000). Many of these small-group and individual activities can take place either face-to-face in situ, or in distributed settings via computer-mediated communications technologies (see Dede, 1991, 1996, 2000; Naidu & Oliver, 1996).

Critical Incident-based Learning

Critical incident-based learning is a pedagogical design in which a *critical incident* provides the anchor for all learning, teaching, and assessment activities (see Naidu &

Oliver, 1999). It is similar to scenario-based learning and PBL, apart from the nature of the event or incident that is used to contextualize all learning and teaching activities.

A hallmark feature of critical incident-based learning is its use of reflection on, and in, action (see Schon, 1983, 1987). Unlike in problem- and scenario-based learning, in critical incident-based learning, learners are required to identify a critical incident from their life or workplace. A typical critical incident is a significant event that has caused someone to rethink or change their perceptions and/or behavior about something and in some way. Practitioners regularly encounter such situations in their workplace, which present them with learning opportunities (see Naidu & Oliver, 1999). However, many of these learning opportunities pass by unnoticed. The aim of this pedagogical design is to teach learners how to recognize these critical incidences as learning opportunities, and how to reflect on them critically while in action (see Naidu & Oliver, 1999; Wilson, 1996).

Design-based Learning

In design-based learning, the *design task* serves as the essential scaffold and anchor for all learning, teaching, and assessment activities (see Hmelo, Holton, & Kolodner, 2000). A design task comprises a number of cognitive tasks. These include information gathering, problem identification, constraint setting, idea generation, modeling, prototyping, and evaluating (Newstetter, 2000). The design task is widely used for skill development and knowledge acquisition in practice-based disciplines such as engineering and architecture.

Like the scenario, problem, or critical incident, the design task offers the learner an opportunity to learn by doing. In order to be able to afford that, a good design task is one that closely resembles real-life tasks in the field. Such a design task seeks to engage and immerse the learner in the complexity and culture of the targeted skill and subject matter content (see Naidu, Anderson, & Riddle, 2000). Depending on the subject matter and the skill that is being taught, design tasks might involve a range of critical learning activities including periods of collaborative group work and individualized self-study. The complexity of carefully articulated design activities makes them excellent vehicles for learning and teaching.

AFFORDANCES OF SITUATED LEARNING DESIGNS

The hallmarks of these situated learning designs are essentially twofold. Foremost, they promote the view that effective, efficient, and engaging learning needs to be *action-based*; and secondly, that learning and teaching also needs to be *situated in some meaningful context* (Naidu, 2010). It is hard to argue how effective, efficient, and engaging learning could be anything other than that.

Learning designs that are action-based require learners to be active partners in the learning and teaching process, as opposed to being passive recipients or consumers of the subject matter. Being an active partner in the learning and teaching process means being actively engaged in carrying out assigned learning activities individually or in groups, taking action, making decisions, solving problems, seeking feedback, reflecting upon the feedback, and improving one's practice, knowledge, and understanding, all as part of the designed learning experience (see Naidu & Bedgood, 2011a).

Learner actions such as these, however, need to be meaningfully contextualized in order for knowledge and understanding to take place, effectively and most efficiently. For this to happen, context is paramount and it needs to be meaningful as well. Learning and teaching is most effective and efficient when it is situated within a meaningful context. The most powerful contexts are those that will most closely reflect the kinds of situations that learners will encounter in their workplace (i.e., those that are authentic). When this is the case, learning and teaching closely resembles an apprenticeship for the learner for the real-world challenge and for the workplace. This kind of learning experience is, by design, integrated in the workplace, and as such it is meaningful, motivating, and relevant (Billett, 2011). Graduates from this kind of learning experience are ready for the workplace immediately upon graduation (Naidu & Bedgood, 2011b). It is hard to imagine why learning and teaching would be anything but like this.

ROLE OF DISTRIBUTED AND NETWORKED TECHNOLOGIES

The growth of the Internet and the World Wide Web, as well as our understanding of social networks (online and offline), and how they influence our lives generally and so pervasively is leading to an increasing interest in their affordances for learning and teaching (see Christakis & Fowler, 2011; Mason, & Rennie, 2008). There are some suggestions that social networks and how information is stored across networked technologies, and how it is accessed via the Internet by learners, alters the nature of learning (see Siemens, 2008). An alternative perspective on the topic suggests that while the distributed nature of information and the knowledge base can and does influence our approaches to learning, the fundamental nature of the cognitive processes associated with learning are not altered as a result (see Kop & Hill, 2008). This conversation seems to be in the same ballpark as the Clark and Kozma debates on the impacts of media on learning with which we are familiar (Clark, 1994; Kozma, 1991).

Whatever position we might have on this subject, it is clear that how information is stored and accessed via networked technologies is influencing, at least, our approaches to learning and teaching, if not our cognitive processes. This is especially so for the learners, but also for the teachers and tutors who are no longer the sole source of information in the contemporary educational environment. Nevertheless, it would be a conjecture to suggest that social networks and networked technologies by themselves influence how we process that information and develop understanding.

Learning is a cognitive process and an outcome of carefully designed learning experiences. These learning experiences comprise independent as well as collaborative learning activities, and they can be self-directed or directed by others. This chapter presents several models of such learning experience designs that have the potential to achieve optimal learning outcomes for students. They are all grounded in the belief that learning is most effective when it is based on learning by doing and problem solving.

Networks and network technologies offer unique opportunities for the execution of these learning experience designs in various ways. These include supporting communication and collaboration between individuals and among groups, in situ and across time and space (see Bower, 2011). However, the possibility of communicating and collaborating by itself is not going to be good enough. Communication and collaboration have to have a clear purpose and explicit outcomes and they will need to be carefully designed and integrated into the learning and teaching transaction (see Baran & Correia, 2009; Wade, Cameron, Morgan, & Williams, 2011).

CHALLENGES AND DIRECTIONS FOR FURTHER WORK

Despite the promises and potential of distance education, contemporary information and communications technologies, and our knowledge of situated cognitive approaches to meaningful learning, distance education practices in many parts have continued to remain a very content-centric and teacher-directed approach to learning and teaching (see Baggaley, 2007; Willems, 2005). Evidence of this is all around us in the form of distance education study materials that do little more than summarize or reproduce content from published text books, technologies that are often inaccessible, and in the case of online distance education, course websites which contain little more than the course schedule, an outline of the subject matter content, lecturer's slides and notes, and sample examination papers (see Baggaley, 2007; Boshier et al., 1997).

Instead of making the most of the potential and unique attributes of distance education and contemporary information and communications technologies, such practices have promoted a model of teaching that is a very poor imitation of conventional classroom practices. Therefore, despite our awareness of the important role of instructional design in distance education, a lot of it continues to be ineffective and delivery centered. It is not often that we pause to think about what we are using to teach, why we are teaching the way we teach, and if our instructional approaches are based on sound educational principles of learning and cognition.

This kind of instructional practice has led to a great deal of frustration for both the learners and the teachers, many of whom have grown increasingly skeptical about the educational benefits of the newer delivery technologies (see Kirkwood, 2000; Rumble, 2000; Schellens & Valcke, 2000). The source of much of this frustration has to do with the failure of many instructional designers to come up with learning designs that best match the learning and teaching context, the subject matter, and the needs of their learners within the constraints of their learning environments. There is no doubt that there are plenty of instances of excellent learning and teaching practices all around us, but clearly there are not enough of them (Baggaley, 2007).

The goal of this chapter is to point out the relevant literature and knowledge that is necessary for the design and development of effective distance learning experiences, or for that matter, any other kind of an educational experience. The learning designs that are described and promoted in this chapter are based on proven principles of human learning including learning by doing, learning by experimentation and failure in a safe learning and teaching environment, and on the role of context and learning scaffolds in learning and teaching. They are good for distance learning as well as other modes of learning. The challenge remains for instructional designers to assert that these are the fundamental principles that must guide learning and teaching practices, and that these principles stand to make most of the opportunities afforded by distance education, as well as cope with its severest challenges.

ACKNOWLEDGMENT

This chapter is a revised version of Naidu, S. (2007). Instructional designs for optimal learning. In M. G. Moore (Ed.), *Handbook of Distance Education, 2nd ed.* (pp. 247–258), Mahwah, NJ: Erlbaum.

The instructional design models that are described in this chapter have been developed in collaboration with several colleagues and the author of this chapter is grateful for their contribution to the development and implementation of these models. These include: *Scenario-based learning* (Som Naidu, Mohan Menon, Chandra Gunawardena, Dayalata Lekamge, and Shironica Karunanayaka) with funding support from Commonwealth of Learning and the Open University of Sri Lanka; *Problem-based learning; Critical incident-based learning* (Andy Koronios and Mary Oliver) with funding support from the Committee for University Teaching and Staff Development, Australia; and *Design-based learning* (Jaynie Anderson and Mathew Riddle) with funding support from the University of Melbourne.

Parts of this revised version have drawn on work that has also been reported in Naidu (2002, 2004a, b). See full reference below.

REFERENCES

Azevedo, A., & Hadwin, A. (Guest Eds.). (2005a). Scaffolding self-regulated learning and metacognition: Implications for the design of computer-based scaffolds [Special Issue]. *Instructional Science: An International Journal of Learning and Cognition, 33*(5–6).

Azevedo, R., & Hadwin, A. F. (2005b). Scaffolding self-regulated learning and metacognition – Implications for the design of computer-based scaffolds, *Instructional Science, 33*(5–6), 367–379.

Baggaley, J. P. (2007). Distance education technologies: An Asian perspective. *Distance Education, 28*(2), 125–131. doi:10.1080/01587910701439191

Bangert-Drowns, R. L., Kulik, C.-L. C., Kulik, J. A., & Morgan, M. T. (1991). The instructional effects of feedback in test-like events. *Review of Educational Research, 61*, 213–238.

Baran, E., & Correia, A.-P. (2009). Student-led facilitation strategies in online discussions. *Distance Education, 30*(3), 339–363. doi:10.1080/01587910903236510

Barrows, H. S. (1994). *Problem-based learning applied to medical education.* Springfield: Southern Illinois University.

Barrows, H. S., & Tamblyn, R. (1980). *Problem-based learning: An approach to medical education.* New York, NY: Springer.

Bernard, R. M., & Naidu, S. (1990). Enhancing interpersonal communication in distance education: Can 'Voice-Mail' help? *Educational and Training Technology International, 27*(3), 293–300.

Bernard, R. M., Naidu, S., & Amundsen, C. L. (1991). Choosing instructional variables to enhance learning in distance education. *Media and Technology for Human Resource Development: Journal of Educational Technology, 4*(1), 3–13.

Bernard, R.M., & Naidu, S. (1992). Post-questioning, concept mapping and feedback: A distance education field experiment. *British Journal of Educational Technology, 23*(1), 48–60.

Billett, S. (2011). Integrating experiences in workplace and university settings: A conceptual perspective. In S. Billett & A. Henderson (Eds.), *Promoting professional learning* (pp. 21–40). Dordrecht, The Nertherlands: Springer.

Boshier, R., Mohapi, M., Moulton, G., Qayyaum, A., Sadownik, L, & Wilson, M. (1997). Best and worst dressed web courses: Strutting into the 21st century in comfort and style. *Distance Education, 18*(2), 327–349. doi:10.1080/0158791970180209

Bower, M. (2011). Synchronous collaboration competencies in web-conferencing environments — their impact on the learning process. *Distance Education, 32*(1), 63–83. doi: 10.1080/01587919.2011.565502

Brown, J. S., Collins, A., & Duguid, P. (1989). Situated cognition and the culture of learning. *Educational Researcher, 18*(1), 32–42.

Burgess. B., & Robertson, P. (1999). *Collaboration: How to find, design and implement collaborative internet projects,* Saratoga, CA: BonusPoint.

Campbell, R. J. (2000, September–October). Descending into the maelstrom of the 21st century with Marshall McLuhan. *Educational Technology, 40*(5), 18–27.

Christakis, N. A., & Fowler, J. F. (2011). *Connected: The amazing power of social networks and how they shape our lives.* London: HarperPress.

Cognition and Technology Group at Vanderbilt. (1990). Anchored instruction and its relationship to situated cognition. *Educational Researcher, 19*(6), 2–10.

Cognition and Technology Group at Vanderbilt. (1991). Technology and the design of generative learning environments. *Educational Technology, 31*(5), 34–40.

Cognition and Technology Group at Vanderbuilt. (1993). Designing learning environments that support thinking. In T. M. Duffy, J. Lowyck, & D. H. Jonassen (Eds.), *Designing environments for constructivist learning* (pp. 9–36). New York, NY: Springer-Verkag.

Clark, R. E. (1983). Reconsidering research on learning from media. *Review of Educational Research, 53*(4), 445–460.

Clark, R. E. (1994). Media will never influence learning. *Educational Technology Research and Development, 53*(2), 21–30.

Collins, A., Brown, J. S., & Holum, A. (1991). Cognitive apprenticeship: Making thinking visible. *American Educator, 15*(3), 6–11, 38–46.

Davis, E., & Miyake, N. (Guest Eds.). (2004). Scaffolding [Special Issue]. *The Journal of the Learning Sciences, 13*(3).

Dede, C. (1991). The evolution of constructivist learning environments: Immersion in distributed, virtual worlds. In B. G. Wilson (Ed.), *Constructivist learning environments: Case studies in instructional design*, (pp. 165–175). Englewood Cliffs: NJ: Educational Technology Publications.

Dede, C. (1996). Emerging technologies and distributed learning. *American Journal of Distance Education, 10*(2), 4–36.

Dede, C. (2000). Emerging technologies and distributed learning in higher education. In D. Hanna (Ed.), *Higher education in an era of digital competition: Choices and challenges* (pp. 71–92). New York, NY: Atwood.

Dick, W., & Carey, L. (1994). *The systematic design of instruction* (3rd ed.). London, England: Scott, Foresman and Company.

Edelson, D. C., & O'Neill, D. K. (1994). The CoVis collaboratory notebook: Supporting collaborative scientific inquiry. In *Recreating the revolution* (pp. 146–152). Proceedings of the National Educational Computing Conference. Eugene, OR: International Society of Technology in Education.

Evensen, D. H., & Hmelo, C. E. (Eds.). (2000). *Problem-based learning: A research perspective on learning interactions*. Mahwah, NJ: Erlbaum.

Flagg, B. N. (1990). *Formative evaluation for educational technologies*. Hillsdale, NJ: Erlbaum.

French, D., Hale, C., Johnson, C., & Farr, G. (1999). *Internet based learning: An introduction and framework for higher education and business*. London, England: Kogan Page.

Gagné, R. M., Briggs, L. J., & Wager, W. W. (1992). *Principles of instructional design* (4th ed.). New York, NY: Harcourt Brace Jovanovich.

Garrison, D. R., & Baynton, M. (1987). Beyond independence in distance education. *The American Journal of Distance Education, 1*(3), 3–15.

Grondlund, N. E. (1985). *Measurement and evaluation in teaching* (5th ed.). New York, NY: Macmillan.

Guba, E. G., & Lincoln, Y. S. (1989). *Fourth generation evaluation*. Newbury Park, CA: Sage.

Heinich, R., Molenda, M., & Russell, J. D. (1993). *Instructional media and the new technologies of instruction*. New York, NY: Macmillan.

Hmelo, C. E. (1998). Problem-based learning: Effects on early acquisition of cognitive skill in medicine. *The Journal of the Learning Sciences, 7*(2), 173–208.

Hmelo, C. E., Holton, D. L., & Kolodner, J. L. (2000). Designing to learn about complex tasks. *The Journal of the Learning Sciences, 9*(3), 243–246.

Jonassen, D. H. (1988). Integrating learning strategies into courseware to facilitate deeper processing. In D. H. Jonassen (Ed.), *Instructional designs for microcomputer courseware* (pp 151–181). Hillsdale, NJ: Erlbaum.

Jonassen, D. H., Hannum, W. H., & Tessmer, M. (1989). *Handbook of task analysis procedures*. New York, NY: Praeger.

Kelly, M. (1994). Course creation issues in distance education. In R. Garrison & D. Shale (Eds.), *Education at a distance: From issues to practice* (pp. 93–94). Malabar, FL: Kreiger.

Kember, D., & Harper, G. (1987). Implications for instruction arising from the relationship between approaches to studying and academic outcomes. *Instructional Science, 16*, 35–46

Kirkpatrick, D. L. (1994). *Evaluating training programs: The four levels*. San Francisco, CA: Berrett-Koehler.

Kirkwood, A. (2000). Learning at home with information and communications technologies. *Distance Education, 21*(2), 248–259. doi:10.1080/0158791000210204

Kirschner, P. A., Kreijns, K., Beers, P. J., & Strijbos, J.-W. (2005). Designing electronic tools for collaborative learning. *Educational Technology, 45*(5), 48–52.

Kop, R., & Hill, A. (2008). Connectivism: Learning theory of the future or vestige of the past? *International Review of Research in Open and Distance Learning, 9*(3), 1–13.

Koschmann, T., Kelson, A. C., Feltovich, P. J., & Barrows, H. S. (1996). Computer-supported problem-based learning: A principled approach to the use of computers in collaborative learning. In T. Koschmann (Ed.), *CSCL: Theory & practice in an emerging paradigm* (pp. 83–124). Mahwah, NJ: Erlbaum.

Kozma, R. B. (1991). Learning with media. *Review of Educational Research, 61*(2), 179–211.

Kulhavy, R. W. (1977). Feedback in written instruction. *Review of Educational Research, 47,* 211–232.

Kulik, J. A., & Kulik, C.-L. C. (1988). Timing of feedback and verbal learning. *Review of Educational Research, 58,* 79–97.

Lockwood, F. (1998). *The design and production of self instructional materials.* London, England: Kogan Page.

Mager, R. F. (1984). *Preparing instructional objectives* (2nd ed.). Belmont, CA: David S. Lake.

Mason, R., & Rennie, F. (2008). *Elearning and social networking handbook: Resources in higher education.* New York, NY: Routledge.

McLuhan, M. (1964). *Understanding media: The extensions of man.* New York, NY: McGraw-Hill.

Moore, M. G. (1987). Learners and learning at a distance: Computer conferencing in distance education. *International Council of Distance Education Bulletin, 14,* 59–65.

Naidu, S. (1989). Computer conferencing in distance education. *International Council of Distance Education Bulletin, 20,* 39–46.

Naidu, S. (1994). Applying learning and instructional strategies in open and distance learning. *Distance Education, 15*(1), 23–41. doi: 10.1080/0158791940150104

Naidu, S. (2002). *Designing and evaluating instruction for e-learning.* In P. L. Rodgers (Ed.), *Designing instruction for technology-enhanced learning* (pp. 134–159). Hershey, PA: Idea Group Publishing.

Naidu, S. (2004a). Learning design as an indicator of quality in teacher education. In K. Rama & M. Menon (Eds.), *Innovations in teacher education — International practices for quality assurance* (pp. 65–76). Bangalore: NAAC.

Naidu, S. (2004b). Supporting learning with creative learning and instructional designs. In J. E. Brindley, C. Walti, & O. Zawacki-Richter (Eds.), ASF Series: Vol. 9. *Learner support in open, distance and online learning environments* (pp. 109–111). Oldenburg, Germany: Carl von Ossietzky University of Oldenburg.

Naidu, S. (2010). Using scenario-based learning to promote situated learning and develop professional knowledge. In E. P. Errington (Ed.), *Preparing graduates for the professions using scenario-based learning* (pp. 39-49). Brisbane, Australia: Post Pressed.

Naidu, S., & Bedgood, D. (2011a). Action-based learning. In N. M. Seel (Ed.), *Encyclopedia of the sciences of learning.* New York, NY: Springer Science and Business Media.

Naidu, S., & Bedgood, D. (2011b). Learning in the social context. In N. M. Seel (Ed.), *Encyclopedia of the sciences of learning.* New York, NY: Springer Science and Business Media.

Naidu, S., & Bernard, R. M. (1992). Enhancing academic achievement in distance education with concept mapping and inserted questions. *Distance Education, 13*(1), 218–233. doi:10.1080/0158791920130205

Naidu, S., & Oliver, M. (1996). Computer supported collaborative problem-based learning (CSC-PBL): An instructional design architecture for virtual learning in nursing education. *Journal of Distance Education, XI*(2), 1–22.

Naidu, S., & Oliver, M. (1999). Critical incident-based computer supported collaborative learning. *Instructional Science: An International Journal of Learning and Cognition, 27*(5), 329–354.

Naidu, S., Anderson, J., & Riddle, M. (2000). The virtual print exhibition: A case of learning by designing. In R. Sims, M. O'Reilly, & S. Sawkins (Eds.), *Learning to choose: Choosing to learn,* Proceedings of the 17th Annual ASCILITE Conference (pp. 109–114). Lismore, Australia: Southern Cross University Press.

Naidu, S., Menon, M., Gunawardena, C., Lekamge, D., & Karunanayaka, S., (2005, November). *Quality teaching and learning in the master of arts in teacher education program at the Open University of Sri Lanka.* Paper presented at the biennial conference of the Open and Distance Learning Association of Australia, Adelaide, South Australia.

Naidu, S., Oliver, M., & Koronios, A. (1999). Approaching clinical decision-making in nursing practice with interactive multimedia and case-based reasoning. *Interactive Multimedia Electronic Journal of Computer Enhanced Learning, 1*(2). Retrieved from http://imej.wfu.edu/

Newsetter, W. C. (2000). Guest editor's introduction. *The Journal of the Learning Sciences, 9*(3), 247–298.

Patton, M. Q. (1990). *Qualitative evaluation and research methods* (2nd ed.). Newbury Park, CA: Sage.

Pea, R. D. (1994). Seeing what we build together: Distributed multimedia learning environments for transformative communications. *The Journal of the Learning Sciences, 3*(3), 285–299.

Pea, R. D. (2004). The social and technological dimensions of scaffolding and related theoretical concepts for learning, education, and human activity [Special Issue on Scaffolding]. *The Journal of the Learning Sciences, 13*(3), 423–451.

Reigeluth, C. M. (Ed.). (1983). *Instructional design theories and models: An overview of their current status.* Hillsdale, NJ: Erlbaum.

Reiser, R. A., & Gagné, R. M. (1983). *Selecting media for instruction.* Englewood Cliffs, NJ: Educational Technology Publications.

Richardson, J. T. E. (2000). *Researching student learning: Approaches to studying in campus-based and distance education*. Philadelphia, PA & Buckingham, UK: Society for Research into Higher Education & Open University Press.

Rigney, J. W. (1978). Learning strategies: A theoretical perspective. In H. F. O'Neil, Jr. (Ed.), *Learning strategies* (pp. 165–205). New York, NY: Academic Press.

Rumble, G. (2000). Student support in distance education in the 21st century: Learning from service management. *Distance Education, 21*(2), 216–235. doi:10.1080/0158791000210202

Salmon, G. (2002). *E-tivities: The key to active online learning*. London, England: Kogan Page.

Salmon, G. (2004). *E-moderating: The key to teaching and learning on-line*. London, England: Kogan Page.

Schank, R. C. (1990). *Tell me a story*. Evanston, IL: Northwestern University Press.

Schank, R. C. (1997). *Virtual learning: A revolutionary approach to building a highly skilled workforce*. New York, NY: McGraw-Hill.

Schank, R. C., & Cleary, C. (1995). *Engines for education*. Hillsdale, NJ: Erlbaum.

Schellens, T., & Valcke, M. (2000). Re-engineering conventional university education: Implications for students' learning styles. *Distance Education, 21*(2), 361–384. doi:10.1080/0158791000210210

Schimmel, B. J. (1983, April). *A meta-analysis of feedback to learners in computerized and programmed instruction*. Paper presented at the annual meeting of the American Educational Research Association, Montréal. Retrieved from ERIC Document Reproduction Service. (ED233 708).

Schmidt, H. G. (1983). Foundations of problem-based learning: Some explanatory notes. *Medical Education, 27*, 11–16.

Schon, D. A. (1983). *The reflective practitioner*. New York, NY: Basic Books.

Schon, D. A. (1987). *Educating the reflective practitioner*. San Francisco, CA: Jossey-Bass.

Scott, A. C., Clayton, J. E., & Gibson, E. L. (1991). *A practical guide to knowledge acquisition*. New York, NY: Addison-Wesley.

Shulman, L. S. (1988). Disciplines of inquiry in education: An overview. In R. M. Jaeger (Ed.), *Complementary methods for research in education* (pp. 3–17). Washington, DC: AERA.

Siemens, G. (2008). *Learning and knowing in networks: Changing roles for educators and designers*. Paper presented to the University of Georgia IT Forum. Retrieved from http://it.coe.uga.edu/itforum/Paper105/Siemens.pdf

Sims, R., Dobbs, G., & Hand, T. (2002). Enhancing quality in online learning: Scaffolding planning and design through proactive evaluation. *Distance Education, 23*(2), 135–148. doi:10.1080/0158791022000009169

Slavin, R. E. (1990). *Cooperative learning: Theory, research and practice*. Englewood Cliffs, NJ: Prentice-Hall.

Slavin, R. E. (1994). Student teams-achievement divisions. In S. Sharan (Ed.), *Handbook of cooperative learning* (pp. 3–19). Westport, CT: Greenwood Press.

Smith, P. L., & Ragan, T. J. (1993). *Instructional design*. New York, NY: Merrill McMillan.

Tait, A., & Mills, R. (2003). *Rethinking learner support in distance education. Change and continuity in an international context*. London, England: RoutledgeFalmer.

Van Patten, J., Chao, C., & Reigeluth. C. M. (1986). A review of strategies for sequencing and synthesizing instruction, *Review of Educational Research, 56*(4), 437–71.

Wade, C. E., Cameron, B. A., Morgan, K., & Williams, K. C. (2011). Are interpersonal relationships necessary for developing trust in online group projects? *Distance Education, 32*(3), 383-396. doi: 10.1080/01587919.2011.610288

Willems, J. (2005). Flexible learning: Implications of "when-ever", "where-ever" and "what-ever". *Distance Education, 26*(3), 429–435. doi:10.1080/01587910500291579

Williams, S. M., & Hmelo, C. E. (1998a). Guest editors' introduction. *The Journal of the Learning Sciences, 7*(3–4), 265–270. doi: 10.1080/10508406.1998.9672055

Williams, S. M., & Hmelo, C. E. (Guest Eds.). (1998b). Learning through problem solving [Special Issue]. *The Journal of the Learning Sciences, 7*(3–4).

Wilson, B. G. (Ed.). (1996). *Constructivist learning environments: Case studies in instructional design*. Englewood Cliffs, NJ: Educational Technology Publications.

18

ACTIVITY DESIGN AND INSTRUCTION IN ONLINE LEARNING

VANESSA P. DENNEN

The first edition of this handbook included a discussion of what was perceived as a pedagogical void in the world of online instruction (Bonk & Dennen, 2003). At that time, the move toward implementing online instruction was far outpacing research. The first generation of online classes tended to center around email. Basic asynchronous discussion board activities or synchronous interactions via text chat tools were included when they were feasible considering technological, administrative, and pedagogical concerns. Content typically was provided via static Web pages.

A common approach for many first wave online instructors was to convert a face-to-face course to an online format, often striving to create an equal or at least equivalent experience. Of course, the lack of visual cues and classroom-based spontaneity yielded challenges for many instructors attempting course conversion and the fidelity of the resulting experience varied. Many of these instructors found that in order to make the design process work well and to produce a motivating and pedagogically sound online course they had to rethink activities and assessments and sometimes even design entirely new ones.

In many ways the pedagogical void noted in 2003 has been filled. New online instructors do not need to look far to find myriad examples of learning activities with solid pedagogical grounding; the literature is full of diverse reports of both teaching cases and empirical studies, representing a broad set of online teaching and learning contexts. However, the void has been filled with a potpourri of theories and studies rather than a single systematic thread of scholarship. In other words, rather than simply refining existing strategies so that they converge on a point, we have seen an expansion of philosophies, examples, and options related to online pedagogy. The challenge, then, has become selection: How do instructors know when to choose a particular approach, activity, or tool?

DIMENSIONS OF THE LEARNING CONTEXT

There are various dimensions of the online learning context that will impact the appropriateness of a particular pedagogical approach. Before designing a new online course, instructors need to ask themselves:

- What are the desired learning outcomes?
- What types of interaction do I hope to foster?
- What are the desired outcomes of those interactions?
- How will both chronological and elapsed time be managed in the course?
- What level of synchronicity will be present?
- What tools might I use, taking into consideration access, learning curve, and user comfort?

Together, these questions can help an instructor identify the variables that will impact pedagogical choices. Designing a course or learning activity without considering these contextual factors and the systemic nature of a course can result in unsatisfactory learning experiences and outcomes. Both interaction and issues of temporality (time, synchronicity) in online courses are discussed in detail below, followed by a collection of ideas for learning activities organized by outcomes. Tools are discussed throughout.

INTERACTION

The interaction possibilities of an online environment have not inherently changed since the inception of the first online classes. However, they have become increasingly sophisticated and complex as technological developments have occurred, Internet access has greatly expanded, and pedagogical creativity and innovation has had time to flourish.

The types of interactions that might take place in an online class context include learner-teacher, learner-learner, and learner-content (Moore, 1989). Others have added teacher-teacher, content-content, and teacher-content to the interaction possibilities (Anderson & Garrison, 1998), but these interaction types are more reflective of professional development and course design issues than within-course interaction. Each is interesting and worthy of discussion in its own way, but here I am choosing to focus solely on the three interaction types that involve learners, since those are the ones instructors should be considering as part of their pedagogical frameworks.

Learner-content interaction, when it exists alone, represents a fairly autonomous type of learning (Moore, 1989). Content may be a static, dynamic, or adaptive interaction partner (see Table 18.1). The use of static content is well established and considered a standard for most classes, but dynamic content is also quite useful when students are studying a living phenomenon. Adaptive content provides a new dimension to leaner-content interactions, allowing feedback that was not previously possible. For large-scale instruction, instructional designers may build unique learning systems that utilize these technologies. For most instructors, however, such systems are beyond the scope of what is reasonable and feasible for them to produce independently for their classes. However, they might assign existing dynamic and adaptive content-based systems to support learner-content interactions in their classes.

Table 18.1 Types of Content with which Learners may Interact

Nature of Content	Description	Example
Static	Content that is unchanged barring a major update either due to medium or nature of publication.	Books, CD-ROMs, journal articles.
Dynamic	Content that is hosted online and potentially updated at any given moment. Requires Internet delivery.	Blogs, wikis, periodicals
Adaptive	A specific type of dynamic content that adjusts specifically to the learner's inputs to provide content that is appropriate to the individual.	Simulations, intelligent tutoring systems

Learner-teacher and learner-learner interactions are key components of constructivist learning principles and related activities. For example, the Community of Inquiry framework (Garrison, Anderson, & Archer, 2010) is built entirely around the idea that learners will interact both with their teacher as well as with each other. Hrastinski (2009) describes the relationship between these interactions and learning in terms of participation, which he defines as "a complex process that includes, for example, doing, talking, thinking, feeling, belonging" (p. 81). Some of these actions are visible, and some are not, but all are components of being a part of learning interactions with a larger group of people.

Learner-Outsider

One new classification of interaction that has arisen is learner-outsider. Learner-outsider interactions occur when the student communicates with people not otherwise affiliated with the class about the class topic. In order for it to count as a learning interaction, some act in which knowledge sharing occurs must take place. The learner may even serve as a knowledge broker in one or both directions. This concept is not inherently new, since students have always shared experiences from outside class with their classes and vice versa, but the combination of online classes and Internet-based communication have made these learning interactions more prevalent in learning and visible to the class setting.

In particular the Web 2.0 movement, discussed in more detail below, has fostered the ability for students to connect and communicate with people outside the class without any prior social network connections. Further, social networking tools allow class members to efficiently mine their existing online social networks for people who may share a previously unknown interest or expertise on the class topic.

A Different View on Interaction

Jefferies, Carsten-Stahl, and McRobb (2007) present a different perspective on interaction in online classes. Rather than looking at the interaction dyads, they suggest that we might consider online learning activities—and really any learning activity—to have one of three interactional foci or orientations: the self, the instructor, or peers. Building off the earlier work of Koschmann (1996) and Leidner and Jarvenpaa (1995), Jefferies et al. discuss these orientations in terms of who has control of the learning environment and map the orientations to both pedagogical theory and typical types of online learning activities.

Both interaction dyads and interactional orientations have much in common, but the concept of orientation brings to the forefront another issue: perspective and intersubjectivity. The teacher and learner's perspective about the orientation of the same activity might differ. For example, a teacher may create a discussion forum with the intent of having students engage in collaborative meaning making only to find that the students entered the discussion with the perspective that they were supposed to be demonstrating their knowledge to the instructor. This mismatch in activity orientation—essentially, a sign that the participants lack intersubjectivity (Vygotsky, 1981; Wertsch, 1985)—means that the outcomes may suffer. For knowledge construction activities to succeed in the online classroom, intersubjectivity (shared understanding of the task and related knowledge) is essential (Bober & Dennen, 2001; Dennen & Wieland, 2007), and shared meanings can only be the outcome of shared activities (O'Donnell & Tharp, 2011).

TEMPORALITY: TIME AND SYNCHRONICITY

Whereas face-to-face classes tend to be organized by class meeting, asynchronous online classes tend to be organized by other units of time, such as the week. Some learners may choose to complete their weekly tasks early in the week, whereas others may wait until the last minute. These timing differences mean that some learners' paths may never have a meaningful intersection during the class. Indeed, the early contributors may not be very aware of the later ones, and the later ones may not perceive the early ones as part of the currently open conversation at the time they participate. And there are further consequences for some contributors based on their timing because posting date has been found to impact the degree of response received on a discussion board (Jeong & Frazier, 2008) and discussion forums take on a particular timing-related momentum that impacts the flow and ultimately the conversation-like qualities and outcomes (Dringus & Ellis, 2010).

Even when learners are not working at opposite ends of a week, time can be a distancing factor. Learners from different time zones may perceive greater challenges to working together, particularly if they are trying to schedule synchronous meetings. Daily schedules can have a similar impact, with some learners available during standard business hours and others not, and some preferring early morning work versus others preferring late evening work.

Synchronicity and computer-mediation also impact perceptions of time. When learners and instructors are connected face-to-face and in real time, their interactions naturally differ from when they are computer-mediated and perhaps also asynchronous. Synchronous interactions are typically more ephemeral than asynchronous ones, although they can be archived. They also tend to be more spontaneous. However, individual message units in synchronous chat tend to be much briefer and are often shallower than messages posted during asynchronous interactions. Such is the nature of the different modalities; people have less time to think and type when they know someone else is waiting for that message to appear on the screen.

Elapsed time—particularly between communication acts—also may impact the effectiveness of different activities and the selection of their mediating tools. In a chat session, different facilitation guidelines may lead alternately to uncomfortable moments

Table 18.2 Equivalent Weeks in Classes by Modality

Modality	Equivalent Meeting Time	What Happens
Face-to-face class	3 hour class meeting (includes break)	Session contains multiple segments with different activities Discussion is constrained to one thread or topic at a time Most, if not all, statements made by students will get a response
Online synchronous class	3 hour live meeting	Session contains multiple segments with different activities Discussion is constrained to one thread or topic at a time Most, if not all, statements made by students will get a response
Online synchronous / asynchronous class	1 hour live meeting + asynchronous discussion	Live session: Contains 1-2 activities Students participate less than during face-to-face or asynchronous (more instructor-centered) Asynchronous discussion: Less participation than in purely asynchronous class
Online asynchronous class	Week-long online discussion	Fewer activities Multiple concurrent threads of discussion Some messages and threads may become lengthy and deep Some messages may not garner any response

of silence as participants wait for someone to type a message or chaotic threading of message units that can be difficult to follow. On a discussion board, although posters in a thread may appear to respond to each other, the elapsed time between messages may render the discussion more of a message posting activity than a truly conversational activity. For this reason, use of incremental deadlines can be helpful (Dennen & Wieland, 2008), essentially scaffolding a more timely and conversational interaction structure for students.

Table 18.2 presents the different ways in which class time might be used during one week of equivalent credit hour classes taught via different modalities.. Note that the online asynchronous class has fewer activities than the synchronous ones, but supports multiple concurrent discussion threads. There is a clear trade-off between immediacy and depth of interaction.

ACTIVITY FRAMEWORKS

Learning activities should be selected with a specific focus on the desired learning outcomes. A given learning activity may not lead in its entirety to a learning outcome and may not involve assessment of that outcome, but the place that it fits within the larger holistic context of a class should be one that contributes to the learner's ability to ultimately achieve the outcome. So, on a more micro level, when selecting individual learning activities, instructors might consider the desired interaction types as well as the desired activity outcomes, all while ensuring alignment with larger course outcomes.

Frequently we hear a student comment on activities done in online classes as "busy work." If students perceive an activity to be busy work, it may well be. Instructors are under pressure to keep learners engaged, and need visible proof of that engagement. Whereas in a face-to-face class that engagement during some weeks might be as simple as asking learners to interact with content by doing readings and attending a lecture—acts that do not require peer interaction and that involve only one-way transmission of information between teacher and student—in an online class the only ways to make engagement visible is to require the learner to leave a mark (e.g., turn in an assignment, contribute to a discussion). Thus, instructors face the challenge of finding a way to enable learners to make that mark on a regular basis (typically weekly in a traditional higher education setting) while at the same time involving the learners in activities that are both meaningful and related to the course learning outcomes. Repeated use of the same activity framework may be perceived by students as boring or busy work, although keeping learning interactions novel, meaningful, continuous, and visible can certainly be an onerous task for instructors.

In this section pedagogical activities have been separated into individual ones and discussion-oriented ones. In many ways, this distinction separates those activities that leave visible proof of engagement from those that do not, although this distinction does not always hold true across categories. Some individual activities, due to their facilitation through a learner management system or other technology-based tracking system, result in indicators that a learner has been active. For example, when a learner completes a simulation or a self-check quiz, there might be an indicator in the gradebook. However, such indicators have limited visibility; although an instructor can see them and tell that a student has been engaged, the students remain in isolation from each other and do not know of each other's progress in the course.

This focus on documented participation in learning activities begs the question: Are learning and participating in online environments intertwined or potentially separate processes? Logical arguments can be made to support either case. Hrastinski (2009) notes that not all learning occurs through visible acts, but suggests that learning and participation should be intertwined, with each impacting the other. The onus is on the instructional designer to find ways for learners to participate in online activities that go beyond marking their presence in a course and that contribute to the learning process.

INDIVIDUAL ACTIVITIES

Individual activities are those completed by the learner in isolation, without the expectation of peer interaction and at most the expectation of instructor feedback. Thus they primarily rely on learner-content interactions. These activities may range from reading material on the low-technology/low interaction end of the category, to watching online videos and listening to podcasts in the middle, to manipulating simulations and taking adaptive tests on the high technology/high interaction end. Instructors typically design and use these activities in a class when the learner either is unfamiliar with the content or, in the case of highly interactive content, may need practice applying the content and would benefit from regular, timely, and specific feedback.

Individual activities typically do not constitute the entirety of an online course for multiple systemic reasons. A course that focused on these individual activities would, essentially, be an online version of a correspondence course. Correspondence courses have historically suffered from high attrition rates (see Billings, 1988, for a discussion of this issue), and online courses have higher attrition rates than their campus counter-parts (Yair, 2007). Although this phenomenon is not yet fully understood, studies have supported the connection between persistence/attrition and variables such as teaching and cognitive presence (Joo, Lim, & Kim, 2011), student satisfaction (Yair, 2007), and a host of institutional, dispositional, and situational factors (Carroll, Ng, & Birch, 2009). Although these factors do not all directly relate to course design, course design might help overcome some of them—particularly the ones related to motivation and self-effi-cacy. A course that focuses solely on learner-content interaction with periodic summa-tive instructor feedback may not be sufficiently compelling or engaging to overcome some of the external forces that make students less likely to complete an online course.

The human feedback and social interaction that are part of discussion-based or group activities are considered motivational factors that will help students feel like they belong to a class and thus encourage persistence. Further, interaction with other learners can impact self-efficacy and help students be timelier in their work as they compare their performance and progress to that of other students. That said, courses that center around individual study can be successful, particularly when the course and instructional materials are well scaffolded, although including some dimension of human interaction is preferred (Pittenger & Doering, 2010). Further, in some instances a highly interactive individual activity such as a simulation with feedback may actually help mitigate some of the struggles faced by instructors of large online classes as they attempt to interact sufficiently with individual students (Proserpio & Magni, 2011).

DISCUSSION ACTIVITIES

Discussion is a category of pedagogical activity with robust interaction potential. Ide-ally, it involves all three of the previously discussed interaction dyads, with learners examining and integrating content into their subsequent communication with both instructor and peers. Additionally, it encourages a multi-focus perspective on the self (How do I understand the material? What questions do I have?), the instructor (How do I demonstrate to the instructor that I need help or that I am learning?), and peers (How do I productively interact with my classmates?). This category of activities may be conducted via a discussion board, but also might make use of blogs, wikis, social book-marking and annotation (e.g., diigo.com), and social video tools (e.g., voicethread.com).

The role of the facilitator in an ongoing discussion should not be diminished, and facilitation need not be solely equated with activities such as responding directly to student posts on a discussion board within a set time frame. Artino (2008) notes that students benefit from individualized and differentiated attention and need support for engaging in online discussion at the higher levels of Bloom's Taxonomy. Even if an instructor is not present in the foreground of the discussion as it unfolds, students need confirmation and guidance from that instructor.

Asynchronous discussion is reliant as much (if not more) on a plan made and commu-nicated in advance as it is on active or concurrent facilitation. In practice, actual critical discourse in online discussion may be sparse (Artino, 2008; Rourke & Kanuka, 2007), an effect that is magnified when student supports are minimal. Thus activities such as debates, which require students to not only post messages in response to an instructor prompt but more importantly to engage in multiple iterations of peer response, need to be designed with clear guidelines and expectations as well as timelines (i.e., will the

Table 18.3 Types of Discussion Activities

Activity Outcome	Teacher Centered	Learner Centered	Sample Activity Types
Information Dissemination	X		Lecture/discussion Ask the expert
		X	Jigsaw Collaborative knowledge base
Assessment and Feedback	X		Response to prompt (typically reading comprehension)
		X	Critique Peer feedback
Meaning making – content oriented		X	Debate Role play Democratic discussion
Meaning making: process oriented		X	Journal Group reflection Debrief discussion
Social		X	Class café Icebreakers Introductions Quizzes and memes Virtual party

class have one long, continuous discussion or will the discussion occur in phases with designated message types for each phase) and desired outcomes. Whereas a classroom instructor might make an announcement and change the course of an activity in the middle, an online facilitator cannot as effectively direct an asynchronous activity as it unfolds.

Table 18.3 provides an overview of types of discussion activities, classifying them by their orientation and noting whether the activity in its most common form tends to be a teacher-centered or learner-centered one.

Information Dissemination Activities

Information dissemination activities tend to be teacher centered and focus on sharing learning content and then allowing for clarification and exploration as desired. For example, an instructor might assign readings, provide lecture notes, or post a podcast and then open a forum in which students may ask questions. Without required participation, overall participation and interaction within such forums tends to be low (Dennen, 2005).

Although the very concept of information dissemination is inherently and traditionally teacher-centered, there are ways in which information dissemination activities might become learner-centered. Typically this requires learners who have some baseline knowledge of the subject matter or who are motivated to learn the course material as well as an instructor who is willing and able to monitor and assist learners on their journey to prepare and share content with their peers. A jigsaw reading activity can be effective for learners who are sufficiently able to read and decode material on their own. In this activity, learners are placed in small groups and each learner is assigned different (but likely related) reading material. Each learner individually does his assigned reading, and then shares the key point with his group. This activity takes a divide-and-conquer approach to reading material, making each individual person's assigned load manageable, but providing the benefit of knowledge from several other readings. The structure of the jigsaw activity has been found to lead to richer cognitive processes than less structured activities (Pozzi, 2010), a finding which supports the idea that students need clear guidelines and expectations when participating in an online forum.

Another activity that promotes information sharing from a learner-centered perspective is building a collaborative knowledge base. In this type of activity, students are encouraged to find and share relevant information with the class, whether that information takes the form of Web pages, videos, articles, or any other content-based media. Collectively, students might work to classify or taxonomize and annotate what they have found so they can share in a meaningful and organized manner. Like jigsaw, this type of activity helps students benefit from the efforts of their peers and allows the class as a group to accomplish more than any one student could reasonable achieve working alone. Traditional discussion boards may be a bit restrictive for these activities, with a threaded structure that does not allow for reorganization of information as new items are added. For this reason, wikis often are considered a good technology for bringing learners together to collaborate on a common document. Alternately, blogs can be used for the same purpose while giving each student a unique platform for sharing what he has found and decentralizing the power structure of a traditional course (Kang, Bonk, & Kim, 2011).

Assessment-Oriented Activities

Assessment of discussion board activities is fairly common, in part because of the need to incentivize learning participation (Dennen, 2008a). Although lurking behaviors may actually contribute to some aspect of student learning (Dennen, 2008b; Nagel, Blignaut, & Cronjé, 2009), participation by at least some learners in the discussion forum is necessary for such learning to be possible. Whether assessment is of a point-for-participation nature or truly considers the content of the learner's contribution may depend on a number of factors. Instructors who are simply looking to generate activity on the behalf of students and who use other forms of assessment (e.g., assignments and tests) may be less inclined to focus closely on discussion board contributions as a measure of learning (as opposed to a measure of participation). Further, the open nature of the discussion board makes it a poor location for assessing knowledge at the lower end of Bloom's taxonomy. The assessment of learned facts and concepts, with its redundancy from learner to learner, is at odds with the very concept of discussion.

The outcome of an online discussion need not be some measure of learning, and indeed it is difficult to measure learning in this way. Consider the classroom-based version of discussion, which is rarely assessed for learning and only occasionally—and rather holistically—assessed for participation; it is difficult to generate a valid measure of individual learning from a process-oriented, interdependent group activity. For example, whose contributions are a greater indicator of learning: the student who asks an insightful question, receives a response, and confirms that she now understands; the student who provides her with a response; or the student who chimes in and agrees with the response? Each student is engaged in the conversation in her own way, and each makes an important contribution to the group, whether that contribution be a question, an answer, or an affirmation. Thus, instructors may use online group discussion as a means to support the process of learning and gain a formative and holistic sense of student knowledge and learning, but without focusing on the artifacts of discussion as indicators of what individual students have learned. Finally, it is difficult for instructors to assess learners as individuals when the learning took place as part of a group interaction and the item(s) being assessed are simply a part of the interdependent group conversation

Assessment *through* discussion board activities—particularly peer assessment or critique—can be a pedagogically useful device for online instructors. Much as students in a classroom might be asked to give an oral presentation or display and defend a piece of original work, in an online class a discussion board might be used to facilitate a similar process. Students can post their presentations, projects, and other related artifacts for their peers to review and comment upon during a set time period. Further, student-authors may be required to respond to the comments and questions that are posted about their work. Note that other tools, such as blogs and voicethread (voicethread. com), might be similarly used to facilitate sharing and critique of student work.

Even though students may prefer instructor feedback, peer feedback can have a positive impact on learner performance in an online class (Ertmer et al., 2007). Peer feedback intertwines formative assessment and peer interaction, and although an instructor need not be visibly involved in the forum where feedback is given, the activity nonetheless requires careful analysis and design to ensure that it is productive for all involved. Ruey (2010) notes that peer feedback activities might be structured so that labor is equitable and distributed among students, ensuring all receive feedback but no individual is inordinately or unfairly burdened with the task. Additionally, students may need guidelines for providing feedback to each other, suggesting how it might be both provided and received or used. For example, guidelines may note that feedback which is specific has a greater chance of resulting in positive changes on behalf of the recipient (van der Pol, van den Berg, Admiraal, & Simons, 2008), or may suggest ways of depersonalizing the feedback so that recipients do not feel attacked. These same guidelines could be used in a classroom setting; the only difference in an online setting is the likelihood of immediate instructor presence should the activity go awry.

Content-Oriented Meaning Making

This category of discussion activities represents frameworks for facilitating collaborative exploration of course-related content in an attempt to make meaning from it. I differentiate it from information dissemination activities because the objective is not quite the same, although certainly the two activity types (information sharing and meaning making) can be combined.

Debate and Argumentation. Debate and argumentation is one approach to having students explore course content. Debate activities have been found to trigger higher levels of cognitive presence than other types of online learning activities such as expert discussion or nominal group techniques (Kanuka, Rourke, & Laflamme, 2007).

When students have to take a stance and argue for or against a concept, they must engage with the content area sufficiently to understand the different perspectives and their underlying evidence or supports. Then, through the activity, learners are required to articulate and defend what they have come to understand as the key points or arguments of one or more sides of the topic. Jeong (2005), in his sequential analysis of debate activities, notes the multiple types of messages that students must contribute (e.g., claims, challenges, evidence) to a forum in order to have a successful debate. The complexity as well as the highly intersubjective nature of such activities means that providing support for students in terms of guidelines or scaffolds for types of messages as well as temporality of messages can be critical to success.

Democratic Discussion. Paulus (2006) notes that argumentation is not the only content-oriented meaning making approach to discussion. She suggests that connection-oriented discussion, in which participants seek to build and verify knowledge rather than to challenge it, is an equally valid approach to engaging students in higher order learning through online discussion. Similarly, Brookfield and Preskill (1999) promote discussion as a way of helping students learn in a democratic society. They suggest that discussion should be used to help students engage in a respectful critical exploration of the multiple perspectives on any given topic. They provide a number of discussion starter strategies, including use of student questions, concrete images, contentious statements, and illustrative quotes. These discussion ideas provide ways of helping students work through shared content

Although their book focuses on discussion in physical classrooms, many of Brookfield and Preskill's (1999) techniques may readily be redesigned to fit either a synchronous or asynchronous online setting. In fact, for some of their starters they suggest doing pre-work via email (e.g., having students submit questions in advance). Others activities, such as snowball (starting discussion in small groups and then bringing it back to the larger group in phases) or rotating stations (students work their way through discussing several smaller topics within a set period of time) lend themselves well to the multi-threaded nature of an asynchronous forum. These discussions would require an active facilitator with a high degree of presence as well as an active peer group in order to flourish.

The elements of choice and learner control are important for enabling democratic discussion as well. Having different topical tracks, much as one might find at a professional conference, is one way of giving students choice. Another is to ask students to submit discussion topics or even suggest topic-related readings in advance of the discussion. Providing choice and learner control also enhances the learner-centered nature of these discussions.

Role Play. Assigning roles to students is a discussion device that can provide support and direction so that students may readily identify a unique contribution they can make to the discussion. Assigned roles might distribute labor or tasks, such as reporter, devil's advocate, and summarizer; such roles are termed functional (Strijbos, Martens, Jochems, & Broers, 2004). In related research, functional roles have been found to deepen student learning (De Wever, Schellens, Van Keer, & Valcke, 2008; De Wever, Van Keer, Schellens, & Valcke, 2009; Schellens, Van Keer, De Wever, & Valcke, 2007). Alternately, role play may engage students in perspective taking by asking them to engage in discussion from the perspective of characters such as historical figures, theorists, or players in a game.

Assigning roles to students alone may not be sufficient to see an effect; students may need designed supports such as scripts and prompts to help them effectively play out their assigned roles (Morris et al., 2010). However, Hoadley (2010) cautions that for as much as an instructor may attempt to design roles, roles and any human interaction inherently has an emergent element that cannot be fully controlled. Thus, the designed and implementation of roles by an instructor should not be considered a guarantee of outcomes and the ability for serendipitous emergent roles and outcomes should be allowed or even fostered.

Process-Oriented Meaning Making Activities

When students are asked to find meaning in a learning experience, the focus is not always the learning outcome or content. Students also might be engaged in discussion of the process in which they engage as they learn or apply new knowledge or skills. Essentially, this category of activities involves outcomes related to learner reflection, self-assessment, and self-efficacy, and also can support the development of metacognitive skills.

Blogs and other journal-like media are highly appropriate tools for supporting this type of learning activity, although traditional discussion boards might also be used. One advantage of blogs is related to ownership and power within the medium, particularly when a hub-and-spoke format is eschewed by the instructor in favor of a decentralized blog network with naturally occurring linkages (H. N. Kim, 2008). A teacher might be considered the owner of a discussion board, whereas individual students can be owners of their own blogs. When learners sense ownership of a virtual space, they are likely to be more comfortable engaging in self-focused discourse. Kang et al. (2011) found that a class that blogs, making full use of the communicative features such as comments and trackbacks, can produce rich, interconnected knowledge that combines content with reflection. Further, students who are asked to blog about other learning activities have been found to go beyond descriptive reflection and engage in critical reflection (Yang, 2009), although peer feedback on these reflections may not always be productive (Xie, Ke, & Sharma, 2008).

Alternately, students might be engaged in group discussion to debrief another learning activity, such as a project. In such cases, the instructor might either help synthesize the diverse experiences of individuals in the course so they can learn from each other's processes, or provide guidance as a team attempts to assess how well they work together. In a team setting, this instructor guidance in the reflective process has been found to be an important component of supporting group performance (P. Kim, Hong, Bonk, & Lim, 2009).

Social Activities

Purely social activities may not seem related to online learning at all, but nonetheless the need exists to acknowledge students as unique individuals and foster interactions that do not always relate directly to the course material. One effect of social presence is the development of class community, which requires a certain degree of comfort with and knowledge of one's co-participants (Laffey, Lin, & Lin, 2008). Learners who cannot see each other and who do not readily feel each other's presence except in a cognitive context—particularly one in which they perceive each other as working in parallel rather than as learning together—may find it difficult to form community. Social activities, in which academic factors like performance and grades are not a concern, can attempt to overcome these barriers.

A shortcoming of online learning is the loss of purely social space and instructor control of whether such spaces might exist. In an asynchronous class, students cannot congregate around and socialize during the temporal margins of the class (before, after, and during break); indeed, those temporal margins really do not exist in such settings. Thus, it becomes necessary to create virtual spaces and activities (e.g., introductions and profiles, icebreakers, class cafés for off-topic discussion, fun quizzes or memes, or virtual parties) within the course that can foster this critical socialization in a setting that is not confounded by instructional purposes. Instructor presence, however, is desirable during these activities and can be a draw for student participation. The instructor can often influence the overall tone of a class by her own degree of social interaction and self-disclosure (Dennen, 2005), thus fostering the types of social cognition that will lead to community.

NEW INFLUENCES AND MOVEMENTS

Online pedagogy does not exist in a vacuum, and thus it continuously reflects developments outside of traditional educational settings. For example, both the open source software and Web 2.0 movements have led to an abundance of new Web-based tools that support collaboration and information sharing, many of which can be used at no monetary cost to the instructor or institution. The open learning movement has done the same for learning materials. Finally, mobile devices provide more continuous course access points, but also challenge the ways in which we think about instructional scope. The resulting influences and movements—edupunk, Web 2.0, open learning, and mLearning—already are having an impact on how instructors design learning activities by influencing the tools and content that they use as well as their expectations regarding and experimentations with both types of interactions and temporality.

The Edupunk Movement

At this point, most educational institutions have officially adopted a course management system that integrates a variety of institutional functions, including pedagogy, administration, and student support. To some degree these tools influence the pedagogical options available to an instructor or the choices that an instructor might make. In particular, instructors with limited time and limited technological ability might abandon some of their pedagogical ideas upon discovering those ideas are not easily or elegantly rendered via the tools being offered to them.

Alternatively, the edupunk movement, perhaps best summarized by Kamenetz (2010), is one in which instructors seek independence from university run and corporate owned learner management systems. As they move away from the tools and perhaps even the pedagogical frameworks that are provided to them, these instructors take more of a do-it-yourself approach to both learning technologies and learning activities. So, while on the one hand there are many instructors who benefit from pedagogical frameworks, templates, examples, wizards, and agents, there also exists a subculture of faculty who are embracing independence, individual control, and, in many cases, innovation. These faculty are not necessarily moving away from the norm to be different or to make a political statement about eschewing popular or corporate technology, but rather because they hold deep beliefs about how they can better meet their students' needs.

Web 2.0

The entrance of Web 2.0-based tools and the growing popularity of social media have not been without impact on what we might now consider more traditional online learning modes (e.g., Web-based training and LMS-based classes). Web 2.0, with its underlying philosophy of user-authors, fits well with a constructivist pedagogy. Indeed, independent of formal, institution-based learning the Web fosters an incredible amount of informal and highly interactive learning driven simply by the collective needs and interests of individual learners.

Classes that jump outside of learner management systems and make use of at large Web 2.0 tools such as blogs, wikis, YouTube, diigo, and a multitude of other forums, expand the range of pedagogical content and interactions. These technologies bring with them richness of possibilities and risks associated with stepping outside of a traditional class setting. In terms of richness, it is easy for both instructors and students to find relevant materials online and repurpose them or create mashups. Outsiders (e.g., people not officially affiliated with the course or the institution) also may be easily invited to join in the learning interactions. In terms of risk, students are not shielded from potential public criticism when they engage in learning interactions that take place on a public stage and which may involve testing ideas and receiving feedback on that stage. Additionally, both learners and instructors must be conscious of the ways in which their online words and actions will live on after the course, and perhaps either be repurposed by others or found when doing an Internet search under their name.

Open Learning

Concurrent with the Web 2.0 movement has been the open learning movement, a movement that has promoted sharing learning resources online so that anyone with Internet access might benefit from them. Bonk (2009) notes that open learning makes learning more global and empowers both individual learners and instructors. Those learners and instructors who have benefitted from the edupunk movement or Web 2.0 learning resources most likely have direct experience with open learning, whether they were aware of the term or not.

Instructors who make use of the wealth of free tools and information available online in their own courses should be encouraged to not only give proper attribution to the people whose openly shared work benefitted their course, but should also consider how they might in turn reciprocate. Options include providing feedback to the original creators, sharing any mashups they have created, or even sharing their own original instructional materials online for others to adopt or adapt. Instructors can license their intellectual work in a variety of ways via Creative Commons (creativecommons.org), which helps maintain attribution and control how others might use or build upon their work.

mLearning

The mobile learning or mLearning movement brings flexibility of access to learning and alternate methods of input and output to the forefront. The intent of mobile learning is not to replicate courses on a mobile device (Quinn, 2011, 2012), but rather to extend learning in new ways. As learners increasingly purchase smart phones and tablets for personal use, they use them in a learning context. The size and nature of these devices encourages learning that is brief, informal, and just-in-time. Mobile applications support interfacing with many LMSes and Web 2.0 tools. Although instructors are not in a position to require learners to acquire these devices, they might increasingly consider how learners might either access the regular online course or augment it—especially in courses with fieldwork components—via mobile devices.

LOOKING FORWARD

Pedagogical activity frameworks for online learning are fairly well established at this time. Contributing factors include the fairly ubiquitous acceptance of integrated LMS-style tools for hosting both administrative and pedagogical functions at the institution and course levels and the commonplace nature of personal computers among people who have access to higher education. Developments continue as educators formalize and test new ideas about how to conduct interactive pedagogical activities in a computer-mediated environment. That noted, there are a few technology-based movements, each of which is equally about a philosophy of learning and interaction as it is about a technology, that are influencing online pedagogy. The future of online pedagogy is likely to continue its current course, with some instructors and institutions seeking to mimic and support face-to-face instruction and others pushing the norms and perhaps redefining some notions of what is possible in a formal learning situation.

REFERENCES

Anderson, T. D., & Garrison, D. R. (1998). Learning in a networked world: New roles and responsibilities. In C. Gibson (Ed.), *Distance Learners in Higher Education* (pp. 97–112). Madison, WI: Atwood.

Artino, A. (2008). Promoting academic motivation and self-regulation: Practical guidelines for online instructors. *TechTrends, 52*(3), 37–45. doi:10.1007/s11528-008-0153-x

Billings, D. M. (1988). Print: A conceptual model of correspondence course completion. *American Journal of Distance Education, 2*(2), 23–35. doi:10.1080/08923648809526621

Bober, M. J., & Dennen, V. P. (2001). Intersubjectivity: Facilitating knowledge construction in online environments. *Educational Media International, 38*(4), 241–250. doi:10.1080/09523980110105150

Bonk, C. J. (2009). *The world is open: How Web technology is revolutionizing education.* San Francisco, CA: Jossey-Bass.

Bonk, C. J., & Dennen, V. P. (2003). Frameworks for research, design, benchmarks, training, and pedagogy in Web-based distance education. In M. G. Moore & B. Anderson (Eds.), *Handbook of distance education* (pp. 331–348). Mahwah, NJ : Erlbaum.

Brookfield, S. D., & Preskill, S. (1999). *Discussion as a way of teaching.* San Francisco, CA: Jossey-Bass.

Carroll, D., Ng, E., & Birch, D. (2009). Retention and progression of postgraduate business students: An Australian perspective. *Open Learning: The Journal of Open, Distance and e-Learning, 24*(3), 197–209. doi:10.1080/02680510903201599

De Wever, B., Schellens, T., Van Keer, H., & Valcke, M. (2008). Structuring asynchronous discussion groups by introducing roles. *Small Group Research, 39*(6), 770–794. doi:10.1177/1046496408323227

De Wever, B., Van Keer, H., Schellens, T., & Valcke, M. (2009). Structuring asynchronous discussion groups: the impact of role assignment and self-assessment on students' levels of knowledge construction through social negotiation. *Journal of Computer Assisted Learning, 25*(2), 177–188. doi:10.1111/j.1365-2729.2008.00292.x

Dennen, V. P. (2005). From message posting to learning dialogues: Factors affecting learner participation in asynchronous discussion. *Distance Education, 26*(1), 127–148. doi:10.1080/01587910500081376

Dennen, V. P. (2008a). Looking for evidence of learning: Assessment and analysis methods for online discourse. *Computers in Human Behavior, 24*(2), 205–219. doi:10.1016/j.chb.2007.01.010

Dennen, V. P. (2008b). Pedagogical lurking: Student engagement in non-posting discussion behavior. *Computers in Human Behavior, 24*(4), 1624–1633. doi:10.1016/j.chb.2007.06.003

Dennen, V. P., & Wieland, K. (2007). From interaction to intersubjectivity: Facilitating online group discourse processes. *Distance Education, 28*(3), 281–297. doi:10.1080/01587910701611328

Dennen, V. P., & Wieland, K. (2008). Does task type impact learner participation? Interaction levels and learner orientation in online discussion activities. *Technology, Instruction, Cognition & Learning, 6*(2), 105–124.

Dringus, L. P., & Ellis, T. (2010). Temporal transitions in participation flow in an asynchronous discussion forum. *Computers & Education, 54*(2), 340–349. doi: 10.1016/j.compedu.2009.08.011

Ertmer, P. A., Richardson, J. C., Belland, B., Camin, D., Connolly, P., Coulthard, G., … Mong, C. (2007). Using peer feedback to enhance the quality of student online postings: An exploratory study. *Journal of Computer-Mediated Communication, 12*(2), 412–433. doi:10.1111/j.1083-6101.2007.00331.x

Garrison, D. R., Anderson, T., & Archer, W. (2010). The first decade of the community of inquiry framework: A retrospective. *The Internet and Higher Education, 13*(1-2), 5–9. doi:10.1016/j.iheduc.2009.10.003

Hoadley, C. (2010). Roles, design, and the nature of CSCL. *Computers in Human Behavior, 26*(4), 551–555. doi:10.1016/j.chb.2009.08.012

Hrastinski, S. (2009). A theory of online learning as online participation. *Computers & Education, 52*(1), 78–82. doi:10.1016/j.compedu.2008.06.009

Jefferies, P., Carsten-Stahl, B., & McRobb, S. (2007). Exploring the relationships between pedagogy, ethics and technology: Building a framework for strategy development. *Technology, Pedagogy and Education, 16*(1), 111–126. doi:10.1080/14759390601168122

Jeong, A. (2005). A guide to analyzing message–response sequences and group interaction patterns in computer-mediated communication. *Distance Education, 26*(3), 367–383. doi:10.1080/01587910500291470

Jeong, A., & Frazier, S. (2008). How day of posting affects level of critical discourse in asynchronous discussions and computer-supported collaborative argumentation. *British Journal of Educational Technology, 39*(5), 875–887. doi:10.1111/j.1467-8535.2007.00789.x

Joo, Y. J., Lim, K. Y., & Kim, E. K. (2011). Online university students' satisfaction and persistence: Examining perceived level of presence, usefulness and ease of use as predictors in a structural model. *Computers & Education, 57*(2), 1654–1664. doi:10.1016/j.compedu.2011.02.008

Kamenetz, A. (2010). *DIY U: Edupunks, edupreneurs, and the coming transformation of higher education.* White River Junction, VT: Chelsea Green Publishing.

Kang, I., Bonk, C. J., & Kim, M.-C. (2011). A case study of blog-based learning in Korea: Technology becomes pedagogy. *The Internet and Higher Education, 14*(4), 227–235. doi:10.1016/j.iheduc.2011.05.002

Kanuka, H., Rourke, L., & Laflamme, E. (2007). The influence of instructional methods on the quality of online discussion. *British Journal of Educational Technology, 38*(2), 260–271. doi:10.1111/j.1467-8535.2006.00620.x

Kim, H. N. (2008). The phenomenon of blogs and theoretical model of blog use in educational contexts. *Computers & Education, 51*(3), 1342–1352. doi:10.1016/j.compedu.2007.12.005

Kim, P., Hong, J.-S., Bonk, C., & Lim, G. (2009). Effects of group reflection variations in project-based learning integrated in a Web 2.0 learning space. *Interactive Learning Environments, 19*(4), 333–349. doi:10.1080/10494820903210782

Koschmann, T. D. (1996). *CSCL, theory and practice of an emerging paradigm.* Mahwah, NJ: Erlbaum.

Laffey, J. M., Lin, G.-Y., & Lin, Y.-M. (2008). Building a social and motivational framework for understanding satisfaction in online learning. *Journal of Educational Computing Research, 38*(1), 1–27. doi:10.2190/EC.38.1.a

Leidner, D. E., & Jarvenpaa, S. L. (1995). The use of information technology to enhance management school education: A theoretical view. *MIS Quarterly, 19*(3), 265–291.

Moore, M. G. (1989). Three types of interaction. *The American Journal of Distance Education, 3*(2), 1–7.

Morris, R., Hadwin, A. F., Gress, C. L. Z., Miller, M., Fior, M., Church, H., & Winne, P. H. (2010). Designing roles, scripts, and prompts to support CSCL in gStudy. *Computers in Human Behavior, 26*(5), 815–824. doi:10.1016/j.chb.2008.12.001

Nagel, L., Blignaut, A. S., & Cronjé, J. C. (2009). Read-only participants: A case for student communication in online classes. *Interactive Learning Environments, 17*(1), 37–51. doi:10.1080/10494820701501028

O'Donnell, C., & Tharp, R. (2011). Integrating cultural community psychology: Activity settings and the shared meanings of intersubjectivity. *American Journal of Community Psychology.* doi:10.1007/s10464-011-9434-1

Paulus, T. (2006). Challenge or connect? Dialogue in online learning environments. *Journal of Computing in Higher Education, 18*(1), 3–29. doi:10.1007/bf03032722

Pittenger, A., & Doering, A. (2010). Influence of motivational design on completion rates in online self-study pharmacy-content courses. *Distance Education, 31*(3), 275–293. doi:10.1080/01587919.2010.513953

Pozzi, F. (2010). Using jigsaw and case atudy for supporting online collaborative learning. *Computers & Education, 55*(1), 67–75. doi:10.1016/j.compedu.2009.12.003

Proserpio, L., & Magni, M. (2011). Teaching without the teacher? Building a learning environment through computer simulations. *International Journal of Information Management.* doi:10.1016/j.ijinfomgt.2011.09.002

Quinn, C. N. (2011). *Designing mLearning: Tapping into the mobile revolution for organizational performance.* San Francisco, CA: Pfeiffer.

Quinn, C. N. (2012). *The mobile academy: mLearning for higher education*. San Francisco, CA: Jossey-Bass.

Rourke, L., & Kanuka, H. (2007). Barriers to online critical discourse. *International Journal of Computer-Supported Collaborative Learning, 2*(1), 105–126. doi:10.1007/s11412-007-9007-3

Ruey, S. (2010). A case study of constructivist instructional strategies for adult online learning. *British Journal of Educational Technology, 41*(5), 706–720. doi:10.1111/j.1467-8535.2009.00965.x

Schellens, T., Van Keer, H., De Wever, B., & Valcke, M. (2007). Scripting by assigning roles: Does it improve knowledge construction in asynchronous discussion groups? *International Journal of Computer-Supported Collaborative Learning, 2*(2), 225–246. doi:10.1007/s11412-007-9016-2

Strijbos, J.-W., Martens, R. L., Jochems, W. M. G., & Broers, N. J. (2004). The effect of functional roles on group efficiency. *Small Group Research, 35*(2), 195–229. doi:10.1177/1046496403260843

van der Pol, J., van den Berg, B. A. M., Admiraal, W. F., & Simons, P. R. J. (2008). The nature, reception, and use of online peer feedback in higher education. *Computers & Education, 51*(4), 1804–1817. doi:10.1016/j.compedu.2008.06.001

Vygotsky, L. S. (1981). The genesis of higher mental functions. In J. V. Wertsch (Ed.), *The concept of activity in Soviet psychology* (pp. 144–188). Armank, NY: Sharpe.

Wertsch, J. V. (1985). *Vygotsky and the social formation of mind*. Cambridge, MA: Harvard University Press.

Xie, Y., Ke, F., & Sharma, P. (2008). The effect of peer feedback for blogging on college students' reflective learning processes. *The Internet and Higher Education, 11*(1), 18–25. doi:10.1016/j.iheduc.2007.11.001

Yair, L. (2007). Comparing dropouts and persistence in e-learning courses. *Computers & Education, 48*(2), 185–204. doi:10.1016/j.compedu.2004.12.004

Yang, S. H. (2009). Using blogs to enhance critical reflection and community of practice. *Educational Technology & Society, 12*(2), 11–21.

19

TECHNOLOGY INTEGRATION

From Implementation to Dynamic Scaffolding

MINCHI C. KIM, KADIR KOZAN, WOORI KIM, AND ADRIE A. KOEHLER

INTRODUCTION

The purpose of this chapter is to discuss key factors that influence technology integration for distance and blended learning environments and to examine fundamental issues for research and practice on technology integration. Successful technology integration requires instructors to be mindful about selecting and customizing technologies to maximize student learning; to be collaborative in incorporating multiple perspectives, interdisciplinary approaches, and community inputs; and to promote sustainable practices that can be continuously revised and enacted. We refer to this process as *dynamic scaffolding for technology integration.* We have broadened the context for technology integration to informal learning environments to address growing interest in and needs for after-school programs and enrichment activities with emergent technologies (social networking sites and games).

FRAMEWORKS FOR GUIDING TECHNOLOGY INTEGRATION

This section presents three recent research-based theoretical frameworks: (1) Hughes's (2005) three levels of technology integration, (2) technology, pedagogy, and content knowledge (TPACK; Koehler & Mishra, 2008, 2009; Mishra & Koehler, 2006), and (3) Kim, Hannafin, and Bryan's (2007) pedagogical framework for teaching and learning with technologies. First, Hughes (2005) suggests three levels of technology integration practice: (a) replacement, (b) amplification, and (c) transformation. Technology as replacement when technology substitutes for other instructional methods to serve the same instructional goal. Technology as amplification involves increasing the efficiency and effectiveness of task performance without changing the task or tasks in question or the overall instructional goal. Technology as transformation can change students' learning experiences and roles in addition to teaching practices and teacher roles. Consequently, research on technology integration should focus on ways to support teachers in moving from replacement to transformation on the continuum.

Second, the TPACK framework (Koehler & Mishra, 2008, 2009; Mishra & Koehler, 2006) emphasizes teacher knowledge for successful technology integration and addresses the relationships among technology, pedagogy, and content. Based on the framework, teacher knowledge consists of technology, pedagogy, and content knowledge bases, as well as, intersections between and among these (e.g., content knowledge, technological pedagogical knowledge). By explaining why a technology would or would not promote learning given a specific content area or pedagogical approach, the TPACK framework provides various rationales for successful technology integration. Finally, Kim et al. (2007) highlight the interconnectedness and alignment of essential factors for technology integration: macro context (at the systemic level, including national and local standards and reforms), teacher level (at the community level, including professional development), and micro context (at the classroom level, including students, teachers, and technologies). They point out that technology integration is often disconnected from national education goals, such as the National Science Education Standards (National Research Council, 1996), and lacks regional support for teachers through face-to-face and online professional development and communities. Kim et al. suggest that research should address how these factors are strategically interrelated and can be best aligned for successful technology integration.

KEY FINDINGS FROM PREVIOUS RESEARCH

1. Content Knowledge

Research has revealed that technology integration in mathematics and science instruction not only supports students' learning of basic content knowledge, but also helps students increase their understandings of underlying mathematical principles and scientific inquiry skills (National Science Foundation, 2007). In a series of large-scale studies conducted in Texas, Roschelle et al. (2010) found that students who used computer-based, interactive representations of mathematical equations (graphs and tables) showed significantly higher knowledge gain than student who did not use the technologically-enhanced representations. These findings were consistent across different levels of students' prior mathematics knowledge, demographics, and diverse characteristics of teachers, including background, content knowledge, and attitudes. They attributed the success of the SimCalc project to its integrative approach involving interactive software allowing students to control and analyze animations of variable changes, a pedagogy encouraging students to make and analyze predictions, and participating teachers' emphasis on teaching advanced mathematics.

2. Motivation and Self-Efficacy

Motivation refers to "the process whereby goal-directed activity is instigated and sustained" (Schunk, Pintrich, & Meece, 2008, p. 4). Educationally motivated students set desired learning goals, engage in certain activities, and increase personal effort to reach desired goals. Many studies have focused on how technology can improve motivation of students in different educational environments, including primary, secondary, and higher education settings (Roblyer & Doering, 2010; Wang & Reeves, 2006). Boster, Meyer, Roberto, and Inge (2002) found that audio and video technology help increase student interest, attention, and curiosity. For example, the use of realistic graphics and vivid colors in learning materials can enhance student retention and motivation. Moreover, utilizing highly interactive technologies, such as virtual educational games (e.g., Second Life, SimCity) and social networking sites (SNSs, e.g., Facebook, MySpace, Ning) has been shown not only to increase motivation, but also to keep students actively engaged in learning (Maushak, Chen, & Lau, 2001).

Self-efficacy, considered as people's judgments of their capabilities to perform a given task (Bandura, 1997), may be "another strong source of motivation" (Driscoll, 2005). Many researchers have reported that students' high self-efficacy enhances their academic achievement and motivation in math, science, and writing (e.g., Bong, 2001; Hsieh, Cho, & Liu 2008; Pajares, 2003). In particular, Hsieh et al. reported that technology-rich collaborative learning in science education can improve student self-efficacy and science achievement because a technology-enhanced learning environment provides students with autonomy to explore learning materials, resources, or guides.

3. Collaborative Knowledge Building

Collaborative knowledge building or learning is "a social interaction" constructed around "a community of learners and teachers, where members acquire and share experience or knowledge" (Liaw, Chen, & Huang, 2008, p. 950), and technology can play a mediating role for enhancing group interactions. Specifically, using technology to promote collaborative knowledge building provides opportunities for (a) increasing connections (e.g., peer-to-peer, peer-to-teacher, and peer-to-knowledge base) and (b) building knowledge as a community resource.

First, Scardamalia and Bereiter (2006) argue that by effectively integrating the Internet and computer technology into teaching and learning practices, instructors give learners the opportunity to be connected with peers and experts in a "knowledge building community" that promotes deep understanding on a topic that goes beyond surface learning or a factual level. One example, Knowledge Forum, allows learners to take their experiences from traditional learning events (e.g., field trips, labs, readings, and projects) and develop, build, and connect ideas related to these experiences in a collaborative database.

Second, learners' personal perspectives and ideas become a resource for the entire class to use in collaborative environments (Matthew, Felvegi, & Callaway, 2009). Matthew, et al. found that requiring undergraduate English education methods students to build a wiki around course content was successful in group-knowledge creation. The specifications of the assignment required learners to build on the work of classmates while assimilating information from multiple sources. Through this wiki-building process, collaboration promoted "the collective knowledge of the group" (Matthew et al., 2009, p. 67).

4. Teacher Roles and Teaching Practice

Meaningful integration of technology in teaching and learning practices requires teachers to not only develop technical skills, but also to redefine their teaching methodologies and beliefs. Research has shown that student learning can be enhanced (a) when teachers incorporate appropriate pedagogies for technology and (b) when teachers are provided an opportunity to reflect on their teaching practices (Gerard, Varma, Corliss, & Linn, 2011).

First, teaching practice and pedagogies can be major determinants in integrating technology to enhance student learning (Loertscher, 2009; Lowther, Inan, Strahl, & Ross, 2008). Loertscher reviewed previous studies focused on using various technologies in teaching and learning and found that "overall, across all uses in all content areas, technology does provide a small, but significant, increase in learning when implemented with fidelity and accompanied by appropriate pedagogical shifts" (p. 48).

Second, teachers' beliefs about teaching and technology also influence technology integration. Ertmer (1999, 2005) discusses two types of barriers that prevent teachers from integrating technology easily into teaching practice: first-order barriers (e.g., lack of resources such as technology and time) and second-order barriers (e.g., teachers' unchanging beliefs about teaching practices and technology). As technology has become more readily available to teachers and students, access to technology has become less of an issue. Providing teachers with the appropriate support and professional development becomes crucial in ensuring that technology is being integrated in ways that encourage a student-centered learning environment.

EXAMPLES OF EMERGING TECHNOLOGIES FOR TECHNOLOGY INTEGRATION

1. Web 2.0

Web 2.0 technology is "an umbrella term for second-generation Web technologies that allow for communication and collaboration of people in Web-based communities" (Newby, Stepich, Lehman, Russell, & Ottenbreit-Leftwich, 2011, p. 189). With several Web 2.0 applications created in the past few years and new applications constantly emerging, teachers have several options for implementing these tools into their teaching and learning processes (Oliver, 2010).

First, Web 2.0 offers educators many choices for enhancing instruction in fairly simplistic and usually inexpensive ways. As Internet access increases, Web 2.0 tools are more readily available than traditional educational software (Nelson, Christopher, & Mims, 2009). Additionally, educators can build on previous experiences of "net generation learners" by using tools with which these individuals are already familiar (Williams & Chinn, 2009). Finally, the diverse capabilities available through a wide selection of Web 2.0 options present educators with tools that promote student creativity, collaboration, and self-exploration.

Much variety exists in the type of Web 2.0 applications available to educators, and many options exist for how teachers use Web 2.0 tools to support learning goals. Oliver (2010) provides an extensive overview of how teachers can employ Web 2.0 technologies in the classroom, sharing specific examples of using Web 2.0 tools by content area. Based on Oliver's (2010) work, Table 19.1 provides an overview of possibilities for using Web 2.0 tools in classroom activities.

Research has shown that integration of Web 2.0 technologies into teaching and learning may promote student engagement and motivation. For instance, Williams and Chinn (2009) developed a marketing project for undergraduate students focused on promoting advertisement for a basketball game that required students to utilize the collaborative, promotional, and marketing features of Web 2.0 tools. Similarly, Ertmer et al. (2011) investigated undergraduates' use of Web 2.0 tools in a "five-week cross-cultural wiki development project" (p. 224). In both instances, students were engaged during the projects and became more literate in Web 2.0 technologies (Ertmer et al., 2011; Williams & Chinn, 2009). Clearly, many other potential uses for Web 2.0 technologies exist, and as teachers become more accustomed to integrating Web 2.0 into their methodologies, best practices will emerge when designing instruction using these tools.

Table 19.1 Overview of Oliver's (2010) Web 2.0 Examples by Content Area

Content Area	Web 2.0 Tool	Examples of Instructional Use
Science	**Gliffy** (diagramming/mapping) **Flickr** (image sharing)	Concept learning
	Mindmeister & **Mindomo** (mind-mapping & visual brainstorming)	Inquiry learning
	Google Spreadsheets and **EditGrid** (collaborative spreadsheets)	Collaborative data collection, Analysis, and Reporting
	Google Docs (collaborative word processing)	
	Prezi and **Prezo** (presentations)	Presentations
	Blackboard (learning management system)	Virtual science fair
English & Language Arts	**Quizlet** (word sets drill & practice)	Vocabulary learning
	Shelfari (book lists and discussions)	Collaborative Web research sharing
	Diigo (Web resource tracking and saving)	
	Gliffy (diagramming/mapping)	Pre-writing/Organizing
	LetterPop (word processing, publication generator)	Writing skills and Literature analysis
	Writewith (collaborative word-processing)	
	ToonDoo (cartoon-based storytelling)	
	Plotbot (collaborative screenplay writing)	
	NowPublic (journalism-type writing)	
	Penzu (private media-enhanced journaling)	
	Story of My Life (media-rich family history)	
Mathematics	**Sketchcast** (virtual sketching and voice recording/sharing)	Technique diagramming
	Free Website Polls (poll and survey generator)	Data collection and Analysis
	Planimeter (map measuring)	Distance and Area calculations
	InstaCalc (shared online calculator)	Problem-solving practice
	Voicethread (movie sharing)	Problem-solving steps
Social Studies	**Timeglider** (media-rich timeline creation)	Historical events
	Many Eyes (visualizations based on datasets)	Dataset analysis
	Google Earth (interactive maps)	Geography exploration
	Footnote (historical document sharing)	Reflection prompts
	Voicethread (collaborative, multimedia slide show)	Reflections, Discussions, and Digital storytelling

(*continued*)

Table 19.1 Continued

Content Area	Web 2.0 Tool	Examples of Instructional Use
Physical Education & Health	PE Central (**Log It**) (pedometer logging)	Fitness planning and Tracking personal health assessment
	Gmaps Pedometer (route/calorie-burning planning)	
	PeerTrainer (exercise and eating tracking)	
	My Pyramid Tracker (exercise and eating tracking)	
	JayCut (video editing)	Healthy behavior promotion/ Public service announcement creation
	SchoolTube (movie outlet)	
	WalkScore (neighborhood "walkability" determiner)	
	My Team Captain (roster management)	Team management
Music & Art	**Nicecast** (Internet radio)	Manage and Broadcast school radio
	ksolo/MySpace Karaoke (musical performance recording)	Performance sharing
	Flickr (image sharing)	Analysis and Reflective activities
	VoiceThread (collaborative, multimedia slide show)	
	GoAnimate (animation generator)	Art and design in animation
	ToonDoo (cartoon-based story telling)	
Foreign Language	**MyStickies** (virtual sticky notes)	Online exploration of international media
	FuzzMail (keystroke recording)	Student comprehension activities
	ESL Video (embeddable video grabber)	
	VoxSwap (social networking)	Interaction with native speakers
	LiveMocha (language learning community)	
Business	**Jing** (screen shot and video capture)	Communication/Presentation skills
	Zazzle (product design and sells)	Small business management
	eXpresso (shared/collaborative spreadsheets)	Accounting/Financial analysis
	Vizu (polling)	Market research

2. Simulations

Definitions and purposes of simulations vary widely, from a static visualization such as a diagram to an interactive visualization (Linn, Chang, Chiu, Zhang, &, McElhaney, 2010) to computational models of real or hypothesized situations in which students manipulate parameters and observe outcomes (Clark, Nelson, Sengupta, & D'Angelo, 2009; Plass et al., 2009). Across these variances, simulations essentially provide a learning environment that is interactive, student-centered, discipline-oriented, and realistic in nature (Conrad & Donaldson, 2011, p. 101).

Researchers have found that simulations can be effective in promoting student complex problem solving, knowledge acquisition, student engagement with peers in learning, and academic achievement (Chang, Chen, Lin, & Sung 2008; Kim et al., 2011; Lunce & Bailey, 2007; Schwarz & White, 2005). For instance, simulations have been utilized extensively in science education because of their affordances of immediate visualization and representation, as well as conceptual cues and procedural supports (Bodzin & Cirucci, 2009; Zacharia & Anderson, 2003). Those affordances enable student to engage in exploring and understanding complicated concepts and principles. For example, the Chem Collective[1] offers diverse simulation collections that include virtual labs and scenario-based learning activities. The virtual modeling and reality of simulation applications can be substitutes for labs and textbooks, allowing students to experience real-time interaction and authentic learning (Kim & Kim, 2011; Shin, 2002). As another example, Schwarz and White (2005) developed the Model-Enhanced ThinkerTools (METT) curriculum, which emphasizes science process skills, understanding of knowledge of science models and modeling, and conceptual understanding of physics. Students who utilized METT showed significantly better knowledge acquisition of modeling and science process skills than the students who did not employ METT.

Numerous Web-based resources[2] for educational simulations have emerged. Despite the proliferation of the simulations, researchers have seldom investigated the challenges that students and teachers confront when simulations are integrated into classroom environments. Research shows that student learning outcomes can be increased with the use of simulations (Kali & Linn, 2009), but it has provided few insights on specific learning and teaching strategies to improve students' engagement, knowledge, decision making, and information management skills (Annetta et al., 2006).

3. Games

A game is defined as "a system in which players engage in an artificial conflict, defined by rules, that results in a quantifiable outcome" (Salen & Zimmerman, 2004, p. 80). Games may enhance teaching and learning of 21st-century skills including "critical thinking and problem solving, teamwork and communication, creativity and innovation, and technology proficiency" (Sardone and Devlin-Scherer, 2010, p. 421). Sardone and Devlin-Scherer further state that digital games incorporate "cognitively complex situations" that offer role assumption, examination and problem solutions (p. 421). Additionally, Prensky (2005) argues that computer and video games may be motivating and engaging. Similarly, research has shown that games may improve motivation, conceptual understanding, process knowledge, spatial knowledge, scientific discourse, and identity in science education (National Research Council, 2011).

Types and educational goals of games vary. For instance, action games can be implemented to improve one's reflexes, adventure games may instigate problem solving and investigation, and strategy games may be used to teach strategy skills. Charsky and Mims (2008) state that games having a historical content, such as *Civilization III* or *Age of Empires*, can be used to compare World War I and World War II. Through online games with social networking features, students can play with other players and learn how to collaborate. Commercial examples of such games are Habbo Hotel,[3] World of Warcraft,[4] and Sims Online.[5] In Quest Atlantis, an educational multiplayer online game, players may undertake different roles to solve realistic problems or engage in different scenarios. In The Taiga Fishkill unit of the game, for instance, players work as environmental scientists fighting a decline in the fish population by offering solutions (Barab, Gresalfi, & Ingram-Goble, 2010).

The main challenge that needs to be addressed by both researchers and practitioners is how to retain and enhance the intrinsically motivating aspects of learning itself within gaming environments (Dede, 2011). More research is warranted to investigate how educational games should be designed with appropriate pedagogies and content knowledge, and support for integration to address practitioners' concerns (Sardone & Devlin-Scherer, 2010). Likewise, more research is needed on how to transform student learning with games to keep students more cognitively active (Barab, Gresalfi, & Arici, 2009).

KEY INFLUENCING FACTORS OF TECHNOLOGY INTEGRATION

This section presents pivotal dimensions of successful technology integration. Kim, Hannafin, and Bryan's (2007) pedagogical framework for teaching and learning with technology identify three dimensions that require a mindful coordination in order to contextualize technologies and technology-enhanced materials and to scaffold student learning: micro context (classroom context), teacher community, and macro context (national, state, and local standards and initiatives). In this section, we examine the micro context.

Context

As the innermost dimension of the framework, micro context refers to a classroom environment where three different types of interaction occur: student-student (peer) interaction, student-teacher interaction, and student-technology interaction. Interaction occurs "when two objects mutually influence one another" and intends to change students' behavior or attitudes toward achieving educational goals (Wagner, 1994, p. 8). The three types of interaction are derived from Hillman, Willis, and Gunawardena (1994) and Moore & Kearsley (1996) classification of four types of interactions (instructor-to-learner, learner-to-learner, and learner-to-content, and learner-to-interface interaction), which added one more dimension (learner-to-interface interaction) to Moore's (1989) original classification.

1. **Student-student (peer) interaction** In traditional classroom teaching, most connections have reflected student-teacher and student-content interactions (Lockwood, 2009). Peer interaction, as a new dimension of distance education in the form of student-student interaction (Moore, 1989), has received considerable attention because it can promote collaboration, constructive discussion, meaningful exchange of feedback, and learning communities (e.g., Balaji & Chakrabarti, 2010; Beldarrain, 2006; Oliver, Omari, & Herrington, 1997). We discuss two issues that influence student-student interaction.

First, student-student interaction is crucial for building online learning communities and requires carefully designed facilitation. Howarth (2006) reported several challenges to increasing student-student interaction. Students, concerned about making mistakes or presenting misunderstandings, may not actively engage in collaborative work. Different levels of motivation and prior knowledge may be obstacles to increasing student-student interaction. Research suggests that discussion can be more effective in small groups than in large-scale group activities (Moore, 1989). Additionally, in distance education settings where students are exposed to abundant resources, technology can guide students to select projects relevant to their interests and help them feel a sense of community (Rovai & Jordan, 2004).

Second, technology can be used to promote constructive discussions among students (Wanstreet, 2009). By providing peer feedback, students can engage in higher-order thinking through the activities of synthesis or analysis. The process of providing feedback also requires students to examine their own conceptions of the topic. Peer feedback derived from student-student interaction shows positive possibilities for "increasing the timeliness of feedback, providing new learning opportunities for both providers and receivers of feedback, humanizing the environment and building community" (An, Shin, & Lim, 2009, p. 750).

2. **Student-teacher interaction**   Traditionally, teachers were considered to be classroom experts who were solely responsible for class activities. However, the role of teachers has changed over time to be more of a co-knowledge constructor in student-centered learning environments (Crawford, 2000). Today's learners, as digital natives, are likely to utilize different forms of technology to communicate with teachers (Prensky, 2001). Therefore, the instructor's perspectives and roles have become more critical in online learning environments. Research suggests several strategies for successfully promoting student-teacher interaction in online learning environments. We examine two of these strategies.

First, interactions between learners and instructors can be enhanced when instructors provide additional support to increase student motivation through deadlines, reminders, and feedback (Bradley & Lomicka, 2000; Moore & Anderson, 2003). Since these types of teacher guides can easily be provided within learning management systems, teachers have access to a multitude of appropriate media to enhance the effectiveness and efficiency of teaching and learning (Wanstreet, 2009, p. 435). For example, a chat room and discussion board in an online learning platform would be a practical way to not only share reflections on readings or other assignments, but also to build a social network and increase social presence between learners and instructors (Garrison, Anderson & Archer, 2000; Morgan, 2011).

Second, technology integration and interactive media can support student-teacher interaction, but instructors must carefully design and plan for interaction with students (Battalio, 2009) and provide learners guidance and support when using technology and media (Moore, 1989). This means instructors must be available, as needed, to talk with and to help students.

With regard to the appropriate level of student-teacher interaction, Roblyer and Wiencke (2003) created a rubric for assessing interactive qualities, focusing on learner-teacher interaction in distance courses. This rubric not only provides substantial feedback on how to make a course more interactive but also allows for a more meaningful examination of the role of interaction in improving student's achievement and satisfaction. This shows that the teacher should consider how the use of interaction may affect student achievement.

3. **Student-technology interaction**   Student-technology interaction addresses the preferences for technology according to the purpose of usage (Lehtinen, 2003). Without the initial interaction with the technology (or interface), students are not able to deal with the content of the online instruction. Through the wide range of online activities mediated by technologies such as e-mail, chat, videoconferencing, and instant messaging that are available within the interface, students have access to needed knowledge and information. Convenient and consistent interface design should be considered

to facilitate student access. We discuss two issues with regard to student-technology interaction.

First, most students today seem to be comfortable with electronic environments and already have considerable online experience that replicates either the campus classroom experience or the interactive methodologies associated with live online courses (Battalio, 2009, p. 450). With such a high level of technological affordances, students could find and use knowledge that is available online (Brown, 2004). Recent studies suggest that the learner-technology interaction may function at the most fundamental level of interaction, since unfamiliarity with the technology leads to difficulties accessing learning materials (Anderson, 2004; Schrum & Hong, 2002).

Second, students require certain skills to effectively and comfortably utilize communication or learning tools to be successful in their student-technology interactions. Hirumi (2002) reported that students should possess the skills necessary to operate the delivery system so that they can successfully interact with "human and non-human resources" (p. 23). More importantly, students' perceptions of technology access clearly influence whether they believe the technology was helpful or inconvenient (Schrum & Hong, 2002). Therefore, the desired outcome of student interaction with technology is that students learn the content and that the use of technology increases their willingness to continue (Thurmond & Wambach, 2004).

EMERGING PERSPECTIVES AND ISSUES FOR RESEARCH ON TECHNOLOGY INTEGRATION

In this section, we investigate three areas that require a collaborative and sustainable coordination to achieve a goal to successfully contextualize technology and technology-enhanced materials and dynamically scaffold student learning in technology-enhanced learning environments. Definitions and examples of scaffolding for technology integration have been discussed elsewhere (Kim & Hannafin, 2011; Kim & Freemyer, 2011). Therefore, we focus on emergent issues that researchers, designers, and practitioners need to consider for technology integration in this section.

Assessment

Technology integration assessment requires multiple levels and forms of formative and summative examination. It measures learners' knowledge gains and provides insights into how to revise teaching and learning practices with technology. Two emerging issues are examined: (a) utilization of multiple formats of assessment, and (b) assessment of teacher learning and technology integration based on theoretical frameworks.

First, technology integration requires a multi-format assessment of learning. Educational assessment has traditionally been concerned with summative learning results (Hickey, Ingram-Goble, & Jameson, 2009). Thus, many forms of assessment have focused on gauging learning outcomes rather than learning processes. Researchers suggest using performance assessments in which learners solve more complex problems and present their rationales for their solutions (Hickey et al., 2009). Alternative assessments address both correct answers and the logical processes involved in problem solving (Shavelson, Baxter, & Pine, 1992). Likewise, such assessments are more complex than traditional multiple choices assessments and can spark a larger reasoning and knowledge level (Ayala, Shavelson, Yin, & Schultz, 2002).

Second, there are few well-established measures of technology integration based on theoretical frameworks (Hofer, Grandgenett, Harris, & Swan, 2011). Many TPACK-based instruments rely on "survey data" in addition to those few based on "content analyses of teachers' written reflections" and "responses to instructional dilemmas" (Hofer et al., 2011, p. 4352). Consequently, Harris, Grandgenett, and Hofer (2010) attempted to develop a more inclusive rubric that incorporates TPACK aspects followed by Hofer et al.'s observational instrument addressing in-class TPACK performance. Moreover, students' interaction with technology may impact teachers' practice, and may become a third-order barrier to technology integration (Kim et al., 2011). Therefore, addressing possible effects of student-technology interaction on technology integration in assessment may also be important.

Design of Technology-Enhanced Curricular Materials

The goal of designing technology-enhanced materials for learning is to make "the most of the opportunities yet effectiveness afforded by technology" in response to leaners' needs and interests (Naidu, 2002, p. 142). Designing technology-enhanced curricular materials is crucial and challenging because of the continuous introduction of emerging technologies. Hence, two critical issues are examined: (a) developing a collaborative and sustainable design model, and (b) helping teachers understand effective ways of contextualizing curricular with technologies.

First, a collaborative and sustainable design model, based on a sound framework, should be established. With a well-illustrated framework supported by elaborated procedures, reliable suggestions, and limitations with evidences, teachers can develop educational curriculum materials that successfully lead to desired learning outcomes (Davis & Krajcik, 2004). Teachers have an understanding of which technologies may be optimal and how they might function in effective and efficient ways. In addition, Schneider and Krajcik (2002) reported that guidelines acquired by other curricular materials help teachers understand and adopt existing ideas or even contrive additional ideas. Valid resources and directions are likely to promote insights into choosing appropriate technologies and designing instruction according to a particular educational setting. Similarly, teachers need more holistic and incremental perspectives on designing their own curricular materials through reflection and pedagogical judgments on established curricular materials (Wang & Paine, 2003).

Second, it is necessary for teachers to comprehend effective ways of contextualizing curricular with technologies to promote student-centered learning. Research has shown that in professional development programs teachers are willing to use new technological tools but have difficulty with linking the new technological affordances to their own existing practice by customizing curriculum (Gerard et al., 2011). Furthermore, teachers are responsible for not only considering students' individualized needs, but also customizing teaching and learning to adapt to different learning styles of students (Rogers, 2000; Willis, 2000).

Informal Learning and Other Settings

Milheim (2007) defines informal learning "as any activity involving the pursuit of understanding, knowledge, or skill that occurs without the presence of externally imposed curricular criteria, typically outside the pre-established curricula of educative institutions" (p. 21). Informal learning often takes place as a result of self-directed behavior and in environments outside of the classroom, such as the community, home, social activities, or peer settings (Freishtat & Sandlin, 2010; National Research Council, 2009; Milheim, 2007). While informal learning often takes the form of collaborative efforts, it can also be individually guided (Lohman, 2006). Two critical issues that should be further researched include (a) exploring additional methods in which technology can be used to engage students in informal learning situations and (b) developing methods using technology that link informal and formal learning environments.

First, research has indicated that technology can be an influencing factor and even a catalyst in informal learning settings (Freishtat & Sandlin, 2010; Lohman, 2006; Milheim, 2007). Also, evidence of the role of technology in influencing informal learning can be found at many different educational levels (Brett & Nagra, 2005; Freishtat & Sandlin, 2010; Looi, et al., 2010; Milheim, 2007) and often in work settings (Lohman, 2006). Specifically, utilizing technology in informal learning can promote ubiquitous communication (Looi et al., 2010), generate multi-sensory learning (Milheim, 2007), provide "immediate access" to information (Milheim, 2007, p. 23), open access to social environments (Brett & Nagra, 2005; Freishtat & Sandlin, 2010), and encourage student-centered learning (Looi et al., 2010). Finding additional ways of using technology in informal settings holds much promise.

Learning through informal methods comes in many forms. For instance, Freishtat and Sandlin (2010) discuss Facebook as a catalyst influencing how youth make connections, form communities, and share information and ideas. At the university level, Brett and Nagra (2005) found that providing college students with a "social learning space," equipped with computers and no rules on talking or eating, led to collaborative study efforts. After reviewing previous research, Milheim (2007) found that the use of technology can be helpful in informal settings with adult literacy students in building self-esteem and facilitating relationship building. Finally, just as technology can enhance informal learning, a lack of technology can be detrimental. After surveying public school teachers on their informal learning experiences, Lohman (2006) concluded that teachers use interactive activities more than independent activities and that providing teachers with "access to adequate computer technology and the internet" (p. 154) can foster such interactive possibilities.

Second, using technology to connect traditional and informal learning environments can enhance learning and deepen understanding. For example, by linking formal and informal learning through mobile devices and online technologies, Looi et al. (2010) designed inquiry-based activities for elementary students. While using the technologies, students responded to a recycling challenge, completed an investigation at a grocery store, reflected on the experience, planned ways to promote recycling, and applied what they had learned from the overall experience. In this case, technology provided a bridge between an informal learning environment and traditional classroom activities.

As these critical issues related to informal learning are further explored, instructional designers and educators should be mindful of designing and supporting informal instruction that is student-centered, interactive, flexible, and goal-driven (National Research Council, 2009). Informal learning environments should also be developed through community-educator partnerships and should incorporate guiding questions and cultural aspects. Pairing technology with informal learning provides opportunities to bridge the gap between informal and traditional learning environments, leading to a more authentic learning environment.

CONCLUSION

How can we ensure that current technologies are consistently and effectively integrated into learning environments? How can we maintain effective technology integration with technologies and learning environments that are continually evolving?

The answer can and should vary, depending on what we mean by technology integration, who we are asking to do it, what goals we want to achieve, what evaluation and assessment measures we plan to use for what purpose. The goal of this chapter was not to provide a quick answer to the questions, but to offer diverse views on how we should approach the questions. We have expanded the context of scaffolding from teacher or technology-initiated support to a dynamic coordination and enactment of various supports that influence student use of technologies for learning. More research is warranted to identify additional factors and reveal how these factors and different sources of support interact with each other in practice.

NOTES

1. Http://www.chemcollective.org/
   TechTrekers (http://www.techtrekers.com/sim.htm);
2. Learn4Good (http://www.learn4good.com/games/simulation.htm);
   Nobelprize (http://nobelprize.org/educational)
3. Http://www.habbo.com/
4. Http://us.battle.net/wow/en/
5. Http://thesims.ea.com/

REFERENCES

An, H., Shin, S., & Lim, K. (2009). The effects of different instructor facilitation approaches on students' interactions during asynchronous online discussions. *Computers & Education, 53*(3), 749–760.

Anderson, T. (2004). Teaching in an online learning context. In T. Anderson & F. Elloumi (Eds.), *Theory and practice of online learning* (pp. 273–294). Athabasca, Canada: Athabasca University.

Annetta, L., Murray, M., Laird, S., Bohr, S., & Park, J. (2006). Serious games: Incorporating video games in the classroom. *Educause Quarterly, 29*(3), 16–22.

Ayala, C. C., Shavelson, R. C., Yin, Y., & Schultz, S. E. (2002). Reasoning dimensions underlying science achievement: The case of performance assessment. *Educational Assessment, 8*(2), 101–121.

Balaji, M. S., & Chakrabarti, D. (2010). Student interactions in online discussion forum: Empirical research from 'media richness theory' perspective. *Journal of Interactive Online Learning, 9*(1), 1–22.

Bandura, A. (1997). *Self-efficacy: The exercise of control.* New York: W.H. Freeman.

Barab, S. A., Gresalfi, M., & Arici, A. (2009). Why educators should care about games. *Educational Leadership, 67*(1), 76–80.

Barab, S. A., Gresalfi, M., & Ingram-Goble, A. (2010). Transformational play: Using games to position person, content, and context. *Educational Researcher, 39*(7), 525–536.

Battalio, J. (2009). Interaction online: A reevaluation. In A. Orellana, T. L. Hudgins, & M. Simonson (Eds.), *The perfect online course: Best practices for designing and teaching* (pp. 443–462). Charlotte, NC: Information Age.

Beldarrain, Y. (2006). Distance education trends: Integrating new technologies to foster student interaction and collaboration, *Distance Education, 27*(2), 139–153.

Bodzin, A., & Cirrucci, L. (2009). Integrating geospatial technologies to examine urban land use change: A design partnership. *Journal of Geography, 108*(4–5), 186–197.

Bong, M. (2001). Between and within-domain relations of academic motivation among middle and high school students: Self-efficacy, task value, and achievement goals. *Journal of Educational Psychology, 93*(1), 23–34.

Boster, F. J., Meyer, G. S., Roberto, A. J., & Inge, C. C. (2002). A report on the effect of the united streaming (TM) application on educational performance. East Lansing, MI: Cometrika, Inc., Baseline Research, LLC., & Longwood University.

Bradley, T., & Lomicka, L. (2000). A Case study of learner interaction in technology-enhanced language learning environments. *Journal of Educational Computing, 22*(3), 347–368.

Brett, P., & Nagra, J. (2005). An investigation into students' use of a computer-based social learning space: lessons for facilitating collaborative approaches to learning. *British Journal of Educational Technology, 36*(2), 281–92.

Brown, K. (2004). Technology: Building interaction. *TechTrends, 48*(5), 34–36.

Chang, K., Chen, L., Lin, Y., & Sung, T. (2008). Effects of learning support in simulation-based physics learning. *Computers & Education, 51*(4), 1486–1498.

Charsky, D., & Mims, C. (2008). Integrating commercial off-the-shelf video games into school curriculums. *TechTrends, 52*(5), 38–44.

Clark, D., Nelson, B., Sengupta, P., & D'Angelo, C. (2009). *Rethinking science learning through digital games and simulations: Genres, examples, and evidence.* Paper presented at The National Research Council Workshop on Gaming and Simulations. Retrieved from http://www7.nationalacademies.org/bose/Clark_Gaming_CommissionedPaper.pdf

Conrad, R., & Donaldson, A. J. (2011). *Engaging the online learner: Activities and resources for creative instruction.* San Francisco: Jossey-Bass.

Crawford. B. A. (2000). Embracing the essence of inquiry: New roles for science teachers. *Journal of Research in Science Teaching, 37*(9), 916–937.

Davis, E. A., & Krajcik, J. S. (2004). Designing educative curriculum materials to promote teacher learning, *Educational Researcher, 34*(3), 3–14.

Dede, C. (2011). Developing a research agenda for educational games and simulations. In S. Tobias, & J. D. Fletcher (Eds.), *Computer games and instruction* (pp. 233–250). Charlotte, NC: Information Age.

Driscoll, M. (2005). *Psychology of learning for instruction* (3rd ed.). New York: Allyn & Bacon.

Ertmer, P. A. (1999). Addressing first-and second-order barriers to change: Strategies for technology integration. *Educational Technology Research and Development, 47*(4), 47–61.

Ertmer, P. A. (2005). Teacher pedagogical beliefs: The final frontier in our quest for technology integration? *Educational Technology Research and Development, 53*(4), 25–39.

Ertmer, P. A., Newby, T. J., Liu, W., Tomory, A., Yu, J., & Lee, Y. (2011). Students' confidence and perceived value for participating in cross-cultural wiki-based collaborations. *Educational Technology Research and Development, 59*(2), 213–228.

Freishtat, R., & Sandlin, J. (2010). Shaping youth discourse about technology: Technological colonization, manifest destiny, and the frontier myth in Facebook's public pedagogy. *Educational Studies (American Educational Studies Association), 46*(5), 503–523.

Garrison, D. R., Anderson, T., & Archer, W. (2000). Critical inquiry in a text-based environment: Computer conferencing in higher education. *The Internet and Higher Education, 2*(2–3), 87–105.

Gerard, L., Varma, K., Corliss, S. B., & Linn, M. C. (2011). Professional development for technology-enhanced science. *Review of Educational Research, 81*(3), 408–448.

Harris, J., Grandgenett, N., & Hofer, M. (2010). Testing a TPACK-based technology integration assessment rubric. In D. Gibson & B. Dodge (Eds.), *Proceedings of Society for Informational Technology & Teacher Education International Conference 2010* (pp. 3833–3840). Chesapeake, VA: AACE.

Hickey, D. T., Ingram-Goble, A. A., & Jameson, E. M. (2009). Designing assessments and assessing designs in virtual educational environments. *Journal of Science Education and Technology, 18,* 187–208.

Hillman, D. C. A., Willis, D. J., & Gunawardena, C. N. (1994). Learner-interface interaction in distance education: An extension of contemporary models and strategies for practitioners. *American Journal of Distance Education, 8*(2), 30–42.

Hirumi, A. (2002). A framework for analyzing, designing, and sequencing planned eLearning interactions. *Quarterly Review of Distance Education, 3*(2), 141–160.

Hofer, M., Grandgenett, N., Harris, J. & Swan, K. (2011). Testing a TPACK-based Technology Integration Observation Instrument. In M. Koehler & P. Mishra (Eds.), *Proceedings of Society for Information Technology & Teacher Education International Conference 2011* (pp. 4352–4359). Chesapeake, VA: AACE.

Howarth, P. (2006). Increasing student interaction. Teaching English BBC British Council [Web Blog Post]. Retrieved from http://www. teachingenglish.org.uk/articles/increasing-student-interaction

Hsieh, P., Cho, Y., & Liu, M. (2008). Middle school focus: Examining the interplay between middle school students achievement goals and self-efficacy in a technology-enhanced learning environment. *American Secondary Education, 36*(3), 33–50.

Hughes, J. (2005). The role of teacher knowledge and learning experiences in forming technology-integrated pedagogy. *Journal of Technology and Teacher Education, 13*(2), 277–302.

Kali, Y., & Linn, M. C. (2009). Designing effective visualizations for elementary school science. *Elementary School Journal, 109*(5), 181–198.

Kim, M. C., Ertmer, P. A., Fang, J., Kim, W., Tomory, A., & Freemyer, S. (2011, April). *Challenges of facilitating technology-enhanced inquiry among high school science students: A multiple case study.* Paper presented at the annual meeting of American Educational Research Association, New Orleans, LA.

Kim, M., Hannafin, M., & Bryan, L. (2007). Technology-enhanced inquiry tools in science education: An emerging pedagogical framework for classroom practice. *Science Education, 91*(6), 1010–1030.

Kim, M. C., & Hannafin, M. J. (2011). Scaffolding problem solving in technology-enhanced learning environments (TELEs): Bridging research and theory with practice. *Computers & Education, 56*(2), 403–417.

Kim, M. C., & Freemyer, S. (2011). Technology integration in science classrooms: Framework, principles, and examples. *Educational Technology, 51*(1), 25–29.

Kim, W. R., & Kim, M. C. (2011, April). *Key characteristics of simulation for inquiry learning in chemistry classes.* Paper presented at the annual meeting of Midwest ATE, Lafayette, IN.

Koehler, M. J., & Mishra, P. (2008). Introducing TPCK. AACTE Committee on Innovation and Technology (Ed.), *The handbook of technological pedagogical content knowledge (TPCK) for educators* (pp. 3–29). Mahwah, NJ: Erlbaum. Retrieved from http://punya.educ.msu.edu/publications/koehler_mishra_08.pdf

Koehler, M. J., & Mishra, P. (2009). What is technological pedagogical content knowledge? *Contemporary Issues in Technology and Teacher Education, 9*(1), 60–70.

Kopcha, T. J. (2010). A systems-based approach to technology integration using mentoring and communities of practice. *Educational Technology Research & Development, 58*(2), 175–190.

Lehtinen, E. (2003). Computer-supported collaborative learning: An approach to powerful learning environments. In E. De Corte, L. Verschaffel, N. Entwistle, & J. Van Merriëboer (Eds.), *Unravelling basic components and dimensions of powerful learning environments* (pp. 35–54). Amsterdam: Elsevier.

Liaw, S., Chen, G., & Huang, H. (2008). Users' attitudes toward Web-based collaborative learning systems for knowledge management. *Computers & Education, 50*(3), 50–61.

Linn, M. C., Chang, H. Y., Chiu, J. L., Zhang, H., & McElhaney, K. (2010). Can desirable difficulties overcome deceptive clarity in scientific visualizations? In A. Benjamin (Ed.), *Successful remembering and successful forgetting: a Festschrift in honor of Robert A. Bjork* (pp. 239–262). New York: Routledge.

Lockwood, C. A. (2009). Building active learning applications and opportunities into a distance-learning leadership course. Retrieved from http://www.cba.nau.edu/Faculty/Intellectual/workingpapers/pdf/Lockwood_ActiveLearning.pdf

Loertscher, D. (2009). Does Technology Really Make a Difference?. *Teacher Librarian, 37*(2), 48–49.

Lohman, M. C. (2006). Factors influencing teachers' engagement in informal learning activities. *Journal of Workplace Learning, 18*(3), 141–156.

Looi, C., Seow, P., Zhang, B., So, H., Chen, W., & Wong, L. (2010). Leveraging mobile technology for sustainable seamless learning: a research agenda. *British Journal of Educational Technology, 41*(2), 154–169.

Lowther, D., Inan, F., Strahl, J., & Ross, S. (2008). Does technology integration "work" when key barriers are removed?. *Educational Media International, 45*(3), 195–213.

Lunce, L. & Bailey, B. (2007). *Using online simulations to enhance preservice teacher understanding of science concepts.* In C. Montgomerie & J. Seale (Eds.), Proceedings of World Conference on Educational Multimedia, Hypermedia and Telecommunications 2007 (pp. 2892–2899). Chesapeake, VA: AACE.

Matthew, K. I., Felvegi, E., & Callaway, R. A. (2009). Wiki as a collaborative learning tool in a language arts methods class. *Journal of Research on Technology in Education, 42*(1), 51–72.

Maushak, N. J., Chen, H, & Lau, H. (2001). *Utilizing edutainment to actively engage K-12 learners and promote students learning: An emergent phenomenon.* (ERIC Document Reproduction Service No. ED 470100)

Milheim, K. (2007). Influence of technology on informal learning. *Adult Basic Education and Literacy, 1*(1), 21–26.

Mishra, P., & Koehler, M.J. (2006). Technological pedagogical content knowledge: A framework for integrating technology in teacher knowledge. *Teachers College Record, 108*(6), 1017–1054.

Moore, M. G. (1989). Three types of interaction. *American Journal of Distance Education, 3*(2), 1–6.

Morgan, T. (2011). Online classroom or community-in-the-making? Instructor conceptualizations and teaching presence in international online contexts. *The Journal of Distance Education, 25*(1). Retrieved from http://www.jofde.ca/index.php/jde/article/view/721/1269

Moore, M. G., & Anderson, W. G. (Eds.), (2003). *Handbook of distance education.* Mahwah, NJ: Erlbaum.

Moore, M. G., & Kearsley, G. (1996). *Distance education: A system view.* Belmont, CA: Wadsworth.

Naidu, S. (2002). Designing and Evaluating Instruction for e-Learning. In P. L. Rogers (Ed.), *Designing instruction for technology-enhanced learning* (pp. 134–159). Hershey, PA: Idea Group Publishing.

National Center for Education Statistics. (2003). *Technology in schools: Suggestions, tools, and guidelines for assessing technology in elementary and secondary education.* Retrieved October 28, 2011 from http://nces.ed.gov/pubs2003/tech_schools/chapter7.asp

National Research Council. (1996). The National Science Education Standards. Washington DC: National Academies Press.

National Research Council. (2009). *Learning Science in Informal Environments: People, Places, and Pursuits.* Committee on Learning Science in Informal Environments, Philip Bell, Bruce Lewenstein, Andrew W. Shouse, and Michael A. Feder, Eds. Board on Science Education, Center for Education, Division of Behavioral and Social Sciences and Education. Washington, DC: The National Academies Press.

National Research Council. (2011). *Learning Science Through Computer Games and Simulations.* Committee on Science Learning: Computer Games, Simulations, and Education, Margaret A. Honey and Margaret L. Hilton, Eds. Board on Science Education, Division of Behavioral and Social Sciences and Education. Washington, DC: The National Academies Press.

National Science Foundation. (2007). *Student results show benefits of math and science partnerships* (07-080). Retrieved from http://www.nsf.gov/ news/news_summ.jsp?cntn_id =109725

Nelson, J., Christopher, A., & Mims, C. (2009). TPACK and Web 2.0: Transformation of teaching and learning. *TechTrends, 53*(5), 80–85.

Newby, T. J., Stepich, D. A., Lehman, J. D., Russell, J. D., & Ottenbreit-Leftwich, A. (2011). *Educational technology for teaching and learning* (4th ed.). Boston, MA: Pearson.

Oliver, K. (2010). Integrating Web 2.0 across the curriculum. *TechTrends, 54*(2), 50–60.

Oliver, R., Omari, A., & Herrington, J. (1997). Exploring student interactions in collaborative Word Wide Web learning environments. In T. Mulder & T. Reeves (Eds.), *Educational Multimedia/Hypermedia and Telecommunications* (pp. 812–817). Charlottesville, VA: AACE.

Pajares, F. (2003). Self-efficacy beliefs, motivation, and achievement in writing: A review of the literature. *Reading, and Writing Quarterly, 19*(2), 139–158.

Plass, J. L., Homer, B. D., Milne, C., Jordan, T., Kalyuga, S., Kim, M., & Lee, H. J. (2009). Design factors for effective science simulations: Representation of information. *International Journal of Gaming and Computer-Mediated Simulations, 1*(1), 16–35.

Prensky, M. (2001). Digital natives, digital immigrants. *On the Horizon, 9*(5), 1–6.

Prensky, M. (2005). Computer games and learning: Digital game-based learning. In J. Raessens & J. Goldstein (Eds.), *Handbook of computer game studies* (pp. 97–122). Cambridge, MA: The MIT Press.

Roblyer, M. D., & Doering, A. H. (2010). *Integrating educational technology into teaching* (5th ed.). Boston MA: Ally & Bacon.

Roblyer, M. D., & Wiencke, W. (2003). Design and use of a rubric to assess and encourage interactive qualities in distance courses. *American Journal of Distance Education, 17*(2). 77–97.

Rogers, P. L. (2000). Barriers to adopting emerging technologies in education. *Journal of Educational Computing Research, 22*(4), 455–472.

Roschelle, J., Schechtman, N., Tatar, D., Hegedus, S., Hopkins, B., Empson, S., … Gallagher, L. (2010). Integration of technology, curriculum, and   professional development for advancing middle school mathematics: Three large-scale studies. *American Educational Research Journal, 47*(4), 833–878.

Rovai, A. P., & Jordan, H. M. (2004). Blended learning and sense of community: A comparative analysis with traditional and fully online graduate courses. *The International Review of Research in Open and Distance Learning, 5*(2), 1–13.

Salen, K., & Zimmerman, E. (2004). *Rules of play: Game design fundamentals.* Cambridge, MA: The MIT Press.

Sardone, N. B., & Devlin-Scherer, R. (2010). Teacher candidate responses to digital games: 21st–century skills development. *Journal of Research on Technology in Education, 42*(4), 409–425.

Scardamalia, M., & Bereiter, C. (2006). Knowledge building: Theory, pedagogy, and technology. In K. Sawyer (Ed.), *Cambridge handbook of the learning sciences* (pp. 97–118). New York: Cambridge University Press.

Schneider, R., & Krajcik, J. (2002). Supporting science teacher learning: The role of educative curriculum materials. *Journal of Science Teacher Education, 13*(3), 221–245.

Schrum, L. & Hong, S. (2002). Dimensions and strategies for online success: Voices from Experienced educators. *Journal of Asynchronous Learning Networks, 6*(1), 57–67.

Schunk, D. H., Pintrich, P. R., & Meece, J. L. (2008). *Motivation in education: Theory, research, and applications* (3rd ed.). Upper Saddle River, NJ: Pearson/Merrill Prentice Hall.

Schwarz, C., & White, B. (2005). Meta-modeling knowledge: Developing students' understanding of scientific modeling. *Cognition and Instruction, 23*(2), 165–205.

Shavelson, R. J., Baxter, G. P., & Pine, J. (1992). Performance assessments: Political rhetoric and measurement reality. *Educational Researcher, 21*(4), 22–27.

Shin, Y. S. (2002), Virtual reality simulations in web-based science education. *Computer Applications in Engineering Education, 10*(1), 18–25.

Thurmond, V., & Wambach, K. (2004). Understanding interactions in distance education: A review of literature. *International Journal of Instructional Technology and Distance Learning, 1*(1), 9–25.

Wagner, E. D. (1994). In support of a function definition of interaction. *The American Journal of Distance Education, 8*(20), 6–29.

Wang, J., & Paine, L. (2003). Learning to teach with mandated curriculum and public examination of teaching as contexts. *Teaching and Teacher Education, 19*(1), 75–94.

Wang, C., & Reeves, T. C. (2006). The meaning of culture in online education: Implications for teaching, learning, and design. In A. Edmundson (Ed.), *Globalized e-learning cultural challenges* (pp. 1–17). Hershey, PA: Idea Group Inc.

Wanstreet, C. E. (2009). Interaction in online learning environments. *Quarterly Review of Distance Education, 7*(4), 399–411.

Williams, J., & Chinn, S. (2009). Using Web 2.0 to support the active learning experience. *Journal of Information Systems Education, 20*(2), 165–174.

Willis, J. (2000). The maturing of constructivist instructional design: Some basic principles that can guide practice. *Educational Technology, 40*(1), 5–16.

Zacharia, Z., & Anderson, O. R. (2003). The effects of an interactive computer-based simulation prior to performing a laboratory inquiry-based experiment on students' conceptual understanding of physics. *American Journal of Physics, 71*(6), 618–629.

20

REALIZING THE PROMISE OF LEARNING OBJECTS

SUSAN MOISEY AND MOHAMED ALLY

INTRODUCTION

Nearly 20 years have elapsed since the term "learning object" first entered the distance education lexicon, and over this relatively brief time period, significant investment and growth has taken place in the development and use of learning objects. With the advent of e-learning and online instruction, learning objects emerged as a promising means for achieving efficiencies and enhanced flexibility in instructional design and course development. The vision they provided was bold and exciting—educators and learners alike could have "anytime, anywhere" access to vast stores of high-quality, proven-effective learning objects to meet a wide array of training and educational needs. Instructors could assemble selected learning objects, customizing them according to student needs and characteristics. Students could access the learning objects on adaptive learning management systems, tailoring the activities according to their personal preferences and individual learning styles. Learning object repositories would serve a range of formal and informal learning needs, providing students with resources for lifelong learning, while promoting educational opportunities and success. To ensure flexible, ubiquitous availability of these resources, learning objects could be accessed in a variety of ways, including from desktop and laptop computers, tablets, and mobile devices. Moreover, given that more than 80% of the world's population is predicted to be accessing the Internet using mobile devices by the year 2015 (Johnson, Smith, Willis, Levine, & Haywood, 2011), effective mobile learning strategies and protocols would be a fundamental part of learning object development and use.

Certainly, the idea of sharing and re-using educational resources is not new. In the past, educators commonly reused learning materials in the same or in different courses, and shared both non-digital and digital learning materials with students and other instructors. However, before the introduction of learning objects, there was no formal or systematic way to share learning materials widely, particularly digital learning materials, or to revise, adapt, and reuse them as needed.

The situation changed with the introduction of learning objects. By cataloguing and housing digital learning materials in repositories, a growing body of instructional resources became available to educators and learners worldwide. Moreover, the open sharing of educational materials significantly added to the abundance of learning resources as increasing numbers of universities and educational organizations made their learning materials available as open educational resources, allowing educators (and students) to use these resources at no cost for teaching and learning purposes (Wiley & Hilton, 2009). As such, learning objects continue to hold great promise for distance education, providing the potential for "mass customization" of individualized instructional materials (McGreal, 2004, p. 3), reducing wasted resources associated with duplicate and redundant learning materials, and providing educators and learners with access to high-quality, instructionally effective learning materials.

WHAT IS A LEARNING OBJECT?

Learning objects—reusable, digital resources designed to facilitate learning—are the product of three diverse disciplines:

1. instructional design, which provides the methodology and means whereby instructional materials are created (e.g., Dick, Carey, & Carey, 2001);
2. computer science, which offers the concept of "objects," parts of program code that can be constructed, assembled, and shared to serve different purposes (Whitten, Bentley, & Dittman, 2001);
3. library science, which provides the concept of cataloging and using labels or "tags" to allow materials to be easily identified or located.

Although learning objects first appeared on the educational and training scene in the mid-1990s, there is still no commonly accepted definition of what precisely constitutes a learning object. In addition, imprecise nomenclature is problematic as learning objects have been variously termed information objects, content objects, learning resources, and knowledge objects, among others (McGreal, 2004). At issue too is the term "learning object" itself (Friesen, 2004). Lack of a clear definition and an inconsistent lexicon creates misunderstanding and confusion, hinders the growth and development of learning objects, and hampers a shared understanding of the concept essential for grounding research in this area.

The Institute of Electrical and Electronic Engineers (IEEE) in its Learning Objects Metadata (LOM) standard document (IEEE, 2002) defined a learning object as "any entity, digital or non-digital, which can be used, re-used or referenced during technology supported learning." McGreal (2004, p. 9) refers to this definition as including "anything and everything," contending that its expansiveness provided little direction for research and practice. Wiley (2002) narrowed the definition somewhat to include only digital resources, defining a learning object as "any digital resource that can be reused to support learning" (p. 7). Further refinements have been proposed (e.g., Hamel & Ryan-Jones, 2002; Sosteric & Hesemeier, 2002), including Polsani (2003), who added more detail, defining a learning object as "an independent and self-standing unit of learning content that is predisposed to reuse in multiple instructional contexts" (section 2.2, para. 4).

Noting the shortcomings of previous definitions, Sicilia and Garcia (2003) added two other characteristics: (a) that learning objects are "digital entities," and (b) that they possess a related "metadata record" describing the potential contexts in which they may be used. Ally (2004) added yet another facet to the definition—that of learning outcomes—proposing a more specific definition of a learning object as "any digital resource that can be re-used to achieve a specific learning outcome" (p. 87), and contending that learning objects must be tied to learning outcomes so that suitable content and assessment can be included and the appropriate delivery medium identified.

Despite the differences in definitions, there appear to be three commonly agreed-upon characteristics of learning objects: they are *digital*, they support *learning*, and they are *reusable*.

With the above characteristics, learning objects can take many forms, the most common being digital text and graphic presentations on specific topics, interactive multimedia activities, streaming audio and video recordings, and assessment tools and test item banks. Things that present information digitally, but that are not tied to a specific learning outcome (such as photographs, diagrams, maps, journal articles, audio and video recordings, and so forth) are often called learning objects, although others would consider them more appropriately termed information objects.

Williams (2004) describes learning objects as combinations of elements or granules, which may include photographs, text, animations, graphics, workshop exercises, assessment questions, articles, video and audio clips, and substantial case studies. The small size or granularity of such objects requires them to be aggregated into a larger size learning object—what Dalsgaard (2005) calls a learning framework—or to be wrapped in what Polsani (2003) calls a learning intention—in order to be useful in instructional situations.

Keller (2008) applies the concept of learning objects to motivation, introducing the term "reusable motivational object" (RMO). Citing previous research (Oh, 2006), he explains how RMOs can be used in combination with learning objects to significantly improve learning outcomes by arousing learners' curiosity or through other means of gaining attention.

The emergence of Web 2.0 and social networking has influenced how learning objects are defined. Wiley (2009) identifies three types of learning objects: content, strategy, and discourse objects. Content objects are "self-contained chunks of information" (p. 353); no contextual information is included in these objects as the instructor is expected to add "contextual scaffolds" such as scenarios or application activities to show how the material relates to the learners. Strategy objects are defined as instructional "procedures, processes, and patterns" (p. 357). Discourse objects are described as a "special class of strategy objects that scaffold interactions among learners" (p. 360); wikis and discussion forums are examples of discourse learning objects.

USES OF LEARNING OBJECTS

The digital format of learning objects allows them to be stored in repositories where they can be searched and retrieved electronically over the Internet and used in different instructional situations. Table 20.1 lists some commonly used repositories. McGreal (2008) describes three main types of learning object repositories: content repositories, which store the objects themselves; linking or metadata repositories, which serve as a portal and provide links to materials located elsewhere; and hybrid repositories which perform both functions.

Table 20.1   Learning Object Repositories

Repositories	Location
Multimedia Educational Resources for Learning and Online Teaching (MERLOT)	http://www.merlot.org
Learning Online Network (LON-CAPA)	http://www.lon-capa.org
Connexions	http://cnx.org
Wisc-Online (University of Wisconsin)	http://www.wisc-online.com
XanEdu	http://www.xanedu.com
National Science Digital Library	http://nsdl.org
MIT Open Courseware	http://ocw.mit.edu/index.htm
Curriki	http://www.curriki.org
National Repository of Online Courses	http://www.montereyinstitute.org/nroc

A great deal of the research into learning objects has addressed technology-related areas, such as repository architecture and search protocols. The expansion of repositories led to the establishment of "meta-repositories" or referatory sites, which allow users to search many repositories simultaneously in order to obtain a complete and comprehensive list of resources (Hart & Albrecht, 2004; Koppi, Bogle, & Bogle, 2005). Ochoa and Duval (2009) conducted a quantitative study of 24 learning object repositories and 15 referatory sites in order to determine size (as of November, 2007) and growth rates and as a way of exploring the "supply" side of the Learning Object Economy. The learning object repositories contained a total of approximately 100,000 items, with an average of 4,000 items each. The learning object referatories contained a total of approximately 300,000 items, with an average of 20,000 items in each site; three of the referatories accounted for two-thirds of the items.

The exponential growth rates of learning object repositories resulting from the open sharing of educational materials have made finding appropriate learning resources a challenge for educators and instructional designers. Various alternatives have been suggested, such as the addition of ontological and pedagogical information to supplement metadata records (Wang, 2008) and the creation of communities of practice (Koper, Pannekeet, Hendriks, & Hummel, 2004), in order to identify appropriate resources to meet specific instructional needs.

Both the content and the process of a learning object may be reused. Usually learning objects are selected for the content they contain and the learning outcomes they elicit. But learning objects can also be reused for their processes, i.e., the underlying code or structure is reused, but the content area is changed. Hodgins (2004) differentiates between "reuse" (i.e., applying the learning object in the same context for which it was designed) and "repurposing" (i.e., applying the learning object in a different context), noting that the latter is more problematic and difficult to achieve.

Various metaphors have been advanced to describe the use of learning objects, and even to assist in their definition. Bennett and McGee (2005) note that "The struggle to define learning objects has occurred through metaphor, which plays a powerful role in helping readers/thinkers translate ideas from one domain to another" (p. 16). Early metaphors like Lego block assemblies, which suggested a somewhat random selection of components, later progressed to that of atom-molecular structures (Wiley, 2002), where objects were aggregated according to their internal structure and potentiality to combine with other objects. Deeming this latter metaphor better, but still insufficient, Paquette and Rosca (2002) posited an "organic" metaphor akin to the cellular structures and processes of the human body, where an ideal learning object "behaves like a complete organism when alone or as a well-integrated being when aggregated as a part. It must have its own autonomy, the connectivity potential to combine physically or through communication, an encapsulation capability through an interface that concentrate its external relationships and some plasticity, that is the ability to adapt to the evolution of the aggregate" (pp. 12–13).

The organic metaphor is unique from its predecessors by the inclusion of communication or interaction as an element. In the organic model, the "whole is more than the sum of the parts," and the result is a dynamic, adaptive, self-organizing structure, unlike the more static models proposed earlier. In the organic model, learning objects are selected and placed within a learning environment that not only promotes learning, but also has the potential to foster a sense of community among learners (Moller, Prestera, Harvey, Downs-Keller, & McCausland, 2002). In their organic, knowledge-building learning environment, learning objects (or knowledge objects as they are termed by the authors) are interrelated with three other elements: scaffolds, discourse action communities, and facilitation. When used in concert with the individual's context, these components "create a rich and open environment that is alive with opportunities, exploration, and meaning-making" (Moller et al., 2002, p. 49). Similarly, Wiley and Edwards (2002) describe an online self-organizing social system with the capacity to solve problems and accomplish specific goals. In this social system, learning objects are "digital tools used to mediate learning" (p. 38), and members of the community evaluate and choose the most appropriate one(s) to access.

BENEFITS OF LEARNING OBJECTS

Digital learning materials have the advantage of being able to be used widely in distance educational environments, particularly in online and mobile learning, where they can be shared and accessed at any time, from any place. The growing interest in the use of learning objects in instruction stems from several factors. Because learning objects are standalone entities, they can be revised or retired without affecting other learning objects. Instructors can draw from a broad range of learning objects, thus allowing flexible assembly of lessons and ease of updating and revisions. Moreover, learning objects may be used with a variety of instructional approaches, (e.g., problem-based learning, collaborative learning) due to the "pedagogically neutral" nature of learning objects, although as Friesen Roberts, and Fisher (2002) note, this latter point has engendered considerable debate.

From an organizational point of view, learning objects allow for efficiencies, avoiding duplication of effort between instructors and among educational institutions, and promoting more consistent instruction within and between courses. Access to learning objects frees instructors from the time-consuming task of content development, providing more opportunity to spend time with students promoting success and supporting learning, in their role as tutors and facilitators of learning (Ally, 2004). The development of authoring systems for learning objects and learning management systems that incorporate learning objects has provided further efficiencies in the development process.

Learning objects also benefit learners, who can search repositories for resources to help achieve specific learning outcomes or for personal interest. The ability to search and select from large stores of digital learning materials facilitates lifelong learning for those with access to learning object repositories. As well, students' use of learning objects increases achievement and promotes success (Bradley & Boyle, 2004), and may facilitate other educational endeavors such as special education and home schooling. Learning object repositories can be accessed from anywhere and at any time using emerging technologies such as tablets and mobile devices which allow for on-the-job and *in situ* learning applications. The relatively small size and short instructional time associated with learning objects makes them suitable for delivery on mobile devices, especially when learners are on the move and/or want to learn while away from their home or office.

Similar, and possibly even greater, benefits exist for business, industry, and the military sector. Learning objects can be used to train staff and support professional development, providing businesses and other organizations with resources to foster a more skilled and educated workforce. Learning objects delivered on mobile devices can easily serve as resources for just-in-time training or updating product knowledge. Concomitant economic benefits, such as greater marketability and increased competitiveness may result from the use of learning objects for staff training and development. The potential of learning objects for the military sector has prompted extensive research and development efforts such as that associated with the SCORM initiative (Shareable Courseware Object Reference Model), which involved the development of a "collection of standards and specifications adapted from multiple sources to provide a comprehensive suite of e-learning capabilities that enable interoperability, accessibility and reusability of Web-based learning content" (Advanced Distributed Learning, 2004).

BARRIERS AFFECTING THE USE OF LEARNING OBJECTS

In order to realize the benefits of learning objects, barriers associated with their development and use need to be overcome. Metros (2005) identified several reasons why learning objects failed to fulfill their original promise: (a) ambiguous definition of what constitutes a learning object; (b) requirement of special expertise and release time for instructors; (c) instructors' discomfort with sharing and reusing course materials; (d) lack of indexing standards, and (e) limited proof that learning objects benefit education.

Moisey, Ally, and Spencer (2006) investigated the barriers and facilitating factors associated with the development and use of learning objects in a graduate-level course on instructional design. They identified similar barriers to those found by Metros (2005) and added several others including the following: difficult-to-navigate repositories; lack of learning objects in some disciplines; poor quality learning objects; inappropriate granularity; lack of a common system and skills for creating metadata; copyright and intellectual property concerns; and attitudinal barriers, particularly lack of confidence in the scholarly and instructional adequacy of the created learning materials and an unwillingness to share them.

Similar findings were reported by Collis and Strijker (2003) based on a survey and interviews with instructors. They found that copyright and intellectual property concerns were a major reason why instructors were hesitant to develop and use learning objects, as was the concern that using others' materials might reflect a lack of expertise on the part of the instructor. Release time, recognition, financial remuneration, specialized authoring software, and technical support were also identified as ways to promote the use and development of learning objects.

ISSUES ASSOCIATED WITH THE USE OF LEARNING OBJECTS

Several issues, including granularity, contextualization, interoperability, and lack of organizational support, affect the development and use of learning objects. As the discussion below shows, the situation is complex and involves many interrelated factors.

Granularity

When a course or a lesson is broken down to create a set of standalone, independent learning objects, how large should these segments be? When creating a learning object to provide students with specific skills or knowledge, how long should it take them to complete the learning activity and achieve the intended outcomes? These questions raise the important issue of granularity.

In terms of the granularity of learning objects, the literature suggests an inverse relationship between size and reusability (Littlejohn, 2003; Sicilia & Garcia, 2003; Wiley et al., 2004). The finer the granularity, the greater the potential to reuse the learning object in different situations; on the other hand, smaller learning objects tend to have less educational value and result in reduced and/or lower-level learning. The granularity of the learning objects contained in a repository can vary greatly, ranging from resources as small as a single diagram or picture to as large as an entire course. While the smaller granular resource is easily reused, it elicits comparatively less learning. In comparison, the larger granulated resource is more difficult to reuse, but results in greater and likely higher-level learning.

The metric for granularity varies, including instructional time, amount of learning achieved, and amount of content covered. Practically speaking, learning objects should be neither so large that they require an inordinate amount of learner completion time, nor so small that they lack meaning or a sense of connectedness. Attempts have been made to specify what constitutes the optimal granularity of a learning object. For example, Polsani (2003) recommends that granularity be limited to a single concept or a small number of related concepts; Hamel and Ryan-Jones (2002) advise limiting the granularity of a learning object to a single educational objective; Wiley (2009) suggests that learning object developers aim for the "sweet spot" by designing objects that "work effectively with our target population without sacrificing too much for the sake of hypothetical future users" (p. 355). The specifications of the University of Wisconsin learning object repository (http://www.wisc-online.com) include granularity as a special condition (McGreal, 2004), indicating that a learning object should take students approximately 15 minutes to complete; however, designations of granularity based on time have been criticized as being subjective and arbitrary (Polsani, 2003).

At present, it would appear that granularity is idiosyncratic, and that the requirements of the situation and preference of the author are the primary determinants of a learning object's size.

Contextualization

A major criticism of learning objects is that they decontextualize learning. To promote reusability, situational information is removed to make the learning object as generic and non-specific as possible. Wiley et al. (2004) discuss the decontextualization of learning objects, noting the inverse relationship between the internal context (and hence size) of a learning object and its reusability. In other words, a more generic learning object will fit into more instructional contexts, whereas a more specific one will fit fewer instructional contexts. However, as Robson (2004) points out, information depends on context to maximize its meaning. He contends that "the greater the contextual match between a LO and the learner, the more effective it is likely to be" (p. 161), and recommends that context be preserved, citing the high cost of (re)contextualization.

In addition to revising or expanding upon a decontextualized learning object, another way of introducing context is to develop additional learning objects so learners can scaffold what they have learned to their own particular situations. In this way, generic learning objects are developed for maximum reuse, accompanied by additional learning objects to address the contexts in which the learning may be applied.

Interoperability

Interoperability is another important consideration affecting the development and use of learning objects. Learning objects should be designed for use with various learning management systems (LMSs) as well as for delivery on different platforms as students are likely to use a variety of technologies (e.g., desktop and laptop computers, tablets, mobile devices) to access learning materials. Intelligent agents can be built into the delivery system to detect the device being used and to format the learning object accordingly (Ally & Lin, 2005).

In particular, learning objects should be developed for delivery on mobile devices as significant numbers of users are accessing the Internet in this way (Johnson et al., 2011). Research has shown that learners are motivated to learn using mobile devices in order to improve their ability to function on the job (Ally, 2009; Ally, Woodburn, Tin, & Elliott, 2010; Kukulska-Hulme, 2010).

The use of mobile devices to access learning objects is convenient and allows learners to situate their learning in the location where it is most effective or relevant, e.g., in the workplace for immediate application. Mobile access to learning objects facilitates just-in-time learning, on-the-job application, and learning in context (Muyinda, Lubega, & Lynch, 2010). Moreover, as many learners already have mobile devices, especially those living in developing countries, there is potential for a significant number of learners to access learning object repositories (Wishart, 2009; Johnson et al., 2011).

Organizational Support

A lack of organizational support is yet another barrier affecting the development and use of learning objects. Few educational institutions are engaged in the wide-scale development and implementation of learning objects due to challenges such as the following:

- development of learning objects to be delivered on different media and technology;
- management of learning objects;
- version control of learning objects;
- updating of learning objects;
- conversion of existing learning materials into learning objects.

For a variety of reasons, faculty members are often reluctant to develop and use learning objects. Intellectual property concerns, attitudinal barriers, lack of time and expertise, unmet needs for technical support, and proper development tools—these are but a few of the reasons why faculty have not embraced learning objects as a means of developing and delivering instruction. To promote the acceptance and use of learning objects, Hart and Albrecht (2004) recommend that organizations consider the following key questions: What are the points of resistance in the use of learning objects? What support is available for the development and use of learning objects? Are the right tools to develop and access learning objects available to staff? How will learning objects from repositories integrate with existing courses? Above all, they emphasize that instructors' attitudes may need to change and that support is required to facilitate the development and use of learning objects.

DEVELOPMENT AND USE OF LEARNING OBJECTS

As with the development of any learning materials, proper instructional design techniques and adherence to learning theories is necessary to ensure that learning objects are high quality, learner-centered, and tied to specified learning outcomes (Ally, 2004; Sosteric & Hesemeier, 2002; Wiley, 2000). They should add value to the learning experience so that learners and instructors alike will choose to use learning objects and be satisfied with their experience. Therefore, the development of learning objects should keep learners and instructors in the forefront throughout the development process (Richards, 2002).

Debate exists over the need for an underlying learning theory or instructional strategy in the design of a learning object. Some theorists (e.g., Ally, 2004; Wiley, 2002) emphasize the importance of developing learning objects from a learning theory base; whereas others contend that learning objects should be "pedagogically neutral" to allow instructors to fit them into a learning strategy of their choice.

Baruque and Melo (2004) propose an eclectic learning theory approach for designing electronic learning materials. Integrating the behaviorist, cognitivist, and constructivist schools of learning, they recommend an iterative process for developing modules using learning objects, in a manner similar to the standard ADDIE instructional design model (e.g., Dick, Carey, & Carey, 2001). In the first phase, analysis, specific learning problems are determined, learner characteristics identified, and existing learning objects sought. In the next phase, design, content is determined, task and content analyses are conducted, and the learning object interface is developed. In the third phase, development, learning objects are created and stored in repositories. This is followed by the implementation phase where the instruction is delivered to learners, and the final phase, evaluation, where formative and summative evaluations are conducted.

Attention to instructional design is important when developing learning objects to ensure their effectiveness and reusability. Learning objects should be interactive, revisable, and adaptive in order to allow for learner differences such as learning style, background, interest, and competency level (Ally, 2004; Lee & Su, 2006). They should be able to be used in different instructional settings and serve a variety of purposes including achieving learning outcomes, remediation, just-in-time learning, as a job aid, or for enrichment. They should be designed for and tested with multiple users before placed in a repository.

Ally (2004) focuses on the "learning" in learning objects, emphasizing that students should experience a change in behavior, knowledge, or attitude as a result of interacting with the learning object. To assure learning, he recommends that a learning object have at least three components, as described below.

1. a pre-learning strategy such as a learning outcome, pre-assessment, advance organizer, or overview to prepare the learner for the learning situation.
2. a presentation strategy, which includes the content, materials, and activities to achieve the outcome for the learning object. Content may include facts, concepts, principles, and procedures in the form of text, audio, graphic, pictures, video, simulations, and animation. A combination of active and passive activities may be used.
3. a post-learning strategy in the form of a summary or a post-assessment to check for achievement of the learning outcome and provide a sense of completion.

Hamel and Ryan-Jones (2002) note that standards do not provide specific guidance for designers on how to plan for or create learning objects. Reviewing the literature on learning object development, they provide a set of five principles to serve as guidelines for authors:

1. Learning objects must be units of instruction that stand alone;
2. Learning objects should follow a standard instructional format;
3. Learning objects should be relatively small;
4. A sequence of learning objects must have a context;
5. Learning objects must be tagged and managed.

Similar to the principles presented above, Longmire (2000) provides the following practical suggestions to guide the development of learning objects:

- use consistent language and terminology;
- present information in easily accessible and comprehensible formats;
- present information for on-screen viewing;
- avoid sequential information across objects (i.e., no backward-forward referencing across objects);
- use a uniform editorial tone across objects;
- include keywords in searchable elements;
- ensure that language and content is appropriate for a broad audience.

Expanding upon the technical writing considerations for learning objects, Bartz (2002) provides practical guidelines for developing the content of learning objects, noting also that learning objects should be independent and not make reference to other learning objects.

Jones (2004) discusses ways of promoting reusability and notes that a learning object should have the following properties to ensure maximum reuse: (a) it should be cohesive, focusing on one topic only; (b) it should be decoupled, having no dependencies on other learning objects; (c) it should be context-free. To ensure optimum reusability, the readability level and language of the learning object should be appropriate for different audiences; information presentations and learning activities suitable for students with different learning styles.

Unfortunately, the advantages associated with reusability are yet to be realized as most learning objects are not reused. In an analysis of a learning object repository, Duncan (2009) found that less than 25% of the modules in the repository analyzed had been reused. Littlejohn, Falconer, and McGill (2008) acknowledge the problem and recommend that learning objects should be designed from the outset with reuse in mind. They note that a learning object's reusability is directly proportional to its durability, ability to engage learners, meaningful contextualization, and suitability to a range of educational models or learning designs. To maximize the reusability potential, learning objects should be designed with the following characteristics:

- easy to source;
- in easily accessible and interoperable formats;
- small granularity;
- easy to repurpose.
- free from legal restrictions (e.g., copyright).

Aggregating Learning Objects

Although learning objects are developed to be used as independent entities, they should also be linkable. Learning objects should be constructed so they can function independently, yet also able to be linked seamlessly to form a coherent module, lesson, or course. The aggregation should also be assembled so that a single learning object may be revised without affecting other objects (Wiley 2000). Some common ways for linking learning objects are described below.

- *Specific to General.* The specific learning objects are presented first, followed by more general learning objects. In some cases, a general learning object can be used as an overview for the lesson.
- *Simple to Complex.* Simple learning objects are completed to set the stage for more complex learning objects. From a learning theory perspective, learners need to attain basic knowledge and skills before they can apply these in real-life situations.
- *Known to Unknown.* Learners use what they already know to gain new skills and knowledge. From a learning theory viewpoint, learners access familiar learning objects to activate existing cognitive structures, making them better prepared to learn the new materials.
- *Spiral.* A learning object can be introduced initially with a low-level activity, and the same learning object presented at a later time with a higher-level activity. The spiral structure can be used to help contextualize learning, For example, a generic learning object presented early in the lesson may be followed by a practical application learning object with a higher-level learning activity that contextualizes the information.

Proposing an organic approach for learning object assembly, Paquette and Rosca (2002) describe several models of aggregation: fusion or juxtaposition; composition through referencing; control and filtering; scripting; and coordination. All but the last are directed toward the assembly of learning objects for a single user. The final model, coordination, describes an aggregation model involving multiple learners where communication and cooperation structures the collection of learning objects.

Learning styles or learner preferences may also play a role in the aggregation of learning objects. When assembling learning objects to create a larger entity (e.g., a lesson, module, or course), a variety of learning objects should be available to accommodate learners with different learning styles or preferences. For example, a "buffet" approach may be used where students self-select the objects they prefer from an array of choices, or a more prescriptive approach may be taken where suitable objects are presented via a learner management system (LMS) after determination of the student's learning style.

Multimedia learning objects offer additional pedagogical benefits due to the multi-sensory stimulation they provide, and can promote higher-level and more efficient learning; however, they also have particular development requirements that need to be addressed. Bradley, Haynes, Cook, Boyle, and Smith (2009) describe the process for developing multimedia learning objects for delivery on mobile devices. They comment upon the particular suitability of multimedia learning objects for the younger generation of students who play games online and access multimedia information on a daily basis using computers, tablets, and mobile devices.

Tools for Learning Object Development and Use

The development of technology and tools to assist the development and use of learning objects is ongoing. Schaffer and Douglas (2004) note that learning and content management systems are becoming increasingly object-oriented, making it easier to develop learning objects and build repositories for different types of learning objects. They foresee that the newer object-oriented systems will allow the integration of knowledge, performance, and learning, where learners and designers are able to access different learning objects as needed. Similarly, Lee and Su (2006) propose the use of object-oriented distributed and heterogeneous data and application systems, which store individual pieces of information that can be assembled into learning objects. Richards (2002) predicts that as the use of learning objects increases and the field matures, intelligent agents will be developed within the learning object system to match and adapt learning objects to meet individual learner needs during the learning process.

Students' Use of Learning Objects

While considerable research has been conducted on the technical attributes, characteristics, and standards for learning objects, comparatively less emphasis has been placed on pedagogical areas. Little investigation has been done into students' use of and experience with learning objects and the effect of learning objects on academic achievement.

Bradley and Boyle (2004) examined the use of learning objects in multiple sections of an undergraduate computer science course. They found that students used learning objects primarily for review and for studying before assessments and exams. Results showed that 12% to 23% more students using the learning objects received a passing grade on the course modules in comparison to those who did not use the learning objects. Ally, Cleveland-Innes, Larwill, and Boskic (2006) investigated learners' experience and satisfaction with learning objects. They concluded that students' selection of repositories and learning objects was based on personal learner needs and expectations for satisfying specific learning outcomes.

LEARNING OBJECT METADATA

Learning objects can only be used if they are able to be located and retrieved from the repositories in which they are housed. Hence, proper labeling or "tagging" is essential to create metadata—"data about data"—to allow instructors, instructional designers, and learners to locate the learning object(s) that best meet their particular needs (McGreal & Roberts, 2001).

Metadata includes domain-specific elements and qualifiers. It functions like an entry or card in a library catalogue, and includes searchable "access points" such as title, author, date, location, and subject (Friesen, Roberts, & Fisher, 2002). Metadata also contains information on areas such as object life cycle, copyright, technical requirements, and intended audience, among others.

Carey, Swallow, and Oldfield (2002) proposed the inclusion of instructional strategy information in metadata, suggesting the use of metadata tags such as the following to explicitly describe the instructional strategy inherent in the learning object: anchor new knowledge in authentic contexts (Anchor); apply theory in practice (Apply); employ multiple styles of learning (Styles); engage in expository or teaching activities (Teach); use trial and error to discover something new (Discover).

To supplement the descriptions in metadata records, Koper (2001) proposed the use of Educational Modeling Language (EML) to provide further detail of the content and processes contained in learning objects. A subset of EML was later integrated into the IMS Learning Design Specification, an occurrence that Paquette (2004) described as "the most important initiative to date to integrate instructional design into the standards movement" (p. 332).

To date, no consensus has been achieved with regard to the content of metadata and the form in which it should be represented. In the mid-1990s, several projects were geared toward the cataloguing of digital objects and the development of systems or "standards" for their identification. The first standard, Dublin Core, was so named as it resulted from a meeting in Dublin, Ohio, which established the Dublin Core Metadata Initiative (http://dublincore.org). Notable projects followed, including the Instructional Management Systems initiative (IMS, http://www.imsproject.org) in North America and the Alliance of Remote Instructional Authoring & Distribution Networks for Europe (ARIADNE, http://www.ariadne.unil.ch); both sought the development of a common system for cataloguing learning objects. In 1998 these consortia made a proposal to the IEEE, which resulted in the LOM standard, the only officially approved standard for learning object metadata to date (IEEE, 2002; Friesen et al., 2002). At about the same time, a Canadian initiative resulted in the CanCore metadata standard (http://www.cancore.ca) and the U.S. Department of Defense adopted the Sharable Courseware Object Reference Model (SCORM, http://www.adlnet.org/scorm/index.cfm) metadata standard.

Several standards for tagging learning objects have been proposed. Most conform to the LOM standard (IEEE, 2002); however, the standard proposed by the IMS Global Consortium (http://www.imsglobal.org) provides a larger, more comprehensive collection of specifications. One of the simplest standards is the CanCore profiling system, which consists of 8 main categories, 15 sub-categories, and 36 elements. CanCore is a subset of the IEEE LOM standard (which includes 76 data elements) and is considered easier to implement and more suitable for educators (Friesen et al., 2002).

Two major schools of thought exist regarding how metadata should be obtained.

Supporters of "internal referencing" believe that the creators of learning objects should also provide the metadata. Advocates of "external referencing" contend that metadata is a job for professionals and that only librarians or information specialists should create metadata (McGreal & Roberts, 2001).

Inter-rater reliability is another concern in the creation of metadata, i.e., the consistency with which different "meta-taggers" will assign the same value or label to an attribute of a learning object. Consistency is important for ensuring maximum reuse of learning objects and maintaining the quality of repositories. Kabel, De Hoog, Wielinga, and Anjewierden (2004) studied the reliability of using indexing vocabularies to annotate fragments of instruction. They found a 75% rate of similarity between the annotations of a group of 28 "inexperienced indexers" with those of an expert, with more agreement on tangible rather than abstract attributes.

The metadata record is in many ways as important as the learning object itself, and its development should be approached with the same diligence and skill. Hamel and Ryan-Jones (2002) recommend developing the metadata as the learning object is being developed. Sicilia and Garcia (2003) emphasize the importance of a complete metadata record to ensure the maximum reusability of a learning object—they argue that the more complete the metadata, the more likely it will be located in a search, and therefore, the greater its likelihood for reuse.

EVALUATING LEARNING OBJECTS

Quality assurance is another major concern identified in the learning object literature (e.g., Collis & Strijker, 2003; Kay & Knaack, 2007; Metros, 2005). Li, Nesbit, and Richards (2006) provide a review of different tools for evaluating learning objects, emphasizing that learning objects should be evaluated before being placed in repositories, and regularly evaluated thereafter to ensure their continued relevance and effectiveness.

A unique characteristic of the MERLOT learning object repository is its peer review system for evaluating the quality of the learning objects it contains. MERLOT contains 14 discipline-specific communities, each with an editorial board guiding peer review policies and practices. Each review is conducted by at least two higher education faculty members who compose a composite review that is posted to the MERLOT Web site. Learning objects are evaluated on three dimensions: quality of content; potential effectiveness as a teaching tool; and ease of use. Each dimension is evaluated separately. In addition to a written review, a one- to five-star rating (5 being highest) is given on each of the three dimensions. An object must average three stars to be posted to the MERLOT site (MERLOT, 2006).

One commonly used tool for evaluating the quality of learning objects is the Learning Object Review Instrument (LORI), which uses the following dimensions to evaluate the quality of learning objects: content quality, learning goal alignment, feedback and adaptation, motivation, presentation design, interaction usability, accessibility, reusability, and standards compliance (Nesbit, Belfer, & Leacock, 2003).

Nesbit, Belfer, and Vargo (2002) proposed a convergent participation model for evaluation of learning objects with eight goals: aid for searching and selecting, guidance for use, formative evaluation, influence on design practices, professional development and student learning, community building, social recognition, and economic exchange. Their evaluation process utilized a panel of members from different stakeholder groups who conduct the evaluation independently and then meet as a group, with a facilitator, to compare their assessments and make adjustments to obtain consensus.

CONCLUSION

Significant investment and growth in the development and use of learning objects has taken place since the mid-1990s, when the concept of learning objects was first introduced. The more recent proliferation of open education resources and increased access by mobile devices has further extended and enhanced the availability and accessibility to learning objects. New challenges have also emerged.

Intelligent, adaptive learning objects are required, with the ability to recognize the device used to present the learning object and contain the expertise of the teacher in order to personalize the learning experience and promote independent learning. More precise and comprehensive ways of describing learning objects are needed, as well as more effective strategies for identifying quality learning objects. Repositories need to be better coordinated and more accessible, with a common and reliable system for meta-tagging and describing learning resources. Finally, to realize the promise of learning objects, more research is needed, particularly in pedagogy-related areas, including the use of open education resources, the reuse and repurposing of learning objects, and the design of learning objects for delivery on mobile devices.

REFERENCES

Advanced Distributed Learning (ADL). (2004). Sharable Content Object Reference Model (SCORM) 2004. Retrieved from http://www.adlnet.org/scorm

Ally, M., Woodburn, T., Tin, T., & Elliott, C. (2010). Mobile access for workplace and language training. In M. Ally & G. Needham (Eds.), *M-Libraries: A virtual library in everyone's pocket* (pp. 117–124). London: Facet Publishing.

Ally, M. (2009). *Mobile Learning: Transforming the delivery of education and training.* Edmonton, Alberta, Canada: Athabasca University Press. Retrieved from http://www.aupress.ca/index.php/books/120155

Ally, M. (2004). Designing effective learning objects for distance education. In R. McGreal (Ed.), *Online education using learning objects* (pp. 87–97). London: RoutledgeFalmer.

Ally, M., Cleveland-Innes, C., Larwill, S., & Boskic, N. (2006). Learner use of learning objects. *Journal of Distance Education, 21*(2), 44–57.

Ally, M., Lin, F., McGreal, R., & Woo, B. (2005, October). An intelligent agent for adapting and delivering electronic course materials to mobile learners. In H. van der Merwe & T. Brown (Eds.), *Proceedings of m-Learn 2005.* Cape Town, South Africa.

Baruque, L. B., & Melo, R. N. (2004). Learning theory and instructional design using learning objects. *Journal of Educational Multimedia and Hypermedia, 1,* 343–361.

Bartz, J. (2002). Great idea, but how do I do it? A practical example of learning object creation using SGML/XML. *Canadian Journal of Learning and Technology, 28*(3), 73–89.

Bennett, K., & McGee, P. (2005). The transformative power of the learning object debate. *Open Learning, 20*(1), 15–30.

Bradley, C., Haynes, R., Cook, J., Boyle, T., & Smith, C. (2009). Design and Development of Multimedia Learning Objects for Mobile Phones. In M. Ally (Ed.), *Mobile learning: Transforming the delivery of education and training* (pp. 157–182). Edmonton, Alberta, Canada: AU Press.

Bradley, C., & Boyle, T. (2004). The design, development, and use of multimedia learning objects. *Journal of Educational Multimedia and Hypermedia, 13*(4), 371–390.

Carey, T., Swallow, J., & Oldfield, W. (2002). Educational rationale for learning objects. *Canadian Journal of Learning and Technology, 28*(3), 55–71.

Collis, B., & Strijker, A. (2003). Re-usable learning objects in context. *International Journal of E-learning, 2*(4), 5–17.

Dalsgaard, C. (2005). *New ways to think about and use learning objects.* Canadian Institute for Distance Education Research (CIDER) presentation, November 3, 2005. Retrieved from http://cider.athabascau.ca/CIDERSessions/sessionarchive

Dick, W., Carey, L., & Carey, J. (2001). *The systematic design of instruction* (5th ed.). New York: Addison-Wesley.

Duncan, S. M. (2009). *Patterns of learning object reuse in the Connexions repository.* Utah State University Graduate Theses and Dissertations, paper 423. Retrieved from http://digitalcommons.usu.edu/etd/423/

Friesen, N. (2004). Three objections to learning objects. In R. McGreal (Ed.), *Online education using learning objects* (pp. 59–70). London: RoutledgeFalmer.

Friesen, N., Roberts, A., & Fisher, S. (2002). CanCore: Metadata for learning objects. *Canadian Journal of Learning and Technology, 28*(3), 43–53.

Hamel, C., & Ryan-Jones, D. (2002). Designing instruction with learning objects. *International Journal of Educational Technology, 3*(1). Retrieved from http://www.ao.uiuc.edu/ijet/v3n1/hamel

Hart, J., & Albrecht, B. (2004). Instructional repositories and referatories. *Educause Research Bulletin, 5,* 1–12.

Hodgins, H. W. (2004). The future of learning objects. In J. R. Lohmann & M. L. Corradini (Eds.), *2002 ECI Conference on e-Technologies in Engineering Education: Learning Outcomes Providing Future Possibilities, Davos, Switzerland.* Retrieved from http://services.bepress.com/cgi/viewcontent.cgi?article=1012&context=eci/etechnologies

Institute of Electrical and Electronic Engineers. (IEEE). (2002). *The learning object metadata standard.* Retrieved from http://ieeeltsc.org/wg12LOM

Johnson, L., Smith, R., Willis, H., Levine, A., & Haywood, K. (2011). *The 2011 Horizon Report.* Austin, TX: The New Media Consortium.

Jones, R. (2004). Designing adaptable learning resources with learning object patterns. *Journal of Digital Information, 6*(1), Article No. 305. Retrieved from http://journals.tdl.org/jodi/article/viewArticle/60/62

Keller, J. (2008). First principles of motivation to learn and e³-learning, *Distance Education, 29*(2), 175–185

Kabel, S., De Hoog, R., Wielinga, B., & Anjewierden, A. (2004). Indexing learning objects: Vocabularies and empirical investigation of consistency. *Journal of Educational Multimedia and Hypermedia, 13*(4), 405–426.

Kay, R., & Knaack, L. (2007). Evaluating the learning in learning objects. *Open Learning, 22*(1), 5–28.

Koper, R. (2001). *Modelling units of study from a pedagogical perspective. The pedagogical meta-model behind EML.* Retrieved from http://eml.ou.nl/introduction/articles.htm

Koper, R., Pannekeet, K., Hendriks, M., & Hummel, H. (2004). Building communities for the exchange of learning objects: Theoretical foundations and requirements. *Journal of Research in Learning Technology, 1* (1), 21–35.

Koppi, T., Bogle, L., & Bogle, M. (2005). Learning objects, repositories, sharing and reliability. *Open Learning, 20*(1), 83–91.

Kukulska-Hulme, A. (2010). Learning cultures on the move: Where are we heading? *Educational Technology & Society, 13*(4), 4–14.

Lee, G., & Su, S. (2006). Learning object models and an e-learning service infrastructure. *Journal of Distance Education Technologies, 4*(1), 1–16.

Li, J., Nesbit, J., & Richards, G. (2006). Evaluating learning objects across boundaries: The semantics of localization. *Journal of Distance Education Technologies, 4*(1), 17–30.

Littlejohn, A. (2003). Issues in reusing online resources. *Journal of Interactive Media in Education, 1.* Retrieved from http://www.jime.open.ac.uk/2003/1

Littlejohn, A., Falconer, I., & Mcgill, L. (2008). Characterising effective elearning resources. *Computers and Education, 50,* 757–771.

Longmire, W. (2000, March). A primer on learning objects. *ASTD Learning Circuits.* Retrieved from http://www.learningcircuits.org/2000/mar2000/Longmire.htm

McGreal, R. (2004). Introduction. In R. McGreal (Ed.), *Online education using learning objects,* (pp. 1–16). London: RoutledgeFalmer.

McGreal, R. (2008). A typology of learning object repositories. *Handbook on information technologies for education and training,* 5–28. New York: Springer. Retrieved from http://www.springerlink.com/index/K801214426K36LJN.pdf

McGreal, R., & Roberts, T. (2001). A primer on metadata for learning objects: Fostering an interoperable environment. *E-Learning, 2*(10), 26–29. Retrieved from http://auspace.athabascau.ca:8080/dspace/handle/2149/231

MERLOT. (2006). *MERLOT peer review.* Retrieved from http://www.merlot.org

Metros, S. E. (2005). Learning Objects: A rose by any other name. *Educause Review, 40*(4), 12–13.

Moisey, S. D., Ally, M., & Spencer, B. (2006). Factors affecting the development and use of learning objects. *The American Journal of Distance Education, 20*(3), 143–161.

Moller, L., Prestera, G., Harvey, D., Downs-Keller, M., & McCausland, J. (2002). Creating an organic building environment within an asynchronous distributed learning context. *Quarterly Review of Distance Education, 3*(1), 47–58.

Muyinda, P. B., Lubega, J. T., & Lynch, K. (2010). Mobile Learning Objects Deployment and Utilization in Developing Countries [Special Issue]. *International Journal of Computing and ICT Research, 4*(1), 37–46.

Nesbit, J. C., Belfer, K., & Vargo, J. (2002). A convergent participation model for evaluation of learning objects. *Canadian Journal of Learning and Technology, 28*(3), 105–120.

Nesbit, J. C., Belfer, K., & Leacock, T. (2003). Learning object review instrument (LORI). *E-learning research and assessment network*. Special Issue http://www.eelera.net

Ochoa, X., & Duval, E. (2009). Quantitative analysis of learning object repositories. *IEEE Transactions on Learning Object Technologies, 2*(3), 226–238.

Oh, S. (2006). *The effects of reusable motivational objects in designing reusable learning object-based instruction* (Unpublished doctoral dissertation). Florida State University, Tallahassee.

Paquette, G. (2004). Educational modeling languages from an instructional engineering perspective. In R. McGreal (Ed.), *Online education using learning objects* (pp. 331–346). London: RoutledgeFalmer.

Paquette, G., & Rosca, I. (2002). Organic aggregation of knowledge objects in educational systems. *Canadian Journal of Learning and Technology, 28*(3), 11–26.

Polsani, P. (2003). Use and abuse of reusable learning objects. *Journal of Digital information, 3*(4). Retrieved from http://jodi.ecs.soton.ac.uk/Articles/v03/i04/Polsani

Richards, G. (2002). The challenges of the learning object paradigm. *Canadian Journal of Learning and Technology, 28*(3), 3–9.

Robson, R. (2004). Context and the role of standards in increasing the value of learning objects. In R. McGreal (Ed.), *Online education using learning objects* (pp. 159–167). London: RoutledgeFalmer.

Schaffer, S. P., & Douglas, I. (2004). Integrating knowledge performance and learning objects. *Quarterly Review of Distance Education, 5*(1), 11–19.

Sicilia, M., & García, E. (2003). On the concepts of usability and reusability of learning objects. *International Review of Research in Open and Distance Learning, 4*(2). Retrieved from http://www.irrodl.org/content/v4.2/sicilia-garcia.html

Sosteric, M., & Hesemeier, S. (2002). When is a learning object not an object?: A first step towards a theory of learning objects. *International Review of Research in Open and Distance Learning Journal, 3*(2). Retrieved from http://www.irrodl.org/content/v3.2/soc-hes.html

Wang, S. (2008). Ontology of learning objects repository for pedagogical knowledge sharing. *Interdisciplinary Journal of E-Learning and Learning Objects, 4*, 1–12.

Whitten, J., Bentley, D., & Dittman, K. (2001). *Systems analysis and design methods*. Burr Ridge, IL: Irwin/McGraw-Hill.

Wiley, D. (2000). *Learning object design and sequencing theory.* (Unpublished doctoral dissertation). Brigham Young University, Provo, Utah.

Wiley, D. (2002). Connecting learning objects to instructional design theory: A definition, a metaphor, and a taxonomy. In D. A. Wiley (Ed.), *The instructional use of learning objects* (pp. 1–35). Bloomington, IN: Agency for Instructional Technology.

Wiley, D. A. (2009). Learning objects and instructional theory. In C. M. Reigeluth & A. A. Carr-Chellman (Eds.), *Instructional-design theories and models: Building a common knowledge base* (pp. 351–262). New York: Routledge.

Wiley, D., & Edwards, E. (2002). Online self-organizing social systems: The decentralized future of online learning. *Quarterly Review of Distance Education, 3*(1), 33–46.

Wiley, D., & Hilton III, J, (2009). Openness, dynamic specialization, and the disaggregated future of higher education. *International Review of Research in Open and Distance Learning, 10*(3). Retrieved from http://www.irrodl.org/index.php/irrodl/article/view/768/1414

Wiley, D., Waters, S., Dawson, D., Lambert, B., Barclay, M., Wade, D., & Nelson, L. (2004). Overcoming the limitations of learning objects. *Journal of Educational Multimedia and Hypermedia, 13*(4), 507–522.

Williams, R. (2004). Context, content and commodities: e-Learning objects. *Electronic Journal of e-Learning, 2*(2), 305–312.

Wishart, C. (2009). The future of mobile learning: The paradigm pioneers of pedagogy. In R. Guy (Ed.), *The evolution of mobile teaching and learning* (pp. 271–289). Santa Rosa, CA: Informing Science Press.

21

EMERGING PRACTICE AND RESEARCH IN BLENDED LEARNING

CHARLES R. GRAHAM

BACKGROUND AND DEFINITION OF BLENDED LEARNING

Discussion of blending learning (BL) is appearing with increased frequency in both the scholarly literature and the popular press. A 2011 literature search by the author found close to 200 dissertations and hundreds of journal articles on the topic (Halverson, Graham, Spring, & Drysdale, 2012). It has also been identified by the American Society for Training and Development as a top trend in the knowledge delivery industry (Rooney, 2003). Historically, blended learning was predominantly found in corporate and higher education contexts, but its use is now increasingly found in K–12 education (Picciano, Seaman, Shea, & Shaw 2012; Staker et al., 2011). Its use in higher education has grown rapidly and is predicted to become the "new traditional model" (Ross & Gage, 2006, p. 167) or the "new normal" in course delivery (Norberg, Dziuban, & Moskal, 2011, p. 207). A 2008 report sponsored by the North American Council for Online Learning (NACOL) stated, "Blended learning is likely to emerge as the predominant model of the future" (Watson, 2008, p. 3).

Despite current popularity of the term blended learning, it is defined with considerable variation across institutional contexts. While researchers have expressed frustration over the unclear definitional contours of this new BL ecosystem (see Oliver & Trigwell, 2005; Picciano, 2009; Teng, Bonk, & Kim, 2009), the fact is that the landscape of BL is still evolving rapidly. Much of the current research has focused on attempting to describe and chart its boundaries. This section will highlight four central issues related to definitions of BL.

1. What is being blended?
2. Should reduced seat time be part of the definition?
3. Should the quantity of online instruction be part of the definition?
4. Should quality factors be part of the definition?

1.1 What is Being Blended?

The primary issue in defining BL is the question of what is being blended? Graham (2006) identified the literature's three most common answers to the question as:

(1) blending online and face-to-face instruction, (2) blending instructional modalities (or delivery media), and (3) blending instructional methods; Oliver and Trigwell (2005) identified six different "mixes" that could be involved; Sharpe, Benfield, Roberts, and Francis (2006, p. 18) identified "eight dimensions of blending." The most common use of the term "BL" denotes a combination of traditional face-to-face and online instruction. Other proposed definitions do not distinguish BL course experiences from either distance learning or traditional face-to-face instruction. For example, mixing content delivery media or pedagogies is common across both distance and face-to-face learning.

1.2 Is Less Seat Time Required?

A second issue focuses on how institutions operationalize the distinction between traditional face-to-face courses and BL courses. At the core of this issue is the point at which a face-to-face course becomes a BL course? Do significant online components constitute BL if students meet for the same amount of time in class? As traditional learning environments increase use of information and communication technologies (ICTs), critical distinctions between face-to-face and distance learning are difficult to base solely on technology use. Some researchers express concern that BL should go beyond merely "'bolting' technology onto a traditional course, using technology as an add-on to teach a difficult concept or adding supplemental information" (Vaughan, 2007, p. 82). Thus some definitions of BL include a reduction in face-to-face contact or seat time (Mayadas & Picciano, 2007; Picciano, 2009; Vaughan, 2007). For example, Picciano's (2009) definition requires that "a portion (institutionally defined) of face-to-face time [be] replaced by online activity" (p. 10).

1.3 How Much Online Learning Is Required?

A third issue commonly raised in defining BL is how much online learning is required to define the experience as BL? Does a face-to-face course with one brief online experience qualify? Conversely, should an online course with a face-to-face orientation be considered BL?

Several authors have acknowledged this issue by defining the boundary between BL and other modalities as a proportion of content delivered online. For example, Allen and Seaman (2007) categorized traditional as having 0% of content delivered online, Web facilitated as 1%–29% online, blended as 30%–79% online, and online as 80% or more. Similarly, Watson, Murin, Vashaw, Gemin, and Rapp (2010) set a threshold of 30% online delivery of content for an environment to be considered blended. A challenge with percentage thresholds is the difficulty in measuring something that is not easily or accurately quantifiable. Additionally, even if a percentage could be accurately determined, what practical difference would exist between courses with 29% versus 30% of content delivered online?

1.4 Should Quality Be Included in the Definition?

A fourth issue prominent in definitions of BL is whether or not quality should be included in the definition. The inclusion of quality in the definition is primarily supported by those who desire to use BL as a tool for transformational change. For example, Garrison and Kanuka (2004) defined BL as "the *thoughtful integration* of classroom face-to-face learning experiences with online learning experiences" (p. 96, emphasis added). Similarly, in 2005 participants in the Sloan-C Blended workshop included in their definition "courses that integrate online with traditional face-to-face class activities in a planned, pedagogically valuable manner" (Picciano, 2005, p. 97, emphasis added). These subjective qualifiers to BL definitions are well intentioned but more aspirational than practical. They stem from a fear that the transformational potential of BL course redesign could be compromised by those not concerned with improving pedagogical quality (Graham & Robison, 2007; Vaughan, 2007)—a fear that is not unfounded. Salomon (2002) warned of education systems' tendency to preserve themselves and their practices: "A most powerful and innovative technology is taken and is domesticated, or if you want—trivialized, such that it does more or less what its predecessors have done, only it does it a bit faster and a bit nicer." (p. 72).

1.5 Can a Vague Definition Actually be Useful?

It may be helpful to think of the term blended learning as a boundary object (Norberg et al., 2011): an element shared across communities of practice, "plastic enough to adapt to local needs and constraints of the several parties employing them, yet robust enough to maintain a common identity across sites.… weakly structured in common use … strongly structured in individual site-use" (Star & Griesemer, 1989, p. 393).

Agreement seems widespread that BL involves a combination of face-to-face and online learning. Beyond that, individual researchers and institutions differ in how they further limit definition boundaries. Some require a reduction in face-to-face seat time, while others may specify levels of online or face-to-face instruction for BL. In a review of the BL literature and implementation practices in the United Kingdom, researchers recognized benefits to a broadly structured definition of BL:

> We noted from the interviews that some institutions have developed their own language, definitions or typologies to describe their blended practices. We suggest that this poor definition [of blended learning] may be a strength and part of the reason why the term is being accepted. The lack of definition allows institutions to adapt and use the term as they see fit, and to develop ownership of it. (Sharpe et al., 2006, p. 17)

In this chapter, BL will simply be defined as learning experiences that combine face-to-face and online instruction.

Models of Blended Learning in Practice

Current emphasis has focused on distinguishing BL from traditional and online coursework. However, future learning systems may be differentiated less on whether they blend than on how they blend (Ross & Gage, 2006). A time may come when the term blended learning becomes obsolete because blending has become the new normal (Cross, 2006; Graham, 2006; Norberg et al., 2011). However, currently a label is helpful to refer to these structurally different environments.

The contemporary BL ecosystem is rich with innovation and creativity. The diversity of blends reflects the range of possibilities for transforming students' learning experience. With time, taxonomies and widely accepted models will provide additional stability for researchers and practitioners. This section of the chapter highlights several prominent examples of emerging BL models. Current models tend to focus on physical dimensions of the learning environments and very general high-level pedagogical approaches.

2.1 K-12 Education Models

BL has been steadily increasing in K-12 contexts (Picciano et al., 2012), partially as an alternative to purely online models and in response to community expectations and funding models that require schools to physically supervise children during the day (Wicks, 2010). Only recently have efforts been made to systematically characterize the K-12 blends as different from prior traditional and distance learning options. Watson (2008) analyzed 10 charter/virtual schools along a spectrum containing seven levels from fully online to traditional face-to-face, varying in the amount of face-to-face versus online instruction as well as optional or required components of both systems. Two years later, Watson participated in expanding the model to include seven defining dimensions:

1. Level of online instruction (unit/lesson, single course, entire curriculum);
2. Time (fixed daily schedule, modified schedule, open entry/open exit);
3. Role of online components (enhance traditional instruction, transform traditional instruction);
4. Teacher role (leads instruction, supports instruction, not involved);
5. Student role (teacher-driven learning, teacher-guided learning, independent learning);
6. Student support (little or none, school-based mentoring, school and home mentoring);
7. Student to teacher ratio (traditional classroom ratio, 2-3 times traditional classroom ratio, instructional helpdesk model).

In 2011, the Innosite Institute released a research report documenting 40 case studies of BL in K-12 contexts across the United States (Staker et al., 2011). The report classified BL models along two dimensions in a 2D graph: the horizontal dimension representing the physical location of the student (brick and mortar to remote) and the vertical dimension representing the location of the course content (offline to online). Within this framework six models were identified (see Table 21.1), and each of the 40 programs was classified as one of the models.

2.2 Higher Education Models

Many institutions of higher education have developed an institution-specific BL categorization. Typically, these models vary along the dimension of how much of a course is taught face-to-face versus mediated by technology (see Table 21.2 for three examples). Picciano (2009) created a two-dimensional representation of blended models with a face-to-face versus online dimension on the horizontal axis and a minimal to infused technology dimension on the vertical axis.

Some of the earliest models of higher education BL resulted from a study of 30 course redesign projects funded by the National Center for Academic Transformation and the PEW Charitable Trusts (Twigg, 2003). The three-year grant program involving universities from across the United States was designed to enhance quality and save funding through redesigning large enrollment courses. Of the 30 course redesigns, 26 used BL approaches to achieve cost savings and quality gains, while 4 adopted a purely online approach (Graham & Allen, 2009). Table 21.3 outlines the five different models that emerged from the PEW redesign projects.

Table 21.1 K-12 Blended Learning Models Identified by Staker, Chan, Clayton, et al. (2011, pp. 7–8)

Model	Description
Face-to-Face Driver	• Face-to-face (F2F) teachers deliver most of the curricula • F2F teacher deploys online learning case by case to supplement or remediate
Rotation	• Students rotate between an online self-paced environment and a traditional teacher-led classroom • the online portion can be remote or on-site at the school • the F2F teacher usually oversees the online work
Flex	• Online platform delivers most of the curricula • F2F teachers provide on-site support as needed
Online Lab	• Online platform delivers the course in a brick-and-mortar lab environment • Students interact with an online instructor around course content • A paraprofessional supervises but provides little content expertise
Self-Blend	• Students choose to take online courses to supplement on-site curricula • Online learning is remote and traditional courses are F2F
Online Driver	• Online platform and remote teacher deliver all curricula • Students work remotely • F2F check-ins are sometimes optional and other times required • Some programs allow for participation in traditional extracurricular activities

Table 21.2 University Categories Defining the Range of Options between Face-to-Face and Online Learning

University of Glamorgan, Wales (Jones, 2006)	University of Waikato, New Zealand (Wright, et al., 2006)	University of Central Florida, USA (Dziuban et al., 2006)
Basic ICT usage – e.g.powerpoint presentations. **E-enhanced** – access to online resources. Use of Bb for announcements, lecture notes, student communication **E-focused** – discussion boards, online assessment tests, interactive learning materials **E-intensive** – whole modules/ awards delivered and moderated online	**Supported online** – courses are taught in the traditional lecture/ tutorial mode, supported by materials provided online **Somewhat online** – there is an online component for on-campus students **Mostly online** – there is a mix of online and some on-campus work in the qualification **Fully online** – students can complete qualifications without coming onto the campus	**E courses** are technology-enhanced courses (this designation has recently been eliminated because there were few if any courses that were not using technology in some way.) **M courses** are blended courses with reduced seat time **W courses** are web courses (completely online)

2.3 Corporate Models

Rossett and Frazee (2006) outlined three general models (see Table 21.4) describing common blends in the corporate environment. The anchor and bookend blend represents a mixture of three common environments: instructor-led classroom instruction, independent online learning, and instructor-guided online learning. The bookend and field blends also highlight a trend supported by BL that integrates learning directly into workplace activities.

Table 21.3 Higher Education Blended Learning Models Identified by Twigg (2003) and Summarized in Graham (2009, p. 378)

Model	Description
supplemental	• Supplemental online materials provided • Online quizzes • Additional online activities • Online activities can take place in a computer lab or at home
replacement	• Reduction of in-class meeting time • Replacement of face-to-face (F2F) classtime with online activities • Online activities can take place in a computer lab or at home.

emporium	• Eliminates class meetings
	• Substitutes a learning resource center with
	  • online materials
	  • on-demand personal assistance

buffet	Student chooses learning options • Lecture • Online • Discovery laboratories • Individual projects • Team/Group activities • And so forth
fully online	• All online learning activities • No required F2F class meetings • (In some cases) optional F2F help

Many corporate training models emphasize integration of informal and formal learning environments, embodied in a move from instructor-led classroom learning to real-time workplace learning supported by online learning tools. Collis (2006) outlined a multi-national company's model that centers each course around a business need or competence gap and focuses on completing a complex work-based activity with face-to-face support from supervisors and online connection to remote experts and peers. Lewis and Orton (2006) described a three-phased BL model at IBM:

Phase 1: 26 weeks of self-paced online learning in the workplace environment
Phase 2: 5 days of face-to-face in-class instruction in the company learning lab
Phase 3: 25 weeks of online learning focused on applying skills in the workplace

Blended Learning Research

Research related to BL is relatively undeveloped compared to research in distance and traditional learning environments. In fact, much of the early work in BL has occurred as an outgrowth of distance learning research. As developed in Section 1, the issues and foci of BL research and ways they complement and are distinct from traditional distance learning research are still being defined. This section of the chapter first explores theoretical frameworks that researchers are using to guide research in BL contexts. Then the Sloan Consortium's five pillars (learning effectiveness, learner satisfaction, faculty satisfaction, access, and cost effectiveness) are used as an organizing framework for reviewing the current BL research.

Table 21.4   Corporate Blended Learning Models Identified by Rosset & Frazee (2006, pp. 10–12)

Model	Description
anchor blend	• Starts with a substantive face-to-face (F2F) classroom experience • Followed by independent online experiences
bookend blend	• An introductory experience online or F2F • A substantive learning experience online or F2F • A conclusion that extends the learning into practice at work
field blend	• The employee is given a range of instructional assets • The employee chooses when and where to use the assets as needed to meet work-related challenges • Many instructional assets are available online • A classroom experience can be part of the mix

3.1 Theory

Theory provides a common language and focus for creating and discussing knowledge in scholarly communities (Dubin, 1978). Behavioral and social science groups have explored extensively what constitutes theory and what role theory plays in the knowledge creation process. Burkhardt and Schoenfeld (2003) noted that "a lack of attention to coherent theory building leaves us looking balkanized and incoherent, the whole … being less than the sum of its parts" (p. 13).

As BL research increases, theoretical frameworks should be developed to address the issues unique to BL environments. Shea (2007) suggested several existing conceptual frameworks that could be used, including the how people learn (HPL) framework that focuses on the development of learner-centered, knowledge-centered, assessment-centered, and community-centered learning environments (Bransford, Brown, & Cocking, 1999). Bunderson (2003) recommended (among other possibilities) the theory of engaged collaborative discourse (Xin, 2002) as a lens for analyzing BL environments. A few researchers have attempted to connect or extend distance education theories to address BL issues. The most comprehensive of these is the work of Garrison and Vaughan (2008) using the community of inquiry (COI) framework with constructs of social, teaching, and cognitive presence to situate and analyze the design of university-level BL (Akyol, Garrison, & Ozden, 2009; Borup, Graham, & Velasquez, 2011; Borup, West, & Graham, 2012). Other researchers have used the theory of transactional distance with concepts of autonomy, dialog, and structure to explain findings in BL contexts (Dron, Seidel, & Litten, 2004; Lim, Fadzil, & Mansor, 2011; Wheeler, 2007).

Other prominent theories applied to the design of BL environments include Keller's (1983) theory of motivation, Giddens' (1984) structuration theory and Laurillard's (1993) conversation theory (see Heinze, Procter, & Scott, 2007; Keller, 2008; Stubbs, Martin, & Endlar, 2006). Structuration theory, which explains the relationship between social structure and individual agency, has been used heavily in information systems research. Conversation theory outlines a multi-stage process describing the communication between instructor and student. Finally, several researchers interested in the adoption of BL as an educational innovation have used Rogers' (1983) diffusion of innovations theory to frame their analyses (Fetters & Duby, 2011; Grgurovic, 2010; Intharaksa, 2009), explaining both the stages of adoption and the factors that affect the rate of adoption of innovations.

While some of the research in BL is solidly grounded in theory, most of the existing research has sought to describe or solve localized challenges without contributing to coherent development of theory. Many studies consider theory only as background information or as a lens to describe findings or outcomes; few attempt to contribute substantively to the conversation about theory. Just as distance learning required theory to focus researchers on psychological rather than physical distance, BL needs theories to focus researchers on the substantive psycho-social issues that make it distinct.

3.2 Learning Effectiveness

The first important question addressed by the BL research relates its effectiveness as an environment for helping students learn. A challenge inherent in this question deals with which characteristics of learning environments have potential to directly impact learning. Media studies resulting in "no significant difference" have taught researchers that while the physical characteristics (affordances) of the environment enable and constrain particular pedagogical methods, the active ingredient in learning is the pedagogy rather than the medium (Clark, 1983). Although the physical characteristics of the learning environments (e.g., online or face-to-face) are not causal factors, they may represent classes of pedagogies distinct enough to enable differences to be measured in meta-analyses where researchers have not yet identified the actual causal factors.

At least five recent meta-analyses have looked specifically at BL as a moderating variable (Bernard et al., 2009; Means, Toyama, Murphy, Bakia, & Jones, 2009; Paul, 2001; Sitzmann, Kraiger, Stewart, & Wisher, 2006; Zhao, Lei, Yan, Lai, & Tan, 2005). A dissertation by Paul (2001) compared the effectiveness of Web-based training (WBT) environments (80 studies) with blended environments combining face-to-face and WBT (15 studies). The study reported a minimal difference in favor of blended over purely online courses, with the mean effect size of the blended condition at +0.27 and the WBT condition at +0.23. In 2005 Zhao et al. conducted a meta-analysis considering a dozen moderating factors, which found that of all the factors, instructor involvement (76 studies) had the most significant impact. They concluded that largely because of instructor involvement "studies that used a combination of technology and face-to-face education resulted in the most positive outcomes" (p. 1863). A meta-analysis in 2006 by Sitzmann et al. compared the effectiveness of Web-based instruction (WBI) and BL with classroom instruction (CI). Results were analyzed separately for outcomes in declarative (104 studies) and procedural knowledge (18 studies); BL was determined to be more effective than CI, with effect sizes of +0.34 for declarative knowledge and +0.52 for procedural knowledge outcomes. The effects of BL on the outcomes were much larger than the effect sizes for pure WBI compared with CI, which were +0.07 for declarative knowledge and -0.15 for procedural knowledge. Additionally, Bernard et al. (2009) conducted a meta-analysis of distance education (DE) courses that compared synchronous DE (5 studies), asynchronous DE (37 studies), and mixed DE (i.e., blended; 7 studies). This study found no significant difference among the three DE modalities, but concluded that the low number of studies available in the non-asynchronous DE categories suggested a need for further research attention.

Most recently, in 2009 the U.S. Department of Education sponsored a meta-analysis looking at contrasts between online and traditional face-to-face learning (Means et al., 2009). The analysis used 50 different contrasts from 45 published studies comparing online and face-to-face instruction. In 21 of the 50 cases, online learners had opportunities for face-to-face contact with an instructor and were therefore considered BL. The primary findings of the study claimed that "classes with online learning (whether taught completely online or blended) on average produced stronger student learning outcomes than did classes with solely face-to-face instruction. The mean effect size for all 50 contrasts was +0.20, p < .001." (p. 18). When the data were disaggregated to compare the effects from the purely online contrasts (29 cases) with the BL contrasts (21 cases), researchers found BL to be superior, with a mean effect size of +0.35 compared to a mean effect size of +0.05 for purely online. Within this framework six models were identified (see Table 21.1), and each of the 40 programs was classified as one of the models. Most recently the six models were further collapsed into four models (Staker & Horn, 2012).

These meta-analyses provided evidence of differences in outcomes of online, blended, and face-to-face learning that are worth studying. However, the causal factors that lead to the improved outcomes are not understood. The analysis of Zhao et al. (2005) suggested that instructor involvement may be a critical factor. The Means et al. (2009) outcomes similarly attributed the largest pedagogical effect to instructor-directed learning environments. However, these studies did not identify aspects of instructor involvement that are important: Is something qualitatively different about the kinds of instructor interactions in a face-to-face or synchronous high-fidelity environment versus interactions in an asynchronous text-based environment? Or is instructor involvement more critical for certain kinds of learning (declarative versus procedural)? The Means et al. study reported opportunity for face-to-face time with the instructor during instruction to be one of the significant moderating variables for online learning. Results from the attempt of the Bernard (2009) study to differentiate between learning declarative knowledge and procedural knowledge seemed to imply that human interaction does not have a significant moderating effect on acquiring declarative knowledge. Others have argued that improved outcomes may have more to do with increased learner time on task in the BL environment (Means et al., 2009; Sitzmann et al., 2006).

While the meta-analyses give a broad view of the impact of BL in experimental studies, many non-experimental studies have also looked at learning effectiveness in BL contexts. The Research Initiative for Teaching Effectiveness at the University of Central Florida (UCF), an early institutional adopter of BL, conducted a multi-year study involving tens of thousands of students examining success rates (defined as C– grade or above) of their online, blended, and face-to-face course offerings. The analysis accounted for college, gender, and modality. They found that while college was the best predictor of success rates, within each college the success rates for BL were higher than both face-to-face and entirely online courses for both genders (Dziuban, Hartman, Moskal, Sorg, & Truman, 2004). Another study looking at success rates of BL offerings at the Rochester Institute of Technology (with a high number of students with hearing impairment) reported 95% of students completing courses with a C– grade or above (Starenko, Vignare, & Humbert, 2007). Many smaller studies have also found positive learning outcomes for BL courses (Boyle, Bradley, Chalk, Jones, & Pickard, 2003; Cottrell & Robinson, 2003; Dowling, Godfrey, & Gyles, 2003; O'Toole & Absalom, 2003; Reasons, Valadares, & Slavkin, 2005; Riffell & Sibley, 2004). Larson and Sung (2009) went beyond academic performance and found that 52% of BL students had an increased interest in the subject matter, more than either the online or face-to-face students.

As mentioned at the beginning of this section, more research is needed to identify the quantity and quality factors of the blended designs that impact achievement and success rates. Shea and Bidjerano (2011) recently completed a study using the COI framework to analyze levels of teaching presence and social presence in blended and online learning environments and the relative impact of these constructs on cognitive presence. The BL students reported higher levels of all three components of the teaching presence construct (instructional design, facilitation of discourse, and direct instruction) and two of the three social presence components (affective communication and open communication with instructor and other students). Researchers have reasoned that this could explain why meta-analyses show students in blended courses outperforming students in purely online courses.

3.3 Learner Satisfaction

Research has also attempted to identify what leads to learner satisfaction in BL courses. Learner satisfaction is complicated, as it is influenced by the expectations, goals, and preferences of the learners as well as the course design and implementation. For example, a learner who expects no instructor interaction and experiences a moderate interaction level might be very satisfied, while a student expecting high interaction might be dissatisfied with the same moderate level.

Vignare (2007) suggested a need to identify and benchmark the elements that lead to satisfaction in BL environments. A couple of studies have attempted to do this. Dziuban, Moskal, and Hartman (2005) used factor analysis to identify two dimensions of satisfaction, which they identify as "learning engagement" and "interaction value." They later identified eight elements that contribute to learner satisfaction in online and blended courses (Moskal et al., 2010). Rothmund (2008) also found a correlation between learner interaction and satisfaction in blended courses. Akyol, Garrison, and Ozden (2009) found that students valued both social presence and teaching presence in their BL experiences.

Because student satisfaction is connected to learner dispositions as well as course design, some researchers have hypothesized that student satisfaction with BL will be moderated by the learner characteristics. For example, the course satisfaction of nontraditional adult learners may be significantly influenced by the convenience, flexibility, and reduced opportunity costs of BL (Moskal et al., 2010). Researchers at the University of Central Florida sought to understand how satisfaction might be influenced by generational markers (e.g., millennials, boomers, genXers) (Dziuban et al., 2005; Dziuban, Moskal, Brophy-Ellison, & Shea, 2007; Dziuban, Moskal, & Futch, 2007). They found significant differences, with millenials feeling the least favorable towards blended environments. Another study used Kolb's (1984) Learning Style Inventory to determine if students with different learning styles had different satisfaction profiles in a blended course (Akkoyunlu & Soylu, 2008). The researchers hypothesized that assimilators (oriented towards information & ideas) would be more satisfied by online components, while divergers (oriented towards people & feelings) would be drawn to the face-to-face components of the blend. The researchers found significant differences between the views of the two groups on all six measured elements of the blended environment. Assimilators scored the online and face-to-face environments as a close first and second place, while divergers placed the greatest value on the face-to-face environment and least value on the online environment. Graff (2003) also looked at learning styles within blended courses and found a significant difference in how learners experienced a sense of community based on learning style. Students with "intuitive" learning approaches (judgments based on feelings) experienced less sense of community than other students in the blended courses. Rovai and Jordan (2004) conducted a study looking at the sense of community developed in fully online, blended, and traditional face-to-face courses. The findings suggest that blended learning experiences build a stronger sense of community among students than either fully online or traditional courses.

Available evidence shows that many learners value both the richness of interactions in a face-to-face environment and the flexibility, convenience, and reduced opportunity costs associated with online learning. Perhaps this combination is why most research finds high levels of student satisfaction with BL options. However, researchers must be cautious because, as with learning effectiveness, it is the pedagogical possibilities (like interaction levels or learner choice) enabled by the modality that can lead to satisfaction. In fact, recent research looking at over a million course evaluations across different course formats showed that "modality does not impact the dimensionality by which students evaluate their course experiences" (Dziuban & Moskal, 2011, p. 236).

3.4 Faculty Satisfaction

The University of Central Florida found that 88% of instructors were satisfied with teaching blended courses and that 81% were "definitely" willing and 13% "probably" willing to teach another blended course (Dziuban et al., 2004). This compares to the 87% faculty satisfaction with teaching purely online courses, with only 67% "definitely" willing to teach purely online again (Dziuban et al., 2004). All faculty involved in a BL pilot program at the University of Wisconsin were happy with their first blended teaching experience and were willing to recommend the approach to others (Aycock, Garnham, & Kaleta, 2002). In contrast, a BL pilot project at the Rochester Institute of Technology found only 41% were willing to teach a blended course again (Vignare & Starenko, 2005).

Faculty satisfaction with course redesign efforts involving online learning was influenced by student-related factors (satisfaction, interaction levels, performance, etc.), instructor-related factors (recognition, reliable technology, collaboration opportunities, professional development, etc.), and institution-related factors (workload, compensation, promotion and tenure issues, etc.; Bolliger;& Wasilik, 2009). Student-related factors were of first concern because faculty are not likely to be satisfied if their students are not having a positive learning experience (Moskal, et al., 2010). Larson & Sung (2009) used student ratings of faculty competence as an indirect measure of faculty satisfaction in blended and online contexts; they reported student ratings of exceptional faculty competence for purely online, blended, and face-to-face modalities at 76%, 44%, and 37%, respectively. Many teachers thrive on the relationships that they build with their students, and those relationships motivate and renew them in their teaching. Certain forms of online learning that involve minimal interaction between teacher and student or in which the instructor feels reduced to being an assignment grader can be unsatisfying for faculty (Hawkins, Barbour, & Graham, 2011, 2012). BL can provide added satisfaction for faculty (particularly faculty used to traditional modes of teaching) because they are able to have some face-to-face relationship building with the students.

As with online learning, researchers recognize that workloads for faculty in BL contexts may increase, especially in the first few years of teaching (Colwell, 2006). Such an increase is partially due to the expectation of increased communication with the instructor via email and other ICT channels, as well as increased time required to learn new technologies and teaching strategies and time required to create and maintain online materials. Faculty who are not compelled to teach blended courses and receive proper preparation are more likely to be satisfied with the outcomes (Vignare, 2007). While sustained professional development may increase faculty workload, it may also facilitate faculty collaboration and teaching success that increase faculty satisfaction. Effective programs specifically created for supporting faculty in BL course redesign can be found at the University of Central Florida (Dziuban et al., 2004), the University of Wisconsin-Milwaukee (Aycock et al., 2002; Garnham & Kaleta, 2002), Rochester Institute of Technology (Starenko, Vignare, & Humbert, 2007; Vignare & Starenko, 2005), and the University of Calgary (Vaughan & Garrison, 2005, 2006).

3.5 Access & Flexibility

Access issues are driving much of the growth of BL around the world. However, little research has specifically investigated access and flexibility. A 2007 survey of 366 U.S. school districts, representing approximately 3,632 schools and 2 million students, identified five primary reasons for online and BL options:

1. Offering courses not otherwise available at the school
2. Meeting the needs of specific groups of students
3. Offering Advanced Placement or college-level courses
4. Reducing scheduling conflicts for students
5. Permitting students who failed a course to take it again (Picciano & Seaman, 2007, p. 9)

All of these reasons are related in some way to providing learners with access to educational opportunities that would be difficult or impossible to provide in the traditional way due to costs. In particular, the online and blended options can address small and rural school needs as well as diverse student needs like advanced placement and credit recovery courses. A BL initiative at Rochester Institute of Technology (RIT) targeted students who were deaf or hard of hearing, as well as English language learners (ELLs) (Long, Vignare, Rappold, & Mallory, 2007). Those subgroups had greater access to classroom participation as discussions were moved from the face-to-face context to asynchronous discussion forums. As a result, satisfaction levels for both subgroups were higher than for the normal student population.

In higher education the opportunity costs for participating in traditional learning options are too high for many potential students who have work, children at home, or other commitments that would make a rigid school schedule inaccessible. Flexible online options reduce the opportunity costs associated with time and place scheduling, but often come at the cost of losing access to a high-touch, relationship-oriented environment with instructors and peers. Data from an international study investigating the use of information and communication technologies in higher education found that change towards more flexible student options is happening at a slow pace (Collis & van der Wende, 2002). BL options provide students with opportunities for benefit/cost tradeoffs relevant to their own circumstances and preferences. Blended options can be of particular interest to institutions that reach out to non-traditional learners in the local communities where they are already well known and trusted; in the literature this idea, referred to as localness, has been an emphasis of Sloan Consortium grant funding (Mayadas & Picciano, 2007; Moloney et al., 2007; Sachs, 2007).

3.6 Cost Effectiveness

Cost effectiveness drives institutions towards adopting BL approaches in higher education (Betts, Hartman, & Oxholm, 2009). The University of Central Florida, for example, has been able to reduce costs with improved scheduling efficiencies and reduced need for physical infrastructure for BL courses (Dziuban et al., 2004, 2011). The National Center for Academic Transformation supported early research to examine whether universities could engage in large-scale course redesign that would simultaneously decrease cost and improve learning outcomes (http://www.thencat.org). They offered $6 million in grants to 30 institutions to engage in course redesign projects and follow detailed cost analysis procedures. Half of the 30 course redesigns involved BL with reduced classroom seat time, seven involved significant technological enhancements with no reduction in seat-time, and eight involved moving completely online with some optional face-to-face class sessions (Graham & Allen, 2009). Twigg (2003) reported collective cost savings across all the projects of $3.6 million each year, with institutional cost reductions ranging from 20% to 84% with an average savings of 40%. Additionally, the projects reported quality improvements such as higher course completion rates, student satisfaction, retention rates, and attitudes towards the subject matter.

Historically, corporations have been more effective at reporting figures related to cost effectiveness than institutions of higher education. However, Blain (2010) reported that only 3% of global companies and 26% of European companies measure return on investment (ROI). Bersin and Associates conducted a large-scale study to identify "what works" in corporate BL (Bersin, 2003), looking closely at BL training programs in 16 large corporations, with an emphasis on determining ROI. Almost all of the BL programs studied generated an ROI of 100% or better. Factors related to cost reduction for the blended programs included reduction in wait time for training, reduction in training hours and associated salary expenses, and reduction in facilities and other training costs. Institutions that have reported significant ROI due to BL training include Avaya (Chute, Williams, & Hancock, 2006), Microsoft (Ziob & Mosher, 2006), IBM (Lewis & Orton, 2006), and Intel (Mahesh & Woll, 2007).

Recommendations for Future Research

With increasing use of blended learning in higher education, corporate training, and K–12 learning contexts, more theoretically grounded research is needed to guide practice. The foundation for creating scholarly knowledge lies in theoretical development, including frameworks that can address any of the three important activities of knowledge creation: explore, explain, or design (Gibbons & Bunderson, 2005). Exploring is the process of identifying, describing, and categorizing, which must include documenting the wide range of different blended learning models and developing taxonomies that enable meaningful systemization of the models for analysis of both physical and pedagogical characteristics of the blends. In addition, theoretical frameworks must explain the how and why behind BL outcomes, which may include extending prominent distance learning theories to the BL context as well as developing new theories specifically created for understanding BL issues. Also, the development of design-based instructional theories will aid practitioners in tailoring BL to their specific needs.

Research shows some general patterns across the three learning modalities (face-to-face, online only, and blended) but still needs to uncover the root causes for improved learning outcomes in BL contexts. Productive areas for exploration include the impact of interaction quantity and quality on outcomes, the relationship between face-to-face and online presence in BL community building, and the correlation between time on task and BL outcomes. Garrison and Vaughan (2008) identified establishing and maintaining cognitive presence in blended communities as the top BL research need related to the COI framework. Other researchers have suggested exploring the relationship between learner characteristics and success with different blends (Dziuban et al., 2007). This will be particularly important as adolescent learners, who lack such adult learning characteristics as high self-regulation, are introduced to BL.

Although a number of studies point to student and faculty satisfaction with BL, more is needed to link the satisfaction data with specific BL design features. Such connections enable better understanding of how BL designs impact not only performance and satisfaction outcomes but also learners' dispositions towards the subject matter, which are likely to significantly impact learner persistence beyond the boundaries of a course.

With a large number of institutions considering how to do BL effectively, there is a need for research that focuses on institutional strategies for successful adoption and implementation of blended learning (Graham, Woodfield, & Harrison, 2013). While access and flexibility are among the most frequently cited purposes for adopting blended learning, very little research has sought to quantify the impact of BL on accessibility as well as on opportunity costs associated with increased flexibility. Similarly, empirical research related to the cost effectiveness of BL is limited, particularly in K–12 and higher education. Research related to both access and cost issues could help institutions, designers, and learners develop and select the models of BL best suited to their needs.

Finally, although BL is often described in terms of blending the physical attributes of online and face-to-face instruction, the psycho-social relationships are the issues at the core of blended learning research and design. Because education is a design-oriented field like engineering or architecture, it must be concerned with tradeoffs involving cost, efficiency, and effectiveness. The foundational challenge of BL research is seeking to understand (1) what humans do very well and (2) what machines do very well, so that the strengths of both can be maximized as they are blended in the service of learning.

REFERENCES

Akkoyunlu, B., & Soylu, M. Y. (2008). A study of student's perceptions in a blended learning environment based on different learning styles. *Educational Technology & Society, 11*(1), 183–193.

Akyol, Z., Garrison, D. R., & Ozden, M. Y. (2009). Online and blended communities of inquiry: Exploring the developmental and perceptional differences. *International Review of Research in Open and Distance Learning, 10*(6), 65–83.

Allen, I. E., & Seaman, J. (2007). *Online nation: Five years of growth in online learning.* Sloan Consortium report.

Aycock, A., Garnham, C., & Kaleta, R. (2002). Lessons learned from the hybrid course project. *Teaching with Technology Today, 8*(6), 9–21.

Bernard, R. M., Abrami, P. C., Borokhovski, E., Wade, C. A., Tamim, R. M., Surkes, M. A., & Bethel, E. C. (2009). A meta-analysis of three types of interaction treatments in distance education. *Review of Educational Research, 79*(3), 1243–1289. doi:10.3102/0034654309333844

Bersin, J. (2003). *Blended learning: What works: An industry study of the business impact of blended learning.* Bersin & Associates Research Report. Retrieved from http://www.bersin.com/Practice/Detail.aspx?docid=5870

Betts, K., Hartman, K., & Oxholm, C. (2009). Re-examining & repositioning higher education: twenty economic and demographic factors driving online and blended program enrollments. *Journal of Asynchronous Learning Networks, 13*(4), 3–23.

Blain, J. (2010). *Current learning trends in Europe and the United States.* Paris, France: Cegos Group.

Bolliger, D. U., & Wasilik, O. (2009). Factors influencing faculty satisfaction with online teaching and learning in higher education. *Distance Education*, *30*(1), 103–116. doi:10.1080/01587910902845949

Boyle, T., Bradley, C., Chalk, P., Jones, R., & Pickard, P. (2003). Using blended learning to improve student success rates in learning to program. *Journal of Educational Media*, *28*(2), 165–178. doi:10.1080/1358165032000153160

Borup, J., Graham, C. R., & Velasquez, A. (2011). The use of asynchronous video communication to improve instructor immediacy and social presence in a blended learning environment. In A. Kitchenham (Ed.), *Blended learning across disciplines: Models for implementation* (pp. 38–57). Hershey, PA: IGI Global.

Borup, J., West, R. E., & Graham, C. R. (2012 in press). Improving online social presence through asynchronous video. *Internet and Higher Education*. doi:10.1016/j.iheduc.2011.11.001

Bransford, J. D., Brown, A. L., & Cocking, R. R. (1999). *How people learn: Brain, mind, experience, and school.* Washington, DC: National Academy Press.

Bunderson, C. V. (2003). Four frameworks for viewing blended learning cases: Comments and critique. *Quarterly Review of Distance Education*, *4*(3), 279–288.

Burkhardt, H., & Schoenfeld, A.H. (2003). Improving educational research: Toward a more useful, more influential, and better-funded enterprise. *Educational Researcher*, *32*(9), 3–14. doi:10.3102/0013189X032009003

Chute, A. G., Williams, J. O. D., & Hancock, B. W. (2006). Transformation of sales skills through knowledge management and blended learning. In C. J. Bonk & C. R. Graham (Eds.), *Handbook of blended learning: Global perspectives, local designs* (pp. 105–119). San Francisco, CA: Pfeiffer.

Clark, R .E. (1983). Reconsidering research on learning from media. *Review of Educational Research*, *53*(4), 445–459.

Collis, B. (2006). Putting blended learning to work. In C. J. Bonk & C. R. Graham (Eds.), *Handbook of blended learning: Global perspectives, local designs* (pp. 461–473). San Francisco, CA: Pfeiffer.

Collis, B., & van der Wende, M. (2002). *Models of technology and change in higher education: An international comparative survey on the current and future use of ICT in higher education.* Report from the Center for Higher Education Policy Studies, University of Twente. Enschede, The Netherlands. Retrieved from http://doc.utwente.nl/44610/

Colwell, J. L. (2006). Experiences with a hybrid class. *College Teaching, 2*(2), 2004–2007.

Cottrell, D. M., & Robinson, R. A. (2003). Case 4: Blended learning in an accounting course. *Quarterly Review of Distance Education, 4*(3), 261–269.

Cross, J. (2006). Foreword. In C. J. Bonk & C. R. Graham (Eds.), *Handbook of blended learning: Global perspectives, local designs* (p. xvii–xxiii). San Francisco, CA: Pfeiffer.

Dowling, C., Godfrey, J., & Gyles, N. (2003). Do hybrid flexible delivery teaching methods improve accounting students' learning outcomes? *Accounting Education*, *12*(4), 373–391. doi:10.1080/0963928032000154512

Dron, J., Seidel, C., & Litten, G. (2004). Transactional distance in a blended learning environment. *Alt-J: Research in Learning Technology*, *12*(2), 163–174. doi:10.1080/0968776042000216219

Dubin, R. (1978). *Theory building.* New York, NY: The Free Press.

Dziuban, C. D., Hartman, J. L., Cavanagh, T. B., & Moskal, P. D. (2011). Blended courses as drivers of institutional transformation. In A. Kitchenham (Ed.), *Blended learning across disciplines: Models for implementation* (pp. 17–37). Hershey, PA: IGI Global.

Dziuban, C., & Moskal, P. (2011). A course is a course is a course: Factor invariance in student evaluation of online, blended and face-to-face learning environments. *The Internet and Higher Education,14*(4), 236–241. doi:10.1016/j.iheduc.2011.05.003

Dziuban, C., Hartman, J., Juge, F., Moskal, P., & Sorg, S. (2006). Blended learning enters the mainstream. In C. J. Bonk & C. R. Graham (Eds.), *Handbook of blended learning: Global perspectives, local designs* (pp. 195–208). San Francisco, CA: Pfeiffer.

Dziuban, C., Hartman, J., Moskal, P., Sorg, S., & Truman, B. (2004). Three ALN modalities: An institutional perspective. *Elements of Quality Online Education: Into the Mainstream* (pp. 127–148). Needham, MA: Sloan Consortium.

Dziuban, C., Moskal, P., & Futch, L.S. (2007). Reactive behavior, ambivalence, and the generations: Emerging patterns in student evaluation of blended learning. In A. G. Picciano & C. D. Dziuban (Eds.), *Blended learning: Research perspectives* (pp. 179–202).Needham, MA: Sloan Consortium.

Dziuban, C., Moskal, P., & Hartman, J. (2005). Higher education, blended learning and the generations: Knowledge is power-no more. In J. Bourne & J. C. Moore (Eds.), *Elements of quality online education: Engaging communities* (pp. 85–100). Needham, MA: Sloan Consortium.

Dziuban, C., Moskal, P., Brophy-Ellison, J., & Shea, P. (2007). Technology-enhanced education and millennial students in higher education. *Metropolitan Universities*, *18*(3), 75–90.

Fetters, M. L., & Duby, T. G. (2011). Faculty development: A stage model matched to blended learning maturation. *Journal of Asynchronous Learning Networks*, *15*(1), 77–83.

Garnham, C., & Kaleta, R. (2002). Introduction to hybrid courses. *Teaching with Technology Today, 8*(6). Retrieved from http://www.associatedcolleges-tc.org/cotf/COTFX/materials/smeatonHybridCoursesnotes.doc

Garrison, D. R., & Kanuka, H. (2004). Blended learning: Uncovering its transformative potential in higher education. *The Internet and Higher Education, 7*(2), 95–105. doi:10.1016/j.iheduc.2004.02.001

Garrison, R. D., & Vaughan, N. D. (2008). *Blended learning in higher education: Framework, principles, and guidelines.* San Francisco, CA: Jossey-Bass.

Gibbons, A. S., & Bunderson, V. (2005). Explore , explain , design. *Encyclopedia of social measurement* (Vol. 1, pp. 927–938). San Diego, CA: Elsevier.

Giddens, A. (1984). *The constitution of society: Elements of the theory of structuration. Elements.* Berkeley: University of California Press.

Graff, M. (2003). Individual differences in sense of classroom community in a blended learning environment. *Journal of Educational Media, 28*(2), 203–210. doi:10.1080/1358165032000165635

Graham, C. R. (2006). Blended learning systems: Definition, current trends, and future directions. In C. J. Bonk & C. R. Graham (Eds.), *Handbook of blended learning: Global perspectives, local designs* (pp. 3–21). San Francisco, CA: Pfeiffer.

Graham, C. R., & Allen, S. (2009). Designing blended learning environments. In P. L. Rogers, G. A. Berg, J. V. Boettcher, C. Howard, L. Justice, & K. Schenk (Eds.), *Encyclopedia of distance learning* (Vol. 2, pp. 562–570). Hershey, PA: IGI Global.

Graham, C. R., & Robison, R. (2007). Realizing the transformational potential of blended learning: Comparing cases of transforming blends and enhancing blends in higher education. In A. G. Picciano & C. D. Dziuban (Eds.), *Blended learning: Research perspectives* (pp. 83–110). Needham, MA: Sloan Consortium.

Graham, C. R., Woodfield, W., & Harrison, J. B. (2013, in press). A framework for institutional adoption and implementation of blended learning in higher education. *Internet and Higher Education.* doi:10.1016/j.iheduc.2012.09.003

Grgurovic, M. (2010). *Technology-enhanced blended language learning in an ESL class: A description of a model and an application of the Diffusion of Innovations theory* (Unpublished Doctoral Dissertation). Iowa State University, Ames.

Halverson, L. R., Graham, C. R., Spring, K. J., & Drysdale, J. S. (2012). An analysis of high impact scholarship and publication trends in blended learning. *Distance Education, 33*(3), 381–413. doi:10.1080/01587919.2012.723166

Hawkins, A., Barbour, M. K., & Graham, C. R. (2012). Everybody is their own island: Teacher disconnection in a virtual school. *InternationalReview of Research in Open and Distance Learning, 13*(2), 122–143.

Hawkins, A., Barbour, M. K., & Graham, C. R. (2011). Strictly business: Teacher perceptions of interaction in virtual schooling. *Journal of Distance Education, 25*(2). Retrieved from http://www.jofde.ca/index.php/jde/article/view/726/1241

Heinze, A., Procter, C., & Scott, B. (2007). Use of conversation theory to underpin blended learning. *International Journal of Teaching and Case Studies, 1*(1/2), 108–120. doi:10.1504/IJTCS.2007.014213

Intharaksa, U. (2009). *Using diffusion of innovation theory to explain the degree of faculty adoption of web-based instruction in a Thai university* (Unpublished doctoral dissertation). Oklahoma State University, Stillwater.

Jones, N. (2006). E-College Wales, a case study of blended learning. In C. J. Bonk & C. R. Graham (Eds.), *Handbook of blended learning: Global perspectives, local designs* (pp. 182–194). San Francisco, CA: Pfeiffer.

Keller, J. M. (1983). Motivational design of instruction. In C. M. Reigeluth (Ed.), *Instructional-design theories and models: An overview of their current status* (pp. 386–434). Hillsdale, NJ: Erlbaum.

Keller, J. M. (2008). First principles of motivation to learn and e3learning. *Distance Education, 29*(2), 175–185. doi:10.1080/01587910802154970

Kolb, D. A. (1984). *Experiential learning: Experience as the source of learning and development.* Upper Saddle River, NJ: Prentice Hall.

Larson, D. K., & Sung, C.-H. (2009). Comparing student performance: Online versus blended versus face-to-face. *Journal of Asynchronous Learning Networks, 13*(1), 31–42.

Laurillard, D. M. (1993). *Rethinking university teaching: A framework for the effective use of educational technology.* London, UK: Routledge.

Lewis, N. J., & Orton, P. Z. (2006). Blending learning for business impact: IBM's case for learning success. In C. J. Bonk & C. R. Graham (Eds.), *Handbook of blended learning: Global perspectives, local designs* (pp. 61–75). San Francisco, CA: Pfeiffer.

Lim, T., Fadzil, M., & Mansor, N. (2011). Mobile learning via SMS at Open University Malaysia: Equitable, effective, and sustainable. *International Review of Research in Open and Distance Learning, 12*(2), 122–137.

Long, G. L., Vignare, K., Rappold, R. P., & Mallory, J. (2007). Access to communication for deaf, hard-of-hearing and ESL students in blended learning courses. *International Review of Research in Open and Distance Learning, 8*(3), 13.

Mahesh, V., & Woll, C. (2007). Blended learning in high tech manufacturing: A case study of cost benefits and production efficiency. *Journal of Asynchronous Learning Networks, 11*(2), 43–60.

Mayadas, A. F., & Picciano, A. G. (2007). Blended learning and localness: The means and the end. *Journal of Asynchronous Learning Networks, 11*(1), 3–7.

Means, B., Toyama, Y., Murphy, R., Bakia, M., & Jones, K. (2009). *Evaluation of evidence-based practices in online learning: A meta-analysis and review of online learning studies.* Washington, DC: Department of Education, Office of Planning, Evaluation, and Policy Development.

Moloney, J. F., Hickey, C. P., Bergin, A. L., Boccia, J., Polley, K., & Riley, J. E. (2007). Characteristics of successful local blended programs in the context of the Sloan-C pillars. *Journal of Asynchronous Learning Networks, 11*(1), 29–47.

Moskal, P. D., Dziuban, C., & Hartman, J. (2010). Online learning: A transforming environment for adults in higher education. In T. T. Kidd (Ed.), *Online education and adult learning: New frontiers for teaching practices* (pp. 54–68). Hershey, PA: IGI Global.

Norberg, A., Dziuban, C. D., & Moskal, P. D. (2011). A time-based blended learning model. *On the Horizon, 19*(3), 207–216. doi:10.1108/10748121111163913

Oliver, M., & Trigwell, K. (2005). Can "blended learning" be redeemed? *E-Learning, 2*(1), 17–26. doi:10.2304/elea.2005.2.1.2

O'Toole, J. M., & Absalom, D. (2003). The impact of blended learning on student outcomes: Is there room on the horse for two? *Journal of Educational Media, 28*(2-3), 179–190. doi:10.1080/1358165032000165680

Paul, D. S. (2001). *A meta-analytic review of factors that influence the effectiveness of Web-based training within the context of distance learning* (Unpublished doctoral dissertation). Texas A&M University, College Station.

Picciano, A. G., Seaman, J., Shea, P., & Swan, K. (2012). Examining the extent and nature of online learning in American k-12 education: The research initiatives of the Alfred P. Sloan Foundation. *The Internet and Higher Education, 15*, 127-135. doi:10.1016/j.iheduc.2011.07.004

Picciano, A. G. (2009). Blending with purpose: The mutimodal model. *Journal of Asynchronous Learning Networks, 13*(1), 7–18.

Picciano, A. G., & Seaman, J. (2007). *K-12 online learning: A survey of U.S. school district administrators.* Needham, MA: Sloan Consortium.

Reasons, S. G., Valadares, K., & Slavkin, M. (2005). Questioning the hybrid model: Student outcomes in different course formats. *Journal of Asynchronous Learning Networks, 9*(1), 83–94.

Riffell, S. K., & Sibley, D. F. (2004). Can hybrid course formats increase attendance in undergraduate environmental science courses? *Journal of Natural Resources and Life Sciences Education, 33*, 1–5.

Rogers, E. M. (1983). *Diffusion of innovations.* New York, NY: Free Press.

Rooney, J. E. (2003). Knowledge infusion: Blending learning opportunities to enhance educational programming and meetings. *Association Management, 55*(6), 26–32.

Ross, B., & Gage, K. (2006). Global perspectives on blended learning: Insight from WebCT and our customers in higher education. In C. J. Bonk & C. R. Graham (Eds.), *Handbook of blended learning: Global perspectives, local designs* (pp. 155–168). San Francisco, CA: Pfeiffer.

Rossett, A., & Frazee, R. V. (2006). *Blended learning opportunities.* American Management Association special report. Retrieved from http://www.grossmont.edu/don.dean/pkms_ddean/ET795A/WhitePaper_BlendLearn.pdf

Rothmund, C. (2008). *Correlation between course interactivity and reported levels of student satisfaction in hybrid courses* (Unpublished doctoral dissertation). Minneapolis, MN: Capella University.

Rovai, A. P., & Jordan, H. M. (2004). Blended learning and sense of community: A comparative analysis with traditional and fully online graduate courses. *International Review of Research in Open and Distance Learning, 5*(2), 13.

Sachs, D. (2007). Pace University, blended learning and localness: A model that works. *Journal of Asynchronous Learning Networks, 11*(1), 15–19.

Salomon, G. (2002). Technology and pedagogy: Why don't we see the promised revolution? *Educational Technology, 42*(2), 71–75.

Sharpe, R., Benfield, G., Roberts, G., & Francis, R. (2006). *The undergraduate experience of blended e-learning: A review of UK literature and practice.* York, UK: The Higher Education Academy. Retrieved from http://www.grossmont.edu/don.dean/pkms_ddean/ET795A/WhitePaper_BlendLearn.pdf

Shea, P. (2007). Towards a conceptual framework for learning in blended environments. In A. G. Picciano & C. D. Dziuban (Eds.), *Blended learning: Research perspectives* (pp. 19–35). Needham, MA: Sloan Consortium.

Shea, P., & Bidjerano, T. (2011). Understanding distinctions in learning in hybrid, and online environments: An empirical investigation of the community of inquiry framework. *Interactive Learning Environments*, 1–16. doi:10.1080/10494820.2011.584320

Sitzmann, T., Kraiger, K., Stewart, D., & Wisher, R. (2006). The comparative effectiveness of web-based and class-room instruction: A meta-analysis. *Personnel Psychology, 59*(3), 623–664. doi:10.1111/j.1744-6570.2006.00049.x

Staker, H., Chan, E., Clayton, M., Hernandez, A., Horn, M. B., & Mackey, K. (2011). *The rise of K–12 blended learning: Profiles of emerging models.* Innosight Institute report. Retrieved from http://www.innosightinstitute.org/innosight/wp-content/uploads/2011/01/The-Rise-of-K-12-Blended-Learning.pdf

Staker, H., & Horn, M. B. (2012). *Classifying K–12 Blended learning.* Innosight Institute report. Retrieved from http://www.innosightinstitute.org/innosight/wp-content/uploads/2012/05/Classifying-K-12-blended-learning2.pdf

Star, S. L., & Griesemer, J. R. (1989). Institutional ecology, 'translations' and boundary objects: Amateurs and professionals in Berkeley's Museum of Vertebrate Zoology, 1907–39. *Social Studies of Science, 19*(3), 387–420. doi:10.1177/030631289019003001

Starenko, M., Vignare, K., & Humbert, J. (2007). Enhancing student interaction and sustaining faculty instructional innovations through blended learning. In A. G. Picciano & C. D. Dziuban (Eds.), *Blended learning: Research perspectives* (pp. 161–178). Needham, MA: Sloan Consortium.

Stubbs, M., Martin, I., & Endlar, L. (2006). The structuration of blended learning: Putting holistic design principles into practice. *British Journal of Educational Technology, 37*(2), 163–175. doi:10.1111/j.1467-8535.2006.00530.x

Teng, Y.-T., Bonk, C. J., & Kim, K.-J. (2009). The trend of blended learning in Taiwan: Perceptions of HRD practitioners and implications for emerging competencies. *Human Resource Development International, 12*(1), 69–84. doi:10.1080/13678860802638842

Twigg, C. A. (2003). Improving learning and reducing costs: New models for online learning. *Educause Review, 38*(5), 28, 30, 32–36, 38.

Vaughan, N., & Garrison, R. D. (2005). Creating cognitive presence in a blended faculty development community. *The Internet and Higher Education, 8*(1), 1–12. doi:10.1016/j.iheduc.2004.11.001

Vaughan, N., (2007). Perspectives on blended learning in higher education. *International Journal on E-Learning, 6*(1), 81–94.

Vaughan, N., & Garrison, D. R. (2006). How blended learning can support a faculty development community of inquiry. *Journal of Asynchronous Learning Networks, 10*(4), 139–152.

Vignare, K. (2007). Review of literature blended learning: Using ALN to change the classroom — Will it work? In A. G. Picciano & C. D. Dziuban (Eds.), *Blended Learning: Research Perspectives* (pp. 37–63). Needham, MA: Sloan Consortium.

Vignare, K., & Starenko, M. (2005). *Blended learning pilot project: Final report for 2003–2004 and 2004–2005.* Online Learning Department Rochester Institute of Technology. Rochester, MA. Retrieved from https://ritdml.rit.edu/handle/1850/276

Watson, J. (2008). *Blended learning: The convergence of online and face-to-face education.* North American Council for Online Learning report.

Watson, J., Murin, A., Vashaw, L., Gemin, B., & Rapp, C. (2010). *Keeping pace with K-12 online learning: An annual review of policy and practice.* Durango, CO: Evergreen Education Group..

Wheeler, S. (2007). The influence of communication technologies and approaches to study on transactional distance in blended learning. *Alt-J: Research in Learning Technology, 15*(2), 103–117. doi:10.1080/09687760701470924

Wicks, M. (2010). *A National primer on K-12 online learning.* Vienna, VA: iNACOL.

Wright, N., Dewstow, R., Topping, M., & Tappenden, S. (2006). New Zealand examples of blended learning. In C. J. Bonk & C. R. Graham (Eds.), *Handbook of blended learning: Global perspectives, local designs* (pp. 169–181). San Francisco, CA: Pfeiffer.

Xin, M.C. (2002). Validity centered design for the domain of engaged collaborative discourse in computer conferencing (Unpublished doctoral dissertation). Brigham Young University, Provo, UT.

Zhao, Y., Lei, J., Yan, B., Lai, C., & Tan, H. S. (2005). What makes the difference? A practical analysis of research on the effectiveness of distance education. *Teachers College Record, 107*(8), 1836–1884. doi:10.1111/j.1467-9620.2005.00544.x

Ziob, L., & Mosher, B. (2006). Putting customers first at Microsoft: Blending learning capabilites with customer needs. In C. J. Bonk & C. R. Graham (Eds.), *Handbook of blended learning: Global perspectives, local designs* (pp. 92–104). San Francisco, CA: Pfeiffer.

22

MODES OF INTERACTION

NORM FRIESEN AND ALEX KUSKIS

This chapter focuses on the pedagogical and technological aspects of interaction in distance education. It reviews a number of types of interaction and suggests areas and approaches to research that will expand our understanding and competence in using new tools, technologies, and techniques.

The rapid growth of social networks like Facebook, both on and off university campuses, together with access to the Internet over portable devices, has more recently confirmed and hastened the expansion of interest to the domain of contextually embedded, self-directed, informal learning (e.g., Jokisalo & Riu, 2009; Bransford et al., 2006). Much of the literature relevant to these domains focuses on student-student and student-teacher interaction. However, the mediated context of distance education has compelled distance educators to consider more seriously interactions between students and diverse educational media (in Moore's 1995 words "the content"). This chapter considers questions concerning the efficacy of equating this student-content interaction in online environments so dominated by social activity.

Another meaning of interaction becomes clear when it is understood in terms of the scientific and technological developments occurring around the Second World War. The emergence of the science of cybernetics (and also of general systems theory) is perhaps the most important of these developments. As defined by its founder, Norbert Wiener (1950), "cybernetics" is "the study of messages as a means of controlling machinery and society, the development of computing machines and other such automata [and it includes correlative] reflections upon psychology and the nervous system ..." (p. 23).

Communication, as Wiener (1950) defines it, is a matter of an exchange of messages "between man and machines, between machines and man, and between machine and machine," in which the human or mechanical nature of the source or receiver is irrelevant:

> When I give an order to a machine, the situation is not essentially different from that which arises when I give an order to a person. In other words, as far as my consciousness goes I am aware of the order that has gone out and of the signal of

compliance that has come back. To me, personally, the fact that the signal in its intermediate stages has gone through a machine rather than through a person is irrelevant and does not in any case greatly change my relation to the signal. Thus the theory of control in engineering, whether human animal or mechanical, is a chapter in the theory of messages. (Wiener, 1950, p. 25)

Such an understanding of communication and interaction, as Packer and Jordan (2000) explain, has "provided the conceptual basis for human-computer interactivity" and is "*de rigeur* for anyone investigating the psychological and socio-cultural implications of human-machine interaction" (p. xvii). It is largely in this systematic and cybernetic form that the term "interaction" has been integrated into the discourses of distance education, lifelong learning, educational technology, and other educational sub-domains: "Much of learning theory and instructional systems design is founded in or explained by analogous reference to concepts borrowed from General Systems Theory" (Larsen, 1985, p. 17). Moore's (1989) seminal article describes three forms of interaction in distance education: between students and teacher, among students themselves, and between students and content. Given the elegant simplicity and broad relevancy of these forms of interaction, they are used to structure much of the remainder of this article. Two additional permutations of Moore's interactive forms, focusing on the teaching role—teacher-teacher and teacher-content interaction—are also considered here. Before we discuss interactive forms derived from Moore, we look at a small number of types of interaction appearing in the literature that fall outside of Moore's framework.

Hillman, Willis, and Gunawardena (1994) describe a type of interaction they call "learner/interface interaction"—defined as the "process of manipulating tools to accomplish a task" (p. 34). Learner/interface interaction focuses on the access, skills, and attitudes necessary for successful technologically-mediated learning. These authors regard learner-interface interaction as distinct from but not unrelated to Moore's three types of interaction. Hillman et al. note that "it is important to make the distinction between the perception of interface as an independent fourth mode of interaction, and the use of the interface as a mediating element in *all* interaction" (p. 34 emphasis added). All forms of interaction in a distance education context are, by definition, technologically-mediated forms of interaction. Thus, Hillman et al.'s interface interaction need not be viewed as a unique form of interaction, but rather as a component of each of the other forms of interaction. One could also argue that even face-to-face interaction is mediated as well—usually with the "medium" being the classroom and institution in which instruction takes place (e.g., see McLuhan, McLuhan, & Hutchon, 1977). For these reasons, we choose not to focus on learner-interface interaction as a separate form of interaction, but do not deny that acquisition of the communication and technical skills associated with it is an integral part of the "hidden curriculum of distance education" (Anderson, 2002).

Building on insights from Fulford and Zhang (1993) and Kruh and Murphy (1990), Sutton (2000) postulates yet another form of interaction termed "vicarious interaction." In distance education, as in classroom-based learning, not all students interact directly with one another or with the teacher during individual classes or even over the duration of an entire course. However, they may interact vicariously. Sutton defines vicarious interaction as occurring "when a student actively processes both sides of a direct interaction between two other students or between another student and the instructor" (p. 4). In a study based on televised courses, Fulford and Zhang (1993) found that student's perceptions of *opportunities* for interaction, rather than *actual* interaction or participation, correlated in important ways with satisfaction with courses. They argue that it is the perception of the opportunity for interaction, rather than actual engagement in it, that results in student satisfaction. Sutton (2000) found that students who interacted vicariously had read, appreciated, and learned from the interactions of others, but they felt no desire to interact themselves and perceived that such interaction would have added little to the course of study. In a more recent study, Mabrito (2007) reported similar findings. However, Kawachi (2003) found no evidence the vicarious interaction leads to improved learning, as did another study by Rovai and Barnum (2003) examining *perceptions* of learning. Without using the term "vicarious learning," and focusing on online learning, Rovai and Barnum noted that "Only active interaction, operationalized by the number of messages posted by students per week, was a significant predictor of perceived learning" (p. 57). And Beaudoin (2002) has noted that although low-visibility students spent significant time in online learning-related tasks, "high-visibility learners" (p. 147), those that interacted, attained higher course grades. Noting such research, our position is that vicarious interaction, because it occurs in combination with other forms of interaction and requires the active interaction of other players to be realized, is not an adequately distinct form of interaction to be viewed as sufficient unto itself.

Interactions between and among students and teachers and their families, workplaces, and communities dramatically influence the context in which formal education takes place. Burnham and Walden (1997) describe this as a fifth form of interaction labeled "learner-environment" interaction. These external interactions are conditioned by broader societal norms and expectations, and are related to a variety of indicators of social status (identified by Burnham & Walden as including gender and race). These larger interactions are complex, sometimes idiosyncratic and generally lie beyond the scope of this paper. However, they cannot be ignored when situating educational interaction in any larger context or community.

In this connection, as Keegan (1980) notes, "In traditional education a teacher teaches. In distance education an institution teaches" (p. 19). Distance students inevitably engage in a variety of institutional interactions in addition to their interactions with the teacher, the content and with each other. They are engaged with registration services, the bookstore, library, help desk, and other services and units. Therefore, learner-institution interaction might be considered a significant type of interaction unto itself (Shin, 2002), and this chapter regards it as such—sometimes referencing it in addition to Moore's three principle interactive forms.

STUDENT-TEACHER AND STUDENT-INSTITUTION INTERACTION

Many of the pedagogical benefits of student-teacher interaction, especially those related to motivation (Wlodkowski, 1985) and feedback (Laurillard, 1997, 2000) can be seen as equally relevant in classroom-based and distance education contexts. Studies of audio (Hampel & Hauck, 2004) and video conferencing (Hearnshaw, 2000; Katz, 2000; Wang, 2004) show that effective student-teacher interaction can take place at a distance, but that the use or absence of these synchronous media, in themselves, has little apparent direct impact on educational outcomes (Russell, 2005). As with related studies of the effects of educational media, the impact of the instructional designs associated with the use of this media seems to have far greater impact on student achievement than the use of any given medium per se (Clark, 1994). Recent work has looked at student-teacher interaction in text-based, distance contexts (Akyol & Garrison, 2009; Garrison, Anderson, & Archer, 2000; Ke, 201; Moore & Kearsley, 2005; Shea, Pickett & Pelz, 2003). This research confirms the educational value of that student-teacher interaction, even when this interaction is confined to textual communications. Dennen, Darabi, and Smith (2007) demonstrate that student satisfaction is tied to students' perceptions that their interpersonal communication needs are being met. The three main factors in meeting these needs are (a) instructors' frequency of contact, (b) their regular presence in class discussions, and (c) expectations being made clear to students. Likewise, Dennen and Wieland (2007) conclude that a consistent, facilitative instructor who anchors discussions around questions and shared artifacts is more likely to produce discourse associated with the co-construction of knowledge.

A major concern for both teachers and administrators is the perception or reality of high workloads and costs associated with student-teacher interaction in distance education. From an administration perspective, Daniel and Marquis (1988) note that the costs associated with interaction between students and teachers "tend to increase in direct proportion to the number of students" (p. 342) in a given class or course. Berge and Muilenburg (2000) report survey results from over 1,000 American distance education teachers that identify concerns with increased time requirements as the largest barrier associated with adoption of networked forms of distance teaching. Is this perception a function of unfamiliarity with media and uncertainties regarding appropriate instructional design, or is it an implicit attribute of technologically-mediated teacher-student interaction? There has now been some research measuring teacher time that does not support the claim that online courses imply an increased work load when compared to their offline counterparts (DiBiase, 2000; Hislop & Ellis, 2004; Lazarus, 2003; McLain, 2005). However, concerns with the high cost of online forms of education continue, and the challenges of measuring and compensating teachers appropriately for time spent in teacher-student interaction remain (Fielden, 2002). Moore's (2000) advice in this regard is sensible (if not always to be unproblematically implemented): The expenditure of teacher time should not be a question of more or less work than in the classroom, but rather "getting better quality out of the same effort" (p. 5).

Whether online course environments are structured using a learning management system like Blackboard or Moodle, and/or some combination of Web 2.0 tools (e.g., blogs and wikis), communication between teachers and students might occasionally require some other interactive communication mode for reasons of confidentiality or for purposes of problem resolution. As Sheer and Fung (2007) demonstrate, email communication can contribute positively to professor and individual student relationships. And sometimes communication is facilitated through asynchronous mediated conversation through the use of telephones or Skype (O'Leary & Quinlan, Jr., 2007).

Garrison et al.'s (2000) Community of Inquiry (COI) model suggests that an important dimension of student-teacher interaction is the reciprocal perception of "social presence." Social presence is defined as "the ability of learners to project their personal characteristics into the community of inquiry, thereby presenting themselves as 'real people'" (Community of Inquiry Model, 2011). For teachers, presence is purposeful and is operationalized in the model as "teaching presence," which Anderson, Rourke, Garrison, and Archer (2001) define as the "design, facilitation, and direction of cognitive and social processes for the purpose of realizing personally meaningful and educationally worthwhile learning outcomes" (p. 90). The result of meaningful teaching presence is expected to be "greater positive affect and higher perceived cognition than [that obtained] by less immediate [or 'present'] instructors" (Baker, 2004, p. 1).

Given the recent rise in the use of social media, and the social nature of Web 2.0 technologies, the emphasis on social presence in the COI model seems prescient. However, with very few exceptions (e.g., Shea et al, 2010), the model has not been applied to social networks and socially oriented Web 2.0 contexts. There appear to be both practical and methodological reasons for this: practically, commercial environments like Facebook or Twitter (whatever their advantages and disadvantages for educational communication) do not provide ready access to a complete set of communication for identification and analysis of patterns of social and teacher presence as do traditional educational systems such as Blackboard. Also, these systems tend to foster a kind of communication that is arguably more germane to processes of leisurely socialization than other forums and technologies specifically designed to foster deliberation and reflection (Friesen, 2010).

STUDENT-STUDENT INTERACTION

The educational potential of collaborative and cooperative learning was not available to students involved in early, correspondence-based distance education. Work on the social construction of knowledge (Brown & Duguid, 2000; Rogoff, 1990), communities of practice (Wenger, 1998; Wenger, McDermott, & Snyder, 2002), situated learning (Lave, 1988), and the applications of these theories to education have resulted in a rich and growing body of knowledge related to student-student interaction and collaborative learning (Brown, 2001; Johnson, Johnson, & Smith, 1991; Slavin, 1995). Most of this research has focused on classroom contexts, largely with school age children. However, adult students—especially those involved in professional development—have also been shown to benefit from student-student interactions –specifically those interactions associated with a sharing of common professional concerns and aspirations (Brookfield, 1987; Schön, 1991). Damon (1984) observes that "intellectual accomplishments flourish best under conditions of highly motivated discovery, the free exchange of ideas and the reciprocal feedback between mutually respected individuals" (p. 340).

Marshall McLuhan famously observed that "the 'content' of any medium is always another medium," usually the medium that came before it (1964, p. 8). This observation can be adapted to collaborative learning in distance education: forms of collaboration originally fostered online were transplanted from conventional educational settings (e.g., "discussions" or "office hours"). Only more recently have distance educators sought to facilitate forms of student-student interaction which are not possible in conventional classroom contexts. Although it is not unambiguously substantiated in research (e.g., Hopkins, Gibson, Solé, Savvides, & Starkey 2008), researchers and practitioners alike believe that interaction between students is a precondition necessary for deep learning. John Dewey anticipated and influenced social constructivist theorists when he described the ideal student's engagement with his or her subject matter as follows: "getting outside of it, seeing it as another would see it, considering what points of contact it has with the life of another so that it may be got into such form that he can appreciate its meaning" (Dewey, 1916, p. 6).

Collaboration between learners or students taking place on computer networks is far from being a new phenomenon. There have been practitioners and advocates of collaborative learning for classroom groups prior to the advent of distance education on the Internet. Smith and MacGregor (1998) define collaborative learning as an umbrella term for educational approaches that involve joint intellectual effort by students, or students working together with teachers. Typical collaborative learning situations involve students working in groups of two or more, together seeking understanding, solutions, meanings, or creating a joint intellectual product, such as an essay, report, or Web resource.

Collaborative learning is associated with a number of beliefs and assumptions, for example: that learning is an active process of creation; that it depends upon rich contexts; that it is inherently social; that it has both affective and subjective dimensions; and that individual students each bring with them diverse skills and experiences that are, together, mutually reinforcing (Smith & MacGregor, 1998). Kennedy and Duffy (2004) contextualize these assumptions for successful online collaborative learning: students must be prepared for such learning by course providers; technical support is essential, especially at the start; teachers must be proficient in supporting this learning; and the institutions themselves must openly support it. Finally, since collaborative learning requires investment of student time and effort, inducements or incentives should be integrated with it. It is widely observed that collaborative learning must be made integral to courses through effective and compelling design and facilitation, otherwise students will simply spend their time on individualized work.

Peer interaction is a critical component of the formal curriculum in many disciplines. The capacity to work together effectively in teams and within professional communities and to communicate effectively with colleagues and clients, is generally regarded as critical to both vocational and personal success. Indeed, many forms of learning can be defined as the process of becoming a member of a community of practice and as requiring the internalization of the methods, language and culture of that community. As Brown and Duguid (2000) assert: "Become a member of a community, engage in its practices, and you can acquire and make use of its knowledge and information. Remain an outsider, and these will remain indigestible" (p. 126). Wenger et al.'s (2002) definition of communities in this regard is useful: A community of practice, they say, is constituted by "groups of people who share a concern, a set of problems, or a passion about a topic, and who deepen their understanding and knowledge of this area by interacting on an ongoing basis" (p. 4). Online professional programs, such as masters programs in business, education, nursing, engineering, and computer science can benefit from being deliberately designed to encourage the formation of such communities of practice, with students adopting and developing the vocabulary, discourse and values of working practitioners.

Moller (1998) proposes that encouraging the formation of community in distance learning contexts has two functions: (a) social reinforcement, through shared identity based on shared values, norms and preferences, resulting in more group cohesion and less attrition, and (b) information exchange, through collaboration and knowledge building. Swan et al (2000) emphasize three factors that contribute to the success of online courses organized to support "knowledge building communities:" "[1] a transparent interface, [2] an instructor who interacts frequently and constructively with students, and [3] a valued and dynamic discussion" (p. 379). Rovai (2002) finds that online students who develop a strong sense of community and perform well also feel less isolated and have greater satisfaction with their academic programs. McInnerney and Roberts (2004) propose three protocols that can be built into online courses to foster a sense of community and productive social interaction: (a) greater use of synchronous communication; (b) inclusion of a community "forming" stage, or warm-up period; and (c) the use of guidelines for successful online communication.

Despite the many pedagogical benefits of interaction among students, some students have been shown to purposely select distance education formats that support independent study, free from the temporal restraints and also interpersonal contact associated with collaborative forms of learning (Daniel & Marquis, 1988; Pagney, 1988). Arnold (1999) argues that by deliberately targeting such student preferences, distance education can "be closer to the content of the learning process and closer to the comprehension and grasp of the problems by individual learners" (p. 5). It is clear that we can no longer assume that distance education is, by definition, either a purely individualized or an entirely collaborative process. When we seek to encourage student-student interaction in distance education programming, we should ensure that instructional designs follow validated best practices, to promote interactions that justify the restrictions that they may impose on student's temporal independence.

In addition to the debate between those who advocate independent forms of distance education and those in favor of explicitly collaborative approaches (e.g., Garrison, 1999), still others argue for the functional equivalency of the three principal modalities of interaction: student-student, student-teacher and student-content. This position has been articulated in conjunction with what Anderson (2003) refers to as the "equivalency theorem" (see also Miyazoe & Anderson, 2010). This theorem consists of the claim that student interactions with teachers, with other students or with content are all ultimately equivalent in terms of their educational efficacy; that "deep and meaningful formal learning is supported as long as one of the[se] three forms of interaction … [occurs] at a high level" (Anderson, 2003, n.p.). A number of studies, including a meta-analysis of existing research (Bernard et al. 2009), shed light on this claim of interactional equivalency. These studies show that all three kinds of interaction are indeed perceived as valuable by students (Rhode, 2009). They also suggest that the importance of the three types of ITs (i.e., those used in the three types of interaction) is found to be associated with increasing achievement outcomes (Bernard et al., 2009). However, these findings do *not* go so far as to support the notion that student-student, student-teacher and student-content interaction are *equivalent* and thus functionally interchangeable. In addition, the literature has yet to show that the use of the term "theorem"—as a "universal" and "demonstrable … proposition or statement" (per the Oxford English Dictionary)—is justified in conjunction with educational interaction in wide and varied fields of educational practice.

In addition to research focusing on collaborative learning and learning in online communities in general, there are numerous studies on various aspects of interactions occurring specifically between students. Indeed, the category of student-student interaction appears to have been investigated far more than the other types of educational interaction discussed here, with many researchers making fine-grained distinctions between types and phases of social interaction between students. For example, Lobel, Neubauer, and Swedburg (2002) hypothesize four distinct stages of interaction in online courses: (a) greeting, (b) gathering, (c) activity, and (d) conclusion. Furthermore, each activity stage also has four distinct phases: (a) adding knowledge to the group, (b) facili-tation, (c) building on the knowledge of others, and (d) reporting back to the group. This kind of detailed theoretical understanding can aid in the instructional design support for learning interaction activities. Molinari (2004) emphasizes the role that social com-munication plays in online group problem-solving courses, where students employed elements she refers to as self-revelation, "tying," and etiquette to construct a foundation for collaborative work. The implication is that instructors need to provide time and space for broader socializing as an enabler of communications with a more specific edu-cational focus. And Merrill and Gilbert (2008) conclude that for problem-based learn-ing superior learning outcomes can be obtained when all phases of the problem-solving exercise are structured around peer interactions. Finally, Garrison and Cleveland-Innes (2005) argue that interaction among students "is not enough" and that teaching pres-ence is necessary to provide "the structure (design) and leadership (facilitation/direc-tion) to establish social and cognitive presence (i.e., community of inquiry)" (p. 144).

No current consideration of interaction among students would be complete without mention of social networking services, particularly Facebook. Indeed, it seems difficult to underestimate the significance and potential of Facebook in educational terms gen-erally: fully half of its users self-identify as students, and half of Facebook users again identify themselves as being between the ages of 18 and 24 (Istrategylabs, 2009). In fact, one study indicates that these users "generally believe that Facebook is intentionally for college students" (Jaschik, 2009, n.p.), perhaps because it was originally designed as such. From the perspectives of marketing, support and pedagogy, Facebook and ser-vices like it represent environments for which students have voluntarily self-selected, in which they have further segregated themselves according to location, institution, etc., and in which they are intrinsically motivated to participate. Educators have advocated "integrating Facebook, Ning, and other sites into K-12 [academic] life" (Davis 2010, n.p.; see also Muñoz & Towner, 2009). Advocates have promoted their use as part of a "con-nectivist" learning theory (Siemens, 2006), which elevates social and communicative interactions and connections to the level of an epistemic category seen as central to learning. This type of learning is characterized not only by greater autonomy for the student, but also by changing roles for the teacher; indeed, a collapse of the distinction between teacher and student altogether (e.g., Couros 2009; Downes, 2005).

It is clear that more research on interaction between students—both on social and explicitly educational platforms—remains to be done. As indicated above, Hopkins et al (2008) assert that the claims made for the potential of student-student interaction, as well as interaction with teachers, to promote higher-order critical inquiry and the social construction of knowledge, require further investigation and evidentiary support.

Student-Content Interaction

Despite the attention that Facebook or other social media have directed towards social interactions between students, interaction with educational content remains central in distance education. In traditional distance education, this has meant study with texts and other media, often supplemented by faculty-created study guides.

Interaction with content in educational contexts can take many forms and serve a variety of functions. Sims (1997) reviews taxonomies of student-media interactions and proposes a "developers classification" that includes object; linear; support; update; con-struct; reflective; simulation; hyperlinked; immersive; and non-immersive virtual forms of interactivity. In a study of the benefits of interactivity within an educational Website, Brady (2004) finds that student-content interactivity positively influenced learning outcomes, satisfaction, and student time-on-task. Tuovinen (2000) classifies these media into five basic categories—sound, text, graphics, video and virtual reality—and pays particular attention to combinations that include sound with any of the other media. He argues that sound and visual images are processed by different parts of the brain and thus combinations of sound with other media are less likely to produce cognitive overload than other combinations. Tuovinen (2000) also adds "multimedia creation" as a separate, more constructive form of student-content interactivity. Benefits of this explicitly creative form of interaction are associated with learning acquired through development of the structure, strategies, and skills needed for effective content creation (Dunlop, 1999).

Clark (2000) has suggested that any evaluation of student-content interaction must recognize that every distance education context consists of two distinct levels of inter-action—the first dealing with attributes of the media that support the interaction, and the second with the instructional or learning design. The temptation to confound these two separate types of student -content interaction, according to Clark, is at the root of many of the terminological and research problems debated in the literature. Although it is conceptually useful to differentiate and even measure these interactions as distinct events, Marshall McLuhan's (1964) famous aphorism that the "the medium is the message" reminds us that the isolated analysis of such events fails to address larger issues related to educational media and their significance. The significance—the message of any instructional medium—often has much more to do with the instructional strategy in which the medium is used, than with the learning outcomes it supports. For example, Diaz (2000) makes a convincing argument that research designs informed by an "instructivist worldview" are not likely to be useful for student-centered and constructivist forms of learning. Research methods that illuminate differences within applications of particular sets of instructional designs are likely to be more productive than those that are designed to compare the effect of interactions across different media and instructional designs.

Myriad Web-based technologies and services like blogs, wikis, YouTube, and Google have been significantly altering the context of student-content interaction. In combination with these technologies and services, work on the development and promotion of Open Educational Resources of various kinds (e.g., Friesen, 2009; Hylén, 2007; Yuan, MacNeill, & Kraan, 2008) provides educators and students with an expanded set of student-content interaction resources. The pioneering work of the MERLOT consortium (http://www.merlot.org) and more recent efforts by open resource and courseware consortia (http://www.oercommons.org; http://www.ocwconsortium.org) have expanded possibilities still further. These projects have created new potential in these areas in large part by making course contents and other educational resources available with few or no legal restrictions on use, reuse, and adaptation. The initial exuberance over the potential of reusable open educational resources (and before them, learning objects) has been tempered by realization that learning or rather, education, is locally and culturally contextualized (Friesen, 2007) and that any one resource's efficacy is dependent upon its use in contexts such as effective learning designs (Koper, 2001). Further, the challenges of opening teachers' practices, and increasing their awareness of the possibilities presented by openly sharing educational resources and courseware have been identified as a significant handicap for the open educational resource community (e.g., D'Antoni, 2008). Nonetheless, it is becoming increasingly easy to find activities and tools designed to enhance student-content interaction, gathered together in various collections on the Web.

There are, of course, many illustrations of the use and development of interactive content—some quite innovative and instructive. For example, Theroux and Kilbane (2004) describe an innovative use of a real-time business case distributed via the Internet to business classes at four universities in the United States and Canada in 2001. A case writer, stationed full-time at given company, published weekly case installments on the Internet, allowing students to view real-time corporate operational data in depth and detail. In addition, students shared their analyses and thinking with company management, influencing the corporate decision-making process. The Internet also enables such student interaction with dynamic real-world content.

A variety of relatively new network services allow students to direct and in some cases, automate aspects of their interaction with content. Among the technologies used are various forms of syndication (RSS, podcasts, etc.). Syndication provides real-time notifications (in machine readable format) of new additions to a Web-enabled resource or collection such as those maintained by a publishing house, generated in a discussion group, or the postings of an individual blogger. These syndicated notices can be searched, sorted, and aggregated by individuals or groups of students or teachers to create customized and personal views of emerging content. A variation on this type of syndication is offered by Twitter, which allows status updates (or "tweets") of a maximum of 140 characters in length to be generated by any one user and also aggregated with any number of other users' tweets. Updates can be collected asynchronously or in real time, and the practical gains that are realized from this new technology range from the effective coordination of scattered protest groups through to the emergence of audiences for the updates of celebrities and academics alike. A broadly comparable set of functions is provided by Facebook's "News Feed," the listing of photo, video, and textual updates and responses that appears as one's homepage on the service. As this Facebook example shows, such a regularly updated selection of contents and contributions is by no means restricted to text-based media—much less messages shorter than 140 characters.

Content may also be designed for very specific instructional purposes, to interact with students at various levels of sophistication. The goal of these adaptive content systems is to customize interaction for individual student needs, including the:

> … ability to set the level of the lesson closely to the student's current and changing level of understanding, to alter instructional strategies and provide remedial tutoring as required, to respond to student input at various levels from keystroke to the overall plan of the solution to the problem, and finally to detect and analyze mistakes in terms of conceptual errors. (Eklund, 1995)

Research determining how content is and can be programmed to interact with the attributes of individual students or users is the subject of much human-computer interaction study (Graff, Lin, Kinshuk, & McGreal, 2011) and also some controversy.

In his book *The Filter Bubble* (2011), Eli Pariser focuses at length on how services like Facebook, Google, and Yahoo use sophisticated and hidden algorithms to customize content (e.g., feeds items, search results, and advertising) according to users' past behaviors and current inputs. Pariser argues that these mechanisms can lead to a kind of "information determinism," a situation in which our past queries, selections and even evasions may "entirely decide" what is made available for selection and interaction in "our future" (p. 90). In his examination, Pariser offers some distinctions and cautions that are relevant in considering the potential (and limitations) of adaptive content in distance education as well. For example, Pariser's discussion makes it clear that there are two kinds of customization that can be offered by this type of content: The kind in which the user is aware of customization and able to control it (e.g., through a profile or by selecting parameters through an online form), and the type that is set automatically and invisibly through his or her past behavior. Significantly for educational concerns, Pariser makes the case that this second type of customization or filtering may limit the user's "autonomy:" "To be free, you have to be able not only to do what you want, but to know what's possible to do" (2011, p. 74). By definition, content that has been adapted, filtered, and personalized based on an individual's previous activities has excluded some possibilities for action. And given that one of the higher aspirations of education has long been personal autonomy (e.g., Biesta, 2002; Kant, 1784), and that the issue of learner autonomy is a constant feature in distance education (Bouchard & Kalman, 1998), this discrepancy will likely continue to pose challenges for educators, developers and researchers.

At the same time, a related and recent development that has attracted significant interest, and that has potential relevance for student-content interaction is represented by research in academic and learning analytics. This refers to "the statistical evaluation of rich data sources to discern patterns that can help individuals at companies, educational institutions, or governments make more informed decisions" (Educause, 2010). Analytic information concerning learning and study patterns, it should be added, can also help individual students, teachers and instructional designers also make informed decisions about their own academic teaching and design activities and strategies. This data or information can be provided to support either of the types of customization suggested by Pariser—whether student-controlled or purely algorithmic. In each case, the rich data sources from which academic and learning patterns can be discerned can have quite conventional sources. These include in particular the learning and content management systems that have long been in place in many university and college contexts, and the records they automatically generate of student activity.

This type of research and development is seeking to provide ways in which users' interactions with various systems can be defined, interrelated, analyzed and understood in terms of typical patterns and profiles. Thus, certain patterns of use (or of non-use) of an online system by one user might fit the profile established by earlier non-completing students, or alternatively, by students who were able to challenge the course before its conclusion. In keeping with the ambitions of student-content interaction, this might result in an automated email and/or text message being sent to the student, as appropriate to his or her situation (e.g., Educause, 2010). Others (e.g., Duval, 2011) have envisioned teachers and students alike being provided with a type of "dashboard" showing "visual overview of their activities and how they relate to those of their peers or other actors in the learning experience" (p. 12). In this way, as Duval claims, students and teachers would no longer be asked to "drive blind" in the context of online educational experiences.

However, it is obvious that the application of academic analytics does not need to conform to the logic of student interaction purely with *content*, but may involve forms of student-institution or student-teacher interaction as well. It may be more effective to send an alert for teacher intervention based on patters indicative of student non-completion or of early completion in a course currently being delivered. It is also important to note that unlike some visions of content personalization or adaptation, the goals generally articulated in conjunction with analytics are to increase student self-awareness and options for self-determination based on information related to previous performance, rather than to "filter out options in advance.

A final comment on student-content interaction relates to the recent phenomenal growth in interest and use of content formatted as educational games or simulations. Of particular interest are (massively) multiplayer interactive games, in which remote players interact simultaneously in three-dimensional environments; these present obvious potential for both student-content and student-student interactions in distance education. The interest of educational researchers in this area has typically been justified not so much in terms of the content of popular game titles, but by pointing to the structure and scale of these games and the industry producing them:

> Much attention has been directed to the use of video games for learning in recent years, in part due to the staggering amounts of capital spent on games in the entertainment industry, but also because of their ability to captivate player attention and hold it for lengthy periods of time as players learn to master game complexities and accomplish objectives. (Dondlinger, 2007, p. 21)

While these two factors are still very much a reality in interactive games, the educational expectations to which they have given rise remain largely unfulfilled. Some, like Klopfer, Osterweil, and Salen (2009) attribute this to "high development costs" for sophisticated games, and a range of other economic and cultural factors, such as the highly competitive game market and "fickle" player "loyalty" (p. 19). At the same time, as these and other authors suggest, there may be deeper structural reasons for the lack of success in educational gaming: namely that what makes games fun is not necessarily compatible with the sometimes less than pleasurable arrangements in education: "Effective use of games and other new technologies" as Klopfer et al. observe, "is likely to be limited unless educational institutions are willing to consider significant changes in pedagogy and content, and rethink the role of teachers and other educational professionals" (p. 19; see also Stutt, 2010). A rethinking of this kind is no small task, and it points in a direction quite different from that of the original enthusiasm concerning the compatibility of computer games with the central educational values of captivating and constructively directing effort and attention. As a result, it remains to be seen the degree to which the perceived potential of this form of student-content interaction will be realized.

Teacher-Content Interaction

A form of interaction that this chapter considers in addition to the three originally identified by Moore is interaction between teachers and content. As indicated above, the selection, development, and application of open educational resources is likely to become an increasingly important component of the teacher's role in both distance and classroom-based education. In keeping with teacher abilities, and the legal restrictions and possibilities associated with a given resource, it may be possible to *customize and adapt it to specific pedagogical requirements. This adaptation may happen through relatively sophisticated means, for example, by setting the external* parameters for Flash® or other software-driven resources. Or it may happen in more humble ways through revision of a wiki page, or of an online document on a word processor or via a service like Google Docs. Since some alternative licenses allow or even require resources, thus modified, to be redistributed, this type of activity is in some cases likely to foster even further teacher-content interaction. It may involve even further instructional personnel in the development, improvement and varying adaptation of a given item. A simple example of this is provided by the translation of MIT open courseware into Mandarin (e.g., Lee, Lin, & Bonk, 2007), one of the principle forms of reuse of this particular content offering; another is provided by the composition, use, and adaptation of wiki resources in WikiEducator and Wikiversity (e.g., see Friesen & Hopkins, 2008). Other examples are covered in a number of recent overviews (e.g., Morgan & Carey, 2009).

Still other tools and environments, from composition and presentation services (e.g., Slideshare.net; Prezi.com) to complex authoring environments, allow teachers to be more active in content creation than in earlier eras when instructional designers and programmers performed much of this work. For example, lectures, student discussions, and debates are easily captured and digitized to create iPod and video-casts that are retrievable by students. Although some have argued for the pedagogical and administrative superiority of content produced by teams of experts, as opposed to "Lone Rangers" or independent teacher-designers (Bates, 1995), the recent explosion of largely instructor-created content, produced with the aid of authoring and delivery systems such as Mediawiki, Moodle, and Blackboard®, illustrates that teachers can (either alone, or with minimal consultative assistance) produce workable curricular content.

One advantage of such homegrown content that is often overlooked is that it can be continually updated and annotated while being put to use. This allows the instructional design processes to continue throughout the delivery timeframe unlike various forms of canned instruction (Tuovinen, 2000). Finally, we can expect these authoring and distribution systems to become more comprehensive, functional and user friendly, as they evolve in both commercial and open source development models. Where more work is needed is in the development of more sophisticated pedagogical tools for the creative interaction of teachers with educational content. Tools are needed that assist teachers in designing and supporting courses based on a variety of pedagogical theories and offering a diversity of customizable learning activities.

Current tools too often limit our perception of the technological affordances of distance education to threaded discussions, provision of hyperlinks, and textual content. It is discouraging to note the lack of pedagogical innovation in many of the allegedly sophisticated content development and delivery tools currently available. For example, the type of threaded discussion forums employed in course delivery today, via platforms such as Moodle and Blackboard, show little pedagogical advance over the conferencing tools used on mainframe systems some 30 years ago (Hamilton & Feenberg, 2005). The hope is that the combination of the example of convenient Web 2.0 and social networking features combined with pedagogically driven innovation may create opportunities for more significant interaction between teacher and content (and between other interactive elements as well). The development of more sophisticated, powerful, and cost-effective systems that can be customized by teachers to enhance interaction in all its forms would be of great value to distance education (Trafford, 2005).

In summary, collections, resources, and tools enabling teacher-content interaction, along with new licensing options, have been proliferating, allowing smaller-scale distance education efforts to continue to flourish. Teachers using these tools are increasingly able to create powerful distance learning programming that supports high levels of interaction of many different qualities and modalities.

Despite some cause for cautious optimism concerning teacher-content interaction, it is clear that concerns of administration and management must be addressed that take into account both the cost and benefit of teachers' creative interaction with content. The major issues to be addressed in connection with teacher-content interaction will continue to be workload, changing skill sets, copyright, and the sometimes contentious relationship between teaching and research, especially in university contexts (Brand, 2000).

Teacher-Teacher Interaction

Internet and Web technologies are providing unprecedented opportunities for various forms of interaction between teachers. Interactive, online forms of social and professional networking are increasingly being leveraged by teachers to stay abreast of developments in both their own disciplines and in distance teaching pedagogy. This interaction between teachers forms the basis of networked scholarly communities of practice within formal education institutions, as well as scholarly societies, or invisible colleges (Genoni, Merrick, & Willson, 2005; Wellman, Koku, & Hunsinger, 2005). Kahnwald (2011) found that the first and most important source of assistance in technical and other challenges comes not from the most informed experts, but from colleagues who are at hand. Koku and Wellman (2004) note that computer-mediated communication provides a technological platform for new kinds of "spatially-based, loosely- bounded, networks of scholars that are more connected than the fitful, amorphous relationships of the past and less physically proximate and bureaucratically structured than contemporary universities" (p. 301). Experience with network-based professional development (Anderson & Mason, 1993), as well as active online social networks of scholarly and other professionals (e.g., http://academia.edu; LinkedIn.com) are illustrative of the potential of this form of teacher-teacher interaction.

We have been seeing the emergence of distance and online teaching portals and networks in which resources, tools, and forums for exchange and interchange between teachers are gathered in a single online location. These portals are supported by professional distance education publishers (i.e., http://Distance-Educator.com), commercial educational software vendors (i.e., www.blackboard.com), postsecondary institutions (i.e., http://www.uwex.edu/disted/home.html; http://www.umuc.edu/ide/) and nonprofit professional research and development organizations (i.e., http://tappedin.org/tappedin/; http://cider.athabascau.ca; http://www.digitallearning.org/about.htm).

INTERACTION CHOICES

Interaction in any of the various modes described above may take place either synchronously or asynchronously and be instantiated in text, audio, video, or in combinations of these communication forms. Unfortunately, too many distance educators and institutions have chosen to restrict themselves to one particular technology and instructional design in defining their own current delivery models and instruction. Just as developments in academic analytics and social networking make it increasingly difficult to separate different forms of interaction (e.g., with content, with others, with the institution), allegiances to one particular technology, design or model are similarly becoming less and less tenable. Teachers and institutions now have the potential to select from a wide variety of forms of mediated interaction. However, such variety creates challenges as educators and administrators are asked, in effect, to make numerous decisions related to the use of media and interactive technologies.

This is made all the more challenging by the lack of unambiguous and useful research results. For example, despite years of study, it is still unclear which students, studying what types of content, under what conditions, and under which instructional design, benefit most from synchronous as opposed to asynchronous interaction. It seems clear that students report positive experiences and achieve learning outcomes using modes of interaction that are either wholly synchronous or asynchronous, as well as both (McInnerney & Roberts, 2004). It is also fairly clear that most modes of interaction discussed above are positively associated student satisfaction and other educational goals (e.g., Rhode, 2009; Bernard, et al., 2009). It may be that the sheer number of variables in real life situations makes any determination of effective combinations of kinds of interaction (together with kinds of content and designs) impossible. It may also be that expectations, costs (from student, teacher, and institutional perspectives), as well as convenience, may be the most significant determinants of combinations of interactive forms. Allowing these factors to alone determine distance education formats and offerings, however, carries an implicit threat to the critical potential of distance education to enhance access to education, which may be endangered. Damarin (2000) has provided a useful set of five principles for decision making based upon the equitable use of technology in education that are designed to reduce rather than exacerbate the digital divide.

Distance educators have traditionally chosen the most inexpensive and widely available media for delivery and excluded alternatives that limit access by requiring student ownership of costly equipment or high access costs. The attraction that opportunities for social interaction hold out for students has justified this approach. As the popularity of services like Facebook and Twitter attest, students show a remarkable willingness to adapt to the constraints of lean media (O'Sullivan & Hoffner, 1998) in return for opportunities to maintain and develop social relations. However, costs and accessibility of voice and video connectivity (in both synchronous and asynchronous) formats continue to fall as availability continues to rise. We can perhaps expect to see increased use of richer media to support interaction in distance education. The recent and widespread adoption of Skype video, voice and text technology by Internet users may already be ushering in an era of richer student-teacher and student-student interaction.

CONCLUSION

To summarize, although interaction among students has been studied most frequently, the various the forms and combinations of interaction discussed here would benefit from systematic and rigorous research using a variety of research tools and methodologies. Greg Kearsley (1995) provided a list of eight questions related to interaction, the answers to which are critical to the development of effective distance education programming. These questions relate to the effects of the frequency of interaction, types of students, subject matter, and learning objectives to which interaction is most critical, as well as the effects of interaction on student satisfaction. These questions can be answered with reference to all the forms of interaction covered here, including those involving complex feedback loops, as is the case in interactions associated with academic analytics. Additional questions related to cost, time requirements, and other workload implications are critical in an era of expanding distance education programming. Unfortunately, the answers to most of these questions remain largely unanswered many years after Kearsley posed them.

The quest for simple solutions that generalize to the many diverse contexts of distance education will likely prove to be futile. A growing mosaic of distance education technologies and practices continues to develop, with no single best way to leverage or even define interaction. Each institution, discipline, region, and user group is certain to continue to develop unique cultural practices and expectations related to their need for and use of interaction in its myriad forms. However, this is not to say that all applications and interactions are equally effective or efficient.

Daniel and Marquis' (1988) seminal challenge to distance educators was to get the mixture right between independence (student-content interaction) and interaction (mainly student-teacher interaction at that early date). In the 21st century, we are doubly challenged to identify the myriad forms and potentialities of interaction, and to understand the equally complex possibilities for their effective combination. Appropriate combinations are expected to result in effective instruction and exciting new educational opportunities; inappropriate combinations may be expensive, exclusive, and exigent. Our responsibility as professional distance educators is to ensure that the modes of interaction we explore, practice, and prescribe are related to the attainment of educational objectives, are open to student diversity, are affordable to both students and institutions, and increase access to education that is potentially deep, meaningful, and fulfilling.

REFERENCES

Anderson, T. (2003). Getting the Mix Right: An updated and theoretical rational for interaction. *International Review of Research in Open and Distance learning*, *4*(2). Retrieved October 30, 2003, from http://www.irrodl.org/content/v4.2/anderson.html

Anderson, T., & Mason, R. (1993). The Bangkok Project: New tool for professional development. *American Journal of Distance Education*, *7*(2), 5–18.

Anderson, T., Rourke, L., Garrison, D. R., & Archer, W. (2001). Assessing teaching presence in a computer conferencing context. *Journal of Asynchronous Learning Networks*, *5*(2). Retrieved December 14, 2005, from http://www.sloan-c.org/publications/jaln/v5n2/v5n2_anderson.asp

Akyol, Z., & Garrison, D. R. (2009). Community of inquiry in adult online learning: Collaborative-constructivist approaches. In T. T. Kidd (Ed.), *Adult learning in the digital age: Perspectives on online technologies and outcomes* (pp. 52–66). Hershey, PA: IGI Global.

Arnold, R. (1999). Will distance disappear in distance education? *Journal of Distance Education*, *14*(2), 1–9.

Baker, J. D. (2004). An investigation of relationships among instructor immediacy and affective and cognitive learning in the online classroom. *The Internet and Higher Education*, *7*(1), 1–13.

Bates, T. (1995). *Technology, open learning and distance education*. London: Routledge.

Beaudoin, M. F. (2002). Learning or Lurking? Tracking the 'invisible' online student. *The Internet and Higher Education*, *5*(2), 147–155.

Berge, Z., & Muilenburg, L. (2000). Barriers to Distance Education as Perceived by Managers and Administrators: Results of a survey. In M. Grey (Ed.), *Distance Learning Administration Annual 2000*. Retrieved January 20, 2006, from http://www.emoderators.com/barriers/man_admin.shtml

Bernard, M. R., Abrami, P. C., Borokhovski, E., Wade, C. A., Tamim, R. M., Surkes, M. A., & Bethel, E. C. (2009). A meta-analysis of three types of interaction treatments in distance education. *The Review of Educational Research, 79*(3), 1243–1289.

Biesta, G. J. J. (2002). *Bildung* and modernity. The future of *Bildung* in a world of difference. *Studies in Philosophy and Education, 21*(4/5), 343–351.

Bouchard, P., & Kalman, L. (1998). Distance education and learner autonomy: Some theoretical implications. *Actes du 15ème colloque de l'Association Canadienne pour l'étude de l'éducation des adultes.* Université d'Ottawa. Retrieved September 2, 2011, from http://doe.concordia.ca/girat/distancePBLK.pdf

Brady, L. (2004). The role of interactivity in web-based educational material. *Usability News, 6*(2) Retrieved November 20, 2005 from http://psychology.wichita.edu/surl/usabilitynews/62/interactivity.htm

Brand, M. (2000). Changing faculty roles in research universities: Using the pathways strategy. *Change, 32*(6), 42–45.

Bransford, J. D., Barron, B., Pea, R., Meltzoff, A., Kuhl, P. Bell, P., … Sabelli, N. (2006). Foundations and opportunities for an interdisciplinary science of learning. In K. Sawyer (Ed.), *The Cambridge handbook of the learning sciences* (pp. 19–34). New York, NY: Cambridge University Press.

Brookfield, S. (1987). Recognizing critical thinking. In S. Brookfield (Ed.), *Developing critical thinkers* (pp. 15–34). Oxford, UK: Jossey-Bass.

Brown, J. S., & Duguid, P. (2000). *Social life of information.* Cambridge, MA: Harvard Business School Press.

Brown, R. E. (2001). The process of community-building in distance learning classes. *Journal of Asynchronous Learning Networks, 5*(2). Retrieved April 30, 2004, from http://www.sloan-c.org/publications/jaln/v5n2/v5n2_brown.asp

Burnham, B., & Walden, B. (1997). Interactions in distance education: A report from the other side. In *Proceedings of the Adult Education Research Conference Oklahoma State University.* Retrieved May 25, 2001 from http://www.edst.educ.ubc.ca/aerc/1997/97burnham.html

Clark, R. (1994). Media will never influence learning. *Educational Technology Research & Development, 42*(3), 21–29.

Clark, R. (2000). Evaluating distance education: Strategies and cautions. *Quarterly Review of Distance Education, 1*(1), 3–16.

Community of inquiry model. (2011, February 16). *EduTech Wiki, A resource kit for educational technology teaching, practice and research.* Retrieved July 5, 2011, from http://edutechwiki.unige.ch/mediawiki/index.php?title=Community_of_inquiry_model&oldid=30824

Couros, A. (2009). Open, connected, social - implications for educational design. *Campus-Wide Information Systems, 26*(3), 232–239.

D'Antoni, S. (2008). Open educational resources: The way forward deliberations of an international community of interest. Retrieved September 2, 2011, from http://oerwiki.iiep-unesco.org/images/4/46/OER_Way_Forward.pdf

Damarin, S. (2000). The 'digital divide' versus digital differences: Principles for equitable use of technology in education. *Educational Technology, 40*(4), 17–22.

Damon, W. (1984). Peer Interaction: The untapped potential. *Journal of Applied Developmental Psychology, 5,* 331–343.

Daniel, J., & Marquis, C. (1988). Interaction and Independence: Getting the mix right. In D. Sewart, D. Keegan, & B. Holmberg (Eds.), *Distance education: International perspectives* (pp. 339–359). London: Routledge.

Davis, M.R. (June 14, 2010). Social Networking Goes to School. *Education Week: Digital Directions.*

Dennen, V. P., Darabi, A. A., & Smith, L. J. (2007). Instructor-learner interaction in online courses: The relative perceived importance of particular instructor actions on performance and satisfaction. *Distance Education, 28*(1), 65–79.

Dennen, V. P., & Wieland, K. (2007). From interaction to intersubjectivity: Facilitating online group discourse processes. *Distance Education, 28*(3), 281–297.

Dewey, J. (1916). *Democracy and education.* New York, NY: Macmillan.

Diaz, D. (2000). Carving a new path for distance education research. *Commentary: March/April.* Retrieved May 21, 2001, from http://horizon.unc.edu/TS/commentary/2000-03a.asp

DiBiase, D. (2000). Is distance teaching more work or less work? *American Journal of Distance Education, 14*(3), 6–20.

Dondlinger, M. J. (2007). Educational video game design: A review of the literature. *Journal of Applied Educational Technology, 4*(1), 21–31. Retrieved October 11, 2011 from: http://www.eduquery.com/jaet/JAET4-1_Dondlinger.pdf

Downes, S. (2005). E-learning 2.0. *eLearn Magazine.* Retrieved October 17, from http://elearnmag.org/subpage.cfm?section=articles&article=29-1

Dunlop, J. (1999). Developing web-based performance support systems to encourage lifelong learning in the workplace. *WebNet Journal, 1*(2).

Duval, E. (2011). Attention Please! Learning Analytics for Visualization and Recommendation. LAK '11: Proceedings of the 1st International Conference on Learning Analytics and Knowledge (pp. 9–17). New York: ACM.

Educause. (2010). 7 things you should know about analytics. Retrieved September 2, 2011 from http://net.educause.edu/ir/library/pdf/ELI7059.pdf

Eklund, J. (1995). Adaptive learning environments: The future for tutorial software. *Australian Educational Computing, 10*(1), 10–14. Retrieved May 21, 2001, from http://nabil.vuse.vanderbilt.edu/nabil/Adaptive_Learning.htm

Fielden, J. (2002). *Costing e-Learning: Is it worth trying or should we ignore the figures?* London: The Observatory on Borderless Higher Education. Retrieved September 2005, from http://www.obhe.ac.uk/products/reports/pdf/August2002.pdf

Friesen, N. (2007). Three objections tolearning objects. In P. McGreal (Ed.), *Online education using learning objects* [Kindle version] (pp. 59–70). London: Routledge.

Friesen, N. (2009). Open educational resources: New possibilities for change and sustainability. *The International Review of Research in Open and Distance Learning, 10*(5). Retrieved September 2, 2011, from http://www.irrodl.org/index.php/irrodl/article/view/664/1388

Friesen, N. (2010). Education and the social web. Connective learning and the commercial imperative. *First Monday, 15*(12) http://www.uic.edu/htbin/cgiwrap/bin/ojs/index.php/fm/article/view/3149/2718

Friesen, N., & Hopkins, J. (2008). Wikiversity; or education meets the free culture movement: An ethnographic investigation. *First Monday, 13*(10). http://www.uic.edu/htbin/cgiwrap/bin/ojs/index.php/fm/

Fulford., C. P., & Zhang, S. (1993). Perceptions of interaction: The critical predictor in distance education. *American Journal of Distance Education, 7*(3), 8–21.

Garrison, D. R. (1999). Will distance disappear in distance education? A reaction. *Journal of Distance Education, 14*(2), 10–13.

Garrison, R., Anderson, T., & Archer, W. (2000). Critical Inquiry in Text-based Environment: Computer conferencing in higher education. *The Internet and Higher Education, 2*(2–3), 87–105.

Garrison, D. R., & Cleveland-Innes, M. (2005). Facilitating cognitive presence in online learning: Interaction is not enough. *American Journal of Distance Education, 19*(3), 133–148.

Genoni, P., Merrick, H., & Willson, M. (2005). The use of the Internet to activate latent ties in scholarly communities. *First Monday, 10*(12). Retrieved December 14, 2005, from http://firstmonday.org/issues/issue10_12/genoni/index.html

Graff, S., Lin, F., Kinshuk, McGreal, R. (2011). *Intelligent and adaptive learning systems: Technology enhanced support for learners and teachers.* Hershey, PA: IGI Global.

Hamilton, E., & Feenberg, A. (2005). The technical codes of online education. *eLearning, 2*(2), 104–121.

Hampel, R., & Hauck, M. (2004). Towards an effective use of audio-conferencing in distance language courses. *Language Learning and Technology, 8*(1), 66–82. Retrieved January 20, 2006, from http://llt.msu.edu/vol8num1/pdf/hampel.pdf

Hearnshaw, D. (2000). Effective desktop videoconferencing with minimal network demands. *British Journal of Educational Technology, 31*(3), 221–227.

Hillman, D., Willis, D. J., & Gunawardena, C. (1994). Learner-interface interaction in distance education: An extension of contemporary models and strategies for practitioners. *The American Journal of Distance, 8*(2), 30–42.

Hislop, G. W., & Ellis, H. J. C. (2004). A study of faculty effort in online teaching. *The Internet and Higher Education, 7*(1), 15–31.

Hopkins, J., Gibson, W., Solé, C., Savvides, N., & Starkey, H. (2008). Interaction and critical inquiry in asynchronous computer-mediated conferencing: A research agenda. *Open learning: The journal of open and distance learning, 23*(1), 29–42.

Hylén, J. (2007). *Giving knowledge for free: The emergence of open educational resources.* Paris, France: OECD Publishing.

Istrategylabs (2009). http://www.istrategylabs.com/2009/01/2009-facebook-demographics-and-statistics-report-276-growth-in-35-54-year-old-users/

Jaschik, S. (January 8, 2009). Online Social Networking on Campus. *Inside Higher Ed.* http://www.insidehighered.com/news/2009/01/08/network

Johnson, D., Johnson, R., & Smith, K. (1991). *Active learning cooperation in the college classroom.* Edina, MN: Interaction Book Co.

Jokisalo, E., & Riu, A. (2009). Informal learning in the era of Web 2.0. *eLearning Papers.* Accessed September 2, 2011, from http://www.elearningeuropa.info/files/media/media19656.pdf

Kahnwald, N. (2011). *Informelles Lernen in virtuellen Gemeinschaften Nutzungspraktiken: zwischen Informa-tion und Partizipation* [Informal learning in virtual communities use practices: between information and participation]. Dissertation completed at the Technische Universität Dresden.

Kant, E. (1784). An answer to the question: What is enlightenment? Retrieved October 15, 2011, from http://www.english.upenn.edu/~mgamer/Etexts/kant.html

Katz, Y. (2000). The comparative suitability of three ICT distance learning methodologies for college level instruction. *Education Media International, 37*(1), 25–30.

Kawachi, P. (2003). Vicarious interaction and the achieved quality of learning. *International Journal on E-Learning, 2*(4), 39–45.

Ke, F. (2010). Examining online teaching, cognitive, and social presence for adult students, *Computers & Education*, 55(2), 808–820.

Kearsley, G. (1995). *The nature and values of interaction in distance education.* In Third Distance Education Research Symposium. College Park, PA: American Center for the Study of Distance Education.

Keegan, D.J. (1980). On defining distance education. *Distance Education, 1*(1), 13–36.

Kennedy, D., & Duffy, T. (2004). Collaboration — a key principle in distance education. *Open Learning, 19*(2), 203–211.

Klopfer, E., Osterweil, S., & Salen, K. (2009). Moving learning games forward: Obstacles, opportunities and openness. The Education Arcade, MIT. Retrieved October 11, 2011, from http://education.mit.edu/papers/MovingLearningGamesForward_EdArcade.pdf

Koku, E., & Wellman, B. (2004). Scholarly networks as learning communities: The case of TechNet. In S. Barab, R. Kling, & J. H. Gray (Eds.), *Designing virtual communities in the service of learning* (pp. 299–337). Cambridge, UK: Cambridge University Press.

Koper, R. (2001*). Modeling units of study from a pedagogical perspective: The pedagogical meta-model behind EML Heerlen.* Open University of the Netherlands. Retrieved June 28, 2002, from http://eml.ou.nl/introduction/docs/ped-metamodel.pdf

Kruh, J., & Murphy, K. (1990, October). *Interaction and teleconferencing — The key to quality instruction.* In AERIC Document Reproduction Service, ED 329418

Larsen, R. E. (1985). What Communication Theories can Teach the Designer of Computer-Based Training. *Educational Technolog*, (July), 16–19.

Laurillard, D. (1997). *Rethinking university teaching: A framework for the effective use of educational technology.* London: Routledge.

Laurillard, D. (2000). New technologies and the curriculum. In P. Scott. P. (Ed.), *Higher education re-formed* (pp. 133–153) London: Falmer Press.

Lave, J. (1988). *Cognition in practice: Mind, mathematics, and culture in everyday life.*Cambridge, UK: Cambridge University Press.

Lazarus, B. L. (2003). Teaching courses online: How much time does it take? *Journal of Asynchronous Learning Networks, 7*(3). Retrieved December 3, 2005, from http://www.sloan-c.org/publications/jaln/v7n3/v7n3_lazarus.asp

Lee, M. M., Lin, M.-F. G., Bonk, C. J. (2007). OOPS, Turning MIT Opencourseware into Chinese: An analysis of a community of practice of global translators. *International Review of Research in Open and Distance Learning* 8(3) 1–21.

Lobel, M., Neubauer, M., & Swedburg, R. (2002). The eClassroom used as a teacher's training laboratory to measure the impact of group facilitation on attending, participation, interaction, and involvement. *International Review of Research in Open and Distance Learning*, 3(2). Retrieved December 12, 2005, from http://www.irrodl.org/content/v3.2/lns.html

Mabrito, M. (2007). Lurking and Learning: A study of vicarious interaction in the online classroom. *The International Journal of Technology, Knowledge and Society, 3*(2) 35–42.

Miyazoe, T. & Anderson, T. (2010). The Interaction Equivalency Theorem. *Journal of Interactive Online Learning, 9*(2), 94–104.

McInnerney, J. M., & Roberts, T.S. (2004). Online learning: Social interaction and the creation of a sense of community. *Educational Technology & Society, 7*(3), 73–81.

McIsaac, M. S., & Gunawardena, C. N. (1996). Distance education. In D. H. Jonassen (Ed.), *Handbook of research for educational communications and technology: A project of the association for educational communications and technology* (pp. 403–437). New York, NY: Simon & Schuster. Retrieved December 23, 2005, from http://seamonkey.ed.asu.edu/~mcisaac/dechapter/

McLain, B. P. (2005). Estimating faculty and student workload for interaction in online graduate music courses. *Journal of Asynchronous Learning Networks, 9*(3). Retrieved December 7, 2005, from http://www.sloan-c.org/publications/jaln/v9n3/v9n3_mclain.asp

McLuhan, M. (1964). *Understanding media: The extensions of man.* Toronto: McGraw-Hill.

McLuhan, M., McLuhan, E., & Hutchon, K. (1977). *City as classroom: Understanding language and media.* Agincourt, ON: Book Society of Canada.

Merrill, M. D., & Gilbert, C. G. (2008). Effective peer interaction in a problem-centered instructional strategy. *Distance education, 29*(2), 199–207.

Molinari, D. L. (2004). The role of social comments in problem-solving groups in an online class. *American Journal of Distance Education, 18*(2), 89–101.

Moller, L. (1998). Designing communities of learners for asynchronous distance education. *Educational Technology Research and Development, 46*(4), 115–122.

Moore, M. (1989). Three types of interaction. *American Journal of Distance Education, 3*(2), 1–6.

Moore, M., & Kearsley, G. (2005). *Distance education: A systems view (2nd ed.).* Belmont, CA: Wadsworth.

Moore, M. G. (2000). Is distance learning more work or less? *American Journal of Distance Education, 14*(3), 1–5.

Morgan, T., & Carey, S. (2009). From open content to open course models: Increasing access and enabling global participation in higher education. *International Review of Research in Open and Distance Learning* 10(5).

Muñoz L. C., & Towner T. L. (2009) Opening Facebook: How to use Facebook in the college classroom. In I. Gibson (Ed.), *Proceedings of Society for Information Technology & Teacher Education International Conference* (pp. 2623–2627). Charleston, SC. Retrieved May 15, 2010, from http://www46.homepage.villanova.edu/john.immerwahr/TP101/Facebook.pdf

O'Leary, P. F., & Quinlan, Jr., T. J. (2007). Learner-instructor telephone interaction: Effects on satisfaction and Achievement of Online Students. *American Journal of Distance Education, 21*(3), 133–143.

O'Sullivan, P., & Hoffner, C. (1998, November). *Across the greatdivide: Melding mass and interpersonal theory through mediated relationships.* National Communication Association Annual Conference. Retrieved May 21, 2001, from http://www.ilstu.edu/~posull/OS&H1998.htm

Packer, R., & Jordan, K. (2000). Overture. In R. Packer & K. Jordan (Eds.), *Multimedia: From Wagner to virtual reality* (pp. xv–xxxviii). New York, NY: Norton.

Pagney, B. (1988). What advantages can conventional education derive from correspondence education? In D. Sewart, D. Keegan, & B. Holmberg (Eds.), *Distance education: International perspectives* (pp. 157–164). London: Routledge.

Pariser, E. (2011). *The filter bubble: What the Internet is hiding from you.* New York, NY: Penguin.

Rhode, J. F. (2009). Interaction equivalency in self-paced online learning environments: An exploration of learner preferences. *Interactional Review of Research in Open and Distance Learning* 10(1).

Rogoff, B. (1990). *Apprenticeship in thinking: Cognitive development in social context.* New York, NY: Oxford University Press.

Rovai, A. P., & Barnum, K. T. (2003). On-line course effectiveness: An analysis of student interactions and perceptions of learning. *Journal of Distance Education, 18*(1), 57–73.

Rovai, A. P. (2002). Sense of community, perceived cognitive learning, and persistence in asynchronous learning networks. *The Internet and Higher Education, 5*(4), 319–332.

Russell, T.L. (2005). *No significant difference phenomenon.* Retrieved December 22, 2005, from http://www.nosignificantdifference.org/

Schön, D. (1991). *The reflective practitioner: How professionals think in action.* Avebury, UK: Ashgate.

Shea, P., Pickett, A., & Pelz, W. (2003). A follow-up investigation of teaching presence in the SUNY Learning Network. *Journal of the Asychronous Learning Network, 7*(2). Retrieved September 17, 2003, from http://www.aln.org/publications/jaln/v7n2/v7n2_shea.asp#shea4

Shea, P., Hayes, S., Vickers, J., Gozza-Cohen, M., Uzuner, S., Mehta, R., … Rangan, P. (2010). A reexamination of the community of inquiry framework: Social network and content analysis. *The Internet and Higher Education, 13*(1–2), 10–21.

Sheer, V. C., & Fung, T. K. (2007). Can email communication enhance professor-student relationship and student evaluation of professor?: Some empirical evidence. *Journal of Educational Computing Research, 37*(3), 289–306.

Shin, N. (2002). Beyond interaction: The relational construct of 'transactional presence'. *Open Learning, 17*(2). 121–137.

Siemens, G. (2006). *Knowing knowledge.* Vancouver, BC, Canada: Lulu Press.

Sims, R (1997). *Interactivity: A forgotten art?* Retrieved January 20, 2006, from http://www.gsu.edu/~wwwitr/docs/interact/

Slavin, R. (1995). *Cooperative learning theory, research, and practice.* Boston, MA: Allyn and Bacon.

Smith, B. L., & MacGregor, J. T. (1998). What is collaborative learning? In A. Goodsell, M. Maher, V. Tinto, B. L. Smith, & J. MacGregor (Eds.), *Collaborative learning: A sourcebook for higher education* (pp. 9–22). University Par: Pennsylvania State University Press.

Stutt, T. (2010). Why educational games fail. *Educational Technology & Change.* Accessed October 11, 2011, from http://etcjournal.com/2010/10/18/why-educational-games-fail/

Sutton, L. (2000). *Vicarious interaction in a course enhanced through the use of computer-mediated communication* (Unpublished doctoral dissertation). Arizona State University, Tempe.

Swan, K., Shea, P., Fredericksen, E., Pickett, A., Pelz, W., & Maher, G. (2000). Building knowledge building communities: Consistency, contact and communication in the virtual classroom. *Journal of Educational Computing Research, 23*(4), 359–383.

Theroux, J., & Kilbane, C. (2004). Experimental online case study for a breakthrough in student engagement: Description and results. *Journal of Asynchronous Learning Networks*, 8(4). Retrieved December 10, 2005, from http://www.sloan-c.org/publications/jaln/v8n4/v8n4_theroux.asp

Trafford, P. (2005, July). Mobile blogs, personal reflections and learning environments. *Ariadne Magazine, 44.* Retrieved January 20, 2006, from http://www.ariadne.ac.uk/issue44/trafford/

Tuovinen, J. (2000). Multimedia distance education interactions. *Education Media International, 37*(1), 16–24.

Wang, Y. (2004). Supporting synchronous distance language learning with desktop videoconferencing. *Language Learning and Technology, 8*(3), 1–37. Retrieved January 20, 2006, from http://www.llt.msu.edu/vol-8num3/pdf/wang.pd

Wellman, B., Koku, E., & Hunsinger, J. (2005). Networked scholarship. In J. Weiss, J. Nolan, & J. Hunsinger (Eds.), *International handbook of virtual learning environments* (pp. 1399–1417) Amsterdam: Springer.

Wenger, E. (1998). *Communities of practice: Learning, meaning, and identity.* Cambridge, UK: Cambridge University Press.

Wenger, E., McDermott, R., & Snyder, W. M. (2002). *Cultivating communities of practice.* Boston, MA: Harvard Business School Press.

Wiener, N. (1950). *The human use of human beings.* New York, NY: The Riverside Press.

Wlodkowski, R. (1985). *Enhancing adult motivation to learn.* San Francisco, CA: Jossey-Bass.

Yuan, L., MacNeill, S., & Kraan, W. (2008). *Open educational resources—opportunities and challenges for higher education.* Retrieved September 2, 2011, from http://learn.creativecommons.org/wp-content/uploads/2008/09/oer_briefing_paper.pdf

23

TEACHING AND LEARNING IN NEGOTIATED AND INFORMAL ONLINE LEARNING ENVIRONMENTS[1]

JANETTE R. HILL, DENISE P. DOMIZI, MINCHI C. KIM, AND HYEONJIN KIM

Grounded in the *Continuum of Learning Environments* perspective (National Research Council, 2009), negotiated and informal learning environments are differentiated in (a) the degree of learners' choices for learning goals, activities, tools, and resources, (a) design of interactions and scaffolds, and (c) types and foci of assessment.

We view informal learning environments as a learning context where learners make more voluntary choices, learners themselves design learning activities to a greater degree, and assessments are more situated, sometimes invisible (or hidden). Each environment also manifests design and learning features associated with underlying epistemological distinctions. In negotiated distance learning environments (NDLEs), learning goals and means are jointly determined, balancing individual with externally established priorities. In informal distance learning environments (IDLEs), learners identify unique learning goals, deploy individual learning approaches, and assume responsibility for assessing their learning. Informal learning takes place in a variety of settings including homes and museums, and during any number of everyday activities (NRC, 2009) whereas the primary contexts for negotiated learning are schools, homeschools, and extracurricular programs, and community-supported enrichment programs. While each has unique theoretical foundations and assumptions, they share common environmental components, including interaction strategies, resources, tools, scaffolds, and assessment strategies. Each is enacted according to its unique epistemological foundations and associated learning goals and contexts.

NEGOTIATED DISTANCE LEARNING ENVIRONMENTS

Negotiated distance learning environments are designed to facilitate the negotiation of learning goals and to promote learner autonomy. Typically, NDLEs manifest constructivist epistemology in that learners construct knowledge by actively engaging in learning activities and meaning making (Piaget, 1972). The nature of knowledge is not fixed; rather, it varies across individuals and communities. The process of knowledge building is enabled by individuals' meaning making and through collaborative interactions with people in a community (Lave & Wenger, 1991; Vygotsky, 1978). Constructivist orientations focus on learner-centered reasoning and knowledge construction, as learners negotiate which components to use and how to use them. Accordingly, constructivist pedagogical models (e.g., problem-based learning, project-based learning, and resource-based learning) support NDLEs. Constructivist pedagogical models share several of the components and characteristics typically associated with scaffolding (Hannafin, Land, & Oliver, 1999; Jonassen, 1999). Unlike direct instruction, scaffolding is a unique and important feature in learning because it facilitates individual meaning-making and goal-setting. Scaffolding also helps learners to practice and develop autonomous learning processes.

Several NDLEs make active use of scaffolding to assist learners. ESTEPWeb (Derry & ESTEP Research Group, 2004) shows how scaffolds can be used effectively to assist users in complex environments. Individuals often become disoriented—lost in hyperspace—while navigating resources in complex learning contexts (Clark, 2003) and need guidance through discourse, driving questions, worksheets, and examples. ESTEPWeb guides pre-service teachers in their study of Learning Sciences using modified problem-based learning. Procedural guidance and opportunities for collaboration are afforded through a variety of tools including Group Whiteboard, My Notebooks, and Discussion Board. Online problem-based scaffolds provide steps that guide students' design work (e.g., step 2, initial proposal), including due dates, guidelines, and templates for writing and submitting ideas (i.e., My Notebook). Online facilitation provides monitoring and formative assessment of individual and group progress by collecting and displaying student performance data while offline facilitation, designed to guide discussions and submissions, is provided by teaching assistants. The pre-service teachers involved in ESTEPWeb reported that both the individual and collaborative activities were useful for their future lesson planning.

NDLE COMPONENTS

NDLEs involve many core components of constructivist learning environments, including interaction, resources, tools, scaffolding, and assessment, all of which are designed to support learner-centered learning activities. The negotiation in learning generally occurs between and among learners, instructors and/or peers (virtual or live), affordances of the environments, and constraints and limitations in available resources and tools. Negotiation also occurs as students establish their learning goals, select and adapt resources to their learning goals, discuss emergent understandings, and reflect on their learning processes. NDLE components vary according to learner type, learning style, preferences, and motivation. Individuals use and adapt various components, such as exploration tools, scaffolding questions, and discussion boards based on their needs.

An example of NDLEs, WebQuests (Dodge, 1995, 2001) have been used for diverse subjects and various levels of learners in both online and face-to-face contexts, including kindergarten through higher education classes in social studies, mathematics, and science (see examples, http://webquest.org). WebQuest's six phases, including introduction, task, information sources, description of process, guidance, and conclusion, guide student learning through inquiry-based or project-based approach. WebQuests enable learners to negotiate the goals of the project and paths to investigate the problem with instructors and peers.

Advances in emergent technologies including social media and virtual worlds have contributed to re-conceptualizing key components of NDLEs. For example, Cifuentes, Xochihua, and Edwards (2011) used Web 2.0 technology such as blogs, wikis, image galleries, interactive desktop videoconferencing, and RSS feeds, in addition to the traditional course management system, Blackboard. Web 2.0 technology serves as a tool for enhancing interaction and scaffolding in NDLEs by facilitating two-way communication, interactive content, and student contributions.

Learning from Interactions

Because of the constructive nature of NDLEs, interactions are often designed to promote problem-solving and self-regulation skills. This shift is apparent in Web-based learning environments, where learning management systems (e.g., Blackboard, Moodle) are designed to help students effectively act on their learning goals (e.g., Kim & Hannafin, 2004; Kitsantas & Dabbagh, 2004; Whipp & Chiarelli, 2004). Dabbagh and Kitsantas (2005) explored student interaction using a learning management system, WebCT (e.g., administrative, collaborative and communication, content creation and delivery, and assessment tools) to facilitate instructional design conceptual understanding and self-regulation. The results indicated that use of WebCT features helped students to develop self-regulation design skills. Content development and delivery experience supported individual goal setting, time management, and help seeking behavior, while technological functions enabled students to pace completion of course assignments.

Learners may also engage with instructors and peers in NDLEs. Instructor interactions are reified as learners read text, find Web resources, and use asynchronous discussion boards (e.g., Garrison & Cleveland-Innes, 2005; Gerber, Scott, & Clements, 2005). The instructor participates in but does not dominate discussions, asking provocative questions, suggesting alternatives, encouraging multiple perspectives, and modeling the practices of their specific community. In discovery learning, for example, instructor planning and structuring can promote problem-solving and interpretation, while unplanned, unstructured activities may engender misunderstandings (Tallent-Runnels et al., 2006). In a recent study, results indicated that students who negotiated and clarified understandings through asynchronous Socratic dialog with an instructor (clarifying students' comments and probing students' assumptions, reasons, and evidence) demonstrated advanced critical thinking skills in their discourse (Yang, Newby, & Bill, 2005).

Uribe, Klein, and Sullivan (2003) investigated online collaboration's influence on student performance, time on task, and attitudes during ill-structured problem solving. Collaborative dyads solved ill-defined problem scenarios better and spent significantly more time on task by sharing via discussion board than the students who worked individually. On the other hand, Heo, Kim, and Kim (2010) reported challenges in promoting student peer interaction during a group-based project for instructional design. The results indicated that students revealed a challenge to promote meaningful interaction between peers even with the group that showed the highest number of postings. They concluded that it essential for online instructors to provide adaptive guidelines and resources for effectively managing projects, finding resources, and reflecting on the process.

Recently, NDLEs have adopted social media as a means to enhance peer-to-peer interactions through social networking and collaborative projects such as wikis (Kaplan & Haenlein, 2009). Social media refers to "a group of Internet-based applications that build on the ideological and technological foundations of Web 2.0 which allows the creation and exchange of user-generated content" (Kaplan & Haenlein, 2010, p. 61). In Cifuentes et al.'s (2011) study, students used Facebook to provide comments on their peers' graphic design work and a wiki to collaboratively construct a visual literacy Web site. Although students initially struggled with posting comments, they eventually became familiar with the process and began to give constructive feedback. Although students have reported benefits of social media in NDLEs, such as timely and effective interactions with peers and instructors, they have encountered technical problems and cognitive overload with the use of them. This may be attributed to learner-interface interaction (Hillman, Willis, & Gunawardena, 1994). The researchers suggested providing different assignments based on learners' prior experiences with social media and creating a separate forum for learners to ask their peers for technical help.

Other researchers (So, Seow, & Looi, 2009) have used mobile devices (e.g., Ultra Mobile Personal Computers, or UMPCs) and have indicated more complex interactions of students, such as location-based interactions and activities. They used UMPC with Google Maps for elementary students' learning in situ. As a result, students created locative contents (i.e., 239 location markers on the Google Maps space) and built collaborative knowledge by interacting with peers and locations. In this blended NDLE, students learned in a real environment and continued their learning interactions in a virtual space with mobile devices and Web 2.0 technology.

Resources

As in constructivist environments, resources in NDLEs play important roles in student learning by providing useful information and knowledge from electronic, print, and human sources (Hannafin et al., 1999). In NDLEs, "the more relevant a resource is to an individual's learning goals, and the more accessible it is, the greater its utility" (Hannafin et al., 1999, p.126). Resources are used in various NDLE contexts, including resource-based learning (Armatas, Holt, & Rice, 2003; Hill, Hannafin, & Domizi, 2005; Macdonald, Heap, & Mason, 2001), problem-based learning (Derry & ESTEP, 2004), case-based learning (Kim, Hannafin, & Kim, 2005), inquiry-based learning (Dodge, 1995), and information seeking (Hill & Hannafin, 1997). In online case-based learning, a variety of resources are available, including Web-based cases, lesson plans, lesson materials, textbooks, and related references. Kim et al. (2005) found that pre-service teachers used resources in a primary or supplementary capacity by evaluating each for their individual lesson goals and designs. This experience enabled pre-service teachers to gain a deeper understanding of complex classroom situations by using and coordinating various resources.

Researchers have reported that learners develop and refine both critical thinking (Dodge, 2001) and metacognitive and self-regulation skills (Hill & Hannafin, 1997; Macdonald et al., 2001) when they seek and use diverse resources to negotiate meaning. However, the benefits of NDLE resources vary according to learners' abilities and strategies (Macdonald et al., 2001). Hill and Hannafin (1997) explored adult learners' strategies while seeking information on the Internet. Participants with high metacognitive knowledge, prior knowledge of content and technology systems, and self-efficacy were best able to refine their searching actions and recognize their orientation within the system. In contrast, browsing and searching among learners with low metacognitive knowledge became readily disoriented and engaged in random searching.

Oliver and Hannafin (2001) reported that learners often failed to use resources in the absence of procedural and metacognitive support. Twelve eighth grade students were asked to find, frame, and solve open-ended scientific problems via the online tools as they reviewed resources using peers, teacher, and online scaffolds. Students whose searching was scaffolded (e.g., through the use of advance organizers) sought information relevant to the problem, while those without scaffolds tended to find little problem-related information, sought information randomly, and did not use keywords effectively. Instructor guidance is critical when using various resources in an environment with high learner autonomy.

Web 2.0 technologies emphasize the social nature of resources on the Web and have shifted "the 'old' model of the Web as a container of information accessed passively by users—into a platform for social and collaborative exchange" (Jovanovic, Gasevic, Torniai, Bateman, & Hatala, 2009, p. 279). For example, learners are able to share and annotate Web resources by using social bookmarking and tagging platforms. However, while the Web is the most prevalent repository for these resources, Web 2.0 technologies, like their predecessors, continue to present challenges regarding their use in NDLEs due to the uncertainty of their relevance to learning goals and the validity of their content (Hill & Hannafin, 1997; Jovanovic et al., 2009).

Tools

Tools in NDLEs allow learners (a) to store, locate, and share information and resources, (b) to engage in higher-order and critical thinking by providing a problem-solving context or virtual world, and (c) to communicate and network with peers, instructors, and other members in a community of practice.

First, students utilize a wide array of Web site and content communities including YouTube and Flickr (Kaplan & Haenlein, 2010) to store, locate, and share resources for learning. With the proliferation of such resources, concerns over non-validated sources, limited classroom time and support for students to navigate and for teachers to monitor (Sharples, Graber, Harrison, & Logan, 2009), age-inappropriate sites have grown (Soloway & Wallace, 1997). Website-filtering (Recker, Walker, & Lawless, 2003), online library systems with filtered resources, and content communities designed for classroom use (e.g., TeacherTube) have become increasingly important as educators seek to support students in finding, filtering, and utilizing learning resources.

Through the Michigan Digital Library Project, Wallace, Kupperman, Krajcik, and Soloway (2000) studied pairs of sixth graders as they sought and used Web-based resources to support inquiry-oriented ecology activities. Video and audio captures of student activities during the 6-day activities indicated that students' information seeking involves "asking and refining questions, exploring, gathering, and evaluating information" (p. 87). Although the goal was to enhance students' interest and understanding of ecology through Web-based research, the students focused on finding information and completing the assignments quickly. Students tended to seek the correct answers rather than exploring, which was described as an intermediate stage between seeking information and answer generation. The researchers concluded that the cognitive complexity involved in seeking and exploring resources requires meta-knowledge and navigation skills to access and use online sources. Metacognitive scaffolds embedded in the exploration tools, for example, can be used to structure and support learning activities hierarchically.

Second, tools in NDLEs support learners actively engaging in higher-order and critical thinking by providing a problem-solving context or virtual world. Tools can provide a structure and learning context in which students identify, investigate, and solve authentic problems. For example, in Web-based Inquiry Science Environments (WISE), students collect scientific evidence from reliable sources (e.g., scientists and government agencies) in order to confront controversial or naïve scientific theories, construct their own queries, and warrant conclusions (Linn, Clark, & Slotta, 2003). Using embedded scaffolds, students learn science in personally meaningful ways, exchange help with peers, and continuously expand their interest in every day science. Learning activities in NDLEs may be linked to and supported by various forms of meta-context such as virtual world (e.g., Second Life), virtual game worlds, and virtual social worlds (Kaplan & Haenlein, 2010), participatory simulations as a microworld (Colella, 2000), interactive animations with multiple knowledge representations (Roschelle et al., 2010) and augmented reality simulations (Squire & Klopfer, 2007).

Third, tools in NDLEs allow learners to communicate and network with peers, instructors, and other members in a community of practice. Those tools, traditionally supported by discussion forums and online journals and recently advanced by numerous forms of blogs, wikis, and social networking sites, may help learners to present their knowledge, receive feedback, and reflect on their learning processes. In Jonassen and Kwon's (2001) study, 18 undergraduate engineering students collaboratively solved problems through face-to-face group meetings and asynchronous computer-mediated communication (CMC). Data were collected from student questionnaires and conversations. Using tools to support analyzing problems, developing solutions, and reflecting on the process, CMC students demonstrated superior problem-solving and richer task-oriented patterns. The researchers attributed improvements to flexibility in learning time and space, which allowed CMC students to spend more time reflecting and thinking critically.

Similarly Daroszewski, Kinser, and Lloyd (2004) found that nursing students who posted weekly online journals demonstrated superior critical thinking, mentoring, and socialization about their practical clinical experiences. Graduate nursing students were directed to write a minimum of three weekly journal entries, which included one original entry and two responses to colleagues' journal entries. Journal entries were analyzed for content, and students completed a 10-item questionnaire. Journal entries indicated that students were building shared understanding and meaning of their peers' clinical settings, while the surveys indicated that students appreciated the opportunity to share and compare experiences and learn more about the different practical settings. In this instance, the opportunity to engage in discourse allowed nursing students to learn from and contribute to a shared pool of experiences.

Harasim (2002) reported success in sharing expertise and co-constructing knowledge through the Global Educators' Network. International scholars from over 60 countries contributed to seminars and discussion on online teaching and learning. Data from interviews, surveys, email communications, and participants' comments were analyzed. The findings revealed that participants generated and linked initial ideas through "intellectual convergence" (p. 182) which enabled them to cooperatively refine, revise, and develop their perspectives. Harasim concluded that the social and friendly nature of the community, which encouraged intellectual and social discourse, contributed to successful knowledge sharing and generating observed.

More recently, researchers have begun to investigate how social media can enhance learning in distance settings. Pachler and Daly (2009) argued that narrative is an essential means with which learners can build collaborative knowledge within blogs and the structure of knowledge is not "pre-defined but evolves through the complex negotiation of narrative nodes that act as catalysts for meaning-making" (p. 15). Luehmann (2008) also reported a middle school teacher's successful use of her blog as a tool to share her teaching practice with her colleagues, provide mentoring support for beginning teachers, and reflect on her own teaching and develop identity as a teacher.

Scaffolds

NDLE scaffolds help to "problematize" (Reiser, 2004, p. 282) ideas and beliefs and corroborate or revise individual knowledge (e.g., conceptual scaffolds; see Hill & Hannafin, 2001), enable learners to conduct formative progress assessments and clarify or adjust goals and tasks (e.g., metacognitive and procedural scaffolds), and encourage alternative views and perspectives to accommodate knowledge (e.g., strategic scaffolds). In NDLEs, scaffolds are provided not from a single source but three different sources that dynamically interact with each other: technology-based scaffolds, instructor-based scaffolds, and peer-based scaffolds (Kim & Hannafin, 2011; Kim, Hannafin, & Bryan, 2007).

First, technology-based scaffolds may augment or supplant mentoring traditionally provided by live instructors. For example, online expert cases provided exemplars for students to relate their own experience to the learning contexts (Kim et al., 2005). Likewise, embedded prompts can facilitate learners' thinking about reasoning processes and problem solving strategies. Ge and Land (2003) studied the effects of peer interaction and question prompts on the problem solving of 117 undergraduate students enrolled in introductory Information Sciences and Technology classes. Students were randomly assigned them to a peer-question, peer-control, individual-question, and individual-control group. The researchers reported a significant relationship between question prompts and problem-solving performance, which they attributed to conceptual and metacognitive scaffolds that helped students identify relevant information, organize plans, generate arguments based upon the information, and evaluate solutions.

Second, instructor-based scaffolds may include feedback assistance and prompts that foster critical thinking. Hill (2002) reported that Could-Should-Must (CSM) messages functioned as procedural scaffolds and outlined necessary activities. Weekly CSM messages were sent to remind students of what they could be, should be and must be doing related to class activities. Hill reported that CSM strategies helped distant learners to build "structural habits" (p. 77), remain on-task, and overcome limited numbers of communication and face-to-face meetings.

Whipp (2003) studied pre-service teachers' use of electronic discussion tools to share ideas and experiences in urban education settings. "Tailored questioning" scaffolds cued critical reflection through online discussion (p. 330). For example, students posted more descriptive and reasoned email responses to the instructor's question regarding whether White teachers could teach African American students effectively. When the instructor employed specific, thought provoking questions tailored to students' interests and their teaching context (e.g., socioeconomic issues), students were better able to contemplate multiple perspectives and express critical ideas.

Chong's (2010) study emphasized the importance of instructor-based scaffolds when students received supervision through blogs from their instructors and wrote a research paper in a hybrid music class. Chong (2010) suggested strategies that instructors can employ to promote student learning with blogging including helping students build ownership, pre-requisite knowledge, and progress map, monitor student progress and provide feedback, and foster peer interactions.

Third, researchers have explored various peer-based scaffolds in distance education. Hoadley and Linn (2000) examined how eighth graders debated and developed scientific understanding about colors using an asynchronous, online discussion board to discuss: "How do the paint chips look different under different lighting?" (p. 844). The authors suggested that performance improved because students shared perspectives through peer discussion. While such studies provide initial evidence of the impact of peer scaffolding, research is needed to promote meaningful interaction among peers in NDLEs.

Assessment

NDLE assessment is formative, dynamic, interactive, and negotiated between instructors and learners. Broad learning goals, defined by the instructional authority, guide students by framing individual objectives and tasks; the negotiation of assessment varies accordingly. Likewise, formats for delivering and supporting assessment range from quizzes, exams, and tests to individual or group projects or electronic portfolios (Mason, Pegler, & Weller, 2004).

Gulikers, Bastiaens, and Kirschner (2004) argue that authentic assessment requires careful consideration of associated dimensions—authentic tasks, physical or virtual context, social context, assessment result, and criteria and standards. NDLE interest has emerged in tools that address lifelong learning, student self-direction, and reflection and revision of one's work. Mason et al. (2004) studied electronic portfolio assessment in student-centered, online graduate courses. Students' e-portfolios contained selected resources and projects from different courses (e.g., writings, PowerPoint slides, and online discussion messages). Mason et al. reported that students integrated experiences from various courses and built authentic, meaningful artifacts in their e-portfolios, and advised instructors to offer explicit guidelines regarding e-portfolio design. Alternative evidence and assessments provided opportunities to focus on personally meaningful topics and to develop strategies for student-centered learning.

Using a Web-based peer assessment system (NetPeas) with undergraduate students, Lin, Liu, and Yuan (2001) examined the relationship between feedback mode (specific and holistic) and thinking patterns (high executive and low executive). They reported that students with high executive thinking patterns improved significantly using peer assessments but students with low executive thinking patterns did not. Predictably, high executive thinkers tended to offer better quality comments while low executive thinkers benefited most from specific than generic feedback.

IMPLICATIONS

NDLEs emphasize active student roles in generating and revising learning goals, selecting tools and resources, and conducting self-assessment. However, comparatively little research exists regarding what or how guidance enhances learners' different activities in a variety of online learning settings. Research is warranted to (a) identify effective guidance types and functions and how guidance interacts with other NDLE components; (b) investigate the guidance needed to support quality interactions between instructors and peers; (c) explore effective ways to balance structured, explicit and open-ended, implicit guidance to support online learning; and (d) examine how different scaffolding strategies, jointly provided by teachers, peers, and technologies in a dynamic learning context, can support or hamper students' use of resources and learning (Kim & Hannafin, 2011; Tabak, 2004).

Given the advent and growth of social media, simulations, and games (NRC, 2011), Prensky (2001) argues that the learning processes and the nature of learning with digital natives need to be reconceptualized. For instance, microblogging, which refers to "communication via the Web by writing short messages restricted to 140 characters" (Ebner, Lienhardt, Rohs, & Meyer, 2010, p. 92), has a potential to engage students in "process-oriented learning" (p. 99) by generating questions, providing responses, exchanging ideas and resources, and reflecting on progress. However, more research is needed to fully examine the potential of such emergent tools and impact on learning and teaching in distance learning settings.

Finally, research is needed to explore how social media, simulations, and games can be successfully integrated into formal education contexts. Researchers criticized the limited empirical evidence on student use of simulations and games and learning outcomes (Ke, 2008; NRC, 2011). How students transfer their experiences and skills with online simulations and games and Web 2.0 to formal education requires further study (Clark, Logan, Luckin, Mee, & Oliver, 2009; Shaffer, 2006). Alternative assessments, that have gained widespread interests with the emergent technologies, require more examinations on their validity for negotiated learning goals influenced by self-regulation and group collaboration in NDLEs.

INFORMAL DISTANCE LEARNING ENVIRONMENTS (IDLES)

According to the National Resource Council's report (2009), informal learning environments "include a broad array of settings, such as family discussions at home, visits to museums, nature centers, or other designed settings, and everyday activities like gardening, as well as recreational activities like hiking and fishing, and participation in clubs" (p. 1). These settings can also include media and online environments.

IDLEs provide opportunities for interaction and collaboration to promote shared understanding. Various tools, resources, and technologies are used to support learner collaboration and engagement. For example, Old Time (OT) music community Sugar in the Gourd (http://forum.sugarinthegourd.com/) is an online space that provides useful links and information about OT music, as well as a discussion forum where members can discuss OT music, post and answer questions, embed YouTube videos, and link to their personal Websites, blogs, or other sites of interest. Waldron (2009) used a cyber-ethnographic approach to study this informal environment, using Wenger's (1998) community of practice as a theoretical framework. She found that members were using and adapting the tools and affordances of the technology in order to learn with and from each other. For example, when one member posted a question about how to create midi files, she received a multitude of responses that included discussions of how different members learn to play songs, pedagogy, technology recommendations, and links to various helpful Websites.

Ebner, Lienhardt, Rohs, and Meyer (2010) were interested in whether microblogs could facilitate informal learning in an economics and management class. They contend that there is an important distinction between formal and informal learning based on environment, motivation, and pedagogical influence, and that most learning is a combination of both formal and informal. With this in mind, they found that their students communicated with and learned from each other through microblogging and solved "real" problems together. Because the free-exchange of their messages were not tied to specific learning goals, they suggest that informal learning did take place.

In an example where an informal learning environment meets a more structured curriculum, the Mote Aquarium's (Sarasota, Florida) SeaTrek Distance Learning Project uses highly interactive videoconferences to facilitate interaction with more knowledgeable others (see http://www.seatrek.org/). Participants interact with educational staff, a presenter, and a technology coordinator during virtual visits, using a combination of live-feed and pre-recorded videos of scientists and animals, PowerPoint slides, the Internet, sound effects, and music. Participants can also engage in activities with knowledgeable affiliates (e.g., scientists) to ask questions and explore concepts.

Researchers have studied the impact of the SeaTrek program on students' perceptions and the usability of the program in schools. Ba and Keisch (2004) observed school-based classrooms and videoconferences from the SeaTrek studio, and interviewed project staff and SeaTrek teams in the schools. They also conducted focus groups and administered online surveys. Students and teachers reported improved content knowledge as well as incidental increases in curiosity about science-related professions, use of multimedia technology, and use of video as an educational tool.

On-demand Resources Support Individual Learning

In order to address diverse learner needs, IDLE resources often vary in form and may represent multiple perspectives (Hill et al., 2005). With the ubiquity of smart phones and other mobile devices, learners now have instant access to resources for both intentional learning situations, as well as those unexpected, situational encounters that occur in everyday life (Clough, Jones, McAndrew, & Scanlon, 2008).

Clough et al. (2008) were interested in how experienced smartphone and PDA users used their devices for intentional informal learning. They found that not only did participants use their devices to support intentional learning, but they were also able to adapt the features on their devices to suit their needs as learners. Further, they found that participants were using their devices as resources for unforeseen situational learning opportunities that arose in situated contexts.

To help facilitate further understanding of how the devices were being used, Clough et al. (2008) adapted Patten, Arnedillo Sanchez, and Tangney's (2006) mobile learning functional framework to be more reflective of informal mobile learning. Categories in the revised framework of informal learning activities that are supported by mobile devices are: referential (i.e., podcasts, dictionaries), location aware (GPS), reflective (reviewing notes, photos, recorded sounds; reading/posting to forums), data collection (taking photos, recording sounds), constructive (taking notes, contributing to Web 2.0), and administrative (calendars, contacts). Continued exploration of mobile learning is an area of needed exploration in IDLEs.

The online version of the Exploratorium (http://www.exploratorium.edu) both supplements and works independently of the physical museum in California. The

Exploratorium is a widely recognized, resource-rich informal learning environment. The Exploratorium Website is a rich repository, both in number and variety of resources available on the site (see www.exploratorium.edu/educate/dl.html), including images, activities, movies, and audio files. During Webcasts, learners observe and hear experts discuss a variety of topics (e.g., space exploration) and interact via a dynamic e-mail system enabled during the broadcast. This enables real-time access to different resources and expert knowledge that can be pursued according to individual interests.

Ford Motor Company's Learning Network (FLN) also makes extensive use of resources. FLN contains more than 400,000 titles, including online courses, e-books, articles, Websites, and thousands of 20-minute learning objects. Consistent with IDLE principles, resources are designed to support learning when and where needed. Although evaluation data have not yet published publicly, Ford representatives suggest that FLN is both positively received and useful for learning (Sosbe, 2003).

Since resources can vary in number and form, IDLEs may require guidance in the appropriate use resources. Libraries, for example, now employ "virtual reference desks" to assist learners in using online resources. Initially, librarians used e-mail or chat rooms to provide support, but with limited success. Advances in Web contact center software have enabled reference librarians to provide services that approximate the experience at a call center (e.g., calling for technical assistance at Apple; Coffman, 2001). Technologies such as Virtual Reference Desk enable librarians to provide the just-in-time assistance when working in a virtual library space.

Varied Tools

IDLE tools must be sufficiently robust to support a range of goals and applications per individual goals and needs. Several dynamic tools are used in The Mixxer to explore the learning of language online (Elia, 2006). As stated on the Website, "The Mixxer is designed to connect language learners around the world so that everyone is both student and teacher" (see http://www.language-exchanges.org). Video conferencing via Skype® is used to connect learners with more knowledgeable others (native speakers), while blogs tools are used to provide a text-based option for gathering knowledge. Learners sign up and then have access to other learners around the world. The dynamic nature of the tools enables learners to extend their experience in ways that enable learning beyond what might have been expected or anticipated.

Manipulation. Tools enabling user manipulation are important for self-study. For example, by using a database learners can gather, explore and manipulate information gathered during the informal experience. The CancerHelp UK Website has been studied in terms of how individuals learn about cancer, cancer treatment, and cancer recovery, and how it meets individually defined needs and goals (Tweddle, James, & Daniels, 2000). Using the database, individuals capture unique data for their personal needs, enabling customized analysis and application in real time.

In a two-phase pilot study, Tweddle et al. (2000) interviewed a total of 23 patients and relatives to assess attitudes toward their Website. During phase one, 14 participants were invited to use the site while being observed, while during the second phase 9 participants representing a mix of gender, age (21–80), and computer experience used the site independently. Results indicated that those who used the site (phase two) independently to search and retrieve information as needed/desired reported positive cognitive and affective outcomes. The authors concluded that manner of site use has important implications for how medical information should be organized and conveyed. By enabling individuals to address personal needs and dynamic questions related to cancer, initial results indicate that CancerHelp met highly situated needs driven by the individual's motivation and need to learn.

Representation. Discussion boards, typically considered a communication tool, can also be used to represent artifacts of understanding. Unlike word processors, they can document the emergence of both individual and shared understanding by reviewing the conversations and reflecting on what has been shared. Gustafson et al. (2001) demonstrated the power of a computer-based patient communication support system with younger women (under the age of 60) with breast cancer, particularly for disadvantaged groups (e.g., African American women, women without insurance). Using a controlled experiment (n = 246), breast cancer patients in the experimental group (n = 147) were given access to Comprehensive Health Enhancement Support System (CHESS) to assist with information provision, decision making, and emotional support. Results indicated that the experimental group reported better information competence and social support, and the disadvantaged group benefited most.

Mobile devices (e.g., PDAs, smart phones) are increasingly used to enable access to representations for informal learning in a variety of contexts. Sung, Hou, Liu, and Chang (2010) explored how elementary students made use of mobile devices for learning during a museum visit. Participants were observed as they explored the museum, making use of information at exhibits as well as a guide available on a mobile device. Results from the study indicated that the problem-solving mobile guide enabled participants to engage in more learner to learner and learner to exhibit interactions than did a more traditional audio-visual mobile guide or paper-based guide. While more research is needed in this emerging area, clearly it is a growing area of interest for informal learning.

Community Scaffolds

In IDLEs, human resources scaffold the development of knowledge and understanding using communication tools (e.g., bulletin boards, chat rooms). CENTERS (CollaborativE INformal InTERaction System) was developed to create opportunities for interaction in an online environment (Contreras-Castillo, Favela, Pérez-Fragoso, & Santamaría-del-Angel, 2004). Participants came from two Mexican universities and included 15 graduate students, 28 undergraduate students, and four teachers enrolled in one of four asynchronous, online courses. The students and teachers were able to identify other participants logged on to the CENTERS system and to interact with them through chat and instant messaging. The researchers reported that the system satisfied the students' need to interact, increased collaboration, helped students learn content knowledge, and helped build social relationships between classmates and their instructors, thereby reducing feelings of isolation.

The CENTERS interface was designed to allow users just-in-time interactions with their peers and instructor. When students were confused, they could send a message to another user logged on to the system. If that student was also confused, they could discuss the issue in a chat room and ultimately ask their teacher for help using those same communication tools. The researchers suggested that the exchanges helped the learners strengthen relationships with classmates and instructor, and to improve understanding of the course material.

Several online mentoring communities scaffold learning informally. MentorNet (www.mentornet.net) is designed to link female students with working professionals in science and math. A 2003 evaluation involved over 2,000 matched mentors and mentees who completed a survey, with a subset completing interviews (see full report at http://www.mentornet.net/documents/files/WomenofColorFinalReportMay2004.pdf). According to Barsion (2004), the vast majority of the participants reported a positive experience with MentorNet for informal learning, including information on careers and fields of study. Participants also reported that mentor support and encouragement were important for their educational experiences. Like CENTERS, MentorNet enables multiples levels of interaction between less and more knowledgeable others.

Individual Assessment

While assessment is important, individual accountability is the primary focus of IDLE assessment. Fundamentally, the uniquely individual goals and aims of participants frame the assessment; each individual determines the extent to which his or her goals and aims have been addressed. Such assessments, however, can prove difficult to identify or validate. Rennert-Ariev (2005) identified several challenges with self-assessment, including the myriad of highly personal and individualized perspectives that influence the assessment. Halliday and Hagar (2002) suggested that context should be considered when judging formal or informal learning processes; context varies with the individual situations and circumstances of individuals.

In IDLEs, learners have reported difficulty identifying their unplanned or incidental learning outcomes. McFerrin (1999) studied a group of 22 students in a graduate level asynchronous online distance education class, and reported that incidental learning, including personal development, including time management, self-directed behaviors, self-confidence, and self-regulation, resulted from the use of the technology itself. These skills were not included in the course objectives, but resulted from activities related to participation. McFerrin found that the students did not differentiate between these incidental outcomes and those that were intended in the course design.

IMPLICATIONS

IDLEs have become increasingly prevalent in the workplace, community, science centers and museums. The research, paradoxically, remains sparse. In many ways, IDLEs remain in their infancy. We need to expand our understanding of how people learn informally at a distance, particularly what people use, how they use it, and what they want to get out of it (see Imel, 2003, for an overview of issues). Of particular interest is the role of individual interaction with different resources, scaffolds, and peers and how these interactions might lead to learning. Given that IDLEs support different interests and goals, individual tools and resources use may appear idiosyncratic; interactions may prove to be uniquely metacognitive and reflective in nature. For designers to understand how to support learning in such environments, rich descriptions of individual use of tools are needed. In addition, we need to better understand the preferences of different types of learners so that appropriate tools, resources, and interactions can be made available.

It could be argued that Web 2.0 brings together many, if not all of the IDLE components we have discussed through "supporting informal conversation, reflexive dialogue and collaborative content generation" (McLoughlin & Lee, 2010, p. 28). With the prevalence of social networking sites, blogs, wikis, online virtual communities, and with the ever-growing number of user-populated sites that support rich media such as YouTube and Flickr, people from around the world with common interests can meet in a virtual space to collaborate and interact, share ideas, build resources, and learn with and from each other (Brown & Adler, 2008). More work is needed in this area to fully understand their contributions to IDLEs.

FUTURE DIRECTIONS FOR NDLES AND IDLES

Communication and networking tools are central to both NDLEs and IDLEs where negotiation of ideas and exploration of individual resources are at a premium. Still, little research exists describing how tools should be employed and structured to support specific learning and thinking interactions (Ravenscroft, 2009; Tallent-Runnels et al., 2006). Continued context-specific research (i.e., NDLE, IDLE) will help facilitate answers to these questions. For example, Thomas (2002) identified a variety of factors that can influence the level of student engagement in high-level thinking. He also indicated that discussion boards do not necessarily support engagement in conversational learning or shared knowledge building. Thus, one avenue of research is to examine how the interface and structure of communication tools can support student engagement in true learning dialogue.

The impact of cultural and informal interactions on learning in the online environment requires further study. For example, peer support plays an important role in NDLEs and IDLEs. Discourse and conversation cues (e.g., emoticons) may help to acculturate students to the culture of, improve their performance in, and enable community building in online learning environments (see Bielman, Putney, & Strudler, 2003). Thus, it is important to examine (a) how peers and community establish, communicate, and refine discourse; (b) how community affiliation and belonging affect learning; and (c) how narrative, used prevalently in Web 2.0 such as blogs and wikis, influences collaborative knowledge and community building and promotes formal and informal interactions in NDLEs and IDLEs (Pachler & Daly, 2009).

A final recommendation is related to the structure of these environments. Students have indicated that access to multiple resources (e.g., course notes, lecture materials, and study aids) enhanced their content knowledge (Newnham, Mather, Grattan, Holmes, & Gardner, 1998). In NDLEs, multiple options enabled learners to assess, select and use resources based on need and suitability (Kim et al., 2005). Research on the process of evaluating, selecting, and using resources for individual goals in NDLEs and IDLEs is needed to determine how resources should be structured and administered while minimizing cognitive overload and confusion. In response to the call for "coordination of formal and informal environments" (NRC, 2009, p. 13), research is also warranted to examine how each component of NDLEs and IDLEs (interaction strategies and activities, tools, resources, scaffolds, and assessment) needs to be aligned with learning goals and supported by different stakeholders.

NOTE

1. We would like to thank Priya Sharma, Kevin Oliver, and Michael Hannafin for their suggestions and ideas which contributed to the original version of this chapter.

REFERENCES

Armatas, C., Holt, D., & Rice, M. (2003). Impacts of an online-supported, resource-based learning environment: Does one size fit all? *Distance Education, 24*(2), 141–158.

Ba, H., & Keisch, D. (2004, May). *Bridging the gap between formal and informal learning: Evaluating the SeaTrek Distance Learning Project: Center for Children and Technology.* New York, NY: Education Development Center

Barsion, S. J. (2004). MentorNet: 2002–2003 program evaluation. New York, NY: SJB Research Consulting. Retrieved from http://www.mentornet.net/documents/files/Eval.0203.Report.pdf

Bielman, V. A., Putney, L. G., & Strudler, N. (2003). Constructing community in a postsecondary virtual classroom. *Journal of Educational Computing Research, 29*(1), 119–144.

Brown, J. S., & Adler, R. P. (2008). Minds on fire: Open education, the long tail, and learning 2.0. *EDUCAUSE Review, 43*(1), 16–20, 22, 24, 26, 28, 30, 32.

Chong, E. K. M. (2010). Using blogging to enhance the initiation of students into academic research. *Computers & Education, 55*(2), 798–807.

Cifuentes, L., Xochihua, O. A., & Edwards, J. C. (2011). Learning in web 2.0 environments: Surface learning and chaos or deep learning and self-regulation? *The Quarterly Review of Distance Education, 12*(1), 1–21.

Clark, R. E. (2003). Research on web-based learning: A half-full glass. In R. Bruning, C. A. Horn & L. M. PytlikZillig (Eds.), *Web-based learning: What do we know? Where do we go?* (pp. 1–22). Greenwich, CT: Information Age.

Clark W., Logan K., Luckin R., Mee, A., & Oliver M. (2009). Beyond Web 2.0: mapping the technology landscapes of young learners. *Journal of Computer Assisted Learning, 25*, 56–69.

Clough, G., Jones, A. C., McAndrew, P., & Scanlon, E. (2008). Informal learning with PDAs and smartphones. *Journal of Computer Assisted Learning, 24*(5), 359–371. doi:10.1111/j.1365-2729.2007.00268.x

Coffman, S. (2001). Distance education and virtual reference: Where are we headed? *Computers in Libraries, 21*(4). Retrieved from http://www.infotoday.com/cilmag/apr01/coffman.htm

Colella, V. (2000). Participatory simulations: Building collaborative understanding through immersive dynamic modeling. *Journal of the Learning Sciences, 9*(4), 471–500.

Contreras-Castillo, J., Favela, J., Pérez-Fragoso, C., & Santamaría-del-Angel, E. (2004). Informal interactions and their implications for online courses. *Computers & Education, 42*(2), 149–168.

Dabbagh, N., & Kitsantas, A. (2005). Using web-based pedagogical tools as scaffolds for self-regulated learning. *Instructional Science, 33*(5-6), 513–540.

Daroszewski, E. B., Kinser, A. G., & Lloyd, S. L. (2004). Online, directed journaling in community health advanced practice nursing clinical education. *Journal of Nursing Education, 43*(4), 175–181.

Derry, S. J., & The ESTEP Research Group. (2004). Estepweb.Org: A case of theory-based web course design. In A. O'Donnell & C. Hmelo (Eds.), *Collaboration, reasoning and technology.* Mahwah, NJ: Erlbaum. Retrieved from http://www.wcer.wisc.edu/stellar/images/PDF/RISE%20Final%20Draft3.pdf

Dodge, B. (1995). WebQuests: A technique for internet-based learning. *Distance Educator, 1*(2), 10–13.

Dodge, B. (2001). Focus: Five rules for writing a great Webquest. *Learning and Leading with Technology, 28*(8), 6–9, 58.

Ebner, M., Lienhardt, C., Rohs, M., & Meyer, I. (2010). Microblogs in Higher Education — A chance to facilitate informal and process-oriented learning? *Computers & Education, 55*(1), 92-100. doi:10.1016/j.compedu.2009.12.006

Elia, A. (2006). Language learning in tandem via Skype. *Reading Matrix: An International Online Journal, 6*(3). Retrieved from http://www.readingmatrix.com/archives/archives_vol6_no3.html

Garrison, D. R., & Cleveland-Innes, M. (2005). Facilitating cognitive presence in online learning: Interaction is not enough. *The American Journal of Distance Education, 19*(3), 133–148.

Ge, X., & Land, S. M. (2003). Scaffolding students' problem-solving processes in an ill-structured task using question prompts and peer interactions. *Educational Technology Research and Development, 51*(1), 21–38.

Gerber, S., Scott, L., & Clements, D. H. (2005). Instructor influence on reasoned argument in discussion boards. *Educational Technology Research and Development, 53*(2), 25–39.

Gulikers, J. T. M., Bastiaens, T. J., & Kirschner, P. A. (2004). A five-dimensional framework for authentic assessment. *Educational Technology Research and Development, 52*(3), 67–86.

Gustafson, D. H., Hawkins, R., Pingree, S., McTavish, F., Arora, N. K., Mendenhall, J., … Salner, A. (2001). Effect of computer support on younger women with breast cancer. *Journal of General Internal Medicine, 16*(7), 435–445.

Hannafin, M. J., Land, S. M., & Oliver, K. (1999). Open learning environments: Foundations, methods, and models. In C. M. Reigeluth (Ed.), *Instructional-design theories and models: A new paradigm of instructional theory* (pp. 115–140). Mahwah, NJ: Erlbaum.

Halliday, J., & Hagar, P. (2002). Context, judgement, and learning. *Educational Theory, 52*(4), 429–443.

Harasim, L. (2002). *What makes online learning communities successful? The role of collaborative learning in social and intellectual development.* Greenwich, CT: Information Age.

Heo, H., Kim, K. Y., & Kim, Y. (2010). Exploratory study on the patterns of online interaction and knowledge co-construction in project-based learning. *Computers & Education, 55*, 1383–1392.

Hill, J. R. (2002). Overcoming obstacles and creating connections: Community building in web-based learning environments. *Journal of Computing in Higher Education, 14*(1), 67–86.

Hill, J. R., & Hannafin, M. J. (1997). Cognitive strategies and learning from the World Wide Web. *Educational Technology Research and Development, 45*(4), 37–64.

Hill, J. R., & Hannafin, M. J. (2001). Teaching and learning in digital environments: The resurgence of resource-based learning environments. *Educational Technology Research and Development, 49*(3), 37–52.

Hill, J. R., Hannafin, M. J., & Domizi, D. P. (2005). Resource-based learning and informal learning environments: Prospects and challenges. In L. T. W. Hin & R. Subramaniam (Eds.), *E-learning and virtual science centers* (pp. 110–125). Hershey, PA: Information Science.

Hillman, D. C., Willis, D. J., & Gunawardena, C. N. (1994). Learner-interface interaction in distance education: An extension of contemporary models and strategies for practitioners. *The American Journal of Distance Education, 8*(2), 30–42.

Hoadley, C. M., & Linn, M. C. (2000). Teaching science through online, peer discussions: Speakeasy in the knowledge integration environment. *International Journal of Science Education, 22*(8), 839–857.

Imel, S. (2003). *Informal adult learning and the Internet. Trends and issues alert.* ERIC Clearinghouse, Adult, Career, and Vocational Education, ED481327

Jonassen, D. (1999). Designing constructivist learning environments. In C. M. Reigeluth (Ed.), *Instructional-design theories and models: A new paradigm of instructional theory* (pp. 215–239). Mahwah, NJ: Erlbaum.

Jonassen, D. H., & Kwon, H., II. (2001). Communication patterns in computer mediated versus face-to-face group problem solving. *Educational Technology Research and Development, 49*(1), 35–51.

Jovanovic, J., Gasevic, D., Torniai, C., Bateman, S., & Hatala, M. (2009). The social semantic web in intelligent learning environments: State of the art and future challenges. *Interactive Learning Environments, 17*(4), 273–309.

Kaplan, A. M., & Haenlein, M. (2009). Users the world, unite! The challenges and opportunities of social media. *Business Horizons 53*, 59–68.

Ke, F. (2008). Computer games application within alternative classroom goal structures: cognitive, metacognitive, and affective evaluation. *Educational Technology Research and Development, 56*, 539–556.

Kim, M. C., & Hannafin, M. J. (2004). Designing online learning environments to support scientific inquiry. *Quarterly Review of Distance Education, 5*(1), 1–10.

Kim, M. C., & Hannafin, M. J. (2011). Scaffolding problem solving in technology-enhanced learning environments (TELEs): Bridging research and theory with practice. *Computers & Education, 56*(2), 403–417.

Kim, M. C., Hannafin, M. J., & Bryan, L. A. (2007). Technology-enhanced inquiry tools in science education: An emerging pedagogical framework for classroom practice. *Science Education, 91*(6), 1010–1030.

Kim, H., Hannafin, M. J., & Kim, M. C. (2005). Online case-based Learning: Components, applications, and assessment. *Distance Learning, 1*(5), 23–31.

Kitsantas, A., & Dabbagh, N. (2004). Promoting self-regulation in distributed learning environments with web-based pedagogical tools: An exploratory study. *Journal on Excellence in College Teaching, 15*(1/2), 119–142.

Lave, J., & Wenger, E. (1991). *Situated learning: Legitimate peripheral participation.* Cambridge: Cambridge University Press.

Lin, S. S. J., Liu, E. Z. F., & Yuan, S. M. (2001). Web-based peer assessment: Feedback for students with various thinking-styles. *Journal of Computer Assisted Learning, 17*(4), 420–432.

Linn, M. C., Clark, D., & Slotta, J. D. (2003). WISE design for knowledge integration. *Science Education, 87*(4), 517–538.

Luehmann, A. L. (2008). Using blogging in support of teacher professional identity development: A case-study. *Journal of the Learning Sciences, 17*(3), 237–337.

National Research Council. (NRC). (2011). Learning science through computer games and simulations. Committee on Science Learning: Computer Games, Simulations, and Education. In M. A. Honey & M. L. Hilton

(Eds.), *Board on Science Education, Division of Behavioral and Social Sciences and Education.* Washington, DC: The National Academies Press. Retrieved August 25, 2011, from http://www.nap.edu/catalog.php?record_id=13078

National Research Council. (NRC). (2009). *Learning science in informal environments: People, places, and pursuits. Committee on Learning Science in Informal Environments.* Washington, DC: The National Academies Press.

Macdonald, J., Heap, N., & Mason, R. (2001). "Have I learnt it?" Evaluating skills for resource-based study using electronic resources. *British Journal of Educational Technology, 32*(4), 419–433.

Mason, R., Pegler, C., & Weller, M. (2004). E-portfolios: An assessment tool for online courses. *British Journal of Educational Technology, 35*(6), 717–727.

McFerrin, K. M. (1999, March). *Incidental learning in a higher education asynchronous online distance education course.* Paper presented at the SITE99: Society for Information Technology and Teacher Education International Conference, San Antonio, TX.

McLoughlin, C., & Lee, M. J. W. (2010). Personalised and self regulated learning in the Web 2.0 era: International exemplars of innovative pedagogy using social software. *Australasian Journal of Educational Technology, 26*(1), 28–43.

McMahon, M. (1997, December). *Social constructivism and the World Wide Web — A paradigm for learning.* Paper presented at the ASCILITE Conference, Perth, Australia.

National Research Council of the National Academies. (2009). *Learning science in informal environments: People, places, and pursuits.* Committee on Learning Science in Informal Environments, National Research Council. Retrieved from http://www.nap.edu/catalog/12190.html

Newnham, R., Mather, A., Grattan, J., Holmes, A., & Gardner, A. (1998). An evaluation of the use of Internet sources as a basis for geography coursework. *Journal of Geography in Higher Education, 22*(1), 19–34.

Oliver, K., & Hannafin, M. J. (2001). Developing and refining mental models in open-ended learning environments: A case study. *Educational Technology Research and Development, 49*(4), 5–32.

Pachler, N., & Daly, C. (2009). Narrative and learning with Web 2.0 technologies: Towards a research agenda. *Journal of Computer Assisted Learning, 25*, 6–18.

Patten, B., Arnedillo Sanchez, I., & Tangney, B. (2006). Designing collaborative, constructionist and contextual applications for handheld devices. *Computers & Education, 46*(3), 294–308. doi:10.1016/j.compedu.2005.11.011

Piaget, J. (1972). *The psychology of the child.* New York, NY: Basic Books.

Prensky, M. (2001). Digital natives, digital immigrants. *On the Horizon, 9*(5), 1–6.

Ravenscroft, A. (2009). Social software, Web 2.0 and learning: status and implications of an evolving paradigm. *Journal of Computer Assisted Learning, 25*, 1–5.

Recker, M. M., Walker, A., & Lawless, K. (2003). What do you recommend? Implementation and analyses of collaborative information filtering of web resources for education. *Instructional Science, 31*(4-5), 299–316.

Reiser, B. J. (2004). Scaffolding complex learning: The mechanisms of structuring and problematizing student work. *Journal of the Learning Sciences, 13*(3), 273–304.

Rennert-Ariev, P. (2005). A theoretical model for the authentic assessment of teaching. *Practical Assessment, Research & Evaluation, 10*(2). Retrieved from http://www.pareonline.net/pdf/v10n2.pdf

Roschelle, J., Schechtman, N., Tatar, D., Hegedus, S., Hopkins, B., Empson, S., … Gallagher, L. (2010). Integration of Technology, Curriculum, and Professional Development for Advancing Middle School Mathematics: Three Large-Scale Studies. *American Educational Research Journal, 47*(4), 833–878.

Shaffer, D. W. (2006). Epistemic frames for epistemic games. *Computers & Education, 46*, 223–234.

Sharples, M., Graber, R., Harrison, C., & Logan, K. (2009). E-safety and Web 2.0 for children aged 11-16. *Journal of Computer Assisted Learning, 25*, 70–84.

So, H.-J., Seow, P., & Looi, C. K. (2009). Location matters: leveraging knowledge building with mobile devices and Web 2.0 technology. *Interactive Learning Environments, 17*(4), 367–382. doi:10.1080/10494820903195389

Soloway, E., & Wallace, R. (1997). Does the Internet support student inquiry? Don't ask. *Communications of the ACM, 40*(5), 11–12.

Sosbe, T. (2003, May). *Ed Sketch: Ford's drive toward quality education. Chief Learning Officer.* Retrieved from http://www.clomedia.com/content/templates/clo_article.asp?articleid=180&zoneid=4

Squire, K., & Klopfer, E. (2007). Augmented reality simulations on handheld computers. *Journal of the Learning Sciences, 16*(3), 371–413.

Sung, Y. T., Hou, H. T., Liu, C. K., & Chang, K. E. (2010). Mobile guide system using problem-solving strategy for museum learning: A sequential learning behavioural pattern analysis. *Journal of Computer Assisted Learning, 26*(2), 106–115. doi:10.1111/j.1365-2729.2010.00345.x

Tabak, I. (2004). Synergy: A complement to emerging patterns of distributed scaffolding. *Journal of the Learning Sciences, 13*(3), 305–335.

Tallent-Runnels, M. K., Thomas, J. A., Lan, W. Y., Cooper, S., Ahern, T. C., Shaw, S. M., & Liu, X. (2006). Teaching courses online: A review of the research. *Review of Educational Research, 76*(1), 93–135.

Thomas, M. J. W. (2002). Learning within incoherent structures: The space of online discussion forums. *Journal of Computer Assisted Learning, 18*(3), 351–366.

Tweddle, S., James, C., & Daniels, H. (2000). Use of a Web site for learning about cancer. *Computers & Education, 35*(4), 309–325.

Uribe, D., Klein, J. D., & Sullivan, H. (2003). The effect of computer-mediated collaborative learning on solving iii-defined problems. *Educational Technology Research and Development, 51*(1), 5–19.

Vygotsky, L. S. (1978). *Mind in society: The development of higher psychological processes.* Cambridge, MA: Harvard University Press.

Waldron, J. (2009). Exploring a virtual music ‚Äòcommunity of practice‚Äô: Informal music learning on the Internet. *Journal of Music, Technology & Education, 2*(2/3), 97–112. doi:10.1386/jmte.2.2-3.97_1

Wallace, R. M., Kupperman, J., Krajcik, J., & Soloway, E. (2000). Science on the web: Students online in a sixth-grade classroom. *Journal of the Learning Sciences, 9*(1), 75–104.

Wenger, E. (1998). *Communities of practice: Learning, meaning, and doing.* New York, NY: Cambridge University Press.

Whipp, J. L. (2003). Scaffolding critical reflection in online discussions - helping prospective teachers think deeply about field experiences in urban schools. *Journal of Teacher Education, 54*(4), 321–333.

Whipp, J. L., & Chiarelli, S. (2004). Self-regulation in a web-based course: A case study. *Educational Technology Research and Development, 52*(4), 5–22.

Yang, Y.-T. C., Newby, T. J., & Bill, R. L. (2005). Using Socratic questioning to promote critical thinking skills through asynchronous discussion forums in distance learning environments. *The American Journal of Distance Education, 19*(3), 163–181.

24

FACULTY PARTICIPATION IN ONLINE DISTANCE EDUCATION

KAY SHATTUCK

This review of the research literature on faculty participation in online education updates the work done previously by Wolcott and Shattuck (2007). Participation is defined simply as teaching online for a U.S. higher education institution. Motivations will be categorized as intrinsic—that is, engaging in the activity is personally satisfying and viewed as a reward in itself—and as extrinsic—that is, responding to external (contextual) stimuli with benefits received from a source other than the activity. The review is organized by motivators (intrinsic and extrinsic) and demotivators for faculty participation in online distance education. An assessment of an evolving emphasis in the faculty participation literature is included. The concluding discussion considers the impact of faculty attitudes, values, and perceptions on decisions to participate in online teaching.

Faculty participation in distance education in U.S. higher education has evolved over the past few decades from being the activity of innovators (Stevenson, 2007) and early adopters (Hagner, 2000; Stevenson, 2007; Twigg, 2001) to that of "early and late majorities" (Stevenson, pp. 141–142). The "Lone Rangers" (Bates, 2002, p. 415) of the 1980s and 1990s were self-motivated and technology-enthusiastic faculty members who built on earlier traditions in utilizing Web technologies in order to open up educational opportunities primarily for non-traditional students. The "Lone Rangers" were joined in the early 2000s by other champions of distance education to better meet the needs of an increasingly diverse set of students. By 2005, many declared that online education had entered the educational mainstream—at least, the mainstream from the institutional perspective of meeting growing student demands—although not in the eyes of many faculty (Allen & Seaman, 2005).

While the early literature on faculty participation focused on psychological motivations for teaching online, the most recent literature adds emphasis to broader contextual sources of motivation. The institutional pressure for instructors to teach online courses is emerging in the literature under topics, such as faculty acceptance (Allen & Seaman, 2010; Shea, 2007), recruitment (Parthasarathy & Smith, 2009), burnout (Bollinger & Wasilik, 2009), and online faculty retention (Chapman, 2011).

Over a decade ago, Hagner (2000) noted that while lack of faculty rewards did not "impede 'early adopters' and 'second-wave' faculty from participating in innovative instruction, rewards are 'crucial' for 'third-wave' faculty members if positive growth" is to be sustained and if continual improvement of teaching for learning is valued. "Third-wave" faculty will stay involved when they see online education "as a way to advance their professional career" (p. 31). Cook and Ley (2004) agreed and noted that "newer research studies indicate a strong trend towards extrinsic motivators as being crucial to faculty decisions to participate (or not) in distance education" (p. 227).

INTRINSIC MOTIVATORS FOR FACULTY PARTICIPATION IN ONLINE LEARNING

According to Wolcott and Shattuck (2007), the primary motivators for faculty participation in online distance education were intrinsic. Seminal work done by Wolcott and Betts (1999) classified five types of intrinsic motives: (a) personal or socially derived satisfactions, (b) personal or professional growth, (c) personal challenge, (d) altruistic, and (e) career-enhancing. Schifter (2002) and Cook (2003) produced similar sets of motives. Four groups of personal motivations for online teaching emerged from faculty narratives collected by Suter (2002): (a) wonder, (b) convenience, (c) professional growth and renewal, and (d) esprit de corps.

Other descriptions of intrinsic motivators include: reaching new audiences, developing new ideas, using new technologies, engaging in intellectual challenge, increasing overall job satisfaction (Betts, 1998; Cook, 2003; Gupton, 2004; Hebert, 2003; O'Quinn, 2002; Schifter, 2000b, 2002); gaining self-fulfillment, enjoying teaching, and undertaking professional challenges (Miller & Husmann, 1999); engaging in self-improvement and promoting professional growth (Tastle, White, & Shackleton, 2005); providing innovative instruction, developing and applying new teaching techniques and skills, keeping abreast of new technologies, and fulfilling a personal desire to teach (Myers, Bennett, Brown, & Henderson, 2004; Rockwell, Schauer, Fritz, & Marx, 1999); making courses more accessible (Kirk & Shoemaker, 1999; Ndahi, 1999); helping students (Christo-Baker, 2004; Keen, 2001; Lin, 2002; Wilson, 2002); and creating opportunities to reach culturally diverse, more mature, and geographically dispersed students (Shea, 2007). Studies done by Schopieray (2006); Stevenson (2007); Shea (2007); Liu, Kim, Bonk, and Magjuka (2007); Cahill (2008); and Chapman (2011) provided additional support illustrating these intrinsic motivators as being the strongest ones for faculty.

EXTRINSIC MOTIVATORS FOR FACULTY PARTICIPATION IN ONLINE LEARNING

Extrinsic motivators are situated in the research as being secondary to intrinsic (personal) motivations to teach online. However, evidence is prevalent that there is a relationship between institutional-level enhancers and motivation. Faculty, although intrinsically motivated, value and desire support services (Bollinger & Wasilik, 2009; Donovan, 2004; Pina, 2005; Ricci, 2002; Shea, 2007; Simonson, Smaldina, Albright, & Zvacek, 2009), training opportunities in technology skills (Cahill, 2008; Iken, 2000; Keen, 2001; Martin, 2003; Tastle et al., 2005), design and instructional support (Lee, 2001), and awareness of sound student support services (Allen & Seaman, 2008; Keen,

2001; Keeton, 2000; Shea, 2007). Pathasarathy (2009) reported that faculty were more likely to deliver online courses when they perceived online education as contributing to a positive image for their school and as allowing their school to meet changing market needs.

Institutions traditionally offer inducements to encourage a particular behavior or activity valued by the organization. External motivators, in terms of incentives to participate in online education, have been related to workload and salary (Christo-Baker, 2004; Martin, 2003; Iken, 2000; Ricci, 2002). Indeed, having the time to develop distance education courses, especially through release from some portion of teaching assignment, was a highly valued incentive for faculty (Ellis, 2000; Keeton, 2000; Keen, 2001; Martin, 2003; Ricci, 2002), but one that was not necessarily provided (Nelson, 2003). Looking at compensation practices and incentives for both developing online education courses and teaching them, Schifter (2004) found little had changed since her 2000 study. Incentives and compensation favored developing over teaching distance education courses.

The complexities of extrinsic motivations will be explored next as motivational variations among online teaching faculty, as motivational considerations of those faculty who teach and those who do not teach online, and as differences between faculty motivations and administrators' assumptions.

Motivational Variations among Online Teaching Faculty

A review of the literature reveals that specific motivations vary across faculty. For example, community college faculty saw distance teaching as part of their job, hence mitigating the influence of external pressures (Miller & Husmann, 1999); while Kirk and Shoemaker (1999) noted, "extrinsic rewards tended to be a greater motivator for younger versus older instructors" (p. 315). Instructors with prior experience teaching online were more motivated by the challenge of online teaching and applications of technology in teaching than were inexperienced instructors. However, Mitchell and Geva-May (2009) found a relationship between academic subject disciplines and willingness to participate in online teaching, but no relationship between willingness to teach online and years of teaching experiences. Faculty in academic subject discipline areas were less likely to accept online learning than those teaching career subjects.

Gender factored into motivation for the faculty surveyed by Lin (2002), who concluded that female faculty members were much more likely to be motivated to teach distance education courses than were males. In 2007, Stevenson concluded that female faculty with less than 10 years of higher education experience were most likely to participate in online instruction (as were faculty 46 years or above). Shea's (2007) survey of 386 faculty in a 36-campus statewide system had similar results. Gupton (2004) also documented significant differences with respect to gender; however, Schifter (2002), Hebert (2003), and Cahill (2008) found no statistically significant relationship between the same variables and participation.

Green, Alejandro, and Brown (2009) explored participation factors that relate to retention of experienced online faculty by surveying full-time tenured, non-tenured, and tenure-track faculty, as well as part-time/adjunct faculty at 23 different universities (n = 135). Overall, respondents were motivated by "situational incentives," including flexibility and opportunities to use technology in addition to intrinsic rewards, such as intellectual challenge. A breakdown of faculty position indicated that tenured- and tenure-track faculty focused on the intrinsic rewards, while full-time, non-tenured and part-time/adjunct faculty found additional motivations in gaining teaching experience, including a "sense of loyalty to university" (p. 9). In a similar vein, Chapman (2011) found that while tenured, tenure-track, and "contingent" (i.e., part-time) faculty were motivated by intrinsic factors, the opportunity for financial rewards was a top incentive—noting that this was inconsistent with previous research. Chapman suggested, "This may be because teaching DE courses is becoming more and more likely to be an expected part of a tenured/tenure-track faculty member's job" (para. 40).

Stewart, Bachman, and Johnson (2010) looked at the relationship between technology acceptance and intentions to teach online. Utilizing an extended version of the Technology Acceptance Model, they found that faculty who enjoyed technology and interactive Web environments were positive about student learning and eager to be involved in online learning. Moreover, they expressed interest in participating in internal and external training opportunities and in involvement with peers in evaluating their courses. They were surprised that "neither comfort with the CMS nor having taught online had a direct or indirect effect on intent to teach online." They offered a possible explanation for that finding, in that "These results may be due to faculty members lacking confidence in their online teaching abilities or experiencing fear from the risks associated with online instruction (e.g., lack of departmental support or faculty acceptance)" (p. 606). The Mitchell and Geva-May (2009) study mentioned above also explored the faculty lag in acceptance of online learning (n = 321, about 10% identified as academic administrators). They hypothesized four variables that might impact faculty acceptance of online learning: (a) intellectual reluctance (whether it matches individual faculty member's values and norms), (b) support (perception of value associated at an institutional level as determined by support services), (c) change (instability caused by changes at a personal [job] level, as well as at the institutional level), and (d) cost-benefit (whether the benefits of online learning outweigh the costs). They concluded that "there is a relationship between attitude and position [faculty significantly more concerned about online learning than administrators], subject of instruction [career more so than academic subjects], and level of experience with OL [more years teaching online, more positive attitude]; but no relationship between attitude and years of experience in a discipline" (p. 85). The study acknowledges that it helps "bring attitudinal influences onto the OLI [Online Learning Implementation] policy agenda" (p. 86).

Motivational Considerations of Faculty Who Teach Online and Those Who Do Not

Stevenson (2007), who replicated Betts'1998 survey, called attention to the fact that although more faculty are teaching online than ever before, the need still outstrips the participation. She noted that the lack of participation by faculty is an issue that should concern educational administrators. She found a positive correlation between the experience of being a student in an online course and willingness to teach online, and a negative correlation between years teaching in higher education and willingness to teach online. Stevenson's findings supported previous research that intrinsic motivations are the key factor for faculty who are already participating in online teaching while nonparticipators indicated that they are more likely to be enticed to teach online with monetary rewards, such as increase in salary and merit pay.

The research consistently indicates that faculty who participate in online teaching are intrinsically motivated, and nonparticipators speculate that extrinsic motives, such as increase in salary and monetary support in the form of overload pay or a stipend, would influence their decision to participate (Betts, 1998; Cook, 2003; Edwards, 2001; Gupton, 2004; O'Quinn & Corry, 2004; Schifter, 2000b, 2002).

Differences between Faculty Motivations and Administrators' Assumptions

Differences between faculty motives to participate, and what administrators believe motivates or would motivate faculty to teach at a distance, are revealed in the research as early as the seminal work of Betts (1998) and later supported by Rockwell et al. (1999), Schifter (2000b), Keen (2001), Hebert (2003), Isham (2004), O'Quinn and Corry (2004), and Gupton (2004). Collectively, those studies found that faculty cited intrinsic reasons for their participation in online distance teaching while administrators speculated that faculty would participate for extrinsic reasons, such as additional money, credit toward tenure and promotion, and release time. There is support from several studies (French, 2001; Gupton, 2004; Schwer, 2001) that administrators and faculty rank workload among the major barriers to faculty participation.

Faculty issues, including incentives, were prominent among issues that impacted department chairs in the implementation of distance education (Mlinek, 2002; Schauer, 2002). More recently, the 2008 Sloan Survey of Online Learning from 2,500 U.S. colleges and universities (Allen & Seaman, 2008) revealed that there was a wide agreement among administration and faculty who teach online about what motivates faculty to participate. Both administrators and faculty agreed that the flexibility in meeting students' needs that online teaching made possible was the primary motivator and that being required to teach online was the least motivating. Administrators and faculty exhibited a notable difference in their perception of compensation as a motivator to teach online: Chief academic officers ranked additional income as second of seven motivators, while faculty ranked it fifth of seven.

Incentives to encourage participation in online distance education are frequently noted in the research. Lee (2001) and Lin (2002) posit that motivation increases with the availability of institutional support mechanisms that can help faculty meet their instructional needs. Keen (2001) also found a strong association between faculty members' belief that there was an organizational climate supportive of distance education and their willingness to use distance education. Lee noted that motivation, satisfaction, and commitment were stronger among faculty as they felt well-supported by their institutions. Along the same lines, Shea, Pickett, and Li (2005) linked satisfaction with provided faculty development and technical support as a predictor of satisfaction in online teaching, as did Shea (2007) when he surveyed 386 faculty in 36 colleges within a large state university system.

The positive impact of availability of training emerges in the literature. Cahill (2008), as well as Simonson et al. (2009) found training a motivator for faculty participation in an online learning program. Liu et al. (2007) extrapolated from faculty interviews that participation in a peer learning community for online instructors would be an inducement. Allen and Seaman (2010) reported that most of the 2,500 reporting U.S. higher education institutions provide some combination of mentoring and internally run training workshops or training courses for faculty to develop teaching skills necessary for online learning.

DEMOTIVATORS TO FACULTY'S PARTICIPATION

The literature continues to identify barriers that discourage faculty participation in distance online education—beginning with the seminal work of Dillon and Walsh (1992), highlighted by Berge, Muilenburg, and Haneghan (2002), and reemphasized by Shea (2007). Four contextual barriers that are tied to extrinsic motivations are consistently cited as negatively influencing faculty decisions to participate in distance education: (a) lack of time, (b) lack of compensation, (c) lack of incentives and/or rewards, and (d) lack of policies and institutional support. Contextual barriers are those deterrents associated with the institutional setting and typically outside of the control of the individual that can impact the motivations of the individual faculty member.

Lack of Time and Compensation

Both time and compensation ranked as the greatest obstacles to faculty desire to teach online at all stages of organizational maturity in distance education as determined by Berge and Muilenburg (2001). Lack of monetary support, such as a stipend, rated highest among deterrents for distance education faculty and division chairs in community colleges surveyed by O'Quinn (2002). More recently, Green et al. (2009) and Shea (2007) noted that workload and time commitments continue to be concerns of surveyed faculty.

Not only is there the widespread contention that online teaching takes more preparation time, but faculty and many administrators also perceive that institutions fail to provide time for course development and management apart from more traditional teaching responsibilities. The lack of administratively provided time, especially release time, was a highly ranked barrier (Christo-Baker, 2004; Curbelo-Ruiz, 2002; Ellis, 2000; Gupton, 2004; O'Quinn, 2002).

Faculty consistently expressed the concern that distance teaching costs them too much time. Specifically, time requirements (as well as lack of compensation for that time) associated with preparing courses (Ndahi, 1999; Rockwell et al., 1999; Tastle et al., 2005; Wolcott & Betts, 1999); learning new teaching or technological skills (Betts, 1998; Halfhill, 1998; Ndahi, 1999); and developing, revising, and teaching the course (Liu et al., 2007; Shea, 2007) are highlighted through the literature. Shea (2007) reported, "Barriers reflect issues associated with inadequate compensation relative to time investment, lack of recognition for and negative reputation of online teaching, complexities of technology and online pedagogy, and reward structure misalignment with online teaching" (p. 85). On the other hand, Pathasarathy and Smith (2009) found in surveying business school faculty, "While we predicted that respondents who perceived delivery time and effort to be greater in the online context would be less likely to adopt online education, the opposite was found to be true (although this finding was only marginally significant)" (para. 33).

Lack of Incentives and Rewards

Faculty participation can be influenced by availability of incentives and rewards for involvement. Studies not only indicate that incentives stimulate participation, but that the lack of incentives and/or rewards works against it (Curbelo-Ruiz, 2002; Ellis, 2000; French, 2001; Nelson, 2003). Liu et al. (2007) noted concern for expected Internet connection costs when traveling as an emerging issue. Further, the issue of intellectual property ownership is a concern, as is the faculty role expanding to performing "help desk" activities (Shea, 2007). Cahill (2008) found when surveying faculty within a university's education department that issues related to the department's professionalism were the strongest inhibitors to participating in e-learning. In fact, she pointed out that "the issues of money, time, and rewards are not motivating factor[s], but they are significant inhibiting factors" (p. 141).

Lack of Policies and Institutional Support

Lack of administrative or technical support services emerges as an important category of barriers affecting adoption of distance education (Bader, 2004; Ndahi, 1999;), as well as participation in it (Berge & Muilenburg, 2001; Schifter, 2000b). Simonson,et al. (2009) noted that faculty expect reliable infrastructure and technology. Other contextual barriers reported in the literature include inadequacy or lack of training (Lin, 2002; Zirkle, 2004; Ndahi, 1999; Schifter, 2000b), lack of funding for materials and other associated expenses (Curbelo-Ruiz, 2002), and lack of clear commitment to or policy on distance education (Ndahi, 1999; Porter, 2003; Sumrall, 2002).

In addition to issues of time and workload, the faculty in a number of studies noted other costs among the factors that either did or would inhibit them from participating. These inhibitors included the perceived lack of quality or academic rigor in online distance education courses (Curbelo-Ruiz, 2002; Lin, 2002; Nelson, 2003; Tastle et al., 2005), the absence or loss of student interaction (Lin, 2002; Nelson, 2003), the perceived restrictive nature of the medium relative to course content and objectives (Nelson, 2003; Sumrall, 2002;), and, more recently, "some unpleasant students" whose interactions are inappropriate for a formal learning situation (Liu et al., 2007, para. 26).

The complexity of higher education systems and traditions cannot be ignored when discussing motivations to teach online. Maguire (2009) posited that "most faculty members do not believe that they have the power to make changes and that this is due to the political nature of the state system of higher education and their faculty union" (para. 15). Others (Edwards, 2001; Hagovsky, 2002; Poe, 2000; Whicker, 2004) likewise noted the lack of incentives for participating in distance education. Pina (2005) reported that offering incentives was the factor rated least successfully implemented in higher education—an indicator, he concluded, of the lack of institutionalization of distance education. This conclusion contrasts with Seaman and Allen's announcement in 2005 that online learning was mainstreamed in the 2,500 surveyed higher education institutions. However, one interpretation of mainstreaming is that it refers to demand and does not necessarily indicate an institution is adequately organized and prepared to deliver a quality educational experience for students.

DISCUSSION: THE IMPACT OF FACULTY ATTITUDES, VALUES, AND PERCEPTIONS

Seaman and Allen (2010) documented that only about one-third of responding faculty from 2,500 U.S. higher education institutions expressed positive opinions about online learning (33% reported in 2006 and 30% reported in 2009). Such a reality check makes it important to discuss the connection of faculty attitudes, values, and perceptions to motivations to participate in online distance education.

A link between attitudes and participation in online learning was suggested by Ulmer, Watson, and Derby (2007) when they acknowledged that faculty with online distance education experience tended to view distance education as positive and enabling student learning. This restates the conclusions found by Lin (2002) that faculty were more likely to participate if they had a positive attitude toward distance education or had a positive distance education experience. Similarly, a link between faculty values and attitudes toward online education can be seen in a study (n = 321) done by Mitchell and Geva-May (2009). They summarized that faculty attitudes serve as a deterrent to an administrative agenda of increasing online learning. Pointedly, they concluded that those interested in increasing faculty participation must refocus and connect with faculty's interests and values rather than rely on technological and administrative perspectives.

Relating extrinsic demotivators (such as time demands of teaching online) and faculty interest and values (intrinsic motivations) would expand understanding of faculty's willingness to participate in online education. Zhen, Garthwait, and Pratt (2008), who used a survey based on a discreet decision model (n = 218), advocated deeper understanding of commonly reported concerns about the time challenges for teaching online. Interestingly, they suggested that "Time or time-related challenges are not factors influencing faculty members' decision," but that "faculty who have the preference and motivation [to teach online] often overcome these time-related barriers." They concluded that faculty who do not use or are not comfortable with online course management systems "yield to these [time-consuming] barriers—Faculty members think Time is the challenge, but that response conceals deeper reasons" (para. 31). Decisions to participate in online teaching were "strongly based on the key variable of faculty general philosophical views and faculty-belief of efficacy" (para. 35). Of course, a cautionary word seems in line here: Care must be taken not to discount or dismiss prevalently reported concerns about time issues as a deterrent to teaching online—the burnout concept is too much a part of the disincentives discussion. That being said, the great value in Zhen et al.'s assessment is that it points out an important link between attitudes, values, and perceptions and their relationship to faculty participation in online learning. If faculty members do not see personal intrinsic value, for example, if they do not perceive their pedagogical values as being accommodated and encouraged when teaching online, they will be more discouraged and might focus on often cited extrinsic demotivators as reasons why they do not wish to teach online.

Three opportunities to connect values and attitudes to extrinsic motivations can be extrapolated from the faculty participation research literature: (a) Training opportunities to associate pedagogical/andragogical values with online learning which hinges on unfamiliar design and teaching nuances, (b) faculty input in online distance education policies and procedures to engage in specific and credible institutional processes by applying teaching and learning values and perspectives, and (c) opportunities to develop and expand a community of practice (Wenger, 1998, 2006) to encourage an exchange of pedagogical/andragogical ideas and experiences, along with peer support of online teaching colleagues.

Training

Timely professional training, especially if leading to certification in online instruction (Chapman, 2011), as well as opportunities to participate in mentoring programs

(Chapman, 2011; Shea, 2007) are incentives for increasing participation in online teaching. Participatory, active learning opportunities in which faculty can see immediate translation and application of their pedagogical/andragogical values into the design and teaching of their courses are incentives. Shea (2007) related a broader, value-added professional benefit for faculty participation in online teaching by emphasizing the "opportunity for more systematic design of online instruction and a corollary positive impact on student learning and on classroom teaching" (p. 75)—that is to say, training opportunities that facilitate faculty understanding and applications of their values in improving student learning in all learning formats.

Faculty Input into Policies and Procedures

Numerous references are made in the participation literature to the lack of institutional- and departmental-level online learning policies. Schopieray (2006) posited the inclusion of faculty voice in the development of departmental and institutional policies and structures as a motivational factor. From that perspective, it is not only the lack of policies, but a disconnect with faculty who can offer pedagogical/andragogical insights into policies and procedures that will impact the operation of online courses, as well as the students enrolled in them. Maguire (2009) agreed and suggested the inclusion in policy-making of part-time/contingent faculty—an often missing or ignored, yet increasingly relied upon, group of educators in higher education.

Greenberg's (2011) study on the benefits and rewards associated with faculty working with instructional design staff to identify quality when developing an online course provides an example of the motivation to teach online. He posited that faculty are more willing to participate in online course development and a peer review process when they believe best practices and the course development instrument are seen as "guidelines" for faculty's professional application rather than "rules" to be prescribed to faculty by administration.

Opportunities for Expanding a Faculty-Centered Community of Practice

Collaborative opportunities for new forms of scholarship on teaching have been suggested by several researchers. Examples include "analyzing student learning for the purpose of improving teaching and learning" (Bernstein & Bass, 2005, para. 2); applying "new [online] methods for documenting and exchanging the intellectual work of teaching" (Hatch, Bass, Ilyoshi, & Mace, 2004, para. 5); using research and practice to guide peer review of online courses for improved student learning (Shattuck, 2007); and encouraging faculty "to enhance practice and contribute to the teaching profession through significant practice-based research" (Sperling, 2003, p. 593). A specific example of the latter is seen in a recent analysis of data collected from faculty participants in an inter-institutional organization of online educators who participated in the 2008–2010 Quality Matters peer reviews (Sener, 2011). Participating in the peer reviews provided the benefits of a peer-to-peer community of practice, specifically, as an opportunity for professional growth, while also providing educators the intrinsically focused improvement of their own course based on collegial exchange and recommendation.

What these examples have in common is an expanding collaboration among colleagues by increasing intellectual and professional exchange (intrinsic motivators) while meeting extrinsic motivations of improving online distance education for their institution. As online learning opportunities continue to grow, perhaps, largely due to demand, Parthasarathy and Smith (2009) suggested:

> There might be additional motivators that are less immediate and that accrue to faculty *through* [italics in original] the institution. Such factors might be labeled *indirect* [italics in original] intrinsic or extrinsic motivators in that faculty believe that when the institution benefits, so do they. (para. 38)

Intrinsic motivations continue in the research literature to be the strongest reported motivators for faculty in higher education to participate in online education. Increasingly, extrinsic motivations are being associated with and understood within the complex motivational system that includes faculty attitudes, values, and perceptions of online distance education. These motivations are increasingly being studied from theoretical models, for example, diffusion of innovation (Shea, 2007), technology acceptance (Stewart et al., 2010), discreet decision (Zhen et al., 2008) and are providing deeper understanding of the dynamics of faculty participation in teaching online.

REFERENCES

Allen, I. E., & Seaman, J. (2005). *Growing by degrees: Online education in the United States, 2005.* Retrieved from http://sloanconsortium.org/publications/survey/growing_by_degrees_2005

Allen, I. E., & Seaman, J. (2008). Staying the course: Online education in the United States, 2008. Retrieved from http://sloanconsortium.org/publications/survey/staying_course

Allen, I. E., & Seaman, J. (2010). Learning on demand: Online education in the United States, 2009. Retrieved from http://www.sloanc.org/publications/survey/pdf/learningondemand.pdf

Bader, J. R. (2004). Faculty perception of issues affecting the utilization of distance education technology: The case of New Mexico State University's College of Agriculture and Home Economics. *Dissertation Abstracts International, 65* (12), 4405A. (UMI No. AAT 3155970)

Bates, A. W. (2002). Supporting faculty. In L. Foster, B. L. Bower, & L. W. Watson (Eds.), *Distance education: Teaching and learning in higher education* (pp. 410–423). Boston, MA: Pearson Custom Publishing.

Bernstein, D., & Bass, R. (2005). The scholarship of teaching and learning. *Academe, 91*(4), 37–43.

Berge, Z. L., & Muilenburg, L. (2001, July/August). Obstacles faced at various stages of capability regarding distance education in institutions of higher education. *TechTrends, 45,* 40–45.

Berge, Z. L., Muilenburg, L. Y., & Haneghan, J. V. (2002). Barriers to distance education and training. *Quarterly Review of Distance Education, 3*(4), 409–418.

Betts, K. S. (1998). Factors influencing faculty participation in distance education in postsecondary education in the United States: An institutional study. *Dissertation Abstracts International, 59*(07), 2376A. (UMI No. AAM 9900013)

Bollinger, D. U., & Wasilik, O. (2009). Factors influencing faculty satisfaction with online teaching and learning in higher education. *Distance Education, 30*(1), 103–116.

Cahill, R. (2008). What motivates faculty participation in eLearning: A case study of complex factors (Unpublished doctoral dissertation). University of St. Thomas, MN.

Chapman, D. (2011). Contingent and tenured/tenure-track faculty: Motivations and incentives to teach distance education courses. *Online Journal of Distance Learning Administration, 14*(3). Retrieved from http://www.westga.edu/~distance/ojdla/fall143/chapman143.html

Christo-Baker, E. A. H. B. (2004). College and university faculty attitudes, incentives and barriers toward distance education. *Dissertation Abstraction International, 65*(09), 3297A. (UMI No. AAT 3146740)

Cook, R. G. (2003). Factors that motivate or inhibit faculty participation in distance education: An exploratory study. *Dissertation Abstraction International, 64*(06), 1953A. (UMI No. AAT 3094001)

Cook, R. G., & Ley, K, (2004). What's driving faculty participation in distance education? Paper presented at the 27th Association for Educational Communications and Technology Conference, Chicago. IL. Retrieved from http://www.eric.edu.gov/PDFS/EDU485097.pdf

Curbelo-Ruiz, A. M. (2002). Factors influencing faculty participation in Web-based distance education technologies. *Dissertation Abstraction International, 63*(04), 1227A. (UMI No. AAT 3049007)

Dillon, C. L., & Walsh, S. M. (1992). Faculty: The neglected resource in distance education. *The American Journal of Distance Education, 6*(3), 5–21.

Donovan, P. R. (2004). Faculty in online distance education: An exploration of four faculty members' experience. *Dissertation Abstraction International, 65*(08), 2957A. (UMI No. ATT NQ93511)

Edwards, Y. V. (2001). Rehabilitation education faculty motivation toward distance education: A national study of CORE rehabilitation faculty. *Dissertation Abstraction International, 62*(06), 2035A. (UMI No. AAT 3018573)

Ellis, E. M. (2000). Faculty participation in the Pennsylvania State University World Campus: Identifying barriers to success. *Open Learning, 15*(3), 233–242.

French, R. C. (2001). Encouraging faculty participation in college and university distance education programs. *Dissertation Abstraction International, 61*(12), 4690A. (UMI No. AAT 9997946)

Green, T., Alejandro, J., & Brown, A. H. (2009). The retention of experienced faculty in online distance education programs: Understanding factors that impact their involvement. *International Review of Research in Open and Distance Learning, 10*(3). Retrieved from http://www.irrodl.org/index.php/irrodl/article/view/683/1306

Greenberg, G. (2011). From the ground up: Conceptions of quality in course design for Web-supported education (Unpublished doctoral dissertation). The Ohio State University, Columbus.

Gupton, K. L. (2004). Factors that affect faculty participation in distance education: An institutional study. *Dissertation Abstraction International, 65*(12), 4488A. (UMI No. AAT 3158437)

Hagner, P. R. (2000, Septembe/October). Faculty engagement and support in the new learning environment. *Educase Review* [Online], 27–37. Retrieved from http://net.educase.edu/ir/library/pdf/ERM0052.pfd

Hagovsky, T. C. (2002). Factors affecting the implementation of distance education initiatives in the Indiana Partnership for Statewide Education. *Dissertation Abstraction International, 64*(08), 2802A. (UMI No. AAT 3099152)

Halfhill, C. S. (1998). An investigation into factors influencing faculty behavior concerning distance learning instruction using the theory of planned behavior. *Dissertation Abstracts International, 59*(11), 4113A. (UMI No. AAT 9910797)

Hatch, T., Bass, R., & Iiyoshi, T, Mace, D. (2004). Building knowledge for teaching and learning. *Change, 36*(5), 42–49.

Hebert, J. G. (2003). Perceived barriers to faculty participation in distance education at a 4-year university. *Dissertation Abstraction International, 64*(09), 3257A. (UMI No. AAT 3106885)

Iken, M. B. T. (2000). Faculty attitudes toward computer-mediated distance education. *Dissertation Abstraction International, 61*(10), 3917A. (UMI No. AAT 9991647)

Isham, E. K. (2004). Faculty and administrators' beliefs about, experience with, and willingness to utilize distance education technologies in medium-sized New Mexico community colleges. *Dissertation Abstraction International, 65*(04), 1224A. (UMI No. AAT 3129894)

Keen, M. A. (2001). Attitudes and beliefs of faculties and administrators in the Ivy Tech State College System on the deployment of technology-mediated, interactive distance education. *Dissertation Abstraction International, 62*(02), 436A. (UMI No. AAT 3004751)

Keeton, C. L. (2000). Institutional structures that influence faculty to participate in distance education. *Dissertation Abstraction International, 61*(10), 3840A. (UMI No. AAT 9993226)

Kirk, J. J., & Shoemaker, H. (1999). Motivating community college instructors to teach on-line: An exploration of selected motivators. .In *Instructing technology* (pp. 310–317). Baton Rouge, LA: Academy of Human Resources Development (ERIC Document Reproduction Service No, ED 431 941).

Lee, J. (2001). Institutional support for distance education and faculty motivation, commitment, satisfaction. *British Journal of Educational Technology, 32*(2), 153–160.

Lee, J. (2002). Faculty and administrator perceptions of instructional support for distance education. *International Journal of Instructional Media, 29*(1), 27–45.

Lin, H. P. (2002). Motivating and inhibiting factors that affect faculty participation in distance education at Idaho State University. *Dissertation Abstraction International, 63*(05), 1799A. (UMI No. AAT 3052734)

Liu, S., Kim, K-J, Bonk, C. J., & Magjuka, R. (2007). What do online MBA professors have to say about online teaching. *Online Journal of Distance Learning Administration, 10*(2). Retrieved from http://www.westga.edu/~distance/ojdla/summer102/liu102.htm

Maguire, L. (2009). The faculty perspective regarding their role in distance education policy making. *Online Journal of Distance Learning Administration, 12*(1). Retrieved from http://www.westga.edu/~distance/ojdla/spring121/maguire121.html

Martin, M. H. (2003). Factors influencing faculty adoption of Web-based courses in teacher education programs within the State University of New York. *Dissertation Abstraction International, 64*(04), 1223A. (UMI No. AAT 3089087)

Miller, M. T., & Husmann, D. E. (1999). Faculty incentives to participate in distance education. *Michigan Community College Journal, 5*(2), 35–42.

Mitchell, B., & Geva-May, I. (2009). Attitudes affecting online learning implementation in higher education institutions. *Journal of Distance Education, 23*(1), 71–88.

Mlinek, D. D. (2002). Differences in the reasons and issues impacting the implementation of technology-based distance education courses and programs as identified by department chairs using the Biglan Model. *Dissertation Abstraction International, 63*(03), 878A. (UMI No. AAT 3045526)

Myers, C. B., Bennett, D., Brown, G., & Henderson, T. (2004). Emerging online learning environments and student learning: An analysis of faculty perceptions. *Educational Technology and Society, 7*(1), 78–86.

Ndahi, H. B. (1999). Utilization of distance learning technology among industrial and technical teacher education faculty. *Journal of Industrial Teacher Education, 36*(4), 21–37.

Nelson, S. J. (2003). Perceptions of agricultural education teacher preparation programs toward distance education. *Dissertation Abstraction International, 64*(07), 2452A. (UMI No. AAT 3098434)

O'Quinn, L. R. (2002). Factors that influence community college faculty participation in distance education. *Dissertation Abstraction International, 63*(03), 879A. (UMI No. AAT 3045485)

O'Quinn, L. R., & Corry, M. (2004). Factors which motivate community college faculty to participate in distance education. *International Journal of E-Learning, 3*(1), 19–30.

Pathasarathy, M., & Smith, M. A. (2009). Valuing the institution: An expanded list of factors influencing faculty adoption of online education. *Online Journal of Distance Learning Administration,12*(2). Retrieved from http://www.westga.edu/~distance/ojdla/summer122/parthasarathy122.pdf

Pina, A. A. (2005). Distance learning: The importance and implementation of factors affecting its institutionalization. *Dissertation Abstraction International, 66*(03), 970A. (UMI No. AAT 3168540)

Poe, M. E. C. (2000). Selected factors affecting attitudes of graduate faculty toward use of two-way audio/two-way video as a primary instructional delivery system. *Dissertation Abstraction International, 61*(07), 2672A. (UMI No. AAT 9980204)

Porter, R. D. (2003). Internet-based distance educators address major distance education barriers in large postsecondary institutions. *Dissertation Abstraction International,65*(04), 1278A. (UMI No. AAT 3130048)

Ricci, G. A. (2002). System infrastructure needs for Web course delivery: A survey of online courses in Florida community colleges. *Dissertation Abstraction International, 63*(02), 569A. (UMI No. AAT 3042973)

Rockwell, S. K., Schauer, J., Fritz, S. M., & Marx, D. B. (1999). Incentives and obstacles influencing higher education faculty and administrators to teach via distance. *Online Journal of Distance Learning Administration* [*Online serial*] *2*(4). Retrieved April 11, 2000, from http://www.westga.edu/~distance/rockwell24.htm

Schauer, J. A. (2002). Role of the department chair in implementing distance education in colleges of agriculture in land-grant institutions. *Dissertation Abstraction International, 63*(03), 840A. (UMI No. AAT 3045534)

Schifter, C. C. (2002). Perception differences about participating in distance education. *Online Journal of Distance Learning Administration, 5*(1). Retrieved January 23, 2006, from http://www.westga.edu/%7Edistance/ojdla/spring51/schifter51.html

Schifter, C. C. (2000a, June). *Distance education facultyiIncentives and compensation: An exploratory study.* Paper presented at the meeting of the National University Teleconferencing Consortium, Toronto.

Schifter, C. C. (2000b, March/April). Faculty motivators and inhibitors for participation in distance education. *Educational Technology,* 43–46.

Schopieray, E. (2006). *Understanding faculty motivation to teach online courses* [Abstract]. (ProQuest AAT 3236419)

Schwer, A. D. (2001). Role of the department chair in the delivery of distance education programs. *Dissertation Abstraction International, 62*(08), 2651A. (UMI No. AAT 3022664)

Sener, J. (2011, November). *Using QM to improve teaching and learning in a screen captured world.* Keynote address presented at the annual conference of Quality Matters, Baltimore, MD.

Shattuck, K. (2007). Quality matters: Collaborative program planning at a state level. *Online Distance Learning Administration, 10*(3). Retrieved from http://www.westga.edu/~distance/ojdla/fall103/shattuck103.htm

Shea, P. (2007). Bridges and barriers to teaching online college courses: A study of experienced online faculty in thirty-six colleges. *Journal of Asynchronous Learning Networks, 11*(2). Retrieved from http://sloanconsortium.org/sites/default/files/v11n2_shea_0.pdf

Shea, P., Pickett, A., & Li, C. S. (2005). Increasing access to higher education: A study of the diffusion of online teaching among 913 college faculty. *International Review of Research in Open and Distance Learning, 6*(2). Retrieved December 2, 2005 from http://www.irrodl.org/content/v6.2/shea.html

Simonson, M., Smaldina, S., Albright, M., & Zvacek, S. (2009). *Teaching and learning at a distance: Foundations of distance education* (4th ed.). Boston: Allyn & Bacon.

Sperling, C. B. (2003). How community colleges understand the scholarship of teaching and learning. *Community College Journal of Research and Practice, 27,* 593–601.

Stevenson, K. N. (2007). *Motivating and inhibiting factors affecting faculty participation in online distance education* (Unpublished doctoral dissertation). East Carolina University, NC.

Stewart, C., Bachman, C., & Johnson, R. (2010). Predictors of faculty acceptance of online education. *MERLOT Journal of Online Learning and Teaching, 6*(3), 597–616. Retrieved from http://jolt.merlot.org/vol6no3/stewartc_0910.pdf

Sumrall, J. G. (2002). Factors which influence faculty attitudes and perceptions of distance education in analytical subject areas. *Dissertation Abstraction International, 65*(06), 2081A. (UMI No. AAT 3135309)

Suter, M. C. (2002). College faculty's transition to online teaching: From classroom space to virtual place. *Dissertation Abstraction International, 62*(12), 4091A. (UMI No. AAT 3037368)

Tastle, W. J., White, B. A., & Shackleton, P. (2005). E-Learning in higher education: The challenge, effort, and return on investment. *International Journal of E-Learning, 4*(2), 241–251.

Ulmer, L.W., Watson, L.W., & Derby, D. (2007). Perceptions of higher education faculty members on the value of distance education. *The Quarterly Review of Distance Education, 8*(1), 59–70.

Wallcott, L. L., & Shattuck, K, (2007). Faculty participation. Motivations, incentives, and rewards. In M, Moore (Ed.), Handbook of distance education (2nd ed., pp. 377–390). Mahwah, NJ: Erlbaum.

Wenger, E. (1998). *Communities of practice: Learning, meaning, and identity.* Cambridge University Press.

Wenger, E. (2006). *Community of practice: A brief introduction.* Retrieved from http://www.ewenger.com/theory/

Whicker, T. R. (2004). Critical issues in internet-based distance learning in community colleges: Perceptions of problems and strategies for solving those problems. *Dissertation Abstraction International, 65*(04), 1209A. (UMI No. AAT 3129911)

Wilson, W. M. (2002). Faculty and administrator attitudes and perceptions toward distance learning in Southern Baptist-related educational institutions. *Dissertation Abstraction International, 63*(04), 1277A. (UMI No. AAT 3050702)

Wolcott, L. L., & Betts, K. S. (1999). What's in it for me? Incentives for faculty participation in distance education. *Journal of Distance Education, 14*(2), 34–49.

Zhen, Y., Garthwait, A., & Pratt, P. (2008). Factors affecting faculty members' decision to teach or not to teach online in higher education. *Online Journal of Distance Learning Administration, 11*(3). Retrieved from http://www.westga.edu/~distance/ojdla/fall113/zhen113.html

Zirkle, C. (2004). Distance education programming barriers in career and technical teacher education in Ohio. *Journal of Vocational Education Research, 29*(3), 157–79.

25

STUDENTS AND TEACHERS AS ETHICAL ACTORS

MELODY M. THOMPSON AND JONATHAN W. WRIGGLESWORTH

Within the broad field of education, discussions of the moral nature of teaching and learning have developed through decades of reflection that in turn connect to centuries of earlier discourse on morality and ethics. The ideas and writings of early distance educators—those dedicated to broadening access to educational programming to unserved or underserved populations of adults—fit well within this discourse tradition. However, many current examples of distance education practice and literature seem less the natural outgrowth of a self-reflective educational enterprise than the offspring of a marriage between rapidly changing socio-economic conditions and institutional expediency. One result has been a lack of attention to ethical issues in the distance education literature. In 2001, the concept paper for the ICDE Special Presidential Session on Ethics in Distance Education and Open Learning stated, "A search of the literature, including documentation available on the World Wide Web, reveals little explicit concern with ethical questions among the community of professionals active in the area of distance education and open learning" (ICDE Dusseldorf 2001, "Full Abstract," ¶ 6).

Since that statement was made, this particular gap in the literature has begun to be filled. Our search for literature with explicit reference to ethics resulted in a number of publications focused on topics related to ethical aspects of distance education. The purpose of this chapter is to review literature focused on two groups of responsible agents— students and teachers—as the basis for reflections on the extent to which the literature provides a foundation for ethical self-reflection, decision-making and practice.

LITERATURE FOCUSED ON STUDENTS

Most of the articles that discuss the ethics of student behavior focus on a taken-for-granted *problem*: cheating or academic dishonesty. A second, less prominent, strand of literature discusses categories of ethical behavior as *issues,* not problems. This latter strand addresses the responsibility of students to be committed learners, that is, to take responsibility for their learning and to behave in ways that contribute fully to others' learning. We will discuss this underemphasized topic first, and then turn our attention to the more widely discussed topic of academic dishonesty.

Commitment to Learning

Haughey (2007) suggests that the act of joining a learning community brings with it an ethical responsibility to oneself, one's fellow students, and the instructor: "In joining a learning community [students] must realize that they assume responsibility for being fully committed as genuine learners to their own and their colleagues' welfare" (p. 142). Thus the emphasis should be on character—what people should *be*—rather than on behavior: what people should *do*. Haughey notes that students' responsibility can be acted out only in a context of mutual accountability, with the instructor and institution providing modeling and support of core values such as honesty and integrity. While the notion of shared responsibility for forming and supporting intellectually stimulating and affectively supportive learning communities is relatively common in the literature, less common is the idea of student engagement as an explicitly *ethical* responsibility. Equally unusual is the idea that thoughtful student feedback about the instructor and the course contributes to the instructor's own learning and "personal fulfilment" (p. 139), making failure to provide such feedback when requested an ethical breach in the student-teacher relationship.

The theme of interdependence is also explicit in Kawachi's (2009) discussion of learners' ethical responsibility both for achieving their own learning and helping others in the group to learn. Arguing against "individualist autonomy as a goal in education" (p. 25), he focuses on positive ethical behaviors in student-student, student-content, student-instructor, and student-technology interactions, that is, on those behaviors that promote motivation toward lifelong learning for self and others. A similar focus on shared responsibility is apparent in Luppicini's (2009) analysis of how conversation builds and sustains online learning communities. Viewing "conversation ethics" as the responsibility of both students and instructors, Luppicini combines insights from technoethics—concerned with the moral and ethical aspects of technology in society—with elements of language theories to propose guiding questions that all participants can use to "advance the co-construction of meaning" (p. 104).

Cultural differences in beliefs about responsibility for learning, in communication patterns, and in power dynamics between dominant and marginalized groups, can limit the generalizability of models or guidelines that prescribe student responsibilities. For example, some ideas about what constitutes ethical student discourse may be rooted in ideologies that grant power to those whose conversational styles reflect the discourse of socially dominant groups at the expense of marginalized groups (Sujo de Montes, Oran, & Willis, 2002). As Anderson and Simpson (2007, p. 133) point out, "power relations such as those formed in face-to-face classes are also enacted as part of the online environment."

A final issue related to student commitment to fellow learners is embedded in the mode of discourse in online courses, in which "conversation" becomes permanent text. While the ability to return to instructors' and classmates' earlier comments has definite advantages, the permanence of these written comments generates ethical concerns. Anderson and Simpson (2007) note the potential for harassment over conflicts or imagined slights reflected in permanently available postings, as well as breaches of confidentiality, possibly as a result of a "distance effect" that reduces students' empathy for each other (Russell, 2004).

Academic Dishonesty

We now turn from potential ethical *issues* to a widely noted ethical *problem*: cheating. Trenholm (2007) notes that while cheating (copying from others, plagiarism, improper collaboration, misrepresentation of identity) is the behavior, the underlying ethical principle that is violated is academic integrity. Cheating is academic dishonesty, and the literature reflects deep concerns about this breach in ethical conduct. Specific topics addressed include the extent of academic dishonesty among distance students, personal motivations and structural causes, and approaches to addressing the problem.[1]

Literature on overall rates of cheating in traditional education provides some context. Although scholars disagree about whether the rates of cheating among students have increased over the last several decades or whether inconsistent terminology has resulted in apparent increases, all agree that cheating among students at all levels of the formal educational system occurs at distressingly high rates (e.g., Baron & Crooks, 2005; Chapman, Davis, Toy, & Wright, 2004; McCabe, 2005).

Currently there is little empirical data on which to base a comparison of cheating in traditional and distance environments. Indeed, a common observation among scholars is that research in this area is limited and largely anecdotal (Baron & Crooks, 2005; Grijalva, Nowell, & Kerkvliet, 2006; Krsak, 2007). As a result, we have insufficient evidence with which to distinguish perception from reality.

Perceptions of increased opportunities for and inclination toward dishonesty by online students occur frequently in the literature. Krsak (2007) asserts that "it is common for faculty to believe that academic dishonesty is easier and more prevalent in online courses" (p. 159), while King, Guyette, and Piotrowski (2009, ¶ 2) suggest that for students enrolled in online programs, "the online environment or milieu contributes to temptation to use dishonesty (in its many forms)...."

Baron and Crooks (2005, p. 40) go so far as to declare "*a general consensus among those involved with higher education* that Web Based Distance Education (WBDE) provides more opportunities for, even promotes more, academic dishonesty than traditional face-to-face (f2f) instruction" (our emphasis). Interestingly, the specific support cited for this very broad statement of a "general consensus" comes from a single study (Kennedy, Nowak, Raghuraman, Thomas, & Davis, 2000) in which 172 students and 69 faculty members were asked their perceptions of the relative ease of cheating in online courses compared to traditional courses. The finding in this study that "both students and faculty believe it is easier to cheat in a distance learning class" ("Discussion," ¶ 1) may contribute to the "commonness" of the idea, but is insufficient for a conclusion of a "general consensus." Ironically, although Baron and Crooks go on to question the validity of the supposed consensus—even labeling such generalizations as dangerous—their own statement will likely be used as support by those who *do* believe that academic dishonesty is more prevalent among distance education students.

The Kennedy et al. (2000) article noted above reflects a quite weak connection between research data and conclusions. The authors use the perceptions of their 241 research participants as the basis for concluding that "as the number of distance learning classes increases so will academic dishonesty ("Discussion," ¶ 1). This assertion is particularly tenuous given the authors' report that students and faculty with experience in online courses perceived less potential impact on academic dishonesty from the online nature of the course.

More recently, King et al. (2009) examined perceptions of extent and ease of dishonest academic behavior by surveying 121 undergraduate business students on their beliefs about cheating in online courses. They report that the majority of students believed that cheating was more prevalent in online courses, while almost three-quarters believed that cheating was easier on line. In contrast to Kennedy et al.'s (2000) earlier study, these researchers found no differences tied to prior experience with online education.

Two studies that went beyond examination of perceptions to measuring actual behavior reported that the prevalence of academic dishonesty in online classes is no higher than in traditional classes. Grijalva et al. (2006) gauged the extent of undergraduate student cheating behavior in an online course at a public university and correlated cheating with specific structural and situational factors. Their analysis indicated "that academic dishonesty in a single online class is not greater than estimates of cheating in a traditional class" (p. 13). A similar conclusion resulted from a study in which rates of Internet plagiarism were manually and electronically (via Turnitin) monitored in an online geography course. Researchers analyzed 429 student assignments in five course sections and concluded that the "finding of a 13 percent rate of plagiarism is in line with rates obtained from other studies that measured actual infractions [in traditional courses]" (Jocoy & DiBiase, 2006, "Discussion," ¶ 1).

Contributing Factors. Although researchers disagree on the extent of academic dishonesty among distance education students, they share beliefs about factors that contribute to such behavior. Most agree, for example, that the factors that motivate traditional students to cheat motivate online students, as well. These well-recognized factors include pressure to achieve, lack of sufficient preparation, and a perception that "everyone's doing it," so that refraining from cheating would be putting oneself at a competitive disadvantage (Grijalvaet al., 2006; King et al., 2009; Krsak, 2007).

Several authors note differences in motivations between demographic groups. For example, Jocoy and DiBiase (2006) point out that adult students whose programs are being paid for by their employers may need to obtain a particular grade in order to receive this support. Culture also plays a role, since ideas about what constitutes academic dishonesty as well as motivations to succeed differ across cultures (Grijalva et al., 2006; Nagy, 2009).

Some scholars have speculated that specific characteristics of the online environment might contribute to the prevalence of cheating. For example, Underwood and Szabo (2003, cited in Jocoy & Dibiase, 2006) suggest that spending more time on the Internet results in "self-reported greater willingness to engage in copy-and-paste plagiarism" ("Introduction," ¶ 2). If this observation is true, then students taking online courses—thereby depending on the Internet for all aspects of their educational activities—would be more likely to plagiarize using online resources.

Other environmental characteristics such as the physical distance between instructor and students—which precludes close oversight—or the psychological distance between participants—which may contribute to a weaker sense of community and mutual responsibility—have also been suggested as factors in distance students' academic dishonesty (Rowe, 2004; Sharma & Maleyeff, 2003). Sharma and Maleyeff (2003) further write of "moral distancing," by which a seemingly "victimless" act quickly and anonymously committed via technology "leads to a distance between the self and the action" (p. 22).

ask how educational opportunities are limited or enhanced for certain populations of learners by the specific materials chosen or produced. They note that while some educators use materials that are free and readily available to anyone with Internet access (e.g., Elias, 2011), many others design their courses around materials that come with considerable costs, thereby excluding some potential students from participation. Still other materials are unsuited to specific learning styles or inaccessible to students with disabilities.

Even seemingly minor content elements such as the examples used to illustrate concepts or the inclusion of idioms unfamiliar to those from other cultures can be culturally exclusive (Bates, 2001). Sankey and St. Hill (2009) report how one large university has confronted the ethical issue of designing for an increasingly diverse non-traditional student population through "transmodal delivery," that is, "the provision to students of a resource-rich multimodal learning environment, allowing students the opportunity to access their course content in a combination of ways" (p. 131). The use of multiple representations of the same content combined with different options for content delivery represents a "new, more ethical approach" to meeting the needs of "today's multiliterate, culturally diverse and dispersed student groups" (p. 149). However, questions remain about the practicability of this approach for small institutions or for faculty who must design their own courses without the support of instructional designers or other technical staff.

Another aspect of content appropriateness arises for students with disabilities. Early assessments of the potential for online programs to provide enhanced access for disabled students were largely positive, noting the various ways in which such programs would make it easier for students to obtain a post-secondary education (Kim-Rupnow, Dowrick, & Burke, 2001). However, Keeler and Horney (2007) suggest that designers and teachers erroneously assume that the online format supported by assistive technology overcomes access difficulties. These scholars state that unless universal design principles have been incorporated into a course, barriers to participation will continue exist.

The Executive Summary of the most recent Managing Online Education (MOE) Survey (Campus Computing Project, 2010, ¶ 1) makes clear that responsibility for appropriate accessibility has been left largely in the hands of designers and teachers: "many institutions may be vulnerable to complaints about … accessibility issues because faculty and academic departments, rather than a central office familiar with the mandates of the Americans with Disabilities Act (ADA), are responsible for ADA compliance." Failure to meet the access requirements of this segment of the student population is an obvious and ongoing ethical concern.

Other questions, both ethical and legal, relate to the complex restrictions on content distribution intended to protect the rights of authors and publishers. To what extent are faculty members aware of—and to what extent do they feel bound by—restrictions on the use and distribution of materials?

One study asked faculty members about specific decisions to "use/not use copied text, images, sounds, animations and video from someone else's Web page with or without obtaining copyright permission, to pay/not pay copyright fees, or to ask/not ask for advice from the institution's copyright and fair use specialists" (Sweeney, 2006, "Background," ¶ 2). Findings showed that most respondents were poorly informed about legislation that regulates the use of copyrighted material in the online environment and also unaware of their institution's policies on copyright compliance. Although recognizing the legally and ethically questionable aspects of such behaviors, in follow-up focus groups many instructors reported inappropriate use of materials, often as the result of pressures felt at the beginning of a semester to get a course ready to open. A positive aspect of the findings was participants' desire to learn more about copyright regulation and to have appropriate information available on line (Sweeney, 2006).

McGreal (2004) looks at the copyright question from a completely different ethical perspective, suggesting that copyright law is now little more than a vehicle for protecting the profits of publishing companies. Although the situation places a heavy burden on institutions in developed countries, from McGreal's point of view the effect on the educational development of poorer countries is much more serious since institutions in poverty-stricken countries cannot afford to pay the fees demanded by the copyright controllers.

This tension between the ethical aspects of the copyright issue and the legal aspects is one that continues to develop as an increasing number of faculty members "push back" against the idea that the Internet provides "free" access to knowledge and information ("The Copyright Rebellion," 2011; Sharpe, 2010). The perceived harm to learning and scholarship that results from overly controlled access to information has prompted considerable resistance, most of which has come in the form of ethical arguments for "open access," as opposed to more pragmatic considerations of how best to bring this goal about (Borgman, 2010). In response, some publishers are defending current practices, claiming that, because of the services they offer, "access to published content is greater and at its lowest cost per use than ever" (Fischman, 2012, The Company Responds, ¶ 5).

Technology Use

Educational technologies are used to support traditional teaching-learning activities: delivery of content, facilitation of discussion, assessment of learning, etc. These common uses will be discussed in detail below in the sections on instruction and assessment. Two other affordances and uses of technologies in Web-based courses present new and significant ethical questions related to preservation of the text-based interactions among course participants and surveillance of student behavior at a level well-beyond what is possible in traditional courses (Anderson & Simpson, 2007; Thompson & Kearns, 2011).

Most course management systems (CMS) allow instructors to collect a wide array of information about students' individual and group activity, often without students being aware of what information is collected and how it is used. Such data and information become part of an ever-expanding permanent record, presumably collected in support of effective teaching and learning. However, Thompson and Kearns (2011) ask how—even whether—the benefits and drawbacks of such uses are evaluated. Are these merely presumed benefits, or is there research to support their value? Further questions focus on students' rights to privacy and confidentiality. Although universities have many policies related to these rights, new uses of technology are in many cases not addressed in such policies, leading to further questions: "[A]re these safeguards addressing the right issue when an even more fundamental issue, informed consent for data gathering, is overlooked? … At what point does our interest in knowing more about a student—in order to make meaningful links to learning—intrude on the student's right to privacy?" (Anderson & Simpson, pp. 134, 135).

Even when the data-gathering or records aspect of the CMS *is* transparent to students, the instructor can add a non-detectable layer of surveillance by creating fictitious or virtual students who appear to others in the class as legitimate participants. While some scholars have recognized the ethical questions inherent in this use of technology (e.g., Nagel, Blignaut, & Cronjé, 2007), others have viewed it as a legitimate way of getting necessary information for the purpose of course improvement (Who is Bill Reed? 2005; Krsak, 2007). The mixed—but largely negative—reactions of students and the sharply divided views of faculty members in reaction to hearing about such practices (Nagel et al., 2007; Parry, 2009) suggest the complexity of actions taken for good—even "ethical"—*ends* but using what some view as unethical and therefore unacceptable *means*.

Teaching or Instruction

One organizing principle for examining the ethical dimensions of teaching in a distance education environment is that of relationship. Haughey (2007, p. 139) proposes that to teach is to lead in the development of responsible relationships between instructor and students: "Teaching is … leadership based upon moral and ethical principles, as opposed to technical ones." Thus, in addition to the obvious responsibility to be knowledgeable in and able to communicate about the appropriate content area, the ethical teacher will lead by example in the development of a learning community characterized by responsibility, authenticity, and presence: "Responsibility reflects the ethic of caring through relationality. Authenticity is based on reciprocity. Presence involves putting the other at the centre while being open oneself to personal change" (Haughey 2007, p. 141).

Hai-Jew (2009, p. 155) suggests that as institutions have broadened their reach to enroll a globalized student population, teachers need to develop an educational ethic that consciously considers the "national, ethnic and racial backgrounds of their learners to offer customized value-added higher education." This outcome necessitates course design based on "cultural sensitivity"—identifying and addressing cultural differences and similarities—and "localization"—considering and making use of the multiple "locales" in which students live (p. 156).

However, many instructors lack experience in integrating such elements into courses. Too common is the situation described by Bates (2001) and Anderson and Simpson (2007), in which instructors use methods and activities that reflect the (usually Western) culture in which a course was developed, with students from other cultures expected to conform to inflexible expectations. For this reason Hai-Jew (2009) suggests faculty may need training on "how to better reach and learn from and about their global students" (p. 184). The extent to which faculty are willing to engage in such professional development is itself a question with ethical dimensions.

Other scholars suggest that teachers also need to be aware of gender diversity as an ethically charged instructional issue. Brey (2006), who sees possibilities for gender inequalities in online courses based on differences in learning styles and facility with computer communication, advises teachers to use teaching strategies and tools "that are sensitive to gender differences in the use of information technology and that do not contain gender biases" (pp. 8-9). Kramarae (2007, p. 177) concurs, noting that "gender needs to be addressed by everyone who wants to offer equal opportunities to all students in distance education."

Assessment of Learning

Assessing learning in any educational context requires skill in developing approaches that effectively measure outcomes as articulated in specific objectives. The "natural and normal" approach in higher education has long been the examination (Rowan, 2000, p. 164). However, differences between distance and traditional post-secondary education suggest the need for other assessment approaches, particularly when program mission and/or learner population are non-traditional: "the development of open and flexible learning, and new attitudes to methods of assessing people's 'worth,' go hand in hand" (Bosworth, cited in Rowan, 2000, p. 163).

Many discussions of alternative assessments reflect a desire to prevent students' unethical behavior, based on the belief that traditional forms of assessment are more amenable to cheating, especially in a distance education environment. However, only a few articles specifically identified alternative assessment as an instructor's *ethical* responsibility—instead casting it as way to discourage or prevent students' *unethical* behavior. In keeping with the focus this chapter, we limit our review to articles that explicitly discuss a teacher's ethical responsibility to design assessments in ways that discourage or prevent academic dishonesty.

Olt (2002) states that there are three possible approaches to minimizing (online) cheating and plagiarism: first, there is the virtues approach. The virtues approach seeks to develop students who do not want to cheat. Second is the prevention approach, which seeks to eliminate or reduce opportunities for students to cheat and to reduce the pressure to cheat. Finally, there is the police approach, which seeks to catch and punish those who do cheat.

Haughey (2007) takes an explicitly ethical and personal approach, situated within the virtues perspective noted in Olt's (2002) statement. He suggests that, rather than relying on standardized approaches, strict rules, and punishments in response to rising rates of cheating, educators should view academic dishonesty in terms of relationships and collective responsibility: "the learner, instructor and institution collectively need to respond by assuming responsibility *as* involved community members, exercising responsibility *to* a particular constituency or constituencies, and demonstrating responsibility *for* a particular area or areas of concern" (p. 142). Specifically, in designing assessments instructors should model ethical expectations for students through understanding their students' contexts, establishing fair workloads, and clearly communicating standards for performance and behavior.

Nagy (2009) focuses on international students' academic dishonesty in her discussion of the "naïve" assumption that all students enrolling in a distance course or program "have the same foundation skills and are thus able to equally conceptualise and utilize technologies to accomplish assessment tasks" (p. 256). She notes that cultural differences penalize students from academic cultures in which a single final examination—for which students can "cram"—rather than graded assignments throughout a course is the common practice. For this reason she suggests that institutions desiring to respond ethically to an increasingly diverse student population should consider offering students multiple assessment pathways as part of the "need for diversity in teaching paradigms" (p. 249).

Some authors offer suggestions for identifying violations of academic integrity in student assessments. Ethical questions surface in these discussions, as well. For example, although authors commonly note the value of plagiarism detection software such as Turnitin (e.g., Jocoy & DiBiase 2006), a few have suggested that use of such services may create a "culture of mistrust" or that this practice may violate students' intellectual property rights through the creation of databases of submitted papers (e.g., Krsak, 2007).

Whatever the *ethical* implications of this latter practice, Lipinski (this volume) provides the most recent *legal* ruling on this question, reporting that while "content created by students is owned by the student-author.... [a] recent appellate decision concluded that use of student papers without permission in a plagiarism detection database is fair use."

A final issue revolves around instructors' ethical responsibility to address instances of suspected academic dishonesty in student assessments. Several sources note the reluctance of faculty members to actively pursue cases of student cheating. Trenholm (2007, p. 293) cites Schneider's (1999) observation that "preventing and punishing cheating languish at the bottom of most professors' 'to do' lists—if they make the list at all." Common reasons for this reluctance include the time needed to pursue investigations, onerous institutional procedures, fear of poor student evaluations, and perceived lack of administrative support for the instructor who dutifully follows institutional policy. On the other hand, students may be less likely to behave dishonestly when they believe that instructors take academic integrity seriously and will document the cases they uncover (Lim & Coulter, 2006; Trenholm, 2007). Thus, while recognizing the difficulties involved, Lim (2009) offers faculty members teaching in open and distance learning systems (ODLS) a clear challenge: "In order for faculty members to nurture their students to become ethical and responsible citizens of society, they need to pursue all suspected cases of ODLS misconduct even in the face of possible hardships" (p. 223).

Developing a Personal Foundation for Ethical Behavior

The last ethical responsibility we examine is the responsibility of faculty members to consciously and intentionally develop a strong foundation for their own ethical behavior. Anderson and Simpson propose (2007) that "applied ethics provides a framework for a disciplined approach to engaging with issues often faced by distance educators" (p. 129), while Haughey (2007) believes that faculty members should be as clear about their own ethical principles as they are about the content they teach. Because ethical issues characterize even the most seemingly mundane aspects of distance educators' work, ethical reflection should be an integral consideration in day-to-day thinking about practice (Thompson & Kearns, 2011).

On the other hand, some scholars have noted that few educators are prepared to meet this challenge. Burge (2007, p. 108) suggests that many educators are "unable to distinguish all the competing rights in an ethical dilemma or [are] unable to reason their own way to a decision." This inability often results from insufficient awareness and/or lack of knowledge. Educators may easily miss the ethical dimensions of various aspects of practice amidst the sometimes conflicting and often difficult-to-negotiate factors in their complex organizational environments. Additionally, few people have studied the elements of moral philosophy, ethics, and ethical decision-making as a foundation for conscious ethical practice (Thompson & Kearns, 2011).

How do educators gain such a foundation? Haughey (2007) observes that a key component of any professional development program—but particularly those intended to develop reflective practitioners—should emphasize the development and articulation of a personal ethical framework. Parscal and Benski (2009) describe a course to prepare instructors to teach on line in which participants examine and discuss the Society for Teaching and Learning in Higher Education's principles for ethical teaching. Results of their qualitative study on the impact of activities "to promote comprehension, application, and ultimately, synthesis of ethical principles" (p. 285) indicate that these activities increase the likelihood that teachers will follow appropriate ethical principles in their practice.

Burge (2007) suggests that reading literature from professions that have grappled with the ethical dimensions of practice can provide useful guidance, as can material from scholarly centers established specifically to provide resources and information on the topic of practical ethics. Her brief review of several classic ethical frameworks and other sources is offered as "a set of tools" for educators desiring to enhance their "ethical fitness" (p. 107). Anderson and Simpson (2007, p. 129) argue for the importance of active engagement in questions of values and "practical morality," noting that educators must use "energetic self-reflection" in applying *general* ethical principles to *particular* cases as a guide for right action.

Thompson and Kearns (2011) agree that finding the balance between overarching ethical principles and the particulars of a given context and situation is the key to developing ethical competency. They see sets of general principles or classic ethical theories as valuable only to the extent that an educator has engaged in—and continues to engage in—the difficult work of developing a moral persona: "What practitioners need is not a universal framework that we can apply personally but rather a coherent and stable *personal* framework that reflects the particular nature of our lives, our values, and our practice contexts" (pp. 262–263). Thompson and Kearns discuss the process of developing a moral persona and offer questions related to specific teaching activities as a way to encourage educators' ethical reflection and development.

LITERATURE AS A FOUNDATION FOR ETHICAL REFLECTION AND PRACTICE

Our review of literature suggests both progress and ongoing challenges in developing an ethical consciousness within the field. The progress is reflected in the large number of publications specifically examining the ethical dimensions of distance education. The challenges are reflected in three characteristics of the literature that currently limit its potential to shape and support ethical decision-making and practice.

First, the level of rigor and sophistication of ethical analysis varies widely across the literature. Although a few authors provide reasoned justifications for their analyses, many others go little further than assertions that a particular behavior or question does, indeed, have ethical dimensions. Often the terms "ethical" or "unethical" are used as synonyms for right or wrong or as markers for issues with an obvious moral content, thus reflecting little more than "plain moral competence": the recognition that our actions are and should be constrained in some way by (unspecified) values and principles in the service of a desire to do what is right (Walker, 2003, p. 8). However, to expand our understanding of particular issues as well as to provide a basis for decision making and action, scholars' ethical reflection and communication needs to be reason-based and tied explicitly to clearly stated values, principles, and goals.

Second, ethical awareness has yet to become an integrated feature of the distance education literature. Most attention has come in the form of "special topic" articles, journals, or books. However, because such issues characterize both the obviously critical and the seemingly mundane aspects of our practice, awareness of and reflection on them should be integrated into our writing as scholars.

Finally, our analysis suggests that certain formal features of many publications—specifically form, tone, and style—constrain thinking about the ethical dimensions of distance education. In considering this aspect of the literature we found a rephrasing Boshier and Onn's (2000, p. 13) question "Who is doing what to whom and why?" useful, asking instead, "Who is talking about whom and how?"

One feature of a sustainable—and *sustaining*—moral community is discourse that values and integrates the voices of all participants. In literature on the ethics of student and faculty behavior, this feature is largely missing, although in different ways and to different degrees in the two sets of literature.

In the literature on student behavior, one voice predominates: that of the educators studying the students as the objects of research. Although research about other aspects of distance education routinely incorporates student voices, those voices are in most cases silent in literature on the ethics of student behavior. The result cannot help but be an impoverished perspective on students as ethical actors in distance education.

In the literature about teaching, we do hear the voice of teachers as active subjects writing to other teachers about ideas assumed to be mutually important. Voice, tone, and word choice signal personal engagement and a conviction that these are issues that educators, as a group, should be pondering *together* through the medium of the literature. What we do not hear are the voices of those being taught (an exception is Harper & Luck, 2009). What are students' ideas about the ethical dimensions of their teachers' actions? If the basis of ethical behavior is in relationships, students should be encouraged to reflect on the ethics of both sides of the teaching-learning relationship, and we suggest that this should be a collaborative reflection among students and their teachers. This gap in the literature suggests that, in most cases, teachers making ethically charged decisions that affect their students are—at most—"taking into consideration" their students' needs, that is thinking *for* them rather than *with* them (Walker, 2003) about issues that affect the shared teaching and learning environment.

CONCLUSION

As is true in many rapidly developing fields, the distance education literature has tended to focus more on the technical aspects of the teaching-learning relationship—doing things right—than on the ethical aspects—doing the right thing. While the latter focus was of great concern to the pioneers of the field, many recent scholars have tended to view this relationship primarily from a methodological or epistemological perspective. However, the welcome expansion of the literature base on the ethical dimensions of distance education challenges all of us to see the ethical aspects of both our day-to-day relationships and our "academic" endeavors as scholars and to integrate that consciousness broadly into our work. While the current literature provides an important resource for meeting these challenges, we need to move forward toward increased sophistication in our ethical reflections and communication, a more systematic integration of an ethical consciousness into our scholarly writing, and both practice and communication about practice that integrates the voices of students *and* teachers. The goal is not to turn students or educators into professional ethicists, but rather to highlight the importance of an ethical consciousness in building and sustaining the fundamental relationships that characterize distance education.

NOTE

1. Most literature focused on academic dishonesty further includes practical suggestions for how course designers and instructors can detect and discourage academic dishonesty, that is, how they can change or prevent specific student behaviors. Given our focus on categories of responsible actors, the primary emphasis in this section of the review will be on students' behavior rather than on what others might do to influence it. Some of this latter material will be reviewed in the section that focuses on what constitutes ethical action by those who design and teach courses.

REFERENCES

Anderson, B., & Simpson, M. (2007). Ethical issues in online education. *Open Learning: The Journal of Open and Distance Learning, 22*(2), 129–138.

Baron, J., & Crooks, S. (2005). Academic integrity in web based distance education. *TechTrends, 49*(2), 40–45.

Bates, T. (2001). International distance education: Cultural and ethical issues. *Distance Education, 22*(1), 122–136.

Borgman, C. L. (2010). Review of *Digitize this book! The politics of new media or why we need open access now. Technology and Culture, 51*(3), 768–770. Retrieved from Project Muse database, http://muse.jhu.edu/journals/tech/summary/v051/51.3.borgman.html

Boshier, R., & Onn, C. M. (2000). Discursive constructions of Web learning and education. *Journal of Distance Education, 15*(2), 1–16.

Burge, E. (2007). Considering ethical issues. *Open Learning: The Journal of Open and Distance Learning, 22*(2), 107–115.

Brey, P. (2006). Social and ethical dimensions of computer-mediated education (preprint version). *Journal of Information, Communication & Ethics in Society 2,* 91–102. http://www.utwente.nl/gw/wijsb/organization/brey/Publicaties_Brey/Brey_2006_Mediated_Education.pdf

Campus Computing Project (2010). *Managing online education survey (w/video).* http://www.campuscomputing.net/item/2010-managing-online-education-survey-wvideo

Carr-Chellman, A. (2005). The new frontier: Web-based education in U.S. culture. In A. A. Carr-Chellman (Ed.), *Global perspectives on e-learning. Rhetoric and reality* (pp. 145–159). Thousand Oaks, CA: Sage.

Chapman, K. J., Davis, R., Toy, D., & Wright, L. (2004). Academic integrity in the business school environment: I'll get by with a little help from my friends. *Journal of Marketing Education, 26*(3), 236–249.

Elias, T. (2011). Universal instructional design principles for mobile learning. *International Review of Research in Open and Distance Learning, 12*(2). Retrieved from http://www.irrodl.org/index.php/irrodl/article/view/965/1792

Grijalva, T., Nowell, C., & Kerkvliet, J. (2006). Academic honesty in online courses. *College Student Journal, 40*(1), 180–185.

Hai-Jew, S. (2009). Why "cultural sensitivities" and "localizations" in global e-learning? In U. Demiray & R. Sharma, *Ethical practices and implications in distance learning* (pp. 155–197). Hershey PA: Information Science Reference.

Harper, D., & Luck, P. (2009). Ethical practice and online learning—A contradiction? In U. Demiray, & R. Sharma (Eds.), *Ethical practices and implications in distance learning* (pp. 305–319). Hershey PA: Information Science Reference.

Haughey, D. (2007), Ethical relationships between instructor, learner and institution. *Open Learning, 22*(2), 139–147.

Heberling, M. (2002). Maintaining academic integrity in online education. *Online Journal of Distance Learning Administration, 5*(1). Retrieved from http://www.westga.edu/%7Edistance/ojdla/spring51/heberling51.pdf

ICDE Dusseldorf 2001 Special Presidential Session. (2001). *Full abstract.* Retrieved from http://www.learndev.org/ICDE2001-Ethics.html#anchor34588

Jocoy, C., & DiBiase, D. (2006). Plagiarism by adult learners online: A case study in detection and remediation. *International Review of Research in Open and Distance Learning, 7*(1). Retrieved from http://www.irrodl.org/index.php/irrodl/article/view/242/495

Kawachi, P. (2009). Ethics in interactions in distance education. In U. Demiray & R. Sharma (Eds.), *Ethical practices and implications in distance learning* (pp. 24–34). Hershey, PA: Information Science Reference.

Keeler, C. G., & Horney, M. (2007). Online course designs: Are special needs being met? *The American Journal of Distance Education, 21*(2), 61–75.

Kennedy, K., Nowak, S., Raghuraman, R., Thomas, J., & Davis, S. F. (2000). Academic dishonesty and distance learning: Student and faculty views. *College Student Journal, 34*(2), 309–314.

Kim-Rupnow, W., Dowrick, P., & Burke, L. (2001). Implications for improving access and outcomes for individuals with disabilities in postsecondary distance education. *The American Journal of Distance Education, 15*(1), 25–40.

King, C. G., Guyette, R. W., & Piotrowski, C. (2009). Online exams and cheating: An empirical analysis of business students' views. *The Journal of Educators Online, 6*(1). Retrieved from http://www.thejeo.com/Archives/Volume6Number1/Kingetalpaper.pdf

Kramarae, C. (2007). Gender matters in online learning. In M. G. Moore (ed.), *Handbook of distance education* (2nd ed., pp. 169–180). Mahwah, NJ: Erlbaum.

Krsak, A. M. (2007, April). Curbing academic dishonesty in online courses. Paper presented at the 2007 TCC (Technology, Conferences, and Community) Worldwide Online Conference. Retrieved from http://tcc.kcc.hawaii.edu/previous/TCC%202007/krsak.pdf

Lim, C. L. (2009). An American perspective of ethical misconduct in ODLS: Who's to Blame? In U. Demiray & R. Sharma (Eds.), *Ethical practices and implications in distance learning* (pp. 216–229). Hershey PA: Information Science Reference.

Lim, C. L., & Coulter, T. (2006). Academic integrity: An instructor's obligation. *International Journal of Teaching and Learning in Higher Education, 17*(2), 155–159. Retrieved from http://www.isetl.org/ijtlhe/pdf/IJTLHE51.pdf

Luppicini, R. (2009). Conversation ethics for online learning communities. In U. Demiray & R. Sharma, *Ethical practices and implications in distance learning* (pp. 98–107). Hershey PA: Information Science Reference.

McCabe, D. L. (2005). Cheating among college and university students: A North American perspective. *Journal of Philosophy of Education, 35*(1), 47–69.

McGreal, R. (2004). Stealing the goose: Copyright and learning. *International Review of Research in Open and Distance Learning, 5*(3). Retrieved from http://www.irrodl.org/index.php/irrodl/article/view/205/819

Nagel, L., Blignaut, S., & Cronjé, J. (2007). Methical Jane: Perspectives on an undisclosed virtual student. *Journal of Computer-Mediated Communication, 12*(4). Retrieved from http://jcmc.indiana.edu/vol12/issue4/nagel.html

Nagy, J. (2009). Market forces in higher education: Cheating and the student-centered learning paradigm. In U. Demiray & R. Sharma (Eds.), *Ethical practices and implications in distance learning* (pp. 249–267). Hershey, PA: Information Science Reference.

Noble, D. (1998). Digital diploma mills: The automation of higher education. *October, 86*, 107–117. Retrieved from JSTOR database, http://www.jstor.org/stable/779110

Olt, M. (2002). Ethics and distance education: Strategies for minimizing academic dishonesty in online assessment. *Online Journal of Distance Learning Administration. 5*(3). Retrieved from http://www.westga.edu/~distance/ojdla/fall53/olt53.html

Parry, M. (2009, May 20). Online professors pose as students to encourage real learning. Retrieved from http://chronicle.com/article/Escalation-in-Digital/129652/

Parscal, T., & Bemski, P. (2009). Preparing faculty to integrate ethics into online facilitation. In U. Demiray & R. Sharma (Eds.), *Ethical practices and implications in distance learning* (pp. 284–294). Hershey PA: Information Science Reference.

Rowan, L. (2000). 'Human' resource management, 'flexible' learning and difference: A feminist exploration. In V. Jakupec & J. Garrick (Eds.), *Flexible learning, human resource and organizational development* (pp. 149–174). New York: Routledge.

Rowe, R. (2004). Cheating in online student assessment: Beyond plagiarism. *Online Journal of Distance Learning Administration, 7*(2). Retrieved from http://www.westga.edu/%7Edistance/ojdla/summer72/rowe72.pdf

Russell, G. (2004). *International Journal of Instructional Technology & Distance Learning, 1*(2). Retrieved from http://www.itdl.org/journal/feb_04/article03.htm

Russell, G. (2009). Ethical concerns with open and distance learning. In U. Demiray & R. Sharma, *Ethical practices and implications in distance learning* (pp. 64–78). Hershey PA: Information Science Reference.

Sankey, M., & St. Hill, R. (2009). The ethics of designing for multimodality: Empowering nontraditional learners. In U. Demiray & R. Sharma (Eds.), *Ethical practices and implications in distance learning* (pp. 125–154). Hershey PA: Information Science Reference.

Sharma, P., &d Maleyeff, J. (2003). Internet education: Potential problems and solutions. *The International Journal of Educational Management. 17*(1), 19–25.

Sharpe, R. (2010). Inequalities in the globalised knowledge-based economy. In J. Burnett, P. Senker, & K. Walker (Eds.), *The myths of technology: Innovation and inequality* (pp. 39–52). New York: Peter Lang.

Speck, B. (2000). The academy, online classes, and the breach in ethics. In R. Weiss, D. Knowlton, & B. Speck (Eds.), *Principles of effective teaching in the online classroom* (pp. 73–81). San Francisco: Jossey-Bass.

Sujo de Montes, L. E. Oran, S. M., & Willis, E. M. (2002). Power, language, and identity: Voices from an online course. *Computers and Composition, 19*, 251–271.

Sweeney, P. (2006). Faculty, copyright law and online course materials. *Online Journal of Distance Learning Administration, 9*(1). Retrieved from http://www.westga.edu/~distance/ojdla/spring91/sweeney91.pdf

Thompson, M. M., & Kearns, L. (2011). Which is to be master? Reflections on ethical decision-making. In E. Burge, C. Gibson, & T. Gibson (Eds.), *Flexible pedagogy, flexible practice: Notes from the trenches of distance education* (pp. 257–270). Athabasca, Canada: Athabasca University Press.

Trenholm, S. (2007). A review of cheating in fully asynchronous online courses: a math or fact-based perspective. *Journal of Educational Technology Systems. 35*(3), 281–300.

Walker, M. U. (2003). *Moral contexts.* Lanham, MD: Rowman and Littlefield.

Who is Bill Reed? (2005). *Online Classroom*, January, 2–3. Abstract retrieved from http://www.magnapubs.com/issues/magnapubs_oc/5_1/news/597081-1.html

Part 4

Policies, Administration, and Management
An Overview
MICHAEL GRAHAME MOORE

If it can be argued that, in formal education, good teaching helps achieve good learning, then it might also be argued (and I say this as one who has assiduously avoided managerial responsibilities!) that both are dependent on the quality of administrators and managers. It is on their perspectives, problems and research-related questions that we focus in Part 4. Where Part 3 ended with a survey of common procedures through, as we said, the unfamiliar prism of ethical analysis, here we start Part 4 with a survey of many of the same common procedures, but this time reported from the more familiar perspective of an experienced distance education administrator. Kearsley's summary distinguishes the responses of managers at two levels, the individual program level, and the institutional level, pointing out that there is considerably more research literature about the former than the latter. The chapter describes the managers' responsibilities in the contexts of course development, staffing, the design and delivery processes, evaluating program outcomes, selecting and maintaining technology, and extending institutional infrastructure to the distant learners.

Following the comment above regarding the dependence of teachers on the quality of management, the argument may be extended a step further, with the proposition that good management is only possible where there is a sound basis for the program in institutional, state and national policy. Policy is the focus for Simonson and Schlosser's contribution. Beginning with an anecdote that compares instituting a distance education program with construction of a physical monument, the authors underscore the vital importance of laying sound policy foundations prior to implementing a program, policies based on clarity of understanding within an institution of its values and its mission, and a vision of the direction for its future and the part to be played by the distance education program. The chapter lists some of the areas about which policy should be developed, echoing the topics addressed in the previous chapter, thus underscoring the close connection between the work of managers and the policy foundation that enable them to do their work—or, as is often the case, the absence of policy that causes them so much frustration as they are compelled to resolve problems and make decisions in an *ad hoc* manner. The policy areas include: academic policy; fiscal, geographic, and governance policies; faculty policies, legal policies, student policies, technical policies, and what the author calls philosophical policies, this being an articulation of the institution's reasons for engaging in distance education, an underpinning of its vision and mission statements.

Unexamined in Simonson and Schlosser's chapter is the seminal policy question, whether to introduce or develop a distance education program in the first place, and what kind of learning needs will justify such a program. This question is addressed by Watkins, Kaufman, and Odunlami in their chapter on strategic planning. A needs assessment model is presented that the authors believe should guide policy makers in acquiring the kind of understanding of needs and opportunities that should precede a decision to introduce or expand a distance education program. Critical components of an institution's policies, introduced in the previous chapter, are brought back into focus here, namely the importance of a well-developed statement of vision and mission, these authors explaining how such statements become "practical guides for staff as they make daily decisions." The chapter proceeds to explain the process of needs assessment, one that should be guided by, and then as an outcome contributing to, the institution's vision and mission. A discussion of the necessity to prioritize and select which specific needs to attend to and which to neglect (taking into account cost factors in particular) as well as making decision about the means of addressing those needs, reminds us of Kearsley's presentation of the responsibilities of management, as well as Simonson and Schlosser's discussion of the importance of visionary policy-makers who enable the manager to make such critically important decisions.

This theme regarding the significance of the administrator, manager, and above all, policy maker in what is ultimately a huge, even revolutionary, paradigm shift in education is taken up in Beaudoin's chapter on leadership. From his literature search for studies of leadership in distance education, reviewing principal journals and a review of books, he is forced to report on the paucity of research in this area. One hopeful area to look for guidance on leadership, and by implication for questions to be subjected to research, is in the various statements of several professional associations and accrediting bodies to define so-called Principles of Good Practice. In the absence of a more precisely articulated theory of leadership, this author suggests such statements offer insights about what constitutes effective leadership practice. Posing the question whether there is a leadership style that is especially appropriate for distance education, Beaudoin proposes a research approach based on analysis of the different types of situations where distance education leaders are most likely to find themselves and recommends study of the concept of transformative leadership, " a particularly compelling model for distance education leaders today", because "organizational practices long entrenched in educational entities urgently require reshaping to adapt to environmental changes."

Beaudoin's drawing attention to the Principles of Good Practice developed by professional associations and accrediting bodies provides an appropriate prologue for the following chapter, in which O'Brien, a senior officer in one of these bodies, describes the role of the regional accrediting agencies. The organizational structure of distance education in the United States cannot be understood without an understanding of the devolved process by which institutions are licensed to operate, nor without such understanding can one understand the context in which policy decisions are made. As O'Brien explains " in order to operate legally, academic institutions must, like other businesses, be licensed by one of the fifty states, each of which sets individual rules governing entities incorporated within its borders." What she calls "the primary mechanism for assuring employers, governments, and most importantly students and their families that degree granting institutions are offering acceptable levels of education" are private accrediting agencies. According to the author the most widely accepted and respected of the accrediting bodies are regional associations, the 50 states having been divided up for historical reasons into six regions. As well as these six regional associations, the specialist Distance Education and Training Council (DETC) is noteworthy, having been the pioneer in evaluating and accrediting distance education in the days of correspondence education, with its accrediting authority established in 1959. It was during the 1980s that the regional agencies began to recognize and implement procedures for examining and evaluating distance education programs. O'Brien explains how the agencies adapted accreditation standards to accommodate distance education and reports (in my view rather optimistically) that "none (of the agencies) now has any problem in finding sufficient numbers of appropriately experienced people to review their standards, staff their visiting teams, and participate on their central commissions." I say optimistic since it has been suggested that what these "appropriately experienced people" often bring to the task of evaluating distance education programs are their very traditional understanding about what is required of a teacher and teaching institution, and when that is the case, the standards they apply are often guided by the question whether the distance learning is the same as 'the real thing." This chapter makes fascinating reading as it unfolds the struggle of the geographically defined agencies to rewrite policies and indeed redefine their roles in a frequently shifting effort to keep up with the borderless character of distance education, including the shift from strict regionalism to national cooperation. A culminating point was the set of regulations drawn up in 2000 and revised in 2006 with its specifications of Best Practices for Electronically Offered Degree and Certificate Programs. Further impetus for this shift came from the need to deal with federal regulations included in the Higher Education Opportunity Act, with most recently (2009) its ludicrous attempt to parse wording to discriminate between the genus distance education and the species correspondence education. Anticipating a later chapter, on professional continuing education, O'Brien's chapter describes the work of specialized (programmatic) accreditors, such as The National League for Nursing Accrediting Commission. .

Closely related to the subject of accreditation is that of program evaluation, the focus of Irele's Chapter 31. Building on Thompson and Irele's (2007) chapter in the previous edition of the *Handbook of Distance Education*, this chapter updates it but also brings a fresh perspective as it considers the still nascent but growing international character of distance education and the effect of that on questions about quality assurance and evaluation generally. Following a discussion about the concept of quality as a basis for evaluation, Irele attempts (for one of the first times) to extend the discussion to the arena of internationally delivered programs. The confounding variable of cultural assumptions and expectations, though not yet researched in the context of evaluation, is one that is obviously very important, and requires study in future. After a summary of the fairly well-known steps to be undertaken in a program evaluation study, Irele proceeds to provide some examples of different evaluation models before returning again to the less well-explored subject of cross-national evaluation, with its various cultural challenges. For a case study, Irele cites a course with students in universities in the United States and China and comments that "as regional accrediting bodies in the United States agree on and disseminate the core dimensions of quality, it can be argued that they should do the same with their international counterparts and stakeholders in general."

The relation of evaluation, accreditation, institutional leadership, policy, indeed the subjects discussed in Part 2 as well as the above, to the two chapters that follow next in Part 3, in which Inglis and then Jung and Lee discuss costs, should be very obvious. Inglis begins by reminding us—and we need to keep this always in mind—that there are two different types of distance education, one being an extension of the classroom and the other based on learning packages, or what Inglis calls resource-based delivery. The terminology is different but the distinction was noted earlier between the virtual class represented by Garrison and Akyol's Chapter 7, and the independent learner (who uses the learning package), represented by Anderson in Chapter 6, and can also be explained in terms of dialogue and structure as in Saba's Chapter 4. In reality most programs in United States are of the classroom type, although usually with at least some element of packaged learning material included. The distinction is important though as we try to understanding the economics of distance education which is, or should be, different to that of conventional education. One critically significant difference between the two approaches is the potential of the package approach to benefit from the economies of scale that are so necessary to obtain the magic combination of both high quality and low cost. Several times since we were introduced to Wedemeyer's and Saba's ideas about a systems approach to teaching, turning it from a craft to a collaborative team activity, we have seen how it is through use of specialist experts and integrated multi-media that distance education can advance the quality of teaching. The core issue is how to support the investments needed to pay for the teams of specialist educators and media producers and the production facilities needed for high quality mediated programs. The answer is to spread the total cost over large numbers of students. How to do this, to have large numbers and also sustain quality instructor-to-learner interaction is a challenge, not only to faculty but even more to the administration and policy-makers. Part of the answer might be to employ a larger proportion of part-time faculty and thus releasing the funds needed for program design and production. Another consideration, if, for example, one wanted to offset the high cost of packing a multimedia simulation into an online classroom, the development cost might be shared with other institutions. Alternatively, packaged materials might be obtained from a learning objects collection or open source repository. Among related cost-effectiveness questions are those concerning the economies of using standardized learning management systems and also use of social media. These two chapters will be seen to derive issues that have arisen in every previous chapter, and in turn have to be brought into play as the reader returns to look at every issue of management and policy, but also course design and teaching. In every aspect of distance education, cost is a major consideration, and the scope of alternative actions at every decision point is heavily dependent on costs of various alternatives.

To round off Part 4, we have an overview of another very contemporary set of issues, this being the legal and copyright issues surrounding intellectual property. Tomas Lipinski explains that laws passed recently have been intended to encourage distance education, but there are "new obligations that educator, student and institution must satisfy before any advantage regarding the use of copyrighted content can be achieved." Four topics within the copyright law are introduced. First are questions about who owns content created by educators and students. Second is knowledge about the rules regarding damage remission when copyright is infringed upon. Third is having sufficient familiarity with the copyright law to know when it is worth the cost of fulfilling these conditions or obligations. Fourth is for educators and students to know the "fair use" doctrine in support of their distance education activities.

The following lines from Lipinski should give a good sense of the flavor of this chapter:

> Content created by students is owned by the student-author. However, an argument can be made that the use of such content in the context of a closed or secure classroom, online or otherwise, is fair use. (Fair use is discussed in detail in a later section of this chapter.) Reposting by the instructor on an open website is likely not fair use, as this is outside the context of the classroom, but use of student work in other contexts in furtherance of the educational mission can be fair use, such as downloading a paper onto a flash drive so the instructor can grade it while traveling or using the paper in a portfolio of projects for future students on a secure site.

This scenario is one that ever reader will be able to identify with, and all will definitely benefit from reading the sections that follow in the chapter, especially the enumeration of the requirements to stay within the boundaries of fair use. An exciting way to end Part 4 is Lipinski's closing sentence: "being sued is a possibility in the distance education setting of the 21st century"!

26

MANAGEMENT OF ONLINE PROGRAMS

GREG KEARSLEY

INTRODUCTION

Online programs require two different levels or types of management: project management and strategic management. Project management deals with the operational details of running a program, whereas strategic management is concerned with macro-level, institutional level, planning considerations. Both types of management might address the same issues, but would do so with different types of concern. For example, project management might involve finding a replacement instructor for one who is ill whereas strategic management might focus on deciding which departments might be funded to recruit new faculty to teach during the next semester or year. The difference in scope might be illustrated by another example. Consider the difference between enforcing a policy on cheating with a particular student versus dealing with cheating overall. The former might involve ensuring that the student is aware of the policy and the consequences of cheating, verifying that cheating occurred, and taking appropriate disciplinary actions. The latter could involve evaluating and implementing anti-plagiarism tools or changing the design of course tests or assignments to make them less susceptible to compromise. Strategic planning is often concerned with assessing future trends (e.g., enrollments, technology) and collecting data to make decisions. It also involves setting goals and priorities with respect to program focus, and resources.

There is relatively little written about managing online programs, and most of what has been published is about strategic rather than project management. Shackleford (2002) and Lynch and Roecker (2007) describe how traditional project management concepts (e.g., scope, task scheduling, risk assessment, quality control, progress tracking, change management) apply to online learning. Abdous and He (2009) explore the use of project management tools to manage online course development. Discenza, Howard, and Schenck (2001). Berge (2000), Panda (2004), Pisel (2008), and MacNeil, Luzius, and Sunkin (2010) discuss strategic planning issues relevant to online programs. See Chapter 28 (this volume) by Watkins, Kaufman and Odunlami for an elaboration of the role and nature of strategic planning in the context of distance education. In this chapter, we'll look at the management of online programs in terms of five major aspects: curriculum, staffing, faculty effectiveness, assessment of program outcomes, technology, and institutional issues. Note that this chapter focuses on higher education, but most of the discussion also applies to K–12 or training settings.

CURRICULUM MANAGEMENT

A large component of managing an online program consists of curriculum management tasks. This involves ensuring that all courses are revised and ready for students at the course start date (usually a semester or quarter). If the course has been taught previously, this means making a copy of the course and updating it with a new schedule as well as any content changes. On the other hand, if this is a new course (or a substantial overhaul of an existing course), then a development timeline will be needed (see Table 26.1), and this will usually involve the collaboration between a faculty developer and an instructional designer and technologist: events that usually call for significant revisions to a course are adoption of a new text (affecting readings and assignments); the switch to a different online learning system, or change in faculty.

The timeline indicated in Table 26.1 assumes that the learning system and technology tools to be used have already been selected and are in use. If this is not the case, then additional time will be needed to evaluate and become proficient with them.

Another dimension of the curriculum management task is quality control of courses, i.e., ensuring that they are well designed and complete. This is usually achieved by having an instructional designer work with faculty in conjunction with the use of design guidelines, course templates and checklists. A more comprehensive approach to establishing course quality is to participate in the Quality Matters peer review process (see http://www.qmprogram.org). This involves the review of courses using a rubric that covers 41 standards, encompassing instructional objectives, assessment, learner interaction, content and resources, technology, support, and accessibility. If the Quality Matters methodology is adopted at the institutional level, it can create a philosophy of continuous quality control among faculty and staff.

A final curriculum development issue is ensuring the full participation of faculty in online course development. Faculty may not be willing to invest the large amounts of time often required to develop online courses without additional compensation or adjustment to their teaching loads. Program directors may need to work with academic administrators (i.e., department heads, deans) to work out suitable adjustments to faculty workloads or salary. This is just one aspect of the various factors that affect faculty participation in online teaching (e.g., Lesht & Windes, 2011).

Table 26.1   Course Development Timeline (Generic Example)

Develop & review syllabus including course objectives, course topics, readings, assignments, tests, grading scheme	2 weeks
Design course/screen layouts and menu structures (create course shell or template)	1 week
Develop course modules including module objectives, reading notes, assignment instructions, grading rubrics, tests, tutorials	1–2 weeks per module
Review all course components for accuracy and correct functionality	1 week

Table 26.2 Online Program Staff (Generic Example)

Director/Coordinator	Manages all aspects of a program. A very small program may be run by an administrative assistant.
Instructional Designer	Works with faculty to create online courses. Usually conducts course or program evaluations.
Technologist	Provides technology support to faculty, staff, students. May belong to IT group.
Administrative Assistant	Handles all administrative processes associated with program. Usually the interface between program and rest of institution
Marketing Specialist	Recruits students and promotes program. May belong to marketing group
Student Advisor	Provides counseling to students in terms of enrollment, financial aid, course scheduling, personal issues

STAFFING

The staff associated with an online program will vary with the size of the distance education program and its complexity. Table 26.2 lists some of the key roles that need to be filled. In a dual mode institution, some of these roles may be provided by groups within the organization besides the distance education program. For example, the Information Technology department may provide the technical support and the marketing department may provide the marketing support. A large program is likely to have its own staff for each of these roles, possibly many individuals for each position. For example, a program with dozens or hundreds of courses is likely to have more than one instructional designer. On the other hand, a small program might not even have a dedicated director, but could be run by an administrative assistant who reports to a Dean or Department head.

It is possible that some staff functions may be outsourced. For example, many online programs depend on an education marketing company to recruit students in exchange for a fee. Likewise, instructional design and technology support may be handled by consultants external to the institution. Many institutions use a learning management system hosted by a vendor (e.g., Blackboard) and in such cases all support for that system is provided by the company.

Inadequate staffing of a program can result in student or faculty dissatisfaction and adversely affect the success of a program. If instructional design support is lacking, courses may be poorly designed which produces confusion or frustration for students and faculty (e.g., unclear assignment instructions). Lack of sufficient technical support can make it difficult for students and faculty to complete course activities (e.g., file upload/download problems). Poor student advising can result in students becoming too frustrated or anxious to continue and dropping out of a program. Indeed, high dropout rates and faculty turnover are indicators of staffing problems.

SUPPORT AND EVALUATION OF FACULTY

Support for faculty is a critical aspect of effective online programs (Betts & Sikorski, 2008; McLean, 2006; Palloff & Pratt, 2001). Faculty often have limited technology or online teaching skills, so a considerable amount of training and technical assistance may be needed. Furthermore, adjunct faculty do not typically have the resources available to on-campus faculty and therefore may need an even higher level of support. Instructors who have inadequate training and support are more likely to do a poor job of teaching and jeopardize the success of the program.

Assessing the effectiveness of faculty teaching is one of the most challenging aspects of managing online programs. While this is no more or less important than the evaluation of on-campus teaching, it is more complex since the teaching behaviors to be assessed (e.g., responsiveness, interaction, maintaining presence) are confounded by the learning system and technology used.

The most common instrument used for faculty assessment is the end- of- course student evaluation. Students are typically asked to rate various aspects of their instructor's performance (see Table 26.3). There is little evidence that these ratings accurately reflect effective teaching practices, although presumably there is some correlation. It seems that the ratings mostly reflect the popularity of instructors and the extent to which they please students. For example, faculty who are very demanding in their grading are likely to get less favorable ratings than instructors who are more liberal.

Most learning management systems track usage, and hence it is possible to collect data on the amount of time that faculty spend online in the various components of their course (e.g., discussion forums, email, assignments). However, efforts by this author to correlate the amount of time spent online with student evaluation ratings have shown no relationship. In other words, faculty who log extensive time online do not appear to be more effective instructors than those who spend less time online. This can be explained by the fact that some instructors do much of their work offline, or are more efficient in their online work and can get more done in less time.

Another method for evaluating teaching effectiveness is to use self assessments. Table 26.4 illustrates the format of such a self assessment. The advantage of this approach is that it provides faculty with an opportunity to reflect on their teaching practice and consider strategies for improvement. However, the value of this approach depends upon how much time faculty are willing to spend on the task and whether they are sufficiently candid.

The ideal way of assessing online teaching effectiveness would be to actually measure the performance of faculty in courses. For example, Roblyer and Wiencke (2003) identified specific criteria for different levels of interaction. It is possible to examine the discussion postings and assignment feedback provided by an instructor and rate them

Table 26.3 Sample Course Evaluation Questions Relating to Instructor Effectiveness

I received feedback from the instructor in a timely manner.

The instructor effectively facilitated discussion within the class.

The instructor made effective use of the online environment for learning.

The instructor was helpful in answering questions.

The amount of interaction that I had with the instructor of this course was satisfactory.

I was satisfied with the quality of instruction provided by this instructor.

Table 26.4 *Sample Faculty Self Assessment Questions*

I participated actively in discussion forums, synthesizing student posts and encouraging continued dialogue.

I responded to all student inquiries within the 48-hr period expected.

I was effective in helping students achieving all course objectives.

The course was conducted so that students always knew what was expected of them.

I frequently discussed recent developments related to the subject matter.

My evaluation of students' work was constructive and rigorous.

Students were intellectually challenged by the course content and activities.

Course workload is appropriate and reasonable.

on such criteria, producing an "interactivity" score. However, such a process would be very time consuming and not practical (unless it could be automated). There is also an ethical/privacy issue associated with examining the details of interactions between faculty and students, and the principle of informed consent should be used.

ASSESSING LEARNING & PROGRAM OUTCOMES

Although assessing the learning outcomes of an online program should be one of the most important management tasks to be accomplished, it is rarely done. The basic problem is that it is very difficult to measure learning outcomes (online or otherwise). It is easy to ask students if they are satisfied with their courses, but this doesn't directly address what was learned. Students can be asked to rate the extent to which they have achieved the specific objectives of a course or the program, but self-assessments are not particularly valid measures of learning. Likewise, grades are not very useful measures of learning since they may not correlate highly with the intended learning outcomes.

Program evaluations often attempt to identify the impact of completing the program on the careers of graduates. Table 26.5 lists some typical questions that a program evaluation asks. However, like the self-assessment of learning outcomes, these ratings may not be very valid.

To improve the validity of self-ratings, supervisors or peers of the graduate can be asked to do the ratings. Usually, the graduate is asked to identify others to provide the ratings. The rating data is averaged across the respondents for a given individual to provide composite and difference scores.

Assessing learning outcomes is only one aspect of evaluating the overall quality of a program. Shelton (2011) reviews 13 models for evaluating the quality on online education programs. In her review she identifies a number of factors common to these models including: (a) institutional commitment, support, and leadership, (b) teaching and

Table 26.5 Sample Program Evaluation Survey Questions

What I learned in the program is highly relevant to my job and/or professional career.

I have already used knowledge/skills acquired from courses in my work.

I believe that the program provides good value for the money and time invested.

Interacting with other students was a valuable part of the program.

Completing the program was a major professional accomplishment for me.

From my perspective, the program was well organized and ran smoothly.

I feel that the content and learning activities of the courses were well chosen.

I found the online learning experience to be enjoyable and satisfying.

I was able to get technical or administrative assistance when I needed it.

learning, (c) faculty and student support, (d) technology evaluation and assessment, (e) cost-effectiveness, and (f) student and faculty satisfaction.

TECHNOLOGY DECISIONS

An ongoing management task for an online program is making decisions about technology to be used (Bates & Sangra, 2011; Collins & Halverson, 2009; Schrum & Levin, 2009). The primary technology involved in most online programs is the learning management system (LMS). The LMS provides the tools most commonly used in online classes including discussion forums, email, tests, assignments, journals, wikis, and most importantly, a gradebook integrated with these tools. These systems also provide user tracking tools, so it is possible to monitor exactly what a student has done in a class. The most commonly used LMS at this time as Blackboard and Moodle although there are many other systems in use.

There are two major decisions that need to be made with respect to use of an LMS. The first is whether to use a system that is hosted by the institution or the vendor. There are pros/cons to either choice. A vendor-hosted system will require less institutional resources (e.g., IT staffing), which is a desirable factor for small colleges or school districts with limited IT departments. On the other hand, a vendor-hosted system will likely cost more in terms of annual license fees and may not offer as much flexibility as an internally hosted system in terms of customizing the system to meet the needs of the institution. Many institutions start off with a hosted solution and then switch to an internally hosted system as they develop their own IT resources.

The second major decision is the way courses are to be developed and implemented using an LMS. In some institutions, faculty are expected to take full responsibility for the creation of their online courses and are given sufficient training to do that. In others, courses are primarily developed by instructional developers working together with faculty as content experts. In many large online programs, courses are taught by adjunct faculty who have not been involved in the development of the courses. In the latter two cases, faculty may have very little knowledge of how to create material in the LMS and only understand the functionality needed to teach with it. So, decisions about what kind of training and access faculty and staff need with respect to the LMS depend upon the instructional model and procedures being employed in a program.

One other important aspect of an LMS is the extent to which it interfaces with the student records system used by the institution (e.g., Banner, PeopleSoft). Data about student enrollments and grades must be passed back and forth between the LMS and the student records database. Ideally, such transfer of information happens automatically and in real time. But in many cases, the data must be manually entered from the LMS to the student records system and vice-versa. This means that the staff involved in doing this must have the necessary training on both systems. It also means there is potential for errors in the manual transfer process which can result in frustrating problems for students, faculty, or staff.

While the LMS is the most important technology component of an online program, it is not likely to be the only one. Faculty and students may need tools for creating Websites, making podcasts, preparing multimedia, or conducting Webinars. Some courses may need to use specialized software such as a mathematical equation editor or a music composition program. There is increasing use of social networking sites in online programs and these sites need to be managed. And faculty, staff, and students will always need basic applications software (e.g., word processing, spreadsheets, slide presentation) as well as Web and network access tools. Although decisions about the latter categories of software tend to be personal decisions these days, institutions may have policies about which tools they will support or license for use on their systems.

Finally, a major technology consideration for any online program at present is the support and use of mobile devices (i.e., phones, PDAs, pads). This presents a new generation of learning environments in which presentation of small "chunks" of information in audio/video form are to be preferred over full screens of text. Likewise, the use of short messages (as in tweets or blog comments) are more suitable than long typed messages typical in discussion forums. So, accommodation of mobile technology is likely to require new techniques for course design as well as online teaching (Brooks-Young, 2010; Quinn, 2011).

Any decisions about technology made by a program would need to be made in consultation with the IT department. In fact, in some institutions, major technology decisions (e.g., choice of an LMS) are made by the IT department or an IT steering committee and all online programs are expected to abide by those decisions. This can be problematic for programs that have needs that are different from the rest of the institution.

INSTITUTIONAL ISSUES

Many institutional issues are associated with the management of an online program, mostly having to do with policies and procedures, particularly in a "dual-mode" institution that also offers on-campus classes. For example, if students have problems with registration, enrollment, or financial aid, can they get timely telephone or online assistance? If students with disabilities need assistance with online learning, can they get that from the university or is this support only provided to on-campus students? What provision is made to include off-campus faculty teaching online courses (who are typically adjuncts) in university faculty meetings?

Most institutional issues revolve around the infrastructure needed for online programs (Meyer & Barefield, 2010; Paolucci & Gambescia, 2007). This includes adequate and reliable computer network capability, online registration and billing systems, remotely accessed library and bookstore services, and online faculty and student support services. Infrastructure primarily means having the staff, facilities, and equipment needed, which translates in financial considerations (e.g., Crawford, Gould, King, & Parker, 2010). Even when the necessary resources are available, there are questions about whether they are well managed and fully available to online students.

A common problem in large institutions is that online programs are located within separate departments or centers with little interaction among programs. For this reason, it is essential to have an institutional committee consisting of all online program managers who meet regularly to coordinate resources and policies across all programs. Such committees should have representation from major service and functional units (i.e., bookstore, library, disabilities, registrar, financial aid, etc.) as well as faculty. Ideally, such committees should report to a senior administrator (e.g., VP or Provost) and not be under the sole auspices of the IT department since this tends to focus the committee too much on technology.

A broader issue is whether an online program is congruent with the mission and goals of the institution. Clearly, an institution in which leadership and/or faculty are not supportive of distance learning represents a problem for any online program in that institution. Equally problematic is an institution that has unrealistic expectations in terms of the revenue or costs associated with online programs. It is not uncommon for an institution to happily accept the revenue generated by online programs but fail to provide the budget and resources needed to run them effectively. Ko and Rosen (2010) discuss the need to match online teaching activities to the level of resources available at the institution.

Other institutional issues associated with distance learning are discussed in other chapters of this this volume; see Hanna (Chapter 43), Simonson and Schlosser (Chapter 27), and Beaudoin (Chapter 29)

ADDITIONAL ISSUES

Apart from these six general areas, there are certain issues that require extra attention in terms of program management. This includes: students with disabilities, international students, field internships, and lab work.

Guidelines for the design of online courses for students with disabilities are widely available (e.g., Coombs, 2010; Rose & Meyer, 2002) but the difficulty lies in implementing such guidelines consistently and thoroughly. It takes extra effort and vigilance to properly prepare an online course for use by individuals with disabilities. For example, all audio/video components need to have a text transcript for students with hearing or visual disabilities; faculty and instructional designers must be continually reminded of this. Likewise, live Web conferences need to provide interpreters or real-time captioning if students with disabilities are to participate and this takes time to organize. While most of these are design factors that should be addressed in course development, not all are. Faculty may provide links to Websites or recommend the use of applications that are not accessible to students with disabilities. Having an office of disability services that can work with students and faculty to address such needs is highly desirable.

Managing a program with international students presents a number of considerations (e.g., Alexander, 2002, Yildiz, 2009). Obviously, differences in time zones need to be accommodated for student/faculty/staff communications. This is particularly an issue if synchronous (i.e., real-time conferencing) is being used in the program. There may be technical issues with internet connections in some countries due to access policies (i.e., some countries may block certain sites or limit the functionality). International students may need extra assistance with administrative aspects such as registration, financial aid, or certification. And there may be curriculum issues with course content or learning activities designed for a domestic student audience that may not be relevant or applicable to other countries. Finally, there may be English language writing issues which affect a student's course performance, although this is a less likely problem today with the proliferation of English language media and Websites.

Field internships can present management issues for an online program if the internships are done remotely and hence all supervision/monitoring must be done at a distance. This usually involves an on-site supervisor who communicates with the online course instructor via email, phone, or Web conferencing and is responsible to ensuring that the student carries out their internship tasks. However, there are often lapses in this supervision process for one reason or another that require intervention by the program staff. Having students keep a detailed time log of their activities and reviewing that log weekly with their course instructor helps to keep internships on track and can reduces the need for involvement by program staff.

Online courses that involve a hands-on lab component (e.g., science or engineering) also present some challenges for program management. To the extent that completion of the labs involves the use of specialized equipment, a plan for getting students remote access to this equipment needs to be formulated, often by organizing access to facilities at local institutions or companies that have the equipment and can provide the training/supervision needed. Some programs have on-campus residence periods to allow for hands-on labs, and, if so, this needs to be organized by program staff. Also, many labs involve use of data collection/analysis or simulation software and licensing/access to this software may need to be arranged by program staff.

As these additional issues illustrate, online programs may involve administrative tasks dictated by the nature of the student population or the disciplines involved.

LEADERSHIP

While the majority of tasks associated with program management are administrative in nature, there are some leadership considerations. Program managers may play a role in the definition of curriculum, the selection of the online learning tools used, the structure of the program, or admission criteria. They may also be involved in decisions about the creation of new programs or how programs fit into the institution, as well as marketing or promotional efforts associated with online learning (Portugal, 2006).

Leadership is also manifested through training and assessment of faculty. Project managers are usually responsible for establishing standards and best practices for faculty through training activities, meetings, and one-on-one communication. They also need to motivate faculty and encourage them to explore new online teaching methods and tools (Tipple, 2010).

The nature of the leadership needed in online programs will vary with the size/status of the program, the nature of the institution, and internal/external changes. As a rule, large programs (e.g., 500+ students) or newly started programs will present greater leadership challenges than those that are smaller or well established. Similarly, programs at institutions that are dedicated to distance learning will usually present fewer leadership issues than those at traditional institutions where conflicts between on-campus and distance learning will need to be addressed. Finally, personnel changes in an organization, increased competition, shifting demographics of the student population, or revenue shortfalls can all entail the need for leadership actions beyond the normal administrative decision-making process.

GUIDELINES

1. The most important element of course development is explicit scheduling of all milestones and communicating that schedule to all faculty and staff involved. Since this schedule is likely to change constantly, it is essential that it be distributed regularly and/or available as a shared file (e.g., Web page).

2. To promote the smooth functioning of a program team, it is essential that all staff members have a clear understanding of their roles and responsibilities. A useful vehicle for doing this is a program handbook distributed to students and faculty that describes each staff position, responsibilities, and contact information. Such a document needs to be maintained as staff roles change and should also be a shared file.

3. Peer interaction among faculty is one of the most effective means for improving teaching effectiveness. Providing structured events (e.g.., Webinars) in which faculty share lessons learned and their use of new tools is a powerful form of professional development. Team teaching assignments in which faculty share responsibilities for the same course are also good peer learning opportunities.

4. While it may be difficult to collect meaningful data on program effectiveness and outcomes, it is critical to do so since there are always likely to be questions about the quality of online learning programs. Collecting multiple types of data (i.e., qualitative and quantitative) is valuable since it tends to provide a more complete understanding of the strengths and weaknesses of a program.

5. Technology decisions often have many ramifications in terms of support, staffing, training, costs, policies/procedures, and internal/external relationships. Therefore, it is essential that as many parties as possible be consulted and have input when technology changes are planned. While this slows down the decision-making process considerably, it helps to ensure that the choices made are more acceptable to all involved in the delivery of the online program(s).

6. Many institutional issues concern resource availability or conflicts over priorities (e.g., staffing, facilities, marketing efforts). The best solution to avoiding such issues is to have as much budget autonomy as possible. Programs that have direct control of their revenue and expenses can make decisions that benefit the program without requiring approval from the rest of the institution.

CONCLUSIONS

Managing an online program is a complicated undertaking that involves a range of issues having to do with curriculum, staffing, faculty, program outcomes, technology, and institutional relationships. Techniques developed for both project management and strategic planning apply. However, a considerable amount of program management involves mundane administrative matters such as student inquiries/complaints, hiring and evaluating employees, budgeting, faculty contracts, technology problems, accreditation reviews , status reports, and coordination meetings with other groups. The predominant activities associated with these tasks are problem-solving, conflict resolution, data collection/analysis, and information synthesis. In other words, managing an online program often has little to do with distance education, per se. On the other hand, a thorough understanding of the nature of online learning and teaching is essential to making good program management decisions.

REFERENCES

Abdous, M., & He, W. (2009). Streamlining the online development process by using project management tools. In A. Orellana, T. Hudgins, & M. Simonson (Eds.), *The perfect online course.* Charlotte, NC: Information Age.

Alexander, S. (2002). Designing learning activities for an international online student body: What have we learned? *Journal of Studies in International Education, 6*(2), 188–200.

Bates, A., & Sangra, A. (2011). *Managing technology in higher education: Strategies for transforming teaching and learning.* San Francisco: Jossey-Bass.

Berge, Z. (2000). *Sustaining distance training: Integrating learning technologies into the fabric of the enterprise.* San Francisco: Jossey-Bass.

Betts, K., & Sikorski, B. (2008). Financial bottom line: Estimating the cost of faculty/adjunct turnover and attrition for online programs. *Online Journal of Distance Learning Administration, 11*(1). Retrieved from http://www.westga.edu/~distance/ojdla/spring111/betts111.pdf

Brooks-Young, S. J. (2010). *Teaching with the tools kids really use: Learning with the web and mobile technologies.* Thousand Oaks, CA: Corwin.

Collins, A., & Halverson, R. (2009). *Rethinking education in the age of technology.* New York: Teachers College Press.

Coombs, N. (2010). *Making online teaching accessible.* San Francisco: Jossey-Bass.

Crawford, C. B., Gould, L. V., King, D. & Parker, C. (2010). Quality and growth implications of incremental costing models for distance education units. *Online Journal of Distance Learning Administration, 13*(1). *Retrieved from* http://www.westga.edu/~distance/ojdla/spring131/crawford131.pdf

Discenza, R., Howard, C., & Schenck, K. (2001). *The design and management of effective distance learning programs.* Hershey, PA: IGI Global.

Ko, S., & Rosen, S. (2010). *Teaching online: A practical guide* (3rd ed). New York: Routledge.

Lesht, F., & Windes, D. (2011). Administrators' views on factors Influencing full-time faculty members' participation in online education. *Online Journal of Distance Learning Administration, 14*(4). Retrieved from http://www.westga.edu/~distance/ojdla/winter144/lesht_windes144.pdf

Lynch, M. M., & Roecker, J. (2007). *Project managing E-learning: A handbook for successful design, delivery and management.* London: Routledge.

MacNeil, D., Luzius, K. & Sunkin, S. (2010). How strategic planning keeps you sane when delivering distance education programs. *Online Journal of Distance Learning Administration, 13*(2). Retrieved from http://www.westga.edu/~distance/ojdla/summer132/macneil_luzius_dunkin132.pdf

McLean, J. (2006). Forgotten faculty: Stress and job satisfaction among distance educators. *Online Journal of Distance Learning Administration, 9*(2). Retrieved from http://www.westga.edu/~distance/ojdla/summer92/mclean92.pdf

Meyer, J. D., & Barefield, A. C. (2010). Infrastructure and administrative support for online programs. *Online Journal of Distance Learning Administration, 1*(3). Retrieved from http://www.westga.edu/~distance/ojdla/Fall133/meyer_barfield133.pdf

Palloff, R., & Pratt, K. (2001). *Lessons from the cyberspace classroom: The realities of online teaching*. San Francisco: Jossey-Bass.

Paolucci, R., & Gambescia, S. F. (2007). Current administrative structures used for online degree program offerings in higher education. *Online Journal of Distance Learning Administration, 10(3)*. Retrieved from http://www.westga.edu/~distance/ojdla/fall103/gambescia103.pdf

Panda, S. (2004). *Planning and management in distance education*. London: Routledge.

Pisel, K. (2008). A strategic planning model for distance education. *Online Journal of Distance Learning Administration, 11(2)*. Retrieved from http://www.westga.edu/~distance/ojdla/summer112/pisel112.pdf

Portugal, L. (2006). Emerging leadership roles in distance education: Current state of affairs and forecasting future trends. *Online Journal of Distance Learning Administration, 9(3). Retrieved from* http://www.westga.edu/~distance/ojdla/fall93/portugal93.pdf

Quinn, C. N. (2011). *The mobile academy: mlearning for higher education*. San Francisco: Jossey Bass.

Roblyer, M. D. & Wiencke, W. (2003). Design and use of a rubric to assess and encourage interactive qualities in distance education courses. *American Journal of Distance Education, 17(2)*, 77–80.

Rose, D. H., & Meyer, A. (2002). *Teaching every student in the digital age: Universal design for learning*. Alexandria, VA: Association for Supervision and Curriculum Development.

Schrum, L., & Levin, B. (2009). *Leading 21st century schools: Harnessing technology for engagement and achievement*. Thousand Oaks, CA: Corwin.

Shackleford. B. (2002). *Project managing E-learning*. Alexandria, VA: ASTD Press.

Shelton, K. (2011). A review of paradigms for evaluating the quality of online education programs. *Online Journal of Distance Learning Administration, 14(1)*. Retrieved from http://www.westga.edu/~distance/ojdla/spring141/shelton141.pdf

Tipple, R. (2010). Effective leadership of online adjunct faculty. *Online Journal of Distance Learning Administration, 13(1)*. Retrieved from http://www.westga.edu/~distance/ojdla/spring131/tipple131.pdf

Yildiz, S. (2009). Social presence in the web-based classroom: Implications for intercultural communication. *Journal of Studies in International Education, 13*(1), 46–65.

27

INSTITUTIONAL POLICY ISSUES

MICHAEL SIMONSON AND CHARLES SCHLOSSER

On October 25, 1965, downtown St. Louis stopped in its tracks and thousands watched as the last piece of the mammoth Gateway Arch was being put into place. The weight of the two sides required braces to prevent them from falling against each other. Fire hoses poured water down the sides to keep the stainless steel cool, which kept the metal from expanding as the sun rose higher. Some horizontal adjustments were required, but when the last piece was put into place and the braces released, it fit perfectly, according to plan, and no one was surprised (Liggett, 1998). The thousands of onlookers applauded as the sun reflected off the bright span. The architects and engineers who were also watching smiled and went back to their offices.

Just like the Arch, an institution's implementation of distance education requires a careful process that includes a systematic plan prior to implementation. Success is almost guaranteed if all the pieces of the plan receive the same attention as the most obvious. The base sections of the Gateway Arch required more engineering savvy and study than any other component. The last and most visible span that connected the two halves received the most attention from the thousands of onlookers, but success was directly related to how the original supports were positioned.

When distance education programs are being considered by an institution, there is often the desire to move directly to policy development, since policies are the most visible component of a new distance education program. However, policies should not be developed in isolation. Rather, distance education policies are a direct consequence of an educational institution's distance education mission, vision, and plan. Policies are developed based on these three initial activities, and consequently, policies are used to produce documents and records, the tools for the policy implementation.

Policy development for distance education is the primary theme of this chapter. Before policies are discussed however, the relationship of policies to other components of an organization's move into distance education should be considered. First, the distance education planning taxonomy of which policies are a part will be discussed (Simonson, Smaldino, Albright, & Zvacek, 2012).

There are five levels to the distance education planning taxonomy:

1. Mission: Institutional mission related to distance education
2. Vision: Institutional vision related to distance education
3. Plan: The distance education plan
4. Policies: The distance education policy manual
5. Documents and Records: Tools for implementation of distance education policies

DISTANCE EDUCATION: MISSION, VISION, PLANNING

Most often, the organizational leader is responsible for establishing and overseeing development of the mission, vision, and plan related to distance education. Sometimes this means a new mission and vision are developed. Often the existing mission and vision statements are modified by adding new phrases. Almost always once the mission and vision are modified, separate distance education plans and policies are necessary.

A leader of a distance education organization is defined as:

> a visionary capable of action who guides an organization's future, its vision, mission, goals, and objectives. The leader guides the organization and its people who have faith in the leader, and have a clear understanding and acceptance of the organization's worthwhile and shared vision and goals. A distance learning leader has competence in knowing, designing, managing, leading and visioning distance education. (Simonson, 2004, p. 48)

Depending on the size of the organization, the leader may independently establish a mission and vision for distance education with the plan and policies developed by others. In larger institutions, mission changes, vision updates, planning documents, and policies are developed by committees of users and stakeholders. In universities, the curriculum committee may set policies for distance education after ad hoc committees modify the university's mission and vision.

In schools, missions, visions, plans, and policies are often set by ad hoc committees of administrators and teachers and approved by the school board. In the private sector, the distance education planning taxonomy including policies is most often developed by staff and approved by executive teams.

Mission and Vision Statements

Mission and vision statements are different. A mission statement should define an organization's purpose and primary goals. Usually mission statements are internal and are used to determine the organization's success. The primary audiences of a mission statement are the administrators and faculty of the institution (Mindtools, n.d.). Mission statements often identify three things: what we do, how we do it, and for whom.

Creation of mission statements often involves these steps:

1. Identify the idea of the institution related to distance education
2. Develop a memorable statement related to distance education
3. Identify key measures of distance education success
4. Refine the language into a concise statement.

Vision statements define the institution's purpose in terms of the values of the program rather than other measures of success. Vision statements are for students and other external stakeholders, but they also set expectations for faculty. Visions are meant to inspire.

Development of vision statements follows these steps:

1. After the mission is developed, identify the human-ness of that mission
2. Identify what is valued most about the distance education-related mission and list the values of the institution
3. Merge the mission and values and develop a statement that inspires, energizes and motivates. (Mindtools, n.d.)

For example, the Florida Virtual School has this set of statements related to its mission, vision, and values:

Mission: To deliver a high quality, technology-based education that provides the skills and knowledge students need for success.

Our Vision: To transform education worldwide—one student at a time.

Our Commitment: The student is at the center of every decision we make.

We have built our school on these beliefs:

- Every student is unique, so learning should be dynamic, flexible and engaging
- Studies should be integrated rather than isolated
- Students, parents, community members, and schools share responsibility for learning
- Students should have choices in how they learn and how they present what they know
- Students should be provided guidance with school and career planning
- Assessments should provide insights not only of student progress but also of instruction and curriculum. (Florida Virtual School, 2011)

THE DISTANCE EDUCATION PLAN

Distance education planning is an activity that provides direction from where an organization is currently to where it thinks it should be in a period of time—often five years. The most obvious consequence of distance education planning is the planning document, a 25- to 50- page report. Often, distance education planning is included in an organization's technology plan—a broader document than a distance education plan.

See, for example, the two most recent U.S. Department of Education technology planning documents: *Toward A New Golden Age In American Education: How the Internet, the Law, and Today's Students are Revolutionizing Expectations* (2004) and *Transforming American Education: Learning Powered by Technology* (2010). Other excellent examples of technology plans that include a strong component of distance education planning were prepared by Milwaukee Area Technical College (2009) and the University of Miami School of Nursing (2010).

In 1996, graduate students at Mississippi State University produced what is still one of the best guides for technology planning. Their *Guidebook for Developing an Effective*

Instructional Technology Plan, Version 2.0 explains a planning model that has the following five phases: recruit and organize a planning team; research; construct the technology plan; formalize the plan; and continually implement, evaluate, and revise.

Distance education and technology plans are the basis for the development of policies (Simonson, 2005), the next section and the primary theme of this chapter.

DISTANCE EDUCATION POLICIES

Policy is defined as a written course of action, such as a statute, procedure, rule, or regulation that is adopted to facilitate program development (King, Nugent, Eich, Mlinek, & Russell, 2000a; King, Nugent, Russell, Eich, & Lacy, 2000b). Distance education is defined as institutionally based formal education where the learning group is separated and where interactive technologies are used to unite the learning group (Schlosser & Simonson, 2009; Simonson, 2009). Distance education policy is the written course of action adopted by institutions to facilitate the development of distance education programs.

IMPORTANCE OF POLICY

Policies provide a framework for the operation of distance education. They form a set of agreed-on rules that explain roles and responsibilities. Policies can be compared to laws of navigation, rules of the road, or language syntax. They provide a standard method of operation, such as "no wake zone," "keep to the right," or "subject and verb must match." Policies give structure to unstructured events and are a natural step in the adoption of an innovation, such as distance education. The institutionalization of a new idea includes the development of rules and regulations (policies) for the use of the innovation (Rogers, 2003). One key indicator that distance education is moving into the mainstream is the increased emphasis on the need for policies to guide its effective growth. The California Polytechnic State University (Cal Poly, n.d.) defines policy this way:

> The formal guidance needed to coordinate and execute activity throughout the institution. When effectively deployed, policy statements help focus attention and resources on high priority issues – aligning and merging efforts to achieve the institutional vision. Policy provides the operational framework within which the institution functions. (para. 3)

The Cal Poly handbook goes on to indicate that policies have widespread application, change infrequently, are expressed in broad terms, have statements of what or why, and answer major operational issues.

POLICY MODELS AND POLICY CATEGORIES

Berge (1998) and Gellman-Danley and Fetzner (1998) have proposed models for distance education policy. These models have been reported and evaluated a number of times in the literature (King et al., 2000a, 2000b; Maguire, 2009) and seem to provide a useful framework for an investigation of distance education policy. One of the best reviews of distance education policies identified and analyzed distance education terminology that was used in faculty handbooks (Delaney, 2009). This study highlighted 31 categories of distance education terms and organized them into a distance education policy framework.

For this discussion, policies for distance education will be divided into seven categories (Gellman-Danley & Fetzner, 1998; King et al., 2000a; 2000b). Key issues related to each of these seven categories will be explained, then examples and sample policies will be offered.

> Policy Area 1: Academic—The key issues in this area deal with academic calendars, accreditation of programs, course quality, course and program evaluation, Carnegie/course units, grading, admission, and curriculum review and approval processes.
>
> Policy Area 2: Fiscal, Geographic, Governance—The key issues in this area deal with tuition rates, special fees, full-time equivalencies, state mandated regulations related to funding, service area limitations, out-of-district versus in-district relationships, consortia agreements, contracts with collaborating organizations, board oversight, administration cost, and tuition disbursement.
>
> Policy Area 3: Faculty—The key issues in this area deal with compensation and workloads, design and development incentives, staff development, faculty support, faculty evaluation, intellectual freedom, and union contracts.
>
> Policy Area 4: Legal—The key issues in this area deal with intellectual property agreements, copyright, and faculty/student/institutional liability.
>
> Policy Area 5: Student—The key issues in this area deal with student support, academic advising, counseling, library services, student training, financial aid, testing and assessment, access to resources, equipment requirements, privacy, and appropriate use of social networking.
>
> Policy Area 6: Technical—The key issues in this area deal with system reliability, connectivity, technical support, hardware/software, and access.
>
> Policy Area 7: Philosophical—This key issues in this area deal with the acceptance of distance education based on a clear understanding of the approach, organizational values and mission, and visions statements.

These seven policy areas will be discussed and the importance of each explained. Of critical importance, and a topic identified often in the literature, is the need for distance education courses to be considered of high quality and comparable to traditionally offered courses. Often the term equivalent (or equivalency) is used when distance education courses are described. Simonson, Schlosser, and Hanson (1999) explain equivalency theory by emphasizing that distant and local learners have fundamentally different environments in which to learn. Just as the triangle and square are considered equivalent if they have the same area even though they are quite different, distant and local learners should be provided equivalent learning experiences that may be quite different but "cover the same area." Learning experiences are anything that happens to the student to promote learning, including what is observed, felt, heard, or done (Simonson et al., 2012).

Equivalent is not the same as equal. Rather, equivalent experiences can be similar or they can be considerably different. The key to equivalency theory is that the totality of learning experiences for each learner should cover the same area, even if the individual experiences might be quite different. The attempt to make learning equal for distant

Table 27.1 Delaney's Distance Education Policy Analysis Framework with Contract Terms (Adapted from Delaney, 2009, p. 99)

Policy Category	Key Issues	Selected Key Terms
Academic	Calendar, course integrity, transcripts, evaluations, admissions, course approvals, accreditation, cancellations, recruiting/marketing	Class size, scheduling, rights of course teaching, office hours, evaluation, competency, quality
Fiscal, Geographic, Governance	Tuition, technology fees, FTE's, space, staffing	Definitions, processes, priorities
Faculty	Compensation and class loads, training, class monitoring, support, evaluation	Compensation, training, equivalency, load, mentoring, release time
Legal	Intellectual property, liability	Intellectual property, sales, contracts
Student	Advising, counseling, library access, materials delivery, student training, testing, accounts, registration, financial aid	Services, fees, equipment, network
Technical	Systems reliability, connectivity, hardware and software, setup, infrastructure, support, scheduling, costs	Technology support, technology costs
Philosophical	Innovation adoption, acceptance of distance education, organizational values	Privacy, professional responsibility

and local learners is an exercise in futility. Instead, instruction designers should create multiple learning experiences that can be assigned or selected by students to permit the attainment of course objectives. Watkins and Schlosser (2000) have proposed a model for course design that applies the concept of equivalent learning experiences. Also, policies for distance education should support the concept of equivalent rather than equal learning experiences.

Delaney's research (2009) identified topics that are often included in policy manuals. This research identified distance education terms found in collective bargaining agreements of colleges. These terms were organized into the seven policy categories and serve as cues to what policy issues should be considered when policy manuals are developed (see Table 27.1).

Next, each of the seven policy categories will be explained in greater detail. These categories may serve as the structure for a policy manual.

Academic Policies
Academic issues are in many respects at the heart of why policies are critical. Academic issues deal with the overall integrity of the course. They deal with students, instruction, curriculum, and program. They probably have the longest and most widespread impact, as students take courses, earn diplomas, and move to other schools or on to higher education. Policies help ensure that institutional integrity is maintained.

A theme that increasingly is being applied to distance education policy development is referred to as an *integrated approach*. This approach advocates using the same procedures for distance education as for other academic issues. Instead of developing new structures and policies for distance education, the intent is to modify existing structures, regulations, rules, and policies to integrate a distance education approach. Flexibility is a necessary ingredient of an integrated approach. Teachers, administrators, and policy-makers should recognize that changes do not reflect a weakening, and that modification is not a threat to integrity. Rather, policy changes necessitated by the development of a distance education program merely demonstrate a natural process and evolution of a school, district, or state to accommodate technology-based instruction. Watkins and Schlosser (2000) discuss Carnegie/course units and explain processes for demonstrating how distance education courses can be compared to traditional face-to-face classes where "seat time" is measured.

First, once an institutional commitment to distance education is made, academic policies should be reviewed and distance education requirements should be integrated into regulations. Specifically, the following academic issues are examples of those to be considered:

- Course schedules and academic calendars, especially for synchronous learning experiences.
- Event, course, and program approval and evaluation
- Student admission
- Grading and assessment of students
- Grade record-keeping and reporting
- Accreditation

Fiscal, Geographic, and Governance Policies
The central issue behind most fiscal, geographic, and governance (FGG) polices is one of ownership: ownership of the course and the curriculum. Ownership is defined in this context as the institution or person that has ultimate responsibility, and whose decisions are final.

Most of the time, the school offering the unit, course, or program has ownership, but if a student is taking only one course as part of a locally offered diploma then in most respects the diploma granting school is the responsible institution. Most often several policies statements need to be in place that relate to various situations where courses are delivered or received.

With ownership comes the question of costs. Certainly the school offering a unit, course, or program has considerable expenses, but so does the receiving school and even the student. In sharing relationships the hope is that costs will average out over a period of time. In other words, if three schools enter into a relationship to share courses, and do so uniformly, the costs of offering and receiving courses will be fairly equal for the three schools. Conversely, if one school does most of the offering of units, courses, or programs then that school will have disproportionate expenses. Policies are needed to clarify how situations such as this are dealt with.

Other fiscal policies for schools offering instruction include those related to tuition, network fees, room and equipment expenses, administration of student files and records, and troubleshooting. Schools receiving courses have costs for room maintenance, library and media support, reception equipment, and student support. Technology fees are often levied to support distance education costs. If fees are implemented, policies need to be in place to determine who collects and distributes this money, and how expenditures are monitored.

Finally, agreements to regularly review costs and to share revenues are important. Often it is difficult to anticipate costs, so if agreements can be made in good faith to yearly or quarterly review expenses and income it is easier to establish working consortia.

Geographic service areas are also difficult administrative issues. Traditionally, schools had clearly designated areas they served, such as districts, counties, states, or regions. With electronic distribution of instruction, these boundaries are invisible. Regulations that set particular geographic limits for schools may need to be clarified or altered when distance education programs are started.

Governance is closely related to finances and geography. For example, which school board is responsible for courses delivered at a distance—the receiving or the sending board? Policies need to clarify this issue before problems in need of resolution emerge.

Faculty Policies
Faculty, or labor-management, issues can easily be the most difficult for policy developers, especially if teachers are unionized. Increasingly, existing labor-management policies are being used to cover distance education. Clearly, faculty need to be recognized for their efforts and expertise in working with distant learners, and until distance education becomes mainstream and expected of all teachers, policies need to be in place that clarify distance teaching responsibilities. Faculty input during policy development is important if policies are to be enthusiastically followed. Often faculty bargaining agreements include information about the conduct of distance education (Delaney, 2009). Simpson (2010) reported that administrators convey the institution's commitment to distance education through the mission statement and faculty reward policies and practices.

Key issues include class size, compensation, design and development incentives, recognition of intellectual property of faculty, office hours, staff development for teachers, and other workload issues. Many recommend that policies regarding labor-management issues be kept flexible since many such issues are difficult to anticipate (Gellman-Danley & Fetzner, 1998; Maguire, 2009). However, faculty issues should be resolved early on in order to avoid critical problems later. Once again, the concept of integration is important. Integrating distance education faculty policy with traditional labor-management policy seems to most often be the best strategy.

Legal Policies
Many faculty and administrators are quite naïve about the legal issues involved in distance education. Policies about copyright and fair use, liability especially for inappropriate use of telecommunications networks, and intellectual property are important to resolve (Twigg, 2000). When units, courses, and programs are offered at a distance they are easily scrutinized and violations are apparent. In addition to developing clear policies related to these issues, many institutions are developing comprehensive staff development/training experiences for faculty who deal with copyright and liability.

Ownership of intellectual property is an important issue for distance education. When courses or portions of courses are packaged for delivery to the distant learner the question of who owns the "package" becomes an obvious issue, more obvious than when students entered a classroom in a traditional school. On one side of the issue are those who emphasize the *property* side of the intellectual property equation. This group argues that the school is the owner of any works produced during working hours, using school resources by faculty. At the other extreme are those who feel the contribution of knowledgeable faculty, the *intellectual* component of "intellectual property," is most important. This camp advocates course ownership by faculty.

Most would agree that both elements are necessary and that neither extreme best serves the school. Often, policies that share profits after expenses with faculty who develop instruction for distant learners are best. The exact split for this sharing should be negotiated and policies developed before courses are offered (Twigg, 2000).

Kranch (2008) provided an excellent summary of the two camps, related to the concept of ownership rights.

> The ownership of the rights to distance learning courses is important because of the value of the intellectual property to both the faculty members and the institution and the resources that both have invested in its creation. Strong arguments can be made for granting intellectual property rights for distance learning course materials to either the academics who produce them or the institution that employs the academics. Arguing for academics retaining the rights are long-standing tradition regarding print and video materials, the personal investment academics make in course materials, the threat to academic freedom perceived in the loss of ownership and the control it represents, and the need to preserve the ability to transport the course materials with the authoring academics as they move to new locations. Arguing for institutional ownership of these intellectual property rights are the "work for hire" provision of copyright law, the resources that the institution provides over and above those used for producing resources for face-to-face courses, the generally uncertain nature of individually-negotiated faculty/institution property rights agreements, and the need to protect the name of the institution associated with the course material. Granting intellectual property rights of distance learning materials to the sponsoring institution best preserves the institution's investment of staff, resources, and name. Including in this ownership the provision that authoring faculty retain the perpetual right of use, augmentation, and remuneration best preserves the faculty member's investment of creativity. With these two principles as the foundation, the interests of both administration and faculty can be served, with the details concerning the use of distance learning property decided by a negotiated committee decision at the local institution. (p. 335)

Student Policies

Student services should be integrated. In other words, policies related to students learning at a distance should be reflected by general student policies. However, regular policies may need to be modified to accommodate the distant learner. Specifically, if asynchronous instruction is being offered, then support services will need to be available when students need them. For example, if a school offers courses such as AP Calculus to students in other schools, then distant students may need to be able to access support services outside of regular school hours. Homework "hotlines" may need to be established and be available to all students, not just distant learners. Library/media center resources should be available to everyone, and computer laboratories should be of equal quality. Polices related to students and their needs are often overlooked, but become more critical in a distance education environment. Institutions are establishing social network policies for students. These policies range on a continuum from restrictive to open, with most falling somewhere between the extremes. Restrictive policies prohibit the use of social networking in any academic activity. Open policies have few, if any, restrictions on how social networking is used within the school or organization.

Student support policies should be clear, flexible, and widely understood, not only by students but also by faculty. Policies related to feedback from instructors should be monitored, and special requirements of distance learners, such as mailing of assignments, use of e-mail, access to Websites, and proctoring of exams should be clear and designed to assist the student be a successful distant learner.

Technical Policies

Often, some organization owns the network used for distance education, or is responsible for its reliability. If a private-sector business is the provider, then clear expectations must be in place, and all members of a consortium should be part of the relationship. If a public agency such as a state education department or education organization is the telecommunications service provider, then very clear chain of command responsibilities should be in place. Often, telecommunications policies are not the same as other policies related to the distance education enterprise since they are not related to the educational mission of the organizations involved and often they are mandated by the private or public provider of services. However, telecommunications procedures should be understood by all involved with managing distance education.

Policies related to student and faculty technical needs, such as the quality of personal computers needed by students who learn at home, should be established. Hardware, software, and connectivity minimum requirements should be clearly explained.

Philosophical Issues

Often overlooked when policies are developed are those that relate to vision, mission, and understanding of distance education. Many advocate that when an educational organization decides to become involved in offering or receiving distance education, its vision and mission statements should reflect this commitment.

Of more direct importance to the success of distance education is the recognition that this approach is credible, high quality, and appropriate. Distance education is an innovation, new to most, and misunderstood by many (Rogers, 2003). Training, administrator support, publicity, and attention to quality are important components of a successful and accepted distance education program. Organizational policies related to these issues should include distance education.

SAMPLE POLICY STATEMENTS

Next, sample policy statements in each of the seven areas will be listed. These samples are generic examples of issues that are often included in college and school distance education policy statements.

Academic
- "... to be an accredited, the school must provide access to 400 instructional units for each student each school year ... schools provide required instructional units

on site or through a combination of local and distance learning programs ... up to 100 instructional units of the 400 unit instructional program requirements of the high school may be met through the use of courses presented primarily through one or more forms of distance learning technologies, such as satellite, regional course sharing, or other audio-video distance learning..."

- "Each course is shown on the high school class schedule ... at least one student is enrolled and participating in each course to be counted ... each student enrolled in a course is assigned to a local certificated teacher who monitors student progress and general appropriateness of the course..."
- "... off-site courses are made available to all students at the school's expense."
- "... at least one student enrolled in each course used towards compliance with the instructional program requirement."
- "... class is scheduled ... each day that school is in session with a certificated teacher present (one teacher may supervise several courses within a single class period)"
- "... the distance education class must be shown on the high school class schedule."
- "... Carnegie class time equivalents will be the same for television courses as for any course."
- "... courses may be taught in-load or as an overload..."
- "... the class size for a distance education courses will be the same as the generally accepted limit for an equivalent traditionally taught course."
- "... the maximum class size for distance learning courses will be 20 for online courses, 30 for telecourses, and 30 for instructional TV courses."

Fiscal/Geographic/Governance
- "Students pay the same fees for distance education classes as for classes delivered on-site."
- "A distance learning committee shall be formed comprised of faculty, administrators and a representation of the faculty senate."
- "The distance learning leadership committee shall consist of a minimum of three full-time faculty and three administrators who will oversee courses and services."
- "A faculty member who has developed a course and who owns the copyright to the course material may be invited by administration to share course material...this is the faculty member's decision."
- "A stipend will be paid to a faculty member teaching a distance education course for the first time."

Faculty
- "Instructors must meet the standards and procedures used by the institutions for regular instructors."
- "Instructors teaching on interactive distance education will be compensated at the rate of $500 per remote site."
- "Instructor training, including system use and suggested teaching procedures, shall be a requisite prior to teaching a course via the distance learning system."
- "The school will provide 12 clock hours of formal training, including at least 8 hours using the network."
- "A faculty member must complete an Internet-based course as a student before developing and offering such a courses...."

- "There will be no reduction in college staff directly related to participation in distance learning."
- "Any videotapes or audiotapes made of distance learning courses shall not be used in evaluating the faculty member without the faculty member's consent."
- "Faculty members teaching a distance education course shall be evaluated in accordance with the same procedures as other faculty members."

Legal
- "… course materials will be reviewed by appropriate school officials to insure copyright regulations are strictly adhered to…"
- "… course materials developed locally will be the property of the originating school, unless special arrangements are made in writing."
- "Intellectual property shall be defined as any trademarkable, copyrightable, or patentable material or thing…"
- "Distance learning shall not cause the elimination of a full-time faculty position."
- "The college must obtain written approval from the faculty member who originally developed the course."
- "The ownership of distance learning materials or processes shall vest in the party or parties designated by a written agreement entered into prior to the production of the materials."
- "… all property rights shall belong to the staff member…"
- "The property rights of projects of staff members shall be shared by the participants in such a manner as they shall agree in writing."
- "If a faculty member chooses to contract away his/her exclusive right to intellectual property of a distance education course, the College shall have the right of first refusal."
- "Course materials created by faculty during their usual working schedule shall be considered works for hire and shall be the property of the College."
- A course offered by the College and the materials developed to meet the requirements for the College approval of a course are considered the property of the College."

Student
- "Students … must have the same services, the same options for continuing education, and the same choices of delivery methods as the traditional on-site students."
- "Direct e-mail interchange between students and faculty shall not be monitored by the College without the prior notice and reasonable suspicion of improper conduct."
- "Library services for distant learners will be equivalent to those of on-campus students."
- "A technology fee will be charged each semester. This fee will be collected from on and off campus students."

Technical
- "… students must remain in sight of the video camera."
- "… students must respect the equipment."
- "… three violations and students are dismissed from the distance education class."

- "… classes missed because of technical problems will be rescheduled and required …"
- "… student use of equipment shall not be monitored without prior notification and without reasonable suspicion of improper conduct."
- "The College shall make a commitment to maintaining/providing adequate technical support for distance learning instruction."
- "The College will provide faculty members who participate with the appropriate training and technical support."
- "The Distance Learning Leadership Committee shall recommend appropriate computer hardware and software, and technical support for distance learning to be provided for delivery of distance learning classes."
- "The College shall arrange for and pay costs of any special training required for faculty to teach distance learning courses. Such training shall not constitute substantial support. Each faculty member who teaches a distance education class will have the opportunity to complete training to improve the quality of distance learning courses."
- "The College shall arrange for and pay the costs of any special training required for faculty who teach distance learning course sections."

Philosophical
- "… is the mission of … school district … using electronic or other technologies to provide high quality educational experiences."
- "… courses delivered to distant learners are considered equivalent to those offered traditionally."
- "Each student, prior to graduation, will enroll and complete at least one course delivered using distance education technologies."
- "Instructional technology shall be used solely to benefit the educational mission of the College."
- "The purpose of distance education is to increase the opportunity for students to take classes, to efficiently utilize District teaching resources, and to provide for quality teaching throughout the entire District."
- "Courses taught by distance learning shall be evaluated regularly by faculty, students, and administration, and rescheduled based upon their effectiveness."

THE POLICY MANUAL

Typically, policies are collected and published in hard copy and electronically. Policy development is handled in a variety of ways depending on the organization. In higher education, a curriculum committee with members from the faculty, administration, and often student body develop and maintain policy manuals. In schools, ad-hoc committees develop local policies and state departments of education often develop standards that relate to course transfer, time, instructor qualifications, and funding.

Organizations develop policies as part of the function of the Office of Human Relations with input from units that participate in distance education staff development, and often from the organization's legal adviser. A typical policy manual (e.g., Alabama A&M, 2010; Northeast Mississippi Community College, 2008) might have a table of contents with these major categories:

SUMMARY

Integrated policies for distance education are preferred (Simonson et al., 2012). In other words, policies that provide guidance and direction to the educational systems should seamlessly include and incorporate the concept of distant delivery of instruction. Students should be defined by their enrollment in a course or program, not by whether they are distant or local learners (Simonson et al., 2012). Initially, distance education policies will probably need to be infused with existing policies. Ultimately, they should be integrated to indicate that distance education is a routine and regularly occurring component of the educational enterprise. Policies are merely tools to facilitate program integrity, quality, and growth.

> In order to plow straight rows, the farmer does not look down at the ground, but at the end of the field.

REFERENCES

Alabama A & M University. (2010). *Distance education procedures manual.* Normal, AL: Author.

Berge, Z. L. (1998). Barriers to online teaching in post-secondary institutions: Can policy changes fix it? *Online Journal of Distance Learning Administration, 1*(2). Retrieved from http://www.westga.edu/~distance/Berge12.html

California Polytechnic State University. (n.d.). Policy vs. procedures: A guideline. Retrieved from http://policy.calpoly.edu/cappolicy.htm

Delaney, S. (2009). Distance education terms in faculty collective bargaining agreements. (Doctoral dissertation, University of Nebraska – Lincoln, 2009). *Dissertation Abstracts International, 70*(7).

Florida Virtual School. (2011). Mission. Retrieved from http://www.flvs.net/areas/aboutus/Pages/Mission.aspx

Gellman-Danley, B., & Fetzner, M. J. (1998). Asking the really tough questions: Policy issues for distance learning. *Online Journal of Distance Learning Administration, 1*(1). Retrieved from http://www.westga.edu/~distance/danley11.html

King, J. W., Nugent, G. C., Eich, J. J., Mlinek, D. L., & Russell, E. B. (2000a). A policy framework for distance education: A case study and model. *DEOSNEWS, 10*(10). Retrieved from http://www.ed.psu.edu/acsde/deos/deosnews/deosnews10_10.asp

King, J. W., Nugent, G. C., Russell, E. B., Eich, J., & Lacy, D. D. (2000b). Policy frameworks for distance education: Implications for decision makers. *Online Journal of Distance Learning Administration, 3*(2). Retrieved from http://www.westga.edu/~distance/king32.html

Kranch, D. A. (2008). Who owns online course intellectual property? *Quarterly Review of Distance Education, 9*(4), 349–356.

Liggett, R. (1998, October 2). A prescription for telemedicine. *Telemedicine Today, 2.*

Maguire, L. (2009). The faculty perspective regarding their role in distance education policy making. *Online Journal of Distance Learning Administration, 12*(1). Retrieved from http://www.westga.edu/~distance/ojdla/spring121/maguire121.html

Milwaukee Area Technical College. (2009). *Academic technology plan.* Milwaukee, WI: Author.

Mindtools. (n.d.). Mission statements and vision statements. Retrieved from www.mindtools.com/pages/article/newLDR_90.htm

Northeast Mississippi Community College. (2008). *Distance learning policy and procedure manual.* Retrieved from http://www2.nemcc.edu/Webmaster/publications/docs/DLManual.pdf

Rogers, E. M. (2003). *Diffusion of innovations* (5th ed.). New York, NY: Free Press.

Schlosser, L. A., & Simonson, M. (2009). *Distance education: Definition and glossary of terms* (3rd ed.). Charlotte, NC: Information Age.

Simonson, M. (2004). Distance learning leaders: Who are they? *Distance Learning, 1*(3), 48.

Simonson, M. (2005). Technology plans and distance education. *Distance Learning, 2*(4), 44.

Simonson, M. (2009). Distance learning. In *Britannica book of the year* (p. 231). Chicago, IL: Encyclopaedia Britannica.

Simonson, M., Schlosser, C., & Hanson, D. (1999). Theory and distance education: A new discussion. *The American Journal of Distance Education, 13*(1), 60–75.

Simonson, M., Smaldino. S., Albright, M., & Zvacek, S. (2012). *Teaching and learning at a distance: Foundations of distance education* (5th ed.). Boston, MA: Pearson.

Simpson, C. M. (2010). Examining the relationship between institutional mission and faculty reward for teaching via distance. *Online Journal of Distance Learning Administration, 13*(1). Retrieved from http://www.westga.edu/~distance/ojdla

Twigg, C. A. (2000). Intellectual property policies for a new learning environment. Retrieved from http://www.thencat.org/Monographs/Whoowns.html

University of Miami School of Nursing and Health Studies. (2010). *Academic technology plan.* Coral Gables, FL: Author.

U.S. Department of Education. (2004). *Toward a new golden age in American education: How the Internet, the law and today's students are revolutionizing expectations. National educational technology plan 2004.* Washington, DC: Author.

U.S. Department of Education. (2010). *Transforming American education: Learning powered by technology. National educational technology plan 2010.* Washington, DC: Author

Watkins, R., & Schlosser, C. (2000). Capabilities-based educational equivalency units: Beginning a professional dialogue. *The American Journal of Distance Education, 14*(3), 34–47.

28

STRATEGIC PLANNING AND NEEDS ASSESSMENT IN DISTANCE EDUCATION

RYAN WATKINS, ROGER KAUFMAN, AND BUSAYO ODUNLAMI

INTRODUCTION

Generally, institutions are more adept at making decisions on *how* to implement activities than deciding *what* results should be accomplished in the first place. Consequently, many institutions develop strategic plans that effectively delineate specific activities (such as expanding distance education offerings) without comparing them against alternative solutions or clearly aligning them with desired results and consequences. Institutions therefore often fail to accomplish their institutional or societal aspirations since they are working from a strategy based on an assumed, or vaguely defined, destination and the premature selection of activities.

Rather than assuming, needs assessments can provide a foundation for strategic planning and subsequent decision making. Needs assessments—systematic processes and tools designed to collect information and guide decisions—measure gaps between desired and current results, and then compare alternative activities that can achieve those aims. Because needs assessments focus on evidence (rather than assumptions) about what should be accomplished, what is being accomplished, and what alternatives can best achieve desired results, they provide institutions with a valuable basis for guiding decisions. Practical needs assessments achieve this by examining and linking three levels of results and consequences: societal contributions, organizational accomplishments, and individual or team achievements (Kaufman 2011; Watkins, West Meiers, & Visser, 2012).

As education professionals (professors, instructors, administrators, trainers, instructional designers, managers, etc.), we experience many new and emerging opportunities to improve educational results. From pedagogical improvements to new information communication technologies (ICTs), we frequently learn about new solutions that are searching of educational problems to solve. Yet, by reversing common practice and defining the results you want to achieve before the processes and resources you might use, you can improve the odds of your decisions leading sustained implementation and valued results (see Nutt, 2008). In this context, strategic planning and needs assessment come forward as central tools for guiding decisions.

Nevertheless, institutions often fail to systematically and scientifically explore whether they have good reasons to create a distance education program. We believe, as does Rumble (1986), that too often "... our first impulse is to search through course catalogs to determine which courses will easily be transformed into online, video, audio, or other digital formats; rarely questioning the *requirement* and/or *usefulness* of the courses or distance education." We wonder, too, why "... those charged with setting up a distance education system are not given the choice to recommend against it" (Rumble, 1986).

Considering distance education, institutional stakeholders should perform solid strategic planning and systematic needs assessments to initially determine what results should be accomplished at the student, program, institutional, and societal levels, and then determine if distance education remains the best alternative to achieve those results. It is time to stop grabbing for pre-mature and/or immediate solutions—solutions perhaps in search of nonexistent problems or opportunities. Rather, it is essential to work with your beneficiaries and partners to create strategic plans that guide decisions and lead to desired results (McCarthy & Samors, 2009).

STRATEGY

For distance education, globalization and technological improvements have increased the requirement for effective strategic planning and decision making (see Rovai & Downey, 2010; McCarthy & Samors, 2009). While distance education used to be a niche market for many programs or colleges, it is now a very competitive environment. Today, the mere fact that your courses are offered at a distance is rarely the distinguishing factor among the options available to students. Flexibility and responsiveness in planning is therefore required to adjust quickly and appropriately to the state of the landscape (e.g., new technology, markets, competition, policies). According to Reeves and Deimler (2011), this requires institutions not only to adapt (i.e., respond) but also to experiment (i.e., innovate). At the same time, stability in vision and mission should anchor your decisions. Consistent focus on achieving desired results for clients and beneficiaries, including society, offers a valuable foundation on which innovation can flourish.

Strategic plans are commonly the point-in-time products of on-going processes within organizations. As Mintzberg (2007) describes, organizational goals typically come in three varieties: those that remain stable over time (e.g., improving learner satisfaction, graduating competent students); those that sounded good previously but go away as more information is learned (e.g., investing in student hardware, partnering with private sector companies); and those that emerge as new information is discovered (e.g., new models of distance delivery, entering overseas markets). As such, at their best strategic plans serve organizations by providing guidance on how the institution can be proactive, responsive, as well as adaptive. At their worst, however, they cause confusion and lead to undesirable results. This leads Bates and Sangra (2011) to suggest that strategic *thinking* is today more important than strategic planning; though we suggest that improving the capacity for both in your institution is the best path to success (Kaufman 2011; Watkins et al., 2012).

While a number of processes support quality strategic planning (such as economic forecasts, market analysis, environmental scans, Strength-Weakness-Opportunity-Threat analysis), needs assessments can provide a useful foundation for these and other planning activities. Offering a systematic and rigorous approach to collecting information, setting priorities, and informing decisions, needs assessments provide the basis for informed and justifiable strategic planning and decision making.

Rumble (1986) urged educators to understand that just because there are *problems* that may be satisfied by distance education methods, this does not necessarily mean that distance education is the best choice for addressing all *problems*. Fortunately, today you have a wide variety of tools available that reduce the possibilities of implementing distance education solutions for inappropriate institutional opportunities or problems. Devote time to a rigorous needs assessment, it is a valuable first step for justifying your decisions (Kaufman, 2000, 2006, 2011).

Before your institution elects to invest financial and other resources in a distance education program, a needs assessment may justify the decision and prepare you to make the difficult decisions that follow (Chaney, Chaney, & Eddy, 2010; Kaufman, 2006, 2011; Watkins, 2006; Watkins et al., 2012). Even so, you may feel pressure to implement solutions prior to justifying your actions. After all, by 2006 more than 40% of colleges and universities already included distance education in their strategic plans (NASULGC-Sloan National Commission on Online Learning, 2007), making it challenging to recommend anything other than distance education solutions without sufficient evidence.

As in corporate settings, educational institutions frequently offer few incentives for stepping back and analyzing the necessary information before making complex decisions. The lack of effective strategic planning and supporting needs assessments is unfortunate because often by the time the impact of a possibly ineffective intervention (e.g., distance education) is known, your institution has used scarce resources and/or the ideal time for addressing the problem/opportunity has passed. To reverse this trend, use systematic planning and assessment to justify your decisions.

NEEDS ASSESSMENTS: GUIDING STRATEGY

A systemic needs assessment can identify, prioritize, and justify the closure of societal, institutional, and individual needs (i.e., gaps in results) in support of effective strategic planning (Kaufman, 1992, 1998, 2000, 2006, 2011). While there are many models for conducting a needs assessment, arguably the most fashionable models include those of Rossett (1987),[1] Robinson and Robinson (1995), Mager and Pipe (1997), Kaufman (1992, 1998, 2000, 2006, 2011), and Altschuld (2010).[2] Each of these approaches can be of value when we realize what each does and does not provide; supplying useful insights otherwise missing from the strategic planning and decision-making processes.

Ideally, your needs assessment will align strategic thinking and planning with tactical and operational decision-making; linking societal, organizational, and individual results. This alignment, we suggest, is of great advantage when making and justifying difficult decisions regarding the future of distance education.

The needs assessment procedures suggested below represent a blend of strengths from a variety assessment models, yet remain structured within a results-focused framework. In addition, the performance criteria generated by a needs assessment provides the bases for design, development, implementation, continual improvement, and evaluation of any solution that is selected—including distance education. Needs assessment thereby links strategic planning to program implementation, evaluation, and continual improvement.

For effective strategic planning, assessment, and decision making, the needs assessment framework we propose is based on three fundamental concepts:

Distance learning is a means, not an end

Needs assessments that differentiate between ends and means can guide strategic decision making. Ends are the results of all that your institution does and delivers, whereas means are the ways in which results are obtained (Kaufman, 1992, 2000, 2006, 2011). Distance learning is as a consequence a means for achieving institutional results. We should first focus on the ends required by the institution for long-term success (based on contributions to both the organization and the external partners) before we make the decision that distance learning is the most effective and efficient means for achieving these results.

All results are not the same

All institutional results should be differentiated depending upon their primary client and beneficiary. While many institutions are proficient at analyzing their inputs and processes, most have spent far less time differentiating the results of they contribute. By differentiating among related results, we can assure that all institutional *products* and *outputs* are aligned with the desired contributions (*outcomes*) of the institution to its external clients and community. Institutions should seek to link the *products* they produce (for example, learners with a defined set of competencies) and the *outputs* they deliver (for example, graduates with a bachelors, masters, or doctoral degree) with the *outcomes* that result (for example, alumni who add value to employer, community groups, and shared society); thus aligning Micro, Macro, and Mega level results (Kaufman, 2000, 2006, 2011; Kaufman, Watkins, & Leigh, 2001; Watkins, 2006).[3]

For effective strategic planning and needs assessment, "need" is a noun and not a verb

In the context of a needs assessment this differentiation in vocabulary is vital. By electing to refer to needs as gaps in institutional results (nouns), you can avoid the alluring selection of solutions, such as distance learning, prematurely. Being able to identify, prioritize, and justify interventions and expenditures on the basis of gaps in results (rather than desired programs or initiatives) is the reward for this slight adjustment to your vocabulary. From those individuals who insist on using need as a verb you will undeniably hear comments like "we *need* a distance learning program" long before the difference in desired and current results has been identified.

Building on these fundamental concepts are the strategic planning processes and procedures for effectively determining if and when a distance education may be an appropriate option for your institution (see Pisel, 2008). The steps that follow will help justify a distance education or alternative effort when appropriate for achieving useful results, as well as define the desired results to which those initiatives should be designed to accomplish.

Step One: Identify and Align the Institution's Vision and Mission

Step one often is (but shouldn't) be an "additional task" for many educational institutions. While most institutions today have multiple mission statements (such as, goals, values, principles, visions) to include in their strategic plan, rarely are these the useful documents they could be for directing decision making (Mintzberg, 1994; Watkins, 2004). In addition, departments and units often have their own missions, which may or may not be in alignment with the institution's vision or even external value-added, used to define their future and their contribution to internal and external stakeholders. This alignment is essential however for providing direction to programs and initiatives that seek to contribute valuable results.

Though many missions statements end up gathering dust on bookshelves, ones that clearly provide for the alignment of individual, team, organizational, and societal results are actually practical guides for staff as they make daily decisions. These practical plans provide useful information on where the institution is going and how decisions at all levels of the institution support those aspirations. At the same time, effective plans are flexible and adaptable to emerging risks and opportunities.

Work to ensure that all your missions (including that of the program, department, school or college, for example) are aligned and contribute to the success of the institution and society. Covey (1996) tells us that "total organizational alignment means that within the realities of the surrounding environment, all components of your organization—including your mission, vision, values, strategy, structure, systems, individual styles and skills, and especially the minds and hearts of your people—support and work together effectively for maximum performance" (p. 21). For institutions conducting a needs assessment, these alignments are essential for defining the desired and/or required results to be achieved (as well as optimal process efficiency and effectiveness). For most public institutions, contributions to society are frequently cited as reasons for their creation in legislative bills; while for private institutions these contributions may be parallel financial goals. The value added to society is however increasingly recognized and required by for-profit organizations as well (Davis, 2005).

If any of your institution's missions—or even the objective of an existing distance learning program—do not guide decisions toward the achievement of the overall vision (best set in measurable, yet ideal terms), then this mission should be revised before any decisions about distance education are made. After all, any activities not linked to the aligned institutional vision (i.e., the beneficial results delivered to external clients and society) and mission objective (i.e., the results that benefit the institution) may lead to the achievement of inappropriate and/or damaging results (Kaufman 1998, 2000, 2006, 2011). The implementation of a distance learning program must, for instance, contribute to the achievement of value added results for learners, the institution, and the community. This alignment is what links programs to the attainment of institutional objectives and assures that they are not merely implementing solutions to unknown problems (Kaufman, 1995).

Your institution may be lacking a vision and/or related mission that set measurable performance criteria for success.[4] If so, then all educational programs should clearly define where they are going and how to tell when they have arrived. Often institutional and program objectives do not include the latter. These measurement standards may sound unnecessary, but they are actually essential. Not only do they define goals and progress toward those goals, they also provide criteria for comparing alternative solutions and later evaluation of implementation.

Step Two: Identify Needs

Needs are discrepancies between current results and those results required for the accomplishment of the institution's vision, mission, program objectives, and individual/team objectives. As such, needs are the measured gaps between desired accomplishments and current achievements. Identifying needs requires both the information obtained in step one (strategic direction that defines what results should be accomplished) as well as the collection of information regarding the current performance and results of the institution. Needs assessments routinely utilize institutional data available in existing reports, accreditation reports, institutional research departments, and other resources, as well as opinion data through the interviews, questionnaires, focus groups, or other procedures to supplement the findings (Freeman, 2004; Kaufman et al., 2001; Watkins et al., 2012; Willis, 1992, 1994).

The combination of both "hard" and "soft" data, as well as qualitative and quantitative data, is essential in determining if distance education is right for your institution (see Table 28.1).

The gathering of information for a needs assessment is best done within a comprehensive framework that ensures that you are aligning all that your organization uses, does, produces, and delivers with valuable contributions to external clients and society. The Organizational Elements Model (OEM) can be a useful tool for organizing the information you collect within a framework that ensures alignment (Kaufman, 1998, 2000, 2006, 2011). The OEM differentiates five levels of institutional planning and assessment:

Mega—planning and assessment with the primary client and beneficiary being society, and results termed as Outcomes.

Macro—planning and assessment with the primary client and beneficiary being the institution, and results termed as Outputs.

Micro—planning and assessment with the primary client and beneficiary being the individuals and teams within the institution, and results termed as Products.

Process—planning and assessment with primary focus on institutional processes an activities.

Inputs—planning and assessment with primary focus on resources and assets.

Table 28.1 Example Data Collections Tools and Techniques for Each Data Type

	Hard	**Soft**
Quantitative	• Performance data • Budgets	• Likert-type scale surveys[1] • Performance ratings
Qualitative	• Focus groups • Analysis of professional list serve • Multi-source performance observations	• Opinion surveys • Individual interviews • Single source performance observations

1 The results of Likert-type scale surveys are often mistakenly thought of as hard data since they result in quantifiable data. This is a good example of why we should consider data on both dimensions (hard-soft and quantitative-qualitative) since a single dimension may lead to confusion and the use of inappropriate statistical techniques and related conclusions.

Table 28.2   Examples of Hard and Soft Data in Relation to the OEM

Level	Hard Data	Soft Data
Mega (Societal value added)	• Tax and charitable contributions of graduates • Student and faculty safety	• Student quality of life • Continuing taxpayer satisfaction with education resulting in funding
Macro (Organizational pay-offs)	• Mission objectives accomplished (such as, increased revenue, graduation rates, job placements, etc.)	• Executive management satisfaction and perceptions of value
Micro (Individual and team results)	• Operating costs Individual/team performance (such as, new degrees conferred, met admissions goals, courses completed by students in emerging markets, etc.)	• Individual/team morale and perceptions of value Learning/learner mastery gains • Student satisfaction with what they learn
Process (Methods and means)	• Cycle time • Length of time taken on a course topic • Number of courses offered online • Use of online library resources	• Learner "attendance" and participation • Learner satisfaction with the learning processes C • lass attendance
Input (Resources and pre-requisites)	• Resource availability • Resource functionality	• Resource adequacy • Resource timeliness

Based on the OEM, institutional data should be collected that reflects each of the interdependent levels (see Table 28.2 for examples).

The Mega level of the OEM specifically details the stakeholder that has traditionally been forgotten or assumed in the development of distance education programs—the society in which all organizations exist (Kaufman, 2000, 2011; Kaufman et al., 2001). Society, as a whole, is not only a beneficiary of that which an institution does and delivers, but for many institutions (especially K-12 schools and universities) society is a primary financial supporter for their efforts. The application of this strategic approach assures that societal contributions are not forgotten in the needs assessment, strategic plans, or the possible implementation of a distance education program.

Many needs assessment approaches suggest that institutions only collect information regarding current processes and achievements; thus relying on the assumptions that desired results are known, agreed upon, and similarly evaluated throughout the institution and among its partners. By collecting data on both current (i.e., What Is) and desired (i.e., What Should Be) results a needs assessment can inform decision-making without relying on an assumption that desired performance is well defined and measured. Utilizing both What Is (WI) and What Should Be (WSB) data, you can identify gaps or discrepancies between What Is and What Should Be (Gap = WSB – WI). Using a consistent scale of measurement (e.g., interval or ratio) these gaps can illustrate real and/or perceived differences between current (WI) and the desired or required (WSB) performance that necessary for individual, organization, and societal success (Kaufman, Guerra-Lopez, Watkins, & Leigh, 2008; Watkins, 2006).

Examine all five elements of the OEM (inputs, processes, products, outputs, and outcomes) to gain a system view of your institution, external clients, and their societal context and realities. By applying the OEM, you are no longer limited to just a Macro view (organization-wide) and a Micro view (sections and/or departments) of your organization.

Step Three: Prioritize and Select Need(s) To Be Addressed

Prioritize and select the needs to be dealt with. In this step of the assessment process, use data and participatory methods to guide decisions. The extent to which data is collected and analyzed will have two effects on the quality of the needs assessment: (a) an extended period of data collection can negate the timeliness of the assessment, and (b) not enough supporting data can invalidate the results of the assessment. The context of the performance problem/opportunity (i.e., the reason why distance education exist or is being considered by your institution) should facilitate how you balance these variables.

Needs assessments are rarely done in the context of unilateral decisions, thus participatory methods are commonly applied to gain "buy-in" and ensure that diverse perspectives are included in the decisions-making. Tools like nominal-group technique, pair-wise comparisons, multi-criteria analysis, and scenarios can all engage a number of partners in making decisions that prioritize gaps (needs) and later inform how they can be closed (Watkins et al., 2012).

The cost of not closing gaps in results is essential to this third step in the assessment process, though often left out during application. A costs analysis can, nonetheless, keep you from enacting a $100,000 distance education solution to a $5,000 problem. Economies of scale can complicate this issue, and guidance to the procedures for this analysis are unique to the context of each institution. A smart starting place for the analysis, however, are the elements previously used to complete the OEM in step two (Kaufman, Watkins, & Sims, 1997). It will be worth your time to at least estimate the costs of each gap between What Is and What Should Be (see Figure 28.1).

A Cost-Consequences Analysis (Kaufman et al., 1997; Muir, Watkins, Kaufman, & Leigh, 1998) is a tool that provides a coarse-grain examination of the cost of closing the gaps, and keeps the needs assessment within the context of the OEM (see Table 28.3). The Cost-Consequences Analysis incorporates, as suggested by Rumble (1986), the cost-efficiency, cost-effectiveness, and cost-benefit analyses.

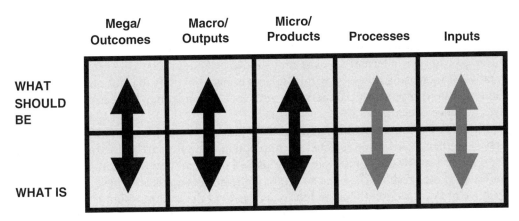

Figure 28.1 The Organizational Elements Model as it relates to needs assessment

Table 28.3 The Questions Posed by CCA and Conventional ROI Frameworks in Relation to their Level of Planning and Decision Making

Level of Planning and Decision Making	Cost-Consequences Questions	Conventional ROI Questions
Mega	Cost to achieve Outcomes vs. Cost of not getting Outcomes? *(cost-utility)*	What did we give vs. What utility of Outcomes did we get?
Macro	Cost to achieve Outputs vs. Cost of not getting Outputs? *(cost-benefit)*	What did we give vs. What benefit of Outputs did we get?
Micro	Cost to achieve Products vs. Cost of not getting Products? *(cost-effectiveness)*	What did we give vs. What effectiveness of Products did we get?
Process	Cost of efficient Processes vs. cost of inefficient Processes? (cost-efficiency)	What did we give vs. What efficiency of Processes did we get?
Input	Cost of the quality Inputs vs. Cost of inferior Inputs? (accounting or auditing)	What did we give vs. What audited Inputs did we get?

As opposed to estimating the cost of not addressing a need, approximating the cost of closing the gaps is more familiar to most educators and administrators.[5] To complete this analysis, however, you must enter step four in order to assign estimated costs for potential solutions (such as distance education and other alternatives).

Step Four: Identify Solution Requirements and Alternative Solutions

Before leaping forward to the identification of alternative solutions—the conventional starting place that most program planning—take time to first define the solution requirements. These requirements establish the criteria by which each alternative solution are judged and later evaluated. Specific solution requirements facilitate the listing of alternative solutions and the selection of the "best" solutions. Solution requirements should include—at minimal—standards for how well solutions meet time, costs, resources constraints, as well as accomplish necessary results.

At least two or three alternatives (i.e., ways and means for meeting identified needs) should be identified for each need (i.e., gap in results) since all problems and opportunities have more than one possible solution. The equifinality principle of systems theory tells us after all that for any need there are always multiple options for achieving desired results.[6]

A distance education program, for example, is just one feasible solution for your institution to consider; alternatives exist and should be sought out. This is the time to get creative. If increasing access to rural students is a goal of your institution, for instance, then satellite campuses or partnerships with local schools may be reasonable alternatives distance education.

Alternative solutions should even be identified in spite of perceived limitations that may keep them from being selected for implementation. Research illustrates that when professionals are aware of multiple solutions to a problem, they are more likely to focus on the goal (i.e., results) than the solution; while professionals who have a limited perspective of available solutions tend to focus more on the solution than the goal (Kruglanski, Pierro, & Sheveland, 2011). In terms of education, this transfer of focus to the results by recognizing expanded options can greatly improve the quality of decisions related to if and when distance education is an appropriate choice.

Creating an extensive list of alternative solutions is also part of a process that improves decision making (Nutt, 2008). Identify the pros, cons, and costs for each possible solution before choosing any activity. This information can then be used to guide decisions, for example, in a multi-criteria analysis or nominal group session (see Watkins et al., 2012). The effort put into analyzing all the possible solutions for any problem will pay off when you make justifiable decisions that can withstand challenges from those sold on an a different choice.

Step Five: Selecting Solutions

Based on the analyses in steps three and four, and assuring alignment with steps one and two, decide if distance education or other alternatives will be valuable tools for accomplishing the results that now define your institution's strategic plans. Deciding upon a single solution may or may not be advisable. For most any problem or opportunity a combination of solutions will typically yield the best results (Watkins, 2006). Costs (such as financial or time) and/or political pressures (for instance, from those saying "we *need* a distance learning program") should not however be drivers of these decisions. The data from the needs assessment should provide you with the essential information for identifying the "right" solutions for your institution. Having systematically implemented a needs assessment will add validity, usefulness, and confidence to your decisions.

As in the previous steps, participatory decision-making methods are often valuable in guiding decisions about what to do in order to achieve results. Work closely with your partners to examine each alternative (and combination of alternatives) to determine what activities will best lead to desired results.

SYSTEMATIC NEEDS ASSESSMENT

The needs assessment process described above offers several distinct advantages if you implement it with rigor:

1. strategic plans can be driven by results-focused needs assessment data rather than knee-jerk responses to current or projected trends in education;
2. decisions are based on accomplishing measurable results for individuals, the institution, and the society. The selection of means and methods may be made on the bases of the costs to meet the needs as compared to the costs to ignore the needs;
3. the rigor of the process can be adjusted for differing context and constraints of the institution;
4. information from the assessment will define both performance and evaluation criteria; and
5. the process leads toward alignment of all that the institution uses, does, produces, and delivers with contributions to students and others in the community.

As institutions are increasing being held accountable for the results of their efforts, time should be taken to assess any performance solution before implementation. These advantages are invaluable, especially when a distance education solution has potentially been prematurely prescribed for you.

Often, distance education programs or initiatives are justified when the strategic plans and needs assessment are complete. The accessibility and reduced long-term costs typically associated with well-planned distance education programs can make them viable option for meeting many institutional objectives. In these cases, the rigorous needs assessment process can provide a level of assurance that distance education will meet its objectives at the Micro, Macro, and Mega levels. Afterwards, there are many useful resources for how to complete the tactical planning leading to the successful implementation of the new distance education program (see Bates & Sangra, 2011; Berge, this volume; Hamel & Prahalad, 1994; Mitroff, Mason, & Pearson, 1994; Pfeiffer, Goodstein, & Nolan, 1989).

PROACTIVE CHANGE

The institutions that will lead distance education in the future will not address the changing realities of education from a reactive perspective. The tactic of waiting to respond to the actions of your competitors, although common in many of today's educational institutions and corporations, can be a death sentence in the educational market place (see Haeckel, 1999; Kaufman & Lick, 2000). And yet predicting the future is not a science. So. how will leaders in distance education ensure a useful and successful future? They will create it!

Proactive change creation moves institutional strategic planning and needs assessment away from a responsive mind-set to one focused on adaptability and creation (see Table 28.4). This change in perspective is essential for determining if and/or when distance education (or any new educational program) may be appropriate for an institution.

Success in the future is likely to be dependent on this ability of an institution to create the future they want as opposed to reacting that produced by others. Those institutions

Table 28.4 Change Creation and Change Management (based on Kaufman & Lick, 2000)

Change Creation	Change Management
Proactive	Reactive
Being pursued	Catching up
Setting the standard	Trying to be competitive
Leading	Following
Long-term focus	Short-term focus (quick fixes)
Vision-driven to add value to all stakeholders	Driven by external events
Internal planning for a better future	Externally imposed disruptions
Change-adaptable or Change-inviting mind-set: A learning organization	Responsive mind-set
Strategic	Tactical
Focuses on all of the institution plus external clients and society	Focus on parts of the institution
A "system" approach	A "systems approach"
Future-creating organization	Responsive and resilient organization
Synergy and co-mentoring	Collaboration
Learning organization	Organizational learning
Works to reinvent a new corporate culture	Works within the current corporate culture

that create markets by meeting the needs of society will have a definite competitive advantage. In higher education we can identify a similar trend with institutions creating markets for distance education and then finding success in meeting the needs of those markets.

FUTURE RESEARCH IN PLANNING FOR DISTANCE EDUCATION

The growth and prosperity of distance education will only continue in the future if educational institutions are focused on adding value to lives of learners and communities (Kaufman & Watkins, 2000). Focus your institution's planning firstly on the required skills and knowledge for learners to attain long-term success and quality of life; then examine how the institutions can best serve those needs. To make this a reality, the educational paradigms that have brought your institution success in the past may have to be reconsidered for their value today and tomorrow.

The transformation of future planning in distance education should be considered within the context of the history of distance education (see Table 28.5). While some trends are more evident in the literature than others, a composite of planning and assessment within distance education provides us with several arenas for future research. These include:

1. the determination of what constitutes a useful distance education program;
2. the determination of what constitutes an effective distance education course/degree;
3. how do institutions validate decisions made regarding the implementation of distance education;
4. how can educational institutions maintain their adaptability to be responsive and responsible and to create the future they and their community desire;
5. what happens to distance education programs when the technologies drive the decision making rather than learner and society value added;
6. when distance education is determined to be the "best" solution for an institution, how can effective and efficient systems by designed;
7. how are effective and efficient distance education systems managed;
8. how can we prove that our distance education program and curriculum adds value, measurably, to internal and external clients and strives continually improve the value we add to all stakeholders.

As a result, investigations into the effective planning for distance education offers many opportunities for researchers.

NOTES

1. There have been serious challenges to "training needs assessments" on the basis that they will, because of their target organizational level, will be wrong 80-90% of the time. See Clark & Estes, 2002; Stolovich, 2002 Triner, Greenberry, & Watkins, 1996.
2. See Watkins, Leigh, Platt, and Kaufman (1998) for a comparison of alternative needs assessment models in terms of what they deliver in scope and content.
3. Differentiating results is not intended to, nor should, imply that some results are more important than others. Results at all levels are important and dependent on the accomplishment of results at other levels for the system to be successful.

Table 28.5 An Analysis of Distance Education Delivery Systems (Kaufman & Watkins, 2000)

	Conventional Instruction	Classic/Historic DL	Current DL	Future DL
Is it learner, teacher, organizationally, or societal focused?	Teacher/ Organizational	Learner	Learner/ organizational	Societal/ organizational/ learner
Is it content driven or usefulness of what is learned-driven?	Content	Content	Content delivery (see Saba, 1999)	Usefulness
Are needs identified? Are needs assessed? Are needs assessed as gaps in result?	Assumed needs	Assumed needs	Assumed needs	Formally determined as gaps in results
Are the courses/programs linked to external usefulness? Are courses/ programs linked with other learning opportunities?	Assumed	Assumed	Assumed	Linked to external value added
Are the courses/programs delivered at an institution or at a remote site, including one's home or workplace?	Institution	Remote site/ home	Remote site/ home (see Matthews, 1999)	All possible (see Welsh, 1999; Moore and Kearsley, 2012)
Are the courses delivered using conventional, telephone, books, and/or workbooks, video, computer, web-based, mobile means? What are the degrees of freedom for the delivery?	Conventional with some audio visual support (see Duning, 1987)	Video, telephone, correspondence materials/boos and workbooks (see Matthews, 1999; Moore and Kearsley, 2011)	Computer, web-based, some video	All used
Is the content of the courses/ programs designed by using a performance system/ instruction - system process?	rarely	rarely	some of the time	always
Is there open interactivity between learner and instructor/ deliverer? Does the learner get immediate feedback concerning performance?	Some of the time	rarely	Some of the time	Always when appropriate
Are the courses/programs evaluated for return-on investment for: a. the learners the b. designers/ deliverers c. the institution, d. the society?	Assumed	Assumed	For learners and, sometimes, the organization (see Moore and Kearsley, 2012)	for all

4. See Abrahams, 1995; Byars & Neil, 1987; Covey, 1996; Garratt, 1995; Nanus, 1992 Senge, 1990.
5. Also consider the "two level business case" approach presented in Kaufman, 2011.
6. More specifically, any need within an "open system," which encompasses most organizations and organizational activities.

REFERENCES

Abrahams, J. (1995). *The mission statement book: 301 corporate mission statements form America's top companies.* Berkeley, CA: Ten Speed Press.

Altschuld, J. W. (Series Ed.). (2010). *The needs assessment KIT* (5 vols.). Thousand Oaks, CA: Sage.

Bates, A., & Sangra, A. (2011). *Managing technology in higher education: Strategies for transforming teaching and learning.* San Francisco: Jossey Bass.

Byars, L., & Neil, T. (1987, July-August). Organizational philosophy and mission statements. *Planning Review.*

Chaney, D., Chaney, E., & Eddy, J. (2010). The context of distance learning programs in higher education: Five enabling assumptions. *Online Journal of Distance Learning Administration, 13*(4).

Clark, R., & Estes, F. (2002). Turning Research into Results: A Guide to Selecting the Right Performance Solutions. Atlanta, GA: The Center for Effective Performance

Covey, S. (1996, March). Organizational alignment. *Quality Digest,* 21.

Davis, I. (2005, May 26). The biggest contract. *The Economist.* 87.

Duning, B. (1987). Independent study in higher education: A captive of legendary resilience? *The American Journal of Distance Education, 1*(1), 37–46.

Freeman, R. (2004). *Planning and implementing open and distance learning systems: A handbook for decision makers.* Vancouver, Canada: Commonwealth of Learning.

Garratt, B. (Ed.). (1995). *Developing strategic thought: Rediscovering the art of direction-giving.* London: McGraw-Hill.

Haeckel, S. (1999). *Adaptive enterprise: Creating and leading sense-and-respond organizations.* Boston: Harvard Business School Press.

Hamel, G., & Prahalad, C. K. (1994). *Competing for the future: Breakthrough strategies for seizing control of your industry and creating the markets of tomorrow.* Boston: Harvard Business School Press.

Kaufman, R. (1992). *Strategic planning plus: An organizational guide* (rev. ed.). Newbury Park, CA: Sage.

Kaufman, R. (1995, Aug. 31). If distance learning is the solution, what's the problem: Beyond DDSS. *DEOS-NEWS* [an electronic publication of the American Center for the Study of Distance Education/*The American Journal of Distance Learning of the Pennsylvania State University*].

Kaufman, R. (1998). *Strategic thinking: A guide to identifying and solving problems* (rev. ed.). Arlington, VA: The American Society for Training & Development; Washington, DC: International Society for Performance Improvement .

Kaufman, R. (2000). *Mega planning: Practical tools for organizational success.* Thousand Oaks, CA: Sage.

Kaufman, R. (2011). *The manager's pocket guide to mega thinking and planning.* Amherst, MA: HRD Press.

Kaufman, R., Guerra-Lopez, I., Watkins, R., & Leigh, D. (2008). *The assessment book: Applied strategic thinking and performance improvement through self-assessments.* Amherst, MA: HRD Press.

Kaufman, R., & Lick, D. (2000). Mega-level strategic planning: Beyond conventional wisdom. In J. Boettcher, M. Doyle, & R. Jensen (Eds.), *Technology-driven planning: Principles to practice.* Ann Arbor, MI: Society for College and University Planning.

Kruglanski, A. W., Pierro, A., & Sheveland, A. (2011). How many roads lead to Rome? Equifinality set-size and commitment to goals and means. *European Journal of Social Psychology, 41,* 344–352.

Kaufman, R., & Watkins, R. (2000). Assuring the future of distance learning. *The Quarterly Review of Distance Education, 1*(1), 59–67.

Kaufman, R., Watkins, R., & Leigh, D. (2001). *Useful educational results: Defining, prioritizing and achieving.* Lancaster, PA: Proactive Publishing.

Kaufman, R., Watkins, R., & Sims, L. (1997). Cost-consequences analysis: A case study. *Performance Improvement Quarterly, 10*(2), 7–1.

Mager, R. F., & Pipe, P. (1997). *Analyzing performance problems* (3rd ed.) Atlanta, GA: The Center for Effective Performance.

McCarthy, S., & Samors, R. (2009). *Online learning as a strategic asset. Volume I: A resource for Ccampus leaders.* Retrieved Jan. 2012: http://www.aplu.org/document.doc?id=1877

Mintzberg, H. (1994). *The rise and fall of strategic planning.* New York: The Free Press.

Mintzberg, H. (2007). *Tracking strategies: Towards a general theory of strategy formation.* Oxford, UK: Oxford University Press.

Mitroff, I., Mason, R. O., & Pearson, C. M. (1994). Radical surgery: What will tomorrow's organizations look like? *Academy of Management Executives, 8*(2), 11–21.

Muir, M., Watkins, R., Kaufman, R., & Leigh, D. (1998). Costs-consequences Analysis: A primer. *Performance Improvement, 37*(4), 8–17.

Moore, M. G., & Kearsley, G. (2012). *Distance education: A systems view* (3rd ed.). New York: Cengage.

Nanus, B. (1992). *Visionary leadership.* San Francisco: Jossey-Bass.

NASULGC-Sloan National Commission on Online Learning. (2007). Online learning as a strategic asset: A survey of presidents and chancellors. Retrieved January 2012, from http://www.aplu.org/NetCommunity/Document.Doc?id=443.

Nutt, P. (2008). Investigating the success of decision making processes. *Journal of Management Studies, 45*(2), 425–455.

Pfeiffer, J. W., Goodstein, L. D., & Nolan, T. M. (1989). *Shaping strategic planning: Frogs, bees, and turkey tails.* Glenview, IL Scott, Foresman & Co.

Pisel, K. (2008). A strategic planning process model for distance education. *Online Journal of Distance Learning Administration, 11*(2).

Robinson, D. G., & Robinson, J. C. (1995), Performance consulting: Moving beyond training. San Francisco: Berrett Koehler.

Rossett, A. (1987). *Training needs assessment.* Englewood Cliffs, NJ: Educational Technology Publications.

Rovai, A., & Downey, J. (2010). Why some distance education programs fail while others succeed in a global environment. *Internet and Higher Education, 13*(3),141–147.

Rumble, G. (1986). *The planning and management of distance education.* New York: St. Martin's Press.

Senge, P. M. (1990). *The fifth discipline: The art & practice of the learning organization.* New York: Doubleday-Currency.

Stolovich, H. (2002). Front-end analysis, implementation planning, and evaluation: Breaking out of the Pamela Syndrome. *Performance Improvement, 41*(4), 5–7.

Triner, D., Greenberry, A., & Watkins, R. (1996). Training needs assessment: A contradiction in terms. *Educational Technology, 36*(6), 51–55.

Watkins, R. (2004). Ends and Means: Aligning e-learning with strategic plans. *Distance Learning Magazine, 1*(5).

Watkins, R. (2006). *Performance by design: the systematic selection, design, and development of performance technologies that accomplish useful results.* Amherst, MA: HRD Press.

Watkins, R., Leigh, D., Platt, W., & Kaufman, R. (1998). Needs Assessment: A digest, review, and comparison of needs assessment literature. *Performance Improvement, 37*(7), 40–53.

Watkins, R., West Meiers, M., & Visser, Y. (2012). *A guide to assessing needs: Tools for collecting information, making decisions, and achieving development results.* Retrieved from http:// www.gapsinresults.com

Willis, B. (1992). *Effective distance education: A primer for faculty and administrators.* Juno: University of Alaska.

Willis, B. (1994). *Distance education strategies and tools.* Englewood Cliffs, CA: Educational Technologies Publications.

29

INSTITUTIONAL LEADERSHIP

MICHAEL F. BEAUDOIN

Although educational structures may appear to be relatively static, they do gradually accommodate selective change, often in response to external factors that eventually force decision makers to consider new options. Few institutional leaders today would not acknowledge that technological innovation is perhaps the single most compelling factor that is driving them toward new organizational arrangements and, for many, it represents the most significant change since their institutions were established. Despite its seemingly inherent resistance to change, and an historical unwillingness to keep pace with corporate innovations, higher education has entered a more industrialized phase, and the resulting changes in structure and systems will demand compatible leadership styles, including approaches that have not typically characterized the management of educational enterprises.

Otto Peters (1994), one of the first to make important contributions to distance education theory, has written extensively of how distance education practitioners have effectively incorporated entrepreneurial elements such as division of labor, marketing, quality control, and other measures that are more akin to operating a business than overseeing an academic entity. Such practices have evolved in many mainstream educational organizations, but some educational planners choose instead to establish entirely new and distinct distance education entities (e.g., British Open University), rather than attempt to transform existing institutions. Roy McTarnaghan, founding president of Florida Gulf Coast University, speaks insightfully in an interview reported in *The American Journal of Distance Education* (Beaudoin, 1998) of establishing that institution as a distance education entity in 1997, noting that such large-scale endeavors must create a distinctive culture with a clearly articulated mission that is shared by all stakeholders, especially faculty, if they are to succeed, rather than attempt to transform conventional systems. The efficacy of introducing distance education into traditional institutional settings and the sustainability of these endeavors continues to engage the interest of scholars. Frederickson (2005) examines this issue on the assumption that mainstream higher education is not receptive, culturally or structurally, to such alternative approaches to the delivery of education. Others have argued that integrating distance education into conventional organizational environments can serve as a strategic initiative that ultimately enhances the viability of such entities.

Noteworthy in this regard is the two-volume study, *Online Learning as a Strategic Asset* (Seman, 2009) a project of the Association of Public and Land-Grant Universities and the Sloan National Commission on Online Learning. It reports results of a study intended as a planning resource for campus leaders. Volume 1 focuses on online learning as a vehicle for advancing an institution's strategic goals; volume 2 examines faculty views and experiences in online teaching. Findings and recommendations are based on 231 interviews at 45 public institutions and nearly 11,000 responses to a faculty survey. The overarching theme is that in an era when many institutions are finally embracing online learning, few recognize the strategic value of such an initiative. This material is especially well suited for administrators who are non-experts in distance education and who require succinct and accessible information to guide their planning. The working premise is that as technology increasingly pervades society, our academic institutions risk becoming obsolete if they do not adapt to changing demographics and market forces. The findings reinforce the argument that no institution today can afford missteps in such a complex enterprise. The history of various attempts to initiate distance education offerings is not especially inspiring, and many failed efforts have dissuaded planners from any further activity. As a consequence, in addition to limiting some universities' ability to become more relevant in the digital age, the lack of progress reinforces those skeptics who remain convinced that the online medium is not a viable or credible means of teaching and learning.

A decade earlier, James Hall (1998) offered a thoughtful analysis of what new, emerging institutional structures might look like, and how leaders within them will be required to function. As traditional and distance education institutions converge, leaders who have been dealing with separate and distinct programs identified with their institutions, will have to manage networked institutions where proprietary lines between programs and students are merging, and participants shift among formal and informal learning venues, with no single institution as a point of reference. As alliances develop and expand, largely prompted by networking technology, and increasingly involving for-profit partners, the mega-university is evolving toward what Hall defines as the meta-university. He argues that bold and creative leadership is required to manage these emerging new structures.

THE LITERATURE ON LEADERSHIP

What resources and means can best cultivate leaders for the work ahead? Those suggesting ways to attract and develop new leadership into distance education might encourage mentoring by senior administrators, attendance at professional meetings, seeking out relevant academic programs of study, and keeping current with literature in the field. But this latter suggestion of consulting the literature as a source of guidance for aspiring leaders presumes that there is a useful body of work available. Duning (1990) undertook an in-depth review of the literature on managerial leadership in distance education; she asserted that this area had attracted far less attention than other dimensions of the field. While there have been descriptions of program planning processes, little examination had occurred of leadership, however defined, within the distance education context. At that point, in assessing the status of scholarly inquiry into the area of distance education management, Duning concluded that the field lacked a theoretical framework to guide our understanding of practice, and that of all the areas of study in distance education, management appeared to be the most neglected. This author thus undertook the task of re-examining the status of this void a decade later to determine if it has been filled; to ask, if not, why; and if it has, to assess if any useful contribution has since been made to theory and practice in this area.

A random sampling of literature in the field was reviewed by conducting a content analysis of titles and abstracts of articles appearing in two American publications (*The American Journal of Distance Education* (*AJDE*), and *DEOSNEWS*, an electronic journal), both published by the American Center for the Study of Distance Education at The Pennsylvania State University. Also examined were issues of a European journal, *Open Learning*, as well as the contents of *Distance Education*, an international journal published by the Open and Distance Learning Association of Australia. Volumes examined in the *AJDE* revealed that, with the exception of one issue (Summer 1998), devoted entirely to distance education leadership (and edited by this author), no other authors wrote on topics with any obvious connection to leadership. *DEOSNEWS* contained only two titles that have any leadership connotations, and although the European and Australian journals included several articles related to staff development and the economics of distance education, no articles appeared on the specific topic of leadership. Thus, we concluded that over a four-year period (1996–1999), several widely read sources of research and writing in distance education theory and practice offered very little on the topic of leadership. We did note at that time, the launch of a new publication, the *Online Journal of Distance Learning Administration* (*OJDLA*), published by West Georgia State University. This publication recently celebrated its 10th anniversary, and is now well established as a flourishing electronic medium for research and writing almost entirely focused on issues relevant to distance education administration that attracts numerous manuscripts for peer review, and is frequently cited.

Another useful means of gauging how popular certain topics seem to be with scholars and practitioners is to review presentations at major national and international distance education conferences. A number of these papers eventually find their way into the literature, and can thus serve as indicators of what issues and ideas are in vogue at the time. An examination was conducted of titles and abstracts of papers presented at the European Distance Education Network research workshop (EDEN; in 2004 [Supporting the Learner], 2006 [Research into Online Distance Education], and 2010 [User Generated Content Assessment in Learning]). The EDEN research workshops (which attract a significant number of major scholars from throughout the world), did not include any papers on management and leadership.

Not unexpectedly, the theme of distance education management and leadership was conspicuously thin (e.g., a perusal of abstracts of the more than 750 papers presented at the Bologna and Australia conferences revealed some presentations on organization and policy, but only a single session directly concerning leadership in distance education. The programs for the 2004, 2006, and 2008 EDEN research workshops (which attract a significant number of major scholars from throughout the world), did not include any papers on management and leadership. Especially noteworthy is West Georgia State University, which again distinguishes itself by sponsoring the only national professional annual meeting in the United States that focuses primarily on distance education administration. It is worth noting that this journal recognizes and publishes the work of emerging scholars contributing new writing on important issues warranting attention. Tipple (2010), for instance, addresses the topic of online education's heavy reliance on adjunct faculty and the need for effective leadership to optimize the productivity and satisfaction of this key group of mentors.

There is an increasingly steady supply of new books on distance education, with some offering a chapter or two on aspects of administration and organization. An examination of new titles on open and distance learning received by this author during his five-year tenure (2005–2010) as book review editor for *The American Journal of Distance Education* yielded few titles dealing primarily with organizing and leading distance education activities. While many books admittedly do present a chapter related to leadership, these are conspicuous, precisely because they are so infrequent. A closer examination of content typically reveals discussions regarding the challenges of implementing a particular program at a specific institution, supported largely by anecdotal data, and providing little insight into how those experiences might be applied to other settings. Yet, it is encouraging to observe the increasing availability of volumes that focus more directly on topics related to the leadership theme. A review of selected databases on open/distance education publications list a few book titles devoted to management-related topics. While these works mainly offer strategies for developing and directing open learning initiatives, rather than formulating more theoretical constructs, the material does help fill the gap in the literature on leadership.

Several books published within the last decade are worth noting briefly. One, of course, is this ambitious volume, the *Handbook of Distance Education*, with both the 2003 and 2007 editions including a substantial section titled "Policies, Administration and Management." Though the several chapters include a wide range of topics from planning to accreditation, all have implications for those responsible for leading distance education programs. Hanna and Latchem's *Leadership and Management in Open and Flexible Learning* (2001) is an especially insightful book offering interesting insights on leadership presented through case studies and interviews. Burge's *Flexible Higher Education-Reflections from Expert Experience* (2007) provides an intriguing perspective on the development of distance education based on the reflections of 44 pioneers who have played leadership roles in the field. Moore and Kearsley (2012), in the third edition of their work on a systems view of online learning, include expanded sections on organizational change, policy useful to distance education planners and decision makers in increasingly global and commercialized settings. This author's own work, *Reflections on Research, Faculty and Leadership in Distance Education* (Beaudoin, 2004) contains several essays on distance education leadership, relating to both research and practice.

It should be recognized that there is a huge body of literature, representing a wide range of quality, covering a broad spectrum of leadership applicable to varied settings and situations, much of which can be appropriately applied to the domain of distance education. A few such titles are: Fullan's *Leading in a Culture of Change* (2001), Kotter's *Leading Change* (1996), Bass' *Leadership and performance beyond expectations* (1985), and Bennis and Nanus' *Leaders: The Strategies for Taking Charge* (1985). Those now involved in or aspiring to leadership roles in distance education would be remiss not to investigate these more generic sources for information, strategies and cautions that are quite germane to their milieu. Of particular note is Donald Schon's *The Reflective Practitioner: How Professionals Think in Action* (1983). Though now somewhat dated, this classic work on reflective practice, has clear implications for distance educators.

He makes a provocative case for developing mature practitioners by encouraging that they actively engage in a process of continuous and systematic reflection of their work during their practice, rather than at a later point when they may no longer be able to make appropriate interventions. This is an especially worthwhile process for an entire generation of distance education practitioners who now have the benefit of significant personal and institutional experience, and are still active. By engaging in "reflection in action," these veterans have the opportunity, as Schon aptly describes it, to define new truths, not only for their own benefit, but for the entire profession as well. This process has the potential to make important new contributions to the field and offer insights to the current generation of leaders.

In summing up this brief review of research, writing, and presentations on leadership, it should be acknowledged that, within the body of work receiving this cursory examination, there may well be more attention given to the leadership theme than we were able to discern, and no doubt some authors would protest that their contributions do address, at least implicitly, certain dimensions of leadership. We suspect that this may be a legitimate claim, yet it can be stated that much of the work reviewed and noted is largely descriptive in nature (e.g., case studies) of specific programs. It must be asked, then, how useful this reportage is in contributing to the body of work on leadership theory and practice or, in truth, to any other important aspects of distance education.

The modest amount of scholarly work related to leadership in distance education is compensated for, to some extent, by material in other areas of educational theory and practice. It is within the arena most closely aligned with distance education (i.e., adult and continuing education) that we can find a quite well-developed body of knowledge relating not only to the planning and management of continuing education activities, but also some attention to the area of leadership. Simerly (1987), for example, has contributed a number of worthwhile studies that can be instructive to distance educators today.

Recognizing that the paucity of material noted in the prior paragraphs represents publications and presentations searched at the time of the 2003 and 2007 editions of this handbook, this author undertook a new search for published work related to distance education leadership in preparing this chapter. Somewhat encouraging is a review of randomly chosen recent issues from a variety of journals devoted to distance education, in which leadership topics occasionally make an appearance. A similar review of journals devoted to educational leadership revealed no articles at all covering distance education administration. Also searched were bibliographies compiled and catalogued as references on leadership in distance education. At first glance, these looked promising; however, upon closer scrutiny, relatively few titles suggest content actually relating to any aspect of leadership in this area. As for the several recent books (2010–2011) covering a variety of topics relating to the planning, management, and evaluation of online education, it is rather startling to see almost no index listings with key words such as leadership, transformative change, and the like. On a final note, it is somewhat distressing, when one does encounter a cache of work in this domain, to detect that it is generally the same half-dozen or so authors who are actively researching and writing about leadership, despite the widespread adoption of online courses and the development of many new programs that presumably should invite interest in this realm.

One might be tempted to conclude, from this review, that the subject of leadership in distance education is being actively avoided, in favor of the usual fare—reports and case studies of specific projects and programs that probe in some detail about the life (and sometimes death) of particular initiatives at selected institutions. Unfortunately, these accounts seldom offer any useful insights about distance education practice that might be generalized for potential relevance and application in other similar settings, and almost never is there any thoughtful analysis about the impact of leadership, or the lack of it, in affecting the outcomes chronicled in these studies. What might be plausible explanations for the persistent minimal interest in this area of study while in other organizational settings, most notably the for-profit corporate sector, there is enormous interest in topics related to organizational leadership, as seen in best-selling books and high priced seminars?

First, those researching and writing in the field may just now be getting beyond the phase in its history where there has been an inordinate amount of interest focused on analyses of how distance instruction compares with more conventional methods and, as new technologies were rapidly deployed, how effectively these various learning environments worked compared to one another. A related factor may be that most who have written in the field thus far have themselves been academics with a preference to devote their writing to pedagogical issues rather than administrative matters. Second, although there has been, in fact, some attention given to the planning and administration of distance education programs for quite some time, most of this work has been confined to accounts of specific case histories, perhaps considered adequate by authors, without getting into the more esoteric domain of leadership. Related to this is the fact that the concept of leadership is not widely recognized as a separate and distinct element of administrative practice or study. This is especially so outside of the United States. Among European authors, for example, leadership is seldom alluded to as a discreet topic for analysis, at least not in the field of education. Third, there are those who simply dismiss the concept as one that is not especially useful for advancing the study or practice of distance education. It is seen as an elusive concept that does not readily lend itself to reliable analysis, or to a set of desirable behaviors applicable to the particulars of each situation. Further, just as some argue that there are no characteristics attributable to distance education that are uniquely its own within the field, they likewise believe the question of leadership within distance education merits no special scrutiny or analysis as a distinct area of study, or even a discreet area of professional practice.

THE NEED FOR LEADERSHIP

What, ultimately, is the usefulness of the body of work accumulated thus far on the subject of distance education leadership? Although most of the work which does exist is largely confined to an occasional book or chapter, conference presentation, journal article, or "Principles of Good Practice," perhaps it can be stated with some confidence that distance education practitioners currently in, or aspiring to leadership roles do have a variety of growing resources available to guide their practice. Assuming that there may be some value to the field of distance education if there is increased attention to leadership issues, what can be done to generate more interest in the topic? At the very least, those planning publications and meetings related to distance education could actively solicit contributions on the subject, and even dedicate entire conferences, journal issues, or books to leadership.

Is there, in fact, any value in attempting to craft, if not a definitive theoretical framework for leadership practice that is unique to distance education, at least a set of guiding principles that, at this moment in which distance education has evolved to a new role and status, can well serve its providers and consumers? Those responsible for mapping new directions for moving distance education to the next stage of its development should be heartened by the efforts of several professional associations and accrediting bodies to define so-called Principles of Good Practice. The New England Association of Schools and Colleges, for example, developed and promulgated a "policy for the accreditation of academic degree and certificate programs offered through distance education" (1998). These quality standards are useful in providing suggested criteria by which we can plan new programs, measuring what we are doing in such areas as matching technology with needs, providing adequate student support, implementing appropriate evaluation measures, etc. In the absence of a more precisely articulated theoretical framework, such principles offer some insights about what constitutes effective leadership practice, and how it ultimately impacts the success or failure of our efforts. These guidelines, if constructed with the benefit of theoretical foundations and thoughtfully articulated, are more effective than simple checklists of helpful hints about what to do and what not to do, as the latter are rather inadequate to address the complex tasks ahead for leaders in this field. Black (2003), for example, offers a useful set of provocative questions intended for institutional leaders and decision makers to use in assessing their respective organizations to guide their efforts at institutional change, not only in higher education but in other contexts as well.

While the most common mode of assessing progress in the development of a body of knowledge in an area of study is the usual review of the literature, other activities related to distance education leadership yields some useful information that can compensate for the limited corpus of written work thus far on the subject. For example, academic programs, symposia, workshops, summer institutes, and other professional development activities, while not necessarily focused on leadership, can contribute to greater awareness and understanding of this area of practice. A number of institutions now offer certificate and graduate level programs of study with curricula in distance education, including courses specifically designed to prepare leaders for the field (e.g., Master of Distance Education, University of Maryland University College; certificate programs offered by University of Wisconsin, Madison). Recently, this author contributed to a leadership institute for distance education managers at community colleges, a promising sign of increased recognition that this area warrants more attention.

It is interesting to speculate on what impact such academic programs might eventually have in creating a distinct body of work that offers a more theoretical approach regarding leadership, rather than the prevailing emphasis on practical applications of administrative techniques. Preparing candidates for careers specifically in distance education through professional education programs has potentially significant implications as, for the first time, the field will acquire a new generation of individuals in leadership roles who did not come up through the ranks during a period when the field was just emerging as a recognizable and viable area of professional practice. In addition to introducing new leadership styles and strategies in their chosen field, this cohort presumably will contribute important new theoretical perspectives as they develop into mature and reflective practitioners and scholars.

Having entered a new millennium in which the promise of ever advancing technologies is likely to present new challenges as well as opportunities, it is tempting to ask if there is perhaps a leadership style that is especially appropriate for distance education. While it may be too bold to suggest a single best approach, it may be useful to identify those situations where distance education leaders are most likely to find themselves, and consider strategic perspectives that might be most compatible and productive in those settings. These include collaborative partnerships such as alliance building with for-profit companies; meta-university arrangements, where networking structures make parochial interests a handicap; new markets requiring a global view beyond one's immediate environs; free-standing virtual entities utilizing asynchronous formats; and more exclusively online delivery systems rather than so-called hybrid arrangements.. These would seem to be a few venues in which there will be need for high performing leaders.

THE TRANSFORMATIVE PROCESS

The notion of transformative leadership, advocated by Bennis and Nanus (1985), among others, is a particularly compelling model for distance education leaders today. This is so because organizational practices long entrenched in educational entities urgently require reshaping to adapt to environmental changes, most notably the emergence of a worldwide market for students, but also an exponential increase in potential competitors for those students. Transformational leaders in education must be capable of helping stakeholders (e.g., administrators, faculty, students, trustees), recognize that there are obvious benefits in doing business in new ways, and that they can no longer afford the luxury of adopting cautious modifications in teaching and learning in an incremental fashion, which academics are so accustomed and comfortable in doing. Irlbeck (2002), Portugal (2006), among others, have argued that the transformational leadership approach is especially effective for distance education leaders. To be sure, there are no facile formulae that can be matched with particular settings that will ensure infallible leadership performance; ultimately, a sense of vision, resoluteness, and the ability to articulate ideas and goals are at the very least, required to succeed.

Advocates and initiators of distance education should no longer be seen, nor view themselves, as mavericks on the fringes of their institutions, but rather as contributors who can play a key role in bringing their institutions to the next stage of development. This new status among those responsible for "alternative" programs is now more common, as institutional decision makers become more aware, often with some alarm, that they may not be as relevant and responsive as their competition is to the demands of diverse new market segments seeking easier access to learning opportunities. Distance educators can capitalize on their institution's growing need to remain competitive in a broader arena, by demonstrating how new delivery systems, once relegated to the margins, can now be central to an institution's strategic planning for success and, in some cases, even survival. And while some might object to the notion of appealing to an organization's self-interest as a means of advancing distance education, the fact is that an innovative new idea very often succeeds, not because it is noble, but because it can serve a valuable purpose, for the provider as well as the user.

Leaders must create conditions conducive to energy, initiative, and innovation in their particular milieu, and bring others along, both above and below them in the organizational hierarchy. This requires, in addition to transformational leadership, what

Hersey, Johnson, and Blanchard (2001) call "situational" leadership, with its ability to diagnose the organization at that moment and determine its stakeholders' readiness for moving in a new direction. In fusing these two approaches, the leader diagnoses the unique situation in the immediate environment, and then transforms it as far along the change continuum as necessary, through a collaborative style. In this way, a climate less resistant to and more receptive toward distance education is created, as the setting and those within it undergo a transition, and are ultimately transformed.

Since few distance educators have the opportunity to create entirely new free-standing entities exclusively designed for online or other delivery systems, but rather labor within institutions positioned somewhere along the continuum between conventional and alternative structures, most eventually face the conundrum of whether or not to promote the notion of a central unit to coordinate distance education activities, and to foster new initiatives. One argument is that, in the absence of a focal point for such endeavors, individual faculty will likely tinker indefinitely and inefficiently on their own with a variety of instructional technology options intended to augment their classroom-based courses, but this approach will not ultimately result in a system-wide adoption of distance education in any comprehensive and cost-effective manner. And those institutions that do incorporate small-scale distance education initiatives, but contract out many specialized functions that allow them to retain their existing infrastructure, are often suspect because they can conveniently tout their involvement in distance education without any real institutional shift in its direction.

Another view is that this incremental process of individual initiatives becoming increasingly prevalent within an institution is that it will eventually lead to a critical mass of participants that ultimately creates the demand for more institutional commitment and support. Proponents of this strategy maintain that it is the pattern that typifies most institutions' progression toward distance education today, and that premature administratively-driven initiatives will only generate further faculty resistance and impede any prospects for longer term change. Bernath (1996) provides interesting insights into this dilemma, citing various European models to illustrate the positive and negative forces at play when attempting to integrate distance education into conventional universities. For opinion leaders in distance education, this particular issue can be one of the most critical, and their insights and advice on the best option will test their credibility and influence within their organizations.

To succeed in any of these contexts, a macro view is critical. Distance education leaders cannot afford to be overly preoccupied with nurturing their own programs and providing the focus for just their own initiatives. They must also insinuate themselves into the academic mainstream and the inner circle of decision makers responsible for considering options for bringing the entire organization to a new place. Bass (1985) advocates a holistic and interdisciplinary approach to leadership to achieve truly transformational change. Yet, many distance education initiatives, even successful ones, are developed largely in isolation, and so remain an anomaly within the broader institutional setting. To achieve their more parochial goals, such leaders utilize a transactional style to gain support, or at least to minimize resistance, rather than attempt a more ambitious collaborative agenda, such as expanding an innovation to possibly affect wider transformational change. Distance educators should no longer see themselves as protectors and survivors of isolated programs for which they have labored mightily, but rather as valued strategic partners who can enable the larger institution, often long seen a obstructionists, to catch up with them and emulate their practices and successes. In short, distance education managers must see themselves, and be seen, as educational leaders who facilitate the articulation, development, implementation, and stewardship of a vision of teaching and learning that is shared and supported by the wider academic community.

But leaders must disabuse themselves of the idea that their programs, however more widely accepted and adopted within their institutions than in the past, are now seen as more legitimate (i.e., equivalent to classroom-based instruction). It is more likely that, in most instances, these alternative delivery methods are now more widely recognized as effective means of capturing a larger market share of prospective new consumers to generate additional revenues. Distance education activists can be convincing advocates because colleges and universities, as in the past, must still plan their future in a continuing context of uncertainty. Since much of that uncertainty in this era has been brought about by the rapid emergence of instructional technology, this phenomenon positions experienced open learning practitioners to be more influential in shaping a strategic agenda for the digital decades ahead than was usually the case in the past.

Much of higher education is still characterized by "Old Millennium" thinking that has functioned for a long time in an old economy (e.g., decisions regarding the number of sections required for a particular course made on the basis of optimizing faculty workloads). In the new economy, where information is the product to be delivered to a broader market in less time and at lower cost, distance education activists must help their organizations ask the right questions and to see that institutions can thrive if they are willing to cultivate an appropriate niche through "New Millennium" thinking.

The challenges facing higher education, and even its most experienced leaders, are formidable, especially when organizations remain stubbornly resistant to change, even when exciting opportunities present themselves (e.g., despite online access to much of the world's lucrative foreign student market, most universities remain oblivious or uninterested, except perhaps for the usual semester abroad program with modest numbers). If their institutions remain unresponsive, distance education planners must diligently seek opportunities to convey a sense of urgency that what they are currently doing (perhaps somewhat unnoticed, yet serving a growing proportion of overall enrollments), represents a model for replication elsewhere if further institutional growth and success is to be realized. But this requires that past and recent successes be documented and disseminated. By doing so, distance education can now, more convincingly than ever before, be cast as an activity to be emulated elsewhere in the organization. This is already happening in the area of instructional design, where many faculty may be unaware of just how much learning from a distance is taking place through their own institution, but are nonetheless eager to acquire new technology tools and training to augment their own classroom-based courses In an earlier era, distance educators typically assumed a warrior mentality to advance their cause; today, they can be more effective as brokers facilitating the expansion or replication of programs and services they had to forcefully advocated for in more contentious times.

Are there particular leadership roles that are more appropriate than others, and are there any "best practices" for leading distance education initiatives and activities? Are certain roles exercised by the previous generation of leaders less relevant now? Perhaps less critical in the repertoire of today's leaders are the roles of advocate, reformer and technician that occupied so much time in the past. Too often, those presiding in decision-making forums engage in deliberations long on technological options, but bereft of fundamental pedagogical issues. The distance education leader, whatever other roles he or she may assume, must always maintain the essential role of educator. This is not to suggest, however, that the distance education leader need not be attentive to the technological side of the enterprise. Indeed, keen attention to the medium is critical, but as Neil Postman (1996) so insightfully points out, it is not so much knowledge of how technology works, as it is how technology impacts its users. Every new technological innovation applied to education at a distance changes things. These changes may be in the intellectual, social, political, economic, or ecological domain, and the effective leader cannot afford to be ignorant of the advantages and also the possible disadvantages of what innovative technology engenders.

DISRUPTION OR INNOVATION?

Clayton Christensen, in his influential work on innovation and change, points out the irony of how many successful organization, headed by effective leaders, are often the most resistant to change simply because they are convinced they already represent the avant-garde element within their arena, having boldly introduced innovative initiatives before others did, leading to profit, prestige and other benefits. If so, what then is the incentive or rationale for contemplating any further change? Christensen refers to this as "the innovator's dilemma" (1997). His notion of disruptive technology is instructive, particularly within the context of the education sector, specifically in higher education, best evidenced in its response to the Internet and the resulting consequence of making teaching and learning possible at anytime and anyplace. Not surprisingly, he points out that the Internet is a technology that has fostered disruption in many organizations, including higher education, with its classroom and campus-based instruction representing established technology, vs. online education, enabled by more innovative technologies. As this is the realm in which nearly every distance education leader functions, they would do well to understand what we might label the dynamics of disruption.

Christensen makes the distinction between disruptive innovation and sustaining innovation. Introducing any authentic innovation is likely disruptive, and leadership's ultimate challenge is to institutionalize it to become a sustaining innovation. Even leading organizations are vulnerable to failure when confronted with disruptive changes in technology or other innovations. Well-managed organizations may fail because they attempt to respond to new technology to satisfy new markets, but lose their position of strength with existing markets. Accepted principles of good management are defined by specific circumstances and thus, seemingly strategic decisions can be right or wrong. This is the innovator's dilemma. Logical decisions critical to success can be the same ones that cause loss of leadership position against competition. Sustaining technologies can ultimately foster improved performance, but are often disruptive initially.

Most innovative challenges are sustaining in nature, but managers of organizations addressing them must recognize what practices are effective in which situations under what conditions, in order to avoid these challenges becoming too disruptive. Such issues as market demand, availability of resources, appropriate technology, etc., can all confound the choices that need to be made. When faced with potentially disrupting technology, mainstream organizations cannot be expected to freely allocate the resources to carve out a competitive position, especially in a small, emerging market. If a university structure is tailored to compete in a certain market (e.g., full-time residential students who are recent high school graduates), it is difficult to be competitive in a totally different one, especially if new infrastructure and marketing is needed to reach a new clientele (e.g., part-time, working, adult learners needing convenient and flexible course scheduling). Christensen argues that creating a different organization is the only way to achieve profit and success with disruptive technology. If a new technology resource (e.g., online courses) appears incompatible with the needs of an institution's mainstream clientele, then that alternative option is likely to be perceived as a threat rather than an opportunity. A potentially viable approach in this instance might be to identify a new market and create a new infrastructure, but organization and their leaders who are successful with the current system, have little tolerance for failure, and so the prospective risk is unpalatable. For this reason alone, many education providers eschew opportunities to implement even relatively modest distance education initiatives. Such are the complex dilemmas that distance education leaders must weigh and resolve, then execute a viable and sustainable plan.

Christensen and Eyring (2011) have more recently applied his notion of disruptive technology specifically on higher education, especially as competition from the for-profit higher education sector has created a new sense of urgency. He notes that online learning technologies can both benefit and disrupt traditional institutions. He notes the irony in the fact that, although the college experience can be transformative for so many people, the learning organization is inherently resistant to transforming itself. Though difficult to abandon a model that has changed little in the past 150 years, if this sector now embraces learning innovations made possible by new technology, he contends that online learning can be truly transformative and create opportunities for universities to not only serve more students, but also lead the country to greater prosperity.

Converting a disruptive innovation to a sustaining one entails significant adaptation, and leadership is the crucial ingredient. Managing a sustaining innovation that the system has become acclimated to is relatively easy, compared to initiating, or even exploring, alluring alternatives. Because disruptive technologies typically require time between investing in them and profiting from them, aside from the distinct possibility that success may never be realized, conventional leaders can easily conjure up numerous arguments for maintaining the status quo. The conflicting demands of disruptive and sustaining technologies requires leaders with the capacity to resolve those tensions, and create a context and culture in which, and by which, the differing challenges faced by innovators become less of a dilemma, and more of a transformative environment for productive and meaningful change.

CONCLUSIONS

Clearly, impressive gains have been made by distance educators and leaders in promulgating online teaching and learning. And so, in the final analysis, can we state with any confidence, that innovative technology has moved from being a disruptive force to a sustaining presence, and that the academy has been truly transformed? Perhaps such an assertion is premature, at least in a broader context, but certainly we can affirm that a generation of distance education leaders has achieved significant change in many settings, and has created favorable conditions for further progress. Hanna (2007) states that is although dramatic changes are occurring in higher education, many driven by distance education, it remains unclear whether transformational change is truly taking place in this sector. Though we can certainly tout impressive advances, are we perhaps witnessing a veneer of instructional technology being overlain on conventional systems and practices that ultimately produces little or no fundamental change? This issue persists as a paramount challenge for distance education leaders to the present day.

What has been referred to as the "institutionalization" of online learning simply will not occur without appropriate institutional leadership. And while decision makers need not be experts in this field, they must at least recognize the potential of online education for their institutions and be willing to create the conditions for innovation in this direction. This will best happen if they manifest transformative leadership. Yet, typically, campus leaders ascend to senior roles via a largely transactional style that is focused more on building relationships within the existing environment than on promoting bold action that transforms their institution and brings it to a new place. If there is any area of engagement that truly requires transformative leadership, it is in the advancement of online education, not to supplant face-to-face instruction but rather to augment conventional approaches.

Many universities thrive on preserving traditional practices, rather than on fostering technology-enhanced pedagogy. When they do recognize that such initiatives are unlikely to threaten their legacy after all, they too often lack any viable mechanisms that can contribute to planned systematic change. And entering the brave new world of distance education is not so much about selecting appropriate technology; rather, it is about managing change. This change process requires that leaders articulate and arrive at an inspirational and doable mission for their organization, that they empower and energize followers to implement that mission, that they be aware of their various stakeholders' values and needs, that they integrate congruent values into the organizational culture, and that they press their institution to improve continuously with minimum disruption and resistance.

For meaningful transformation to ultimately occur, both veteran and emerging leaders must be prepared for the roles we have described. They must rely not only on instinct or anecdotes derived from past experience, but also from new insights informed by valid data. They must devote greater attention to leadership as a discreet area of study and practice for the important work ahead. The continuing contribution of distance educators demands a clear vision of where we want to go and where we want to lead others.

REFERENCES

Bass, B. (1985). *Leadership and performance beyond expectations.* New York: The Free Press.

Beaudoin, M. (Guest Ed.). (1998). Interview: Speaking personally with Roy McTarnaghan. The American *Journal of Distance Education, 12*(2), 73–78.

Beaudoin, M. (2004). *Reflections on research, faculty and leadership in distance education.* Oldenburg, Germany: Oldenburg University Press.

Bennis, W., & Nanus, B. (1985). *Leaders: The strategies for taking charge.* New York: Harper and Row.

Bernath, U. (1996). Distance education in mainstream higher education: A strategic issue at conventional universities. In M. Thompson (Ed.), *Internationalism in distance education: A vision for higher education.* (ACSDE Research Monograph No. 10, pp. 45–51). University Park: The Pennsylvania State University.

Black, L. (2003). *Adult and distance education management: An Aaplication of the metaphor "organizations as organisms"* Retrieved January 7, 2012, from http://www.westga.edu/%7Edistance/ojdla/winter64/black64.htm

Burge, E. (Ed.). (2007). *Flexible higher education-reflections from expert experience*. New York: Open University Press.

Christensen, C. (1997). *The innovator's dilemma: When new technologies cause great firms to fail*. Cambridge, MA: Harvard Business School Press.

Christensen, C., & Eyring, H. (2011). *The innovative university: Changing the DNA of higher education from the inside out*. San Francisco: Jossey-Bass.

Duning, B. (1990). The literature of management. In M. Moore (Ed.), *Contemporary issues in American distance education* (pp. 30–43). Oxford, UK: Pergamon Press.

Frederickson, D. (2005). *A traditional institution moves to acknowledge its dual-track: Mainstreaming distributed/distance learning in one institution?* Retrieved 7 January, 2012, from http://library.athabascau.ca/mais-project/DarleneFrederickson.pdf

Fullan, M. (2001). *Leading in a culture of change*. San Francisco: Jossey-Bass.

Hall, J. W. (1998). Leadership in accreditation and networked learning. *The American Journal of Distance Education, 12*(2), 5–15.

Hanna, D. (2007). Organizational change in higher distance education. In M. Moore (Ed.), *Handbook of distance education* (pp. 501–514). Mahwah, NJ: Erlbaum.

Hanna, D., & Latchem, C. (2001). *Leadership and management in open and flexible learning*. London: Kogan Page.

Hersey, P., Johnson, D., & Blanchard, K. (2001). *Management of organizational behavior: Leading human resources*. Englewood Cliffs, NJ: Prentice Hall.

Irlbeck, S. (2002, October). Leadership and Distance Education in Higher Education: A US perspective. *The international Review of Research in Open and Distance Learning, 3*(2). Retrieved from http://www.irrodl.org/index.php/irrodl/article/view/91/170

Kotter, J. (1996). *Leading change*. Boston. Harvard Business School Press.

McCarthy, S., & Samors, R. (2009). Online learning as a strategic asset, Vol. 1: A resource for campus leaders. Washington DC: Association of Public and Land-Grant Universities. Retrieved from http://www.aplu.org/NetCommunity/Document.Doc?id=1877

Moore, M., & Kearsley, G. (2012). *Distance education: A systems view of online learning* (3rd ed.). Belmont, CA: Wadsworth.

New England Association of Schools and Colleges, Commission on Institutions of Higher Education. (1998). *Policy for the accreditation of academic degree and certificate programs offered through distance education*. Bedford, MA: Author.

Peters, O. (1994). *Otto Peters on distance education—The industrialization of teaching and learning* (D. Keegan, Ed.). London: Routledge.

Portugal, L. (2006, Summer). Emerging leadership roles in distance education: Current state of affairs and forecasting future trends. *Online Journal of Distance Learning, 4*(3). Retrieved from http://www.westga.edu/~distance/ojdla/fall93/portugal93.htm

Postman, N. (1996). *The ends of education*. New York: Vintage Books.

Research into Online Distance Education and E-Learning Making the Difference. (2006). EDEN research workshop, Castelldefels, Spain. Retrieved from http://www. secretariat @ eden-online.org

Schon, D. (1983). *The reflective practitioner: How professionals think in action*. London: Temple Smith.

Seaman, J (2009). *Online learning as a strategic asset, Vol. 2: The paradox of faculty voices*. Washington DC: Association of Public and Land-Grant Universities. http://www.aplu.org/NetCommunity/Document.Doc?id=1879

Simerly, R. G. (1987). *Strategic planning and leadership in continuing education*. San Francisco: Jossey-Bass.

Supporting the Learner in Distance Education and E-Learning. (2004). EDEN research workshop, Carl von Ossietzky University of Oldenburg, Oldenburg, Germany. Retrieved from http://www. secretariat @ eden-online.org

Tipple, R. (2010, Spring). Effective leadership of adjunct online faculty. *Online Journal of Distance Learning Administration, 13*(1). Retrieved from http://www.westga.edu/~distance/ojdla/summer06/tipplel93.htm

User Generated Content Assessment in Learning — Enhancing Transparency and Quality of Peer Production. (2010). EDEN research workshop, Budapest University of Technology and Economics. Budapest, Hungary. Retrieved from http://www. secretariat @ eden-online.org

30

ACCREDITATION

Assuring Quality and Fostering Improvement[1]

PATRICIA M. O'BRIEN

INTRODUCTION

This chapter describes the role of accreditation in assuring the quality of distance education offered by colleges and universities. The chapter focuses primarily on the efforts of the regional accrediting associations in the United States, although the work of specialized accreditors is also acknowledged. Following a brief historical overview of accreditation, the chapter describes the early work of the Distance Education and Training Council (DETC) to assess distance education programs, then goes on to review how the regional associations developed an approach to the review of distance education and to describe the current practice of the regional associations. The chapter concludes with a few remarks about the impact of federal regulations on accreditors' review of distance education.

Although this chapter focuses exclusively on accreditation in the United States, quality assurance agencies around the world are also encompassing distance education within their purview. For example, Chapter B3 of the U.K. Quality Code for Higher Education used by the British Quality Assurance Agency (QAA) includes "Indicators of Sound Practice" for "flexible and distributed learning." More details can be found at: http://www.qaa.ac.uk/Publications/InformationAndGuidance/Documents/Quality %20Code%20-%20Chapter%20B3.pdf

HISTORICAL BACKGROUND

Unlike most other countries in the world, the United States has never had a Ministry of Higher Education directly regulating the quality of its postsecondary institutions of learning; such control is not among the powers granted to the federal government by the U.S. Constitution. Instead, in order to operate legally, academic institutions must, like other businesses, be licensed by one of the 50 states, each of which sets individual rules governing entities incorporated within its borders. For the most part, such rules describe the minimal inputs necessary for initiating an institution of higher education rather than set any criteria for the effectiveness of their educational outcomes. Because of the variety of these requirements, private accreditation associations, have, for more than 100 years, provided the primary mechanism for assuring employers, governments, and, most importantly, students and their families, that degree-granting institutions are offering education at an acceptable level of quality (Brittingham, 2009). As Brittingham notes, accreditation serves two purposes: to evaluate current practice and provide public assurance of the quality of higher education and to foster ongoing improvement of accredited colleges and universities. Accreditation certifies that an institution of higher education (a) has clearly defined purposes appropriate to an institution of higher learning, (b) has assembled and organized those resources necessary to achieve its purposes, (c) demonstrates through evidence that it is achieving its purposes, and (d) has the ability to continue to achieve its purposes.

There are three types of accrediting associations in the United States:

1. Programmatic or specialized associations that accredit programs of study; examples include the Association to Advance Collegiate Schools of Business (AACSB) and National Council for Accreditation of Teacher Education (NCATE);
2. National associations that accredit faith-based or career-focused institutions; examples include Association for Biblical Higher Education (ABHE) and Accrediting Council for Independent Colleges and Schools (ACICS);
3. Regional associations that accredit degree-granting colleges and universities.

The most widely accepted and respected of the accrediting bodies in the United States are the following six regional associations: (a) the Higher Learning Commission (North Central Association), (b) the Middle States Association of Colleges and Schools, (c) the New England Association of Schools and Colleges, (d) the Northwest Commission on Colleges and Universities, (e) the Southern Association of Schools and Colleges, and (f) the Western Association of Schools and Colleges (see http://www.chea.org for detailed information about these associations, including their geographic scope, standards, processes, and personnel). These currently accredit approximately 3,500 degree-granting institutions of higher education. The range of institutions encompasses public and independent institutions (both not-for-profit and for-profit); research universities and community technical colleges; secular and religious schools; those with exclusively on-site or on-line offerings.

The specific regional association by which an institution is recognized is generally determined by the geographic location in which it is chartered, the 50 states having been divided up for historical reasons into six regions. In some instances, these correspond with common usage (e.g., the New England Association accredits institutions in the six New England States) but in others instances, they do not (e.g., the Higher Learning Commission accredits institutions in 19 states, ranging from West Virginia to Arizona and North Dakota). By common agreement, a remote campus of an institution accredited by a region other than that in which the remote campus is located conforms to the standards of the region of the home campus. A representative of the accrediting body responsible for the remote campus region may be included on the team which visits the home campus for an accreditation review. Further, five of the regional accrediting associations extend membership (i.e., accreditation) to a growing number of institutions outside the geographical borders of the United States, both public and private.

Although nongovernmental in nature, the regional associations—and some national associations—are linked to the federal government through a process called "recognition" by the United States Department of Education (USDOE). Recognition by the USDOE establishes the agency as a reliable authority on the quality of education offered by the institutions it accredits and enables students at those institutions to participate in Title IV federal financial aid programs. To maintain recognition, agencies undergo a review every five years. (For more about federal recognition, see http://www2.ed.gov/admins/finaid/accred/index.html).

The Council for Higher Education Accreditation (CHEA), the umbrella organizations for institutional and programmatic accreditation, also provides a recognition function for accrediting agencies. Recognition by CHEA certifies that the agency meets the standards for academic quality, improvement, and accountability. (For more about CHEA recognition, see http://www.chea.org). Recognition of an accrediting agency by the USDOE and/or CHEA provides assurance of the trustworthiness of the accreditation process—in other words, that the agency is not an "accreditation mill"—and accreditation of an institution by a recognized association provides assurance of the quality of education offered by the institution_in other words, that it is not a "degree mill" (CHEA, 2012).

THE DISTANCE EDUCATION AND TRAINING COUNCIL

In addition to the degree-granting institutions served by the regional accrediting associations, however there are non-traditional institutions that grant programs through modalities other than face-to-face education. At the start of the 20th century, these were largely correspondence schools and, as the number of such schools and programs grew, so did the need to find effective mechanisms through which to assure the quality of the education offered through such programs. In 1926, owing to the proliferation of various entities that were offering credentials to students who completed a course of study while not physically at the institution but through the mail, the Distance Education and Training Council (DETC; http://www.detc.org) was formed under the name National Home Study Council.

DETC describes itself as a "voluntary association of correspondence schools" that is "dedicated to fostering quality assurance, protection of the rights of students and institutional self-improvement through voluntary accreditation via peer evaluation" (DETC, 2011, p. 9). In 1955, the DETC established an independent accrediting commission, which achieved recognition by the USDOE four years later. DETC is also currently recognized by the Council for Higher Education Accreditation (CHEA), and since 1973 had been continuously recognized by CHEA's predecessors, the National Commission on Accreditation, the council on Postsecondary Accreditation, and the Commission on Recognition of Postsecondary Accreditation. DETC accredits over 100 institutions, some of which offer degrees, others of which offer short-term programs via distance education.

Recognition of DETC as an accrediting body made it possible for consumers to have some assurance as to the legitimacy of certain correspondence schools. However, despite its recognition by the U.S. Department of Education and CHEA and its predecessors, DETC is still not able to assure students enrolled in its member programs and institutions that they will have their credentials recognized by certain employers or governments (municipal, state, or national) or be able to transfer their credits to regionally accredited institutions. Ultimately, decisions about the transfer of credit are left to the receiving institution. Decisions by regionally accredited colleges and universities not to accept credits from DETC-accredit programs reflect, to some extent, the fact that although certain DETC programs may offer advanced academic degrees, others are postsecondary, but not necessarily appropriate, to higher education. Indeed, although the Council currently accredits more than 60 degree-granting distance programs, other institutions among its membership offer programs lasting only a few weeks.

REVIEW OF DISTANCE EDUCATION BY THE REGIONAL ACCREDITING ASSOCIATIONS

Technically, any distance education offered by an institution is included in its regional accreditation, since accreditation is never partial, and if an institution is accredited, all of its offerings are included in that accreditation. Nevertheless, for the first three fourths of the 20th century, the regional accrediting associations concentrated almost exclusively on quality control of the site-based education offered by their members. By the end of the 20th century, however, the regional accrediting associations and their commissions on higher education recognized that there was a need for them, at a minimum, to provide guidelines in the area of distance education. They acted, first individually and then as a unified group, to establish regulations that would allow their members to include distance education offerings within their overall institutional accreditation.

Part of the impetus for action by the regional associations came from federal regulations. As noted above, the regional accrediting associations are recognized by the U.S. Department of Education. The criteria for recognition are established as part of the reauthorization of the Higher Education Opportunity Act, and those criteria include responsibilities for accrediting agencies to assure the quality of programming offered through distance education. In the regulations, distance education programs are identified as one of the substantive changes accreditors must review before such programs are offered for the first time. The regulations also stipulate distance education must be reviewed at the time of the institution's comprehensive evaluation for re-accreditation.

As early as 1986, the Higher Learning Commission (then known as the North Central Association of Schools and Colleges), the largest of the regional associations, had evaluated and granted membership to what was then known as National Technological University, which offered degrees in engineering to working professionals through courses designed and delivered by full-time faculty from regionally accredited institutions whose engineering programs were accredited by the American Board of Engineering Technology (ABET).[2] In so doing, the Higher Learning Commission established the importance of focusing on the effectiveness with which an entity delivers education rather than on the physical location at which the credits are earned.

Consequently, when the number and variety of courses, programs, and complete degrees offered through electronically mediated technology began to proliferate in the last decade of the 20th century, the regional accrediting associations had experience and precedent to draw on as they considered the ways in which such offerings conformed to the specific standards of the relevant accrediting association. That is, even without the impetus provided by the federal recognition process, the six regional associations had begun to consider how they could expand and explicate their standards in order to include such offerings within the accreditation of their member institutions.

What was being confronted reflected the changes in the academy brought about by distance education, which has transformed the ways in which professors teach, students learn, and researchers collaborate (Christensen, Horn, Caldera, & Soares, 2011). Amidst such changes, it is not at all surprising that the regional accrediting associations faced and wrestled with the question of whether regionalism, although it had served the country so well and for so long, was now, in fact, obsolete, as argued most recently by Dickeson (2006). It quickly became evident that because new distance learning providers were in a position to seek a charter, and therefore accreditation, from more than one association, it would be necessary to ensure that accreditation standards made it impossible, or at least difficult for institutions to engage in accreditation shopping—that is, looking for the easiest association by which to be accredited.

By the end of the 20th century, on-line learning had become ubiquitous in higher education, and growth in distance education continues into the 21st century. The National Center for Education Statistics reported that in 1995, distance education courses—and in some cases, whole programs (The National Center for Education Statistics, 2009)—were being offered by more than a third of all two-year and four-year institutions. Five years later, that percentage jumped to 56%, and, by 2006, two-thirds of postsecondary institutions (66%) in the United States were offering distance education courses and/or programs. Eduventures, a research and consulting company, has tracked the dramatic growth in on-line enrollments from just under 7,000 in 1995 to 165,370 in 2000, to almost a million (991,211) in 2005, to an estimated 2.5 million in 2010. Eduventures predicts that by 2015, on-line enrollments will reach close to 3.5 million (Garrett, 2009).

So, although even today some institutions are still offering programs exclusively through a "traditional" approach to learning, the majority of institutions are delivering at least some portion of their educational program through the on-line modality. As institutions began to institute their extended menu of distance education offerings, they wanted the assurance of external quality control mechanisms even as they were understandably loath to add yet another specialized accrediting association to those already active on their campuses. A number of organizations to which these institutions also belonged and which were interested in preserving the quality of higher education offerings developed sets of rules and guidelines to assist members in their activities. Some, like the Western Interstate Commission on Higher Education (WICHE), established a separate body—for example, such programs as the Western Cooperative for Educational Telecommunication—devoted to the development of guiding principles and consultation on on-line instruction (http://wcet.wiche.org). Others, however, such as the American Council on Education, developed suggested procedures as just one of the many services they offered their members.

In addition, beginning in the last decade of the 20th century, institutions sought guidance from their regional accrediting associations about quality control of such offerings. In response to members' needs and to the requirements of federal regulations, the regional associations developed policies to address distance education and modified their standards to reflect the "new" instructional modalities.

ADAPTING REGIONAL ACCREDITATION STANDARDS TO INCORPORATE DISTANCE EDUCATION

The regional accrediting associations decided they could expand their existing standards to include distance education within institutional accreditation for two main reasons. First, the existing standards emphasized educational outcomes and required that institutions command the resources (both human and other) for their effective achievement. Indeed, the assessment of educational outcomes, which had long been established as an indicator of institutional quality, was receiving increased attention as higher education, more expensive than ever, found itself increasingly consumer- and market-driven. In adjusting to that reality, the regional associations had already adopted standards of appropriate flexibility to evaluate entities where they could focus more on the quality of those who designed and delivered the courses than on their employment status (full-, part-time, or adjunct).

Second, in modifying standards to encompass distance education, the regional associations were following the long tradition of adapting to changing social needs that had allowed them over time to include within their membership community colleges, teachers colleges, and single-purpose graduate programs, all of which had originally been excluded from the associations.

In examining the standards already applied to site-based institutions, the accreditors recognized that they would have to make some adaptations to accommodate the particular necessities of distance education. For example, although accrediting standards require institutions to admit those students who can benefit from the programs offered, they do allow an institution to have an open admission policy if it supplies appropriate remediation for those who need help in order to work at the collegiate level. For distance education, this requirement had to be extended to include the technological expertise needed by the student in order to complete a program. The requirements for library and information resource personnel likewise had to be expanded to mandate student access to a help desk.

In addition to formulating standards for the review of distance education offerings, the regional associations were aware that they also had to carefully consider the identification and training of those would who implement such regulations, both as on-site visitors and as members of their central decision-making bodies. Although the cohort from whom they drew was at first quite limited, none now has any problem in finding sufficient numbers of appropriately experienced people to review their standards, staff their visiting teams, and participate on their central commissions. And, indeed, in any given year, more than half of teams representing regional accrediting associations visited institutions that included distance learning among their offerings.

THE MOVE FROM STRICT REGIONALISM TO NATIONAL COOPERATION

The regional associations, however, were slowly coming to understand that even within the constraints of regionalism, certain national standards had to be agreed upon. In discussing and determining the standards they adopted to measure quality in distance education programs, they entered into fairly new territory, for never before had these accrediting associations been willing to yield their regional sovereignty to achieve a nationwide consensus. As a group, the regional associations had already subscribed to the WICHE guidelines as they then were, and several of the associations had adopted policies governing their own membership. Others were well along in adopting such standards before 1993, when it became clear that what was needed was a joint statement of expectations to which any institution seeking regional accreditation would have to conform. A task force was therefore formed, composed of staff representatives of the six regional associations, with an observer from CHEA, their umbrella organization. Before adopting encompassing standards, its first task was to review all existing relevant documents from both the regional accreditors and other organizations. Reviewing documents from outside organizations, the task force concluded that, although suitable as a starting point for their work, the existing guidelines were too broad for use by the regional associations, as those guidelines applied equally to degree-granting and non-degree-granting programs. The task force eventually suggested a set of expanded criteria, which, after consideration by the members of each association, were accepted with minor linguistic changes by the commissions.

Although the individual accrediting associations ascribed to the general principles contained in the joint guidelines, the actual wording adopted by each reflected the language and approach characteristic of the individual association. The issue of institutions without a regional base became prominent with the establishment and eventual accreditation in 2003 of Western Governors University, which serves students in 19 states that encompass four of the six accrediting regions. In response to its founding, a separate Interregional Accrediting Committee, comprising representatives from those four regional accrediting associations (Northwest, Higher Learning Commission, WASC-Senior, and WASC-Junior) was established to conduct the review for initial accreditation. Subsequent evaluations for reaccreditation have been undertaken by the Northwest Commission on Colleges and Universities, which is considered to be the University's "home" accrediting body because the main offices of Western Governors University are located in Utah, which falls under the review of the that commission.

By 2000, as the number and complexity of distance education programs continued to increase, the regional commissions realized that they had to rewrite their policy yet again to develop one document to which all could ascribe without modification. In August, 2000, they published a draft of the "Statement of Regional Accrediting Commissions on the Evaluation of Electronically Offered Degrees and Certificate Programs." Renamed "The Statement of Commitment by the Regional Accrediting Commissions for the Evaluation of Electronically Offered Degree and Certificate Programs," http://www.sacscoc.org/pdf/commadap.pdf), this document placed technologically mediated instruction squarely within the context of regional accreditation and marked the first time the regional commissions jointly issued a set of regulations rather than developing guidelines to be restated in terms suitable for each region. The statement outlined the approach of the regional associations to quality assurance and improvement of distance education, an approach expressed as a set of commitments to: the traditions, principles, and values of regional accreditation; to cooperation, consistency, and collaboration; and to supporting good practice.

The Statement of Commitment was supplemented by a statement of "Best Practices for Electronically Offered Degree and Certificate Programs." These practices were divided into five separate components, each of which addressed a particular area of institutional activity relevant to distance education:

1. Institutional Context and Commitment
2. Curriculum and Instruction
3. Faculty Support
4. Student Support
5. Evaluation and Assessment

Each component began with a general statement followed by individual numbered paragraphs addressing specific matters describing those elements essential to quality distance education programming. Those, in turn, were followed by protocols in the form of questions designed to assist institutions and evaluators in determining the existence of those elements.

For example, the statement on Curriculum and Instruction read: "Methods change, but standards of quality endure. The important issues are not technical but curriculum-driven and pedagogical. Decisions about such matters are made by qualified professionals and focus on learning outcomes for an increasingly diverse student population." The first "essential element" articulated for Curriculum and Instruction was: "As with all curriculum development and review, the institution assures that each program of study results in collegiate level learning outcomes appropriate to the rigor and breadth of the degree or certificate awarded by the institution, that the electronically offered degree or certificate program is coherent and complete, and that such programs leading to undergraduate degrees include general education requirements." Questions comprising the protocol for that element included: "Does the program design involve the demonstration of such skills as analysis, comprehension, communication, and effective research?" "Are related instructional materials appropriate and readily accessible to students?"

Each association made its own determination of how to use the Statement of Commitment and Best Practices. Typically, institutions were asked to reference these documents when preparing substantive change reports on distance education and when writing interim reports or self-studies prepared in advance of comprehensive evaluations. The documents were provided to members of evaluation teams visiting institutions that offered programs via distance education and to the Commissions as they made their decisions.

C-RAC GUIDELINES FOR THE EVALUATION OF DISTANCE EDUCATION

Although the Statement of Commitment and Best Practices served the accrediting commissions and their members well, they were seen as very much a work in progress, a set of regulations that might need to be rethought and further developed as new methodologies evolved. In the late 2000s, the Council of Regional Accrediting Commissions (C-RAC) decided the time had come to update the documents guiding their review of distance education.

The new document, which is currently in use, is entitled *Guidelines for the Evaluation of Distance Education (On-line Learning)*. The document is based on a 2006 report prepared by the General Accounting Office, *Evidence of Quality in Distance Education drawn from Interviews with the Accreditation Community* and is available on-line at http://cihe.neasc.org/downloads/Pp90_Guidelines_for_the_Evaluation_of_Distance_Education__On-line_Learning_.pdf

The document comprises nine hallmarks of quality in distance education:

1. On-line learning is appropriate to the institution's mission and purposes.
2. The institution's plans for developing, sustaining and, if appropriate, expanding on-line learning offerings are integrated into its regular planning and evaluation processes.
3. On-line learning is incorporated into the institution's systems of governance and academic oversight.
4. Curricula for the institution's on-line learning offerings re coherent, cohesive, and comparable in academic rigor to programs offered in traditional instructional formats.
5. The institution evaluates the effectiveness of its on-line learning offerings, including the extent to which the on-line learning goals are achieved, and uses the results of its evaluations to enhance the attainment of goals.
6. Faculty responsible for delivering the on-line learning curricula and evaluating the students' success in achieving the online learning goals are appropriately qualified and effectively supported.
7. The institution provides effective student and academic services to support students enrolled in online learning offerings.
8. The institution provides sufficient resources to support and, if appropriate, expand its online learning offerings.
9. The institution assures the integrity of its online learning offerings.

The *Guidelines* also offer examples of the types of evidence institutions might cite to demonstrate fulfillment of the quality hallmarks. For the first hallmark, for example, the institution is asked to demonstrate that its mission statement "explains the role of on-line learning within the range of the institution's programs and services" and that "senior administrators and staff can articulate how on-line learning is consonant with the institution's mission and goals."

Like the Statement of Commitment and Best Practices before them, the *Guidelines* are used by institutions when preparing a report to seek approval when distance education is offered for the first time and when preparing periodic accreditation review reports (e.g., a comprehensive self-study or an interim report), by teams when they conduct accreditation visits, and by the accrediting commissions when reviewing institutional reports.

REVIEW OF DISTANCE EDUCATION BY PROGRAMMATIC ACCREDITORS

In addition to the work of the regional accrediting associations, many of the specialized (programmatic) accreditors also include the review of distance education in their standards, policies, and procedures. The National League for Nursing Accrediting Commission (NLNAC, 2008), for example, has identified the following "critical elements" for the review of distance education:

- Congruence with governing organization mission
- Instructional design and delivery method of the course(s)

- Preparation and competence of the faculty
- Quality and accessibility of the support services
- Accessibility, currency, and relevancy of learning resources
- Currency and appropriateness of the offerings relative to the method of delivery
- Provision for faculty/student and student/student interaction
- Ongoing evaluation of student learning
- Provision for verification of student identity (p. 49)

The Commission on Dental Accreditation of the American Dental Association includes references to on-line programs in its accreditation standards for all types of dental education. Hanlon (2004) reviewed the impact of these standards and their use by evaluators with experience in distance learning.

The standards of the Association to Advance Collegiate Schools of Business (AACSB) include the expectation that institutions offering their programs via distance education will be able to demonstrate "technology support and assistance for students and faculty, security and confidentiality safeguards, accountability for learning, and technology to provide sufficient interactive components for quality education." The association also expects that distance education programs will provide "significant learning interaction opportunities" between faculty and students and acknowledges that the assessment of student learning in on-line programs "may require other metrics and may depend more heavily on demonstration of the learning outcomes." (AACSB, 2011, pp. 29–30).

THE IMPACT OF FEDERAL REGULATIONS ON ACCEDITORS' REVIEW OF DISTANCE EDUCATION

As noted earlier, part of the impetus for the review of distance education by accrediting association came from federal regulations included in the Higher Education Opportunity Act. Around the time the regulations were being developed, Congress completed its latest reauthorization, and the negotiated rulemaking that followed reauthorization resulted in several regulations regarding accreditors' oversight of distance learning. These regulations addressed correspondence education, the content of accreditation standards, training of the evaluators who conduct accreditation reviews, and verification of students' identity. These regulations are available at: http://edocket.access.gpo.gov/2009/pdf/E9-25186.pdf

The 2009 regulations, for the first time, drew a distinction between distance education and correspondence education and included a definition of correspondence education (Part IV, p. 55426). The primary difference between distance and correspondence education has to do with the frequency and nature of the interaction between faculty and students—in the case of correspondence education, interaction is less frequent and is typically initiated by the student. Accreditors are responsible to determine which type of education an institution offers (distance or correspondence) and to assess the quality of the education. The regulations also stipulate that accreditation standards "effectively address the quality of an institution's distance education or correspondence education" (Part IV, p. 55427). There is no requirement that accrediting commissions have separate standards for distance education, but distance education must receive explicit mention in the standards. In response to this regulation, accrediting commissions revised their standards and policies to include correspondence education as well as explicit mention of distance education.

The regulations also include the requirement that accreditors prepare their evaluators to discharge "their responsibilities regarding distance and correspondence education" (Part IV, p. 55427). In response, accrediting commissions modified their training materials and workshops to heighten the attention given to distance education and to introduce the concept of correspondence education.

Finally, the regulations stipulate that accreditors must ensure that institutions have in place effective procedures to verify the identity of distance and correspondence education students—that the student who registers is the same student who participates in, completes, and receives the grade for a distance (or correspondence) education course. Accreditors are also required to verify that institutions make clear in writing that their procedures protect student privacy and notify students at the time of registration or enrollment of any additional costs associated with the verification procedures (Part IV, p. 55427). In response, accrediting commissions revised their standards and/or developed policies to reflect these requirements. In fact, the last of the *Guidelines for the Evaluation of Distance Education (On-line Learning)* includes the requirements concerning verification of student identity.

In 2010, the U.S. Department of Education completed a second round of negotiated rulemaking, which resulted in additional regulations for accreditors; the regulations are available at http://edocket.access.gpo.gov/2010/pdf/2010-26531.pdf. One of these concerns the award of academic credit and includes a definition of a credit hour:

> an amount of work represented in intended learning outcomes and verified by evidence of student achievement that is an institutional established equivalence that reasonably approximates not less than—
>
> One hour of classroom or direct faculty instruction and a minimum of two hours of out of class student work each week for approximately fifteen weeks for one semester or trimester hour of credit, or ten to twelve weeks for one quarter hour of credit, or the equivalent amount of work over a different amount of time. (Part II, p. 66946)

Accreditors are required to verify that institutions' policies concerning the award of credit are consistent with this definition and that the policies are applied in courses offered in all formats and modalities, including distance education. Institutions are expected to provide evidence, through course schedules, course outcomes, and syllabi, that the amount of work required of students is consistent with the definition.

MAINTAINING THE BALANCE BETWEEN COMPLIANCE AND IMPROVEMENT

The requirement that these regulations be incorporated into accreditation standards, policies, and procedures has led to concerns about federal intrusion into the accreditation process (Eaton, 2010). Some are concerned that the increasing number of federal regulations has led to an imbalance between the dual purposes of accreditation—quality assurance and quality improvement. There are concerns that the responsibility of accreditors to assure quality, including compliance with federal regulations, may be eclipsing the value of accreditation as a process through which institutions can foster improvement. Moving forward, it will take the commitment of both institutions and accrediting associations to assure that accreditation does not become simply a bureaucratic exercise but rather remains a vital process of self-regulation and peer review that functions as much to foster improvement as it does to assure quality.

NOTES

1. The author wishes to acknowledge the contributions of Amy Lezberg, the author of this chapter in previous editions of the Handbook of Disatnce Learning and of the 1998 article, "Quality Control in Distance Education: The Role of Regional Accreditation." Her work provided a solid foundation for the current text.
2. In 2005, National Technological University merged with Walden University and became NTU School of Engineering and Applied Science at Walden University. As of 2011, NTU is no longer accepting new applications, and Walden University is teaching out the NTU's programs.

REFERENCES

Association to Advance Collegiate Schools of Business. (2011). *Eligibility procedures and accreditation standards for business education.* Retrieved on February 15, 2012, from http://www.aacsb.edu/accreditation/standards-2011-revisions-jan2011.pdf

Brittingham, B. (2009). Accreditation in the United States: How did we get to where we are? In P. O'Brien (Ed.), *Accreditation: Assuring and enhancing quality* (pp. 7–27). San Francisco, CA: Jossey Bass.

Christensen, C. M., Horn, M. B., Caldera, L. E., & Soares, L. (2011). *Disrupting college: How Disruptive innovation can deliver quality and affordability to postsecondary education.* Washington, DC: Center for American Progress.

Council for Higher Education Accreditation. (2012). *Important questions about accreditation, degree mills, and accreditation mills.* Retrieved on February 15, 2012, from http://www.chea.org/degreemills/default.htm

Dickeson, R. (2006). *The need for accreditation reform.* Retrieved on August 11, 2011, from http://www2.ed.gov/about/bdscomm/list/hiedfuture/reports/dickeson.pdf

Distance Education and Training Council. (2011). *Accreditation handbook.* Retrieved on August 4, 2011, from http://www.detc.org/accreditationhandbook/index.html

Eaton, J. (2010, July 20). Accreditation's accidental transformation. *Inside Higher Education.* Retrieved on October 10, 2011, from http://www.chea.org/pdf/Inside%20Higher%20Ed%20Op-Ed.pdf

Garrett, R. (2009). *Online higher education market update.* Boston: Eduventures Inc.

Hanlon, L. . (2004). Accreditation of distance learning in the field of dentistry. *American Journal of Distance Education, 18*(3), 151–167.

Lezberg, A. (1998). Quality control in distance education: The role of regional accreditation. *American Journal of Distance Education, 12*(2), 26–35.

National Center for Education Statistics. (2009). *Distance education at postsecondary institutions.* Retrieved August 4, 2011, from http://nces.ed.gov/pubs2009/2009044.pdf

National League for Nursing Accrediting Commission. (2008). *Accreditation manual.* Retrieved on February 15, 2012, from http://www.nlnac.org/manuals/NLNACManual2008.pdf

Part II: Department of Education: 34 CFR Parts 600, 602, 603, et al. Program integrity issues; Final Rule. Federal Register 75: 209 (October 29, 2010) 66832–66975.

Part IV Department of Education 34 CFR Parts 600 and 602 Institutional eligibility under the Higher Education Act of 1965, as amended, and the secretary's recognition of accrediting agencies; Final rule." Federal Register 74: 206 (October 27, 2009) 55414–55435.

31

EVALUATING DISTANCE EDUCATION IN AN ERA OF INTERNATIONALIZATION

MODUPE E. IRELE

In their UNESCO report, Altbach, Reisberg, and Rumbley (2009) observe that distance education has emerged "as an extremely important option for higher education expansion and delivery in many quarters" (p. 123) and ascribe the new importance of distance education to "rapid and groundbreaking" (p. 123) advancements in information and communications technologies. Similarly, the National Center for Education Statistics (NCES; 2011) notes that universities in the United States and overseas are leveraging advanced technologies to put education within the reach of many more individuals around the world.

This increase in the number of learners comes not just from higher education but also from the corporate world. As more learners from the work force seek additional qualifications, universities face significant competition from a variety of providers. In response to such competition, universities see online delivery as a means of increasing enrollments and see corporate bodies as viable sources of new recruits and the funding with which to service them. For their part, corporate bodies reach out to universities for their research and academic expertise reflecting what the Economist Intelligence Unit has described as, "a surge in research-driven public and private sector relationships (Economist Intelligence Unit, 2008, p. 12).

As these kinds of partnerships increase in a globalized setting where "the production and dissemination of knowledge are no longer the restricted purview of higher education" (Parker, 2008, p. 310), universities and other training institutions will need to "demonstrate the quality of their services in ways that are intelligible to all their stakeholders, including potential students and their employers; faculty and staff; regulators; and government agencies" (Parker, 2008, p. 305). This will usually involve well-structured and properly-executed evaluation activities.

THE PRESENT FACE OF DISTANCE EDUCATION

NCES' 2007-2008 (NCES, 2011) statistical reports reveal that within the United States, there were about 4.3 million undergraduates enrolled in distance education courses, a

4% increase on the 2003–2004 data. The report also states that an additional 22% of the graduate population participated in distance learning at the postgraduate level. Outside of the United States, similarly impressive growth can be noticed especially through the Mega universities which enroll students in the hundreds of thousands. As explained in a UNESCO report, it is indeed

> … extremely difficult to calculate the numbers of students engaged in distance education worldwide but the existence of nearly 24 mega-universities a number of which boast over one million students speaks to a quantitatively significant phenomenon. (Altbach, Reisberg, & Rumbley, 2009, p. xviii)

These developments reflect an increasing number of international partnerships. Major examples come from countries such as Australia and the United Kingdom that are exporting higher education through electronic technology (Eaton, 2002). Other examples can be found in partnerships among elite higher education institutions such as the Massachusetts Institute of Technology's partnership with the UK's Cambridge University and Stanford, Yale, and Princeton's partnership with Oxford University to create an online college for alumni (Peters, 2003, p. 11). Also, in line with the e-Europe Plan, all European Union member states' universities were by the end of 2005 to offer on-line access for their students (Walker, 2005).

Central to this spurt of growth is, of course, technology. As Butcher aptly points out, we now have "technologically clever ways of replicating traditional, face-to-face education models" (quoted in Altbach et al., p. 125). Although student interaction has for some time been simulated through chat and discussion boards embedded in learning management systems such as WebCt and Blackboard, the opportunities for such discussions have significantly increased through the use of internet spaces such as Facebook and MySpace which allow for more informal discussions in authentic contexts and on topics of personal interest to learners (International Council for Distance Education, 2009). These new situations are reducing even more the "transactional distance" (Moore, 1997) between students and instructors.

This more recent use of social networking web sites has proved to be particularly beneficial in cross-border courses and programs. As global citizenship education becomes much more pervasive and important, team and group building in virtual space has become a key feature of international programs (Wang, 2011, p. 243). Instead of the traditional semester or year spent abroad, students are learning how to interact with foreign students and their culture through online videoconferencing, for example, Skype. Course designers are now attempting to build social presence through the integration of more informal tasks and assignments (Walker, 2005; Wang, 2011).

These developments are making distance education programs simultaneously more exciting but more vulnerable to scrutiny, and making the case for focused evaluation much stronger.

THE CASE FOR DISTANCE EDUCATION PROGRAM EVALUATION

Program evaluation in general serves many purposes including helping to prove the worth of the program, and to improve the program (Barger, 2008).

The worth of distance education programs is still not universally accepted despite the fact that it has been around for well over a century. There are those who are suspicious of it because they have little or no familiarity with it (Twigg, 2001), while others remain uncertain about the long term effects and usefulness of the new technologies associated with it given the, "actual effects … have not always measured up to the 'sweeping expectations' that have characterized their arrival on the scene" (Guri-Rosenblit quoted in Altbach et al., 2009, p. 124). Deepening the uncertainty, moreover, is the speed with which the technological terrain changes and causes concern about practitioners' competence in using it (Bates, 2000, p. 198). Consequently, when faced with these new technology-based programs, administrators and technology providers still demand assurance regarding their quality and merit. Well conducted evaluation studies, whose results are carefully and accurately documented and presented thus are required to allay these fears.

Evaluation exercises conducted in response to the above concerns were initially focused on presenting data that demonstrated that distance education programs were "as good as" resident instruction programs (Thompson & Irele, 2007). However, distance education is evolving its own unique characteristics that set it apart from traditional classroom-based education (Peters, 2003, p. 21), and so the evaluation of its programs and course offerings requires clearly identified and articulated quality criteria on which to base appropriate and relevant evaluation studies.

But quality is "a complex and difficult concept, one that depends on a range of factors, arising from the student, the curriculum, the instructional design, technology used, [and] faculty characteristics" (Meyer, quoted in Shelton, 2011, p. 1). Efforts to evaluate the quality and merit of programs begin with a clear understanding of what makes for quality in this field and because distance learning reaches beyond local and regional boundaries, there is a need for stakeholders to have a common understanding of the indicators of quality in distributed learning situations (Twigg, 2001). These quality criteria will form the bases for evaluating international programs to determine whether they meet, or correspond with, the needs of domestic learners and, of course, vice versa, whether domestic programs correspond with the needs of international learners.

It may therefore be helpful to first consider the discussions around quality issues before considering evaluation processes and implementation.

CONSTRUCTING THE CONCEPT OF QUALITY IN DISTANCE EDUCATION AS A BASIS FOR EVALUATION

As discussed above, the notion of quality in distance education is complex, consisting as it does of an array of interdependent infrastructures and personnel (Lockee, Moore, & Burton, 2002). Cleary (2001) explains that in higher education, quality is a construct

> relative to the unique perspectives and interpretations of different stakeholder groups (students, alumni, faculty, administrators, parents, oversight boards, employers, state legislatures, local governing bodies, accrediting associations, transfer institutions, and the general public). (p. 20)

Sherry (2003) provides a tabular framework for understanding the quality constructs elaborated by the eight regional accreditation agencies in the original *Guidelines for Distance Education* from the institution's, faculty's or learner's perspective or simultaneously, across the three perspectives. She compares each of the constructs (curriculum and instruction, evaluation and assessment, facilities and finances, student services, library and library resources) with Chickering and Gamson's (1987) indicators of effective teaching and learning in traditional education, and against Brookfield's (1990) insights into adult learning. The tabular framework reveals how, in the three works, quality in distance education was closely aligned with that in traditional education.

As distance education's own special pedagogy began to be better understood, the regional accrediting commissions evolved this statement with regard to the evaluation and assessment of distance education that points to the breadth of expectations from evaluation activities:

> Both the assessment of student achievement and the evaluation of overall programs take on an added importance as new techniques evolve. For example, in asynchronous programs, the element of seat time is essentially removed from the equation. For these reasons, the institution conducts sustained, evidence-based and participatory inquiry as to whether distance learning programs are achieving objectives. The results of such inquiry are used to guide curriculum design and delivery, pedagogy, and educational processes and may affect future policy and budgets perhaps having implications for the institution's role and mission. (Lezberg, 2003, p. 433)

Listing example organizations, Thompson and Irele (2007) point out that a number of organizations, have been working to develop distance education program standards to "guide the development, delivery and evaluation of distance education programs and processes in a rapidly changing educational environment" (p. 429). Choosing to highlight the institutions mentioned below, they describe the guidelines as being "consistent in their focus on issues related to course design, learning outcomes, technology, learner and faculty support, institutional commitment, and assessment and evaluation (p. 430):

- American Council on Education (1996), *Distance Learning Evaluation Guide*
- The Pennsylvania State University (1998), *An Emerging Set of Guiding Principles and Practices for the Design and Development of Distance Education*
- American Distance Education Consortium (2000), *ADEC Guiding Principles for Distance Teaching and Learning*
- *The Sloan-C*™ (2002), Elements of Quality: The Sloan-C™ Framework
- Western Cooperative for Educational Telecommunications (1999), *Principles of Good Practice for Electronically Offered Academic Degree and Certificate Programs.*

Focusing on program instructional design, Lockee, Burton, and Potter (2010) compare standards for distance education programming from 10 organizations in higher, K–12, and professional education:

- Distance Learning Accreditation Board
- Monterey Institute
- Sloan Consortium (Sloan-C)
- Southern Regional Education Board
- Institute for Higher Education Policy
- Southern Association for colleges and Schools
- The Accrediting Bureau of Health Education Schools

- Accrediting Commision of Career Schools and Colleges of Technology
- Accrediting Council for Independent Colleges and Schools
- Distance Education and TrainingCouncil, Accrediting Commission

Lockee and her colleagues (2010) note six common themes: instructional design; a comparative perspective with regard to campus-based instruction; mandatory interaction; media selection issues; faculty training requirements; and student support. Notwithstanding these commonalities, they found the wording of the standards, particularly that of the themes of instructional design, mandatory interaction and faculty training, did not sufficiently address issues directly related to instruction for distant-taught programs, For example, in the instructional design theme, the term "instructional design" was conspicuous by its absence.

According to Shelton (2011a) though, the literature has focused on "the quality of teaching and pedagogy far more than that of program quality" (p. 7) probably because whole programs typically move online later than the individual courses. She also notes from the literature that attempts to evaluate quality were often made through accreditation, an efficient and effective course development process, and effective pedagogy. Furthermore, while some stakeholders expected quality programs to have attributes that overcame the perception that distance education was inferior to traditional education (Benson, cited in Shelton, 2011a, p. 2) others saw quality as a combination of retention rate, academic outcomes and success in online student and faculty support (Shelton & Saltsman, cited in Shelton, 2011a).

Despite the diversity of approaches to evaluating quality however, and while accepting the difficulty of grasping this concept for all program elements, Shelton (2011a) argues that there is no "excuse to ignore the need for assessing and demonstrating quality online education" (p. 2). She reviewed 13 articles and studies that appeared between 2000 and 2009 which she considered "best represent the different efforts available to define and evaluate the quality of online education programs" (Shelton, 2011, p. 2). Based on her review of these 13 approaches (or as she calls them "paradigms"), she uncovered the following six common dimensions of quality, starting with the most commonly cited:

- Institutional commitment, support and leadership
- Teaching and learning
- Faculty support, student support; course development
- Technology, evaluation and assessment
- Cost effectiveness , management and planning
- Student and faculty satisfaction

EXTENDING THE DISCUSSION OF QUALITY CRITERIA TO THE GLOBAL ARENA

A review of the international literature uncovers similar but perhaps extended quality criteria compared to those that pertain in the United States.

According to Parker (2008), "The formulation of quality assurance systems for online education, while most often regulated at a regional or national level, has in recent years been driven by international developments" (p. 313). Summarizing the quality standards proposed for online learning in Australia, England, Canada, and the United States, she says the commonalities "at a basic level ... include providing clear statements of educational goals; sustaining the institutional commitment to support learners; and engaging in a collaborative process of discovery, which contributes to improving the teaching and learning environment" (p. 306).

Other international developments include a focus on protecting distance education learners from fraudulent or unaccredited providers (Parker, 2008). But the student or consumer perspective is often absent in the development of quality standards used as the basis for evaluation in the United States (Frydenberg, cited in Thompson & Irele, 2007). Furthermore, with greater heterogeneity in the nationalities of students participating in distance education programs worldwide, there will be a need for "consumer information that assists students in making judgments about the quality of institutions and programs based on, among other factors, accredited status" (Eaton, 2002, p. 10). Indeed, international students are already being encouraged to take a proactive "buyer beware" (Parker, 2008) evaluative perspective when choosing online programs. U.S. providers should be aware of this trend as they may not get the opportunity to know the needs of international prospects if they wait for data from the more reactive student satisfaction survey (administered at the end of the program) to assess and refine the quality of their programs.

Lockee, Perkins, Potter, Burton, and Kreb's (2011) review of 17 national and international organizations' quality standards provides further insights into regional approaches to quality standards. Of the 17 organizations, 10 were national and had been reviewed in the 2010 study discussed earlier in this chapter. The seven international organizations were

- Canadian Recommended E-Learning Guidelines
- European Institute for E-Learning
- Open and Distance Learning Quality Council
- European Foundation for Management Development
- Australasian Council on Open, Distance and e-Learning
- Open ECBCheck
- French Forum for Open and Distance Learning

In their 2011 study, Lockee and colleagues noted three important differences in the way the domestic and international institutions approached the six themes (instructional design, comparative perspective with regard to campus-based instruction; mandatory interaction; media selection issues; faculty training requirements; and student support): (a) The foreign guidelines were more detailed in their treatment of quality criteria relating to instructional design but were not as insistent on the need for interaction. (b) The foreign institutions were more concerned that faculty members obtain training in the pedagogy of distance education as opposed to training in the use of technology. (c) The foreign institutions were also not as concerned about establishing parity between distance education and campus-based experiences of instruction but rather, they wanted distance education programs to offer students the same value and opportunities as were offered by other types of programs and courses. Such differences within individual thematic areas suggest that even relatively small shifts in emphasis (let alone whole differences in criteria) may lead foreign learners to evaluate their learning experiences differently from U.S. learners and this may lead to unanticipated answers for U.S. program providers and evaluators.

The impact of culture on the quality of courses and programs has become another important evaluation criterion for cross-border distance education offerings. Townley, Geng, and Zhang (2003) state that offshore programs that ignore valid cultural differences and may "lose much of their effectiveness" (p. 84). They point out that cultural and familiar uses of language can significantly undermine students' abilities to succeed. In the cross-border program between a Chinese and a U.S. university that they describe, Chinese students noted that "sometimes the words and expressions used by the U.S. students do not accord with what we have learned" (p. 88).

Edmundson (2009) observes similar challenges in the corporate world of training where companies "fail to recognize the impact of cultural differences on the program's success" (p. 1).

> However, e-learning courses are cultural artifacts, embedded with the cultural values, preferences, characteristics and nuances of the culture that designed them, and inherently creating challenges for learners from other cultures. (Edmundson 2009, p. 1)

A focus on learning outcomes should remind those involved in the evaluation of distance education programs in the United States. that, for international programs, there are likely to be special indicators of quality that are key to the success of foreign students but not to that of domestic students.

THE EVALUATION PROCESS

Thompson and Irele (2007) list three important steps in the planning and implementation of an evaluation project. The first step is for the evaluator to "clarify the purpose of the evaluation in meeting stakeholders' information needs and what, specifically will be evaluated" (p. 424).

Evaluators must, therefore, be clear about whose perspective they are taking when engaging in an evaluation activity (Twigg, 2001). Perspectives can be those of administrators, accrediting agencies, vendors, students, and employers. Another useful way of categorizing perspectives is to divide them into those of providers or consumers, given that "the accreditation process and many of the quality assurance methods used in the academy pre-date the consumer culture that has become widely accepted in today's society" (Twigg, 2001, p. 2). Using this system of categorization, the providers' category would include subcategories such as accrediting agencies while the consumers' category would include subcategories such as students and employers, among many others, whose perspectives, too, would have to be considered.

To clarify what, specifically will be evaluated, evaluators should determine whether success will be expressed in terms of "increased enrollments," "high retention rates," "outstanding learner performance," "increased job potential of graduates," or "higher satisfaction from current employers?" (Lockee et al., 2002, p. 26). They must decide how the data will be used and avoid trying to answer too many questions with one evaluation activity or answer too many general questions.

As a next step, the evaluator chooses the most appropriate data collection methods and tools; some of the relevant tools are participant observations, questionnaires, interviews, online monitoring of responses, and advance prototyping or pilot testing (Moore & Kearsley, 1996; Ruhe & Zumbo, 2009). Also pertinent are surveys, student personal diaries, learning assessment instruments such as tests, essay questions, and portfolios (Cyrs, 2001).

In the third step the evaluator writes an evaluation report that gets the right information into the right hands (Thompson & Irele, 2007). Reports should be impartial, clearly describe the program being evaluated, be timely, and disclose the full set of evaluation findings to the persons affected by the evaluation and those with expressed legal rights to receive the results. The report should include an attention-getting headline, a description of the major issues related to the headline, present data related to the issues, and a recommendation or summary of the findings (Reeves & Hedberg, cited in Thompson & Irele, 2007).

DISTANCE EDUCATION EVALUATION MODELS AND EXAMPLE PROJECTS

As distance education gains prominence within higher education and more evaluation models specific to the field emerge, such models can serve as road maps to guide evaluation practice (Mertens cited, in Ruhe Zumbo, 2009, p. 24). Three of such recent models of distance education evaluation are highlighted and discussed below.

The first model is Ruhe and Zumbo's (2009) or Unfolding Model which the authors describe as a guide for professional program evaluation in distance education because it is "grounded in the science of test assessment and educational measurement" (p. 75). Messick's (cited in Ruhe & Zumbo, 2009) framework for determining test validity provides the basis for the Unfolding Model as his categories are considered to overlap with others commonly used in distance education evaluation, such as relevance, cost-benefit, values, and unintended consequences.

The model itself has four facets grouped along two bases. Represented as a four-cell model, the top row contains the two facets of "scientific evidence" and "relevance and cost-benefit," which together form the scientific basis. The bottom row is the consequential basis and contains the two facets of "underlying values" and "unintended consequences." Each cell unfolds "to show further information needed for an evaluation study" (Ruhe & Zumbo, 2009, p. 18), hence the name Unfolding Model. With the model, evaluators can bring all four facets to the fore in their evaluation activities, including values and unintended consequences both of which, the authors believe, are not often privileged in other evaluation models. They emphasize that the four facets overlap and that evaluators should not expect to neatly fit their analyses into any of the four.

The unfolding model involves the use of multiple types of data (both quantitative and qualitative) collected from varied sources and analyzed from different value perspectives. However, Bates (2009) considers that the authors do not provide assistance on how to measure whether the values or goals specific to e-learning and distance education have been achieved.

Shelton offers another model, *Quality Scorecard for the Administration of Online Education Programs*, which can be used to "demonstrate to accrediting bodies elements of quality within the program as well as an overall level of quality" (Shelton, 2011b). The scorecard is based on the Institute of Higher Education Policy's 24 benchmarks and was developed through a Delphi study involving 43 experts. It contains 70 elements of quality divided into nine categories. Each element has a potential score of between 0 and 3 depending on whether the quality was (1) not observed, (2) insufficiently observed, (3) in moderate use, or (4) meets criterion completely. To avoid undue subjectivity, the rating for each item is to be supported with evidence. When completed the scorecard produces an overall numeric score between 0 and 210. The nine categories, not listed in order of any priority or weighting, are:

1. Institutional support (four questions worth a maximum score of 12);
2. Technical support (six questions worth a maximum score of 18);
3. Course development and instructional design (12 questions worth a maximum score of 36);
4. Course structure (eight questions worth a maximum score of 24);
5. Teaching and learning (five questions worth a maximum score of 15);
6. Social and student engagement (one question worth a maximum score of 3);
7. Faculty support (six questions worth a maximum score of 18);
8. Student support (17 questions worth a maximum score of 51);
9. Evaluation and assessment (11 questions worth a maximum score of 33).

According to Shelton, the scorecard is expected to "… facilitate a more consistent method by which administrators and educators may evaluate and improve the overall quality of their institutions' online education programs (2011a, p. 9).

A third model incorporates international perspectives gleaned from the world of training. Developed by Edmundson (2009), it proposes five cultural adaptations to strengthen the quality of programs offered to international learners—translation, localization, modularization, origination, and cultural analysis.

Through translation the vocabulary is changed to that of the target language. The challenge is to be aware of and avoid verbal nuances such as contractions and word sets ending in prepositions (for example, "go over"). Localization has to do with visual and textual differences between cultures. Designers need to be aware of taboos, gestures, and symbols that may have negative connotations in the target culture. Modularization involves using alternative learning objects or activities that accomplish the same learning objectives. This will require using appropriate technology platforms that support the plugging in of learning objects, in this case cross-cultural learning objects. Origination refers to starting from scratch with the full participation of the learners to help identify and explain critical cultural differences and proffer appropriate solutions to them.

When carrying out a cultural analysis, characteristics of the target learners are compared and contrasted with those of the course (e.g., content, pedagogical approaches, and media used) and then one of the four adaptations (as is relevant) can be applied to the situation to solve the most critical differences in the most cost-efficient way. Testing may be implemented through surveys, focus groups, and individual observation.

THE IMPACT OF COST ON THE QUALITY OF DISTANCE EDUCATION PROGRAMS

Notwithstanding the availability of quality criteria and evaluation models, Sherry (2003) observes that quality-based issues are not always at the forefront of decisions about distance education (p. 436). Indeed, one single factor, cost, often has a dramatic effect on the quality and even delivery of distance education programs. This tension between cost and quality of distance education may be surmised in the cost-benefit approach often taken when evaluating costs in distance education programs. Ehrmann (2002) observes that cost and benefits are generally evaluated separately, with the unfortunate but frequent result that "the cheaper program option will automatically be considered better" (p. 7). Also, start-up requirements may often be cost prohibitive for many organizations (Bartley & Golek, 2004), Thus, programs that would otherwise meet the quality criteria are often let go when the costs of implementing them are considered too high (Thompson & Irele, 2007).

CASE STUDY: A MULTI-MODAL APPROACH TO PROGRAM EVALUATION

As Shelton (2011a) remarks, there are limited accounts of program evaluations in the literature. It can therefore be informative to look at examples of evaluation activities. Following are two case studies that provide insight into the evaluation issues discussed above.

Describing an online Geographic Information System program, Walker (2005) provides an example of a multi-modal evaluation study done in what he and Ruhe and Zumbo (2009) describe as the contemporary tradition of evaluation. The evaluation combined three approaches taken from Worthen, Sanders, and Fitzpartick (1997) six evaluation approaches (objectives-oriented, consumer-oriented, management-oriented, expertise-oriented, adversary-oriented, and participant-oriented), to provide multiple stakeholders' perspectives, using multiple data collection methods. The program objectives were to (a) identify weaknesses in order to improve effectiveness (b) ensure parity with face-to-face classes, and (c) provide information for program renewal. The three approaches used were: management-, expertise-, and participant-oriented approaches. The data collection methods were (a) student and instructor surveys regarding their respective perspectives on the online psychosocial learning environment, (b) content analysis comparing the online version of classes to face-to-face versions, (c) basic cost comparisons in online versus face-to-face classes, (d) aggregated academic outcomes, (e) student retention, and (f) benchmarking against other GIS certificate programs.

The multiple mode approach allowed the department to focus on those areas of departmental and institutional importance. The use of multiple instruments helped the evaluators to target and to collect the specific type of data they required. For example, the same survey was administered to both students and faculty to collect data about their perspectives regarding the psychosocial learning environment. The evaluators were thus able to note that the students' rated their satisfaction regarding interaction and collaboration significantly lower than did the instructors. Also, learner outcomes were addressed through a comparative analysis of the grades of the face-to-face students and those of the online students. However, it is interesting to note that the online students' grades showed them doing either very well or quite badly with 10% failing and more dropping out; there were very few in the middle ranges.

Walker's (2005) description demonstrated that by matching the strategies and methods for collecting data to the perspective-orientation, a more rounded view of program strengths and weaknesses was obtained. As he summarized, the combination of methods provided "administrators and decision-makers with an overall program outlook informed by non-biased data that should aid in more objective decisions" (p. 11). However, while differences in course content between the face-to-face classes and the online classes were noted, course design which is one of the hall marks of quality noted above, was not evaluated. Also not evaluated was the technology used, which is another indicator of quality often mentioned in quality guidelines. These omissions reflect Lockee et al.'s (2011) concerns that the guidelines reviewed paid insufficient attention to instructional design and the use of technology.

CASE STUDY: EVALUATION TIPS FROM AN INTERNATIONAL DISTANCE EDUCATION COURSE

Conspicuously limited in their number in the literature are discussions about quality criteria for distance education programs offered internationally. With more and more programs being planned for and delivered to an international audience, evaluators could do with a pool of indicators and/or questions to guide them in obtaining the right information for optimum program quality and effectiveness. Individual international distance education courses can provide data that hint at quality indicators and evaluation questions that could usefully be integrated into the evaluation activities of other international courses and programs.

Townley et al. (2003) describe an international distance education course in Library Information Systems that was composed of 32 students: eight American and 24 Chinese, with each set participating from their respective universities in the United States and China. While one of the three course goals was focused on the specific content area of knowledge management, the other two goals were that (a) students and faculty learn how to learn in an international and virtual classroom, and (b) students and faculty develop skills and learn methods that were effective in communicating across cultures. The course was delivered via a combination of WebCT software, videotaped lectures and videoconferencing technologies "to create a virtual environment for learning" (Townley et al., 2003, p. 84).

The course was conducted in English (spoken and written), and most of the texts were written in English with a few texts translated into Chinese. Two instructors were used—one American and the other Chinese, both with knowledge of the other country. On the U.S. side, a Chinese graduate assistant was on hand to help with translation and other language-related issues. On the Chinese side, the instructor was already familiar with the senior students having previously worked at the university for a couple of years. Also, those students who had been in his classes served to explain U.S. teaching styles to their new classmates. The course used a combination of synchronous and asynchronous meeting times for team building and group discussions. Four mixed-nationality teams of eight students were formed.

The authors' descriptions of this course hint at possible areas that evaluators of international programs could investigate to obtain data for improving stakeholders' experiences of distance-delivered programs and build a pool of quality criteria for such programs.

A couple of emerging hints relate to language. First, with regard to group membership, the administrators soon realized that an enrollment ratio of three Chinese students to one American was best and allowed the groups to communicate without being overwhelmed by the other. The Chinese students, in particular, felt more comfortable expressing themselves; because the Chinese were not fluent in and thus not as comfortable speaking English, having more students on the team who could explain and extend the ideas to the others was very helpful (Townley et al., 2003, p. 87). Furthermore, differences in the use of language affected the learning process and outcomes, with the Chinese students being confused by the Americans' use of slang and idiomatic language. Because the Chinese were more proficient in written than spoken English, individual assignments were slated for WebCT. The students were comfortable using this environment as they could provide more polished and detailed responses to other students' communications.

The second hint relates to the effect of culture on course design. Operating from a collectivist culture, the Chinese had organized a pre-class discussion and ironed out knotty issues related to the group assignment before the arrival of the Americans for the synchronous class meeting. Coming from a more individualistic tradition, the Americans were not prepared for the assignment to already have been somewhat completed; they had anticipated an in-class discussion during which decisions would be made. This led to some tension especially at the beginning of the course before a workable process was negotiated among the groups.

The above hint underscores the different views about interaction noted in the U.S. and international institutions' quality guidelines reviewed by Lockee et al. (2011b). Elements in course design meant to promote interaction should be concerned with the effect of culture on learning preferences. Whether or not there is a need for course redesign can be determined through open-ended questions inviting qualitative answers. In the case of the Chinese-American course, there was liberal use of open-ended questions to elicit students' responses about the effect of culture on the effectiveness of the course.

Other important evaluation questions hinted at have to do with the effect of translation and interpretation on the quality of materials and understanding of texts and communication. One could also seek to know how the blend of technologies worked (or didn't work) and what systems are in place to reduce or eliminate undesirable cultural influences? As Townley et al. (2003) stress, "learning how to interact with a different culture is as important as learning subject content in terms of learning outcomes" (p. 89). This point underscores the need for detail-level evaluation questions that address the implementation of quality criteria in international distance education programs.

CONCLUSION

Evidence from the literature allows us to accept that distance education is now firmly entrenched in the mainstream of U.S. higher education and within a global market where U.S. and foreign universities and corporations exchange their academic wares across their nations' borders.

In the wake of these developments, the role of evaluation is critical as "institutions that offer distance-delivered courses and programs share a compelling need to determine their quality" (Lockee et al., 2002, p. 21). There are clear indications of an emerging consensus about core components of quality for domestically delivered distance education programs. These have served to form the frameworks for the implementation of evaluation activities. However, there are similarly clear indications that these criteria of quality may not stretch far enough for internationally delivered programs. Missing in particular is the dimension of culture which affects course design, student/teacher interaction and collaboration, and appropriate technology platform and interface.

As regional accrediting bodies in the United States agree on and disseminate the core dimensions of quality, they should do the same with their international counterparts and stakeholders in general.

Meanwhile, as quality criteria are established and can serve as the bases of what has merit and worth in distance education programs, evaluation of such programs is likely to be easier to implement regardless of who initiates it or whose perspective is driving it. With the variety of models of distance education evaluation now developed, evaluators can choose from a selection of approaches and methods those that will guide the evaluation process although none is comprehensive in terms of the situations and questions it can address.

Further work needs to be done to tease out the components of quality that can be meaningfully integrated into international distance learning programs. Having a pool of questions or clearly delineated areas of a score card that draw attention to the needs of an expanding global community of learners will be useful. Clearly, this will be no mean task, especially with the ever-changing terrain of distance education's technologies and pedagogies. Nevertheless, stakeholders have a collective responsibility to assure the quality of the programs offered at home and abroad so that no community is disadvantaged and programs have a greater chance of succeeding.

REFERENCES

Altbach, P. G., Reisberg, L., & Rumbley, L. E. (2009). *Trends in global higher education: Tracking an academic revolution.* Paris: UNESCO.

American Council on Education. (1996). *Distance learning evaluation guide.* Washington, DC: American Council on Education.

American Distance Education Consortium. (2000). *ADEC guiding principles for distance teaching and learning.* Retrieved March 2005 from http://www.adecedu/admin/papers/distance-teaching_principles.html

Barger, B. (2008). The anatomy of program design for an online business management course. *College Teaching Methods and Styles Journal, 4*(1), 99–106.

Bartley, S. J., & Golek, J. H. (2004). Evaluating the cost effectiveness of online and face-to-face instruction. *Educational Technology & Society, 7*(4), 167–175.

Bates, A. W. (2000). *Managing technological change. Strategies for college and university leaders.* San Francisco: Jossey-Bass.

Bates, A. W. (2009, May 4). *Reviews of 'Evaluation in distance education and e-Learning'.* Retrieved December November 16, 2011, from Online learnng and distance education resources: http://tonybates.ca/2009/05/04/reviews-of-evaluation-in-distance-education-and-e-learning

Brookfield, S. D. (1990). *The skillful teacher: On technique, trust and responsiveness in the classroom.* San Francisco: Jossey-Bass.

Chickering, A. W., & Gamson, Z. F. (1987). Development and adaptations of the seven principles for good practice in undergraduate education. *New Directions for Teaching and Learning , 4*, 75–81.

Cleary, T. S. (2001). Indicators of quality. *Planning for higher education, 29*(3), 19–28.

Cyrs, T. E. (2001). *Evaluating distance learning programs and courses.* Retrieved from http://www.zianet.com/edacyrs/tips/evaluate_dl.htm

Eaton, J. (2002). *Maintaining the delicate balance: Distance learning. higher education accreditation and the policy of self-regulation.* Retrieved October 20, 2011, from http://www.educause.edu/Resources/MaintainingtheDelicateBalanceD/160432

Economist Intelligence Unit. (2008). *The future of higher education:How technology will shape learning.* Retrieved http://www.nmc.org/pdf/Future-of-Higher-Ed-(NMC).pdf

Edmundson, A. (2009, May). *Culturally accessible e-learning: An overdue global business imperative.* Retrieved December 15, 2011, from ASTD Learning Circuits, http://www.astd.org/LC/2009/0509_edmundson.htm

Erhmann, S. (2002). *Evaluating (and improving) benefits of educational uses of technology.* Retrieved January 26, 2006, from http://www.wcet.info/projects/tcm/whitepapers.asp

International Council for Distance Education. (2009). *Global trends in higher education, adult and distance learning*. Retrieved from http://www.icde.org/Global+Trends+in+Higher+Education,+Adult+and+Distance+Learning.9UFRvY0L.ips

Lezberg, A. K. (2003). Accreditation: Quality control in higher distance education. In M. G. Moore, & W. G. Anderson (Eds.), *Handbook of distance education* (pp. 425–434). Mahwah, NJ: Erlbaum.

Lockee, B., Burton, J. K., & Potter, K. R. (2010, September 29). *Examining standards for distance education systems*. Retrieved February 20, 2012, from http://www.aect.org/publications/whitepapers/2010/ICER1.pdf

Lockee, B., Moore, M., & Burton, J. (2002). Measuring success: Evaluation strategies for distance education. *Educause Quarterly , 1*, 20–26.

Lockee, B., Perkins, R., Potter, K., Burton, J., & Kreb, S. G. (2011, August 4). Defining quality in distance education: Examining national and international standards for online learning. *27th Annual Conference on distance teaching and learning*. Madison, WI.

Moore, J. (2002). Elements of quality: The Sloan-C framework. *Learning Abstracts, 5*(12).

Moore, M. G. (1997). Theory of transactional distance. In D. Keegan, *Theoretical principles of distance education* (Vol. 3, pp. 22–38). New York: Routledge.

Moore, M. G., & Kearsley, G. (1996). *Distance education: A systems view*. Belmont, CA: Wadsworth.

National Center for Education Statistics. (2011). *The condition of education 2011*. Retrieved form http://nces.ed.gov: US Department of Education

Parker, N .K. (2008). The quality dilemma in online education revisited. In T. Anderson (Ed.), *Theory and practice in online learning (pp. 305–340)*. Retrieved http://www.aupress.ca/index.php/books/120146

Peters, O. (2003). *Distance education in transition: New trends and challenges*. Oldenburg, Germany: Bibliotheks- und Informationssystem de Universitat Oldenburg.

Ruhe, V., & Zumbo, B. D. (2009). *Evaluation in distance education and e-learning: The unfolding model*. New York: Guilford Press.

Shelton, K. (2011a). A review of paradigms for evaluating the quality of online education programs. *Online Journal of Distance Learning Administration, 5*(1). Retrieved from http://www.icde.org/Online+Journal+of+Distance+Learning+Administration

Shelton, K. (2011b). *Quality scorecard for the administration of online education programs*. Retrieved February 2012, from http://www.sloanconsortium.org/quality_scoreboard_online_program

Sherry, A. C. (2003). Quality and its measurement in distance education. In M. G. Moore, & W. G. Anderson (Eds.), *Handbook of distance education* (pp. 435–459). Mahwah, NJ: Erlbaum.

The National Center for Education Statistics. (2003, July 18). *Distance education at degree-granting post secondary institutions*. Retrieved from http://nces.ed.gov/surveys/peqis/publications/2003017

The Pennsylvania State University. (1998). *An emerging set of guiding principles and practices for the design and development of distance education*. Universisty Park: Author.

Thompson, M., & Irele, M. E. (2007). Evaluating distance education programs. In M. M. Moore, *Handbook of distance education (2nd ed.)* (pp. 419–436). Mahwah, NJ: Erlbaum.

Townley, C. T., Geng, Q., & Zhang, J. (2003). Using distance education to internationalize library and information science scholarship. *Libri , 53*, 82–93.

Twigg, C. A. (2001). Quality assurance for whom? Providers and consumers in today's distributed learning evironment. *The Pew learning and technology program.*Washington, DC: Pew Institute.

Walker, S. L. (2005). Objective evaluation in an online geographic Information system certificate program. *Turkish Online Journal of Distance Education, 6*(1). Retrieved from https://tojde.anadolu.edu.tr/tojde17/articles/walker.htm

Wang, C. (2011). Instructional design for cross-cultural online collaboration: Grouping strategies and assignment design. *Australasian Journal of Educational Technology, 27*(2), 243–258.

Western Cooperative for Educational Telecommunications. (1999). *Principles of good practice for electronically offered academic degree and certificate programs*. Retrieved January 13, 2007, from http://wcet.info/services/publications/balancing/principles.asp

Worthen, B. R., Sanders, J. R., & Fitzpatrick, J. L. (1997). *Program evaluation: Alternative approaches and practical guidelines* (2nd ed.). New York: Longman.

32

THE CHANGING COSTS OF DELIVERY OF DISTANCE EDUCATION PROGRAMS

ALISTAIR INGLIS

When online learning first became popular, it was widely believed that delivering courses online would offer a major opportunity to reduce costs. Quite soon however, it became apparent that cost savings were not as easily achieved in practice (Fielden, 2002; Rumble, 2001). Delivery of courses online typically incurs much higher costs initially, owing to the need to set up new infrastructure and processes, and to develop new teaching materials and train staff in new methods of teaching. However, as time has gone by, institutions have become more familiar with the cost factors they have to manage. They have seen potential for cost reduction through substitution rather than duplication of online services, greater re-use and sharing of e-resources, increased peer learning, and more standardised production of materials (Laurillard, 2007).

In earlier editions of the *Handbook of Distance Education*, the focus of the chapter corresponding to this (Inglis, 2003, 2007) was on comparing the costs of online distance education delivery with the costs of other methods of distance education delivery. However, with the widespread and increasing adoption of online delivery and the decreasing use of earlier delivery methods, the relevance of such comparisons has diminished. Distance educators are now much more interested in the way the costs of different methods of online delivery compare. At the same time, interest in the economics of online distance education in general appears to have waned. The number of publications addressing this topic that are published each year has fallen and researchers have been finding fewer questions to investigate. A 2009 review of research published between 2000 and 2009 in the five most prominent journals in distance education found only 12 articles in the area of costs and benefits, and none was published later than 2005 (Zawacki-Richter, Bäcker, & Vugt, 2009). A few have appeared subsequently, though, in other journals (see, for example, Crawford, Gould, King, and Parker, 2010; Gordon, He, & Abdous, 2009; Laaser, 2008; Laurillard, 2007). Yet there are still important issues to be investigated (Guri-Rosenblit & Gros, 2011) and good reasons why distance educators' interest in the costs and economics of online distance education should be maintained. Developments in technology, changes in the way in which technology is being used, and changes in pedagogy all carry important cost implications which will impact the opportunities that educators will have in future to improve the quality of programs delivered at a distance. As Arafeh (2004) argued, technologies should not be adopted just because they are new but because they offer clear added value.

Developments in technology over the past decade have wrought substantial changes to the landscape of online learning. Whereas previously institutions were centralising their delivery of online infrastructure through the establishment of learning management systems, now institutions are turning to the "cloud" (He, Cernusca, & Abdous, 2011); whereas previously institutions were seeking ways of training their teaching staff to develop professionally-looking online resources, now attention has shifted to the possibilities of adopting and adapting open educational resources (Butcher, 2011). Against this rapidly changing background, the question for educational managers remains the same: how is it possible to steer a course through the maze of technological and strategic options without putting the financial security of their institution at risk. In such a fluid situation, it is not possible to put forward fail-safe solutions. Instead one must be content to identify general principles which may then be contextualised to the situation at hand.

Part of the difficulty that is encountered in trying to compare costs is the variety of ways in which they are measured—for example, in terms of overall costs, costs per student per workload hour, costs per student per contact hour, or some other measure.

In this chapter, the basic principles that affect costs in distance education will be discussed, but special attention will be given to some of the more important factors that recently have begun to affect cost relationships in significant ways.

DISTINCTION BETWEEN CLASSROOM-BASED AND RESOURCE-BASED MODELS COURSE DELIVERY

In considering costs in relation to distance education, it is important to distinguish between two qualitatively different ways of understanding distance education. In most parts of the world, distance education is conceived of as a mode of delivery in which teaching and learning is mediated via packages of self-instructional learning resources. This has been described as a *resource-based model* of distance education delivery (Inglis, Ling, & Joosten, 2002). In the case of the resource-based model, learning occurs mainly through interaction between the learner and the learning materials. However, in the United States, distance education is often conceived of in terms of a mode of delivery in which teaching-learning interactions are synchronous and mediated via technology. This has been referred to as *classroom-based model* of distance education delivery. Classroom-based delivery involves learning that takes place through dialogic interaction between student and tutor and student and student. Of course, in the case of online learning, the classroom is virtual. Both approaches to distance education delivery have elements of the other. However, the distinction remains and has significant implications for the costs of delivery of educational programmes.

Distance education has attained the importance it has as a result of distance educators embracing the need for attention to quality. This was not always the case. Fifty years ago distance education was characterised by high failure and high attrition rates and was seen as very much a "second best" mode of delivery. The planners of the UK Open University realised that to bring down attrition rates they needed to improve the quality of teaching.

Quality was also seen as a critical consideration for *online* distance education, but for somewhat different reasons. In a context where both the technologies and mode of delivery were new, there was a concern that the impacts of the change in delivery method on teaching and learning could not all be predicted. Consequently, the concerns about quality were motivated by a desire to avoid the pitfalls that could not be anticipated.

The planners of the UK Open University recognised that the way to obtain the resources to invest heavily in improving the quality of teaching was by taking advantage of the considerable economies of scale that are achievable in distance education. It was this realisation that led to the success of the Open University which spurred on the enormous growth in distance education in the 1970s and 80s.

Economies of scale are achieved by altering the relationship between fixed and variable costs. In distance education, examples of fixed costs include the costs of infrastructure, while variable costs include the costs of assessing students' assignments, the costs of provision of student support. Economies of scale can be obtained at two levels (Ashenden, 1987). At the course level, they can be obtained by spreading the fixed costs associated with the design and development of learning packages over a larger course intake. At the institutional level, economies of scale are obtained by spreading the costs of institutional infrastructure needed for delivery of programs across a larger cohort of distance education students. The cost per student of provision of institutional infrastructure is reduced by using infrastructure acquired to enable programs to be delivered at a distance, to expand the intakes into the programs.

Economies of scale are achievable in a similar way in *online* distance education. In this case the fixed costs also include the information and communications technology infrastructure costs and the variable costs include also the costs of bandwidth.

MODELS OF ONLINE DISTANCE EDUCATION

When Twigg (1994) proposed the development of a new National Learning Infrastructure in the United States, she described a delivery model in which student numbers were boosted by achieving savings in the cost of delivery through the use of technology to support a shift to resource-based learning. This was an example of the classic model pioneered by the UK Open University of obtaining economies of scale through a shift from classroom-based to resource-based delivery. Other even earlier attempts to promote such an approach are mentioned in earlier chapters of this volume, including, for example the American open university in the form of the University of Mid-America (McNeil, 1980) and Wedemeyer's Open School (see Chapter 2 in this volume).

Murray Turoff, one of the pioneers of computer-mediated communication, proposed a different type of model for a virtual university (Turoff, 1996). This retained a classroom-based delivery model, but took it online. Turoff believed that the way in which the potential of technology should be exploited was not to increase student intakes or increase efficiency, but only to improve the quality of teaching. He saw the savings need to do this being obtained in the area of institutional infrastructure. The Twigg and Turoff models represent the two ends of a continuum, in relation to the costing of online learning.

The development of online learning coincided with a shift in thinking within higher education towards a social constructivist view of learning which placed much greater importance on student-student and student-teacher interaction. Proponents of this social constructivist view of learning became advocates of a classroom-based model of online delivery which emphasised online discussion, online collaboration, and the notion of co-construction of knowledge. Weller (2004) pointed out the challenge that this presented for institutional administrators: pedagogical approaches that combine discussion and collaboration with online learning have both high fixed costs and high variable costs.

THE BASIS ON WHICH COSTS ARE COMPARED

Comparing the costs of alternative ways of delivering courses is not straightforward. To begin with, it is generally difficult to obtain meaningful cost data. Laurillard (2007) explained the difficulties due to the lack of consistency across institutions in measuring costs, the lack of consistency within institutions in comparing the costs of new technology with the costs of traditional methods of delivery, the failure of researchers to explain inconsistencies in the findings of costing studies, and the lack of agreement on how to compare the benefits of new technology against traditional methods. The difficulty in obtaining meaningful cost data increases when one moves into the international arena. Actual costs vary from country to country but they don't vary consistently; for example, labour costs are much higher in first world countries that in third world countries. The costs of technology and telecommunications, however, are generally higher in third world countries than in first world countries. Furthermore, relative costs are not stable. They are subject to exchange-rate variations that at times can be quite large.

Even if it were possible to know the actual costs of two alternative ways of delivering a course, this information is of limited value unless one can also compare the relative values of outputs. It is generally accepted that in an educational context outputs can best be compared in terms of the quality of student learning. Bartolic-Zlomislic and Bates (1999), drawing on the work of Cukier (1997), assessed the benefits flowing from a major course development venture in terms of a range of outcome measures including measures of performance-driven benefits such as student/instructor satisfaction, learning outcomes, and return on investment; measures of value-added benefits such as increased access, flexibility, and ease of use, and measures of value-added benefits such as the potential for new markets.

Because of the complexity of the costing of online learning, the difficulty of establishing cost-benefit relationships, and the fact that costs change continually over time, it is much more important in trying to compare the actual costs of different delivery methods to understand the way in which costs are impacted by other variables than to have a detailed knowledge of the actual costs themselves.

THE CONFOUNDING EFFECTS OF HIDDEN COSTS

A difficulty that arises in trying to compare the costs of online delivery with the costs of other forms of delivery is that there are invariably some costs that remain unaccounted for. These hidden costs can distort the basis of comparison. The costs of long-established methods of delivery are usually well understood, whereas the costs of emerging methods of delivery are often not all known. Comparisons of this type therefore tend to understate the costs of newer methods of delivery while fully accounting for the costs of existing methods. The effect is to place new methods of delivery in a more favourable light.

The work of Paul Bacsich and his colleagues (1999) has helped to identify the contribution to overall costs of hidden costs. These researchers subdivided hidden costs into three separate categories: institutional costs, costs to staff, and costs to students. They classified as institutional costs, the costs of collaboration, the costs of monitoring informal staff student contact, the costs of copyright compliance, and the costs of costing. Staff costs are those costs borne by staff, even though in some cases they ought in principle to be borne by the institution. Amongst the staff costs, they included the costs of time spent in development of learning materials out-of-hours and the costs of use of privately purchased computers and consumables. Amongst the costs to students, they included the costs of cartridges needed to print out learning materials. While the existence of hidden costs is accepted, researchers do not agree on what the hidden costs are. For example, Morgan (2000) included, as hidden costs, the costs of maintaining the central administrative services, such as the central finance office and the president's office, the costs of construction and maintenance of Websites, and the costs of evaluation.

SHIFTING COSTS ONTO THE LEARNER

As indicated above, it is now widely recognised that online learning does not yield the types of savings for institutions that were originally expected, and that therefore to support online learning institutions need to be actively managing costs. From the range of delivery options, an institution needs to choose the combination that will yield the best outcomes taking into consideration whatever the limit is on aggregate cost. Moonen (1994) argued that for costs to be reduced in the long run, some must be passed on to the student. This may be achieved in a number of ways. For example, Turoff (1996) in his costing model for a virtual university proposed shifting most of the computer and communications costs on the learner.

Expecting students to bear costs that previously were borne by the institution represents a sort of "sleight of hand" when it comes to measuring the costs of different delivery models. It doesn't actually amount to reducing costs at all. However, there are some circumstances in which such a shift of costs is reasonable and even logical. If developments in technology result in the take-up of particular technologies becoming so widespread that students can be expected to possess the technology, then taking advantage of that fact may be to the student's benefit. The advent of mobile phones is a case in point. The penetration of mobile phones into homes has now become so widespread that even in poor African countries mobile phones are commonplace. Therefore, depending on the type of phone plan to which a person subscribes, support received via mobile phone, despite offering much greater convenience, may not impose any added cost on the learner.

Inglis (1999) found that in comparing the actual costs of offering a print-based course with the expected costs of offering the same course online, telecommunications represented a significant proportion of costs. While the cost, and even the availability of telecommunications, still remains an issue in some developing countries, particularly in Africa, the spread of broadband for entertainment purposes and the widespread take-up of high-speed capped broadband plans have eliminated telecommunications access as a cost consideration for most students.

CONSIDERATION OF COSTS IN A TRAINING CONTEXT

Online distance education is increasingly being used in business to lower costs and improve training outcomes. However, the way in which training costs are analysed in a business context is somewhat different from the way they are analysed in a public education context. Costs are measured in relation to the activities of the business rather than in terms of financial expense.

One cost factor that has been repeatedly identified as a major contributor to costs in a training context is the cost of travel, including the cost of time spent in travel (Moonen, 1997; Ravet & Layte, 1997). This is a factor that is not generally considered when comparing the costs of different modes of delivery of university programmes as this is typically a cost borne by the student. In business, much training continues to be delivered face-to-face and a significant proportion of that training at a location distant from a person's place of employment.

Businesses judge the value of training on the basis of the return on the initial investment (ROI) rather than just on the magnitude of the initial investment (Cukier, 1997). ROI can be calculated as the percentage of the profit generated from the investment after taking taxation into account or as time taken to recover the Initial investment. However, the basis on which the return is calculated may affect the comparison. Barnett and Mattox (2010) explain that measures of success, including ROI, are determined by both learning and business needs and Cross (2001) points out that training managers are apt to measure returns in terms of attainment of learning outcomes whereas business unit managers are more likely to measure returns in terms of business outcomes.

RECENT DEVELOPMENTS IN TECHNOLOGY AND THEIR IMPACT ON COSTS

One consequence of the much greater reliance that is placed today on information and communications technology for the delivery of distance education programmes is that the economics of distance education have become much more closely tied to these developments. For this reason, when comparing costs of alternative modes of delivery, it is important to consider which are the most significant trends in relation to information and communications technologies that are impacting costs.

The emergence of online learning represented a major advance in the application of information and communications technology to education. However, recently another surge in development has been seen. Several new trends in the way in which technology is being used in education, with important implications for online distance education, have become apparent. The first, of course, has been the rapid adoption of social networking media, such as Facebook and Twitter and other services like them. These may not represent mainstream delivery media but form part of the technological environment in which learners operate and therefore offer the potential to be woven into learning activities. More directly relevant to course delivery are the growing range of Web 2.0 tools such as blogs, wikis, which have opened the possibility of introducing new types of teaching-learner interactions into distance education Whether these technologies will advance teaching and learning to the extent that the advocates for them claim is yet to be demonstrated. However, their availability is unquestionably altering the way in which the delivery of distance education is understood. It is also having an impact on costs by increasing the range of options available to distance educators and the consequent investment in technological infrastructure, staff development and course development.

A decade ago, institutions began centralising support for online learning by implementing central learning management systems. This approach was consistent with the principle of obtaining economies of scale by spreading the costs of infrastructure across the largest number of students. However, developments in the marketplace leading to what many institutions perceived to be a near-monopoly situation, together with the appearance of a number of successful open-source solutions, led many to re-evaluate their technology strategies (Bates, 2011). As a result many institutions have moved across to open source solutions. The reasons for adopting open source solutions have been varied.

The reasons for moving to open sources solutions have been mixed. Although some institutions saw the relief from having to pay annual licence fees as a significant saving, those that have examined their costs closely, have generally concluded that licence fees don't represent an important cost factor. On the other hand, switching LMSs carries a considerable cost because of the need to convert courseware and train staff. For a switch to be justified, the additional cost must therefore be balanced by other benefits. For some institutions, the most attractive benefit is being able to customise the LMS. However, customisation itself carries a cost. The difficulty in making a cost-benefit assessment in relation to choice of LMS is that the field does not stand still. Such assessments can usually only be made against products already in the market, not against products that are yet to appear.

A more recent development has been the emergence of cloud computing (He et al., 2011). The advent of cloud computing has a bearing on costs because as well as providing access to increased economies of scale, it shifts the balance between fixed and variable costs—replacing the capital costs of IT infrastructure with recurrent costs of service provision. This alters the way in which costs vary with increase in student numbers, enabling breakeven points to be reached with lower student numbers. However, a stronger justification for moving to cloud computing may lie in improvements to the quality of services than in decreases in costs (Goldstein, 2010). Cloud computing also offers institutions much greater flexibility in introducing innovations.

As institutions have developed greater understanding of the characteristics of the technologies supporting online learning they have discovered ways of lowering the cost of using technology. This is the normal pattern in other industries. Use of technologies becomes more efficient with time. An OECD study that compared costs across 19 institutions in 13 countries in the Asia-Pacific region, it was found that universities saw potential for increased efficiencies through facilitating increased peer or automated learning, drawing on the learning objects model to increase the re-use of materials, and standardising courses (OECD, 2005). It is to be expected that institutions will be more likely to recognise opportunities for reducing costs by reflecting on the way in which improvements can be made to the ways in which they are operating than by trying to imagine new ways of operating. Nevertheless, developments such as the shift towards cloud computing also offer substantial opportunities for reducing costs and it therefore behoves managers of distance education operations to investigate these opportunities.

EMERGENCE OF THE OPEN EDUCATIONAL RESOURCES MOVEMENT

The development that promises to have the greatest impact on costs of online distance education courses over the coming years is the emergence of the open educational resources (OER) movement. The term "open educational resources" arose from the 2002 UNESCO Forum on the Impact of Open Courseware for Higher Education in Developing Countries (UNESCO, 2002). The OER movement originated from an earlier movement seeking to promote the development of reusable learning objects (Saum, 2007). However, while the goals of the learning objects movement and the OER movement are similar—lowering the cost of courseware development by encouraging reuse—the methods being pursued to achieve this are quite different. The learning objects movement was focused on modularity, digital rights management, and—most importantly, in this context—the development of learning objects economies (Friesen, 2009). By contrast, the OER movement has been focused on encouraging sharing as a way of reducing costs.

Frequently, OER are described as digital resources. Kanwar, Kodhandaraman, and Umar (2010, p. 67) explained that OER are seen as "(1) free and freely available, (2) suitable for all levels of education, (3) modular, (4) reusable, and (5) online", and that this definition assumes that OER are reusable learning objects. However, Butcher (2011) says that OER may be in any medium and that what defines OER is simply their copyright status. Atkins, Brown, and Hammond (2007) define OER as:

> … teaching, learning, and research resources that reside in the public domain or have been released under an intellectual property license that permits their free use or re-purposing by others. (p. 4)

Use of OER does not preclude the use of copyright resources nor development by an institution of its own resources; OER may simply form part of a mixed collection of resources (Butcher, 2011).

In considering the impact of OER we must give consideration to what is meant by "resources" in this context. In much of the discussion of OER, the resources being considered are the types of materials that support lectures, such as lecture notes and PowerPoint presentations (Butcher, 2011). However, the materials supplied to students learning at a distance are often much more sophisticated. With the growth in the multimedia considerable investment was made into the development of interactive learning environments. A wide range of pedagogical models is therefore encompassed by the term "learning resources". It is true that some distance education resources bear a closer similarity to textbooks than to a "tutorial-in-print" (Rowntree, 1974). These would not, however, be regarded as examples of good practice. The OER movement has so far made little distinction between these different types of resources despite the very considerable cost implications that such distinctions carry. Resources are considered to be the packages of materials supplied to students irrespective of what they are comprised. However, these authors point out that the OER concept has evolved over the past decade, starting out as lecture notes placed online (as per the MIT Open Courseware Initiative), developing into self-instructional materials designed for structured learning (as per the UK Open University's Open Learn Project) and then developing to the collaborative development of shared courses (as per the Virtual University for Small States of the Commonwealth).

However, institutional attitudes are not so important in developing countries as the attitudes of funding agencies. For funding agencies, the adoption of OER offers a means of amplifying the return on investment in learning resource development.

Notwithstanding the growing interest in OER, the movement still faces a threat to its survival from the fact that the current models for OER development are not sustainable in the long term. Most OER development is donor supported, and when donor funding is withdrawn activity typically ceases (Kanwar et al., 2010). Whether the movement can evolve to become one that is economically sustainable is yet to be seen.

One development gives reason for some optimism about the future of the OER movement. While the cause of developing nations has depended for support on organisations such as the Commonwealth of Learning, UNESCO and the Hewlett Foundation, the Labor-Education initiative of the Obama administration (Carey, 2011) offers more substantial resources behind the concept. This initiative provides for community colleges competing for US$2 billion funding to produce educational resources that must be made freely available under a Creative Commons licence to institutions anywhere in the world. With funding on this scale, it seems inevitable that the OER concept will be brought into the mainstream and if that is the outcome then the implications for the ways in which institutions go about learning resource development could be substantial.

THE RELATIONSHIP BETWEEN COST AND QUALITY

Attempts to contain or manage costs can have important bearing on the quality of educational delivery. Costs should not be considered in isolation from quality. The reason for the UK Open University's original pursuit of economies of scale was to support the substantial investment needed to develop high quality learning resources and provide a range of innovative student support services. The University's choice of the resource-based delivery model was, consequently, not driven just by the aim of maximising flexibility but also by the aim of enhancing quality. Not everyone has held the view that that learning at university level is best facilitated via a resource-based model. Turoff (1997) argued that by the time that subject matter is sufficiently well understood that it can be presented in the form of learning packages, it is too out of date to be relevant at the university level. However, development of the Internet and the World Wide Web has made the development and dissemination of up-to-date educational resources easier.

Quality is measured not just in terms of the topicality and depth of subject matter that a course covers, but also in terms of the effectiveness with which students learn—which is in turn a function of the design of a course and the way in which it is delivered. In the debate that has been taking place regarding the future of OER, the focus has been largely on licensing rather than pedagogical issues (Butcher, 2011). However, for OERs to make a lasting impact, they need to meet pedagogical quality criteria.

Use of OER alters the cost-benefit relationship in delivery of distance education courses on both the cost and benefit side of the equation and may reduce or eliminate one of the major contributors to the cost of delivery of courses—i.e. the cost of courseware development. However, given that the resources used to deliver a course may be a combination of OER, self-developed and copyright materials, the impact on cost will depend on what the mix of resources is. As noted, Butcher (2011) argues that use of OER represents a powerful force for improving the quality of teaching and learning in distance education. In many cases that will be so, however, whether or not it will be so in a particular case will depend very much on an institution's starting point. For an institution that has already made a substantial investment in the development of learning resources, shifting to use of OER may not offer much by way of an improvement in the quality of teaching and learning. It may on the other hand contribute to an improvement in the quality of educational provision by providing access to resources that are of a standard that an institution might not be able to develop itself. OER are particularly attractive to institutions in developing countries where the funding for development of learning resources is scarce and the need for expansion of educational opportunities is greatest.

The proposition that taking up the use of OER offers an effective means of enhancing quality seems to fly in the face of the strong case that has been mounted by those of social constructivist persuasion that the way to improve learning is to increase student-student interaction by moving towards the greater use of a (virtual) classroom-based delivery model. However, the situation is complex, because in a context where technological infrastructure is relatively weak or very costly, use of resource materials offers a means of ensuring that students are still supported in their learning. This is another reason why OER are particularly attractive to institutions in developing countries.

Development of resources designed for facilitating learning rather than simply for informing is a much more time-consuming endeavour and an endeavour which has far greater cost implications. The distinction between facilitating learning and informing is often overlooked or its importance downplayed. Resources intended to facilitate learning need to be designed to scaffold the development of learners' understanding and their development of other capabilities. This involves incorporation of suitable learning activities into the learning resource—a process that requires considerable development effort. By contrast, resources intended merely to inform need only be meaningful to those for readers for whom they are intended. The development of resources designed to facilitate learning is, consequently, more resource-demanding. However, separate from the OER developments, the well-developed resource repositories, some of which were established well before the emergence of the OER as a significant movement in distance education, have been strengthening the processes by which the quality of the resources they hold and these steps taken to strengthen quality assurance will also benefit efforts to improve quality of OER (Stella, 2010).

WHAT CONCLUSIONS CAN WE DRAW?

As explained at the beginning of this chapter, one of the keys to understanding the impact of costs in distance education is to understand the way in which economies of scale are achieved. While the manner in which courses are delivered may have changed considerably, the ways in which economies of scale are obtained have remained essentially the same. Economies of scale are potentially achievable in situations where the ratio of fixed costs to variable costs is high. Many fixed costs are associated with the design and development of courses, and particularly with the design and development of learning resources. The quest for greater economies of scale favours adoption of a resource-based delivery model.

However, up to this point, costs have been discussed as though courses are relatively homogeneous in their designs and this is frequently not the case. Moreover, there are some good reasons why institutions should be seeking to adopt more heterogeneous designs. By doing so they may, at the same time, be able to improve quality and contain costs.

Courses comprise a variety of components. The cost of development of individual components can vary greatly. Managing the overall costs of development and delivery may therefore involve separately managing individual components. For example, the way to gain the benefit of well-designed multimedia simulations may be by combining them with much more easily developed resources. The cost of development of multimedia simulations is commonly recognised as being very high. However, the cost-per-student of incorporating a multimedia simulation into a course can be brought down by sharing the cost of development with a group of institutions or by obtaining the simulation from a learning objects collection. The increasing popularity of the OER concept is likely to give new impetus to efforts to solve the technological and pedagogical problems encountered when the concept of reusable learning objects was earlier proposed as a way of bringing down the cost of high quality courseware.

The trend away from institutional provision of online learning infrastructure to use of third-party services will reduce an institution's ability to achieve economies of scale at the institutional level. Infrastructure capital costs will be replaced by annual service subscription costs. Paradoxically, though, further economies may still be achievable. The reason for this is that the potential for obtaining economies of scale will be passed on to the service providers. They, in turn, should reflect this in lowered subscription costs. Whether or not this happens will depend on the operation of market forces.

Moving to cloud computing carries additional risks, including security, privacy, reliability, vendor dependency, and compliancy with legal requirements (Goldstein, 2010; He et al., 2011). Some of these risks are related to third-party provision of service, and some to a change in the point of delivery. These risks will be unlike risks that institutions will previously have managed and therefore it will be important to develop an understanding of the risks in order that they can be managed appropriately and effectively. This is an area where institutions could work together to develop a shared understanding. Depending on the way in which risks are managed, the actions taken to mitigate the risks may themselves carry a significant cost and institutions should take this factor into account in deciding when, whether and how to move to outsourcing.

The emergence of the OER movement can be expected to yield some cost savings, although the extent of the savings is yet to be established. Its impact will depend in part on the types of services that grow up to support the sharing of resources. The investment of time spent in locating suitable resources can be as costly as the investment of time in developing resources if the resources are scarce or there is no readily available means of identifying what resources are available in a particular discipline area. So the development of directories and databases will be important in determining the impact that this movement has.

One cost factor that does not appear to have attracted much attention up to this point is the cost of innovation. Many distance education providers are investing heavily in technology-based innovation, not to save costs, but to demonstrate their commitment to keeping up with the latest developments. This type of activity can be regarded as research and development and as such is normally carried out in order to identify ways of saving costs or improving service. However, educational institutions are often not very successful at institutionalising pedagogical innovation and if investments in research development are not institutionalised then practically the whole of the initial investment becomes an added cost.

WHAT MORE WOULD IT BE USEFUL TO KNOW ABOUT THE RELATIVE COSTS OF ONLINE LEARNING?

At a time when the costs of online delivery are becoming better understood, the developments in social media, Web 2.0 technologies, cloud computing, together with the OER movement, are once again raising the level of uncertainty about the costs of delivery for those in institutions who are charged with the responsibility for managing costs and improving quality. While educational managers are probably in a better position to anticipate the likely impact on costs of some of these more recent developments than they were when online learning first emerged as an important force in education, now, they are probably not as well prepared to anticipate their impact on quality. So the challenges for educational managers remain considerable. Managing the costs of online learning is of doubtful value if the consequence of keeping costs contained results in a reduction in quality. It is for this reason that the relatively superficial consideration of quality by many of those engaged in the debate about the merits of OER is a matter of concern.

In earlier editions of this volume, it was predicted that the increasingly important issues of productivity and costs were likely to lead towards alignment of the practice of distance education in the United States and the practice of distance education elsewhere in the world (Inglis, 2003, 2007). In the United States, there is some evidence of the recognition of the value of learning resources, such as the championing by Educause of the National Learning Infrastructure Initiative (NLII; Twigg, 1994) and the establishment of learning resource repositories, such as MERLOT (www.merlot.org), to take advantage of economies of scale. However, the remote classroom model continues to be embraced quite strongly. Elsewhere, meanwhile, the ascendancy of Web 2.0 technologies has resulted in a somewhat more noticeable shift in the opposite direction. Nevertheless, many questions remain to be answered and new issues are surfacing:

- Are students' needs in relation to engagement for learning the same as or different from their needs for engagement in social interaction and what are the implications for the costs of the type of learning environments institutions provide?
- If learner-learner interaction is essential to offering students a quality learning experience, then how can online distance education continue to expand if obtaining economies of scale are only obtained by employing resource-based delivery models?
- Will the increase in the magnitude of variable costs to fixed costs that is occurring as a consequence of a shift from institutionally-provided IT services to cloud-based services raise or lower the institutional cost of service provision?
- Is the growing array of technological options now becoming available for supporting online distance education increasing flexibility at the expense of complexity and cost?

- What new potential risks are likely to be encountered to cloud-based delivery of distance education programs and what steps ought an institution to be taking to mitigate those risks?

REFERENCES

Arafeh, S. (2004). *The implications of information and communications technologies for distance education: Looking toward the future* (Final Report, P11913). Arlington, VA: SRI International.

Ashenden, D. (1987). *Costs and cost structure in external studies: A discussion of issues and possibilities in Australian higher education.* Canberra: Australian Government Publishing Service.

Atkins, D. E., Brown, J. S., & Hammond, A. L. (2007). *A review of the Open Educational Resources (OER) movement: Achievements, challenges and new opportunities.* Menlo Park, CA: Hewlett Foundation.

Bacsich, P., Ash, C., Boniwell, K., Kaplan, L., Mardell, J., & Carvon-Atach, A. (1999). *The costs of networked learning.* Sheffield, UK: Sheffield Hallam University.

Barnett, K., & Mattox, J. R. (2010). Measuring success and ROI in corporate training. *Journal of Asynchronous Learning Networks, 14*(2), 28–44.

Bartolic-Zlomislic, S., & Bates, A. W. (1999). *Assessing the costs and benefits of telelearning: A case study from the University of British Columbia.* Retrieved from http://research.cstudies.ubc.ca.nce/indiex.html

Bates, T. (2011). Understanding Web 2.0 and its implications for e-learning. In M. Lee & C. McLoughlin (Eds.), *Web 2.0-based e-Learning: Applying social informatics for tertiary teaching* (pp. 21–42), Hershey, PA: IGI Global.

Butcher, N. (2011). *A basic guide to Open Educational Resources (OER).* Vancouver, Canada: Commonwealth of Learning.

Carey, K. (2011, May 15). The quiet revolution in open learning. *The Chronicle of Higher Education.* Retrieved from http://chronicle.com/article/The-Quiet-Revolution-in-Open/127545/

Crawford, C. B., Gould, L. V., King, D., & Parker, C. (2010). Quality and growth implications of incremental costing models for distance education units. *Online Journal of Distance Education Administration, 13*(1). Retrieved from: http://www.westga.edu/~distance/ojdla/spring131/crawford131.html

Cross, J. (2001). A fresh look at ROI. *Learning circuits.* Retrieved from http://www.learningcircuits.org/2001/jan2001/cross.html

Cukier, J. (1997). Cost-benefit analysis of telelearning: Developing a methodology framework. *Distance Education, 18*(1), 137–152.

Fielden, J. (2002, August). Costing e-learning: is it worth trying or should we ignore the figures? *The Observatory on Borderless Higher Education, Report.* Retrieved from http://www.obhe.ac.uk

Friesen, N. (2009). Open educational resources: New possibilities for change and sustainability, *International Review of Research in Open and Distance Education, 10*(5). Retrieved from http://www.irrodl.org/index.php/irrodl/article/view/664/1388

Goldstein, P. J. (2010). Demystifying the cloud: Implications for IT funding in higher education. *ECAR Research Bulletin* 4. Boulder, CO: Educause Center for Applied Research.

Gordon, S., He, W., & Abdous, M. (2009). Using a web-based system to estimate the cost of online course production. *Online Journal of Distance Education Administration, 12*(3). Retrieved from http://www.westgo.edu/~distance/ojdla/fall123/gordon123.pdf

Guri-Rosenblit, & Gros, B. (2011). E-learning: Confusing terminology, research gaps and inherent challenges. *The Journal of Distance Education, 25*(11). Retrieved from http://www.jofde.ca/index.php/jde/article/view/729

He, W., Cernusca, D., & Abdous, M. (2011). Exploring cloud computing fpr distance education. *Online Journal of Distance Learning Administration, 14*(3). Retrieved from http://www.westga.edu/~distance/ojdla/fall143/he_cernusca_abdous143.html

Inglis, A. (1999). Is online delivery less costly than print and is it meaningful to ask? *Distance Education, 20*(2), 220–239.

Inglis, A. (2003). A comparison of online delivery costs with some alternative distance delivery methods. In M. G. Moore & W. Anderson (Eds.), *Handbook of distance education* (pp. 727–740). Mahwah, NJ: Erlbaum.

Inglis, A. (2007). Comparing costs of alternative delivery methods. In M. G. Moore (Ed.), *Handbook of distance education* (2nd ed., pp. 437–448) Mahwah, NJ: Erlbaum.

Inglis, A., Ling, P., & Joosten, V. (2002). *Delivering digitally: Managing the transition to the knowledge media* (2nd ed.). London: Kogan Page.

Kanwar, A., Kodhandaraman, B., & Umar, A. (2010). Toward sustainable open education resources: A perspective from the global south, *The American Journal of Distance Education, 24*(2), 65–80.

Laaser, W. (2008). Economics of distance education reconsidered. *Turkish Online Journal of Distance Education, 9*(3). Retrieved from: https://tojde.anadolu.edu.tr/tojde31/pdf/article_10.pdf

Laurillard, D. (2007). Modelling benefits-oriented costs for technology enhanced learning. *Higher Education, 54*(1), 21–39.

McNeil, D. R. (1980). UMA: progress of an experiment. In M. N. Chamberlain (Ed.), *Providing continuing education by media and technology* (pp. 315–339).San Francisco: Jossey-Bass.

Moonen, J. (1994). How to do more with less? In K. Beattie, C. McNaught, & S. Wills (Eds.), *Interactive multimedia in university education: Designing for change in teaching and learning* (pp. 155–164). Amsterdam: Elsevier.

Moonen, J. (1997). The efficiency of telelearning. *Journal of Asynchronous Learning Networks, 1*(2), 68–77.

Morgan, B. M. (2000). *Is distance learning worth it? Helping determine the costs of online courses* (Unpublished masters thesis). Marshall University; Huntington, West Virginia.

OECD. (2005). *E-learning in tertiary education: Where do we stand?* Paris: Author.

Ravet, S., & Layte, M. (1997). *Technology-based training. A comprehensive guide to choosing, implementing and developing new technologies in training.* London: Kogan Page.

Rowntree, D. (1974). *Educational technology in curriculum development.* London: Harper Row.

Rumble, G. (2001). Just how relevant is e-education to global education needs? *Open Learning, 16*(3), 223–232.

Saum, R. (2007). An abridged history of learning objects. In P. Northrup (Ed.), *Learning objects for instruction: Design and evaluation* (pp. 1–15). Hershey, PA: IGI Global.

Stella, A. (2010). Quality and quality assurance in higher education: The opportunities and challenges of OER, UNESCO: COL Workshop, Taking OER beyond the OER Community: Towards Quality in Higher Education, Windhoek, Namibia.

Turoff, M. (1996). Costs of the development of a virtual university. *Journal of Asynchronous Learning Networks, 1*(2), 17–27. Retrieved http://www.aln.org

Turoff, M. (1997, April). *Alternative futures for distance teaching: The force and the darkside.* Invited Keynote Presentation, UNESCO/Open University International Colloquiem, Virtual Learning Environments and the Role of the Teacher. Milton Keynes, UK: The Open University.

Twigg, C. A. (1994). The need for a National Learning Infrastructure, *Educom Review, 29*, 4–6. Retrieved from http://www.educause/nlii/keydocs/monograph.html

UNESCO. (2002). Forum on the impact of open courseware for higher education in developing countries final report. Retrieved from http://unesdoc.unesco.org/images/0012/001285/128515e.pdf

Weller, M. (2004). Learning objects and the e-learning cost dilemma. *Open Learning, 19*(3), 293–302.

Zawacki-Richter, O., Bäcker, E. M., & Vugt, S. (2009). Review of distance education research (2000 to 2008): Analysis of research areas, methods and authorship patterns. *International Review of Research in Open and Distance Learning, 10*(6), 21–49.

33

COST-EFFECTIVENESS OF ONLINE EDUCATION

INSUNG JUNG AND SUNG LEE

INTRODUCTION

In general, the literature has shown that "distance education can be more cost-effective than face-to-face education and that costs are predominantly dependent upon student enrollment and the fixed costs of course development and delivery" (Cukier, 1997, p. 138). But cost-effectiveness of distance education is often influenced by several other factors such as technology choice (Rumble, 2003), amount of interactions (Inglis, 1999), and type of learner support (Hülsmann, 2004). This chapter is an attempt to provide an overview of cost-effectiveness studies in distance education by examining various factors affecting cost-effectiveness of both early distance education delivered mostly by one-way technologies and online education carried out via interactive network technologies.

COST-EFFECTIVENESS OF EARLY DISTANCE EDUCATION

Capper and Fletcher (1996) analyzed previous studies on cost-effectiveness of distance education and identified factors influencing costs in distance education. Those factors include: number of courses offered (since the cost of developing a course is one of the major expenses in distance education, the most cost-efficient approach is to offer fewer courses for larger numbers of students), frequency of course revision, type of media used, type and amount of student support, and attrition rate. They concluded that even though cost-effectiveness of distance education is supported in most of the studies, costs vary substantially from one situation to another and are influenced by a number of factors. Generally, cost-effectiveness of distance education increases as the number of students increase, and the number of courses declines because labor costs in distance education directly corresponds to the number of enrolled students (Berge & Donaldson, 2008).

A substantial number of studies analyzed in Capper and Fletcher's (1996) report supported cost-effectiveness of distance education. A study which was conducted in Sri Lanka showed that distance education was by far the most cost-effective—4.5 to 6 times more cost-effective than residential training programs offered in colleges of education or in service teacher training programs. The main reason for this cost-effectiveness of distance education was that the teachers in the distance education programs continued with their full teaching loads, whereas the other groups did not. As appeared in this study, savings on salary costs and travel costs for program participants have been reported as one of the main sources of cost-effectiveness of distance education.

There were cost-effectiveness studies which focused more on effectiveness of distance education than on the costs and analyzed general cost-effectiveness of distance education via various technologies. Early cost-effectiveness studies on videoconferencing report substantial cost-benefits (Hosley & Randolph, 1993; Showalter, 1983; Trevor-Deutsch & Baker, 1997). Ludlow (1994) revealed that even though its costs were higher than other classroom-based programs, interactive satellite-delivered training courses were cost-effective due to increased enrollments, increased student access to quality programs and resources, and other benefits.

Hall (1997) compared CD-ROM-based training to classroom-based training in a high-tech company and reported that over the three-year pilot period, costs for the CD-ROM-based course were 47% less than those for classroom-based courses. Moreover, the improved instructional design, a variety of instructional models and other strategies contributed to more effective learning and reduced training time.

After analyzing a series of studies on cost-effectiveness of distance education, Moore and Thompson (1997) found that cost-effectiveness depended more on costs in relation to education value, rather on costs alone. Thus, when one analyzes the cost-effectiveness of distance education, not only cost efficiency but also quality, service and speed of distance learning need to be considered. With these considerations in mind, Moore and Thompson reported several studies on cost-effectiveness of technologically mediated instruction using various technologies in a variety of contexts. As early examples of the studies, reports of Christopher (1982) and Showalter (1983) were analyzed. Christopher found that the Teleteach Expanded Delivery System was more cost-effective than resident instruction for providing training to Air Force students at remote sites. Showalter reported that a 55% cost benefit in delivering continuing education to professionals via an audioconferencing system. The cost benefits of audioconferencing were also reported in some other studies in K-12 context (Schmidt, Sullivan, & Hardy, 1994).

In addition, studies that specifically compare cost-effectiveness of a distance education course via videoconferencing to a traditional classroom-based course were reported. Those studies emphasized substantial savings through decreased travel costs by bringing training to the workplace (Moore & Thompson, 1997).

However, based on the analysis of studies prior to 1998, Zhao, Lei, Yan, Lai, and Tan (2005) conclude that distance education appeared to be less effective compared with face-to-face education, while studies after 1998 found the opposite. This may be explained by the fact that distance programs are getting better with more powerful delivery media and more sophisticated support systems due to the technology changes.

While the aforementioned studies are useful in providing a comparative look at identifying the costs and effectiveness of early distance education, they often exclude "costs of development or costs borne by students" and "use competing methodologies" which make them difficult to compare (Bakia, 2000). Because of the methodological limitations of cost-effectiveness studies, findings from these studies need to be viewed as suggestive rather than definitive.

Since the emergence of interactive network technologies, online education has become a popular mode of distance education.

COST-EFFECTIVENESS OF ONLINE EDUCATION

The many benefits associated with online education are well discussed in the literature. Several educators or decision makers believe that the primary benefit of online education is that costs can be distributed over a large number of students, resulting in economies of scale for educational institutions (Inglis, 1999; Kearsley, 2000; Whalen & Wright, 1999). Inglis (2007) argued that these economies of scale in online education can be obtained by spreading the fixed costs of design and development of Web-delivered resource materials across a larger course intake and the costs of the information and communication technology infrastructure needed to support online delivery across a large total online cohort.

As discussed in several articles (McDonald & Gibson, 1998; Relan & Gillani, 1997; Salmon, 1999; Saravani & Clayton, 2009; Sharma, 2011), online technologies are known to be capable of providing an interactive learning environment which supports people in communicating with others in different places and time zones to fulfill their education or training needs. The Internet, as one of online technologies, is viewed as an innovative distance education approach for delivering instruction to learners in different places and/or difference time and for improving learner-learner, learner-instructor interaction. Related research and case studies show that virtual education via the Internet provides an opportunity to develop new learning experiences for learners by managing self-directed learning and sharing information and ideas in a cooperative and collaborative manner (Daugherty & Funke, 1998; Hiltz, 1994; Huddlestone & Pike, 2008; Jonassen, Prevish, Christy, & Stavrulaki 1999). Moreover, online education provides new learners with access to quality online degree programs that will not only provide important credentials, but also offer them a strong sense of accomplishment, personal satisfaction and overall life enrichment (Oakley II, 2004).

To analyze the cost-benefits of online education, Cukier (1997) summarized four of the cost-benefit methodologies examined in the previous studies and argued for an integrated approach to the cost-benefit analysis of network-based learning. Four approaches to cost-benefit analysis include: a value-based approach, a mathematical modeling approach, a comparative approach, and a return on investment (ROI) approach.

A value-based approach considers the pedagogical needs and values of an educational institution in analyzing cost-benefits of online education. For instance, an educational institution which sees small group interaction as important learner experience will be more likely to view interaction as a benefit to be analyzed whereas an institution whose goal in adopting online education is to reach as many students as possible will view expansive delivery and limited interaction as benefits in introducing online education. A mathematical modeling approach focuses on the costs and benefits that can be easily quantifiable. For example, a study which examines both the costs and benefits of videoconferencing used in two different ways will be interested in cost assessments for the teleconferencing, the costs savings resulting from remote delivery in two ways: where the instructor travels to the students; and where the students travel to the instructor, and benefits of each method. In this study, cost-benefits of videoconferencing in two different delivery situations will be quantified for comparison.

A return on investment approach attributes an economic value to benefits and seeks to measure monetary gains of adopting a new technology in education. This approach has been adopted in more recent studies including Sharma (2011), Wentling and Park (2002), Wilson, Wilson, and Thangavel (2007), and Yi, Zuo, and Wang (2007).

The proposed approach to cost-benefit analysis of online education, called an integrated approach, focuses on integrating major concepts in these four previous approaches. When this integrated approach is adopted, analyses of costs must address categories of capital and recurrent costs, production and delivery costs, and fixed and variable costs. And when estimating benefits of online education, performance-driven benefits such as learning outcomes, cost savings, students & teacher satisfaction, and opportunity costs; value-driven benefits such as flexibility, access, interaction, user-friendliness, and adaptability of materials; and value-added benefits such as reduction in capital investment, reduction in pollution, increased job creation, new business opportunities, reductions in social community costs, and creation of secondary markets must be analyzed. Cukier (1997) emphasized that the analysis of costs and benefits should be conducted separately and the approach should be multi-leveled. Cukier's idea can be found in some quality assurance mechanisms for e-learning. For example, Clayton and Saravani (2009) proposed a quality assurance model which is multi-leveled and combines the effectiveness and impact analysis and the ROI approach.

Based on Cukier's (1997) frameworks of cost-benefit analysis, six case studies have been conducted by the NCE-Telelearning project team in Canada and two of them are available online. Cost measures assessed in the two case studies (Bartolic-Zlomislic & Bates, 1999; Bartolic-Zlomislic & Brett, 1999) include: (a) capital and recurrent costs, (b) production and delivery costs, and (c) fixed and variable costs. The cost structure of each technology is analyzed and the unit cost per learner is measured. The costs assessed in Bartolic-Zlomislic and Brett's study did not include overhead costs as these were unknown. Benefit data include: (a) performance driven benefits, (b) value driven benefits, and (c) societal or value added benefits. Both quantitative and qualitative data were collected and included students, faculty and staff, and administrator perspectives.

A case study by Bartolic-Zlomislic and Brett (1999) analyzed costs and benefits of an entirely online graduate course at the Ontario Institute for Studies in Education of The University of Toronto in changing the software from Parti, a UNIX-based mail and conferencing software, to WebCSILE, a Web-based software. The result of the study projected that their online program will make a small notional profit of $1,962 Canadian per year during five years and 19 students will be needed to break-even. It concluded that it is possible to develop highly cost-effective online courses within a niche market, at relatively moderate cost to learners. It also recognized that, despite the change in software from Parti to WebCSILE, the largest cost of the online course was tutoring and marking time spent by the instructors due to the nature of the course, which emphasized active online discussions. These costs could be lowered if the format of the course was changed to a less constructivistic environment. The instructors and students reported that additional skills to the contents of the course were learned, such as computer and writing skills. A case study from the University of British Columbia (Bartolic-Zlomislic & Bates, 1999) also reported similar results. The researchers found that the annual break-even enrollment based on the projected costs and revenues over four years was 44 students.

A study by Inglis (2007) is an attempt to examine the costs of shifting from print-based course to online course and to seek the rationales for moving to online delivery. Inglis showed that online delivery was less economical, when measured on a cost per student basis, than print-based delivery for four different intake levels (50/100/150/200 students). The distribution costs (such as ISP charges and individual support) for online courses represented a major component of overall costs. The author predicted that while there is an appreciable likelihood that the costs of mounting the subject online would be considerably higher than the estimates made during the planning phase, the likelihood of the costs being lower is small. The results of this study, in part, reflect the fact that in traditional print-based distance education most of the economies of scale that are obtainable in the design, development and delivery stages have already been obtained. Several strategies to balance costs with benefits in online education are suggested.

There are other empirical studies that specifically compare the cost-benefits of online courses to traditional face-to-face courses. Bakia (2000) reported a study conducted by the Rochester Institute of Technology which compared the operational costs of asynchronous instruction using a variety of online technologies including email, Internet, Web materials, and telephone conferencing in traditional classrooms, and distance courses. Given the exclusions of planning and production costs and investments in technical infrastructure, the study reported cost-effectiveness of asynchronous instruction used in distance courses. It also found that faculty used equal or more time in distance courses and reported using their time differently.

Jung (2005) compared the cost-effectiveness of an online method with a face-to-face teaching in an in-service teacher training class. She found that online teacher training was more cost-effective than face-to-face teacher training, mainly due to the lower opportunity cost of the participants. Similarly, another study conducted by Whalen and Wright (1999) reports that Web-based training is more cost-effective than classroom teaching mainly due to the reduction in course delivery time and the potential to deliver courses to a larger number of students in Web-based training. In particular, asynchronous teaching on the Web showed cost-effective compared with synchronous teaching on the Web because of the cost of having a live instructor and the greater student salary costs due to the extra time required to deliver the course.

Hodges (2009) reported the effectiveness of distance education delivered on the Intranet. Some identified benefits of intranet learning system include (a) 94% of users see an increase in compliance, (b) users save up to 93% of the costs of traditional training, (c) instructors save up to 30 hours per week, and (d) managers save up to 15 hours per week.

The most commonly cited benefits of online education include lower course fees, reducing travel costs, and minimization of lost work productivity on the job (Clarke, Lewis, Cole, & Ringrose, 2005; Grollman & Cannon, 2003; Shankar, 2007; Wilson et al., 2007; Wurtmann & Galli-Debicella, 2008). However, what people often fail to see is the high fixed costs involved in online education development and delivery. The large initial expenditures in new equipment and training for the developers can take a substantial amount of investment and time to implement effectively (Bartley & Golek, 2004). While online education can offer better economies of scale, it comes with a heavier price tag than originally assumed. Several studies acknowledge that extensive additional cost—for example, maintenance and upgrading of hardware and software and continuous staff training—is often involved with the implementation of online education. As Laaser

(2008) warned, the cost of the learning platform itself therefore has to be considered only as a minor cost item. In this regard, in order to maximize benefits and minimize costs, different online education strategies need to be adopted by a learning institution considering economics of scale and the flexibility of learning method. Sharma (2011) showed that a self-directed asynchronous approach can be highly flexible and achieve great economies of scale whereas a cooperative synchronous method is low in both flexibility and economies of scale.

Another area where caution is needed in analyzing cost-benefits of online education is that the point at which each program breaks even is different depending on the number of students. The appropriate number of students should not be determined by economies of scale only, but considering educational philosophy, course design, and the number of students who can be accommodated by the technology (Wentling & Park, 2002). Bates (2000) suggested between 20 and 40 students as an appropriate number of students for online education per year per course and Bishop (2000) argued for 25 students as an appropriate size for both fiscally viable and pedagogically sound. Wentling and Park (2002) recommended 22 students as an optimal cohort size for online education in a case study of university program using breakeven analysis.

A report of cost-effectiveness of online courses in a mega-university shows that the development and delivery costs for online education decrease over time (Jung & Leem, 2000). And when compared with a traditional distance education course, which used TV and textbooks, an online course had higher completion rate (55.2% in the traditional course and 93.1% in the online course) and thus lower cost per completer. The students in two different courses show significant differences in learning achievement and technology literacy level.

From the studies reviewed in this section, we understand that the scale, design, and production quality, an institution's pedagogical value, and rapidly changing costs of hardware and software all influence cost-effectiveness of online education. Some studies have focused on identifying more specific factors affecting cost-effectiveness of online education. The following section introduces their tentative findings.

FACTORS AFFECTING COST-EFFECTIVENESS OF ONLINE EDUCATION

Even though the technology is becoming more widely available and affordable, limited infrastructure and experience, high costs, and slow Internet speeds are still one of the major obstacles in online education in both developed and developing countries. In addition to technologies, several other factors that affect cost and/or effectiveness of online education are identified in previous studies.

- Number of students in a course (Weller, 2004)
- The length of course lifetimes(Rumble, 2001)
- Number of courses offered (Capper & Fletcher, 1996; Rumble, 2001)
- Amount of multimedia component in online courses (Whalen & Wright, 1999)
- Amount of instructor-led interaction (Inglis, 1999; Rumble, 2001)
- Type of online education platforms (Bartolic-Zlomislic & Bates, 1999; Laaser, 2008)
- Choice of synchronous vs. asynchronous online interaction (Sharma, 2011; Whalen & Wright, 1999)

- Completion rate (Jung & Leem, 2000)
- Organizational structures such as single-mode and mixed-mode systems (Rumble, 2003)

Yi et al. (2007) argue that the critical factors to be taken into consideration while evaluating the investment in online education are the investment scale, the investment structure and the resources. On the benefits side, the key factors that they proposed are the benefits from the application of the technology and the benefits from the quality instruction.

Considering these factors, some cost-saving strategies were identified in previous studies. For example, online education system often requires a huge database system of online courses and materials. Since the cost of developing a database is high, most online education institutions have experienced financial difficulties in establishing a large database for their students. As a strategy to reduce the cost in operating online education, many institutions have "unbundled" educational functions—such as online course development, distribution, tutoring, assessment, general administrative affairs and learner supports (Farrell, 1999)—which are increasingly shared among specialized institutions.

Unlike analog systems, digital databases can be linked through computer networks, shared globally, revised by users, and then transformed into meaningful knowledge. The Cyber Teacher Training Center in Korea, for example, is establishing a database of online teacher training programs in cooperation with other Korean teacher training institutions. Online training programs in this database can be used, revised and implemented in different ways by different centers, and sharing allows each training center to reduce its costs for program development (Jung, 2000).

Partnerships reduce the burden of online education institutions by distributing costs across partners. An example of a sound partnership is the partnership between Singapore's first privately-funded university, the non-profit Singapore Institute of Management which allowed for the adoption and adaptation of UK Open University courses. This partnership has now evolved into an accreditation relationship with the establishment of SIM University (Latchem & Jung, 2009).

By forming appropriate partnerships with businesses, online education institutions diminish their investment risks. Collaborations with education institutions can also be mutually advantageous by permitting the exchange of technology and human resources and the sharing of courses. Each institution can develop online courses in its areas of specialization and exchange access to those courses with its partner institutions. Partnerships can also be formed with education institutions or companies in foreign countries.

Cost-effectiveness of online education can be achieved either by reducing the costs or improving the effectiveness of online education. Recent studies in the cost-effectiveness of online instruction seem to focus more on identifying factors affecting learning process, satisfaction and achievement in online instruction than on comparative cost-effectiveness of online courses over traditional courses. Instructional design, social and students' personal factors have been identified as three major factors contributing to success in online learning (Jung & Rha, 2000).

Instructional design factors such as flexible course structure, quick and frequent feedback, visual layouts, and multiples zones of content knowledge influenced online interaction and learner satisfaction (Bartley & Golek, 2004; McLoughlin, 1999; Sun, Tsai, Finger, Chen, & Yeh, 2008; Suzuki, 2007; Vrasidas & McIsaac, 1999), and thus improved effectiveness of online education. For instance, McLoughlin (1999) attempted to present an approach to the design of a culturally responsive Web environment for Indigenous Australian students and to illustrate how cultural issues and decisions were incorporated into pedagogical design of an online course. He found that design strategies such as providing the multiples zones of content knowledge, adopting participatory course structure, and creating dynamic online learning communities were effective in improving students' learning and satisfaction. Suzuki (2007) reported the effectiveness of the competency-based online program which combines core reading material with related Weblinks and online quizzes and requires weekly participation in threaded discussions, reports from the students on their learning and other assignment work to ensure that they are actively learning and deepening their understanding.

Social factors also affect the effectiveness of online learning. Anderson and Harris (1997) identified factors predicting the use and perceived benefits of the Internet as an instructional tool. Interpersonal interaction among learners and social integration were among the most influential factors, which is also supported by McDonald and Gibson (1998) and more recently by Cacciamani (2010). In addition, the study of Gunawardena and Zittle (1997) revealed that social presence exhibited by participants contributed more than 60% of learner satisfaction with computer conferencing courses. Specifically, Gunawardena and Zittle examined how effective social presence—the degree to which a person is perceived as real in mediated communication environment—is as a predictor of overall learner satisfaction in a computer-mediated conferencing system. The results of the study reveal that social presence contributes about 60% of learner satisfaction with computer-conferencing courses. It is suggested that design strategies that enhance social presence need to be integrated in computer-mediated learning environments in order to improve the effectiveness of online education.

Students' personal factors also play important role in online learning. For example, students' prior knowledge with technology or subject affected learning in online courses (Hill & Hannafin, 1997; Wishart & Blease, 1999; Zhao et al., 2005). Zhao et al. (2005) revealed that an author's involvement, students' grade, attitude, beliefs, satisfaction and participation, and a teacher's observation have a significant impact on the effectiveness of online education. With higher scores of these factors, the students showed higher achievements in online education than in face-to-face education. Biner, Bink, Huffman, and Dean (1995) found several personality factors such as self-sufficiency, introversion, and relative lack of compulsiveness were related to achievement among the telecourse students. Learners being autonomous individuals constructing their own knowledge (Jonassen et al., 1999; Yen & Liu, 2009) and involving actively in their learning (Johnson, Hornik, & Salas, 2008; Shneiderman, Borkowski, Alavi, & Norman 1998) also tended to maximize their own learning. On the other hand, some studies such as Selim (2007) reveal that instructor's characteristics also affect the effectiveness of online education.

With the fast development of information and communication technologies, we are now observing changes in teaching-learning modes and wide spread of online education at all educational levels throughout the world. It is thus important for educators and policy makers to understand the factors affecting those changes and their effectiveness so strategies can be appropriately explored to improve overall cost-effectiveness of online education.

FUTURE DIRECTIONS

More valid and reliable empirical data are needed on issues of costs and learning improvement for definite conclusions on the cost-effectiveness of online education (Jung, 2003). Some specific questions for future studies on cost-effectiveness include:

- Does the use of a standardized learning management system reduce costs without diminishing the quality of education?
- How much can online resource sharing improve the cost effectiveness of online education?
- How do different design strategies of online courses affect cost-effectiveness?
- What are possible ways of improving cost-effectiveness, while maintaining high interactivity?
- How can recent technologies, including social media, contribute to the improvement of cost-effectiveness of online education?
- How can economics of scale be achieved in specific contexts?
- How often must online education courses be updated or revised to maximize cost-effectiveness?
- Which factors should be considered when defining of cost-effectiveness?

The increased number of technology options have brought more opportunities than ever for distance education. Online education programs offer possibilities that would not otherwise be available because of costs, time or location constraints, especially to working adults. In addition, traditional institutions that have never provided distance education are now adopting online technologies to increase the flexibility and openness of their programs. Even though most agree that advanced technologies have made education and training more flexible and open, many learners still are unable to access the necessary technologies. There is a fear that the gap between the "haves" and the "have-nots" has widened and continues to do so. Issues of removing or lessening the disparity of access need to be addressed in cost-effectiveness studies of online education.

Educators and researchers must also continue to explore more sophisticated means of improving quality and cost-effectiveness of online education. Future studies should address questions such as:

- What are the effective design strategies to help learners maintain and manage their learning goals and processes while browsing online resources? (instructional strategies)
- How can we assist learners to more actively process information and construct meaningful knowledge? (moderating strategies)
- How can virtual education motivate the learner? (motivational strategies)
- What are the most effective and efficient means of providing guidance and feedback to learners during their learning process? (support strategies)
- What are the most effective testing strategies in virtual education to ensure that learners have integrated the desired knowledge and skills?(assessment strategies)
- How and to what extent should institutions cooperate with each other in terms of sharing e-learning resources? (partnership strategies)

Over the past few years, some of these questions have been answered. However, we need more empirical studies to explore both the effects and costs of specific design strategies on students' learning and motivation.

REFERENCES

Anderson, S. E., & Harris, J. B. (1997). Factors associated with amount of use and benefits obtained by users of a statewide Educational Telecomputing Network. *Educational Technology Research and Development, 45*(1), 19–50.

Bates, A. W. (2000). *Managing technological change: Strategies for college and university leaders.* San Francisco: Jossey-Bass.

Bakia, M. (2000, January/February). Costs of ICT use in higher education: What little we know. *TechKnow-Logia,* 49–52.

Bartley, S. J., & Golek, J. H. (2004). Evaluating the cost effectiveness of online and face-to-face instruction. *Educational Technology & Society, 7*(4), 167–175.

Bartolic-Zlomislic, S., & Brett, C. (1999). *Assessing the costs and benefits of telelearning: A case study from the Ontario Institute for Studies in Education of the University of Toronto.* Retrieved from http://citeseerx.ist.psu.edu/viewdoc/download?doi=10.1.1.4.5268&rep=rep1&type=pdf

Bartolic-Zlomislic, S., & Bates, A.W. (1999). *Assessing the costs and benefits of telelearning: A case study from the University of British Columbia.* Retrieved from http://www.c3l.uni-oldenburg.de/cde/econ/readings/bates99.pdf

Berge, S. L., & Donaldson, C. (2008). Cost-benefit of online learning. In W. J. Bramble & S. Panda (Eds.), *Economics of distance and online learning* (pp. 179–194). New York: Routledge.

Bishop, T. (2000). UMUC's online MBA program: A case study of cost-effectiveness and the implications for large-scale programs. *Online Education, 2,* 173–182.

Biner, P. M., Bink, M. L., Huffman, M. L., & Dean, R. S. (1995). Personality characteristics differentiating and predicting the achievement of televised-course students and traditional-course students. *American Journal of Distance Education, 9*(2), 46–60.

Cacciamani, S. (2010). Towards a knowledge building community: From guided to self-organized inquiry. *Canadian Journal of Learning and Technology, 36*(1). Retrieved from http://www.cjlt.ca/index.php/cjlt/article/view/582l

Capper, J., & Fletcher, D. (1996). *Effectiveness and cost-effectiveness of print-based correspondence study.* A paper prepared for the Institute for Defense Analyses. Alexandria, VA.

Christopher, G. R. (1982). The Air Force Institute of Technology — The Air Force reaches out through media: An update. In L. Parker & C. Olgren (Eds.), *Teleconferenicng and electonic communications* (pp. 343–344). Madison: University of Wisconsin-Extension.

Clarke, A., Lewis, D., Cole, I., & Ringrose, L. (2005). A strategic approach to developing e-learning capability for healthcare. *Health Information and Libraries Journal, 22*(2), 33–41.

Cukier, J. (1997). Cost-benefit analysis of telelearning: Developing a methodology framework. *Distance Education, 18*(1), 137–152.

Daugherty, M., & Funke, B. (1998). University faculty and student perceptions of web-based instruction. *Journal of Distance Education, 13*(1), 21–39.

Farrell, G. M. (1999). Introduction. In G. M. Farrell (Ed.), *The development of virtual education: A global perspective* (pp. 87–98). Vancouver: The Commonwealth of Learning.

Grollman, W. K., & Cannon, D. (2003). E-learning: A better chalkboard. *Financial Executive,* 45–47.

Gunawardena, C. N., & Zittle, F. J. (1997). Social presence as a predictor of satisfaction within a computer-mediated conferencing environment. *American Journal of Distance Education, 11*(3), 8–26.

Hall, B. (1997). *Web-based training: A cookbook.* New York: Wiley.

Hill, J. R., & Hannafin, M. (1997). Cognitive strategies and learning from the World Wide Web. *Educational Technology Research and Development, 45*(4), 37–64.

Hiltz, S. R. (1994). *The virtual classroom: Learning without limits via computer networks.* Norwood, NJ: Ablex.

Hosley, D. L., & Randolph, S. L. (1993). *Distance learning as a training and education tool.* Kennedy Space Center, FL: Lockheed Space Operations Co. ERIC Document Reproduction Service No. ED 335 936.

Huddlestone, J., & Pike J. (2008). Seven key decision factors for selecting e-learning. *Cognition Technology and Work, 10,* 237–247.

Hülsmann, T. (2004, March). The two-pronged attack on learner support: Costs and the centrifugal forces of convergence. Paper presented at *The Third EDEN Research Workshop and International Conference: Support-*

ing the Learner in Distance Education and E-Learning, Oldenburg, Germany. Retrieved from http://www.c3l. uni-oldenburg.de/cde/support/fa04/Vol.%209%20chapters/H%fclsmann.pdf

Inglis, A. (1999). Is online delivery less costly than print and is it meaningful to ask? *Distance Education, 20*(2), 220–239.

Inglis, A. (2007). Comparing costs of alternative delivery methods. In M. G. Moore (Ed.), *Handbook of distance education* (*2nd ed.*, pp. 437–449). Mahwah, NJ: Erlbaum.

Johnson, R. D., Hornik, S., & Salas, E. (2008). An empirical examination of factors contributing to the creation of successful e-learning environments. *International Journal of Human-Computer Studies, 66*(5), 356–369.

Jonassen, D., Prevish, T., Christy, D., & Stavrulaki, E. (1999). Learning to solve problems on the Web: Aggregate planning in a business management course. *Distance Education, 20*(1), 49–63.

Jung, I. S. (2000). Korea's experiments in virtual education. *Technical Notes, 5*(2). Washington, D.C.: World Bank.

Jung, I. S. (2003). Cost-effectiveness of online education. In M.G. Moore, & W.G. Anderson (Eds.), *Handbook of distance education* (pp. 717–726). Mahwah, NJ: Erlbaum.

Jung, I. S. (2005). Cost-effectiveness of online teacher training. *Open Learning, 20*(2), 131–146.

Jung, I. S., & Leem, J. H. (2000, February). *Comparing cost-effectiveness of web-based instruction and televised distance education*. A paper prepared for the Institute of Distance Education of the Korea National Open University. Seoul, Korea.

Jung, I. S., & Rha, I. (2000). Effectiveness and cost-effectiveness of online education: A review of literature. *Educational Technology, 52*(3), 34–44.

Kearsley, G., (2000). *Online education: Learning and teaching in cyberspace.* Belmont, CA: Wadsworth.

Laaser, W. (2008). Economics of distance education reconsidered. *Turkish Online Journal of Distance Education, 9*(3), 121–129.

Latchem, C., & Jung, I.S. (2009). *Distance and blended learning in Asia*. New York: Routledge.

Ludlow, B. L. (1994). *A comparison of traditional and distance education models. In rural partnerships: Working together.* ERIC Document Reproduction. Service No. ED 369 599.

McDonald, J., & Gibson, C.C. (1998). Interpersonal dynamics and group development in computer conferencing. *American Journal of Distance Education, 12*(1), 7–25.

McLoughlin, C. (1999). Culturally responsive technology use: Developing an on-line community of learners. *British Journal of Educational Technology, 30*(3), 231–244.

Moore, M. G., & Thompson, M. M. (1997). The effects of distance learning: Revised edition. *ACSDE Research Monograph, 15.* University Park: The Pennsylvania State University.

Oakley II, B. (2004). The value of online learning: Perspectives from the University of Illinois at Springfield. *Journal of Asynchronous Learning Networks, 8*(3), 22–32. Retrieved from http://sloanconsortium.org/system/files/v8n3_oakley.pdf

Relan, A., & Gillani, B.B. (1997). Web-based instruction and traditional classroom: Similarities and differences. In B. H. Khan (Ed.), *Web-based instruction* (pp. 41–46). Englewood Cliffs, NJ: Educational Technology Publications.

Rumble, G. (2001). The costs and costing of networked learning, *Journal of Asynchronous Learning Networks 5*(2), 75–96.

Rumble, G. (2003). Modeling the costs and economics of distance education. In M. G. Moore, & W. G. Anderson (Eds.), *Handbook of distance education* (pp. 703–716). Mahwah, NJ: Erlbaum.

Salmon, G. (1999). Computer mediated conferencing in large scale management education. *Open Learning, 14*(2), 34–43.

Saravani, S. J., & Clayton, J. (2009). Ensuring quality and measuring effectiveness, impact and capability of e-learning in the workplace, *The Cambridge International Conference on Open and Distance Learning 2009*, 135–143. Retrieved from http://www2.open.ac.uk/r06/documents/CambridgeConferenceMainPaper2009. pdf

Schmidt, K. J., Sullivan, M .J., & Hardy, D. W. (1994). Teaching migrant students algebra by audioconference. *The American Journal of Distance Education, 8*(3), 51–63.

Selim, H. M. (2007). E-learning critical success factors: An exploratory investigation of student perceptions. *International Journal of Technology Marketing, 2*(2), 157–182.

Sharma, K. (2011). Financial implications of implementing an e-learning project. *Journal of European Industrial Training, 35*(7), 658–686.

Shneiderman, B., Borkowski, E. Y., Alavi, M., & Norman, K. (1998). Emergent patterns of teaching/learning in electronic classrooms. *Educational Technology Research and Development, 46*(4), 23–42.

Showalter, R. G. (1983). *Speaker telephone continuing education for school personnel serving handicapped children: Final project report 1981–82.* Indianapolis: Indiana State Department of Public Instruction, Indianapolis Division of Special Education. ERIC Document Reproduction Service No. ED 231 150.

Sun, P. C., Tsai, R. J., Finger, G., Chen, Y. Y., & Yeh, D. (2008). What drives a successful e-Learning? An empirical investigation of the critical factors influencing learner satisfaction. *Computers and Education, 50*(4), 1183–1202.

Suzuki, K. (2007, July). *Learner-centered design in higher education by ICT with IDT.* Keynote address at the 8th International Conference on Information Technology Based Higher Education and Training, Kumamoto, Japan.

Trevor-Deutsch, L., & Baker, W. (1997). *Cost/benefit review of the interactive learning connection.* University Space Network Pilot. Ottawa, Canada: Strathmere Associates International Ltd.

Vrasidas, C., & McIassc, M. S. (1999). Factors influencing interaction in an online course. *American Journal of Distance Education, 13*(3), 22–36.

Weller, M. (2004). Learning objects and the e-learning cost dilemma. *Open Learning, 19*(3), 293–302.

Wentling, T., & Park, J. H. (2002). *Cost analysis of e-learning: A case study of a university program.* Retrieved from http://citeseerx.ist.psu.edu/viewdoc/download?doi=10.1.1.86.5844&rep=rep1&type=pdf

Whalen, T., & Wright, D. (1999). Methodology for cost-benefit analysis of Web-based telelearning: Case study of the Bell Online Institute. *American Journal of Distance Education, 13*(1), 23–44.

Wilson, R. Wilson, M., & Thangavel N. (2007). Cost-benefit analysis of e-learning. *Principal Journal on Information Sciences and Computing, 1*(1), 1–8.

Wishart, J., & Blease, D. (1999). Theories underlying perceived changes in teaching and learning after installing a computer network in a secondary school. *British Journal of Educational Technology, 30*(1), 25–42.

Wurtmann, B., & Galli-Debicella, A. (2008). E-learning time: Benefits, misconceptions and challenges. *Training Magazine.* Retrieved from http://www.trainingmag.com/MSG/CONTENT_DISPLAY/TRAINING/E3IC%20734785DA6216CB04D57F7%2063B92B6788

Yen, C., & Liu, S. (2009). Learner autonomy as a predictor of course success and final grades in community college online courses. *Journal of Educational Computing Research, 41*(3), 347–367.

Yi, L. Y., Zuo, M. Z., &Wang, Z.X. (2007, July). A model for analyzing and evaluating the return on investment in e-learning. Paper presented at the Seventh IEEE International Conference on advanced learning technologies, Nigata, Japan..

Zhao, Y., Lei, J., Yan, B., Lai, C., & Tan, H. S. (2005). The costs and costing of networked learning. *Teachers College Record, 107*(8), 1–83.

34

LEGAL AND RECENT COPYRIGHT ISSUES

TOMAS A. LIPINSKI

INTRODUCTION

Four topics within the copyright law should be of concern to the distance educator and student. First, ownership issues regarding content created by educators and students can complicate delivery of that content into the distance learning space. Once ownership issues are resolved or at least accommodated, a second step is for all participants to understand and, where possible, to position themselves and their institution to use the rules regarding damage remission to their advantage. The ability to qualify for such remission may make some individuals and institutions unattractive defendants. Third, familiarity with the specific provisions of the copyright law related to distance education may lead to the conclusion that the benefit of such provisions are not worth the cost of fulfilling the conditions or obligations upon which use of the provisions is predicated. Finally, and as a result of this reality, educators and students may turn increasingly to fair use to support their distance education activities. This chapter proceeds to update (from the discussion of the topic in the previous edition of the handbook, Lipinski, 2007, and to a lesser extent Lipinski, 2003) and review these topics.

SORTING OUT COPYRIGHT OWNERSHIP ISSUES: STUDENT, FACULTY, OR INSTITUTION?

The discussion of copyright ownership issues regarding instructor-created (outlines, study guides, other handouts, tests, articles, and other publications, etc.) and to a lesser extent student-authored (term papers and other assignments, discussion board and other postings, etc.) content was discussed in detail in the first (Lipinski, 2003) and second editions (Lipinski, 2007) and is not repeated here. However, several additional points and case law update are presented.

Ownership and Use of Student-Created Content

Content created by students is owned by the student-author. However, an argument can be made that the use of such content in the context of a closed or secure classroom, online or otherwise, is fair use. (Fair use is discussed in detail in a later section of this chapter.) Reposting by the instructor on an open Web site is likely not fair use, as this is outside the context of the classroom, but use of student work in other contexts in furtherance of the educational mission can be fair use, such as downloading a paper onto a flash drive so the instructor can grade it while traveling or using the paper in a portfolio of projects for future students on a secure site. A recent appellate decision concluded that use of student papers without permission in a plagiarism detection database is fair use (*A.V. v. iParadigms, Ltd.*, 2009). However, use of student papers without permission on a term-paper-for-sale Web site is not (*Weidner v. Carroll*, 2010). This use did not serve a positive educational goal such as catching the student plagiarizer. Quite the opposite, it promoted it! Likewise use without permission of student created artwork in a commercial advertisement is also likely not fair use (see, *Rainey v. Wayne State University*, 1998, p. 965: "alleged unauthorized use of the of plaintiff's ["a masters student in the fine arts program at WSU"] paintings in a brochure distributed at the 1997 North American Auto Show").

Legal support for use of student created content in the context of the distance education classroom might be found in the concept of implied license. Whether an implied, nonexclusive license exists in a particular situation turns on three factors: (a) whether the parties were engaged in a short-term discrete transaction as opposed to an ongoing relationship; (b) whether the creator utilized written contracts providing that the copyrighted materials could only be used with the creator's future involvement or express permission; and (c) whether the creator's conduct during the creation or delivery of the copyrighted material indicated that the use of the material without the creator's involvement or consent was permissible (*John G. Danielson, Inc. v. Winchester-Conant Properties, Inc.*, 2003). These elements are satisfied in the educational context as the student classroom experience is ongoing, typically without indication from the student that reasonable uses are prohibited and the fact that a pattern of creation (as part of an assignment or exam) and use (for grading, portfolio, etc.) is repeated over and over again throughout the academic year. An implied license can be based on the legal concept of estoppel. Estoppel is "[a]n affirmative defense alleging good-faith reliance on a misleading representation and an injury or detrimental change in position resulting from that reliance" (*Black's Law Dictionary*, 2009, n.p.). In other words, by enrolling in the class it is reasonable to conclude that the student may use instructor content and the instructor may use student content to further the goals of educational interchange. Like fair use, estoppel is a fact dependant analysis requiring adjudication. Reliance upon it requires some legal risk.

One method of avoiding uncertainty is to require at some point prior to the beginning of the programmatic experience consent from the student for use of his or her content in the context of the classroom and perhaps the broader educational environment, in an online art gallery or exhibit of student projects and performances for example. This could be accomplished by a click-to-agree mechanism the student encounters when he or she first logs into the institutional computing network for example. The assent mechanism could be part of the general acceptable use policy (AUP) most institutions employ in some form or another and to which students are required to sign or otherwise agree to abide by. In the alternative, this assent could be performed on a semester-by-semester or course-by-course basis within the campus course management system.

The AUP is an opportunity to advise students of their general obligation under the copyright law not to engage in infringing activity (as well as not to break laws or violate other institutional codes of behavior). Such policy often indicates what sanctions the institution will impose for conduct that deviates from the agreed upon (through use of e-signature or "click-to-agree" confirmation) standards.

Disclosure of such copyright information and sanctions is now required by section 1092 of title 20 of the United States Code as part of the annual institutional disclosures made to students under federal financial aid programs. The disclosures must now include a general copyright warning, information on the legal penalties for copyright infringement and documentation of the institution's policies including sanctions regarding illegal file sharing using campus facilities (20 U.S.C. § 1092(a)(1)(P)(i)-(iii)). Other statutory triggers regarding the use of policies, notices, and copyright information was discussed in detail in Lipinski (2007), in specific sections 110 (Lipinski, 2005) and 512 (Lipinski, 2006).

Courts have upheld click-to-agree mechanisms under contract law principles. "Creating an enforceable contract requires only an offer and acceptance and sufficient consideration to render that agreement enforceable. The consideration can come from a variety of sources, not just from property rights" (Nimmer, 2010, at § 11.2, n.p.). In the Web environment, "courts have consistently held that the use of a website for such purposes of purchasing a ticket manifests the user's assent to the Terms of Use, and that such terms constitute a binding contract as long as the terms are sufficiently conspicuous" (*Druyan v. Jagger*, 2007, p. 237, citations omitted). In the educational Web context, the benefit of access to institutional computing facilities might be viewed as separate consideration (in addition to tuition), whereby the AUP represents the terms of use offered to the student (and others such as employees), and the click-to-agree acknowledgment acceptance of those terms (see also, *Feldman v. Google, Inc.*, 2006, p. 237; *Southwest Airlines Co., v. Boardfirst, L.L.C.*, 2007, pp. *20–*21; *Ticketmaster L.L.C. v. RMG Technologies, Inc.*, 2007, p. 1108).

Ownership and Use of Instructor-Created Content

Determining who owns instructor work-product is bit more complicated. To be sure the instructor is the creator but under the copyright law that is not the same as the owner: "It is clear here-and is not contested by defendants-that Shaul [the instructor]is the creator of the teaching materials in question" (*Shaul v. Cherry Valley-Springfield Central School District*, 2004, p. 185). The general rule under section 201 is that work made in the course of one's employment is owned by the employer, as it constitutes a so-called "work made for hire" 17 U.S.C. § 201(a). There is an exception when there is evidence of an agreement to the contrary: "the parties have expressly agreed otherwise in a written instrument signed by them" 17 U.S.C. § 201(b). The sole alternative to the work of an "employee" under the copyright law is one made by independent contractor. When the creator is an independent contractor, he or she is the owner of the work. This might occur when the instructor-employee creates an additional (beyond the scope of his or her normal duties) course to be used by other institutions as part of his or her institution's desire to enter the race for "course-in-a-box" type products marketed to other educators and other institutions.

Some works undertaken in this independent contractor capacity could actually be designated as a work made for hire: "a work specially ordered or commissioned for use as a contribution to a collective work, as a part of a motion picture or other audiovisual work, as a translation, as a supplementary work, as a compilation, as an instructional text, as a test, as answer material for a test, or as an atlas, if the parties expressly agree in a written instrument signed by them that the work shall be considered a work made for hire" 17 U.S.C. § 101. In complicated cases, using a contract to sort out ownership issues is advisable. Otherwise the default rule of employer-as-owner as described above applies.

An additional twist to these rules occurs where courts create an exception for instructors at institutions of higher education for scholarly (papers, articles, books, etc.) and instructional (outlines, tests, etc.) content. A case decided but not published since the previous edition reiterates this position: "This evidence [referring to the university documentation under discussion] is arguably indicative of the general practice and understanding, by both faculty and also possibly by University counsel, that teaching materials fell within the general rule of traditional academic works for which ownership would be vested in the author of the materials" (*Bosch v. Ball-Kell,* 2006, p. *4). This decision is from the leading appellate jurisdiction (the Seventh Circuit, covering the states of Wisconsin, Illinois, and Indiana) recognizing a faculty exception to the statutory work made for hire rules. This case establishing the judicial exception is *Hays v. Sony Corporation of America* (1998), where the court evaluated the pros and cons of institutional versus instructor ownership, at least in the context of the university setting: "The argument would be that academic writing, being within the scope of academic employment, is work made for hire, per se; so, in the absence of an express written and signed waiver of the academic employer's rights, the copyright in such writing must belong to the employer. But considering the havoc that such a conclusion would wreak in the settled practices of academic institutions, the lack of fit between the policy of the work-for-hire doctrine and the conditions of academic production, and the absence of any indication that Congress meant to abolish the teacher exception, we might, if forced to decide the issue, conclude that the exception had survived the enactment of the 1976 Act" (*Hays v. Sony Corporation of America,* 1998, p. 417–418). The *Hays* decision was based on a case decided the year previous by the same court (*Weinstein v. University of Illinois,* 1987).

Other cases from other jurisdictions have cited and followed the decisions in either *Hays* or *Weinstein* or both (see, for example, *Pittsburg State University/Kansas National Education Association v. Kansas Board of Regents/Pittsburg State University,* 2005, p. 346). In denying ownership rights to K–12 instructors, one court acknowledged that such rights apply in higher education: "the 'academic tradition' granting authors ownership of their own scholarly work is not pertinent to teaching materials that were never explicitly prepared for publication by Shaul, as opposed to published articles by university professors" (*Shaul v. Cherry Valley-Springfield Central School District,* 2004, p. 186). The instructor-ownership right to academic work product, whether for the classroom or for scholarship, applies to instructors at institutions of higher education alone, and to instructors, not all employees. In *Foraste v. Brown University* (2003, p. 239, at n. 5) the court, citing both Hays and Weinstein, denied ownership rights to a university photographer but nonetheless made comment that it recognized such a right would exist for the university's instructors. An opposite older position appears now in the minority (*University of Colorado v. American Cyanamid,* 1995, 1999, 2000; *Vanderhurst v. Colorado Mountain College District,* 1998). Unless the institution resides in a jurisdiction where the courts have refused to recognize an instructor, ownership exception to the statutory default of employer ownership, instructors at institutions of higher education should argue for ownership rights in content created in the context of the distance education classroom, as well as other teaching and scholarly content created in the course of their employment. Use the decided cases that support such rights as persuasive authority to convince the institution or a court that such rights should be extended in your jurisdictions as well. An alternative strategy is to consider use of a contractual mechanism to express the ownership desires of the parties.

DAMAGE REMISSION: LESSONING THE STING OF INFRINGEMENT

Issues of liability (direct, contributory, and vicarious) and monetary damage awards (actual, statutory, and attorney's fees and costs) were detailed in the previous version of this chapter (Lipinski, 2007) and are not repeated here. Limitations on statutory damages were also discussed (section 504), including the remission of all damage awards under section 512 (the so-called taken-down provision) and in specific relating to institutions of higher education under subsection (e) of section 512 (see also, Lipinski, 2006).

To review, under section 504(c)(2) "[t]he court shall remit statutory damages in any case where an infringer believed and had reasonable grounds for believing that his or her use of the copyrighted work was a fair use under section 107, if the infringer was: (i) an employee or agent of a nonprofit educational institution, library, or archives acting within the scope of his or her employment who, or such institution, library, or archives itself, which infringed by reproducing the work in copies or phonorecords …" 17 U.S.C. § 504. This immunity applies to both the employee as well as the institution. Once the immunity applies, all statutory damages must be remitted. The more the institution can position itself and its employees to benefit from this provision by understanding what lawful reproduction rights each possesses, what is fair use and what is not, the better. This is a significant deterrent to litigation and positions non-profits and their employees as very unattractive defendants!

Section 512 details the take-down or disabling requirements when entities receive notice (actual or constructive, depending on the circumstances) of infringing conduct. Section 512(e) provides guidance for institutions of higher education, allowing the institution additional circumstances when it need not heed such notice. Section 512(c)(1) (a) and section 512(d)(1) indicate that in order for the monetary damage limitation to apply the service provider must not possess actual knowledge that the material or an activity using the material on the system or network is infringing or, in the absence of such actual knowledge, not be aware of facts or circumstances from which infringing activity is apparent or upon obtaining such knowledge or awareness, acts expeditiously to remove, or disable access to, the material. Actual knowledge can come from a notice received from the copyright owner or his or her representative. Such notice must contain the required elements identified by the statute.

The first element of proper notice is "[a] physical or electronic signature of a person authorized to act on behalf of the owner of an exclusive right that is allegedly infringed" (17 U.S.C. § 512(c)(30(A)(i)). While the communication must be written, the first proviso suggests that its form can be an electronic writing or message. Next, the work that is infringed must be identified as well as the alleged material that infringes upon it (17 U.S.C. § 512(c)(30(A)(ii) and (iii)). These are two related but obviously separate pieces of information. Next, proper contact information must be provided. An incomplete or inadequate notice places a duty upon the service provider to contact the copyright owner and ask for clarification from the copyright owner, in effect offer the copyright owner a chance to perfect an inadequate notice. Without this contact or follow-up an incomplete (c)(3) notice may be used to trigger a similar removal or disabling requirement as it might provide sufficient general knowledge or awareness under either (c)(1) (A)(i) and (ii) or (d)(1)(A) and (B). Proper contact information is that "information reasonably sufficient to permit the service provider to contact the complaining party, such as an address, telephone number, and, if available, an electronic mail address at which the complaining party may be contacted" (17 U.S.C. § 512(c)(30(A)(iv)).

Oddly, the notice and removal or disabling provision of section 512 does not anticipate that the alleged infringement be proved in a court of law. However, to prevent copyright owners from willy-nilly erring on the side of accusation, forcing removal or disabling of copyrighted material unnecessarily, section 512(c)(3)(A)(v) requires that the copyright include "[a] statement that the complaining party has a good faith belief that use of the material in the manner complained of is not authorized by the copyright owner, its agent, or the law" 17 U.S.C. § 512(c)(30(A)(v). So too, section 512(f), also creates separate liability for misrepresentations that are "knowingly materially" made, subject to civil remedy including damages, costs, and attorney's fees. However, there a bit of legal wiggle room between a copyright owner that in good faith believes his or her works are being infringed and one who "knowingly materially misrepresents" that it is so infringed.

Recent case law suggests that the good faith statement by the owner or his or her representative claiming that use of the work is infringing must include some assessment of possible defenses such as fair use. In *Lenz v. Universal Music Corp.*, (2008) the court observed: "Accordingly, in order for a copyright owner to proceed under the DMCA with 'a good faith belief that use of the material in the manner complained of is not authorized by the copyright owner, its agent, or the law,' the owner must evaluate whether the material makes fair use of the copyright. An allegation that a copyright owner acted in bad faith by issuing a takedown notice without proper consideration of the fair use doctrine thus is sufficient to state a misrepresentation claim pursuant to Section 512(f) of the DMCA. Such an interpretation of the DMCA furthers both the purposes of the DMCA itself and copyright law in general." (*Lenz v. Universal Music Corp.*, 2008, pp. 1154-1155) Assuming this assessment has been made, a proper notice can trigger a take-down or access disabling response or in cases of a failed notice obligations nonetheless to undertake some action. This is the second reason why an understanding of fair use is critical in the distance education setting (the first was that the statutory damage remission of section 504 is dependent upon the existence of a reasonable belief that the reproduction complained of was fair use). Understanding fair use can assist an institution in determining whether the section 512 notice to take-down or disable content is adequate in that the sender of the notice should have considered fair use as a possible defense. The institution may believe the use complained of to be fair and so decides to let the material remain accessible or perhaps pursue legal remedy under section 512(f). If the removal is not expeditious, the protection of the statute may nonetheless be lost. However, if fair use applies, then neither take-down or disabling is necessary nor protection from damages under section 512 needed. The interplay of fair use and section 512 demonstrates the dynamic influence this concept provides in the distance education setting.

SPECIFIC PROVISIONS RELATED TO DISTANCE EDUCATION

Another reason why an understanding of fair use is important relates to the usefulness of other provisions of the copyright law or lack thereof. Section 110(2) grants additional display and performance rights to qualifying educational institutions, i.e., those that are nonprofit and accredited. Distance educators might desire to record their teaching session (a video broadcast, a Web-stream, etc.) for later review by students. That recording might also capture not only the teacher's performance of the content (the lecture) but the copyright content as well (e.g., pages from a text book, an illustration or map, a video clip to which the instructor offers explanation, etc.). The recording then also reproduces content protected by copyright. An instructor might also like to record his or her presentations ahead of time and make the class session available to students 24/7. The lecture might also include copyrighted content, such as a several pages from a text book, illustrations, maps, or a video clip (a "reasonable and limited portion") to which the instructor offers explanation, etc.). Section 112 allows educators to make such ephemeral archive (of the distance education stream for example) as well as preparation copies. These provisions come with an array of compliance-oriented obligations that many educators and institutions find burdensome and so fair use appears a more attractive recourse. Section 110 and 112 were covered in the previous edition of this chapter (Lipinski, 2007; for a detailed study of the provisions, see Lipinski, 2005)

REGULATORY EXEMPTION FOR USE OF DVDS IN EDUCATION

Suppose an instructor or student would like to use a DVD clip as part of an online classroom discussion. Suppose also that the DVD is protected by CSS but that the instructor or student knows how to "get around" that control using DeCSS. Circumventing an access control that a copyright owner places on his or her work such as CSS violates section 1201(a)(1). Trafficking in the anti-circumvention access or use "device" is also a violation under section 1201(a)(2) and (b). These rules, as well as a statutory exception, allow circumvention of an access control for purposes of curriculum development (17 U.S.C. § 1201(d)(4)). These provisions were discussed in Lipinski (2007) and in great detail in Lipinski (2006).

Recent regulatory activity created an exemption to the anti-circumvention rules that may be very useful to instructors and students alike. As part of a current three-year cycle or rule-making in 2010 (the rules were a year late and should have been issued in 2009), the Librarian of Congress exempted the following: "Motion pictures on DVDs that are lawfully made and acquired and that are protected by the Content Scrambling System when circumvention is accomplished solely in order to accomplish the incorporation of short portions of motion pictures into new works for the purpose of criticism or comment, and where the person engaging in circumvention believes and has reasonable grounds for believing that circumvention is necessary to fulfill the purpose of the use in the following instances: (i) Educational uses by college and university professors and by college and university film and media studies students …" 37 C.F.R. 201.40 (2010). Observe that while all instructors in higher education can circumvent under this exemption, only students of film and media may do so. Furthermore, instructors at the K-12 level cannot use this exemption whatsoever! New rules are expected in 2012.

FAIR USE IN THE WEB-BASED OR WEB-SUPPLEMENTED CLASSROOM

Instructors and students may arrive at the conclusion that the exemptions provided by sections 110 and 112 or that the damage remission of 504 and 512 offer little solace in

540 • Tomas A. Lipinski

the often zero-risk climate of the non-profit educational entity. It may be that the qualifying obligations are too confusing or burdensome to implement. Or it may be that the scenario envisioned by sections 110 and 112 simply does not apply to your facts, e.g., you are a for-profit online school. These problems dissolve when turning to fair use as the concept can be applied to any setting. Remember, fair use is not a defense to a section 1201 violation, though it might be a part of making the case for a regulatory exception under the current three-year cycle of rule-making.

Using fair use in a frequent and efficient manner requires having some sense of the four fair use factors (each must be applied in every case) and how courts apply those factors. Fair use is a fact-dependant analysis so the more cases (fact scenarios) known the more informed will be the decision-making when applying the factors to a new set of facts. The remaining sections of this chapter focus upon an overview of fair use, the recent case law and scenarios most relevant to educators and students (for a detailed discussion, see Lipinski, 2010).

The Four Fair Use Factors: An Overview

Fair use operates as a form of privilege in law, to undertake what otherwise in its absence would be an infringing use. Fair use is an equitable doctrine. Courts refuse to establish bright line tests. Section 107 provides a minimum set of factors to consider when determining whether or not on the whole the use should be deemed fair. There are four fair use factors: (a) the purpose and character of the use, including whether such use is of a commercial nature or is for nonprofit educational purposes; (b) the nature of the copyrighted work; (c) the amount and substantiality of the portion used in relation to the copyrighted work as a whole; and (d) the effect of the use upon the potential market for or value of the copyrighted work. These four factors are prefaced by a statutory preamble that lists a number of possible fair uses: "Notwithstanding the provisions of sections 106 and 106A, the fair use of a copyrighted work, including such use by reproduction in copies or phonorecords or by any other means specified by that section, for purposes such as criticism, comment, news reporting, teaching (including multiple copies for classroom use), scholarship, or research, is not an infringement of copyright." However, a categorical determination, e.g., all uses in "teaching" are fair uses, is rejected by the very next sentence. "In determining whether the use made of a work in any particular case is a fair use the factors to be considered shall include ..." The final sentence of section 107 reflects an amendment necessitated by a federal circuit court decision (*Salinger v. Random House, Inc.*, 1987) that suggested that use of an unpublished work could never be a fair use: "The fact that a work is unpublished shall not itself bar a finding of fair use if such finding is made upon consideration of all the above factors" 17 U.S.C. § 107. Evaluation of any particular circumstances must involve therefore recourse to all four factors and each factor's various sub-parts.

First Factor: The Purpose and Character of the Use

The first factor looks to the purpose and character of the use and by command of the statute inquires whether the use is of a "commercial nature or is for nonprofit educational purposes" 17 U.S.C. § 107. Courts have had little opportunity to discuss the contours of what constitutes "nonprofit educational purposes" but do consider whether a use is commercial or noncommercial, with the former weighing against a finding of fair use. "The language of the statute makes clear that the commercial or nonprofit educational purpose of a work is only one element of the first factor enquiry into its purpose and character … the mere fact that a use is educational and not for profit does not insulate it from a finding of infringement, any more than the commercial character of a use bars a finding of fairness" (*Campbell v. Acuff-Rose Music*, 1994, p. 579). In other words an educational use even in a nonprofit setting can still be infringing! "[T]he crux of the profit/nonprofit distinction is not whether the sole motive of the use is monetary gain but whether the user stands to profit from exploitation of the copyrighted material without paying the customary price" (*Harper & Row Publishers, Inc. v. Nation Enterprises*, deemed 1985, p. 561). In other words an educational use even in a nonprofit setting can still be commercial.

A commercial use may be offset, so to speak, by a use that is transformative. Nontransformative uses tend to supersede the original work or operate as a market substitute, thus do not favor fair use. Transformative uses have the opposite effect. Fair use promotes uses that are complementary but not those that are substitutive: "we may say that copying that is complementary to the copyrighted work (in the sense that nails are complements of hammers) is fair use, but copying that is a substitute for the copyrighted work (in the sense that nails are substitutes for pegs or screws), or for derivative works from the copyrighted work … is not fair use" (*Ty, Inc. v. Publication International Ltd.*, 2002, p. 517). An example of a complementary work is a workbook or study guide. It is not a substitute for the original textbook or classic novel but is rather enhancing or complementary to it, the same way a book review is complementary, although a scathing review is not very complimentary.

Second Factor: The Nature of the Work

The second fair use factor considers the nature of the work. While many sub-factors such as age, price, etc., of the work could be hypothesized courts focus on two sub-factors when determining whether the nature of the work favors or disfavors a fair use or the degree to which it favors or disfavors fair use. The first sub-factor assesses the publication status of the work. Fair use favors less the use of unpublished works or, said another way, courts tend to be more protective of unpublished works. This occurs for two reasons. First, the historical context of copyright reveals the right of "first publication" as a significant right of the copyright holder. Second, since copyright is an economic right, in the circumstance of an unpublished work, the copyright holder has not yet experienced the benefit of the marketplace. A second, more important question is whether the work, based on its creative content, falls on the "thick" or the "thin" side of copyright protection. Courts have placed scientific and technical information, journal literature from the hard sciences such as chemistry or physics, for example, on the far end of copyright protection, or so-called thin copyright, as opposed to poetry or works of fiction, on the opposite end. This is not to be taken as a slight against authors of those works. Courts rather focus on the factual nature of the "thin" work. For example, in *American Geophysical Union v. Texaco, Inc.* (1994, p. 925), the scientific journal articles photocopied were "essentially factual in nature" but the chapter excerpts from various social science and humanities monographs used to compile the course-packs in *Princeton University Press v. Michigan Document Services* (1996, p. 1389) were "creative material." In both cases the overall use was deemed not fair. Likewise, the nature of the newspaper articles posted to an electronic bulletin board in *Los Angeles Times v. Free Republic* (2000, p. *55) were "predominantly factual" and though the "defendants' fair use claim is stronger than it would be had the works been purely fictional" the use over-all did not favor a finding of fair use.

Third Factor: The Amount and Substantiality of the Portion Used in Relation to the Work as a Whole

In recent years this factor is less about rigid "how much can I take" and more about whether the amount taken is reasonable in light of a good transformative purpose. Past educator and student fixation on numbers or percents is now counterproductive. The significant question is whether the user is taking only as much as is necessary to accom-plish that good (first factor) purpose. Using images or text in a searchable-retrievable archive of documents may indeed require that 100% of the work be used. The third fac-tor includes both a quantitative and a qualitative assessment. Determining the "amount" of the use is accomplished by examining the work "as a whole" and comparing to this the amount actually used. In one case, the district court found that *Rachel Weeping* [the alleged infringing second book written by Burchaell] includes 4.3% of the words in *Pregnant by Mistake* [the alleged, infringed first book]" (*Maxtone-Graham v. Burtchaell*, 1986, p. 1257). A second assessment is made to determine if the user nonetheless takes a substantial portion of the work in another sense: even though the proportion of the amount of the work used is small, does the use nonetheless appropriate the most signifi-cant part of the work, its essence, or as courts have deemed it, the "heart" of the work? This inquiry is made because if the heart is taken, it is akin to a wholesale taking as it appropriates the creative core of the work such as revealing the surprise ending in the trailer for a movie (*Video Pipeline, Inc. v. Buena Vista Home Entertainment, Inc.*, 2004, p. 201), the signature guitar or base line in a popular song (*Campbell v. Acuff-Rose Music*, 1994, p. 569), or a controversial political decision explained in one's memoirs (*Harper & Row Publishers, Inc. v. Nation Enterprises*, 1985). In either assessment, courts are con-cerned that using too much of the work will undermine the need for the original. This relates to the next factor, the market impact.

Fourth Factor: The Effect of the Use upon the Potential Market for or Value of the Work

When assessing the market impact or effect upon the value of the work, again, several considerations are required. First, the concept of market is not singular, e.g., sales rev-enue lost as reproduction of the work made purchase of an additional copy unneces-sary. Assessing the impact the use may have on future primary markets and secondary ("reprint") as well as derivative markets must also be made. The decision to enter a secondary market, e.g., release of the first season of a popular television or cable series on DVD, is the copyright holder's, as is the right to develop derivative markets, e.g., video game based on a blockbuster movie or vice-versa. These concepts are reflected in a recent controversy involving a print version of the popular Web-based Harry Pot-ter Lexicon. No one would argue that publication of a reader's guide is a substitute for reading the original Harry Potter as there is "no plausible basis to conclude that publi-cation of the Lexicon would impair sales of the Harry Potter novels" (*Warner Brothers Entertainment, Inc. v. RDR Books*, 2008, p. 550). However, the publication of the planned guide might impair the market for Rowling's two companion books (*Quidditch through the Ages* and *Fantastic Beasts & Where to Find Them*): "publication of the Lexicon could harm sales of … companion books. Unless they sought to enjoy the companion books for their entertainment value alone, consumers who purchased the Lexicon would have scant incentive to purchase either of Rowling's companion books ... information ... in these short works has been incorporated into the Lexicon almost wholesale" (*Warner Brothers Entertainment, Inc. v. RDR Books*, 2008, p. 550). However, the Lexicon was not a derivative work: "By condensing, synthesizing, and reorganizing the preexisting material in an A-to-Z reference guide, the Lexicon does not recast the material in another medium to retell the story of *Harry Potter* [as a theatrical staging of the series off-Broadway would do for example], but instead gives the copyrighted material another purpose ... Under these circumstances, and because the Lexicon does not fall under any example of derivative works listed in the statute, Plaintiffs have failed to show that the Lexicon is a derivative work" (*Warner Brothers Entertainment, Inc. v. RDR Books*, 2008, p. 539). Section 101 defines a derivative work as "a work based upon one or more preexisting works, such as a translation, musical arrangement, dramatization, fictionalization, motion picture version, sound recording, art reproduction, abridgment, condensation, or any other form in which a work may be recast, transformed, or adapted." A recent circuit court decision explained further the goal of the fourth factor: "The adverse effect with which fair use is primarily concerned is that of market substitution. Uses which are complementary, on the other hand, are more likely to be found fair because most authors would not want those uses to be impeded by a license requirement" (*Peter Letterese and Associates, Inc. v. World Institute of Scientology Enterprises, Inc.*, 2008, pp. 1315–1316). The meaning of market "effect" under section 107 may not be the same as its literal or ordinary meaning. The effect on the market that results from critique is not a concern of the copyright law.

The best way to learn about fair use is to look at the cases. The following lists presents several dozen fair use decisions organized in hopefully useful and relevant (to the educational environment) clusters. Each case is listed with a short summary of the facts and the results. Each cluster is accompanied by a summary statement or assessment that can guide educators and students alike in future use of content protected by copyright.

Fair Use in Practice: Textbooks, Readers, and Other Publications

Copy shop, course-pack, subject reader, or anthology compilation and reproduction are typically not fair use as the use is not considered transformative, even though for the classroom such use avoids paying the customary reprint price:

Blackwell Publishing, Inc. v. Excel Research group, Inc. (2009) (copy shop serving University of Michigan students, accepted course-packs from professors, allowed students access to the master copy in order to make their own copy of readings using copy-shop equipment and offering bindery service for student copies as well not fair use).

Princeton University Press v. Michigan Document Services (1996) (reproduction of chapters in a course-pack not fair use):

Merely reprinting or posting content to a web site is not transformative and not fair use:

Society of the Holy Transfiguration Monastery, Inc. v. Gregory (2010) (Web posting by Denver Archbishop Gregory of translations made by monastery members of ancient Greek religious texts was not transformative and not fair use).

Lowry's Reports, Inc. v. Legg Mason, Inc. (2003) (reproduction of newsletters by financial advising corporation not fair use).

American Geophysical Union, et al. v. Texaco, Inc. (1994) (photocopy of scientific journal articles for file cabinet archive of employee not fair use).

Harper & Row Publishers, Inc. v. Nation Enterprises (1985) (publication by *The Nation* magazine of an excerpt from former President Ford's soon to be published memoirs not fair use).

Preparation of a sequel or entertainment product based upon another work is not fair use as these products are within the expected market for derivative works of the copyright owner, a right of the copyright owner to enter or forego.

Salinger v. Colting (2009, 2010) (use of Mr. C. character in *60 Years* not a fair use of the Holden Caulfield character from *Catcher in the Rye*).

Castle Rock Entertainment, Inc. v. Carol Publishing Group (1998) (creation of trivia games drawn from scripts of *Seinfeld* television show not fair use).

Fair Use in Practice: Criticism, Evaluation, Analysis of Interviews, and Other Primary Data

Criticism, review, evaluation, analysis of other content is a transformative, often complementary fair use but take only as much as is necessary! Taking too much tends to undermine this alleged "good" purpose and also tips the third factor against the use; worse, taking too much also negatively impacts the market as it tends to substitute for the original or part of it.

Chicago Board of Education v. Substance, Inc. (2003, 2004) (criticism of standardized tests a good purpose but publication of entire test in order to demonstrate flaws not fair use, the value of the test (ability to use the test in the future) undermined).

NXIVM Corp. v. Ross Institute (2004) (use of seminar material to critique its content fair use even though sales of the seminar plummeted).

Sundeman v. Seajay Society, Inc. (1998) (reproduction of complete copy, near complete copy, and paraphrase or quote of 4%–6% of an unpublished manuscript for purposes of scholarship and research, among other purposes was fair use).

Mastone-Graham v. Burtchaell (1986, 1987) (use of published interviews in a new book with a different slant fair use).

Fair Use in Practice: Outline, Training Materials, Workbooks

Use of content in outlines, training materials etc. tend not to be derivative works and can be fair use as these items often complement or enhance use of the original work, but if too much is taken courts will conclude the use is not fair as this tends to substitute for the original work.

Peter Letterese and Associates, Inc. v. World Institute of Scientology Enterprises, Inc. (2008) (use of excerpts from sales training book by Scientology Church to create instructional materials for new members based around the prior work not fair use, but use of excerpts in internal administrative manuals fair use).

Gulfstream Aerospace Corp. v. Camp Systems International, Inc. (2006) (reproduction of repair manual in service program documentation fair use).

SCQuARE Intern., Ltd. v. BBDO Atlanta, Inc. (2006) (creation of abbreviated training manual based on content from previous seminars developed under contract not fair use).

Worldwide Church of God v. Philadelphia Church of God, Inc. (2000) (reproduction of Mystery of the Ages text by church founder for training and instruction by spin-off church not fair use).

Greaver v. National Association of Corporate Directors (1997) (use of material in similar seminar outline not fair use).

Rubin v. Brooks/Cole Pub. Co. (1993) (inclusion of "love Scale" in college psychology textbook fair use).

Fair Use in Practice: Illustration, Example, or Documentation

Taking the entire work can be fair use when done for purposes of illustration, example, documentation, or to place an event in its historical context.

Gaylord v. U.S. (2010) (creation of postage stamp from photograph derivative of actual Korean War Veteran Memorial and not fair use of sculptor's original 19-statue monument. The stamp is a non-transformative, commercial use, with an "identical" purpose and character of the actual memorial (to commemorate the sacrifice of those who served) though no adverse market impact: "someone seeking to take a photograph ... or otherwise create a derivative work would not find the stamp to a suitable substitute" for the memorial itself).

Bouchat v. Baltimore Ravens, LP (2010) (use of early Ravens flying B logo drawing in NFL "highlight" film not transformative, use of same logo in lobby team headquarters on "museum-like" display of a set of first season tickets and in two large photographs of team's first season, first-round draft picks (holding up jersey displaying logo) is fair use, demonstrating historical event of team's founding and first season).

Sofa Entertainment, Inc. v. Dodger Productions, Inc. (2010) (use of seven-second clip from *Ed Sullivan Show* with its host introducing the first national television appearance of musical group Four Seasons in Broadway play *Jersey Boys* to "serve as a historical reference point" is fair use).

Lennon v. Premise Media Corp. (2008) (use of segment from song *Imagine* in documentary "pro-religion" film fair use).

Healthcare Advocates, Inc. v. Harding, Earley, Follmer & Frailey (2007) (copy of screenshots from Internet Archive repository for use in litigation defense fair use).

Bill Graham Archives v. Dorling Kindersley Ltd. (2006) (minimized but complete image of several concert posters to illustrate timeline in rock music documentary book of band Grateful Dead fair use).

Antioch Co. v. Scrapbook Borders, Inc. (2003) (reproduction of stickers in a "how-to" book not fair use as the copyright owner also marketed "how-to" scrapbook).

Hofheinz v. AMC Productions, Inc. (2001) (use of movie clips and other content in documentary about iconic 1960s teen beach and rebellion movie studio fair use).

Images Audio Visual Productions, Inc. v. Perini Building Co., Inc. (2000) (reproduction of construction photographs for use in arbitration proceedings not fair use).

Los Angeles Times v. Free Republic (2000) (use of entire news stories though thin copyright on current events discussion board took too much, was not transformative and not fair use).

Higgins v. Detroit Educational Television Foundation (1998) (voiced-over gangster rap song excerpt in documentary film decrying gang and drug lifestyle fair use).

Fair Use in Practice: Access Tools such as Guides, Indexes, etc.

When works are used to create indexes, guidebooks, etc., these functional works are deemed transformative, as long as the amount taken is necessary to accomplish a good purpose such as full-text searching of the content, otherwise this amount tends to substitute rather than enhance the need for the original.

> *Warner Brothers Entertainment, Inc. v. RDR Books* (2008) (Lexicon of the fictional world of Harry Potter, while not derivative, took too much from series and two companion books, not fair use).
>
> *Ty, Inc. v. Publication International Ltd.* (2002, 2003) (use of photographs of sculptural works (Beanie Babies) in a collector's guide fair use, use of photographs of sculptural works to illustrate scenes in children's book not fair use).
>
> *Kelly v. Arriba Soft Corp.* (2003) (complete though thumbnail copies of Internet photographs in image index Website fair use).
>
> *Twin Peaks Productions, Inc. v. Publications International Ltd.* (1993) (detailed episode guide to television show not fair use).

Fair Use in Practice: Archiving and Preservation

Large-scale and complete archiving and access of protected content can be fair use when the benefit serves some broader societal benefit where the amount is necessary in order allow for that benefit to be achieved.

> *A.V. v. iParadigms, Ltd.* (2009) (use of student papers in plagiarism detection database fair use). Compare, *Weidner v. Carroll* (2010) (injunction against defendants who "operated term paper websites which specifically sold named Plaintiffs published papers on the website without their permission").
>
> *Perfect 10 v. Google, Inc.* (2007) (cache of images fair use in order to facilitate search for images on the Web).
>
> *Field v. Google, Inc.* (2006) (cache of images fair use in order to facilitate search for images on the Web).

TOWARDS THE FUTURE OF COPYRIGHT IN THE DISTANCE EDUCATION CLASSROOM

Owners and users of copyrighted material will continue to debate the limits of fair use as well as the applications of other provisions of the copyright law. Two pending cases may offer guidance for future editions of this handbook but for now the best that can be said is conjecture. In *Cambridge University Press v. Patton* (2012), the court concluded that the first factor favored the university as the reproduction of chapters while nontransformative was for "strictly nonprofit educational purposes." The second factor also favored fair use as "informational in nature." The fourth factor depended on whether or not the publishers could show evidence of an excerpt market and if that market was constant or increasing. If revenues were nonexistent, insignificant or trailing off, then this factor tended to favor fair use as well. In several of the 74 excerpts assessed by the court often a determining factor was the third "how much" factor. Where the court established the following measure: Where a book has no chapters or less than 10 chapters then a fair amount is 10%. Where a book contains 10 or more chapters the amount that is within fair use is one chapter or its equivalent. The court counted all pages including the index. In any scenario, this use was further conditioned the excerpt being accessed only by students in the class, only for the term of the class, prohibited from further distribution, and that students were informed of copyright law. The decision did not involve the use of complete journal articles which are likely to have a reprint market under the fourth factor, at least for recent article and could likely constitute 100% of the work, in terms of the third factor. See also, *Cambridge University Press v. Becker* (2010a, b, 2011). As of the writing of this chapter, an appeal of the decision to the Eleventh Circuit was filed on September 11, 2012.

In a practice common in distance education, reproduction of motion media and subsequent streaming a recently filed case pushes the boundaries of fair use as the educational films are reproduced and streamed in their entirety beyond the limits of section 112 and section 110. In *A.I.M.E. v. Regents of the University of California* (2011, at ¶ 44), "The process of digitally streaming video programs implicates a number of exclusive copyright rights of educational video publishers and exclusive distributors like AVP, including the right to reproduce or copy a work, the right to publicly perform a work, the right to publicly distribute a work and the right to publicly display a work." After initial negotiations broke down, the plaintiffs alleged that the "Defendants' exploitations of AVP Shakespeare DVDs are the proverbial tip of the iceberg … A review of this list reveals that the scale of the Defendants' copyright infringing activities is massive." *A.I.M.E. v. Regents of the University of California* (2011, at ¶ 77-78. Whether either litigation results in a decision that will be useful to distance educators remains to be seen. These two cases demonstrate that being sued is a possibility in the distance education setting of the twenty-first century, and until precedent clearly favors such use the threat of litigation remains.

NOTE

* Prepared by Tomas A. Lipinski, J.D., LL.M., Ph.D.: This summary is designed to provide accurate and authoritative information in regard to the subject matter covered. However, this information is NOT provided as a substitute for legal advice. If legal advice or expert assistance is required, the services of a competent legal professional should be retained. Reference to statute sections are to Title 17, United States Code, unless otherwise noted.

CASES

A.I.M.E. v. Regents of the University of California, Case No. CV 10-09378 CBM (MANx) (filed October 24, 2011) (second amended complaint).

American Geophysical Union, et al. v. Texaco, Inc., 60 F.3d 913 (2d Cir. 1994).

Antioch Co. v. Scrapbook Borders, Inc., 291 F. Supp. 2d 980 (D. Minn. 2003).

A.V. v. iParadigms, Ltd., 562 F.3d 630 (4th Cir. 2009).

Bill Graham Archives v. Dorling Kindersley Ltd., 448 F.3d 605 (2d Cir. 2006).

Blackwell Publishing, Inc. v. Excel Research group, Inc., 661 F.Supp.2d 786 (E.D. Mich. 2009).

Bosch v. Ball-Kell, 2006 WL 2548053 (C.D. Ill. 2006) (unpublished).

Bouchat v. Baltimore Ravens, LP, 619 F.3d 301 (4th Cir. 2010).

Cambridge University Press v. Becker, Civil Action No. 1:08-CV-1425-ODE (N.D. Ga. September 30, 2010a).

Cambridge University Press v. Becker, Civil Action No. 1:08-CV-1425-ODE (N.D. Ga. December 28, 2010b).

Cambridge University Press v. Becker, Civil Action No. 1:08-CV-1425-ODE (N.D. Ga. March 17, 2011)

Cambridge v. Becker, 2012 WL 1835696 (N.D. Ga.).

Campbell v. Acuff-Rose Music, 510 U.S. 569 (1994).

Castle Rock Entertainment, Inc. v. Carol Publishing Group, 150 F.3d 132 (2d Cir. 1998)

Chicago Board of Education v. Substance, Inc., 354 F.3d 624 (7th Cir. 2003), cert. denied 543 U.S. 816 (2004).

Druyan v. Jagger, 508 F.Supp.2d 228, 237 (S.D.N.Y. 2007).

Field v. Google, Inc., 412 F. Supp. 2d 1106 (D. Nev. 2006).

Feldman v. Google, Inc., 513 F. Supp. 2d 229, 237 (E.D. Pa. 2006).

Foraste v. Brown University, 290 F. Supp. 2d 234 (D.R.I 2003).

Gaylord v. U.S., 595 F.3d 1364 (Fed. Cir. 2010).

Greaver v. National Association of Corporate Directors, 1997 WL 34605245 (D.D.C., 1997) (unpublished).

Gulfstream Aerospace Corp. v. Camp Systems International, Inc., 428 F.Supp.2d 1369 (S.D. Ga. 2006).

Harper & Row Publishers, Inc. v. Nation Enterprises, 471 U.S. 539 (1985).

Hays v. Sony Corporation of America, 847 F.2d 412 (7th Cir, 1988).

Healthcare Advocates, Inc. v. Harding, Earley, Follmer & Frailey, 497 F. Supp. 2d 627 (E.D. Pa. 2007).

Higgins v. Detroit Educational Television Foundation, 4 F. Supp. 2d 701 (E.D. Mich. 1998).

Hofheinz v. AMC Productions, Inc., 147 F. Supp. 2d 127 (E.D.N.Y. 2001).

Images Audio Visual Productions, Inc. v. Perini Building Co., Inc., 91 F. Supp. 2d 1075 (E.D. Mich. 2000).

John G. Danielson, Inc. v. Winchester-Conant Properties, Inc., 322 F.3d 26 (1st Cir. 2003).

Kelly v. Arriba Soft Corp., 336 F.3d 811 (9th Cir. 2003).

Lennon v. Premise Media Corp., 556 F. Supp. 2d 310 (S.D.N.Y. 2008).

Lenz v. Universal Music Corp., 572 F. Supp. 2d 1150 (N.D. Cal. 2008).

Los Angeles Times v. Free Republic, 29 Media L. Rep. 1028 (C.D. Cal. 2000).

Lowry's Reports, Inc. v. Legg Mason, Inc., 271 F.Supp.2d 737 (D. Md. 2003).

Maxtone-Graham v. Burtchaell, 803 F.2d 1253 (2d Cir. 1986), cert. denied 481 U.S. 1059 (1987).

Metro-Goldwyn-Mayer Studios Inc. v. Grokster, Ltd., 125 S.Ct. 2764 (2005).

NXIVM Corp. v. Ross Institute, 364 F.3d 471 (2d Cir. 2004).

Perfect 10 v. Google, Inc., 487 F.3d 701 (9th Cir. 2007).

Peter Letterese and Associates, Inc. v. World Institute of Scientology Enterprises, Inc., 533.F.3d 1287 (11th Cir. 2008).

Pittsburg State University/Kansas National Education Association v. Kansas Board of Regents/Pittsburg State University, 122 P.3d 336 (Kan. 2005).

Princeton University Press v. Michigan Document Services, 99 F.3d 1381(6th Cir. 1996), cert. denied, 520 U.S. 1156 (1997).

Rubin v. Brooks/Cole Pub. Co., 836 F. Supp. 909 (D.Mass.1993).

Salinger v. Colting, 641 F.Supp.2d 250 (S.D.N.Y. 2009), aff'd on other grounds 607 F.3d 68 (2d Cir. 2010).

Salinger v. Random House, Inc., 811 F.2d 90 (2nd Cir.), cert. denied 493 U.S. 1094 (1987).

SCQuARE Intern., Ltd. v. BBDO Atlanta, Inc., 455 F. Supp. 2d 1347 (N.D. Ga. 2006).

Shaul v. Cherry Valley-Springfield Central School District, 363 F.3d 177 (2d Cir. 2004). Society of the Holy Transfiguration Monastery, Inc. v. Gregory, 2010 WL 4923907 (D. Mass.).

Sofa Entertainment, Inc. v. Dodger Productions, Inc., 2010 WL 4228343 (C.D. Cal.)

Sony Corporation of America v. Universal Studios, Inc., 464 U.S. 417 (1984).

Southwest Airlines Co., v. Boardfirst, L.L.C., 2007 U.S. Dist. LEXIS 96230 (N.D. Texas 2007).

Sundeman v. Seajay Society, Inc., 142 F.3d 194 (4th Cir. 1998).

Ticketmaster L.L.C. v. RMG Technologies, Inc., 507 F.Supp.2d 1096, 1108 (C.D. Cal. 2007).

Twin Peaks Productions, Inc. v. Publications International Ltd., 996 F.2d 1366 (2d Cir. 1993).

Ty, Inc. v. Publication International Ltd., 292 F.3d 512 (7th Cir. 2002), cert. denied 537 U.S. 1110 (2003).

University of Colorado v. American Cyanamid, 880 F. Supp. 1387 (D. Colo. 1995), aff'd in part, vacated in part and remanded 196 F.3d 1366, 1376 (Fed. Cir. 1999), cert. denied 529 U.S. 1130 (2000).

Vanderhurst v. Colorado Mountain College District, 16 F. Supp. 2d 1297 (D. Colo. 1998).

Video Pipeline, Inc. v. Buena Vista Home Entertainment, Inc., 342 F.3d 191 (3d Cir. 2003), cert. denied 540 U.S. 1178 (2004).

Warner Brothers Entertainment, Inc. v. RDR Books, 575 F.Supp.2d 513 (S.D.N.Y. 2008).

Weidner v. Carroll, 2010 WL 310310 (S.D. Ill.) (unpublished).

Weinstein v. University of Illinois, 881 F.2d 1091 (7th Cir. 1987).

Worldwide Church of God v. Philadelphia Church of God, Inc., 227 F.3d 1110 (9th Cir. 2000).

REFERENCES

Black's Law Dictionary (9th ed.). (2009). St. Paul, MN: West Group.

Lipinski, T. A. (2003). Legal issues in the development and use of copyrighted material in web-based distance education. In M. G. Moore & W. G. Anderson (Eds.), *Handbook of distance education* (pp. 481-505). Hillsdale, NJ: Erlbaum.

Lipinski, T. A. (2005). *Copyright law and the distance education classroom*. Lanham, MD: Scarecrow Press.

Lipinski, T. A. (2006). *The complete copyright liability handbook for librarians and educators*. New York, NY: Neal-Schuman.

Lipinski, T. A. (2007). Legal issues in the development and use of copyrighted material. In M. G. Moore (Ed.), Handbook of distance education (pp. 451-469). Hillsdale, NJ: Erlbaum.

Lipinski, T. . (2010). A functional approach to understanding and applying fair use. *Annual Review of Information Science and Technology 45*, 525-621.

Nimmer, R. T. (2010). *Information law*. St. Paul, MN: West Group.

Part 5

Audiences and Providers
An Overview
MICHAEL GRAHAME MOORE

In Part 5, 10 chapters report distance education from the perspective of specific consumer groups and program suppliers, focusing in turn on elementary and high schools, community colleges, training in the corporate sector, continuing professional education, and the armed forces. Introduced for the first time in this edition, the above chapters are followed by a review of the practice, potential, and problems of teaching at a distance for doctoral study and then a chapter that focuses on one field that has proven to be especially challenging for distance educators, the study of sciences. Part 5 closes with two chapters that focus on higher education, and the nature of the cultural and organizational changes underway in universities worldwide, with the second of this pair of chapters extending these questions even beyond the university level, to provide a provocative and challenging set of hypotheses about the future as a fitting conclusion to this particular edition of the *Handbook*.

To begin Part 5, two chapters, one by Clark and the other Barbour describe distance education in regard to children in the elementary and secondary schools (K–12). We previously presented one specific aspect of K–12 distance education, in Cavanaugh's chapter on student achievement. Here Clark's chapter summarizes the history from the 1920s through to the development of today's virtual schools, including a classification of the different types of virtual school, and discusses professional development for school teachers before laying out "some perennial issues" and comments about the future of K–12 distance education. Barbour takes up the account of virtual schools and dedicates his whole chapter to this topic, including a more expanded typology. Other features of this chapter include effectiveness, in which obviously he complements Cavanaugh, teacher roles, and the research in design, delivery, and student support.

Following this discussion of pre-college schooling, Jaggers provides a representation of distance education in the community colleges. As she says, "community colleges have long been interested in distance education" in order "to serve their largely non-traditional student populations." In the past, community colleges outstripped other educational sectors in teaching through high quality productions of video telecourses, and now, building on that tradition, almost every community college offers online courses. This chapter extends some familiar themes encountered in previous chapters, such as course completion and grade achievement, taking into account the special challenges of the community college's comparatively underprepared and often under-resourced student population. However, this author's conclusions are similar to others heard previously: "colleges need to provide online instructors with resources and training to implement high-quality online curricula and pedagogies that engage students and help them build their self-directed learning skills; create student readiness assessments that result in tailored feedback and student training; and put in place peer-review-driven continuous quality improvement processes. Some of these recommendations would radically reshape the way that institutions are organized, including the role of the faculty member."

The next three chapters share a common interest in the application of distance education in work settings, the emphasis being on training adults needing to sustain and enhance their technical, business and professional knowledge and skills. First, Berge offers a chapter about the part played by distance education in meeting the training needs of modern business corporations. Echoing Jaggars' conclusion, this chapter also introduces the theme of organizational change, and reflecting some of what we read in Part 4, Berge begins by pointing out the key responsibilities of educational managers, to " constantly align and realign the strategic plan of the organization." Rising to the top among the pressures requiring such changes in the training strategy of most corporations is the shift from national to global markets. "It cannot be emphasized too strongly that in the global economy today, distance training and education must solve *critical business needs* for it to be sustainable in the organization." Critical business needs include making training more cost-effective but also turning the organization into a learning organization. The starting point in the corporate environment is identifying the business purposes and goals of initiating and supporting a distance learning program. Berge's chapter includes a discussion of barriers to successful distance education in the training context, not too dissimilar from what has been encountered elsewhere in the *Handbook* in reference to higher and K-12 education. As in those other contexts, Berge emphasizes the difficulty is not in converting training materials into an electronic format, but in trying to change corporate tradition and attitudes". Well worth reflecting upon with regard to policy and management of all sectors of education as well as training is Berge's description of the steps that organizations should go through as they work through the change process, (even though it "usually looks like 'two steps forward and one back'").

Kuhne continues the theme of distance education as a means of coping with the continuously changing state of knowledge, as he addresses its use in continuing professional education (CPE). Although defining "professional" in its most inclusive sense, the chapter focuses primarily on the continuing education of health professionals, specifically doctors and nurses, and also on CPE of accountants, with a briefer review of CPE for insurance agents, lawyers, social workers. The conclusion—which suggests there are many opportunities for research related to other professions as well as those that were featured here—is that "distance education could soon become the preferred way of enabling professionals to keep abreast of changing profession-specific knowledge and skills, maintain and enhance their professional competence, assist their progress from novice to expert practitioners, and advance their careers through promotion and other job changes."

Following the discussion of the corporate and continuing professional education sectors, we next have a contribution about professional development and training in the U.S. armed forces, who have consistently been among the world's leaders in the application of communications technologies in continuing education and training—from the 1960s, when the United States Armed Forces Institute was the largest distance teaching organization in the world, up to the present, when we read about such high profile initiatives as The National Guard's Emergency Management Nexus in Second Life or the Defense Education & Training Network. Statistics alone are impressive when one reads about the military sector. Kenyon, Twogood, and Summerlin tell us, for example that one major program, the Advanced Distributed Learning Service has 725,000 active users and over 2300 courses, course completions average about 600,000 per month, with January 2011 registering over 1 million course completions. The Air Technology Network of the Airforce has grown into a network of 6 broadcast centers broadcasting over 350 courses per year resulting in approximately 129,000 student hours within Air Force, and 228,000 student-hours government-wide. The Advanced Distributed Learning Initiative includes the development of "sharable content object reference model," and is thus the principal forum for the development of learning objects, a cutting edge initiative we looked at in Chapter 20 of this book. The armed forces today, as in the past, retained certain qualities that make them ideal environments for distance education. These include a full range of both simple and highly advanced communications technologies, a decision-making structure that makes it possible to implement policies requiring substantial training investments, and the opportunity to deliver at scale which makes the substantial investments cost effective. There is some research on the teaching and learning effectiveness of these systems, but the extent of this research pales into insignificance by comparison with the scale of implementation, and provides innumerable opportunities for students who want to do research, civilian as well as military.

Among such students, quite likely there will be many in pursuit of doctoral degrees in education. Some might even be pursuing their degrees as distance learners, and this is the subject of Chapter 41, in which Evans and Green provide (for the first time in any of the *Handbook* editions) a review of the practice and problems of doctoral study online. The focus here is not only on study for the PhD, but also professional doctorates in fields like education, library and information science, and nursing, requiring original research and scholarship aimed at enhancing knowledge of value in professional or workplace settings, rather than advancing disciplinary knowledge. Written by Australian and U.S. co-authors, the chapter provides an international perspective and an opportunity to compare the approach to doctoral study at a distance in two different educational cultures. One statistic that stands out indicates the importance of the trend for distance education to grow into a dominating form of doctoral study; 72% of American students pursuing a doctorate in education work full time and fewer (25%) were (2007–08) enrolled full time. It is telling that the two largest providers of programs for the part-time doctoral student are the for-profit institutions, much more ready to respond to needs and a growing market than the public institutions, which nevertheless, it can be confidently predicted, will take up this field of practice in increasing numbers in the next decade.

Teaching and learning science at a distance has been the most challenging academic subject for distance educators, with various strategies adopted to deal with the especially critical need to provide students with laboratory experiences. Kennepohl's chapter explains the caution of the science community with regard to non-traditional methods of teaching, and the innovations that are becoming accepted, from the oldest—the "home experiment kit," to applications of virtual reality, and accessing remote laboratory facilities by wireless and similar technologies.

The final two chapters of Part 5 introduce and discuss questions about the place of distance education in the future of higher education, and the transformational changes that can be imagined as well as the changes in how institutions are organized to accommodate change. In Chapter 43 Hanna begins with a reminder of the global crisis of inaccessibility to higher education, with universities worldwide facing the challenge of meeting dramatically increasing demand, while also experiencing reduced financial support. How will the university of the future respond to this and other challenges? "Will its activities continue to be concentrated in campuses, conveying the idea that the "university is a place," or will its focus increasingly be "independent of place" and focused on the widest possible forms of knowledge sharing and discovery? "As these questions illustrate, dramatic changes in higher education are underway and distance education programs and technologies are major drivers of transformation. The changes occurring today are more than simple procedural changes or ways of conducting business; they likely represent fundamental shifts in values, assumptions, culture, and missions. With the current environment of instant and pervasive connections to storerooms of knowledge located all over the world, in multiple languages, with fewer and fewer barriers to access, we see a third set of emerging new models, where students are dynamically connected through the Internet and other advanced technologies with each other, with faculty mentors, and with institutional academic support structures in ways not imagined just a few years ago. Choices regarding pedagogy, technology, culture, and strategy are increasingly complex and blurred."

Blurring of boundaries is the theme of the final chapter. Like Hanna, Visser begins his chapter with an analysis of the problems of access to education in less developed countries, reminding us of the leading part played by distance education in international development, "driven by the desire to overcome the shortcomings of established schooling practices."

Based on his own experience in UNESCO's educational development projects, Visser's is a critical perspective, one that sees "discrepancy between the established practice of distance education and the overriding purposes for educational development." Such discrepancy can be attributed in part at least to over-narrow views about the meaning of learning, and this author leads us in a reflection on the meaning of learning as it relates to contemporary society. He closes with a discussion about the potential of open educational resources in contributing to "much needed fundamental reshaping of the learning landscape." Visser's chapter is a very personal critique of distance education in its contemporary form (as he understands it), and in its style is a departure from the literature reviews that make up other chapters. However, it is our hope that in closing the volume with this polemic, we will leave the reader with food for thought, hoping also that it will lead some readers to respond, preferably with research-based arguments, about the future of our field.

35

THE EVOLUTION OF K–12 DISTANCE EDUCATION AND VIRTUAL SCHOOLS

TOM CLARK

This chapter describes the evolution of K–12 distance education, from earlier forms and methods up to the emergence of virtual schools. A virtual school is an educational organization that offers K–12 courses through Internet- or Web-based methods. In many ways, the virtual school movement is an outgrowth of the independent study high school movement that began in the 1920s. Perennial issues, effective practices and lessons learned in prior incarnations of K–12 distance education remain relevant for K–12 online education policy and practice today.

FROM INDEPENDENT STUDY TO VIRTUAL LEARNING

K–12 distance education is an evolving phenomenon in the United States, where students between the ages of 5 and 18 are usually enrolled in elementary, middle, and high schools, from Kindergarten through 12th grade. Over 54 million students were enrolled in public or private K–12 schools in the United States in 2009 (U.S. Department of Education, 2011). Distance education courses and supplemental instruction for K–12 learners incorporate print, audio, video, multimedia, and online technologies. The primary purpose of K–12 distance education, expanding access to curriculum and providing educational choices, has changed little over time.

The Evolution of K–12 Distance Education Technologies

A succession of technologies was used to deliver distance education in the 20th century (see Table 35.1). In this section, print-based methods are described first, followed by audio, video, and Web-based methods.

Emergence of K–12 Independent Study

The role of independent study programs as the forerunner of virtual schools is nowhere more apparent than at the University of Nebraska-Lincoln. The university began a supervised correspondence study program in 1929. In 1932 Nebraska received a $5,000 grant from the Carnegie Foundation for curriculum enrichment in small high schools

Table 35.1   Timeline of K-12 Distance Education and Instructional Technologies

Date	First Documented Use in K–12 Education
1910	Instructional film
1923	Supervised correspondence study
1930	Educational radio
1933	Educational television
1956	Telecourse study
1961	Airborne instruction
1965	Computer based learning
1967	Audio conferencing
1973	Educational satellite instruction
1984	Computer mediated communication
1985	Satellite network instruction
1989	Microwave/ITFS network instruction
1993	Web based instruction

through its supervised study method (Broady, 1932). This pilot funding led to what was an enormous federal grant at the time—$100,000 a year for 10 years—from the federal Works Progress Administration. Nebraska's Independent Study High School went on to achieve state accreditation for its diploma program in 1967 and regional accreditation in 1978 (Young & McMahon, 1991). In the 1990s, Nebraska used a federal grant to launch one of the first virtual high schools.

Supervised Study Model.   From the beginning, a key way in which K–12 independent study differed from postsecondary study was in the use of supervision. The Nebraska plan for enriching the curriculum of small high schools through a supervised extension service has become the model for much of Nebraska's subsequent work in independent study. In supervised correspondence study, "the local high school secures the lessons, provides periods in the regular school day for study, supervises the pupils' work, and returns the lessons to the correspondence study center," which prepares and grades the lessons (Broady, Platt, & Bell, 1931, p. 9).

This plan had its basis in an earlier experiment. Superintendent Sydney C. Mitchell devised the Benton Harbor Plan for supervised vocational correspondence study in 1923 (Mitchell, 1923).

From 1923 to 1930, over 100 U.S. high schools started supervised correspondence study programs (Harding, 1944). In 1929, the University of Nebraska became the first university to offer supervised high school correspondence study. Over two dozen other universities and a few state education agencies subsequently developed independent study programs. "Independent study" is the term commonly used these days to denote correspondence study.

Estimating the Scope of K–12 Independent Study.   Until the 1990s, print-based independent study was the mainstay of K–12 distance education. The National

University Extension Association (NUEA) began tracking academic high school study by correspondence in its member institutions in 1929. Bittner and Mallory (1933) bemoaned the "difficulty of securing uniformity in methods of counting students and enrollments" (p. 270). The first numbers published by NUEA were for 1934–1935, when 75% of enrollments were at the University of Nebraska-Lincoln. During World War II, a teacher shortage and early enlistment spurred a jump in high school enrollments by high school students and soldiers. After the war, high school enrollments in NUEA institutions dropped until the mid-1950s.

Enrollments increased 40% in the 1980s (NUCEA, 1991) then flattened out in the 1990s. Enrollments rebounded to an all-time high of 175,000 in 2004–2005 (D. Gearhart, personal communication, March 31, 2006). However, about 45% of these enrollments were in online courses, double the percentage four years earlier. As print-based independent study enrollments declined, some programs phased out that option.

Emergence of Technology-Based Methods

Print media such as textbooks continued to play a role in K–12 distance education throughout the 20th century, but by the early 21st century, electronic methods had largely replaced print.

Audio-Based K–12 Distance Education. The first major electronic media used in distance education, educational radio, saw limited use in U.S. K–12 education, mostly in the 1920s and 1930s for supplemental instruction. The Communications Act of 1934 that established the Federal Communications Commission (FCC) did not reserve educational frequencies for radio. The Ohio School of the Air was the first educational radio system. Begun in 1921, it served as a model for other states, but lost funding in 1937 (Saettler, 2004). The Wisconsin School of the Air, the nation's longest running educational radio system, operated from 1930 through 1975. It focused on specific educational needs, supplementing the curriculum in small rural schools by offering elective topics not available locally, such as music. At its peak in 1966, classes receiving School of the Air instructional broadcasts in Wisconsin K–8 public schools enrolled about 330,000 students (Bianchi, 2002). Grounding their efforts in Dewey's progressive education philosophy, School of the Air lesson designers focused on the strengths of the radio medium, such as stimulation of active involvement and imagining. They built opportunities for community participation through contests, festivals, and events, and forged personal connections between students and radio instructors. These approaches remain relevant for K–12 online learning today (Bianchi, 2002).

Educational telephone has also had limited applications in K–12 education. Statewide educational telephone networks such as Wisconsin's ETN began to appear in the late 1970s. The audioconferencing portion of the Learn Alaska Network was its only successful component, provided programming for K–12 and other audiences in remote areas (Bramble, 1988).

The 1980s saw use of a variety of low-bandwidth networking technologies that combined audio and computer conferencing, such as freeze-frame video, audiographics, and Videotex (Hudson & Boyd, 1984). Today, audio is still an important component of online courses. Podcasting and digital audio are in use at all educational levels to provide supplemental access to educational content (Hew, 2009).

Video-Based K–12 Distance Education. The first use of educational film in K–12 instruction may have occurred in the Rochester, New York public schools in 1910 (Saettler, 2004). K–12 educational television programming began in 1933 at the University of Iowa's Experimental Visual Broadcasting Station W9XK, with supplemental 15-minute evening broadcasts to groups of children, such as Boy Scouts seeking to meet merit badge requirements About 389 such programs were broadcast between 1933 and 1939 (Kurtz, 1959). In its Sixth Report and Order in 1952, the FCC reserved TV channels for educational use, facilitating the creation of a national network of educational stations. Later rulings reserved space for education on cable TV and direct-to-home satellite systems. As a result, out-of-school educational broadcasting for children was continued through popular programs such as *Sesame Street* on PBS stations beginning in the 1970s. Supplemental in-school experiences have also been a major focus. In 1998, about 80% of U.S. public television stations provided educational programming to elementary or secondary schools (Corporation for Public Broadcasting, 1999).

In general, the use of educational broadcast television in the United States for full courses designed for K–12 learners has been rare. High school students seeking early college credit may enroll in telecourses offered by community colleges, either directly or through dual enrollment programs (Clark, 2000). In 2005, PBS discontinued its Adult Learning Service, which provided networked feeds of telecourses to postsecondary institutions. At its peak in 2001, it facilitated 450,000 telecourse enrollments a year (Behrens, 2005). Its successor, Annenberg Learner (www.learner.org), continues to license video content to educational institutions for integration into courses and provides professional development content for K–12 teachers.

A compilation of 421 comparative studies of achievement in instructional television and conventional courses by Chu and Schramm (1975) included 64 elementary level studies and 92 at the secondary level. Overall, about three in four studies showed "no significant difference." Differences between treatment effects were more commonly seen in secondary-level studies that looked at the academic outcomes of high school students. A majority (57%) of secondary studies showed no significant difference, but a higher percentage showed television instruction to be more effective (26%) than conventional instruction (17%). While most elementary studies (78%) showed no significant difference, a higher percentage found television instruction more effective (16%) than conventional instruction (6%). This situation was reversed at the college level, where three in four studies showed no significant difference, but a lower percentage of studies showed television instruction to be more effective (11%) than found conventional instruction to be more effective (14%). In other words, at the elementary and secondary levels, where there was a difference, it favored instructional television. Chu and Schramm concluded that "by and large, instructional television can be more easily used for primary and secondary students than for college students" (p. 6).

Educational satellite emerged in the 1970s as a method of providing high-quality video-based instruction without the use of terrestrial transmitters. It represented an evolution from airplane-based transmitters, such as the Midwest Program on Airborne Television Instruction, launched in 1961 by Purdue University to provide supplemental instruction to K–12 learners in six Midwestern states with $16 million in year 1 funding from the Ford Foundation. Technical and policy issues led to MPATI's demise.

It was converted to a videotape library in 1968, which proved valuable to the Public Broadcasting Service when it launched in 1969 (Jajkowski, 2004). In 1973, 10 years after the first satellite was placed in a stationary geosynchronous orbit, the Applications Technology Satellite F (ATS-F) telecast inservices for rural K–12 educators (Grayson, Norwood, & Wigren, 1973). In 1985, the first national satellite network created to serve K–12 education was founded. The TI-IN Network was privately operated and delivered courses and staff development programming developed at Education Service Center 20 in San Antonio, Texas. By 1986, it had 150 receive sites in 12 states and offered 18 high school courses and staff development opportunities (Pease & Tinsley, 1986). In 1988, TI-IN and similar networks began to receive federal funding through the U.S. Department of Education's Star Schools Program, the first modern-day federal program for K–12 distance education (Kirby, 1998). About 40% of K–12 unit schools, typically the smallest and most rural districts, reported use of satellite television in 1999 (Howley & Harmon, 2000).

Beginning in the 1980s, terrestrial education networks were established with a succession of technologies to provide two-way video and other services. Hezel Associates (1998) annually documented distance learning practices in the 50 states from 1987 through 1998. The Education Network of Maine, developed in 1989, combined two-way video via microwave with microwave broadcasts (ITFS) or compressed video to outlying sites. Oregon's EDNET, also begun in 1989, consisted of separate satellite, compressed video, and computer networks. The Utah Education Network, serving both K–12 and higher education, came online in 1991 using a microwave backbone and compressed video to other sites. Closed-circuit educational telecommunications networks using compressed or full-motion videoconferencing systems for two-way video, two-way audio emerged in the early 1990s and began replacing microwave and ITFS systems. Hundreds of small videoconferencing networks appeared, linking K–12 schools and educational consortia.

Later state networks used fiber optic technologies to deliver video, data, and voice services that supported video-based distance education, computer networking, and telephony. The Iowa Communications Network is the most extensive and unique example. By 2006, this state-owned and financed network connected over 700 two-way full-motion video classrooms in K–12 schools. Similar networks were built in other states during the 1990s, usually with financing and ownership by the regional telephone company.

There has been declining interest in adding new capacity to educational networks in recent years. For example, the Iowa Communications Network connects about the same number of classrooms today as it did in 2006. However, broadband networks like the ICN serve many other purposes, such as providing high-bandwidth Internet connectivity needed by schools for online and blended learning. Satellite educational networks cannot match these capabilities, making them less adaptable as learning paradigms change. Most have ceased operations.

Comparison studies included in later meta-analyses found no significant differences in achievement of two-way video learners and face-to-face learners (for example, Hinnant, 1994; Libler, 1991; Wick, 1997). The involvement of local distance education coordinators, administrators and teachers was critical to build broad based support for two-way video course implementation (Johnson, 1996).

Computer-Based K–12 Learning. Suppes, Jerman, and Groen (1966) experimented with computer-based learning in fourth grade classrooms at Stanford in 1965. Elementary school experiments with Plato III also began at University of Illinois around this time (Van Meer, 2003). In the 1980s and 1990s, many schools began to provide computer-assisted learning, typically in computer labs where students were supervised in individualized learning.

The development of USENET in 1980 and SMTP email and the Internet Protocol Suite in 1982 made possible the standardized exchange of text information and communications over the Internet between computers. Computer conferencing also emerged, allowing computer users to interact in real time. Goodman (1992) describes an online role playing simulation of the Arab-Israeli conflict moderated by University of Michigan's School of Education. High schools first participated in this ongoing project in 1984 (http://aic.conflix.org). Berge and Collins (1998) compiled examples of the supplemental use of computer-mediated communication (CMC) in a wide variety of K–12 contexts. Multimedia tools emerged in the 1980s and 1990s that could be used to create interactive, engaging computer-based content and learning environments. All of these technologies and approaches helped set the stage for the virtual school movement, which is described at length later in this chapter.

Growth of Technology-Based Distance Education

Enrollments in technology-based K–12 distance education courses grew rapidly in the 2000s. The U.S. Department of Education (2008) surveyed a representative sample of public school districts nationwide in 2002–2003 and 2004–2005. It estimated 507,000 enrollments in technology-based distance education courses through U.S. public school districts in 2004–2005, which represented an increase of more than 50% since 2002–2003. The most frequently cited course providers were postsecondary institutions (47%), other school districts (33%) and the state's own sanctioned or sponsored virtual school (24%). In 2004–2005, districts that reported technology-based distance education enrollments were more likely to report that at least some of the courses were online (58%) than video-based (47%). Only two years earlier, two-way interactive video courses were reported more frequently. Online and video-based enrollments were not counted separately in this survey, which was limited to enrollments via public schools.

K–12 online learning grew rapidly throughout the 2000s. There were an estimated 300,000 K–12 enrollments in online courses via public and private schools in 2002–2003 (Newman, Stein, & Trask, 2003), up from an estimated 40,000–50,000 in 2000–2001 (Clark, 2001). Based on a Sloan Consortium survey, Picciano and Seaman (2009) estimated that in 2007–2008 about 666,000 K–12 students were enrolled in online courses. This represented a 47% increase in two years. By 2010–2011, there were well over 1 million enrollments in fully online K–12 courses. While a defensible estimate of total enrollments is not available, state sanctioned or sponsored virtual schools reported over 536,000 course enrollments, while full-time multi-district schools had about 250,000 enrollments. Enrollment growth in these two program types was over 25% in a year. Single-district, consortium and postsecondary-led program enrollments were not estimated (Watson, Murin, Vashaw, Gemin, & Rapp, 2010).

Postsecondary online learning also continues to grow, fueling calls for K–12 students to experience online learning before college. By fall 2010, over 6.1 million college students were taking at least one course online. When compared with a year earlier, online college course enrollments grew by 10% (Allen & Seaman, 2011). K–12 blended learning is also growing rapidly. While estimating 666,000 K–12 online enrollments in 2007–2008, Allen and Seaman (2011) also estimated that 350,000 students were enrolled in courses that blended online and face to face learning. Most online learning programs in the growing single-district sector are blended rather than fully online (Watson et al., 2011).

EMERGENCE OF THE VIRTUAL SCHOOL

The emergence of virtual schools for K–12 learners in the 1990s represents the latest in an ever-accelerating series of technological advances in the field of K–12 distance education. Some authors made prescient statements about virtual schools during the "pre-Web" era. In December 1987, Morten Paulsen, a Norwegian distance education expert, penned an article titled, "In Search of a Virtual School." Referring to both K–12 and postsecondary education, Paulsen asserted, "the virtual school will dominate future distance education. It is possible to create a virtual school around a computer-based information system … at present, computer conferencing is the only technology that can serve as a basis for creating a 'virtual school'." (pp. 71–73). Paulsen believed that in contrast to previous distance learning systems, computer-conferencing systems had the capability to handle the professional, didactic, administrative, and social tasks necessary to run a virtual school. But the technology was not yet ready.

By 1994, there were already several virtual school experiments underway that combined Internet tools such as email, chat, and FTP, with computer-based content to deliver mainly text-based online instruction. Several were private schools that still offer online learning today. Utah Department of Education's Electronic High School began in 1994 as a broker for a blend of technology-delivered high school courses from in-state and out-of-state providers.

Federal and state funding played a major role in the growth of the virtual school movement. The University of Nebraska-Lincoln CLASS Project was federally funded in 1996, as was the Hawaii e-School later that year, and Concord Consortium's Virtual High School in 1997. The Utah Department of Education began its Electronic High School as an internal initiative in 1994, while the Florida Virtual School began in 1997 as a cooperative effort between two Florida school districts funded through a state grant.

Early virtual school efforts typically focused on supplemental study at the high school level. For example, the Virtual High School consortium reported about 500 enrollments at 27 member high schools in 1997–1998 (U.S. Department of Education, 2000a). Its successor, the VHS Global Consortium (2011) has continued this focus on providing high school level courses. It reported over 15,000 enrollments at 676 member schools in 2010–2011.

Virtual high schools gave way to virtual schools, as online learning expanded to other educational levels. Of 32 virtual schools or consortia responding to a survey (Clark, 2001), all reported offering high school courses, but a surprising 51% offered middle school courses as well. Today, many virtual schools offer online courses at all K–12 levels, on a full-time or supplemental basis (Watson et al., 2010).

In 2004, Watson, Winograd, and Kalmon conducted the first in a series of national studies for the *Keeping Pace with Online Learning* series, which has become a standard reference work in the field of K–12 online learning. After contacting officials in 22 states about K–12 online learning, they ultimately profile practices in 11 selected states, then considered the implications of their research for policy and practice. They found that K–12 online learning programs were growing rapidly. Practices were being developed in the absence of clear state-level guidance, as states had not yet created policies specific to K–12 online learning. In subsequent annual studies, Watson and his colleagues profiled program practices in all 50 states, while providing analysis on policy issues and trends, such as growth in state virtual school and full-time online learning enrollments, the emergence of blended learning, and the recent rapid growth of single-district online and blended learning programs (Watson et al., 2011).

Virtual School Types

Virtual K–12 schools may be classified in many ways, each of which may serve valid purposes. One simple method is by organizational control (Clark, 2001). As seen in the previous section, virtual schools may be part of or an outgrowth of independent study high school programs at universities. Some are sponsored or sanctioned as statewide programs by state entities, while others are full-time virtual charter schools or online learning programs with a statewide reach. Virtual schools may be operated by local school districts or regional education agencies, or by private schools. Virtual schools are also operated by educational consortia. For-profit educational service providers may also manage or operate virtual schools.

Postsecondary Programs. As explained earlier, as university-based independent study high schools went online, they developed many of the early online high school programs, most of which continue to operate today. In spring 1996, the University of Nebraska was the first organization to obtain federal funding to build a virtual high school through its CLASS Project. The university used a $2.5 million proof of concept funding from the U.S. General Services Administration and a five-year, $17.5 million U.S. Department of Education Star Schools Program grant to develop custom software and build a complete Web-based high school curriculum. In 1999, the university spun off Class.com, one of the early K–12 online educational management organizations. The University of Nebraska continues to offer a full online curriculum via its Independent Study High School (http://highschool.unl.edu). Other major providers include BYU Independent Study, Indiana University, University of Missouri, University of Oklahoma, and University of Texas. Recent enrollment growth has been limited in most of these programs. While online dual enrollment is probably growing rapidly, especially in community colleges, current surveys are not designed to track it.

State-Level Virtual Schools. In 2002, only 14 states had a virtual school operated or sanctioned by the state to serve as the state's virtual school (Clark, 2002). By 2011, state virtual schools or state-led online learning initiatives existed in 40 states, and state virtual schools collectively had about 536,000 course enrollments. State virtual schools play essential roles as change agents, capacity builders, and service providers. State virtual schools in Florida and North Carolina have grown rapidly and benefit from FTE-based financial models similar to conventional public school districts. However, most state virtual schools have recently seen limited growth, and their roles are being re-examined, in light of budget cuts and the expanding role of local school districts and other providers (Watson et al., 2010, 2011). Some states have online initiatives that are not statewide virtual schools, but provide learning services statewide, such as the University of California College Prep initiative, begun in 1999 (Clark, 2002).

Virtual Charter School Full-Time Programs. In 2011, 30 states had at least one full-time K–12 online learning program serving multiple districts, enrolling an estimated 250,000 students. (Watson et al., 2011). In the large majority of cases, but not all, these full-time programs are charter schools. Most are operated by local or regional education agencies. In most states where charter schools are permitted, state aid typically follows the student to the district operating the charter school and pays for attendance. For-profit entities often provide educational services on behalf of the charter entity. However, many virtual charter schools operate independently. One of the longest running is Basehor-Linwood Virtual School, established by a Kansas school district in 1997. Like many other virtual schools, it has expanded its offerings over time and now offers fee-based credit recovery.

A limited number of national for-profit service providers operate statewide full-time online schools, typically on behalf of local charter school entities. The largest are K-12 Inc., which served about 83,000 Full Time Equivalent (FTE) students, and Connections Academy, now part of Connections Learning, which served about 35,000 FTE students in 2010–2011. These national providers probably serve about 60% of full-time online learning students (Watson et al., 2011). K-12 was co-founded in 1999 by William Bennett, former U.S. Secretary of Education. It began by operating virtual charter schools for early elementary grades in five states. It added grade levels each year until it offered every grade level from K through 12. Connections Academy has followed a similar growth model since its founding in 2001.

Full-time online learning appeals to those families interested in homeschooling or home instruction. In spring 2007, an estimated 1.5 million students nationwide were homeschooled, or nearly twice as many as in 1999. Homeschoolers represented about 2.7% of all K–12 students in 2007 (U.S. Department of Education, 2009). By definition, homeschooled students who enroll in a full-time online charter school become public school students.

School District-Led Programs. K–12 online learning programs led by local education agencies are the fastest growing type of online learning program (Watsonet al., 2011). Well-established programs often began with a narrow focus and grew in mission and scope over time. For example, HISD Virtual School in Houston, Texas, began with online AP courses, then added a middle school curriculum to help students prepare for AP. Today, it offers fee-based supplemental high school courses, credit recovery courses, a blended online and on-site evening school option for school leavers, a full-time online program with Connections Academy, and supplemental courses via Texas Virtual School Network. Today, many district-led programs follow blended learning models. Miami Dade County Public Schools' iPrep Academy provides local supervision of online study in FLVS Virtual Learning Labs, while students at Carpe Diem Collegiate High School rotate between online introductory and face to face applied sessions in each course (Horn & Staker, 2011).

Virtual Private Schools. A wide range of for-profit and nonprofit private K–12 schools offer K–12 online learning programs. Accredited virtual private schools with long track records include the Keystone School, part of one of the oldest proprietary high schools in the nation, the Christa McAuliffe Academy, which now offers a School of Arts and

Sciences internationally, and Laurel Springs School, an online college prep academy. Private schools with accreditation by AdvanceEd, which represents the six regional accreditation agencies, or state approval as a recognized diploma-granting educational program, have greater acceptability among employers and university admission offices for their diplomas.

Online Learning Consortia.   Consortia also played an important role in the growth of virtual schooling. The best known of these is the Virtual High School, founded in 1997 by the Hudson (Massachusetts) Public Schools and the Concord Consortium, now operated by the nonprofit VHS Global Consortium. This is a unique cooperative in which participating schools contribute a "netcourse," and, in return, receive 50 student enrollments per year in courses offered by the Consortium. Other long-running consortia such as Colorado Online Learning have adopted similar approaches. Some extend existing P-20 dual-credit partnerships, such as the Connecticut Distance Learning Consortium, while others, such as the Western Consortium for Accelerated Learning Opportunities, seek to expand access to online courses in multiple states.

Educational Management Organizations.   Course, content, and platform providers, many of them for-profits, played an important role in the growth of the virtual school movement, and are at the table in policy discussions today. Many virtual schools obtain their learning management systems and their web-based course content from these education management organizations (EMOs), although it is also common today for virtual schools to develop their own courses. A number of EMOs have become builders and operators of virtual schools. For example, for-profit K-12 Inc. acts as an EMO for charter school entities, while nonprofit Florida Virtual School provides EMO services for local, regional, and state education agencies.

DISTANCE AND VIRTUAL PROFESSIONAL DEVELOPMENT OR K–12 EDUCATORS

Distance learning for pre-service teacher education and inservice professional development has a long history in the United States (Schmidt & Faulkner, 1989). The first teachers or normal college to offer correspondence study appears to have been Western State Normal School (later Western Michigan University) in Kalamazoo, Michigan, beginning in 1905 (Bittner & Mallory, 1933). Maul (1929) identified 59 of 157 teacher's colleges and normal schools responding to a 1928 survey as offering college courses by correspondence.

Local and regional education agencies are traditional providers of staff development, while regional universities traditionally provide college credit courses applicable to certification and recertification. Distance and virtual learning provides access for pre-service and inservice teachers to new providers, regardless of traditional education service area boundaries.

In the late 1990s, shortages of certified teachers spurred the development of distance and online education programs for the alternative certification for educators. Online professional development providers also emerged, registering with states to offer continuing education opportunities that counted toward recertification. U.S. Department of Education programs have supported a number of online professional development projects, such as PBS Teacherline, which offered 100 online professional development courses in 2005. In 2005–2006, about one in four U.S. public school teachers responding to a national survey had participated in online courses or modules (Hezel Associates, 2007).

The growing number of K–12 online learning programs has created a new role for online professional development: the training of online teachers. Dawley, Rice, and Hinck (2010) surveyed 830 teachers in virtual schools, finding that 94% received training for online teaching from their virtual school, while only 30% received it from a university.

PERENNIAL ISSUES IN K–12 DISTANCE AND VIRTUAL LEARNING

While some perennial issues represent enduring challenges, others result from misconceptions or a lack of understanding about K–12 distance and online learning practice.

Government Funding and Policymaking. The federal government has traditionally seen educational technology and distance learning as tools for use in education reform and school improvement efforts. In the United States, K–12 education is locally controlled but governed at the state level with some federal assistance. Federal influence is limited (Clark & Else, 1998). As described earlier, a number of federal grant programs have supported the development of distance and virtual learning. State "pass-through" grants funded through federal programs have been used for widespread experimentation at the local and regional level, and have funded many state-level initiatives. For example, under the No Child Left Behind Act of 2001, most federal funding for educational technology was consolidated into state block grants under the Enhancing Education Through Technology Program (EETT). From fiscal year (FY) 2002 through FY 2008, this program disbursed about $3.4 billion in educational technology funding. The summative evaluation report (SRI International, 2009) showed that teacher technology use and classroom-level student technology access grew in EETT districts. By FY 2007, 81% of teachers in EETT funded districts reported receiving technology professional development in the past year, while 63% reported students had high-speed Internet access in their classrooms, with no significant difference between high and low poverty schools. At the same time, states were less able to document progress toward EETT goals. By FY 2007, only 27 states had created standards for teacher technology competency, only 24 states had measures for technology integration, and only 6 had completed statewide assessments of eight grade student technology proficiency.

The first major federal policy document focusing on K–12 distance learning in the United States is *Linking for Learning* (Office of Technology Assessment, 1987). The report's authors concluded that state education agencies act both as gatekeepers and catalysts, and that federal and state regulations significantly affect the development of distance education.

In the last few years, with the future of federal funding and NCLB reauthorization uncertain, non-profit associations of the states such as the National Governors Association (NGA) and Council of Chief State School Officers (CCSSO), philanthropic organizations such as the Gates Foundation, and non-profit interest groups such as the International Council for K–12 Online Learning (iNACOL) have stepped up to act as catalysts and provide policy leadership. Core student learning competencies in math and literacy (www.corestandards.org) have been developed by NGA and CCSSO, and adopted by 45 states as of 2011. The Next Generation Learning Challenges (www.next-genlearning.org) developed by EDUCAUSE with Gates Foundation funding seek to tap the potential of technology to improve college readiness and completion via math and literacy competencies and whole-school blended learning.

Earlier in the evolution of K–12 distance education, state seat time requirements linked to state aid for local districts spurred development of supervised versions of independent study and distance education. However, these gatekeeper policies now hamper the further development of competency-based online and blended learning approaches. The CCSSO and iNACOL advocate state adoption of policies to enable competency-based learning aligned with Common Core State Standards (Sturgis, Patrick, & Pittenger, 2011). Sturgis and Patrick (2010) see competency-based learning as key to increasing high school graduation rates and college and career readiness among underachieving high school students.

In-state teacher certification requirements are another gatekeeper issue impacting K–12 distance and online learning. In 2011, all 30 states with a state virtual school required in-state teacher certification for online K–12 teachers (Stoops, 2011). Another issue is that standard teacher certification does not address the quality of distance and online teaching. Standards for quality online teaching adopted and revised by iNACOL (2010) represent a consensus of practitioners and policy makers. The State of Georgia (2006) created an online teaching endorsement which requires completion of three online courses built around online teaching competencies. Several other states now have considering similar endorsements.

Access and Equity.   Access to distance education and educational technology has been seen by states and the federal government as a way in which K–12 schools can address important equity issues. Some researchers have studied technology access for special populations, such as the compliance of distance learning systems with the Americans with Disabilities Act (Meyen, Lian, & Tangen, 1998) and barriers to technology access for K–12 learners with disabilities (U.S. Department of Education, 2000b). Rose and Blomeyer (2007) reviewed the legal requirements for equitable access to online learning programs for students with disabilities and other underserved groups. Support for technology infrastructure building is one way policy makers have sought to equalize educational opportunities since the 1990s. Internet access became so ubiquitous by 2005 that the annual federal survey was discontinued, as nearly 100% of public schools had Internet access, compared to 35% in 1994. Gaps in student access to technology also narrowed greatly. In 2005, the ratio of students to Internet-connected computers was just over 4 to 1 in high-poverty schools, and 3 to 1 in low-poverty schools. In 1998, ratios were much higher in high poverty schools (17 to 1) than in low-poverty schools (10 to 1) (Wells & Lewis, 2006).

The dialogue about technology access in schools has now shifted to whether schools can provide the 1 to 1 computing capabilities needed to offer blended learning environments to students. Blended learning represents the convergence of online schooling and technology integration in face-to-face education (Watson, 2008). This rapid rise in connectivity can be attributed in part to the Schools and Libraries program (www.usac.org), a federal program established in 1996 to develop Internet infrastructure in schools and libraries that is commonly known as E-Rate. In 2010, it provided $2.3 billion in support to applicants.

Curriculum equity has become a rallying point for those seeking to redress historical inequities in education. The virtual school movement was fueled in part by a lawsuit against the state of California over access to Advanced Placement high school courses that can increase college opportunities for K–12 learners (Hill, 2000). Another curriculum equity issue is the use of distance and virtual learning in academic tracking. In a 1984 survey, only 25% of school counselors at small high schools in Texas reported recommending correspondence study to students needing additional credits. Most correspondence students they referred were D and F students (Barker & Petersen, 1984). On the other hand, a later survey of principals at small Texas schools showed that 80% limited enrollment in satellite videoconferencing courses to A and B students (Barker, 1987). Vocationally oriented high school correspondence study has been shown to reduce dropout rate and increase GED completion for school leavers (Bucks County Public Schools, 1972). In the 1980s, computer-based learning became a common tool in working with at-risk learners. Today, more high school students are taking online courses for credit recovery than to supplement their course of study (Picciano, Seaman, & Day, 2010). K–12 online learning courses often demonstrate a bimodal distribution, in which low-achieving and high-achieving students predominate, and fewer students are in the middle (Dickson, 2005).

As noted earlier, the Wisconsin School of the Air saw hundreds of thousands of enrollments in rural K–8 schools in supplemental instruction by radio. Participation in satellite-based distance education was highest in rural and small schools. Over half of the schools participating online in the Virtual High School in 1999–2000 had enrollments under 800 students (U.S. Department of Education, 2000a). Small rural school districts see the availability of online courses as an important lifeline that allows them to offer course options and expand their curriculum (Picciano & Seaman, 2009). Instead of replacing these conventional schools, supplemental virtual school programs have strengthened them. The growing use of blended or hybrid learning that combines online and face-to-face instruction also serves to reinforce the importance of local bricks-and-mortar schools in K–12 online learning.

Societal Attitudes.   The attitudes of parents and community members play an important role in determining K–12 student participation in distance and virtual learning. A national Phi Delta Kappa poll of 1002 adults in 2011 (Bushaw & Lopez, 2011) showed mixed yet evolving attitudes toward online and technology-based learning. Those polled demonstrated strong support for the use of computer technology in high schools to prepare students for college or career (96%) or to increase class availability in small/rural schools (93%).

However, the public appears to strongly support students spending the school day at a bricks-and-mortar school, even if it affects academic outcomes. About 40% supported and 59% opposed allowing high school students to attend a bricks-and-mortar school for fewer hours each week if they were using computer technology to learn at home. Around 46% preferred hiring a more effective teacher who could only teach online, while 50% supported hiring a less effective teacher who could teach the class in person.

Concerns about education market forces.   As described earlier in this chapter, many of the educational management organizations participating in the development and operation of virtual schools are for-profit companies. K–12 distance and virtual learning is part of a multibillion-dollar education market in which the interests of venture capitalists and shareholders must be weighed along with those of students, parents, and local communities. A significant portion of technology investments in schools has come through in-kind donations from for-profits, which often work closely with education agencies and play a role in public policy making and planning.

Some have expressed concern that for-profit companies are driving policy development for K–12 online learning. However, a variety of other entities appear to be influencing policy development. In the long term, the constant turnover in distance education technologies and methods makes it challenging for any stakeholder group to gain a lasting advantage.

Concerns about Student Outcomes

A perennial issue in K–12 distance learning has been whether distance learners achieve outcomes at least equal to conventional learners. Childs (1949) studied 1,800 Nebraska high school students enrolled in conventional study and 1,250 enrolled via correspondence study In most areas tested, the correspondence students scored significantly higher than conventional students of equal age and ability level. Attrition studies had less positive results. In 1956, Childs and the other researchers found that only 58% of students enrolling in high school courses at 24 NUEA member institutions actually completed them, although the completion rate rose to 69% for those completing one lesson (Childs, 1966). Completion rates were better at University of Nebraska, averaging 65% to 75% from 1932 through 1990 (Young & McMahon, 1991). Completion rates are still an issue in online learning today.

Strong effect sizes in favor of computer-assisted instruction in comparison studies suggest that well-designed technology-enhanced learning environments can boost K–12 student achievement. However, the vast majority of studies at all educational levels show no significant difference (Russell, 2001). The main value for the field of conducting comparison studies and meta-analyses continues to be one of building credibility for distance and online education with stakeholders.

However, it should be noted that standardized academic content area tests do not measure all significant learning impacts (Hawkes, Cambre, & Lewis, 1999). Smith and Dillon (1999) observe that in most studies comparing distance learning with conventional learning, the learning strategies or methods used within the distance learning and conventional courses are not the same, so there is not really a simple comparison of delivery methods. Rather than advocating studies that control for both media and method, they call for studies that use achievement and other outcomes to demonstrate the most effective combinations of instructional methods and media. In doing so they are building upon the work of Kozma and others. Kozma (2000) summarizes a number of major technology interventions and the variety of alternative research methodologies used to demonstrate their effectiveness, noting that many of the technology treatments are "naturally and intentionally confounded" (p. 10). Curriculum, teaching, assessment, and technology components cannot be disentangled for study in isolation.

A limited number of K–12 distance education research studies can be considered scientifically based, as they follow rigorous experimental or quasi-experimental designs that allow researchers to say whether a treatment actually caused the observed effect. Only these kinds of studies meet the standards of rigor needed for inclusion in meta-analytic studies of academic achievement (Cavanaugh, 1999). Some rigorous qualitative studies also appear in the literature. Case study research can be used to generate valid, testable hypotheses and theories suitable for further empirical research (Eisenhardt, 1989).

In a prior edition of this *Handbook of Disatnce Learning*, the present author issued a call for research on distance and online learning, to demonstrate the impact on K–12 academic student performance, delineate factors that increase success rates, and determine the most effective combinations of media and methods. This call is answered elsewhere in this volume. For a systematic review of recent research studies, see Chapter 11 of this volume, where Cavanaugh presents research on student achievement and success factors in K–12 distance and online education, and Chapter 36, where Barbour describes a variety of research underway on K–12 online learning.

REFLECTIONS ON THE FUTURE OF K–12 DISTANCE EDUCATION

Government funding for educational technology has changed the playing field. The public is often unaware of large funding streams like E-Rate, which provides over $2 billion annually from small charges on their monthly phone bills. Over a period of 15 years, E-Rate has made possible robust technology infrastructure in schools nationwide, while other federal and state programs have funded teacher training and technology in many schools. This government funding laid the groundwork for today's rapidly growing online and blended learning programs.

A lack of common metrics makes it hard to measure student and program success. Over 75 years ago, distance education researchers bemoaned the difficulty of securing uniformity in student data elements. Little has changed since then. If state education agencies added course-level data elements for online learning and blended learning to their statewide student record systems, it would be a major step forward.

Should the focus be on expanding educational access or improving results? The traditional role of distance education is to expand access, and this role endures. It continues through supplemental K–12 online learning, which increases access to AP and other electives for students in small and rural schools, and new options for School Choice. Outcomes may improve when students can receive credit recovery and stay on track for graduation—a potential benefit that is sometimes hampered by states' seat time requirements.

Can online and blended learning really address equity concerns? Historically, schools often used satellite courses for high-achieving learners and independent study for low-achieving ones. A bimodal distribution is apparent among online learners today. To avoid making online learning a new form of tracking, schools should use it to help underperforming students catch up and graduate. A comprehensive system of supports is often needed for these learners to succeed, which is best addressed via blended learning in the local school.

Are full-time and elementary-level online learning programs good for students? The evolution of distance education provides some insights here. High school independent study programs graduated many students, but also had high dropout rates, which suggests they are not for everyone. Homeschooling has also grown, but it is unlikely that more than 5% of K–12 students will be home schooled anytime soon. Experiments with full-time K–12 public schooling via distance education and online learning have had mixed results.

Are online and blended learning programs a good idea for schools? There is a long track record of distance and online education helping schools meet individual student needs. Even in schools with no prior experience with K–12 online learning, blended programs can naturally build upon existing programs such as one to one computing, computer assisted instruction, and data driven decision making. They may be the future of K–12 education.

REFERENCES

Allen, I. E., & Seaman, J. (2011). *Going the distance: Online education in the United States, 2011*. Needham, MA: Babson Survey Research Group and Quahog Research Group, LLC.

Barker, B. O. (1987,January). *An evaluation of interactive satellite television as a delivery system for high school instruction*. Paper presented at the annual meeting of the Southwest Educational Research Association, 10th, Dallas, TX. (ERIC Document Reproduction Service No. ED 277 534)

Barker, B. O., & Petersen, P. D. (1984). *A research report on small high schools in the United States in regards to curricular offerings, micro-computer usage, and correspondence courses*. Salt Lake City, UT: Brigham Young University, Division of Continuing Education. (ERIC Document Reproduction Service No. ED 239 825)

Behrens, S. (2005). *PBS drops its middleman role in college telecourses*. Retrieved from http://www.current.org/education/ed0507adult.shtml

Berge, Z. L., & Collins, M. P. (Eds.). (1998). *Wired together: The online classroom in K–12*. Cresskill, NJ: Hampton Press.

Bianchi, W. (2002). The Wisconsin School of the Air: success story with implications. *Educational Technology & Society, 5*(1), 141–147.

Bittner, W. S., & Mallory, H. F. (1933). *University teaching by mail; a survey of correspondence instruction conducted by American universities*. New York: Macmillan.

Bramble, W. J. (1988, Winter). Distance learning in Alaska's rural schools. *Learning Tomorrow, 4*, 241–256. (ERIC Document Reproduction Service No. ED302210)

Broady, K. O. (1932, February). Supervised correspondence study given new impetus. *Nebraska Education Journal*. Abstracted in P. D. B. Perlham, *Teaching by correspondence: an annotated bibliography* (p. 13). Sacramento: California State Department of Education, 1936.

Broady, K. O., Platt, E. T., & Bell, M. D. (1931). *Practical procedures for enriching the curriculums of small schools*. Lincoln: University of Nebraska.

Bucks County Public Schools. (1972). *Supervised independent study program. Annual report*. Doylestown, PA: Bucks County Public Schools. (ERIC Document Reproduction Service No. ED072213)

Bushaw, W. J., & Lopez, S. J. (2011, September). The 43rd annual Phi Delta Kappa/Gallup poll of the public's attitudes toward public schools. *Phi Delta Kappan*, pp. 41–58.

Cavanaugh, C. S. (1999). *The effectiveness of interactive distance education technologies in K–12 learning: A meta-analysis*. Tampa: University of South Florida. (ERIC Document Reproduction Service No. ED 430 547)

Childs, G. B. (1949). A comparison of supervised correspondence study pupils and classroom pupils in achievement in school subjects (Unpublished doctoral dissertation, University of Nebraska, Lincoln). Abstracted in *Annotated bibliography of correspondence study 1897–1960* (p. 173). Washington, DC: National University Association, 1960.

Childs, G. B. (1966). Review of research in correspondence study. In C. A. Wedemeyer (1966), *The Brandenburg memorial essays on correspondence instruction: II* (pp. 126–140). Madison: University of Wisconsin Extension.

Chu, G. C., & Schramm, W. (1975). *Learning from television: What the research says* (Rev. ed.). Washington, DC: National Association of Educational Broadcasters.

Clark, T. (2000). *Virtual high schools: state of the states. A study of virtual high school planning and operation in the United States*. Macomb, Illinois: Center for the Application of Information Technologies. Retrieved from http://www.imsa.edu/programs/ivhs/pdfs/stateofstates.pdf

Clark, T. (2001). *Virtual schools: status and trends*. Phoenix, AZ: WestEd. Retrieved from http://www.wested.org/online_pubs/virtualschools.pdf

Clark, T. (2002). Virtual and distance education in American schools. In M. G. Moore & W. A. Anderson (Eds.), *Handbook of distance education* (pp. 673–699). Mahwah, NJ: Erlbaum.

Clark, T., & Else, D. (1998). *Distance education, electronic networking, and school policy*. Fastback 441. Bloomington, IN: Phi Delta Kappa. (ERIC Document Reproduction Service No. ED 425 711).

Corporation for Public Broadcasting. (1999). Elementary and secondary educational services of public television grantees: highlights from the 1998 station activities survey. *CPB Research Notes*, No. 116. (ERIC Document Reproduction Service No. ED 428 746).

Dawley, L., Rice, K., & Hinck, G. (2010). *Going virtual! 2010: The status of professional development and unique needs of K-12 online teachers.* Retrieved from http://edtech.boisestate.edu/goingvirtual/goingvirtual3.pdf

Dickson, W. P. (2005). *Toward a deeper understanding of student performance in virtual high school courses.* Study funded by North Central Regional Education Laboratory. Retrieved from http://www.mivu.org/LinkClick.aspx?fileticket=I5uq2DZ7Y%2BI%3D&tabid=373

Eisenhardt, K. M. (1989, October). Building theories from case study research. *The Academy of Management Review, 14*(4), 532–550.

Goodman, F. L. (1992). Instructional gaming through computer conferencing. In M. D. Waggoner (Ed.), *Empowering networks: Computer conferencing in education* (pp. 101–126). Englewood Cliffs, NJ: Educational Technology Publications.

Grayson, L. P., Norwood, F. W., & Wigren, H. E. (1973). *Man-made moons: Satellite communications for schools.* Washington, DC: National Education Association.

Harding, L. W. (1944, May). Correspondence instruction. *Education Digest, 9,* 8–11.

Hawkes, M., Cambre, M., & Lewis, M. (1999). *The Ohio SchoolNet telecommunity evaluation results: interactive video adoption and resource needs.* Oak Brook, IL: North Central Regional Educational Laboratory. (ERIC Document Reproduction Service No. ED 433 003)

Hew, K. F. (2009, June). Use of audio podcast in K-12 and higher education: a review of research topics and methodologies. *Educational Technology Research and Development, 57*(3), 333–357.

Hezel Associates. (1998). *Educational telecommunications and distance learning: The state-by-state analysis, 1998–99.* Syracuse, NY: Author.

Hezel Associates. (2007). *PBS TeacherLine national survey of teacher professional development, 2005–2006.* Syracuse, NY: Author.

Hill, D. (2000). Test case. *Education Week, 19*(25), 34–38.

Hinnant, E. C. (1994). Distance learning using fiber optics: A study of student achievement and student perception of system quality (Doctoral dissertation, Mississippi State University, 1994). *Dissertation Abstracts International, 5(10),* 3164A.

Horn, M/ B., & Staker, H. (2011). *The ride of K-12 blended learning.* Innosight Institute. Retrieved from http://www.innosightinstitute.org/blended_learning_models

Howley, C. B., & Harmon, H. L. (2000). K-12 unit schooling in rural America: a first description. *Rural Educator, 22*(1), 10–18.

Hudson, H. E., & Boyd, C. H. (1984). *Distance learning: A review for educators.* Austin, TX: Southwest Educational Development Laboratory. (ERIC Document Reproduction Service No. ED246872).

iNACOL (2010). *National standards for quality online teaching.* Retrieved November 1, 2011, from http://www.inacol.org/research/nationalstandards/iNACOL_TeachingStandardsv2.pdf

Jajkowski. S. (2004). *MPATI: The flying classroom.* Retrieved from http://www.chicagotelevision.com/MPATI.htm

Johnson, C. F. (1996). Distance education: Factors that affect implementation in secondary schools (Doctoral dissertation, University of Wisconsin, Madison, 1996). *Dissertation Abstracts International, 57*(4), 1S50A.

Kirby, E. (1998). Administrative issues for high school distance education. *Online Journal of Distance Learning Administration, 1*(2). Retrieved November 1, 2011, from http://www.westga.edu/~distance/ojdla

Kozma, R. (2000). Reflection on the state of educational technology research and development. *Educational Technology Research and Development, 48(1),* 5–15.

Kurtz, B. E. (1959). *Pioneering in educational television, 1932–1939.* Iowa City: State University of Iowa.

Libler, R. (1991). A study of the effectiveness of interactive television as a primary mode of instruction in selected high school physics courses (Doctoral dissertation, Ball State University, 1991). *Dissertation Abstracts International, 52*(6), 2116A.

Maul, C. (1929). Administrative practices in correspondence study departments of teachers colleges and normal schools (Unpublished masters thesis). University of Kansas, Lawrence. Abstracted in Perlham, P. D. B., Teaching by correspondence: An annotated bibliography (p. 41). Sacramento: California State Department of Education, 1936.

Meyen, E. L., Lian, C. H. T., & Tangen, P. (1998). Issues associated with the design and delivery of online instruction. *Focus on Autism and Other Developmental Disabilities, 13*(1), 53–60.

Mitchell, S. C. (1923, June). For the 90 per cent. *School Review,* 439–444.

National University Continuing Education Association. (1991). *Independent study program profiles 1989– 1990. Final report.* Washington, DC: NUCEA, Research and Evaluation Committee. (ERIC Document Reproduction Service No. ED328723)

Newman, A., Stein, M., & Trask, E. (2003, September). *What can virtual learning do for your school?* Boston: Eduventures.

Office of Technology Assessment. (1987). *Linking for learning: a new course for education.* Washington, DC: Author.

Paulsen, M. F. (1987, December/January). In search of a virtual school. *T. H.E. Journal*, pp. 71–76.

Pease, P. S., & Tinsley, P. J. (1986, October). *Reaching rural schools using an interactive satellite based educational network.* Paper presented at the annual conference of the National Rural and Small Schools Consortium in Bellingham, WA. (ERIC Document Reproduction Service No. ED281681)

Picciano, A. G., & Seaman, J. (2009). *K–12 online learning: A 2008 follow-up of the survey of U.S. school district administrators.* Needham, MA: BABSON Survey Research Group & The Sloan Consortium.

Picciano, A. G., & Seaman, J. & Day, S. (2010). *Online learning in Illinois high schools: has the time come?* Needham, MA: BABSON Survey Research Group.

Rose, R., & Blomeyer, R. L. (2007). *Access and equity in online classes and virtual schools.* NACOL Research Committee Research Brief. Retrieved from http://www.inacol.org/research/docs/NACOL_EquityAccess.pdf

Russell, T. L. (2001). *The no significant difference phenomenon.* Montgomery, AL: IDECC.

Saettler, L. P. (2004). *The evolution of American educational technology.* Charlotte, NC: Information Age.

Schmidt, B. J., & Faulkner, S. L. (1989, Fall). Staff development through distance education. *Journal of Staff Development, 10*(4), 2–7.

Smith, P. L., & Dillon, C. L. (1999). Comparing distance learning and classroom learning: Conceptual considerations. *American Journal of Distance Education, 13*(2), 6–23.

Smith, R. E. (1990). Effectiveness of the interactive satellite method in the teaching of first-year German: A look at selected high schools in Arkansas and Mississippi (Doctoral dissertation, University of Mississippi, 1990). *Dissertation Abstracts International, 52*(2), 0517A.

Southern Regional Education Board. (2006). *Multi-state online professional development.* Retrieved April 19, 2006, from http://www.sreb.org/programs/EdTech/MOPD/about.asp

SRI International (2009). *Evaluation of the Enhancing Education through Technology program: final report.* Washington, DC: U.S. Department of Education, Office of Planning, Evaluation and Policy Development, Policy and Program Studies Service.

State of Georgia (2006). *Online teaching endorsement program.* Retrieved November 1, 2011, from http://rules.sos.state.ga.us/docs/505/3/85.pdf

Stoops, T. (2011, July 6). *Virtually irrelevant: how certification rules impede the growth of virtual schools.* Spotlight No. 412, John Locke Foundation. Retrieved from http://www.johnlocke.org/acrobat/spotlights/Spotlight412VirtualSchools.pdf

Sturgis, C., & Patrick, S. (2010). *When success is the only option: designing competency-based pathways for next generation learning.* Quincy, MA: Nellie Mae Education Foundation.

Sturgis, C., Patrick, S., & Pittenger, L. (2011). *It's not a matter of time: highlights from the 2011 competency-based learning summit.* Washington, DC: iNACOL/CCSSO.

Suppes, P., Jerman, M., & Groen, G. (1966). Arithmetic drills and review on a computer-based teletype. *Arithmetic Teacher, 13*, 303–309.

United States Department of Education. (2000a). *e-learning: putting a world class education at the fingertips of all children.* Washington, DC: U.S. Department of Education, Office of Educational Research and Improvement.

United States Department of Education. (2000b). *What are the barriers to the use of advanced telecommunications for students with disabilities in public schools?* (National Center for Education Statistics No. 2000042). Washington, DC: Author.

United States Department of Education. (2008). *Technology-based distance education courses for public elementary and secondary school students: 2002–03 and 2004–05.* (NCES 2008-008). Washington, DC: National Center for Education Statistics.

United States Department of Education. (2009). *1.5 million homeschooled students in the United States in 2007.* (NCES 2009-030). (Issue Brief). Washington, DC: National Center for Education Statistics.

United States Department of Education. (2011). *Condition of education 2011.* (NCES 2011-033). Washington, DC: National Center for Education Statistics.

Van Meer, E. (2003, November 5). PLATO: from computer-based education to corporate social responsibility. Iterations. http://www.cbi.umn.edu/iterations/vanmeer.html

VHS Global Consortium (2011). *VHS member profile.* Maynard, MA: Author. Retrieved from http://www.govhs.org/Pages/AboutUs-Home

Watson, J. (2008). Blended learning: the convergence of online and face to face education. iNACOL Promising Practices in Online Learning series. Retrieved from http://www.inacol.org/research/promisingpractices/NACOL_PP-BlendedLearning-lr.pdf

Watson, J., Murin, A., Vashaw, L., Gemin, B., & Rapp, C. (2010). *Keeping pace with K-12 online learning. A review of state-level policy and practice.* Durango, CO: Evergreen Education Group.

Watson, J., Murin, A., Vashaw, L., Gemin, B., & Rapp, C. (2011). *Keeping pace with K-12 online learning. A review of state-level policy and practice.* Durango, CO: Evergreen Education Group.

Wells, J., & Lewis, L. (2006). Internet access in U.S. public schools and classrooms: 1994–2005 (NCES 2007-020). U.S. Department of Education. Washington, DC: National Center for Education Statistics.

Wick, W. R. (1997). An analysis of the effectiveness of distance learning at remote sites versus on-site location in high school foreign language programs (Doctoral dissertation, University of Minnesota, 1997). *Dissertation Abstracts International, 58(2),* 0360A.

Young, R. G., & McMahon, M. (1991). University-sponsored high school independent study. In B. L. Watkins & S. J. Wright (Eds.), *The foundations of American distance education: A century of collegiate correspondence study* (pp. 93–108). Dubuque, IA: Kendall/Hunt.

36

THE LANDSCAPE OF K–12 ONLINE LEARNING

MICHAEL K. BARBOUR

Distance education at the K–12 or primary and secondary level has a history that is almost as long as distance education within higher education (see Chapter 35 in this volume for a fuller history). K–12 online learning is a more recent phenomenon. In the United States the first K–12 online learning program was developed by the private school Laurel Springs School's online program around 1991, followed in 1994 by the Utah Electronic High School and the first cyber charter school, Choice 2000 in California (Clark, 2003; Darrow, 2010). The first entirely online schools were the Virtual High School Global Consortium (VHS) and the Florida Virtual School (FLVS), both created in 1997 (Friend & Johnston, 2005; Pape, Adams, & Ribeiro, 2005). Three years later Clark (2000) reported statewide virtual schools in Florida, New Mexico, and Utah, and three more in the planning stages (i.e., Illinois, Kentucky, and Michigan). The following year Clark (2001) indicated there were at least 14 states with existing or planned virtual schools. The growth in students participating in K–12 online learning increased in a similar fashion. Clark (2001) estimated that there were approximately 40,000 and 50,000 students—representing less than 0.001% of the K–12 student population—enrolled in one or more K–12 online learning courses during the 2000–2001 school year. Ten years later Watson, Murin, Vashaw, Gemin, and Rapp (2011) reported K–12 online learning activity in almost all 50 states, while Ambient Insights (2011) indicated that there were approximately 4 million students—representing approximately 6% of the K–12 student population—enrolled in K–12 online learning courses during the 2010–11 school year.

Jurisdictions outside of the United States have seen similar patterns of development and growth. K–12 online learning in Canada began in British Columbia with the creation of two programs around 1993: the New Directions in Distance Learning (Dallas, 1999) and the EBUS Academy (Winkelmans, Anderson, & Barbour, 2010). Within three years, there were programs in Manitoba, Ontario, Alberta, and Newfoundland and Labrador (Barker & Wendel, 2001; Barker, Wendel, & Richmond, 1999; Haughey & Fenwick, 1996; Stevens, 1997). In the first national examination of K–12 online learning in Canada, the Canadian Teachers Federation (2000) estimated there were approximately

25,000 K–12 students—representing approximately 0.005% of the K–12 student population—enrolled in one of more online course during the 1999–2000 school year. Ten years later there were approximately 182,000 students—representing approximately 4.2% of the K–12 student population— students enrolled in one or more distance education courses (Barbour 2011b).

DESCRIBING K–12 ONLINE LEARNING

Historically, in the United States there have been specific descriptors for K–12 online learning. Virtual schools have been those in which students took one or more courses in a supplemental manner, while cyber schools were programs that had students engaged in full-time online instruction (although the recent International Council for K–12 Online Learning (iNACOL) Online Learning Definitions Project uses the terms synonymously). One of the first classifications of K–12 online learning programs was Clark (2001), who outlined seven different categories based on the entity responsible for the administration of the program (see Table 36.1).

However, even within the United States, it is becoming more difficult to place K–12 online learning programs into specific categories. For example, the Odyssey Charter School is a charter school, but its enrollment is generally restricted to a single school district because of its requirement that students physically attend the school for one half a day per week (Barbour & Plough, 2009). Beginning with the 2009 edition of the *Keeping Pace with K–12 Online Learning* report, Watson, Gemin, Ryan, and Wicks (2009) introduced a matrix of dimensions for describing K–12 online learning programs (see Table 36.2). At present it is these dimensions that are used to describe K–12 online learning programs.

Table 36.1 Clark's (2001) Seven Categories of K–12 Online Learning Programs

Type	Description
State-sanctioned, state-level	Schools that operate on a statewide level, such as the FLVS or the Illinois Virtual School (IVHS).
College and university-based	Independent university high schools or university-sponsored delivery of courses to K–12 students, such as the University of Nebraska-Lincoln Independent Study High School or the University of California College Prep Online.
Consortium and regionally-based	Schools operated by a group of schools or school districts that pool their resources to participate, such as the VHS.
Local education agency-based	Schools operated by a single school or school district, such as the Gwinnett County Online Campus or the Cobb County eSchool.
Virtual charter schools	Schools created under legislation in many states, such as Connections Academy, also commonly known as cyberschools.
Private virtual schools	Schools operated in the same manner as a brick and mortar private school, such as the Christa McAuliffe Academy in Washington state.
For-profit providers of curricula, content, tool and infrastructure	Commercial companies acting as vendors for the delivery of courses or the use of course materials, such as APEX Learning or Aventa Learning.

Table 36.2   Watson et al.'s (2009) Dimensions for Describing K–12 Online Learning Programs

Dimension	Variables
Comprehensiveness Reach	District; multi-district; state; multi-state; national; global
Type	District; magnet; contract; charter; private; home
Location	School; home; other
Delivery	Asynrchonous; synchronous
Operational control	Local board; consortium; regional authority; university, state; independent vendor
Type of instruction	Fully online; blending online and face-to-face; fully face-to-face
Grade level	Elementary; middle school; high school
Teacher-student interaction	High; moderate; low
Student-student interaction	High; moderate; low

LITERATURE AND RESEARCH RELATED TO K–12 ONLINE LEARNING

While online learning at the K–12 level has been practiced for approximately two decades, the availability of literature and, in particular the published research, to inform that practice has not kept pace. Barbour (2011a) reviewed 262 articles from the main distance education journals for Australia, Canada, New Zealand, and the United States from 2005 to 2009, and found only 24 articles (or less than 10%) related to K–12 distance education.

However, this is changing. Cavanaugh, Barbour, and Clark (2009) indicated that of the 226 publications included in their review of the literature there were only 29 items were from 1997 to 2000, but there were 69 items published from 2006 to 2009. To date there have been three major reviews of the literature related to K–12 online learning. The first was Rice (2006), who conducted a review of the literature from 1995 to 2005; Barbour and Reeves (2009) examined literature related to K–12 online learning from 1994 to 2008; Cavanaugh et al. (2009) examined open access literature from 1997 to 2008.

Literature on K–12 Online Learning

In their review of the open access literature, Cavanaugh et al. (2009) stated that the published literature related to K–12 online learning was primarily "based upon the personal experiences of those involved in the practice of virtual schooling" (¶ 5). Within this largely practitioner-focused literature, Cavanaugh et al. describe it as being mainly literature about "statewide and consortium/multi-district virtual schools, the roles of teachers and administrators, the promise of virtual schooling and its initial rationale for implementation, administrative challenges, the technology utilized, and interact with students" (Conclusions and Implications, ¶ 1).

In their book *Virtual Schools: Planning for Success*, Berge and Clark (2005) described five potential benefits of and five challenges facing to K–12 online learning.

- Potential benefits: higher levels of motivation; expanding educational access; providing high-quality learning opportunities; improving student outcomes and skills; allowing for educational choice; and administrative efficiency

Table 36.3 Summary of the Benefits of Virtual Schooling (Barbour & Reeves, 2009, p. 409)

Benefit	Reference
Higher levels of motivation	Kellogg & Politoski (2002)
Expanding educational access	Berge & Clark (2005); Cavanaugh (2001); Freedman, Darrow, Watson & Lorenzo (2002); Fulton (2002); Hernandez (2005); Kellogg & Politoski (2002); Zucker (2005)
Providing high-quality learning opportunities	Berge & Clark (2005); Butz (2004); Elbaum & Tinker (1997); Fulton (2002a); Kaplan-Leiserson (2003); Kellogg & Politoski (2002); Thomas (1999; 2000; 2003); Tinker & Haavind (1997)
Improving student outcomes and skills	Berge & Clark (2005); Zucker & Kozma (2003)
Allowing for educational choice	Baker, Bouras, Hartwig & McNair (2005); Berge & Clark (2005); Butz (2004); Fulton (2002); Hassell & Terrell (2004)
Administrative efficiency	Keeler (2003); Russo (2001); Vail (2001)

- Challenges facing: high start-up costs associated with virtual schools; access issues surrounding the digital divide; approval or accreditation of virtual schools; and student readiness issues and retention issues

In their review of the literature, Barbour and Reeves (2009) used these potential benefits and challenges to classify the existing literature (see Tables 36.3 and 36.4).

It is important to point out, as Barbour and Reeves did themselves, that the benefits listed were only potential benefits. As Barbour (2010) further underlined:

[Barbour and Reeves] were careful to remind readers that while online learning may allow for educational improvements such as a high levels of learner motivation, high quality learning opportunities or improvement in student outcomes, it certainly did not guarantee any of these potential benefits would be realized simply by the introduction of online learning. (p. 7)

Table 36.4 Summary of the Challenges of Virtual Schooling (Barbour & Reeves, 2009, p. 411)

Challenge	Reference
High start-up costs associated with virtual schools	Berge & Clark (2005); Morris (2002)
Access issues surrounding the digital divide	Berge & Clark (2005)
Approval or accreditation of virtual schools	Berge & Clark (2005)
Student readiness issues and retention issues	Ballas & Belyk (2000); Barker & Wendel (2001); Berge and Clark (2005); Bigbie & McCarroll (2000); Cavanuagh, Gillan, Bosnick, Hess & Scott (2005); Clark, Lewis, Oyer, & Schreiber (2002); Espinoza, Dove, Zucker & Kozma (1999); Haughey & Muirhead (1999); Kozma, Zucker & Espinoza (1998); McLeod, Hughes, Brown, Choi & Maeda (2005); Zucker & Kozma (2003)

As the research to date has shown, none of these potential benefits have been proven by empirical studies using reliable and valid methodology.

Research on K–12 Online Learning

There is general agreement about the themes that have been dominant in the limited amount of research conducted on K–12 online learning to date. Rice (2006) described the research as either being comparisons of student performance between those enrolled in online and face-to-face environments or examinations of the qualities and characteristics of the online learning experience; with the comparative research being the dominant of the two groups. Similarly, Cavanaugh et al. (2009) indicated that the research fell into two categories: effectiveness and issues related to student readiness and retention, most focusing on the effectiveness category.

An examination of the findings related to comparison of student performance in K–12 online learning environments and the traditional classroom shows mixed results (see Table 36.5).

However, these general findings do not tell the complete story. For example, Mulcahy and Barbour (2010) later speculated that weaker students may have been self-selecting a less rigorous curriculum in order to avoid taking online courses (a finding that was also supported by Mulcahy, Dibbon, & Norberg, 2008). This kind of skewing of the potential sample from the K–12 online learning is quite common in the studies listed above (see Table 36.6).

This kind of student selectivity in the K–12 online learning samples should not be surprising to anyone familiar with its practice. With the exception of the past three to five years, the literature related to K–12 online learning has provided a fairly consistent description of K–12 online learners (see Table 36.7).

Rice (2006) summarized this problem by indicating the research into the effectiveness of K–12 online learning as being "challenged with issues of small sample size,

Table 36.5 Summary of Research Related to the Effectiveness of K–12 Online Learning

Study	Finding
Ballas & Belyk (2000)	performance of virtual and classroom students in Alberta were similar in English and Social Studies courses, but classroom students performed better overall in all other subject areas
Bigbie & McCarroll (2000)	over half of the students who completed FLVS courses scored an A in their course and only 7% received a failing grade
Barker & Wendel (2001)	students in the six virtual schools in three different provinces performed no worse than the students from the three conventional schools
Cavanaugh et al. (2005)	FLVS students performed better on a non-mandatory assessment tool than students from the traditional classroom
McLeod et al. (2005)	FLVS students performed better on an assessment of algebraic understanding than their classroom counterparts
Barbour & Mulcahy (2008)	little difference in the overall performance of students based upon delivery model
Barbour & Mulcahy (2009a)	no difference in student performance based upon method of course delivery

Table 36.6 Methodological Issues with the K–12 Online Learning Samples in Comparative Studies

Study	Sample
Ballas & Belyk (2000)	participation rate in the assessment among virtual students ranged from 65% to 75% compared to 90% to 96% for the classroom-based students
Bigbie & McCarroll (2000)	between 25% and 50% of students had dropped out of their FLVS courses over the previous two-year period
Cavanaugh et al. (2005)	speculated that the virtual school students who did take the assessment may have been more academically motivated and naturally higher achieving students
McLeod et al. (2005)	results of the student performance were due to the high dropout rate in virtual school courses

Table 36.7 Description of K–12 Online Learner from the Research

Study	Sample
Kozma et al. (1998)	vast majority of VHS students in their courses were planning to attend a four-year college
Espinoza et al., 1999	VHS courses are predominantly designated as 'honors,' and students enrolled are mostly college bound
Haughey & Muirhead (1999)	preferred characteristics include the highly motivated, self-directed, self-disciplined, independent learner who could read and write well, and who also had a strong interest in or ability with technology
Roblyer & Elbaum (2000)	only students with a high need to control and structure their own learning may choose distance formats freely
Clark et al. (2002)	IVHS students were highly motivated, high achieving, self-directed and/or who liked to work independently
Mills (2003)	typical online student was an A or B student
Watkins (2005)	45% of the students who participated in e-learning opportunities in Michigan were either advanced placement or academically advanced students

dissimilar comparison groups, and differences in instructor experience and training" (p. 431, emphasis added). She concluded "that the effectiveness of distance education appears to have more to do with who is teaching, *who is learning*, and how that learning is accomplished, and less to do with the medium" (p. 440, emphasis added).

Cavanaugh, in Chapter 11 of this Handbook, concludes that the research into the effectiveness of K–12 online learning "suggests that as distance education is currently practiced, student learning on average in well-designed online elementary and secondary environments appears to be equivalent to learning in a well-designed classroom environment" (p. 172). The potential problems with the K–12 online learning samples from the studies included in those meta-analyses above should call into question that conclusion. This is particularly true when some have indicated that there is a growing segment of K–12 online learning students who would fall into the category of at-risk students (Barbour, 2009, 2011a; Klein, 2006; Rapp, Eckes, & Plurker, 2006; Watson, Gemin, & Ryan, 2008).

EXAMINING K–12 ONLINE LEARNING TEACHER ROLES

One aspect of K–12 online learning that scholars have agreed upon is the fact that the growth of K–12 online learning has resulted in changes to the traditional role of the teacher. In a traditional classroom environment, the teacher is responsible for designing the instructional activities that get employed with the students, presenting the content or actually teaching the material, and helping to facilitate students while they are completing any independent work. In an online environment it is often the case that different individuals perform each of these tasks.

Davis, Niederhauser, Compton, Lindstrom, and Schoeny (2005) were probably the first researchers to specifically delineate individual virtual school teacher roles as a part of their "Teacher Education Goes Into Virtual Schooling" (TEGIVS) project. As a follow-up to a series of online teaching case studies entitled "The Good Practice to Inform Iowa Learning Online," Iowa State University secured funding from the U.S. Department of Education's Fund for the Improvement of Post Secondary Education (FIPSE) and partnered with the Universities of Florida and Virginia, Graceland University and Iowa Learning Online to create TEGIVS. The purpose of TEGIVS was "to build on that work [i.e., the Good Practice to Inform Iowa Learning Online project] to incorporate virtual schooling into pre-service teacher education" (Davis et al., 2005, p. 342). The TEGIVS project would introduce and orient new and current teachers to three roles in the K–12 online learning environment: virtual school designer, virtual school teacher, and virtual school site facilitator (also called mentor teacher, mediating teacher or learning coach—depending on the literature; Davis, 2007).

In a special issue of the *Journal of Technology and Teacher Education* devoted to K–12 online learning, Ferdig, Cavanaugh, DiPietro, Black, and Dawson (2009) further delineated the different roles that teachers might undertake in the K–12 online learning environment into eight separate responsibilities. The Davis (2007) and Ferdig et al. (2009) K–12 online learning teacher roles are described, and compared, in Table 36.8. While the Ferdig et al. (2009) classification is the more developed, within the literature the Davis (2007) has become the more commonly used.

Research into the Design of K–12 Online Learning

There are only a handful of studies that have examined the design and delivery of virtual schooling, most with methodological limitations. For example, Barbour (2005, 2007) first proposed 10—and later seven—principles of effective online course design for adolescent learners (such as those found in K–12 online learning environments). These principles were developed based on interviews with six course developers and teachers in a single Canadian virtual school. The researcher did not undertake any additional data collection and analysis that would have allowed him to triangulate his findings. It is also important to note the virtual school where Barbour conducted this study used a primarily synchronous form of delivery (almost unique among K–12 online learning programs in North America), where teachers and students rarely use the asynchronous course content (Barbour & Hill, 2011).

In a separate line of inquiry, Barbour and Cooze (Barbour & Cooze, 2004; Cooze & Barbour, 2005, 2007) examined the potential for designers of K–12 online courses to focus on specific student learning styles. The researchers concluded that students who were visual learners (traditional modalities); possessed interpersonal, bodily-kinesthetic,

Table 36.8 Teacher Roles in Online Learning Environments

Davis' roles	Davis' responsibilities	Ferdig et al.'s roles	Ferdig et al.' responsibilities
Designer	Design instructional materials. Works in team with teachers and a virtual school to construct the online course, etc.	Instructional Designer	The creator of the online course in accordance with content standards using effective strategies for the learners and the content
Teacher	Presents activities, manages pacing, rigor, etc.. Interacts with students and their facilitators. Undertakes assessment, grading, etc.	Teacher	The educator with primary responsibility for student instruction within an online course including interaction with students and assigning course grades
		Online Facilitator	The person who supports students in a virtual school program. The facilitator may interact with students online or may facilitate at the physical site where students access their online course.
Facilitator	Local mentor and advocate for students(s). Proctors & records grades, etc.	Local Key Contact	The professional who assists students in registering and otherwise accessing virtual courses
		Mentor	The academic tutor or course assistant for students
		Technology Coordinator	The person who facilitates technical support for educators and students
		Guidance Counselor	The academic advisor for students
		Administrator	The instructional leader of the virtual school

logical-mathematical, and visual-spatial intelligences (Gardner's multiple intelligences, or were assimilators (Kolb's theory of experiential learning) were naturally the better online learning; and that course designers should focus on including course elements that would assist learners who did not posses these characteristics. Unfortunately, research into learning styles has been found to be quite unreliable (Coffield, Moseley, Hall, & Ecclestone, 2004), and is seen by some researchers as a form of pseudo-science (Reeves, 1993). Similarly, Keeler (2006) also focused on the influence of learning styles on online course design for secondary students.

Using a sample course from the University of Oregon's Center for Electronic Studying, Keeler, Richter, Horney, Anderson, and Ditson (2007) discussed how differentiated instruction and universal design could be used to create a course for students with learning disabilities. The following year, Grabinger, Aplin, and Ponnappa-Brenner (2008) also described how universal design in online learning environments could be used to address the needs of students with cognitive impairments. In one of the few examples of empirical research, Keeler and Horney (2008) conducted an analysis of 22 online high school courses using the validated *Instrument of Instructional Design Elements of High School Online Courses* (Keeler, 2003). Their analysis found 38 design elements, from five categories (i.e., accessibility, Web site design, technologies used, instructional methodologies, and support systems) were important with online instruction for students with disabilities (Keeler, 2004; Keeler & Anderson-Inman, 2004a,b). However, their instrument was limited to description of the online course (i.e., asynchronous curricular material), and failed to account for the quality of that material.

To address these limitations, and the need to serve a wider range of students because of online learning graduation requirements, (iNACOL; as the professional association representing K–12 online learning programs) conducted a review of published K–12 online course design standards that resulted in the release of the *National Standards for Quality Online Courses* (iNACOL 2007a). In the introduction to these standards, it states:

> In partnership with the Southern Regional Education Board (SREB), NACOL is adopting the Standards for Quality Online Courses as a primary source, with an additional rubric for inclusion of 21st century skills, with reference to the Partnership for 21st Century Skills. (p. 2)

The Partnership for 21st Century Skills is in reference to a report on *Virtual Schools and 21st Century Skills* that was commissioned by iNACOL and the Partnership for 21st Century Skills in 2006 (see iNACOL & Partnership for 21st Century Skills, 2006). To date, there has not been any published research to test the validity and reliability of, or even support for the SREB standards. However, even though these standards have not been subjected to the rigorous process that most "national standards" undergo, jurisdictions such as Texas have adopted these standards for the design of their K–12 online learning programs.

Research into the Delivery of K–12 Online Learning

Within the field of K–12 online learning there has been almost universal agreement that the practice of teaching in an online environment is different and requires a different set of skills than teaching in a traditional face-to-face environment. Roblyer and McKenzie (2000) argued that some of the skills like good communication and classroom organization skills, were characteristics common to both successful online teachers and successful classroom teachers. Yet, Davis et al. (2007) also argued "effective virtual teachers have qualities and skills that often set them apart from traditional teachers" (p. 28). Further, Davis and Roblyer (2005) made the case that many of the skills needed to teach in an online environment were consistent to those skills traditionally taught by teacher education programs, but that there were also skills needed to be successful in the online classroom that were absent from brick-and-mortar environments.

The differences between teaching in an online and face-to-face environment go beyond the individual skills involved. For example, Easton (2003) argued that online teachers need to undergo a paradigm shift in how they perceived time and space, managed instructional activities and assessments, and engaged with students. This was consistent with Lowes (2005), who indicated that those teaching in the online environment needed to use different strategies when planning on "how to reach and evaluate, students when you cannot interact with them face-to-face on a daily basis" (p. 12). Finally, Morris (2002), who was writing about those teaching in technology-mediated environments (like online classrooms), argued that those teachers needed to have a strong proficiency with technology and understanding of the curriculum, as well as possess strong communication and organizational skills, and be excited about online learning as a method of educational delivery.

Unfortunately, the available research into the delivery of K–12 online learning has yet to fully define—or even begin to scratch the surface—on what constitutes effective online teaching. While Cathy Cavanaugh in her Chapter 11 (this volume) on "Student Achievement in Elementary and High School" describes research into student characteristics, course design factors, teacher preparation and development, course facilitation, and technological approaches that all have implications for the effective delivery of K–12 online learning opportunities; unfortunately this research has similar methodological limitations that are found into the research on effective design of K–12 online learning. For example, DiPietro, Ferdig, Black, and Preston (2008) reported best practices in asynchronous teaching based upon the perceptions of online teachers at a single statewide, supplemental virtual school. These self-reports were not validated through observation of their teaching or through student performance in their courses. Also, the teachers who were interviewed were those that had been identified by the virtual school itself as being "good online teachers." Later, DiPietro (2010) described five beliefs of "successful" asynchronous pedagogic practices based on interviews with virtual school teachers, along with samples of course content shared by the teachers, at a single statewide supplemental virtual school. Similar to the earlier study, there was no independent verification that the beliefs of these teachers were actually acted upon in their online teaching, and students were again excluded from the data collection process.

Similarly, Murphy and Coffin (2003) described their unsystematic observations of synchronous instruction with teachers from a single virtual school (and primarily from a single subject area). Nippard and Murphy (2007) relied only upon the observations of 12 recordings of synchronous classes without other methods of data collection to triangulate the findings. Studies by Murphy and her colleagues (Murphy & Rodríguez-Manzanares, 2009a, b; Murphy, Rodriguez-Manzanares, & Barbour, 2011) investigated virtual school teachers' perceptions of student motivation in the online environment, teachers' ability to be learner-centered, and teachers' perceptions of the affordances of synchronous and asynchronous learning tools. These three studies were limited to interviews with the same 42 virtual school teachers from across Canada. Again, there was no effort to triangulate these qualitative findings using other data sources.

In addition to developing standards for online course design, iNACOL also conducted a review of published K–12 online teaching standards that resulted in the release of the *National Standards for Quality Online Teaching* (iNACOL, 2007b). Like their other set of "national standards," there has been no research published to support the selection of the individual standards included. There has also yet to be any attempt to validate these standards using empirical research methods. Recently, authors have attempted to seek evidence from within the literature to support these national standards (e.g., Ferdig et al., 2009) or have surveyed online teachers to determine their perceptions of these national standards (e.g., Smith, 2009). However, there still has not been a systematic validation of these standards or the associated instruments to measure these standards released by iNACOL.

Further, McCombs and Vakili (2005) developed a learner-centered framework containing online learning practices based upon the American Psychology Association's (APA) 14 learner-centered principles (i.e., APA Work Group of the Board of Educational Affairs, 1997). Critics had begun to argue that "distance education provides a unique context in which to infuse learner-centered principles" (Wagner & McCombs, 1995, p. 32), and that the "fourteen individual statements [were] helpful but not enough" when it came to distance education environments, like online learning (Bonk & Cunningham, 1998, p. 32). In a review of the research literature related to the delivery of education using online learning, McCombs and Vakili (2005) used the APA's original four domains to propose 37 online learning practices: metacognitive and cognitive (10 practices), affective and motivational (10 practices), developmental and social (9 practices), and individual-differences factors (8 practices).

These 37 practices included suggestions such as "provide access to real-time data and experts in the fields of study and to real-world tasks," "incorporate initial and ongoing needs assessments that provide choice of activities and create optimally challenging environments," "create hyperlinks to resources and discussions to aid in scaffolding learning," or "provide multiple ways of displaying materials electronically—to use one example from each of the four domains (pp. 1591–1594). However, like many such proposed frameworks—particularly within the field of K–12 online learning—there has yet to be empirical evidence to validate any of these practices.

Research into the Support of K–12 Online Learning

Research into effective strategies to support K–12 online learning is also scant and methodologically limited. The Educational Success Prediction Instrument (ESPRI), reported by Roblyer and Marshall (2002–2003), was developed to "help predict which high school students would be likely to succeed in online courses and provide a basis for counseling and support for other students interested in becoming online learners to help them become more successful" (p. 241). Roblyer and Marshall conducted a validation study of the ESPRI and found that the instrument had a reliability level of 0.92 with a sample of 135 online learning students, which included students with disabilities. In a follow-up to their initial study, Roblyer, Davis, Mills, Marshall, and Pape (2008) again found the ESPRI had a reliability level of 0.92, this time with a sample of 4,100 online learning students, which again included students with disabilities. Roblyer (2005) stated that the next step in this line of inquiry was "to develop preparation materials to help students whose ESPRI results indicate potential for problems in online learning" (¶ 8). Roblyer et al. (2008) also found GPA to be as reliable a predictor of student success in the K–12 online learning environment as the ESPRI.

While little has been written about the various roles facilitators or mentor teachers undertake, limited research has indicated this individual has a critical role on students' success in online learning (Barbour & Mulcahy, 2004; Roblyer, Freeman, Stabler, & Schneidmiller, 2007). Barbour and Mulcahy (2004) found that teachers at the school level provided substantial levels of support in a wide range of areas, including supervisory and administrative duties, technical troubleshooting, and providing content-based assistance. However, these findings were based on only five teachers performing this role in the first year of operation for a single, Canadian virtual school. In a follow-up to that initial study, Barbour and Mulcahy (2009b) found that the amount of time these school-based teachers spent supporting the students engaged in online learning had actually increased. The authors also found that as students with a wider range of abilities are enrolling in online courses the local school-based teachers have to spend more time monitoring students' progress and assisting the academically weaker students. Similarly, in their evaluation of a statewide virtual school, Roblyer et al. (2007) found that school-based teachers "directly working with students day by day [were] key to the success of the [K–12 online learning] program" (p. 11). However, beyond the findings in these two individual province-wide/statewide supplemental programs, there has not been additional research into the role of local teachers in supporting K–12 students engaged in online learning.

The most systematic investigation into the support for students engaged in K–12 online learning was led by the National Center for Rural Education Support at the University of North Carolina – Chapel Hill. A team of researchers explored the impact of web-based professional development for school-based facilitator personnel and whether that training affected student performance and retention. The online professional development focused on several issues identified as common challenges for virtual school facilitators (e.g., the first day of school, how to talk about and support online assignments, potential student fears, helping to develop time management skills, assisting with the problem of too much work, what to do when students become disengaged, how to ease students who are worried about their grades, etc.; Irving, Hannum, Farmer, de la Varre, & Keane, 2009). The multi-year study included students enrolled in a variety of K–12 online learning programs from multiple states. The researchers found online students that had facilitators who completed the professional development had a higher level of retention (Hannuma, Irvin, Lei, & Farmer, 2008). Finally, the researcher also stated that effective facilitators should have "a good, working relationship, who were consistently responsive in their interactions with the teacher, and engaged with and interested in their students" (de la Varre, Keane, & Irvin, 2010, pp. 202–203); and facilitators should also assist the online teacher by projecting teacher presence (de la Varre, Keane, & Irvin, 2011).

RECOMMENDATIONS REGARDING FUTURE RESEARCH

There is no shortage of issues within the realm of K–12 online learning that need to be examined. As a part of their synthesis of a series of North Central Regional Educational Laboratory funded quantitative K–12 online learning studies, Smith, Clark, and Blomeyer (2005) recommended seven different areas for future research:

1. interpreting "equal of better' achievement findings;
2. understanding and improving student persistence;
3. instructional models that lead to student process skills;
4. issues related to student satisfaction and motivation;
5. identifying and remediating characteristics for successful online learning;
6. leveraging the features of online learning systems; and
7. discriminating online learning based upon a variety of educational contexts.

Similarly, as a part of her review of the K–12 distance education literature, Rice (2006) recommended researchers should focus on:

- improving the quality of research that examines the critical components of learning directly related to younger learners;
- continuing to expand on the development of prediction instructions that help identify successful learner attributes;
- developing organized student evaluation systems to facilitate consistent data collection;
- investigating the relationship between student supports and at-risk student needs in relation to distance education;
- investigating the social and cognitive aspects of distance education and the effect of knowledge construction; and
- developing valid and reliable tools for identifying interactive qualities in course design and instruction. (p. 442)

In their review of the literature Cavanaugh et al. (2009) recommended researchers establish best practices for online teaching, improve the identification and remediation of factors related to success for online learners, investigate the nature of support provided to online learners (particularly the lower performer) by how school-based teachers. Finally, Barbour and Reeves (2009) called for future research to focus on "factors that affect student success in virtual school environments" (p. 412).

However, Barbour and Reeves (2009) went even further in their discussion of how future research into K–12 online learning should be conducted, recommending a design-based research approach. This research approach is characterized by several critical characteristics that could be applied to studies of K–12 online learning:

- it addresses pressing complex problems in real contexts in close collaboration with practitioners;
- it integrates known and hypothetical design principles with technological affordances to render plausible solutions to these real world problems; and
- it requires iterative cycles of rigorous and reflective inquiry to test and refine innovative learning environments as well as to identify and refine new design principles.

Design-based research goes through the following stages: "analysis of practical problems by researchers and practitioners in collaboration," "development of solutions informed by existing design principles and technological innovation," "iterative cycles of testing and refinement of solutions in practice," and "reflection to produce design principles and enhance solution implementation" (Reeves, 2006, p. 59). Theory is infused throughout the design-based research process. Theory-based design principles are centric in design research. Design-based researchers constantly engage in design and redesign, striving to maximize the possibility of designing better solutions to the problems of practitioners while seeking opportunities to better understand the implications of design principles.

Educational research, particularly educational technology research, is plagued with examples of teams of researchers descending upon schools and school districts, helping to implement innovative technologies and pedagogies—often of more interest to the research team than the local staff, only to have the local staff at the school revert to more familiar practices after the external support is removed when the research team leaves (Fishman, Marx, Blumenfeld, Krajcik & Soloway, 2004; Fogleman, Fishman, & Krajcik,

2006). Design-based research, in contrast to more traditional methods, begins with the involvement of the local stakeholders in clarifying the challenges to be addressed and the prototype interventions to be used. At the same time, there is a focus on the development of theory to explain what occurs in the local context. Finally, design-based research requires multiple cycles of reflection and improvement to ensure that changes become part of the routine of those involved in the system, for example teachers at the school level.

To date, the only exception to this pattern is the VHS, which was established through a five year federal grant, with an expectation of external evaluation. SRI International, based upon seven goals identified in conjunction with their VHS partners, conducted several annual evaluations (e.g., Espinoza, Dove, Zucker, & Kozma, 1999; Kozma, Zucker, & Espinoza, 1998; Kozma et al., 2000), content-specific investigations in focus areas where VHS was not meeting their initial goals (e.g., Elbaum, McIntyre, & Smith, 2002; Yamashiro & Zucker, 1999), and a final evaluation (e.g., Zucker & Kozma, 2003). The VHS and their staff were full participants in this research process: assisting in the identification of issues to be examined, the design of the research, the implementation of the recommendations, and then beginning the process again to ensure that recommendations actually addressed the original problem. This cyclical research process that the VHS and SRI International engaged in was able to resolve many of the initial issues in the implementation of what was then a new model of educational delivery. In fact, much of the research-based evidence about K–12 online learning we have today still comes from the design research approach these groups had engaged in.

Essentially, the VHS were able to "focus on finding out how to improve education with different types of students in specific places at particular times of their development" (Reeves, 1999, p. 6). The findings from the design research approach utilized by VHS and SRI International should form the starting point for additional research into the design, delivery, and support of K–12 online learning in similar K–12 online learning settings. Blomeyer (2002) even provided an example of a potential design-based research study within the K–12 online learning environment that could also be considered scientifically-based research.

> Students from a population of interest may be randomly assigned to sections of an online course segment, with different instructional features, to identify effective treatments prior to comparisons with students in conventional study. (p. 14)

A study of this nature, if the participant group had identified it as a problem and the research was conducted over multiple cycles, would address several of the priority areas listed above. As a design-based research project, it should address the specific problem experienced by the participant group and form a set of design principles that could be used as a starting point the next time a K–12 online learning program experiences a similar challenge.

REFERENCES

Ambient Insight. (2011). *2011 Learning technology research taxonomy: Research methodology, buyer segmentation, product definitions, and licensing model.* Monroe, WA: Author. Retrieved from http://www.ambientinsight.com/Resources/Documents/AmbientInsight_Learning_Technology_Taxonomy.pdf

American Psychology Association Work Group of the Board of Educational Affairs. (1997). *Learner-centered psychological principles: A framework for school reform and redesign.* Washington, DC: Author.

Baker, J. D., Bouras, C., Hartwig, S. M., & McNair, E. R. (2005). K12, Inc. and the Colorado Virtual Academy: A virtual charter school. In Z. L. Berge & T. Clark (Eds.), *Virtual schools: Planning for success* (pp. 133–142). New York, NY: Teachers College Press.

Ballas, F. A., & Belyk, D. (2000). *Student achievement and performance levels in online education research study*. Red Deer, Canada: Schollie Research & Consulting. Retrieved from http://web.archive.org/web/20051031044348/http://www.ataoc.ca/files/pdf/AOCresearch_full_report.pdf

Barbour, M. K. (2005). The design of web-based courses for secondary students. *Journal of Distance Learning, 9*(1), 27–36.

Barbour, M. K. (2007). Teacher and developer perceptions of effective web-based design for secondary school students. *Journal of Distance Education, 21*(3), 93–114. Retrieved from http://www.jofde.ca/index.php/jde/article/view/30

Barbour, M. K. (2009). Today's student and virtual schooling: The reality, the challenges, the promise... *Journal of Distance Learning, 13*(1), 5–25.

Barbour, M. K. (2010). Researching K-12 online learning: What do we know and what should we examine? *Distance Learning, 7*(2), 7–12.

Barbour, M. K. (2011a). The promise and the reality: Exploring virtual schooling in rural jurisdictions. *Education in Rural Australia, 21*(1), 1–20.

Barbour, M. K. (2011b). *State of the nation study: K-12 online learning in Canada*. Vienna, VA: International Council for K-12 Online Learning. Retrieved from http://www.inacol.org/research/docs/iNACOL_CanadaStudy_201111.pdf

Barbour, M. K., & Cooze, M. (2004). All for one and one for all: Designing web-based courses for students based upon individual learning styles. *Staff and Educational Development International, 8*(2/3), 95–108.

Barbour, M. K., & Hill, J. R. (2011). What are they doing and how are they doing it? Rural student experiences in virtual schooling. *Journal of Distance Education, 25*(1). Retrieved from http://www.jofde.ca/index.php/jde/article/view/725

Barbour, M. K., & Mulcahy, D. (2004). The role of mediating teachers in Newfoundland's new model of distance education. *The Morning Watch, 32*(1-2). Retrieved from http://www.mun.ca/educ/faculty/mwatch/fall4/barbourmulcahy.htm

Barbour, M. K., & Mulcahy, D. (2008). How are they doing? Examining student achievement in virtual schooling. *Education in Rural Australia, 18*(2), 63–74.

Barbour, M. K., & Mulcahy, D. (2009a). Student performance in virtual schooling: Looking beyond the numbers. *ERS Spectrum, 27*(1), 23–30.

Barbour, M. K., & Mulcahy, D. (2009b). Beyond volunteerism and good will: Examining the commitment of school-based teachers to distance education. In I. Gibson, R. Weber, K. McFerrin, R. Carlsen, & D. A. Willis (Eds.), *Proceedings of the Annual Conference of the Society for Information Technology and Teacher Education* (pp. 779–784). Norfolk, VA: Association for the Advancement of Computing in Education.

Barbour, M. K., & Plough, C. (2009). Social networking in cyberschooling: Helping to make online learning less isolating. *Tech Trends, 53*(4), 56–60.

Barbour, M. K., & Reeves, T. C. (2009). The reality of virtual schools: A review of the literature. *Computers and Education, 52*(2), 402–416.

Barker, K., & Wendel, T. (2001). *e-Learning: Studying Canada's virtual secondary schools*. Kelowna, Canada: Society for the Advancement of Excellence in Education. Retrieved from http://web.archive.org/web/20040720185017/http://www.saee.ca/pdfs/006.pdf

Barker, K., Wendel, T., & Richmond, M. (1999). *Linking the literature: School effectiveness and virtual schools*. Vancouver, Canada: FuturEd. Retrieved from http://web.archive.org/web/20061112102653/http://www.futured.com/pdf/Virtual.pdf

Berge, Z. L., & Clark, T. (2005). *Virtual schools: Planning for success*. New York, NY: Teachers College Press.

Bigbie, C., & McCarroll, W. (2000). *The Florida high school evaluation 1999–2000 report*. Tallahassee: Florida State University.

Blomeyer, R. L. (2002). *Online learning for K-12 students: What do we know now?* Naperville, IL: North Central Regional Educational Laboratory. Retrieved from http://www.ncrel.org/tech/elearn/synthesis.pdf

Bonk, C., & Cunningham, D. (1998). Searching for learner-centered constructivist, and sociocultural components of collaborative educational learning tools. In C. Bonk & K. King (Eds.), *Electronic collaborators: Learner-centered technologies for literacy, apprenticeship, and discourse* (pp. 25–50). Mahwah, NJ: Erlbaum.

Bush, J., & Wise, B. (2010). *Digital learning now*. Tallahassee, FL: Foundation for Excellence in Education. Retrieved from http://www.excelined.org/Docs/Digital Learning Now Report FINAL.pdf

Butz, C. (2004). *Parent and student satisfaction with online education at the elementary and secondary levels* (Unpublished doctoral dissertation). University of Nevada at Las Vegas, Las Vegas.

Canadian Teachers Federation. (2000). *Facts sheets on contractual issues in distance/online education*. Ottawa, Canada: Author.

Cavanaugh, C. (2001). The effectiveness of interactive distance education technologies in K-12 learning: A meta-analysis. *International Journal of Educational Telecommunications, 7*(1), 73–88.

Cavanaugh, C., Barbour, M. K., & Clark, T. (2009). Research and practice in K-12 online learning: A review of literature. *International Review of Research in Open and Distance Learning, 10*(1). Retrieved from http://www.irrodl.org/index.php/irrodl/article/view/607

Cavanaugh, C., Gillan, K. J., Bosnick, J., Hess, M., & Scott, H. (2005). *Succeeding at the gateway: Secondary algebra learning in the virtual school*. Jacksonville: University of North Florida.

Cavanaugh, C., Gillan, K. J., Kromrey, J., Hess, M., & Blomeyer, R. (2004). *The effects of distance education on K–12 student outcomes: A meta-analysis*. Naperville, IL: Learning Point Associates. Retrieved from http://www.ncrel.org/tech/distance/k12distance.pdf

Clark, T. (2000). *Virtual high schools: State of the states — A study of virtual high school planning and preparation in the United States*: Center for the Application of Information Technologies, Western Illinois University. Retrieved from http://www.imsa.edu/programs/ivhs/pdfs/stateofstates.pdf

Clark, T. (2001). *Virtual schools: Trends and issues—A study of virtual schools in the United States*. San Francisco, CA: Western Regional Educational Laboratories. Retrieved from http://www.wested.org/online_pubs/virtualschools.pdf

Clark, T. (2003). Virtual and distance education in American schools. In M. G. Moore & W. G. Anderson (Eds.), *Handbook of distance education* (pp. 673–699). Mahwah, NJ: Erlbaum.

Clark, T., Lewis, E., Oyer, E., & Schreiber, J. (2002). *Illinois Virtual High School Evaluation, 2001–2002*. Carbondale, IL: TA Consulting and Southern Illinois University. Retrieved from http://www2.imsa.edu/programs/ivhs/pdfs/IVHS_FinalRpt.pdf

Coffield, F., Moseley, D., Hall, E., & Ecclestone, K. (2004). *Learning styles and pedagogy in post-16 learning. A systematic and critical review*. London: Learning and Skills Research Centre. Retrieved from https://crm.lsnlearning.org.uk/user/order.aspx?code=041543

Cooze, M., & Barbour, M. K. (2005). Learning styles: A focus upon e- learning practices and pedagogy and their implications for success in secondary high school students in Newfoundland and Labrador. *Malaysian Online Journal of Instructional Technology, 2*(1). Retrieved from http://pppjj.usm.my/mojit/articles/pdf/April05/02-Michael%20Barbour.pdf

Cooze, M., & Barbour, M. K. (2007). Learning styles: A focus upon e-learning practices and pedagogy and their implications for successful instructional design. *Journal of Applied Educational Technology, 4*(1). Retrieved from http://www.eduquery.com/jaet/JAET4-1_Cooze.pdf

Dallas, J. (1999). *Distance education for kindergarten to grade 12: A Canadian perspective*. A presentation at the Pan-Commonwealth Forum, Brunei. Retrieved from http://www.col.org/forum/PCFpapers/PostWork/dallas.pdf

Darrow, R. (2010). *A comparative study between online charter high schools and traditional high schools in California* (Unpublished doctoral dissertation). California State University, Fresno.

Davis, N. E. (2007, February). *Teacher's Education Goes into Virtual Schooling*. Paper presented at the FIPSE Comprehensive Conference. Retrieved from http://ctlt.iastate.edu/~tegivs/TEGIVS/publications/VS%20Symposium2007.pdf

Davis, N. E., Niederhauser, D., Compton, L., Lindstrom, D., & Schoeny, Z. (2005, March). *Virtual schooling lab practice: Case studies for teacher preparation*. Paper presented at the Society for Information Technology and Teacher Education International Annual Conference Phoenix, AZ.

Davis, N. E., & Roblyer, M. D. (2005). Preparing teachers for the "schools that technology build": Evaluation of a program to train teachers for virtual schooling. *Journal of Research on Technology in Education, 37*(4), 399–409.

Davis, N., Roblyer, M., Charania, A., Ferdig, R., Harms, C., Compton, L., & Cho, M. (2007). Illustrating the "virtual" in virtual schooling: Challenges and strategies for creating real tools to prepare virtual teachers. *Internet and Higher Education, 10*(1), 27–39.

de la Varre, C., Keane, J., & Irvin, M. J. (2010). Enhancing online distance education in small rural US schools: A hybrid, learner-centred model. ALT-J: Research in Learning Technology, 18(3), 193-205.

de la Varre, C., Keane, J., & Irvin, M. J. (2011). Dual perspectives on the contribution of on-site facilitators to teaching presence in a blended learning environment. Journal of Distance Education, 25(3). Retrieved from http://www.jofde.ca/index.php/jde/article/view/751/1285

DiPietro, M. (2010). Virtual school pedagogy: The instructional practices of K-12 virtual school teachers. *Journal of Educational Computing Research, 42*(3), 327–354.

DiPietro, M., Ferdig, R. E., Black, E. W. & Preston, M. (2008). Best practices in teaching K–12 online: Lessons learned from Michigan Virtual School teachers. *Journal of Interactive Online Learning, 7*(1). Retrieved from http://www.ncolr.org/jiol/issues/getfile.cfm?volID=7&IssueID=22&ArticleID=113

Easton, S. (2003). Clarifying the instructor's role in online distance learning. *Communication Education, 52*(2), 87–105.

Elbaum, B., McIntyre, C., & Smith, A. (2002). *Essential elements: Prepare, design, and teach your online course.* Madison, WI: Atwood Publishing.

Elbaum, B., & Tinker, R. (1997). *A review of secondary netcourses and virtual schools.* Concord, MA: Concord Consortium.

Espinoza, C., Dove, T., Zucker, A., & Kozma, R. (1999). *An evaluation of the Virtual High School after two years in operation.* Arlington, VA: SRI International. Retrieved from http://ctl.sri.com/publications/downloads/evalvhs2yrs.pdf

Ferdig, R., Cavanaugh, C., DiPietro, M., Black, E., & Dawson, K. (2009). Virtual schooling standards and best practices for teacher education. *Journal of Technology and Teacher Education, 17*(4), 479–503.

Fishman, B., Marx, R., Blumenfeld, P., Krajcik, J.S., & Soloway, E. (2004). Creating a framework for research on systemic technology innovations. *Journal of the Learning Sciences, 13*, 43–76.

Fogleman, J., Fishman, B., & Krajcik, J. (2006). Sustaining innovations through lead teacher learning: A learning sciences perspective on supporting professional development. *Teaching Education, 17*(2), 181–194.

Freedman, G., Darrow, R., Watson, J., & Lorenzo, G. (2002). *California virtual school report: A national survey of virtual education practice and policy with recommendations for the State of California*: Lorenzo Associates, Inc. Retrieved from http://web.archive.org/web/20061207213241/http://www.edpath.com/images/VHSReport.pdf

Friend, B., & Johnston, S. (2005). Florida Virtual School: A choice for all students. In Z. L. Berge & T. Clark (Eds.), *Virtual schools: Planning for success* (pp. 97–117). New York, NY: Teachers College Press.

Fulton, K. (2002). *Preserving principles of public education in an online world.* Washington, DC: Center on Education Policy. Retrieved from http://web.archive.org/web/20060524121739/http://www.ctredpol.org/democracypublicschools/preserving_principles_online_world_full.pdf

Grabinger, S. R., Aplin, C. & Ponnappa-Brenner, G. (2008). Supporting learners with cognitive impairments in online environments. *TechTrends, 52*(1), 63–69.

Hannum, W. H., Irvin, M. J., Lei, P.-W., & Farmer, T. W. (2008). Effectiveness of using learner-centered principles on student retention in distance education courses in rural schools. *Distance Education, 29*(3), 211–229.

Hassell, B. C., & Terrell, M. G. (2004). How can virtual schools be a vibrant part of meeting the choice provisions of the No Child Left Behind Act?. *Virtual School Report.* Retrieved from http://www2.ed.gov/about/offices/list/os/technology/plan/2004/site/documents/Hassel-Terrell-VirtualSchools.pdf

Haughey, M., & Fenwick, T. (1996). Issues in forming school district consortia to provide distance education: Lessons from Alberta. *Journal of Distance Education, 11*(1). Retrieved from http://www.jofde.ca/index.php/jde/article/view/242/454

Haughey, M., & Muirhead, W. (1999). *On-line learning: Best practices for Alberta school jurisdictions.* Edmonton, Canada: Government of Alberta. Retrieved from http://www.phrd.ab.ca/technology/best_practices/on-line-learning.pdf

Hernandez, F. J. (2005). Equity and access: The promise of virtual schools. In Z. L. Berge & T. Clark (Eds.), *Virtual schools: Planning for success* (pp. 20–34). New York, NY: Teachers College Press.

International Council for K-12 Online Learning. (2007a). *National standards for quality online courses.* Vienna, VA: Authors. Retrieved from http://www.inacol.org/resources/nationalstandards/NACOL%20Standards%20Quality%20Online%20Courses%202007.pdf

International Council for K-12 Online Learning. (2007b). *National standards for quality online teaching.* Vienna, VA: Authors. Retrieved from http://www.inacol.org/resources/nationalstandards/NACOL%20Standards%20Quality%20Online%20Teaching.pdf

International Council for K-12 Online Learning & Partnership for 21st Century Skills. (2006). *Virtual schools and 21st century skills.* Vienna, VA: Authors. Retrieved from http://www.21stcenturyskills.org/documents/VSand21stCenturySkillsFINALPaper.pdf

Irvin, M. J., Hannum, W. H., Farmer, T. W., de la Varre, C., & Keane, J. (2009). Supporting online learning for Advanced Placement students in small rural schools: Conceptual foundations and intervention components of the Facilitator Preparation Program. *The Rural Educator, 31*(1), 29–36.

Kaplan-Leiserson, E. (2003). We-learning: Social software and e-learning. *Learning Circuits.* Retrieved from http://www.astd.org/LC/2003/1203_kaplan.htm

Keeler, C. (2003). *Developing and using an instrument to describe instructional design elements of high school online courses* (Unpublished doctoral dissertation). University of Oregon, Eugene.

Keeler, C. (2004). *Assessment in online environment: A cross-school description of secondary courses.* A paper presented at the annual meeting of the American Educational Research Association. San Diego, CA. Retrieved from http://coe.nevada.edu/ckeeler/teachingportfolio/researchinterests.html#Assessment_in_Online_Environments:_A

Keeler, C. (2006). *Designing online Courses to meet diverse learning style preferences.* A paper presented at the annual meeting of the American Educational Research Association. San Francisco, CA. Retrieved from http://coe.nevada.edu/ckeeler/teachingportfolio/researchinterests.html#Learning_Styles

Keeler, C., & Anderson-Inman, L. (2004a). *Instructional design elements of high school online courses: An instrument.* A paper presented at the annual meeting of the American Educational Research Association. San Diego, CA. Retrieved from http://coe.nevada.edu/ckeeler/teachingportfolio/researchinterests.html#Instructional_Design_Elements_of_High

Keeler, C., & Anderson-Inman, L. (2004b). *A cross-school description of instructional design and delivery elements of high school level online courses.* A paper presented at the annual meeting of the American Educational Research Association Annual Meeting. San Diego, CA. Retrieved from http://coe.nevada.edu/ckeeler/teachingportfolio/researchinterests.html#A_Cross-School_Description_of

Keeler, C. G., & Horney, M. (2007). Online course designs: Are special needs being met? *American Journal of Distance Education, 21*(2), 61–75.

Keeler, C. G., Richter, J., Horney, M. A., Anderson, L., & Ditson, M. (2007). Exceptional learners: Differentiated instruction online. In C. Cavanaugh & R. Blomeyer (Eds.), *What works in K-12 online learning* (pp. 125–178). Eugene, OR: International Society for Technology in Education.

Kellogg, L., & Politoski, K. (2002). *Virtual schools across America: Trends in K-12 online education.* Los Angeles, CA: Peak Group Research Corporation.

Klein, C. (2006). *Virtual charter schools and home schooling.* Youngston, NY: Cambria Press.

Kozma, R., Zucker, A., & Espinoza, C. (1998). *An evaluation of the Virtual High School after one year in operation.* Arlington, VA: SRI International. Retrieved from http://ctl.sri.com/publications/downloads/evalvhs1yr.pdf

Kozma, R., Zucker, A., Espinoza, C., McGhee, R., Yarnall, L., Zalles, D., & Lewis, A. (2000). *The online course experience: Evaluation of the Virtual High School's third year of implementation, 1999–2000.* Arlington, VA: SRI International. Retrieved from http://ctl.sri.com/publications/downloads/VHS_Online_Experience.pdf

Lowes, S. (2005). *Online teaching and classroom change: The impact of virtual high school on its teachers and their schools.* New York, NY: Institute for Learning Technologies, Columbia University. Retrieved from http://www.ilt.columbia.edu/publications/lowes_final.pdf

McCombs, B., & Vakili, D. (2005). A learner-centered framework for e-learning. *Teachers College Record, 107*(8), 1582–1600.

McLeod, S., Hughes, J. E., Brown, R., Choi, J., & Maeda, Y. (2005). *Algebra achievement in virtual and traditional schools.* Naperville, IL: Learning Point Associates.

Mills, S. (2003). Implementing online secondary education: An evaluation of a virtual high school. In C. Crawford, N. Davis, J. Price, R. Weber, & D. A. Willis (Eds.), *Proceedings of Society for Information Technology & Teacher Education International Conference 2003* (pp. 444–451). Chesapeake, VA: Association for the Advancement of Computing in Education.

Morris, S. (2002). *Teaching and learning online: A step-by-step guide for designing an online K-12 school program.* Lanham, MD: Scarecrow Press.

Mulcahy, D., & Barbour, M. K. (2010, May). *Duck and cover: Are rural students taking basic courses to avoid taking them online?* A roundtable presented at the annual meeting of the American Educational Research Association, Denver, CO.

Mulcahy, D. M., Dibbon, D., & Norberg, C. (2008). *An investigation into the nature of education in a rural and remote region of Newfoundland and Labrador: The straits.* St. John's: The Harris Centre, Memorial University of Newfoundland.

Murphy, E., & Coffin, G. (2003). Synchronous communication in a web-based senior high school course: Maximizing affordances and minimizing constraints of the tool. *American Journal of Distance Education, 17*(4), 235–246.

Murphy, E., & Rodriguez-Manzanares, M. (2009a). Learner-centredness in high-school distance learning: Teachers' perspectives and research-validated principles. *Australasian Journal of Educational Technology, 25*(5), 597–610. Retrieved from http://www.ascilite.org.au/ajet/ajet25/murphy.html

Murphy, E., & Rodriguez-Manzanares, M. (2009b). Teachers' perspectives on motivation in high-school distance education. *Journal of Distance Education, 23*(3), 1–24. Retrieved from http://www.jofde.ca/index.php/jde/article/view/602

Murphy, E., Rodriguez-Manzanares, M., & Barbour, M. K. (2011). Asynchronous and synchronous online teaching: Perspectives of Canadian high school distance education teachers. *British Journal of Educational Technology, 42*(4), 583–591.

Nippard, N., & Murphy, E. (2007). Social presence in the web-based synchronous secondary classroom. *Canadian Journal of Learning and Technology, 33*(1). Retrieved from http://www.cjlt.ca/content/vol33.1/nippard.html

Pape, L., Adams, R., & Ribeiro, C. (2005). The Virtual High School: Collaboration and online professional development. In Z. L. Berge & T. Clark (Eds.), *Virtual schools: Planning for success* (pp. 118–132). New York, NY: Teachers College Press.

Rapp, K. E., Eckes, S. E., & Plurker, J. A. (2006). Cyber charter schools in Indiana: Policy implications of the current statutory language. *Education Policy Brief, 4*(3). Retrieved from http://ceep.indiana.edu/projects/PDF/PB_V4N3_Winter_2006_CyberCharter.pdf

Reeves, T. C. (1999). *A research agenda for interactive learning in the new millennium.* A keynote address to the World Conference on Educational Multimedia, Hypermedia & Telecommunications, Seattle, WA.

Reeves, T. C. (2000, April). Enhancing the worth of instructional technology research through design experiments and other development research strategies. A paper presented at the Annual Meeting of the American Educational Research Association, New Orleans, LA.

Reeves, T. C. (1993). Pseudoscience in computer-based instruction: The case of learner control research. *Journal of Computer-Based Instruction, 20*(2), 39–46.

Reeves, T. C. (2006). Design research from the technology perspective. In J. V. Akker, K. Gravemeijer, S. McKenney, & N. Nieveen (Eds.), *Educational design research* (pp. 86–109). London: Routledge.

Rice, K. L. (2006). A comprehensive look at distance education in the K-12 context. *Journal of Research on Technology in Education, 38*(4), 425–448.

Roblyer, M. D. (2005). Who plays well in the virtual sandbox? Characteristics of successful online students and teachers. *SIGTel Bulletin,* (2). Retrieved from http://web.archive.org/web/20060930130650/http://www.iste.org/Content/NavigationMenu/Membership/SIGs/SIGTel_Telelearning_/SIGTel_Bulletin2/Archive/2005_20067/2005_July_-_Roblyer.htm

Roblyer, M. D., Davis, L., Mills, S. C., Marshall, J., & Pape, L. (2008) Toward practical procedures for predicting and promoting success in virtual school students. *American Journal of Distance Education, 22*(2), 90–109.

Roblyer, M. D., & Elbaum, B. (2000). Virtual learning? Research on virtual high schools *Learning & Leading with Technology, 27*(4), 58–61.

Roblyer, M. D., Freeman, J., Stabler, M., & Schneidmiller, J. (2007). *External evaluation of the Alabama ACCESS initiative: Phase 3 report.* Eugene, OR: International Society for Technology in Education. Retrieved from http://accessdl.state.al.us/2006Evaluation.pdf

Roblyer, M. D., & Marshall, J. C. (2002–2003). Predicting success of virtual high school students: Preliminary results from an educational success prediction instrument. *Journal of Research on Technology in Education, 35*(2), 241–255.

Roblyer, M. D., & McKenzie, B. (2000). Distant but not out-of-touch: What makes an effective distance learning instructor? *Learning and Leading With Technology, 27*(6), 50–53.

Russo, A. (2001). E-learning everywhere. *The School Administrator.* Retrieved from http://www.aasa.org/SchoolAdministratorArticle.aspx?id=10698

Smith, R. D. (2009). Virtual voices: Online teachers' perceptions of online teaching standards. *Journal of Technology and Teacher Education, 17*(4), 547–571.

Smith, R., Clark, T., & Blomeyer, R. L. (2005). *A synthesis of new research on K-12 online learning.* Naperville, IL: Learning Point Associates. Retrieved from http://www.ncrel.org/tech/synthesis/synthesis.pdf

Stevens, K. (1997). The place of telelearning in the development of rural schools in Newfoundland and Labrador *Prospects, 4*(4). Retrieved from http://www.cdli.ca/Community/Prospects/v4n4/telelearning.htm

Thomas, W. R. (1999). *Essential elements for web-based courses for high school students.* Atlanta, GA: Southern Regional Education Board. Retrieved from http://publications.sreb.org/1999/99T03_EssentialElements.pdf

Thomas, W. R. (2000). *Essential principles of quality: Guidelines for web-based courses for middle and high schools.* Atlanta, GA: Southern Regional Education Board. Retrieved from http://publications.sreb.org/2000/00T04_EssentialPrinciples.pdf

Thomas, W. R. (2003). *Essential principles of high-quality online teaching: Guidelines for evaluating K-12 online teachers.* Atlanta, GA: Southern Regional Education Board. Retrieved from http://publications.sreb.org/2003/03T02_Essential_Principles.pdf

Tinker, R., & Haavind, S. (1997). *Netcourses and netseminars: Current practice and new designs.* Concord, MA: Concord Consortium. Retrieved from http://archive.concord.org/publications/pdf/netcours.pdf

Vail, K. (2001). Online learning grows up: No longer an experiment, virtual school is here to stay. *Electronic School.* Retrieved from http://web.archive.org/web/20080608145221/http://www.electronic-school.com/2001/09/0901f1.html

Wagner, E., & McCombs, B. (1995). Learner-centered psychological principles in practice: Designs for distance education. *Educational Technology 35*(2), 32–35.

Watkins, T. (2005). *Exploring e-learning reforms for Michigan: The new educational (r)evolution.* Detroit, MI: Wayne State University. Retrieved from http://web.archive.org/web/20051208000848/http://www.coe.wayne.edu/e-learningReport.pdf

Watson, J. F., Gemin, B., & Ryan, J. (2008). *Keeping pace with k–12 online learning: A review of state-level policy and practice.* Evergreen, CO: Evergreen Consulting Associates. Retrieved from http://www.kpk12.com/downloads/KeepingPace_2008.pdf

Watson, J. F., Gemin, B., Ryan, J., & Wicks, M. (2009). *Keeping pace with K–12 online learning: A review of state-level policy and practice.* Evergreen, CO: Evergreen Education Group. Retrieved from http://www.kpk12.com/downloads/KeepingPace09-fullreport.pdf

Watson, J., Murin, A., Vashaw, L., Gemin, B., & Rapp, C. (2011). *Keeping pace with K-12 online learning: An annual review of state-level policy and practice.* Evergreen, CO: Evergreen Education Group. Retrieved from http://kpk12.com/cms/wp-content/uploads/EEG_KeepingPace2011-lr.pdf

Watson, J. F., Winograd, K., & Kalmon, S. (2004). *Keeping pace with K-12 online learning: A snapshot of state-level policy and practice.* Naperville, IL: North Central Regional Educational Laboratory. Retrieved from http://www.kpk12.com/cms/wp-content/uploads/KeepingPace_2004.pdf

Winkelmans, T., Anderson, B., & Barbour, M. K. (2010). Distributed learning in British Columbia: A journey from correspondence to online delivery. *Journal of Open, Flexible and Distance Learning, 14*(1), 6–28.

Yamashiro, K., & Zucker, A. (1999). An expert panel review of the quality of Virtual High School courses: Final report. Arlington, VA: SRI International.

Zucker, A. (2005). *A study of student interaction and collaboration in the Virtual High School.* Naperville, IL: Learning Point Associates.

Zucker, A., & Kozma, R. (2003). The Virtual High Shool: Teaching generation V. New York, NY: Teachers College Press.

37

ONLINE LEARNING IN COMMUNITY COLLEGES

SHANNA SMITH JAGGARS

Public community colleges educate more than 7 million students per year, comprising over 40% of postsecondary enrollments (U.S. Department of Education, 2011a). As open-access institutions, community colleges strive to provide opportunities to a wide variety of students, many of whom cannot afford the cost or time required to attend traditional four-year colleges. Compared with public four-year institutions, community college students are more likely to be 25 or older, to attend school part-time, and to be employed full-time (U.S. Department of Education, 2011b). The majority of students entering community college are also academically underprepared in English or mathematics (Attewell, Lavin, Domina, & Levey, 2006; Bailey, Jeong, & Cho, 2010), for a variety of reasons: some were poorly-served by their high school education; some are recent immigrants who need assistance with English reading and writing skills; and some are older students who have been away from school for an extended period and have forgotten much of the content they once learned. Moreover, the majority of community college students are the first in their family to attend college (Choy, 2001), and as such, may have a limited understanding of how to navigate the cultural and logistical barriers of higher education, including how to be successful in college-level coursework (e.g., see Pascarella, Pierson, Wolniak, & Terenzini, 2004; Rosenbaum, Deil-Amen, & Person, 2006).

In order to serve their largely non-traditional student populations, community colleges have long been interested in distance education. They began to expand distance education options in the 1970s, moving beyond correspondence-by-mail courses to telecourses and live interactive television, and in the 1990s, to online coursework (Mullins, 2003). As the 20th century gave way to the 21st, online learning enrollments increased more quickly at two-year colleges than at four-year colleges; by 2007, over 97% of two-year colleges offered online courses, compared to only 66% of all postsecondary institutions (Parsad & Lewis, 2008).

This chapter reviews the literature on online learning in the community college setting, focusing on patterns of student online course-taking, student performance in online versus face-to-face courses, and factors affecting online course performance.

PATTERNS OF ONLINE COURSE-TAKING
IN THE COMMUNITY COLLEGE

Today, most community colleges offer a mix of face-to-face and online courses, which allows some students to take advantage of the flexibility of online course sections, while others choose to maintain a fully face-to-face course schedule. Recent studies of students' course-taking patterns across the Virginia and Washington public community college systems indicate that nearly half of students take at least one online course across their first four or five years of enrollment (Jaggars & Xu, 2010; Xu & Jaggars, 2011a). As might be expected, online courses are more popular among community college students who are balancing multiple life demands (e.g., are 25 or older, have dependents, or are employed full-time). However, those who choose an online course are also more likely to be White, from higher-income neighborhoods, academically prepared at entry, and fluent in the English language (Jaggars & Xu, 2010; Xu & Jaggars, 2011a). Thus, the typical student taking an online course in the community college may be juggling work and family responsibilities, but is also equipped with a relatively strong academic background.

Given that most community colleges offer an array of courses online, it may be surprising that over half of their students do not take advantage of online options. However, for some community college students, online coursework is not yet a viable option. While the "digital divide" has perhaps disappeared in terms of overall Internet use, low-income households are still at a significant disadvantage in terms of the relatively sophisticated infrastructure required to participate in online learning. In 2009, only 42% of households with incomes less than $30,000, 46% of adults who had at most a high school degree, 52% of African Americans, and 47% of Hispanics had high-speed Internet access at home (Rainie, 2010). These numbers have not grown substantially since 2006 (cf. Rainie, Estabrook, & Witt, 2007). Accordingly, it is not clear whether online courses are expanding postsecondary access among low-income populations. For example, in a study of 15 community colleges in six states (Cox, 2005), several colleges did not expect their new online courses to bring in a new population of students, due to the poor technological infrastructure of the surrounding community.

Among community college students who do take online courses, few take *all* of their courses online. While 22% of community college students were enrolled in an online course in 2007–2008, only 3% were enrolled in an entirely-online degree program (Radford, 2011). Similarly, among students entering Virginia community colleges in the fall of 2008, only 3% took all of their courses online in their first semester; and throughout their college career, most "online" students maintain a mix of online and face-to-face course enrollments (Jaggars & Xu, 2010; Xu & Jaggars, 2011a). From the quantitative data alone, it is difficult to determine whether students prefer this mix-and-match strategy, or whether they would prefer to take more courses online and are thwarted by a lack of available offerings; and indeed, there is some evidence for both perspectives.

College administrators tend to believe that student demand for online courses continues to outpace current offerings, a belief that seems borne out by the continuing and strong increase in online course enrollments each year. And certainly some students prefer online courses to face-to-face courses (even conveniently-scheduled ones), and some may wish they could take all their courses online. In particular, the flexibility of online coursework is a boon for students balancing work, family, and school responsibilities (e.g., see Radford, 2011); and such students may create a loud clamor for the expansion of online learning options.

However, it is not clear that all students who enroll in online courses necessarily prefer them to face-to-face sections. For example, Cox's aforementioned study (2005) found that "At several sites, the bulk of student enrollment in online courses occurred after on-site sections had filled, suggesting that students would have preferred to take the face-to-face versions" (p. 1770). In some cases, a student may simply seek a section offered at a time that matches his or her schedule; in the absence of such face-to-face options, the student will fall back on an online section.

Finally, some students prefer to mix face-to-face courses into their online experience, or prefer to take all their courses face-to-face. In a recent series of interviews conducted with students participating in online courses at two Virginia community colleges (Jaggars, 2012), many students had distinct preferences regarding which types of courses they would take online and which types of courses they would not. For example, one student said,

> There's no way I could do algebra online. I'm barely making it through algebra right now, face-to-face, so I know I could not do it online.... I wanted to have as much credits as I could get this semester, so my advisor told me certain classes I could take. And then she said, "Well these are online," and I figured that they are mostly reading—which they are, health is mostly reading. And college composition, it's reading and writing. I figured I could do those online.

STUDENT PERFORMANCE IN ONLINE COURSES

The preponderance of research comparing college students' performance in online versus face-to-face courses has focused on relatively well-prepared students attending fairly selective universities (Jaggars & Bailey, 2010), while only a handful have focused on community college students. Overall, the studies conducted in the community college setting across the past decade (Blackner, 2000; Carpenter, Brown, & Hickman, 2004; Chambers, 2002; Davis, 2007; Harlee, 2006; Jaggars & Xu, 2010; Kleinman & Entin, 2002; Musgrove, 2002; Rosenfeld, 2005; Summerlin, 2003; Waschull, 2001; Xu & Jaggars, 2011a; Zavarella, 2008) tend to indicate that students are more likely to withdraw from online courses mid-semester, but among those that complete the course, grades and other academic outcomes are fairly similar between online and face-to-face sections. However, the most recent of these studies suggest that earlier research underestimated the extent to which online and face-to-face courses differ in terms of student outcomes (Jaggars & Xu, 2010; Xu & Jaggars, 2011a).

Course Completion

Course completion is a fundamental measure of success for community college students. While relatively high-income university students can afford to withdraw mid-semester from courses that do not engage or interest them, low-income community college students can ill-afford to pay full tuition for a course that they do not successfully complete. Moreover, students who withdraw from a course mid-semester run the very real risk of never returning to successfully complete the course, thereby prohibiting progression to the next course in the sequence (see, e.g., Bailey et al., 2010).

Nearly every study comparing course completion rates between online and face-to-face community college courses has concluded that online completion rates are substantially lower. This trend seems consistent across a variety of different academic subjects and course levels, including developmental mathematics (50% online vs. 85% face-to-face completion in Beginning Algebra, and 33% online vs. 63% face-to-face completion in Intermediate Algebra, Blackner, 2000; 51% face-to-face vs. 73% online completion with C or better in Intermediate Algebra, Summerlin, 2003; and 61% online vs. 80% face-to-face completion in Basic Algebra, Zavarella, 2008); developmental writing (raw percentages unavailable, but adjusted odds of completion were nearly five times higher in face-to-face courses, Carpenter et al., 2004); college-level English, mathematics, and history courses (83% online vs. 89% face-to-face completion, Rosenfeld, 2005); computer and business courses (73% online or telecourse vs. 81% face-to-face completion, Harlee, 2006; 53% online vs. 94% face-to-face completion, Kleinman & Entin, 2002) and on aggregate across all courses in six Ohio community colleges (77% online vs. 90% face-to-face completion, Chambers, 2002). However, a study of an introductory psychology course at a two-year technical college found equivalent raw withdrawal rates in the two types of sections (91% online vs. 88% face-to-face completion across two terms; Waschull, 2001).

Some online-learning advocates argue that high online withdrawal rates are due not to the course format, but to the non-traditional characteristics of online students (Howell, Laws, & Lindsay, 2004; Hyllegard, Heping, & Hunter, 2008). And indeed, most comparison studies have not included adequate controls for the distinctly different characteristics of students who choose online courses. To confront this issue head-on, Jaggars and Xu conducted studies in two quite different states: Virginia (Jaggars & Xu, 2010) and Washington (Xu & Jaggars, 2011a). Each study involved dozens of community colleges, tens of thousands of students, and hundreds of thousands of courses; each study tracked students who initially enrolled in 2004 for four years (in Virginia) or five years (in Washington). The analysis focused only on students who had taken at least one online course in their community college career, greatly reducing the possibility that results would be driven by pre-existing differences between students who choose to enroll in online courses versus those that do not. In Virginia, raw face-to-face completion rates were 81% while online completion rates were 68%; in Washington, the same rates were 90% versus 82%.[1] To adjust these raw rates for possible biases, the authors then limited the focus to only introductory mathematics and English (key courses required of almost all students), and entered a wide array of course-level, semester-level, and student-level control variables. In both states, the inclusion of the additional controls did not diminish the estimated effect of online modality on course withdrawal. Indeed, a subsequent analysis of the Virginia data (Xu & Jaggars, 2011b) demonstrated that the inclusion of strict controls may *increase* rather than decrease the estimated gap between online and face-to-face courses. Finally, in order to ensure that results were not outdated in their focus on a 2004 cohort, analyses were replicated by focusing on students who entered each system in 2008 and tracking the students for one year, an approach which yielded very similar results.

Overall, the results of the Virginia and Washington studies strongly indicate that community college students who choose to take a course online are less likely to successfully complete that course than if they were to take it face-to-face. Among students who do complete a given course, however, do students in online and face-to-face sections have similar course grades?

Course Grades

Most studies of community college online performance have concluded that, among students who persist to the end of the semester, online and face-to-face students have similar probabilities of earning a good grade. Several studies have found no difference in online versus face-to-face grades or exam scores (Blackner, 2000; Kleinman & Entin, 2002; Musgrove, 2002; Rosenfeld, 2005; Summerlin, 2003; Waschull, 2001), while one study found higher grades online (Carpenter et al., 2004) and two others found lower grades online (Chambers, 2002; Harlee, 2006).

However, all of these studies share a key methodological problem: If two sections of a course have very different completion rates, then they may be quite different in their composition of students at the end of the semester. Thus, a simple comparison of learning outcomes between course completers may not be valid. For example, a study of developmental writing at a large comprehensive community college (Carpenter et al., 2004) found that students who completed the online course were more likely to earn a good grade in comparison to those who completed the face-to-face course; however, students were also significantly more likely to withdraw from the online course. The authors acknowledged that the higher grades in the online course could be an artifact of its substantially higher withdrawal rates. To further explore this possibility, they examined each student's academic placement test scores, which were measured prior to course entry. Results indicated that students with *lower* placement scores were more likely to withdraw from the online section, while students with *higher* scores were more likely to withdraw from the face-to-face section, thus leaving the online section with students who were better prepared. This pattern gives weight to the notion that differential withdrawal rates can result in misleading comparisons between students who complete online and face-to-face courses.

To eliminate the potential confounding effect of unequal withdrawal in the analysis of learning outcomes, Xu and Jaggars (2011b) performed an additional analysis with the aforementioned Virginia state data, using a propensity score method that matched each student who completed a given course online with an otherwise extremely-similar student who completed the same type of course face-to-face. This analysis represents the *only* study in this review that explicitly addressed and removed the potential influence of unequal withdrawal, and it found that online students who completed the course were significantly less likely to earn a good grade (C or above) than were face-to-face students.

Subsequent Progression

For community college students, retention into subsequent semesters, as well as progression to the next course in the program sequence, are critical issues. The majority of students enter community college academically underprepared; many of these students fail to exit the developmental sequence and progress to introductory college-level "gatekeeper" courses, and thus are stalled early on the path to a credential (Bailey, Jaggars, & Cho, 2010; Bailey, Jeong, & Cho, 2010). Yet despite the importance of progression, few studies have examined the impact of online courses on subsequent course enrollment and eventual college completion. Summerlin (2003), who focused on a community college developmental mathematics course, compared a sample of online students (N = 79) to a randomly-drawn sample of face-to-face students (N = 143) and noted that students taking developmental mathematics online were less likely to subsequently pass college-level algebra, but the study provided no further controls in that analysis. In the previously discussed Virginia and Washington studies (Jaggars & Xu, 2010; Xu & Jaggars, 2011a), which used a wide array of controls, the authors found that:

- Students who took online coursework in early semesters were less likely to return to school in subsequent semesters. For example, among the Virginia 2004 cohort, those who took one or more online courses in the first fall semester were significantly less likely to return in the spring, with adjusted retention rates 5 percentage points lower than those of students who took a fully face-to-face curriculum (69% vs. 74%).
- Students who took developmental English and mathematics courses online were much less likely to subsequently succeed in college-level English and mathematics. For example, adjusted enrollment rates into college-level English among the Virginia 2004 cohort were almost 30 percentage points lower among those who took their developmental English course online compared to those who took their developmental course face-to-face.
- Students who took a higher proportion of credits online were less likely to attain a credential or to transfer to a four-year institution. For example, in the Virginia 2004 cohort, those who took only a few credits online had award/transfer rates that were six percentage points higher than those who took a substantial number of credits online.

The evidence from Virginia and Washington suggests that online learning may undercut progression among community college students. This is not surprising in light of the fact that students are less likely to successfully complete a course if they take it online. While some students may retake the course in an attempt to complete it and move forward, others may give up on the course entirely—which is a major barrier if the course is required to complete one's chosen program of study.

Factors Affecting Online Course Performance

The body of research evidence discussed above suggests that poor online performance rates in community colleges are not simply due to the characteristics of students who choose to enroll in those courses. That is, independent of students' prior skills, the online format of the course itself might pose difficulties for students. What, then, might be the specific course characteristics that affect student performance? The theoretical and research literature suggest at least three possibilities: increased "social distance," a relative lack of structure inherent in online courses, and technical difficulties.

Social Distance

Numerous educational theorists argue that in order to improve retention rates, institutions need to build students' sense of belonging and commitment; this might be accomplished by encouraging social relationships through communities of learning and by otherwise helping students feel that the institution "cares" (Karp, 2011). Similarly, distance education theorists argue that in order to engage and motivate students, distance courses must explicitly build social or emotional connections between students and instructors, as well as among students (e.g., Fontaine, 2010; Garrison, Anderson, & Archer, 2003). And indeed, a sense of "social presence," or the projection of an authentic persona that connects to others involved in the course, correlates strongly with online student course satisfaction, performance, and retention (Boston et al., 2009; Gunawardena & Zittle, 1997; Liu, Gomez, & Yen, 2009; Picciano, 2002; Richardson & Swan, 2003).

Studies of community college students' experiences, however, suggest that many online courses lack a sense of social presence. A study by the Virginia community college system noted that 43% of students complained of inadequate levels of feedback and interaction in their online courses (Virginia Community College System, 2001). Similarly, in a qualitative study of online students enrolled in four high-risk community college courses (HRCs), students' primary complaint was a sense of isolation in their online course (Bambara, Harbour, Davies, & Athey, 2009). As the authors noted in terms of student-instructor interaction:

> HRC participants did not see anyone, and they did not have a sense that anyone was present. David explained, "I don't feel like there was an instructor presence.... I don't feel like there was anything that I was learning from the instructor. The instructor was simply there as a Web administrator or as a grader." (pp. 224–225)

Students also felt a lack of interaction with one another:

> What our participants found was aptly described by Samantha as follows: "No interaction between the students, student interaction is nonexistent! I know nothing about these people!" They had no sense of community within the HRCs, no peer interaction. Geraldine remarked, "I was just sort of on this island, all by myself." David echoed her sentiments when he said, "I felt like, specifically in that [HRC] class, I was alone and adrift." (p. 225)

The lack of social presence and interaction in some online courses may be due to a lack of instructor time and training. To provide high-quality curricula and instruction, faculty need strong support from the institution. Well-regarded online courses are often designed through a team-based approach, with faculty collaborating with an instructional designer, and often with additional support staff (e.g., Alvarez, Blair, Monske, & Wolf, 2005; Hawkes & Coldeway, 2002; Hixon, 2008; Knowles & Kalata, 2007; Puzziferro & Shelton, 2008; Thille, 2008; Xu & Morris, 2007). Yet in Cox's (2005) study of 15 community colleges, most faculty were left to design online courses on their own, and training for online instructors was primarily focused on technical aspects of the online course management system. As one teacher explained:

> I took a course on Web CT ... and it was glaringly obvious from the moment I walked in that the course was taught by someone who knew the technology inside out and backwards, but had no sense of how to communicate that material. No sense of what classroom assessment is about or how to get input from the students. (p. 1780)

Similarly, a recent survey of community college English teachers (Millward, 2008) found that while most colleges offer training to online instructors, faculty were dissatisfied with the training programs' focus on technology rather than pedagogy. Moreover, 43% indicated that they received no compensation for the time they spent on training. Overall, the survey found, as Millward summarizes, that instructors "are asking for more access, more training, more time for innovation and implementation, and more research" (p. 391). A survey of North Carolina community college online instructors (Pagliari, Batts, & McFadden, 2009) also found disheartening results, concluding that "it is apparent that the two-year institutions within the state of North Carolina still need to dedicate time and effort to the training of their faculty who teach online and also create an infrastructure that assists and promotes training."

In Cox's (2005) study, none of the colleges offered faculty the degree of expert support they needed to redesign curricula and pedagogical strategies for the online context. Worse, some institutions had policies that actively undercut faculty engagement in online learning, such as not counting online courses as part of a normal teaching load, or enrolling twice the number of students in online as compared to face-to-face sections. As a result, one college's online coordinator said:

> Probably the same range of practice that we have in our face-to-face courses is being replicated online, when that might have been an opportunity not just to teach people technology, but to have them think about engaging students and what kinds of things you can do better online, rather than just post your lecture, or whatever it is that might be happening. (p. 1779)

Until colleges provide faculty with support for intensive online course development, and require intensive pedagogical training for online faculty, it is unlikely that students will feel the strong sense of connection to their instructor and other students that may help motivate and inspire them to succeed in an online course.

Lack of Structure

In a study of public and private two-year colleges, Rosenbaum and colleagues (2006) argue that private schools have better student outcomes with a similarly disadvantaged population because they provide a more strongly structured experience for their students. For example, private two-year colleges often have simpler and more streamlined curricula, incorporate intensive and intrusive advising into the student experience, and bundle students into cohorts. Building on Rosenbaum et al.'s argument, Scott-Clayton (2011) pulled together literature from education research and behavioral economics to set forth evidence for a "structure hypothesis": that community college students are often overwhelmed by the complexity of the college experience, and will benefit from support structures that help them consistently make appropriate choices.

Yet distance learning, beginning with correspondence courses, has traditionally been a less-structured alternative to the face-to-face classroom. Most online courses are asynchronous (Parsad & Lewis, 2008), allowing students to access course materials and work on assignments at times that are most convenient to them, and to use idiosyncratic strategies to access, navigate, digest, and apply the material. While this flexibility is a boon to some students, the relative lack of structure in online courses may lead others to get lost, procrastinate, or fall behind on assignments.

Distance education theorists argue that a low-structure approach is more appropriate for some learners than others. Moore and Kearsley (2004) note that some students have a strong capacity to structure their own learning and thrive when they are able to take control, while others need much more guidance in order to succeed. The work of community college researchers who focus on student support infrastructures (e.g., Karp, 2011; Rosenbaum et al., 2006; Scott-Clayton, 2011) suggests that a first-generation low-income community college student is likely to need more guidance, at least initially, than would a high-income university student. For example, Scott-Clayton points out that many low-income students may have been reared under a "natural development" philosophy. As Lareau (2003) explains, children from the natural development school tend to be more passive in their approach to institutions such as school; they may have difficulty diagnosing their own needs and making those needs known to people in authority. In contrast, higher-income children are often reared under the "concerted cultivation" philosophy, which encourages children to be self-directed and forthright advocates for their own needs. Pursuing that line of thinking, it seems reasonable that a young student from a higher-income family might have little difficulty diving into a relatively-unstructured online course for the first time, organizing his or her own learning and reaching out to the instructor with any questions or concerns. In contrast, a young student from a lower-income family might initially be uncertain as to how to structure their own learning, and feel uncomfortable reaching out for help. Thus, rather than expecting that community college students will instantly adapt to a new and perhaps confusing low-structure online environment, institutions and their instructors may need to explicitly help students learn how to succeed in an online course. Such "scaffolding" activities might include providing clear expectations and instructions, as well as using activities and processes that teach metacognition, system knowledge, and self-efficacy (Hannafin, Hill, Oliver, Glazer, & Sharma, 2003).

Technical Difficulties

When researchers talk to students about their online course experience, technical problems (both unavoidable system-based problems and difficulties caused by the user's lack of familiarity with the system) surface as a frequent complaint (e.g., Bambara et al., 2009; El Mansour & Mupinga, 2007; Hara & Kling, 1999; Mupinga, Nora, & Yaw, 2006; Navarro & Shoemaker, 2000; Rivera, McAlister, & Rice, 2002; Wang, 2008). For example, in Zavarella's (2008) community college study, the predominant reasons for student withdrawal from online courses were technical problems, computer-based learning issues, or other factors explicitly related to the online nature of the course.

To the extent that student technical difficulties spring from outdated at-home technology, they can also have an impact on the pedagogical quality of the course. In a study of a rural community college (Hurt, 2008), online faculty reported that slow dial-up Internet access was a significant problem in their area. As the author notes, "the very slow connection speed offered by dial-up can make a very tedious task something as simple as navigating Blackboard to obtain a daily announcement" (p. 8). Consequently, most instructors limited their online courses to text files, eschewing the use of "videos, recorded presentations, simulations, models, or any type of large files that would require someone on dial-up a great deal of time to download" (Hurt, 2008, p. 8).

Technical difficulties can also spring from students' lack of familiarity with technology. While many online advocates suggest that today's students are highly tech-savvy, that may not necessarily be true of low-income populations. For example, in Hurt's (2008) study, instructors initially stated that students' lack of technical skills was not a problem. In a later round of interviews, however, further probing revealed that technology problems are indeed an issue for some students. As Hurt (2008) reports, "Another person who had claimed that technology deficiencies were no longer a problem said in the second interview that 'those people' drop out of the class" (p. 9). Unfortunately, while almost all campuses provide some type of technical support service for students, such services are not always open at the hours when students may be working online: a recent survey estimates that only 33% of two- and four-year institutions offer round-the-clock technical support (Green, 2010).

Providing comprehensive technical support to online students, however, may require a level of time and money that would be difficult for resource-strapped colleges to muster. As a consequence, most community colleges have taken a different approach: screening into online courses only those students who are likely to succeed without extensive supports. For example, the Washington State community and technical college system encourages students to take a voluntary assessment that provides students with feedback as to whether an online course is a good option for them (Xu & Jaggars, 2011a). Such assessments are meant to communicate the expectations of online course-work and to improve students' self-awareness of how their academic assets match (or do not match) the features and challenges of online learning. These measures, however, do not appear very effective; one study pointed out this could be due to the fact that students are self-assessing and may not be aware of their own strengths and weaknesses (Millward, 2008).

Another possible reason for the assessments' lack of effectiveness may be that they are poorly tailored to the individual. For example, similar to many other individual community colleges' and systems' approaches, the Washington assessment provided students with very general advice. As an illustration, a student who indicated that his or her technology skills were "very basic" would be told to "Contact your college, they may offer courses to help you build your skills." In Xu and Jaggars' (2011a) report to the Washington system, the authors suggested creating an assessment that provides tailored feedback to prospective online students. For example, in response to a student's self-report of "very basic" technology skills, the system could guide students to specific technology courses or workshops available at the student's own campus in the upcoming semester. Colleges could also require new online students to complete a tutorial with practice exercises, demonstrating that the student can accomplish basic technical skills.

IMPROVING ONLINE (AND FACE-TO-FACE) OUTCOMES

The specific suggestions included in the preceding sections may help ensure that students are properly prepared for online courses, make strong connections with faculty and other students, and are scaffolded with supports that help them further build the self-directed learning skills that they need to succeed in online courses and in the broader academic and professional world. However, as Jenkins (2011) discusses in his review of institutional improvement in the community college sector, strategies that substantially improve student success are unlikely to be adopted on a wide scale across the institution unless the college engages in a systematic long-term improvement process.

Currently, most colleges have only a weak system in place for evaluating the quality of online teaching and learning. As Cox (2005) notes, at the typical community college:

the assessment of the online program or of the individual online courses focuses on the technological components, rather than the processes of teaching and learning that constitute the online courses and the online program. Indeed, a consistent feature across every college was the scarcity (or more frequently, the complete absence) of assessment data for online courses.... Furthermore, at nearly every college, although administrators expressed deep concern with the consistently low retention rates in online courses, none of the colleges had analyzed the problem. (pp. 1778–1779)

Jenkins (2011) suggests that in order to create a more complete system of assessment and culture of improvement, community colleges need to cultivate leadership for improved student success throughout the institution, and empower faculty to establish common learning outcomes and assessments for academic programs. Departments can then set ambitious standards for course learning outcomes, and continuously assess and improve the extent to which students meet these outcomes. Jenkins (2011) points out that colleges can create time and space for this critical faculty-driven work by redefining professional development and departmental service, and focusing those activities more sharply on defining, aligning, and improving departmental learning outcomes.

The American Public University System provides a model of how such a continuous quality improvement system could work (Ice, 2009). On a semesterly basis, the system identifies online programs and instructors with significantly higher scores and examines their work for innovative or exemplary practices that could potentially be implemented by lower-scoring programs and instructors. Perhaps most importantly, program directors review individual faculty outcomes with each instructor, constructively discuss potential ways to improve scores, and incorporate these reports into quarterly audits.

Of course, a quality improvement process should not be limited to online courses alone. Face-to-face courses would also benefit from continuous assessment and revision. Online program administrators, however, may have an advantage in terms of pushing a continuous improvement agenda for two reasons. First, online learning is relatively new to many faculty, and their experience with it is still evolving. Moreover, according to a recent survey (Green, 2010), a vast majority of colleges have either recently completed or expect to soon implement a reorganization of online learning. It may be more politically viable to introduce a new quality improvement approach within the still-shifting context of online learning than within the relatively traditional context of face-to-face learning. And second, online course management systems offer the possibility of far more advanced learner analytics than is possible in face-to-face learning, and these sophisticated data might feed more readily into a continuous improvement approach. For example, the Open Learning Initiative captures transactional data on all student learning activities and uses the resulting data to revise each course for the following semester (Thille, 2008).

CONCLUSION

The conclusion that community college students perform more poorly in online courses than in face-to-face courses does not imply that face-to-face courses are an ideal standard for comparison. Community college administrators estimate face-to-face course completion rates to be approximately 76% (Instructional Technology Council, 2010), which certainly leaves room for improvement. In his 1999 book, *Honored but Invisible*, Grubb pointed out that community college instructors are often instructionally isolated, with few resources and supports to help them systematically improve their teaching. More recent research suggests that this situation has changed little over the past decade (Grubb, 2010). Moreover, institutions have much more work to do to support underprepared students—whether in online or in face-to-face courses—to succeed (Karp, 2011). The literature reviewed in this chapter makes several recommendations to help institutions improve students' online performance. It is worth nothing that many of these recommendations apply to face-to-face coursework as well.

Online learning affords flexibility and convenience to students and also allows institutions to be more flexible in their approach to education, in both narrow ways (e.g., offering more sections of a course than can be accommodated by the college's physical classroom space) and very broad ways (e.g., enrolling new students each month into competency-based programs, à la Western Governors University). Yet students also encounter challenges in online coursework as it is typically implemented—including technical difficulties, a sense of isolation, a relative lack of structure, and a general lack of support—that may contribute to poor performance, particularly among community college students. To help ameliorate these problems while still allowing for increased flexibility, some educators advocate the expansion of hybrid coursework, which is thought to provide students with the "best of both worlds." For example, most courses redesigned under the National Center for Academic Transformation process are modified to become hybrid courses or technology-assisted face-to-face courses, rather than to become online courses (Twigg, 2003). However, hybrid courses appear to be relatively rare in the community college context (Jaggars & Xu, 2010; Xu & Jaggars, 2011a). This low prevalence may be due to the fact that hybrid courses do not offer complete freedom from geographic and temporal constraint, and thus do not hold out the same promise for improved access to postsecondary education. Accordingly, online learning has an important role in community college education—a role that will likely continue to grow in scope and consequence.

In order for online learning to meet its promise of improving postsecondary access and success among low-income and underprepared community college students, colleges need to provide online instructors with resources and training to implement high-quality online curricula and pedagogies that engage students and help them build their self-directed learning skills; create student readiness assessments that result in tailored feedback and student training; and put in place peer-review-driven continuous quality improvement processes. Some of these recommendations would radically reshape the way that institutions are organized, including the role of the faculty member. However, in order for colleges to meet increased expectations for student success, such changes may be necessary—not only in the online classroom, but also in the traditional face-to-face classroom.

NOTES

1. "Course completion" was defined as completing the course with a D or above, rather than withdrawing from or failing the course.

REFERENCES

Alvarez, D. M., Blair, K., Monske, E., & Wolf, A. (2005). Team models in online course development: A unit-specific approach. *Educational Technology & Society, 8*(3), 176–186.

Attewell, P., Lavin, D., Domina, T., & Levey, T. (2006). New evidence on college remediation. *The Journal of Higher Education, 77*(5), 886–924.

Bailey, T., Jaggars, S. S., & Cho, S.-W. (2010, February). *Exploring the gap between developmental education referral and enrollment.* Paper presented at the Achieving the Dream Strategy Institute, Charlotte, NC.

Bailey, T., Jeong, D. W., & Cho, S.-W. (2010). Referral, enrollment, and completion in developmental education sequences in community colleges. *Economics of Education Review, 29*(2), 255–270.

Bambara, C. S., Harbour, C. P., Davies, T. G., & Athey, S. (2009). Delicate engagement: The lived experience of community college students enrolled in high-risk online courses. *Community College Review, 36*(3), 219–238.

Blackner, D. M. (2000). *Prediction of community college students' success in developmental math with traditional classroom, computer-based on-campus and computer-based at a distance instruction using locus of control, math anxiety and learning style* (Unpublished doctoral dissertation). University of North Texas, Denton, TX. Available from ProQuest Dissertations and Theses database. (UMI No. 3064379)

Boston, W., Diaz, S. R., Gibson, A. M., Ice, P., Richardson, J., & Swan, K. (2009). An exploration of the relationship between indicators of the community of inquiry framework and retention in online programs. *Journal of Asynchronous Learning Networks, 13*(3), 67–83.

Carpenter, T. G., Brown, W. L., & Hickman, R. C. (2004). Influences of online delivery on developmental writing outcomes. *Journal of Developmental Education, 28*(1), 14–18.

Chambers, T. E. (2002). *Internet course student achievement: In Ohio's two-year community and technical colleges, are online courses less effective than traditional courses?* (Unpublished doctoral dissertation). Bowling Green State University, Bowling Green, OH. Available from ProQuest Dissertations and Theses database. (UMI No. 3079264)

Choy, S. (2001). Essay: Students whose parents did not go to college: Postsecondary access, persistence, and attainment. In *The Condition of Education, 2001*, Washington, DC: U.S. Department of Education, National Center for Education Statistics.

Cox, R. D. (2005). Online education as institutional myth: Rituals and realities at community colleges. *Teachers College Record, 107*(8), 1754–1787.

Davis, D. E. (2007). *Best of both worlds: Do hybrid courses have better outcomes than distance only courses in the North Carolina community college system?* (Unpublished doctoral dissertation). North Carolina State University, Raleigh, NC. Available from ProQuest Dissertations and Theses database. (UMI No. 3279320).

El Mansour, B., & Mupinga, D. M. (2007). Students' positive and negative experiences in hybrid and online classes. *College Student Journal, 41*(1), 242–248.

Fontaine, G. (2010). Presence in "Teleland." In K. E. Rudestam & J. Schoenholtz-Read (Eds.), *Handbook of online learning: Innovations in higher education and corporate training* (2nd ed., pp. 30–56). Thousand Oaks, CA: Sage.

Garrison, D. R., Anderson, T., & Archer, W. (2003). A theory of critical inquiry in online distance education. In M. G. Moore & W. G. Anderson (Eds.), *Handbook of distance education* (pp. 113–127). Mahwah, NJ: Erlbaum.

Green, K. (2010). *Managing online education.* Encino, CA: The Campus Computing Project. Retrieved from http://www.campuscomputing.net/sites/www.campuscomputing.net/files/ManagingOnlineEd2010-Exec-SummaryGraphics.pdf

Grubb, W. N. (with Worthen, H., Byrd, B., Webb, E., Badway, N., Case, C., Goto, S., & Villeneuve, J. C.) (1999). *Honored but invisible: An inside look at teaching in community colleges.* New York, NY: Routledge.

Grubb, W. N. (2010, September). *The quandaries of basic skills: Views from the classroom.* Paper presented at the National Center for Postsecondary Research Developmental Education Conference, New York, NY.

Gunawardena, C. N., & Zittle, F. J. (1997). Social presence as a predictor of satisfaction within a computer-mediated conferencing environment. *American Journal of Distance Education, 11*(3), 8–26.

Hannafin, M., Hill, J. R., Oliver, K., Glazer, E., & Sharma, P. (2003). Cognitive and learning factors in web-based distance learning environments. In M. G. Moore & W. G. Anderson (Eds.), *Handbook of distance education* (pp. 245–260). Mahwah, NJ: Erlbaum.

Hara, N., & Kling, R. (1999). Students' frustrations with a web-based distance education course. *First Monday, 4*(12). Retrieved from http://firstmonday.org/htbin/cgiwrap/bin/ojs/index.php/fm/article/view/710/620

Harlee, D. G. (2006). Student success in traditional and distance learning courses: A comparative analysis of technical college undergraduates in South Carolina (Unpublished doctoral dissertation). Capella University, Minneapolis, MN. Available from ProQuest Dissertations and Theses database. (UMI No. 3226237)

Hawkes, M., & Coldeway, D. O. (2002). An analysis of team vs. faculty-based online course development: Implications for instructional design. *The Quarterly Review of Distance Education, 3*(4), 431–441.

Hixon, E. (2008). Team-based online course development: A case study of collaboration models. *Online Journal of Distance Learning Administration, 11*(4). Retrieved from http://www.westga.edu/~distance/ojdla/

Howell, S. L., Laws, R. D., & Lindsay, N. K. (2004). Reevaluating course completion in distance education. *Quarterly Review of Distance Education, 5*(4), 243–252.

Hurt, J. (2008). The advantages and disadvantages of teaching and learning on-line. *Delta Kappa Gamma Bulletin, 74*(4), 5–11.

Hyllegard, D., Heping, D., & Hunter, C. (2008). Why do students leave online courses? Attrition in community college distance learning courses. *International Journal of Instructional Media, 35*(4), 429–434.

Ice, P. (2009). *Using the Community of Inquiry Framework survey for multi-level institutional evaluation and continuous quality improvement* [Sloan-C 2009 Effective Practice Award winner, website description]. Retrieved from http://sloanconsortium.org/

Instructional Technology Council. (2010). *Distance education survey results: Trends in eLearning: Tracking the impact of eLearning at community colleges.* Washington, DC: Author.

Jaggars, S. S., & Bailey, T. (2010). *Effectiveness of fully online courses for college students: Response to a Department of Education meta-analysis.* New York, NY: Columbia University, Teachers College, Community College Research Center.

Jaggars, S. S., & Xu, D. (2010). *Online learning in the Virginia community college system.* New York, NY: Columbia University, Teachers College, Community College Research Center.

Jaggars, S. S. (2012, April). *Beyond Flexibility: Why students choose online courses in community college.* Paper presented at the 2012 Annual Meeting of the American Educational Research Association, Vancouver, BC.

Jenkins, D. (2011). *Redesigning community colleges for completion: Lessons from research on high performance organizations* (CCRC Working Paper No. 24, Assessment of Evidence Series). New York, NY: Columbia University, Teachers College, Community College Research Center.

Karp, M. M. (2011). Toward a new understanding of non-academic student support: Four mechanisms encouraging positive student outcomes in the community college (CCRC Working Paper No. 28, Assessment of Evidence Series). New York, NY: Columbia University, Teachers College, Community College Research Center.

Kleinman, J. N., & Entin, E. B. (2002). Comparison of in-class and distance-learning students' performance and attitudes in an introductory computer science course. *Journal of Computing Sciences in Colleges, 17*(6), 206–219.

Knowles, E., & Kalata, K. (2007). A model for enhancing online course development. *Innovate, 4*(2). Retrieved from http://www.innovateonline.info/pdf/vol4_issue2/A_Model_for_Enhancing_Online_Course_Development.pdf

Lareau, A. (2003). *Unequal childhoods: Class, race, and family life* (1st ed.). Berkeley, CA: University of California Press.

Liu, S. Y., Gomez, J., & Yen, C.-J. (2009). Community college online course retention and final grade: Predictability of social presence. *Journal of Interactive Online Learning, 8*(2), 165–182.

Millward, J. (2008). An analysis of the national "TYCA Research Initiative Survey Section III: Technology and Pedagogy" in two-year college English programs. *Teaching English in the Two Year College, 35*(4), 372–398.

Moore, M. G., & Kearsley, G. (2004). *Distance education: A systems view* (2nd ed.) Belmont, CA: Wadsworth.

Mullins, M. M. (2007). Community colleges. In M. G. Moore & W. G. Anderson (Eds.), *Handbook of distance education* (2nd ed., pp. 491–500). Mahwah, NJ: Erlbaum.

Mupinga, D. M., Nora, R. T., & Yaw, D. C. (2006). The learning styles, expectations, and needs of online students. *College Teaching, 54*(1), 185–189.

Musgrove, A. T. (2002). *An examination of the Kolb LSI and GEFT and their relationship to academic achievement in web-based and face-to-face nursing courses* (Unpublished doctoral dissertation). Florida Atlantic University. Available at ProQuest Dissertations & Theses database. (UMI No. 3055363)

Navarro, P., & Shoemaker, J. (2000). Performance and perceptions of distance learners in cyberspace. *American Journal of Distance Education, 14*(2), 15–35.

Pagliari, L., Batts, D., & McFadden, C. (2009). Desired versus actual training for online instructors in community colleges. *Online Journal of Distance Learning Administration, 12*(4). Retrieved from http://www.westga.edu/~distance/ojdla/winter124/pagliari124.html

Parsad, B., & Lewis, L. (2008). *Distance education at degree-granting postsecondary institutions: 2006-07. First look.* (NCES 2009-044). Washington, DC: U.S. Department of Education, Institute of Education Sciences, National Center for Education Statistics.

Pascarella, E. T., Pierson, C. T., Wolniak. G. C., & Terenzini, P. T. (2004). First-generation college students: Additional evidence on college experiences and outcomes. *The Journal of Higher Education, 75*(3), 249–284.

Picciano, A. G. (2002). Beyond student perceptions: Issues of interaction, presence, and performance in an online course. *Journal of Asynchronous Learning Networks, 6*(1), 21–40.

Puzziferro, M., & Shelton, K. (2008). A model for developing high-quality online courses: Integrating a systems approach with learning theory. *Journal of Asynchronous Learning Networks, 12*(3–4), 119–136.

Radford, A. W. (2011). *Learning at a distance: Undergraduate enrollment in distance education courses and degree programs.* Washington DC: U.S. Department of Education, National Center for Education Statistics.

Rainie, L. (2010). *Internet, broadband, and cell phone statistics.* Washington, DC: Pew Internet. Retrieved from http://pewinternet.org/Reports/2010/Internet-broadband-and-cell-phone-statistics.aspx

Rainie, L., Estabrook, L., & Witt, E. (2007). *Information searches that solve problems.* Washington, DC: Pew Internet.

Richardson, J. C., & Swan, K. (2003). Examining social presence in online courses in relation to students' perceived learning and satisfaction. *Journal of Asynchronous Learning Networks, 7*(1), 68–88.

Rivera, J. C., McAlister, M. K., & Rice, M. L. (2002). A comparison of student outcomes and satisfaction between traditional and web based course offerings. *Online Journal of Distance Learning Administration, 5*(3). Retrieved from http://www.westga.edu/~distance/ojdla/fall53/rivera53.html

Rosenbaum, J. E., Deil-Amen, R., & Person, A. E. (2006). *After admission: From college access to college success.* New York, NY: Russell Sage.

Rosenfeld, G. (2005). *A comparison of the outcomes of distance learning students versus traditional classroom students in the community college* (Unpublished doctoral dissertation). Florida Atlantic University. Available at ProQuest Dissertations and Theses database. (UMI No. 3173536)

Scott-Clayton, J. (2011). *The shapeless river: Does a lack of structure inhibit students' progress at community colleges?* (CCRC Working Paper No. 25, Assessment of Evidence Series). New York, NY: Columbia University, Teachers College, Community College Research Center.

Summerlin, J. A. (2003). *A comparison of the effectiveness of off-line Internet and traditional classroom remediation of mathematical skills* (Unpublished doctoral dissertation). Baylor University, Waco, TX. Available at ProQuest Dissertations and Theses database. (UMI No. 3086388)

Thille, C. (2008). Building open learning as a community-based research activity. In T. Iiyoshi & M. S. V. Kumar (Eds.), *Opening up education: The collective advancement of education through open technology, open content, and open knowledge* (pp. 165–180). Cambridge, MA: MIT Press.

Twigg, C. A. (2003). Improving learning and reducing costs: New models for online learning. *Educause Review, 38*(5), 28–38.

U.S. Department of Education (2011a). *The Condition of Education, 2011,* Table A-39-1. Washington, DC: U.S. Department of Education, National Center for Education Statistics. Retrieved October 18, 2011, from http://nces.ed.gov/programs/coe/current_tables.asp

U.S. Department of Education (2011b). *The Condition of Education, 2011,* Tables A-39-1 and A-45-1 (author's calculations). Washington, DC: U.S. Department of Education, National Center for Education Statistics. Retrieved October 18, 2011, from http://nces.ed.gov/programs/coe/current_tables.asp

Virginia Community College System. (2001). *Virginia community college system organizational strategy for distance learning: Final report.* Richmond, VA: Author.

Wang, L. (2008). Developing and evaluating an interactive multimedia instructional tool: Learning outcomes and user experiences of optometry students. *Journal of Educational Multimedia and Hypermedia, 17*(1), 43–57.

Waschull, S. B. (2001). The online delivery of psychology courses: Attrition, performance, and evaluation. *Teaching of Psychology, 28*(2), 143–147.

Xu, D., & Jaggars, S. S. (2011a). *Online and hybrid course enrollment and performance in Washington State community and technical colleges* (CCRC Working Paper No. 31). New York, NY: Columbia University, Teachers College, Community College Research Center.

Xu, D., & Jaggars, S. S. (2011b). The effectiveness of distance education across Virginia's community colleges: Evidence from introductory college-level math and English courses. *Educational Evaluation and Policy Analysis, 33,* 360–377.

Xu, H., & Morris, L. V. (2007). Collaborative course development for online courses. *Innovative Higher Education, 32*(1), 35–47.

Zavarella, C. A. (2008). *Computer-based instruction and remedial mathematics: A study of student retention at a Florida community college* (Unpublished doctoral dissertation). University of South Florida, Tampa. Available at ProQuest Dissertations and Theses database. (UMI No. 3326039)

38

DISTANCE TRAINING AND EDUCATION IN THE CORPORATE SECTOR

ZANE L. BERGE[1]

One way to view management's role is that managers must constantly align and realign the strategic plan of the organization so that mission-critical functions match the core capabilities and core competencies of the enterprise. If we begin to analyze this statement, we find several concepts that need to be explored: *strategic plan, mission-critical functions, core capabilities,* and *core competencies.* Distance education forces managers to think of each of these in new ways. Even how strategic planning is accomplished successfully in the global economy of the 21st century is different from in the past.

Managers and leaders who are charged with distance training and education functions decide on what courses and programs to produce and what media/infrastructure will be used to implement these programs. Their decisions are guided by organizational mission and business needs, usually determined by market research or policy (Berge, 2001; Berge & Giles, 2008; Berge & Kearsley, 2003). This means aligning *projects and programs* that involve distance training and education activities with *strategic plans.* Said simply, managers are using distance training and education to *solve business problems* through managing and planning (Berge & Smith, 2000; also see Kearsley, Chapter 26, this volume). That having been said, we are only beginning to identify in useful ways what the capabilities and competencies are that are needed in distance training and education.

GLOBAL ECONOMY IS CHANGING HOW WE DO BUSINESS

The recent transition from an industrial economy to a knowledge-based economy has companies competing to control intellectual assets, not physical assets (Clerc, 2008; McCrea, Gay, & Bacon, 2000; Napierala, Weiss-Selig, & Berge, 2005; Nyberg, 2011; Seufert, 2001). Over a decade ago (see Table 38.1), some of the main l changes being felt within most larger organizations were identified (Moe, Bailey, & Lau, 1999) and are still true today. With the increased rate at which the amount of information is doubling, it becomes important that the right information reaches the right people when it is needed.

Table 38.1 Shifts in the Economy

Old Economy	New Economy
A Skill	Life-Long Learning
Labor vs. Management	Teams
Business vs. Environment	Encourage Growth
Security	Risk Taking
Monopolies	Competition
Plant, Equipment	Intellectual Property
National	Global
Status Quo	Speed, Change
Top-down	Distributed

Many changes have to do with philosophy, and, in turn, organizational culture. For instance, it used to be that university students could, for the most part, in four years or four years plus graduate work, expect to gain the skills and knowledge necessary to prepare them for a lifetime of work in their chosen field. Of course, today's university educators do not harbor any illusions. Each professor knows that it is increasingly important to teach students how to learn, so that the effects of the ever decreasing half-life of knowledge can be ameliorated with lifelong learning as a goal. The same is true of learners in the workplace:

> A consideration of training at a distance forces a re-examination about the ways people learn and are trained.… Corporate employees in the future will need to take control of their own growth and development, demanding training time and money as part of their rewards for supplying their services. Adult education principles of self-directed and life-long learning will become a major part of compensation packages. Collective bargaining agreements in the future will probably require levels of training for employees that do not exist today. Companies desiring a competitive advantage will "jump on the band wagon" and establish policies and procedures to take advantage of distance learning to deliver these services … The rapidly changing workplace of the future will demand that trainers move toward this vision with a spirit of adventure. Training professionals at all levels will need considerable imagination, common sense and creativity to cope with the changes that undoubtedly await us. Corporate success depends upon having and keeping talented people. The shortage of such people is widely accepted, and training (including distance education), at long last, is beginning to be recognized as part of the solution. (Dooley, Dooley, & Byrom, 1998, p. 353)

Along with these changes in how training and education is perceived, are cultural changes throughout the organization and the people associated with it (see Table 38.2). For instance, as more employees have technology systems at home and as pressure increases for individuals to take control of their own learning throughout their lifetime, there can be a blurring of the distinction between what is learning and what is work (Berge et al., 2005; Takiya, Archbold, & Berge, 2005).

Employees know that they must continuously learn or will be at a competitive disadvantage in the marketplace, and therefore demand the organization support their

Table 38.2   Shifts in Training

Old Economy	New Economy
Four-Year Degree	Forty-Year Degree
Training as Cost Center	Training as Competitive Advantage
Learner Mobility	Content Mobility
Correspondence & Video	High-tech Multimedia Centers
One-Size Fits All	Tailored Programs
Just-in-Case	Just-in-Time
Isolated learners and learning events	On-going virtual learning communities

learning. McCrea et al. (2000) state that management's mission is to develop an "enterprise-wide process of continuous and globally distributed learning that directly links business goals and individual learning outcomes" (p. 16). While the concept of "just enough" training may be useful (Zielinski, 2000), there is no such thing as just enough learning.

BUSINESS NEEDS FOR DISTANCE TRAINING AND EDUCATION

Training resources need to be used to accomplish the organization's strategic objectives. The usual approach, however, is for the various areas of an organization to look at the training function *after* the goals, objectives, and plans are in place. Essentially, business units or departments place their "orders" for training. This approach often leaves the training function scrambling for time and resources. This situation almost always results in a training function that cannot provide all the services requested of it, with those services that are supplied often being ineffective. Thus, training must provide its support with the constraints of a budget that has little relationship to need (Brace & Berge, 2006).

Having a strategy that links distance training and education to the organization's business goals is important (Galagan, 2000; Watkins, Kaufman, & Odunlami, Chapter 28, this volume). There are compelling reasons for distance training and education in the workplace. Needs for which organizations are turning to distance training to help solve business problems involve cost reduction—such things as reducing time to market, travel expenditures, time spent in training; and lower opportunity costs of lost productivity. But in addition to cost reduction, distance training and education can also increase effectiveness and efficiency in ways that may not reduce costs directly, but are necessary to meet mission-critical functions of the organization. Some of these will be discussed below in a section called "Key Business Drivers."

Significant Business Needs

Essentially, one can view distance training serving three significant business needs:

- meeting the challenge of uncommon organizational change
- sustaining competitive advantage
- achieving organizational goals

It cannot be emphasized too strongly that in the global economy today, distance training and education must solve *critical business needs* for it to be sustainable in the organization.

Meeting the Challenge of Uncommon Organizational Change. Short of bankruptcy, there may be no business event that serves as a more imperative catalyst for change than a corporate merger. The cultural context in which people work is made clear when a merger juxtaposes different cultures and challenges everyone to change and grow. For example, Friend and Hepple (2001) described the merging of SBC Communications with AT&T and the affect on their regional telecom training centers:

> Working across time zones with widely varying systems, practices, and cultures challenged the merged SBC. Eliminating redundancies resulted in savings for the CFL (Center for Learning) and its SBC internal clients. However, staffing varied continuously through restructuring, job changes, outsourcing, and new hiring. As employee experience levels fluctuated, the need for faster, more effective, and flexible training had never been greater. (p. 52)

Another type of tumultuous change can come from a mandate—whether from a government authority or from the organization's chief executive. The cultural and organizational changes necessary to deal with these events are one of the principal reasons distance education has found success in meeting training and educational needs within many organizations.

Sustaining Competitive Advantage. In the middle of this Knowledge Age, the economy requires a continuously learning workforce. Rapid technological change and a core of knowledge workers who must stay abreast of these changes are considered key to sustaining a competitive advantage in the workplace. As organizations invest in building learning systems that serve the individual and the corporation for success in our new economy, distance training and education help meet the challenge of their competition and set the standards in the marketplace. An example is Motorola University. With a globally dispersed workforce and clientele, and sparse subject-matter experts in high demand, distance training programs were an immediate step in Motorola's development of human capital. Motorola eliminated time constraints and travel regarding training and education. This allowed them a competitive advantage over many of their competitors (Wiggenhorn, 2007).

Achieving Organizational Toals. As the global economy changes the way business is transacted and as technology is a contributing factor to change, the competition for markets and customers continues to be a significant challenge. Distance training and education is looked upon as a way of investing in people throughout the organization. Not only does this make a smarter, faster, and more efficient workforce, but it generally produces a happier one as well. Providing educational support and training for employees is one way of showing that management cares, and at the same time it increases workers' performance, motivation, and morale (Anonymous, 2010). In the end, this type of investment in human capital reduces staff turnover, extends retention rates, and thereby adds value in the achievement of organizational goals.

Key Business Drivers

The key drivers affecting the business unit using distance training and education include: (a) reducing direct costs to the employer as mentioned above; (b) lack of time for trainees and trainers; (c) the fast-paced and quickly changing industries, with rapid development-to-delivery cycles, which does not allow a window for training; (d) developing training for high volumes of employees; (e) access to training for employees who are spread across a geographically diverse area; (f) maintain consistency of quality training throughout the organization: and (g) the need to become a learning organization.

Cost to Employer. Many times, there are high costs to the organization associated with having a majority of training delivered in the traditional classroom. If trainers are not on-site, line managers must fund travel budgets and assume the loss of productivity for travel time for participants. With traditional training methods, companies generally spend more money, up to two-thirds of the training expenses, on transporting and housing trainees rather than on actual training programs (Mottl, 2000; Urdan & Weggen, 2000). Alternatives include outsourcing or having a trainer travel to each site. Other alternatives include having trainers travel to participants and therefore potentially reduce the overall corporations training cost. According to *Training Magazine's* (2011) Industry Report, technology is a force in training. While this survey includes only United States firms, approximately 22% of training hours were delivered via online or computer-based technologies—fairly stable from the previous year. An additional 1.3% of training hours were delivered via social networking or mobile devices (down from 7.2% the previous year). To the extent distance education and training increases, some of the direct costs mentioned here can be reduced, albeit other problems may increase.

Lack of Time for Trainees. While cost is a major issue for the organization, the lack of time is a critical factor for the employees. Time to attend to personal technical skill development, while concurrently needing to attend to business deliverables that are on rapid development-to-delivery cycles, often seems impossible to everyone concerned (Branch, Lyon, & Porten, 2001).

Rapid Development-to-Delivery Cycles. By the time training is designed, developed, and scheduled, the employee may no longer need it. As competition and demand in today's society cause more rapid development-to-delivery cycles, there is a smaller window for training to occur with each of those products and services (Dobbs, 2000). Latten, Davis, and Stallings (2001) explained:

> Our client base was quickly surpassing the existing training infrastructure. Mergers and organizational changes were creating an environment where key business decisions were being made faster than ever. The result, an increased demand for training as a result of new business strategies and processes. The need for training to reach growing numbers of participants, faster and in their place of business was at an all time high. We knew that traditional classroom training was not a possible solution for meeting the current business challenges. Both cost and reduced cycle times were obstacles that traditional classroom training could not easily address. (p. 164)

In many cases, learning opportunities have to be modular, just-in-time, and highly relevant to compete with other tasks and opportunities that are critical to the success of the organization (Rogers & Becker, 2001). Many organizations face mergers, mandates, and increased business from other sources to the point that new initiatives occur faster than ever. As project timelines accelerate to meet the growing demands, the impact on training is there is less time to build trainer expertise and less time to reach larger numbers of participants (Latten et al., 2001).

High Volumes of Employees. Large organizations are especially challenged in providing training, in trying to reduce costs with limited resources, and in providing a consistent message. Training at national or regional facilities becomes impossible when thousands or hundreds of thousands of employees need to be trained uniformly very quickly (Wankel, 2001).

Training Employees Who are Spread across a Geographically Diverse Area. When there are a great number of employees to train, and especially when they are dispersed geographically, equitable training delivery is difficult and costly.

Distance training and education usually makes economic sense and can also make sense in these cases by making training content available in convenient, adult-sized bites, rather than in week-long sessions at remote locations. Persons charged with training can target specific audiences, regardless of geographic location, or make subject matter experts available based on need rather than ease of access to location (Dessinger & Conley, 2001; Walker, 1998).

Reduced Training Budgets at a Time When More Training is Needed. Budgets continue to be squeezed and managers are required to do more with less. Payne and Payne (1998) described such a scenario at the Federal Aviation Administration:

> The FAA's technical training budget was cut by Congress from over $135M in 1992 to just over $77M in 1996, a 43% decline (Federal Aviation Administration, 1997). This dramatic reduction in the training budget resulted in the number of FAA students receiving technical training declining from over 28,000 to just over 16,000, a corresponding drop of 41% (Federal Aviation Administration, 1997). A congressional mandate during this same period caused the FAA to go through a downsizing activity that reduced the size of the agency by 11%. This downsizing asked fewer FAA employees to do more during an era of a severely constrained and a continually declining training budget as the mission of the Agency did not change. The problem the FAA faced was finding ways to reduce the overall cost of providing training while increasing the training opportunities for employees. The FAA needed to solve this problem in a manner that was not prohibitively expensive in its start-up costs and that could begin to show a return on the investment almost immediately. (p. 202)

This type of phenomenon is more common each day.

Need to Become a Learning Organization. As mentioned earlier, university professors know they cannot teach all that students will need to know in a field for a lifetime. Many workplace organizations are starting to understand that the same thing is true about training. This is why Peter Senge's work regarding becoming a "learning organizations" resonated as it has (Senge, 1990; Zemke, 1999). At the heart of the learning organization is a change in philosophy—from instruction and training to learning—and a key element in distance training is the students taking responsibility for their own learning. Workers who neglect to invest in their own intellectual capital do so at their own risk, given they can no longer rely on a single set of skills for a lifetime of work (Ruttenbur, Spickler, & Lurie, 2000). So, employees today demand that organizations make a continuous investment in their professional development (McCrea et al., 2000, p. 11). All this significantly changes the roles and functions of both instructors and learners.

Planning and Managing Distance Training and Education

The challenge of planning and implementing distance education programs includes both pedagogical changes and organizational issues. The management team must systematically analyze organizational needs. The team must include at least one person to champion technology-enhanced learning, who has high enough rank and who is at the level in the organization that can match learning goals with the strategic goals for the business unit. The team must also have a person or persons in charge of infrastructure and support services, and other managers and staff with a stake in promoting successful technology-enhanced learning. The charge to this management team may include the following:

- identify the business purposes and goals of initiating and supporting a distance learning program;
- collect and summarize information on current distance education programs and the strategic plans of various business units considering the use of distance training and education;
- evaluate strategies and technologies for delivering distance education programs (advantages, disadvantages, costs) and reach agreement on which strategies and technologies will be proposed;
- define what is needed to deliver technology-enhanced learning programs effectively including equipment and facilities; competencies and training; policy development and culture change;
- investigate successful models at other organizations;
- specify needs and incentives for instructors, designers, and developers who become involved in developing and implementing technology-enhanced learning;
- estimate costs and resource commitments;
- identify potential barriers to successful implementation of the recommended strategies and technologies and suggest how to manage these;
- establish a process for at least annual review of new technologies and other aspects of the distance programs to assess their potential for improving the delivery of distance training and reducing associated costs;
- report findings and recommendations to senior decision-makers; define needs for particular academic programs (Berge & Schrum, 1998).

Obstacles To Distance Training and Education

There are many individual barriers to distance training and education (Berge & Kendrick, 2005). Based on survey responses, a subsequent factor analysis clustered 64 barriers into the following 10 factors: (a) administrative structure, (b) organizational change, (c) technical expertise, (d) social interaction and quality, (e) faculty compensation and time, (f) threatened by technology, (g) legal issues, (h) evaluation/effectiveness, (i) access, and, (j0) student support services (Muilenburg & Berge, 2001).

Administrative Structure. Lack of credibility for distance education within a particular administrative structure, and lack of money, can be problems for distance education. Competing with, or using, new business models can cause difficulties, too. When partnerships are formed among different units within an organization, or among different organizations, lack of agreement concerning such issues as revenue sharing, regulations, tuition and fees, as well as scheduling, FTEs (full-time equivalents), and issuance of credits can become obstacles to distance education.

Organizational Change. Most organizations are resistant to change. Without a shared vision for distance learning, a strategic plan, and key players within the organization who are knowledgeable and supportive of distance learning, implementing a distance learning program is a slow and difficult process. Difficulty in convincing stakeholders of the benefits of distance learning, the often slow pace of implementation, or the lack of an identifiable business need are all barriers to distance education.

The difficulty is not in converting training material into an electronic format, but in trying to change corporate traditions and attitudes (Dooley et al., 1998, p. 353).

Technical Expertise, Support, and Infrastructure. It is difficult to keep up with the fast pace of technological change. Many instructors lack the knowledge and skills to design and teach distance learning courses, yet their organizations lack support staff to assist with technical problems, to develop distance learning course materials, or to provide distance learning training. The technology-enhanced classrooms or laboratories and the infrastructure required to use them may not be available.

Social Interaction and Quality. Participants in distance learning courses can feel isolated due to lack of person-to-person contact. Some educators and students are uncomfortable with the use of student-centered and collaborative learning activities on philosophical grounds, or because these methods are usually a change from the traditional social structure of the classroom. There are concerns about the quality of distance learning courses, programs, the possible lack of prerequisite skills and knowledge of students, and student learning. The outcomes of student learning in distance education, as well as the testing and assessment of student outcomes, are concerns.

Faculty Compensation and Time. In all stages of design, development, and evaluation, distance education courses almost always require a greater time commitment than the same instructional objectives or goals when using an in-person classroom. Therefore, faculty compensation, incentives, workload, and release time become important issues if the system in use assumes traditional, in-person classrooms. Lack of grants to fund distance learning projects is also a problem.

Threatened by Technology. Some people fear that an increase in the use of distance learning technologies may decrease the need for teaching faculty. Feeling intimidated by technology may also threaten an instructor's sense of competence or authority. Either or both of these psychological factors may lead a person to feel that their job security is threatened.

> Trainers (line evaluators, contractors, and Institute staff) perceived their classroom days were over. They had relished the role of "sage on the stage" and were reluctant to relinquish that gratifying identity. With technology perceived as the "enemy" in human interaction and spontaneity, many felt the joys of interacting with peers and colleagues would rapidly decline in this new medium reminiscent of the "high tech, low touch" theory. They struggled to envision the possibilities of building positive educational relationships online or through video conferencing. (Longnecker, 2001)

Legal Issues. The increasing use of the Internet to deliver distance learning raises concerns about copyright, fair use policies, intellectual property rights, and other legal issues such as piracy, problems with hackers, and viruses.

Evaluation/Effectiveness. There is concern over a lack of research supporting the effectiveness of distance learning as well as a lack of effective evaluation methods for distance learning courses and programs.

Access. Many students lack access or there are concerns over equal access to courses offered via technologies such as Web-based instruction. Instructors also lack access to the necessary equipment and courses.

Student Support Services. Provision of student services such as advisement, library services, admissions and financial aid is a critical facet of any distance learning program. There are also concerns about how to monitor the identity of distance learning students.

Stages of Organizational Capability

When considering the distance delivery of training and education and viewing the organization collectively, it is useful to think of the enterprises' current "stage." As with any innovation, the process usually looks like "two steps forward and one back."

> The promise of distance learning remains unfulfilled in many organizations. In spite of many good intentions, extensive pilots and trials, and a great deal of perception building efforts, these organizations fail to recognize some key planning and implementation steps that can make the difference in 'Sustaining Distance Learning'. (Howard, 2001, p. 270)

A brief model that described stages of organizational maturity, or capabilities, with regard to the delivery of distance training and education (Schreiber, 1998) was presented:

- Stage 1: Separate or sporadic distance learning events occur in the organization.
- Stage 2: The organization's technological capability and infrastructure can support distance learning events. When distance education events occur, they are replicated through an interdisciplinary team which responds to staff and management needs and makes recommendations regarding the organization and management of distance learning among the workforce.

- Stage 3: The organization has established a distance learning policy, procedures are in place and planning occurs. This means that a stable and predictable process is in place to facilitate the identification and selection of content and of technology to deliver distance training.
- Stage 4: Distance training and education has been institutionalized in the organization as characterized by policy, communication, and practice that are aligned so that business objectives are being addressed. The business unit has established a distance education identity and conducts systematic assessment of distance training events from an organizational perspective.

Of course, these stages represent points along a continuum; the capability stages an organization moves through if planning to institutionalize distance training and education, are neither linear nor discrete. While it is convenient to describe an organization as generally being at a particular stage, this does not mean the absence of all elements from earlier stages, nor does it mean that all units within the organization are at that same stage.

In general, success early in Stage 1 is characterized by the use of effective project management processes. Later, in late Stage 1 and in Stage 2, the emphasis shifts to *program* management. In late Stage 2 and Stage 3, along with the continuation of program management, a good amount of organizational development and the cultural change efforts are necessary to sustain distance training and education implementation and use at the organizational level. Stage 4 in an organization's distance delivery capability relies on effective strategic planning to guide cultural change and resource reallocation for success and on the ability to link program planning and perspectives to organizational strategic planning and perspectives. Keep in mind that there are often two levels of analyses. There are activities, processes, and work at the program level, such as evaluation and marketing. There are also these same functions at a higher, organizational level.

Excessive problems arise when the implementation of distance education exceeds the level of organizational core capabilities and core competencies to support those activities—that is, when there is a lack of strategic and tactical planning.

SUMMARY OF THE STAGES OF ORGANIZATIONAL CAPABILITY

Not all organizations, perhaps not even most organizations, should consistently strive toward a goal of achieving a higher stage of technology use or the highest stage of integrating distance education as part of the way business is conducted. There is nothing wrong with an organization's distance training and education being a series of events, or one or more separate programs. Program implementation initially relies on sound project management, and, regardless of whether the organization changes to a more integrated stage of distance training or not, solid program planning and management will always continue to be a key to effective and efficient program presentation. What matters most is that the appropriate level of capability for distance education is strategically planned for at the respective organizational level, and that the allocation of resources matches that level of capability.

Linking the Organizational Perspective with Distance Training Programs

Strategic planning consists of all the means that an organization can use to redefine itself and to realize a plan (see Watkins et al., Chapter 28, this volume). Since the fundamental objective of a strategic plan is to chart a course from where the organization is now to where it wants to be at an agreed point in the future (i.e., at the end of the planning cycle), knowing a particular stage of organizational capability would be useful to identify common barriers to implementation of distance training and education at that level along the continuum.

The overarching goal of strategic planning is to cause a common vision of the desired future within the organization, with performance objectives integrated into operations and strategies, and with training—providing those involved with the skills to contribute (Watkins & Callahan, 1998). One way to view such planning is as a systematic way of identifying and capitalizing on the strengths within the enterprise. At the same time, planning is done to identify and provide for the needs of the organization, a part of this is overcoming barriers that are obstacles to the organization. Serious consideration must be given to the critical issues (core competencies and core capabilities) and barriers (both perceived and real) that will be confronted when implementing distance training and education within the organization.

There are a variety of strategic planning models that have been described for business, non-profit, and educational organizations (see, for example, Bean, 1993; Burkhart & Reuss, 1993; Cafferella, 1994; Goodstein, Nolan, & Pfeiffer, 1992). Regardless of the particular model or process an organization uses for such planning, major issues that must be planned for include: educational process, student recruitment and enrollment management, higher education development and student development services, human resources, research, information, physical planning and development, financial management & planning, development, national role, collaboration, and institutional culture (Howell, Williams, & Lindsay, 2003; Lion & Stark, 2010; Meyer & Barefield, 2010). Strategic planning is not defined by a methodology, a process or a system but from the entire context and system in which strategic planning occurs.

> [Strategic planning] could be considered a concerted effort to achieve an ensemble of decisions and actions which form and guide an organization to be what it is, to do what it does and to know why it does it (Bean, 1993). By utilizing a future-looking approach, strategic planning emphasizes the future implications of decisions made in the present. (Hache, 1998)

With a clear vision of the future of the organization, strategic planning is used to create and define the environment—with its boundaries and parameters—in which distance training and organizational learning will take place. The idea is to create a mission and objectives, gather extensive data, analyze and diagnose information regarding the internal and external environment, and decide on the strategies, actions, and evaluations that have as high a possibility of success in implementation, while avoiding expensive pitfalls (Albrecht & Bardsley, 1994).

The tools used to link strategic planning to program management include: communication systems and management of those systems, budgeting, infrastructure, workforce development, and revisions to policies and procedures (see Figure 38.1).

PROGRAM PERSPECTIVE		ORGANIZATIONAL PERSPECTIVE
PROJECT/PROGRAM MANAGEMENT	TOOLS FOR CHANGE	STRATEGIC PLANNING
EXERCISING PROFESSIONAL RESPONSIBILITY	BUDGET	INTEGRATION WITH THE ORGANIZATIONAL MISSION AND VISION
	INFRASTRUCTURE	
ENGAGING RELEVANT CONTEXTS		GUIDING BELIEFS/PRINCIPLES
	COMMUNICATION	
DESIGNING THE PROGRAM		EXTERNAL ENVIRONMENTAL SCAN
	WORKFORCE DEVELOPMENT	
		INTERNAL ORGANIZATIONAL STRENGTHS
MANAGING ADMINISTRATIVE ASPECTS	POLICY	

Figure 38.1 Linking the program perspective with an organizational perspective: Using project and program management, tools for change, and strategic planning.

Communication

Distance training and education depends on the marriage of computer and communication *systems*. It should be managed as a system, in which the communication aspect of the technologies is emphasized. The technologies typically used in corporate, distance learning settings emphasize conferencing capabilities, which underscores the communication dynamic that is typically encountered in classroom settings (Wagner, 2000).

Establishing a Budget

The organization must decide what equipment and resources are considered infrastructure and what are considered operational expenses. A review of cost analyses for all distance training programs may show that a program(s) will appear to lose money if technology infrastructure costs are included in the program budget. Still, a program budget, to give a true indication of costs, must cover all areas including support services (e.g., instructional development; registration; materials development), infrastructure, and instructor training and development (Berge & Schrum, 1998). Essentially, the budget and resource allocation issues in distance training and education involve course design or course purchase, course development and delivery, learner support, and administration costs of the program.

Determining Functional Infrastructure

Some infrastructure resources and functions should be common across all distance training, and others are more useful when decentralized across business units or location. While decentralization may appear to unnecessarily duplicate efforts and costs, it may more closely align expertise with program needs. Centralization of services may allow managers of all distance training and education programs more direct access to top decision makers and encourage a more efficient use of resources. The risk is in overburdening specific programs with bureaucracy and overhead, while not meeting specific program needs. Generally, centralization is favored for the following functions: marketing, instructional design and development support, technology help desk and infrastructure, professional/faculty development, evaluation, promotion and incentive structures, and registration.

Workforce Development

It is hard to imagine anything more important to program implementation than recruiting and retaining expert trainers and support staff. Are all instructors equally suited to teach in distance training and education programs? The answer is generally, "No." Would it be wise to begin with a small cohort of willing trainers? If time and energy are spent in training this cohort, and it is given support for its development and implementation, its successes will often inspire others.

In some organizations an initial group of enthusiastic instructors have been trained in effective distance teaching methods, and the individuals comprising the group then become mentors for the next group of instructors. Ongoing support is given to these instructors through workshops, online discussion groups, and strategic feedback. Occasionally, an instructor works as an apprentice to a practitioner who is teaching a distance course, and the following term is mentored as he or she practices what was learned.

A timeline is helpful to new distance training instructors as they begin to conceptualize their tasks. Answers to the following questions, and the availability of specific training as needed, will go a long way toward retaining new distance instructors. What business needs are being targeted? At what point should the syllabus be in place? What materials need to be developed and tested? Is the hardware and software already in place and functional? What are the options when something goes wrong?

Revising Policies and Procedures

The management team can provide leadership in policy revision and remove barriers to the mainstreaming of distance training and education. Each incentive or disincentive, the reporting and accountability structures, and the determination of major resource allocations have a role in changing the organizational culture. Leadership is required to effectively interpret changes in the social, political, economic, and training/educational environment. Several critical issues unique to program planning for distance training emerge.

Policies and procedures are normally framed within organizational policies or outside mandates. Such policies are tools for leading an organization in ways that are thought by management to be useful—either in defining a vision or orchestrating cultural change within the organization. A key to ensuring that mandates or missions are carried out and that organizational policies are implemented is development of a strategic plan. This plan becomes one of the primary instruments of organizational policy and provides the framework for allocating and managing resources and accommodating organizational change and development (Berge & Schrum, 1998; Khakhar, 2001; Pisel, 2008; Riza, 2007).

CONCLUSIONS

In the global economy of the 21st century, learning organizations are under increasing pressure to show training and development are directly contributing to the profitability of the organization. This must be done at a time when employees are often scattered around the world, and when the expense of bringing learners to a central location and keeping them from their job for extended periods of time is no long an option, both from a cost perspective and from a time-to-market standpoint. This chapter focused on the organizational perspective with a few hints of dramatic changes to the roles and functions of instructors and learners.

Distance training and education is an important part of increasing performance in the workplace. To remain competitive, more emphasis will have to be placed on distance learning. It is through sound management and planning that distance training and education can effectively and efficiently meet the business needs of the organization.

NOTE

1. I wish to thank Liz Huegelmeyer for her help in editing this version of the chapter.

REFERENCES

Albrecht, R., & Bardsley, G. (1994). Strategic planning and academic planning for distance education. In Barry Willis (Ed.), *Distance Education: Strategies and Tools* (pp. 67–86), Englewood Cliffs, NJ: Educational Technology Publications

Anonymous. (2010, December 17). Distance learning success. Retrieved from http://distance-learning-success. blogspot.com/2010/12/investing-in-training-isnt-just-good.html

Bean, W. (1993). *Strategic planning that makes things happen.* Amherst, MA: HRD Press.

Berge, Z. L., & Giles, L. (2008). Strategic planning for e-learning in the workplace. In L. Tomei (Ed.), *Adapting information and communication technologies for effective education* (pp. 257–270). Hershey, PA: IGI Global. doi:10.4018/978-1-59904-922-9.ch020

Berge, Z. L., & Kearsley, G. (2003, November/December). The sustainability of distance training: Follow-up to case studies. *The Technology Source.* Retrieved from http://www.technologysource.org/article/sustainability_of_distance_training/

Berge, Z. L., & Kendrick, A. A. (2005, February). Can interest in distance training be sustained in corporate organizations? *International Journal of Instructional Technology & Distance Learning, 2*(2). Retrieved from http://www.itdl.org/Journal/Feb_05/article05.htm

Berge, Z. L., & Schrum, L. (1998). Strategic planning linked with program implementation for distance education. *CAUSE/EFFECT, 21*(3), 31–38.

Berge, Z. L., & Smith, D. (2000). Implementing corporate distance training using change management, strategic planning, and project management. In L. Lau (Ed.), *Distance learning technologies: Issues, trends and opportunities* (pp. 39–51). Hershey, PA: Idea Group.

Berge, Z. L. (Ed.). (2001). *Sustaining distance training: Integrating learning technologies into the fabric of the enterprise.* San Francisco, CA: Jossey-Bass.

Berge, Z. L., Bichy, C., Grayson, C., Johnson, A., Macadoff, S., & Nee, K. (2005). Where does work end and home life begin? In P. Rogers, C. Howard, J. Boettcher, L. Justice, K. Schenk, & G. Berg (Eds.), *Encyclopedia of distance learning* (pp. 2038–2043). Hershey, PA: Idea Group.

Brace, T., & Berge, Z.L. (2006). Strategic planning for distance training. In M. Khosrow-Pour (Ed.), *Encyclopedia of ecommerce, e-government, and mobile commerce* (pp. 1052–1057). Hershey, PA: Idea Group. doi:10.4018/978-1-59140-799-7.ch169

Branch, A., Lyon, A., & Porten, S. (2001). Hewlett-Packard's regional training center – site information & learning centers (SILC). In Z. L. Berge, (Ed.) *Sustaining distance training: Integrating learning technologies into the fabric of the enterprise* (pp. 235–254). San Francisco, CA: Jossey-Bass.

Burkhart, P. J., & Reuss, S. (1993). *Successful strategic planning: A guide to nonprofit agencies and organizations.* Newbury Park, CA: Sage.

Cafferella, R. S. (1994). *Planning programs for adult learners: A practical guide for educators, trainers and staff developers*. San Francisco, CA: Jossey-Basss.

Clerc, F. (2008, January). From traditional intellectual property to profitable intellectual capital management. Retrieved from http://www.spencerstuart.com/yourcareer/management/1239/

Dessinger, J., & Conley, L. (2001). Beyond the sizzle: Sustaining distance training at ford motor company dealerships. In Z. L. Berge (Ed.) *Sustaining distance training: Integrating learning technologies into the fabric of the enterprise* (pp. 178–198). San Francisco, CA: Jossey-Bass.

Dobbs, K. (2000, June). Who's in charge of e-learning? *Training, 37*(6), 54–58.

Dooley, L.M ., Dooley, K. E., & Byrom, K. (1998). Distance training under construction at H. B. Zachry Company. In D. A. Schreiber & Z. L. Berge (Eds.). *Distance training: How innovative organizations are using technology to maximize learning and meet business objectives* (pp. 351–368). San Francisco, CA: Jossey-Bass.

Federal Aviation Administration. (1997, September). *Survey of educational technology*. Washington, DC: Training Program Office, AHR-14 USA, Department of Transportation.

Friend, N., & Hepple, T. (2001). Lessons from merging SBC's Regional Telecom Learning Centers. In Z. L. Berge (Ed.) *Sustaining distance training: Integrating learning technologies into the fabric of the enterprise* (pp. 48–69). San Francisco, CA: Jossey-Bass.

Galagan, P. A. (2000, May). Getting started with e-learning: An interview with Dell computer's John Cone about pulling the big lever. *Training & Development, 54*(5), 62–64.

Goodstein, L. D., Nolan, T. M., & Pfeiffer, J. W. (1992). *Applied strategic planning: A comprehensive guide*. San Diego, CA: Pfeiffer & Company.

Hache, D. (1998, Summer). Strategic planning of distance education in the age of teleinformatics. *Online Journal of Distance learning Administration, 1*(2). State University of West Georgia, Distance Education Center. Retrieved from http://www.westga.edu/~distance/Hache12.html

Howard, B. (2001). Supporting an enterprise distance learning program at NYNEX. In Z. L. Berge (Ed.) *Sustaining distance training: Integrating learning technologies into the fabric of the enterprise* (pp. 270–290). San Francisco, CA: Jossey-Bass.

Howell, S. L., Williams, P. B., & Lindsay, N. K. (2003). Thirty-two trends affecting distance education: An informed foundation for strategic planning. *Online Journal of Distance Learning Administration*, 6(3), Retrieved from http://www.westga.edu/~distance/ojdla/fall63/howell63.html

Khakhar, D. (2001). *A framework for open distance learning — organization and management*. London, England: Portland Press. Retrieved from http://www.portlandpress.com/pp/books/online/vu/pdf/vu_ch3.pdf

Latten, S., Davis, M., & Stallings, N. (2001). Sustaining distance education and training First Union: Transitioning from the classroom. In Z. L. Berge (Ed.) *Sustaining distance training: Integrating learning technologies into the fabric of the enterprise* (pp. 164–177). San Francisco, CA: Jossey-Bass.

Lion, R. W., & Stark, G. (2010). A glance at institutional support for faculty teaching in an online learning environment. *Educause Quarterly, 33*(3), Retrieved from http://www.educause.edu/EDUCAUSE Quarterly/EDUCAUSEQuarterlyMagazineVolum/AGlanceatInstitutionalSupportf/213685

Longnecker, J. L. (2001). Attracting, training, and retaining instructors for distance learning at the US General Accounting Office. In Z. L. Berge (Ed.) *Sustaining distance training: Integrating learning technologies into the fabric of the enterprise* (pp. 85–105). San Francisco, CA: Jossey-Bass.

McCrea, F., Gay, R. K., & Bacon, R. (2000, January 18). Riding the big waves: A white paper on the B2B e*learning industry. San Francisco, CA: Thomas Weisel Partners.

Meyer, J. D., & Barefield, A. C. (2010). Infrastructure and administrative support for online programs. *Online Journal of Distance Learning Administration*, 8(3), Retrieved from http://www.westga.edu/~distance/ojdla/Fall133/meyer_barfield133.html

Moe, M. T., Bailey, K., & Lau, R. (1999, April 9). *The book of knowledge: Investing in the growing education and training industry* (p. 45). Report #1268. New York, NY: Merrill Lynch & Co., Global Securities Research & Economics Group, Global Fundamental Equity Research Department. .

Mottl, J. N. (2000, January 3). Learn at a distance: Online learning is poised to become the new standard. *InformationWeek Online*. Retrieved from http://www.informationweek.com/767/learn.htm

Muilenburg, L. Y., & Berge. Z. (2001). Barriers to distance education: A factor analytic study. *The American Journal of Distance Education, 15*(2), 7–24.

Napierala, K., Weiss Selig, L., & Berge, Z. L. (2005). The role of training and development in using knowledge networks to build intellectual capital. *Journal of Knowledge Management Practice*. Retrieved from http://www.tlainc.com/articl81.htm

Nyberg, A. (2011, March 11). A challenging transition to the knowledge-based knowledge economy [Web log message]. Retrieved from http://www.cipforum.org/blogs/2011/03/11/a-challenging-transition-to-the-knowledge-based-knowledge-economy

Payne, L. W., & Payne, H. E. (1998). Interactive video teletraining in the Federal Aviation Administration. In D. A. Schreiber & Z. L. Berge (Eds.), *Distance training: How innovative organizations are using technology to maximize learning and meet business objectives* (pp. 201–222). San Francisco, CA: Jossey-Bass.

Pisel, K. P. (2008). A strategic planning process model for distance education. *Online Journal of Distance Learning Administration*, 6(2), Retrieved from http://detaskforce.illinoisstate.edu/downloads/planningprocess-model_000.pdf

Riza, A. (2007). Strategic planning at the state's education institutions serving "open and distance education", which are of nonprofit concern. *Turkish Online Journal of Distance Education*, 8(1). Retrieved from http://tojde.anadolu.edu.tr/tojde25/pdf/article_14.pdf

Rogers, N. E., & Becker, S. L. (2001). From training enhancement to organizational learning: The migration of distance learning at the American Red Cross. In Z. L. Berge (Ed.) *Sustaining distance training: Integrating learning technologies into the fabric of the enterprise* (pp. 329–350). San Francisco, CA: Jossey-Bass.

Ruttenbur, B. W., Spickler, G., & Lurie, S. (2000, July 6). *e-Learning: The engine of the knowledge economy.* New York, NY: Morgan Keegan & Co. Inc.

Schreiber, D. A. (1998). Organizational technology and its impact on distance training. In D. A. Schreiber & Z L. Berge (Eds.), *Distance training: How innovative organizations are using technology to maximize learning and meet business objectives* (pp. 3–18). San Francisco, CA: Jossey-Bass.

Senge, P. M. (1990). *The fifth discipline: The art and practice of the learning organization.* New York, NY: Doubleday.

Seufert S. (2001). E-Learning business models, Strategies, success factors and best practice examples. In R. Defillippi & C. Wankel (Eds.), *Rethinking management education* (pp. 100–124). Greenwich, CT: Information Age.

Takiya, S., Archbold, J., & Berge, Z. L. (2005, April). Flexible training's intrusion on work/life balance. *The Turkish Online Journal of Distance Education*, 6(2). Retrieved from http://tojde.anadolu.edu.tr/tojde18/articles/article5.htm

Training Magazine. (2011, November/December). 2011 training industry report. *Training Magazine, 48*(6), 22–35.

Urdan, T. A., & Weggen, C. C. (2000). *Corporate e-learning: Exploring a new frontier.* San Francisco, CA: W.R. Hambrect and Company. Retrieved from http:// www.spectrainteractive.com/pdfs/CorporateELearingHamrecht.pdf

Wagner, E. D. (2000, Fall). Emerging technology trends in elearning. *Line Zine.* Retrieved from http://www.linezine.com/2.1/features/ewette.htm

Walker, S. (1998). Online training costs and evaluation. In D. A. Schreiber & Z. L. Berge (Eds.), *Distance training: How innovative organizations are using technology to maximize learning and meet business objectives* (pp. 270–286). San Francisco, CA: Jossey-Bass.

Wankel, M.J. (2001). The United States Postal Service's integration of distance training and education initiatives to meet organizational goals. In Z. L. Berge (Ed.) *Sustaining distance training: Integrating learning technologies into the fabric of the enterprise* (pp. 291–311). San Francisco, CA: Jossey-Bass.

Watkins, K., & Callahan, M. (1998). Return on knowledge assets: Rethinking investments in educational technology. *Educational Technology, 38*(4), 33–40.

Wiggenhorn, B. (2007, December 19). Develop a competitive advantage at your own pace. *Fast company.* Retrieved from http://www.fastcompany.com/articles/archive/bwiggenhorn.html

Zemke, R. (1999, September). Why organizations still aren't learning. *Training, 36*(9), 40–49.

Zielinski, D. (2000, March). Can you keep learners online? *Training, 17*(3), 64–75.

39

CONTINUING PROFESSIONAL EDUCATION

GARY W. KUHNE

Distance education has long been recognized as valuable for delivering continuing professional education (CPE) within various professions. The second half of the 20th century saw a variety of creative and productive efforts to offer CPE through audio and video conferencing, computer conferencing, correspondence, and satellite. However, the portion of the resources that were allotted to distance education remained quite small. One example could be seen within continuing medical education (CME) where only 3% of activities in 2000 were provided by distance education (ACCME Annual Reports 2001).

The first decade of the 21st century however, has witnessed a dramatic surge in the use of distance education due to the expansion of online technologies. Various writers have used dramatic terms to describe this phenomenon, including such terms as "rapid expansion" within continuing medical education (Cook, Levinson, Garside, Dupras, Erwin, & Montori, 2010a), "major trend" within continuing medical and allied health professions (Harden, 2005), "creating a revolution" within continuing professional education in medicine, nursing, and allied health (Cook, Levinson, Garside, Dupras, Erwin, & Montori, 2008), and "expanding at an exponential rate" within continuing dental education (Feeney, Reynolds, Eaton, & Harper, 2008). When describing the popularity of online distance education for continuing education of social workers, Dezendorf, Green, and Krul (2004) stated that distance education-based CPE will "fundamentally alter the marketplace," away from traditional face-to-face providers.

When seeking to understand the contemporary CPE realities, it is important for us to appreciate that the domain of continuing professional education is very broad, encompassing all the formal and informal organized institutional educational efforts targeting practitioners needing to maintain both professional certification and continuing competencies to practice medicine, law, ministry, allied health professions, accounting, and a variety of other professions . The very breadth of the CPE field and the impressive range of CPE research currently taking place within each profession, as well as the variety of issues and applications of distance education within such groups, make it impossible to update the state of the CPE world comprehensively in a single chapter. To give some sense of the amount of knowledge growth, consider that Cook et al. (2010b) identified over 2,700 studies between 1990 and 2008 on Internet-based CPE within the health professions alone and were forced to limit their own meta-review of the research to just selected themes and issues.

In the attempt to gain some sense of the broad issues and trends , this chapter will begin by identifying some CPE considerations that bridge all occupations. Then, a more extensive examination of research and issues within one major arena of CPE, continuing medical education (CME), will be presented to provide a representative picture of the contemporary landscape of CPE. This will be followed by a more limited summary of research within continuing nursing education (CNE) and continuing professional education for accountants, to demonstrate that some of the same distance education research findings and themes are emerging in other professions. Finally, a brief sampling of current realities, trends, and research on distance education-based CPE within other professional contexts will be presented.

THE NATURE OF CONTINUING PROFESSIONAL EDUCATION AS A DOMAIN OF PRACTICE

Participating in continuing professional education enables practitioners in the professions to achieve a number of important occupational aims including keeping abreast of changing knowledge and skills, maintaining and enhancing their competence, assisting their progress from novice to expert practitioners, and advancing their careers through promotion and other job changes (Evans, 2008; Houle, 1980; Queeney, 2000). With increasing attention to the social context of learning within education research and theory over the past decade, it is not surprising that various authors have advocated the inclusion of "community of learning" concepts into the definition of CPE. For example, Chalmers and Keown (2006) suggest that CPE should also include efforts to foster the development of viable professional learning communities that create lifelong learning orientations. Another example of building on the social context of learning is seen in Desilets and Dickerson (2010) when they suggest that continuing professional development requires that the provider be aware of both internal and external influences that can impact professional practice, and consider such influences when planning and evaluating CPE activities. Beyond discussions over the proper purpose for CPE, deciding which occupations actually fit under the term "profession," and thus qualify as a legitimate focus for CPE, has been a subject of debate for many decades (Evans, 2008; Houle, 1980; Queeney, 2000; Tobias, 2003). The answers suggested for inclusion form an occupational continuum running from those occupations recognized as possessing professional knowledge bases, scientific-research foundations, and general-public recognition of status (such as law, medicine, university professors, and clergy) to nearly any occupation committed to professionalizing processes (Evans, 2008; Houle, 1980;). These professionalizing processes involve making consistent efforts to improve the competency and proficiency of their members, as well as developing meaningful quality-control mechanisms to police the occupation and maintain proficiency in the eyes of the general public. While debate continues regarding the actual extent of professional occupations, most current CPE literature tends to be toward the more inclusive end of the continuum and regards groups as diverse as accountants, allied-health professionals, social workers, and realtors as falling within the professional domain. Using this broader definition of "profession," more than 25% of the U.S. workforce could be viewed as proper recipients of CPE (Cervero, 2001). Based upon the more inclusive view, observers estimate that billions of dollars are spent annually by professionals and their employing organizations on CPE and CPD. This figure begins to make sense if we consider the costs tied to one form of informal CPE within a single professional group, i.e., the use of medical "apps" by healthcare professionals (i.e., programs on smart phones, iPhone and iPads), which has created an estimated $84 million industry in 2010 alone (Ardito, 2011). Another example of the magnitude of the market is found within data from the Accrediting Council For Continuing Medical Education (ACCME, 2010), which shows that the 2009 income for its 707 national CME providers was over $2 billion. If other medical education providers could be included, as well as providers of CPE to all other professions, the $84 billion figure begins to look very conservative.

The significant growth of CPE in recent years has been fostered by a number of factors, including the inherently changing nature of professional knowledge. In many fields the "half-life" of knowledge is less than five years (Cervero, 2001). Next, the professions themselves are inclined to foster CPE as a way to maintain excellence and increase competitive advantage, and for these reasons, most professions mandate such continuing-education. Calls for accountability from the general public, professional associations, consumer-advocacy groups, and state legislatures also help foster CPE. Closely related to professional accountability concerns are increased interests in public health and safety, as well as the growing threats of malpractice litigation. Underlying all of these factors is a public belief that CPE is the best answer for maintaining the competency needed by professionals (Nowlen, 1988). The issue of whether such confidence is justified is a major area of debate within CPE, although beyond the focus of this chapter.

A wide variety of educational providers are attracted to the CPE market. They include scholarly societies, professional associations, regulatory agencies, government agencies, employers, private entrepreneurs, universities and colleges, foundations, and proprietary schools (Queeney, 2000). What is the proper delivery mode for CPE has been an important question for some years (Cervero, 1998, 2000). Cost factors play heavily in the consideration of delivery formats. Professionals cannot calculate the cost of attending CPE solely on the basis of travel expenses and conference fees. For many professionals, the time they spend away from the practice for education and training is time unable to be "billed" for professional services. Thus, the true costs must include such lost income for CPE.

One important result of this cost reality has been the increasing use of distance education, a growth that has been remarkable for its magnitude over the past decade. While programs are offered in a variety of forms, including video conferencing, computer conferencing, and Web-based delivery, it is the online, Web-based learning approach that dominates the current landscape (Cook, Levinson, Garside, Dupras, Erwin, & Montori, 2010b).

DISTANCE EDUCATION IN CONTINUING MEDICAL EDUCATION

The American Medical Society (AMS, 1993) defines continuing medical education as those educational activities serving to maintain, develop, or increase the knowledge, skills, professional performance, and relationships that comprise the services offered by a physician to the public. Medical schools in the United States began offering CME in the late 1920s, with mandatory CME programs beginning in 1934 (National Library of Medicine Online, 2004). Mandatory CME became widespread by the end of the 1960s, and 41 states currently mandate some form of continuing medical education for relicensure. There are some 2,500 CME providers in the United States (Pijanowski, 1998), although this number drops to less than 1,500 if only those able to offer programming on an interstate basis are considered (http://www.ama-assn.org/ama/pub/education-careers/continuing-medical-education/).

Traditionally, the AMA has specified that CME take the form of formal educational programs (normally face-to-face), offered by traditional CME providers in a format consisting of a series of programs lasting up to five days (Davis, Lindsay, & Mazmanian, 1994). Part of the current revolution in offering CPE through distance education is revealed in the fact that the AMA guidelines regarding "life activities" now accepted include live Internet teleconferences, (http://www.ama-assn.org/ama/pub/education-careers/continuing-medical-education/frequently-asked-questions.page). Thus the primary professional association for medicine has now affirmed as a guiding principle that virtual attendance of online and other Web-based educational programs is accepted on par with face-to-face offerings, as long as the offerings meet other specified design criteria.

Another picture of the dramatic growth in CPE through distance education is seen in data referred to earlier from the Accrediting Council For Continuing Medical Education (ACCME, 2010. As previously states, in 2009, total income for 707 national CME providers was over $2 billion. These 707 providers provided almost 100,000 accredited CME activities to over 17,000,000 participants. These activities include live courses, and Internet-based (IB) activities. Another picture of growth is seen by comparing ACCME reports from 2000 and 2009. Internet-based educational offerings accounted for only 3% of total educational activities in 2000, but grew to over 34% of total activities in 2009 (ACCME Annual Reports 2001 and 2010). In those nine years, the availability of Internet-based activities increased 10 fold, and the Internet is predicted to become the dominant delivery method of CPE in the near future (Aranella, Yox, & Eckstein, 2010;, Bennett, Casebeer, Zheng, & Kristofco, 2004; Cook et al., 2008; Harris, Sklar, Amend, & Novalis-Marine, 2010; Rossett & McDonald, 2006). An important factor in the expansion of distance education is tied to the AMA recent approval of Internet point of care (POC) or "just in time" learning in which a physician engages in self-directed learning on the Internet to answer a specific clinical question or patient care challenge, completing a reflective process documenting the question, identifying the relevant sources of information, and describing how the information will be applied in clinical practice (AMA, The Physician's Recognition Award and credit system, 2010). Another example, is seen in a recent initiative by the American Board of Internal Medicine (ABIM) to replace a paper and pencil multiple choice examinations with an Internet portfolio process for a maintenance of certification requirement (Green, Reddy, & Holmboe, 2009).

While meeting regulations regarding continuing certification is a major motivation for continuing professional education research demonstrates that other motivational factors also exist. For example, Pijanowski (1998) suggests that CME is driven by professionals seeking ways to address stress and pressure caused by the shift to managed health care as well as by the desire to reduce practice tensions caused by the increased threat of lawsuits, changes in ethnic and demographic composition of patients, and technological changes. The need of many doctors to address bioethical challenges in their practice is also a factor (Wentz, Jackson, Raichle, & Davis, 2003).

Beyond the varieties of motivations for CME, Manning and DeBakey (2001) suggest a paradigm shift is occurring within CME, a shift in which CME is refocusing on the individual needs of physicians in their everyday practice setting. The program emphasis within this paradigm shift in CME emphasizes programs that reflect:

- Learner-centered adult-learning orientations;
- Personal-needs assessments and identification of learning style preferences;
- Elaboration of specific physician competencies;
- The use of learning contracts, reflective learning, and practiced-based learning.

One example this paradigm shift in CME is seen in the fact that the term "hours" in CME has been replaced with the term "credits" to eliminate the static and negative concept of "seat time" or "hours" equating to learning. Such a paradigm shift has even led the AMA to change the name of its Division of Continuing Medical Education to the Division of Continuing Physician Professional Development (AMA, 2010).

The shift described above within contemporary CME programs into a more learner-centered, technology-based, individualized approaches has perhaps been the primary driving force speeding the move toward increased use of distance education (Wentz et al., 2003). Harden (2005) suggests that the rapid growth of the Internet and e-learning is altering the very nature of CME as program designers make increased use of reusable learning objects, virtual practice with virtual patients, learning-outcomes frameworks, self-assessments, guided-learning resources, and collaborative or peer-to-peer learning. Harden goes even further to suggest that online learning opportunities provide a bridge between the cutting edge of CME and often outdated education procedures embedded in institutions and professional organizations. In a similar vein, Wiecha, Heyden, Sternthal, and Merialdi (2010) found that the use of virtual worlds have become an important element in the educational technology landscape of CME and offer the chance for a new medical education pedagogy that will produce professional learning outcomes well beyond traditional formats for CME.

One interesting side note on the dramatic shifts within CME to using distance education formats has been the reluctance to replace lecture as a preferred educational teaching strategy even within distance education formats for continuing education. Nowlen (1988) and Cervero (2000) both remind us that the research clearly suggests lecture alone produces the lowest level of behavioral change, particularly in professional practice settings. Harden's (2005) suggestion that program designers make increased use of reusable learning objects, virtual practice with virtual patients, learning-outcomes frameworks, self-assessments, guided-learning resources, and collaborative or peer-to-peer learning, provides the field with a practical way out of the lecture cul-de-sac. The reluctance to leave lecture is tied to the dominance of this teaching strategy in much preparatory education for professionals, as well as the relatively conservative nature of physicians approaching CME. Harris, Novalis-Marine, & Harris (2003), in a study of different online CME programs within three different groups of California physicians, found that physicians who used online CME courses tended to be younger than average and more likely to be female. Yet the growing body of research evidence has caused even conservative physicians to dramatically change their attitudes toward distance education-based CME and non-traditional approaches to CME. The rapid growth in online learning has helped to break the dominance of lecture in CME if for no other reason than the constructivist, interactive nature of most online program design models.

Another way to substantiate the growing use of online formats within CME is to comparing the data from descriptive research studies over the past decade. The decade began with studies such as reported by Carriere and Harvey (2001) that examined the state of distance continuing medical education in North America. Their study drew upon three surveys of the members of the Alliance of Continuing Medical Education and revealed that while considerable interest existed in distance education, the majority (68%) of recognized CME providers had not yet developed any distance education programming. Contrast this picture with the current picture of CME providers identified with the AMA in which it is clear that most are now offering online education. Also in 2007, the Medical Education Collaborative (MEC) published a report titled *Addressing the Needs of Physician Learners* analyzing the findings of their survey of physician CME preferences. Although physicians may prefer traditional formats, they participate in Internet-based CME almost as frequently as live educational forums (21% vs. 24%). Crenshaw et al. (2010) point out that over 96% of physicians in the United States use the Internet to answer clinical questions and thus it is reasonable to assume the acceptance of online CME can only grow in keeping with this trend..

Another significant line of research in the use of distance education for CME has concentrated on the comparison of learning outcomes between distance education and more traditional formats. In a meta-review of 76 studies published between 1966 and 2002, Chumley-Jones, Dobbie, and Alford (2002) found online CPE to be at least as effective as other instructional methods for knowledge gains. Wutoh, Boren, and Balab (2004) examined 16 research studies on online learning in CME in terms physician performance and health care outcomes. Six of the studies confirmed positive changes in participant knowledge over traditional formats, while three studies showed a positive change in practices. The remainder of the studies showed no difference in knowledge levels between Internet-based interventions and traditional formats of CME. The results affirmed that online CME programs are at least as effective as traditional formats. Curran and Fleet (2005) also reviewed evaluation outcomes of Web-based medical education and concluded that while learner satisfaction was high, limited studies were available for actual impacts on practice change and health outcomes. More recently, Cook et al. (2008), in a meta-analysis of research studies on Internet-based learning in health professions, discovered multiple studies confirming that Internet-based educational offerings are associated with favorable outcomes across a wide variety of learners, learning contexts, and clinical topics. The data strongly suggests the effectiveness of such offerings is similar to traditional methods of program delivery. Curran, Lockyer, Sargeant, Fleet, and Silver (2006) found in another meta-analysis of the research fond repeated evidence that a distance education CME instructional format was found to be effective in enhancing knowledge, confidence, and self-reported practice change outcomes across a variety of clinical subject matter areas. In another study confirming this equivalency reality, Ryan et al. (2007) looked at effectiveness of an online alternative to an existing face-to-face CME workshop in preparing practitioners for accreditation as a pharmacotherapies prescriber for opioid dependence and discovered that the online CME mode was equally as effective as the face-to face mode and was also rated highly by participants.

Another significant line of research in the use of distance education for CME has concentrated on the comparison of learner satisfaction between distance education and more traditional formats. Much research evidence exists for high levels of learner satisfaction with distance education formats. Sargent et al. (2004) investigated physicians' satisfaction with interpersonal interactive online continuing medical education. Because they highly valued interpersonal interaction with peers during face-to face learning, physicians tended to critique online CME in terms of their experience of such interactions. Most physicians indicated they had equally rich discussions with peers within the online environment, although they noted that such interactions were influenced by the quality of the programs and the presence of skilled facilitators. They also affirmed their satisfaction with online learning in terms of the degree of self-pacing possible and the opportunity for self-reflection prior to interaction. Prior experience with online learning was a strong influence over perception of effectiveness—in other words, those with no prior experience with online programs were reluctant to trust that mediated interaction could be as satisfying as face-to-face education. In another more recent meta-analysis of research studies, Cook, Levinson, Garside, Dupras, Erwin, & Montori (2010b) found more than 50 reports of research into programs with doctors, nurses, pharmacists, and allied health professionals that provides evidence that interactivity, the use of practice exercises, and feedback improve both learning and satisfaction in continuing medical education. The use of online discussions (both synchronous and asynchronous) produced significantly higher learner satisfaction. Intensive feedback from instructors and fellow learners was highly desired.

One final note: When drawing conclusions from the published research on distance education use in CME (or any CPE context), it is important to recognize that CME is offered in a variety of distance education formats. Confusion can arise in interpreting research literature if care is not taken to specify the specific format analyzed in the study. For example, conclusions on effectiveness of distance education in CME without defining the specific format employed can produce confusing findings—findings tied to a live video-conference could be very different from finding tied to an asynchronous online course. To further complicate the picture, even studies using the same format studies (i.e., comparing online courses) do not necessarily compare the same pedagogical variables. A well-designed, interactive online course would have very different learning outcomes from an online course that is little more than lecture notes and readings scanned into a Web page with periodic use of "talking heads" video lectures. In other words, a well-designed distance education program is going to provide different learning outcomes than a poorly designed program. Recognizing these limitations, Olson and Shershneva (2004) suggest the need to develop quality standards for each form of distance education employed. When considering Web-based designs in CME, they suggest drawing upon the standards already adopted by such groups as American Federation of Teachers, Distance Education and Training Council (DETC), Institute for Higher Education Policy, Alfred P. Sloan Foundation, and the Western Cooperative for Educational Telecommunications (WCET).

As noted at the beginning of this section, CME provides a representative picture of the uses, results, and issues with distance education-based CPE within many contemporary professions. Certainly the dramatic growth, the proven effectiveness in terms of learning outcomes, the high levels of learner satisfaction, and the growing use of various tools for increasing personalization of learning are clear across many professions.

A BRIEFER LOOK AT DISTANCE EDUCATION USE WITHIN CONTINUING NURSING EDUCATION AND CPE FOR ACCOUNTANTS

Continuing Nursing Education (CNE) is defined as the ongoing, continuing professional education in which nurses learn new knowledge, skills, and attitudes, and assistance in knowing how to integrate these into their nursing practices (Bell, Chelf, & Geerdes, 2000; Farrah, 1998; Mamary & Charles, 2000). Nursing as a profession has historically demonstrated openness to new delivery modes and even made use of distance education (correspondence courses) as far back as the late 19th century (Armstrong, Gessner, & Cooper, 2000; Stein, 1998). By the second half of the 20th century, telephone audio courses became common in CNE, with video conferencing soon added. By the late 1970s computers began to be used, particularly at Ohio State University (Chumley-Jones et al., 2002).

The transition from onsite to online formats in CNE accelerated during the final decade of the 20th century (Ali, Hodson-Carlton, & Ryan, 2002; Bothel, 2001; Mueller, 2002). The dramatic growth over the past decade has reflected the growth of online CME we examined in the previous section. One example of such growth is seen the fact that the number of fully online RN-BSN programs in the United Stated grew to 96 by 2007 and 129 by 2009 (Bigony, 2010). Nguyen, Zierler, and Nguyen (2011), in survey of 193 nursing faculty from nursing schools in the western United States, found that more than half made frequent use of distance education, and two-thirds felt competent with distance learning tools. Furthermore, Jones and Wolf (2010) found that the concept of teaching online has gained widespread acceptance at various universities and academic institutions, providing a viable alternative to traditional forms of CNE. Adegbola (2011) found the continuing use of audio-teleconferencing provided valuable frameworks for collaborative learning in CNE and proved useful to foster self-reflection and the development of learning communities. The value of distance education formats for CNE has been confirmed in a variety of studies. Beatty's (2001) study with nurses in rural Pennsylvania demonstrated the value of developing online alternatives for CNE. Most of the nurses faced a variety of obstacles in seeking face-to-face CNE, including travel distance, time, fear of traveling alone in a city, navigating city traffic, family concerns, weather, late night classes, and concern at having no previous experience with professional networks. The distance education alternatives were both appreciated and beneficial to the subjects of the study. In 2004 Cobb carried out a meta-analysis of 17 research articles that focused on the evaluation of online CNE, and revealed that online CNE was gaining in popularity, and most CNE online participants found the experience of participating in such programs both rewarding and an effective learning format. Similarly, Piernik-Yoder (2004) examined the use of distance education to meet continuing education requirements by allied health care professionals in the state of Texas. While the study found that overall allied professionals' use of distance education to meet CE requirements was low, the perception of distance education-based CNE was very positive among those who had previously experienced using distance education to meet CE requirements. Huckstadt and Hayes (2005) examined 73 registered nurses enrolled in online continuing education courses and discovered that the majority of the nurses were enthusiastic about their online learning experience and would like to have other courses designed and delivered in this manner.

The positive view of distance education among nurses pursuing CNE was also confirmed by a study of nurse practitioners in Canada (Andrusyszyn, Cragg, & Humbert, 2005). While holding relatively positive attitudes toward multiple delivery methods, the nurses' preferred method to learn was through print-based programs. Convenience, self-direction, and timing of learning were found to be more important than delivery method or learning style, findings which suggest a similar current study would find online CNE particularly valued. Another similar study examined the use of Webcasting (technology used to deliver audio and video presentations via the Internet, usually in a synchronous format) for graduate nursing education at West Virginia University School of Nursing (DiMaria-Ghalili, Ostrow, & Rodney, 2005). Both students and faculty viewed the program favorably, and, within eight months, Webcasting, as a delivery format, was integrated throughout the nursing program. Jukkala, Henly, and Lindeke (2008) found particular openness to online formats among nurses living in remote or rural areas.

A number of research studies within CNE have examined Web-based programs in terms of knowledge gains. Fike, McCall, Raehl, Smith, and Lockman (2009) investigated possible differences in learning outcomes for students enrolled in competency-based anatomy and pharmaceutical calculations courses through distance education compared with face-to-face lectures. The mean examination final scores and course grades did not significantly differ and the researchers concluded that both formats provided equitable learning opportunities and roughly equivalent learning outcomes. Wright (2008) found that the overall knowledge gains by nurses for diabetes management knowledge was essentially the same whether the teaching took place within the regular classroom setting or whether the education was delivered via computer-based training.

But these recent findings on learning outcomes simply affirmed and aligned with earlier important CNE studies. Prows, Hetteberg, Hopkin, Latta, and Powers (2004) found statistically significant improvements in posttest scores for similar courses offered in Web-based versus face-to-face formats. Jeffries (2005) measured knowledge gains in online CNE courses and found that 100% of the learners passed the required exams, successfully completed the online course, and demonstrated acceptable levels of knowledge gain. Atick and Rankin (2002) found that nurses' posttest scores for a specific CNE course offered in both residential and distance formats were not significantly different for the Web and paper version of the course. They further found that participation in the Web-based version of the course enhanced the nurses' computer skills, an important learning outcome, since so much of nursing practice and health care is becoming computerized. Olson, Stedman-Smith, and Fredrickson (2005) examined 70 nurse practitioners in a Web-based CNE program concerning environmental health care concepts. Changes in learning from pretest to posttest demonstrated acceptable knowledge gains and 91% of the nurses felt the course content helped them to gain further professional knowledge concerning environmental health. Nearly 86% felt the online course helped them to improve their ability to conduct environmental exposure histories. Finally, Phillips (2005) found that learning outcomes in online CNE were improved by the use of active learning strategies such as asynchronous discussions and the use of case studies. Phillips also found that feedback from peers, educators, and technology greatly influenced learner satisfaction.

More recently, Kittleson (2009) reviewed 140 research studies of online learning in CNE and found evidence that the rigor and quality of such courses often exceeded that of face-to-face offerings, and provided an alternative that more and more practitioners were taking to meet CNE requirements. Randolph, Rogers, and Ostendorf (2011) focused on a study conducted in 2005 and 2008 to evaluate self-reported competency achievement by occupational health nursing program graduates. A key finding was that distance education learners had higher competency scores compared to on-campus graduates.

One issue impacting the move toward online CNE is the computer literacy of nurses. Such literacy and use of computers has definitely been growing. Hegge, Powers, Hendrickx, and Vinson (2002), studying registered nurses in South Dakota, found that 75% of nurses had computers at home while 76% had computers at work, yet fewer than 20% used computers for nursing CE. They suggested one key to increased participation in online CNE is better orientation of nurses to use new technology. Compare this with Nguyen, Zierler, and Nguyen's 2011 study, cited early, which shows that now more than two-thirds of the nursing faculty have experience and competence in online and distance education delivery of educational programs, a percentage that reveals a much improved computer literacy among the nurse students. The study also found that 69% of the nursing faculty still wanted more training to improve their distance education teaching and design efforts. This finding confirms earlier research, such as reported by Ali et al. (2005), that examined the needs of nursing faculty as CNE transitioned from traditional classroom instruction to an online community of learning. They found that faculty development in online education is a critical component of effective CNE and that redesigning and rethinking faculty roles must become a priority in order to improve the value of distance-based CNE. Certainly Southernwood's (2008) conclusion that access to appropriate distance learning materials, facilitated student interaction and adequate tutorial support may provide the most effective and efficient option for today's healthcare professionals needing CNE.

CONTINUING EDUCATION OF CERTIFIED PUBLIC ACCOUNTANTS

Mandatory continuing education within accounting was first suggested in 1967, with Iowa becoming the first state to require CPE as a requirement for relicensure in 1971. Currently 52 of the 54 legal jurisdictions that issue CPA licenses require continuing professional education for re-licensure. CPA re-licensure certification requires 120 hours of CPE every three years (http://www.aicpa.org/About/FAQs/Pages/FAQs.aspx#aicpa_answer6) with annual, biennial. or triannual renewal periods depending upon state jurisdiction (American Institute of Certified Public Accountants [AICPA], 2004, 2011; Streer, Clark, & Holt, 1995). The debate over such education has intensified following the introduction and adoption of a 150 hours requirement among most of the 55 jurisdictions that regulate public accounting (Crawford, 2011). The strategy for taking the required hours has changed dramatically in the past decade. According to Thomas and Harper (2001), even into the 1990s, continuing professional education in the accounting field took the form of participants being awarded credit for attending a requisite number of session hours in face-to-face education programs. Such credit was granted for attendance, regardless of whether any learning took place. In the late 1990s, AICPA began to suggest that a competency-based model be followed and credit be considered for programming beyond traditional classroom time, such as teaching or authoring courses, and self-directed learning activities such as reading professional journals, leadership in professional organizations, research on professional topics, and mentoring activities (Stevens, 1999). This modifying of traditional expectations encouraged CPE providers to consider a variety of formats and delivery strategies, including distance education approaches (Perdue & Valentine, 1998).

One important study conducted for the Georgia Society of Certified Public Accountants found that respondents believe distance education, including use of the Internet, was an effective way to learn (Perdue & Valentine, 1998). In another study of distance education use for CPE within accounting, Ernst and Young (Kahan, 1998) found that programs delivered via the Internet, audio and video tapes, and CD-ROM were favorably received by practitioners. Practitioners who took courses on interactive, multimedia continuing professional education products performed far better on-the-job than those attending seminars and conferences and finished their work at a faster pace. Others found a rather conservative attitude among practitioners. Nacinovich (1998) found that organizations offering distance education-based continuing professional education courses to CPAs tended to find poor market reception, although the research was limited to self-study forms of distance education and not interactive online courses. In a similar study, Foy (1998) found limited acceptance of many self-study forms of continuing professional education such as CD-ROMs or audio tapes.

By the end of the first decade of the 21 century, the change had become "revolutionary" in the same way we found in CME and CNE. Perhaps the most dramatic evidence of such change is reflected in the fact that the AICPA has created an online curriculum (AICPA, 2011). The IFRS Certificate Program is a curriculum of 25 online, on-demand, self-study training courses. CPAs who successfully complete all courses receive a Certificate of Educational Achievement and approximately 42 hours of continuing education credit. Dosch (2010), in a review of online management programs in accounting, has underscored the expansion of this delivery tool The offering of online continuing professional education courses was seen as a key to controlling costs associated with the increasing required educational hours; essentially all providers of CPE for accountants were developing a least some online presence.

Another factor that has contributed to the growth of online learning options within accounting CPE is the pressure of daily time demands for the typical practitioner. Kahan (1998) cites research that indicates that CPAs feel overwhelmed in managing their day-to-day practices and that meeting the mandated continuing professional education contributes further to the problem. This leads many practitioners to choose continuing professional education alternatives that minimize time away from the practice, such as subscribing to a series of video programs.

A POTPOURRI OF FINDINGS ON DISTANCE EDUCATION IN A VARIETY OF PROFESSIONS

This section of the chapter provides a glimpse of the current picture of distance education research within a variety of other professional occupations. A survey of insurance agents and brokers in the states of California, Oregon, and Washington indicated that only 1% of insurance agents took an online course (Chartered Property Causality Underwriters [CPCU], 2001). The study indicated that the low interest in Internet training was due to the value given to networking and personal interaction opportunities in a classroom setting. Although current online learning was low, 22% of respondents indicated that they would take online courses in the future. A more recent study by the Independent Insurance Agents and Brokers of America (IIABA) indicated that 95% of the agents surveyed believed cost-savings and not losing time from work were good reasons to consider taking CPE online (Ruquet, 2004). As the opportunity for online CPE grows, Ruquet warns insurance agents of the importance to choose distance education-based options carefully, due to lack of quality of some providers.

Umble and Dooley (2004) surveyed a number of professions and human resource development (HRD) settings regarding the use of educational technologies and distance education. They concluded many programs lack quality and often are limited in extent because they are designed in ways that are ultimately unsustainable. There seemed to be limited use of program planning models and very little effort to take into account the needs of all internal and external stakeholders. Hyer, Taylor, and Nanni (2004) discuss the problem of satisfying regulator requirements based upon fixed-hour curriculums and the use of online learning formats within geriatric risk-management settings.

In a study of Canadian rehabilitation professionals utilizing distance education for CPE, Liu, Cook, Varnhagen, and Miyazaki (2004) found the majority were very satisfied with programs delivered by satellite, video conferencing, and online. Online CPE programming for social workers in the United States has grown in popularity to the point that further development of online CPE threatens to fundamentally alter the marketplace for CPE away from traditional face-to-face providers (Dezendorf et al., 2004).

Dedman (2008), in a study of more than 600 instructors overseeing field placement of social workers, found that the vast majority (95%) were either currently receiving online training or were open to that delivery method. In fact, while concerns were voiced about the lack of warmth of such program delivery, the online option was seen as an ideal solution to the problem of how to train busy professionals volunteering to supervise social work students. Styra (2004) found that psychiatrists in Canada have embraced many aspects of the Internet for health care information, online journals, and e-mail, although they are slow to fully accept online CME offerings. Winters (1998) suggested distance education-based CPE offers hope for overcoming the isolated nature of pastoral ministry.

The use of distance CPE alternatives is developing among lawyers. In states mandating continuing legal education, lawyers are required to complete between 12 and 15 hours per year (including 3 hours of ethics) of continuing professional education credits for relicensure (American Bar Association, ABA Online, 2004). In 2001, the ABA endorsed the inclusion of new technologies (computer-based training, Web-based training) for approval in continuing legal education. The ABA's position is that lawyers have different learning styles, and as such, should have the option to undertake continuing legal education based upon their own individual needs. The ABA also emphasizes that learning should be self-directed and learner-centered. According to the ABA, over 50% of the states with continuing legal education requirements now approve learner-centered and self-directed computer-based and Web-based CPE. Today, some states have gone even further, advancing a holistic approach to continuing legal education rather than the traditional didactic-content driven courses. According to Keeva (2004), Minnesota has approved "soft-skill" type courses in the areas of self-reflection, stress, resiliency, and career satisfaction for continuing legal education.

SOME CONCLUDING THOUGHTS ON DISTANCE EDUCATION WITHIN CPE

The next five years should produce a growing body of research within a variety of professions on the best practices, course design issues, learning outcomes, and viability of distance education-based CPE. Hopefully, the professions will decide to draw upon such research findings across professions rather than maintain the isolated focus on a single profession that has plagued much of the history of modern CPE. Distance education could soon become the preferred way of enabling professionals to keep abreast of changing profession-specific knowledge and skills, maintain, and enhance their professional competence, assist their progress from novice to expert practitioners, and advance their careers through promotion and other job changes.

REFERENCES

ABA Online. (2004). *ABA Online. American Bar Association.* Retrieved from http://www.abanet.org

Accreditation Council for Continuing Medical Education. (2001). *Annual report data for 2000.* Chicago, IL: Accreditation Council for Continuing Medical Education.

Accreditation Council for Continuing Medical Education. (2010). *Annual report data for 2009.* Chicago, IL: Accreditation Council for Continuing Medical Education.

Adegbola, M. (2011). Taking learning to the learner: Using audio teleconferencing for postclinical conferences and more. *Creative Nursing, 17*(3), 120–125.

AICPA Online. (2004). *AICPA Online. American Institute of Certificated Public Accountants.* Retrieved from http://www.aicpa.org/members/index.htm

AICPA. (2011). AICPA introduces IFRS certificate program based on comprehensive, integrated curriculum, online study. *Education Business Weekly,* 19. Retrieved from http://search.proquest.com/docview/8603103 95?accountid=13158

Ali, N. S., Hodson-Carlton, K., & Ryan, M. (2002). Web-based professional education for advanced practice nursing: A consumer guide for program selection. *The Journal of Continuing Education in Nursing, 33,* 33–38.

Ali, N. S., Hodson-Carlton, K., Ryan, M., Flowers, J., Rose, M. A., & Wayda, V. (2005). Online education: Needs assessment for faculty development. *The Journal of Continuing Education in Nursing, 36*(1), 32–38.

American Medical Association. (1993). *The Physician's Recognition Award: 1993 information booklet.* Chicago: American Medical Association.

American Medical Association. (2010). Continuing medical education for licensure reregistration. Retrieved from http://www.ama-assn.org/ama1/pub/upload/mm/40/table16.pdf

Andrusyszyn, M., Cragg, C. E., & Humbert, J. (2005). Nurse practitioner preferences for distance education methods related to learning style, course content, and achievement. *Journal of Nursing Education, 40,* 163–170.

Armstrong, M. L., Gessner, B. A., & Cooper, S. S. (2000). Pots, pans, and pearls: The nursing profession's rich history with distance education for a new century of nursing. *The Journal of Continuing Education in Nursing, 31,* 63–70.

Aranella, c., Yox, S., & Eckstein, D. S. (2010). Expanding the reach of a cancer palliative care curriculum through web-based dissemination: A public-private collaboration. *Journal of Cancer Education, 25,* 418–421. doi:10.1007/s13187-010-0066-1

Ardito, S. C. (2011). Mobile apps for the health professional. *Searcher, 19*(6), 46-50. Retrieved from http://search. proquest.com/docview/875640436?accountid=13158

Atick, L., & Rankin, J. (2002). A Descriptive study of registered nurses'experience with web-based learning. *Journal of Advanced Nursing, 40*(4), 457–465.

Beatty, R. M. (2001). Continuing professional education, organizational support, and professional competence: Dilemmas of rural nurses. *The Journal of Continuing Education in Nursing, 32,* 203–209.

Bell, D. F., Chelf, J. H., & Geerdes, P. (2000). An outcomes model prototype: Integrating continuing education learning into practice. *Journal of Continuing Education in Nursing, 31*(3), 111–115.

Bennett, N. L., Casebeer, L. L., Zheng, S., & Kristofco, R. (2006). Information-seeking behaviors and reflective practice. *Journal of Continuing Education in the Health Professions, 26*(2), 120–127. Retrieved from http://dx.doi.org/10.1002/chp.60

Bigony, L. (2010). Can you go the distance? Attending the virtual classroom. *Orthopaedic Nursing, 29*(6), 390–392.

Bothel, R. (2001). Bringing it all together. *Online Journal of Distance Education Administration, 4*(1). Retrieved from http://www.westgate.edu/%Edistance/ojdia/spring41/spring41.html

Carriere, M. F., & Harvey, D. (2001). Current state of distance continuing medical education in North America. *The Journal of Continuing Education in Health Professions, 21*, 150–157.

Cervero, R. M. (1988). *Continuing learning in the professions.* San Francisco: Jossey-Bass.

Cervero, R. M. (1998). Forward. In W. H. Young (Ed.), *Continuing professional education in transition: Visions for the professions and new strategies for lifelong learning* (pp. ix–x). Malabar, FL: Kreiger.

Cervero, R. M. (2000). Trends and issues in continuing professional education. In V. W. Mott & B. J. Daley (Eds.), *Charting a course for continuing professional education: Reframing professional practice* (pp. 3–12). San Francisco: Jossey-Bass.

Cervero, R. M. (2001). Continuing professional education in transition, 1981–2000. *International Journal of Lifelong Education, 20*(1–2), 16–30.

Chalmers, L., & Keown, P. (2006) Communities of practice and professional development, *International Journal of Lifelong Education, 25*(2), 139–156.

Chartered Property Causality Underwriters Society's Pacific Northwest and Lake Washington Chapters. (2001). The Internet: CE choice for the future? *CPCU Journal, 54*, 19–29.

Chumley-Jones, H. S., Dobbie, A., & Alford, C. L. (2002). Web-based learning: Sound educational method or hype? A review of the evaluation literature. *Academic Medicine, 77*(10), S86–S93.

Cobb, S. C. (2004). Internet continuing education for health care professionals: An integrative review. *Journal of Continuing Education in the Health Professions, 24*, 171–180.

Cook, D., Levinson, A., Garside, S., Dupras, D., Erwin, P., and Montori, M. (2008). Internet-Based Learning in the Health Professions: A Meta-analysis. *Journal of the American Medical Association (JAMA), 300*(10), 1181–1196.

Cook, D., Levinson, A., Garside, S., Dupras, D., Erwin, P., & Montori, M. (2010a). Instructional design variations in Internet-based learning for health professions Education: A systematic review and meta-analysis. *Academic Medicine, 85*(5), 909–922.

Cook, D., Levinson, A., Garside, S., Dupras, D., Erwin, P., & Montori, M. (2010b). The Impact of E-Learning in Medical Education. *Academic Medicine, 81*(3), 207–212.

Cook, D. A., Garside, S., Levinson, A. J., Dupras, D. M., & Montori, V. M. (2010). What do we mean by web-based learning? A systematic review of the variability of interventions. *Medical Education, 44*(8), 765–774. doi:10.1111/j.1365-2923.2010.03723.x

Crawford, D. L. (2011). Practitioner and educator preferences regarding accounting curriculm meeting the 150-hour requirement. *Academy of Educational Leadership Journal, 15*(4), 47–66.

Crenshaw, K., Curry, W., Salanitro, A., Safford, M., Houston, T., Allison, J., & Estrada, C. A. (2010). Is physician engagement with web-based cme associated with patients' baseline hemoglobin A1c levels? The rural diabetes online care study. *Academic Medicine, 85*(9), 1151–1517. doi:10.1097

Curran, V., & Fleet, L. (2005). A review of evaluation outcomes of Web-based continuing medical education. *Medical Education, 39*(6), 561–567.

Curran, V, Lockyer, J., Sargeant, J., Fleet, L., & Silver, I. (2006). Evaluation of Learning Outcomes in Web-Based Continuing Medical Education. *Academic Medicine, 81*(10), S30–S34.

Davis, D., Lindsay, E., & Mazmanian, P. (1994). The effectiveness of CME interventions. In D. A. Davis & R. A. Fox (Eds.), *The physician as learner: Linking research to practice.* Chicago: American Medical Association.

Dedman, D. (2008). *Social work field instructor's perceptions of on-line training* (Unpublished doctoral dissertation). Western Michigan University, Kalamazoo.

Desilets, L., & Dickerson, P. (2010). Continuing Nursing Education: Enhancing Professional Development. *Journal of Continuing Nursing in Nursing, 41*(3), 100–101.

Dezendorf, P., Green, R., & Krul, R. (2004). CE online: Use it or lose it. *Professional Development: The International Journal of Continuing Social Work Education, 7*(1), 24–34.

DiMaria-Ghalili, R. A., Ostrow, L., & Rodney, K. (2005). Webcasting: A new instructional technology in distance graduate nursing education. *Journal of Nursing Education, 44*, 11–18.

Dosch, J. (2010). Teaching management accounting online. *Cost Management, 24*(2), 44–48.

Evans, L. (2008). Professionalism, professionality and the development of education professionals. *British Journal of Educational Studies, 56*(1), 20–38.

Farrah, S. J. (1998). Variables influencing the likelihood of practice change after continuing nursing education participation. *Dissertation Abstracts International, 60*, 1598.

Feeney, L., Reynolds, P., Eaton, K., & Harper, J. (2008). A description of the new technologies used in transforming dental education. *British Dental Journal, 204*(1), 19–28.

Fike, D., McCall, K., Raehl, C., Smith, Q., & Lockman, P. (2009). Achieving equivalent academic performance between campuses using a distributed education model. *American Journal of Pharmaceutical Education, 73*(5), 1–88.

Foy, N. F. (1998). *Continuing professional education needs of NYNEX Certified Management Accountants and implications for the Institute of Certified Management Accountants' mandates.* New York: Columbia Teachers College.

Green, M. L., Reddy, S. G., & Holmboe, E. (2009). Teaching and evaluating point of care learning with an internet-based clinical question portfolio. *Journal of Continuing Education in the Health Professions, 29*(4), 209–219. doi:10.1002/chp.20039

Harden, R. M. (2005). A new vision for distance learning and continuing medical education. *The Journal of Continuing Education in Health Professions, 25*, 43–51.

Harris, J. M., Novalis-Marine, C., & Harris, R. B. (2003). Women physicians are early adopters of online continuing education. *The Journal of Continuing Education in Health Professions, 23*, 221–228.

Harris, J. M., Jr., Sklar, B. M., Amend, R. W., & Novalis-Marine, C. (2010). The growth, characteristics, and future of online CME. *Journal of Continuing Education in the Health Professions, 30*(1), 3–10. Retrieved from http://www.blackwell-synergy.com/doi/abs/10.1002/chp.20050

Hegge, M., Powers, P., Hendrickx, L., & Vinson, J. (2002). Competence, continuing education, and computers. *The Journal of Continuing Education in Nursing, 33*, 24–32.

Houle, C. O. (1980). *Continuing learning in the professions.* San Francisco: Jossey-Bass.

Huckstadt, A. and Hayes, K. (2005). Evaluation of interactive online courses for advanced practice nurses. *Journal of the American Academy of Nurse Practitioners, 17*(3), 85–89.

Hyer, K., Taylor, H., & Nanni, K. (2004). Designing health care risk management online: Meeting regulators' concerns for fixed-hour curriculum. *Gerontology and Geriatrics Education, 24*(4), 77–94.

Jeffries, P. R. (2005). Development and testing of a hyperlearning model for design of an online critical care course. *Journal of Nursing Education, 44*(8), 366–372.

Jones, D., & Wolf, D. (2010). Shaping the future of nursing education today using distant education and technology. *ABNF Journal, 21*(2), 44–47.

Jukkala, A., Henly, S., & Lindeke, L. (2008). Rural Pprceptions of continuing professional education. *The Journal of Continuing Education in Nursing, 39*(12), 555–563.

Kahan, S. (1998). Using CPE to bring in business. *The Practical Account, 31*, 1.

Keeva, S. (2004). CLE for the whole person. *ABA Journal, 90*, 76.

Kittleson, M. (2009). The future of technology in health education: Challenging the traditional delivery dogma. *American Journal of Health Education, 40*(6), 310–316.

Liu, L., Cook, A., Varnhagen, S., & Miyazaki, M. (2004). Rehabilitative professionals' satisfaction with continuing education delivered at a distance using different technologies. *Assistive Technology. Special Issue: Distance Learning, 16*(2), 104–115.

Mamary, E. M., & Charles, P. (2000). On-site to online: Barriers to the use of computers for continuing education. *Journal of Continuing Education in the Health Professions, 20*(3), 171–175.

Manning, P. R., & DeBakey, L. (2001). Continuing medical education: The paradigm is changing. *The Journal of Continuing Education in Health Care Professions, 21*, 46–54.

Mueller, C. L. (2002). Teaching at a distance via the Web. *Excellence in Nursing Education Research, 3*(2), 1–4.

Nacinovich, M. (1998). CPE: Lights, camera, action? *Accounting Technology, 14*(3), 38–43.

National Library of Medicine Online. (2004). *History of continuing medical education.* Retrieved from http://www.ncbi.nlm.nih.gov

Nowlen, P. M. (1988). *A new approach to continuing education for business and the professions: The performance model.* New York: Macmillan.

Nguyen, D. N., Zierler, B., & Nguyen, H. Q. (2011). A survey of nursing faculty needs for training in use of new technologies for education and practice. *Journal of Nursing Education, 50*(4), 181–189.

Olson, C. A., & Shershneva, S. B. (2004). Setting quality standards for Web-based continuing medical education. *The Journal of Continuing Education in Health Professions, 24*, 100–111.

Olson, D., Stedman-Smith, M., & Fredrickson, A. (2005). Environmental health and nursing: Piloting a technology-enhanced distance learning module. *AAOHN Journal, 53*(8), 353–359.

Perdue, K. J., & Valentine, T. (1998). Beliefs of certified public accountants toward distance education: A statewide Georgia survey. *The American Journal of Distance Education, 12*(3), 29–41.

Phillips, J. M. (2005). Strategies for active learning in online continuing education. *The Journal of Continuing Education in Nursing, 36*, 77–83.

Piernik-Yoder, B. (2004). *The use of distance education to meet continuing education requirements by allied health professionals in the state of Texas.* Available from Proquest Dissertations and Theses database. (UMI No. 3141864)

Pijanowski, K. (1998). Continuing medical education in transition: The evolution of a new paradigm. In W. H. Young (Ed.), *Continuing professional education in transition: Visions for the professions and new strategies for lifelong learning* (pp. 143–169). Malabar, FL: Kreiger.

Prows, C. A., Hetteberg, C., Hopkin, R. J., Latta, K. K., & Powers, S. M. (2004). Development of a Web-based genetics institute for a nursing audience. *Journal of Continuing Education in Nursing, 35*(5), 223–231.

Queeney, D. S. (2000). Continuing professional education. In A. L. Wilson & Hayes, E. R. (Eds.), *Handbook of adult and continuing education* (pp. 375–391). San Francisco: Jossey-Bass.

Randolph, S. A., Rogers, B., & Ostendorf, J. S. (2011). Evaluation of an occupational health nursing program through competency achievement: On-campus and distance education, 2005 and 2008. *AAOHN Journal, 59*(9), 387–399.

Rossett, A., & McDonald, J. A. (2006). Evaluating technology-enhanced continuing medical education. *Medical Education Online, 11*, 1–8.

Ruquet, M. E. (2004). Agents warned to avoid CE mills for training. *National Underwriter Company, 108*, 25.

Ryan, G., Lyon, P., Kumar, K., Bell, J., Barnet, S., and Shaw, T. (2007). Online CME: An effective alternative to face-to-face delivery. *Medical Teacher, 29*(8), e251–e257.

Sargent, J., Curran, V., Jarvis-Selinger, S., Ferrier, S., Allen, M., Kriby, F., et al. (2004). Interactive online continuing medical education: Physicians' perceptions and experiences. *The Journal of Continuing Education in Health Professions, 24*, 227–236.

Southernwood, J. (2008). Distance learning: The future of continuing professional development. *Community Practitioner, 81*(10), 21–23.

Stein, A. M. (1998). History of continuing nursing education in the United States. *Journal of Continuing Education in Nursing, 29*(6), 245–252.

Stevens, M. G. (1999). Changing the direction of CPE. *The Practical Accountant, 32*, 1.

Streer, P. J., Clark, R. L., & Holt, M. E. (1995). Assessing the utility of continuing professional education for certified public accountants. *Research in Accounting Regulation, 9*, 211–222.

Styra, R. (2004). The Internet's impact on the practice of psychiatry. *Canadian Journal of Psychiatry, 49*(1), 5–11.

Thomas, P. B., & Harper, B. S. (2001). CPE: Changing with the profession. *The CPA Journal, 71*, 2.

Tobias, R. (2003) Continuing professional education and professionalization: travelling without a map or compass? *International Journal of Lifelong Education, 22*(5), 445–456.

Umble, K. E., & Dooley, L. M. (2004). Planning human resource development and continuing professional education programs that use educational technologies: Voices that must be heard. *Advances in Developing Human Resources. Special Issue: Boundary Spanning: Expanding Frames of Reference for Human Resource Development and Continuing Professional Education, 6*(1), 86–100.

Wentz, D. K., Jackson, J. J., Raichle, L., & Davis, A. (2003). Forces for change in the landscape of CME, CPD, and health systems-linked education. In D. Davis, B. Barnes, & R. Fox (Eds.), *The continuing professional development of physicians: From research to practice* (pp. 25–48). New York: AMA Press.

Wiecha, J., Heyden, R., Sternthal E., & Merialdi, M. (2010). Learning in a Virtual World: Experience With Using Second Life for Medical Education. *Journal of Medical Internet Research, 12*(1). Retrieved from http://www.ncbi.nlm.nih.gov/pmc/articles/PMC2821584/

Winters, M. L. (1998). The ministry: A concert of concerns. In W. H. Young (Ed.), *Continuing professional education in transition: Visions for the professions and new strategies for lifelong learning*. Malabar, FL: Kreiger.

Wright, M. (2008). *Staff nurses' level of diabetes and diabetes management knowledge after a diabetes lecture-based and computer-based educational intervention* (Unpublished doctoral dissertation). University of Alabama at Birmingham.

Wutoh, R., Boren, S. A., & Balab, E. A. (2004). E-learning: A review of Internet-based continuing medical education. *The Journal of Continuing Education in Health Professions, 24*, 20–30.

40

DISTANCE EDUCATION IN THE ARMED FORCES

PEGGY L. KENYON, GARY TWOGOOD, AND LINDA A. SUMMERLIN

For many years, the United States Armed Forces have been interested and active in the field of distance learning. Though the methods of distribution have evolved, the earliest examples were seen in the publication of training materials for use in battlefield locations during World War I. Many years later, facing aggression from the enemies of Japan and Germany during World War II, troops were given quick fundamental instruction at home, and then shipped off to face the enemy abroad. To supplement their training on the front lines, the military turned to researchers in education. This resulted in some of the earliest tools in instructional media and delivery of distance education. Various pamphlets, guides, cartoons and films covered a wide range of topics—from how to disassemble an M-16 rifle, to how to protect soldiers from communicable disease. This practical and vital training was produced with the intent of being delivered directly to the soldier, sailor, or airman in the field to accomplish the training mission.

In the ensuing years, military distance education has become a reliable method of bringing access to training and education for the men and women in uniformed and civilian service, anytime and anywhere it is needed.

MILITARY DISTANCE LEARNING

The Army Correspondence Course Program

Until 1978, Army distance learning consisted mainly of the distribution of training materials to the soldiers in the field or while on duty at home. Even though it did tremendous service to enhance learning, there was little student support and the program was not accredited. Around that same time period, The Army Correspondence Course Program (ACCP) came to be managed by the Army Institute of Professional Development (AIPD) and received its first accreditation by the Distance Education Training Council. The AIPD was recognized as an institution that incorporated best business practices and offered support and other services to assist students in achieving their educational goals.

This early, formal, and newly accredited program, consisted of text-based instructional material used to train, assess, and award credit (Duncan, 2005). Each day thousands of books bound in yellow jackets were mailed to students who completed the material and then returned specific items to be hand-scored. Despite the formal name of ACCP, to many soldiers it was known simply as the "Yellow Books" and was an important tool in career progression. For soldiers, the points gained toward promotion, and the courses completed, became a part of their official military personnel file and served to highlight personal commitment to professional self-development.

The Army Correspondence Course Program was changed for the digital age around 1990, when it was offered as Web-based content. As technology began to mature and computers became prominent in the workplace, as well as the soldier's home, the design of distance learning began to change. With a mission to establish "classrooms without walls" hundreds of hours of content were digitized for Web delivery (Duncan, 2005).

A second move to modernize the program occurred in 2007 to make the Web-based content more student-centered, engaging, and interactive. This current movement makes the best use of guided simulations, gaming scenarios, and real-time feedback. This effort is still underway.

At this time, the fully accredited Army Correspondence Course Program offers both individual and group study options and is open to Reserve and Active Army components as well as to Department of the Army civilians. The program has had over 100,000 annual enrollments and continues to be a successful way to train the force (Duncan, 2005).

The United States Armed Forces Institute

The Air Force was an early adopter of Distance Learning. In 1942, the United States Armed Forces Institute (USAFI) was established in Madison, Wisconsin. It worked with the University of Wisconsin and 70 other academic institutions to provide educational opportunities for thousands of members of the armed services, a mission of special significance during World War II and the post-war period. This allowed coursework to be completed, through distance learning, during the service member's actual duty day.

The Air Force definition of distance learning is one of physical distance between learner and instructor following a structured curriculum. Using traditional written material and one-way technology such as television, audio, and film, distance learning provided a means to deliver instruction to learners around the world.

The Air Force Extension Course Institute

The Extension Course Institute (ECI) and the United States Armed Forces Institute (USAFI) used the same course delivery model around 1950. The Air Force ECI was established to provide correspondence courses to airmen and was the only Air Force correspondence school. Similar to the Army's ACCP, the ECI's original mission was to provide nonresident Career Development Courses (CDCs) for both active duty and reserve Air Force personnel. These included formal upgrade training, supplemental training, and career broadening courses. Career advancement in the Air Force required airmen to complete ECI courses, and on the job training (OJT) performance, to be eligible for promotion.

During the early years, thousands of copies of each course were printed and stored in a warehouse at Gunter AFB, Alabama. The batch printing process required estimates of how many copies would be required, in a fervent hope that there wouldn't be major changes in content before new copies needed to be ordered. As might be expected, ECI was an expensive program. Waste was unavoidable because requirements for copies changed frequently. Changes in content often generated out of cycle reprint requirements with additional postage dramatically increasing the cost. By the 1980s, processes were improved to allow printing on demand which drastically reduced the amount of material to be stored. Out of cycle reprints were minimized and the currency of the content was improved. While waste was minimized, postage remained a major expense.

The Air Force continued upgrading capabilities well into the late 1990s by converting ECI courses to CD-ROM delivery. The use of CDs allowed the use of video clips, complex graphics, and audio to greatly enhance the user experience. An additional benefit was a huge reduction in postage charges. Also during the latter part of this decade, and realizing the common place nature of the computer and its benefits to the student, the Air Force Distance Learning Office (AFDLO) was established. At AFDLO, with a small staff of only seven people, standards and policy were established for Air Force distance learning and the championing of much needed funding for implementation of a program of this magnitude.

In February 2000, the Air Force Institute for Advanced Distributed Learning (AFIADL) was formed out of a merger of ECI, the Air Force Distance Learning Office and the Air Technology Network. AFIADL emerged as an all encompassing agency that enabled the Air Force to provide learning anytime, anywhere, through enterprise delivery and student management systems. The AFIADL worked diligently to make the necessary upgrades that would continue to modernize the program.

Converting CD-ROM delivery to an online format has been a modernization effort that was completed in 2011. The 254 courses that were previously offered via CD now reside on Air University's Advanced Distributed Learning Services (ADLS) site. These courses are in PDF format that allow users to highlight, take notes, and print selected portions of the lesson. Additionally, students may download the entire course to DVD or their personal computer, so they can have access while away from military domains. The obvious advantages for updating content, providing anytime/anywhere access for users, and cost savings, in terms of postage, make this format an advantage.

The Navy's Center for Personal and Professional Development

Just as the Army and Air Force evolved from paper-based correspondence courses of the past 40 years, the Navy followed suit. The same distribution, postage, and updating issues appeared over the years and dissipated as technologies enabled content to be distributed, at first via CD-ROM, and then, eventually, online.

In the late 1990s, the Navy also entered the arena of technology-enabled distance learning. This endeavor was intended to deliver quality education and training to the right people at the right time as part of their career-long training continuum. As a result, a network of automated electronic classrooms, video tele-training, and learning resource centers were used to carry out these tasks. There were five phases to the implementation of this plan: developing an enterprise strategic plan, refining that plan, designing and developing system architecture to support it, evaluation of the prototype, and launching those enhancements. The five-phase program was eventually fielded in May of 2001 via military and nonmilitary Web sites. There were also plans to have classified information on its own protected site.

In the meantime, courses were converted to the new format. In the beginning, 50 Navy-specific courses were converted, as were 580 general business and management courses and 800 other technical courses. It was a herculean, therefore slow process. Housing the courses on the Navy's learning management system was part of this process.

By the year 2000, and in response to the increasing need for Sailors to have access to higher education in pursuit of their GED and/or college degree, the Navy College's Distance Learning Partner program was developed. Since its inception, partnerships with colleges and universities have added to the distance learning opportunities, with each degree making maximum use of professional military training and experience to fulfill degree requirements.

On May 30, 2008, the Navy entered into its current distributed learning program, which focuses on increasing efficiencies. The Center for Personal and Professional Development serves as the central authority for Navy training for leadership, profession and personal development, as well as training and support. It provides the tools, opportunities, and solutions to foster an environment for each student to maximize their potential. With effective technology-driven training delivery, this organization provides the competencies needed in support of mission readiness.

DISTANCE LEARNING VERSUS DISTRIBUTED LEARNING

In the late 1990s, the Department of Defense (DoD), acting on a White House initiative, launched the Advanced Distributed Learning (ADL) program. This program changed the emphasis of distance learning—where teachers were physically separated from the learner, to distributed learning—where separation might occur but face-to-face classroom presence, on a limited basis, could also be part of the paradigm (Fletcher, Tobias, & Wisher, 2007). It has been called one of the most significant events in the DoD's commitment to distance education (Duncan, 2005). The ADL vision was for human knowledge, stored as digital content, to be accessible to all and have the ability to be used in a variety of instructional settings. The change marked a difference in the way distance learning would be designed, developed, and packaged for delivery. It marked the shift away from paper-based, television, to emerging technologies, including the use of the Internet.

The Advanced Distributed Learning Initiative

The White House's initiative, during the late 1990s, prompted the ADL to develop standards for Web-based content. Even though the DoD took months to update guidance for course developers, the intent was to provide a way for developers to share content, methods, and code, while ensuring tax dollars were not wasted on duplicated efforts. The DoD planned for online search routines to discover content. The DoD also enlisted the ADL to published requirements for accessibility, interoperability, durability, and reusability of Web-based content. To implement DoD guidance, the ADL initiative developed an idea called the Shareable Content Object Reference Module (SCORM). This model allowed these search routines along with the accessibility, interoperability, durability, and reusability that was required. Unfortunately, implementation was not easy. Even though the concept called for content to be separated into small pieces—such as lessons, topics, or tasks, which would allow pieces to be reassembled into different ways, the files ended up being too large. Keeping content piece small has proven to be more difficult to implement than was anticipated by the DoD.

The early concept of course design with SCORM was compared to Lego blocks. Each piece would represent a small, standalone, reusable piece of instructional content. These small, "tagged" pieces would populate a database available for discovery by all other military services and government agencies. This way, the items that would be needed, could be retrieved and reused by any of these entities, therefore saving time and money. Although a promising concept, the large database of reusable chunks has yet to be realized. All branches of the military have active programs producing SCORM-compliant courses, however, each implement the standards in different ways. The Army chose a business model that did not define the size or level of content tagging. As a result, most developers opted to tag at the course level. That meant reusability was limited, and unlikely to be used by other services, or government agencies, at the large, full-course level.

For DoD, the acceptance and use of SCORM continues to be at issue. Therefore, the promise of interoperability between delivery systems and the hope of reusability have not been fully realized. The granularity, or size of learning objects to be shared, is not adequately defined or standardized among organizations. The governance and location of repositories for these learning objects has not been fully addressed. Even more fundamental has been the question of whether or not all Web-based content needs to be SCORM-compliant. These issues have prompted a review and revision of DoD guidance.

The Army Distributed Learning Program

General Reimer, the former Chief of Staff of the Army, approved the concept plan for The Army Distributed Learning Program (TADLP) on April 19, 1996. His vision was to look into the possibility that, in time, resident courses would consist of officer and non-commissioned officer professional education courses. All other courses, which included military occupational specialties, would be presented by a combination of resident training and distributed learning. This program provided the overarching long-range programming, planning, funding, and acquisition strategy needed for DL to become a pillar of Army training.

The Army Distributed Learning Program combines resources of the active Army and reserve component to deliver instruction to soldiers, worldwide. It uses information technology to develop, implement, and evaluate instruction, enhancing and extending traditional methods of learning. TADLP is an integral component of the institutional, operation, and self-development training domains.

The Army Distributed Learning Program is comprised of Army-wide courseware development, the Army eLearning program, The Army Learning Management System (ALMS), and distributed learning classrooms (fixed and deployable). TADLP supports the DoD intent to deliver "learner-centric" training, when and where required, increasing and sustaining readiness throughout the active Army and reserve component.

The Army National Guard, had its own distributed learning initiative supporting the four pillars of their system: courseware, technology, instructor training, and learner support services. Their approach to development of courseware differed from the Army in that they believed development should be designed specifically for the delivery platform (Bond, Poker, & Pugh, 1999). Today, this focus has shifted, as technology has evolved and delivery platforms have changed, which now offer greater flexibility.

Advanced Distributed Learning Service

The Air Force Advanced Distributed Learning Service (ADLS) was established in February of 2000, by combining three distinct organizations: the Air Force Distance Learning Office (AFDLO), the Extension Course Institute (ECI), and the Air Technology Network

Program Management Office (ATN PMO). It served to carry out the mission to provide voluntary non-resident courses for both active duty and reserve Air Force personnel and providing career-broadening advanced distributed learning courses to people throughout the DoD and civil service. Having a place to control these learning products became important as demand grew.

Computer-based training was a vast improvement over publishing textbooks and mailing them to students. As more courses were delivered via CD-ROM, certain issues began to arise. One of the major problems was in version control. Whenever an update was needed, a new CD-ROM was reproduced and distributed to organizations. This resulted in improper filing of the old, outdated version, with the unintentional result of a user being given the wrong copy. With emergence of the Internet, publishing and mailing items to students was resolved. Upgrades in versioning software helped students get the most current versions of the training they required. Costs were lowered and centralization of material helped everyone gain access to, and have the ability to update, material, quickly and more easily than ever.

The Air Force migrated into the eLearning era using distributed learning funds generated by the Air Technology Network (ATN, 2009). In October of 2004, the Air Education and Training Command (AETC) initiated an effort to deliver and track their courses online using a learning management system (LMS). The projected population was 44,000 users. Consequently, demand wildly exceeded expectations. By the end of 2005, over 100,,000 users were actively pursuing their training requirements by using this system. This success was noted, and the ADLS was selected by Air Staff in June 2006 to host all computer-based Air Force ancillary and readiness/deployment training. By the end of that same year, ADLS had 640,000 registered users. Unfortunately, the huge number of users stressed the system, which was only designed to support the original 44,000 users, so it crashed. With heroic measures, service was restored within three days. Server restrictions caused access times to be slow and interruptions frequent. Ultimately, service was adequately restored and improved with the addition and architectural reconfiguration of servers.

The Air Force's Air Force ADLS currently delivers, tracks, and reports SCORM-based course content 24 hours a day, 7 days a week. After establishing an account from a ".mil" environment, content is accessible anytime, anywhere. ADLS also has a unique feature (site partners), which allows organizations or agencies to manage their own courses and users, thus behaving as stand-alone learning management system. When a user logs on to one of these sites, they are accessing courses unique to that particular site. Typically, the sites contain content relating to functional career areas. Currently ADLS has 19 site partners.

Management of ADLS is centrally administered with decentralized execution. Configuration control of ADLS is done in conjunction with its partners. If a change is desired, a user or manager submits a System Change Request (SCR), which is recorded by the ADLS program management staff. The change requests are prioritized and presented at a quarterly configuration control board meeting. The partners review the list, and the prioritization, recommending approval or disapproval. The SCR list is then given to ADLS programmers to develop and implement. Constant communication ensures SCRs are clearly defined and that the submitter knows the status.

ADLS currently has 725,000 active users and over 2,300 courses. Course completions average about 600,000 per month, with January 2011 registering over 1,000,000 course completions. The staff to support this mission consists of four people manning the help desk from 0600–2000 Monday–Friday, and 0800–1200 on Saturday.

PROGRAMS AND INITIATIVES

The Future of Print and the Use of Electronic Publications

For the Air Force, print will continue to be used extensively. In spite of a DoD drive to convert as many courses as possible to online, the Air University maintains that it will not select media that are less than optimal to reach its many learning objectives. For some objectives, print still offers the most effective way for students to read large amounts of text. It is believed by the university that print is truly the only "anytime-anywhere" medium. With security issues, DOD firewalls, Computer Based Instruction (CBI) development costs, and lack of bandwidth assure print has a long future in Air Force distance learning. It will continue to be used as a supporting medium for most courses, whether they are using interactive television (ITV), audio conferencing, CBI, or online. As soon as technology and quality-control permits, some text materials will be delivered electronically for onsite printing and binding.

Satellite Delivery of Distance Learning

The Army's distance learning, via one-way satellite delivery, has evolved over the years. Like the Air Force's experience with emerging (and changing) technologies, the Army also experienced a period of time where instruction was broadcast via satellite, effectively. As technologies allowed other methods of more effective distance learning to occur, older technologies became less attractive, less effective, and less used. For example, with the advent of digital television transmission, analog service was no longer a viable option.

While the use of one-way satellite delivery for distance learning of resident training had declined, the opposite was true for distributed learning. The Army's Deployed Digital Training Campus (DDTC), a transportable networked classroom supporting 20 students simultaneously with workstations, uses network collaboration tools, Video Tele-training (VTT). This medium allows access to the World Wide Web via satellite communications, Interactive Multimedia Instruction, and access to the Army Learning Management System and other Web-based training products and simulations.

The primary objective of the DDTC is to provide the same level of training capabilities to soldiers serving in deployed units as soldiers located at home station. The DDTC is a deployable system enabling group or individual instruction through VTT or collaboration. It allows professional development training through access to current distributed-learning products and constructive simulations-based training. The DDTC provides a means for the current institutional training base to deliver proponent approved Distributed Learning products and services to deployed forces. It also provides a flexible means to meet surge training requirements. The DDTC provides the capability to access structured formalized training (such as individual Web-based courses and VTT sessions) as well as access to unstructured training through live and online collaboration. It facilitates the transformation of the institutional training base from a centralized resident training environment to a blended resident and distributed training environment. This blended approach lays the foundation for a more flexible institutional training philosophy necessary to support the Army's current wartime training needs and ongoing future force transition.

The Army supports delivery of distributed learning to its reservists with their Digital Training Facilities (DTF) program. The original commitment was to provide a DTF within 50 miles of all reservists. Over time, and with the proliferation of the Internet, the program had to close some facilities but still offers access to top-of-the-line equipment and connections allowing access to the Internet and training classes. At this time there are 223 DTFs at 91 installations in the United States, Germany, Belgium, Italy, and Korea.

Computer-Based Instruction

Computer-based instruction is also known as interactive courseware (ICW) and interactive multimedia instruction (IMI). All branches of the military have programs using these modes of delivery. Most have evolved to Web-based delivery. With the demand for more and more multimedia, and the resulting strains on bandwidth, the program offers options using CD-ROM and digital video disk (DVD). The portable CBI option is also appealing to certain populations, such as Army reservists, who may not have access to computers with connectivity.

The Air Force also has found value in their CD-ROM/DVD offerings and will continue to use the courses that have already been produced. With the development of data-casting, many of these courses will be available for delivery by satellite to local servers without having to modify them to meet the constraints of public Internet delivery. It is expected, however, that with time and funding cuts, many of these legacy CD-ROM courses will migrate to SCORM standards.

eLearning

The Army offers free, individual Army training for every active Army, National Guard, reservist, ROTC cadet, and department of the Army civilian, through its e-Learning program. There are thousands of courses available. Some offer certification, are prep programs or offer other learning opportunities in trade, business, or leadership skills. The program also provides subject matter experts and mentors to support students in their self-development. Other supportive services offered include access to digital books, eLibraries, and online research tools. Language training, one of the most popular features of the eLearning program, is also available to the student, when they need it, 24 hours a day.

New Initiatives in Distributed Learning

Distributed learning content must be developed for delivery on a variety of platforms. It should contain reconfigurable items, such as: video, game-based scenarios, digital tutors, and assessments that are tailored for learners. Content could incorporate the use of social media, massively multiple online games (MMOGs), and other emerging technologies. It leverages the power of information and communication technologies (such as, simulation, interactive multimedia instruction (IMI), video tele-training, e-learning, and others) and can be either real-time (synchronous) or non-real time (asynchronous).

Distributed learning will also continue to support stand-alone learning. IMIs that are self-paced, and offer learning without an instructor, need to serve soldiers and civilians positioned in remote areas, especially where there is little or no bandwidth.

Virtual Worlds

In late 2008, the Air Force began to explore the capabilities of the virtual world with an initiative they christened MyBase. The military was interested in exploring virtual worlds to reduce the time and costs associated with bringing airmen into resident training and to create more realistic experiences for users than those provided by traditional IMI. The Navy Undersea Warfare Center also piloted the use of Second Life for operational testing, training, collaboration, product development, and design.

The National Guard developed their presence in Second Life as Emergency Management (EM) Nexus, a training and preparedness program. EM Nexus is part of the Joint State Response Training System, aimed at civilian responders, emergency operations centers and joint operations centers. It is a hybrid delivery that combines the functionality of a virtual world with the ability to link to external distance-learning applications.

The United States Training and Doctrine Command (TRADOC) set up a virtual experience for civilians to explore a career in the Army. The virtual space included career counseling, presentations on military life, and school benefits. Although there is still interest in the efficacy of virtual worlds for military training, the level of interest is currently mixed.

Mobile Learning

The Army's mobile learning initiative began with the establishment of the Connecting Soldiers to Digital Apps pilot in September 2009. The pilot was to explore the value of using smart phones to provide soldiers with applications for select administrative, training, and tactical functions. The CSDA set additional goals to evaluate new training approaches that allow soldiers to learn anytime, anywhere.

The Army sees the next generation learner as part of the Digital Generation, totally comfortable with the latest media technology. Using this logical extension of distributed learning, there are plans by the Army to supplement classroom learning by extending and partially transferring training content into the soldier's hands through smart phone and other mobile technologies. It provides a means to augment traditional learning with hands on application of new processes or procedures learned in residence. The Army believes that students learning from hand-held technologies are picking up the course material much faster and with greater retention resulting in significantly higher graduating scores. This method of learning potentially saves time and money in training our soldiers.

The program was widely accepted in the beginning but slowed when challenged by questions of security, cost, content, and networks began to surface. In particular, the program is hampered by concerns over information assurance—to ensure information and data being carried in the smart phone is being protected from inadvertent loss or disclosure. Although most training content is unclassified, there is concern that the content, in aggregate, may be sensitive.

As a result of a white paper published on Air Force Future Learning Technology, a number of areas of emerging technology were investigated for potential implementation into the Air Force distance learning capability. Among them were mobile learning and virtual worlds.

Hand-held mobile devices have become the center of attention to supplement more traditional training methods. The Air Force is conducting studies to determine whether mobile learning can be used as a supplemental training device or should be limited to performance support applications. Studies need to be conducted to ensure LMSs are optimized for delivery to mobile devices. Content development also needs to be investigated to maximize compatibility between server-based and mobile-delivered training materials.

As the budget, personnel availability, operations tempo, and technology continue to be ever changing, the Air Force will continue to explore distance learning applications as a way to reduce costs and accommodate personnel issues through the appropriate application of evolving technology.

The Army Distance Learning Program Modernization

The modernization of The Army Distance Learning Program Modernization (TADLP) is an effort to revolutionize the way the Army develops and delivers training and education. This shift is an aggressive and ambitious endeavor that requires a significant change in the current culture. It will also take tremendous teamwork and coordination to adapt and move forward the capabilities that remain relevant while abandoning those that no longer support current and future learning requirements for soldiers and civilians.

The modernization of the Army's Distributed Learning Program is a bold strategy that establishes a continuum of learning throughout the career of the Army professional. It proposes new programs, plans, and policies, risk-taking in leveraging new learning and neurosciences, learning strategies, and application of learning technologies in curriculum/courseware design and delivery that will enable the execution of rigorous, relevant, and tailored content at the point of need.

TADLP will offer a single portal to digital resources and connect learners to mentors. It will also provide streamlined access to peer-based learning interactions, facilitators, and content repositories that provide learning that allows for career assignment, advancement, change, and the pursuit of personal educational goals.

The TADLP learning framework is learner centric, provides a career-long continuum, is continuously accessible, offers transparent infrastructure to the user, and supports the learner with Subject Matter Experts (SMEs), facilitators, digitized learning media, Knowledge Management Structures, policies, and resourcing models.

In recent years the rapid development of computer and communication technologies have established new instructional opportunities in distributed learning. Disruptive technologies—the displacement of a previously used technology—have revolutionized advances and driven transformation, providing the learner: content self-discovery capability, peer-to-peer interaction and dissemination of experience-based learning. TADLP will use these opportunities to allow active learning using automated and adaptive information extraction, assimilation, and other technology management, to provide Soldiers the ability to become adaptive, critical thinkers, able to solve complex problems in uncertain operational environments.

TADLP will facilitate a Continuous Adaptive Learning Model (CALM) through its robust capability to develop and update engaging technology-delivered DL content. This content can be used in the schoolhouse as part of a blended learning approach, distributed for sustainment training, or accessed via performance support applications.

New Training and Education Models for Military Distributed Learning

The behaviorist pedagogy has focused the military learning model since the late 1960s. Behavioral learning theory begins with a concept of changing behaviors as a result of the soldiers' response to stimuli. This has been especially attractive for use in training (as opposed to educational) programs as the learning outcomes associated with training are usually clearly measured and demonstrated behaviorally (Anderson & Dron, 2011). According to behaviorist theory, it is the desired outcome, the new behavior, or changes in behavior that is the focus of instruction. This definition fit the military's focus on training tasks: a specific, measurable response to a specific stimulus. These theoretical ideas led directly to instructional designs such as computer-assisted instruction, and instructional systems designs.

In line with this behaviorist approach, the Army learning model for instructional development was the Systems Approach to Training (SAT). It served the needs of the Army from about 1973 until just recently, when the model was changed to the Analysis, Design, Development, Implementation and Evaluation (ADDIE) process. The previous SAT process followed similar standard design processes, but had an emphasis on the systems approach. To meet the needs of distributed learning with its emerging technologies and blended learning components, the ADDIE process offers emphasis in areas that require greater flexibility while keeping rigorous and relevant training and education needs paramount.

Integrating Social Media and Distance Learning

In the past, the model for military distance learning assumed learners chose DL because of their learning preference. The model was defined by a lack of social presence and the presentation was stand alone without teachers or other students considered.

The learners who chose DL were thought to be autonomous in their learning style, comfortable alone with a book or with computer-based learning. The model persisted for many years in spite of research that indicated the opposite. Anderson and Dron (2011) noted differences between the performance outcomes based on the interaction with an instructor or other learners; with high levels or low levels of social presence.

With the popularity of new Web technology, collaboration between teachers and students offers as much or as little social presences as is required by personal preference. For the first time in 40 years, the Army is changing from their favored behaviorist model of learning

With the revolutionary Army Learning Concept for 2015, the Army asked "How must the Army change its learning model from one that barely satisfies today's needs to one that promotes operational adaptability, engages learners, enables the Army to outpace adversaries, and meets the Army's learning requirements in 2015?" (Army Learning Concept, 2015) Anderson and Dron (2011) define this as the so-called fourth and fifth generation distance technologies that incorporate Web technology to create "intelligent flexible learning." It should be noted that none of these generations has been eliminated over time; rather, the repertoire of options available to DL designers and learners has increased.

The Army was searching for a new model to fit the "next generation learner must be adaptive on several levels if it is to support the qualities of operational adaptability in the force. First, the Army learning model must develop adaptable Soldiers and leaders who have the cognitive, interpersonal, and cultural skills necessary to make sound judgments in complex environments, from the tactical to strategic level" (TRADOC Pamphlet 525-8-2, 2010, p. 16).

The Army's new learning model requires an "adaptive development and delivery system, not bound by brick and mortar, but one that extends knowledge to Soldiers at the operational edge, is capable of updating learning content rapidly, and is responsive to Operational Army needs" (TRADOC Pamphlet 525-8-2, 2010, p. 16). The Army defines the operational edge in terms of placing learning content in the hands of the learner, anytime, anywhere.

Perhaps the most challenging of all is the concept of sustained adaptation. This concept uses routine feedback from soldier performance to drive adjustments to curriculum content and learning products. This isn't an adjustment made by training developers; these are adjustments made by technology. Sustaining adaptation includes a capacity to routinely explore and integrate advanced technologies and learning methods to remain competitive and engage learners.

By design, the 2015 learning model must promote adaptable qualities in soldiers and leaders and be sufficiently adaptable to adjust to shifting operational demands. The solution is a continuous adaptive learning model, a framework comprised of elements that together create a learner-centric, career-long continuum of learning that is continuously accessible and provides learning at the point of need in the learner's career. Transparent to the learner, but integral to the model, is a supporting infrastructure that includes subject matter experts and facilitators from the centers of excellence (CoEs), a digitized learning media production capability, knowledge management structures, and policies and resourcing models that are flexible enough to adapt to shifting operational and learner demands. The model's underlying infrastructure is critical to enabling the shift from a course-based, throughput-oriented, instructor-led model to one that is centered on the learner. Through this adaptive development and delivery infrastructure, the learning model provides maximum opportunities for individual learning that are grounded in schoolhouse experiences, and continue through the career span in a soldiers' career.

The Future of Military DL

Although distance learning has great potential to reduce training costs, provide more training events, and focus on specific training requirements, there are some who still resist implementation. Often it is resource availability or policy gaps that delay the implementation of expanding distance learning content. Although there is a requirement and a desire for distance learning in many areas, the funding and manpower to make it always lags behind. In2011, as a result of resource constraints, Army training and education developers were directed to increase the type and number of courses developed for distributed learning. It is likely the other services will also seek new ways to design and develop distributed learning and stay within a tightening budget.

In her comments to the Army training and education community, Helen Remily, the TCM-TADLP commented on the state of DL. We are "embarking on a revolutionary modernization in the way the Army develops and delivers learning content an aggressive and ambitious endeavor that requires a significant transformation of our current culture" (U.S. Army, 2012, p. 1). She called on all stakeholders to adapt new and emerging technologies and be prepared to retain the relevant and abandon what no longer supports the new Army Learning Model. Military DL will remain efficient and effective while engaging soldiers, sailors, airmen, and civilians into the 21st century.

REFERENCES

Anderson, T., & Dron, J. (2011). Three generations of distance education pedagogy. *The International Review of Research in Open and Distance Learning.* Retrieved from http://www.irrodl.org/index.php/irrodl/article/view/890/1663

Bond, C., Poker, F., & Pugh, J. (1999, August). The National Guard distributed learning initiative, a system's approach. *Conference Proceedings, the 15th Annual Conference of Distance Teaching and Learning* (pp. 45–49). Madison, WI: The University of Wisconsin System.

Connecting Soldiers to Digital Applications. (2009). Retrieved from http://www.arcic.army.mil/csda.html

Distributed Learning System. (n.d.). Digital Deployed Training Campus Overview. Retrieved July 21, 2011, from https://www.dls.army.mil/DDTC_overview.html.

Duncan, S., (2005). The U.S. Army's impact on the history of distance education. *The Quarterly Review of Distance Education, 6*(4), 2005, 397–404.

Fletcher, J. D., Tobias, S., & Wisher, R. A. (2007). Learning anytime, anywhere: Advanced distributed learning and the changing face of education. *Educational Researcher, 36,* 96–102.

Welcome to ATN, Air technology network. (2009, June 5). Retrieved September 2011 from http://atn.afit.edu

U.S. Army. (2012, April 18). *The Army distributed learning program modernization strategy* (Strategic Plan 2012-2015). Washington, DC: Author.

U. S. Training and Doctrine Command Pamphlet 525-8-2 (2010, September 14), V 1.0,.

41

DOCTORATES FOR PROFESSIONALS THROUGH DISTANCE EDUCATION

TERRY EVANS AND ROSEMARY GREEN

INTRODUCTION

Distance education has a long history of providing learning and training across a comprehensive range of fields and educational sectors for children, adolescents, adults, and the elderly. One small, but significant, part of this provision has been in doctoral education, the most advanced area of university study. However, the distance education literature has made little reference to this field, although interest is emerging in this area, especially as more mid-career professional people undertake doctorates, whether PhDs or so-called professional doctorates. Evans (2008) reported, "a review of the literature on distance education shows that doctorates have rarely been a topic of consideration [and] the literature on doctoral education shows that distance education has rarely been a topic within it" (p. 304). Little has changed since Evans conducted his review. While research, data, and writing on both distance education and doctoral education grow and become increasingly easier to access (due, in no small part, to online data sets and reports), the two fields have not yet merged. However, in practice, a symbiotic connection between distance education and doctoral education has taken place over in the past two decades or more. This chapter reviews the issues and practices surrounding doctoral education at a distance, especially for those in major professional fields of study—education, library, and information science, and nursing, for example—and considers the future implications for what appears to be a growing aspect of distance education practice. This review draws particularly on our experiences, research and writing on U.S. and Australian practices in distance-based professional doctoral education. These are illustrative of the two major North American and British traditions of doctoral education in the English-speaking world.

In order to review this field, it is important to be clear about what is included as doctoral education for this purpose. We are influenced by international standards and discussions on these matters and include graduate programs leading to the award of a doctoral degree based solely or substantially on original research and scholarship that is deemed to have made a significant and original contribution to knowledge. This includes

PhDs, of course, and those many professional doctorate courses that require, as part of their courses, original research and scholarship for professional or workplace, rather than disciplinary, purposes. In this sense, the UK Council of Graduate Education argued that, "Professional Doctorates need to be seen and treated as research degrees that produce doctoral thinkers and doers in specified areas of professional practice and by different means" (Powell & Long, 2005, p. 27). The importance of research in all doctorates is seen as fundamental in many parts of the world, although in the United States this is less the case for professional doctorates; in some U.S. professional doctorate programs research is not seen as fundamental and research training is limited and not practiced (Archbald, 2011; Offerman, 2011). For example, the American Association of Colleges of Nursing articulates a distinction between professional and research-focused doctorates.

> The DNP is designed for nurses seeking a terminal degree in nursing practice and offers an alternative to research-focused doctoral programs. DNP-prepared nurses are well-equipped to fully implement the science developed by nurse researchers prepared in PhD, DNSc, and other research-focused nursing doctorates. (AACN, 2011b)

The above contrasts with international policies on doctorates. For example, the European University Association (EUA) asserts, "the most predominant and essential component of the doctorate is research" (2005, p. 8). The League of European Research Universities (LERU) recommended to the European Commission and others that they "Acknowledge the distinctiveness of doctoral training, which is intimately tied to the research process" (2007, p. 14). This is also the case in Australia where the Government's Australian Qualifications Framework (AQF) states that a doctoral graduate "... will have systematic and critical understanding of a complex field of learning and specialised research skills for the advancement of learning and/or for professional practice" (AQF, 2011, p. 61). Likewise, the Council of Australian Deans and Directors of Graduate Studies (DDOGS) argues: "The Council considers that research is the fundamental substance of a doctorate. It does not accept that a best practice doctorate can be earned solely or substantially on the basis of coursework" (DDOGS, 2008, p. 3).

For this chapter, however, the importance of a significant research element in a doctoral course rests on its implications for distance education practice. That is, doctoral coursework at a distance may be seen as an extension of many other areas of distance education coursework practices in terms of curriculum and educational design, assessment etc.; whereas, facilitating, supporting, advising/supervising and examining students' research at a distance require different understandings and practices from those of "conventional" distance education.

These different understandings and practices are not radically different from some particular areas of distance education practice, for example, those where students are supported and supervised to complete individual projects or fieldwork practice. The doctoral students' experiences are, however, necessarily individual and original during their research and dissertation (thesis) writing; therefore, distance educators and their universities need to develop and adopt particular practices to ensure each student undertakes research appropriately, ethically, and of a substance and standard to be worthy of a doctorate. In this chapter we have separated the discussion into a review of the background to doctoral education at a distance and then a discussion of its future.

THE BACKGROUND OF DOCTORAL EDUCATION AT A DISTANCE

Doctoral Education Research for Part-Time Students

Professional people undertaking doctorates typically (but not exclusively) do so part-time; that is, they usually work in their professions while undertaking their doctorates as a secondary activity. The notion of part-time doctoral study is quite precise in some nations, and somewhat less so in others. For example, in Australia "part-time" and "full-time" doctoral candidature (as it is termed) are defined and used by government, universities and other agencies in their funding, reporting and resource allocations. Specifically, the Australian Government funds tuition for full-time domestic candidates for four years maximum, whereas domestic part-time candidates are funded at half the annual rate but for twice as many years (eight) (Evans, Evans, & Marsh, 2008). Universities report their numbers of candidates each semester to the responsible government department together with key characteristics, including full-time or part-time candidature, and whether candidates are enrolled on-campus or off-campus. These data are made available publicly and, as one might expect, most off-campus candidates are also part-time and, in the terms of this chapter, are "distance students." However, the doctoral candidate population exhibits considerable diversity (see, Evans & Pearson, 1999; Pearson, Cumming, Evans, Macauley, & Ryland, 2008, 2011; Pearson, Evans, & Macauley, 2008), and even the "simple" matter of what it means to be a part-time or full-time candidate or an on-campus or off-campus candidate is not always easy to assume. (For example, Evans has advised doctoral candidates who are enrolled formally as part-time and off-campus, although they are also full-time staff members working at the university for whom their doctoral study is also part of their work.)

In North America, where federal, state, and provincial governments partially fund university education, categories related to full-time and part-time doctoral study vary, as evident in data provided by the U.S. National Center for Education Statistics (Choy & Cataldi, 2011; Hussar & Bailey, 2011; Snyder & Dillow, 2011). In some instances, such distinctions do not exist for government funding and administrative purposes, although the practical consequences are part of universities' departmental doctoral processes and courses. American graduate students rely upon their own resources—current earnings, savings, and employer and family contributions—to meet their expenses. Grant aid, a major form of financial assistance from federal, state, institutional, or private sources, may be awarded in various forms, such as "grants, scholarships, fellowships, traineeships, tuition waivers, or tuition reimbursement by an employer" (Choy & Cataldi, 2011, p. 14). Many doctoral students rely upon stipends available through research, teaching, or administrative assistantships; usually full-time enrollment is a prerequisite for graduate stipends. In the United States, assistantship recipients are customarily chosen by academic departments, which, in many instances, receive federally funded research grants that support such assistantships.

Part-time doctoral study itself is not often discussed in the literature on higher education or distance education. Neumann and Rodwell (2009) see that such students are "invisible" in the institutional and policy sense. Typically, U.S. data sources categorize distance enrollment, part-time enrollment, and numbers of doctoral students separately (Choy & Cataldi, 2011; Hussar & Bailey, 2011; Snyder & Dillow, 2011). However, where numbers of doctoral students enrolled in online or hybrid programs are reported from the institutional, regional, or national level, we infer that the majority of these students are part time. There is more literature, however, on related topics where part-time doctoral study is an explicit or implicit feature. In particular, this is the case where individual doctoral programs are reported, especially those in professional fields to which we turn in the next section. Barnacle and Usher (2003) and Evans (2002) have addressed the features of part-time study in terms that show the potential benefits to society from having professionals undertake research training through doctorates focused on topics that that are directly related to professional practice. Evans (2010a, 2011) has written specifically on how students can manage part-time doctoral study around their work and family commitments that are important matters for most mid-career professional people. He has also written for supervisors (advisors) on how to understand and work productively with such students.

Doctoral Education in Professional Contexts and Disciplines

Coursework-based doctorates and higher-degree-by research (HDR) doctorates in several disciplines are well suited for delivery at a distance, either partially (as in hybrid or blended programs) or entirely. American doctorates require a substantial period of taught coursework, followed by an original research project, whereas "the research project dominates and defines Australian doctorates" (Green, 2009, p. 12). With the growth in professional doctorates, taught coursework is becoming increasingly more common in Australian doctoral work. The fields of education, nursing, and library and information science (LIS) offer germane examples of doctoral programs that have successfully incorporated distance education models. Doctoral programs in education, nursing, and LIS are customarily populated by professional adults, typified as practitioners who seek, "a university-based foundation for their practice" (Archbald, 2011, p. 11). In these and other professional fields, work experience is highly valued (Lee, 2011) and sometimes "required before the doctorate is awarded" (Thurgood, Golladay, & Hill, 2006, p. 21).

Education

The doctorate in education is customarily linked to the profession of teaching, although doctoral students and graduates cover an array of topics and practices related to education and its management (see, for example, Leonard, Becker, & Coate, 2004; Malfroy, 2011). In both nations, described in this chapter, the doctorate in education broadly spans two degrees, the discipline-based PhD and the practitioner-oriented EdD. The Australian PhD and EdD are more research-intensive (Green, 2009; McWilliam et al., 2002). Candidates in U.S. and Australian doctoral education programs often enter doctoral programs as experienced, professional teachers and educational administrators. The median age of the U.S. doctoral candidate in education is 41.5 years of age, the highest median among fields of study measured by the U.S. Department of Education (Snyder & Dillow, 2011); in Australia the mean is 45 years (Pearson et al., 2008). These students commence research with known and immediate problems found in professional practice on which they can build applied research that is significant and relevant to their students, colleagues, and the profession at large (Beutel et al., 2010; Green, 2009; Offerman, 2011).

Education is a large enterprise, "a sprawling field of study, broad reaching and multidisciplinary" (Richardson, 2006, p. 245). The field has produced "more doctorates every year from 1962 to 1999 than any other major field" (Thurgood et al., 2006, p. 15). During 2007–2008, "15 percent of doctoral students were working on a Ph.D. in education,

Doctor of Education (EdD), or other education doctorate" (Choy & Cataldi, 2011, p. 5); many, if not most, continued to teach or otherwise work while enrolled as doctoral students. Addressing the tendency of education doctorates to continue working while attending school part time, Richardson (2006) notes that a large number of these doctoral students must either support themselves through graduate school or rely upon workplace funding; education doctoral candidates are enrolled part time and continue to work while studying. In response, many schools of education schedule classes at night or on weekends (Richardson, 2006) and offer hybrid or fully distance-based programs. Compared with enrollees in other graduate degree programs during 2007–2008, a greater proportion of U.S. students pursuing a doctorate in education worked full time while enrolled (72%), and fewer (25%) were enrolled full time. Twenty-one percent of doctoral education students, a relatively large percentage when compared with other disciplines, received financial assistance from their places of employment during 2007–2008 (Choy & Cataldi, 2011). These data shed light on the negotiations that doctoral students, particularly those in education and other practitioner-based fields, must make in their working, personal, and academic lives.

Currently, U.S. schools of education are adopting online modalities at a rate slightly higher than graduate schools of other disciplines. Between 2004 and 2008, schools of education offering online courses grew steadily in number each year. In 2006, 71% of these schools reported offering one or more credit-bearing online courses at the undergraduate or graduate level. Institutions known for their online programs reported the largest numbers of conferred doctorates in education for the 2004–2005 year: Nova Southeastern University, 432 (ranked first for doctorates earned); Capella University, 167 (ranked second); Argosy University, 136 (ranked fifth) (Eduventures, 2008). Capella and Argosy are for-profit universities and members of a cohort of educational institutions that invest heavily in distance learning. Nearly two-thirds of U.S. for-profit institutions indicate that online learning is critical to their long-term planning (Allen & Seaman, 2010).

Teachers, administrators, and other practitioners enrolled in doctoral education programs appreciate the need for research that contributes to both professional knowledge and practice. These learners focus on locating and appropriating the intersections between practice and scholarship, practice and theory, practice and research (Green & Macauley, 2007). "When they engage with information and information systems, they seek efficiency, effectiveness, ease and appropriateness, and, above all, customization to their personal learning styles and research interests" (pp. 322–323). Although these findings target doctorate in education students, their attributes as intentional learners are widely observable in other professional doctorate students.

Nursing

As professions and academic fields, "education and nursing demonstrate a reciprocal relationship of practice and research. [Doctoral research within both fields] is actualized in professional practice where it is also evaluated" (Green 2009, p. 136). Like the doctorate in education, Australian and American nursing doctorates fall into the research-heavy PhD (and DNSc) and the professional doctorate. The "prof-doc" counterparts of the DNP in the United States are the DN, DNurs, and DM in Australia (Green, 2009). In the United States especially, curricula for both the professional doctorate and the PhD emphasize didactic learning. In both countries, the professional nursing doctorate requires a higher level of experiential and clinical competencies than does the PhD, reflective of practitioners-students' imperative to contribute to disciplinary knowledge as well as patient and community well-being. "DNP-prepared clinicians [are expected to] develop culturally appropriate, data-driven, innovative programs that address stakeholder concerns while building on previous research to effect organizational and societal change" (Brown-Benedict, 2008, p. 454).

Of all fields, nursing acutely demonstrates a critical linkage between the doctorate and the profession. The nursing workforce shortage is widespread internationally, and the literature points to an urgent need for nurses, especially doctorally prepared nursing faculty, to train practicing nurses. Nursing programs are seriously short of faculty, and impending faculty retirements within the next decade are expected to exacerbate this lack of qualified instructors (Candela et al., 2009). Efforts to increase the numbers of nursing graduates and doctoral programs are hindered by low enrollments, high attrition rates, and, consequently, low graduation rates. Student age plays a role as well, for nurses who choose to undertake a doctorate "often do so late in their careers" (Effken, 2008, p. 557), leaving less time to develop fully as nursing educators. As are their U.S. counterparts, Australian nursing faculty are increasingly pressured to undertake doctoral level preparation, and "many are seeking doctoral studies on a part-time basis while continuing to be employed as academics" (Redman, 2007, p. 62). The nursing profession continues to respond aggressively to the need for doctorally prepared nurses. Recently, the American Association of Colleges of Nursing (AACN, 2011a) announced an encouraging trend upward in nursing program enrollments overall, fueled in part by a growth in distance-based doctoral coursework and programs. In the United States, the professional doctorate is growing quickly; the numbers of DNP programs increased from 20 in 2006 to 153 in 2010; 106 programs are in the planning stages. During the 2009–2010 academic year, 533 research-focused doctorates and 1,282 practice-focused doctorates in nursing were awarded (AACN, 2011a). Similarly, longitudinal research into Australian doctoral education (Evans & Macauley, 2010) has identified a marked growth in nursing doctorates relative to other professional doctorates.

In 2006, the U.S. Department of Health and Human Services announced that it had prioritized the training of health educators in new technologies and distance education methods, with critical implications for professional and advanced health education delivered at a distance. As the number of doctoral nursing programs increases, delivery of such programs is shifting noticeably toward partial or complete online formats (Candela et al., 2009). Like most adult professionals who elect to undertake doctorates at a distance, nursing candidates respond to the flexibility, convenience, and ways of accessing instructors and academic resources that no longer require close proximity. These are especially relevant factors for graduate students who must juggle multiple responsibilities (Candela et al., 2009; Green, 2009; Offerman, 2011).

Library and Information Science

The PhD is the only doctoral degree in Library and Information Science (LIS); there is no professional LIS doctorate. In Australia, Charles Sturt University offered a professional doctorate in the field using distance education, however, enrollments were not sufficient to sustain the program. The Masters degree dominates the field of library and information science as the terminal degree in many nations and is conferred in greater numbers than PhDs. The U.S. PhD in LIS follows a traditional curriculum that includes coursework, a comprehensive examination preliminary to dissertation research, and the completed dissertation; a practicum may also be required. Since 1926, when the first doctorate in library science was offered at the University of Chicago, 38 North American universities have offered doctoral degrees in LIS. During decade spanning 1998–2007, 841 LIS doctorates were awarded by American universities (Sugimoto, Russell, & Grant, 2009). Wallace (2009) reports 998 students enrolled in doctoral programs accredited by the American Library Association in 2008. Typical of most data retrieved for this chapter, distinctions among part-time, full-time, distance-based, and on-campus enrollment are not available. Twenty-seven of Australia's 39 universities produced 114 LIS-related PhDs, earned by LIS educators, researchers, and practitioners between 1962 and 2006 (Macauley, Evans, & Pearson, 2010). However, these figures do not necessarily mark a growth in the numbers of LIS educators who hold PhDs in library and information science. Australian and American researchers alike have noted a declining percentage of LIS faculty earning a PhD in library science as, increasingly, members of the LIS professoriate are reported to hold doctorates in computer science, education, and other disciplines (Jaeger, Golbeck, Druin, & Fleischmann, 2010; Macauley et al., 2010; Sugimoto et al., 2009).

Not surprisingly, librarian practitioners and LIS educators are among the earliest adopters of educational technology. Since the 1980s, college and university libraries have provided the first campus sites, both physical and virtual, for 21st-century information tools (Macauley & Green, 2008). The library profession and LIS education in the United States, Australia, and Europe whole-heartedly embrace the movement toward online education, its practices, pedagogies, and technologies. In 2005, a number of LIS schools and other academic units with tracks in education, communication, informatics, information technology, and information science united to form the iSchools caucus, an international organization dedicated to promoting the information field throughout the 21st century and broadly concerned "with questions of design and preservation across information spaces, from digital and virtual spaces such as online communities, social networking, the World Wide Web, and databases to physical spaces" (iSchools, 2011). Practicing librarians and information specialists seeking advanced degrees "generally comprise the largest enrollment base of these schools" (Harris, 2009, p. 171). iSchools institutions dominate the list of most productive LIS-related doctoral programs, and the caucus has been termed a "phenomenon." Even so, the LIS and information community have yet to engage in substantial dialogue regarding implications of the iSchools approach (Sugimoto et al., 2009), a virtual embodiment that challenges and extends the potential for professional doctoral education across multiple disciplines.

DOCTORAL EDUCATION AT A DISTANCE

Evans (2008) reports that Nova University in Florida appears to be the first university to formally offer a doctoral program mainly at a distance in the early 1970s (http://www.fischlerschool.nova.edu/experience-fse/history-and-growth). However, the Nova doctorates are based substantially on coursework together with a small applied research dissertation. White (1980) argues that such doctoral programs at a distance were criticized from outside of distance education largely, it seems, on the basis that "real" doctorates can only be undertaken as full-time students nestled within the academy. Pearson and Ford (1997) show that the academy in Australia has actually accommodated doctoral research that has been off-campus and part time for many years, indeed since the first PhDs at the University of Melbourne in 1948. Simpson (2009) notes that there were similar practices in the UK, especially through the University of London's external programs and relations with colleges and fledgling universities in the UK and in the British Commonwealth (pp. 222–223). In effect, there were people enrolled as PhD students who undertook their study off-campus and part time while engaged in employment; sometimes this was in a research position in a government or business organization, or in a professional occupation, such as, a veterinarian or agricultural officer.

Although these latter types of doctoral programs were rarely considered as "distance education" in the sense that this term was used from the 1970s, the practices and procedures are ones that provide the basis for more contemporary doctoral work with part-time candidates. In Australia, for example, Evans (2008) reports that external (distance) study (almost entirely part time) has been a formal part of Australian university practices since the 1980s when the government recorded such enrolments. The major Australian universities offering doctorates at this time were Deakin University and the University of New England, which were the major distance education (dual-mode) universities at the time.

The doctoral enterprise has proven highly successful in both countries, and the trend toward steadily increasing enrollments in American and Australian doctoral programs (and distance-based doctoral instruction) continues into the 21st century. Australian universities awarded 5,796 research doctorates in 2009, approximately a 380% increase since 1991 (Macauley et al., 2011). Graduate enrollments in the United States during the last half of the 20th century have soared and continue to increase steadily (Archbald, 2011). A total of 63,712 doctoral degrees were earned in American universities during the 2007–2008 academic year, a 38.5% increase over the prior decade. The U.S. Department of Education predicted that approximately 97,900 doctoral degrees will be earned at U.S. institutions in 2019–2020, a 54% increase (Hussar & Bailey, 2011). Furthermore, when all disciplines are represented, the projected numbers of American doctorates earned by men will increase by 39%, while a 68% increase for women is anticipated. This prediction alone has a broader implication for growth in numbers of women achieving doctorates across all disciplines, via all forms of delivery.

The 2000 report *Re-envisioning the PhD* (Nyquist & Wulff, 2000) emphasizes the need to increase doctoral students' exposure to technology and prepare doctoral students for a wider variety of professional options. The U.S. PhD has long been considered an elite, advanced degree awarded to privileged students "for extended study as they prepared for careers as scholars and researchers" (Nettles & Millett, 2006, p. 1), most of whom resided on campus and studied full time. These assumptions have nearly reached obsolescence as forces from within and external to higher education reshape doctoral education. Technological developments, changes in workforce composition, global economies, commodification of higher education, and competition for students (Altbach, Gumport, & Johnstone, 2001; Archbald, 2011; Livingston, 2009; Thurgood et al., 2006) have profoundly influenced the intention, design, and delivery of the doctorate in Australia, North America, and worldwide. Simultaneously, technological developments which are "altering forever the ways in which we utilize information and communicate with each other" and widely varied methods for delivering distance learning "affect teaching and learning (including research) at all levels" (LaPidus, 2001, p. 275). Those in the growing population of professionals seeking an advanced degree recognize that personal and professional circumstances preclude students leaving their current employment, relocating, or undertaking a lengthy commute to campus. Administrators and educators have responded, and "graduate education is now being designed in more systematic ways to reflect clearer links between one's education and career" (Livingston, 2009, p. 27).

Online study now assumes a major role in doctoral education worldwide. Consequently, "the mid-career adult wanting to advance in his or her present field, enter a new field, or embark on a journey of intellectual growth and enrichment" now has enhanced accessibility to doctoral faculty, courses, and academic resources (Archbald, 2011, p. 13). As the pool of nontraditional students continues to grow, distance education provides an appealing venue for attracting and retaining new students in doctoral programs (Christensen, Anakwe, & Kessler, 2001; Livingston, 2009). A recent review of the research on distance education reported in North American doctoral dissertations for the decade 1998–2007 found that the earlier studies in their sample focused on distance education as an educational phenomenon; much of the research set out to compare traditional to online learning modes and technologies (Davies, Howell, & Petrie, 2010). By 2007, a shift toward research interest in learners' and instructors' experiences with, and perceptions of, distance education was noted. Conceivably, the decrease in studies that compare face-to-face instruction with distance-based instruction signals a greater acceptance of distance learning as an integrated, viable means of education (Davies et al., 2010).

THE FUTURE OF DOCTORAL EDUCATION AT A DISTANCE

Advising / Supervising

International, national, and institutional documents and policies are slowly recognizing that PhD programs are not (just) apprenticeships for academic appointments, i.e., the destination for about 40% of PhD graduates in most industrialized nations. In 2005, the European University Association produced a report entitled *Doctoral Programmes for the European Knowledge Society* in which it noted:

> With changing demographic trends in Europe, doctoral training may be seen as part of "life-long learning" in line with the Lisbon objectives. This, however, requires a more flexible approach with regard to both the organisation and duration of doctoral studies for part-time candidates. (EUA, 2005, p. 24)

Furthermore, a UNESCO report on postgraduate education—*Trends and Issues in Postgraduate Education: Challenges for Research*—acknowledged that doctorates "in high demand often focus on specific work-related fields as they can lead to professional advancement" (2007, p. 7). The European University Association reached similar conclusions.

> … (A) doctoral candidate was, in most cases, a person with a deep interest in research and a future career in academic research and teaching. This is not true anymore, although society still tends to maintain the stereotype of people with doctoral degrees as scholars living on the isolated worlds of academia … there (is) a growing number of students who pursue doctoral training for professional; knowledge and skill development (for) industry, government and administration, medical and health provision, legal and financial services, NGOs, etc. There are

many students who (undertake) doctoral training for personal development ... and to widen their employment opportunities ... The doctoral candidate today is a very diverse figure. Doctoral ... programmes are reflecting and tackling this reality through finding the right balance between research, which remains the core element of doctoral education, and the necessary orientation to the wider labour market. (EUA, 2005, pp. 26–27)

These circumstances require that advisors and supervisors adopt approaches to supervision that reflect the professional qualities and seniority of their students. They also require understanding that the research being conducted is often fundamentally concerned with the students' professional lives and careers which produces both positive and negative tensions that advisors and supervisors need to recognize and accommodate (Evans, 2010a, 2010b). It is important that part-time professional students are not "invisible" (Neumann & Rodwell, 2009) to advisors and supervisors and are valued as professionals (Lee, 2011). Distance educators have wrestled with many of these types of problems over the years and have deployed correspondence, radio, television, telephone, and now online media to give students a place in the academy. The potential for fruitful conversations is high between experienced distance educators and doctoral advisors, supervisors, coordinators, and deans of graduate studies. The judicious use of online and social media could well produce highly productive doctoral networks connecting universities and the professional contexts in which their doctoral students are located (Evans, Hickey, & Davis, 2005). Of course, the fundamental goal is the achievement of a timely and good quality doctorate, but other goals may be achieved, such as, (future) collaborative applied research, product and service development, and community engagement. Advising or supervising a doctoral student in a professional field can be seen as developing a productive relationship with a nascent "ambassador" for the university and its research.

Information Gathering and Literature Reviewing

Macauley and Green (2008) observed that the proliferation of research sources in digital formats has brought about a fundamental shift in information- and literature-seeking behaviors. Students across all disciplines, at all levels of study, behave as distance learners when gathering literature sources, regardless of whether they are enrolled on campus or online. Academic libraries worldwide provide Web-based library catalogs and databases, full text journal and monograph collections, and electronic tutorials for their distance learners; in doing so, libraries have opened more opportunities for students in any geographic location. "The student reading an online journal in the physical library experiences the same interaction and engagement with information as a colleague who accesses the same journal at a site away from campus" (Macauley & Green, 2008, p. 373). Given the escalation of online collections, resources, and instructional modes conveniently accessible from anywhere, at any time, students are increasingly inclined to seek information from the virtual environment rather than visit the physical library (Green, 2009; Macauley & Green, 2008). Information seeking in this manner requires and accommodates learner autonomy, characteristic of students who undertake professional doctorates at a distance. These practitioners "are accustomed to handling large amounts of information, then decoding, filtering, and synthesizing for others" (Green & Macauley, 2007, p. 325). The fields of education, nursing, library and information science, and other professions require that practitioners exhibit advanced proficiencies in gathering, evaluating, and applying evidence-based literature. Many professional doctorate students arrive at the doctoral process having consumed research actively throughout their careers. Consequently, as Green and Macauley put it, "their familiarity with the literature and research of their profession[s] inclines them toward seeking, organizing, and evaluating practice-oriented information" (p. 325).

The literature reviewing process is central to the doctoral enterprise, common to doctorates in the United States and Australia, across all disciplines. Whether doctoral candidates enroll in research-intensive or practice-oriented programs, they can expect to be inducted into the discursive norms, as well as, "the canonical, epistemological and craft knowledge of their disciplines" (Green, 2009, p. 19) by engaging with the literature. At the same time, professional doctorate candidates commence their explorations of the literature intending to investigate a problem related to their professional practice (Offerman, 2011). U.S, and Australian doctoral students often receive different orientations into the literature and literature reviewing practices. Those studying in U.S. doctoral programs are acculturated "more gradually via extended coursework, deliberate instruction and formal training" (p. 96), which takes place in the physical or virtual classroom. A significant proportion of content-based and applied knowledge, as well as theoretical, epistemological, and ontological foundations of the disciplines, is learned through taught coursework. Much of this coursework is specific to the discipline, while other taught courses may concentrate more broadly on research methods; this is the case in the social sciences and health sciences especially. Research methods courses that incorporate advanced information literacy and literature review instruction are often offered early in doctoral program as a means of grounding incoming students in disciplinary language, norms, and practices. These courses are well suited to online delivery or a blended format, and they may be co-taught by a faculty member and specialist librarian (Green, 2006, 2009). In some American graduate programs, early courses such as these focus on the process of associating of literature reviewing with formulating research questions for doctoral investigation. Students are explicitly taught the essential skills of appraisal and critical analysis of the literature, developing in these students the "capacity to negotiate research literatures ... required for disciplinary participation and, ultimately, disciplinary (re)production" (Green, 2009, p. 108).

Because Australian doctoral curricula require little or no coursework, students must commence reviewing the literature intensely and independently during the earliest days in order to establish research and disciplinary foundations. Where programs do incorporate seminars and learning activities shared by an intact cohort, new doctoral candidates are introduced to information literacy work and literature reviewing in the first academic terms. Within this framework, students are initiated into disciplinary literatures and discourse, while forming learning communities and receiving support for academic progress (Beutel et al., 2010; Green 2009).

Successful doctoral students inevitably reach the point of focused gathering, reading, appraising, then writing from and about the literature specific to their topics, at which time the status of being on-campus or off-campus, full time or part time becomes indistinguishable. In essence, the concentrated activities necessary for preparing one's self and for conducting original, advanced research simultaneously individualize and segregate doctoral learners. Green (2009) finds that, in some instances, students can ameliorate the sense of isolation endemic to doctoral work by becoming attuned to the dialogue held with the literature and positioning themselves within those conversations.

Supporting Doctoral Students

Distance education has often been highly proactive in the provision of forms of support for its students, and the work of Mills and Tait is notable in this regard (see, for example, Tait & Mills, 2003). The emergence of internet-based means of communication over the past two decades, and especially educational and social software of the past decade, has provided new scope and opportunities. For example, Rapanotti, Barroca, Vargas-Vera, and Minocha (n.d.) describe how their part-time research students at the UK Open University are supported via a Second Life entity that they have created for these purposes. In New Zealand a network to support Māori doctoral students has been established which addresses their needs whether on-campus or at a distance (Kidman, 2007). It supports Māori graduate students wherever they are in the world through a Web-based service (http://www.mai.ac.nz/). Again, the potential is high for blending good distance education policies and practices with the needs of doctoral education for professional people.

Educators and learners now have decades of experimentation, experience, and growth on which to continue building and improving off-campus programs. The body of best practices that have proven successful over time is seen in an array of recommendations and strategies, many relevant to the means by which doctoral students communicate with each other, academic faculty and staff, and research mentors. The cohort model is common in the United States and, increasingly, Australia, particularly in professional doctorate programs in education and nursing. Members of doctoral cohorts experience an enhanced sense of community—academic, professional, and personal—that, in turn, accommodates cooperation and reciprocity. Increasingly, cohorts are formed as elements of hybrid programs, those in which face-to-face instructional sessions complement learning activities that occur at a distance, in real time or asynchronously. Instructional designers and distance educators are attuned to the value of active learning strategies and authentic activities that recognize diverse learning styles, facilitated by Web 2.0 technologies, social networking, and Web-based communication applications such as GoogleChat and Skype (Broome, Halstead, Pesut, Rawl, & Boland 2011; Candela et al., 2009; Effken, 2008; Offerman, 2011).

CONCLUSION

In many respects the future for doctoral education at a distance, especially in professional contexts, seems assured. The growth in demand from Masters qualified professional people who wish to extend their knowledge and expertise as applied researchers in their fields has been high. Other than due to the vagaries of economic circumstances and government policies, there is no reason to expect this demand to decline, especially in the developed nations. The pursuit of new knowledge in these knowledge-based economies calls for people who are able to produce (and apply) such new knowledge to contemporary problems, concerns and demands. This suggests that the future is good for universities that are able to offer doctoral programs to professional people who need to study part time and who wish to focus on topics and applications related to their professions. Much of this provision needs to draw on distance education expertise in order to be successful, although one may expect that forms of blended provision (on-campus, online seminars, residential schools, etc.) could be most common. As has often been the case in good quality distance education, a focus on students' contexts and needs is paramount. In the case of doctoral students working in professional fields, this involves seeing them as more than "mere students" and as highly experienced and highly educated people with considerable expertise in their fields who need guidance and mentoring to develop their research skills through doctoral research projects. It is largely about a supervisory / advisory pedagogy of respect—respect for what they know and can do, rather than a dismissiveness of such.

Because doctoral work may be seen as contributing significantly to national, social, and economic benefit, then such doctoral work represents a worthwhile investment for the future. This chapter considers the particular institutional investments that are required to provide high quality distance education experiences and support for doctoral students in their professional contexts. It draws on the related literature from both distance education and doctoral education to support its propositions for good policy and practice.

REFERENCES

Allen, I. E., & Seaman, J. (2010). *Class differences: Online education in the United States, 2010.* Newburyport, MA: Sloan Consortium and Babson Survey Research Group.

Altbach P. G., Gumport, P. J., & Johnstone, D. B. (Eds.). (2001). *In defense of American higher education.* Baltimore MD: Johns Hopkins Press.

American Association of Colleges of Nursing. (2011a). *Despite economic challenges facing schools of nursing, new AACN data confirm sizable growth in doctoral nursing programs.* Retrieved from http://www.aacn.nche.edu/Media/NewsReleases/2011/enrollsurge.html

American Association of Colleges of Nursing. (2011b). *Leading initiatives: Doctor of Nursing Practice.* Retrieved from http://www.aacn.nche.edu/dnp

Archbald, D. (2011). The emergence of the nontraditional doctorate: A historical overview. *New Directions for Adult and Continuing Education, 129,* 7–19. doi: 10.1002/ace.396

Australian Qualifications Framework Council. (2011). *Australian qualifications framework.* South Australia: Ministerial Council for Tertiary Education and Employment. Australian Qualifications Framework Council. Retrieved from http://www.aqf.edu.au

Barnacle, R., & Usher, R. (2003). Assessing the quality of research training: The case of part-time candidates in full-time professional work. *Higher Education Research & Development, 22,* 345–358.

Beutel, D., Gray, L., Beames, S., Klenowski, V., Ehrich, L., & Kapitzke, C. (2010). An exploratory study of online social networking within a doctorate of education program. *International Journal of Learning, 17,* 67–79.

Broome, M. E., Halstead, J. A., Pesut, D. J., Rawl, S. M., & Boland, D. L. (2011). Evaluating the outcomes of a distance-accessible PhD program. *Journal of Professional Nursing, 27,* 69–77. doi:10.1016/j.profnurs.2010.09.011

Brown-Benedict, D. J. (2008). The doctor of nursing practice degree: Lessons from the history of the professional doctorate in other disciplines. *Journal of Nursing Education, 47,* 448–457.

Candela, L., Carver, L., Diaz, A., Edmunds, J., Talusan, R., & Tarrant, T. A. (2009). An online doctoral education course using problem-based learning. *Journal of Nursing Education, 48,* 116–119.

Choy, S. P., & Cataldi, E. F. (2011). *Graduate and first-professional students: 2007–08.* (NCES 2011-174). Washington DC: US Department of Education. National Center for Education Statistics. Retrieved from http://nces.ed.gov/pubsearch/pubsinfo.asp?pubid=2011174

Christensen, E. W., Anakwe, U. P., & Kessler, E. H. (2001). Receptivity to distance learning: The effect of technology, reputation, constraints, and learning preferences. *Journal of Research on Computing in Education, 33,* 263–279.

Council of Australian Deans and Directors of Graduate Studies. (2008). *Framework for best practice in doctoral research education in Australia.* Retrieved from http://www.ddogs.edu.au/

Davies, R. S., Howell, S., L., & Petrie, J. (2010). A review of trends in distance education scholarship at research universities in North America, 1998–2007. *The International Review of Research in Open and Distance Learning, 11*(3). Retrieved from http://www.irrodl.org/index.php/irrodl/article/view/876/1602

Eduventures. (2008). *Common indicators for schools of education, Part II: Characteristics and benchmarks for schools of education.* Boston MA: Eduventures. Schools of Education Learning Collaborative. Retrieved from http://www.eduventures.org

Effken, J. A. (2008). Doctoral education from a distance. *Nursing Clinics of North America, 43,* 557–566. doi: 10.1016/j.cnur.2008.06.007

European University Association. (2005). *Doctoral programmes for the European knowledge society.* Brussels: European University Association. Retrieved from http://www.eua.be

Evans, T. D. (2011). Managing part-time candidature with work and family commitments. In C. Denholm & T. D. Evans (Eds.), *Doctorates downunder: Keys to successful doctoral study in Australia and New Zealand.* (2nd ed., pp. 179–185) Melbourne, Australia: ACER Press.

Evans, T. D. (2002). Part-time research students: Are they producing knowledge where it counts? *Journal of Higher Education and Research and Development, 21,* 155–165.

Evans, T. D. (2008). Transforming doctoral education through distance education. In T. D. Evans, M. Haughey, & D. Murphy (Eds.), *International handbook of distance education* (pp. 303–317). Bingley, UK: Emerald.

Evans, T. D. (2010a). Supervising part-time doctoral students. In M. Walker & P. Thomson (Eds.), *Doctoral supervisor's companion. Supporting effective research in education and the social sciences* (Vol. 2, pp. 131–137). New York: Routledge.

Evans, T. D. (2010b). Understanding doctoral research for professional practitioners. In M. Walker & P. Thomson (Eds.), *Doctoral supervisor's companion. Supporting effective research in education and the social sciences* (Vol. 2, pp. 66–75). New York: Routledge.

Evans, T. D, Evans, B., & Marsh, H. (2008). Australia. In M. Nerad, & M. Heggelund (Eds.), *Toward a global PhD? Forces and forms in doctoral education worldwide* (pp. 171–203). Seattle, WA: Center for Innovation and Research in Graduate Education, University of Washington.

Evans, T. D, Hickey, C., & Davis, H. (2005). Research issues arising from doctoral education at a distance. In T.D. Evans, P. Smith, & E. Stacey. (Eds.), *Research in distance education 6.* Geelong: Deakin University. Retrieved from http://www.deakin.edu.au/education/rads/conferences/ publications/ride/2004/index.php

Evans, T. D, & Macauley, P. D. (2010). Australian PhD theses in selected professional and academic disciplines 1987–2006 and the implications for future research capacity. *Journal of the World University Forum, 3,* 103–116.

Evans, T. D., & Pearson, M. (1999). Off-campus doctoral research in Australia: Emerging issues and practices. In A. Holbrook & S. Johnston (Eds.), *Supervision of postgraduate research in education* (pp. 185–206). Coldstream, Victoria: Australian Association for Research in Education.

Green, R. (2009). *American and Australian doctoral literature reviewing practices and pedagogies* (Unpublished doctoral dissertation). Deakin University, Geelong, Australia.

Green, R. (2006). Fostering a community of doctoral learners. *Journal of Library Administration, 45,* 169–183.

Green, R., & Macauley, P. D. (2007). Doctoral students' engagement with information: An American–Australian perspective. *portal: Libraries & the Academy, 7,* 317–332.

Harris, R. (2009). "Their little bit of ground slowly squashed into nothing": Technology, gender, and the vanishing librarian. In G. J. Leckie & J. E. Buschman (Eds.), *Information technology in librarianship: Critical approaches* (pp. 165–180). Westport CT: Libraries Unlimited.

Hussar, W. J., & Bailey, T. M. (2011). *Projections of education statistics to 2019.* (NCES 2011-017). Washington DC: National Center for Education Statistics, Institute of Education Sciences, U.S. Department of Education. Retrieved from http://nces.ed.gov/pubs2011/2011017.pdf

iSchools. (2011). *The power to transform lives.* Retrieved from http://www.iSchoolss.org

Jaeger, P. T., Golbeck, J., Druin, A., & Fleischmann, K. R. (2010). The first Workshop on the Future of iSchools Doctoral Education: Issues, challenges, and aspirations. *Journal of Education for Library & Information Science, 51,* 201–208.

Kidman, J. (2007). Supervising Māori doctoral candidates. In C. Denholm & T. Evans (Eds.), *Supervising doctorates downunder: Keys to successful doctoral study in Australia and New Zealand* (pp. 164–172). Melbourne, Australia: ACER Press.

LaPidus, J. B. (2001). Graduate education and research. In P. G. Altbach, P. J. Gumport, & D. B. Johnstone (Eds.), *In defense of American higher education* (pp. 259–276). Baltimore, MD: Johns Hopkins University.

Lee, A. (2011). Professional practice and doctoral education: Becoming a researcher. In L. Scanlon (Ed.), *"Becoming" a professional: An interdisciplinary analysis of professional learning* (pp. 153–169). New York: Springer.

Leonard, D,. Becker, R., & Coate, K. (2004). Continuing professional and career development: The doctoral experience of education alumni at a UK university. *Studies in Continuing Education, 26,* 369–385.

League of European Research Universities. (2007). *Doctoral studies in Europe: Excellence in researcher training.* Leuven, Belgium: Author.

Livingston, M. P. (2009). *Dissertation writing in nontraditional distance doctoral programs: Approaches to challenges of dissertation completion* (Unpublished doctoral dissertation). Nova Southeastern University, Fort Lauderdale FL.

Macauley, P. D, Evans, T. D., & Pearson, M. (2010). Australian PhDs by LIS educators, researchers and practitioners: Depicting diversity and demise. *Library & Information Science Research, 32*, 258–264. doi:10.1016/j.lisr.2010.07.007

Macauley, P. D, Evans, T. D., & Pearson, M. (2011). *Classifying Australian PhD thesis records by ANZSRC field of research codes. Report on a Study for the Research Excellence Branch, Australian Research Council.* Canberra: Australian Research Council Research Excellence Branch.

Macauley, P. D, & Green, R. (2008). The transformation of information and library services. In T. D Evans, M. Haughey, & D. Murphy (Eds.), *International handbook of distance education* (pp. 367–383). Bingley, UK: Emerald.

Malfroy, J. (2011). The impact of university–industry research on doctoral programs and practices. *Studies in Higher Education, 36*, 571–584. doi:10.1080/03075079.2011.594594

McWilliam, E., Taylor, P. G., Thomson, P., Green, B., Maxwell, T., Wildy, H., & Simons, D. (2002). *Research training in doctoral programs: What can be learned from professional doctorates?* Canberra, Australia: Department of Education, Science and Technology.

Nettles, M. T., & Millett, C. M. (2006). *Three magic letters: Getting to Ph.D.* Baltimore MD: Johns Hopkins Press.

Neumann, R., & Rodwell, J. (2009). The "invisible" part-time research students: A case study of satisfaction and completion. *Studies in Higher Education, 34*, 55–68. doi:10.1080/03075070802601960

Nyquist, J., & Wulff, D. H. (2000). *Re-envisioning the PhD: Recommendations from national studies on doctoral education.* University of Washington, Seattle. Retrieved from http://depts.washington.edu/envision/project_resources/national_recommend.html

Offerman, M. (2011). Profile of the nontraditional degree student. *New Directions for Adult and Continuing Education, 129*, 21–30. doi:10.1002/ace.397

Pearson, M., Cumming, J., Evans, T., Macauley, P., & Ryland, K. (2008). Exploring the extent and nature of the diversity of the doctoral population in Australia: A profile of the respondents to a 2005 national survey. In M. Kiley & G. Mullins (Eds.), *Quality in postgraduate research: Research education in the new global environment - conference proceedings* (pp. 90–114). Canberra: Australian National University. Retrieved from http://www.qpr.edu.au/papersdatabase.php?orderBy=author&byYear=2008

Pearson, M., Cumming, J., Evans T., Macauley, P., & Ryland, K. (2011). How shall we know them? Capturing the diversity of difference in Australian doctoral candidates and their experiences. *Studies in Higher Education, 6*, 527–542. doi:10.1080/03075079.2011.594591

Pearson, M., Evans T., & Macauley, P. (2008). Growth and diversity in doctoral education: Assessing the Australian experience. *Higher Education, 55*, 357–372. doi:10.1007/s10734-007-9059-3

Pearson, M., & Ford, L. (1997). *Open and flexible PhD study and research.* Canberra, Australia: Department of Employment, Education, Training and Youth Affairs Evaluation and Investigations Program. Retrieved from http://www.dest.gov.au/sectors/higher_education/publications_resources/profiles/archives/open_flexible_phd_study.htm

Powell, S., & Long, E. (2005). *Professional doctorate awards in the UK.* Lichfield, UK: UK Council for Graduate Education.

Rapanotti, L. , Barroca, L., Vargas-Vera, M., & Minocha, S. (n.d.). *Deep think: A Second Life campus for part-time research students at a distance.* Milton Keynes, UK: Open University. Retrieved from http://virtualmphil.open.ac.uk/

Redman, R. W. (2007). Critical challenges in doctoral education: Highlights of the biennial meeting of the International Network for Doctoral Education in Nursing, Tokyo, Japan, 2007. *Japan Journal of Nursing Science, 4*, 61–65. doi:10.1111/j.1742-7924.2007.00081.x

Richardson, V. (2006). Stewards of the field, stewards of an enterprise. In C. M. Golde & G. E. Walker (Eds.), *Envisioning the future of doctoral education: Preparing stewards of the discipline. Carnegie essays on the doctorate* (pp. 251–267). San Francisco: Jossey-Bass.

Simpson, R. (2009). *The development of the PhD in Britain, 1917–1959 and since.* New York: Edwin Mellen Press.

Snyder, T. D., & Dillow, S .A. (2011). *Digest of education statistics 2010* (NCES 2011-015). Washington, DC: National Center for Education Statistics, Institute of Education Sciences, U.S. Department of Education. Retrieved from http://nces.ed.gov/pubs2011/2011015.pdf

Sugimoto, C. R., Russell, T. G., & Grant, S. (2009). Library and information science doctoral education: The landscape from 1930–2007. *Journal of Education for Library and Information Science, 50*, 190–202.

Tait, A., & Mills, R. (Eds.). (2003). *Rethinking learner support in distance education: Change and continuity in an international context.* New York: Routledge.

Thurgood, L., Golladay, M., & Hill, S. (2006). *U.S. doctorates in the 20th century.* (NSF 06-319). Arlington, VA: National Science Foundation, Division of Science Resources Statistics. Retrieved from http://www.nsf.gov/statistics/nsf06319/pdf/nsf06319.pdf

UNESCO. (2007). *Trends and issues in postgraduate education: Challenges for research. Final report of the UNESCO Forum on Higher Education, Research and Knowledge.* Paris: UNESCO. Retrieved from http://unesdoc.unesco.org/images/0016/001607/160744e.pdf

U.S. Department of Health and Human Services. (2006). *U.S. grants and funding.* Washington DC: U.S. Department of Health and Human Services. Retrieved from http://www.hhs.gov/grants/index.shtml

Wallace, D. P. (2009). The iSchools, education for librarianship, and the voice of doom and gloom. *Journal of Academic Librarianship, 35,* 405–409. doi:10.1016/j.acalib.2009.07.001

White, M.A. (1980). Graduate degrees by external studies: The Nova University programmes in Florida. *Distance Education, 1,* 188–197.

42

TEACHING SCIENCE[1] AT A DISTANCE

DIETMAR K. KENNEPOHL

INTRODUCTION

There has been a well-documented and progressive decline in student participation in mathematics and science at both school and university levels in several industrialized countries around the world (James, 2007). Nevertheless, the overall demand for learning science has also taken on a renewed urgency (Commission on Mathematics and Science Education, 2009; UNESCO Education Sector, 2011) and is globally exceeding the capacity of established educational routes. Together the challenges of participation and capacity are becoming more pressing as we consider science education in the 21st century. Online distance delivery offers practical alternatives to traditional on-campus education, but teaching science online and at a distance can be more demanding than (and certainly is not as common as) many other disciplines. There are a variety of reasons for this, of which the most obvious is dealing with the practical and applied components (laboratory, clinic, field work). This chapter will take a look at higher education teaching and learning in science with special emphasis on practical work.

SCIENCE CULTURE

Every discipline and sub-discipline has its own particular epistemology, language, culture, and its own way of doing things. Students are not merely learning facts and concepts, they usually undergo an apprenticeship within their discipline. That is, they effectively learn within the context of being, for example, an electrical engineer or a microbiologist or a mathematician. So, in considering teaching and learning in science, it becomes important to appreciate some features that may be particular to the science culture (Matthews, 1994).

Science is both content (body of knowledge) and process (way of knowing). The approach to teaching and learning often tries to reflect scientific methodology or process. That is, students are expected to state a problem, ask questions, make observations, keep records, offer explanations, create a design or carry out an experiment, and

670

communicate findings with others. The vehicle to learning is problem solving and scientific inquiry, and this forms the model for navigating and dealing with hypotheses, facts, laws, and theories. It is therefore not surprising that the practical components are at the heart of most science programs, or that more research activities are being introduced at the undergraduate level (Taraban & Blanton, 2008). Still, this discovery-, problem- or inquiry-based approach has always been difficult to do on a large scale without falling back into a more expository (demonstration) mode. However, the larger problem in science is the tyranny of content. Most science and engineering courses are packed with content, activities, multiple tasks and choices that often lead to cognitive overload and an actual decrease in learning (Impelluso, 2009; Sweller, Ayres, & Kalyuga, 2011). This volume and complexity of content and concepts is a great challenge, but the actual order in which the learner tackles these is also important and, in some cases, can make learning more difficult. The sciences have a long tradition of scaffolding and building up basic skills first before getting to the heart of and usually the interesting bits of the discipline itself. "The teaching of math and science suffers from being all scales and not enough music" (Tobias, 1990, p. 42).

THE APPROACH TO LEARNING SCIENCE

As suggested above, the teaching of science has a well-founded constructivist and experiential perspective (Bailey & Garratt 2002). In the context of the aforementioned content and process components in science, science educators (both on campus and at a distance) use many of the same tactics for teaching and learning as their colleagues in other disciplines. That is, long established principles like student engagement, interaction, prompt feedback, time on track, creating respectful/open learning environments, and clear expectations are valued and employed (Chickering & Gamson, 1987). Still, doing this online and at a distance can present some additional challenges. Miller (2008) provides a good overview of some approaches and addresses myths surrounding online teaching in the sciences. However, there are three areas that warrant particular attention for the sciences namely (a) concept inventories and misconceptions, (b) integrating information and communication technologies (ICTs), and (c) laboratories.

Determining a student's concept knowledge was first made popular in the area of physics (Hestenes, Wells, & Swackhamer, 1992), but is now being actively investigated by science educators in numerous other disciplines. The idea of the concept inventory is to carry out measurements with a multiple choice test before and after a course to identify where and how much learning has occurred. Surprisingly, in one physics course some negative learning was actually reported (Savinainen & Scott, 2002). Nevertheless, both the culprit and opportunity is seen as learner misconceptions (Duit, 1999). The concept inventory provides the diagnostic window to target specific misconceptions in the course, which can eventually be turned into learning opportunities. The suggested approach is to lead learners through a sort of conceptual conflict (Hewson & Hewson, 1984) whereby they first predict what should happen, then are confronted with factual data, and finally are asked to analyze and resolve any discrepancies with the original prediction. This process closely parallels scientific methodology. Success greatly depends on judging the amount of intervention by the teacher. Practice has shown that merely telling students what the correct concept entails, without having them work through it themselves, is ineffective (Guzzetti, Snyder, Glass, & Gamas, 1993). Conversely, having students figure it

inquiry based instruction. Domin argues that having the student only experience one or two instructional styles gives "an incomplete depiction of the scientific enterprise" and active participation in all three of Kuhn's phases is encouraged (Domin, 2009).

A variety of methods are being used to deliver the practical components of a course to distance learners, including (a) supervised face-to-face sessions offered in a concentrated format on campus or at regional sites or in the field, (b) home study laboratory kits, (c) virtual laboratories (includes video demonstrations), and (d) remote laboratories. The first type, with the exception of having more flexible locations and times, is almost exactly what one would find at a residential institution. However, the other three would be viewed by most science educators as alternative delivery modes.

The gold standard has essentially been the face-to-face model and anything other than this traditional approach is subject to intense scrutiny. This perspective is commonly held despite reports in the literature that the alternative modes are essentially equivalent and in a few cases better than face-to-face (Corter, Esche, Chassapis, Ma, & Nickerson, 2011; Doulgeri & Matiakis, 2006; Fiore & Ratti, 2007; Lindsay & Good, 2005; Smetana & Bell, 2011). Indeed, critics of alternate modes cite either a need for a "proper" laboratory environment, with all of its atmosphere, noises, smells, and the haptic experience of experimenting, or a supposed lack in alternative modes of direct student-student and student-instructor interactions. While both laboratory environment and human interaction can and do lead to both formal and informal learning, we know that other forms of interaction in other environments can equally well lead to learning (Anderson, 2003).

Home-Study Laboratories

One strategy is to have learners carry out laboratory work off-campus on their own. Examples of this include (a) the use of laboratory kits, (b) practicing kitchen science (using common household items), and (c) undertaking self-directed fieldwork. The first two approaches are most common and have been used for some time around the globe, including in Australia (Hall, Jones, & Palmer, 2006; Lyall & Patti, 2010; Mosse & Wright, 2010), Africa (Kriek & Grayson, 2009), United Kingdom (Burnley, 2008; Ross & Scanlon, 1995, pp. 137–145), Canada (Al-Shamali & Connors, 2010; Kennepohl, 2007), and the United States (Jeschofnig & Jeschofnig, 2011; Reeves & Kimbrough, 2004). In contrast, although self-directed fieldwork is done in the earth sciences and some life sciences, evidence of this approach in the literature is meagre (Cloutis, 2010). One of the preferred approaches to fieldwork has been the "urban trail" model where students explore their local environments using some generic guidance (Dove, 1997). With the development of GPS technologies and access to mobile devices there is an expectation that self-directed fieldwork will become a richer experience and increase in popularity.

Although home-study laboratories have many of the aims, concerns, and approaches in common with traditional residential laboratories, there are some notable differences. The most obvious is that they offer the learner great autonomy in space and time, which is consistent with the notion that distance learners tend to be self-directed, seeking control of their own learning outcomes (Moore, 1983; Paulsen, 1993). While students enjoy the freedom offered by home-study laboratories, they are also isolated. This brings us to the second notable difference. The home-study laboratories possess a strong student-content component with student-teacher and student-student interactions being limited to remote communications (e-mail and phone). Anderson's equivalency theorem suggests that deep and meaningful learning should still be supported with this type of mix (2003). The third notable difference is the context of the home-study laboratory itself. The teaching laboratory experience is not only an important vehicle for learning, it also contextualizes how a scientist might think and operate. Home-study experiments are brought directly into the home and therefore science is no longer viewed as something that is only done in the laboratory. That science is all around us and a part of our world is an important message that a lot of science educators try to convey to their students. Home-study laboratory work is an excellent way of doing this and arguably should be part of any undergraduate science program.

In addition to these differences, there are other important factors to weigh when considering using home-study laboratories including cost, logistical complexity, added capacity and experimental sophistication. It is often assumed that home-study is substantially cheaper and easier compared with running residential laboratories. At least one recent audit of institutional costs for chemistry laboratories showed that the residential mode was more economical than the home-study mode (Shaw & Carmichael, 2010). The particular model of home study can also influence who carries the expense. For example, employing kitchen experiments or having students purchase commercially assembled kits provides savings for the institution, but moves the cost to the learner (Jeschofnig & Jeschofnig, 2011, pp. 57–65). While kitchen science can provide a solid non-threatening introduction to laboratory work, it is also particularly problematic if over used. It can be aggravating for the learner to assemble the needed materials (Jeschofnig & Jeschofnig, 2011, p. 58) and it may not meet the expected level of sophistication for a post-secondary science course (Kennepohl, 2007). Still, when compared with the face-to-face option, distance students seem to prefer the flexibility of doing laboratory work at home, which is reflected in reports of dramatic increases in course enrolment and laboratory participation when employing the home-study option (Al-Shamali & Connors, 2010).

However, for numerous reasons including access to specific required equipment, facilities, chemicals, and specimens, as well as safety concerns, not all laboratory work can be accommodated through home study. However, other alternatives do exist.

Virtual Laboratories

Simulations have been with us long before modern computers were on the scene, with a long history in such fields as medicine (Satava, 2008) and the military (Oriesek & Schwarz, 2008, pp. 10–11). However, it was the development of flight simulators that popularized the idea using simulations for training and learning. Currently, training simulations are used in many areas including operating vehicles and marine craft, healthcare, air traffic control, different military applications, industrial processes, production, logistics, business, finance, economics, history, science, engineering, and education among others. Some simulators are incredibly complex and realistic, but also very expensive. As educators, we are more interested in the affordable and accessible simulations available as learning tools for our students.

Many science educators have found this to be a great way to teach students (especially new students), because the overall cognitive load is smaller than in the equivalent real life situation (Kirschner, 2002; Sweller et al., 2011). There is certainly a natural assumption that the more life-like the virtual environment is (i.e., higher fidelity between real and virtual), the more learning will occur. While this is an intuitive assumption, it is not always true. A very realistic simulation is often better suited in training and challenging the expert, while the beginner is usually better off with a simplified version of reality. While this is good news for keeping costs down, some designers underscore the importance of having sufficient reality cues present in the simulation to engage the learner (Swan, 2008). In short, the challenge for the educator is to determine in specific situations exactly what sub-set of reality provides the desired learning environment.

A major strength of the virtual laboratory is that it allows a great deal of student autonomy. Computer simulations can provide continuous and automatic feedback and the learner is in control within a safe environment—not just physically safe, but having the knowledge that work will not be lost, or can easily be redone. Furthermore, one can speed up or slow down different components of the work, which provides time to explore and relieves the student of tedious work not directly related to learning. In the "sandbox" of the virtual laboratory one can explore all sorts of "what if" scenarios without consequence, which might be impractical in a real practicum. Many of the design features employed in gaming, especially those that engage the learner, can work quite well in the virtual laboratory, allowing opportunity to exploit the strong connection between play and learning (Kolb & Kolb, 2010). Other advantages of the virtual laboratory include increasing IT literacy, the ability of the system to track students, and potentially automate some of the assessment. Conversely, there are also several disadvantages. While there is room for exploration by the learner, a simulation cannot deal with alternate models because one is bound by what is programmed into the simulation. Often some sort of technical and/or teacher support is required. As with the home-study laboratories, there is also isolation from direct human contact and, again, there is a limit to what can be accommodated (not everything is readily simulated). One curious disadvantage of the virtual laboratory is that it is very difficult to simulate non- ideal situations and errors that are so easily found in real life.

Remote Laboratories

Scientists and engineers not only employ remote control when an experiment or instrument is physically inaccessible (e.g., because of location or danger), they also find it an excellent method for sharing expensive equipment and facilities. Remote control over the Internet for teaching experiments was first established in the early 1990s (Cox & Baruch, 1994; Penfield & Larson, 1996). The number of examples of remote access for teaching laboratories in the natural and physical sciences is small, with the bulk of contributions coming from the areas of robotics, computing, and engineering. A worldwide inventory of about 120 remote controlled laboratory sites done in 2006 indicates that about 60%–70% was in engineering, 30% in physics (this includes electronics labs), and less than 10% occur in other disciplines (Gröber, Vetter, Eckert, & Jodl, 2007).[3] Together, a summary of remote laboratory sites found online (Le Couteur, 2009), an online bibliography of literature (DiscoverLab, 2007), and a review of platforms and applications (Kolias, Anagnostopoulos, & Kayafas, 2008) give a good initial overview of the range of teaching experiments available.

In contrast to virtual laboratories, remote access allows learners to physically carry out real experiments online. Students obtain real results using real substances and make real conclusions, just as they would if they were in the laboratory with the equipment. Remote laboratories represent the best alternative to working in a real laboratory, and are being employed in four ways: (a) to allow observations of natural phenomenon or experiments;

(b) to carry out measurements; (c) to manipulate instruments or physical objects in experiments; and (d) to facilitate collaborative work at a distance (Kennepohl, 2010).

Similar to the home-study and virtual laboratories, the student-student and student–instructor interactions are usually reduced or altered in the remote laboratory. There is also the additional challenge of making the student comfortable and functional within the remote laboratory environment itself. Early accounts focussed mostly on the technology, feasibility, and the ability to have the learner connect with and control an experiment remotely. In later studies, there was more emphasis on pedagogy and learning design. Teachers certainly have many of the same aims and employ many of the same strategies as in the traditional proximal laboratory. So, in addition to the necessary infrastructure (system architectures, policies, logistics), they also discovered that successful remote laboratories are self-contained, intuitive and designed with a seamless pedagogical front-end to facilitate the high level of student learning and skills-development to allow experiments to be carried out at a distance (Azad, Auer, & Harward, 2011). The opportunity to do real experiments as opposed to simulations cannot be understated and has often been stressed by researchers in the area (Cooper, 2005; Kennepohl, 2010; Machotka, Nedić, Nafalski, & Göl, 2010). Since these remote laboratories exist in the physical world with real experiments on real samples, there is also the possibility of operational problems, errors, and non-ideal results. In moderation, this is beneficial for the student and should be seen as an opportunity to encourage learning.

A common problem faced by science educators is securing the financial commitment to build and maintain remote laboratories. There are certainly examples of many initial efforts on various Web sites that reflect a keen interest. Unfortunately, the fact that many of those remote laboratory Web sites are currently not functional points to the exploratory nature of this mode of delivery and a serious underestimation of what is needed to maintain working experiments. Fortunately, various interinstitutional collaborations, communities, and consortia are emerging to share the cost and the benefits of remote laboratories, as well as some commercial interests offering remote laboratory services. For example, the STaRBURSTT (Science Teaching and Research Brings Undergraduate Research Strengths Through Technology; www.as.ysu.edu/~adhunter/STaRBURSTT/index.html) CyberInstrumentation Consortium in the United States has a network over several institutions of single crystal x-ray diffraction instruments. In Europe, LiLa (Library of Labs) is an initiative of eight universities and three enterprises (Richter, Tetour, & Boehringer, 2011) and RCL (Remote Control Laboratories), based at the University of Kaiserslautern, in addition to providing physics experiments for its own students, is working with partners to do training and outreach (Eckert, Gröber, & Jodl, 2009). Other sites like MARVEL (Virtual Laboratory in Mechatronics: Access to Remote and Virtual e-Learning) at the University of Bremen (Müller & Ferreira, 2005) and NetLab in Australia (Machotka et al., 2010) have opened their laboratories for others to use. Certainly to avoid developing everything from scratch and unnecessary duplication, one can envisage future networks of remote laboratories sharing or hosting experiments.

Getting the Right Mix of Laboratories

Studies indicate that particular components of learning are better suited to different modes of delivery (Lindsay & Good, 2005). In a comparative study of different laboratory models Elawady and Tolba (2009) describe the current situation as an "unresolved debate" with each type of laboratory having its own "advocates and detractors." While the question of "which is best?" may not be definitively settled, the more interesting and promising work is being done around combining the different modes to optimize convenience and learning (Corter et al., 2011; Ma & Nickerson, 2006; Pyatt & Sims, 2011). For example, students could prepare and leave samples on-campus and then carry out the instrumental analysis from home as a remote laboratory, or they might carry out some initial experiments with a home-study kit and then complete the last few experiments on-campus. However, the most common combination has been using computer simulations to prepare the student for the face-to-face laboratory just like training a pilot with a flight simulator. The "virtual-plus-real" combination often works better than either on its own (Jaakkola & Nurmi, 2008; Zacharia, Olympiou, & Papaevripidou, 2008). It is interesting to note that the best order for the combination is not always from simulation to reality. In at least one case, switching the order, starting with reality and then carry out virtual work afterwards, produced better results (Smith & Puntambekar, 2010).

ON THE HORIZON

Many technological tools are emerging which can not only be employed directly by the science educator (Dede & Barab, 2009), but will fundamentally change our approach to learning. These include the increased availability of mobile devices and interest in m-learning (Ally, 2009; Chao, 2011). Portable GPS-enabled gadgets have found strong support in areas such as health, medicine (Premkumar, 2011), and in several field-sciences (Gaved, McCann, & Valentine, 2009; Miyata, Ishigami, & Sannomiya, 2011), as well as occupations requiring both physical mobility and the ability to access and move information. Examples outside of these disciplines include mobile phones used as flash cards (Sauder et al., 2009) in biology and chemistry and accessing remote laboratories (Orduña, García-Zubia, López-de-Ipiña, & Irurzun, 2011). It is certainly expected that as mobile devices and their networks become even more affordable and sophisticated they will be further incorporated into science courses. One interesting development of mobile devices is their popularity in informal science settings (Scanlon, Jones, & Waycott, 2005). Considering that the average university graduate's science knowledge already comes mostly from informal sources (outside the classroom), it will be curious to see the impact of m-learning on the science literacy of the general population.

Indeed, the aspiration to "science for all," with its goal of universal and open access to science has really benefitted from distance education and new technologies. Of particular interest is the whole movement around open educational resources (OERs), which has presented us with a new way of doing things that should realize savings and increase access (Baraniuk, 2008; D'Antoni, 2009). Within science education, there are related movements that complement and reinforce OERs, including resource-sharing in remote laboratories (discussed earlier), as well as e-science and cyberinfrastructure-enhanced science initiatives (Atkins, Brown, & Hammond, 2007, pp. 47–50). Given the expense of creating or buying resources in the science-related disciplines, coupled with the fact that scientific principles are very transportable, OERs seem like a natural option.

Connectivity to both content and people in digital networks is very exciting (Jones & Sclater, 2010), and science educators are just now starting to explore the possibities, with cautious optimism. The initial appeal here is student engagement and interest, because there is an impression that the new generation of learners are digital natives who are not only attracted to this, but are expecting it. However, the stronger draw for science educators is the ability to have students collaborate (and learn to collaborate) ideally using a scientific inquiry approach, which is analogous to what one would find in scientific research networks. At the same time, this digital connectivity affords the learner numerous opportunities and choices independent of many traditional barriers, well known to distance educators (Boschmann, 2010). However, there is concern here that without some framework or guidance, the high degree of freedom and large number of choices could potentially inhibit learning (especially at the undergraduate level).

One advantage of having learners in a digital environment is that the activities generate a lot of data that can be tracked and analyzed. Marketing and business firms have been collecting and analyzing information on their customers for years. The area of learning analytics is promising to offer teachers and institutions a similar way to inform their decisions around teaching and learning (Siemens & Long, 2011). The insight offered from actual performance, choices and preferences of learners, in addition to instructor intuition or student evaluations, will be profound in shaping future learning environments. At the moment, learning analytics are being used in a rudimentary ways, such as determining an individual's preferred learning style or identifying students that are at risk in a course. However, we may not be that far away from having courses literally adapt to the student, rather than the other way around.

Teaching science-related disciplines online and at a distance is both different and difficult. The approach needs to take into account the nature of science, the scientific community, as well as practical considerations for that crucial laboratory component, which for the distance educator may be the most challenging part. ICTs are having a great impact on how we teach and learn and the sciences are no different in that respect. The new technologies have become more than tools, they are requiring us to change the way we teach—to do those things we have always wanted to do. We can move from content to activities and have self-directed learners who can collaborate and understand how to use information and not just memorize it. Together with the student, we have the opportunity to create flexible and accessible learning environments for the individual.

> I never teach my pupils; I only attempt to provide the conditions in which they can learn.
>
> —Albert Einstein

NOTES

1. This chapter will use the term "science" to refer in general to all science and technology related disciplines including health sciences and engineering.
2. Teaching laboratory includes any practical course component including clinical and field work.
3. The authors will shortly be releasing an updated report and analysis of over 350 remote sites.

REFERENCES

Ally, M. (Ed.). (2009). *Mobile learning: Transforming the delivery of education and training.* Edmonton, Canada: AU Press.

Al-Shamali, F., & Connors, M. (2010). Low-cost physics home laboratory. In D. Kennepohl & L. Shaw (Eds.), *Accessible elements: Teaching science online and at a distance* (pp. 131–146). Edmonton, Canada: AU Press.

Anderson, T. (2003). Getting the mix right again: An updated and theoretical rationale for interaction. International *Review of Research in Open and Distance Learning, 4*(2). Retrieved from http://www.irrodl.org/index.php/irrodl/article/view/149/230

Atkins, D. E., Brown, J. S., & Hammond, A. L. (2007). *A review of the open educational resources (OER) movement: Achievements, challenges, and new opportunities.* San Francisco, CA: The William and Flora Hewlett Foundation.

Azad, A. K. M., Auer, M. E., & Harward, V. J. (Eds.). (2011). *Internet accessible remote laboratories: Scalable e-learning tools for engineering and science disciplines.* Hershey, PA: IGI Global.

Bailey, P. D., & Garratt J. (2002). Chemical education: Theory and practice. *University Chemistry Education, 6,* 39–57.

Baraniuk, R. G. (2008). Challenges and opportunities for the open education movement: A Connexions case study. In T. Iiyoshi & M. S. V. Kumar (Eds.), *Opening up education: The collective advancement of education through open technology, open content, and open knowledge* (pp. 229–246). Cambridge, MA: The MIT Press.

Bennett, S. W., & O'Neale, K. (1998). Skills development and practical work in chemistry. *University Chemistry Education, 2,* 58–62.

Boschmann, E. (2003). Teaching chemistry via distance education. Journal of Chemical Education, 80, 704–708.

Boschmann, E. (2010). Institutional consideration: A vision for distance education. In D. Kennepohl & L. Shaw (Eds.), *Accessible elements: Teaching science online and at a distance* (pp. 247–266). Edmonton, Canada: AU Press.

Burnley, S. (2008). Satisfying sustainability skills needs at a distance. *International Journal of Performability Engineering, 4,* 371–384.

Byers W. (2002). Promoting active learning through small group laboratory classes. *University Chemistry Education, 6,* 28–34.

Casanova, R. S., Civelli, J. L., Kimbrough, D. R., Heath, B. P., & Reeves, J. H. (2006). Distance learning: A viable alternative to the conventional lecture-lab format in general chemistry. *Journal of Chemical Education, 83,* 501–507.

Chao , L. (Ed.). (2011). *Open source mobile learning: Mobile Linux applications.* Hershey, PA: IGI Global.

Chickering, A. W., & Gamson, Z. F. (1987, March). Seven principles for good practice in undergraduate education. *American Association for Higher Education Bulletin,* 3–7.

Cloutis, E. (2010). Laboratories in the earth sciences. In D. Kennepohl & L. Shaw (Eds.), *Accessible elements: Teaching science online and at a distance* (pp. 147–166). Edmonton, Canada: AU Press.

Commission on Mathematics and Science Education. (2009). *The opportunity equation: Transforming mathematics and science education and the global economy.* New York, NY: Carnegie Corporation. Retrieved from http://opportunityequation.org/uploads/files/oe_report.pdf

Cooper, M. (2005). Remote laboratories in teaching and learning — Issues impinging on widespread adoption in science and engineering education. *International Journal of Online Engineering, 1,* 1–7.

Corter, J. E., Esche, S. K., Chassapis, C., Ma, J., & Nickerson, J. V. (2011). Process and learning outcomes from remotely-operated, simulated, and hands-on student laboratories. *Computers & Education, 57,* 2054–2067.

Cox, M. J., & Baruch, J.E.F. (1994, October). *Robotic telescopes: An interactive exhibit on the World-Wide Web. Proceedings of the 2nd International Conference of the World-Wide Web, Chicago.* University Park: The Pennsylvania State University Press. Retrieved from http://citeseerx.ist.psu.edu/viewdoc/download?doi=10.1.1.5 1.9564&rep=rep1&type=pdf

D'Antoni, S. (2009). Open educational resources: Reviewing initiatives andissues. *Open Learning: The Journal of Open, Distance and e-Learning, 24,* 3–10.

Deacona, C., & Hajek, A. (2011). Student perceptions of the value of physics laboratories. *International Journal of Science Education, 33,* 943–977.

Dede, C., & Barab, S. (2009). Emerging technologies for learning science: A time of rapid advances. *International Journal of Science Education, 18,* 301–304.

DiscoverLab (2007). Publications and reference materials about the WWSL and related Projects. Retrieved February 25, 2009, from: http://www.discoverlab.com/publications.html

Domin, D. S. (1999). A review of laboratory instruction styles. *Journal of Chemical Education, 76,* 543–547.

Domin, D. S. (2009). Considering laboratory instruction through Kuhn's view of the nature of science. *Journal of Chemical Education, 86,* 274–276.

Doulgeri, Z., & Matiakis, T. (2006). A web telerobotic system to teach industrial robot path planning and control. IEEE Transactions on Education, 49, 263–270.

Dove, J. (1997). Perceptual geography through urban trails. *Journal of Geography in Higher Education, 21,* 79–88.

Duit, R. (1999). Conceptual change approaches in science education. In W. Schnotz, S. Vosniadou, & M. Carretero (Eds.), *New perspectives on conceptual change* (pp. 263–282). Oxford, UK: Pergamon.

Eckert, B., Gröber, S., & Jodl, H.-J. (2009). Distance education in physics via the Internet. *American Journal of Distance Education, 23,* 125–138.

Elawady, Y. H., & Tolba, A. S. (2009). Educational objectives of different laboratory types: A comparative study. *International Journal of Computer Science and Information Security, 6*(2), 89–96.

Fiore, L., & Ratti, G. (2007). Remote laboratory and animal behaviour: An interactive open field system. *Computers & Education, 49,* 1299–1307.

Gaved, M., McCann, L., & Valentine, C. (2009). ERA (Enabling Remote Activity): A KMi designed system to support remote participation by mobility disabled students in geology field trips. Tech Report kmi-06-15 v1.1. Milton Keynes, UK: Open University. Retrieved from http://kmi.open.ac.uk/publications/pdf/kmi-06-15.pdf

George, S. (2003). Robert A. Millikan Award Lecture (August 2002): Global study of the role of the laboratory in physics education. *American Journal of Physics, 71,* 745–749.

Gröber, S., Vetter, M., Eckert, B., & Jodl, H.-J. (2007). Experimenting from a distance—remotely controlled laboratory (RCL). *European Journal of Physics, 28,* S127–S141.

Guzzetti, B. J., Snyder, T. E., Glass, G. V. & Gamas, W. S. (1993). Promoting conceptual change in science: A comparative meta-analysis of instructional interventions from reading education and science education. *Reading Research Quarterly, 28*(2), 117–155.

Habermeier, H.-U. (2007). Education and economy—An analysis of statistical data. *Journal of Materials Education, 29*(1–2), 55–70.

Hall, W., Jones, J. T., & Palmer, S. (2006). Providing a practical education for off-campus engineering students. *British Journal of Engineering Education, 5,* 49–57.

Hestenes, D., Wells M., & Swackhamer, G. (1992). Force concept inventory. *The Physics Teacher, 30,* 141–158.

Hewson, P. W., & Hewson, M. G. A. (1984). The role of conceptual conflict in conceptual change and the design of science instruction. *Instructional Science, 13,* 1–13.

Impelluso, T. J. (2009). Assessing cognitive load theory to improve student learning for mechanical engineers. *The American Journal of Distance Education, 23,* 179–193.

Jaakkola, T., & Nurmi, S. (2008). Fostering elementary school students' understanding of simple electricity by combining simulation and laboratory activities. *Journal of Computer Assisted Learning, 24,* 271–283.

James, K. (2007). Factors influencing students' choice(s) of experimental science subjects within the International Baccalaureate Diploma Programme. *Journal of Research in International Education, 6,* 9–39.

Jeschofnig, L., & Jeschofnig, P. (2011). Teaching lab science courses online. San Francisco, CA: Jossey-Bass.

Jones, C., & Sclater, N. (2010). Learning in an age of digital networks. *International Preservation News, 55,* 6–10.

Jordan, S. (2011). Using interactive computer-based assessment to support beginning distance learners of science. *Open Learning: The Journal of Open, Distance and e-Learning, 26,* 147–164.

Kennepohl, D. (2007). Using home-laboratory kits to teach general chemistry. *Chemistry Education: Research and Practice, 8,* 337–346.

Kennepohl, D. (2010). Remote control teaching laboratories and practicals. In D. Kennepohl & L. Shaw (Eds.), *Accessible elements: Teaching science online and at a distance* (pp. 167–187). Edmonton, Canada: AU Press.

Kennepohl, D., Guay, M., & Thomas, V. (2010). Using an online, self-diagnostic test for introductory general chemistry at an open university. *Journal of Chemical Education, 87,* 1273–1277.

Kirschner, P. A. (2002). Cognitive load theory: Implications of cognitive load theory on the design of learning. *Learning and Instruction, 12,* 1–10.

Kirschner, P. A., & Meester, M. A. M. (1988). The laboratory in higher science education: Problems, premises and objectives. *Higher Education, 17,* 81–98.

Kolb, A. Y., & Kolb, D. A. (2010). Learning to play, playing to learn: A case study of a ludic learning space. *Journal of Organizational Change Management, 23,* 26–50.

Kolias, V., Anagnostopoulos, I., & Kayafas, E. (2008). Remote experiments in education: A survey over different platforms and application fields. *Proceedings of the 11th International Conference on Optimization of Electrical and Electronic Equipment—OPTIM 2008* (pp. 181–188). New York, NY: Institute of Electrical and Electronics Engineers.

Kriek, J., & Grayson, D. (2009). A holistic professional development model for South African physical science teachers. *South African Journal of Education, 29,* 185–203.

Kuhn, T. S. (1970). *The structure of scientific revolutions* (2nd ed.). Chicago, IL: University of Chicago Press.

Lagowski, J. J. (2005). A chemical laboratory in a digital world. *Chemical Education International, 6,* 1–7.

Le Couteur, P. (2009). Review of literature on remote & web-based science labs for BCcampus articulation and transfer of Remote and Web-based Science Lab Curriculum Project. Retrieved from http://rwsl.nic.bc.ca/Docs/Review_of_Literature_on_Remote_and_Web-based_Science_Labs.pdf

Lindsay, E. D., & Good, M. C. (2005). Effects of laboratory access modes upon learning outcomes. *IEEE Transactions on Education, 48,* 619–631.

Lyall R., & Patti, A. F. (2010). Taking the chemistry experience home — Home experiments or "kitchen chemistry." In D. Kennepohl & L. Shaw (Eds.), *Accessible elements: Teaching science online and at a distance* (pp. 83–108). Edmonton, Canada: AU Press.

Ma, J., & Nickerson, J. V. (2006). Hands-on, simulated, and remote laboratories: A comparative literature review. *ACM Computing Surveys, 38*(3), 1–24.

Machotka, J., Nedić, Z., Nafalski, A., & Göl, Ö. (2010, February). Collaboration in the remote laboratory NetLab. In Z. J, Pudlowski (Ed.), *1st WIETE Annual Conference on Engineering and Technology Education, Pattaya, Thailand* (pp. 22–25). Melbourne, Australia: World Institute for Engineering and Technology Education.

Matthews, M. R. (1994). *Science teaching: The role of history and philosophy of science.* London: Routledge.

Mawn, M. V., Carrico, P., Charuk, K., Stote, K. S., & Lawrence, B. (2011). Hands-on and online: scientific explorations through distance learning. *Open Learning: The Journal of Open, Distance and e-Learning, 26,* 135–146.

Miller, K. W. (2008). Teaching science methods online: Myths about inquiry-based online learning. *Science Educator, 17,* 80–86.

Miyata, H., Ishigami, M., & Sannomiya, M. (2011). Development and evaluation of the flower identification database for mobile with a geo-tagged picture map. *International Journal of Mobile Learning and Organisation, 5,* 192–205.

Moore, M. G. (1983). On a theory of independent study. In D. Sewart, D. Keegan, & B. Holmberg (Eds.), *Distance education: International perspectives* (pp. 68–94). London: Croom Helm/St. Martin's Press.

Mosse, J., & Wright, W. (2010). Acquisition of laboratory skills by on-campus and distance education students. In D. Kennepohl & L. Shaw (Eds.), *Accessible elements: Teaching science online and at a distance* (pp. 109–129). Edmonton, Canada: AU Press.

Müller, D., & Ferreira, J. M. (2005). Online labs and the MARVEL experience. *iJOE International Journal on Online Engineering, 1,* 1–5.

National Research Council (2003). *BIO2010: Transforming undergraduate education for future research biologists.* Washington, DC: The National Academies Press.

Orduña, P., García-Zubia, J., López-de-Ipiña, D., & Irurzun, J. (2011). Accessing remote laboratories from mobile devices. In L. Chao (Ed.), *Open source mobile learning: Mobile Linux applications* (pp. 233–246). Hershey, PA: IGI Global.

Oriesek, D. F., & Schwarz, J. O. (2008). *Business wargaming: Securing corporate value.* Basingstoke, UK: Gower Publishing.

Paulsen, M. F. (1993). The hexagon of cooperative freedom: A distance education theory attuned to computer conferencing. *DEOS - The Distance Education Online Symposium, 3*(2). Retrieved from: http://www.ed.psu.edu/acsde/deos/deosnews/deosnews3_2.asp

Penfield Jr., P., & Larson, R. C. (1996). Education via advanced technologies. *IEEE Transactions on Education, 39,* 436–443.

Premkumar, K. (2011). Mobile learning in medicine. In A. Kitchenham (Ed.), *Models for interdisciplinary mobile learning: Delivering information to students* (pp. 137–153). Hershey, PA: IGI Global.

Psillos, D., & Niedderer, H. (Eds.). (2002). *Teaching and learning in the science laboratory.* The Netherlands: Kluwer Academic.

Pyatt, K., & Sims, R. (2011). Virtual and physical experimentation in inquiry-based science labs: Attitudes, performance and access. *Journal of Science Education and Technology, 21*(1), 133–147.

Reeves, J., & Kimbrough, D. (2004). Solving the laboratory dilemma in distance learning general chemistry. *Journal of Asynchronous Learning Networks, 8*(3), 47–51.

Richter, T., Tetour, Y., & Boehringer, D. (2011, Sepember). Library of labs: A European project on the dissemination of remote experiments and virtual laboratories. In J. Bernardino & J. C. Quadrado (Eds.), *Proceedings of World Engineering Education WEE2011* (pp. 555–562). Lisbon, Portugal: European Society for Engineering Education. Retrieved from http://www.sefi.be/wp-content/papers2011/T12/220.pdf

Ross S., & Scanlon E. (1995). *Open science: distance teaching and open learning of science subjects.* London, UK: Paul Chapman.

Rudd, V., (1994). Happy birthday to yOU. *Education in Chemistry, 31,* 87.

Satava, R. M. (2008). Historical review of surgical simulation—A personal perspective. *World Journal of Surgery, 32,* 141–148.

Sauder, D., Timpte, C., Pennington, R., Tsoi, M. Y., Paredes, J. B., & Pursell, D. (2009). Adapting to student learning styles: Using cell phone technology in undergraduate science instruction. In G. Siemens and C. Fulford (Eds.), *Proceedings of World Conference on Educational Multimedia, Hypermedia and Telecommunications 2009* (pp. 3066–3071). Chesapeake, VA: AACE. Retrieved from http://www.editlib.org/p/31917

Savinainen, A., & Scott, P. (2002). Using the Force Concept Inventory to monitor student learning and to plan teaching. *Physics Education, 37,* 53–58.

Scanlon, E., Jones, A., & Waycott, J. (2005). Mobile technologies: Prospects for their use in learning in informal science settings. *Journal of Interactive Media in Education, 21*(5). Retrieved from http://www/jime.open.ac.uk/2005/25

Shaw, L., & Carmichael, R. (2010). Needs, costs, and accessibility of DE science lab programs. In D. Kennepohl & L. Shaw (Eds.), *Accessible elements: Teaching science online and at a distance* (pp. 191–211). Edmonton, Canada: AU Press.

Siemens, G., & Long, P. (2011). Penetrating the fog: Analytics in learning and education. *EDUCAUSE Review, 46*(5). Retrieved from http://www.educause.edu/EDUCAUSE+Review/EDUCAUSEReviewMagazineVolume46/PenetratingtheFogAnalyticsinLe/235017

Smetana, L. K., & Bell, R. L. (2011). Computer simulations to support science instruction and learning: A critical review of the literature. *International Journal of ScienceEducation, 34*(9), 1337–1370.

Smith, G. W., & Puntambekar, S. (2010, July). Examining the combination of physical and virtual experiments in an inquiry science classroom. Computer Based Learning in Science (CBLIS) Conference, Warsaw, Poland. Retrieved from: http://www.compasswiki.org/images/b/b6/C16_Smith.doc

Smith, J. I., & Tanner, K. (2010). The problem of revealing how students think: Concept inventories and beyond. *CBE-Life Sciences Education, 9,* 1–5.

Sunal, D. W., Wright, E. L., & Sundberg, C. (Eds.). (2008). *The impact of the laboratory and technology on learning and teaching science K-16.* Greenwich, CT: Information Age.

Swan, A. (2007). Open access and the progress of science. *American Scientist, 95,* 197–199.

Swan, R. H. (2008). Deriving operational principles for the design of engaging learning experiences (doctoral dissertation). Retrieved from ProQuest Dissertations and Theses Database. (AAT 3319394).

Sweller, J., Ayres, P., & Kalyuga, S. (2011). *Cognitive load theory.* New York, NY: Springer.

Taraban, R., & Blanton, R. L. (Eds.) (2008). *Creating effective undergraduate research programs in science: The transformation from student to scientist.* New York, NY: Teachers College Press.

Tobias, S. (1990). *They're not dumb, they're different: Stalking the second tier.* Tucson, AZ: Research Corporation.

UNESCO Education Sector. (2011). Current challenges in basic science education. Retrieved from http://unesdoc.unesco.org/images/0019/001914/191425e.pdf

Zacharia, Z. C., Olympiou, G., & Papaevripidou, M. (2008). Effects of experimenting with physical and virtual manipulatives on students' conceptual understanding in heat and temperature. *Journal of Research in Science Teaching, 45,* 1021–1035.

43

EMERGING ORGANIZATIONAL MODELS IN HIGHER EDUCATION

DONALD E. HANNA

THE CONTEXT FOR EMERGING ORGANIZATIONAL MODELS AND CHANGE

Access to higher education has never been more important. Being able to access knowl-edge from any location, at any time, for any age, and in many ways, has become a requirement for individual, community, economic, and collective well-being. At the same time, governments around the world are under severe stress as they struggle to provide sufficient publicly funded support to expand higher education.

Public universities in many countries of the world are facing reduced funding and increased demand. In the United States, according to Lyall and Sell (2005), public higher education is gradually being privatized, with much less government support being pro-vided per student served. Following the global financial crisis of 2008 and 2009, this trend of reduced public support for higher education has accelerated. Financial support from governments has dropped as a percentage of institutional support, and students are paying more for access. Since 1990, tuition and fees have increased faster than any other segment of the consumer price index, including health care. Students in the United States are borrowing more to finance their education, and default rates on student loans have increased significantly in 2011 (Deritis, 2011). For the first time ever in 2010, debt from loans to students attending higher education in the United States exceeded total U.S. credit card debt.

Not-for-profit private universities, a major component of the higher education system in the United States but much less prominent in other countries, are facing increas-ing competition from both public and for-profit institutions. Not-for-profit institutions constitute a wide diversity of types of institutions, ranging from elite institutions like Harvard, Stanford, and MIT, to small and struggling residential institutions. During the past decade, some of these small institutions, with regional accreditation status, have become takeover targets for large for-profit educational corporations[1] that are building rapidly growing online degree programs.

Because of significant investments primarily in growing online degree programs, for-profit universities in the United States have grown rapidly during the past two decades both in numbers and enrollments. These universities have utilized government loan programs for students to build enrollment, especially targeting low-income students and military personnel who are eligible for these programs. They have employed distance learning instructional strategies and taken advantage of rapidly advancing electronic technologies to achieve both administrative and instructional efficiencies.

A GLOBAL CRISIS OF ACCESS

The global context for higher education is becoming more competitive. Universities worldwide are facing the common challenge of meeting dramatically increasing demand, and with the recent economic crises experienced by many parts of the world, with few exceptions, they are also experiencing reduced financial support.

In countries experiencing high population birth rates, young populations are increasingly unable to find a place in an institution of higher education. Rapidly growing economies have created burgeoning demand for and access to learning (e.g., China, India, Southeast Asia). In still others, poor economies have resulted in reduced funding capacity of government (parts of Africa and other developing regions). In 1996, Daniel (1996, p. 4) forecast this impending crisis of access, stating that simply to keep up with the participation rates worldwide in higher education at that time, there would need to be one new residential university of 20,000 students built each week through the year 2025. Clearly this is a goal that has not been achieved.

To close this critical access gap, Daniel (1996) chronicled the development of national open universities such as the UKOU, Indira Ghandi Open University, Andalou University, and the China TV University System as important future players in global higher education. These institutions and others like them were built as open and distance learning institutions, and they have experienced rapid growth. Daniel and Macintosh (2003) suggested that both traditional residential universities and these rapidly developing would need to incorporate emerging technologies to improve, but that they must remain committed to developing improved strategies for learning and tutoring rather than rely solely on emerging new technologies.

Overall, the context for higher education globally has changed significantly in the past two decades, and these changes have enormous implications for all higher education organizations and systems. Distance education, in form, reach, contexts, technologies employed, and organizational sponsorship, has entered the mainstream in a big way, with an enormous worldwide consequence of new challenges and probable major organizational change for all universities.

CHANGING ORGANIZATIONAL CONTEXTS, STRATEGIES, AND TACTICS

Many scholars have written about the coming transformation (radical change of structure, processes, and culture) of higher education and the global pressures for change. Gladwell (2002) indicates that major change often happens through many series of small seemingly insignificant changes that at some point coalesce into an event that is simply too big to escape notice, one that documents that true transformation, i.e., radical change, has in fact occurred.

Christensen (2006) and Christensen and Eyring (2011) suggest that new technologies act as either sustaining or disruptive both to business and to educational organizations, and that this concept can be applied to global higher education. Sustaining technologies enable the improvement of products or programs, but without substantially changing how the organization functions. Schlechty (2001) identifies this as a first order change, one that essentially alters tasks without altering processes or culture. According to Christensen, a disruptive technology changes the organization more dramatically, first by radically altering the processes used. For example, in the case of higher education, national open universities and earlier correspondence education programs began by moving the teaching and learning process out of the face-to-face classroom environment, first to distance education by mail (correspondence) and then more recently to online learning. This initial step constituted the first step of a potentially disruptive technology. According to Gladwell, preliminary changes may eventually lead to a "tipping" point, in which overall organizational and cultural change is clearly recognized as dramatic. Christensen suggests that disruptive technologies begin by providing inferior quality products by usual standards of measurement. Their initial contribution is that they provide a basis for offering significantly different benefits at a lower cost. In the case of open and distance learning, the initial benefits derived were expanded access, independent of geography and other limiting life roles. And in general, these benefits were provided to learners at lower cost. According to Christensen, many customers and providers in established markets initially reject the new technology and set of processes as inadequate and of much lower quality. This clearly was the case in much of academia in the early years of distance learning, whether observed at the center of national open universities, or on the periphery of traditional higher education institutions. Over time, new organizations emerge that organize around adapting emerging technologies; these organizations then begin to apply these technologies to emerging markets previously viewed as relatively unimportant by core providers. Christensen suggests that as this new market demand is met using these "disruptive" technologies, program and process advances begin to occur, enabling improvements that provide a level of quality that meets the expectations of the mainstream market. Eventually, previously core providers and mainstream learners perceive the disruptive technology as providing an equivalent or even superior product, because of the value added benefits of flexibility, access, convenience, and improved core resources. Based on an evolving lower cost structure, with added value, the disruptive technology offers both competition to and potential replacement of previous core programs, and enables revolutionary change of the type suggested by Gladwell's tipping point, and by Schlechty's third order change of structure, culture, and values.

To summarize the rapidity with which distance learning has altered the global landscape for higher education, prior to about 1980, distance learning programs were operated largely at the margins of residential universities. These programs included both face-to-face courses offered at off-site locations, and courses offered via correspondence learning (via mail) and interactive video (via satellite or microwave transmission). Distance learning programs were focused almost exclusively on meeting the needs of adult students, and did not seriously impact the core mission of providing residential experiences for 18- to 22-year-old students.

The changing context for learning, especially in the past decade, has required that distance education, and more importantly, the technologies employed in distance education learning environments, become a core strategy for most universities. Recent trends and studies in the United States show that learners expect institutions of higher education to be responsive to their individual needs, which increasingly means providing course schedules and formats that are convenient, easily accessed, and independent of a fixed times and locations (Allen & Seaman, 2004, 2010). Enrollments in online courses increased by 21% between 2009 and 2010. This compared with an increase of 2% for residential campus enrollments during the same period. Sixty-three percent of institutions surveyed said that online learning was an essential and even critical part of their future strategy; and almost 30% of enrollments overall are in online courses.

THE MATURATION OF NATIONAL DISTANCE EDUCATION UNIVERSITIES

Daniel (1996) outlined the emergence of national distance education universities, headlined by the United Kingdom Open University, The Open University of China (formerly China Central Radio and TV University), Andalou University in Turkey, Indira Ghandi Open University, and the Hong Kong Open University. These and many other national (and state or provincial) distance education universities have grown rapidly in response to growing demand for higher education. As online technologies emerged, these universities have increasingly migrated programs to the Internet to provide increased access to degree programs, often extending this access beyond national borders. As an example, the Open University of Catalunya (http://www.uoc.edu/portal/english/), founded in 1994 as an entirely online university and based in Barcelona, offers degree programs in the Catalan language, and also in Spanish, to more than 46,000 students, extending its reach throughout Spain and beyond to Central and South America.

THE EMERGENCE OF FOR-PROFIT UNIVERSITIES

During the past several decades, numerous for-profit universities have been established in the United States in order to take advantage of lucrative high-end learning markets created by the accelerating pace of change, the changing structure of the global economy, and the widespread availability of government student loans. The largest and best known for-profit university, the University of Phoenix, owned by Apollo Group (APOL, NYSE), started as a face-to-face university offering professional programs to adults during the evening in major cities throughout the West. They added an online dimension in 1990 in which enrollment relatively quickly surpassed face-to-face enrollments. The University of Phoenix total enrollment temporarily topped 600,000 students in 2010, although its enrollment in 2011 fell. This drop in enrollment corresponded in time with increased scrutiny of the financial and academic practices of for-profit providers in recruiting students and providing financial aid loans, along with a greater focus on evaluating success and degree completion rates of online students enrolling in for-profit institutions. Like the University of Phoenix, most for-profit universities have added online programs, and these online programs have grown substantially as the market has expanded. The number of for-profit universities that have adapted significant face-to-face on-the-ground operations to the Internet is significant; some of the largest include:

1. DeVry University, headquartered in Chicago, Illinois, and owned by DeVry, Inc. (DV, NYSE). Estimated 2010 enrollment was reported as more than 95,000 students. (See http://www.businesswire.com/news/home/20101207005640/en/DeVry-Announces-Fall-2010-Enrollment).

2. Strayer University, headquartered in Baltimore, Maryland, and owned by Strayer, Inc. (STRA: NASDAQ). Estimated 2010 enrollment was reported as more than 57,000 students, of which more than 33,000 were enrolled 100% in online courses (http://www.businesswire.com/news/home/20110217005396/en/Strayer-Education-Reports-Fourth-Quarter-Full-Year).

3. Argosy University, headquartered in Pittsburgh, Pennsylvania, and owned by Education Management Corporation (EDMC, NASDAQ). Estimated 2010 enrollment was reported as more than 33,000 students, of which more than 11,000 were enrolled 100% in online courses.

In addition to these major for-profit players, during the past decade in the United States, numerous educational entrepreneurs have jumped into the distance education market by purchasing small not-for-profit residential institutions that were already regionally accredited, and transforming them into large distance education providers. Three prominent examples of this trend include:

1. Grand Canyon University, located in Phoenix, Arizona, and owned by Grand Canyon Education (NASDAQ, LOPE). Reported 2010 enrollment was more than 41,000 students, with all but 3,800 students enrolled online.

2. Ashford University, located in Clinton, Iowa, owned by Bridgepoint Education Inc. (BPI, NYSE); 2010 year-end enrollment at was reported as more than 77,892 students, up from 53,688; almost all of this growth is attributed to online enrollments. The University of the Rockies, located in Colorado Springs, CO, is also owned by Bridgepoint. University of the Rockies offers graduate programs, primarily in psychology; its online offerings are growing dramatically.

3. Kaplan University, located in Davenport, Iowa, is owned by the Iowa College Acquisition Company, a subsidiary of the Washington Post Company (WPO, NYSE). Enrollment in 2010 was reported at more than 64,000 students.

Added to this complex and growing mix of institutions are several for-profit universities organized exclusively around making programs available only online, although short-term residency experiences may be required for some programs. Two of the most prominent are:

1. Capella University, located in Minneapolis, Minnesota, and owned by Capella Education Company (NYSE: CPLA). Capella offers bachelors, masters, and Ph.D. programs in a number of fields. Headcount enrollment exceeded 38,000 in 2010.

2. Walden University is located in Minneapolis, Minnesota, and owned by Laureate Education, Inc., based in Baltimore, Maryland. Laureate is a private corporation that owns more than 50 for-profit educational institutions located throughout the world. Enrollment in Walden University programs is estimated to be more than 40,000 students; enrollment in other Laureate institutions worldwide is an additional 10,000 plus. Former U.S. President Bill Clinton serves as honorary Chancellor of Laureate Education.

In mass, these institutions tend to serve lower income students, new immigrants, and lifelong learners, sometimes with minimal preparation, all audiences not well-served by existing residential institutions. Growth rates of the for-profit higher education sector during the past 10 years are phenomenal, especially when measured against the meager 2% growth for public universities during the same period of time.

STRATEGIC ALLIANCES

Collaborations or strategic partnerships that bring together two or more universities are increasingly a means of enhancing the competitive positions of existing universities. In the 1990s, university-business strategic alliances were formed to build organizational capacity to deliver new services and programs and to reach new audiences. These collaborations and alliances exhibited many elements and forms, and involved blending organizational missions, goals, programs, capabilities, and personnel to create new learning strategies and opportunities. More recently, the creation of consortia and partnerships that support individual university program development, such as the World University Network, American Distance Education Consortium, the Sloan C-Consortium, the European Association of Distance Education Teaching Universities, and Quality Matters, all have combined to provide platforms for distance learning and online education program improvement.

Kaufman (1991) suggests that consortia and alliances are effective in times of complexity and competition in at least three ways. First, they spread risk; second, they enable the organization to incorporate new ideas; and third, they help the organization to bypass cultural prohibitions against previously heretical ideas or practices.

Formal strategic alliances in distance learning began rather modestly in the early 1980s in the United States, and were generally formed between organizations (university to university or university to business) in a single country. Such alliances are now becoming global in nature. While these types of international alliances appear impressive on the surface, the organization of full-scale collaborative degree programs has yet to materialize. A major challenge is whether significant cultural differences, operational understandings, and educational practices across culture and international borders can be overcome, and whether members can arrive at a common vision, mission, and direction.

An exception to this in the United States is Western Governors University (http://www.wgu.edu). WGU is an example of an early strategic alliance designed to gain market advantage and serve students more effectively. Originally formed by the western states governors in 1996 around the concept of becoming a clearinghouse and marketing vehicle for distance learning courses for universities throughout the West, WGU leaders quickly learned that something more was needed to attract both partners and students, and as a result, they settled on the concept of competency-based degrees, requiring measures of and assessment of competencies for each degree offered. This has enabled the university during the first decade of the 21st century to occupy a relatively unfilled (but very likely to grow in the future) programming niche in distance learning, that of certifying learning rather than offering courses. In 2011, WGU was awarded the United States Distance Learning Association (USDLA) 21st Century Award for Best Practices in Distance Learning, in recognition of their competency-based learning model and their success in expanding access to higher education.

In this competitive environment, with the pace of change accelerating, with learners becoming more knowledgeable and sophisticated, with greater diversity and numbers of organizations coming into existence, and with the high cost of investing in new technologies, strategic planning and careful organizational development in distance education is critical. An understanding of learning models and pedagogical choices, and the academic, financial, and marketing implications of the choices, is essential.

EVOLVING LEARNING MODELS AND CONCEPTS OF DISTANCE EDUCATION

Until just a few years ago, distance education was designed to provide the same learning opportunities that were available in on-campus settings to individual students separated from the campus by distance. Distance education was conceptualized as involving a teacher interacting asynchronously with a single student. Separated by distance, the teacher and student engaged in a structured two-way exchange (Moore, 1973; Peters & Keegan, 1994) mediated by print and electronic technologies. Wedemeyer (1981) emphasized the independence of learner action within this model, and Keegan (1990, p. 44) specifically excluded the learning group as a primary context for distance education learning and teaching, although he acknowledged the possibility of "occasional meetings for didactic and social purposes." This model of learning was adopted in university correspondence or independent learning courses in the United States at the turn of the 20th century, and was expanded dramatically with the development of open universities in the latter half of the century. In the United Kingdom, Europe, Australia, New Zealand, and many other countries, print-based materials, audiocassettes, and other learning resources were used to create a common framework for the learner to access university courses and degree programs at times and schedules convenient to them.

With the creation of the national open universities based upon the independent learner model and organized to deal with an explosion in demand for higher education, distance education was organized as an industrial form of education, where mass distribution, standardization, division of labor, and assembly-line procedures were defining characteristics (Peters & Keegan, 1994). Referring to the development of the national open universities, Evans (1999) defines these focused efforts as "single-mode" distance teaching universities, as contrasted with "single-mode" campus-based universities, or the mixed-mode universities described by Rumble (1986).

More recent definitions of distance education programs included the extension of traditional classrooms to new locations where a teacher is connected synchronously with students in classrooms. Widely utilized in the United States, the most common form of this definition was the connection of off-campus learners via audio-conferencing, video-conferencing, or computer-conferencing at scheduled times. These traditionally structured and institutionally framed definitions of distance education, and the resulting pedagogical strategies, are heavily dependent upon teacher directed instructional goals and activities. As such, they still largely represent Schlechty's first dimension of change, that of the adoption of procedural changes that alter how the task of teaching is accomplished. These instructional models have become quite limiting as the Internet and the World Wide Web have developed.

With the current environment of instant and pervasive connections to storerooms of knowledge located all over the world, in multiple languages, with fewer and fewer barriers to access, a third set of emerging new models, where students are dynamically connected through the Internet and other advanced technologies with each other, with faculty mentors, and with institutional academic support structures in ways not imagined just a few years ago. Choices regarding pedagogy, technology, culture, and strategy are increasingly complex and blurred. Theories of learning have evolved from a focus on the content and process of incorporating knowledge into a cognitive frame-work and behavioral measurements of learning, to engaging learners in creative ways that build upon learner motivation, participation, and ability to learn flexibly and effi-ciently, with a structure that enables questions, searching, and sorting of a mountain of information and perspectives immediately available to the learner. In effect, the transi-tion has been from a measurement of what one knows, to a focus on how one learns and applies knowledge. As a result, effective distance learning environments have changed from a focus upon the knowledge, teaching performance and competence of the teacher first and foremost, to emphasize the engagement of the student with both the content and with other students, the systematic creation of opportunities within and outside of the "classroom" both to learn and to demonstrate or model what has been learned, and assessment strategies that enable the growth and development of the learner in more personally meaningful and measurable ways. Brown and Adler (2008) refer to this transformational change as one that goes from: "I think, therefore I am" to "We partici-pate, therefore we are."

Learning via distance education has changed from being the product of an "indus-trial process of mass distribution of knowledge," to becoming a process whereby the learner's needs for knowledge are addressed through customized and highly personal strategies that are initiated by the learner with assistance from and in consultation with the teacher. To summarize the change in application of learning theory outlined above to the new environments of distance learning, interaction with the learner is key; learn-ing opportunities begin with the needs of the learner rather than the specific knowledge to be conveyed by the teacher.

THE IMPACT OF NEW TECHNOLOGIES ON DISTANCE LEARNING

Changes in distance education practice based upon changing educational theories noted above have been dramatic if not profound. For most of the 20th century, distance educa-tion involved the technologies of pen and pencil, paper, the typewriter, and the postal ser-vice, which provided the sole link between the individual instructor and the individual student. Electronic technologies and social networking software have changed this inter-action. With the development of radio and then television, it became possible to transmit educational courses, programs, and content widely using these mass media distribution channels. More recently, Internet 2 and Web 2.0 have enabled even broader access to university courses. This educator's personal visits to remote areas and schools, sometimes fueled by solar power and generators, in Australia, Thailand, South Africa, and several Caribbean countries, confirm that learners in remote areas of countries throughout the world are connected with universities in ways unimaginable a few years ago.

The rapid deployment of the Internet has radically altered previous technological environments for distance learning, opening up many new possibilities for connecting learners and teachers. The Internet has made possible the World Wide Web, with powerful and very rapidly expanding means of distributing and sharing knowledge on a global basis. As examples, Google, Google Scholar, and Google Earth (http://www.google.com), and Wikipedia (http://wikipedia.org) are four knowledge seeking and sharing services that have been available less than 10 years, but they have impacted our ways of accessing, storing, and sharing information in profound ways. The open education resources movement has advanced rapidly, and there are many inexpensive ways of creating virtual interactions among people across international borders. Skype (http:/www.skype.com), for example, enables worldwide audio, text, and video interactions between online users at a fraction of the cost of previous interactive technologies. It is now literally possible to be a learner or a teacher of university level instruction without being present at, or even affiliated with, a university, and still be connected to one's colleagues or to other learners on a daily real-time way. Three highly successful recent examples of this capacity are the Khan Academy (www.khanacademy.com), Sebastian Thrun's successful offering in 2011 of a course in computer science from Stanford University (http://www.udacity.com) that enrolled more than 160,000 students worldwide, and even Voice of America's Jessica Beinecke's channel teaching American slang to Chinese mandarin speakers (http://www.unsv.com/material/OMG-Meiyu/).

The Internet is a "disruptive" technology regarding higher education, and there is little disagreement that its arrival has opened up many new possibilities for providing rich learning opportunities accessible in revolutionary ways. These new and previously almost unimaginable possibilities are increasingly driven directly by learner needs rather than through institutional funnels. The idea of a university described by Jude in Thomas Hardy's novel, *Jude the Obscure*, as being circumscribed and protected by a wall ("it was a wall, but what a wall!") is obsolete.

Growing experiences with online Web-based platforms in distance education and in campus-based programs are changing the strategies for learning at a distance to be more group-oriented and interactive. Early adopters are also attempting to document or demonstrate the financial advantages of online instruction. Today, being connected to world class educational resources independent from institutions of higher education is entirely within the realm of possibility for learners separated by distance, and the connection with others and to increasingly sophisticated sources of content is becoming central to the learning process.

Technologies such as the smart phone, with tens of thousands of applications and increasing, provide a growing body of open educational resources accessible from anywhere. Low cost audio and video connections are changing the nature of both the classroom, and whether or not a classroom, and even a teacher, is really needed. It may be that the next question is whether or not a university organized around a campus and detailed course offerings is necessary. If technology is focused on empowering the student rather than on extending the reach of the teacher, what implications does this have for institutions of higher education? Indeed there are emerging models that suggest that universities, as we have thought about them in the 20th century, may be far less important than previously thought. Anya Kamenetz (2010) goes so far as to suggest that learners depart from formal university programs and define their own learning plans. She suggests, that with the increased cost of attending formal universities, whether residential or online, learners no longer can afford formal higher education. And, she points out that with development of the Internet and the World Wide Web, learners may no longer need the formal direction that universities have provided in the past. While a radical view at the moment, such perspectives are gaining traction with the rapid expansion of the open education resources movement. For example, the Open Education Resources Foundation (http://wikieducator.org/OERF:Home), a partnership created in 2011 aimed at developing new methods of sharing intellectual and teaching resources freely across cultural and institutional boundaries, argues that demand for learning is simply too great, and access too unequally distributed, for institutions to continue to hoard such resources.

TRANSFORMATIONAL CHANGE AND ORGANIZATIONAL MODELS

Looking towards the future, will the university continue to focus on producing academic degrees and credits as its primary measure of learning? Or will other measures become prominent? Will its activities continue to be concentrated in campuses, conveying the idea that the university is a place, or will its focus increasingly be independent of place and focused on the widest possible forms of knowledge sharing and discovery? How will the productivity of the university of the future be measured? Will its distance education efforts gradually become its most prominent future?

As these questions illustrate, dramatic changes in higher education are underway and distance education programs and technologies are major drivers of transformation. The changes occurring today are more than simple procedural changes or ways of conducting business; they likely represent fundamental shifts in values, assumptions, culture, and missions. As a result of these shifts, new assumptions and understandings about what a university is and is not will develop over time. Already, many universities are becoming more focused around what the student is experiencing, and less centered around the internal organizational framework of the university. To put it another way, more attention is being paid to the experience of the client, and, over time, the nature of the academy is likely to change dramatically as a result.

CONCLUSION

Understanding the complex dynamics of cultural values, conflict, and organizational change in universities is critical to building a framework for the future of distance education. Transformational change involves changing the nature of the work of the university, reorienting its purpose, and refocusing its intent, and involves deep changes in the culture of the organization.

As demand for higher education has increased globally, universities are operating in a more competitive and business-like environment than ever before. New technologies are both enabling and forcing changes in learning and teaching. Learners expect to be able to learn in locations convenient to them in a flexible manner. They expect quality resources to be provided in multiple formats. In many cases, distance learning is the driver for providing leadership for implementing new ideas, approaches, and models and for leading organizational change within residential universities.

According to Schwahn and Spady (1998), change is a continuous process, highly chaotic in nature, but necessary for organizational renewal and even survival. Radical third order change is "disruptive to the existing order," as Christensen, Schlechty, and others have noted (Christensen, 2006; Christensen & Eyering, 2011; Schlechty, 2009; Armstrong, 2000). Distance learning and the new Web 2.0 technologies are radically changing and transforming educational practice in higher education. Brown and Adler (2008) go so far as to discuss these changes not as technological or even organizational in nature, but as a fundamental transformation in how people will learn in the future.

The goal of this chapter was to provide the reader with an understanding of the fundamental issues and concepts concerning the historical development of distance learning within higher education organizations, and a glimpse of organization models for the future. It will be useful in interpreting other chapters in this handbook from the perspectives of teaching, learning, policy, administration, strategy, economics, and marketing.

NOTES

1. See Bridgepoint Education Corporation: http://bridgepointeducation.com/; Apollo Group: http://www.apollogrp.edu/about.aspx; Grand Canyon University: http://www.gcu.edu/; Kaplan University: http://www.kaplan.edu/; Laureate International Universities: http://laureate.net/

REFERENCES

Armstrong, L. (2000). Distance learning: An academic leader's perspective on a disruptive product. *Change, 32*(6), 20–27.

Allen, E. I., & Seaman, J. (2004). *Entering the mainstream: The quality and extent of online education in the United States, 2003 and 2004.* Wellesley, MA: The Sloan Consortium.

Allen, E. I., & Seaman, J. (2010). *Class differences: Online education in the United States, 2010.* Wellesley, MA: The Sloan Consortium.

Brown, J. S., & Adler, R. P. (2008). Minds on fire: Open education, the long tail, and learning 2.0. *Educause Review, 43*(1), 16–32.

Christensen, C. M. (2006). *The innovator's dilemma: The revolutionary book that will change the way you do business.* New York: Collins Business Essentials.

Christensen, C. M., & Eyring, H. J. (2011). *The innovative university: Changing the DNA of higher education from the inside out.* San Francisco: Jossey Bass.

Daniel, S. J. (1996). *Mega-universities and knowledge media: Technology strategies for higher education.* London: Biddles Ltd.

Daniel, S. J., & Macintosh, W. (2003). Leading ODL futures in the eternal triangle: The mega-university response to the greatest moral challenge of our age. In M. G. Moore (Ed.), *The handbook of distance education* (pp. 811–828). Mahwah NJ: Erlbaum.

Deritis, C. (2011). *Student loan's failing grade.* Retrieved February 14, 2012, from http://image.exct.net/lib/fefb127575640d/m/2/Student+Lendings+Failing+Grade.pdf

Evans, T. (1999). From dual-mode to flexible delivery: paradoxical transitions in Australian open and distance education. *Performance-Improvement-Quarterly, 12*(2), 84–95.

Gladwell, M. (2002). *The tipping point: How little things can make a big difference.* Boston: Little Brown.

Kamenetz, A. (2010). *DIY U : Edupunks, edupreneurs, and the coming transformation of higher education.* White River Junction, VT: Chelsea Green.

Kaufman, H. (1991). *Time, chance, and organizations: Natural selection in a perilous environment* (2nd ed.). Chatham, NJ: Chatham House.

Keegan, D. (1990). *Foundations of distance education* (2nd ed.). London: Routledge.

Lyall, K. C., & Sell, K. R. (2005). *The true genius of America at risk: The de facto privatization of public higher education.* Westport, CT: Praeger/Greenwood.

Moore, M. G. (1973). Toward a theory of independent learning and teaching. *Journal of Higher Education, 44,* 661–679.

Peters, O., & Keegan, D. (1994). *Otto Peters on distance education : the industrialization of teaching and learning.* New York: Routledge.

Rumble, G. (1986). *The planning and management of distance education.* London: Croom Helm.

Schlechty, P. C. (2001). *Inventing better schools: An action plan for educational reform.* San Francisco: Jossey-Bass.

Schlechty, P. C. (2009). *Leading for learning: How to transform schools into learning organizations.* San Francisco: Jossey-Bass.

Schwahn, C. J., & Spady, W. G. (1998). *Total leaders: Applying the best future-focused change strategies to education.* Arlington, VA: American Association of School Administrators.

Wedemeyer, C. A. (1981). *Learning at the back door: Reflections on non-traditional learning in the lifespan.* Madison: University of Wisconsin Press.

44

LEARNING IN A WORLD OF BLURRED BOUNDARIES

JAN VISSER

INTRODUCTION

Reflecting in 1992 on the turbulent history of global communications, Arthur C. Clarke foresaw a world in which we have "reached the stage when virtually anything we want to do in the field of communications is possible: the constraints are no longer technical, but economic, legal, or political" (p. 213). Developments 20 years thence inspire hope that some of those restraints are becoming more relaxed and that Clarke's vision may indeed come true and thus make it easier for learners around the world to get unhindered access to learning opportunities.

I have been a participant-observer of the development of distance education in the majority world[1] since I started working in Africa more than 40 years ago and continued to do so for the subsequent two decades. My professional responsibilities and interests gradually grew to encompass the so-called developing world in general, thus bringing Asia and Latin America into purview as well. Technological developments, taking off during the 1980s and accelerating ever since, have been a major force in changing the world's learning landscape,[2] increasingly affording opportunities to learn across geographical boundaries. It led UNESCO in 1993 to follow suit on a recommendation to its Executive Board to pursue establishing a world system of open education called Learning Without Frontiers (UNESCO Executive Board, 1993a,b).

It is perhaps only now, as increasingly more relevant open (and low cost) resources for learning become available via the Internet, that the original vision of Learning Without Frontiers can start taking shape. If so, it should gradually lead mainstream thinking about distance education to adopt a global perspective, rather than one that is dominated by the experiences and interests of the minority world. It should also lead to taking a more relaxed view of what exactly defines the field. Distance education is then best seen as one among multiple facilitating mechanisms through which people learn. Ideally, such mechanisms should be well integrated among themselves. The question of what defines distance education then becomes less relevant,[3] which is a good thing as it allows learners to develop greater autonomy to smoothly navigate an increasingly more comprehensive and resource rich learning landscape.

My choice of issues and references to the literature in this chapter is informed by, and perhaps biased towards, the above described experiences and their ensuing vision of the future. But let us start at the beginning. My experience with distance education started in the context of international development cooperation with third world countries.

INTERNATIONAL DEVELOPMENT COOPERATION

The development of distance education outside the places where it first took hold in Australia, Europe, and North America was largely prompted, at least initially, by what is commonly referred to as "international development cooperation." The meaning and connotations associated with that concept have changed significantly over time. In fact, the history of international development cooperation is more than 60 years old, but the origin of its pre-history may be located hundreds of years earlier, when the efforts of navigators and new conceptualizations by scientists started changing dominant ideas about the world and perceptions of the place of humans within it (e.g., Boorstin, 1985; Koestler, 1959). Those who had the economic power, and thus had access to the technology of the day, discovered that they were not alone in the world and that other peoples—mostly seen as essentially different and invariably inferior—co-inhabited the planet. Thus, different forms of often exploitative cohabitation emerged. Colonization was born. That period mostly ended during the third quarter of the last century. Emancipation and decolonization, largely driven by the formerly oppressed, led to the recognition among those who eventually relinquished power that not everything in the world was right. In fact, it laid bare great inequalities that conflicted with long held moral convictions—convictions that had, until then, been solely applied (and even then only partially) to the societies of those who held the convictions. Such inequalities, it was realized, were immoral and they threatened stability. A new world order was called for.

Initial ideas about development focused on technology transfer. The world was seen as polarized between developed and underdeveloped nations, terms that were later replaced by industrialized and developing nations, countries in transition being a third category, which was added later. A simple rationale lay beneath the development philosophy. Countries that saw themselves as developed thought they had little to learn from those that required development; instead, they felt compelled to share their expertise with those countries whose different state of development was assumed to have resulted from the absence of such expertise. There was thus a formidable urge on the part of some to teach and an assumed great need on the part of hundreds of millions of others to learn. While the development discourse reflecting this philosophy has become more nuanced over time, much of its basic assumptions are still very much alive.

The above remarks provide a backdrop for the subsequent discussion of the role of distance education as a contributing factor to attempts to build a better world. The following four statements are offered as an advance organizer for that discussion:

1. The development effort undertaken over the past 60+ years has largely focused on creating and improving education systems, modeled after those of the industrialized West.
2. Educational needs in developing nations (defined as implied by the previous statement) have been so enormous—compared to the available resources—that traditional modalities could never meet the challenge. The search for alternatives, including distance education, was a natural consequence of this recognition.

3. The visions underlying the concepts of development and education tend to explain the world, its history, and the possibilities to shape its future, in linear terms. They furthermore assume that the knowledge systems of the developed world are superior to local or indigenous knowledge systems. The history of international development during the past 60+ years justifies questioning the validity of these visions.

4. When the international development effort took off, the prevailing global issues and concerns were limited in scope and biased towards the problems that had upset the world during the 1930s and 40s. It took another half century to discover that the world was infinitely more complex than we had ever thought. A more comprehensive picture of global issues and concerns has started to emerge over the past two decades. However, we far from understand fully how to deal with its implications from a learning point of view.

SCOPE OF THIS CHAPTER

This chapter looks at distance education in the perspective of a world that increasingly faces issues and concerns of planetary import and dimensions, a topic closely linked to the very reasons why distance education became an important international development issue. I shall particularly focus on the discrepancy between the established practice of distance education and the overriding purposes for educational development. This will lead to a critique of the field as it currently stands, a critique, though, that is equally valid for many other modalities of educational practice.

The above referred critique of distance education is linked to the larger question of the meaning of learning. I shall elaborate on the need to revisit the meaning of learning as it relates to the demands of our time and conclude with a section that explores the potential of the current interest in the development of open educational resources for a much needed fundamental reshaping of the learning landscape.

PROMPTS TO DEVELOPING DISTANCE EDUCATION IN RESOURCE POOR COUNTRIES

The development of distance education in the developing world has largely been driven by the desire to overcome the shortcomings of established schooling practices. The literature of the period when distance education started to position itself as a serious alternative to or complement of school-based offerings in the third world would often contrast distance education—or, as it used to be called, correspondence education and, in some other cases, radio or TV education—with so-called traditional or conventional education (e.g., Edström, Erdos, & Prosser, 1970; Erdos, 1967; Faure et al., 1972; Perraton, 1976; Young, Perraton, Jenkins, & Dodds, 1980).

Different considerations motivated the emergence of distance education as a significant alternative. Chief among them was—and continues to be (e.g., Creed & Perraton, 2001)—the growing concern that a large proportion of the world's population remained deprived of opportunities to learn, while those same opportunities were commonly available to others. At the same time there was the expectation that new media would usher in an era of until then unimagined possibilities to overcome the barriers of the past.

Hope and vision were accompanied by the desire to gather evidence in support of the claims that media, and the instructional design principles underlying their use, could indeed help overcome the formidable obstacles faced by educational leaders and planners in developing countries. Most notable was a worldwide research project undertaken by UNESCO's International Institute for Educational Planning (IIEP) in 1965/66 (UNESCO—IIEP, 1967a, 1967b). Other prominent sources reflecting the thinking of that time regarding the educational use of media are Schramm's (1977) *Big Media, Little Media*; Jamison and McAnany's (1978) *Radio for Education and Development*; and Jamison, Klees, and Wells's (1978) *The Costs of Educational Media: Guidelines for Planning and Evaluation.*

During the same period, the instructional design field was coming of age with such classics as Gagné's *The Conditions of Learning* (first published in 1965) and Gagné and Briggs's *Principles of Instructional Design* (first published in 1974), giving confidence that the process of making people learn, and ensuring that their learning achievements would match their originally identified learning needs, could not only be controlled but also managed within a considerably wider range of parameters than those traditionally considered. Particularly, it became clear that such a process was not necessarily or exclusively dependent on the physical presence of a human facilitator.

The above factors taken together provided a powerful reason to search for the solution of the world's educational problems outside of the conventional schooling practice. Naturally, it also raised questions about the comparative quality of the contemplated alternatives and their perceived validity, leading to the concern with parity of esteem.

Two inadequacies of traditional education are usually highlighted in such sources as mentioned above. The first of these inadequacies has to do with the inability of existing schooling systems to meet the basic learning needs of all. This problem was highlighted by Julian Huxley, UNESCO's first Director-General, at the time the Organization was created (see UNESCO, 2000). It has serious societal and personal consequences (e.g., Sharma, 2003). Six decades and a half later it still exists. Noticeable advances have been made of late, as becomes clear when comparing earlier statistics (UNESCO Institute of Statistics, 2005) with recent ones (UNESCO, 2011), but improvements are not fast enough to combat prospected tendencies for the numbers of out of school children to rise again. Females are affected more than males.

The other major shortcoming of the schooling system, recognized in at least part of the literature cited earlier (e.g., Faure et al., 1972; Young et al., 1980), had and has to do with the schooling tradition itself, particularly the kind of learning it instills in students, the social consequences of expectations it generates, and the often limited relevance of what is being taught for those who learn, considering their real-life needs.

GLOBAL ISSUES AND CONCERNS

The import of the above inadequacies should be appraised against the backdrop of Article 26 of the Universal Declaration of Human Rights (see sidebar). Education, in the view of the declaration, transcends the mere concern with the acquisition of particular skills and pieces of knowledge. The second paragraph relates education to both personal growth and the ability to live in harmony with oneself, one's environment and one's fellow human beings. Consequently, the deficit of the school system should not be interpreted solely in terms of the lack of opportunity to acquire such competencies as the ability to read and write, but rather in terms of how education contributes to our ability to interact constructively with the world around us and to attend to fundamental concerns about how we live together.[4] Naturally, the declaration refers to such concerns in terms that reflect the date of its adoption, 1948.

Article 26

1) Everyone has a right to education. Education shall be free, at least in the elementary and fundamental stages. Elementary education shall be compulsory. Technical and professional education shall be made generally available and higher education shall be equally accessible to all on the basis of merit.

2) Education shall be directed to the full development of the human personality and to the strengthening of respect for human rights and fundamental freedoms. It shall promote understanding, tolerance and friendship among all nations, racial or religious groups, and shall further the activities of the United Nations for the maintenance of peace.

3) Parents have a prior right to choose the kind of education that shall be given to their children.

From: Universal Declaration of Human Rights
(1948; cited in UNESCO, 2000, p. 16)

We live in a different world now. The world population has almost tripled in the 64 years that have since passed. We live closer together than ever before, physically as well as in terms of ease of communication and pervasiveness of social networking by multiple means. Techno-science has progressively become an ever more important driver—if not the principal driver—of social change, not only in the industrialized world but increasingly in ways that affect the world at large. Meanwhile, past problems still exist. Attention to issues of world peace; respect for human rights and fundamental freedoms; cross-cultural understanding; appreciation of diversity and tolerance of difference is as much needed now as it was in 1948. But other, equally or even more important, issues have emerged. Inequitable access to increasingly limited resources such as food; injustice in the distribution of wealth and power around the globe; water stress; insufficiencies of the traditional ways of producing energy; degradation of ecosystem services; disintegration of societal coherence; unbridled urbanization; unchecked pollution; climate change; and dramatic loss of biodiversity are but some of the critical issues that will be increasingly among the concerns of future generations if humanity is to survive, survival being something that cannot be naturally assumed (e.g., Barnosky et al., 2011). The above issues are all an integral part of a polycrisis the solution of which is a *conditio sine qua non* for sustaining human life on earth (Crutzen 2002; Morin & Kern, 1999; Sachs, 2007). It calls for a fundamental reconceptualization of the very nature of learning and the practice of making learning happen.

RESHAPING THE ARCHITECTURE OF THE LEARNING LANDSCAPE

Interestingly, such a call to step back and take a critically fresh look at what we are doing when it comes to facilitating human learning comes at a time when, independently, "new insights from many different fields are converging to create a new science of learning that may transform educational practices" (Meltzoff, Kuhl, Movellan, & Sejnowski, 2009, p. 284). The review by Meltzoff et al. concludes that "convergence of discoveries in psychology, neuroscience, and machine learning has resulted in principles of human learning that are leading to changes in educational theory and the design of learning environments" and that a "key component [in this context] is the role of 'the social' in learning" (p. 288).

Reshaping the architecture of the learning landscape should (a) create greater openness for exploring and negotiating learning opportunities, integrating informal and formal learning; while (b) taking into account the needs of societies, communities and individual learners to learn across and along the lifespan; (c) understanding the meaning of learning in an inter- and transdisciplinary as well as transcultural perspective; (d) recognizing the essential dialogic nature of learning and the role played by the social in learning; (e) aware of the vital function of self-organization in the constitution of, often transnational and transgenerational, learning communities. This lengthy description can only hint at the wealth of resources available in and the rich complexity of a vast, largely uncharted and unexplored, terrain.[5]

Reshaping the architecture of the learning landscape should go hand in hand with the reconceptualization of learning itself. Given the constellation of problems that characterize human existence at the start of the third millennium, it should lead to habits of thought that are rooted in consciousness of the planetary dimensions and import of key challenges and opportunities currently faced by humanity and to the ability to generate what Morin (1982, 2005) has called "complex thought," weaving together what has come apart over time as knowledge became more and more specialized and separate disciplines developed. Similar calls can be found in the work of Nicolescu (2002) and Wilson (1998). J. Visser (2006) discusses implications for the development of higher education in the digital age.

In the transformation of educational practice, as suggested by Meltzoff et al. (2009), particular attention should go to exploring the ecological nature of learning, bringing into perspective that learning relates to adaptive human behavior at a level higher than the "deliberate acquisition of specific skills, knowledge, habits and propensities" (J. Visser, 2008, p. 16). It should seek to broaden the definition of learning (e.g., J. Visser, 2012; Y. L. Visser, Rowland, & J. Visser, 2002). Research should thus be informed by theory that considers the complexity of the learning landscape as well as the integral nature of meaningful learning. Conversely, it should contribute to such theory development. Besides, as Meltzoff et al. (2009) conclude, innovative "educational practice ... [should be] leading to the design of new experimental work" (p. 288). Technological developments that facilitate self-organized social networking, such as the increasingly ubiquitous use of handheld communication devices (e.g., Scanlon, Jones, & Waycott, 2005) and the Semantic Web (e.g., Anderson & Whitelock, 2004) provide interesting opportunities for making inroads into such research and practice, as does the work by Cortazzi and Jin (2002) and others on cultural synergy.

DISTANCE EDUCATION'S INTEGRAL ROLE WITHIN THE LEARNING LANDSCAPE

A survey of the learning landscape (J. Visser, 2012) reveals that it is populated with learners and learning communities, which engage in multiple forms of learning, undertaken with diverse purposes in mind or at times undergone spontaneously without a previously defined purpose. Such learning takes place via different means in varying temporal and spatial contexts. Distance education is one among many other modalities through which learning can be facilitated. As such it plays a role that is integral to all else that defines the learning landscape. Thinking of distance education—or e-learning for that matter—as something special, which sets it apart from the concern with education in general, is therefore unhelpful. The same holds obviously true for other domains of educational intervention, such as the formal schooling system. It will become increasingly important to think of what connects the different domains in the learning landscape, rather than what distinguishes one domain from the other.

For the same reason, formal and informal learning must be conceived of as interconnected domains, surrounded, at most, by fluid boundaries. They are both integral to a continuous learning landscape. Research into the meaning of learning via the Learning Stories Project of the Learning Development Institute (Learning Development Institute—MOL, n.d.; J. Visser, Berg, Burnett, & Y. L. Visser, 2002; Y. L. Visser & J. Visser, 2000;) has revealed a clear trend among participating research subjects for learners to be seen as inhabitants of not just one, but a wide variety of learning spaces, the large majority of which are *not* inspired by the idea that learning and schooling are one and the same thing (J. Visser, Y. L. Visser, Amirault, Genge, & Miller, 2002; M. Visser, & J. Visser, 2003). In fact, the most dramatically meaningful learning experiences reported were often associated with emotions, an area that receives little attention in formal education. Meaningful learning experiences almost invariably occur outside the formal learning context. The Science of Learning Center dedicated to the study of Learning in Informal and Formal Environments (LIFE Center, n.d.) displays on its Web site[6] a visualization of the proportions of time we spend, on average, learning formally and informally during our lifetime. According to the analysis made by the LIFE Center,

> school-aged children[7] spend about 19% of their time in formal settings such as school, and the remaining 81% time in informal settings. Second, at many developmental ages most of our learning occurs in informal settings. Young children from birth to 5 years of age learn primarily in informal settings; and as adults, we learn in informal workplace environments. Much of human learning is done in informal learning environments....

In line with the earlier referred review by Meltzoff et al. (2009), the analysis by the LIFE Center also finds that a "key factor in informal learning settings is their highly social nature."

A third area in which it is becoming increasingly crucial to recognize the integrity of the global learning landscape concerns the division between the majority and the minority world. Grave inequalities continue to exist and people in the two worlds live in starkly dissimilar material and varied social and cultural circumstances, justifying that serious specialized attention be paid to building and sharing of knowledge about the development of distance education in the third world at large (e.g., Perraton, 2007, or, even more so, Young et al., 1980); a particular continent such as Africa (e.g., Butcher, Latchem, Levey, & Mawoyo, 2011); or a sub-continent or region, such as sub-Saharan Africa (e.g., Leary & Berge, 2007). However, despite varying material conditions, lifestyles, worldviews, adopted values and held beliefs; regardless of conflicts of interest; notwithstanding fierce competition for the earth's scarce resources; and even though we do not trust at first sight each other's intentions, there is much that we share. We share the possibility to learn from each other's experience and accumulated knowledge and wisdom; we share the opportunity to interact with each other and learn together in ways that, thanks to technological developments, were simply unthinkable a mere two to three decades ago; and we share the responsibility to collectively and individually contribute to meeting the challenges and overcoming the problems of our time.

WHAT KIND OF LEARNING

The problems referred to in the last sentence of the previous paragraph are far from minor. In fact, never in human history have they been as vastly complex and all encompassing as they are now. They have become publicly visible relatively recently and none of them can be tackled in isolation. Their complex nature is such that consequences cannot easily be foreseen. Addressing them thus requires ways of thinking that are fundamentally different from the past. They require human beings to be able to function in entirely unpredictable situations. For physics Nobel laureate Leon Lederman (1999) this "points to a search for educational processes that will strive for the capability of adapting, and even thriving in areas of new problems and new opportunities" (p. 3), whence the call to

> look across all disciplines, across the knowledge base of the sciences, across the wisdom of the humanities, the verities and explorations of the arts, for the ingredients that will enable our students to continually interact with a world in change, with the imminence of changes bringing essentially unforeseeable consequences. (p. 3)[8]

The above rationale applies as much to the formal school in its different guises as to any alternative or complement to the schooling system, such as distance education. However, it would be a mistake to look at any particular option—whether the school or any of its alternatives—in isolation. The role and importance of any integrated component of the learning landscape should be contemplated and appreciated in the context of all other components. The functionality of a particular component can often be seen to depend on the functionality of other components with which it interacts. Thus, by way of example, the effectiveness of media-facilitated learning depends on prior exposure to media use in, for instance, the family environment and formal schooling. Conversely, learning within a formal schooling context can gain in effectiveness if parallel avenues for enrichment are open via media such as the Internet. As to distance education per se, the primary question to be asked is not how its development might improve access to and participation in education and at what cost, but rather: How can distance education contribute to a better world? Put this way, the question combines the concern to open up possibilities for learning to the as yet unreached with the need to do so in ways that will be responsive to questions about the purposes of education, the meaning of learning, and the critique of the existing schooling tradition.

LEARNING: THE COMPREHENSIVE PICTURE

One of the greatest impediments to rethinking education and reshaping the architecture of the learning landscape is the difficulty we experience in overcoming the preconceptions about learning with which most of us grow up (J. Visser & Y. L. Visser, 2000). The need to broaden our views of learning has been amply discussed in a series of transdisciplinary debates, promoted and conducted under the auspices of UNESCO and the Learning Development Institute since 1999 (J. Visser et al., 1999; Learning Development Institute—MOL, n.d.).

Further insight can be derived through disciplined inquiry into learning as perceived by those who learn. Such inquiry typically focuses on the entire human being or on the activity of an entire collaborative entity in a cultural-historical perspective. It thus involves units of analysis the order of magnitude of which transcends the habitual research perspective, which tends to focus on learning tasks that are narrowly defined in scope and time and that may involve only very specific learning behaviors assumed to be undertaken by isolated individuals. Cole (1991) makes a similar point regarding the need to redefine the unit of analysis in the study of socially shared cognitions. Insights derived from the learning stories[9] referred to earlier in this chapter provide a relevant example of research that takes a broad view of learning. The research in question focuses on the learning of individuals. John-Steiner (2000) goes beyond the individual level and makes the collaborative team or partnership the unit of analysis in her study of creative collaboration. Still more broadly defined units of analysis are possible. Marshall (2000), for instance, makes an entire institution the unit of analysis in a learning story of the Illinois Mathematics and Science Academy.

We learn from all the above studies that meaningful learning requires a focus on:

- the development of felt ownership of knowledge;
- the emotional integration of any particular learning experience in an individual's perceived lifespan development;
- the generative nature of learning;
- the real-life context as the natural habitat for learning;
- the interaction with the learning of others as a basis for one's own learning;
- the power of learning to turn negative self-perceptions into positive ones;
- persistence as a strategy to manage life's challenges;
- "the balance between individuality and social connectedness." (Feldman, 2000, p. xii)

The latter issue is particularly relevant in connection with the global concerns referred to earlier in this chapter. It calls for looking beyond the content of education and asking pertinent questions about *how* we learn. Meaningful learning was found to be particularly facilitated when initially negative conditions could be transformed into positive challenges; when role models were present or emotionally significant support was available in the environment of the learner; or when there were opportunities for independent exploration of one's learning and metacognition.

AN INCREASINGLY OPEN WORLD

> The races of mankind will never again be able to go back to their citadels of high-walled exclusiveness. They are today exposed to one another, physically and intellectually. The shells which have so long given them full security within their individual enclosures have been broken, and by no artificial process can they be mended again.
>
> Rabindranath Tagore (1930)[10]

The prevailing focus in the distance education discourse has for a long time been on such issues as cost-effectiveness, economies of scale, and parity of esteem, all of them defined with reference to the traditional school context. This has left the thinking about distance education in the fold of the dominant classroom model. Despite the advent of powerful new technologies and the increasing realization that the problems of today are essentially different from yesterday's problems, there is a disturbing lack of imagination in how discourse and practice remain locked into the conceptions of the past. The abundant use of such terms as "online classroom" and "virtual school" is but one expression of how powerful a place the ideas of school and classroom continue to occupy in our language, and thus our thought processes. Even when new terms are introduced, such as "e-learning," the reality behind them is often as sadly representative of the unaltered past—dressed for the occasion in new clothes—as the choice of the term itself is testimony to the absence of creative thinking.

The time when the case for distance education still needed to be argued in terms of this modality's validity vis-à-vis face-to-face education has long gone by. Distance education has gained recognition and enjoys esteem. There is no longer a pressing need to think of it primarily as an alternative to traditional education. Instead, the time has come to redirect our thinking towards the creative exploration of how the experience gained in the development of distance education can be harnessed to build the learning societies of the future, serving the multiple purposes of lifelong and life-wide learning in a global perspective, a perspective that recognizes that we can all learn from each other, irrespective of where we live.

Rabindranath Tagore, quoted at the beginning of this section, wrote at a time when his native India was still a colony under British rule. After it attained independence in 1947, it became classified as a developing country. In the third and second millennium BCE the civilization of the Indus Valley had a thriving economy. India was home from 427 to 1197 to Nalanda University, the oldest known university in the world. "The university died a slow death about the time that some of the great European universities, including those in Oxford, England, and Bologna, Italy, were just getting started, and more than half a millennium before Harvard or Yale were established" (Garten, 2006, p. 1). India has now once again reached a stage of advanced economic development that places it among the four so-called BRIC countries—Brazil, Russia, India, and China, countries that can no longer be ignored by the powerful minority world. At the same time, economies in the West are in crisis and many of its universities face problems similar to one that Nalanda University was facing at the time of its demise: declining financial support. Besides, universities around the world struggle to come to terms with the challenge that the reality faced by students when they graduate is no longer consistent with *how* and *for what* they are being prepared (e.g., Cyranoski, Gilbert, Ledford, Nayar, & Yahia, 2011; Jaschik, 2012; McCook, 2011). The 1930 quote from Tagore at the beginning of this section captures perfectly well the situation we are in today, much more so even than what Tagore concluded about the world more than 80 years ago. Time has come to start thinking of the world as a planet-wide ecology of learning and complex cognition in which the exchange of ideas and the generation of new knowledge are largely mediated by technological means and facilitated by the free, or at least affordable, access to open resources.

AN INCREASINGLY COMPLEX WORLD

The history of the development of civilizations around the world—the case of the Indus Valley civilization referred to above is but an example—is a reminder of the temporality of the ways in which cultures and power structures interact with each other over time. Against the backdrop of historical and evolutionary time frames, the realities with which we live during our lifetime are nothing but ephemeral. The world has always been in constant flux. The rate at which change manifests itself has gradually increased ever since our first major invention some 10,000 years ago: agriculture. Agriculture spread out from the Fertile Crescent where it originated. In the process, it revolutionized the world. It led to subsequent technological revolutions that triggered yet other such upheavals. Consequently, at the present stage the rate of change has reached levels, in multiple domains, that are higher than ever before. In such a turbulent world, which Jeffrey Sachs in his 2007 Reith Lectures appropriately qualifies as "bursting at the seams," the divisions of the past have largely become irrelevant. Traditional boundaries have become blurred. Moreover, any of the major problems and challenges the world faces are intimately linked with other problems, none of which can be addressed in isolation, applying the linear approaches that still worked in the past (Morin, 1999). The complex nature of the problem space of the 21st century is its defining characteristic.

COMPLEX COGNITION FOR A COMPLEX WORLD

Learning in the 21st century must reflect the nature of the world in which learning individuals operate. Learning has the ultimate purpose of allowing us to interact constructively with change. It must recognize that we are ourselves part of the change we collectively create. The idea that we learn to prepare ourselves for a job or career that defines how we fulfill our lives belongs to another age. We learn as we go along, together, and observe how well we fare, jointly, negotiating our ever changing circumstances amidst the fragile equilibria that hold our world together. In such a world, cognition does not merely serve the mastery of skills. Despite the emphasis in current educational discourse on competency-based learning, it is important to realize that learning does not end with the attainment of the desired competencies. In fact, learning never ends in a world in which every single individual—and all of us together—must constantly harmonize our existence with the existence of other beings, human and non-human.

We must thus develop a vision of learning that is ubiquitous; unrelated to conditions such as age, time, space and circumstance of learning individuals; manifests itself not only in the behavior of individuals but at diverse levels of complex organization; and that, in whatever context it takes place, does so as part of a pattern of interrelated learning events occurring in a learning landscape of beautiful complexity. Cognition is, and has always been, an ecological phenomenon. Notions such as "interrelationship" and "evolving communities" are an essential part of it. The ability to survive amidst complexity crucially depends on the capability to make sense of regularity among randomness. This is, according to Gell-Mann (1994), the essence of learning. It is also key to any life form's chances of survival in an environment populated with other forms of life.

My use of the term "learning landscape" in this chapter may be taken to be metaphorical. Like the real landscape, the learning landscape is the result of, on the one hand, the natural—that is ecological—interplay of different learning entities seeking to establish themselves in the midst of others and, on the other, of the consciously planned action on the part of some actors to reshape and adjust what nature tends to produce. I use the term "landscape" deliberately because of its connotations, some of which are more poetic than operational. This, then, brings into play, in addition to the usual parameters of effectiveness and efficiency of the learning environment, also its aesthetic and ethical qualities. The planners and leaders whose actions impact on the learning landscape may well want to consider this extended meaning of the metaphor and look for beauty and harmony in the learning landscape as a major indicator for the quality of the ecology of cognition. It is probably no exaggeration to say that, so far, the work of governmental educational planning agencies, as well as of related entrepreneurial and institutional efforts, to create the infrastructural conditions for the facilitation of learning, leaves considerable room for improvement in terms of the need to be environmentally aware of what else happens in the learning landscape. This observation obviously includes much of the distance education effort as well.

The term "learning landscape" reflects the idea of complex cognition, a concept I first proposed in November 2000 during an internal seminar at the Santa Fe Institute. Cognition is a complex phenomenon in the sense that it evolves according to the laws that govern the behavior of complex adaptive systems. The conditions that underlie such behavior are well known and the literature is vast (see for some of the founding notions, e.g., Gell-Mann, 1995; Holland, 1995). The stock market, the weather, and biological systems are often quoted examples of it.

The notion of distributed cognitions approximates the idea of complex cognition. However, as Salomon (1993) points out, the meaning attributed to the term "distributed cognitions" varies considerably, depending on the theoretical perspective adopted by different researchers. On one end of the spectrum, there is the view that "cognition *in general* should be … conceived as principally distributed," the "proper unit of psychological analysis … [being] the *joint … socially mediated action* in a cultural context" (p. xv). This view contrasts with the common perception that cognitions reside inside individuals' heads. On the other end of the spectrum, one finds the conception that "'solo' and distributed cognitions are still distinguished from each other and are taken to be in an interdependent dynamic interaction" (p. xvi). This juxtaposition of views is resolved in the concept of complex cognition, which makes the distinction irrelevant, integrating the diverse points of view in a single notion. Cognition is individually owned *and* socially shared at the same time.

A NEW HORIZON?

We live in interesting times. The future of educational development may soon be less dependent on the top-down creation and management of learning infrastructure. As a consequence, the learning landscape may change in fundamental ways. Michel Serres's[11] vision of establishing a world system of open education may finally come true, in a sense. If so, it will not be created singlehandedly by UNESCO, to which it was suggested 20 years ago, nor by any other such organization, whether intergovernmental or national. If indeed a world in which learning has no frontiers is a viable idea, it will materialize thanks to the joint effort of such organizations as UNESCO and the Commonwealth of Learning, which are committed and are both playing prominent roles in the Open Educational Resources (OER) movement, together with the Open Education Resource Foundation (OERF)[12]; the Open Education Resource university[13] partnership (Bates, 2011a; OERu, 2011; Stacey, 2011); volunteering educational institutions, many currently at the tertiary level; and countless individuals.[14]

If things go the way we may hope they will, the world system of open education will not, as Serres thought, be *established*. Instead, it will *come forward* as the result of the interplay of the interests to learn and let learn of the now more than seven billion inhabitants of planet Earth and the 9.3 billion with which we will share this planet in 2050. Self-organization, not organization, will drive the process. Essential educational resources will be free and openly available to all. Learners can use them "as is" and make their own autonomous choices. If properly licensed as Free Cultural Works, those who see it as their mission to help others learn can reuse those materials, revise, remix and redistribute them. Learning will no longer be primarily the outcome of teaching, whether face-to-face or at a distance, thus creating space for peer-to-peer learning. Likewise, learning will cease to depend on traditional curricular structures or be bound by customary divisions of fields of knowledge into separate disciplines and sub-disciplines. Communities of learning will emerge thanks to the self-organization of those who want to learn and thus become independent of the organizational efforts of those who want to educate. The division between informal and formal learning will be a thing of the past so that the learning landscape will be made up of interconnected learning spaces, regardless of whether they have intentionally been created for learning's sake or if they just happen to make learning possible, such as online gaming, watching TV, or something so simple as going for a walk, alone or together. Learners will learn together in a culturally synergistic manner in spite of ethnic and national divisions (Cortazzi & Jin, 2002; Jin & Cortazzi, 1993; Wang, 2010). Societies' role in ensuring education for all will then, in the first place, involve the creation of propitious conditions for learners and teachers at all levels to organize themselves within the learning landscape, caring for its well-being and growth.

Are we still far removed from the realization of these seemingly idealistic visions of the future? It depends. Utterances to the effect that prediction is very difficult, especially when it is about the future are reported to have been made throughout history. My favorite source for it is Niels Bohr. We can discern patterns and tendencies that give us confidence about what might be possible, but we cannot know what seven billion people will do in the circumstance. It is even more difficult to say in what way powerful individual entities will move and to what extent their course of action can be influenced by constituents. But, we can envision scenarios and they may as such be influential in shaping the future. Thus, Egan (2008) sketches a scenario that runs from 2010 to 2060 for comparably far reaching educational reform (and it isn't primarily based on technology). A 50-year time frame seems to be a reasonable expectation for any such comprehensive and fundamental change to materialize. More is at stake than merely resolving technological issues that still hinder universal access to digital material and more is required than creating, continually developing and maintaining an abundant collection of open educational resources in different media formats. The most important transformation lies in the change of meanings, values, attitudes, and practices among members of the communities of learning in both the formal and informal realms. Emerging interest to look beyond OER towards the development of open educational practices (OEP) (e.g., Kehrwald, 2011; OPAL, 2011) is an encouraging development in this regard.

Bates (2011b) refers to the formation of the OERu as "perhaps the most noticeable" development in 2011. Note that much has happened over the 10-year period prior to Bates's observation. MIT's announcement on April 4, 2001, that it would make nearly all its course materials freely available online (MITnews, 2001) was a landmark event. It sparked similar action by other universities, which joined the effort later. Initiatives emerged as well to make open educational resources available at primary and secondary level or in ways that cut across different levels.[15] When looking back at the past 10 years of its OpenCourseWare (OCW) initiative, MIT concludes that it has put nearly 2100 MIT courses online that have been used by more than 100 million people (MITnews, 2011).

Besides the above freely available open educational resources, there is also a growing output of commercially available video or audio recorded lecture series, available at prices that compare with the cost of buying a good book. These courses are specifically designed for use in the absence of any structured online support.[16] Thanks to these efforts, one sees a resurgence of interest in the art of lecturing. A similar recognition of the value of the artfully crafted and skillfully delivered lecture transpires from TV Ontario's (TVO) "Big Ideas" programming.[17] TVO used to state explicitly in announcing its weekly installments of the program that it is "devoted to the art of the lecture and the importance of ideas in public life." Paul Kennedy's *Ideas* series,[18] broadcast by the Canadian Broadcasting Corporation (CBC), as well as the annual Reith Lectures,[19] produced by the British Broadcasting Corporation (BBC) since 1948, are equally good examples of this freely available educational resource that in modern educational discourse is often despised and referred to as outdated and no longer of this time because of the format's poor interactivity. Such negative appreciation obviously ignores that, while reading a good book or when listening to a good lecture, the learning dialogue with the unreachable author takes place in the learner's head.

Solutions are in the works as well to create alternative routes to accreditation that bypass the need to be enrolled at an institution. Most notable in this regard are the efforts of the OERu partnership (OERu, 2011) and MIT's recent most online learning initiative (Parry, 2011), the latter of which caters to, among other things, the individual assessment of any student's work, allowing "students who demonstrate their mastery of subjects to earn a certificate of completion awarded by *MITx*" (MITnews, 2011). However valuable, relevant, and important these developments are, there is the risk that the continued principal focus on formal learning in these efforts takes attention away from the equally valid and urgent necessity to expand the OER movement to respond much more extensively and deeply to the need for the development of informal learning and non-accredited structured learning.

CONCLUDING THOUGHTS

The reality of learning is changing fast. It is changing in ways that may make it inappropriate, superfluous, or irrelevant to still include in the title of a possible fourth edition of this handbook—should it be decided to publish one—the notion of distance education, with its historical connotations of emulating the traditional formal schooling practice and striving for equivalent experiences (Simonson & Schlosser, Chapter 27, this volume). Of the past of research and theory building regarding distance education, the concept of transactional distance (Moore, Chapter 3, this volume) is probably the one important idea that should be retained, but it may have to be reconceptualized within a world of blurred boundaries in which the resources of learning are open to all, freely accessible, and licensed such that new knowledge and learning can build, unhindered by arbitrary restrictions, on prior intellectual and artistic achievement, increasingly in the context of self-organized communities of learning.

These changes, if indeed they materialize, call for new research. Such research should be informed by the essentially complex nature of the emerging global learning landscape and the fluidity of the patterns of interaction between the diverse learning spaces, in both the formal and informal domains, that constitute the fabric of this global environment. Creativity will be required in developing novel methods of inquiry in the development of such research.

NOTES

1. The term "majority world" refers to the poorer countries, those that are less developed from the perspective of mainstream Western economic development ideals. These are the countries where most people of the world live. Alternative designations are "third world countries"—an anomalous phrase since the concepts of first world and second world have become obsolete following the end of the cold war—and "developing nations"—an equally awkward concept as it suggests that the minority wealthier part of the world does no longer develop. Geographically, the majority world is predominantly found in Africa, Latin America, and Asia, but the concept does equally apply to pockets in the wealthier parts of the world. Historically it has remained difficult to delineate these (gradually shifting) conceptual boundaries.
2. Changes in the learning landscape are to be attributed to more factors than just the rapid and pervasive technological development. A more comprehensive overview can be found in *Learners in a changing learning landscape: Reflections from a dialogue on new roles and expectations* by J. Visser and Visser-Valfrey (Eds.) (2008).
3. An alternative perspective on why we should not be overly concerned with questions about definition of the field can be found in the concluding paragraphs of the introductory chapter of Perraton's (2007) *Open and Distance Learning in the Developing World.*
4. Note that, almost 50 years later, the issue of learning to live together was explicitly identified in the Delors Report as one of the four pillars on which education for the 21 century should be built (Delors et al., 1996).
5. The following references are provided to allow for further exploration of what is involved in the suggested reshaping of the architecture of the learning landscape. The work of the Center for *Learning in Informal and Formal Environments* (LIFE Center, n.d.) and the steady stream of publications emanating from the LIFE Center stand out regarding the integration of the learning landscape. The multi-author volume on *Learners in a changing learning landscape: Reflections from a dialogue on new roles and expectation* (J. Visser & Visser-Valfrey, 2008) is an additional source of interest. Research on and explorations of the meaning of learning in a life-wide and lifelong context have been among the concerns of the present author (J. Visser, 2008, 2012). Initial inroads into exploring the issue of self-organization in open online learning were made by Wiley and Edwards (2002). Wiley (2006) revisited the issue four years later, the same year when Jakubowicz (2006) also published on this issue. *The International Review of Research in Open and Distance Learning* recently dedicated a special issue to "Emergent Learning, Connections, Design for Learning" (Sims & Kays, 2011). The literature about complexity in education is equally relevant in this regard. A good starting point here is the set of Web pages on Complexity and Education (n.d.) maintained by the University of Alberta, which contain many useful references to both books and articles. Additional sources of interest are Doll, Fleener, Trueit, & St. Julien (2005); Mason (2008); and Morrison (2006). The issue of dialogism has been explored extensively by Shotter (e.g., 2007, 2008, 2009, 2010) for several decades. The references given here are to some of his more recent contributions. The Network for Transdisciplinary Research maintains a comprehensive structured database of literature in the field of transdisciplinary research (Database Bibliography Transdisciplinarity, n.d.).
6. See http://life-slc.org/about/about.html.
7. Note that the reference is to children in the Western world.
8. Lederman's thoughts are reminiscent of the observation by another physics Nobel laureate, Albert Einstein, made in 1946 at the start of the nuclear age, namely that "everything has changed, save the way we think." (Quoted by Lawrence Krauss on the occasion of the 2012 Bulletin of the Atomic Scientists 'Doomsday Clock' announcement. Retrieved from http://www.thebulletin.org/content/media-center/announcements/2012/01/10/doomsday-clock-moves-1-minute-closer-to-midnight).
9. Note that the Greek root of the word story, as well as of history, ἱστορία (historia), means inquiry.
10. See Tagore and Ray (2007, Vol. 5, p. 76).
11. Michel Serres is the French philosopher who, as a member of the Ad Hoc Forum of Reflection on UNESCO's Role in the Last Decade of the Twentieth Century (UNESCO Executive Board, 1993a,b), suggested that UNESCO establish a world system of open education.

12. See http://wikieducator.org/OERF:Home.
13. See http://wikieducator.org/OER_university/Home.
14. Note that at the time of writing, more than one thousand individuals—in diverse ways involved or interested in education, from 87 different countries—are participating in a massive open online workshop about Open Content Licensing (http://wikieducator.org/Open_content_licensing_for_educators/Home).
15. Specific instances are the WikiEducator platform (http://www.wikieducator.com); the KhanAcademy (http://www.khanacademy.org/); MathsExcellence (http://www.mathsexcellence.co.za/); Siyavula (http://siyavula.org.za/about/); For the Love of Science (http://www.learndev.org/ScienceWorkBooks.html); and SugarLabs (http://www.sugarlabs.org/) to name but a few examples.
16. Most noteworthy in this genre is the output of the Teaching Company (www.teach12.com), which produces college level courses, taught by professors who have distinguished themselves as scientists and teachers. The affordability of these courses positions them as an interesting alternative of or complement to open educational resources. Somewhat comparable are lecture series offered in Dutch by the Home Academy (https://www.home-academy.nl/). A wider range of such courses may well be available in yet other languages. I am aware of at least one instance of the use of the video version of one of these commercially available courses in a developing country context by a self-organized group of faculty members of different universities, meeting once a week and involving substantial peer-to-peer learning.
17. See http://bigideas.tvo.org/.
18. See http://www.cbc.ca/ideas/.
19. See http://www.bbc.co.uk/radio4/features/the-reith-lectures/archive/.

REFERENCES

Anderson, T., & Whitelock, D. (2004). The educational semantic web: Visioning and practicing the future of education [Special issue]. *Journal of Interactive Media in Education, 2004*(1). Retrieved from http://www-jime.open.ac.uk/article/2004-1/181

Barnosky, A. D., Matzke, N., Tomiya, S., Wogan, G. O. U., Swartz, B., Quental, T. B., ... Ferrer, E. A. (2011). Has the Earth's sixth mass extinction already arrived? *Nature, 471*(7336), 51–57.

Bates, T. (2011a). *Introducing the OERu — and some questions.* Retrieved from http://www.tonybates.ca/2011/10/05/introducing-the-oeru-and-some-questions/

Bates, T. (2011b). *E-learning in 2011: A retrospective.* Retrieved from http://www.tonybates.ca/2011/12/13/e-learning-in-2011-a-retrospective/

Boorstin, D. J. (1985). *The discoverers: A history of man's search to know his world and himself.* New York, NY: Random House.

Butcher, N., Latchem, C., Levey, L., & Mawoyo, M. (Eds.). (2011). Special issue on distance education for empowerment and development in Africa. *Distance Education, 32*(2), 149–302.

Clarke, A. C. (1992). *How the world was one: Beyond the global village.* London, UK: Victor Gollancz.

Cole, M. (1991). Conclusion. In L. B. Resnick, J. M. Levine, & S. D. Teasley (Eds.), *Perspectives on socially shared cognition* (pp. 398–417). Washington, DC: American Psychological Association.

Complexity and Education (n.d.). Web site on *Complexity and Education* of the University of Alberta. Retrieved from http://www.complexityandeducation.ualberta.ca/complexityinedref.htm.

Cortazzi, M., & Jin, L. (2002). Cultures of learning: The social construction of educational identities. In D. C. S. Li (Ed.), *Discourses in search of members, in honor of Ron Scollon* (pp. 49–78). Lanham, NY: University Press of America.

Creed, C., & Perraton, H. (2001). Distance education in the E-9 countries: The development and future of distance education programmes in the nine high-population countries. Paris, France: UNESCO. Retrieved from http://unesdoc.unesco.org/images/0012/001231/123157e.pdf

Crutzen, P. J. (2002). Geology of mankind. Nature 415(6867), 23–23.

Cyranoski, D., Gilbert, N., Ledford, H., Nayar, A., & Yahia, M. (2011). *Nature, 472*(7343), 280–282.

Database Bibliography Transdisciplinarity. (n.d.). The database Bibliography Transdisciplinarity. Bern: Swiss Academies of Arts and Sciences. Retrieved from http://www.transdisciplinarity.ch/e/Bibliography/

Delors, J., Al Mufti, I., Amagi, I., Carneiro, R., Chung, F., Geremek, B., ... Zhou N. (1996). Learning: The treasure within. Report to UNESCO of the International Commission on Education for the Twenty-first Century. Paris, France: UNESCO.

Doll, W., Fleener, M. J., Trueit, D., & St. Julien, J. (Eds.). (2005). *Chaos, complexity, curriculum and culture: A conversation.* New York, NY: Peter Lang.

Edström, L. O., Erdos, R., & Prosser, R. (Eds.). (1970). *Mass education: Studies in adult education and teaching by correspondence in some developing countries.* Stockholm, Sweden: The Dag Hammerskjöld Foundation.

Egan, K. (2008). *The future of education: Reimagining our schools from the ground up.* New Haven, CT: Yale University Press.

Erdos, R. F. (1967). *Teaching by correspondence* (a UNESCO Source Book). London, UK: Longmans, Green & Co Limited; Paris, France: UNESCO.

Faure, E., Herrera, F., Kaddoura, A-R., Lopes, H., Petrovsky, A. V., Rahnema, M., & Ward, F. C. (1972). *Learning to be: The world of education today and tomorrow.* Report to UNESCO of the International Commission on the Development of Education. Paris, France: UNESCO.

Feldman, D. H. (2000). Foreword. In V. John-Steiner, *Creative collaboration* (pp. ix–xiii). New York, NY: Oxford University Press.

Gagné, R. M. (1965/1985). *The conditions of learning* (1st/4th ed.). New York, NY: Holt, Rinehart and Winston.

Gagné, R. M., & Briggs, L. J. (1974). *Principles of instructional design.* New York, NY: Holt, Rinehart and Winston.

Garten, J. E. (2006, December 9). Really old school. *New York Times.* Retrieved from http://www.nytimes.com/2006/12/09/opinion/09garten

Gell-Mann, M. (1994). *The quark and the jaguar: Adventures in the simple and the complex.* New York, NY: W. H. Freeman and Company.

Gell-Mann, M. (1995). What is complexity? *Complexity, 1*(1), 16–19.

Holland, J. H. (1995). Can there be a unified theory of complex adaptive systems? In H. J. Morowitz & J. L. Singer (Eds.), The mind, the brain, and complex adaptive systems. *Proceedings Volume XXII, Santa Fe Institute, Studies in the Sciences of Complexity* (pp. 45–50). Reading, MA: Addison-Wesley.

Jakubowicz, P. (2006, November) *Complexity theory and online learning.* Paper presented at the Asia-Pacific Educational Research Association International Conference, Hong Kong. Retrieved from http://numerons.in/files/documents/24Complexity-Theory-and-Online-Learning.pdf

Jamison, D. T., & McAnany, E. G. (1978). *Radio for education and development.* Beverly Hills, CA: Sage.

Jamison, D. T., Klees, S. J., & Wells, S. J. (1978). *The costs of educational media: Guidelines for planning and evaluation.* Beverly Hills, CA: Sage.

Jaschik, S. (2012, January 9). Dissing the dissertation. *Inside Higher Ed.* Retrieved from http://www.insidehighered.com/news/2012/01/09/mla-considers-radical-changes-dissertation.

Jin, L., & Cortazzi, M. (1993). Cultural orientation and academic language use, in D. Graddol, L. Thompson, & M.Byram (Eds.), *Language and culture* (pp. 84–97). Clevedon, UK: Multilingual Matters.

John-Steiner, V. (2000). *Creative collaboration.* New York, NY: Oxford University Press.

Kehrwald, B. (Ed.). (2011). Open educational practices [Special issue]. *Journal of Open, Flexible and Distance Learning, 15*(2). *Retrieved from http://journals.akoaotearoa.ac.nz/index.php/JOFDL*

Koestler, A. (1959). *The sleepwalkers: A history of man's changing vision of the universe.* London, UK: Hutchinson.

Learning Development Institute—MOL (n.d.). The *Meaning of Learning (MOL)* focus area of activity of the Learning Development Institute. Retrieved from http://www.learndev.org/MoL.htm.

Leary, J., & Berge, Z. (2007). Successful distance education programs in sub-Saharan Africa. *Turkish Online Journal of Distance Education, 8*(2), 136–145. Retrieved from https://tojde.anadolu.edu.tr/tojde26/pdf/article_12.pdf

Lederman, L. M. (1999, April). On the threshold of the 21st century: Comments on science education. In (J. Visser, Chair), *The symposium on overcoming the underdevelopment of learning.* Symposium conducted at the Annual Meeting of the American Educational Research Association, Montreal, Canada. Retrieved from http://www.learndev.org/dl/lederman_f.pdf

LIFE Center (n.d.). *Learning in Informal and Formal Environments.* Science of Learning Center. Retrieved from http://life-slc.org/

Marshall, S. P. (2000, October). The learning story of the Illinois Mathematics and Science Academy. In (J. Visser, Chair), *The Meaning of Learning Project of the Learning Development Institute.* Presented at the International Conference of the Association for Educational Communications and Technology, Denver, CO. Retrieved from http://www.learndev.org/dl/DenverMarshall.PDF

Mason, M. B. (Ed.). (2008). *Complexity theory and the philosophy of education.* Oxford, UK: Wiley-Blackwell.

McCook, A. (2011). Rethinking PhD's. *Nature, 472*(7343), 280–282.

Meltzoff, A. N., Kuhl, P. K., Movellan, J., & Sejnowski, T. J. (2009). Foundations for a new science of learning. *Science, 325*(5938), 284–288.

MITnews (2001). *MIT to make nearly all course materials available free on the World Wide Web.* Retrieved from http://web.mit.edu/newsoffice/2001/ocw.html

MITnews (2011). *MIT launches online learning initiative: 'MITx' will offer courses online and make online learning tools freely available.* Retrieved from http://web.mit.edu/newsoffice/2011/mitx-education-initiative-1219.html

Morin, E. (1982). *Science avec conscience* [Science with conscience]. Paris, France: Fayard.

Morin, E. (1999). *Seven complex lessons in education for the future.* Paris, France: UNESCO. Retrieved from http://unesdoc.unesco.org/images/0011/001177/117740eo.pdf

Morin, E., & Kern, A. B. (1999). *Homeland earth: a manifesto for the new millenium.* Cresskill, NJ: Hampton Press.

Morin, E. (2005). *Introduction à la pensée complexe* [Introduction to complex thought]. Paris, France: Éditions du Seuil.

Morrison, K. (2006, November). *Complexity theory and education.* Paper presented at the Asia-Pacific Educational Research Association International Conference, Hong Kong. Retrieved from http://edisdat.ied.edu.hk/pubarch/b15907314/full_paper/SYMPO-000004_Keith%20Morrison.pdf

Nicolescu, B. (2002). *Manifesto of transdisciplinarity.* New York, NY: SUNY Press.

OERu (2011). *Open Education Resource university: Towards a logic model and plan for action.* Retrieved from http://wikieducator.org/images/c/c2/Report_OERU-Final-version.pdf

OPAL (2011). *Beyond OER: Shifting focus to open educational practices.* Report by the Open Educational Quality Initiative. Retrieved from http://duepublico.uni-duisburg-essen.de/servlets/DeriveServlet/Derivate-25907/OPALReport2011-Beyond-OER.pdf

Parry, M. (2011, December 19). MIT will offer certificates to outside students who take its online courses. *The Chronicle of Higher Education.* Retrieved from http://chronicle.com/article/MIT-Will-Offer-Certificates-to/130121/

Perraton, H. (Ed.). (1976). *Food from learning: The International Extension College 1971–1976.* Cambridge, UK: International Extension College.

Perraton, H. (2007). *Open and distance learning in the developing world.* London, UK: Routledge.

Sachs, J. (2007). Bursting at the seams. *Reith Lectures 2007.* Retrieved from http://www.bbc.co.uk/radio4/reith2007/

Salomon, G. (Ed.) (1993). *Distributed cognitions: Psychological and educational considerations.* Cambridge, UK: Cambridge University Press.

Scanlon, E., Jones, A., & Waycott, J. (2005). Mobile technologies: Prospects for their use in learning in informal science settings. *Journal of Interactive Media in Education, 2005*(25). Retrieved from http://oro.open.ac.uk/6529/1/scanlon-2005-25.pdf

Schramm, W. (1977). *Big media, little media: Tools and technologies for instruction.* Beverly Hills, CA: Sage.

Sims, R., & Kays, E. (Eds.). (2011). Emergent learning, connections, design for learning [Special issue]. *International Review of Research in Open and Distance Learning, 12*(7). Retrieved from http://www.irrodl.org/index.php/irrodl

Sharma, Y. (2003). Written out of the script. *The New Courrier, No. 2.* Retrieved from http://unesdoc.unesco.org/images/0013/001300/130036e.pdf#130045

Shotter, J. (2007). Vico, Wittgenstein, Bakhtin and the *background*: What is there before anything is. *Analysis and Metaphysics, 6,* 195–223.

Shotter, J (2008). Dialogism and polyphony in organizational theorizing: Action guiding anticipations and the continuous creation of novelty. *Organization Studies, 29*(4), 501–524.

Shotter, J. (2009). Moments of common reference in dialogic communication: A basis for unconfused collaboration in unique contexts. *The International Journal of Collaborative Practices, 1*(1), 31–39. Retrieved from http://ijcp.files.wordpress.com/2009/06/shotter-english.pdf

Shotter, J. (2010). Situated dialogic action research: Disclosing 'beginnings' for innovative change in organizations. *Organizational Research Methods, 13*(2), 268–285.

Stacey, P. (2011). *Open Educational Resource University (OERU).* Retrieved from http://edtechfrontier.com/2011/02/22/open-educational-resource-university-oeru/

Tagore, R., & Ray, M. K. (2007). *The English writings of Rabindranath Tagore in 8 volumes – Volume 5: Essays.* New Delhi, India: Atlantic Publishers and Distributers.

UNESCO (2000). *World education report 2000 – The right to education: Towards education for all throughout life.* Paris, France: UNESCO Publishing. Retrieved from http://www.unesco.org/education/information/wer/PDFeng/wholewer.PDF

UNESCO (2011). *EFA Global Monitoring Report.* Paris, France: UNESCO Publishing. Retrieved from http://unesdoc.unesco.org/images/0019/001907/190743e.pdf

UNESCO Executive Board. (1993a). *Consideration of the results of the deliberations of the Ad Hoc Forum of Reflection.* Paris, France: UNESCO. Retrieved from http://unesdoc.unesco.org/images/0009/000958/095846eo.pdf

UNESCO Executive Board (1993b). Decisions adopted by the Executive Board at its 142nd session. Paris, France: UNESCO. Retrieved from http://unesdoc.unesco.org/images/0009/000958/095807e.pdf

UNESCO Institute of Statistics. (2005). *Children out of school: Measuring exclusion from primary education.* Montreal, Canada: UNESCO Institute of Statistics. Retrieved from http://www.uis.unesco.org/template/pdf/educgeneral/OOSC_EN_WEB_FINAL.pdf

UNESCO—IIEP (1967a). *New educational media in action: Case studies for planners – I, II, & III.* Paris, France: United Nations Educational, Scientific and Cultural Organization.

UNESCO—IIEP (1967b). *The new media: Memo to educational planners.* Paris, France: United Nations Educational, Scientific and Cultural Organization.

Visser, J. (2006). Universities, wisdom, transdisciplinarity and the challenges and opportunities of technology. In M. F. Beaudoin (Ed.), *Perspectives on higher education in the digital age* (pp. 187–205). New York, NY: Nova Science Publishers.

Visser, J. (2008). Constructive interaction with change: Implications for learners and the environment in which they learn. In J. Visser & M. Visser-Valfrey (Eds.), *Learners in a changing learning landscape: Reflections from a dialogue on new roles and expectations* (pp. 11–35). Dordrecht, The Netherlands: Springer.

Visser, J. (2012). Reflections on a definition: Revisiting the meaning of learning. In D. N. Aspin, J. Chapman, K. Evans, & R. Baqnall (Eds.), *Second international handbook of lifelong learning* (pp. 163–179). Dordrecht, The Netherlands: Springer.

Visser, J., Berenfeld, B., Burnett, R., Diarra, C. M., Driscoll, M. P., Lederman, … Tinker, R. (1999, April). *Overcoming the underdevelopment of learning.* Symposium held at the Annual Meeting of the American Educational Research Association, Montreal, Canada. Retrieved from http://www.learndev.org/aera.html.

Visser, J., Berg, D., Burnett, R., & Visser, Y. L. (2002, February). *In search of the meaning of learning: A social process of raising questions and creating meanings.* Workshop held at the Annual Convention of the Association for Educational Communications and Technology, Long Beach, CA.

Visser, J., & Visser, Y. L. (2000). On the difficulty of changing our perceptions about such things as learning. In (J. Visser, Chair) *Search of the meaning of learning* at the International Conference of the Association for Educational Communications and Technology, Denver, CO [Presidential Session]. Retrieved from http://www.learndev.org/dl/DenverVisserVisser.PDF

Visser, J., Visser, Y. L., Amirault, R. J., Genge, C. D., & Miller, V. (2002, April). *Second order learning stories.* Paper presented by at the annual meeting of the American Educational Research Association (AERA), New Orleans, LA.

Visser, J., & Visser-Valfrey, M. (Eds.). (2008). *Learners in a changing learning landscape: Reflections from a dialogue on new roles and expectations.* Dordrecht, The Netherlands: Springer.

Visser, J, Visser, Y. L., Amirault, R. J., Genge, C. D., & Miller, V. (2002, April). *Second order learning stories.* Paper presented at the Annual Meeting of the American Educational Research Association (AERA), New Orleans, LA.

Visser, M., & Visser, J. (2003, October). *"We closed our books and put them away." Learning stories from Mozambique—A critical reflection on communicating about the reality and future of learning.* Paper presented at the International Conference of the Association for Educational Communications and Technology (AECT), Anaheim, CA, October.

Visser, Y. L., Rowland, G., & Visser, J. (Eds.). (2002). Broadening the definition of learning [Special issue]. *Educational Technology, 42*(2).

Visser, Y. L., & Visser, J. (2000, October). *The learning stories project.* Paper presented at the International Conference of the Association for Educational Communications and Technology, Denver, CO.

Wang, L. (2010). *Chinese postgraduate students in a British university: Their learning experiences and learning beliefs* (Unpublished doctoral dissertation). Retrieved from http://etheses.dur.ac.uk/196/1/Lihong_Wang_PhDThesis.pdf

Wiley, D. (2006). Online self-organizing social systems: Four years later. In R. Luppicini (Ed.), *Online learning communities* (pp. 289–298). Charlotte, NC: Information Age.

Wiley, D. A., & Edwards, E. K. (2002). Online self-organizing social systems: The decentralized future of online learning. *Quarterly Review of Distance Education, 3*(1), 33–46.

Wilson, E. O. (1998). *Consilience: The unity of knowledge.* New York, NY: Alfred A. Knopf.

Young, M., Perraton, H., Jenkins, J., & Dodds, T. (1980). *Distance teaching for the third world: The lion and the clockwork mouse.* London, UK: Routledge & Kegan Paul.

LIST OF CONTRIBUTORS

Zehra Akyol is a researcher in the field of educational technology. Her research interest includes teaching and learning in online and blended learning contexts, factors affecting and technologies supporting the development of communities of inquiry and meta-cognition.

Mike Allen (Ph.D., Michigan State University) is professor in the Department of Communication at UW-Milwaukee and has published more than 100 meta-analysis in the area of social influence.

Mohamed Ally is chair and professor in the Centre for Distance Education at Athabasca University. He completed his Ph.D. at the University of Alberta in Canada. Dr. Ally's research areas include distance education, e-learning, mobile learning, and use of ICT for education for all.

William Anderson is Director of Distance Learning at the University of Otago. His research is in the areas of online learning communities and interaction online, the design of online learning environments, teaching and learning strategies in online environments, and the nature of the student experience of learning online.

Michael K. Barbour is an Assistant Professor at Wayne State University in Detroit, Michigan, where he teaches Instructional Technology and Qualitative Research Methodology. Research interests focus on the effective design, delivery, and support of online learning to K-12 students in virtual school environments, particularly those in rural jurisdictions.

Michael F. Beaudoin is Professor of Education, University of New England, and Adjunct Professor, University of Maryland University College's Masters of Distance Education program. He has held senior administrative positions at several institutions, is the author of over 100 publications and presentations in distance education, leadership, and related topics.

Zane L. Berge is Professor and former Director of the Training Systems graduate programs at the UMBC Campus, University System of Maryland. Berge's publications involving educational technology and distance education include work as a primary author, editor, or presenter of 10 books and over 300 chapters, articles, and conference presentations.

Linda M. Black was Founding Director of a U.S. Navy Information Systems training center and leader of the Competency Based Assistance Team for the U.S. Navy. She was Dean of Distance Education Initiatives at Mountain State University and adjunct professor teaching distance education courses in The Pennsylvania State University's Adult Education Program.

Nancy Burrell (Ph.D., Michigan State University) is Professor and Chair in the Department of Communication at University of Wisconsin-Milwaukee where she also is Director of the Campus Mediation Center.

Cathy Cavanaugh is Associate Professor of Educational Technology at the University of Florida. She served as a Fulbright Senior Scholar to Nepal in 2010 and received the Research Award from the International Association for K–12 Online Learning in 2009. She serves as an advisor to the European Commission Lifelong Learning Programme.

Tom Clark, President of TA Consulting has led evaluations for programs ranging from a $9.1 million Star Schools grant for K-12 online learning, to a postsecondary FIPSE grant for medical educators. Publications include *Virtual Schools: Planning for Success* (2005) with Zane Berge. He was an advisor for U. S. Department of Education's Evaluating Online Learning (2008).

Susan Crichton is an associate professor at University of British Columbia Okanagan Campus. She researches appropriate technologies to enable social justice and equity of access for learners in challenging contexts, and is currently exploring the use of hand-held technologies in rural and urban settings in Canada and East Africa.

Robert F. Curry is Director of Advising for Distance Learning at Old Dominion University. He was a chapter author for the first and second editions of *The Handbook of Distance Education*. Dr. Curry has degrees from Furman University, the University of Georgia, and the College of William and Mary.

Vanessa P. Dennen is an Associate Professor of Instructional Systems at Florida State University. Her research investigates the nexus of cognitive, motivational, and social elements in computer-mediated communication, concentrating on: learner participation in online activities and interactions, norm development, and informal learning within online communities of practice.

William C. Diehl is a consultant and works with higher education institutions, non-profits, government agencies, and corporations on a range of projects. He is the Interviews Editor for *The American Journal of Distance Education*, an instructor for The Pennsylvania State University, and founder of The International Museum of Distance Education.

Denise P. Domizi is the Associate Coordinator of TA and Faculty Development at the Center for Teaching and Learning at the University of Georgia. Her research interests include informal learning environments, contextual influences on learning, and learner-centered instructional strategies in both face-to-face and online environments.

Terry Evans is a Professor of Education at Deakin University, Australia. He edited (with C. Denholm) the *Doctorates Downunder* series of books for students, supervisors, and graduates (2006, 2007, 2009, 2012), and (with M. Haughey and D. Murphy) *The International Handbook of Distance Education* (2008).

Elaine Fabbro is the Head, Information Literacy & Public Services, at Athabasca University Library. She is the co-author of *Exploring the Digital Library: A Guide for Online Teaching and Learning*, and has presented at a number of conferences on various aspects of library services for distance learners.

Norm Friesen is the Canada Research Chair in E-Learning Practices at Thompson Rivers University in British Columbia. He is author of *Re-Thinking E-Learning Research: Foundations, Methods and Practices"* (2009) and *The Place of the Classroom and the Space of the Screen"* (2011).

D. Randy Garrison is a professor in the Faculty of Education at the University of Calgary and has researched teaching and learning in adult, higher and distance education contexts. His books include *An Introduction to Distance Education: Understanding Teaching and Learning in a New Era* (2010) and *E-Learning in the 21st century* (2nd ed.) (2011).

Charles R. Graham studies technology-mediated teaching and learning, focusing on the design and evaluation of blended and online learning environments. He also researches the use of technology to enhance traditional teaching and learning. Charles co-edited the *Handbook of Blended Learning*.

Rosemary Green is Graduate Programs Librarian and Associate Professor at Shenandoah University in Winchester, VA, where she coordinates library services and information literacy instruction for on-campus and off-campus graduate students. She also teaches graduate research methods courses in education, music, and occupational therapy.

Charlotte N. Gunawardena is Regents' Professor of Distance Education and Instructional Technology in the Organizational Learning and Instructional Technology Program, at the University of New Mexico. She has published on distance education for over twenty years, consulted internationally, and currently researches the socio-cultural context of online learning communities.

Donald E. Hanna is Professor of Educational Communications with the University of Wisconsin-Extension, and Professor of Engineering Professional Development at the University of Wisconsin-Madison. His research and teaching focuses on organizational change, online learning, technology, and quality in higher education.

Michael J. Hannafin is Professor of Educational Psychology and Instructional Technology at the University of Georgia where he directs the Learning and Performance Support Laboratory. His research focuses on the design and support for student-centered learning.

Tiffany M. Herder works as a Senior Instructional Designer for Capella University collaborating with faculty and cross-functional staff to create high quality learning experiences. Her research interests include learner engagement in collaborative online environments.

Janette R. Hill is a Professor in the Department of Lifelong Education, Administration, and Policy at the University of Georgia (UGA) where she also serves as Department Head. Her current research focuses on the study of emerging/Web-based technologies, community building in virtual environments, resource-based learning, and information/knowledge management systems.

Alistair Inglis is Deputy Pro Vice-Chancellor at Curtin University Sarawak. He is Deputy Editor of the International research journal, *Distance Education.* He has worked extensively in distance, open, and flexible learning and has published on a range of topics including costs of distance education, instructional design, and quality in distance education.

Modupe E. Irele is co-founder of Key Learning Solutions, an organization that focuses on developing core academic skills and competencies among Nigerian teachers and college-bound students. She is an adjunct Assistant Professor in The Pennsylvania State University World Campus where she teaches graduate students online in the Adult Education Program .

Shanna Smith Jaggars is a Senior Research Associate at the Community College Research Center at Teachers College, Columbia University. She has led quantitative studies of online course outcomes in community colleges in two states, and co-directed a qualitative study of online learning focused on Virginia community colleges.

Kay Johnson has been involved in distance education since joining Athabasca University in 2000. In addition to her current work teaching and writing courses to develop students' information literacy and academic skills, she was the Library's Head of Reference and Public Services for seven years.

Insung Jung is a Professor at the International Christian University in Tokyo and an advisor and former director of the International Board of Standards for Training, Performance and Instruction. She is co-author and co-editor of *Distance and Blended Learning in Asia* and *Quality Assurance and Accreditation in Distance Education and E-learning.*

Roger Kaufman is Professor Emeritus at Florida State University. He is the author of 40 books and more than 200 articles on strategic planning and needs assessment. His most recent book is *A Manager's Pocket Guide to Strategic Planning and Thinking.*

Greg Kearsley is the Director, Online Graduate Programs in Education at the University of New England. He has been involved in the design, development, and teaching of online courses for more than 30 years. He is the co-author of *Distance Education: A Systems Approach* with Michael G. Moore and has written over 20 other books about technology and education.

Dietmar K. Kennepohl is Professor of Chemistry and Associate Vice President Academic at Athabasca University. Most of his teaching experience has been in a distributed and online setting. He holds both university and national teaching awards. His current research interests include chemical education, main group, and green chemistry.

Peggy L. Kenyon is a Division Chief with The Army Distributed Learning Program located in the Office of the TRADOC Capabilities Manager at Ft. Eustis, VA, responsible for technical standards for distributed learning products. She has an MBA and an Ed.S in Education and is completing a dissertation in Education Technology with Walden University.

Hyeonjin Kim is an Assistant Professor in the Department of Education at Korea National University of Education. Her research interests include design of technology-enhanced learning environments and learning (activity) processes in technology environments.

Minchi C. Kim is an Assistant Professor of Learning Design and Technology in the Department of Curriculum and Instruction at Purdue University. Her research addresses designing and scaffolding students' problem solving with technology-enhanced learning environments, advancing pedagogical frameworks for learning and teaching in technology-rich contexts, and integrating emergent technologies.

Woori Kim is a doctoral student of Learning Design and Technology in the Department of Curriculum and Instruction at Purdue University. Her research focuses on the effects of e-learning and technology integration both in a short-term and in a long-term

Shelley Kinash is an Associate Professor and the Director of Quality, Teaching, and Learning at Bond University in Queensland, Australia. She has been an academic for 18 years, in Canada and Australia. Her Ph.D. research was on blind online learners and she is currently researching mobile learning, universal design for learning and assurance of learning.

Adrie A. Koehler is a doctoral student of Learning Design and Technology in the Department of Curriculum and Instruction at Purdue University. Her research focuses on the beginning teacher experience. Specifically, she is interested in how beginning teachers can be supported through the use of emerging technologies.

Kadir Kozan is a doctoral student of Learning Design and Technology in the Department of Curriculum and Instruction at Purdue University. His main research interest is how to match educational technology or technology integration with human cognition in order to enhance learning.

Gary W. Kuhne is the Co-Professor-In- Charge of the Adult Education Program at The Pennsylvania State University and the Lead Faculty for the World Campus M.Ed. in Adult Education. Dr. Kuhne is President of the Institute for the Study of Ministry Dynamics and a consultant to business and industry, government agencies, higher education institutions, and churches.

Alex Kuskis has divided his career between education and business. He has held management positions in book publishing and the computer industry and taught, both online and on campus at several universities, including Toronto, Manitoba, Royal Roads, and presently, Gonzaga University, for which he teaches online M.A. courses in media studies.

Sung Lee is the President of Gyenong Gi-Do Provincial Institute for Lifelong Learning, S. Korea. His research has focused on evaluation and measurement of educational effectiveness and cost-effectiveness.

Tomas A. Lipinski is Executive Associate Dean at the Indiana University School of Library and Information Science, Indiana University Purdue University Indianapolis. His current project is a book on licensing resources.

Edward Mabry (Ph.D., Bowling Green University) is Associate Professor in the Department of Communication at UW-Milwaukee and conducts research in the area of technological group communication.

Susan Moisey is an Associate Professor in the Centre for Distance Education at Athabasca University where she teaches masters- and doctoral-level courses in instructional design and learning theory. Her research interests include alternative instructional design models, online learning strategies, distance learners with disabilities, and inclusive education.

Michael Grahame Moore is Distinguished Professor of Education at The Pennsylvania State University. He is the founder and editor of *The American Journal of Distance Education*. His many publications include *Distance Education: A Systems* View (with G. Kearsley; 3rd ed.), 2012.

Som Naidu is Associate Professor and Director of Learning & Teaching Quality Enhancement and Evaluation Services at Charles Sturt University, Australia. He is

Executive Editor of the journal *Distance Education*, Assistant Editor of the journal *Interactive Learning Environments* and co-series Editor of the Routledge book series on *Open and Flexible Learning*.

Patricia M. O'Brien is Deputy Director of the higher education commission of the New England Association of Schools and Colleges (NEASC), the regional accrediting association for New England. Prior to NEASC, she worked at Bridgewater State University and Emmanuel College. Her degrees are from Wellesley College and Harvard University.

Busayo Odunlami is a management consultant specializing in technology implementation and deployment for organizational knowledge and development projects. His degrees include Information and Systems Engineering (Lehigh University) and Social-Organizational Psychology (Columbia University). Busayo is a member of the World Bank's African Region Learning Team.

Kikuko Omori (M.A., University of Kansas) is a doctoral student in the Department of Communication at UW-Milwaukee. Her area of research considers how educational technology become adapted by cultures for use.

Von V. Pittman recently retired after working more than 35 years, at four state universities. He has developed programs in every distance education format. In addition, he has taught courses in communications, higher education, and American history, and has written widely in the history of distance and continuing education.

Farhad Saba is Professor Emeritus of Educational Technology at San Diego State University. His current research, scholarly writing and consulting continue to be focused on key theoretical concepts in the field and application of systems approach to developing the theory of distance education.

Charles Schlosser is a program professor in the Instructional Technology and Distance Education program at Nova Southeastern University. He earned his Ph.D. from Iowa State University. He is co-editor of the *Quarterly Review of Distance Education*, co-editor of the book series *Perspectives in Instructional Technology and Distance Education*, and managing editor of the journal *Distance Learning*.

Kay Shattuck serves as director of research for Quality Matters, a faculty peer review program. She is also affiliated with The Pennsylvania State University's World Campus Faculty Development program and an adjunct assistant professor with the university's College of Education where she has been teaching online since 2000.

Rick L. Shearer is the Director of World Campus Learning Design at the Pennsylvania State University. Over the past 25 years he has developed courses for CBI, educational television, traditional print, two-way interactive video, and online. His research interests cover systems dynamic modeling of distance education, learner control, and dialogue/interaction analysis.

Michael Simonson is a program professor at Nova Southeastern University in the Instructional Technology and Distance Education program. He earned his Ph.D. from the University of Iowa. Simonson has authored four major textbooks and has over 150 scholarly publications. He is editor of the *Quarterly Review of Distance Education*, and *Distance Learning* journal.

Liyan Song is an associate professor in the Department of Educational Technology and Literacy at Towson University. Her research interests include the design and assessment of distance education and technology integration in schools.

Tina M. Stavredes is a Harold Able Distinguished faculty and the Chair of the Psychology Department in the School of Undergraduate Studies at Capella University. She has also held several leadership roles in online learning serving non-traditional students.

Linda A. Summerlin has, since July, 2008, been with the U.S. Army as a TRADOC Fellow, earning her Master's Degree in Instructional Technology and rotating throughout the Army's major training programs and centers of excellence.

Melody M. Thompson is an Associate Professor in The Pennsylvania State University's Adult Education Program. Her research focuses on the ethical dimensions of online education and the history of adult education. Past positions include Director, Planning & Research for the World Campus and Director, American Center for the Study of Distance Education (ACSDE).

Erik Timmerman (Ph.D., University of Texas) is Associate Professor at the University of Wisconsin-Milwaukee. His research examines communication technology use and outcomes.

Gary Twogood is AETC/A3IA Product Integration Manager at Randolph Air force Base, TX. He has been involved with Air Force Distance Learning since 1995. He is responsible for providing assistance to customers who want to load courses on the Air Force's Advanced Distributed Learning Service (ADLS).

Jan Visser, UNESCO's former Director for Learning Without Frontiers, is President and Senior Researcher at the Learning Development Institute (http://www.learndev.org). He is both a theoretical physicist and cognitive scientist with published research in both fields. Dr. Visser is also a musician (who builds his own instruments) and an avid walker.

Ryan Watkins is an associate professor at George Washington University in Washington, DC. He is an author of 10 books and more than 90 articles. His most recent book is *A Guide to Assessing Needs*, published by the World Bank and available for free online at www.gapsinresults.com.

Richard E. West is an assistant professor of Instructional Psychology and Technology at Brigham Young University. His research interests include online collaborative learning and the design and support of environments to promote collaborative innovation.

Jonathan W. Wrigglesworth is a doctoral candidate in The Pennsylvania State University's Adult Education Program. His research interests are in the areas of online learning communities, social networks and social activism, and the ethical dimensions of online education. He has held teaching positions at several universities in Asia and the Middle East.

INDEX